Twentieth-Century
Literary Criticism

Guide to Gale Literary Criticism Series

For criticism on	Consult these Gale series
Authors now living or who died after December 31, 1999	*CONTEMPORARY LITERARY CRITICISM (CLC)*
Authors who died between 1900 and 1999	*TWENTIETH-CENTURY LITERARY CRITICISM (TCLC)*
Authors who died between 1800 and 1899	*NINETEENTH-CENTURY LITERATURE CRITICISM (NCLC)*
Authors who died between 1400 and 1799	*LITERATURE CRITICISM FROM 1400 TO 1800 (LC)* *SHAKESPEAREAN CRITICISM (SC)*
Authors who died before 1400	*CLASSICAL AND MEDIEVAL LITERATURE CRITICISM (CMLC)*
Authors of books for children and young adults	*CHILDREN'S LITERATURE REVIEW (CLR)*
Dramatists	*DRAMA CRITICISM (DC)*
Poets	*POETRY CRITICISM (PC)*
Short story writers	*SHORT STORY CRITICISM (SSC)*
Literary topics and movements	*HARLEM RENAISSANCE: A GALE CRITICAL COMPANION (HR)* *THE BEAT GENERATION: A GALE CRITICAL COMPANION (BG)* *FEMINISM IN LITERATURE: A GALE CRITICAL COMPANION (FL)* *GOTHIC LITERATURE: A GALE CRITICAL COMPANION (GL)*
Asian American writers of the last two hundred years	*ASIAN AMERICAN LITERATURE (AAL)*
Black writers of the past two hundred years	*BLACK LITERATURE CRITICISM (BLC-1)* *BLACK LITERATURE CRITICISM SUPPLEMENT (BLCS)* *BLACK LITERATURE CRITICISM: CLASSIC AND EMERGING AUTHORS SINCE 1950 (BLC-2)*
Hispanic writers of the late nineteenth and twentieth centuries	*HISPANIC LITERATURE CRITICISM (HLC)* *HISPANIC LITERATURE CRITICISM SUPPLEMENT (HLCS)*
Native North American writers and orators of the eighteenth, nineteenth, and twentieth centuries	*NATIVE NORTH AMERICAN LITERATURE (NNAL)*
Major authors from the Renaissance to the present	*WORLD LITERATURE CRITICISM, 1500 TO THE PRESENT (WLC)* *WORLD LITERATURE CRITICISM SUPPLEMENT (WLCS)*

ISSN 0276-8178

Volume 267

Twentieth-Century Literary Criticism

**Criticism of the
Works of Novelists, Poets, Playwrights,
Short Story Writers, and Other Creative Writers
Who Lived between 1900 and 1999,
from the First Published Critical
Appraisals to Current Evaluations**

Kathy D. Darrow
Project Editor

GALE
CENGAGE Learning

Detroit • New York • San Francisco • New Haven, Conn • Waterville, Maine • London

GALE
CENGAGE Learning®

Twentieth-Century Literary Criticism, Vol. 267

Project Editor: Kathy D. Darrow

Editorial: Dana Barnes, Sara Constantakis, Matthew Derda, Kristen Dorsch, Dana Ferguson, Jeffrey W. Hunter, Michelle Kazensky, Jelena O. Krstović, Michelle Lee, Marie Toft, Lawrence J. Trudeau

Content Conversion: Katrina D. Coach, Gwen Tucker

Indexing Services: Laurie Andriot

Rights and Acquisitions: Elaine Kosta, Edna Shy, Sheila Spencer

Composition and Electronic Capture: Gary Oudersluys

Manufacturing: Cynde Lentz

Product Manager: Mary Onorato

For product information and technology assistance, contact us at **Gale Customer Support, 1-800-877-4253.**
For permission to use material from this text or product, submit all requests online at **www.cengage.com/permissions.**
Further permissions questions can be emailed to **permissionrequest@cengage.com**

Gale
27500 Drake Rd.
Farmington Hills, MI, 48331-3535

LIBRARY OF CONGRESS CATALOG CARD NUMBER 76-46132

ISBN-13: 978-1-4144-7047-4
ISBN-10: 1-4144-7047-9

ISSN 0276-8178

Printed in the United States of America
1 2 3 4 5 6 7 16 15 14 13 12

Contents

Preface vii

Acknowledgments xi

Gale Literature Product Advisory Board xiii

Preface

Since its inception *Twentieth-Century Literary Criticism* (*TCLC*) has been purchased and used by some 10,000 school, public, and college or university libraries. *TCLC* has covered more than 1000 authors, representing over 60 nationalities and nearly 50,000 titles. No other reference source has surveyed the critical response to twentieth-century authors and literature as thoroughly as *TCLC*. In the words of one reviewer, "there is nothing comparable available." *TCLC* "is a gold mine of information—dates, pseudonyms, biographical information, and criticism from books and periodicals—which many librarians would have difficulty assembling on their own."

Scope of the Series

TCLC is designed to serve as an introduction to authors who died between 1900 and 1999 and to the most significant interpretations of these author's works. Volumes published from 1978 through 1999 included authors who died between 1900 and 1960. The great poets, novelists, short story writers, playwrights, and philosophers of the period are frequently studied in high school and college literature courses. In organizing and reprinting the vast amount of critical material written on these authors, *TCLC* helps students develop valuable insight into literary history, promotes a better understanding of the texts, and sparks ideas for papers and assignments. Each entry in *TCLC* presents a comprehensive survey on an author's career or an individual work of literature and provides the user with a multiplicity of interpretations and assessments. Such variety allows students to pursue their own interests; furthermore, it fosters an awareness that literature is dynamic and responsive to many different opinions.

Every fourth volume of *TCLC* is devoted to literary topics. These topics widen the focus of the series from the individual authors to such broader subjects as literary movements, prominent themes in twentieth-century literature, literary reaction to political and historical events, significant eras in literary history, prominent literary anniversaries, and the literatures of cultures that are often overlooked by English-speaking readers.

TCLC is designed as a companion series to Gale's *Contemporary Literary Criticism,* (*CLC*) which reprints commentary on authors who died after 1999. Because of the different time periods under consideration, there is no duplication of material between *CLC* and *TCLC*.

Organization of the Book

A *TCLC* entry consists of the following elements:

- The **Author Heading** cites the name under which the author most commonly wrote, followed by birth and death dates. Also located here are any name variations under which an author wrote, including transliterated forms for authors whose native languages use nonroman alphabets. If the author wrote consistently under a pseudonym, the pseudonym is listed in the author heading and the author's actual name is given in parenthesis on the first line of the biographical and critical information. Uncertain birth or death dates are indicated by question marks. Single-work entries are preceded by a heading that consists of the most common form of the title in English translation (if applicable) and the name of its author.

- The **Introduction** contains background information that introduces the reader to the author, work, or topic that is the subject of the entry.

- The list of **Principal Works** is ordered chronologically by date of first publication and lists the most important works by the author. The genre and publication date of each work is given. In the case of foreign authors whose works have been translated into English, the English-language version of the title follows in brackets. Unless otherwise indicated, dramas are dated by first performance, not first publication. Lists of **Representative Works** by different authors appear with topic entries.

■ Reprinted **Criticism** is arranged chronologically in each entry to provide a useful perspective on changes in critical evaluation over time. The critic's name and the date of composition or publication of the critical work are given at the beginning of each piece of criticism. Unsigned criticism is preceded by the title of the source in which it originally appeared. All titles by the author featured in the text are printed in boldface type. Footnotes are reprinted at the end of each essay or excerpt. In the case of excerpted criticism, only those footnotes that pertain to the excerpted texts are included. Criticism in topic entries is arranged chronologically under a variety of subheadings to facilitate the study of different aspects of the topic.

■ A complete **Bibliographical Citation** of the original essay or book precedes each piece of criticism. Source citations in the Literary Criticism Series follow University of Chicago Press style, as outlined in *The Chicago Manual of Style,* 15th ed. (Chicago: The University of Chicago Press, 2003).

■ Critical essays are prefaced by brief **Annotations** explicating each piece.

■ An annotated bibliography of **Further Reading** appears at the end of each entry and suggests resources for additional study. In some cases, significant essays for which the editors could not obtain reprint rights are included here. Boxed material following the further reading list provides references to other biographical and critical sources on the author in series published by Gale.

Indexes

A **Cumulative Author Index** lists all of the authors that appear in a wide variety of reference sources published by Gale, including *TCLC.* A complete list of these sources is found facing the first page of the Author Index. The index also includes birth and death dates and cross references between pseudonyms and actual names.

A **Cumulative Topic Index** lists the literary themes and topics treated in *TCLC* as well as other Literature Criticism series.

A **Cumulative Nationality Index** lists all authors featured in *TCLC* by nationality, followed by the numbers of the *TCLC* volumes in which their entries appear.

An alphabetical **Title Index** accompanies each volume of *TCLC.* Listings of titles by authors covered in the given volume are followed by the author's name and the corresponding page numbers where the titles are discussed. English translations of foreign titles and variations of titles are cross-referenced to the title under which a work was originally published. Titles of novels, dramas, nonfiction books, and poetry, short story, or essay collections are printed in italics, while individual poems, short stories, and essays are printed in roman type within quotation marks.

In response to numerous suggestions from librarians, Gale also produces a paperbound edition of the *TCLC* cumulative title index. This annual cumulation, which alphabetically lists all titles reviewed in the series, is available to all customers. Additional copies of this index are available upon request. Librarians and patrons will welcome this separate index; it saves shelf space, is easy to use, and is recyclable upon receipt of the next edition.

Citing *Twentieth-Century Literary Criticism*

When citing criticism reprinted in the Literary Criticism Series, students should provide complete bibliographic information so that the cited essay can be located in the original print or electronic source. Students who quote directly from reprinted criticism may use any accepted bibliographic format, such as University of Chicago Press style or Modern Language Association (MLA) style. Both the MLA and the University of Chicago formats are acceptable and recognized as being the current standards for citations. It is important, however, to choose one format for all citations; do not mix the two formats within a list of citations.

The examples below follow recommendations for preparing a bibliography set forth in *The Chicago Manual of Style,* 15th ed. (Chicago: The University of Chicago Press, (2003); the first example pertains to material drawn from periodicals, the second to material reprinted from books:

Cardone, Resha. "Reappearing Acts: Effigies and the Resurrection of Chilean Collective Memory in Marco Antonio de la Parra's *La tierra insomne o La puta madre.*" *Hispania* 88, no. 2 (May 2005): 284-93. Reprinted in *Twentieth-Century Literary Criticism.* Vol. 206, edited by Thomas J. Schoenberg and Lawrence J. Trudeau, 356-65. Detroit: Gale, 2008.

Kuester, Martin. "Myth and Postmodernist Turn in Canadian Short Fiction: Sheila Watson, 'Antigone' (1959)." In *The Canadian Short Story: Interpretations,* edited by Reginald M. Nischik, pp. 163-74. Rochester, N.Y.: Camden House, 2007. Reprinted in *Twentieth-Century Literary Criticism.* Vol. 206, edited by Thomas J. Schoenberg and Lawrence J. Trudeau, 227-32. Detroit: Gale, 2008.
The examples below follow recommendations for preparing a works cited list set forth in the Modern Language Association of America's MLA Handbook for Writers of Research Papers, 7th ed. (New York: MLA, 2009. Print); the first example pertains to material drawn from periodicals, the second to material reprinted from books:

Cardone, Resha. "Reappearing Acts: Effigies and the Resurrection of Chilean Collective Memory in Marco Antonio de la Parra's *La tierra insomne o La puta madre.*" *Hispania* 88.2 (May 2005): 284-93. Rpt. in *Twentieth-Century Literary Criticism.* Eds. Thomas J. Schoenberg and Lawrence J. Trudeau. Vol. 206. Detroit: Gale, 2008. 356-65. Print.

Kuester, Martin. "Myth and Postmodernist Turn in Canadian Short Fiction: Sheila Watson, 'Antigone' (1959)." *The Canadian Short Story: Interpretations.* Ed. Reginald M. Nischik. Rochester, N.Y.: Camden House, 2007. 163-74. Rpt. in *Twentieth-Century Literary Criticism.* Eds. Thomas J. Schoenberg and Lawrence J. Trudeau. Vol. 206. Detroit: Gale, 2008. 227-32. Print.

Suggestions are Welcome

Readers who wish to suggest new features, topics, or authors to appear in future volumes, or who have other suggestions or comments are cordially invited to call, write, or fax the Product Manager:

Product Manager, Literary Criticism Series
Gale
27500 Drake Road
Farmington Hills, MI 48331-3535
1-800-347-4253 (GALE)
Fax: 248-699-8884

Acknowledgments

The editors wish to thank the copyright holders of the criticism included in this volume and the permissions managers of many book and magazine publishing companies for assisting us in securing reproduction rights. Following is a list of the copyright holders who have granted us permission to reproduce material in this volume of *TCLC*. Every effort has been made to trace copyright, but if omissions have been made, please let us know.

COPYRIGHTED MATERIAL IN *TCLC*, VOLUME 267, WAS REPRODUCED FROM THE FOLLOWING PERIODICALS:

Claudel Studies, v. 13, 1986 for "Satan with and without a Face in Georges Bernanos" by Stephen Maddux. Copyright © 1986 by Stephen Maddux. Reproduced by permission of the author.—*International Journal of Women's Studies,* v. 4, May/June, 1981 for "Rebecca Harding Davis: Domesticity, Social Order, and the Industrial Novel" by Jean Pfaelzer. Copyright © 1981 by Jean Pfaelzer. Reproduced by permission of the author.—*Journal of American Culture,* v. 3, fall, 1980. Copyright © 1980 by Basil Blackwell Ltd. Reproduced by permission of Blackwell Publishers.—*L'Esprit Créateur,* v. 4, winter, 1964. Copyright © 1964 by Johns Hopkins University Press. Reproduced by permission.—*Renascence,* v. 30, fall, 1978. Copyright © 1978, Marquette University Press. Reproduced by permission.—*Symposium,* v. 25, winter, 1971. Copyright © 1971 by Taylor & Francis. Reproduced by permission of Taylor & Francis Group, LLC, http://www.taylorandfrancis.com.

COPYRIGHTED MATERIAL IN *TCLC*, VOLUME 267, WAS REPRODUCED FROM THE FOLLOWING BOOKS:

Avery, George C. From *Inquiry and Testament: A Study of the Novels and Short Prose of Robert Walser.* University of Pennsylvania Press,1968. Copyright © 1968 by University of Pennsylvania Press. Reprinted with permission of the University of Pennsylvania Press.—Balthasar, Hans Urs von. From *Bernanos: An Ecclesial Existence.* Ignatius Press, 1996. Copyright © 1996 by Ignatius Press. Reproduced by permission.—Benjamin, Walter. From *Robert Walser Rediscovered: Stories, Fairy-Tale Plays, and Critical Responses,* by Robert Walser. University Press of New England, 1985. Copyright © 1985 by University Press of New England. Reproduced by permission.—Bernofsky, Susan. From *The Robber,* by Robert Walser. University of Nebraska Press, 2000. Copyright © 2000 by University of Nebraska Press. Reproduced by permission of the University of Nebraska Press.—Blumenthal, Gerda. From *The Poetic Imagination of Georges Bernanos: An Essay in Interpretation.* The Johns Hopkins Press, 1965. Copyright © 1965 by Johns Hopkins University Press. Reproduced by permission.—Bush, William. From *Georges Bernanos,* for "Images, Patterns and Themes." Twayne Publishers, Inc., 1969. Copyright © 1969 by William Bush. Reproduced by permission of the author.—Bush, William S. From *Monsieur Ouine* by Georges Bernanos. University of Nebraska Press, 2000. Copyright © 2000 by University of Nebraska Press. Reproduced by permission of the University of Nebraska Press.—Dowling, David. From *Capital Letters: Authorship in the Antebellum Literary Market.* University of Iowa Press, 2009. Copyright © 2009 by University of Iowa Press. Reproduced by permission.—Frederick, Samuel. From *Digressions in European Literature: From Cervantes to Sebald.* Palgrave Macmillan, 2011. Copyright © 2011 by Palgrave Macmillan. Reproduced by permission.—Gass, William H. From *"Masquerade" and Other Stories,* by Robert Walser. The Johns Hopkins University Press, 1990. Copyright © 1990 by The Johns Hopkins University Press. All rights reserved. Reproduced by permission.—Goodling, Sara Britton. From *Twisted from the Ordinary: Essays on American Literary Naturalism.* The University of Tennessee Press, 2003. Copyright © 2003 by The University of Tennessee Press. Reproduced by permission of The University of Tennessee Press.—Harris, Sharon M. From *Rebecca Harding Davis and American Realism.* University of Pennsylvania Press, 1991. Copyright © 1991 by University Pennsylvania Press. Reprinted with permission of the University of Pennsylvania Press.—Hebblethwaite, Peter. From *Bernanos: An Introduction.* Bowes and Bowes, 1965. Copyright © 1965 by Random House Group Ltd. Reproduced by permission of Random House Group Limited.—Heffernan, Valerie. From *Provocation from the Periphery: Robert Walser Re-examined.* Königshausen & Neumann, 2007. Copyright © 2007 by Königshausen & Neumann. Reproduced by permission.—Heppenstall, Rayner. From *The Double Image: Mutations of Christian Mythology in the Work of Four French Catholic Writers of To-day and Yesterday,* Secker & Warburg, 1947. Copyright © 1947 by Reed International Books Ltd. Reproduced by permission.—Keane, Susan M. From *Image and Theme, Studies in Modern French Fiction: Bernanos, Malraux, Sarraute, Gide, Martin Du Gard.* Department of Romance Languages and Literatures, Harvard University, 1969. Copyright © 1969 by Harvard University. Reproduced by permission.—Lasseter, Janice Milner. From *Haw-*

Gale Literature Product Advisory Board

The members of the Gale Literature Product Advisory Board—reference librarians from public and academic library systems—represent a cross-section of our customer base and offer a variety of informed perspectives on both the presentation and content of our literature products. Advisory board members assess and define such quality issues as the relevance, currency, and usefulness of the author coverage, critical content, and literary topics included in our series; evaluate the layout, presentation, and general quality of our printed volumes; provide feedback on the criteria used for selecting authors and topics covered in our series; provide suggestions for potential enhancements to our series; identify any gaps in our coverage of authors or literary topics, recommending authors or topics for inclusion; analyze the appropriateness of our content and presentation for various user audiences, such as high school students, undergraduates, graduate students, librarians, and educators; and offer feedback on any proposed changes/enhancements to our series. We wish to thank the following advisors for their advice throughout the year.

Georges Bernanos
1888-1948

(Full name Paul Louis Georges Bernanos) French novelist, essayist, short story writer, and playwright.

The following entry provides an overview of Bernanos's life and works. For additional information on his career, see *TCLC,* Volume 3.

INTRODUCTION

Bernanos is considered an important French author and thinker of the early twentieth century. He is primarily remembered for his political essays, as well as several provocative novels, including *Sous le soleil de Satan* (1926; *Under the Sun of Satan*), *Journal d'un curé de campagne* (1936; *The Diary of a Country Priest*), and *Monsieur Ouine* (1943; *The Open Mind*). In these and other writings, the author responded to the atrocities and violence of his era, including World War I, the Spanish Civil War, and World War II, and exposed the ever-present struggle between good and evil in society and the individual. Raised in the Catholic Church, Bernanos maintained his faith throughout his life, often promoting a return to traditional Christian values as an answer to society's decline; he also greatly valued the innocence of childhood, which was a primary thematic focus of his work. Critically acclaimed during his lifetime, Bernanos is still respected for his impeccable prose style, formal innovations, and powerful spiritual vision. Writing in 1947, Rayner Heppenstall described him as "a serious and at times an exquisite artist," a "superb rhetorician," and "a profound judge of motive," asserting that his prose "is massive and simple in its weight, fluid and direct in its address."

BIOGRAPHICAL INFORMATION

Bernanos was born Paul Louis Georges Bernanos on February 20, 1888, in Paris, to Marie-Clémence Moreau and Emile Bernanos. An ill child, he nearly died at the age of eighteen months; his subsequent recovery his devoutly Catholic parents attributed to the intercession of the Virgin Mary. Beginning in 1898, Bernanos attended the Jesuit school at 391 rue de Vaugirard, and later the preseminary school of Notre-Dame-des-Champs in Paris, where he developed a love for French composition. After failing his first and second *baccalauréat,* he enrolled in the Collège Sainte-Marie at Aire-sur-la-Lys, where he completed secondary studies in philosophy in 1906. That fall, Bernanos began studying at the Faculté de Droit at the Université de Paris and over the next three years completed his license in law and literature. During this time, the author became involved with the nationalistic Action Française youth guard and participated in various demonstrations, some of which were violent. As early as 1907, his first short stories appeared in royalist publications. In 1909, his studies were completed and Bernanos was called for obligatory military service, but his health failed during the training process, and he was released in 1910 to recuperate. After a brief return to Paris, Bernanos traveled to the provinces in 1913 to edit the journal *L'Avant-garde de Normandie,* where he published essays and short stories. In Rouen, the author met Jehanne Pauline Marie Talbert d'Arc, who became his wife in 1917.

At the onset of World War I, Bernanos returned to service and saw trench warfare firsthand. He was discharged in 1919 and moved to the seaside at Berck, where he began work on his first novel, *Under the Sun of Satan,* which was published in 1926 to widespread acclaim. For much of this period, the author was unemployed, and he and his growing family were forced to rely on outside family members for support. In 1922, Bernanos found a job as a traveling insurance agent, but with the success of *Under the Sun of Satan* he quit his job and devoted his time to writing a second novel, *L'imposture* (1927; *The Impostor*). Although his publisher provided the author with a monthly stipend, Bernanos continued to experience financial duress and completed his third novel, *La joie* (1929; *Joy*), in a state of panic. Shortly thereafter, the author was notified that his monthly income would cease until he repaid his debts. The family settled for three years in La Bayorre, but as financial pressures mounted during the 1930s, they were forced to leave everything behind and move to Majorca, Spain. Bernanos produced several works over the next decade, including a detective novel and the acclaimed *The Diary of a Country Priest*. The author returned to France with his family in 1937 and published *Les grands cimetières sous la lune* (1938; *A Diary of My Times*), which chronicled his experience of the Spanish Civil War. In 1938, with the dream of establishing a family farm abroad, Bernanos left Europe and settled briefly on a ranch in Brazil, where he completed *The Open Mind,* a novel he had begun a decade before. In 1945, however, he returned to France and continued to write over the next few years, despite his failing health. On July 5, 1948, Bernanos died in Neuilly-sur-Seine, France, of liver cancer.

MAJOR WORKS

Bernanos's first novel, *Under the Sun of Satan,* was also one of his most successful works. Inspired in part by the author's experiences in the trenches during World War I, the novel examines human despair in three parts and demonstrates the ruthless power of the demonic in the affairs of humankind. One part of the narrative concerns Mouchette, a pregnant sixteen-year-old, who kills her lover for failing to live up to her romantic ideals. Another section of the work describes the last day in the life of the old saint of Lumbres, who is blessed with the gift of reading souls and who realizes on his deathbed that he has blasphemed in asking for miracles. The central part of the novel, however, focuses on a young priest called to sainthood, who is eventually seduced by Satan. The disparate threads of the plot are drawn together when Mouchette encounters the young priest, whose despair matches her own, and finally takes her own life. *The Diary of a Country Priest,* for many scholars, is one of Bernanos's finest achievements. While the central conflict of the novel is the tension between the idealistic protagonist-priest's spiritual struggle and his relationship with his parishioners, Bernanos also demonstrates the ways in which the divine and material worlds are at odds in the work, and shows the disparity between appearances and truth. As the priest deals with self-doubt, he becomes increasingly entangled in the secrets and dramas of his flock, and his best efforts to minister are often misinterpreted. Deemed a failure, the protagonist eventually learns he has cancer, a discovery that eventually leads to clarity and enlightenment. At the end of the novel, the priest utters his last words, "Tout est grâce," or "Everything is grace." *The Open Mind,* also published in English under its original French title, *Monsieur Ouine,* centers on the protagonist Monsieur Ouine, a professor who, as his name implies, says "yes" and "no" at the same time. Ouine presides maliciously over the nearby town of Fenouille, where Steeny, a fourteen-year-old boy, lives with his mother and her companion. On the night that Ouine seduces Steeny, another man is found murdered, which throws the town into chaos, and eventually culminates in multiple suicides and a lynching. The final chapter of the novel, written at the same time as the Nazi occupation of France, deals with the death of Ouine. Some scholars have suggested that the novel can be read as an allegory of Hitler's conquest of Europe, while others have pointed toward more universal themes in the work, such as the corruption and dissolution of society as a result of pervasive evil. *The Open Mind,* as well as other writings, reflect Bernanos's concern for the despair of children and the loss of innocence in the modern world.

In addition to novels, Bernanos also produced important essays during his literary career. *A Diary of My Times* chronicles the author's experiences living in Majorca during the late 1930s and his opinions regarding the Spanish Civil War. The French title of the work, which literally translates as "The Great Moonlit Cemeteries," reflects Bernanos's memory of an experience, when he discovered a pile of corpses that were doused with gasoline and set on fire. In addition to recording atrocities that he had witnessed, the author also rejected the position of conservatives within the Catholic Church, who considered Francisco Franco's war against the Spanish republic justified, instead arguing that the crisis was the result of the disintegration of Christian values in modern society. In other sections of the work, Bernanos asserted that there was no human compassion on either side of the conflict, and he correctly predicted that more widespread violence would sweep over Europe in the years to come. *A Diary of My Times* is also significant for its often-quoted preface, in which Bernanos reflects on his philosophy concerning childhood, a state he admired for its pure innocence. In *Nous autres Français* (1939), Bernanos attempted to articulate his thoughts regarding French honor, while he explored similar themes in *Lettre aux Anglais* (1942; *Plea for Liberty: Letters to the English, the Americans, the Europeans*). Another collection of essays, *Le chemin de la Croix-des-Ames* (1948), charts the author's reaction to daily news bulletins during World War II, while *Les enfants humilies: Journal 1939-1940* (1949), described as a "war diary," offers Bernanos's personal response to the onset of World War II.

CRITICAL RECEPTION

Throughout his career, Bernanos enjoyed popularity and the admiration of critics for both his novels and nonfiction works. His first novel, *Under the Sun of Satan,* achieved both critical and popular success, and three years later, his third novel, *Joy,* was awarded the Prix Fémina. Despite the critical success of these early works, Bernanos constantly struggled with financial despair throughout his career, and he wrote many books, such as those of the early 1930s, out of desperation for money; for this reason, many of these works are generally viewed as his least successful as an author. In 1936, however, he produced *The Diary of a Country Priest,* which many critics regard as his most accomplished novel. Widely praised at the time, the work was awarded the Grand Prix du Roman de l'Académie Française. Bernanos won new admirers in 1938, with the publication of *A Diary of My Times,* including Paris publisher Gaston Gallimard and Simone Weil, the French philosopher and activist, who in a long letter to Bernanos asserted that he alone had revealed the truths of the Spanish Civil War. In 1926, 1937, 1940, and 1946, the author was offered the Légion d'Honneur, but in each case he refused. Likewise, in March of 1946, when François Mauriac welcomed Bernanos into the Académie, the author again politely refused the honor. Bernanos's reputation flourished during the 1940s, and he was increasingly in demand as a lecturer in Europe and North Africa. At the time of his death in 1948, he was still perceived as a valued figure of French letters. Writing in 1949, Ernst Erich Noth [see Further Reading] described Bernanos as a "visionary," but argued that he also "gives testimony of his own time."

In the decades following Bernanos's death, scholars have continued to study the thematic and formal concerns of his work. During the 1950s and 1960s, a number of critics, including Donat O'Donnell [see Further Reading], Thomas Molnar, and Peter Hebblethwaite, examined Christian themes in Bernanos's writings. O'Donnell related the author's work to the Faustian tradition in literature and argued that his entire career was an effort "to convey to his readers his own burning conviction of the existence and power of the Devil," while Molnar focused on Bernanos's depiction of modern society as a "soulless collective force," which suffered as a result of its separation from God. Hebblethwaite emphasized Bernanos's stance as a Catholic writer but noted that his belief in the "sanctity" of life and his compassion for humanity make him relevant to modern readers. Both Hans Urs von Balthasar and Susan M. Keane highlighted the importance of dream in Bernanos's writings, while William Bush, in his 1969 study, contended that the "primacy of childhood" and the "suffering" of the innocent adolescent are the central themes of his work. A number of commentators, such as J. E. Flower [see Further Reading] and Arnold L. Weinstein, have praised Bernanos's formal techniques. Weinstein, writing in 1971, reflected on techniques the author used to create "chaos" in his writings, in order to "render the moral tensions of his work with immediacy" and challenge the reader to find meaning and order in experience. More recently, Stephen Maddux studied the evolution of Bernanos's characterization of Satan and the protagonist-priest throughout his career, while Bush, in his introduction to a newly translated 2000 edition of *Monsieur Ouine*, emphasized the author's facility with mixing narrative genres, including allegory, the detective novel, and the "story of initiation." As recent scholarship demonstrates, Bernanos continues to garner attention and admiration for his unique and visionary writings, and he has maintained his position as an important figure of modern French literature. Writing in 2007, Ralph McInerny remarked that Bernanos, "from the outset of his literary career, had an almost unique ability to provide his reader with an unforgettable sense of the stakes of life," concluding that his work "can be seen as a corrective to the banality of much modern fiction."

PRINCIPAL WORKS

Sous le soleil de Satan [*Under the Sun of Satan*] (novel) 1926

L'imposture [*The Impostor*] (novel) 1927

La joie [*Joy*] (novel) 1929

La grande peur des bien-pensants, Édouard Drumont (essay) 1931

Jeanne: Relapse et sainte [*Sanctity Will Out*] (essay) 1934

Un crime [*A Crime*] (novel) 1935

Journal d'un curé de campagne [*The Diary of a Country Priest*] (novel) 1936

Nouvelle histoire de Mouchette [*Mouchette*] (novella) 1937

Les grands cimetières sous la lune [*A Diary of My Times*] (essays) 1938

Nous autres Français (essays) 1939

Scandale de la vérité (essays) 1939

Lettre aux Anglais [*Plea for Liberty: Letters to the English, the Americans, the Europeans*] (letters) 1942

Monsieur Ouine [*The Open Mind*] (novel) 1943

La France contre les robots [*Tradition of Freedom*] (essays) 1944

Le chemin de la Croix-des-Ames (essays) 1948

Dialogues des Carmélites [*The Carmelites*] (play) 1949

Les enfants humiliés: Journal 1939-1940 (essays) 1949

Un mauvais rêve [*Night Is Darkest*] (novel) 1951

La liberté, pour quoi faire? [*Last Essays*] (lectures) 1953

Français, si vous saviez, 1945-1948 (essays) 1961

The Heroic Face of Innocence (short stories) 1999

CRITICISM

Rayner Heppenstall (essay date 1947)

SOURCE: Heppenstall, Rayner. "The Priest as Scapegoat." In *The Double Image: Mutations of Christian Mythology in the Work of Four French Catholic Writers of To-day and Yesterday*, pp. 29-44. London: Secker & Warburg, 1947.

[*In the following essay, Heppenstall describes Bernanos's fiction as both "primitive, pre-Christian" and "post-Christian" in its appeal to "the theories of Freud and his successors," and he discerns at the core of the author's mythology "the figure of the scapegoat priest, on whom we load all our sins and send him out into the wilderness and who is the point at which primitive belief assumes the Christian paraphernalia."*]

Certain notions that I had entertained for a long time about the work of Georges Bernanos in particular were crystallised for me when I read the following in a paper by D. W. Winnicott and Clare Britton on *The Problem of Homeless Children*: 'Each child, according to the degree of his distrust, and according to the degree of his hopelessness about the loss of his own home (and sometimes his recognition of the inadequacy of that home while it lasted), is all the time testing the hostel staff as he would test his own parents. Sometimes he does this directly, but most of the time he is content to let another child do the testing for him. An important thing about this testing is that it is not something that can be achieved and done with. Always somebody has to be a nuisance. Often one of the staff will say: "We'd be all right if it weren't for Tommy . . .", but in point of fact the others can only afford to be "all right" because Tommy is being a nuisance, and is proving to them that the home can stand up to Tommy's testing, and could therefore presumably stand up to their own.'

It is curious how the psychological emphasis has shifted off 'repression' since the war. The feeling of insecurity and a lack of childhood discipline are now regarded as the chief source of our ills. If Dr. Winnicott were an army psychiatrist or any kind of official spokesman, I might be suspicious of his emphasis on 'discipline'. But I happen to know him for a peculiarly disinterested man with no axe to grind. Not even an anti-Freudian axe. For all the separate conclusions to which his extensive field-work in peace-time and war-time has brought him, Dr. Winnicott still regards himself as a Freudian and officiates for the British Institute of Psycho-Analysis.

His general view is that a child requires to have its original feeling of infinity closely delimited and its life confined within a circle. If the laws established by a child's parents prove unreliable, if the child can break them with impunity, the feeling of infinity becomes an abyss of nothingness and sets up acute distress and indeed despair in the child. He looks elsewhere for his circle of authority and tests the law personified by his teachers and later by the police. 'The young delinquent', says Dr. Winnicott in another paper on *Delinquency Research,* 'values and loves the policeman.' And he points out that 'the thief's inability to keep and enjoy what is stolen is well known. The boy who steals apples from an orchard and who eats the apples himself is not ill, is not a delinquent. He is just greedy, and his greed is relatively conscious. The anti-social child steals apples and either wastes them or gives them away. Intermediate is the boy who eats them and is sick, the sickness being a bodily form of feeling guilty.'

I am afraid that these considerations may seem a little remote from the subject proposed in the title of this essay. I offer them in elucidation of the first statement I have taken from Dr. Winnicott. This is entirely germane to my purpose.

What I had been thinking about Bernanos was that all the priests who are central characters in his novels are employed as scapegoats in a quite primitive, magical sense. Then I began to compare Bernanos with other Catholic writers and with non-Catholic writers, and after a while it began to seem to me that all the key characters in fiction were scapegoats in one sense or another. Indeed, I began to wonder whether the whole of our narrative and dramatic literature were not a concerted effort to find and employ scapegoats.

I fancied that somewhere there must exist a heavy thesis by a German professor in which all this is set forth, but I have been unable to find it. Instead, I found 'Tommy' in Dr. Winnicott's Oxfordshire hostel, a link between primitive ritual and sophisticated literature, and I felt that the argument had already become a great deal less far-fetched. I opened *The Golden Bough* with an easy mind. The original scapegoat was Jewish. 'On the Day of Atonement, which was the tenth day of the seventh month, the Jewish high-priest laid both his hands on the head of a live goat, confessed over it all the iniquities of the Children of Israel, and having thereby transferred the sins of the people to the beast, sent it away into the wilderness.' Fraser is full of the most enchanting details of the use of animal and inanimate creatures for the private and communal expulsion of sin or sickness among the peoples of every part of the world, but of course a human scapegoat is the most efficient. 'The devices to which the cunning and selfish savage resorts for the sake of easing himself at the expense of his neighbour are manifold.' It is uncertain to what extent Fraser ever realised that 'the cunning and selfish savage' is ubiquitous and eternal. He never let on. He was a wise man and quietly finished his work. The dig at religious mythology was comparatively safe. 'The accumulated misfortunes and sins of the whole people are sometimes laid upon the dying god, who is supposed to bear them away for ever, leaving the people innocent and happy.' But I must not go on quoting from *The Golden Bough*. It is probably accessible to every reader of these pages. Before I move to literary territory, I would like simply to point out that a journalistic misuse of the word 'scapegoat' is widely current to-day and that it is no part of the word's original sense to imply blame. To-day we have lost the sense of our own guilt. It is always 'they' and never 'we' who have sinned. In this respect we have fallen below the moral and indeed the psychological level of 'the cunning and selfish savage'. Anti-Semitism and Vansittartism do not properly employ Jews or Germans as scapegoats. They impute sin to the victim and name it as the cause of the people's misfortunes. The function of a true scapegoat is beneficial, and scapegoats are to be loved.

The night a new priest arrives in the village, a man is murdered. The new priest, sensitive, pale and mysteriously ill, turns out in the end to be a girl. The murdered man was the expected priest. The girl commits suicide after a confession. Lesbian practices lay at the root of her disorder. In other words, she had broken a very serious *tabu.* The priest paid the price of her guilt and unhappiness. After masquerading as a priest and thus taking his function to herself, she also must die. That is the plot of **The Crime,** the earliest, least sophisticated and perhaps even least mythological of Bernanos' novels and the only one in which the subject-matter is explicitly that of a thriller. However, no novel by Bernanos is without a body.

Bernanos is best known in this country for **The Diary of a Country Priest** and **A Diary of My Times** (*Les Grands Cimetières sous la Lune*). These were translated and published in England in 1936 and 1937. **The Diary of a Country Priest** had a popular success. But **The Crime** and **The Star of Satan** had been published in translation some years before and quickly remaindered. I bought both books in 1939 for sixpence and ninepence respectively from Woolworth's and from a tobacconist's lending library.

A Diary of My Times is not a work of fiction and does not concern us here. The work of Georges Bernanos divides cleanly into two parts, the fiction (whose theme is constant and obsessive) and the polemics. **A Diary of My Times** is a protest against the massacres perpetrated by Franco's men in Majorca. By it, Bernanos gained a great deal of credit among non-Catholics during the Spanish Civil War.

In **The Diary of a Country Priest,** a young priest already sick dies at his post. He dies for and from the sins of his village. These sins drain away through him, and in the end he chokes up (his only other food is dry bread and sour wine). The sin which finishes him off is the sin of excessive love of the creature on the part of the *châtelaine.* In terms of primitive *tabu,* this was a form of lingering incest wish. The young priest brings it to light and subjugates it in the manner of a psychoanalyst with a gift for the theatre (but the scene is also reminiscent of a medieval conjuration of demons), and that is the end of him. His cancer proliferates at an unheard-of rate, and he dies.

L'Imposture and its sequel, **La Joie,** concern a priest who has lost his faith. He is presented rather unsympathetically, but it is implied that contemporary city life (he functions in Paris) has choked his channels of grace. He is in fact an inefficient scapegoat. Full of his own sins, how can he absorb the sins of others? The fact that he is a city priest is already symptomatic. To go to a remote village is a stage on the journey to the wilderness. This priest is refusing to take that journey. In Paris, an old man dies because of the priest's inability to bring down help from God or, contrariwise, to draw away the old man's sins. Then the priest leaves Paris for a re-

mote village, but lives obstinately at the *château.* Here, in **La Joie,** he exerts a remoter influence upon a young, beautiful and well-born girl who is in an acute state of grace. The connection is not stated, but it appears to the imagination to be in some way as a result of this influence that the girl is presently murdered by the Russian chauffeur who cannot endure the spectacle of so much God-given joy and who has observed the girl at her prayers. Perhaps it is that the girl herself must be the scapegoat because the priest cannot or will not. However, not only has the murder itself a distinctly erotic flavour, but the seeing the girl at prayer is also done in the style of Susannah and the Elders, as if prayer were a thing peculiarly not to be observed by members of the opposite sex.

The Star of Satan presents a feminine type whose sin Bernanos looks upon with profound compassion and whose story he tells again in the **Nouvelle Histoire de Mouchette,** where, however, expiation is secured by non-clerical means. Mouchette is the girl ill-treated at home who goes wrong at a tender age, normally with older men who are her social superiors.

Again the connection is curiously inexplicit. But in some mysterious way the Mouchette of **The Star of Satan** is redeemed by the struggles of a clumsy young priest both with his own stubborn (caprine?) soul and with an exterior devil who causes him to lose himself at night (in the wilderness?) and to walk round in circles. The young priest in **The Star of Satan** flagellates and wears about his middle a rope so tight that it eats into his flesh.

A class of scapegoats with whom Bernanos has merely implicit dealings are witches. With the master of all covens, however, the prince of evil, the key-scapegoat, he makes overt play. And indeed Bernanos is the only known case of a novelist causing the devil himself to appear in the middle of a perfectly serious novel. In the **Star of Satan,** the devil personally presents himself to the Curé de Lumbres at night on that country road in the guise of a talkative wayfarer and causes the young priest to lose his sense of direction and fail in a mission, only to be confronted with a greater mission at the first light of dawn.

As I say, Bernanos does not explicitly broach the subject of witchcraft. His work nevertheless contains elements which only a knowledge of the secret paths of witchcraft will elucidate. Similarly, he does not explicitly broach the subject of *Poltergeister* and yet treads repeatedly on *Poltergeist* territory. Is the *Poltergeist* a scapegoat? In the sense that people blame their *alter ego,* the beast in themselves which is 'brought out', the 'something' which is 'bigger' than they are, he is. For he is clearly a disturbance caused in the environment by the individual who is pestered.

Let us note, at any rate, that Bernanos' portrait of the devil closely resembles the friendly little man in black or grey who recurs incessantly throughout the two hundred years of witchcraft trials. Let us also note that Mouchette is the type of *Poltergeist* girl in early puberty of which the most notable contemporary representative was Marguerite Rozier of Lyons, whose phenomena were first exhibited in 1930. Perhaps most significant of all is the fact that the young priest of *The Star of Satan* is modelled upon the Curé d'Ars and that the Curé d'Ars was troubled all his life by rappings, displacement of objects and inexplicable outbreaks of fire, which have made him as classic a *Poltergeist* figure as the Rev. Samuel Wesley and which Mr. Gerald Heard attributes to a form of electrical energy generated by intense prayer.

Let us be quite frank and admit that an element of Bernanos' appeal to his reader is pornographic. Flagellation, transvestism, the seduction of fourteen-year-olds by middle-aged rakes, the sadistic murder of pure girls of good family by proletarian debauchees who are foreigners and peeping Toms into the bargain . . . these are the familiar ingredients of rubber-shop literature, with or without the shutters of the confessional, the priestly robe, the candle-lit study and the clouds of incense.[1] Yet Bernanos is a serious and at times an exquisite artist. He is a superb rhetorician, a profound judge of motive, a man tender and generous (as only a Latin seems able to be) in his attitude to public affairs[2] and a considerable scholar. His narrative technique is possibly unequalled in our time. The prose is massive and simple in its weight, fluid and direct in its address. There is no other writer who could make a spasm of conscience last fifty pages and be neither dull and unconvincing, nor yet fantastic and buzzing with conceits.

The type of Christian faith which M. Bernanos exemplifies is dignified, modest and quite free from either sensationalism or hysteria. From his polemical writing, he must be judged to be a liberal moralist disinclined to debate points of theology with his religious superiors but of a resolute independence in his casuistry. He derives the manner of his eloquence from Léon Bloy and Charles Péguy, but displays none of Bloy's private anguish, none of his highly coloured, analogical and indeed allegorical theologising, and none of Péguy's affectations of a pre-Tridentine simplicity. The direct descendant of Bloy is Berdyaev, a Russian. The direct descendants of Péguy are Gill, Chesterton, Pepler, the bucolic, tankard-draining, hand-loom-weaving, one-acre-and-a-cow English Arcadians. In France itself, the Mendelian laws of intellectual descent operate with greater complexity, though from Péguy we derive J.O.C., the *Jeunesse Ouvrière Catholique,* and the manual thought of M. Denis de Rougement. Like Bloy, Bernanos lives in the world and attacks *les bien-pensants,* but his fantasy has been chastened by Péguy.

Like both, he is a French patriot. Unlike both, he shows no special predilection for the poor. So far as an infidel can judge, he stands in far less danger of excommunication than did either of his predecessors.

But a man gives away his predicament in dreams. In a body of work as cleanly divided as Bernanos', his fiction will represent the dream-life as T. S. Eliot's poetry does. A number of Eliot's prose doctrines are refuted in his verse, and much of Bernanos' rhetoric is given the lie by fictions produced when the censor was nodding and the will rampant.

The work of Georges Bernanos is at bottom primitive, pre-Christian. At the same time, its appeal is also post-Christian and not at all uncongenial to an audience conditioned by the theories of Freud and his successors. As music plays directly upon the rhythms of the heart-beat and the bowels, Bernanos, though he uses Christian stage-properties and Christian prestige, plays upon the most deeply flowing mass-impulses of mankind. Bernanos (in his fiction) is a witch-doctor. He is also a psycho-analyst for whom, and for his patients, primitive magic is still operative and primitive *tabus* still valid. The excitement attached to watching a girl pray is a marked instance. And always in the centre of the stage stands the figure of the scapegoat priest, on whom we load all our sins and send him out into the wilderness and who is the point at which primitive belief assumes the Christian paraphernalia.

There is a little recognised form of heresy or predisposition towards heresy which consists in taking the part for the whole or an attribute for the reality. All forms of idolatry indeed are in some sense identical with the erotic tendency known as fetishism. The heretic in such a case may never give overt expression to an heretical doctrine. He substitutes an ancillary for the central mystery and adores something other than incarnate God. It is not far from the truth to say that Bernanos adores the priestly function. Adores? At least he is obsessed with it. And the erotic analogy persists. The feeling changes with the object. The fetishist cannot be truly said to love the shoe or the fur-coat in the sense in which he ought to have loved its possessor.

Is it perhaps that for the intelligent, contemporary Catholic the priest is a figure he cannot accept? It must be obvious to an intelligent Catholic that priests are commonly stupid and that many of them mislead their flocks. Does he, therefore, wish to attach to them a primitive, magical and quasiphallic significance in order to fit them into his world-picture at all? To working-class Protestants in provincial towns, the Catholic priest is at once a figure of ridicule and fear. I was brought up to believe that when a Catholic priest visits the house of one of his parishioners, he leaves his umbrella on the door-step as a sign that nobody, least of all the husband, must enter.

Certainly, the rank-and-file, secular priest is the central figure in Catholicism, and certainly Catholic intellectuals are embarrassed by him. He must be either sentimentalised, deplored or haloed with primitive mystery. He is more popular with anti-clerical writers than with his co-religionists. The lecherous, tormented priests of Liam O'Flaherty, the bumbling idiots of Joyce, are more alive than anything in *croyant* literature. Léon Bloy ignored the secular priest, though he wrote of Trappists and Carthusians. Graham Greene has one book, *The Power and the Glory*, which I imagine to have been directly inspired by Bernanos. The priest here is placed in a country which Greene visited, hated and failed to understand, and he is a bibulous fellow of weak character but an efficient scapegoat. Otherwise, Greene ignores all priests, secular and cloistered. His liveliest cleric is an unfrocked Anglican.

In Greene's novels, the plumbing system of grace is in full flow, but the scapegoats are laymen, preferably criminals and almost certainly lapsed Catholics. But the machinery of fear is altogether more elaborate and sophisticated in Greene. Fear itself is his obsession, fear his theme. In *Brighton Rock,* which has been commonly regarded as Greene's masterpiece, it is explicitly stated that the forces of good and evil must be felt with maximum impact and that a bad Catholic is superior to a good pagan for this reason. In other words, faith increases the *frisson*. The chief argument for belief is that, if you do not believe, you cannot be damned.

Tommy can be truly said to misbehave himself on behalf of the other children. From the children's point of view, he is a true scapegoat. 'The others can only afford to be "all right" because Tommy is being a nuisance.' But the children are not the whole community. There are also the members of the staff who say, 'We'd be all right if it weren't for Tommy'. The wilderness into which the other children send Tommy is the wilderness of adult disapproval, and unfortunately the wilderness in this case has a point of view of its own. To the child community, Tommy is a scapegoat. To the adult community, he is a young criminal.

It is probable that there must always be a similar ambiguity in the rôle of scapegoat in a highly developed and complex society. I have already remarked on the journalistic misuse of 'scapegoat' to mean 'those on whom one lays the blame'. The Jews for the anti-Semite, the Germans for Lord Vansittart, the war itself for the man in the street, the *bourgeoisie* for orthodox communists, the machine for the Arcadians . . . are all fulfilling some of the functions of a true scapegoat, but the fact is unrecognised by those who employ them. The scapegoat's function, of which all men feel the need, has receded into unconsciousness, and 'the cunning and selfish savage' of the twentieth century has succumbed to the final indignity of hating the useful saviour-beast on whom he lays the burden of his sins.

On the other hand, a class of scapegoats who formerly met with unmitigated disapproval have in the modern world received something like adulation from certain groups in society. Now here we have a situation like that in Dr. Winnicott's hostel. The criminal of the gangster films is 'Tommy'. Who are 'the other children'? Can it be that they are the orphans of industrial capitalism, the working classes and the dispossessed in general? As a matter of demonstrable fact, they are. The upper and middle-classes do not read *No Orchids for Miss Blandish*. They read Edgar Wallace or the academic thriller, in which the police or the private detective are the heroes, though we must not forget the vogue of Raffles among the displaced members of the officer class who sold vacuum-cleaners after the last war.

It is evident that the German professor who writes that heavy thesis will have to be a Marxist. To-day is not the only hey-day of the property criminals. We remember Villon and other *poètes maudits*. The greatest popular hero this country ever had was a property criminal, Robin Hood, who retired to the wilderness of Sherwood Forest. The type of mild and amiable scapegoat hero in a more settled age was Robinson Crusoe.

But these are impure types. The criminal scapegoat, the scapegoat hero and another, the scapegoat-fool . . . are the only considerable mythological figures so far employed in Hollywood. The fool has his own history. Mr. Polly was the type of many scapegoat-fools in the English novel, Rip van Winkle in the American. Both were inferior to Chaplin on the films. The Germans may be said to have created the scapegoat leader or in other words to have formed themselves up in a column with the goat at their head and all marched into the desert together.

This is in fact the only method by which a scapegoat may be employed for revolutionary purposes. To have an efficient scapegoat makes for contentment and good behaviour. From their own point of view, our rulers do well to encourage the proletarian adulation of gangsters on the films, if not indeed to allow a substantial criminal class to flourish within the social framework on the American pattern. The members of the hostel staff will no doubt bear this in mind.

A final point of mythological interest. The human scapegoats of the ancient world, although frequently the representatives of God, were invariably chosen for some physical peculiarity, deformity or condition of sickness. Moreover, to give them a positive, fertilising function in addition to their primary task in the expulsion of evil, they were in some communities chastised upon the genital organs 'with squills and branches of the wild fig'. Contemporary creators of literary scapegoats have unconsciously returned with increasing clarity to these original types.

Especially has the criminal scapegoat tended of late towards abnormality. Graham Greene's simplest exemplar, the killer in *A Gun for Sale,* has a hare-lip of which he is constantly and bitterly conscious. In the film, in which Alan Ladd plays the part, this lip is changed for a wrist deformed by the killer's mother with a flat-iron. Pop-eye in William Faulkner's *Sanctuary* and Slim in *No Orchards for Miss Blandish* are both impotent. Pop-eye avails himself of a common fertility symbol, the corn-cob. The boy in *Brighton Rock* is not impotent, but he experiences great difficulty. He is a creature of markedly low physique.

The Bernanos priests are at once ill, of stubborn conscience and socially inept or marked out to be outcasts. The good ones are untrained country youths whose scrupulosity tortures them very nearly to the point of madness. There is also a peculiar fitness in the priest's black robe.

If we take the view that human society ought to develop in the direction of greater individual responsibility, we shall of course deplore all scapegoats and (with Fraser) regard their history as 'an endless number of very unamiable devices for palming off upon someone else the trouble which a man shrinks from bearing himself'. But if we are in favour of the natural man or if we despair of exterminating in ourselves 'the cunning, selfish savage' and the homeless child, yet it is still clearly preferable that scapegoats should be volunteers, as they frequently were in the ancient world and as they are at the New Year festival in Lhasa to-day. In this respect, M. Bernanos exhibits a fine willingness. The degree of his self-identification with his victims is unusual. Many people in this country believed that **The Diary of a Country Priest** was a true diary and, although we are unused to priests with moustaches, that the person on the jacket wrapped in a great muffler and with burning, phthisic eyes was the dying priest himself. It is he in fact, the author, who will take away your sins. It may be observed, however, that, in making this offer, M. Bernanos is doing no more than his duty as an intellectual to-day. For, despite the long and distinguished succession of *poètes maudits,* there never was an age in which of itself the possession of exceptional gifts of intelligence or sensibility so qualified a man for employment in the vicarious expulsion of evils.

The bulk of this chapter was written before the publication in England of **The Open Mind** (1945). The original, **Monsieur Ouine,** had appeared in Buenos Aires two years previously, but no copy of it came my way.

The Open Mind is in many ways the least satisfying novel Bernanos has given us. It is clear that the translator is partly at fault. His attempt to be highly idiomatic has covered the book with a thin coating of totally inappropriate English public-school slang. Whatever splendour the language of the original may have had is lost. However, the trouble lies deeper than this.

The Bernanos mythology has gone to pieces. The flat ground of boredom and of sins whose chief characteristic (as says the saint of Lumbres in **The Star of Satan**) is their awful monotony, has broken up into a volcanic region of murder and insanity. The priest's mission is ineffectual, and indeed no priest is introduced until towards the end. The closest approximation to a true scapegoat is Monsieur Ouine himself, a radical intellectual. If the inert, malignant parish of the earlier novels was indeed a parable of the world, this village of Fenouille is evidently a world at war.

In the first place, no previous novel of Bernanos has contained so many characters. It is clear that the author did not know on whom to fix his spotlight. At first it appears that we are to see all through the eyes of 'Steeny', a middle-class boy whose widowed mother and English governess seem to be involved in some kind of Lesbian relationship with each other. But the spotlight quickly shifts to the crazy *châtelaine,* an aging tom-boy who drives a huge mare, sleeps with the young men of the village, destroys her husband with sloth and discouragement, alternately abducts young 'Steeny' and attempts to run him down with her mare, and goes to the police with accusations against Monsieur Ouine, her husband's friend, who has a room in the *château,* who is dying (but this is not at first made clear, so that we may regard his death as one of those mysterious, expiatory deaths with which Bernanos has made us familiar) and by whom she is at once fascinated and outraged. Monsieur Ouine becomes 'Steeny's' confidant and monitor, though what he teaches him is uncertain unless it be to know himself (Monsieur Ouine is a character from the same mould as the Irish doctor in an American masterpiece, Djuna Barnes's *Nightwood,* with which indeed there are other parallels in this book). But again the spotlight shifts. It is turned upon a Flemish farmer, his crippled grandson and his grand-daughter whose husband, a poacher, is suspected of the murder of a little cowherd. The Old 'Un appears to decide for these two that they shall commit suicide. They do. The mayor is next pushed to the centre of the stage, a man with a big, over-sensitive nose, who is smitten with remorse over his youthful excesses and spends his days frantically scrubbing himself to get rid of the smell of sin. He goes mad and later escapes to the presbytery in his pyjamas. He, the priest and the *châtelaine* all make extraordinary speeches at the funeral. The priest and the mayor are laughed at. The *châtelaine* so incenses the crowd by scratching the face of one of their number and allowing her mare to kick another in the chest that they fall upon her, overturn her carriage and beat her to death. All this takes place amid a fury of veiled accusations and anonymous letters.

Elements of the original mythology are still to be found lying about the book, and indeed the theme of this chapter becomes explicit and self-conscious at one point. 'Hatred of priests', says the author *in propria persona,* 'is one of the most profound human emotions, and among the least clearly understood. Doubtless it is as old as humanity. If the present age has contrived to raise it to an almost magic level of subtle efficacy, that is because the abasement or disappearance of other powers has made of the priest, apparently so closely related to the very structure of our society, a being more eccentric, harder to classify, than any of those magic greybeards whom the ancient world kept sequestered in temples, in close commerce only with the gods. To-day the priest is all the more strange and hard to classify, in that he will not admit that he is exceptional, nearly always himself the dupe of gross surface appearances, fooled by the ironic respect of some, the servile championship of others.' There are still other creatures prepared for sacrifice, even if it is only within the framework of the class-struggle. Of the *châtelaine,* just before her death at the hands of the crowd, we read, 'Probably they did not know they hated her. Or perhaps they saw, and yet could not recognise, in mysterious shape, their own abject state. And she, whose equals refused to meet her, suspected by everyone, was a kind of victim left by her class to the other to be devoured, a hostage forfeited in advance. Even so, the village still awaited that blunder which should really deliver her into their hands, some funny, catcall-provoking incident which would justify anything. The world of to-day is full of such mysterious hostages.' But the machinery by which the sacrificial process takes place has been shattered. There is no effective hostage.

The Pagan Empire is personified by Dr. Malépine, a smart rationalist full of psychiatrical jargon. The priest's accusation against him and against rationalists in general is that they have 'sealed up God's name in poor men's hearts'. 'In future,' says the priest, 'the poor will no longer have words to name what they lack.' The priest feels defeated by his parish, and his vision extends to the world. 'This village and many others like it. . . . Yes, when they break out in flames you may see all kinds of strange beasts emerging, whose names humanity forgot long ago, always supposing it ever gave them any'. And again, in less apocalyptical language, 'The moment will come when to preach hope, in a world organised for despair, will be tantamount to throwing a live coal into a powder-cask.' Monsieur Ouine, a teacher of resignation and modern languages, dies empty. He has achieved perfect balance, like a dead tree.

The myth is destroyed. Prospero's staff is broken and his books at the bottom of the sea. This marks the end of a remarkable cycle of novels and it may be the beginning of a new cycle. *The Open Mind* is disordered by something which looks like a breakdown of faith. It might have been a better novel if it had been held together more firmly by faith. At the same time, it might also have been a better novel if it had contained no faith, if it had been held together by despair, which a number of our contemporaries have shown to be an excellent medium.

Notes

1. Let us also be scrupulously fair and admit that Bernanos is sparing of his incense. Perhaps no other Catholic writer has so little of it blowing about his pages. Indeed, he rarely takes us inside a church at all. The candle-lit study, hall and passages of the presbytery are his favourite *mise en scène.* It is also as well to point out that the appeal of pornography is by no means a superficial one. The evil of pornography is like the evil of public oratory and lies in the fact that it appeals too directly and with insufficient control to the deepest instincts, and this is the level attacked also by mythology.

2. What other Catholic came so well out of the Spanish affair? Only Maritain. At the same time, it should be noted that there was a rough division by orders. Where Jesuit influence prevailed (and this appeared to include the rank and file of secular priests), Franco's disgusting crusade was taken at its face value. On the whole, and notably in this country, the Dominicans and those whom they directed were more judicious.

Hans Urs von Balthasar (essay date 1954)

SOURCE: Balthasar, Hans Urs von. "The Dream of the Imagination." In *Bernanos: An Ecclesial Existence,* translated by Erasmo Leiva-Merikakis, pp. 121-53. San Francisco: Ignatius Press, 1996.

[*In the following essay, taken from his book-length study of Bernanos originally published in German in 1954, Balthasar emphasizes the central importance of dreams and human imagination in the author's work, stating that, for him, dreams are the vehicles by which the poet and pious individual experience the connection between temporal and eternal existence, and achieve a proper awareness of the physical world as "mere appearance." The critic adds, however, that dreams in Bernanos's work can also be directed towards evil and a world where no "authentic communication" can take place because "the sinner has fallen in love narcissistically with his own closed-off microcosm."*]

The word *dream* is present everywhere in Bernanos. It appears both in the novels and in the critical writings. It covers such an enormous range of experience that it is almost too much for a single concept to encompass. If we seek in Bernanos for an *existential*, it is in the dream that it becomes tangible. Everything in Bernanos—both the best and the worst—is to be found under the sign of the dream. For this reason we may at first be inclined to dismiss as meaningless, or at least as illimitable, a concept that can mean so many things. This would be unjust. For even though in this case, as elsewhere in Bernanos, no philosophical theory may be elaborated on the relationship between existence and the power of the imagination, nevertheless the lines traced by his treatment of the dream, as they cross one another time and again, yield a clear pattern that constitutes the background before which the whole drama of this life and work is played out. As usual, what we must first do here is listen carefully to what Bernanos says and means, all the while trying to detect one first level of coherence by identifying various groups of motifs and different layers of signification. Nothing here must be forced; everything must be kept loose and interpreted as living signs: that is, we must not attempt to separate Bernanos' "abstract thought" from the concrete reality of his characters' and his own lived experience.

1. The Dream of Existence and Eternity

The basic and comprehensive meaning of "dream" in Bernanos may be construed from the prophetic form of reason, and therefore of existence, which we have discussed. To be human means to undergo the adventure of eternity, which has its decisive and central turning point in death. To be human, therefore, means both things at once: to understand oneself in one's uniqueness as a being oriented through death *toward* eternity (as a being who is *becoming* eternal) *and* to see and understand oneself nevertheless within temporality *from* the perspective of eternity (as a being who already, and continually, is becoming *eternal*). Consequently, our every situation, our every decision, and even our every real thought possesses a gleaming quality that reveals man's relatedness to the eternal or, even more, the very foundation of eternity. This confers on existence a perspectivism identical with the fact that man is spirit, and this perspectivism can always and necessarily be experienced and interpreted in two ways that run counter to each other. When man is conscious of himself as living within temporality, then the manner in which eternity dawns through all his acts must appear like the opening up of the depths of a dream, of a space of consciousness that looms into man's temporal reality with all the intensity of the memory of a physically experienced dream, or like the sensation of a dream image that is present but that the sleeper cannot draw up into the sphere of waking consciousness. "The average man", wrote Bernanos, "is by no means proud of his soul. The only thing he wants to do is deny it. He denies it with immense relief, as one wakes from a terrible dream."[1] Conversely, the sense of eternity's depth can acquire

such preponderance as the source of everything most real and significant in a person, it can so become the very basis of meaning and the locus of ideation, that, considered from this perspective, all the phenomena of temporality begin to be experienced as steeped in an unreality peculiar to themselves: as mere images in a dream.

We might at first be tempted to trace these motifs in Bernanos to some aspect of the Romantic and Idealist traditions, such as Albert Béguin has described in his book *L'Âme romantique et le rêve*.[2] But, despite a surface similarity, the core of the dream experience in Bernanos is something quite different, something more primal and without apparent derivation. We can already see this from the fact that there is nothing "Romantic" about Bernanos in the ordinary sense of the word, no trace of reverie or vague nostalgia. Everything about him has a manly clarity, hardness, and resolve. We would be more on track if for an instant we thought of some connection with Freud, not Freud the interpreter of dreams, but Freud the researcher into the depths of the soul. Bernanos is familiar with, and closely follows, this method of depth analysis; but he does not stop there. This, too, is for him the path to the expression of something deeper: the self-transcendence of the whole of existence into an eternity for or against God; and this depth of resolve, which reaches down to the very source of the underground waters of eternity, is what is present in a man's every act and state of consciousness.

The expression of such depths may be detected in the normal pattern of Bernanos' narrative technique: it is as if the most important decisions have already been made in advance; and the temporal course of events, which in fact results *from* a decision already made in eternity (although seeming to develop *toward* that decision), appears by comparison to be but the delayed rumble of a thunder whose lightning has rent the sky elsewhere. In **Under Satan's Sun** we read: "The marquis' glance hesitated for a second, surveyed him from head to foot, then suddenly hardened. The pale blue of his pupils turned green. At this moment Germaine could have read her destiny in them."[3] "Her disappointment was so strong, her disdain so immediate and decisive, that in reality the events that are to follow were, so to speak, already inscribed in her."[4] "Through her noisy despair she felt a vast silent joy emerging like a presentiment. . . . From that moment on, her impending destiny could be read in the depths of her insolent eyes."[5] "But the fatal sign was already written on the wall."[6]

Similar passages may be found in **Mouchette's New Story**: "The revolt beginning to snarl in her is a blind and mute demon. But does it deserve the name of revolt? Rather, it may be called the sudden feeling, shattering like a lightning bolt, that she is turning her back on the past, that she is venturing her first step, the decisive step toward her destiny".[7] The interior dimension becomes even more manifest in the episode of Mouchette's suicide: "The gesture of suicide really frightens only those who are never tempted in that direction, those who will surely never be tempted, because that black abyss welcomes only the predestined. The person who already possesses the will to murder ignores this for the time being and will realize it only at the last moment. The last glimmer of consciousness in a suicide, if he is not a madman, must consist of stupor—a frantic amazement."[8]

We must note that the term "predestined" does not here have its conventional theological meaning; rather, it denotes the condition of a soul that has long lived on and been nourished by a reality that is fully unveiled to the soul only at the very end. And yet, because this veiled mystery belongs to eternity, it cannot remain totally hidden from temporal consciousness, which apprehends it by means of a "presentiment" everywhere at work in Bernanos. Mouchette's father had, "for the first time, the presentiment of a near and inexplicable danger".[9] The Abbé Menou-Segrais is agitated by "the foreboding of a strange and inevitable event".[10] The country priest remarks: "A serene man would smile at my anguish. But, can one control a presentiment?"[11] Mainville feels he is "discerning . . . something like the shadow and presentiment of a misfortune",[12] and later he is again "seized by a kind of dark foreboding".[13] The motif recurs everywhere: "You can tell a mediocre person by this feature: generally, he is quite insensitive to the announcement of impending catastrophes, while the presentiment of a misfortune is for a strong soul a thousand times more anguishing than the misfortune itself. To have a presentiment is not the action of a mediocre man. . . . A certain degree of optimism is what, in imbeciles, provides the exact measure of their cowardice."[14]

At this crossroads we recognize the convergence of many of the main tracks of Bernanos' thought. Dying, for instance, means for him "going to the bottom" of things; dying constitutes the decisive act of self-recognition and of cognition as such. Then, too, there is the truth that one cannot be one's own spectator while living one's life but ought to be just that at the moment of dying. On the other hand, however, Bernanos insists that the anticipation of the death agony during life can be a man's—and certainly a writer's—highest organ of cognition. Finally, we see that, for Bernanos, the remembrance of youth is an inexhaustible source of dreams for existence, something that enables our fluid existence to remember its eternal origins.

But let us return to the subject of dreams.

We are now in a position to understand why, referring to a shallow philosophy of progress, Bernanos can say that it "risks slowly drying up in souls, along with the religious sense, the faculty of dreaming, which is the very source of hope".[15] And, concerning his hero Drumont, he comments: "How could he say everything? There is in him this power of dreaming that burdens the life of a man and overwhelms him with its immense weight, making the transition to the humblest and most ordinary act (like writing a letter, paying a visit, settling accounts) something extremely painful, cutting."[16] The ability to dream is here one and the same thing as the fundamental act of thinking, which is why thinking can precisely be described as a *machine à rêves,* a "dreaming machine".[17] The dreaming faculty is also one with the power of the imagination to create the horizons in which the individual images and concepts then find their place. As so often, it is in a letter to Jorge de Lima that Bernanos makes the most decisive statements concerning this subject:

> I write you today to thank you for your fine article on **Monsieur Ouine.** You put it in a marvelous category: that of oniric, or dream, literature. I would be so pleased if the first random critic didn't term it "surrealist". Nothing is more real or more objective than dreams. But there are many narrow-minded people who admit only Zola's brand of reality. How dumb the world is, so dumb it makes you cry, but you never forget it can be saved by infinite Mercy. Why can't they understand how logical things can become oniric, and logically, for instance in hypnosis and in novels? This is because nothing is as lucid as a dream. And is there anything more conscious than the intoxication of art? Ah, my dear Jorge! Life is full of imagination, and from it come the good images, like those of a luminous intelligence such as yours. From here I send you the warm greetings of an awakened sleeper.[18]

> ([*Lettres à Jorge de Lima*])

In the novel **A Crime,** the problem of the oniric imagination arises in the character of the genial little judge. This man sees the lines of convergence of fragmentary clues beginning to glimmer in his spirit's depths—his "subconscious"—focusing on an imaginary center that he cannot perceive consciously. In fact, this depth is the true depth of reality, of his authentic life:

> "Here, I have a question for you", he asks the inspector. "Do you dream?" "You ask if I dream?" "I mean: Do you now and then have dreams?—Not the kind of dream that is only a chaos of images, the kind that the sleeper himself can hardly believe in. I mean real dreams, the kind of dream that is so logical and believable that it seems to last beyond the time of sleeping. These are the dreams that have a place in our memory and belong to our past. . . . Yes, my dear fellow: . . . sometimes it happens that I doubt the reality of certain very recent facts simply because they match my . . . my dreams too well, which are nothing but plain dreams. I couldn't call them by any other name."[19]

> ([*Un Crime*] [*A Crime*])

But did this man not continue "in full light of day, with a creature of flesh and blood, the conversation he had begun the previous night with an imaginary character, a ghost—nothing"?[20] "'For three days now I haven't been able to recognize myself', the little judge admitted sadly. 'I dream awake: that's the word! It's a rather unusual state. . . . Suppose, my dear fellow, that an idea comes to me in a dream. All right, it happens to everyone. If I open my eyes, swish! . . . , the idea flies off. But then it clings there, somewhere, in some nook in my brain, like a bat clinging to the beams of the ceiling.'"[21]

By dreaming and giving free rein to his imagination, the judge comes within reaching distance of the unlikely solution that could never have been found through mere analysis. His work here resembles that of the writer, which we will later discuss expressly. Both judge and writer are for Bernanos exponents of a reason that is functioning correctly. The waking dreamer is aware of the fact that his whole temporal existence by no means corresponds to ultimate wakefulness; but he has neither the power nor the motive to perceive the oniric aspect of existence as an intolerable barrier, a glass house whose walls he must shatter at all costs. It is not at all the case that he is about to smother imprisoned in this dream world. His situation, rather, is that of a person who knows the way out and already possesses it in advance in his intimate depths: for such a person, as a result, both time and eternity reciprocally take on the character of a dream. (The same basic experience, parenthetically, may be found in Sartre's *Les Jeux sont faits,* only here the this-worldly and the other-worldly characterize one another and grind each other down dialectically, while in Bernanos the two distinct realities open up to the religious depths of existence.)

In the face of eternity, nothing earthly can claim to possess ultimate reality. To his friend Paulus Gordan, Bernanos writes: "The only precaution I recommend is not to take either me or my books too seriously, or my trials either: these may be great, but Providence allows me to see them as such only when they are past."[22] The course of life resembles the wavy line traced by dolphins in the sea. Their bodies half-emerge out of the water, only to dive back down at once. Our life proceeds from dream to dream: dream at the surface, dream in the depths, this-worldly dream and other-worldly dream. Dreams are the blossoming projection of the imagination, the experience that confers splendor and depth on the thinness of our existence. Thus, one of his characters finds "what is banal and inferior wrapped in the magic of a dream—of the one and only dream of a poor life that had never experienced anything of consequence except this one matter of conscience that was its undoing, this one and only doubt, this one and only magic spell!"[23] But, conversely, the miserliness of existence, which keeps it from developing into fullness, also belongs to the realm of dreams: "These mud-stained folk . . . go and come as in a dream, eking out the little that remains to them in their store of memo-

ries. . . . What a short step from this diminished life to death itself!"[24]

Within this twin-sighted expanse, the dream is at one with the consciousness of a living being. The more spirit a being possesses, the more it dreams. When viewed in Monsieur Ouine's distorting mirror, this truth can lead to the following reflections:

> "What do you expect, Madame Marchal?", said Philippe. "An imbecile shouldn't dream of becoming a musician or a poet. Monsieur Ouine says that death is always caused by a dream." . . .
>
> "Die of a dream? What are you babbling about there, Monsieur Philippe? You're only repeating words without understanding them."
>
> Philippe shrugged his shoulders and said: "If people didn't dream, . . . I suppose they'd live to be old, much older than usual. Maybe they'd live forever."
>
> "What about animals, Monsieur Philippe? Don't they also die?"
>
> "Animals dream in their own way. If we could read in their brain, we would surely see that they too desire what they don't have, and they don't exactly know what. This is what dreaming is."
>
> "So then Monsieur Ouine doesn't dream?"
>
> "Yes", said the child. "But he didn't allow himself to for a long time. I don't want anything, he used to say, nothing good and nothing bad. Nowadays he claims that he's opened up to dreams like an old rotten boat is open to the sea."[25]

This experience remains profoundly ambiguous and hence, in the end, indifferent, not in the sense of Idealist and æsthetic indifference, but in the sense that it is the matter of the decisive choice that will orient this final indeterminateness of existence either toward God or toward the world of pure dreams as ultimate goal. In the latter case, we would arrive at the essence of evil, the "evil dream". The heroine of **A Crime** gives us a precise indication of when the threshold has been crossed: "Who could carry us farther away and more reliably than our dreams? . . . dreams into which none but ourselves ever enters. . . . But only few people know how to dream. To dream is to lie to oneself, and in order to lie to oneself one must first learn how to lie to everyone."[26] And she addresses these final deceitful words to the boy she has already deceived: "The world is full of people who don't conceal anything because they have nothing to hide. They are nothing. . . . But you kept silent. And yet silence itself would not for long have been for you an effective protection. The moment would have come when you'd have had to wear a mask, or, rather, masks, an infinity of masks, one mask for every day of your life."[27]

When we interpret existence, thought, and the spirit itself on the basis of the imagination, then we risk the very strong and almost unavoidable temptation of seeing life as a lie, of embracing life by embracing it as a lie that one seeks and loves for its own sake. As we shall see, Bernanos interpreted the essence of evil in this sense; but by no means did he view existence itself as a necessary lie simply because it rests on the imagination: on the contrary, Bernanos vigorously opposed any attempt at a demonic systematization of existence. At its root, the imagination remains indifferent; it can be elevated to the highest level of art and religion, or it can be put to the worst and lowest uses. There exists a "fatal hour when the imagination, which is at once powerful and childlike, accelerates its rhythm and begins to poison thought instead of making it fruitful".[28]

For the moment, let us leave the phenomenon of the imagination with these considerations of its lack of differentiation, which also connotes its limitlessness. In the next chapters we will see how certain realities emerge with ever more dominance to impose bounds and limits *from the outside* on the oniric nature of the present life. For, in and of itself, life does not feel any such limitations. For now let us just say that the definitive *interior* limit of life's character as dream is death, which Bernanos describes magnificently as the "liberation of the truth caught within it": "And if I could die for the truth, then I would be freeing myself along with it, and I could escape with the truth into *the Light without dreams*."[29] And, while God is being described with this phrase, we must not forget the complementary truth: that hell is the end of the "evil dream" whose internal logic is progressive self-destruction leading, precisely, to hell as natural extremity. The final description of Mouchette is that she is "defeated, hurled out of her dream, . . . stripped of everything, even of her dream";[30] and Ouine portrays in sinister fashion the self-destruction of the evil dream: "What could you possibly need my secrets for? . . . Their complexity now appears to me as vacuous as the complexity of dreams. Is it even secrets we're still dealing with here? I would like to be able to hate them, but I neither hate them nor love them. Without my knowing it, their malice has slowly given out. They are like those wines that are too old, without taste, of a pale pink, which before dying have eaten through the cork of the stopper and even gnawed at the bottle's glass sides."[31]

2. THE POET'S DREAM AND REALITY

Bernanos always viewed his poetic vision under the image of the dream. It is in the image of the dream that the poet[32] himself may find the characteristics of a reality that emerges creatively out of nothingness, with all the proximity and concreteness of what has been experienced: only in the dream is there access to such a reality. And, if the writer succeeds in casting such an experience in adequate form, then the access to it is extended to all those who are gifted with the same capacity to dream. Proper to the work of art is an interior

space of immediate and tremendous truth, a sphere that has no continuity with the flatness of everyday truth; but the poet must pay for the existence of this truth with his very substance. Thus, Bernanos says in connection with Drumont: "He grew old too late and too abruptly, all of a sudden, following the example of so many heroes, or, to speak his own language, of so many *vocati*, those 'called' souls and *sacrificial beings, born and matured in their dream, who draw a vision of the world out of themselves, out of themselves alone, from their own interior life.* It may be that this vision is mistaken in more than one point; but it has such astounding verisimilitude that it confounds the analysts and the prudent, making them for a moment lose all trust in their numbers and statistics."[33]

For Bernanos, the event of literary creation is something inextricably bound up with the total history of the writer's existence. His work is the *anamnesis* and the creative provocation (in the literal sense of "calling forth") of what in him is closest to eternity, to God, of what in him is most intimately nestled in the kingdom of purity: in a word, his work is the memory of his *childhood*. The child knows everything. For the forgetfulness and sense of loss of the later years—beginning with all that is buried under and overshadowed in our maturity—the child remains the inexhaustible dream source: it is the child in the poet who produces all the true and real figures that are born from the poet's soul and that vie in reality with any living person.

What Bernanos says in this connection is unfalteringly precise, both as theory and as personal confession. Let us listen to him: "As for my books, what's good about them comes from far off, from my youth, from my childhood, from the deep wellsprings of my childhood."[34] "Childhood is always magical."[35] When the lady of a manor near Fressins believed she recognized in the figure of the count in *The Diary of a Country Priest* the very image of her father and wrote her objections to Bernanos, he replied with a confession that lays open the sources of his creative activity:

I began *The Diary* one evening last winter, having absolutely no idea where I was going with it. How many novels have I begun in this way, which never got past page twenty because they weren't taking me anywhere! No matter! As soon as I take pen in hand, what at once begins emerging before me is my childhood, a very ordinary childhood like all the others; and yet, it is from it that I draw everything I write as from an *inexhaustible fountain of dreams*: the faces and landscapes of my childhood, all mixed up, confused, shuffled helter-skelter by this peculiar unconscious memory that makes me what I am—a novelist and, God willing, also a poet. You can understand this, can't you? . . . This is what happened with your father. . . . You're not wrong in assuming that, when I wrote down the name of Torcy, the memory of your father was present to me; but this memory is everywhere, often unbeknownst to me, in the first part of my book. . . . How can I help it? From a certain moment on, I'm not inventing anything: I simply retell what I am *seeing*. People I have loved pass before me on the screen, and I recognize them only a long time afterward when they have already stopped acting and speaking. Or it happens that I don't recognize them at all, because they've been transformed little by little, forming, in conjunction with others, part of an imaginary creation more real to me than any living person.[36]

And these real creations, all of them born from the poet's maternal soul, now inhabit the souls of thousands and thousands of others, and here too they are more real and more active than most so-called real living persons, for they are children of an authentic fruitfulness of the spirit. These real figures, moreover, are in solidarity with both the eternal weal and the woe of the poet who created them, for better or for worse. Michelangelo cannot reach his eternal bliss without his Adam and his Lorenzo de' Medici, any more than Bernanos without his children, who are the imperishable reality he succeeded in creating, because they arose from that source of eternity in him that was a childhood intimately bound to God:

> Unknown companions, dear old brothers: one day we'll arrive together at the gates of the Kingdom of God. You are indeed a weary band, a harassed band. You are white with the dust of the roads. Dear hardened face, I've not been able to wipe off your sweat! Your eyes have seen both good and evil; they have fulfilled their task, they have braved both life and death: they have never surrendered their vision! When we meet again, old brothers, I will find you just so: just as I dreamed of you in my childhood. For it was to meet you that I had set out—I was running toward you. At the first turn in the road I would have seen the glowing red flames of your eternal watchfires. My childhood belonged only to you. And on one certain day, a day known to me, I was perhaps worthy to become the head of your unyielding band. May God not will that I should ever again see the roads where I lost trace of you, at the hour when adolescence lengthens its shadows, when the juices of death come to flow into the heart's blood and course all through our veins! Roads of the Artois country, at the very end of autumn; roads wild and pungent like beasts, roads rotting in the November rain, clouds galloping like horses, rumblings in the heavens, dead waters. . . . I would arrive home, push the iron gate, and bring my boots reddened by the storm close to the fire. Dawn came well before my fictional characters—still barely formed, memberless embryos—returned to their haunts deep in the silence of my soul: Mouchette and Donissan, Cénabre, Chantal, and you, the only one of my creations whose face at times I thought I clearly saw, you, to whom I did not dare to give a name—beloved curé of an imaginary Ambricourt. Were you then my masters? Could you possibly be such even today? Ah, I know well how vain such a return to the past is. My life is indeed already full of the dead. But the deadest of the dead is the little boy I once was. Still, when the hour comes, it is he who once again will take his place at the head of

my life; it is he who will gather up the years of my poor life, down to the last one. And, like a young commander rallying his disorderly troop of veterans, it is he who will be the first to enter the House of the Father.[37]

> ([*Les Grands cimetières sous la lune*] [*The Great Cemeteries under the moon*])

We know with what incredible effort and slowness Bernanos worked, with how alert a reason, how unflagging a devotion: the best image would be that of a sweating peasant. And, one more thing, he worked in continual despair: "Do whatever I may, I shall never, never turn my wretched person to better advantage or bring in a greater harvest. Such a thing, alas, is easy only in dreams."[38] This great appeal to childhood as a source of dreams by no means implies a feeling of distance from the earth but rather an almost superhuman obligation. Thus it is with total seriousness that, while expressing his heartfelt gratitude to a critic he admires, Claude E. Magny, Bernanos says of himself: "I am a novelist, that is, a man who lives his dreams, or relives them without knowing it. Therefore, I may be said to have no 'intentions', in the sense normally given this word. But you make me better understand this world in which at one time I pushed forward, from page to page, in the darkness, guided by an instinct similar in kind, perhaps, to the sense of orientation birds have."[39] Vallery-Radot is right when he states: "Bernanos did not create literature. What he did as he wrote was truly to give his soul, his flesh, and his blood, because all of his heroes—both the worst and the best—are his very own ghosts that he bears within him."[40] It would here, then, be appropriate to see a distant analogy to the Eucharist within the human realm: for it is not in vain that the image of the pelican may be applied both to Christ and to the writer. Julien Green's assertion that the writer's attitude toward his characters is like God the Father's toward his creatures once again casts light on the impenetrable mystery of Christian literature: for the soul of the poet must be pure indeed in order to give birth to unclean creatures and follow them intimately on their dark paths without itself becoming impure but rather helping to redeem the foulness of the prodigal son by its own purity.

This is where we see the barrier emerge that flings the writer back from the dream of God-likeness (so fondly dreamed by Claudel: the poet as vicar of the Logos!) and into the ambiguities of the æsthetic dream. For the poet does more than simply deplete his own life by pouring it into the phantoms in his books. (And, parenthetically, will he truly be able to make his marionettes intercede for him when his turn comes to render an account before the one who is the only real Creator?) No: he will have to ask himself seriously, perhaps with fear and trembling, whether he has not denied his fellow-men the real substance of his Christian love by the sheer force of bestowing it upon his dreams. Indeed, he will have to ascertain whether, in his conspiracy with the sinners and criminals he has invented, he has not already trespassed the allowable limits and, in a manner more pregnant with consequences than he realizes, scattered in the world an evil seed whose rank growth he can no longer contain. On this matter we must be clear that what is involved is not the Romantic problematic of the golem or the demonic visions of an E. T. A. Hoffmann: our concern, rather, is with the sober Christian realization that the creation of literature is an activity within the realm of existence for which an account must be given.

In this connection we reflect on the figure of the old Ganse in *An Evil Dream,* a writer in the mold of Balzac or Zola, prolific as a nature goddess, who with unscrupulous sensuality has squandered his life by pouring it into his work. Now in his old age his imagination is running dry, and he is at a loss as to where to turn. His dreams continue to proliferate uncontrollably like a sputtering motor running on empty; but his interior life is devastated, since he has allowed all of his human substance to pass over into the universe he has created. He would perhaps be willing to grant himself some peace in order to buy time

> if it weren't that, by an atrocious irony, his overheated imagination could not stop multiplying to the point of absurdity, as in a nightmare, these unfinished creatures mingled with tatters of stories. The swarming of these creatures in his brain gave the wretched man the illusion, ceaselessly reborn, of the creative power he had lost. Thus it is that he began ten different novels, hellbent on finding his way—his way out. . . . But, as he felt this interior solitude expanding about him—the solitude that is the damnation of the depleted artist—he clung with all his strength, like a shipwrecked man, to the collaborator he had long grown used to. Her mere presence evoked at once his real life and his dreamed-of life.[41]

Precisely this "collaborator", however, Simone Alfieri, about whom Ganse has begun a new book that is to fuse reality and dream definitively, happens to be the heroine of *An Evil Dream,* the double murderess who commits her crimes simply by following the internal logic of evil. She is the imagination of the old Ganse become reality; she is his golem, "his likeness", and "his mirror",[42] the living proof that the writer's dreams have an enormously dangerous resonance in the realm of reality.

Years before, Bernanos had already wrestled with this theme in the eerie novella *Madame Dargent.* It is significant enough that with his very first opus, produced in 1922, the novelist is already treading the terrain of great literature. The wife of a famous writer is on her deathbed, but she cannot die because in her death the whole of her life is becoming present, visible to her like an exact reflection in the water. She had loved her husband. As for him, however, after loving her for a brief while, he had again turned to the characters in his novels, nourishing their intensity by all kinds of flirtatious and parallel affairs. What could the poor woman do to enter into the locked dream-world of the man she loved? She transformed herself into his characters. "I am yourself, do you hear me?—*yourself!* . . . What you have dreamed of, I have lived. . . . My portion in life, what I have been, is all those women you have dreamed up, dearer to you than the living! Madame Guebla, Monique, Mademoiselle de Sergy, old Gambier's granddaughter, the heroines of your plays and novels. . . . I had indeed read your books! How I pursued all these women in your books! With what famished curiosity! Despite all your talent, you had only given them a dubious existence, a slight, intangible form. But I gave them something better: a body, real muscles, a will, an arm." In her delirious dream she slowly begins revealing what all of this means: she has killed the boy whom her husband had ostensibly adopted but who in fact was the child of a mistress; and she has also killed this woman. When, in his unbelief, the novelist demands proof of her deeds, she hurls at his feet the pearl necklace he had seen his mistress wearing a hundred times. In death the horrible truth is revealed, the truth of an illustrious writer's existence: "Take your share of my burden!", the dying woman cries out. "A secret, *this secret,* is what's holding me back in life! I must tell it, must confess it, must scream it out. I must expel it from me, must void myself of it!" He then strangles her, to reduce to silence something too terrible. But the last sentence of the novella gives us only a tentative sum-up: "But who knows? More than one murderous image that the writer has rid himself of still stirs in a book ten centuries afterwards."[43] Here the act of literary creation stands in close proximity to adultery: the woman is merely giving external fulfillment to the internal consequences of her husband's deeds. And such proximity borders on the demonic region of the æsthetic, as defined by Kierkegaard.

The novella *Madame Dargent* is the best commentary on *An Evil Dream.* Aside from the oniric character of sin, to be examined later, we may say that the latter book centers at once on the psychological situation of detachment already mentioned by Bernanos: that is, the way a writer's figures acquire a living autonomy by becoming detached from the soul of their creator. There are certain "turning points in a book" where the author "no longer feels he is master of the characters he has slowly seen forming under his eyes. He remains simply a spectator of a drama whose meaning has just suddenly escaped him."[44] And yet he remains responsible for this meaning: after all, it is he who has started the characters off on the way they now must follow to the end with total consistency, without bothering to consult him. Ganse's collaborator is full of his creatures; she is "choking on them": "Yes, I am really smothering. If I take much longer in becoming myself again, I'll never be able to do it. After all, imperfect as these creatures may be, they belong to you, they are something that came from you. Don't deny it: they give you a little comfort in spite of everything. . . . They live in me: they just move in, they multiply in me without difficulty—go ahead, laugh! And I don't have any hope, not the least hope—what am I saying? not the tiniest bit of hope!—of drawing them out of myself to take my turn in unloading them into a novel."[45]

Involved here is a nonphysical, perverted act of procreation that renders the real act of love impossible ("you have killed my taste for love", Simone says at one point to Ganse)[46] but that nonetheless produces a real birth in the world: "I will soon bring you the solution [*dénouement*] you've been searching for for six months", Simone reassures Ganse.[47] What is meant is the murder she is pondering: "This scares you a little, doesn't it? Come on, admit it! I look like I've come out of one of your machines! Here you are suddenly having a conversation with one of your characters, and you have no way of making her get back into your outline for the book. There she is, walking off by herself!"[48] No one but Ganse leads her to commit the murder.[49]

It is true, to be sure, that both the novel and the novella operate within a world from which faith is absent. And it could be that the step into reality, taken by a believing writer who has truly surrendered to God, would lead in the exactly opposite direction. Was it not, after all, for the sake of the saints that Bernanos lived and wrote? And did these saints not emerge with radiant freshness from his imagination? While writing *Joy* he confesses: "I am living with two delightful saints [Chantal de Clergerie and the Abbé Chevance], two real saints I invent as I go along. Everything is so luminous that I can think of nothing else, and my heart is enthralled."[50] And he can extricate these true dreams from the tangle of illusions and mirages of false dreams:

As far back in my past as I can go, I can't remember having had many illusions. An illusion is a cheap dream, a rag-doll dream, the kind of dream that too often is grafted onto a precocious experience, the dream of the future accountants of this world. Yes, I too have had my dreams; but I more than knew they were dreams. An illusion is a stillborn dream, a midget dream, to scale with a child's size. But I would have nothing but wildly unbounded dreams—otherwise, what's the good of dreaming? And this is precisely why they didn't disappoint me. If I were to live again, I'd try my best to have even bigger ones, because life is infinitely greater and more beautiful than I had imagined, even in dreams, and I am smaller. I have dreamed of saints and heroes, skipping all the intervening forms of our species, and now I realize that these intervening forms barely exist and that only the saints and the heroes count. The intervening forms are like bland porridge, a real potpourri: take a sampling from anywhere

at random and you'll know what all of it tastes like. And such a gelatinous mass wouldn't even deserve a name if the saints and the heroes didn't give it one, didn't give it their own name, which is Man. In short, it's by virtue of the saints and the heroes that I am: it's they who from my earliest days sated me with dreams and kept me from illusions. . . . Everyone pressured me to become a practical young man, otherwise I would starve to death. But in actuality it's my dreams that nourish me. Bigots, military men, and grownups in general have been absolutely useless to me. I've had to find other patron saints, like Donissan, Menou-Segrais, Chantal, Chevance. It's from the hand of these, my heroes, that I eat my daily bread.[51]

([*Les Enfants humiliés*] [*The Humiliated Children*])

Who could question this proud and childlike confession on Bernanos' part or doubt that he did indeed nourish his dream figures with his heart's blood? Once again, only he himself is here entitled to draw the boundaries, to set up the marker pointing to the danger that can lurk in the dream of sanctity, the danger Bernanos held before himself as a warning in the unmistakable form of his frightful Abbé *Cénabre*, the unbelieving and, indeed, possessed priest who was an analyst of mystical states. Writing about saints is his vocation and his passion. But one sentence of *The Imposture* reveals his whole evil secret all at once: "This author's art, or, rather, his happy formula, when plumbed to the bottom, may be defined as follows: to write about sanctity as if charity did not exist."[52] In this case, everything becomes counterfeit, because "the only sure means of knowing is to love."[53] We must listen to the devastating analysis that Bernanos makes of Cénabre's literary activity. Here, he is obviously pillorying the methods of that mystic *cum littérateur*, Henri Bremond; but it is also certain that, in so doing, he is far from forgetting himself:

It's not possible to read him without a feeling of discomfort; but only one of these very saints he has mutilated could wrest his secret from him. . . . No matter how simple and soothing, how enveloping and insistent his art always was, they always refused themselves to its wiles. Just the preface of his last book is fifty pages long, and these are full of prudent silences, reservations, and veiled hints, as if the poor man, in his fear, were backing away as much as possible, to avoid the inevitable confrontation. For, as soon as the rebellious witness appears, the careful balance is broken. . . . The pages multiply, and the book drags on interminably, like a cruel dream punctuated with starts. And all of a sudden the author . . . wakes up, abruptly losing his composure, and plunges again into the dispute with a kind of rage. This makes the reader feel uneasiness mingled with astonishment. From where this sudden anger? What happens is that, when violence is inflicted on the truth, a frightful irony rises through the lying words much as the stench gives away the presence of a corpse. For all others, this irony is imperceptible; but the arrogance of the Abbé Cénabre cannot fail to know its bite. Anxious to flee from himself, and in addition smitten with his imaginary characters, whom he substitutes almost unconsciously for the real ones and whom he strains to regard as the real ones, Cénabre finds himself, alas, always only himself, at the end of his crooked road. What his saints lack is precisely what has justly been refused to him. His every effort to conceal this only reveals his own deficiencies a little better. What can we say . . . ? In order to give some consistency to his ghosts he has stripped himself of his treasure: the precious lies that would have camouflaged him as they have camouflaged so many others to the end. . . . He sees himself naked.[54]

Precisely this realization that his heroes and saints have torn off all his soul's clothing is what provides the transition to Cénabre's discovery of the fact that he no longer believes and to his act of opening up to the evil spirit.

The writer's great danger, from which his profession always separates him only by a hair's breadth, is *the vice of vices*, the essence of original sin, which is also the cause for the downfall of Cénabre, Ganse, and Ouine—the sin of Eve in paradise and of all her guilty children: *curiosity,* or, expressed in a more theological way, knowledge without love, the kind of knowledge that is not paid and vouched for with one's existence and suffering, the forced anticipation of the vision God wants to bestow through grace but into which impatient man bites as he bit into the forbidden apple. We know that everything in Bernanos is oriented toward vision: the vision of God's hidden mysteries, the vision of concealed sanctity, the vision of souls as they are before God, and also the vision of evil and hell exactly as they are in the eyes of the Redeemer. For this very reason the sin against such vision can be portrayed by Bernanos only in all its immeasurable enormity. But how close this sin of curiosity is to the literary creative act! We read the following concerning Cénabre:

> The only truly fertile joys he ever derived from belief were precisely those of a curiosity wholly focused on the problem of this supernatural life, whose reality he would never dream of denying today any more than in the past. Indeed, at present [in the last years of his possession], no less than in the past, he was exasperated by the crudeness and inherent poverty of the theses of rationalism, of the ridiculous and pretentious daydreaming of psycho-physiology, or, still worse, of the school of psychiatry in fashion. The only problem that interested him, then, had already been stated and would always remain so.[55]

Thus, although he had in the meantime become an unbeliever, he continued to lead "this secret, impenetrable life, in which his strange genius had spent itself animating the characters born of his dream—his holy men and women."[56]

The same occurs with Ganse and his collaborator, who lives the evil dream to the end, a dream out of which curiosity precipitates like a quintessence: "She could barely remember the chain of circumstances—interconnected among themselves by the delirious logic of a dream—that had brought her to that point or for what purpose she had come there. The only sensation that subsisted in the midst of this terrible swooning of her soul was the kind of professional curiosity she had learned in the school of old Ganse",[57] "that pinch of curiosity, of impatience, which she knew so well and which she had felt every time at decisive moments".[58]

Monsieur Ouine, finally, is the work in which the theme of the *identity of curiosity and damnation* is developed to its conclusion. And if the figure of André Gide stands at the source of the character of Ouine, it is precisely because, for Bernanos, Gide represents the archetype of the curious man: "The only virtue of this great man is a curiosity that is so greedy, so cruel even, that it seems to be a form of lust."[59] Ouine calls curiosity "the most powerful instrument of dissolution", and he carries it "to the point of hatred".[60] The greedy curiosity of Ouine and Cénabre (and both are here but mouthpieces of Bernanos) extended only to the hidden world of the spiritual. The dying Ouine says: "Curiosity is eating me up. It digs up and gnaws away at the little left me. Such is my hunger. Why wasn't I curious about *things*? My hunger has been only for souls. But why am I saying 'hunger'? I've lusted after them with another desire that doesn't deserve the name of hunger. . . . With what jubilation I've entered these modest consciences, so little different from one another in appearance, so common, like little brick houses without luster, blackened by habit, by prejudice, by stupidity. . . . They would all of a sudden surrender their secret to me, but I didn't hurry to take it."[61]

Curiosity is the great danger Bernanos always keeps in front of his eyes so as not to succumb to it: "Thanks to God, I think I have never really felt that low form of congeniality called curiosity. The great calamity—among many others—of those unfortunates who received from Providence a critical spirit like a bunch of thorns in the heart is their condition of being curious by necessity, or, if I may be so bold, by vocation."[62] Bernanos, then, knew exactly what he was doing when he distinguished between dream and illusion. Without having explicitly named it, he was evidently aware of the fact that *the dream is delimited* by a higher reality, and this fact keeps us from concluding that saints and heroes are nothing but protuberances of the writer's dreaming soul, intensified versions of his own self, mirror images of himself, whose truth lies only in the psychological substance of dreams. A disdainful guffaw was his consistent reaction to such "ridiculous and pretentious daydreaming on the part of psychophysiology and psychiatry", burdened as they are with the "thorns of the critical spirit". Nothing is more real than *the saint* who, in his quality as saint, breaks out beyond literature's dream sphere: he is the "rebellious witness" against Cénabre's attempt at æstheticizing spirituality, so real that he strips the æsthete mercilessly of all his dreamy tinsel and leaves him standing there "naked".[63]

Even if every other vision of the world were based on the imagination, and in that sense had its origin in dreams, still there would exist *one* vision that would absolutely transcend this description and operate in a region above it: that is the vision or intuition the saint has into souls, the supernatural *charism of cardiognosis* (or "ability to read in men's hearts") normally possessed by both Bernanos' priests and his other saints. This is the unexpected and yet *logically derived absolute point that informs all of Bernanos' vision, even on the literary plane.* What is involved is, not æsthetic intuition as defined by Schelling (the identity of the ideal and the real), but the participation—conferred by grace and realized within the ecclesial community and for its benefit—in the truly real vision of invisible spiritual reality as God himself sees it. The nebulous dream zone, which is to say, the whole zone of man's relative faculty to think and imagine, is transcended, so that the saint soars beyond it to become immersed in the resplendent blue skies of visionary certainty. In the end, literary creation aspires only to be a humble and prayerful participation, paid for with suffering, in the saint's charism of reading into men's hearts. Bernanos knows what he is doing when he dares to grasp the moment when this inner eye opens in the spirit of a saint:

> Like the radiance of a hidden glimmer, like an inexhaustible source of brightness flowing through him, an unknown sensation, infinitely subtle and pure, without any admixture, was moving through him, little by little, toward the principle of life and as it went was transforming him in his very flesh. Just as a man dying of thirst opens up totally to the water's keen coolness, he did not know whether what had in some sense pierced him from side to side was pleasure or pain. Did he at that instant know the price of the gift that was being given him, or this gift itself? Through so many tragic struggles, in which his will seemed at times to waver, he still retained this power of sovereign lucidness throughout his life, and yet he was never clearly aware, no doubt, of the power he had. The reason is that nothing resembled less the human experience of slow investigation, going from observed fact to observed fact, with continual hesitations and almost always stopping midway—when human experience, that is, is not hoodwinked regarding the extent of its own cleverness. The Abbé Donissan's interior vision preceded every hypothesis and imposed itself by its own weight. But, once this sudden evidence had overwhelmed the spirit, the understanding already acquired could discover the reason for its certainty only very slowly, by way of a detour. The same is the case with a man who awakens before an unknown landscape he discovers suddenly in the dazzling noon light: even though his eyes have already taken in the whole horizon, he himself emerges only gradually from the depths of his dream.[64]

This text, of an admirable philosophical density and clarity, provides us with an unambiguous criterion: *Truth lies in the saint's way of seeing.* "Sanctity" here is to be understood, not only in a moral sense, but as an existentially lived ecclesial ministry that communicates the competence of judging together with Christ and also consequently, as a prerequisite to such judgment, the faculty of seeing souls just as they are. Nor are we speaking here of an exceptional and purely subjective privilege in which the community does not participate and in which it therefore has no interest; we are speaking, rather, of a function for the benefit of all. This becomes intelligible provided (as we will later show) we do not dichotomize between the institutional offices of the Church and the sanctity of the Church but rather see them as the two poles, in tension with one another, of one and the same archetypal sphere. The individual Christian existence of the average Catholic is subjected to the criterion of this vision of sanctity in a twofold manner. First, he is confronted with the criterion of sanctity in the sacramental and objective form that the Word of God also has in the Church: seen and judged by God's Word, a Catholic's existence is laid bare to its very foundation (cf. Heb 4:12-13). And, second, he is also confronted with the criterion of sanctity in the existential, subjective form of the holy person. This person, the saint, can walk through an average Catholic existence and polarize it—like a confused jumble of steel splinters—in the direction of the truth, a truth that such a Catholic could not otherwise have found. Such radical reorientation can become a terrible judgment, humanly speaking, and a seemingly excessive challenge for the Christian paralyzed with banality. These two poles of sanctity were brought close together by Bernanos already in *Under Satan's Sun* in order to emphasize the fact that they belong together: Donissan suffers in his official function as confessor, which puts him in a position of exercising his gift of clairvoyance in this office, as if the objective power of vision that every priest possesses by virtue of his office had only coincidentally become subjective as well in Donissan's case. From this perspective, sanctity is a reflection of the Church's infallibility becoming manifest within the sphere of experience.

Let us consider the passage in which the intensity of Donissan's interior vision is most powerful, the passage where we see Mouchette, the sinner, judged and consumed by Donissan's words during confession. He tells *her* her sins and describes exactly what he sees in her:

> What she was hearing was not a judge's verdict or anything that surpassed her understanding—that of a dark and wild little animal. No: what she was hearing (and told with a terrible sweetness) was her own story, the story of Mouchette, not at all dramatized by some theatrical director and enriched with strange and peculiar touches, but quite the contrary: her own story in summary, reduced to nothing, seen from the inside. That particular sin that is eating us up: how little substance it leaves our life with! What she saw being consumed in the fire of his words was . . . herself, and she could

conceal nothing from the pointed and sharp flame that penetrated into the last nook, into the last fiber of her flesh. In rhythm with the rising and falling of that formidable voice that resounded in the bowels of her being, she felt the heat of her own life increase or decrease. The voice was at first distinct, using everyday words, and her terror welcomed it like a friendly face in a frightening dream. Then the voice became more and more commingled with the interior testimony—the wrenching whisper of a conscience polluted at its own deep source—to such an extent that the two voices blended to form but a single lament, like a solitary gushing of crimson blood.[65]

The words spoken in sacramental confession are mightier than any conscience. They awaken to a salutary remorse the slumbering conscience entangled in its own lies, and they take it up into something greater than itself: the truth, which, in order to make free, must first capture with sovereign authority a conscience kicking and screaming with animal savagery: "The way I have seen you makes it impossible for you to escape me, despite all your cunning. . . . Out of yourself you have drawn only empty dreams, which always met with disappointment. . . . You think you're free? *That* you could only have been in God."[66] Mouchette will henceforth be unable to escape imprisonment by the Word. In the end it is a matter of indifference whether, in a paroxysm of fear, she attempts to commit all possible crimes and thus deliver herself to Satan's power, or she finally capitulates and accepts the Word of grace as one conquered by it. She is the creature marked by the Word, the woman who has had the Word's brand burned into her like a head of cattle: she has now become a possession of her Master. And this introduces the second aspect: the event of her being judged because a saint, in passing, has touched her life. For this, too, we have a text of unsurpassable lucidity:

> Certain simple men, who are born for some quiet work, are suddenly thrust by an extraordinary encounter into the heart of things, as by one single stroke of lightning that is quickly extinguished. They must then make a supreme effort: we see them apply themselves—to the last minute of their incomprehensible life—as they strive to recall and recapture the thing that never recurs, the thing that fulminated their back that one instant. This spectacle is so tragic and so profoundly bitter that the only comparable thing is the death of a little child. Vainly do they retrace their past step by step, memory by memory; vainly do they spell out their life, letter by letter. The reckoning is there before them, and yet the story no longer makes sense. They have become strangers, as it were, to their own adventure: they can no longer recognize themselves within it. The tragic element has pierced them from side to side, so as to kill someone else standing beside them. How could they remain insensitive to this injustice perpetrated by fate, to the evil-doing and stupidity of chance? Their greatest efforts will make no more progress than the shiver shaking an innocent and unarmed animal: *when they die they undergo a fate beyond their powers.* For, regardless of how far an average spirit may

reach—even if we allow that through symbols and appearances he may now and then have touched the real—still it cannot be that he has usurped the lot of the strong, which is not so much the knowledge of the real as it is the feeling of our incapacity to seize it and keep it whole: the ferocious irony of the true.[67]

We are here made privy to the lethal character of redemptive truth and to the reason why God seldom bestows it other than within the fire-proof containment of the sacraments: otherwise, men would perish in their dream world under the cataract of this light. Nevertheless, the imaginative Christian writer humbly ventures to make himself malleable to this truth and attempts to see souls with the eyes of the saint. He looks at the first Mouchette through the eyes of Donissan; and, on his own responsibility, he dares to look at the second Mouchette through these same eyes, although he no longer names them expressly. And, at bottom, it is the writer's humility that keeps him from assuming her visible redemption himself.

3. The Evil Dream and Sanctity

We have just seen, in the example of this episode involving Mouchette, how Bernanos can consider simultaneously, under the category of the dream, the most positive and the most negative reality: most positive is the act of literary creation, and most negative is the world of evil. According to Bernanos (and here we are tempted to think of Schopenhauer), the dream is all at once the exponent and the existential instance of this-worldliness as judged (that is, as exactly measured and adjusted) by real truth: the dream is the revelation of the world in all its character as mere appearance, a character of which man at times becomes conscious by way of a presentiment without, nevertheless, his being able to tear away the veil. The authentic poet dreams in the direction of the truth; but the Evil One, on the contrary, loves appearances for their own sake, and he weaves himself into the dream of evil as into a cocoon: he dreams in the direction of nothingness. Here the particular form of "dream logic" itself becomes symbolic: for here we can observe how the sinner yearns—secretly or openly—to abolish all the ontological laws dictated by a waking logic, as well as the dreamer's will to ensconce himself in the dream and displace the threshold of awakening. This is an essentially solitary world, since in the dream there can take place no authentic communication, and this too is pregnant with meaning: the sinner has fallen in love narcissistically with his own closed-off microcosm, or, better, his "microchaos"; and so, he populates the theater of the world solely with the chimeras of his own fantasy.

"Out of yourself you have drawn only empty dreams, which always met with disappointment."[68] This statement of Donissan to Mouchette should be writ large over Bernanos' trilogy of evil: *A Crime, An Evil Dream,* and *Monsieur Ouine,* for it defines precisely what the three books have in common.

In *A Crime* we witness the web spun by mendacity, loved and sought after for its own sake and accepted despite its inevitable end: "Yes, I have loved lies. I don't mean useful lies, that abject form of lying that is only a means of self-defense like any other, employed with regret and shame. . . . I have loved lying as such, and it has rewarded me handsomely. It has given me the only freedom I could enjoy without constraints, because, if the truth sets us free, still it places on our deliverance conditions that are too hard for my pride to accept, and lying imposes no conditions at all. There is one thing: in the end it kills you. It is killing me now."[69]

In *An Evil Dream,* Madame Alfieri, quite different from the Evangéline of *A Crime,*[70] has an even more conscious experience of the "delirious logic of dreaming"[71] and the "inexorable unfolding of nightmares":[72] these involve at once a painfully and obsessively exact process of calculating and a nonchalance and carelessness that define the enjoyment of the devious and the illogical for their own sake. Simone Alfieri finds her "satisfaction" in dreams, and Olivier, who tears this net of dreams, then becomes entangled in the web that sin continues to spin as Simone invites him to share her dreaming solitude.[73] For her, lying is "a marvelous evasion, a relaxation that always works, a rest, a forgetting", for "she was one of those—more numerous than we think—who love lying for its own sake, who employ lies with profound cleverness and insight, those also who truly value lying only when true and false mingle in it so intimately that they become one thing and come to have a life of their own, creating another life within ordinary life."[74] Along this path, however, Simone becomes the prey of the dreams that consume her, and, since this is precisely what she wants and strives for, in the end self-hatred is revealed as the source of all her motivations:

> The only hatred she had ever truly known, lived, and drunk to the dregs was hatred of herself. How clear it all was now! Why was she realizing it so late? She had hated herself since childhood, at first without knowing it, then with a sly and hypocritical ambition, the kind of frightful solicitude with which a poisoner surrounds the victim she one day intends to slay. . . . She had never forgiven herself, and would never forgive herself, for having failed where many other women succeeded who were worth much less than herself: but these others had known how to act, while she had only had dreams, without ever succeeding in controlling them. Her dreams had invaded her life, smothered her soul and will. Ever since the first awakening of adolescence, they were sucking up her energies, depleting her life's sap.[75]

This condition, of course, was a marvelous windfall for Lipotte, the psychoanalyst: "[We are dealing]", he says, "with a bad[76] dream of childhood long since forgotten,

forgotten for twenty, thirty, forty years, a dream that has made you suffer all along under twenty different names, and not one of these names is its true one."[77] And Simone admits: "Yes, by a hair's breadth I would have gone on in calm and blissful ignorance of my true self. . . . So many girls . . . are quite satisfied with little vices, with bad dreams that are chalked up to nerves—the same dreams that did the job at age thirteen and will continue to do the job until we die."[78] But then came her first marriage, her first murder, and, with it, the great lie. *An Evil Dream,* however, wants to go farther: it wants to capture, within the category of the dream, the feeling for life of a whole generation of modern youth, of all those young people who at base no longer love anything, least of all themselves, and who, with an uncanny indifference to both life and death, renounce existence willingly in the same way they had only just enjoyed it, with dissipation and boredom as starting points.[79]

In *Monsieur Ouine* both themes are carried to their conclusion: the analysis of sin and that of the *Zeitgeist* under the sign of unreality, and this both for the individual personalities (at whose center Ouine stands, but all others find their place in his constellation) and for the collective. In a manuscript passage omitted from the printed version of the book, we witness a burial service and requiem Mass at which the "dead parish"[80] unwillingly assists. It is a text in which this second aspect of the unreality of the collective receives particularly striking expression: "As the priest . . . took off his black chasuble and seemed to head for the pulpit (actually he went only as far as the communion rail), a muffled grumbling rose from the depths of the church. It was not so much a murmur of impatience as the kind of groan that escapes a sleeper buried in his dream."[81] Ouine gives the explanation for it, he who, in his "half-sleep, rich in dreams",[82] himself appears to be a material out of which all possible dream images may be formed: "The amazing thing is that you can imagine him in any situation whatsoever, true or false, ordinary or unusual, tragic, comic, or absurd: he lends himself to everything, he is matter for all possible dreams."[83] This is the same Ouine who, at the end of his dream adventure with souls, will have to call everything into question: "Have I really done what I have just said? . . . Or have I only desired it? Have I dreamed it?"[84] Even the extraordinary Jambe-de-Laine is a dreamer at bottom ("Does she dream?"),[85] and particularly Steeny, who is brother to the young men in *An Evil Dream,* entered with full consciousness into the world of sin as into a dreamable world obedient to the laws of dreams: "The world of laziness and dreams that had once submerged his weak forebear—the fabulous horizon, the lakes of oblivion, the magnificent voices—abruptly opened up for him, too, and he felt himself strong enough to live there among so many ghosts, glared at by their thousands of eyes, until he had to take the ultimate misstep: with us here, there is no chance of winning; the only thing you can do is fall. Monsieur Ouine himself will fall."[86]

The eloquent symbol for the dream character of the whole trilogy is homosexuality, a theme with an oblique, shadowy presence in all three novels: homosexuality as the perversion of love into self-love or lack of love, which amounts to the same thing, for a love-partner of the same sex is but a duplication and a mirror of the self. For Bernanos, sexual inversion is the efficacious sign or "sacrament" of sin and therefore the best means for making it visible. Moreover, the spiritual reality behind this sign is nothing other than unreality, nothingness itself: the attempt to displace the one and only reality instituted by God and usurp its place. Thus, the dream stands here, no longer for the projection of an idea by the soul, but rather for the evacuation of all meaning, the dilution of being, a vacuum, a distorting mirror, and the dissolution not only of a person's substance but, more comprehensively, even of the form in which this substance can express itself. There exists a (philosophical) idealism of godlessness that is the adequate expression for the loss of being through sin.

Bernanos underwent a certain evolution in his manner of portraying this "nothingness". He was convinced that evil cannot be portrayed from the outside, from a bystander's perspective, and that a certain internal experience is required for this that is not at all, in itself, necessarily evil: such an experience, in the last analysis, is based on Christ's own descent into temptation and hell. Bernanos, consequently, was always careful not to describe evil simplistically from the standpoint of the world of light and love, or hell from the standpoint of heaven. Thus, in his first attempt, Bernanos tried his hand at understanding the unreality of evil as a function of the underlying reality of Satan, and he interpreted all lies by reference to the ultimate "truth" of Satan, the "Father of Lies", whom he endeavored to bring into full evidence by making him emerge naked out of all his phantoms and disguises. By this procedure Bernanos accomplished one thing: by flying in the face of a shallow rationalism, he compelled the reader to acknowledge the reality of hell and its particular form of existence. In the soul of Mouchette, Satan was at first nothing but a "dream, . . . barely distinguishable from other dreams"; but he soon becomes an indisputable certainty, "real and living, companion and executioner, now lamenting and languishing—a fountain of tears; now insistent, brutal, eager to coerce; then again, at the decisive instant, cruel, devouring, all of him present in a painful and bitter burst of laughter, at first a servant but now the master."[87]

For Donissan himself, Satan becomes the reality to which all dreams have referred: "Alas, everything is no more than a dream, and the shadow of a dream!", the Evil One whispers to Donissan. "Everything was only a dream, except for your slow ascent toward the real world, your birth, your growing expansion. Raise yourself up toward my mouth, and listen to the word that contains all knowledge!"[88] We again see something similar in *The Imposture,* in which the image of the demon, present from the outset, emerges ever more clearly through the fog: Cénabre "already knew that this humiliating laughter [of his] was only the external manifestation of a certain and abundant reality, a concrete life, to which he had always wanted to remain a stranger. In his inability to deny the evidence, he was reduced to delaying its sudden, inevitable outburst."[89]

But already here, and increasingly so with every new novel, Bernanos became ever more conscious that he was portraying evil with means that were ultimately in contradiction to it: these means derived from an abundant life of the spirit, whereas what should have been shown was the death of the spirit, and from the harmonious coherence of the spirit, whereas what should have been conveyed was the dissolution of all logic. Is not the demonic, precisely, the breaking-off of all communication? The projection of the reality of the divine world of grace (which now lies behind, having become invisible) forward into the world of perdition and hell creates a univocal view of reality that is too naïve because purely imaginative, and as such it can no longer withstand the deeper logic of evil. Contrary to Bernanos' deeper intention, the appearance of Manichaeism in the early works necessarily emerged at the point where he wanted to portray *simultaneously* both the character of Satan's kingdom as dream (that is, its character as absolute, intrinsic appearance) *and* its univocal truth and reality as standing in ontological communion with the kingdom of grace. One of these terms had to cancel out the other; and, in fact, it was the second element—uncritical and purely imaginative—that questioned and finally displaced the first category, which is speculative and in itself by far the more important. This is why the first element henceforth disappears more and more behind the second element; but this does not occur as a retraction of the absoluteness and definitiveness of damnation but as a way of surpassing the first manner of portraying evil by driving it to its ultimate consequences. Only in the "trilogy" does evil become fully incarnate by being considered from within, and hell is no longer merely the buttress of "dreams" but the consummation of the spirit's disintegration.

But there then arises the *question about the reality from whose perspective dream can be judged as dream and, hence, confined to its unreality.* In *The Imposture* and in *Joy,* it is doubtless the saint who, in the midst of the phantasmal masquerade of the Evil One, constitutes the counterpole of reality. (This is dramatized in the central portion of *The Imposture* by the satyr-play on bourgeois Catholicism and in *Joy* by the devil's five marionettes.) What happens, however, when the saint himself disappears, either by being utterly reduced as a character (like the Curé de Fenouille) or by disappearing altogether (as in **An Evil Dream, A Crime,** and **Mouchette's New Story**)? Where can we then find a distancing standard of judgment? In this case, it can no longer be manifested directly; the world of perdition is indeed shut off from heaven; it acknowledges no criterion that can judge it; if such a thing were attempted, the demonic viewpoint would only laugh at it as a childish endeavor. There is no priest to reach into the night of the second Mouchette or into the suicidal world of Philippe and Olivier, and, even when Ouine does converse with his parish priest, not the slightest communion in the truth results. *At this point the writer himself assumes the role of the priest. As he walks with his shadowy heroes through Hades, he, Orpheus, is still very much alive.* And the steps he takes toward nothingness do measure out a real distance from it. When a Christian turns his back on heaven in order to walk with his brothers, he yet has a relationship with God even by way of his back! Donissan is the man who looks away from heaven in order to look toward hell: "As for me", he says, "ever since my childhood I have lived less hoping for the glory we will one day possess than sorrowing for the glory we have lost."[90] He has heavenly bliss behind him—like the Christ Child as he comes down from heaven and must turn his glance toward the Cross and hell, and like the Crucified himself, who creates the most expressive and (on earth) unsurpassable form of his relationship to his Father precisely out of his abandonment by God. In the final analysis, the reality by which the dream of evil must be measured is the Cross. The Crucified renounced heaven in order to be annihilated along with sinners; and, precisely for this reason, the Cross is the reality that measures and judges both nothingness and hell. No one can experience a deeper and more comprehensive abandonment by God than the eternal Son of the Father. The ever-deeper reality that shatters the dream of sin is not the imagined figure of Satan but the Cross, which has been fashioned in such a way that it reaches the very bottom of the abyss. Donissan himself knew this,[91] and Bernanos too, with the passing of time, had nothing else left to him. Sin has no depth—this he would come to see clearly at the end of his life—because it "makes us live at the surface of ourselves. We will again go back into ourselves only to die, and there is where he awaits us."[92]

Notes

1. *Liberté*, 232.
2. "The Romantic Soul and the Experience of Dreams", 1939.
3. *Soleil*, 13.
4. Ibid., 37.
5. Ibid., 41.
6. Ibid., 74.
7. *Mouchette*, 142-43.
8. Ibid., 220-21.
9. *Soleil*, 33.
10. Ibid., 100.
11. *Curé*, 163.
12. *Rêve*, 41-42.
13. Ibid., 124.
14. *Croix*, February 1943, 183.
15. *Peur*, 194.
16. Ibid., 126.
17. *Rêve*, 89.
18. *To Jorge de Lima*, November 15, 1943; *Lettres inédites*, 57.
19. *Crime*, 177-79.
20. Ibid., 188.
21. Ibid., 191-92.
22. *To Paulus Gordan*, in *Bul.* 5, 6.
23. *Soleil*, 274.
24. *To His Wife*, 1917 or 1918; *Erbarmen*, 30.
25. *Ouine*, 221-22.
26. *Crime*, 225.
27. Ibid., 224.
28. *Joie*, 173.
29. *Enfants*, 257. (The italics are von Balthasar's.—Trans.)
30. *Soleil*, 197.
31. *Ouine*, 236.
32. "Poet" and "poetic", here translating the German *Dichter* and *dichterisch*, are used in a general sense to refer to the creative writer. These words do not in this context refer to the writer of poetry as opposed to the writer of prose. In this sense, Bernanos is a "poet", which says a great deal more about him than the simple term "writer".—Trans.
33. *Peur*, 257. (The italics are von Balthasar's.—Trans.)
34. *To Paulus Gordan*, in *Bul.* 5, 6.
35. *To Assia Lassaigne*, November 3, 1945; *Bul.* 6, 11. In Bernanos, the word "magical" has a very pure resonance, connoting "full of enchantment".

36. *To Madame de La Noue,* 1935; *Bul.* 1, 5. (The italics are von Balthasar's.—TRANS.)

37. *Cimetières,* iv-v.

38. *To Vallery-Radot,* September 1933; *Bul.* 9, 2.

39. *To Claude E. Magny,* August 18, 1946; *Bul.* 4, 7.

40. *Souvenirs,* in *Bul.* 2-3, 28.

41. *Rêve,* 101-2.

42. Ibid., 62.

43. *Nouvelles,* 279-88.

44. *Rêve,* 233-34.

45. Ibid., 83.

46. Ibid., 84.

47. Ibid., 88.

48. Ibid., 91.

49. See ibid., 104.

50. *To Massis,* August 15, 1927; *C. du R.,* 44.

51. *Enfants,* 199-200.

52. *Imposture,* 29.

53. *Croix,* August 1940, 39.

54. *Imposture,* 30-31.

55. *Joie,* 297.

56. Ibid., 304.

57. *Rêve,* 233.

58. Ibid., 246.

59. *Croix,* February 1, 1945, 483.

60. *Ouine,* 146.

61. Ibid., 241 (corrected text).

62. *Sur la poésie: Préface pour les poèmes de Jorge de Lima* (Rio de Janeiro, 1939); in *Bul.* 15-16, 11-12.

63. *Imposture,* 30-31.

64. *Soleil,* 193.

65. Ibid., 203-4.

66. Ibid., 207.

67. Ibid., 275-76. (The italics are von Balthasar's.—TRANS.)

68. Ibid., 207.

69. *Crime,* 231.

70. In *A Crime,* the heroine was bound by an accursed love to Evangéline Souricet, grand-niece by marriage of the heroine's victim. It was to assure Evangéline her inheritance that the heroine killed. This heroine then became Simone Alfieri in *An Evil Dream,* and here she found another Evangéline, but in the form of a character in a novel. It is this woman, poorly imagined by Ganse, who becomes embodied in Simone and gives free rein to Simone's will to murder.—Note of the French trans.

71. *Rêve,* 233.

72. Ibid., 237.

73. Ibid., 160.

74. Ibid., 193.

75. Ibid., 243.

76. The text plays on the ambiguity of the French word *mauvais,* which in normal usage means "bad", but "evil" in the more precise moral and theological sense.—TRANS.

77. *Rêve,* 108.

78. Ibid., 81.

79. See ibid., 132; and "Notes et Variantes" of the critical edition, 283.

80. *Monsieur Ouine* was published in German under the title *Die tote Gemeinde. La Paroisse morte* (The dead parish) is apparently a title Bernanos himself also considered for this novel.—TRANS.

81. *Bul.* 11, 13.

82. *Ouine,* 18.

83. Ibid., 43.

84. Ibid., 242.

85. Ibid., 79.

86. Ibid., 21-22.

87. *Soleil,* 201.

88. Ibid., 271.

89. *Imposture,* 75.

90. *Soleil,* 238.

91. Ibid., 284-85.

92. *Agenda,* January 24, 1948; in *Bernanos,* 147.

Bibliographical References in the Footnotes

We here give the date of first publication, followed by the publisher and date of the edition referenced. Square brackets enclose the abbreviated title of the work.

Finally, we give the literal English translation of the works' titles as used in the present volume.

I. Works of Fiction and Hagiography

Madame Dargent (1922). Plon, 1955. [*Madame Dargent*]

————*Madame Dargent*

Sous le soleil de Satan (1926). Plon, 1926. [*Soleil*]

————*Under Satan's Sun*

L'Imposture (1927). Plon, 1929. [*Imposture*]

————*The Imposture*

La Joie (1928). Plon, 1929. [*Joie*]

————*Joy*

Un Crime (1935). Plon, 1935. [*Crime*]

————*A Crime*

Journal d'un curé de campagne (1936). Plon, 1936. [*Curé*]

————*Diary of a Country Priest*

Nouvelle Histoire de Mouchette (1937). Plon, 1937. [*Mouchette*]

————*Mouchette's New Story*

Nouvelles (containing *Dialogues d'ombres, Madame Dargent, Une Nuit*). (1955). Plon, 1955. [*Nouvelles*]

Monsieur Ouine (1943). Plon, 1946. [*Ouine*]

————*Monsieur Ouine*

Un Mauvais rêve (1959). Plon, 1950. [*Rêve*]

————*An Evil Dream*

II. Critical Works and Lectures

La Grande peur des bien-pensants (1931). Palatine, 1947. [*Peur*]

————*The Great Fear of the Right-Thinking*

Le Chemin de la Croix-des-Ames (1942-1945). Gallimard, 1948. [*Croix*]

————*The Way of the Cross-of-Souls*

Les Enfants humiliés (1949). Gallimard, 1949. [*Enfants*]

————*The Humiliated Children*

La Liberté, pourquoi faire? (1953). Gallimard, 1953. [*Liberté*]

————*What for, Freedom?*

III. Other References

Cahiers du Rhône. Seuil, 1949: *Georges Bernanos: Essais et témoignages.* [*C. du R.*]

Bernanos par lui-même. Seuil, 1954. Ed. by Albert Béguin. Col. "Ecrivains de toujours". [*Bernanos*]

Bulletin trimestriel de la Société des Amis de Georges Bernanos. Starting in December 1949. [*Bul.*]

Georges Bernanos. *Das sanfte Erbarmen: Briefe des Dichters.* Intro. by A. Béguin; selected and trans. by Hans Urs von Balthasar. Einsiedeln: Johannes Verlag, 1951. [*Erbarmen*]

Georges Bernanos, *Lettres à Jorge de Lima.* Privately printed. Rio de Janeiro, 1953.

Thomas Molnar (essay date 1960)

SOURCE: Molnar, Thomas. "'A Touchstone of Christianity'." In *Bernanos: His Political Thought and Prophecy*, pp. 173-202. New York: Sheed and Ward, 1960.

[*In the following essay, Molnar summarizes Bernanos's Christian vision of the modern world, conveyed in both his fiction and prose writings, which regards the modern state, whether totalitarian, socialist, or democratic, as a soulless collective force that has usurped the individual's freedom and circumvented his or her unique relation to God, and which ultimately must be saved by the heroic efforts of the "saboteur" saint.*]

In a letter to Dom Besse, in 1919, Bernanos had noted: "Writing, for me, is the condition of my moral life." Whoever is willing to penetrate his world, the inner climate of his novels and of his polemical writings, must be struck by the incredible moral and spiritual tension which is the rule there and which reveals the truth of his statement. But moral life is not merely an individual affair: it must have the human universe as the atmosphere in which it is immersed, with which it creatively communicates. Bernanos labored passionately to sustain the moral condition of the world, and this labor he considered a challenge for each man.

We would not understand anything of his career as a writer if we ignored this capital point. Bernanos was not a pale intellectual, content to register events and distill from them some far-fetched conclusions, but a man bodily and spiritually living in this world, identifying himself *absolutely* with its condition, *viscerally* reacting to its progression, to the risks and dangers it runs, to the signs of its cure and redemption. Bernanos, like the curé of Ambricourt, *divines* the world and people in it, he knows them with the artist's intuition, but even more with a certain supernatural knowledge which penetrates swiftly—arrow-like—and comes to grips with the essential.

Such a view of the world is only given to those who are supernaturally interested in it, that is, in its salvation. If Bernanos' views are often baffling and seem frequently irrelevant—"he does not conclude" was people's verdict at his post-war lectures—it is because he does not appear in the guise of an expert: historian, sociologist, politician—not even in the garb of a philosopher. Rather, he is one of us—and I do not mean an "average man"—he probes our condition from within, follows the inner wayfarer in his peregrination, sometimes verbose, sometimes losing the main thread of the dialogue he conducts, but always relevant about the one palpitating subject: man as he is underneath systems, interests, slogans, poses.

The proof of the tremendous seriousness with which Bernanos looked at the world is that he knew the most atrocious of temptations that can assail a Christian. "The demon of my heart often asks—'what is the use?'" he remarked in **Les Grands Cimetières** [**Les Grands Cimetières sous la lune**], and Professor Lima tells me that in their last conversation in Brazil, Bernanos echoed these words again, affirming that all hope for saving modern man must be given up. This was not to be his last word, and the abbé Pézeril was in his right to call him, in a magnificent funeral oration, "a touchstone of Christianity," *a man of hope.* Bernanos himself was careful to distinguish between hope and optimism, indicating that the former is a virtue, "a basic determination of the soul," while optimism is "false hope, for the use of cowards and imbeciles."[1] In a most telling phrase, he defined the highest form of hope as "despair overcome" (*désespoir surmonté*), putting thus into a formula the profoundest secret of his heart.

This is to say that he considered the world and its spiritual condition vital, so vital, in fact, that he was tempted—this is the meaning of his quoted words—to give himself up in despair over its disease. The Christian, it is true, lives *beyond* this world, in the expectation of another; but his hope must find an object here on earth too, otherwise his faith becomes formalistic, selfish and distorted. Who can know the inner combat in which Bernanos engaged his demon?

THE MACHINE PARADISE

When he returned from Brazil and established himself in France, it was with an enlarged sphere of interest and horizon that Bernanos set to work. His central preoccupations had remained the same: the saint among dry souls, the human person among robots, the victims surrounded by exploiters of all kinds. But new themes were now embroidered on the original fabric: the problem of man's freedom on an increasingly mechanized and organized planet, the struggle of the inner man against the reflexes imposed on him by technology, the fundamental paganism of the modern State.

If France had formed the exclusive frame of reference of Bernanos' writings before the war, his newly made acquaintance with another continent and civilization prompted him, after 1945, to focus his interest on global developments. Indeed, in comparison to the interlocking ties of the whole of western civilization—so dramatically demonstrated by the war—France, even Europe, seemed now small and limited, although by no means less important and more negligible. But this new perspective imposed itself on Bernanos as on so many others. His relative proximity, during the Brazilian stay, to the United States, then the new foundations of South American life and civilization, gave him better instruments to judge the old continent and a better sense of proportion for observing the conflict between old and new.

By civilization Bernanos meant the spirit which informs an age, underlies the reflexes of the people, sets their goals and organizes the web of their relationships. More than that, "a civilization is a compromise between what is good and what is evil in man, a defense system against his instincts."[2] This idea brings to mind the concept of equilibrium, served, consciously and unconsciously, by all the forces of which a civilization consists: individuals and the State, the interests of the person and those of the collectivity, freedom and law, progress and tradition. This tension is a fact of life which the Catholic concept of man had incorporated and further refined by the demands it made on the individual. Thus Christian civilization and all those which have preceded it, as well as the "European" civilization which has followed without breaking its organic ties with it, have formed themselves on the same image.

The emergence of the machine has broken this continuity and has ushered in a crisis not only of the present civilization, but of civilization in general. Why is a technical civilization a denial of the very principles which have governed so far the co-existence of men and their covenant with God?

One of the most searching Catholic answers to this question is given by Romano Guardini. In *The End of the Modern World,* Father Guardini contrasts the classical-medieval world-view in which man was a servant of Creation, with the post-Renaissance centuries and their exaltation of man as a master of nature. He then proceeds to show how modern man has been driven to ride technology (as the unhappy hunter rides the tiger in the Chinese tale) which he cannot tame. The more thorough his technological domination over nature, the less he can avoid constructing a new order of things, quasi-independent of nature, but so coherent and so self-sufficient as to constitute a new nature, as it were. In this artificial world, "the crucial events of life—conception, birth, sickness and death—have lost their mystery. They have become biological or social phenomena dealt with by science or by a series of techniques." "Human nature is withering beneath the destructive hands of modernity"; the alienated man is thus born, no longer interested in his universe existentially, with his mind and heart and senses, but bent upon acquiring power; the tragedy of his present condition is that "while gaining infinite scope for movement, man is losing his own position in the realm of being."[3]

Guardini locates the point of no return, not in the materialistic nineteenth century when "technology developed only slowly at the hands of a non-technologized mentality," but in the recent decades. This diagnosis is correct and important: from Descartes to Renan, from Bacon to H. G. Wells, mastery over nature and the happiness of mankind were proudly flown together on the flag of Utopia. Only very near to us in time have technology and mechano-human manipulative devices entered upon an unholy alliance in which the line of separation between the human being and his tools is not always and not clearly distinguishable.

This does not mean that the machine is in itself innocent. Machines are no more tools, Bernanos writes, because they cannot be owned and managed by the individual worker. They require teamwork and their very operation imposes a distance between the manipulators and their products. The theme of the production line often comes up in Bernanos' war-time and post-war writings; yet he recognizes that technological mentality is not merely the *product* of the machine, it is also the *symptom* of a society losing its natural reflexes. He would have agreed with Guardini that the process had started around the beginning of the century; around 1900, the European states still had a human appearance; they lined up behind a human figure, the Tsar, the Emperor, the President of the Republic. People cherished the State because they found in it either the conditions of their prosperity and personal expansion, or, at least, the promise of these things. Every conquest of the State was chalked up for the cause of freedom, order and social peace, no matter how distant in many cases. Nobody noticed (except a Dostoievsky, a Nietzsche, a Lord Acton) that the "humanity" of the state was decreasing and that a huge bureaucratic apparatus would receive the heritage thus relinquished. The World War, post-war upheavals and revolutions, unemployment, the emergence of mass-parties slowly forced the State to abdicate, "not in favor of the 'masses' which, on the contrary, became more defenseless, but for the benefit of a small aristocracy of engineers and policemen."[4]

This development could not have been foreseen. "Suppose," Bernanos writes, "that one asked an educated man in the thirteenth, fifteenth or even the seventeenth century, what his idea of the future society was?—He would have answered right away that this civilization will be peaceful, at once very close to nature and prodigiously refined, cultured . . . Millions had been preparing this kind of world. Today we understand their error: the invasion of machines has taken our society by sur-

prise, so that it collapsed under the weight. This is because such an invasion had never been envisaged."[5]

Man succumbed to this invasion because he took his liberty for granted and was unwilling to pay a continued price for it. Freedom was anyway taken to be synonymous with the rule of man, the preparation of the earthly paradise; whatever helped to bring it about—and the machine seemed to be the most powerful among the instruments of happiness—was blessed by the citizen who, moreover, entertained the illusion that, through the means of democracy, he had an effective control on this development and over his own destiny. As long as this was only an image, a dream, the trap laid by the machine was not noticed. The image and the dream were, in fact, the sentimental aspects of an ideology, the ideology of progress, which acted as a stimulant and was, therefore, a beneficial force.

The machine has quickly put an end to this honeymoon mood between man and his planet, because it presented its own intolerant conditions, its own logic and its own image of happiness, that is, efficiency. It represents a tremendous force since it is a mirage of wealth and power, the mechanical embodiment of spirits from ancient folktales, serving man's appetites and serving them here, now, and in fantastic proportions. Compared to the machine nothing else is important; even the ideological vehicle which had facilitated its conquest is dismissed; "every day brings us new proof," Bernanos remarked, "that the age of ideologies is long passed, in New York as well as in Moscow or in London. We see the British imperial democracy, the American plutocratic democracy, and the Marxist Empire walk, if not hand in hand, at least towards the same goal . . . that is, towards maintaining a system inside which they all have acquired wealth and power."[6]

The age of ideologies may be considered as a sort of last stop before the "machine paradise to which we shall arrive in a state of degradation, like beasts." Even the ideologies and their conflicts had been preferable to the universal orthodoxy of machine-civilization when, in the name of efficiency and mechanical perfection, the dreariest of all tyrannies will establish itself. As a Christian, he knew that perfection is not of this world, and that for human beings to claim it is the surest sign of beastliness and Mammon worship.

The ideologies promised *freedom* and *happiness*; can machine-civilization, which is their heir, be counted upon to usher in their reign?

Freedom, in its only understood, that is, collective form, today is known as democracy. Needless to say, Bernanos never counted himself among the democrats; in his judgment, this system was as mechanical as many other aspects of the modern world, and, moreover, it was an irrational way of taking a guess at what the best policy might be under given circumstances. The Gallup-poll and various other opinion-gathering procedures, further caricatural refinements of the democratic principle, support unwittingly Bernanos' skeptical attitude. But let us admit, he says, that modern man, conditioned to the *democratic* ways, has become also enamored of *technology*: can he have both? Can he vote for this or that technician, as he presumed he could for this or that politician?

First of all, he has no competence to judge so-called experts and to choose among them. The very terms "technology" and "technologue" indicate that this domain is beyond the natural understanding and common sense of the citizen and that its extent may only be measured by other technologues. In the second place, in view of the fact that "modern society will increasingly be an aggregation of technical problems which have to be solved," everything, from the formulation of the problem to the blueprinting of the solution and the calculation of its cost—in money, time, work, human sacrifice—will be strictly within the expert's competence. "Do you then imagine," Bernanos asks, "that the working of those thousand and one wheels, each dependent on the other and running faster than lightning, will wait on the convenience of the honest fellows who come together at electoral meetings to cheer this or that parliamentary program . . . Technique's every step forward is a step away from the Democracy that was the old-time worker's dream."[7]

But of course the disappearance or formalization of democracy is not all. Freedom, under various other forms, cannot be preserved under a mechanical civilization. Chateaubriand, to mention only one, had foreseen, a hundred years before Bernanos, the coming loss of privacy and the decreasing importance of the individual. He had written, in the epilogue to his *Mémories d'Outre-tombe*: "The folly of the age is to achieve the unity of the peoples while turning the whole species into a single unit. Granted. But while we are acquiring these general faculties, is not a whole chain of private feelings in danger of perishing?" Chateaubriand, a child of the individualistic eighteenth century, was confronted only by powerless ideologues of the type of Saint-Simon and Comte and dreaming social prophets like Michelet; but Bernanos and ourselves, his contemporaries, have measured the progress of a totalitarianism of a different sort, under dictatorships as well as under mass-democracy; we risk no longer merely to lose "a chain of private feelings" in a world where people are conditioned daily to have identical reactions and hysterias, but the complete loss of our individuality in most of its manifestations.

"The disciplines imposed by technique have slowly ruined, or at least considerably weakened the reflexes of the individual against the collectivity", wrote Bernanos.[8]

We must bear in mind that this was, for him, not a mere historical accident, reparable or irreparable, but a sin against God's most precious gift. Political, social and intellectual freedom are, after all, aspects of the creature's strongest link to the Creator, the source of his personality and the stamp of his dignity. To sign it away is not merely to re-enact the drama of Faust, but a sure indication of an inner unbalance, the severance of roots, after which there is only the petrification of the soul and of the faculties it commands and vivifies. This is why Bernanos can say that "one cannot understand the least thing about modern civilization if one does not first realize that it is a universal conspiracy to destroy the inner life";[9] and why he refers, a few pages further, to machine civilization as a "cancer," "a profound, aberrant crisis, a deviation, a perversion of human energy."[10]

However, for many modern thinkers *happiness* is still achievable in the service of the State, the collectivity, or even outside them; and it is possible even without the breath of *freedom* to enliven it. Immense forces crush the individual, they say, and in order to struggle effectively against them, the collectivity alone can and must be counted upon. It is therefore in the interest of the individual, it is indeed the very meaning of his freedom, that he should alienate this freedom—temporarily or forever—and subordinate himself to community-set aims. The result will be a *new happiness,* stripped of the egoistic features of the old, the happiness of public immersion, of being part of the whole, of being absorbed in the *Nirvana of togetherness.*

This new concept of happiness, related to technological progress, is guaranteed by the State. The State uses the machine and imposes the equality and the organization which the forces liberated by the machine require if they are to be prevented from running wild. Mechanical perfection will, indeed, emancipate the worker from everyday drudgery, but will also relocate him to bureaucratic posts where he will no more understand the meaning of his activity than on the assembly line. In addition, it is highly doubtful that his relationship to his superiors will improve; the same distance as before will be maintained between the unskilled worker or clerk, displaced by the machine, and the few thousand specialists who will keep his destiny in their hands. The argument that the masses, freed from the most painful type of manual work and physical exertion, will now have enough time for leisure, that they will be more "cultured" and better "informed," is so thoroughly contradicted by the facts we have been witnessing for the past few decades, that it must be relegated to the rubbish heap of other "progressive" dreams.

In several of Bernanos' novels there appears a twentieth-century version of Monsieur Homais, whether as a journalist, a half-educated student or an escaped seminarian; in each case he is not only weak and mediocre, but vicious as well, a creature whose insignificance of intellect is matched only by the insincerity of his soul. Bernanos could never persuade himself that small-time intellectuals are anything but parasites. "What can the world expect of cultural equality?" he asked. "What an illusion to believe in the fraternity of idling intellectuals!"[11] He saw in them, indeed, pale copies of the diabolical figures which Satan in an egalitarian age uses to tempt man by what is most shameful in him. According to Bernanos, as Mounier remarks, the present world does not deserve any prowess on the part of Satan who apportions his efforts by the power of the resistance offered. Mediocre people cannot sin, and are, therefore, not tragic; *their only form of revolt is indifference.*

The most pernicious among modern evils is, then, *mediocrity.* Bernanos who ultimately trusted the individual alone, found the latter's indifference and lack of resistance far more dangerous than the more awesome forms of modern techniques of oppression. The mediocre and indifferent ones are, by definition, indistinguishable from each other, since all they aspire to achieve is to be part of the whole, to let things take their course, to be one among the many. In them the soul is dead, their existence consists of elementary reactions to animal needs. The only function they fulfill in society is *to be counted*—to form the units of statistics, to constitute the mass. "A world dominated by Force is an abominable world," Bernanos exclaimed, "but a world dominated by Number is ignoble. Force sooner or later becomes a challenge and invites revolt. It calls for heroes and martyrs. The abject tyranny of Number is a slow infection which provokes no fever. Number creates a society after its own image, a society of human beings, who are not equal but identical, recognizable only by their fingerprints."[12]

How could one speak of happiness in their case, provided we mean by happiness something worthy of God's creatures? Since they offer no resistance, the gigantic forces of the age pass through them and determine their fate as well as their concept of happiness. These forces, that is, the technicians who manipulate them, dispose of enormous means to carry out their plans and transform mankind into a "colony of industrious animals." If work itself will become lighter from a strictly physical point of view, the filling of leisure hours will represent real difficulty since the "industrious beast" will be deprived of imagination, real creativity, even of a desire to indulge in anything but the collectively approved forms of entertainment.

Thus Bernanos saw clearly the problem of modern man in industrial mass societies, the problem which is becoming more acute every day: the freedom of empty or half-furnished minds who turn to destruction, nihilism, or the most vulgar and superficial forms of commercial

and State-devised distraction. He identified correctly also the personnel moving into the posts vacated by the elite, the "engineers of the soul" as Stalin called them. "Committees of psychologists will argue with committees of moralists and committees of theologians until the citizen's every last indefeasible right will be warranted by half a score of governmental offices, open daily from 9 to 5, excepting, of course, for Sundays and holidays."[13] The only sort of inner life these experts will allow will be "a modest and moderate form of introspection, directed by the doctor and tending to produce an optimistic frame of mind."[14] The last word, after all, will be *happiness* as promised; only it will be the happiness of the unfree, soulless, directed man, working and playing under supervision and reduced to the state of a robot.

THE WARDEN STATE: THE ORDER OF A GRAVEYARD

If human beings turn into robots, so must necessarily the State which is no longer informed by the spirit of freedom; contrary to what one would assume at first glance, the disciplining of robots is a more difficult task than the settling of conflicts among rational and free men. Robots being small wheels in a machinery, the latter must be immensely powerful if it is to work smoothly. Nor can it—that is, the State—be absolutely sure that today's robots might not become tomorrow's rebels, since, after all, not inert matter but human beings are involved in the present historic crisis. As we shall see, Bernanos envisages such a possibility, that is, the revolt of freedom in the desolate cemetery of the machine paradise.

He considered it an irrefutable point that machines, ever larger, more perfect and supremely efficient, must become the monopoly of the State. No legislation, no semblance of private capitalism, no billion-dollar corporations with all their machine-given power and wealth, may remain outside the ubiquitous State, although arrangements may be reached in the form of this or that compromise. Ultimately, however, the machine must work for the State, and the individual owner—insofar as big corporations can at all be called "individual owners"—becomes, at best, a huge middle man between the State and the public.

Power thus accumulated in the hands of the "warden State"—the name given by Bernanos to the nameless collectivity—can be assimilated into a dictatorship. Not the dictatorship of one man—this has never been the case—but of the party of the Technocrats, far more powerful because more cohesive than a party of ideologues and politicians who, after all, like to interpret ideas and who therefore disagree. The Technocrats do not disagree, at least not on essentials. For them, universal dictatorship is an absolute, short of which they cannot stop because the technocratic mentality, like the machine it copies, tolerates no obstruction, no contradiction to its efficiency.

One can still argue, as the majority of men do, that the technocrats, their technique and power, will exercise control over the material world only; machines take the place of the servant, reduce the hours of work, open so-far unsuspected ways of subduing a hostile nature. These services of technology and science, the argument runs, facilitate rather than obstruct the superior kind of life because they make leisure and culture possible; schools, theatres, libraries, travel and tourism are available to the millions who thereby enrich themselves and prepare for yet higher forms of freedom and the good life.

Bernanos fought this argument with special violence. "Watch out!" he cried, "among all the techniques there is a technique of discipline for which the mere obedience of the past is not satisfactory. Obedience used to be obtained by all kinds of empirical methods, so that one may say that it was less a discipline that a moderate disorder. Technique, on the other hand, will sooner or later insist on forming its own collaborators, who will belong to it body and soul, who will accept without discussion the technical concept of order, life and the reason for living. In a world which is entirely devoted to Efficiency and Production, it is imperative that each citizen, from his birth, should be consecrated to the same gods. Technique cannot be called into question since the solutions it imposes are by definition the most practical."[15]

If it cannot be called into question, much less can it be opposed. The fact that the old forms of aristocratic and monarchic abuses were successfully combatted and destroyed by a militant and meaningful *liberalism,* makes us believe that now, when the descendants of those liberals favor an all-powerful State, we should continue trusting and acclaiming them. But virtuous action in the past represents no guarantee of virtue for the future, much less infallibility. Indeed, it may have been corrupted by its very success. The all-powerful State, with the help of its machines and robots, will tolerate no contradiction and no opposition, even with the liberal label on it. "In proportion as the causes of disorder will double or triple, technique will increase its means of defense and repression tenfold, a hundredfold. Order will be maintained, but it will be the order of a cemetery. It will be maintained in the name of a Society of which only the administrative framework and the police will have survived—a skeleton."[16]

This will be the end; meanwhile, the State grows and expands; it takes care of its citizens and thinks for them. It says: since I do these things for you and plan to do more, why don't you trust me with your freedom? What possible use can you make of liberty? I shall be free for you, I shall be free alone. Thus the Pagan State is conceived, says Bernanos, which is the same thing as the pagan god. "And what will it matter," he adds, "under which name we must adore it—Democracy or Dictatorship?"[17]

THE FREE MAN

Throughout the Bernanosian analysis it is clear that the writer is speaking not only as a citizen, a critic, a Frenchman, a contemporary to fateful events, but first and foremost as a Christian. Characteristically, he called the coming State not a "brave new world", "1984," "post-historic world," "post-western civilization,"—but the *pagan state.* As a Christian, feeling *one* with Christian history and tradition, he knew what the pagan state was and the menace it once represented. In fact, he conceived of the present threat as greater than in the first centuries of Christianity: nobody can say of the first Christians that they were mediocre and that they shunned risks. Today, however, people—and this includes Bernanos' fellow-Catholics—are mediocre, they seek security and the comfort of the soul. The pagan state of the future will be immeasurably stronger than Nero's and Diocletian's had been, and Bernanos knew that it would persecute Christians and free men for the same reasons.

But the modern state is not so much a danger in itself as a means of measuring the corruption of the underlying reality: of the individual and the collectivity. One of Bernanos' recurring themes was the idea that just as the abdication of elites within society makes way for pseudo-elites and ultimately for a generalized wickedness, so, on another plane, the abdication of society itself, its scorn for humanness, is responsible for the cancer-like growth of the State. The images Bernanos uses to express this observation are, again, similar to those he used in the description of the abbé Cénabre; when the abbé's spiritual vocation ran down like a bad clock, there began at once the invasion of moral and corporal degradation; uncleanliness, like maggots on a corpse in another image, attack immediately like an enemy who had been waiting at the gate and who had been kept out only by a constant, unceasing effort and vigilance.

With regard to the progress of evil in the abbé Cénabre, I have used the word "carapace" under which his decomposition remained invisible (except to the abbé Chevance and Chantal). Bernanos used a similar image to paint the new, sinister role of the State. "Human society is in the process of dissolution. Totalitarian organization is to this society in dissolution what wooden or metal braces would be to a body which is rotting away. The braces become more and more rigid, take more and more room in proportion as the body occupies less, until the day when the orthopedic apparatus replaces completely the body which is then reduced to naught."[18] (Let us bear in mind that Bernanos meant mass-democracy no less than Hitlerism and Bolshevism when he spoke of totalitarian regimes.)

Society in a state of putrefaction, the "sclerosis of individual consciences," the "liquidation of history," "spiritual entropy," "man amputated of God," are sources, signs and consequences of the phenomena observed by Bernanos. He did not make these observations systematically, nor did he order them in a logical or historical sequence. The principal virtue of his analysis—and the sureness and depth of his diagnosis—derive from his underlying assimilation of society to the individual, society's sense of freedom and honor to the individual's moral conscience, society's resignation to the individual's despair, its corruption to his turning against God. In short, Bernanos, throughout his social-polemical works, remained a novelist, retaining the novelist's psychological insights, and the novelist, in turn, never ceased to be a Christian. Thus the ultimate answer Bernanos proposes is always a Christian answer: like the curé of Ambricourt and Chantal de Clergerie whose sanctity cuts through the Gordian knot of evil, so the saint, the authentically free man, is to save the world from the tyranny engulfing it.

As we have seen, this does not mean that Bernanos was spared the temptation of despair. I have mentioned his idea that real heroism is hopelessness overcome; the experience must have been familiar to him. His writings show abundantly that he was almost constantly balanced between resignation and hope—so much so that the superficial reader may even accuse him of incoherence. However, this same frequent absence of logical reasoning is proper to all those thinkers whose philosophy is of the existential kind, and who do not seem to be able to decide whether to follow the indications of intelligence or that of faith. For the first tells them that man, once he is engaged in a process of abdication, builds system after system in justification of his preference for un-freedom; while the second reminds them that there is always in man an indestructible residue of spiritual longing by which, and with God's help, he chooses the fullness of life.

This "inconsistency" was the substance of the thought of Pascal, Kierkegaard, Nietzsche and Shestov, to mention only a few, and it received a particular emphasis with Bernanos in whose case the philosophical difficulty was further complicated by an interest in political events and prophecies, the future of France and the fate of western civilization. Thus he is perfectly truthful and consistent when he finds no saving grace for the modern world, and yet puts all his feverish hope into the individual's last stand. "People agree with me," he wrote towards the end of his life, "that this civilization is de-

ceptive and dangerous; they cannot accept the idea that it may be unreformable. They reassure themselves by thinking that man will end up some day by redecorating the interior of this civilization . . . Their error is that they never wonder if the experiment in process could not be followed in spite of man, because of the enormous means it commands."[19]

Yet, there are many texts and passages of his speeches from the same period in which he dismisses any determinism and necessary decline, and points up signs of an unexpected side-street which does not lead to a dead end. Before an audience at the Sorbonne, he advised the students not to think that mankind is "a locomotive launched on its rails" and following an inevitable course; rather, he said, "compare it to a work of art that the artist begins to shape again and again." This comparison is, of course, an old one, for the image of the clay, formless but taking shape under the sculptor's fingers, has been a favorite of believers of all kinds. In Bernanos, it shows, together with and inseparable from the more somber predictions, that in his extreme sensitiveness he registered the progress of every ripple on the ocean of life and tried to guess its final destination.

It is not surprising that he found most ripples expanding in the wrong direction. Again, it was his rational side which suggested to him that once man gives away a parcel of his freedom, he may never reconquer it. In a passage of the *Lettre aux Anglais*, he explains his anguish over the irreversible trend away from the individual: "Man is not made to live alone, and the strayed members of the flock invariably end by coming back to it. Whereas if man one day sacrifices the rights of the Person to some collectivity, he will never find them again, for that collectivity will ceaselessly grow in power and material efficiency . . . You will tell me that the democratic Collectivity will never make any attempt against the sacred rights of the Person. Forgive me, but how can I be sure of any such thing? Why should not the majority tomorrow impose upon me its own moral code if mine stands in the way of its profits?"[20]

Yet, the man of faith provides the answer, namely in the same *Lettre aux Anglais*: "I do not deny," he writes, "that human society seems to evolve towards a kind of universal collectivism, but this is because the forces of defense of the human person are as if struck by stupor. Nevertheless, these forces exist and their reaction will be like a thunderbolt. What is needed to spark it? The passionate will of a few thousand men, free and proud."[21]

Note that these "few thousand men" do not have to form a political elite, in fact they do not have to form a group, a party, a network: they do not have to be linked in any way. Their power of reaction is their "freedom and pride" which would be vague requirements, indeed, if Bernanos had not so often given flesh and bone to these words in his novels and through his own behavior. What he means then is not an organized opposition to the modern world, because he knows, or rather feels with a sure instinct that the most acute danger of this world is, precisely, that in it even freedom must organize, must build a heavy apparatus and finally strengthen the very image of man it means to combat. No, in Bernanos' judgment the Technical State will "have no enemy but *the man who is not like other men*,[22] or, more simply, the man who does not believe in Technique."[23] Why is he a danger to machine-civilization? Because "the modern world is a mechanism with such complicated interlocking parts, that the presence of one single free man exposes it, sooner or later, to a peril similar to that which a planet, miraculously exempt from the laws of gravitation, would create in the solar system."[24] Such free men, Bernanos says on another occasion, using another image, would be "the grains of flint which, because of the ever-present danger they create, use up the zeal of the machinery's engineer and hold in check its appetite."[25]

THE SAINT

Is this free man, hypothetical or actual, a mere *saboteur*, a bitter opponent who finds pleasure, however justified, in placing obstacles in the way of the machine's heavy feet, in delaying the inevitable march of the Technical State? Or is he the Bernanosian *saint*, disposing of an inexhaustible reservoir of fighting spirit, but also of insight and charity, used not for malice and destruction, but for opposing, endlessly, freedom to indolence, love to routine? It is true that, carried away by his famous tempests of fury, Bernanos had frequent moments when he charged, bull-like, all those who seemed to oppose his own version of honesty, good faith and courage; his friends, acquaintances, audiences, interviewers, confessors, all testify that nobody was spared on such occasions: academicians, men of letters, generals, ministers, chiefs of state, political parties, frivolous ladies, prelates were brought up to the eye of the needle, only to find that they could not pass. Back in France, after 1945, he used to declare that the freest man today was the one who refused all participation, because every group, party or interest was selfish and corrupt. But there was another Bernanosian reaction too: once before, Bernanos, we have seen, had referred to the saint "thrown across the path" of modern cynicism and hypocrisy: it was the abbé Donissan in **Under the Sun of Satan** whose lonely and tormented figure was called upon to shock post-war France into a recognition of the devil lurking on sideroads and defying the unwary. In the teeth of a universal danger it is again the saint who will prove himself God's champion.

First, as the Poor and as the Child. Like Léon Bloy, Bernanos understood the profound Christian truth that *poverty* cannot be suppressed only displaced. With other Catholic philosophers, he saw in Marxism a doctrine which humiliates the poor and robs him of his dignity by enrolling him in the proletarian horde and assuming that he lives by bread alone. The colossal system of "changing the world" implies, in his eyes, a ruthless regimentation, the degradation of all higher ambition in view of the supreme recompense: filling the stomach. The poor, he maintained, are jealous of their individuality and do not mean to stand on their hindlegs for a bone. Marxism does not offer them a more dignified life, that is, a recognition and justification of their higher aspirations, but, on the contrary, insists on reducing all men to the level of proletars, by denying their spiritual nature. Marxism, of course, is not alone to blame: industrial capitalism had long before deformed the full image of man and had made of him, through its own angle of vision and interests, the *homo economicus,* Bernanos' (and Tocqueville's) "industrious beast." Marx, opposing the British textile manufacturers and coal mine operators, had fallen into their error.

The Child too is, for Bernanos, a prefiguration of the saint. I have shown, in the first chapter, in what sense his conception of the child is opposed by the modern concept of educators, psychologists and business interests, all of which converge upon the child in order to make of him a small adult, a target of salesmen, researchers and experimenters. These representatives of the modern adult world are impatient to integrate him in the circuit of their own affairs; the child must be made an accomplice and a victim of efficiency, he must serve science and production, he must not be a point at which society becomes incalculable, wastes time, and risks raising a generation indifferent to its own strange predilection for self-harassment.

But the real saint is more than the child and the poor, although he partakes in the virtues of both and also in that special grace that God seems to bestow on them. The role of the saint, a supernatural role, is to serve as a mysterious entity in the divine plan to counter-balance evil. All the physical and spiritual strength of Donissan was needed to stand up to the devil's challenge; the curé of Ambricourt, weak and sickly as he was, wielded fantastic power over those entrusted to him; Chantal, the fragile flower of a day, burned up in her quiet glow the poison of the maniacs and shallow souls around her. The saint who faces the modern world must represent God's interests in a different, yet similar situation; grace must overflow in him so that he may offer himself not on every front, for he is but a limited man, but with the help of that special virtue by which spirit can be infused into an inert body, by which the non-material may be everywhere at once. Bernanos firmly believed that only Christians had a chance to save the modern world: "Christianity divinizes man. Less than that is not enough for the balancing of the enormous advantage that Collectivity has over the Person. If we do not claim membership in the human order, we shall fall under the iron law of the Giant State . . . . The triumph of man in this world will be obtained only through a flawless self-discipline."[26]

Bernanos does not speak of the self-discipline of the ascetic and of the monk, although, as the example of the abbé Donissan and of the curé of Ambricourt shows, he justified self-mortification as an offering to God for the sins of others and also as a means of gaining more spiritual authority over them. But the ideal type for him always remained the militant saint—Joan of Arc, Saint Louis—to whom it never occurred to tend his supernatural virtues as some rare flower, but who engages it in the thick of the battle. The saints in his novels are amazingly *robust* spiritually and give themselves with prodigality, never once thinking of sparing their God-given energy. Yet their exceptional qualities are not barriers between them and the rest of the mortals. Since they form the true elite—of the Church and of mankind—there is no limit to their willingness to risk their life and entire being. Hence, they do more rather than less, they are constantly at their task, and do not separate themselves from the others in the knowledge of their apartness. The saints are witnesses that the world is blessed by God and that sanctity is, therefore, not the exceptional but the normal; Mounier rightly remarks that Bernanos has eliminated any rare or sublime quality from his saints: "he pushes them with both hands towards banality and shapes them like very down-to-earth figures. Their task is to be well understood by all."[27]

This saint who is so deeply rooted in the earth, is *in* the world while serving a supernatural plan. But, of course, he has no program, no system. Indeed, he is embarrassed by the fact that others, with mixed respect and suspicion, credit him with superior intelligence and complicated designs. How innocent is Chantal's cry when she is reminded that her presence among her father's strange guests poses problems: "Am I a problem? . . . You too think so? But what problem?"

The misunderstanding is only apparent. The saint, in reality, is simple because his inner being is turned towards the very source of simplicity. It is again Chantal who says: "One ought to be like crystal, like pure water. One ought to be transparent so that God might be seen through us." It is always the others who see a *problem* in the saint's presence because he obstructs their deviousness.

But the misunderstanding and the conflict are, of course, never-ending and manyfold: in the great figures of his novels Bernanos saw not only the heroes of spiritual battles but also true revolutionizers of man's existence. This is why the saints are the best qualified to take up arms in man's defense: they are "fellows who . . . would let themselves be made into mincemeat before

giving Caesar anything more than his due."[28] In this way the *saint*—that is, in his relationship to society, the *free man*—assumes two roles, both of which are deliberately left undefined with any precision: one is what we may call the "saboteur," the "flint among the wheels of the machine"; the second is the "resistant," who is irreducible and unassimilable by the technological mentality and by the State.

It must be stressed once more that Bernanos had too clear an insight into the nature of freedom to impose a "pattern of freedom" and a course of action for his saint; the saint is what he is because he is a *man,* that is, literally incalculable to the clumsy machinery that the State uses in its classification of the citizen's inner life and external behavior. This does not mean that his actions are random actions, dictated by whim and deliberate non-conformity; he is rather like Bernanos himself, that is, at peace with his conscience because he follows truth as he sees it.

Also like Bernanos, the "saboteur," the "resistant" is a solitary man; naturally, he is *in* the world, as I have said before, and he freely shoulders the duties accruing to him in society. If he preserves his freedom, it is not in the Gidean sense of "disponibility," of never choosing at the crossroads of life. On the contrary, he has chosen once and for all; his apparent changes measure only the shifts among his fellow-men. But he is a solitary man as opposed to the mass-man of our age. He is the element of freedom which vitiates the social calculus, the one atom whose path cannot be described in advance.

To say that the saint is a saboteur is not to say that he lacks charity and that he finds pleasure in upsetting progress. Of "progress," of course, Bernanos had very definite views and, as can be expected, less than favorable.[29] But precisely because it seemed to him that his fellow-men lost their sane judgment in sacrificing their freedom and life for the ephemeral monsters of progress, he imposed a third mission on his saints: he wanted them to redeem not only the misguided, but, above all, the evil guides.

The final proof of Bernanos' perfect grasp of the modern world—and of his flawless Christianity—is that he identified the creators of modern civilization—the liquidators and the human maggots—with the supernaturally *poor* who must be saved before everybody else. Mounier calls this insistence on saving the guilty "a desperate invitation to fraternity unto death, launched to the brother who is blinded by the evil spirit."[30] I do not think that this appeal of Bernanos was born in despair; on the contrary, in my view it shows great confidence to make room for the prodigal brother in the Father's tent. Bernanos who attacked without respite the "imbeciles," and the greatest of them all, the builders of Babel, of the earthly paradise, knew well that their lack of faith was crushing them with the whole weight of the universe. Only the saints are able to relieve the burdens of the greatest sinners.

The word "prophet" comes involuntarily to one's mind when speaking of Bernanos—for several reasons: his *indignation* before the spiritual state of the modern world, his loud and eloquent *denunciation* of certain people and classes and his readiness to show the road of a radical regeneration, that is his *forgiveness.* These are, however, the qualities of the prophet, and are not, on every point, reconcilable with those of the polemicist. As a result, we find Bernanos often guilty of remaining within the sphere of generalities, neglecting the duty of illustrating the problems he raises, as if the fire of the truth he proclaims—and with which we agree—were sufficient to illuminate the unelaborated details of his subject. At other times, however, the image he uses is so expressive that it replaces, by itself, a painstaking documentation, and gives us the supreme satisfaction of seeing, in a flash, from within. Among contemporary French writers perhaps Bergson alone had a similar gift.

Another defect of Bernanos is that he frequently interrupts his discussion in order to pour his wrath on adversaries, after which he grafts yet other issues on the newly-found one: the result is a network of unrelated topics, all brilliant as far as they go, but weakened in persuasive power. Gaëtan Picon aptly remarks that Bernanos conceived his novels as "total expressions"; it is quite clear that he had the same view of his polemical works as well: even when they are intended to focus on one issue, they soon turn into "total expressions" of the writer's world view.

All this followed from the fact—emphasized so many times in this book—that Bernanos remained a novelist even in his polemical writings. But when I say a "novelist," I must give that word an extended meaning, as in the case of a Dostoievsky or a Proust, who were also immersed in their stories as in a concentrated form of life. But while with Dostoievsky and Proust—certainly the latter—the novel was a substitute for life and took precedence over life, Bernanos envisaged the writer's problem the other way around: he was primarily interested in life, and his novels and polemics were two ways of illustrating this interest. Most emphatically he did not write *romans à thèse,* fictional versions of his beliefs and convictions; his fictional characters and the real characters whom he observed, described, analyzed and criticized were, for him, men and women belonging to the same universe; they would have been capable of exchanging roles and continuing to live in the framework either of the novels or of real life.

There are two reasons for this: one is Bernanos' amazing knowledge of the human being, a knowledge which always starts from the deepest depth of the soul. Once his grasp of the inner man is secured, it is relatively easy for him to show everything as following from this inner reality: behavior and words are attached to the soul's secret like a dog, held on leash, to his master. It is this insight that Bernanos trusted under all circumstances, whether observing real life or writing his stories.

The second reason is the identity of the atmosphere that he creates in the novels and in the polemical writings. Even behind and around trivial acts there is drama and tension because, in the Bernanosian view, the soul is always involved and we are never indifferent. Or, if we are, it is a form of Satan's temptation, that is another potential drama. The world of politics, the life of nations, conflicts of class or group interests set the same forces into motion as life on a personal level since nations, classes, even the State and the machine also have souls, are bathed in the atmosphere of sin, perdition and redemption.

This concept of life, fictional *and* real, is faithfully rendered by his style which, in turn, was the exact manifestation of his personality. Stanislas Fumet, who had encouraged his early steps as a writer and helped publish his first novel, wrote of his style: "He conceived of writing as of an attack. Sentences upon sentences, overwhelming, overwhelmed, scintillating; here a zone of obscurity, there a patch of light." To this we may add the observation that he had learned a great deal from Drumont, from Léon Bloy and Péguy, the three men with whom he undoubtedly forms a *group* on several counts. From Drumont he inherited the style of the charging bull, the relentless pursuer of the opponent; from Bloy the apocalyptic visions and vaticinations; and from Péguy the poetry of the soul, expressed in calmly developed images, impressed on the reader (and better still, on the hearer) by means of abundant repetitions like in old epic poems.

These gifts and shortcomings he put in the service of a grand ideal, the regeneration of mankind. No doubt his understanding of the nature of evil—the first condition of such a regeneration—was exceptional: there is no writer today who could compose a scene like the confrontation of the Countess by the curé of Ambricourt on the eve of her death. The same subtlety and forcefulness as were displayed by the curé were Bernanos' eminent weapons in fighting his own battles against the devil whose ways and strategy he understood with a truly supernatural insight. This is why he forms in us not only a conceptual understanding of the great issues and dramas of this age, but a palpitating reality as well, which makes us shudder and leaves us terror-stricken, or raises us to pity and love, and which, finally, makes it clear why we are part of the world he describes. His images and visions are, of course, magnificent, whether morbid or elevating, hopeful or hellish: but it is the total spiritual comprehension of the world—a catholic comprehension—which makes them so expressive of reality and which, in turn, convinces us of reality's higher dimension: truth.

But how can one speak of truth when Bernanos was a partisan who, all his life, rejected caution and revised his judgments more than once? Yet, the word is not out of place: *truth,* in the sense of an incredibly generous spiritual grasp of things human, and *truth* in the sense of bringing his political understanding up to the level of his charity. I have remarked earlier that we may suspect in Bernanos' inner life some tremendous combats with his demon, the temptation of despair, and that it must have cost him an immense energy to love the "imbeciles," the soul-corrupters, the Pharisees he had detected under so many disguises: the respectable bourgeois, the gullible Machiavellian, the false priest, the soulless technician, the seeker of a spiritual alibi in "social concern." But precisely: the more he understood of the world, the more essential he found that it should be saved without exclusions. There is, when all is said and done, a Tocqueville's political wisdom in him, transfigured by a stronger faith still that we must seek the conditions of *total* regeneration. In spite of his love and admiration of certain forms of the life and images of the past, he ridiculed those who accused him of "medieval" mentality; he lived very much in this world and age, but saw no reason why this age should be exceptional: he understood that in his forsakenness, modern man is even more a child of God, a child calling out—silently and shamefacedly—to his Father.

This generous understanding—again Tocqueville's grasp of the age of democracy and liberalism comes to one's mind—made it possible for Bernanos to evolve from the position of a twentieth-century Drumont to a unique position, without labels, but stamped with the sign of hope. To follow his own distinction: not optimism but hope. Given this humility, the great events of his life—and of his political consciousness—the break with Maurras, the testimony of Majorca, life in Brazil, the shock of the "stolen Resistance" (as victory had been stolen in 1918), all were liberating and deepening experiences, ranged on a continuous line and permeated with the same conviction, the inspiration behind Bernanos' political concern. This conviction is religious in nature because its source is the belief that the saints are capable of saving the more indolent members of the mystical body. Similarly, within society or the nation, the elite must labor for the material and moral well being of the people. Failure in this task is treason, the only guilt Bernanos never seems to forgive because, in his view, it is the point of origin of other sins against the people by an abdicating elite which, nevertheless, clings to the power it does not deserve.

In this respect there is, indeed, little difference between the elite which betrays its mission and the priest who loses his vocation. They display the same symptom: inability to address and guide those who would naturally trust them; the priest drives the penitent to despair, the elite sows confusion among the people. Bernanos' great polemical works: **La Grande Peur des Bien-Pensants, Les Enfants humiliés, Les Grands Cimetières sous la lune, Scandale de la vérité** and his post-1945 articles, are all denunciations of elites which failed in the dialogue in 1871, in 1918, in 1936, in 1940 (Vichy), in 1945 (the Resistance). He remained convinced to the end that the people—*le petit peuple*—would have understood them.

Thus every political experience nourished his substance, and was turned by him into a profound concern. Had he not retained the simplicity of childhood, his preoccupations would have made him a cynic; had he not been a man of absolute faith, they would have overcome him. He escaped these temptations because he never doubted God's mercy; and he never doubted his own vocation: this is why, in Mauriac's parting words, he became, in the last years of his life, "an old molossus with bloodshot eyes, biting at the shins of fat sheep and foolish ewes."

Notes

1. *La Liberté pour quoi faire?*, p. 15.

2. *Ibid.*, p. 189.

3. Romano Guardini, *The End of the Modern World* (New York: Sheed and Ward, 1956).

4. "Nous sommes en guerre," in *Carrefour,* July 16, 1947. Bernanos means here the State as a traditional entity, as the product of history, the organizer and civilizer of society. We shall see farther on what he thought of the modern State.

5. *La France contre les Robots,* pp. 133-34.

6. *Ibid.,* pp. 24-25.

7. *Tradition of Freedom,* p. 148.

8. *La Liberté pour quoi faire?*, pp. 106-7.

9. *Tradition of Freedom,* p. 105.

10. *Ibid.,* p. 114.

11. *Nous autres, Français,* p. 162.

12. *La France contre les Robots,* pp. 182-183.

13. *Lettre aux Anglais,* p. 183.

14. *Tradition of Freedom,* p. 156.

15. *La France contre les Robots,* pp. 194-195.

16. *Lettre aux Anglais,* p. 154.

17. *Plea for Liberty,* p. 242.

18. "Nous sommes en guerre," in *Carrefour,* July 16, 1947.

19. *Last Essays,* p. 100.

20. Quoted in *Plea for Liberty,* p. 262.

21. Pp. 192-93.

22. My italics.

23. *Tradition of Freedom,* p. 199.

24. Quoted in *Cahiers du Rhône,* [*Essais et témoinages* (Ed. du Seuil, 1949).]

25. *Plea for Liberty,* p. 247.—Indeed, what self-respecting man has not been at least tempted to cheat at the myriad of tests he is supposed to fill out, answer, check, and spend hours on, either by sabotaging the test or by guessing the answers that the tester wants to receive.

26. *Lettre aux Anglais,* p. 205.

27. [Em. Mounier,] "Un Surnaturalisme historique," in *L'Espoir des désespérés* [Ed. du Seuil, 1953),] p. 216.

28. *Lettre aux Anglais*; quoted in *Plea for Liberty,* p. 267.

29. "'Morning coffee in Paris, aperitive at Chandernagor, and dinner in San Francisco'—can you realize it! Oh, in the next inevitable war the flame-thrower tanks will be able to launch their fire at two thousand meters instead of only fifty, your sons' faces will be instantly boiled and their eyes pop out of their orbits. But when peace is signed, you will again congratulate each other on mechanical progress." *La France contre les Robots,* pp. 137-38.

30. "Un Surnaturalisme historique," etc. p. 208.

Books by Bernanos

AMERICAN EDITIONS OF BERNANOS' POLITICAL ESSAYS:

Plea for Liberty (Pantheon, 1944)

Tradition of Freedom (Roy, 1950)

The Last Essays (Regnery, 1955)

POLITICAL WORKS:

La Grande Peur des Bien-Pensants (Grasset, 1931)

Les Grands Cimetières sous la lune (Plon, 1938)

Scandale de la vérité (Gallimard, 1939)

Nous autres, Français (Gallimard, 1939)

Lettre aux Anglais (Gallimard, 1946)

La France contre les Robots (Robert Laffont, 1947)

Les Enfants humiliés (Gallimard, 1949)

La Liberté pour quoi faire? (Gallimard, 1953)

THE MORE IMPORTANT NOVELS OF BERNANOS:

Sous le Soleil de Satan (Plon, 1926)

Under the Sun of Satan (New York: Pantheon, 1949)

L'Imposture (Plon, 1927)

La Joie (Plon, 1929)

Joy (New York: Pantheon, 1946)

Journal d'un Curé de Campagne (Plon, 1936)

Diary of a Country Priest (New York: Macmillan, 1948)

Nouvelle Histoire de Mouchette (Plon, 1937)

Monsieur Ouine (Plon, 1946)

Albert Sonnenfeld (essay date winter 1964)

SOURCE: Sonnenfeld, Albert. "The Hostile Phantoms of Georges Bernanos: *Sous le Soleil de Satan* and *M. Ouine.*" *L'Esprit Créateur* 4, no. 4 (winter 1964): 208-21.

[*In the following essay, Sonnenfeld discerns in Bernanos's two novels* Under the Sun of Satan *and* The Open Mind *critical responses to works by Anatole France and André Gide, both of whom the author harshly criticized for their anti-Catholic writings, and notes the elements in both novels that parody characters and events in France's and Gide's works.*]

If in the beginning was the Word then all other words are but echoes. To an observer who had discerned certain stylistic influences in his early paintings, Degas affably replied with the query: "Vous avez déjà vu quelqu'un naître seul?" The works of art which form his intellectual hereditary traits are truly the progenitors of the artist. They are the great, often hostile, phantoms haunting the imagination of the potential creator; he cannot escape their shadowy presence. "Toute invention est réponse," André Malraux proclaimed, and it is precisely as a reply to the "voices of silence" that every work of art must, at least implicitly, be an act of criticism. The two fundamental and most easily discernible critical responses to the echoes of the Word are *pastiche* and *parody*. They are possible both simultaneously and consecutively. When Baudelaire, in *Le Cygne,* writes "Veuve d'Hector, hélas! et femme d'Hélénus!", his use of the rhyme *us* and of proper names combines with the strategic position of *hélas* and the equilibrium of the 4:2//2:4 rhythm to form a pastiche of Racine.[1] In other words, Baudelaire is implying that there is a quality in the style of his predecessor worth imitating in this particular context and, far more indirectly, that the style of Lamartine, say, would not be apposite here. Parody is much more explicit: its lineage is easier to trace since it is often a stylistic attack against a particular work which must be recognizable if the parody is to be successful. The minute we read "Eh bien! tous ces marins et tous ces capitaines," we know (even if the poet had not given us his source) that Tristan Corbière is parodying Hugo's *Oceano Nox*: "O combien de marins! combien de capitaines . . ." The casual *Eh bien!* and the deprecatory *tous ces* function as a criticism of the ecstatic Hugolian *O combien de.*

What we normally consider *originality* in art is the suppression of the identifiable model or target, of the direct linkage to an earlier work of art which marks parody and most pastiche as dependent rather than independent creation.[2] The artist becomes inventor, expressing, in Malraux's words, "une volonté obscure et fanatique de rupture avec l'art dont il est né." It is with this *rupture* that art begins, Malraux continues; no art is possible without it. But even in *original* art, I believe, invention remains response; no one, despite Rimbaud, has created the world or the word anew. The two fundamental critical postures of pastiche and parody, which on this more general level one might call *imitation* and *revolt*, maintain, albeit obliquely, the work of art's condition as an echo or critical response. Every artistic or philosophical decision governing the creation of the work is in effect, whether conscious or not, a form of imitation or revolt or both. That Nerval should choose the sonnet form in *Les Chimères,* for example, denotes a revolt against the expansive forms of his Romantic contemporaries and an imitation of an earlier tradition. Gide's predilection for the first-person *récit* links him to Constant while divorcing him from his Naturalist predecessors. Curiously, in the "original" work of art the degree of dependency found in pastiche and parody has been reversed. Pastiche, with its often elusive debt to a model, becomes in the work of *imitation* the Elysian hunting-ground of the diligent cataloguer of sources; it will not concern us further here. But parody, so intimately bound to its target that it rarely attains autonomous excellence, is endowed in the work of *revolt* with such autonomy that it is frequently impossible to trace the original target which irritated the author into creation. Thanks to the Symbolists' extraordinary self-consciousness about the creative act, many of us have long limited our view of the author as critic to such works, *Ars poetica* and *Künstlerroman* for instance, which treat directly of art and the artist. Bewildering as it may seem in the abstract, however, any work of art may constitute an act of literary criticism, a credo or a nego of sorts; and that act of criticism may itself have been a primary force in the creation of the work of art.

No author could be more alien to the modern tradition of the creator-critic (exemplified by Henry James, T. S. Eliot, Gide, and countless others) than Georges Bernanos. No one seems less preoccupied by esthetic problems: "Nul n'est moins *art pour art,* nul n'est moins amateur que moi," he wrote to his spiritual director Dom Besse. Bernanos has nothing but contempt for the "littérature des littérateurs qui se fait et se défait en vase clos, bien que transparent, comme certaines expériences de chimie." He protests at having to submit his writings piecemeal for editorial emendation: "Si j'en avais fait autant pour le Soleil de Satan, Dieu sait quelles corrections imbéciles on m'aurait ainsi imposées—ou suggérées—qui auraient fait de ce bouquin un de ces romans *bien construits* . . ." When last year I inquired whether in Bernanos' unpublished correspondence there were any discussions of his conception of the art of the novel, with particular reference to Dostoevsky,[3] I was assured by the executor of the Bernanos estate that the author of **M. Ouine** was not a man of letters! He was, nevertheless, an avid reader. His polemic works (especially the articles collected in **Le Crépuscule des Vieux**) are replete with the names of major figures in modern literature; he judges them all, condemns most of them, but almost never on esthetic criteria. What counts for Bernanos is the writer's spiritual condition, his moral influence, the Catholic relevance of his subject matter ("Ce n'est pas ma chanson qui est immortelle, c'est ce que je chante"). How else can one explain Bernanos' admiration for Barbey d'Aurevilly and Léon Bloy, his disdain for Proust and Gide? This almost desperate priority accorded matter over manner no doubt explains the striking technical flaws in many of his early novels. When writing **Sous le Soleil de Satan,** he explained in 1940, "j'avais le choix entre convaincre et séduire. J'ai choisi de convaincre et non de plaire." And so that brilliant first novel is patently flawed by the constant, tasteless interventions of Bernanos the polemicist: facile ironies at the expense of the secularism of the Third Republic; deformation of characterization to prove a point; irrelevant digressions; above all, the introduction at the novel's end of an apparently gratuitous caricature of Anatole France in the person of Antoine Saint-Marin of the French Academy, "le dernier des Grecs," a character who seemingly has nothing to do with the main lines of the story of Mouchette and Father Donissan.

That the caricatural portrait of Antoine Saint-Marin was no afterthought becomes obvious in the light of Robert Vallery-Radot's account of the composition of the novel. Bernanos' friend and initial sponsor, to whom the novelist had read his creation aloud, tells us that the three sections of **Sous le Soleil de Satan** were written in the following order: 1. *Le Saint de Lumbres* (now the final section, which concludes with the portrait of Saint-Marin); 2. *Histoire de Mouchette* (now the prologue or opening chapter); 3. *La Tentation du Désespoir* (now the second section, devoted to the early career of Father Donissan). If we reread the novel according to the initial order of creation, we have the uneasy feeling that the despised Saint-Marin is gazing malevolently and yet protectively at the melodramatic convulsions of Mouchette as well as at the metaphysical combat waged against Satan by Father Donissan, the future Saint of Lumbres. This is as it should be, for Antoine Saint-Marin, that is, Anatole France, angered Bernanos into creating this novel; it is only fair that he be present in the great novel that he unknowingly inspired.

The true motivation for Saint-Marin's strange pilgrimage to the church of the Saint of Lumbres is never fully explained, but it is obvious that he is driven by intellectual curiosity, not by spiritual necessity. There might even be material for a new book. For over fifty years, the celebrated writer had exercised "la magistrature de l'ironie," respecting nothing, least of all the truth: "nul être pensant n'a défloré plus d'idées." Like Anatole France, he prides himself on his Hellenism and was hailed as "ce nouveau miracle de la civilisation méditerranéenne." The young grammarians who form his entourage of subservient admirers have nothing but praise for his style. "Sa simplicité savante, sa phrase aussi rouée qu'une ingénue de théâtre . . ." His public adores the tone of intimate impertinence, the way in which he dispenses the treasures of a "scepticisme de boulevard" as though it were ancient wisdom. The reputation of the self-styled "professeur de doute" had, like that of Anatole France, been consecrated by membership in the French Academy. Bernanos takes cruel delight in depicting Saint-Marin's lechery, his dependence on drugs, his un-Christian fear of death. But the words which recur most frequently in this memorable caricature are *skepticism* and *irony*, as clearly applicable to Anatole France as the appellation "vieux jongleur" which Bernanos perhaps uses to remind the reader of France's *Le Jongleur de Notre-Dame*.[4] This accumulation of recognizable traits does not make *Sous le Soleil de Satan* into a frivolous *roman à clef*, however. For Georges Bernanos, Anatole France was the symbol of everything that was hateful in a dechristianized modern France living in the false light of Satan's sun: "Notre république athénienne a fait son Dieu d'Anatole France," he wrote in *Le Crépuscule des Vieux*. And in an important letter to F. Lefèvre, he condemned the historical role of the author of *L'Histoire contemporaine*:

> C'est ainsi qu'on propose Anatole France à l'admiration du monde. Prenant prétexte d'une réaction contre une nouvelle anarchie romantique, le dix-huitième siècle essaie de rentrer derrière ce vieillard ereinté. Remède pire encore que le mal! Car l'ivresse artificielle du rationalisme finit toujours par aboutir à un accès de *delirium tremens*. Et l'on voit tout à coup paraître à travers le désert d'une littérature rendue stérile, le sauvage, l'homme de la nature, le primate plein de songes et ruminant la ruine totale de la planète avec un cœur d'enfant: le Genevois Rousseau.

In an interview given shortly after the publication of *Sous le Soleil de Satan,* Bernanos, far from denying the origins of Saint-Marin, launched into a new tirade:

> Je n'ai pas voulu me borner à une caricature d'Anatole France, mais puisqu'on parle de lui, tant mieux. Cela devrait contenter, d'ailleurs, ses rares disciples, dans un moment où leur maître glisse à une indifférence, à un oubli mille fois plus dur à un tel homme que le mépris. Son œuvre est vile. Ce n'etait qu'un jeu, dit-on. Mais quel jeu? Jouer avec l'espérance des hommes, c'est duper la faim et la soif du pauvre. Il y a peut-être aujourd'hui dans le monde tel ou tel misérable désespéré parce que l'auteur de *Thaïs* avait de l'esprit, savait sa langue. Cela, c'est la faute que rien ne rédime, c'est le crime essentiel, absolu. La haine même fait place à une espèce d'horreur sacrée si l'on songe que cette consommation de l'espérance n'a servi qu'à donner, pendant plus d'un demi-siècle au cruel vieillard, des félicités de professeur libertin. Non! Je ne le hais plus. Je voudrais simplement emprunter pour lui à l'Evangile sa malédiction la plus mystérieuse: il serait bon que cet homme ne fût jamais né.

It is obvious that the last lines of this vituperation echo, almost verbatim, passages in the portrait of Saint-Marin in *Sous le Soleil de Satan.* But far more essential is the attack on France, not as the defender of Dreyfus or as contributor to *Le Temps,* but as the author of *Thaïs,* a work whose elegance may have so undermined Catholicism in the mind of a reader as to cause him to lose faith and hope; all this in the name of witty entertainment. This is why Antoine Saint-Marin is referred to with annoying and obsessive frequency as "l'auteur du *Cierge Pascal*": the religious title of a novel which has clearly received ironic treatment from Saint-Marin may well be synonymous with *Thaïs.* "Si vous n'avez point vu l'ermite," the doctor from Chavranches tells Saint-Marin to console him at Father Donissan's absence, "au moins connaissez-vous l'ermitage? Quelle curieuse maison! Quelle solitude!" As the author of *Le Cierge Pascal* approaches the confessional where the contorted dead body of the Saint of Lumbres is hidden, he thinks aloud: "Je tiens mon saint!" If indeed Saint-Marin had written his book about the hermit of Lumbres, he would have written *Thaïs*; Father Donissan would have become Father Paphnuce.

Thaïs is, of course, a virtual anthology of parodies ranging from Plato's Banquet to Flaubert's *Tentation de Saint-Antoine.* For Bernanos, it is primarily an attack on faith itself, on the Community of Saints, and he would view it as a spurious mockery of the very type of priest who interested him most in his first works: the athlete of God, as he calls him, the fisher of souls. In his eclectic and masterfully elegant style, Anatole France tells the story of Father Paphnuce, abbé of Antinoé and the most uncompromising ascetic in the desert of the Thebaid. No one observed more rigorous fasts, no one wore rougher hairshirts, no one whipped himself as mercilessly to preclude even the possibility of demonic visitations. Among Paphnuce's talents, France writes ironically, was the ability to distinguish dreams sent by God from those inspired by Satan. And so, despite the memories of his own Augustinian youth, Paphnuce sets out for Alexandria to convert the courtisan Thaïs whose image, stimulated by the priest's repressed sexual longings, the author intimates, had been haunting his "divinely" inspired dreams. Thaïs herself was born of poor, idolatrous tavern-keepers, and after a childhood of abuse in an atmosphere of drunken debauchery runs away to become a dancer. She is not unready to listen to Paphnuce's arguments, for she has begun to worry about aging; nor has she forgotten the Christian slave, Ahmès, who had her baptised. But it is The Banquet and the subsequent orgy which lead her to obey Paphnuce's entreaties to renounce her life of sin by following him into the desert to a convent: "Vois c'est le soir, ô ma sœur. Les ombres bleues de la nuit couvrent les collines. Mais bientôt tu verras briller dans l'aurore les tabernacles de vie; bientôt tu verras s'allumer les roses de l'éternel matin." One can image Bernanos' reaction upon encountering in this ironic context a cluster of images which for him was replete with the most personal and intense religious significance. The author of *Sous le Soleil de Satan* returned incessantly to the image of night and dawn, so much so that Lucifer was for him "la fausse Aurore"; to console the sinner he wrote: "Quand on va jusqu'au bout de la nuit, on rencontre une autre aurore." The final section of *Thaïs* is the most blatantly satirical. "Saint" Paphnuce returns to the hermitage in the Thebaid, still haunted by the visions of Thaïs which by now have become far less ambiguous. The devil himself has entered Paphnuce's life, but ironically at the moment he joins the ranks of the possessed, crouching on top of a phallic column, he becomes a saint in the public's view. Thousands flock to witness the hermit's ultimate act of self-mortification; a commercialized pilgrimage, not unlike Lourdes, flourishes on the spot. Finally, upon hearing that Thaïs is dying in an aura of sanctity Paphnuce resolves to yield to the devil's blandishments only to learn to his horror that the sisters view him as a diabolic vampire.

This rudimentary but necessary plot summary cannot help but evoke certain resonances familiar to the student of *Sous le Soleil de Satan.* Like Paphnuce, Father Donissan is an obsessively rigorous ascetic, whipping himself cruelly, wearing hairshirts and fasting. Indeed, one of the sights which Saint-Marin finds most intriguing at Lumbres is of "la croix, le fouet de cuir, la muraille rouge . . ." Unfortunately, Bernanos' priest does not have the uncanny ability, with which Anatole France roguishly endowed his hero, to distinguish divine messages from demonic temptation. Donissan, like Paphnuce, sees Satan everywhere, above all in his own soul, and each of his intended "miracles" (especially the exorcism of Mouchette and the attempted resurrection of

the little Havret boy) turns out to have been the result of diabolic complicity. "J'ai fait aussi dans mon temps quelques folies," Donissan admitted to a priest who was reading him a chapter from the *Lives of the Desert Fathers.* Paphnuce's extravagances, we remember, are based on the prodigious acts of the desert fathers. Discussing the perplexity of some of his readers when faced with the new novelistic treatment accorded the priest in *Sous le Soleil de Satan,* Bernanos speculated ironically: "On pourrait imaginer d'écrire mon livre sur un plan romantique. L'abbé Donissan y serait en lutte ouverte avec son évêque l'abbé Menou-Segrais, un prêtre voluptueux et borné, Mouchette, une courtisane sanctifiée par le vice, qui donnerait des leçons au pape et referait devant le chapitre de la cathédrale le monologue de *Ruy Blas.*" The latter part of this hypothetical reworking of his first novel could also apply to *Thaïs,* of course. Even as Bernanos really created her, Mouchette is in the mould of France's heroine. She is the daughter of non-believing parents (her father is a brewer while Thaïs' idolatrous father ran a sailors' tavern) and soon becomes the victim of the Marquis de Cadignan's sexual appetites. From this initial violation of her innocence, she falls into ever greater depravity complicated by severe mental disorder, until possible salvation appears in the person of Father Donissan. Unlike Paphnuce's unctuous appeal for Thaïs' conversion, clearly a parody of edifying Church pamphleteering ("quel tressaillement agitera la chair de ton âme quand tu sentiras les doigts de lumière se poser sur tes yeux . . ."), Bernanos' priest undertakes a full-fledged exorcism. Unlike Thaïs' facile conversion and passive ascension toward sainthood, Mouchette's very salvation is in doubt despite her possible conversion *in articulo mortis,* when she cuts her own throat in a rage of satanic despair. Finally, both Father Paphnuce and Father Donissan become "saints," and their respective hermitages become the sites of miracles and subsequently the goal of pilgrimages.

It would be foolish to insist on further analogies of detail between the two novels. What interests us here is an act of creation dictated by a hostile phantom. Though direct comparisons between *Sous le Soleil de Satan,* the life of the Curé d'Ars, the *Diaboliques* of Barbey d'Aurevilly and the strident polemic novels of Léon Bloy seem to most Bernanos readers a more fertile terrain for source-hunting, it was the bitter memory of his reaction to *Thaïs* which secretly governed the creation of his first novel. Both books are divided into three parts devoted, though not in the same order, to the torments of the demon-haunted priest, the precipitous fall and possible redemption of a sexually corrupted woman, the final, equivocal sanctification of the priest-hero. Since *Thaïs* is itself a parody, Bernanos could not content himself with parodying France's attack on the hermit priest, though of course *L'Imposture* was to show he was capable of vicious parody. Instead, he wrote what one might call a counter-parody. Where Anatole France made fun of the demon-haunted Paphnuce, Bernanos took him seriously and transformed his nightmarish existence into a spiritual drama worthy of Dostoevsky. Both priest-heros are extremists, however, and the image of the priesthood protected by a Donissan is, as Father Blanchet has pointed out so clearly in his *Le Prêtre dans le roman d'aujourd'hui,* thoroughly disconcerting to literal-minded Catholic priests. Where the French sceptic parodied the Romantic *Madeleine repentie* trope in his adaptation of the Golden Legend of Thaïs, Bernanos treated the fall and possible redemption of Mouchette with high seriousness, creating a parable of the impossibility of innocence on Satan's earth ("le prince de ce monde"). Where France cleverly mocked the commercialized pilgrimages of Fatima and Lourdes, Bernanos, equally contemptuous of popular cure hunting, portrayed a genuine, if misguided, "saint." In **Sous le Soleil de Satan** Bernanos was still groping with the rudiments of novelistic craft (as indeed he was to until the **Journal d'un Curé de Campagne**); the esthetically unpardonable creation of Antoine Saint-Marin, who detracts from the potency of the effect of Donissan's death, was perhaps the novelist's unconscious admission that his first novel was written not only under Satan's sun but in the half-light of Anatole France's irony. "The sneer from Voltaire to Anatole France," Claudel wrote to Jacques Rivière, "has always seemed to me to be the sign of the damned. As soon as man is possessed by the hatred of God, he is unable to prevent himself from laughing."[5] Georges Bernanos hated the laughter of Anatole France's *Thaïs,* but he could not escape it. Invention, especially in a first work, is response, and Bernanos answered the endlessly recurring echoes of a hostile voice in his own strident tone.

"Ceux à qui il [Bernanos] parla à cette époque de son roman se souviennent qu'il le présentait comme une satire d'André Gide—l'homme qui dit à la fois *Oui* et *Non.* De cette première intention, il ne restera à peu près rien dans l'œuvre réalisée, où il est trop évident que le personnage de Ouine doit tout à des sources purement intérieures." These revealing words from Albert Béguin's postface to his masterful critical edition of **M. Ouine** give us a valuable clue to the critical-creative reflex which governed the composition of Bernanos' most complex novel. If, as Béguin alleges, almost nothing of the original personal satire of Gide remains, it is because Bernanos had by now (he worked on the novel from 1931 to 1940) become a skillful novelistic technician who would never allow a work of art to be flawed by the gross caricature of a writer and one of his works, as had been the case in **Sous le Soleil de Satan.** Despite Béguin's allegation, I find that the work, if not the personality, of Gide remains the target of Bernanos' wrath, that **M. Ouine** can fruitfully be considered as an intricate parody of various Gidian ideas, themes and even phrases: in short, that the novel which

Bernanos called "le fumier de Job" is a response to the hated voice of the author of *L'Immoraliste.* For Gide's very name is anathema to Bernanos; in the articles of the 1920's and 1930's collected in **Le Crépuscule des Vieux** and in his other polemic works, Bernanos rails constantly against Gide and his disciples: "Nous les vîmes alors revenir en foule à M. Gide, et se suspendre au vieux tronc vermoulu comme un essaim de mouches grises d'automne dès la première gelée blanche."

The image of Gide which dominates Bernanos' vituperations is that of the teacher, the corruptor of youth, the didactic poet of *Les Nourritures Terrestres,* and the arbiter of literary taste: "J'affirme que la peste noire n'anéantirait pas plus tôt le genre humain que ces forces obscures et féroces que les charmants petits dilettantes sortis de la poche de M. Gide caressent impunément de leurs doigts délicats." Bernanos sees French youth, "munis de leur petit brevet d'immoralisme," becoming servile imitators of their master's homosexuality while remaining afraid of life itself: ". . . ces fruits tardifs de l'automne gidien, si l'hiver les épargne, n'échapperont pas au soleil d'avril, rentreront avant que d'avoir pu éclore dans le cadavre où ils furent couvés." Gide's self-proclaimed pedagogical mission as a liberator of youth from moral constriction so infuriates Bernanos that he speaks of "l'entremetteur spirituel d'une petite troupe d'archanges révoltés contre les lois, et il lui faut désormais moucher et torcher toute une marmaille, comme un surveillant de classe enfantine." In addition, Bernanos insists constantly on Gide's virtual decrepitude, his intellectual sterility; "cette vieille empoisonneuse," he called him in an article in *l'Action Française.* "Une momie [conservée] dans les aromates," "comme ces animaux élémentaires auxquels un seul orifice tient lieu de bouche et d'anus, ce qui semble le dernier mot de la sincérité gidienne," "ce haut cas de perversité intellectuelle"; these are some of the epithets Bernanos applies to the author of *Les Faux-Monnayeurs.* But, above all, he attacks Gide's unwillingness to take a stand, to assume the Bernanosian risk ("les vieilles gens craignent moins l'erreur que le risque," we read in **Sous le Soleil de Satan**), to accept Pascal's wager: "Qu'est-ce qu'un gidisme sans mystère?" "Le goût de l'immoraliste dévot ne fut jamais que de troubler les âmes par une équivoque savante, au joint de l'intelligence et de la sensualité, à ce point précis où naît la honte, dont cet homme étrange semble affamé." Gide is the man who says both *Oui* and *Non: Ouine.*

In the light of these vicious polemics, it is revealing that Bernanos stresses **M. Ouine**'s role as spiritual mentor, as self-designated pedagogue. He is a retired professor of modern languages who, we learn early in the novel, has devised a new method of teaching concerning which he is corresponding with the minister of education. He recalls with pleasure that "pas un de mes élèves, jadis, qui n'ait fait le projet de me suivre . . .

au bout du monde." His chosen disciple in the dead parish of Fenouille is the young boy Philippe who considers Ouine "le compagnon prédestiné de sa vie, l'initiateur, le héros poursuivi à travers tant de livres." Philippe's "nouveau maître," as he calls M. Ouine, expresses himself constantly in Gidian aphorisms: "cette chambre . . . c'est moi qui ai voulu son dénuement"; "chacun de nous peut aller jusqu'au bout de soi-même"; "comme ces gelées vivantes, au fond de la mer, je flotte et j'absorbe. Nous vous apprendrons ce pauvre secret. Oui, vous apprendrez de moi à vous laisser remplir par l'heure qui passe." Like Gide, or at least like Bernanos' conception of him, M. Ouine's essential moral posture is ambiguous. The Dean of Lescure remarks that he has never heard from Ouine a word for or against religion: "il semble ne s'intéresser qu'au problème moral." Late in the novel, the author comments that Ouine was incapable of renouncing "une seule de ces heures dont chacune avait marqué un progrès vers la délivrance, la liberté totale . . . il se rappelait n'avoir jamais réellement détesté qu'une contrainte, celle dont le principe était en lui, la conscience du bien et du mal, pareille à un autre être dans l'être—ce ver." Moreover, in a rather insidious manner, Bernanos allows himself to make certain allusions to Gide's work (". . . qui de nous n'a cherché la brebis perdue, rapporté l'agneau sur ses épaules?" Ouine remarks); or to Gide's person ("M. Valéry, par exemple, l'ancien receveur général. Votre maître et lui étaient jadis camarades," someone tells Philippe). There are disturbing undertones of homosexuality in Ouine's relationship with Philippe ("ses belles mains nettes, ses mains qui font indifféremment le bien et le mal, comme celle [*sic*] d'un dieu," Jambe-de-Laine tells the boy) and in the insinuation that Ouine is responsible for the murder of the crippled cowherd.

More revealing than a list of details identifying Ouine with Gide is a study of the evolution of the teacher-disciple relationship. In Gide's work this is, of course, a recurring pattern: Ménalque and Nathanaël in the *Nourritures,* Ménalque and Michel in *L'Immoraliste,* Edouard and Bernard in *Les Faux-Monnayeurs.* In **M. Ouine,** what Bernanos has done is to dramatize the pernicious influence that *an old immoralist might have had on a young Gide.* Philippe's childhood surrounded by women cannot help but recall *Si le grain ne meurt* and *La Porte étroite.* He lives with his mother and an English governess of sorts named "Miss"; his father is either dead or has disappeared (so much is ambiguous in **M. Ouine**). But instead of the modest, tranquil and harmonious existence of an Anna Shackleton, Bernanos, attacking Gide, hints at a lesbian relationship between Philippe's mother and "Miss" and, moreover, makes the Englishwoman's dealings with Philippe, whom she calls "Steeny" after her favorite English novel, appear more than slightly compromising. That this analogy is not mere speculation is shown by a key symbol. Madame de Néréis, the insane châtelaine of Wambescourt with

whom Ouine is staying, comments on Philippe's resemblance to his master and to prove her point pulls out an old picture of Ouine as a student:

> Que diable Philippe peut-il avoir de commun avec ce ridicule garçon? Le regard sans doute . . . Et tout à coup, comme à travers le papier flétri, une double petite ombre bouge, recule, recule encore, se rétrécit à la mesure de deux prunelles imperceptibles, presque effacées, de deux points pâles qui fixent Steeny avec une espèce de tristesse impérieuse . . . Mes yeux! pense-t-il, juste mes yeux!

Philippe tears up the picture, but Madame de Néréis continues to insist on its importance, recounting that Ouine had said of the boy: "Je viens de me revoir moi-même, comme un mort regarde dans le passé . . . Le petit garçon que j'étais, je l'ai vu, j'aurais pu le toucher, l'entendre."

With astonishing rapidity Ouine's young disciple becomes a virtual replica of the master himself. Steeny's predisposition toward becoming a new Gide is such that in the course of his first meeting with Ouine he already expresses himself in thoroughly Gidian terms: "je me méfie de Dieu—telle est ma façon de l'honorer"; or, "je suis ma pente, voilà tout." After his first initiation into Ouine's doctrines, Steeny goes beyond mere aphorisms and makes a full-blown, Gidian proclamation:

> La vie pour nous, ça ne doit pas être un but, c'est une proie. Et pas une seule, des milliers et des milliers de proies, autant que d'heures. Il s'agit de n'en rater aucune, avant la dernière, la dernière des dernières, celle qui nous échappe toujours,—couic! Une chose qui bouge, et tu sautes dessus. Dès lors, pourvu que tu t'empares de l'animal, qu'importe si c'est par ruse ou par force? Tu peux le poursuivre ou l'attendre, l'affûter, le tirer posé ou branché, le prendre au gîte. Ou encore l'avaler au passage comme une truite, à contre-courant, qui engoule le frai. "Je vous apprendrai, m'a-t-il dit, à vous remplir de l'heure qui passe! . . ."

The ill-fated cowherd who hears this Ménalque-like admonition to live for the present significantly answers: ". . . je suis sûr que vous venez de parler exactement comme lui [Ouine], je n'aurais pas reconnu votre voix." Like Bernard Profitendieu, indeed like the departing Prodigal himself, Steeny exults in being fatherless: ". . . plus d'ancêtres, le monde commence. J'aime mieux ça." He will take to the open road ("Je n'ai jamais aimé que les routes"), but he runs straight from his home to the monastically furnished room of M. Ouine, "ce demi-dieu bedonnant," as Bernanos contemptuously labels him.

The author of **M. Ouine** castigated Gide's work as "les délectations d'une imagination qui fut toujours des plus médiocres, aujourd'hui frappée d'impuissance, incapable d'évacuer ses rêves . . ." The death of M. Ouine is Bernanos' cruelest revenge on the man he considered to be the perverter of French youth. The retired professor of languages, who had functioned as a kind of anti-priest or saint in reverse, causing moral disintegration, suffering and even crime, dies fully aware of his own insignificance: "C'est moi qui ne suis rien." To his bewildered disciple, he tells the extraordinary myth of the empty bottle, drawing his symbol from the very bottle which he had shared with Steeny in a bizarre ceremony of consecration in evil in the early pages of the novel. "Je suis vide aussi," Ouine admits. He had thirsted for souls like a bogus God, he had won disciples, contaminated an entire parish ("La Paroisse morte" was Bernanos original title for the novel); but in so doing, Ouine, like the Gide of Bernanosian polemics, lost his own soul. "Je crois," Bernanos told F. Lefèvre in 1925, "que l'enfer imaginaire où jouent les personnages de M. Gide se rétrécit à mesure que s'approfondit un enfer intérieur, qu'il nous appartient pas de sonder." In *M. Ouine,* Bernanos sounded the depths of the Gidian hell.

Neither Anatole France nor André Gide are central to the drama of salvation and damnation which was Bernanos' main preocupation in both *Sous le Soleil de Satan* and *M. Ouine,* and, indeed, in all of his novels. It would be idle to pretend that his "sources" dominated all aspects of the two novels treated here. But Georges Bernanos was a writer who often wrote through reaction. In a letter to Anna de Noailles dated 1926, Bernanos said: "Je ne puis plus seulement ouvrir l'un de vos livres sans rougir de vous avoir laissé ignorer qu'ils sont depuis longtemps mes ennemis familiers . . . et qu'un des buts de ma pauvre vie est de vous renoncer parfaitement." The tension between polemicist and novelist in Bernanos' writing was such that he often began with a counterattack on an enemy before creating his own memorable characters. *L'Imposture* is a bad novel precisely because it is almost exclusively caricatural; only the presence of Abbé Chevance saves that work from the oblivion of personal polemics. Celebrated in literary and political circles for his violent fits of rage, Bernanos heard the hostile voices first. His instinctive reaction as a pamphleteer was to denounce; as a novelist, however, he unconsciously turned to a most imaginative form of criticism: parody. His boldest inventions reveal themselves to be responses. Ironically, the hated Anatole France and the despised André Gide must be acknowledged as patron saints of two of Georges Bernanos' finest novels.

Notes

1. This is not to denigrate Baudelaire's originality here, which consists precisely in invoking Racine in a poem about exile, Andromaque, and the melancholy alienation inspired by the view of the "new" Paris.

2. Cf. Proust's remark in *A l'Ombre des jeunes filles en fleur* (I, p. 155): "Toute nouveauté ayant pour condition l'élimination préalable du poncif auquel nous étions habitués et qui nous semblait la réalité même . . ."

3. See this writer's forthcoming piece "Dostoevsky and Bernanos," in *Renascence.*

4. Bernanos not only detested the whole notion of "God's Fool," but the facility implied in the notion of the artist as "jongleur." "Il est si facile," he wrote bitterly, "de faire de jolis livres pour de jolis yeux dans une jolie maison." And in December 1945: ". . . le métier d'écrivain n'est plus un métier, c'est une aventure, et d'abord une aventure spirituelle. Toutes les aventures spirituelles sont des Calvaires."

5. Cf. M. Ouine's comment, "il y a une malice dans le rire, un poison."

Peter Hebblethwaite (essay date 1965)

SOURCE: Hebblethwaite, Peter. "The Search for Heroes." In *Bernanos: An Introduction,* pp. 9-24. London: Bowes and Bowes, 1965.

[*In the following essay, Hebblethwaite describes Bernanos as "a Catholic writer," despite the author's claim against this label, and he details his qualities as a writer that make him relevant to modern readers, especially his presentation of the "sanctity" of life and his compassion for humanity.*]

In his lengthy *Lettre aux Anglais,* which has so far gone without a reply, Georges Bernanos introduced himself:

> My work is myself. It is me at home. I speak to you, pipe in mouth, my jacket still damp from the last shower, my boots steaming in front of the fire. I do not even trouble to go into another room to talk to you. I do my writing in the living room, on the table at which, later on, I shall be having supper with my wife and children.
>
> (English trans., p. 15.)

The letter is dated January 1942, it had been started a year before, and Bernanos was in Brazil. The tone of voice is familiar and friendly. We may have heard from an English critic that Bernanos 'uses language like flame-thrower',[1] or that he was misguided enough to drag the Devil into one of his novels; but he does not sound like a demagogue or an eccentric, and dialogue with him should be possible. We can perhaps, belatedly, answer his letter.

It could, of course, be argued that Bernanos sent his letter to the wrong address and that his is one of those typically French voices which do not carry across the

Channel. Bernanos is not a writer who speaks to a ready-made public, but one of those who create the taste by which they will be appreciated. He wrote to his publisher in 1934:

> There are writers who create their own public. Even where there is an initial success, a *coup de surprise,* the most difficult task remains to be done, and after the honeymoon come the partial failures, the misunderstandings, the quarrels and the reconciliations.[2]

So far, and on this side of the Channel, Bernanos has not so much been misunderstood as ignored; reconciliation is not needed because there has been no quarrel. To enable us to measure the width of the chasm which has to be bridged before a relationship can begin, I will quote a passage from Bernanos alongside one from George Orwell.

Here is Orwell, in his essay on 'The Art of Donald McGill':

> If you look into your own mind, which are you, Don Quixote or Sancho Panza? Almost certainly you are both. There is one part of you that wishes to be a hero or a saint, but another part of you is a fat little man who sees very clearly the advantages of staying alive with a whole skin. He is your unofficial self, the voice of the belly protesting against the soul . . . His tastes lie towards safety, soft beds, no work, pots of beer, and women with 'voluptuous' curves.[3]

Here now is Bernanos, in his semi-autobiographical *Les Enfants humiliés*:

> No matter how far back I go in my life, I don't remember having many illusions. An illusion is a dream on the cheap, a dream too often grafted onto precocious experience, a dream of future clerks. I had my dreams, true, but I knew they were dreams. An illusion is the abortion of a dream, a dwarf-dream, cut down to the size of a child; but I wanted my dreams to be boundless—what use have they otherwise? If I had to begin life over again, I would try to make them greater still, because life is infinitely greater and more beautiful than I had imagined, even in my dreams; and I infinitely smaller. I dreamed of saints and heroes, neglecting the intermediate forms of humanity, and I discover that the intermediate forms of humanity scarcely exist, that only the saints and heroes really count. The intermediate forms are a sort of pulp, a spineless mush—when you have taken a handful you know the rest, and this jelly would not deserve a name if the saints and heroes did not give it one, did not bestow on it the name of 'man'. It is thanks to the saints and heroes that I am anything at all; they have long ago given me my fill of dreams and saved me from illusions.

> (*Les Enfants humiliés,* pp. 199-200.)

At first glance Orwell seems so much more attractive because so much less pretentious. He gives us the old familiar choice between body and soul, not without a certain complicity with Brother Ass. But Orwell never

quite lost the habit of seeing the working-classes through the cosy fug of an Edwardian music-hall, and in presenting the 'body' in terms of proletarian tastes he is indulging in a form of social blackmail; his intention clearly is that the reader should recognise his own secret, unavowed self. There is a good deal of bluff in Orwell's attitude, and Bernanos would have called the bluff. For Bernanos is not interested in the body-soul duality, or rather he begins where it leaves off. This is why he objected so strongly to Mauriac, 'the tortured author of so many books in which despair of the flesh sweats on every page, like muddy water from the walls of a cellar'. (*La Liberté, pour quoi faire?* p. 130.[4]) The judgement is typical of Bernanos in that it is unfair to Mauriac and revealing about himself. Orwell seems to regard heroism or sanctity as remote and distinctly unlikely possibilities; he is more interested in the fat little man. Bernanos, with his gaze riveted on the saints and heroes, appears to dismiss the rest of humanity with a gesture of scorn; and since we are included in 'the intermediate forms', we feel perhaps inclined to shut our ears. But Bernanos is not declaring his contempt for ordinary people. He is rejecting mediocrity wherever it is found; and mediocrity means for him the refusal of risk, the refusal of commitment, an attitude in which the fear of being disturbed predominates. Mediocrity can wear a bowler hat or a cloth-cap, and it can also hide under a mitre; whatever its headgear, Bernanos is opposed to it. His novels are one important attempt in the twentieth century to break with mediocrity and to restore status to the hero.

The hero, in drama and in the novel, was in eclipse. M. Bénichou[5] spoke of the 'demolition of the hero' in French literature of the seventeenth century: the self-assured heroes of Corneille gave way to the tortured, hesitant protagonists of Racine, undermined by a love that has become a malady. The work of demolition went on into the nineteenth century with redoubled vigour. Emma Bovary, for example, is great only in her dreams, and in England Thackeray aptly subtitled his *Vanity Fair* 'a novel without a hero'. The naturalists were even less interested in the hero. 'Naturalism,' wrote Huysmans in his repentant preface to the 1884 edition of *A Rebours,* 'did not admit of the exception, at least in theory. It confined itself to depicting ordinary existence and tried to create characters who would be as like as possible to the average.' That the hero in the older sense should gradually vanish is perhaps a consequence of democracy; the unheroic hero, the common man, muddling through somehow, has become typical of the twentieth century, and he can be as misunderstood and tragic a figure as any Greek prince burdened with the affairs of state. The artist hero in Proust, his ironical brother in Thomas Mann and the political heroes of André Malraux are attempts to restore to the hero his fading glory. Some of them attempt still more: they offer a way of salvation, propose a way of escape from the crushing banality of modern life. Without being naïvely proposed as models, they suggest that the possibilities of human nature are more wide-ranging than is commonly supposed. They open windows, let in air.

Bernanos' contribution is the creation of a new literary type: the saint-hero.[6] Here, of course, the ambiguities, literary and theological, come crowding in. A remark of Pascal illustrates the difficulties facing a novelist who deals with sanctity: 'It requires grace to turn a man into a saint, and anyone who doubts it does not know what a saint is or what a man is.'[7] The novelist who 'knows what a saint is' may try to make grace perceptible in the form of sudden conversions or other breaks in the psychological unity of his novel. Or he may forget 'what a man is', and then the saint will begin to look like a superman. The result, in either case, will be unconvincing. Bernanos, with his first hero, Abbé Donissan in **Sous le soleil de Satan,** tries to have it both ways. On the one hand, we have a meeting with Satan and an attempted miracle, and in the intervals too much stress is placed on Donissan's strength of will, on his spiritual athleticism. The novel is a splendid failure. But in **La Joie** and, more impressively still, in **Journal d'un curé de campagne,** the human is transformed from within by grace, and grace seems natural without losing its quality of 'otherness'. The last words of the diary are:

> How easy it is to hate oneself. True grace is to forget. Yet if pride could die in us the supreme grace would be to love oneself in all simplicity—as one would love any of those who have loved and suffered in Christ.
>
> (**Journal d'un curé de campagne,** p. 363.)

Poverty, self-forgetfulness, charity, humility—these are the attributes of Bernanos' fictional saints, and they are not the attributes of heroes as we usually conceive them. But through them a new and overlooked form of heroism is restored: the heroism of sanctity. Huysmans again provides an important pointer: 'Virtue being, one must admit, an *exception,* was therefore excluded from the naturalist project. Not having the Catholic notion of fall and temptation, we did not realise the strivings and sufferings which virtue had to go through. Spiritual heroism meant nothing to us.' Provided we substitute sanctity for 'virtue'—with its too exclusively ethical associations—this passage describes the project of Bernanos.

The three novels I have mentioned present the risk of sanctity. Bernanos wrote five more novels. In **Un Crime, Un Mauvais rêve** and **Monsieur Ouine** evil appears to dominate, and these novels are the sombre background against which his saints are seen. **L'Imposture** can be considered as Bernanos' Faust, and **La Nouvelle histoire de Mouchette** is a short *récit* on the death of innocence. All Bernanos' novels were written, though not all were published, in the period between the two wars. He wrote in 1936:

> The world wars of today which seem to show such prodigious human activity, are in fact indictments of the growing apathy of humanity. In the end, at certain stated periods, huge flocks of resigned sheep will be led to the slaughter.
>
> (**Journal d'un curé de campagne,** p. 180.)

The social and political characteristics of the period, reflected obliquely in the novels, are tackled directly in numerous other works of uneven quality which combine polemics, autobiography, satirical portraits and historical *aperçus* with highly individual religious meditation; they are of less interest to an English reader who, though sensitive to the prose, may have difficulty in identifying the targets of Bernanos' abuse. The strange, hallucinating world of the novels will be my main concern.

Bernanos, as will already be apparent, is preoccupied in his novels with religious problems, but he was not a 'theologian' still less a 'philosopher'. He would have greeted his appearance in a volume called *The Novelist as Philosopher*[8] with his characteristic roar of laughter—his friends always refer to it as volcanic. Nor would he claim to be a mystic. He was a man of faith who knew his catechism. Like Graham Greene, though for different reasons, he does not like to call himself a Catholic novelist:

> May God preserve us from poets who are apologists! If there is one thing to be ashamed of it is to see methods of propaganda, taken from politics, divide truths into those which can and those which cannot be said, into the convenient and the inconvenient, the regrettable and the consoling, the dangerous and the harmless—as if there were truths without risk. That is why I refused the name of Catholic novelist and why I said that I was a Catholic who wrote novels, no more, no less . . . If you cannot harmonise without strain and contortions your faith and your art, then keep silent.[9]

The publication of **Les Grands cimetières sous la lune,** based on his experiences in Majorca in 1936-37, with its pitiless attack on the blessing given by the Spanish hierarchy to Franco's cause, shows that Bernanos meant what he said. The *enfant terrible* kept his independence. Yet though he always preserved his liberty of thought and action, he did not departmentalise his mind; he never separated his meditation on the life of Christ from the business of writing novels. And in a sense his claim that he is not a Catholic writer is disingenuous.

It is disingenuous because he shows in his novels about sanctity the way the life of Christ is worked out in men and women of our time. Bernanos is thus an unusual figure in the literature of the twentieth century, a voice apart. He believed that prayer was a condition of lucidity about ourselves and the world. His Curé de campagne notes:

For one who has the habit of prayer, reflection is often merely an alibi, a cunning way of finding confirmation for one's plans. Reasoning will always obscure what we wish to keep in the shadows. A worlding can think out the pros and cons and sum up his chances. No doubt. But what are our chances worth? We who have admitted once and for all into each moment of our puny lives the terrifying presence of God?

(*Journal d'un curé de campagne*, pp. 6-7.)

Most people agree that a point of view, a centre of co-herence, is essential to a novelist. Bernanos has a point of view, but it is something more than simply an angle from which things are seen; it becomes a shaft of light. Prayer is the faltering approach to a God's-eye view of the world and ourselves. The deficiencies Miss Iris Murdoch finds in much modern fiction are answered in the novels of Bernanos: 'We no longer see man against a background of values, of realities which transcend him. We picture man as a brave naked will surrounded by an easily comprehended empirical world. For the hard idea of truth we have substituted the facile idea of sincerity.'[10]

This does not mean that Bernanos' novels are didactic tracts, but it does mean that he is committed. His repeated affirmation, *Je ne suis pas un écrivain*, is not just a piece of literary coquetry. It is his protest against the writer who is exiled from his own works. Without exception the novelists who appear as characters in his novels are elegant word-spinners with nothing to say because they have divorced literature from life and refused commitment. In his criticism of them we catch an echo of the voice of Pascal, rebuking Montaigne for his 'nonchalance du salut'. Saint-Marin, a character unmistakably modelled on Anatole France, sums up all that Bernanos detests in the 'literary world' and, by contrast, expresses his own convictions:

The efforts of fifty years, his splendid career . . . do they count for so little? Let the fools prate on about Art if they will. This wonderful juggler with words knows only its slavery. The world, which thinks it knows him, knows only what conceals him. The musical gossip whose only theme has been himself has never expressed himself. He is exiled from his own books.

(*Sous le soleil de Satan*, p. 347.)

Bernanos is ever-present and omnipresent in his own books. Not that this should evoke the romantic image of the poet-pelican, feeding his young on his own heart's-blood. Bernanos is not concerned with petty self-revelations, but he demands of literature that it should involve the whole man, commit him decisively. He wrote in 1945:

The profession of writing is no longer a profession but an adventure—and primarily a spiritual adventure. All spiritual adventures are Calvaries.[11]

But this fidelity to the truth within did not blind him to the world outside. He preferred to write on café tables, he explains,

so as not to be the dupe of imaginary creatures, so as to rediscover, with a glance at an unknown passer-by, the right proportion of joy and pain.

(*Les Grands cimetières sous la lune*, p. III.)

Why, asked Mauriac, whose own carefully protected existence contrasts with Bernanos' incessant nomadism, choose such an inconvenient place of work?[12] Bernanos had already answered the question:

I write on café tables because I cannot for long go without the human voice and the human countenance, of which I have tried to speak nobly.

(Ibid., p. II.)

The greatness and uniqueness of Bernanos is that, at his best, he remains close both to humanity and to grace.

What public, then, does Bernanos hope to reach, or create? The question is a highly relevant one for a Christian writer in a post-Christian society. Gaëton Picon, one of the best critics of Bernanos, has given one answer:

If the work of Bernanos were nothing more than the expression of Christian thought, we non-Christians would have to regard it as a closed garden. But no one can escape its power because it animates with incomparable strength a world simultaneously unusual and familiar, visionary and everyday.[13]

Bernanos does not come trailing clouds of incense. At the same time belief in the supernatural order colours his whole work. In *Les Grands cimetières sous la lune*, Bernanos makes an agnostic mount the pulpit steps and address the puzzled Christians in this way:

You are not very interested in agnostics, but they are enormously interested in you . . . It is tempting to observe you from close at hand, to try you out. For after all, you are supposed to believe in hell. Does the look you cast upon us reveal something of the pity you would certainly not refuse to someone condemned to death by a court? Oh naturally we don't ask for a stupid display of pity, but even so, to imagine that a certain number of people with whom one has danced, ski'd, played bridge, will gnash their teeth and curse God for all eternity, that should after all change a man. In short, we agnostics think you are interesting. But in fact you are not, hardly at all, and we have a feeling of being let down. We feel humiliated because we had hoped in you, that is, doubted ourselves, our unbelief. So it is true that you believe in hell. You expect us to go there. It is astonishing that, in these conditions, you should have absolutely no sense of the pathos of the situation.

(*Les Grands cimetières sous la lune*, pp. 251-252.)

Bernanos' hypothetical agnostic is much severer than most Christian theologians would be; but it remains true that since defeat and catastrophe can never be final for a Christian, the only form of tragedy he ultimately recognises is the tragedy of damnation. It is also true, as Orwell tartly remarked on *The Heart of the Matter,* that 'when people really believed in hell, they were not so fond of striking graceful attitudes on its brink'.[14] Bernanos, at least, is not posing gracefully. Nor does he suppress his beliefs or make tactical concessions in order to win readers. In the *Lettre aux Anglais* he has an apology which is also an affirmation:

> I would not like to annoy my readers who do not believe by speaking of the Devil, but after all journalists and politicians allow themselves to designate him frequently under the name of Evil or the Forces of Evil. Why should I be more timid than they are?
>
> (*Lettre aux Anglais,* p. 197.)

At the very least, Bernanos might be conceded a willing suspension of disbelief.

Moreover, he has earned the right to a hearing because, besides speaking from his experience as a Christian, he remains close to humanity and reflects the pressures of his age. He is not a remote island cut off from the mainland of the twentieth century, in the manner of Claudel. A Bernanos is only possible where there is a pluralistic culture, where there is constant dialogue between unbelief and belief; and he is only possible in an age in which Christianity has largely ceased to mould institutions, in which belief in the supernatural has gone and all that remains are its ethical derivatives, such as the desire for justice, indignation at oppression and respect for the claims of the human person in a world no longer on the human scale. Many people try to dismiss the supernatural because they fear a truncating of themselves, a loss of personality; they think the choice is between God and personal fulfilment. Bernanos would reply, with his Curé de Torcy:

> Paganism was no enemy of nature, but Christianity alone can exalt it, can raise it to man's own height, to the peak of his dreams.
>
> (*Journal d'un curé de campagne,* p. 25.)

That does not, of course, end the dialogue. Bernanos shares the aspirations towards justice, but he also tracks them down to their source. There is something more. *Angoisse,* when it is not just a vogue-word to be toyed with over the sherry glasses, expresses the horror at the void left in human existence when God has been declared absent. Bernanos knew *angoisse* and diagnosed its presence in so many of our attitudes, the sense of insecurity, the increasing powerlessness of the individual to affect policy, all those nameless fears which are summed up in the fear of the bomb—whose moral consequences Bernanos foresaw.[15] Orwell's 'fat little man' may 'see very clearly the advantages of staying alive with a whole skin', his tastes may be inclined to safety and soft beds, but even supposing that he could afford a fall-out shelter, it will not be enough to dispose of his anxieties. Bernanos, in the end, speaks to those who have lost hope, those who are at the end of their tether.[16] In the preface to his projected but never completed *Vie de Jésus,* written in Brazil, he addresses the spiritually destitute:

> I would like to write this book for the poorest of men. I would also like to write it in their language, but that is not permissible. One cannot imitate either poverty or the language of poverty. One has to be poor oneself to share, without sacrilege, in the sacrament of poverty.
>
> Christ came into this world, and he came for everyone, not simply for those who were poor. Around his crib were gathered shepherds and kings, but neither the shepherds nor the kings were poor. It may be that the penitent thief was poor, but we are not sure of it. Contrary to what many moralisers believe, true poverty does not find a way out in crime; it issues neither into good nor evil; true poverty knows no way out. The only way out of the poverty of the truly poor is in God. . . .[17]

This little-known passage can stand at the head of Bernanos' novels. There is a strong sense of the spoken word about it; the obsessive repetitions, reminiscent of the flow of Péguy, the refusal to separate the world of nature from the world of grace which leads to an unexpected use of language (*le sacrement de la misère*), the tilting at the moralists, the deliberate, childlike directness, above all the overriding generosity and compassion—all these are characteristic of Bernanos. 'One reads Bernanos for the sound of his voice,' noted an English critic,[18] but here the sound of the voice is inseparable from what is being said.

There is something Russian in Bernanos' sympathy with outcasts, with the spiritually and materially wretched, with *enfants humiliés* of all kinds. It is not an accident that his anonymous Curé of Ambricourt, who was his own favourite character, should have read *The Childhood of Maxim Gorki.* The Curé writes in his diary:

> If one has known real poverty and its mysterious, incommunicable joys, Russian writers can bring tears to the eyes . . . If the Church could make saints out of whole nations, she would have made Russia the patron saint of Want (*Misère*).
>
> (*Journal d'un curé de campagne,* pp. 63-64.)

Bernanos' originality among French novelists lies first of all in his presentation of the adventure of sanctity; but he has also learned, in the same school as his saint-heroes, compassion, a quality rare enough to make him worth investigating.

Notes

1. Raymond Mortimer, in *New Writing and Daylight,* Summer 1943.

2. Quoted by Albert Béguin in *La Table Ronde,* October 1950.

3. *Critical Essays,* 1946, pp. 96-97.

4. Mauriac quotes this judgement on himself in *Mémoires Intérieurs,* and adds the eirenic comment: 'Not one of those who were the victims of Bernanos' outrageous treatment (among the Christians at least) has harboured a grudge against him. . . . Our relations with Bernanos were in the nature of intercession.' (English translation, p. 189.)

5. In *Morales du Grand Siècle,* Paris, 1948.

6. 'Priest-hero' would exclude Chantal of *La Joie.* In any case the 'priest-hero' already had a long if unflattering literary history. Cf. Pierre Sage, *Le 'bon Prêtre' dans la Littérature française, d'Amandis de Gaule au Génie du Christianisme,* Geneva and Lille, 1951. The type remains constant up to Châteaubriand: the 'good priest' is a hermit hidden in the woods to whom young lovers can safely look for guidance. The nineteenth century adds Abbé Bournisien and sees him from the outside, as part of the sociological *milieu.*

7. *Pensées,* edited by L. Lafuma, translated by Martin Turnell, London, 1962, No. 769.

8. *Studies in French Fiction* 1935-1960, edited by John Cruickshank. It is only fair to add that Mr. Ernest Beaumont, in his excellent chapter on Bernanos, is not unduly worried by the label 'philosopher'.

9. *Bulletin de la Société des Amis de Georges Bernanos* (referred to henceforward as *Bulletin*), Nos., 15-16 pp. 13-14.

10. 'Against Dryness,' in *Encounter,* 88, January 1961, p. 18.

11. *Bernanos par lui-même,* edited by Albert Béguin, p. 149.

12. *Mémoires Intérieurs,* English translation, p. 195.

13. *Georges Bernanos,* Paris, 1948, p. 100.

14. Review in *New Yorker,* 17th July 1948.

15. Cf. *La France contre les Robots,* p. 77: 'What makes me despair of the future is that the rending and the burning of several thousands of innocent people should be a task that a respectable man can accomplish without staining his shirt-cuffs—or even his imagination.'

16. Bernanos admired Conrad and especially *Heart of Darkness.* At one time he thought of appropriating Conrad's title *The End of the Tether (Au Bout du Rouleau)* for the novel eventually called *Un Mauvais rêve.* Cf. *Bulletin,* No. 1, p. 10.

17. *Bulletin,* No. 6, pp. 1-2.

18. David Tylden-Wright, *The Image of France,* Secker and Warburg, 1957, p. 103.

Bibliographical Note

I. NOVELS OF BERNANOS

Sous le soleil de Satan, Plon, 1926.

L'Imposture, Plon, 1927.

La Joie, Plon, 1929.

Un Crime, Plon, 1935.

Journal d'un curé de campagne, Plon, 1936.

Nouvelle Histoire de Mouchette, Plon, 1937.

Monsieur Ouine, Atlantica, Rio de Janeiro, 1943; Plon, 1946. (The text of these editions is defective; for completions and corrections cf. Club des Libraires de France, 1955.)

Un Mauvais rêve (1935), Plon, 1950.

OTHER EDITIONS

All except *Un Mauvais rêve* have been published by Plon in the *Livres de Poche* collection.

Œuvres Romanesques, suivies de Dialogues des Carmélites, preface by Gaëton Picon, text edited and annotated by Michel Estève, Bibliothèque de la Pléiade, 1961.

II. OTHER WORKS OF BERNANOS

Lettre aux Anglais, Atlantica, Rio de Janeiro, 1942; Gallimard, 1948.

La France contre les Robots, Rio, 1944; Laffont, 1947.

POSTHUMOUSLY PUBLISHED

Les Enfants humiliés (written 1940), Gallimard, 1949.

La Liberté, pour quoi faire? Gallimard, 1953.

For unpublished texts, early drafts and biographical material the *Bulletin de la Société des Amis de Georges Bernanos* (M. Camille Sautet, 51 rue de la Chapelle, Paris 18e) is essential.

III. NOVELS OF BERNANOS IN ENGLISH TRANSLATION

Star of Satan (Sous le soleil de Satan) trs. Pamela Morris, The Bodley Head, London, 1940; Macmillan, New York, 1940.

Under the Sun of Satan, trs. H. L. Binsse, Pantheon Books, New York, 1949.

Joy (La Joie), trs. Louise Varèse, The Bodley Head, London, 1948; Pantheon Books, New York, 1946.

The Crime (*Un Crime*), trs. Anne Green, R. Hale & Co., London, 1936; Dutton, New York, 1946.

The Diary of a Country Priest (*Journal d'un curé de campagne*), trs. Pamela Morris, The Bodley Head, 1937; Doubleday (Image Books), New York & Toronto, 1954; Collins (Fontana Books), London, 1956.

The Open Mind (*Monsieur Ouine*), trs. Geoffrey Dunlop, The Bodley Head, London, 1945.

Night is Darkest (*Un Mauvais rêve*), trs. W. J. Strachan, The Bodley Head, London, 1953.

IV. OTHER WORKS OF BERNANOS IN ENGLISH TRANSLATION

Diary of my Times (*Les Grands cimitières sous la lune*), The Bodley Head, London, 1938; Macmillan, New York, 1938.

Plea for Liberty (*Lettre aux Anglais*), trs. H. L. Binsse and Ruth Bethell, Pantheon Books, New York, 1944; Dennis Dobson, London, 1945.

NOTE

All references, except where otherwise stated, are to the original French editions of Bernanos' works by permission of the publishers.

Gerda Blumenthal (essay date 1965)

SOURCE: Blumenthal, Gerda. "Rotten Vessels." In *The Poetic Imagination of Georges Bernanos: An Essay in Interpretation*, pp. 18-41. Baltimore: The Johns Hopkins Press, 1965.

[*In the following essay, Blumenthal interprets Bernanos's novel* The Open Mind, *highlighting the manner in which the author links images of water and death or corruption in the work, and how Ouine, "the prototype of all of Bernanos' satanic figures," ultimately experiences "the divine irony" of his evil existence: "He has become no god but a mere mirror of the Serpent's vacant, craving eye."*]

> *L'ennui de l'homme vient à bout de tout, monsieur l'abbé, il amollirait la terre*
>
> ### *Monsieur Ouine*
>
> *Je pense à ces poches flasques et translucides de la mer.*
>
> ### *Journal d'un curé de campagne*

The process of dissolution and liquefaction is nearly ubiquitous in the Bernanosian universe. The drowning of the children is its most violent and sudden manifestation; but perhaps more sinister are the innumerable instances in which we see characters and places disinte-

grating slowly, as if infected by some form of cancer or gangrene. They begin to swell up, ooze water, gradually lose their shape, and finally turn into porous, amorphous masses which sink to the bottom of the sea.

In the seemingly chaotic but actually superbly controlled movement of *Monsieur Ouine,* this deadly process occurs in its full range and is tracked to its origin, which forms the novel's largely invisible center of gravity—the thirst of the satanic water, in the form of the infinitely active, mesmerizing glance of Ouine. Through this glance, which becomes one with the satanic eye of the sea, Bernanos evokes the sea's ultimately futile yet ruinous craving to usurp the divine "secret" of life by drawing it out of the living creatures of earth. Here, in contrast to the *Nouvelle Histoire* [*Nouvelle Histoire de Mouchette*], this rape is conceived as a slow, insidious invasion and pollution of the earth's life-giving springs by the destructive water, as a result of which aberrant, tumorous growths start mushrooming all over with irresistible force.

In the microcosm of Fenouille, the reader encounters all at once a landscape, its dwellings, and its people in that putrid stage of decomposition in which water seeps out everywhere and the air is filled with an evil smell. Bernanos referred once to his extraordinary last novel as "Job's dungheap" and a "lugubre urinoir."[1] This is at least on one level a very apt description. Torrential rains are, throughout the novel, washing out roads, rotting pastures, and swelling the pond in which the little cowherd is found dead. Black water seeps from under the stone floors of the castle—symbol of Fenouille's nobility—and gives to the room in which Anthelme de Néréis is dying the "living force of certain plant leprosies."

> Loin de la détruire, il semble que l'eau ne ferait qu'en gonfler la semence, profondément enfouie sous pierre.[2]

The pillars of its sacred place, the dark and dank church, "sweat out an icy, stagnant water which makes the hands greasy."[3]

The evil water has contaminated the population, right down to the children, to the point where Steeny himself, the key figure among the novel's all-important three children, suddenly sees himself in despair as a contaminated well:

> . . . une part de lui-même avait été, lui vivant, frappée de mort, abolie. Par quelle blessure mystérieuse, par quelle brèche ouverte de l'âme avait-elle glissé au néant? Il semblait qu'avec elle se fût évanouie toute sécurité, toute certitude et que la conscience, ainsi qu'une citerne crevée ne laissât plus désormais monter à la surface qu'une eau limoneuse, chargée d'angoisse.[4]

Finally, and above all, there is Ouine himself, the "soft and humid" false father of Fenouille, whose bone structure has disappeared "as if his skin no longer covered anything but a sort of soft fat"[5] and who in dying resembles "a rotten old ship opening up to the sea."[6]

Water and death are linked inseparably in this work. There appears to be no trace of a pure spring left in Fenouille, the "dead parish." Hence the mayor's despondent reflection, near the end of the novel, that water is powerless, that only fire can put an end to the mire which has swamped the village. "There is no filth, no smell that can resist fire. We don't know of any water that's as pure as fire, right? . . . I should have known that water could do nothing to help me, that there is nothing better than fire."[7]

Yet ironically, and here lies the profound originality of this work, the poisonous miasma which rises from the soil to breed violence, insanity, and death in Fenouille, derives its deadly power from a calm, icy *abîme de néant,* in which a great dreamer of purity, Ouine, has taken refuge from the impurities and the turbulence of earth.

The antagonist's basic motif, the great satanic motif that Bernanos develops in **Monsieur Ouine,** is the spirit's revulsion at the *souillure* of incarnate life—its weight, its smells, its share of death and corruption. Like the fallen Angel to whose spell he has succumbed, Ouine is offended by the scheme of creation in which spirit and finite, mortal matter are linked indissolubly. He refuses to wrestle with the to him despicable "fatalities" of existence and chooses instead to vindicate his dream of Paradise in his own fashion, by circumventing them. In his bitter hatred of the earth, he has detached himself from it by assuming the role of an outsider, or stranger, a dispassionate, benign spectator not subject to its contamination. His retreat is evoked as a deliberate gliding down to the depths of the sea, where none of the shocks and reverberations which agitate the earth are felt and where his defiant spirit can observe and taste life in a state of purity, in the water's magic mirror.

"I no longer meet anything head on," Ouine confides to Steeny in their first encounter, in which he imparts to the boy his loathing of all living things and their ineradicable tendency to deteriorate and die. "Like those living jellyfish at the bottom of the sea, I float and absorb."[8] One may question Bernanos' discretion in attributing this savage perception of himself to Ouine—here as elsewhere, the writer's imagination has run ahead of the possibilities of dialogue—but the image itself is significant. Slippery and effeminate, the old language professor has repudiated the active, masculine effort of facing up and giving shape to the world and appears indeed hardly to stir from his peaceful abode, the little pink room in the Néréis' castle. At the same time, in order to satisfy his obsessive thirst for life—characteristic Ber-

nanosian symptom of a being submerged by satanic hatred—he has become an infinitely active extension of the Serpent's eye which feeds on the lives of others.

Ouine is the prototype of all of Bernanos' satanic figures. Himself seduced in his childhood by a false father figure, one of his teachers, he has in turn become a vengeful seducer. Unlike Mouchette, he has survived the blight of his childhood's dream of Paradise and is maintaining the illusion of living by feeding on the substance of other living beings, whom he in turn is able to entice away from their love of earth and into the deep waters of satanic hatred. Through the power of his glance, Satan's bottomless reaches of nonbeing absorb the earthbound reality of life and simply dissolve it.

Throughout the novel, the fundamentally ambiguous, counterfeit nature of this glance, which is the secret of the antagonist's power of seduction, is accentuated. As Ouine's name suggests, he destroys what he appears to affirm. Just as water reflects the landscape at its edge in reverse, so Ouine, the false priest of Fenouille, is a counterfeit figure of love and innocence. His sexual ambiguity—does he rape the little cowherd? was he ever in love with Jambe-de-Laine?—suggests childlike innocence. His unctuous manner suggests the priest; his detachment from worldly concerns, the poverty and selflessness of the saints. Above all, his "passion for souls" is a cruel counterfeit of a father's love. Whereas the vision of a Donissan, a Chevance or a curé d'Ambricourt encompasses in a flash the mysterious struggle of a soul in distress, orients it anew towards its goal, and reconciles it to itself, that is, *inspires* it, Ouine's avid eye arrests its victim in an ironic reflection which reveals to the latter all his latent *dégoût* and self-hatred and, thus overwhelming him, sucks him in or *l'aspire*. The anguished and warped inhabitants of Fenouille—Bernanos' greatest evocation of the modern world in its state of inner disarray—are an easy prey for Ouine's mesmerizing glance. They open themselves up to him and, as they surrender to his gaze their deepest terrors, find not only themselves emptied of the last vestige of pride and purpose which has sustained them but the world of others turned into a chain of tarnished mirrors endlessly reflecting their own hateful self-image.

> Il ne dit jamais de mal de personne, et il est très bon, très indulgent. Mais on voit au fond de ses yeux je ne sais quoi qui fait comprendre le ridicule des gens. Et ce ridicule ôté, ils n'intéressent plus, ils sont vides. La vie aussi est vide. Une grande maison vide, où chacun entre à son tour. A travers les murs, vous entendez le piétinement de ceux qui vont entrer, de ceux qui sortent. Mais ils ne se rencontrent jamais. Vos pas sonnent dans les couloirs, et si vous parlez, vous croyez entendre la réponse. C'est l'écho de vos paroles, rien de plus. Lorsque vous vous trouvez brusquement en face de quelqu'un, il n'y a qu'à regarder d'un peu près, vous reconnaissez votre propre image au fond d'une de ces glaces usées, verdies, sous une caresse de poussière.[9]

Ironically, the treacherous glance which is thirsting for its victims' "secret," that is, the mysterious spring of life which is the source of the created world's beauty and vitality, is debarred from what it craves by its very act of invading and polluting it. What it takes hold of time and again is not the human earth's sublime though vulnerable creative *élan,* its divine gift, the promise of Paradise, but only their reverse: earth's dream of death, and its longing to return to the uncreated abyss. It is ultimately in vain that Ouine, after having induced in his victims a *vertige* of self-hatred and scorn of earth, holds out to them a dazzling reflection of the sea, in which the tasteless and colorless "thirsty" water of the abyss takes on the vibrant beauty of a redeemed and purified earth. To this reflection they succumb. But the beings whom his satanic glance succeeds in absorbing so disintegrate in the process that they bring nothing to fill the gaping emptiness. Their vital substance is simply lost, lost both to creation and to Satan whose thirst it cannot but cheat by its elusiveness. In the dying Ouine's monologue which, near the end of the novel, Steeny hears in a prophetic dream that marks the boy's liberation, Ouine is forced to face up to the divine irony whereby the deceiver must in the end see himself as deceived: in defying his earthly condition and seeking Paradise in the water's unbounded realm of reflection—symbol of the Serpent's false promise of power and immunity—he has permitted himself to be dissolved into nothingness. He has become no god but a mere mirror of the Serpent's vacant, craving eye.

> La curiosité me dévore. . . . A ce moment elle creuse et ronge le peu qui me reste. Telle est ma faim. Que n'ai-je été curieux des choses! Mais je n'ai eu faim que des âmes. Que dire faim? Qu'est-ce que la faim? Je les ai convoitées d'un désir, auquel le mot faim ne convient pas, la vraie faim grince des dents, le regard de la faim brûle comme du feu. . . . Je les regardais jouer et souffrir ainsi que celui qui les a créées eût pu les regarder lui-même. . . . je me sentais leur providence, une providence presque aussi inviolable que l'autre. . . .
>
> Ai-je vraiment fait ce que je viens de dire? . . . L'ai-je seulement voulu? L'ai-je rêve? N'ai-je été qu'un regard, un oeil ouvert et fixe, une convoitise impuissante?[10]

Nevertheless, the impact of the satanic eye on the human landscape is ravaging. Out of the depth of the earth and its inhabitants, Ouine's glance draws forth a veritable flood of malice and hatred in which the entire village is caught up. Each seeks to rid himself of his own unbearable ennui by foisting it on others, until Fenouille's population becomes

> . . . ce lac de boue toujours gluant sur quoi passe et repasse vainement l'immense marée de l'amour divin, la mer de flammes vivantes et rugissantes qui a fécondé le chaos.[11]

The first major victim of the satanic spell which Ouine's eye has cast over Fenouille is the possessed creature who is the village's *châtelaine.* We learn that Jambe-de-Laine—the villagers' injurious nickname for Mme. de Néréis—installed Ouine in the château shortly after her marriage to the weak, sensuous Anthelme de Néréis and has been serving him with slavish devotion. Revolted by the baseness and vulgarity of the village into which she has come to live as a result of her marriage, she sees in the serenely detached Ouine a kind of avenging deity who will obtain retribution for her and bring her into a purer, calmer world:

> . . . quiconque l'approche n'a justement plus besoin d'aimer [she tells Steeny], quelle paix, quel silence! L'aimer? Je vais vous dire, mon coeur: comme d'autres rayonnent, échauffent, notre ami absorbe tout rayonnement, toute chaleur. Le génie de M. Ouine, voyez-vous, c'est le froid. Dans ce froid, l'âme repose.[12]

The sign that she has been caught in the icy depth of Ouine's satanic hatred—"A clear and icy water, that is what hatred is," she tells the boy—is the "magic glance" by means of which she in turn draws out of her husband and all the young men who have succumbed to her spell their basest impulses.

Drained of her joy and will to live by her satanic master, Jambe-de-Laine has become another link in the chain of the *abîme's* reflections, another unfathomable eye condemned to invade and to "drink" with satanic glee the poisoned source of the lives of others. ". . . there is enough substance in a single man to feed a whole life—and what life can boast of having drained another to the end, to the bottom, to the dregs?"[13]

But something is still alive in Jambe-de-Laine and stirs violently. Unlike Ouine, whose motionless fluidity suggests the final stage of earth's return to water, the figure of the *châtelaine* is seen oscillating between the water's deadly magic and an authentic struggle for life. Her "incredibly pure profile" reveals vestiges of great nobility; her demented bearing suggests a mortally wounded creature's last effort to wrench itself free of the trap. We see her alternately as a spider, a wild beast, a monstrous broken toy, a creature pursued by ghosts, but most significantly "a trapped animal . . . which, after a night, a day, and another night of immense effort, having dragged behind it the trap and chain, faces the always fatal second dawn and, though still on its feet, enters the death agony."[14] These images, and the symbolic wild mare behind which we see the *châtelaine* careering down the roads, in their ambivalent evocations of both a destroyer and a victim, confirm Jambe-de-Laine's deeply equivocal role in the novel. She both defies life by serving Ouine and throwing herself and her victims into his avid *gueule,* and in turn, in moments of clearsightedness, she hates and defies the evil old man and finds the strength to denounce him and warn his victims of the snare. This ambivalence manifests itself most clearly in her relationship to Ouine's choicest prey, the boy Steeny.

The special object of the antagonist's gaze, in this novel again, is a child. The child is not only the most defenseless victim; he is, above all, the purest embodiment of the secret of life which the Serpent has forfeited and seeks in vain to recapture. Significantly, the novel's violent but at first hidden movement of fermentation erupts into the open after the central event has taken place: the unaccounted-for rape and murder of the little cowherd whom Ouine has sent off in the night with a message to Steeny's mother and followed and who is found the next morning naked and strangled in the pond. "Childhood is the salt of the earth," Ouine exclaims with great emphasis after the funeral. "Let it lose its savor, and soon the world will be nothing but rot and gangrene."[15] No sooner, indeed, has the child been buried, than murders, suicides, and insanity sweep through Fenouille. At last the mayor himself becomes insane with self-loathing and fear and vanishes from the scene. The fate of the children in the novel's "world of old men" is the most haunting theme of *Monsieur Ouine,* but that is at least in part because it is related so closely to the inevitable decay of a world that does not treasure and protect its children. Despite all appearances to the contrary, it is their innocence, Bernanos keeps reminding the reader, which is holding the world together and keeping it from turning back on itself completely. Whereas we see the rest of the village's inhabitants arrested and mesmerized by their own image reflected in Ouine's glance and pulled back into the fundamentally inhuman, anonymous *dégoût,* or hatred of life, which is like the backwash of the stream of creation, the children's quest of the Father's Kingdom is a movement accomplished in blindness to themselves and in a clear, intuitive discernment of the goal. After the little boy's funeral, Ouine has indeed reason to gloat and to assume, with ill-concealed satisfaction, that Fenouille has been left defenseless against its inner pollution: "It would now produce poison with anything, the way diabetics produce sugar."[16]

The young priest echoes the sinister prophecy:

> Vous verrez surgir de toutes parts des maires de Fenouille qui tourneront contre eux, contre leur propre chair, une haine désormais aveugle, car les causes resteront enfouies au plus profond de la mémoire héréditaire. . . . Au train où va le monde, nous saurons bientôt si l'homme peut se réconcilier avec lui-même au point d'oublier sans retour ce que nous appelons de son vrai nom l'antique Paradis sur la terre, la Joie perdue, le Royaume perdu de la joie.[17]

However, two children are left in Fenouille after the cowherd's death: Guillaume and Steeny. Both are fatherless and, in an almost all-encompassing sense, disinherited. They have nothing to sustain them but each other's friendship and the unfulfilled promise of their dream of Paradise. Yet such is the power of their dream and of the mystery of life which they incarnate that in the end it breaks the Serpent's snare and turns his triumph into defeat. First shocked into an awareness of the true nature of Ouine's "calm" water by the little cowherd's violent death, Steeny, on whom we see Ouine's glance fasten in an attempt at seduction that now has all the dimensions of the Bernanosian satanic rape, is able to overcome the antagonist. Even in this work, in which the writer puts before us his most disconsolate vision of the world as a "dead parish," rotting in self-exile and unable to draw pure water from any source, the source is there. The children, both living and dead, continue to point the way. The dramatic and poetic core of *Monsieur Ouine* is very clear: it is the critical encounter between the serpent, Ouine, and a dove, in the figure of the adolescent Philippe or Steeny, whose eager, pulsating life is caught, early in the novel, in the cold depth of Ouine's glance and who very nearly perishes in it.

Every character, episode, and image in the novel bears directly on the boy's fate. From the opening pages, the stage is set for an overwhelming drama, in which the virile, heaven-bound spirit of the boy is setting out to discover and join his missing father—human correlative and symbol of the divine Father—and is almost turned back by the effeminate, dissolving spirit of fear and death. We see that spirit close in on the boy through a chain of satanic eyes or mirrors that extends from his mother to the governess, to Jambe-de-Laine, to the host of corrupt and cowardly villagers, to Ouine's glance, which is the "jaw" of death.

We find the boy brooding in a house which, in the absence of his father who long ago disappeared mysteriously, has been transformed by his mother into a jealously guarded island which will preserve her from the "perfidious water" of the sea. Her infallible weapon against the challenges and perils of living is an evasive gentleness that absorbs every active force and reduces it to impotence.

> 'La douceur a raison de tout.' . . . Et c'est vrai que rien n'a résisté à cette douceur, jamais. . . . Comment ne pas l'imaginer sous les espèces d'un animal familier? Entre elle et la vie, le rongeur industrieux multiplie ses digues, fouille, creuse, déblaie, surveille jour et nuit le niveau de l'eau perfide. Douceur, douceur, douceur. A la plus légère ombre suspecte sur le miroir tranquille, la petite bête dresse son museau délié, quitte la rive, rame de la queue et des pattes jusqu'à l'obstacle et commence à ronger sans bruit, assidu, infatigable.[18]

There is a muted hint that her ingenious gentleness once wove its snare of silence around the enemy of her peace, the impassioned Philippe, her husband, and destroyed him. He is "the vanished, the sunken, the eternally absent one."[19] Now she recognizes in her growing son Philippe the same hated driving force that surges ahead, threatening her tranquillity, and she is calmly determined to defy it again in him. Everything about the house is stifling the boy. It is indeed the very negation of a "father's house"—"Why do guys always talk about their father's house?"[20] he wonders. It has become a gilded cage, a Lesbian love-nest for the two women from which the world, and the boy in particular, are subtly excluded.

The dual theme of the boy's dream of finding his father and his almost instant arrest is stated immediately and forcefully. We see Philippe, or Steeny as his mother calls him to blot out his father's memory, immobilized by terror as the insinuating glance and the sly hands of Miss, his mother's companion, take hold of him and seek to provoke him to punishable aggression. He wrenches himself free, crying: "No! No!" Sick at heart, he looks out of the window, longing to escape and to go off in search of his father whom, despite what he has been told, he firmly believes to be alive. But all he can see is the tiny village and, beyond it, "the tiny yellow road, coiled in on itself like a snake and leading nowhere."[21] He is ready to do anything, throw himself into any breach, only to be free and set out on his search. At that moment, as if summoned by magic, Jambe-de-Laine appears and invites him to visit her guest, Ouine, at the château. As the boy, who is perplexed by her unusual appearance but delighted to be able to escape, gets into her carriage and they race towards the to him unfamiliar place, he wonders, with a strange sense of foreboding, where this adventure will lead him, "*vers quelle fatalité?*"[22] The child's foreboding turns out to be well founded. The image of the circular road prefigures the satanic snare into which his blind revolt is throwing him. The paternal, slightly ridiculous figure of the old professor, who, puffed up with fat despite an advanced case of tuberculosis, welcomes him in the little pink room in the château, is the satanic shadow or double of the father the boy is searching for and now believes he has found.

Ouine's concern for him is but a thinly disguised craving. For years, he confides to Steeny, he has been watching the boy from a distance, longing to know him:

> Que de fois je vous ai vu traverser la route pour monter vers Hagron en tuant des merles! Et du premier regard j'avais reconnu cette marche inégale, tour à tour impérieuse ou lente, et ces sursauts que vous avez, comme d'un appel augural, ces haltes brusques, absurdes en plein soleil . . . ah! c'était bien bien là l'image que j'ai caressée tant d'années, une vie, une jeune vie humaine, tout ignorance et tout audace, la part réellement périssable de l'univers, seule promesse qui ne sera jamais tenue, merveille unique![23]

To Ouine, the boy represents his own lost childhood and its glorious promise. "I have just seen myself again," he has told Jambe-de-Laine, "as a dead man sees the past. The little boy I once was, I have seen him, I could have touched and heard him."[24]

In a satanic movement of repetition and reflection, Ouine now fastens on the boy the same gaze his own seducer once fastened on him—"on his own glance that of another, unknown, empty and fixed as that of a dead man."[25] As Ouine talks about life with the boy, a sense of enchantment overcomes Steeny. He feels far removed from everything. The imagery of the passage evokes the satanic metamorphosis of solid walls into an enveloping, caressing tide:

> Le merveilleux silence de la petite chambre paraît seulement s'ébranler, virer doucement autour d'un axe invisible. Il croyait le sentir glisser sur son front, sur sa poitrine, sur ses paumes ainsi que la caresse de l'eau. A quelle profondeur descendrait-il, vers quel abîme de paix? Jamais encore au cours de cette journée capitale, il ne s'était senti plus loin de l'enfance, de l'univers maintenant décoloré de l'enfance, des joies et des peines d'hier, de toute joie, de toute peine.[26]

Reading bitterness and defiance in Steeny's eyes, Ouine begins a discourse in which this defiance is projected and magnified to a point where it becomes an overwhelming defiance of life itself. Everything in life, he tells the boy, and youth in particular, ends up corrupted and destroyed because life is nothing but a process of decay, a return to nothingness.

> Tout s'altère, se corrompt, retourne à la boue originelle. . . . Ah! Philippe, chaque pas que vous faisiez en avant, sous l'averse de feu, *chaque pas que vous faisiez le soir au-devant de votre ombre,* arrachait de moi une crainte, un scrupule. . . .[27]

As the boy listens in awe and drinks glass after glass of the Madeira which his host keeps pouring for him, the shadow of death spreads over him in the form of Ouine's huge silhouette on the wall. Throughout the novel, his hovering shadow signifies the child's ensnarement by the intoxicating dream of water. Under his false father's shadow, he feels immune: nothing can touch him any longer, nothing matters. "Oh absurd dream!—Steeny thought he had found the predestined companion of his life, the initiator, the hero whom he had pursued through so many books." He is "drunk with overcome pain, security, and pride."[28] In Ouine's presence, life is seen as hideous, but it no longer has the power to hurt him.

> Philippe croyait sentir, non sans un vague effroi, le même silence se refermer autour d'eux, silence vivant qui paraît n'absorber que la part plus grossière du bruit, donne l'illusion d'une espèce de transparence sonore. Car c'est bien en effet, à la magie de l'eau, à ses souples enveloppements, un miracle éternel de l'eau que rêve Philippe.[29]

That night Steeny falls asleep in Ouine's room. In the deeply organic universe which the Bernanosian vision evokes in this work, in which no part of his teeming human landscape is touched without setting off deep reverberations throughout the whole, the triumph of the satanic dream of returning to death is confirmed by the murder that takes place that same night of another child, the little cowherd. It is a pitch-black night in which "torrents of water" inundate the roads and the cowherd loses his way to the village. The next morning,

> . . . la même pluie lourde, sans aucune brise, tombait d'aplomb sur le sol fumant. Très loin, vers l'est et comme au bord d'un autre monde, l'aube orageuse formait lentement ses nuées, à travers une poussière d'eau.[30]

Ironically, Ouine's strangle hold on the boy tightens progressively as the grim reality of the "perfidious water" and of living beings putrid with inner corruption impinges more and more strongly on Steeny's aroused consciousness. He sees Anthelme dying from a gangrenous infection, which is but an outer manifestation of the nobleman's weak and dissolute being, and he learns, first from the dying man and then from Miss, the truth about his father's fate. It is worse than death: after having been believed dead for five years, the father was found in an asylum in Germany and simply left there. He either became insane or was locked up for desertion in the war. In keeping with the novel's over-all character of an unsolved riddle, the father's fate is not fully clarified for the reader. All that is certain is that he is one of Bernanos' unforgiven and unforgiving "dead," whom human cruelty and indifference have simply erased from the earth and thrown into the deep sea of oblivion, from which their dream of revenge keeps rising to poison the living. Guillaume, the crippled boy to whom Steeny has run early in the morning, unable to bear the horror of what he has heard and seen, reflects on the curse which seems to lie on the village. In a penetrating vision, he sees these unloved dead and their aborted lives, who have been claimed by the abyss, tugging at the earth from below with hatred:

> Le désordre universel, s'ils en étaient la cause? Moi, je les vois très bien à la frontière qu'ils ont franchie trop tôt, malgré eux, et qui s'efforcent de la repasser—les coups qu'ils portent ébranlent le monde.[31]

Guillaume, whose intuitive perception is re-enforced by a passionate devotion to his friend, warns Steeny of the backwash of hatred and self-repudiation to which his father and his whole lost generation who served as cannon-fodder in the war have succumbed and to which Steeny has now been left prey.

> Votre avidité, votre dureté, votre passion de revanche— cette rage à vous contredire, à vous renier, comme si vous aviez fait déjà de grandes choses, des choses mémorables, et qu'elles vous eussent déçu. . . . Tenez, votre admiration pour M. Ouine, votre idée d'un héroïsme à rebours. . . .[32]

But the successive revelations of evil have overwhelmed Steeny. He is unable to face up to them, even with the support of his little friend who urges him "never to turn

his head back, but only to think of tomorrow." In a highly symbolic passage, we see him caught that day in a suicidal *vertige,* in which his and Guillaume's dream of heroic conquests and discoveries is defeated and transformed into the consoling vision of Ouine's aquatic paradise.

Prompted by his own intuition and his friend's warning, the boy tries to resist his new hero and take flight. He begins to dream of the open road, symbol of human striving and hope.

> La belle route! la chère route! Vertigineuse amie, promesse immense. L'homme qui l'a faite de ses mains pouce à pouce, fouillée jusqu'au coeur, jusqu'à son coeur de pierre, puis enfin polie, caressée, ne la reconnaît plus, croit en elle. La grande chance, la chance suprême de sa vie est là, sous ses yeux, sous ses pas. Brèche fabuleuse, déroulement sans fin . . . arche sublime lancée sur l'azur. . . . Qui n'a pas vu la route à l'aube, entre ces deux rangées d'arbres, toute fraîche, toute vivante, ne sait ce que c'est que l'espérance.[33]

"Today . . . today," it tells him. But another voice answers, "Why not tomorrow? Tomorrow would be too late. . . . In twenty-four hours, one could lose his life, he said to himself in a state of intoxication." He is arrested by a vivid hallucination in which the "radiant image of death" holds out to him "a brand new, shining life—untouched, immaculate—miraculously restored to him."[34] At that very moment, Jambe-de-Laine's wild mare comes racing straight toward him and misses him by the breadth of a hair. Everything begins to whirl around him: the road slides into a heaving sea.

> La route s'est mise à remuer doucement, doucement sous lui, ainsi qu'une bête dorée . . . tout ce qu'il peut faire, mon Dieu, c'est de garder son équilibre, de tenir en équilibre, sur ses épaules, cette tête vide. . . . Peine perdue! C'est tout le paysage à présent qui glisse jusqu'au creux de la houle, chavire.[35]

The novel's pervasive theme of human betrayal and corruption and their impact on the boy, whom they threaten to deliver into the satanic snare set for him by Ouine, are sharply restated in this episode by means of a metaphor. A former woodcutter of the forest of Saint-Vaast happens to witness Jambe-de-Laine's assault on the boy, in which, we gather, she is simultaneously trying to kill the boy and to destroy herself in order to put an end to her sinister bondage to Ouine. Both the *châtelaine* and Steeny are depicted metaphorically in the young trees of the exploited and devastated forest:

> La vieille forêt vendue, revendue, vendue encore, passant de mains en mains au fond d'études sordides et tout à coup, son sort fixé, jetée bas en vingt semaines, écrasée, broyée, débitée par trains entiers jour et nuit, jusqu'au dernier charroi triomphant à travers le village, la musique, les drapeaux, puis le silence qui retombe sur les jeunes taillis éventrés, tout nus, grelottant au vent d'hiver. . . .[36]

After this episode, which leaves the boy weak with terror, the focus shifts back to the village, which is described as "stewing in its crime." It appears to be unable to purge itself of the evil that has taken possession of it, as any healthy organism would, even a large city which "when night falls sweats out through all its pores the filth of the day that has ended and sweeps it into its ditches and gutters, until it becomes one slimy mass slowly flowing out to sea through its immense subterranean rivers."[37] The rancor of the village keeps rising. Suspicion falls on the young poacher and son-in-law of Vandomme, Eugène, and he is arrested and charged with the child's murder. Drawn with obvious love, this Eugène is one of Bernanos' high-spirited young rebels, who appear predestined to serve as scapegoats for the world's rotten old men. Unable to prove his innocence, challenged by his stiff-necked old father-in-law to save the honor of the family, Eugène, together with his young wife Hélène, commits suicide in his hut the night before the arrest. The death of these two is characterized by the same movement of gliding and sinking we have seen in the **Nouvelle Histoire.** Here again, it marks the transformation, through despair, of the vital, impelling dream of Paradise, of an earth redeemed by grace, into the engulfing dream of death.

> . . . j'ai rêvé tous ces temps-ci [Hélène tells him] d'une grande forêt très haute, rien que des troncs comme des colonnes, tout droits, tout noirs, et je croyais voir la mer à travers, très loin, une grange bleue. . . . Du moins, je croyais que c'était la mer, puisque je ne l'ai jamais vue.[38]

But when she is on the point of pulling the trigger in despair, she surrenders to a water which is no longer the azure gulf, reward for an accomplished journey, but a deep place of refuge from a world that is unbearably evil:

> Jamais elle ne s'était sentie plus molle, plus souple, toute docilité, toute caresse. Il lui semble qu'elle flotte sans pesanteur au fond d'une eau calme où nul remous ne peut l'atteindre. La pensée même de la fin prochaine ne lui parvient qu'amortie et décolorée à travers cette épaisseur limpide. Ah! faire vite ce qui doit être fait, glisser de cette paix dans l'autre. . . .[39]

The double suicide of the young people is conceived, much like the cowherd's murder for which in a mysterious way it serves to atone, as an immolation. It is another slaughter of innocents by the village, intended to appease the satanic storm that has caused its "lakes of filth" to overflow. But with every victim it devours the water keeps rising; its thirst appears bent on absorbing and dissolving all that is still intact. On the day of the child's funeral the crowd's malice reaches its height in the presence of the small white coffin which finally confronts it tangibly with its own pollution. The priest's glance tries in vain to rest on a solid face or shape in the vast heaving mass in front of him: everywhere it

slips.[40] In the cemetery, the crowd is a "somber flood." "With the roar of waters when the sluice gates are opened,"[41] it closes in, first on the priest, almost pushing him into the freshly dug grave, then on Jambe-de-Laine. She dies a few days later, more, we are told, of her own will to die than of the physical injuries they have inflicted on her.

The *châtelaine's* death, like that of the two Mouchettes or of Eugène and his wife, places us before one of the central mysteries of the Bernanosian drama: these suicides are in reality murders. In destroying themselves, the victims of satanic violation or rape merely consummate the destruction wrought on them by the Antagonist. Their surrender to the water, far from expressing a rejection of the Father and of their dream of Paradise, is in fact a last desperate act of hope—hope that in destroying the hateful reflection of themselves and of the world, which they see in the sea's mirror, they will overcome the obstacle that stands between them and the Father. There is a poignant suggestion that those deaths do indeed, despite the delusion which underlies them, break the satanic mirror, with its dreadful vision of life as living death, and restore their victims to innocence. If this is so, then the thirsty water is cheated of its prey; for what awaits those children of reckless hope at the moment of death is the true confrontation they have been seeking all along: the earth's reconciliation with the *gouffre d'azur* of the Father's love, source and fulfillment of all life.

All these deaths have a redemptive function in the novel. They serve to wrench Steeny out of the jaw of death by arousing him sharply. As the boy's gaze becomes clearer and stronger, it slowly subdues the treacherous power of the Antagonist's eye, until finally the roles are reversed. In the end, it is Steeny who witnesses the defeat of his mentor. What he sees is that the only one who dies, in the ultimate sense of dissolving irrevocably into nothingness, is his "hero" himself, the murderer and usurper of life. Ouine, whose glance has fed on others throughout his lifetime, is forced at the moment of death to turn this glance on himself. What is finally revealed to him is that the life he has coveted and believes he has made his own has eluded him; that he has nothing, is nothing, and is returning to nothingness. Even Jambe-de-Laine, he bitterly concedes to the boy, has eluded him:

> —Elle s'est échappée, voilà le mot, elle s'est élancée hors de toute atteinte—échappée n'est peut-être pas le mot qui convient? Elle s'est élancée comme une flamme, comme un cri.[42]

At the end of **Monsieur Ouine,** a profound silence reigns again. The satanic storm has spent itself, after unleashing a flood of evil that has left the village devastated, and we are back in the dead center of the storm's eye, the little pink room where the old language professor is dying. The tuberculosis which finally kills him is, like the tumors and cancers that feed everywhere on Bernanos' deceived humanity, the visible sign of the encroachment of delusion on reality, of the thirsty flood within the bowels of the earth that, like "a life within a life," eats away the earth's strength and substance. Now it is Steeny's turn to watch his dying mentor with deep attention. Sober, rid of his intoxication at last, he is able to face up to the Serpent's eye and see it for what it is: not a haven of peace but a roaring abyss.

Just before Ouine dies, we see the boy's release from the professor's strangle hold and the re-emergence of the dream of Paradise out of the depths of the dream of death. Still spellbound by his idol and deeply grieved at the sight of Ouine's approaching death, Steeny suddenly recalls a memory. It prefigures perfectly his impending liberation from his false haven and the resumption of his quest for the true Father. As he looks out of the window from Ouine's room where he has been spending days and hours on end, he remembers how, to escape from his mother and Miss, he used to spend hours by the empty dovecot right by the house. It had been closed to the birds for fifteen years.

> Quinze ans! Il imaginait le départ des oiseaux, leur détresse. Des heures, des jours, des mois peut-être, ils avaient dû cerner la vieille tour close de leur vol, de leurs cris, de leurs ombres. . . . Puis ils étaient partis un matin, vers quelque pays fabuleux.[43]

Within an hour or two after Ouine has died, the boy who has once again had too much wine and has fallen asleep by his mentor's bed has a final prophetic dream. In this dream, Ouine and the Serpent are one. He hears Ouine moaning with rage and frustration as he is sucked into the gaping void of his own insatiable desire:

> Je désirais, je m'enflais de désir au lieu de rassasier ma faim, je ne m'incorporais nulle substance, ni bien, ni mal, mon âme n'est qu'une outre pleine de vent. Et voilà maintenant, jeune homme, qu'elle m'aspire tout entier, je me sens fondre et disparaître dans cette gueule vorace, elle ramollit jusqu'à mes os.
>
> —Pouah! [the boy replies] vous parlez de votre âme comme la grenouille pourrait parler du serpent.
>
> —Cet animal me fascine en effet, poursuivit imperturbablement M. Ouine. Est-ce sa faim que je sens, ou la mienne. . . . Oh! mon garçon, si ce n'est ici qu'un rêve, ce rêve est bien étrange.[44]

Among the last words that Steeny hears Ouine murmuring "in a tone of enormous greed" are "a whole life, a long life, a whole childhood, a new childhood."[45] In his dream, the boy still sees Ouine's immense shadow hovering over him, but now it fills him with "a vague, indefinable pity, with the kind of sorrowful serenity which comes after the crisis of a great illness, when the awaited dawn that will bring recovery is still below the horizon."[46]

The event of Ouine's death and of the child's emergence is summed up poetically by Bernanos in the image of a poisonous liquid which, through exposure to the open air, has lost its power. "The vials are empty, the poisons evaporated in the air, diluted, innocuous." The deadly water of Satan's thirst, divested of its magic, is "tasteless, colorless, neither hot nor cold . . . it would quench no fire. . . ." Ouine tells the boy in his dream, "My thirst and this water are one and the same."[47] And Steeny sees him wondering, wrathfully, who would ever want to drink this "thirsty" water with him.

Notes

1. Albert Béguin, *Bernanos par lui-même*, p. 166.

2. *Monsieur Ouine*, p. 82.

3. *Ibid.*, p. 158.

4. *Ibid.*, p. 121.

5. *Ibid.*, p. 226.

6. *Ibid.*, p. 222.

7. *Ibid.*, pp. 203-4.

8. *Ibid.*, p. 25.

9. *Ibid.*, p. 218.

10. *Ibid.*, pp. 241, 242.

11. *Journal d'un curé de campagne*, p. 172.

12. *Monsieur Ouine*, p. 88.

13. *Ibid.*, p. 89.

14. *Ibid.*, p. 82.

15. *Ibid.*, p. 169.

16. *Ibid.*, p. 168.

17. *Ibid.*, p. 208.

18. *Ibid.*, p. 4.

19. *Ibid.*, p. 3.

20. *Ibid.*, p. 44.

21. *Ibid.*, p. 9.

22. *Ibid.*, p. 15.

23. *Ibid.*, p. 25.

24. *Ibid.*, p. 87.

25. *Ibid.*, p. 147.

26. *Ibid.*, pp. 21-22.

27. *Ibid.*, p. 25. Italics mine.

28. *Ibid.*, p. 19.

29. *Ibid.*, p. 23.

30. *Ibid.*, p. 31.

31. *Ibid.*, p. 48.

32. *Ibid.*, p. 40.

33. *Ibid.*, p. 71.

34. *Ibid.*, p. 72.

35. *Ibid.*, pp. 77-78.

36. *Ibid.*, p. 75.

37. *Ibid.*, p. 163.

38. *Ibid.*, p. 152.

39. *Ibid.*, p. 153.

40. *Ibid.*, p. 167.

41. *Ibid.*, p. 174.

42. *Ibid.*, p. 242.

43. *Ibid.*, p. 217.

44. *Ibid.*, pp. 234-35.

45. *Ibid.*, p. 236.

46. *Ibid.*, p. 237.

47. *Ibid.*, p. 239.

Bibliography

I. WORKS OF GEORGES BERNANOS

Journal d'un curé de campagne. Paris: Plon, 1936.

Un Mauvais Rêve. Paris: Plon, 1951.

Monsieur Ouine. Paris: Plon, 1946.

Nouvelle Histoire de Mouchette. Monaco: Editions du Rocher, 1946.

II. MAJOR CRITICAL STUDIES OF BERNANOS.

BÉGUIN, ALBERT. *Bernanos par lui-même.* Paris: Editions du Seuil, 1954.

William Bush (essay date 1969)

SOURCE: Bush, William. "Images, Patterns and Themes." In *Georges Bernanos,* pp. 53-61. New York: Twayne Publishers, Inc., 1969.

[*In the following essay, Bush emphasizes the central, recurring themes and "patterns" in Bernanos's fiction, claiming that the "primacy of childhood" and the "suffering" of the innocent adolescent, more than the struggles of his priest-heroes, form the core concern of his writings.*]

The theme of childhood dominates Bernanos' fiction.[1] The most common manifestation of this theme is seen in the recurrent pattern of a suffering adolescent crushed by circumstances beyond his comprehension. Two other images of childhood are also frequently evoked throughout the author's work: first, that of childhood innocence which, as it were, rises up as a protective force in the hour of need in adult life; secondly, the beautiful, evangelical image of becoming a child again, especially, in Bernanos, as one confronts death.

The primacy of childhood as theme will, of course, be challenged by a good majority of those critics who have mistaken the frequently encountered image of the priest for Bernanos' major theme.[2] While it is certainly true that Bernanos, armed with an unusually powerful and penetrating psychological insight which permitted him to probe the depths of the interior life of all his major characters, has spared no aspect of the inner life of the priest, and while good priests and bad priests alike, both equally convincing in their struggles, come to life for the reader, yet to regard the character of the priest as the central theme necessarily excludes half of Bernanos' fiction. Thus, although his best known and perhaps his most successful novel is, and will remain, *Diary of a Country Priest,* and although both his second and third novels, *L'Imposture* and *Joy* respectively, turn around the drama of the redemption of a single non-believing priest, yet the priest is absent from *Mouchette* and is of only secondary importance in *M. Ouine, Night Is Darkest* and, in a sense, in *A Crime.* Moreover, even in his first novel, *Under the Sun of Satan,* which usually rather shocks the reader as he encounters the temptations of the priest-saint in his battles with Satan both within and without himself, Bernanos had already felt the need to balance his priest by the presence of a "humiliated child," a crushed, disappointed adolescent.

Even when the author attempted to deal with other themes, the mystery of childhood kept intruding. In both *Night Is Darkest* and, to a certain extent, in *M. Ouine,* Bernanos dealt with the washed-out, used-up generation which survived World War I. Yet, even so, in both of these books the author envisaged what each of the major characters had suffered in his youth, what humiliations had been overcome and how this victory is continually paid for in adult life. The same phenomenon can be observed in Bernanos' one detective novel, *A Crime,* a book he wrote only for money and in which he took no pride. In this strange story the murderess kills both an old woman and the priest, a new arrival in the village who has not yet been seen by anyone. The murderess strips the young man, dons his cassock, and masquerades as the new priest while the old woman's killer is being sought. Thus, although the priest as an image is present, it is truly neither a novel about a priest nor, for that matter, about a man; rather, it is about a criminal woman whose greatest grace is her un-happy childhood, a childhood which can even be said to be cursed since she herself is the child of a defrocked nun and, quite probably, a priest. Finally, *Mouchette,* Bernanos' last conceived novel—only the last great chapter of *M. Ouine* would be written after it—deals only with the theme of humiliated adolescence: the young heroine is raped and finally commits suicide.

Death by suicide is, indeed, another common pattern for Bernanos' adolescents. Yet, strangely enough, their suicides are always born of their honor which, rather than surrender, they prefer to risk in a last supreme ef-fort of taking their own life. The first Mouchette in *Un-der the Sun of Satan* cuts her throat, then asks to be carried to the church to die. In *A Crime,* the altar boy; in *Night Is Darkest,* Philippe; in *Mouchette,* the hero-ine; all these adolescents seek death after a shattering disappointment. For Bernanos honored risk and be-lieved it to be the great characteristic of heroes, saints and martyrs as well as a virtue especially belonging to youth. His "children" thus consistently answered the disappointment which assaulted them by risking every-thing in one last gesture.

Characters other than Bernanos' adolescents, however, also resort to suicide: the non-believing priest, Abbé Cénabre, goes through the motion of shooting himself while his former penitent, Pernichon, actually succeeds in an attempt at taking his own life. The drug-addicted Russian chauffeur in *Joy* kills himself after slaughtering the novel's heroine, Chantal de Clergerie; both the mur-deress in *A Crime* and her defrocked-nun mother kill themselves; the lovers in *M. Ouine* die in a double sui-cide; finally, the non-believing doctor in *Diary of a Country Priest* shoots himself.[3] If one objects that so much suicide seems rather excessive, it must be re-called that, in trying to portray the deeper truths of the mystery of human life, Bernanos became aware of the preoccupation of contemporary man whose civilization continues to plunge him towards a mass suicide.

Yet there is also an aesthetic aspect in Bernanos' choice of the adolescent as his central figure since such a youth is an excellent image of man as he encounters the truth of life and death. Indeed, the disappointments of ado-lescence seem to become only more intense in later life as they change form and gradually bring man, still suf-fering from hopes unfulfilled, to death. Thus, although Bernanos' rational search for a perfect hero seemed to have drawn him towards the priest, his intuitive sense insisted on a more universal—if less exalted—image: the suffering adolescent.[4]

Perhaps it is Bernanos' preoccupation with the human aspects of man that caused him to choose these ever-recurring images and patterns. He condemned German heroism—that of a superman such as Siegfried—and contrasted it with French heroism—that of Roland, the epic hero who dies defeated, but in a manner becoming to his humanity as God's vassal. Bernanos' orientation towards the human limitations of man are to be seen also as part of his extraordinarily deep penetration of the mysteries of Christianity. At a moment when con-versions to Catholicism were very much in fashion, Bernanos jokingly remarked on his publisher's bio-graphical form that he was a Catholic but did not have the honor of being a convert, intimating thereby what he always was to maintain: the Church was home to him, and he expressed himself in the Church as would a member of any large family. Indeed, the image of the family is also part of his very human approach not only to existence itself, but also to his patriotism and to his whole experience of God.

The experience of God is perhaps the most strikingly unusual theme of Bernanos' work. If one may say that *any* experience of God is mysticism, then one must surely say that there is a very great mystical side to Bernanos. Not that his mysticism soared off to ethereal heights; on the contrary, it was the most down-to-earth, day-by-day application of what was, for Bernanos, ab-solute truth: God had become man. With his very keen historical sense Bernanos realized that France's history, from Clovis to Louis XVI, was a result of his country-men's application of this belief to their daily lives, to their institutions, to their way of thinking, acting, speak-ing and writing.

Referring to Bernanos' religion, many have tried to summarize it by saying that it is a religion of the "Be-atitudes," and surely a certain truth is in that statement. Bernanos himself disclaimed all knowledge of formal theology other than what he had learned at his mother's knee: his catechism. But neither the catechism nor the Beatitudes answer completely the question raised when a noted German-Swiss theologian, Hans Urs von Balth-azar, dedicates a large volume to Bernanos,[5] discussing the theological implications of his work in great detail. Nor do the Beatitudes and the catechism explain the surprise that nuns and priests experience as they find that this layman and father of six children had an inti-mate insight into their own spiritual struggles and temp-tations. What, then, more than the Beatitudes and the catechism is there behind Bernanos' Christianity?

The answer to this question bears, of course, on what Bernanos was and on what God was for him. One has only to read his youthful letters written to Abbé Lagrange, his former professor, to realize that Bernanos' interior life—that life of prayer and promises to God, that life of constant reference to, and communication with, the Absolute—was already, at the age of sixteen, highly developed. And it was in the depths of this highly developed interior life that were to be conceived all of Bernanos' major characters, whether saints or sinners.

The fusion in Bernanos of both height and depth as one looks at man would seem to lie behind the comparison of his work with that of Dostoyevsky who, like Bernanos, was not content to show merely the depths of man's degradation, but also the spiritual heights to which he could soar.

Surely from Bernanos' interior life came his preoccupation with the agony of Christ in the Garden of Gethsemane, an image given considerable scope in *Joy* and *The Carmelites.* Both Péguy, much admired by Bernanos, and Pascal can be said to have treated this same image before him in an equally probing manner and in contrast to de Vigny's unchristian treatment. As he was entering his last hours on the night of July 4, 1948, Bernanos observed, "Now I am caught in the Holy Agony." This was the statement upon whose significance he had so amply meditated in *The Carmelites,* the work he had completed the very day he became definitively bed-ridden a few months before his death.

The path leading from suffering innocence to the agony in the garden is, therefore, the one the reader must take in encountering Bernanos' work. To a great extent it is, of course, still an image of the suffering innocence one encounters in the Garden of Gethsemane, and there can be no doubt that Bernanos sought to raise the implications of the suffering innocent to the cosmic heights of expiatory suffering of which the crucifixion of Christ is, for the Christian, the supreme image.

One can even note a certain evolution in Bernanos' work around this Christian theme of expiation.[6] His first three novels, *Under the Sun of Satan, L'Imposture* and *Joy* all show saints suffering for sinners, a classic Catholic concept dear to Claudel. Bernanos, however, abandoned it in his last five novels, leaving in them the resolution of "who suffers for whom" in the hands of God alone. Trusting more and more in the mystery of "God's sweet mercy," as he liked to put it, Bernanos thus moves towards a more definitive exaltation of the *mystery* of God's workings rather than towards a definition of the mystery.

The realization that the suffering of the innocent is not only an image of the human condition but also of the agony of Christ in Gethsemane is bound eventually to raise the question of the relationship between man's personal attitude towards himself and that of his role in the garden of suffering innocents. Bernanos learned at some point that hatred of self is the most dangerous of temptations, the one that leads straight into despair. In his first novel this temptation pushes the priest-hero to a ferocious self-flagellation with a chain. Again, in acceptance of herself and her impotence Chantal de Clergerie, the holy young girl who accomplishes the redemption of the non-believing priest of *L'Imposture* and *Joy,* attains her union with God. The statement of

this truth in *Diary of a Country Priest* as the author closes his journal is striking:

> Yet if all pride were dead in us, the real grace of graces would be to love ourselves, humbly, just as we might love any suffering member of the body of Jesus Christ.

Blanche de la Force has to learn this truth through the humiliating necessities brought about by her fearsome nature. The hatred of self is at the root of the madness which drives the Mayor of Fenouille in *M. Ouine* to kill himself. Bernanos' work, therefore, seems to imply that in order to arrive at being a child again, man must learn to stop hating himself—for otherwise he is in danger of hating both God in himself as well as what God wants to accomplish in man through what He has given him.

As strange as it may seem at first glance, the setting Bernanos chose for the majority of his novels is of importance spiritually as well as aesthetically. Half of Bernanos' novels are set in the wet, woody haunts of France's Artois region, in the *département* of Pas-de-Calais. There the odors of wet clay and decaying leaves blend with the smell of the *genièvre* with which the peasants lace their bowls of coffee, sipped through a sugar cube held between their teeth. Bernanos' spirituality has a distinctively Flemish robustness about it which often shocks the more legally-minded, scrupulous Catholic.[7] Since the local priests were frequent guests at the Bernanos "château," the young boy had adequate opportunity to imbibe a very sane spirituality from these northern ecclesiastics. It hardly seems exaggerated to venture the observation that any harm he may have suffered from his early education with the Jesuits[8] in Paris was probably set into a healthy balance by his familiarity with a less probing, but equally intelligent, form of Christianity.

If Bernanos' predominant image of struggling for good is that of learning to accept oneself, the images of the extensive domination of evil in his world are manifold. The idea of the lie which one lives is not only the theme in *L'Imposture* and in *A Crime*; it is also a constantly recurring characteristic of his sinners. Coupled with it is a curiosity, a desire to penetrate the secrets of others, only for the sake of knowing. The two psychiatrists in Bernanos' work (one in *Joy,* another in *Night Is Darkest*), Ouine, the eponomic hero of *M. Ouine,* and Ganse, the foundering novelist of *Night Is Darkest,* all wish to *know*.

But curiosity does not stop with these characters. Indeed it is curiosity which pushes the priest-hero of *Under the Sun of Satan* to attempt to raise a dead child since he wants to *know* who the real master is—God or Satan—and if all his own suffering has been for nothing. It is true that other, more commonly expected marks of evil are also frequent in Bernanos' sinners. The use of drugs and alcohol as well as homosexuality are characteristic of a good number of his more troubled characters. Nonetheless, the most constant sin—which, for Bernanos, constitutes the "sun of Satan"—remains, however, *knowing,* "knowing in order to destroy, then renewing the desire in the midst of the destruction."⁹*M. Ouine* is Bernanos' most finished incarnation of this very basic human sin which has not changed, according to Bernanos' anthropology, since the serpent tempted the mother of the race by saying, "Eat of this fruit and ye shall be as gods, discerning good and evil."¹⁰

But the struggle with evil in Bernanos is not limited, in either his thought or his work, to great sinners or great saints alone. By far the most common manifestation of the struggle is, according to Bernanos, to be found in the mediocre.¹¹ Against mediocrity Bernanos penned many elegant pages in his non-fiction, and this, the most common characteristic of the human race, is also frequently incarnated in his novels. Although never actually heroes of the novels, the mediocre do take some of the more important secondary roles: the cartesian priest in *Under the Sun of Satan* who pushes Donissan towards the aborted miracle of raising the dead child; the academician who discovers Donissan's body in the confessional. Again, there are the journalist Pernichon who kills himself in *L'Imposture,* M. de Clergerie, the father of the heroine of *Joy,* and the novelist Ganse in *Night Is Darkest.* Bernanos felt that this part of humanity is especially favored by modern bourgeois democracy where risk is frowned upon and the most basic concern is no longer honor, but security. Indeed, concern with money and position in life are the primary concerns of the dominant class in the modern world of European civilization, a world that scorns both the peasants and the working classes.

Bernanos' implacable faith in the monarchy as the only hope for France was, in fact, rooted in his sympathy for the peasants and working classes. He conceived of the king as the image of the people, as their protector against exploitation by the penny-wise bourgeois who would run the republic for his own best interests. For Bernanos, France's honor alone was to be considered. It appears also that his belief in the monarchy may well be tied to the Christian dogma of the Incarnation, since he believes that national truth, like divine truth, becomes clear only when it is incarnate. For Bernanos, the king's interests must always lie there where the interests of his people lie, otherwise the king is overthrown. But, in his eyes, the interests of the rulers of the bourgeois republic lie, all too often, where their personal gain lies.

Because Bernanos held economic interests in such scorn, it is not surprising that he should not only look upon poverty as honorable, but actually develop, some-

what in the manner of Léon Bloy and Charles Péguy, a mysticism concerning the role of poverty in the cosmic order. Thus the poor, who are always hoping for enough to meet their immediate needs, have hope, whereas the rich have no need to hope. Again, the poor who stand on the brink of despair but still do not yield to the demon who beckons them, give an authentic image of man's spiritual condition, of his unconquerable hope.

Bernanos' occasional portraits of peasants and lower-class people in his novels show much of the author's sympathetic orientation towards them. The charwoman mistress of the defrocked priest in *Diary of a Country Priest* is, in a sense, a saint in her acceptance of the risks involved in her love for her companion: she freely accepts the almost unbearable situation in which she finds herself and dares even to find a cosmic communion with all of man's misery when things become too dificult. The mother of the second Mouchette, sitting down only to die while her husband's and sons' drunken snores mingle with the cries of the latest-born, can only invoke for the reader, as for Bernanos, "the sweet mercy of God."

In strong contrast to this sort of "natural sanctity" of the lower classes is the spiritual struggle of Bernanos' "saintly" heroes. Donissan, the priest-hero of *Under the Sun of Satan,* Chevance in *L'Imposture,* Chantal de Clergerie in *Joy* and the curé of Ambricourt in *Diary of a Country Priest* provide the primary examples of this bernanosian saint. In the evolution of these heroes one can see Bernanos moving towards one primary goal: acceptance of one's impotence before God. If this struggle is most acutely accentuated in *Under the Sun of Satan,* it finds complete resolution in *Diary of a Country Priest,* having been enunciated in detail by Bernanos in *Joy* where, in fact, Chantal de Clergerie's "joy" is defined as "the certitude of her own impotence."¹²

All of Bernanos' novels can be said generally to turn around man's struggle with evil and his response to the presence of God in him. Whether in the humiliated adolescents, great sinners or great saints, whether in the mediocre or the poor, there is a Pascalian theme through all of Bernanos' work: man's misery and his potential grandeur as a being created in God's image, redeemed by God Incarnate and sustained by the life-giving Spirit of God. And, regardless of where Bernanos begins, regardless of what stage of his character's life he deals with, he invariably causes his creatures to look back to their childhood, as it were, to provide the needed balance to the destructive drama of daily existence as the author pushes them towards death. Thus, it may be said that Bernanos would have concluded that in the search for childhood man reveals both his present misery and his past—and future—glory, that lost glory which was once his in the first garden and which has been restored to him through the agony of Christ in another garden.

Notes

1. Albert Béguin in LM underlined this theme. Since it has been further studied by other students of Bernanos: Marie-Agnès Fragnière, *Bernanos fidèle à l'enfant,* Editions universitaires (Fribourg: 1963), 155 pp.; Yves Bridel, *L'Esprit de l'enfance dans l'Oeuvre romanesque de Georges Bernanos,* Minard, 1966, 272 pp.; SE pp. 103-125, a chapter also published in *Revue des Lettres Modernes,* Autumn 1960, pp. 333-355 (*Etudes bernanosiennes* no. 1, pp. 109-131).

2. Even Albert Béguin in LM tends to defend this idea that the priest is the central figure in Bernanos' novels. See LM, pp. 68-83.

3. See Guy Gaucher, *Le Thème de la Mort dans les Romans de Bernanos,* Lettres Modernes, 1955.

4. SE, pp. 103-125.

5. Hans Urs von Balthazar, *Bernanos,* Verlag Jacob Hegner (Köln & Olten: 1954), translated into French by Maurice de Gandillac as *Le Chrétien Bernanos,* Seuil, 1956. The French edition suppresses the 22 pages of biography of the original German text.

6. See SE.

7. The character of the curé of Torcy in *Diary of a Country Priest* is not only avowedly Flemish, but also typical of one side of Bernanos' own personal spirituality. A similar phenomenon of identification can be seen in the character of Sr. Constance in *The Carmélites.*

8. While it is true that Bernanos was apparently happy at the Jesuit *collège* on the rue de Vaugirard where he was a day student only, he was not happy as a boarding student at Notre-Dame-des-Champs. Albert Béguin in LM confused these two institutions since he assumed that Bernanos' remarks against the Jesuit system were aimed at the Vaugirard school. It is understandable, however, that such a mistake could occur since the superior of Notre-Dame-des-Champs was also a Jesuit and no doubt ran his school according to the severity of Jesuit discipline. He it was who suggested to Bernanos' parents that their son be sent to a commercial school.

9. OE, p. 237: Connaître pour détruire, et renouveler dans la destruction sa connaissance et son désir—ô soleil de Satan!—désir du néant recherché pour lui-même, abominable effusion du coeur!

10. Genesis III: 5.

11. See SE, pp. 33-59, where a whole chapter is devoted to the mediocre and *imbéciles* in Bernanos' thought.

12. OE, p. 681. Car à présent, l'idée, la certitude de son impuissance était devenue le centre éblouissant de sa joie.

Annotated Bibliography

PRIMARY SOURCES

All books were published in Paris, unless otherwise stated. Principal editions only are listed here. Publication in periodicals is indicated within parentheses.

BERNANOS' FICTION

Sous le Soleil de Satan

———. 1926: Plon.

———. 1961: Gallimard, in *Oeuvres romanesques.*

In English

The Star of Satan, trans. by Veronica Lukas, John Lane (London: 1927).

Under the Sun of Satan, trans. by Harry L. Binsse, Pantheon (New York: 1949).

L'Imposture

1927: Plon.

1961: Gallimard, in *Oeuvres romanesques.*

La Joie

———. (1928: *La Revue universelle*)

———. 1929: Plon.

———. 1954: Club du meilleur livre (édition critique d'Albert Béguin).

———. 1961: Gallimard, in *Oeuvres romanesques.*

In English

Joy, trans. by Louise Varese, Pantheon (New York: 1946); Bodley Head (London: 1948).

Un Crime

———. 1935: Plon.

———. 1961: Gallimard, in *Oeuvres romanesques.*

In English

The Crime, trans. by Anne Green, R. Hale & Co. (London: 1936). This same translation was published in the United States as *A Crime,* E. P. Dutton (New York: 1936).

Journal d'un curé de campagne

———. (1935-36: *La Revue hebdomadaire*)

———. 1936: Plon.

Gallimard, in *Oeuvres romanesques.*

————. 1964: Le livre de poche "Université" (étude et notes de Michel Estève).

In English

Diary of a Country Priest, trans. by Pamela Morris, Boriswood (London: 1937). This same translation was published in the United States under the same title in 1954 by Image Books, reprinted in England by Collins in 1956.

Nouvelle histoire de Mouchette

————. 1937: Plon.

————. 1961: Gallimard, in *Oeuvres romanesques.*

In English

Mouchette, trans. by J. C. Whitehouse, Holt, Rinehart and Winston (New York: 1966).

M. Ouine

————. 1943: Atlantica (Rio de Janeiro).

————. 1946: Plon.

————. 1955: Club des Libraires de France (édition critique d'Albert Béguin).

1961: Gallimard, in *Oeuvres romanesques.* This text is that established by Béguin in the 1955 edition.

In English

The Open Mind, trans. by Geoffry Dunlop, John Lane (London: 1945).

Un mauvais rêve

————. (1950: *La Table Ronde*)

————. 1950: Plon. Both a normal and a critical edition were issued at the same time, both prepared by Albert Béguin.

1961: Gallimard, in *Oeuvres romanesques.*

In English

Night Is Darkest, trans. by W. J. Strachan, Bodley Head (London: 1953).

Dialogues des Carmélites

————. 1949: La Baconnière (Neuchâtel) and Seuil.

————. 1961: Gallimard, in *Oeuvres romanesques.*

In English

The Fearless Heart, trans. by Michel Legat, Bodley Head (London: 1952). The same translation was published in the United States by the Newman Press (Westminster, Md.: 1952).

The Carmelites, trans. by G. Hopkins, Collins (London: 1961).

COLLECTED WORKS

Oeuvres romanesques, suivies de *Dialogues des Carmélites,* Gallimard (1961), Bibliothèque de la Pléiade. Péface de Gaëtan Picon. Texte établi par A. Béguin. Biographie et notes par Michel Estève. This volume, since its publication, is the standard one. The early fiction as well as the youthful letters of Bernanos to Abbé Lagrange are included. The notes are rich with a wealth of relevant letters and texts.

OTHER PRIMARY SOURCES

Other major primary sources where texts by Bernanos may be found include the following:

BULLETIN de la Société des Amis de Georges Bernanos of which 58 numbers have appeared since its first issue in 1949.

Georges Bernanos, Essais et témoignages réunis par Albert Béguin, La Baconnière (Neuchatel) and Seuil (1949).

SECONDARY SOURCES

BOOKS IN FRENCH

Unless otherwise stated, all books were published in Paris.

ALBERT BÉGUIN, *Bernanos par lui-même,* Seuil (1954). This little volume is still the best introduction available both to the man and to his thought, though its author died 1957 and much work has been done since. But the hypotheses found in this book are still, for the most part, to be explored.

————, *Georges Bernanos,* Essais et témoignages réunis par Albert Béguin, La Baconnière (Neuchatel), and Seuil (1949). An invaluable source of information giving letters, memories of friends, literary and political history and the very beautiful account of Bernanos' death by Abbé Pezeril.

YVES BRIDEL, *L'Esprit d'enfance dans l'oeuvre romanesque de Georges Bernanos,* Minard (1966). A very thoroughgoing thematic study which might serve as an introduction.

WILLIAM BUSH, *Souffrance et Expiation dans la Pensée de Bernanos,* Minard (1962). A thematic study giving especial emphasis to Bernanos' spiritual evolution.

MARIE-AGNÈS FRAGNIÈRE, *Bernanos fidèle à l'enfant,* Editions Universitaires (Fribourg: 1964). A short study on the theme of childhood and its role in Bernanos' work.

GUY GAUCHER, *Le Thème de la Mort dans les romans de Bernanos,* Minard (1955). A short but very solid thematic study. Contains some unpublished letters of Bernanos.

HANS URS VON BALTHAZAR, *Le Chrétien Bernanos* (traduit de l'allemand par Maurice de Gandillac), Seuil (1956). This translation of the noted German-Swiss theologian's monumental volume on Bernanos remains, to date, the most imposing study consecrated to Bernanos. While very complete in one sense, it still misses the essentials, having been conceived around a given context: the seven Sacraments. Such an arbitrary division of Bernanos' world can only lead to arbitrary conclusions. The French translation surpressed the biographical section in the original German published by Hegner Verlag (Cologne & Olten: 1954).

REVIEWS DEVOTED TO BERNANOS

BULLETIN de la Société des Amis de Georges Bernanos, (distributed by M. J. Minard, 73 rue de Cardinal-Lemoine, Paris V) of which 58 numbers have appeared since its first issue in 1949.

"Etudes bernanosiennes," periodic issues of *La Revue des Lettres Modernes* devoted exclusively to Bernanos and edited by Michel Estève. Since its first number in 1960 seven issues have appeared.

Notes and References

ABBREVIATIONS

Unless stated otherwise, all books in these notes and references were published in Paris.

In addition, the following abbreviations will be used:

GB   *Georges Bernanos,* Essais et Témoignages réunis par Albert Béguin, Les Cahiers du Rhône, Le Baconnière, Neuchatel, and Seuil, 1949.

LM   Albert Béguin, *Bernanos par lui-même,* Images et textes inédits présentés par Albert Béguin, Seuil, 1954.

OE   Geogres Bernanos, *Oeuvres romanesques suivies de Dialogues des Carmélites* (Bibliothèque de la Pléiade), Préface par Gaëton Picon, Texte et variantes établis par Albert Béguin, Notes par Michel Estève, Gallimard, 1961.

SE   William Bush, *Souffrance et Expiation dans la Pensée de Bernanos,* Minard, 1962.

Susan M. Keane (essay date 1969)

SOURCE: Keane, Susan M. "Dream Imagery in the Novels of Bernanos." In *Image and Theme, Studies in Modern French Fiction: Bernanos, Malraux, Sarraute, Gide, Martin Du Gard,* edited by W. M. Frohock, pp. 11-37. Cambridge, Mass.: Department of Romance Languages and Literatures, Harvard University, 1969.

[*In the following essay, Keane studies the "close association between dream-image and metaphor" in Bernanos's novels, focusing especially on how these "ve-*

hicles" of expression reinforce the central themes in the author's work and contribute to "the creation of a dream-like world."]

Few writers have been less willing than Bernanos to discourse with readers on their own terms. He does not speak his interlocutor's language, but his own; and he refuses to install familiar landmarks in his imaginative world. The very landscapes are strange and frightening: perspectives are unstable, roads are interminable, and buildings are endowed with a kind of sinister life. Human relationships are equally disconcerting; characters are isolated from one another by mysterious barriers, or communicate in signs that they understand better than we do. Conversation, which in another novelist might provide some echo of the common world, offers none here; Robert Kemp has remarked that in the novels "tout le monde parle Bernanos."[1] If the reader is to find any common ground with Bernanos, it is not in the exterior world of concrete, objective realities, but in the responses that the writer's imagination awakens in his own. He is forced into adapting his own subjectivity to a new angle of vision.

It is in the light of this problem that we ought to approach the question of imagery in Bernanos. It is possible to define an image generally as an analogical statement transmitting a sense impression; but in practice the use of material elements in figurative language presents as many variations as there are writers. Many authors draw a clear boundary between literal and analogical language; Bernanos is not one of them. For some writers, the concept of imagery implies vivid evocation of something palpable and concrete; Gautier, for example, could explain his artistic principles by saying, "Je suis un homme pour qui le monde extérieur existe." Bernanos is almost a polar opposite of Gautier. For him, the exterior world seems to serve chiefly as a stimulus to the imagination. The reader is far more conscious of a subject than of objects. Thus, whereas it is fairly simple for an attentive reader to visualize Gautier's statue or still-life, it is frequently difficult to envision precisely what Bernanos is describing, because he is far less interested in the object itself than in its effect upon the consciousness. A great many of his images are concerned with the experience of sensation rather than its causes:

> Cela vous vient comme une idée . . . comme un vertige . . . de se laisser tomber, glisser . . . d'aller jusqu'en bas—tout à fait—jusqu'au fond—où le mépris des imbéciles n'irait même pas vous chercher . . .
>
> (*SSS* [*Sous le soleil de Satan*], p. 97)[2]

> Je n'ai rien vu, rien entendu, je ne pensais même à rien. Cela m'a comme frappé dans le dos.
>
> (*J* [*La Joie*], p. 715.)

Even when the vehicle of an image is easily seen to be water, or fire, or some other definable object, the reader is still conscious of strong feeling—and not merely perception—on the part of a subject:

> Ce qu'elle voyait se consumer au feu de la parole, c'était elle-même, ne dérobant rien à la flamme droite et aiguë, suivie jusqu'au dernier détour, à la dernière fibre de chair.
>
> (*SSS,* p. 200.)

> La Pensée que cette lutte va finir . . . n'est entrée en moi que peu à peu. C'était un mince filet d'eau limpide, et maintenant cela déborde de l'âme, me remplit de fraîcheur.
>
> (*JCC* [*Journal d'un curé de campagne*], p. 1255.)

When the exterior world is perceived, it is with a sense of alienation; the subject's astigmatism distorts and estranges familiar things:

> Et soudain, pareil à ces paysages trop lumineux, trop vibrants, que submerge d'un coup le crépuscule, et qui réapparaissent lentement, méconnaissables, semblent remonter de l'abîme de la nuit, l'étroit univers familier dans lequel elle était née, où elle avait vécu, prenait un aspect nouveau.
>
> (*J,* pp. 562-563.)

> Le village m'apparaît bien différent de ce qu'il était en automne, on dirait que la limpidité de l'air lui enlève peu à peu toute pesanteur, et lorsque le soleil commence à décliner, on pourrait le croire suspendu dans le vide, il ne touche pas à la terre, il m'échappe, il s'envole.
>
> (*JCC,* p. 1208.)

> Mais il s'éloigna de son pas pesant, et aussitot Mouchette crut voir son image falote glisser avec une rapidité prodigieuse comme aspirée par le vide.
>
> (*NM* [*Nouvelle Histoire de Mouchette*], p. 1344.)

In these images, the subject cannot really be said to be *observing* an analogy; in a sense, he is submitting to one. He is not consciously creating metaphors, any more than the dreamer creates the images that haunt his sleep. For the Bernanosian character, there is a close correspondence between mental image and metaphor; his imagination is less creative than receptive.

The images we have cited express the point of view of characters in the novels of Bernanos; but their essential passivity is similar to that which the writer observed in himself. "Cette image me hante" is a sentence found more than once in the polemical works.[3] A letter written to his fiancée during World War II shows that he sometimes felt himself to be a target for images, rather than a creator of them:

> C'est presque en vain que l'âme s'efforce de prendre conscience d'elle-même, au milieu de cette immobilité du néant; rien ne l'agite ici que les images décevantes et passionnées de son bonheur ancien, images mille

> fois pressées et flattées de tant de mains caressantes, pauvres images en exil et fanées comme les pages d'un livre trop de fois lu!
>
> (*BPLM,* p. 102.)

This tendency also affects his definition of his work as a writer. In a letter to the critic Claude-Edmonde Magny, he said: "Je suis un romancier, c'est-à-dire un homme qui vit ses rêves, ou les revit sans le savoir. Je n'ai donc pas d'intentions, au sens qu'on donne généralement à ce mot" (*OR* [*Oeuvres romanesques*], p. 1857). The work of writing a novel was, for him, "un de ces longs voyages à travers les images et les rêves qui s'achèvent toujours prosaïquement chez l'éditeur" (*GSSL* [*Les Grands Cimetières sous la lune*], p. ii).

The writer's own testimony, then, would seem to indicate the existence of a strong involuntary element in the production of figurative language; for him, the relationship between mental image and metaphor seems to have been a fairly direct one. Gaëtan Picon lends support to this idea when he speaks of Bernanos' images as being "moins obtenues que reçues," and remarks that they do not make the reader aware of the artistic effort that may be involved in their creation.[4] He, too, considers that they are somewhat passive in nature. More direct evidence is provided by the fact that the images found in the novels of Bernanos are echoed in his polemical works and his letters: images of water and mud, animals and minerals, occur in *Les Grands Cimetières sous la lune* and *Les Enfants humiliés* as well as in *Sous le soleil de Satan* and *Monsieur Ouine.*[5] The sources of many of these images are traceable to Bernanos' childhood in Artois, and the writer attributes his involuntary use of certain themes to the tenacity of these early associations. In an eloquent passage in *Les Enfants humiliés,* he contrasts his own compulsions with the feelings of *déracinés* for their native country:

> Ils me font rigoler avec leur nostalgie de paysages français! Je n'ai pas revu ceux de ma jeunesse, je tiens à la Provence par un sentiment mille fois plus fort et plus jaloux. Il n'en est pas moins vrai qu'après trente ans d'absence—ou de ce que nous appelons par ce nom—les personnages de mes livres se retrouvent d'eux-mêmes aux lieux que j'ai cru quitter. Ici ou ailleurs, pourquoi aurais-je la nostalgie de ce que je possède malgré moi, que je ne puis trahir? Pourquoi évoquerais-je avec mélancolie l'eau noire du chemin creux, la haie qui siffle sous l'averse, puisque je suis moi-même la haie et l'eau noire?
>
> (*EH* [*Les Enfants humiliés*], pp. 37-38.)

The obsessive element which Bernanos recognizes in his own experience is extended in various ways into the lives of his characters. Like their creator, they tend to become overwhelmed by mental images at moments of strain. Donissan, the hero of *Sous le soleil de Satan,* experiences grave psychological distress just before his last battle; his pain and confusion are reflected in images (*SSS*, pp. 233-238). The apostate priest Cénabre, when he realizes that he has lost his faith and when he is about to regain it, passes through a somewhat similar state (*I* [*L'Imposture*], p. 368; *J*, p. 715).

Frequently, the obsession of a character assumes the proportions of hallucination or vision. Donissan has a mysterious encounter with a horse-trader who may be the devil in disguise; the reader is never sure at what point reality leaves off and hallucination begins (*SSS*, pp. 167—184). Chevance, the reluctant witness of Cénabre's apostasy, wanders through the streets of Paris looking for him; it soon becomes apparent that the whole journey is the product of a dying man's delirium (*I*, pp. 505-524). Chantal de Clergerie, who has strangely fallen heir to Chevance's responsibility for Cénabre, has mystical visions involving both priests (*J*, pp. 678-679; 685-686). Monsieur Ouine, at the point of death, has a long conversation with Steeny, a young disciple; it later turns out that the boy was drunk at the time and probably imagined the whole encounter (*MO* [*Monsieur Oine*], pp. 1540-1561). All of these episodes are characterized by long successions of images whose vehicles often change rapidly, as in dreams. If there is any logic in these passages, it is oneiric rather than rational: what Bernanos calls the "succession d'un cauchemar" (*I*, p. 426).

It is at first somewhat surprising that mystical images should be similar to those resulting from delirium or drunkenness. As a Catholic writer, and one of the less rationalistic members of his faith, Bernanos is a firm believer in the validity of mystical experience. At the same time, he recognizes that mysticism, like dreaming or delirium, is a state in which rational elements are no longer in control of the human consciousness. However inevitable or valuable such states may be, they are also somewhat dangerous. A man may be destroyed by his dreams; and the curé of Torcy, in the *Journal d'un curé de campagne,* points out that even mystics, absorbed in the presence of God, are not safe:

> Que veux-tu, mon petit, j'ai mes idées sur la harpe du jeune David. C'était un garçon de talent, sûr, mais toute sa musique ne l'a pas préservé du péché. Je sais bien que les pauvres écrivains bien-pensants qui fabriquent des Vies de saints pour l'exportation, s'imaginent qu'un bonhomme est à l'abri dans l'extase, qu'il s'y trouve au chaud et en sûreté comme dans le sein d'Abraham. En sûreté!
>
> (*JCC*, p. 1041.)

But these disturbing forms of experience never cease to exert a powerful fascination for Bernanos. It may be said that dreams provide the key to understanding this writer's figurative expression; but, if this statement is to be reliable, then the definition of *dream* must be a very broad one, embracing any condition in which the mind is prey to non-rational forces.

This close association between dream-image and metaphor has concrete results in the presence of certain metaphorical vehicles in the novels. The themes most frequently recurring[6] are: sensation; water in various forms; animals; light and darkness; sickness and death. Many metaphors are also concerned with children. Other vehicles, less notable for their frequency than for their occurrence at significant moments, are mirrors, roads, circles, obstacles, and stones. It has been remarked that these vehicles, which remain extraordinarily constant throughout the novels, have nothing particularly original about them. Indeed, the reader who is disconcerted by the strangeness of Bernanos' world may find that he at least recognizes the materials of which it is made.[7] These materials are the property of all human experience, and especially of that part of it which lies below the surface of consciousness. Even when the vehicles themselves are not particularly oneiric—some images are concerned with historical figures, for example—the perspective in which they are treated leaves little doubt as to the world to which they belong. In the following pages, we shall consider examples of some of these themes, and their role in the creation of a dream-like world.

In many cases the vehicles are definable only in terms of sensation rather than of objects. We have already noted Bernanos' general tendency to insist upon feelings rather than their sources. This tendency makes itself felt to varying degrees, however. It is difficult, for example, to refer to a sensation of sight and to ignore what is seen. To a lesser degree, a description of hearing also implies a description of what is heard, however vaguely. But in the case of touch (or pain, or vertigo), it is possible to be much more self-centered and oblivious to the outside world. It is not, perhaps, surprising that many images having to do with this kind of sensation are particularly appropriate for evoking states of dreaming or madness. It is worth noting as well that a similar perspective is characteristic of some mystical writing. Abbé Bremond, widely respected as an authority on the subject, says that "les plus hauts mystiques insistent plus longuement sur les ténèbres au sein desquels ils s'unissent à Dieu que sur une appréhension claire de celui qu'ils étreignent. Ils parlent beaucoup plus des touches divines que de celui qui les touche." He cites, as examples of images used by mystics, "un certain parfum," "une odeur de paradis," "un poids secret." He also speaks of the sense of being pushed by something, of being like a sponge in a vast ocean, of feeling the presence of a bird whose wings brush one's face.[8] The images mentioned here find precise echoes in those of Bernanos.[9] The implication here is not, of course, that Bernanos found his thematic repertory in a few pages of Bremond, but that these metaphors belong to a much more universal repertory of oneiric and mystical figures of speech. We can expect that images of sensation will be adaptable to a variety of contexts and carry many different implications.

The sensation of falling, which characterizes the dreaming or half-waking state, is typical of this category. It recurs frequently in the novels, and in a number of moral and spiritual situations. In *Nouvelle Histoire de Mouchette,* it is used to evoke a feeling of lassitude and hopelessness:

> Elle obéit à une loi aussi fixe, aussi implacable que celui qui régit la chute d'un corps, car un certain désespoir a son accélération propre.
>
> (*NM,* p. 1320-21.)

A similar image in *Sous le soleil de Satan* carries a more specific theological reference to despair:

> Ce n'est plus ce cloître qu'il désire, mais quelque chose de plus secret que la solitude, l'évanouissement d'une chute éternelle, dans les ténèbres refermées.
>
> (*SSS,* p. 327.)

What is implied here is a fall into the spiritual abyss, away from God. The saints of Bernanos, whose strength is often combined with a kind of apparent weakness, also discover the abyss of light, the fall *into* God. The heroine of *La Joie* experiences this paradoxical sensation:

> Elle croyait glisser lentement, puis glisser tout à fait dans le sommeil . . . Seulement elle tombait en Dieu.
>
> (*J,* p. 568.)

> Dix fois, vingt fois peut-être, elle avait failli céder au vertige, rouler jusqu'au bord du gouffre de lumière, et n'avait sagement achevé son oraison qu'au prix d'un effort intolérable. Mais n'était-elle pas tombée à son insu?
>
> (*J,* p. 577.)

This image of falling into God was one which Bernanos may well have found in the works of Bremond.[10] It seems to have haunted him to the end of his career. It appears first in *La Joie,* and is given a favored place in *Dialogues des Carmélites.*[11] It is used ironically in *Un Mauvais Rêve* (p. 971) and *Monsieur Ouine*:

> Je n'ai nullement songé à nier l'existence de mon âme, et aujourd'hui même je ne saurais la mettre en doute, mais j'ai perdu tout sentiment de la mienne, alors qu'il y a une heure seulement, je l'éprouvais ainsi qu'un vide, une attente, une aspiration intérieure. Sans doute a-t-elle achevé de m'engloutir? Je suis tombé en elle, jeune homme, de la manière dont les élus tombent en Dieu.
>
> (*MO,* p. 1560.)

The spiritual life is also described more conventionally in terms of an ascent toward God, but even in these cases there is an attempt to imbue the traditional metaphor with strong feeling:

> Ainsi l'homme surnaturel est à l'aise si haut que l'amour le porte et sa vie spirituelle ne comporte aucun vertige.
>
> (*SSS,* p. 198.)

> Oh! naturellement, rien n'est si facile que de grimper là-haut: Dieu vous y porte. Il s'agit seulement d'y tenir, et, le cas échéant, de savoir descendre.
>
> (*JCC,* p. 1041.)

It is notable that ascent, as well as descent, is usually a passive process in Bernanos' metaphors. The man who succeeds in scaling figurative heights through his own efforts is rare indeed; even the mountain-climber is not fully aware of what he is doing:

> J'étais comme un homme qui, ayant grimpé d'un trait une pente vertigineuse, ouvre les yeux, s'arrête ébloui, hors d'état de monter ou de descendre.
>
> (*JCC,* p. 1161.)

Images of involuntary flight, or of extraordinary ease of movement, can also indicate that rational forces are not in control. Donissan, the unconscious prey of diabolical forces, is "alerte, dispos, léger, ainsi qu'après un bon sommeil dans la fraîcheur du matin" (*SSS,* p. 164). In *Monsieur Ouine,* the insane mayor of Fenouille muses in this fashion before a public speech:

> Il parlera quand il voudra, il parlera presque à son insu, avec une facilité, une légèreté aérienne. Il parlera comme on vole.
>
> (*MO,* p. 1496.)

These images, which imply a kind of rejoicing in an illusion of power, are among the most sinister in Bernanos. Such a degree of ill-founded confidence means that the victim is, for the moment at least, totally deceived by his dreams. When reason succeeds in breaking through, a character is able to be somewhat skeptical about unexpected feelings of lightness and ease. Chantal de Clergerie, perhaps more than any other creature of Bernanos, is characterized by images of flying things: she is compared to a bird, an angel, a flower blown by the air (*J,* pp. 666; 543-544.) At the same time, she is seriously troubled by her own spiritual flights. Simone Alfieri, under a very different kind of compulsion, is astonished and disconcerted by the facility with which she manages to invent alibis for a projected crime (*MR* [*Un Mauvais Rêve*], p. 992).

Sensations of lightness do not always connote ease; they can be medical symptoms, as we see in the words of the dying Mme Dargent:

> Mes pauvres os sont creux, légers comme des plumes—au-dedans et au-dehors il n'y a que du vide—oui! tout est vide et flottant, hors de cette affreuse tête de plomb.
>
> (*MD* [*Madame Dargent*], p. 6.)

Chevance, in the delirium which precedes his death, has the same symptom, as does the mother of the second Mouchette, (*I*, pp. 507-508; *NM*, p. 1314). Olivier Mainville, in *Un Mauvais Rêve,* experiences a lightness like that of a drugged man (*MR*, p. 977). The weightlessness of the dying Ouine has moral rather than medical connotations; recognizing that nothing is left of what was once his character, he says, "je n'ai plus de poids" (*MO*, p. 1560). Even here, however, he is still speaking with the voice of a patient describing symptoms. This perspective is perhaps significant for the interpretation of other metaphorical vehicles in Bernanos. A sick man, describing his condition, often creates images to do so; but he has very little interest in the beauty or inherent qualities of the vehicles he uses. He is concerned only with the accuracy with which they can describe the effect of a sensation upon his consciousness. Bernanos' characters are often sick men themselves; but even when they are not, this highly subjective angle of vision frequently prevails in their metaphors. Their choice of vehicles results more from inner compulsion than from objective appreciation. Aesthetic considerations are secondary.

Images of sound are a case in point. Although Bernanos occasionally evokes the chords of a symphony or the melodies produced at random by a pianist, he is more interested in the voices and music that exist within the mind, often despite efforts to the contrary. Terror, for example, is comparable to a loud cry:

> Je m'éveillais brusquement avec, dans l'oreille, un grand cri—mais estce encore ce mot-là qui convient? Evidemment non.
>
> (*JCC*, p. 1099.)

> C'est que je me suis crue morte, moi aussi, figurez-vous. C'est comme un cri, un très grand cri, mais que je n'entendais pas par les oreilles, vous comprenez?
>
> (*MO*, p. 1415.)

A more continuous kind of sensation is typified by a constant murmur or chant. The little invalid in *Monsieur Ouine* compares his chronic suffering to the murmur of voices:

> Souffrir, voyez-vous, cela s'apprend. C'est d'abord comme un petit murmure au fond de soi, jour et nuit. Jour et nuit, qu'on dorme ou qu'on veille, n'importe! Il arrive parfois que vous croyez ne plus l'entendre, mais il suffit de prêter l'oreille: la chose est toujours là qui parle, dans sa langue, une langue inconnue.
>
> (*MO*, p. 1384.)

In *Nouvelle Histoire de Mouchette,* there is a clear equivalence between music and obsession. The novel's heroine is unable to feel any order in the world surrounding her, and perceives events only through a confused rumble of sounds:

> La fuite de l'école, l'attente au bord du chemin, sa course errante à travers les taillis dans la grande colère du vent et le flagellement de la pluie, la rencontre de M. Arsène—cela n'arrive pas à faire une véritable histoire, cela n'a ni commencement ni fin, cela ressemblerait plutôt à une rumeur confuse qui remplit maintenant sa pauvre tête, une sorte de chant funèbre.
>
> (*NM*, p. 1301.)

It is when Mouchette is finally overcome by this obsessive murmur that she drowns herself. She is unable to maintain any kind of distance between herself and what she hears, or to organize it in any way; she is the passive victim of her sensations.

In Mouchette, as well as in other characters, Bernanos magnifies tendencies which he has perceived in himself. Obviously, he is able to organize his private world; otherwise, he would never have been an artist. But his choice of images does not seem to be particularly free. Like his characters, he has less interest in the vehicles as such than in their capacity to describe a given state of consciousness; and, indeed, certain vehicles seem themselves to form part of that state of consciousness.

One such compulsive theme is water. The water image is one that attracted Bernanos long before he thought of becoming a writer; we see it in letters he wrote as a schoolboy:

> Un rien m'agite et me fait rêver, mais ce mouvement-là dure trois jours, quatre jours, un mois, et l'eau s'apaise et redevient dormante, ainsi qu'avant, tant que je ne souffre point . . .
>
> (**Lettres à l'abbé Lagrange,** *OR*, p. 1734.)

> Prêchez-moi, grondez-moi, je tends l'oreille, je suis devant vous comme une terre sans eau—c'est David qui l'a dit le premier . . .
>
> (*Ibid.*, pp. 1735-1736.)

The young Bernanos is aware of the Biblical allusions called forth by his use of the water symbol; but it is perhaps significant that he never stops to analyze the symbol itself. The novelist Bernanos does not do so either. Unlike Claudel, for example, he has little or nothing to say about the multiple levels of meaning contained within the water symbol. Rather, he reaches out almost instinctively for whatever vehicle best expresses his angle of vision. And for him, as for other writers, water lends itself to the expression of many aspects of the dream world. Water metaphors can help to create the atmosphere of instability which is often typical of the oneiric perspective. They also lend themselves to descriptions of the soul and the subconscious. (Even the language of cliché tells us of the *depths* of the soul and the still waters that run deep.) The schoolboy letters of Bernanos reflect this equation between soul and water, and it appears in the novels as well.

The water metaphor is particularly adapted to the idea of impenetrable depth, and also to that of impurity— properties which, for Bernanos, are also attributable to the human soul. Cénabre, at the moment of yielding to temptation, is conscious of the "eaux dormantes et pourries de l'âme" (*I,* p. 355). The curé of Ambricourt discerns "une eau trouble, une boue," in the gaze of a parishioner (*JCC,* p. 1125). The father of Chantal de Clergerie takes this view of the soul:

> Chacun de nous a son secret, ses secrets, une multitude de secrets, qui achèvent de pourrir dans la conscience, s'y consument lentement, lentement . . . Toi-même, ma fille, oui, toi-même; si tu vis de longues années, tu sentiras peut-être, à l'heure de la mort, ce poids, ce clapotis de la vase sous l'eau profonde.
>
> (*J,* p. 592.)

It is evidently in contrast to images such as these that Bernanos means us to understand the description of the Virgin Mary by the curé of Torcy:

> Car enfin, elle était née sans péché, quelle solitude étonnante! Une source si pure, si limpide, si limpide et si pure, qu'elle ne pouvait même pas y voir refléter sa propre image, faite pour la seule joie du Père—ô solitude sacrée!
>
> (*JCC,* p. 1193.)

For Bernanos, sinfulness is less an aggregate of bad deeds than an innate state of being, something lurking in the depths of the soul. The Virgin was the only creature whose unconscious motives were pure; clear water, or a state of untroubled grace, is something generally denied to men.

In examples such as that we have just cited, it is quite possible to find doctrinal meanings in Bernanos' water images. But there are dangers in extending this procedure too far. The metaphors of Bernanos are not illustrations of intellectual perceptions, but analogies seized at a much more instinctive and ambiguous level. Water may be a symbol of grace; but water and mud may also signify, much more vaguely, "that-which-is-to-be-feared," or that which engulfs rationality and consciousness. They can frequently be equated with the broad concept of dreams which forms one of the bases for this essay.

The character who has yielded totally to his dreams is reduced to floating aimlessly about. The hallucinations of Mme Dargent involve drifting in lakes and oceans (*MD,* p. 7), and M. Ouine says of himself: "Comme ces gelées vivantes, au fond de la mer, je flotte et j'absorbe" (*MO,* p. 1368). Both of these characters have withdrawn into a solipsistic state and are incapable of reacting to any reality outside themselves. There are other cases in which the personality is not yet absorbed by irrational elements, but the possibility or danger is clearly

present. A character in *Monsieur Ouine* compares herself, in a moment of terror, to a sinking ship: "je coulais à pic, comme un navire sabordé" (*MO,* p. 1416). Cénabre, on the verge of madness, evokes the same image:

> Tout tremblant encore de l'effroyable assaut, le regard exténué, la bouche amère, il reprenait possession, une à une, des idées et des images que la soudaine explosion de terreur avait éparpillées ainsi que des feuilles mortes: il essayait de raisonner avec ces pauvres débris sauvés du désastre, ainsi qu'un navire englouti à demi utilise ses derniers foyers.
>
> (*J,* p. 715.)

In a more spiritual context, Chantal de Clergerie sinks into mystical states, despite her own efforts to the contrary:

> Littéralement, elle crut entendre se refermer sur elle une eau profonde, et aussitôt, en effet, son corps défaillit sous un poids immense, accru sans cesse et dont l'irrésistible poussée chassait la vie hors de ses veines.
>
> (*J,* p. 681.)

The second Mouchette, whose drowning is physical rather than figurative, may also be said to have yielded to her obsessions; it is notable that several times during the hours before her death she unconsciously mimes the gestures of a drowning person:

> Mais aujourd'hui, d'un mouvement irréfléchi comme d'un noyé qui s'enfonce, elle a pris à pleins bras le paquet de chiffons fumant d'urine et de lait aigre . . .
>
> (*NM,* p. 1299; see also pp. 1329-1330.)

The same gestures are made by the first Mouchette, when the abbé Donissan forces her to recognize that her pride and sense of independence have been based upon illusions, that, instead of being a free spirit, she is a victim. This recognition produces a state of shock:

> Alors elle se dressa, battant l'air de ses mains, la tête jetée en arrière, puis d'une épaule à l'autre, absolument comme un noyé qui s'enfonce.
>
> (*SSS,* p. 207.)

This gesture, too, is a prelude to suicide.

The helplessness implicit in these images of drowning is also expressed by images of mud, with the difference that, whereas water may signify certain desirable qualities, it is almost impossible for mud to represent anything essentially good. It is used, quite naturally, as a symbol of humiliation or disgust. To become engulfed in it is to have given up on life. Those who are tired of life welcome it, as they would welcome even shame:

> Car le seul repos véritable qu'ait jamais connu, parmi des êtres qu'il déteste ou qu'il méprise, son cœur sauvage, c'est le dégoût. Incapable de justifier par des rai-

sons la révolte de sa nature, son refus à peine conscient, elle se venge ainsi à sa manière de son incompréhensible solitude, comme à la limite de la fatigue, il arrive qu'elle se couche exprès à la place la plus boueuse de la route.

> (*NM*, p. 1338; see also *SSS*, p. 109; *JCC*, p. 1203.)

For the curé of Fenouille, the dead souls of his parishioners appear, almost palpably, as lakes of mud (*MO*, p. 1488). A similar metaphor occurs to the curé of Ambricourt, when he envisions the souls of the damned as "ce lac de boue toujours gluant sur quoi passe et repasse vainement l'immense marée de l'amour divin" (*JCC*, p. 1139). We have already noted images of the polluted waters of the soul, and of the "vase sous l'eau profonde"; the souls envisioned by the two curés are those who have yielded to such elements.[12]

Thus far, we have been considering water in its most drastic aspect, as the element that engulfs, and usually destroys. Sometimes, though, water represents an element in which a character can exist, and perhaps maintain a certain autonomy. His world is strange and distorted, and he himself is isolated. His perceptions are those of the dream world, transformed by water and mist, but they are still perceptions. The second Mouchette has the impression, at one point, of living in a kind of aquarium, disconcerting but not altogether unpleasant:

> . . . l'air lourd, visqueux, imprégné de cette buée grasse qui sort des tourbières, transmet la vibration aussi fidèlement qu'une eau profonde.
>
> (*NM*, p. 1278.)

The curé of Ambricourt, bewildered by an interview that is not going as he expected, focuses on the landscape and finds that it has assumed a watery unreality:

> Par la fenêtre ouverte, à travers les rideaux de linon, on voyait l'immense pelouse fermée par la muraille des pins, sous un ciel nocturne. C'était comme un étang d'eau croupissante.
>
> (*JCC*, p. 1146.)

Sometimes, as in cases of madness, the perspective is more thoroughly deformed. The insane grandmother in *La Joie* sees the world in this way:

> Puis le même brouillard qu'elle connaissait commença de recouvrir lentement les êtres et les choses, de moins en moins saisissables, pareils à leur propre reflet dans l'eau.
>
> (*J*, 656.)

The perception of this unstable kind of landscape is likely to result in an acute sense of alienation. The victims of this astigmatism are the prisoners of their own subjectivity; human presences, in this sort of environ-

ment, are extremely difficult to grasp. In *L'Imposture*, for example, a bewildered and desperate character sees his interlocutor in this way:

> A présent la tête énorme semblait flotter de l'une à l'autre épaule, telle une épave sur une eau morte.
>
> (*I*, p. 437.)

It is notable that Bernanos, who almost never describes faces clearly, evokes a number of images of faces seen through glass or water:

> Celle qu'il avait tant de fois caressée dans ses livres, et dont il croyait avoir épuisé la douceur, la mort— d'ailleurs partout visible sous sa froide ironie comme un visage sous une eau claire et profonde—cent fois rêvée, savourée, il ne la reconnut pas.
>
> (*SSS*, p. 282.)

> La grace divine (depuis des mois, il n'en sentait même pas l'absence) se montrait encore une fois: c'était comme la face d'un cadavre au fond des eaux, c'était comme un cri plaintif dans la brume.
>
> (*I*, p. 348.)

The image of the face seen through water expresses loneliness and incommunication: distances between persons cannot be breached, no matter how near the other may appear to be. When the face perceived is one's own, the combination of recognition and strangeness is apt to produce fear, or at least anxiety. Madame Dargent is terrified when she finds her own reflection in a hallucinatory pool (*MD*, p. 7). The heroine of *Un Mauvais Rêve*, about to commit a crime, is startled when she comes by accident upon her image in a mirror:

> La glace usée ne laissait paraître qu'une sorte de nappe diffuse, rayée d'ombre, où elle croyait voir monter et descendre sa face livide, ainsi que du fond d'une eau trouble.
>
> (*MR*, p. 1017.)

A fear mixed with fascination is felt by the curé of Ambricourt, when he cautiously approaches the task of writing a spiritual journal; and he, too, is haunted by a face that he half recognizes:

> Mon regard semblait glisser à la surface d'une autre conscience jusqu'alors inconnue de moi, d'un miroir troublé où j'ai craint tout à coup de voir surgir un visage—quel visage; le mien peut-être? . . . un visage retrouvé, oublié.
>
> Il faudrait parler de soi avec une rigueur inflexible
>
> (*JCC*, p. 1036.)

The curé, a compulsive but somewhat reluctant author, is the only one of Bernanos' writer-characters to be presented in a favorable light. His imaginative processes are evidently similar to his creator's: Bernanos has the same troubled fascination with his own image, and the same experience of a kind of involuntary creation of characters. If we are to believe the testimony of the polemical works, the use of water or mirrors to reflect faces is not a carefully conceived technique, in order to make solid realities more vague. On the contrary; it expresses the way in which Bernanos sees, or rather feels, the presence of his characters. They were never solid realities in the first place; they were the companions of his dreams. A striking indication of his attitude toward them is provided by the famous passage in *Les Grands Cimetières sous la lune* where he addresses them directly: "Compagnons inconnus, vieux frères . . ." In the following lines, he evokes the way in which his half-formed creations haunted his imagination, even when he was a child:

> L'aube venait bien avant que fussent rentrés dans le silence de l'âme, dans ses profondes repaires, les personnages fabuleux encore à peine formés, embryons sans membres, Mouchette et Donissan, Cénabre, Chantal, et vous, vous seul de mes créatures dont j'ai parfois cru discerner le visage mais à qui je n'ai pas osé donner de nom—cher curé d'un Ambricourt imaginaire. Etiez-vous alors mes maîtres? Aujourd'hui même, l'êtes-vous?

> (*GCSL* [*GCSL*], p. iv.)

When Bernanos speaks about discerning the face of the curé of Ambricourt, his angle of vision recalls the image of the face seen through water. The sense of a vague, haunting presence is here, and so is the unstable perspective. This time, though, the water-mirror motif is absent, and the oneiric element is mentioned quite specifically. This is true in other instances in Bernanos' works. Olivier Mainville, in *Un Mauvais Rêve,* sees other people only through the distorted lens of his own dreams:

> "Tu dégueules?" lui cria en passant un marmot à face blême, minuscule, pareil à un jouet de cauchemar.

> (*MR,* p. 974.)

In *Monsieur Ouine,* the old peasant Devandomme is alienated from his acquaintances by his private obsessions and tragedies; he, too, envisions others in a nightmarish way:

> Millediû! les vitres de l'estaminet sont toutes noires de dos d'homme et quand il passe ils se tournent tous à la fois, blêmes à travers la fumée des pipes, blêmes comme ces visages qu'on voit en rêve.

> (*MO,* p. 1482.)

These examples would seem to reinforce our assumption that vehicles, in and of themselves, are of secondary importance for Bernanos. Water is an important elsement in what Bachelard would call the "material imagination" of Bernanos, but it is far from being the only important theme that suits his purpose. Other ve-

hicles are of considerable help in creating the oneiric atmosphere that is characteristic of this writer's world. Light is one such vehicle; and, indeed, light and water are sometimes confused in a single impression. The Bernanosian saint often sinks into a "gouffre de lumière" that contains properties of both elements. A minor character in *Sous le soleil de Satan* envisions the spiritual life in this way:

> Je crois que le chrétien de bonne volonté se maintient de lui-même dans la lumière d'en haut, comme un homme dont le volume et le poids sont dans une proportion si constante et si adroitement calculée qu'il surnage dans l'eau s'il veut bien seulement y demeurer en repos.

> (*SSS,* p. 124.)

Light, like water, is often a force that requires passive submission; instead of being an aid to the senses, it can bombard them. Mme Dargent feels that her thoughts are being made clearer by a "lumière crue, aveuglante, implacable" (*MD,* p. 6). The brilliance of the summer sun, in *La Joie,* is notable above all for its cruelty:

> Et c'était bien, en effet, à la morsure, à des milliards et des milliards de petites morsures assidues, à un énorme grignotement que faisait penser la pluie raide tombée d'un ciel morne, l'averse des dards chauffés à blanc, l'innombrable succion de l'astre.

> (*J,* p. 649.)

Even in cases where light is an aid, rather than a hindrance, to seeing, there is little discernment of color and line. Bernanos recognizes his own tendency to visualize things in terms of light and shade; in one letter, he speaks of the creatures of his imagination who "passent sur l'écran" in what seems to be a cinematographic fashion (*OR,* p. 1847). Scenes such as that which opens *Sous le soleil de Satan* tend to reduce a landscape to the play of light and shade:

> Voici l'heure du soir qu'aima P.-J. Toulet. Voici l'horizon qui se défait—un grand nuage d'ivoire au couchant et, du zénith au sol, le ciel crépusculaire, la solitude immense, déjà glacée—plein d'un silence liquide . . . Voici l'heure du poète qui distillait la vie dans son cœur, pour en extraire l'essence secrète, embaumée, empoisonnée.

> Déjà la troupe humaine remue dans l'ombre, aux mille bras, aux mille bouches; déjà le boulevard déferle et resplendit . . . Et lui, accoudé à la table de marbre, regardait monter la nuit, comme un lis.

> (*SSS,* p. 59.)

Here, the medium of light serves a function similar to that of water, by endowing what is seen with the vagueness and instability of the dream world.

Like the water symbol, the theme of light is apt to call forth theological interpretations. Echoing a long religious tradition, Bernanos tends to associate fire and light with the presence of God, and darkness and cold with the presence of evil. The theological implications of these themes are particularly important in *Sous le soleil de Satan,* where the light-symbol is sometimes used ironically, and in *L'Imposture* and *La Joie,* originally planned as one novel under the title "Les Ténèbres." But, although Bernanos is following a tradition of religious symbolism here, he is also capable of communicating a strong individual bias. The conventional pattern co-exists with personal, affective connotations, as in this example from Monsieur Ouine:

> Qui n'a pas vu la route à l'aube, entre ses deux rangées d'arbres, toute fraîche, toute vivante, ne sait pas ce que c'est que l'espérance.
>
> (*MO,* p. 1409.)

The same association between morning and hope is present in a letter to a friend:

> La chasse nous a menés très loin, bien plus loin que nous ne pensions aller, le soir tombe, et il s'agit de faire face aux ténèbres, et aux bêtes de l'ombre. Il faut que nous formions le camp, il faut que nous tenions jusqu'au matin. O mort si douce, ô seul matin!
>
> (*BPLM,* p. 120.)

The choice of symbols here would seem to be due to personal inclination or instinct rather than adherence to tradition.

Conventional symbolism is also a fairly minor factor in Bernanos' animal metaphors. Albert Béguin was much impressed by what he called the "bestiary" of Bernanos,[13] and, indeed, this category is the most numerous of any found in the novels. It is somewhat misleading, however, to use the term "bestiary," with its implication of neat rational equivalences. Memory, rather than reason, accounts for their choice. A great number of the images have to do with the domestic animals, minor pests, and small game to be found in many country regions of France, and certainly in that part of Artois where Bernanos spent much of his childhood. The animals belong to the landscape that he never saw in later life, but which had nonetheless become part of him. Like the metaphors of water and light, animal images in Bernanos can be located first and foremost in the country of the mind.

Sometimes landscape and animals are united in the same metaphor, so that the countryside becomes something endowed with sentient life. In *Sous le soleil de Satan,* trees blown by the wind grumble like bears (*SSS,* p. 83). In *Un Mauvais Rêve,* the city of Paris is seen by Olivier Mainville as "une bête familière," noisy and seemingly harmless, but unexpectedly voracious (*MR,* p. 897). In a slightly less sinister evocation, Steeny, M. Ouine's young disciple, sees the road stretching before

him as "une bête dorée" (*MO,* p. 1414). The curé of Ambricourt, looking over the village which constitutes his parish, feels that his gaze is being returned:

> On dirait qu'elle me tourne le dos et m'observe de biais, les yeux miclos, à la manière des chats.
>
> (*JCC,* p. 1061.)

Here, animal life is used in the same way as some of the water and light images: to express a perspective in which objects are not stable or predictable. The practice of "animalization" of the inanimate may perhaps be seen as a variation upon the traditional rhetorical device of personification. It tends, however, to be more disturbing than personification, perhaps because the procedure has become less frozen by tradition, perhaps because the irrational is intrinsically more frightening than that which can think. This fear may well have some connection with the fact that animals frequently serve as a concrete symbol of what is sub-human in every person. Sometimes a kind of animal presence is detected in the soul: witness the letter in which Bernanos speaks of doing battle with the "bêtes de l'ombre." Cénabre is vaguely aware of "toutes ces choses aveugles et rampantes au fond de sa conscience" (*I,* p. 446). Simone Alfieri, on the point of taking a drug, is afraid of "ce premier accès d'euphorie qui réveille au fond de l'être on ne sait quelle petite bête sournoise, capricieuse, experte à toutes les trahisons" (*MR,* p. 988).

More often, though, this sub-human aspect is made apparent through the use of animals in characterization. The historian Clergerie has a "tête de rat" (*J,* p. 535), and it is obvious that the metaphor has moral as well as physical connotations. The same image is applied to the choirboy in *Un Crime* (*C* [*Un Crime*], p. 815) and to the unfrocked priest in the *Journal d'un curé de campagne* (*JCC,* p. 1243). A sweet but fundamentally destructive disposition is compared to the nibbling of a small rodent (*MO,* pp. 1352-1353). M. Ouine, who is physically and morally the least attractive of Bernanos' characters, evokes comparison with creatures that are barely alive:

> Mon âme n'est qu'un outre plein de vent. Et voilà maintenant, jeune homme, qu'elle m'aspire à mon tour, je me sens fondre et disparaître dans cette gueule vorace.
>
> (*MO,* p. 1552.)

These images are chiefly notable because they arouse a fairly strong degree of revulsion; other images used in characterization, however, emphasize the wretchedness of the person concerned. Those who are oppressed by others are compared to hunted animals, or beasts led to the slaughter; those who are caught in impossible situations, are compared to trapped animals. There is still an element of the grotesque in some of these images, as in this description of Jambe-de-laine:

Elle . . . se jeta en avant, comme pour rattraper son équilibre. Philippe pensa à un gigantesque oiseau blessé qui marche sur les ailes.

(*MO*, p. 1357.)

But there is only pathos in the comparison of the murdered Chantal de Clergerie to "un oiseau mort," (*J,* p. 722) or in this complaint of the curé of Ambricourt:

Mon Dieu, j'ai présumé de mes forces. Vous m'avez jeté au désespoir comme on jette à l'eau une petite bête à peine née, aveugle.

(*JCC,* p. 1144.)

Occasionally, animal imagery is used to evoke more positive qualities. Chantal, who seems to attract "flying" images, is compared to a lark (*J,* p. 659) and to a gray pheasant (*J,* p. 666). The curé of Ambricourt is praised for his faithful, dog-like eyes (*JCC,* p. 1092). But aside from such exceptions—and they are relatively few in comparison with the total number of animal images—the "bestiary" serves above all to point out what is less than human in the characters of the novels. These images are not notable for the ideas they express, but for their emotional impact: the reader is above all conscious of the feelings of pity, fear, or revulsion that many animals arouse. The juxtaposition of human and animal elements reminds us of the metamorphoses that occur in dreams and in folklore: transformations that are horrifying, because they involve a change from a higher to a lower level of life.

If animal images can be used to emphasize what is subhuman in a character, plant images may represent a soul that has hardened into a kind of immobility. Old Devandomme, in *Monsieur Ouine,* is likened to a tree (*MO,* p. 1462). Chantal de Clergerie has a vision of Cénabre in which the apostate priest is seen as the dead Judas,

fruit noir d'un arbre noir, à l'entrée du honteux royaume de l'ombre, sentinelle exacte, incorruptible, que la miséricorde assiège en vain, qui ne laissera passer aucun pardon, pour que l'enfer consomme en sûreté sa paix horrible.

(*J,* p. 685.)

In these examples, the plant represents something which, if it does not lack life, at least lacks feeling; as the second example shows us, Bernanos considers that this is a state bordering upon damnation.

The extreme degree of metamorphosis is that which transforms feeling into stone: Medusa is more terrifying than Circe. It is true that Bernanos seems to have felt somewhat ambivalent about images of stone and firmness. He sympathizes with old Devandomme's efforts to "demeurer ferme à travers ce qui bouge" (*MO,* p.

1461); and in his attitude, we can discern some vestige of that of the young schoolboy who had an overwhelming dread of softness.[14] Nevertheless, it remains true that images of hardness and stone are usually endowed with fairly sinister overtones. Donissan, reflecting on a moment of hardness, says, "Je me damnais . . . je me sentais durcir comme une pierre" (*SSS,* p. 236). Bernanos said of his second novel, "*L'Imposture* est un visage de pierre, mais qui pleure de vraies larmes" (*BPLM,* p. 173). The same might be said of the novel's protagonist. Cénabre, as he becomes more closed in upon himself, also becomes rigid and immobile: his tears are like water piercing through stone (*I,* p. 376), and his features seem carved out of stone (*J,* p. 692). Steeny is frightened when he feels his own features take on a kind of immobility (*MO,* p. 1451-1452).[15] Even Ouine himself, who usually attracts images of softness, prides himself on the diamond-like constancy of his faith in himself (*MO,* p. 1470). For the curé of Ambricourt, the souls in hell are "ces pierres embrasées qui furent des hommes" (*JCC,* p. 1157). To be fixed and immobile, once and for all, is to have no escape from oneself. This total withdrawal from life is not without some analogy with that which we described with respect to water images despite the fact that water and stone are dissimilar vehicles. The rock-like Ouine is also the creature who has become immersed in his own dreams.

Immobility can also be characteristic of things exterior to a subject: obstacles that loom up in one's path, causing fear, or frustration, or both. The immobile, frightening shadow of a priest is seen twice in the novels, and under very different circumstances: Simone Alfieri, stumbling away from the scene of her crime, encounters the young curé she met earlier in the day; Chantal de Clergerie, emerging from a vision involving the abbé Cénabre, sees him standing motionless before her (*MR,* p. 1005; *J,* p. 687). The immovable obstacle can also be something really inanimate, like a wall. The young poacher in *Monsieur Ouine,* forced into a sitation whose only issue is suicide, feels that his way is blocked by "un sentiment simple et terrible dont il ignore le nom, un mur nu, lisse comme verre" (*MO,* p. 1478). The second Mouchette is frustrated by forces she does not understand; her wretchedness is "aussi infranchissable que les murs d'une prison" (*NM,* p. 1302). In the *Journal d'un curé de campagne,* hell is "la porte à jamais close," the one situation from which there is no exit (*JCC,* p. 1047, also p. 1255). In some cases, the constraint upon liberty surrounds the individual even more closely, and becomes a part of him. Mme Dargent, looking back upon the silent humiliation of her life, says, "J'étais scellée vive, dans un béton inexorable" (*MD,* p. 80). The oneiric quality of these obstacles is made explicit in this image from *L'Imposture*:

> Dans quel rêve, dans quel cauchemar frénétique s'agite-t-on ainsi pour voir se rétrécir autour de soi l'espace libre, se fermer toutes les issues?
>
> (*I*, p. 345.)

If the wall evokes the isolation of the individual, and his imprisonment in his own dreams, a breach in the wall must represent a degree of awakening or of liberty. The consequences of this breach are not always pleasant: however harmful the wall of isolation may be, it can represent a kind of security to the individual. When a break in his defenses is made, catastrophe may follow. Thus, despair enters the mind of the second Mouchette through a kind of breach (*NM*, p. 1343). In *L'Imposture,* the wall symbolizes the self-deception with which the abbé Cénabre has been surrounding himself for some time; when he is finally forced to see the meaning, or lack of meaning, of his spiritual life, the wall is broken:

> Par la brèche mystérieuse, le passé tout entier avait glissé comme une eau, et il ne demeurait, sous le regard inaltérable de la conscience, que des gestes plus vains que des songes . . .
>
> (*I*, p. 334.)

For Bernanos, however, even such disastrous consequences seem preferable to a totally isolated mode of existence. In most cases, walls exist to be broken. For Chantal de Clergerie, a breach is an opening upon the world of the divine (*J*, p. 681). Cénabre is finally redeemed by the destruction of the wall surrounding his personality (*J*, p. 719). In the *Journal d'un curé de campagne,* this description is given of the moment in which the wall of solitude surrounding a human being for many years is at last broken:

> Il me semblait qu'une main mystérieuse venait d'ouvrir une brèche dans on ne sait quelle muraille invisible, et la paix rentrait de toutes parts . . .
>
> (*JCC*, p. 1162.)

Toward the end of the novel, the curé of Ambricourt says to a rebellious young parishioner:

> Jetez-vous donc en avant tant que vous voudrez, il faudra que la muraille cède un jour, et toutes les brèches ouvrent sur le ciel.
>
> (*JCC*, p. 1226.)

The element of frustration which is basic to wall images is also apparent in images of circles. The words *cercle enchanté,* which are relatively frequent in Bernanos, are used to indicate a situation in which the spirit is trapped in some way. In *L'Imposture,* a man commits a social error, and cuts himself off from the society in which he lives; he is said to have broken "le cercle enchanté des convenances" (*I*, p. 403). Such disparate characters as Cénabre, Chantal, and Simone Alfi-

eri make attempts to break through the enchanted circle (*I*, p. 464; *J*, 572; *MR*, p. 999). In some cases, a narrowing circle denotes an increasingly desperate situation. The image is applied to Chevance when he realizes that he is about to die (*I*, p. 523), and to M. Ouine, when he has refused salvation for the last time:

> Il savait seulement que là-haut, derrière les tilleuls et les ifs, avait été sa dernière chance. Elle n'était plus. Le cercle enchanté, rétréci chaque jour, ne se laisserait plus rompre.
>
> (*MO*, p. 1470.)

The exasperation of circular journeys is also evoked in the novels. The first Mouchette, for example, cannot bear the thought of a way of life which would bring her nothing new:

> A quoi bon s'engager une fois dans votre chemin, qui ne mène nulle part? Que voulez-vous que je fasse d'un univers rond comme une pelote?
>
> (*SSS*, p. 70.)

In *La Joie,* it is said to be better to attack one's problems directly than to circle around them (*J*, pp. 611-612). The characters in the novels sometimes literally travel in circles. The most notable example is in the long passage in which the abbé Donissan, seeking to make a simple journey from one parish to another, is led around in circles by a mysterious force that turns out to be diabolical (*SSS*, p. 162ff).

The frustrating journey is a commonplace in the dream world, and it does not need to be circular in order to be futile. Sometimes, the infinity of the road ahead is itself a problem. Olivier Mainville, in *Un Mauvais Rêve,* is haunted by visions of a limitless road which will allow him to escape the problems of his life:

> Tandis que nous poursuivions cette conversation, je croyais voir distinctement, par-dessus l'épaule de Philippe, une longue route droite, éclatante, infinie, entre deux rangées d'arbres énormes, d'un vert pâle aux reflets d'argent, dont j'entendais frémir les cimes.
>
> (*MR*, p. 951.)

But the end of this road remains undefined. The last time the reader sees him, Oliver is running away with no more purpose than a small child.

For Olivier, the road represents a concrete temptation, and his flight is a real one. For other characters, the road stands for a more figurative kind of journey. Cénabre, when he acknowledges his apostasy to himself, sets out on a "route terrible à suivre, inconnue," and is forced to continue on a "route implacable" (*I*, pp. 327, 349). Steeny, in *Monsieur Ouine,* sees the road as a symbol of liberty: "La belle route! la chère route! Vertigineuse amie, promesse immense!" (*MO*, p.

1406). The curé of Fenouille finds that the one image that consoles him when he is discouraged is that of a beggar, pursued along the road by dogs (*MO*, p. 1515). Even when there is no compulsion to flight, however, Bernanos' characters are fond of roads. Chantal de Clergerie imagines how Christ himself must have loved, in his native countryside, "les routes grises, dorées par l'averse" (*J*, p. 864). The curé of Ambricourt, when he learns that he is about to die, realizes how much he will miss familiar roads (*JCC*, pp. 1421-1422).

This love of roads was obviously shared by the writer himself. In the preface to *Les Grands Cimetières sous la lune,* he apostrophizes the "chemins du pays d'Artois, à l'extrême automne, fauves et odorantes comme des bêtes, sentiers pourrissants sous la pluie de novembre . . ." (*GCSL*, p. iv). The compulsion to some kinds of flight was doubtless also part of his make-up. Life, to him, was a journey; and the most superficial acquaintance with his biography will show that this was literally, as well as metaphorically true.[16] But the writer's strong attraction to roads is, in a sense, self-defeating; there is no clear consciousness of goals to be achieved; the "promesse immense" is constantly held out, but we are not made aware of the moment at which it is kept. The paths of dream-journeys lie within the individual consciousness, and rarely lead anywhere in particular. Bernanos extends this property to the actual and figurative journeys of real life; for him, most purely human goals are relatively worthless, overshadowed by dreams and illusions. The only real journey's end is death.

The theme of death is an extremely frequent one in the novels; it is hard to think of any other writer who includes so many deathbed scenes in a relatively short body of work. The macabre aspects of death are not neglected; even as a child, Bernanos was haunted by visions of "le petit trou noir où je serai un jour, en tête à tête avec mille choses désagréables" (*OR*, p. 1733). This obsession extends to his characters. The mayor of Fenouille, in *Monsieur Ouine,* is overcome by a self-disgust which, he thinks, must be analogous to that which a cadavre feels for itself (*MO*, p. 1518). A delinquent child tells the curé of Ambricourt that, when she has misbehaved, she punishes herself by pretending that she is dead (*JCC*, p. 1207). But, if death is given a nightmarish immediacy in some passages, it is idealized in others. It constitutes the one opportunity for escape from obsessive dreams, into the "lumière sans rêves" (*EH*, p. 257). "O mort si fraîche, ô seul matin" is a refrain that occurs more than once in Bernanos' writings.[17] And, in the prologue to *Les Grands Cimetières sous la lune,* the idea of death is combined with those of homecoming at journey's end, and childhood recovered:

> Certes, ma vie est déjà pleine de morts. Mais le plus mort des morts est le petit garçon que je fus. Et pourtant, l'heure venue, c'est lui qui reprendra sa place à la

tête de ma vie, rassemblera mes pauvres années jusqu'à la dernière, et comme un jeune chef ses vétérans, ralliant la troupe en désordre entrera le premier dans la Maison du Père.

> (*GCSL*, p. v.)

It is perhaps too easy to accuse Bernanos of proposing escapist goals here; the objects of hope, in this passage, are that part of the past which is least recoverable and that moment of the future which is least controllable by man. The ordinary objectives of adult human life in the real world are totally disregarded. But this is precisely because Bernanos has a somewhat ambiguous attitude toward what most people call the "real world." We have noticed, in the novels, a degree of confusion between literal and oneiric events; a similar confusion exists at moments when Bernanos treats historical reality. One might almost say that he manages to give an oneiric structure to contemporary history.

Albert Sonnenfeld, in a recent study, attributes the dream-like view of history to a number of twentieth-century Catholic writers. He thinks that they are under a kind of compulsion to interpret the modern world in accordance with their childhood dreams of glory:

> "Perhaps it is only in childhood that books have any deep influence on our lives," Greene wrote. Is it childhood reading which explains the recurrence of castles, knights and monastic priests in so many Catholic novels? Of one thing I am sure. The modern Catholic novelist, like the German Romantics, the former faced with two world wars and the consequent despoliation of traditional social and religious values, the latter confronted by the French Revolution and Napoleonic wars, longs for a simple, orderly world, for the world of childhood and of childhood fantasies.[18]

To dismiss Bernanos' polemical writings as childhood fantasies is to accord them less than their full value; nonetheless, Sonnenfeld is probably right when he characterizes some of the writer's philosophical opponents as his "hostile phantoms."[19] Admirers of Bernanos have not underestimated his capacity to lend a mythical dimension to contemporary history. The writer recognizes this tendency himself when he describes the Battle of Britain in the *Lettre aux Anglais*: "Votre victoire est un rêve d'enfant, réalisé par des hommes" (*LAA* [*Lettre aux Anglais*], p. 10). And the childlike perspective is deliberately assumed in *Nous autres Français,* where he bitterly accuses the ruling classes in the language of a reluctant schoolboy: "Vous avez mis les peuples au collège" (*NAF* [*Nous autres Français*], pp. 153, 164-167). Even in the case of visible contemporary events, it is impossible to dissociate dreams from reality.

The fact that the dream-world is inescapable, and yet dangerous, is responsible for a great deal of the tension that exists in Bernanos' novels. Struggles between human beings have little importance for his characters;

their chief adversaries are their obsessions. Donissan's antagonist is the inner light that may be either celestial or infernal; Cénabre's, the impulse to pride that threatens to paralyze or petrify his soul; Ouine's, the unreal world in which he has consented to exist. The characters in **Un Mauvais Rêve** are driven into isolation by their separate dreams. Even the dream-states of mysticism are feared and resisted; hence the wariness of Chantal, confronted with a mystical experience whose nature she does not recognize. The curé of Ambricourt, communicating with his parishioners, deals not with their actions but with their ruling obsessions: "Nous juger sur ce que nous appelons nos actes est peut-être aussi vain que de nous juger sur nos rêves" (**JCC,** p. 1100).

The conflict between dreams and rational forces is apparent in those of Bernanos' characters who, like their creator, are writers in spite of themselves. To a certain degree, their work consists in transmuting mental images into metaphors, and it is evident that the process is by no means an easy one. The curé of Ambricourt is bemused by a mental image in which his parish is personified, and has its own face and expression. He tries to use the metaphor in a sermon:

> J'ai eu l'idée d'utiliser ce passage, en l'arrangeant un peu, pour mon instruction du dimanche. Le *regard de la paroisse* a fait sourire et je me suis arrêté une seconde au beau milieu de la phrase avec l'impression, très nette hélas! de jouer la comédie. Dieu sait pourtant que j'étais sincère! Mais il y a toujours dans les images qui ont trop ému notre cœur quelque chose de trouble.
>
> (*JCC,* p. 1052.)

The curé of Fenouille, preaching the funeral sermon of a murdered child, is less prudent; he allows himself to be carried away by his own images, and his lack of restraint precipitates disaster:

> Son humble regard pâlissait tandis que ses bras, avec une lenteur solennelle, se levaient à son insu, comme d'un nageur épuisé qui ne se défend plus, coule à pic. Trop simple d'esprit, trop peu poète pour avoir mesuré la puissance des images et leur péril, celle qu'il venait d'évoquer s'emparait de lui avec une force irrésistible. Il voyait, il touchait presque ces montagnes d'excréments, ces lacs de boue.
>
> (*MO,* p. 1488.)

For the two curés, a metaphor is less to be sought out than to be restrained. A strong effort is required if the forces of imagination are to be controlled and dominated; and it is evident that Bernanos feels that this kind of effort is required of any real artist. A passage in **La France contre les robots** makes this idea clear:

> Un véritable romancier qui commence un livre part à la conquête de l'inconnu, il ne domine son œuvre qu'à la dernière page, elle lui résiste jusqu'au bout comme le taureau estoqué qui se couche aux pieds du matador, tout ruisselant de sang et d'écume.

> Rien n'est plus facile que de se persuader soi-même qu'on est vivant, très vivant, il suffit de gesticuler beaucoup, de parler d'échanger des idées comme on échange des sous, une idée appelant l'autre, comme les images, dans le déroulement des songes. Hélas! dès qu'on s'examine un peu on trouve très aisément en soi ces sources d'énergie corrompue, stérile. Un artiste les connaît mieux qu'un autre car tout le travail de création est précisément de les refouler, de les dominer, de faire taire coûte que coûte ce ronron monotone.
>
> (**FCR** [*La France contre les robots*], pp. 136, 142.)

For Bernanos, if not for every writer, the artist's work consists in measuring himself against his obsessions. The dream world is an adversary that must be dominated; images are like wild animals that must be tamed:

> Je travaille dans la nuit la plus opaque, je me bats avec les images et les mots d'une bataille extraordinaire; chaque page écrite me coûte un monde.
>
> (*BPLM,* p. 101.)

Paradoxically, it is perhaps because these efforts of Bernanos do not altogether succeed that his works have interested many readers. The dreams of his creatures do not always remain this side of incoherence; and, as we are made aware of a character's struggle with dreams or hallucinations, we are always conscious of the artist's struggle to dominate his own imagination. There is little sense of triumphant order, either in the events of the novels or in the style of the novelist. We are far more aware of tensions than of resolutions. If Bernanos attracts us, it is not because he communicates a sense of serenity but because he invites—or requires—us to share in his exertions.

Notes

1. *Nouvelles littéraires,* 14 March 1946, quoted by Jean Scheidegger, *Georges Bernanos romancier* (Paris: Attinger, 1956), 142.

2. The following abbreviations refer to those of Bernanos' works which are included in the Pléiade edition (*Oeuvres romanesques,* Paris, 1961): *MD, Madame Dargent; DO, Dialogue d'ombres; SSS, Sous le soleil de Satan; I, L'Imposture; J, La Joie; MR, Un Mauvais Rêve; C, Un Crime; JCC, Journal d'un curé de campagne; NM, Nouvelle Histoire de Mouchette; MO, Monsieur Ouine; DC, Dialogue des Carmélites.* The edition as a whole is referred to as *OR.* In addition, certain abbreviations refer to the writer's articles and polemical works: *GCSL Les Grands Cimetières sous la lune* (Paris: Plon, 1938); *NAF, Nous Autres Français* (Paris: Gallimard, 1939); *LAA, Lettre aux Anglais* (Rio: Atlantica, 1942); *EH, Les Enfants humiliés* (Paris: Gallimard, 1949); *LPQF, La Liberté pour quoi faire?* (Paris: Gallimard, 1953); *CCA, Le Chemin de la Croix-des-âmes* (Paris: Gallimard,

1948), *FCR, La France contre les robots* (Paris: Club français du livre, 1955); *FSVS, Français, si vous saviez* (Paris: Gallimard, 1961). The notation *BPLM* stands for *Bernanos par lui-même*, ed. Albert Béguin (Paris: Seuil, 1961).

3. See, for example, *FSVS*, p. 35, and *LPQF*, p. 211.

4. Gaëtan Picon, *Georges Bernanos* (Paris: Marin, 1948), p. 107.

5. The images in the well-known preface to *GCSL* tend to support this statement. We might also consider the following, almost random examples: ". . . la monstrueuse enfance reniée, forte comme une bête, indomptable, avec un cœur de taureau" (*EH*, p. 93). "Il faut si peu d'eau croupie pour entretenir une mauvaise pensée" (*EH*, p. 112). ". . . ces régions de l'être où la mémoire individuelle ne se distingue plus de la mémoire héréditaire, se perd en elle ainsi qu'un ruisseau babillard dans les eaux noires et profondes" (*CCA*, p. 219). ". . . cette espèce de justice qui est à la véritable justice ce que le minéral est à l'être vivant organisé, le cristal à l'homme" (*LPQF*, p. 112).

6. This observation of frequency is based upon my own doctoral thesis, "Images and Themes in the Novels of Georges Bernanos: An Index with Commentary" (Harvard University, 1967). In the novels and short stories of Bernanos, there are well over 500 images of animals, about 375 of fire, light and their contraries, about 300 of water in various forms, about 200 of sickness and death, and 200 of various kinds of sensation. There are about 160 images of children. Among the less frequent categories are obstacles (100), roads (90), mirrors (40), circles (30), stones (20). Statistics of this kind can never pretend to absolute mathematical accuracy; for this reason, the figures have been quoted in round terms.

7. This combination of familiarity and incoherence, which is especially apparent in *Monsieur Ouine*, is treated by W. M. Frohock in *Style and Temper: Studies in French Fiction, 1925-1960* (Cambridge: Harvard Univ. Press, 1967), pp. 45-61.

8. Henri Bremond, *Histoire littéraire du sentiment religieux en France* (Paris: Bloud et Gay, 1916-1933), XI, 405-408. This reference to Bremond is doubtless somewhat incongruous in an essay whose subject is Bernanos. There was little love lost between the two men, and it is probable that Bremond was the model for the apostate Cénabre. But the two men also seem to have had a certain respect for, or interest in, each other's works. Bernanos' friend Mgr Pézeril has told me that the novelist was thoroughly familiar with the *Histoire du sentiment religieux*. Bremond, on his side, expressed himself as being struck by the "divination étonnante" in Bernanos' portrayal of the mystic Chantal de Clergerie (*Nouvelles littéraires*, early June 1929, quoted by Henri Massis, "Coups de bec et bruits de plume," *Bulletin des lettres*, CLII [15 November 1953], 399-400).

9. The following examples seem especially similar to those cited by Bremond: "L'odeur que je veux dire n'est pas véritablement une odeur, ça vient de plus loin, de plus profond, de la mémoire, de l'âme, est-ce qu'on sait? L'eau n'y fait rien, faudrait autre chose" (*MO*, p. 1440). "Mais le rude maître n'était plus qui recueillait à mesure sa joie mystérieuse pour qu'elle n'en sentît pas le poids surnaturel" (*J*, p. 554). "Je n'ai rien vu, rien entendu, je ne pensais même à rien. Cela m'a comme frappé dans le dos" (*J*, p. 715). "Comme ces gelées vivantes, au fond de la mer, je flotte et j'absorbe" (*MO*, p. 1368). "Vous êtes dans l'ombre d'une aile gigantesque qui va se refermer sur nous" (*DO*, p. 48).

10. The following passage from *La Joie* seems explicable only in terms of a passage in Bremond. It marks the first appearance in the novels of the *tomber en Dieu* image.

"C'étaient les heures de jadis, si pareilles à celles de l'enfance, et il n'y manquait même pas la merveilleuse attente qui lui donnait autrefois l'illusion de courir à perdre haleine au bord d'un abîme enchanté. Au bord des Pyrénées, sur un sentier vertigineux, regardant par la portière du coche le gouffre rose où tournent les aigles, la petite fille préférée de Sainte Thérèse s'écrie joyeusement, 'Je ne puis tomber qu'en Dieu!'" (*J*, p. 552.)

The "petite fille" referred to here cannot be found in the biography of Saint Teresa of Avila, nor in that of Sainte Thérèse of Lisieux, in whom Bernanos was particularly interested. But she corresponds closely with Mme Jourdain, a wealthy young widow who helped the Spanish Carmelites establish their first foundation in France, early in the Seventeenth Century. Bremond describes the journey of the founders from Spain to France:

"On eut beaucoup de peine à passer les montagnes et à franchir les précipices qui se trouvaient sur le chemin. [. . .] Au bord de ces abîmes béants, Mme Jourdain disait avec allégresse: 'Je ne saurais tomber qu'en Dieu!'" (*Histoire littéraire du sentiment religieux*, II, 295). Since Bremond found this anecdote in a private publication of the Carmelites, it seems most probable that his work was Bernanos' source.

11. *DC*, p. 1672. In the face of the danger confronting her community, Sœur Constance laughs and says, "Mais nous, ma Sœur, nous ne pouvons tomber

qu'en Dieu!" This young nun belongs to a category of childlike personalities, particularly frequent in Bernanos' later works. At the same time, she bears a certain family resemblance to Bremond's Mme Jourdain: both are Carmelite novices, and both manage to combine innocence and joyfulness with a kind of inner distinction.

12. Georges Poulet considers this metaphor to be a key to Bernanos' conception of the human condition: man is trapped in a hopeless predicament, as if in a lake of mud, and can only escape through the radical intervention of divine grace. (*Le Point de départ*, Paris, Plon, 1964, pp. 51-58.)

13. "Contribution au bestiaire de Bernanos," *Bulletin de la société des amis de Bernanos* (July 1958), pp. 9-23.

14. This *peur du flou* is treated at some length by Poulet (*loc. cit.*).

15. These metamorphoses into stone find an unexpected echo in a novel by the writer's son, Michel Bernanos: *La Montagne morte de la vie* (Paris: Pauvert, 1967). The work is concerned with a young sailor's voyage to unknown lands. It becomes apparent very early that the protagonist is engaged in a nightmare situation from which there is no issue; the only possible progression is from horror to horror, passively endured as dreams are. The voyage ends in the discovery of a mountainous desert, peopled by strange statues. In the last pages, the young sailor and his companion become like the statues and are changed into stone. The book ends in this way: "Le seul souvenir qui me reste, depuis des siècles que je vis dans la pierre, est le doux contact de larmes sur un visage d'homme," (p. 151).

16. This point is mentioned by Henri Debluë in *Les Romans de Georges Bernanos ou le défi du rêve* (Neuchâtel: La Baconnière, 1965), p. 59.

17. The letter already quoted is echoed in *Jeanne relapse et sainte* (Paris: Plon, 1934), p. 67.

18. "Twentieth-century Gothic: Reflections on the Catholic novel," *Southern Review*, I (Spring 1965), 391.

19. "The Hostile Phantoms of Georges Bernanos: *Sous le soleil de Satan* and *Monsieur Ouine*," *L'Esprit Créateur*, IV (Winter 1964), 208-221.

Arnold L. Weinstein (essay date winter 1971)

SOURCE: Weinstein, Arnold L. "Bernanos' *Monsieur Ouine* and the Esthetic of Chaos." *Symposium* 25, no. 4 (winter 1971): 392-407.

[*In the following essay, Weinstein explores Bernanos's use of various literary and stylistic techniques in his novel* The Open Mind *to create "chaos," in order to* "render the moral tensions of his work with immediacy" *and* "impose" *on the reader* "the task of ordering life and finding meaning in experience." *In addition, the critic demonstrates the appropriateness of this* "structural principle" *in the novel,* "for it furthers the suspense of the murder story" *and* "causes the reader to confront 'first hand' . . . the intense but 'unlabeled' emotive character relationships."]

Monsieur Ouine is a strange and compelling novel. Much of its fascination seems to derive from one source: chaos. Within the French tradition and even in the Bernanos canon, there are few works so imbued with the principle of disorder. Among the perplexing factors which it presents are (1) a murder that is neither witnessed by the reader nor solved within the story, (2) a series of mysteries and ambiguities ranging from uncertain sexual relations between characters to bewildering use of personal pronouns and descriptive adjectives at the beginning of chapters, (3) abundance of direct quotations coming from unannounced characters and referring to omitted or hitherto unseen events, (4) apparent discontinuity and ellipsis in specific dialogues and entire chapters, and (5) absence of linear chronology or sequence between contiguous passages. In dealing with *Monsieur Ouine,* as with novels like *Absalom, Absalom!* or *La Route des Flandres*, we must first understand why the story is told in this fashion before picking it apart solely with a view toward theme, image or symbol. Some critics, notably W. M. Frohock,[1] have suggested that the novel's ultimate cohesiveness derives from a pervasive and consistent image network of disease, decay and animality. While these image patterns do indeed cohere as in a poem, nonetheless there is much to be learned from a study of presentation.[2] In a book that evidently flouts the conventions of storytelling, any critical assessment should account for that break from tradition. Is there a coherent pattern or structural principle that informs the composition of this novel? How is it related to Bernanos' thematic concerns? If we study the narrative strategy of *Monsieur Ouine,* in detail and at large, will we be able to relate the two stories that Bernanos is telling: the "realistic" detective story and the "symbolic" moral drama?

The effects of abrupt direct quotation, ambiguous pronouns and elliptic presentation can be best observed through the study of a long representative passage:

> La voix s'éteint par degrès, n'est plus qu'un ronronnement vague que scande mystérieusement chaque bref sursaut de la bougie, dans un halo d'or. "Steeny, méchant Steeny!" Est-ce donc Miss qui, une fois de plus, referme sur lui ses cruels bras? Mais c'est en vain qu'il prête l'oreille pour entendre éclater le grand rire farouche, triomphal: une main prudente, inconnue, creuse soigneusement l'oreiller autour de sa nuque brûlante. Comme la toile est fraîche! . . . Hein? Quoi? Revenir demain? [. . .]

—Écoutez, monsieur Ouine, ai-je dormi?

Il répète longtemps tout bas, pour lui seul, la même question sans oser ouvrir les yeux. Le vieil homme est loin maintenant, Dieu sait où—dans quel coin de cette maison morte? Il aime mieux l'imaginer plus loin encore, à travers champs, sur la route douce. La route! . . . La route? . . . Qui parle de route? Non pas celle-ci, non pas l'une de ces routes pâles, mais la sienne, sa Route, qu'il a tant de fois vue en rêve, la route ouverte, infinie, gueule béante . . . La route! La route! Et face à il ne sait quelle brèche immense, pleine d'étoiles, il s'endort, les poings fermés.

—Je lui ai donné ma parole d'honneur, répète Steeny pour la deuxième fois.

La même pluie lourde, sans aucune brise, tombait d'aplomb sur le sol fumant. Très loins vers l'est et comme au bord d'un autre monde, l'aube orageuse formait lentement ses nuées, à travers une poussière d'eau.

—C'est bon, c'est bon, fit le petit boiteux Guillaume, j'ai compris, mais ne parlez pas trop fort, Philippe; il est rentré ce matin couvert de boue, une oreille arrachée, il a perdu son fusil. Les gardes lui ont donné la chasse de Dugny à Théroigne. Ah! si vous l'aviez vu vider le pot de bière tout d'un trait, à la régalade. Quelle soif! De temps en temps, hors d'haleine, il baissait un peu la cruche, et je l'entendais mordre la grès, en gémissant . . . Mon Dieu, mon Dieu, Philippe, pourrais-je jamais l'aimer?

—Tu ferais aussi bien de le tuer, dit Steeny gravement. Et aussitot, il éclata de rire et prit la main de son ami.

—Ne riez pas! supplia l'infirme. Vous me faites peur réellement, Philippe. Moi qui ne crains personne, pas même cet affreux bâtard, il y a des jours . . . il me semble que vous tirez sur moi de toutes vos forces, je vais tomber, mon cœur se vide.

—Eh bien! lâche-moi, mon vieux, je puis bien tomber tout seul.

—Jamais, dit l'enfant d'une voix sourde, jamais!

De qui, de quel ancêtre, de quel maître farouche tenait-il ce petit visage barbare, avec ses pommettes mongoles, la dépression profonde des orbites sous le double arc frontal, la bouche impérieuse, presque sauvage, et ces crins noirs?[3]

([*Oeuvres romanesques*])

This passage, or combination of passages, has been quoted in its entirety so that both the techniques for beginning passages and the frequency of transition between them can be displayed. In the first section the narrative voice is neither an objective third-person point of view nor a subjective interior monologue; it is Bernanos' version of "style indirect libre" which can be best understood as an interior voice often reflecting the character's thoughts, often going beyond the character to embrace larger segments of the narrative.[4] The beginning statement does not tell us, but forces us to *feel* that Steeny is falling asleep. The novelist concerned with immediacy or presentational impact will always make use of "vulnerable" situations where the mind is losing control over the events to be described. Such moments, particularly favored by certain American novelists (c.f. Faulkner's depiction of the idiot's sickness in *The Sound and the Fury*),[5] are relatively infrequent in the more cerebral, analytic French tradition. These uncertain states of consciousness (falling asleep, slight drunkeness, shock, pain) are privileged moments in this novel, because they herald into a "realistic" decor instants of irrational or supernatural vision. "Steeny, méchant Steeny!" is a classic example of the unannounced quotation; through a process of association (natural to Steeny, for he is falling asleep; unnatural for the reader, for he must recall, reconstruct), these three words evoke Miss, Michelle and the entire stifling home relationship. The "est-ce donc Miss . . ." confirms the evocation.

The transition between sections obviously reflects Steeny's loss of consciousness. Again direct quotation is used instead of descriptive narrative: "Écoutez, monsieur Ouine, ai-je dormi?" Next the interior voice resumes the narrative and describes Steeny's feelings in a manner that is lyrical in tone, symbolic in meaning but—on the whole—comprehensible in its presentation. Those familiar with the fictional world of Bernanos know that the word *route* is full of poetic resonance and symbolizes the promise of childhood.

The opening line of the next section is a pure enigma: "Je lui ai donné ma parole d'honneur, répète Steeny pour la deuxième fois." Again we experience both the surprise value and ambiguity of direct speech; although we know who is speaking, we have no idea when Steeny is speaking, where he is speaking, to whom he is speaking, or about whom ("lui" is totally ambiguous) he is speaking. Moreover, we seem to have missed the first statement, as Steeny is repeating it for the second time. Above all, we have no idea what he is talking about, for we have witnessed no promises given. Now there is no law that says a writer must explain every line to his reader. In French classical theater, *exposition* consists precisely in gradually bringing the spectator up to date; the device of beginning *in medias res* is frequently used in novels to achieve a kind of immediacy. Most novelists, however, quickly clarify and "situate" the material that is enigmatic or unexplained: Bernanos, in this novel, chooses both to charge these mysterious introductory remarks with emotion and to delay putting them in context. In short, we assaulted with the bare fact that a promise has been made. The following lines give us the temporal and spatial setting in very vague terms which manage to conceal any link with the preceding narrative: "La même pluie lourde . . ." The mysterious promise will be affirmed seven pages later ("Écoute, Guillaume . . . j'ai manqué à ma parole . . .") and finally witnessed (in a flashback) two pages after that.

Guillaume, the friend of Steeny, is equally adroit in the use of ambiguous discourse. We have no notion who "il" is ("il est rentré ce matin . . .") and do not even know who Guillaume is. We nonetheless receive a great deal of concrete information: the suspicious return of the unknown individual, the feelings of Guillaume toward him, the enigmatic relation between Steeny and Guillaume. We are confronted with the reality of an action, but we do not possess the necessary information to render it intelligible. Aside from prologing the mystery, these ambiguities manage to involve the reader, to force upon him facts and character revelation which he can neither analyze nor reject. By stripping the dialogue of explanatory remarks, Bernanos gives us the "raw" expression of an instantaneous feeling without the necessary rational orientation; we possess an emotive reality, but cannot interpret it. As was the case with Steeny's promise, the ambiguities are clarified some pages later. It will become clear that Guillaume is Philippe's moral conscience (pp. 1380-81), that "il" is Eugène, and that the mysterious return is a major clue in the murder investigation.

At the close of the extract quoted, we see the opening lines of the commentary on the facial expression of Guillaume: "De qui, de quel ancêtre, . . ." Here, then, is the beginning of the long-awaited background which will shed light on the dialogue. For Bernanos, the ultimate explanation of character resides either in childhood or in the past. Hence, the narrative voice leads us to "old Vandomme," Hélène, Eugène and the history of the Vandomme family. At the close of the flashback the dialogue is resumed with Guillaume's request: "Racontez-moi, racontez-moi, supplia l'infirme. Et d'abord êtes-vous bien sûr d'avoir compris?" (p. 1380). In spite of the formal break in the text, it takes the reader a moment to realize these words refer not to the history of the Vandomme family, but precisely to the mysterious events involving Steeny's promise. Now that the reader has gained insight into Guillaume's family background, he can bring this sense of the past to bear on the continuation of the original dialogue. As the dialogue progresses, many of the earlier mysteries and ambiguities are resolved: the secret of Anthelme, the promise made to Ginette, etc.

How can one describe this technique, and what are its implications? By using isolated or abrupt direct quotations, uncertain pronouns and incomplete facts, Bernanos elicits from the reader a reaction that exceeds mere passive reception. The reader is assaulted; he is confronted with enigmatic, elliptic fragments of reality—of factual or emotional nature—and the missing names or explanations come later. Bernanos was not a technician of the novel.[6] Like Faulkner, however, he intuitively sought new forms of presentation that would vitalize and render the moral tensions of his work with immediacy. The process of solving mysteries, filling in ellipses, affixing semantic labels to the stuff of experience, is *not* a literary technique: It is the life process which we experience every minute of our lives. Rather than giving us a self-contained, digested, classical artifact, Bernanos has imposed on us, as well as upon his characters, the task of ordering life and finding meaning in experience. This structural principle is particularly appropriate in **Monsieur Ouine,** for it furthers the suspense of the murder story (key facts are withheld), and, more importantly, it causes the reader to confront "first hand" and with immediacy the intense but "unlabeled" emotive character relationships. The reader himself— and not merely the narrator—must reconstruct, interpret, understand.

There are many stylistic devices that oblige us to piece together this narrative, and ellipsis is only one facet of Bernanos' use of direct speech in **Monsieur Ouine.** Ambiguous pronouns constitute another anomaly: "'Au fond, pense Philippe, *leur* nature m'embête'" (p. 1408) (italics added); and "'Hélas! non, *elle* ne comprend pas. Ne peut pas comprendre . . .'" (p. 1442). The effect of introductory quotation may also be a simple one of surprise appearance: "'Hop! Steeny . . . par ici Steeny, mon petit ange . . .'" (p. 1390); or "'eh bien quoi! sans vous commander, monsieur Steeny, vous pourriez me prêter la main, je ne suis pas assez forte pour le manier'" (p. 1561). Other introductory quotes ostensibly announce a mere change of scene, but their position in the passage intensifies their symbolic implications: "'As-tu fini de te frotter la peau, Arsène?'" (page 1436); and "'Baissez la lumière, mon enfant, dit M. Ouine, nous jouirons encore de ce déclin du jour'" (p. 1527).

Direct speech is jolting and unsettling in other conjunctures; e.g., the explicit reference to an act we have missed: "'Prenez garde seulement de vous étourdir, remarqua le vieil homme impassible. Vous en êtes à votre cinquième ou sixième verre de vin'" (p. 1373). Another example of the descriptive narrative trailing the quotation occurs when Jambe-de-Laine asks Philippe to give her the all-important package which fell out of the carriage:

> "Rendez-moi ce paquet, Philippe . . ." La robe de Mme de Néréis est fendue à la taille, découvre une pauvre combinaison de jersey; un pan de soie traîne dans l'eau jaune. Ginette aurait-elle peur? Sa bouche esquisse une grimace douloureuse et le rouge des levres a coulé jusqu'au menton.

> "Dans votre main . . . là . . . voyons, Philippe!" Tiens, c'est vrai qu'un cahot a jeté hors de la voiture une chose informe, qu'il a rattrapée au vol.

> (p. 1391)

In both of these instances, the reader is deprived of his privileged stance as ubiquitous onlooker; his own perception of events is manipulated by either the fancy of the narrative voice or the stunned consciousness of the characters themselves.

There is also a great deal of recalled direct speech which approximates a chorus effect. We learn about M. Ouine and Jambe-de-Laine from cryptic recollections of the towns people. Much of what we know about the events themselves is telescoped by quoted reminiscences. These scenes are related in a style resembling the frozen past of a reporter ("La chose faite, personne n'a su dire comment elle s'était faite, par quel miracle" [p. 1482]), and there is much quotation from the townspeople—the equivalent of interviews—and, of course, the sermon itself. The direct speech of the townspeople is significantly given in retrospect in the past tense. The conjunction of direct quotation (creating immediacy, bringing the scene closer) and the past tenses (adding a fatal, "already happened" perspective to an event not yet described) creates a certain effect of helplessness in the reader. He is informed that something catastrophic has happened but he has yet to encounter it in the narrative: "'Nous étions seulement curieux de ce qu'elle allait faire, dira plus tard Clodiot, le fagotier. On s'attendait plûtot à rigoler'" (p. 1499); and "'Pour sortir du cimetière, dirent-ils, elle n'avait qu'à s'en aller tranquillement, nous ne lui voulions pas de mal. Ou même parler. D'ordinaire sa langue était assez bien pendue'" (p. 1500).

Such extensive and varied use direct speech admittedly goes beyond the realm of structure and can be considered as a separate stylistic device; yet one hesitates to place it under "voice," since the evocative or shock value of the direct quotation is conveyed either by the position in the passage or by the absence of explanatory background. Direct quotation adds to the mystery and must be seen as an element of presentation.

The second step of our analysis is to discover whether the arrangement of individual often fragmentary scenes within the larger "chapters" is based on a coherent principle. As has been shown, most of the passages open abruptly with either direct quotation or uncommented experiential presentation. The very first page of the book presents a striking example:

> Elle a pris ce petit visage à pleines mains—ses longues mains, ses longues mains douces—et regarde Steeny dans les yeux avec une audace tranquille. Comme ses yeux sont pâles! On dirait qu'ils s'effacent un peu, se retirent . . . les voilà maintenant plus pâles encore, d'un gris bleuté, à peine vivants, avec une paillette d'or qui danse. "Non! non! s'écrie Steeny. Non!" Et il se jette en arrière, les dents serrées, sa jolie figure crispée d'angoisse, comme s'il allait vomir. Mon Dieu!
>
> (p. 1349)

The reader is thrown into the unlabeled, uninterpreted emotive reality of a character relationship. Gaëtan Picon has remarked that most of Bernanos' novels open with "une attaque brusque." Yet the technique in *Monsieur Ouine* is more radical. We are not merely dropped in the middle of a situation; we are, rather, hurled into powerful, uncommented experiential presentation. A glance at the opening lines of *L'Imposture* should reveal the differences between the earlier and the later method:

> —Mon cher enfant, dit l'abbé Cénabre, de sa belle voix lente et grave, un certain attachement aux biens de ce monde est légitime, et leur défense contre les entreprises d'autrui, dans les limites de la justice, me semble un devoir autant qu'un droit. Néanmoins, il convient d'agir avec prudence, discrétion, discernement . . . La vie chrétienne dans le siècle est toute proportion, toute mesure: un équilibre . . .
>
> (p. 311)

Clearly, we are dealing with a more complex phenomenon in *Monsieur Ouine*. The opening of *L'Imposture* is abrupt but totally coherent. In our novel, the reader is both confused and attracted by the situation until he is led by the interior voice into the past. The gesture of Miss and the frantic reaction of Steeny can be *understood* only after the reader acquires some background information (the history of the "douceur" of Michelle, the savage virility of Steeny's father who becomes the antecedent of the ambiguous "englouti," "absent éternel," "disparu" of the opening pages). Thus, the flashback provides a framework in which to place the raw events already witnessed. The second "chapter" opens equally abruptly with a voice crying "Hé bien, Steeny, tout seul?" (p. 1356). Although the ensuing dialogue has a surface (and syntactical) coherence, the reader can only feel—not interpret—the allusions and descriptions concerning Ginette: "sa pauvre tête folle," "le misérable visage torturé," "des yeux de bête traquée", and, of course, the presumed reaction of Michelle: "D'où vient-il? Dîner chez Ginette! Mais il est fou!" Presentation of character and event is, of course, not like algebraic equations. Some degree of ellipsis, or telescoping, or allusion, is almost always present, and few descriptions are wholly explicit and self-supporting. Moreover, it is a respectable convention to describe characters in a suggestive manner, pointing to or presupposing a context that will be later dealt with. "Sa pauvre tête folle," and "le misérable visage torturé" generate interest about Ginette, tell us that this character harbors a story. In the traditional Balzacian novel such a story or context precedes the dramatic treatment of the character. In this novel the "mystery" of Ginette encroaches on the very narrative framework, i.e., Steeny's response to Ginette (on which our optic depends) is curiously blurred. In *Monsieur Ouine* the character relationships cannot be defined; the intense and sometimes ferocious interactions between Steeny and Miss, Steeny and Guillaume, Steeny and Monsieur Ouine, are rendered with such immediacy and intimacy as to suggest a kind of affective impressionism, a purely sensuous or emotive apprehension without contours or grids. The novel consists of compelling, despotic personal exchanges which, like hot flashes or sudden vertigo, both resist analysis and dictate conduct. One senses a world of emotional absolutes, a system of spiritual and visceral forces that is operative behind the facade of conventional character roles. Bernanos' world view is cogent and imperious, but it wrestles fitfully with traditional labels. In a manner strangely analogous to Eliot's judgment of *Hamlet,* the emotional intensity goes far beyond its visible causes. The upshot is often bewildering, consisting of enigmatic, puppet-like, spasmodic behavior patterns. In an earlier century Bernanos would have doubtless written allegories, for the unseen forces are more real to him than the apparent forms they inhabit. Bernanos depicts the experiential life of his characters at such close range that we have no distance and our vision becomes blurred. Some sense of clarity does emerge, however, and throughout *Monsieur Ouine* the pattern seems to be the one noted in the opening passage. Dialogue or enigmatic description yields to background material; in this case, the story of Ginette: Anthelme and his tranformation, the reputation of Ginette and the presence of M. Ouine in the château. Even though the flashback is ironically presented by way of the townspeople's opinions, we nevertheless bring a wealth of information to the continuing dialogue and present action. In the passage concerning Steeny and Guillaume analyzed above, the same sequence occurs. A page of highly ambiguous, elliptic dialogue is followed by the interior narrative voice which leads us into the past of Guillaume, where we become acquainted with Old Vandomme, Hélène, Eugène and the mysterious "petit homme vert" with his tales of Vandomme glory. Again the flashback itself presents a certain amount of ambiguity (vague adjectives and uncertain terms such as "le vieux," "l'étranger," "le fils," "la bru," "l'autre"), but some clarity and an emotive framework are nonetheless gained. When the flashback is broken, Guillaume's first words are, as we have seen, "Racontez-moi, racontez-moi." This link between flashback and continued dialogue reveals, however, a component of imaginative or lyrical structure hardly suspected. The flashback closes with the suspicious death of the lieutenant who proclaimed the glory of the Vandomme family; in spite of the irony, his tale and the style in telling it ("Ah! mes amis, redoutez ce sang généreux . . .") represent the noble past, the age of honor and heroes. Although the mysterious character's death throws the veracity of the legend into doubt, all of the Vandommes draw their courage and dignity from this "might have been." The words following this death are Guillaume's "Racontez-moi, racontez-moi" which refer, in reality, to Steeny's experience at the bedside of the dying Anthelme and—more importantly—to his meeting with and impressions of Monsieur Ouine. In short, each sequence deals with search for a father, a figure of stature. This search is a recurrent motif in the novels of Bernanos, and it is the trademark of his childlike heroes. The confusion (for

the reader) between the Vandomme story, Anthelme's revelation that Philippe's father is alive, and discovery of M. Ouine, is a rich and suggestive one. As Steeny explains at length to Guillaume that the heroic models of the present are insipid and empty, that the veritable Hero of today is M. Ouine, the reader senses the poetic value of the chapter's arrangement. The spiritual isolation of Old Vandomme among the townspeople who are "d'une autre espèce"; the gulf between his values and those of his daughter, Hélène ("La famille paternelle lui reste inconnue, aussi fabuleuse qu'une tribu d'Afrique" [pp. 1376-77]); his correctness and dignity contrasted with the violent disorder of Hélène's passion for Eugène; the haunting memory of a past that is perhaps fictional, but certainly glorious; the slightly ludicrous death of the lieutenant—each one of these contrasts is a poetic foreshadowing of Steeny's assertion that M. Ouine is the Maître in an age without heroes.

The same technique is operative for other characters. We are introduced to the emotional turmoil of Hélène's mind, before we fully understand the nature of her relation with Eugène and her father. We are likewise led from a fragmentary present to an explanatory past with regard to Miss (pp. 1445-46). The priest also reveals some of the motives of his conduct by mentioning his painful childhood, although one cannot speak of experiential presentation in this case. The technique is visible in the case of M. Ouine himself, and it is most revealing. Much of what seemed enigmatic in his behavior becomes clear after the narrative voice has related his pitiable childhood and the perversion of his instinct for love (pp. 1471-73).

Because practically all the flashbacks deal with either the innocence and pain of childhood (the history of Michelle, the implied suffering and corruption of Jambe-de-Laine, the pain endured by Miss, the priest, and M. Ouine) or the dignity of the past (the history of the Vandomme family, the reminiscences of Malvina at the close of the novel), the technique of temporal shifting provides a spiritual framework for the present events. Because these explanations *follow* the ambiguous, elliptic presentation of the immediate story, the reader is compelled to experience the chaotic events of the present before acquiring a rational understanding of them. The absence of moral harmony is conveyed stylistically before evocation of the past labels and confirms it. Moreover, the ambiguity and disorder of the narrative delay communication of facts and increase suspense in the mystery. Cumulatively, the novel's sequence of disordered confrontations begins to take its toll, and there is a movement toward ultimate chaos. As the individual character relationships converge (together with their explanations as revealed by flashbacks), the reader senses that the forces of chaos are mounting: that there is something rotten in the town of Fenouille is stated over and over. In the detective story, which is, in some sense, the purely verbal or semantic dimension of a many-faceted spiritual phenomenon, there is a movement toward final clarity, the disappearance of all ambiguity: the solving of the murder.

If we look at the overall appearance of the novel, we see the simultaneous movement from chaos to clarity and from single violence to mass violence evident in the style. As the missing pieces start falling into place (the ambiguous pronouns and enigmatic relationships are clarified), we witness the ominous accumulation of flashbacks, bristling references to a healthy past, tragic remembrances of wounded childhood. Precisely this juxtaposition of experiential present and explanatory past helps create the general stylistic disorder of the first half of the novel—a disorder perfectly attuned to transmit the fury, infirmity or madness of the separate character relationships. Yet, at the very center of these chaotic relationships which seem to have only their violence in common—the private, rotten world of Miss, Michelle and Steeny; the isolation and grotesque lack of harmony between Eugène, Hélène, Old Vandomme and his family history; the desperate nature of Guillaume's relation to Steeny the obscure corruption and decay of the Néréis château concerning Anthelme, Jambe-de-Laine and M. Ouine; the pitiable story of Arsène, his nose, his past and his wife; the crucial, but undefined relations between Steeny and Jambe-de-Laine, Steeny and M. Ouine—lies an action concealed by the novelist, but fatally uniting the characters: the murder of the cowherd. This solitary act of violence is not shown, but we experience in its place, as a furious lyrical echo, the reign of chaos or the death of spirit in every character relationship.

The scenes in the church and the cemetery are the climax of the story: clarity for the detective story and chaos for the spiritual tale that accompanies it. By realizing that the murder of the cowherd is the very crystallization of the moral decay in Fenouille, the priest, in effect, solves the mystery: "". . . Que je bénisse aujourd'hui ce malheureux petit mort, à quoi ça pourrait bien vous servir? Il a été l'instrument innocent de votre perte, c'est votre péché à tous, je ne bénirai pas votre péché!'" (p. 1490). Because this act has been concealed and bears the seal of no one character, it serves as a fitting common denominator for the violence of the parish. In announcing to his congregation that they are all guilty of the murder, the priest clarifies and transcends the preceding ambiguities. In symbolically solving the murder, he grotesquely restores his dead parish to life and unifies into a collective holocaust the isolated eruptions of violence that we have hitherto witnessed. As the blacksmith later remarked:

". . . En somme, depuis des jours, le village barbotait dans son crime; chacun pour soi, chacun pour son compte, ça aurait dû s'arranger petit à petit. Le mal-

heur a voulu qu'on aille tous à cette messe, tous à la fois, tous ensemble. C'est comme une vapeur qui nous aurait monté d'un coup à la tête. Positivement, lorsque le curé a parlé, l'air s'est mis à manquer, monsieur, parole d'honneur! L'air était devenu chaud et gras comme celui de notre fournil quand je tue mon cochon."

(pp. 1483-84)

It is extremely significant that the presentation of the scene in the church is a controlled one; the stylistic disorder so apparent in the recounting of individual character relationships has yielded to an ordered means of presentation. The sermon itself is delivered with little disorder or interruption; filled with violent images, repetitions, accumulations, parataxis, isolation of expressive adjectives, and breathless tempo, is is nonetheless coherent and lucid. The priest's sermon is the first attempts to explain, to interpret the chaotic violence that has erupted in Fenouille. The priest's effort is both too late and too early: too late because the parish has already been undermined, too early because the ultimate eruption of violence—the expression of the ultimate solidarity of the townspeople—is yet to break out. Again the style will mirror the change: a new kind of disorder is introduced. We begin to perceive an alarming discontinuity in the discourse. The order maintained in the church is rapidly disintegrating. The Inspector of the Academy is unable to deliver his insipid speech; Arsène makes his fated attempt at confession and each time we perceive the same four tragic words eloquently expressing unity and solidarity: "Messieurs, mes chers concitoyens"; The deputy Viduval is able to emit only "Messieurs, Messieurs . . ."; the deputy Merville delivers a thundering "Dispersez-vous!" and is met by a "grognement de colère." The peak of chaos is, of course, the arrival of Ginette. Just as the violence of the earlier scenes is being repeated, so her entrance is presented in the corresponding experiential style:

Tout à coup, ce fut comme si le tumulte indistinct, la rumeur sourde se fût brisée en une multitude de notes différentes . . . Et toutes les têtes, non pas d'un seul mouvement, mais à la manière des épis d'une pièce de blé déjà haute lorsqu'un changement brusque du vent la rebrousse d'une extrémité du champ à l'autre, se tournèrent vers l'allée centrale que le recul des spectateurs laissait vide.

"Jambe-de-Laine! Jambe-de-Laine!"

(p. 1497)

At this very point the reader perceives the great mare and the carriage and still another simultaneous roar of the crowd: "Jambe-de-Laine! Jambe-de-Laine!" before the character herself appears.

Jambe-de-Laine is the catalyst; she precipitates the final mass murder which we and everybody else witness this time. Or do we? The outbreak of violence is made overwhelmingly clear, but the nature of the attack is highly obscure. The deed itself remains little more experiential than its hidden ancestor, the murder of the cowherd.

It has now become apparent that the gradual clarification of ambiguities and the outbreak of communal violence are bound together in causality. Solving the small murder was the stimulus for the large one. The unseen act—recreated through style and content in the entire first half of the novel—is indeed the core of the book; as the layers of ambiguity and ellipsis are pealed away, the reader approaches the heart of the dilemma. In the church the priest removes the final veil, and the reality of the murder—if not the "ownership" of it—is at last assumed by the congregation. The realistic story of an isolated, unseen murder and the symbolic presentation of a town's spiritual death become one in the transition from individual crime to mass chaos, from the church to the cemetery.

Now the violence is over. The style of the rest of the novel is lucid; the final task of order and interpretation faces the reader as well as the characters. Arsène's role in the novel becomes particularly significant at this juncture. As mayor, the elected representative of the parish, he is exemplary of its decay, a living symbol of the breakdown at Fenouille. The community staunchly resists him by casting him in the archetypal role of the scapegoat: Consumed by his guilt and the general spiritual corruption Arsène, is considered insane. In attempting to explain this "madness," each character posits, in effect, his interpretation of all the disorder in the novel. The individual attempts to understand, to explain, constitute the last phase of the novel's progression. With regard to plot and style, these last dialogues reflect an effort to impose order on the chaos that has preceded.

Malvina's explanation is a simple one:

> —Les hommes deviennent tous fous, fit-elle avec un profond soupir. Faut qu'il y ait, comme on dit, quelque chose dans l'air, un poison, je ne sais quoi. Voyez-vous, docteur, en mon temps—je parle de ma jeunesse, bien sûr—les vieux n'avaient pas la moitié du vice de ceux d'aujourd'hui. Pour moi, le mal vient de là. Le monde est en train de pourrir par les vieux.

(p. 1511)

The doctor refuses to see in the entire situation anything more transcendent than physiological or psychic disturbances. Arsène is merely a "nerveux"; his illness is a "bizarre tumeur de l'esprit." The priest recognizes in Arsène symptoms of a disease which must necessarily befall a society that has renounced God:

> ". . . Oui, monsieur, l'heure vient (peut-être est-elle déjà venue?) où le désir de la pureté qu'on croit avoir muré au fond de la conscience et qui y a perdu jusqu'à son nom va faire éclater son sépulcre. Et, si toute autre

issue lui est fermée, il en trouvera une dans la chair et le sang—oui, monsieur—vous le verrez paraître sous des formes inattendues et, j'ose le dire, hideuses, horribles . . ."

(p. 1509)

The explanations by the doctor and the priest illuminate a dialectic central to Bernanos' work. Only in *Monsieur Ouine,* however, does the contrast between the scientific psychological mode and the spiritual vision of God affect the very form of the novel. The priest opposes the reductive labels of the doctor with a vision that, like the paintings of Hieronymus Bosch, perceives the world of spirit in physical forms. The priest describes the universe that Bernanos is seeking to render in *Monsieur Ouine*:

> Ce village, et beaucoup de villages qui lui ressemblent, reprit le curé de Fenouille toujours calme, tous ces villages jadis chrétiens, lorsqu'ils commenceront à flamber—oui—vous en verrez sortir toutes sortes de bêtes dont les hommes ont depuis longtemps oublié le nom, à supposer qu'on leur en ait jamais donné un.

(p. 1508)

To be sure, the recurrent images of sewage and rotting and animality give the reader some notion of the spiritual world Bernanos is depicting.[7] However, Bernanos must find means to suggest the awful power and impact of such monstrous transformations. A twentieth-century novelist simply cannot describe pictorially a gargoyle and leave it at that. Bernanos has attempted to convey the intensity of such a vision; he has depicted characters buffeted by forces, performing enigmatic acts, attracted to and repelled by one another as if in fits of seizure. Therefore, the words of the priest and the doctor imply two esthetics as well as two modes of response. Bernanos has *presented* his story to implement the optic of the priest.

It is thus significant that the final interpretation of the chaos comes from the person who brought it forth: M. Ouine. The explanation itself is given with the clarity of a rhetorical exposition: after describing the nature of his malefic influence, M. Ouine proceeds to a lucid conclusion:

> Leur Créateur ne les a pas mieux connues que moi, aucune possession de l'amour ne peut être comparée à cette prise infaillible, qui n'offense pas le patient, le laisse intact et pourtant à notre entière merci, prisonnier mais gardant ses nuances les plus délicates, toutes les irisations, toutes les diaprures de la vie. Telles étaient ces âmes. Voilà ce que je fis de Néréis, ce pauvre enfant malchanceux. Voilà ce que je fis de Jambe-de-Laine, dans cette vieille maison qui devra conserver ma mémoire, dont chaque pierre s'est imprégnée de mon plaisir.

(p. 1559)

On the face of it, such an "explanation" is somewhat less than satisfying, and many critics have noted the strange inadequacy of Monsieur Ouine as villain or as character. It is perhaps through style, in particular our distinction between the rational—scientific and experiential—spiritual mode, that we may best account for the retired professor. The contrastive reactions of the doctor and the priest enable us—in terms of style and meaning—to discern a hierarchy of responses in **Monsieur Ouine.** It is therefore no surprise that the Observer (lucid, dispassionate, ironic) does not usually fare well with Bernanos.[8] Once the moral integrity of the Observer is thrown into doubt, the act of writing soon follows, and literature as a whole threatens to be contaminated. How does one learn about people in order to tell their story? Certain qualities in **Monsieur Ouine** are rarely found in the French tradition they are immediacy, irrationality, opacity, which indicate that. Bernanos has given serious treatment to Sartre's *boutade* that omniscient writing *à la Mauriac* can only come from God.

Recognizing the problematic, exploitative dimension of analytic writing, Bernanos moves into a strange proximity with two very different American writers. Hawthorne and James are obsessed with the dilemma of conveying the intimate workings of individual consciences and, at the same time, honoring the sanctity of the human heart. The detached, poisonous, and ultimately sinful *knowledge* of Monsieur Ouine reminds us of the writer's guilt, a guilt and inadequacy that inform the very narrative strategy of such works as *The Aspern Papers* and *The Blithedale Romance.* The retired professor illustrates the modern spiritual malady par excellence: absence of compassion and the desire to observe, understand and manipulate other human beings. Ouine tries to usurp the lucidity and power of God. His cold detachment constitutes both a sin and a posture virtually synonymous with that of the writer. But the final enigma in Bernanos is always death: that supreme agony constitutes the worth and tally of a man's life. In this crucial instance Monsieur Ouine's vision falters, and he can experience only hunger and emptiness.[9] He is literally absorbed into his own emptiness and disappears rather than dies.

It does not seem fanciful to emphasize the connection between Monsieur Ouine's stance in life and the manner in which Bernanos has told his story. The immediacy of experience—even when harmful or destructive—and the mystery of passion, may yield a more authentic picture than the ravenous, often inhuman appetite for clarity. The living parish, like the balanced life, must acknowledge and hallow the affective and spiritual needs of the individual, while at the same time preserving some sense of form, harmony, and community. The community is threatened when passion becomes self-gratification, when selflessness and purity are forgotten, and the twin reigns of violence and abstraction stamps out love. **Monsieur Ouine** is about such a breakdown. The author has used mystery and

suspense to draw the reader into his decaying world. Bernanos has brilliantly utilized the art form of the detective story, predicated on hidden guilt and communal ignorance, to evoke the emerging chaos of modern life and to convey to the reader a "living" feeling of his dead parish.

Notes

1. *Style and Temper: Studies in French Fiction,* 1925-1960. (Cambridge, Massachusetts, 1967), pp. 45-61.

2. A purely syntactical analysis such as that of Pierre Maubrey, *L'Expression de la passion intérieure dans le style de Bernanos romancier* (Washington, 1959), does little to elucidate the specific problems of *Monsieur Ouine*; this novel differs from the earlier works of Bernanos because of ambiguity, ellipsis and discontinuity in the presentation and structure of the narrative—not because of new syntactical devices. Likewise, Gerda Blumenthal's study of Bernanos' novels. *The Poetic Imagination of Georges Bernanos* (Baltimore, 1965), pp. 18-41, suggests a broad symbolic network of water images but is unconcerned with structure. Henri Dubluë, *Les Romans de Georges Bernanos* (Neuchâtel, 1965), p. 173, best indicates the direction we are taking when he says: "Si tous les personnages du livre sont homicides, on comprend qu'il est vain de connaître nominalement l'assassin du petit vacher. Sa mort est la conséquence du désordre profond de la paroisse morte. Et la confusion du récit est l'expression nécessaire de ce désordre." This last sentence is our point of departure. Finally, we are seeking to account for and to justify the narrative confusion that William Bush, *L'Angoisse du mystère: Essai sur Bernanos et Monsieur Ouine* (Paris, 1966), *passim,* attributes to the novelist's lack of control over his material and/or the unfortunate circumstances during which *Monsieur Ouine* was written.

3. *Œuvres romanesques* (Pléiade edition, Paris, 1961), pp. 1374-76. Future quotations will be from this edition and appear parenthetically.

4. See Gaëtan Picon's preface to the Pléiade edition, pp. xix-xxvi, for a discussion of the concept.

5. See Philip Rahv, "The Cult of Experience in American Writing," *Literary Opinion in America,* ed. Morton D. Zabel (New York, 1951).

6. See Rima Drell Reck, *Literature and Responsibility* (Baton Rouge, 1969), pp. 116-141, for pertinent comments on Bernanos' concept of the writer.

7. See Frohock, pp. 45-61.

8. See the treatment of Saint Marin in *Sous le soleil de Satan.*

9. See the note of Michel Estève, Pléiade ed., p. 1880, for discussion of the images that express this hunger.

John Lye (essay date fall 1978)

SOURCE: Lye, John. *"The Diary of a Country Priest* and the Christian Novel." *Renascence* 30, no. 1 (fall 1978): 19-31.

[*In the following essay, Lye posits reasons for "the failure of the novel form" to dramatize the process of becoming a devout Christian, and, against this line of thought, he emphasizes Bernanos's "relative success" at depicting "the spiritual life of a Christian" in his novel* The Diary of a Country Priest, *which he describes as "a moving representation of a life lived at the junction of imminent and transcendent truth."*]

The Diary of a Country Priest by Georges Bernanos[1] is an unusual novel in that it successfully dramatizes the spiritual life of a Christian. For both formal and cultural reasons the novel has rarely turned to this task, and when it has, has done poorly. Most novels which have attempted to represent Christian spirituality appear sentimental and inauthentic; generally they have been novels of manners, novels of argument, or conversion novels which complete their task when the protagonist has reached an elementary stage of faith. For most such "religious" novels Christianity is a set of emotional responses or intellectual arguments; at their best they may reach toward two levels richer in human experience, the moral truth of the Christian vision or the mythic patterns it provides and draws upon. The complexity, richness and maturity of spiritual experience so persuasively evoked in such works as St. Augustine's *Confessions* is in novels seldom achieved. Newman's *Apologia Pro Vita Sua* will always be read; not so his *Loss and Gain: The Story of a Convert.* The most successful writer of Christian novels, Fyodor Dostoevsky, brilliantly illumines and defends the logic and humanity of Christianity. His novels dramatize the intellectual and social issues of the day, the tragedy of human passions as well as their potential (though often foolish) nobility, the hunger of men for intellectual and moral truth, the triumph of Christian action and value. It is unfair to blame Dostoevsky for what he does not do; but he does not illumine the spiritual innerness of a Christian. His great strugglers are not Christians; his great Christians are marked by wise simplicity, deep innocence, selflessness, patience. They represent the idea of Christian maturity. Tolstoy attempts a closer approach to the realities of Christian life in the great conversion scene in the last chapters of *Anna Karenina.* Here the sincere and pure-souled Levin, reflecting on a peasant's witness of the farmer Fokanych's righteousness, stumbles wide-eyed into the heart of Christianity in a beautiful, lucid scene; yet after going back high-hearted into common life he finds that he has, within a short time, gotten angry at the coachman, been cool to his brother, talked thoughtlessly to a guest. By the end of the novel, by living back into his theoretical and practical concerns and his domestic life, Levin comes to the conclusion that he will still be foolish and sinful in countless small ways, but that his whole life "is no longer meaningless as it was before, but has an incontestable meaning of goodness, with which I have the power to invest it." This calm assurance is the book's conclusion; for all his power of realism Tolstoy is, like Dostoeovsky, illustrating the moral and intellectual truth of the faith, and Levin is an innately good person who finally recognizes the spiritual principles of his being. There is a whole arena of human experience which is chronicled by spiritual *apologiae* and detailed by mystics and saints, adumbrated by monastery rules, dealt with in countless books of instruction and exhortation and witnessed to by confessionals, that process of living into God's will, maturing in Christ, struggling against the fallen state and other malignities; and into this arena these great works, and the countless less great, virtually do not enter. It is into this arena that Bernanos' *Diary* plunges. My intention is to suggest some reason for the failure of the novel form to imitate such spiritual innerness, and to explain Bernanos' relative success.

The Christian lives at the meeting-place of doctrine and life, of revealed and experienced truth, in a universe that is ontologically distinct from that of secular man. Two major problems for Christian fiction are the representation of transcendent as well as immanent truth, and the convincing inclusion of doctrine. Immanent truth exists "in the world," is provable by experience, and needs always to be so proven, to be experienced to be understood. It is best illuminated in the crucible of the world's complexities and the imagination's riches, and is the typical subject of the novel form. Transcendent truths are truths which have been revealed to man. One could not deduce from experience the truth of John 3:16, "For God so loved the world that he gave his only begotten Son, that whosoever believeth in him should not perish, but have everlasting life." (Jesus to Nicodemus); but once this is revealed it reorganizes the world, changes ontology, alters human action. Transcendent truths must be precisely stated. As opposed to immanent truths, they must be believed in order to be experienced. I realize that this distinction between truths could be attacked; it could be claimed, for instance, that as "immanent truth" is not "in" molecular structures, it must be transcendent. But to deny the dichotomy as men experience it is to end trapped in an idealist or materialist world. Berdyaev illustrated the truth of the complexity of Christian man's amphibian state when he boasted of Dostoevsky that "he restored to man the spiritual depth of which he had been bereft when it was moved [by the Orthodox Church] to the inaccessible heights of a transcendent plane."[2]; the Christian reality is not the transcendent plane but the junction of immanence and transcendence.

In order to support the nature of such experience there must be, in fiction as in life, doctrine—the Word of God as taught by the church. On the one hand, an artist cannot control his creativity by a set of doctrinal statements; only if his work has allegiance to the real experience of men can it flourish. On the other hand, without doctrine the transcendent truth cannot be made clear. What is necessary is that the ontological truths of Christianity, which are of their nature moral, be embodied in human action with the accompanying support of doctrinal statement. Both doctrine and the transcendent realities it illumines are difficult to introduce into the novel form, for the novel has its mimetic base in perceived physical and psychic realities; since its inception it has been given over to psychological and sociological realism, to a world which ontologically is wholly immanent. It is possible to introduce doctrine through allegory and symbolism, and a sense of the transcendent through a sense of the sublime, but these techniques tend to vitiate the "felt life"[3] of the novel, and so erode its formal base. When the emotional results of Christian experience are introduced without the necessary support of a union of doctrine and immanence they tend to give the impression of an inauthentic sentimentality. The novel does deal with "religious" experience, a confrontation with the ultimate realities of man's life, but these themes are most successful when they suggest that there is no meaning, or that meaning must be wrested by natural man from his own despair and the world's indifference—direct denials of transcendent truth and of the theological meaning of hope.

Through his craft, his vision and his tradition, Bernanos has in **The Diary of a Country Priest** managed a convincing novel of Christian innerness, a moving representation of a life lived at the junction of immanent and transcendent truth. The protagonist of the novel, the Curé d'Ambricourt, has visions, feels and acts upon the presence of God, exercises some of the "gifts of the Spirit" (I *Cor.*:12), and acts as God's instrument in bringing salvation to at least one of the characters. The whole pattern of the curé's life is, as he and we come to see, under God's guidance and grace. The book deals resolutely with the large problems of the moral and spiritual meaning of the universe; it deals with, for instance, the role of the Church in the world, the spiritual and imaginative desolation of modern man, the problems of suffering and poverty, the nature of evil, the nature and action of God, the innocence and spoliation of children, the goodness of the world itself. The action of the novel is an explication of the truth of the Beatitudes, and it dramatizes the mysteries of the bearing of the burdens of others and of becoming a living sacrifice (*Gal.* 6:2, *Rom.* 12:1). With all this it is a novel of vividly realized felt life and psychological truth, and it retains the person and struggles of an individual in the world as its emotional centre.

There are several statements in the novel which may be taken as indicators of its aesthetic intent. The novel's mentor-figure, the Curé de Torcy, remarks to the curé about Claudel and religious writers generally, "writers are all the same: when they get to holy things they wallow in the sublime—they lay it on thick. Sanctity has nothing to do with being sublime" (p. 178). The "sublime" is an evocation of a sense of transcendent power through an appeal to the awesome, beautiful, stirring aspects of the created world. The transcendence evoked depends upon an emotional response and is, as a transcendence, impersonal and removed from man's state— the emotional correlation of the philosophic God of the enlightenment. The "sanctity" that de Torcy is after is the progress of an individual soul towards a personal and moral God. The God the protagonist serves is not, he says, a "geometric or moralistic God" (p. 77), not "a pagan god or the god of intellectuals—and for me it comes to much the same" (pp. 149-150). An aesthetic result of the imitation of the workings of a loving God who "not only judges our life but shares it, takes it on Himself" (p. 77), is that such a reality cannot be evoked by schematized or allegorical structures, but must be dealt with through the lives of individuals. Further, as the curé says of lust, "lust must be seen, not understood" (p. 110)—the moral realities must be incarnated in human actions, not merely paraded in words for the intellect. The reality the novel must pursue is one of vivid and individualized felt life.

Two traditions in which Bernanos is writing aid him greatly in his task, the anti-bourgeois tradition of the French novel and the tradition of Catholic thought which places the heart of evil not in passionate crimes but in narrow and recalcitrant self-centeredness. Satan has, writes the curé, tried to get ahold of the mind of God, but has wholly misunderstood it in his hate; so as the essence of all good is love, the essence of sin is lust, "a mysterious wound in the side of humanity; or rather at the very source of its life" (p. 109). Behind poverty and suffering in the world are "rich men," "hard and grasping" people, poor as well as rich, "out for power more than possession" (p. 58); their "eternal itch for gains" is, writes the curé, "doubtless . . . no more than a veiled, hypocritical, perhaps unconscious form of the horrible craving, too base to admit, which still obsesses them" (p. 85). Evil emerges in individuals most often as wilfull obliquity, grasping pettiness, a crust of evasions, emotional immaturity, a whole web of opacities and rapacities carefully nurtured and concealed which yield the frightening complexities of mediocrity. This mediocrity, narrowness, graspingness, is closely associated in the book with the bourgeois mind and the sins of bourgeois culture. Bernanos gains from the very deft portrayal of the failures of bourgeois culture of the tradition of French realism, and through his conception of evil is able to combine an openness to the ontological realities of the Christian faith with the dissenting criticism of middle-class hypocrisy and narrowness which is central to the whole history of the novel form. Great wrong-doers, large-spirited and impassioned or noble-minded rebels, are far closer to God than the mediocre, because they have an openness, an honesty; the curé can "commune with" the suffering of Chantal, Delbende, Mme la Comtesse, Olivier, as he cannot commune with the closed hearts of Surplice Mitonnet, Mlle Louise, Dufréty. Through its admiration for the courage of great and honest and suffering hearts the novel espouses an ideal of romantic heroism which is very attractive to most readers and which wins their allegiance to the hard-earned faithfulness of de Torcy and the curé. This sense of heroic goodness and courage is deepened by the novel's conception of moral action and faith as states of being. Purity, for instance, is "one of those mysterious but obvious conditions of that supernatural knowledge of ourselves in the Divine which we speak of as faith" (p. 112). Bernanos avoids the trap of "moral action," the easy association between Christian righteousness and bourgeois values which has turned so many earnest Christian novels into near-parodies; by its idea of heroism, by its dramatization of morality as a state of being, a disposition towards God and man and self, and by its association of evil with mediocrity and the bourgeois, Bernanos has made peace with the social stance of the novel form and has opened the way for a Christian view of the roots of action.

The novel gains greatly in power and credibility, too, from its affiliations with other formal and generic structures—the confession or spiritual *apologia,* the meditation, the theodic and the tragic. It is close to the confession form by virtue especially of the diary form, as well as by virtue of its material. The diary form allows for "recollection," a deeply evaluative self-presence described by Bernanos' contemporary, Gabriel Marcel, as becoming capable "of taking up my position—in regard to my life; I withdraw from it in a certain way, but not as the subject of pure cognition; *in this withdrawal I carry with me that which I am and which perhaps my life is not.* This brings out the gap between my being and my life."[4] This evaluative self-presence is at the heart of the quality of "witness," that sense of the authenticity of recorded life which infuses great confessions and is at the heart of the success of *The Diary [The Diary of a Country Priest].* The method of selection of the confession and the diary is the quality of inner meaning, and so just that quality is enlivened by the form. The work is close to the meditation by its subjects of good, evil, suffering and such, by the quality of witness, and particularly by virtue of the tone and man-

ner, the poignant brooding voice of the prose and the poetic and spiritually attuned consciousness of the curé. The diary form contributes too in that juxtaposed entries form relations to one another without direct signals and so add to the sense of a subtle interknittedness that the meditative and poetic manner creates. These formal affiliations add a strong sense of authentic experience to the novel, help to control the elements of mystery, spirituality and tragic consciousness, and help open the reader to the possible truth as well as the complexity of the subject matter. The theodic character of the work, its desire to explain evil, suffering, the nature and intentions of God, adds an authenticity in its willingness to face up to the real problems of men, and also contributes to a sense of an imaginatively integral universe. The sense of the tragic in the book, enabled by a conception of redemptive suffering and an acute awareness of the anguish of man's fallen state, adds to the sense of the heroic, deepens the reader's allegiance to the meaningfulness of the action, and avoids the sense of callow optimism that the Christian "answer" to man's condition so often suggests.

These formal and generic affiliations help Bernanos to portray the mystery of personality and deed through a sense of authentic and reflective presence in a tragic and complex universe. The novel is highly dramatic as well; long speeches and confrontations are given stagings which keep the reader intent on the moral and psychological realities of the characters, lust is seen and so is understood, we are present in the book in an existential fashion. And while the nature of the universe becomes more apparent, the reader is kept from making neat formulations; it is part of the book's understanding that good and evil cannot be easily unentwined by men, and that men need to be loved rather than judged. In the terms of Marcel, Bernanos keeps the material of the novel on the level of mystery rather than on the level of problem, and hence keeps it open to transcendence.[5]

At the center of the novel stands the person of the curé and the relation that the reader has to him. His is the soul through which we are brought to a sense of the reality of God, and through his experience (and our experience of his experience) we can see the truth of the moral and spiritual revelations of the Christian ontology; doctrine is validated in felt life. As the reader enters the book he is plunged immediately into an intelligent and intuitive consciousness. In the first paragraph he writes of his parish, of good and evil today, and of the character of M. le Curé de Norenfontes. Of Norenfontes he writes, "He is a good priest, deeply kind and human, who at diocesan headquarters is even considered a bit of a free-thinker, on the dangerous side" (p. 7); the values of the curé are evoked here and, subtly, their opposition to officialdom. The curé goes on to remark that "His outbursts fill his colleagues with glee, and he stresses them with a look meant to be fiery, but which gives me such a deep sensation of stale discouragement that it almost brings tears to my eyes"; one has a sense here of the curé's intuitive nature, his ability to discern and sympathize with the spiritual suffering of another, a sense emphasized by the apparent insensitivity of the other priests to the real situation of Norenfontes. The reader is quickly taught to read on this level of intuition and spiritual discernment, guided by the curé but also by the tensions, unnoticed by the curé, between his awareness and that of others, which tensions form part of the considerable operation of irony in the book. The tone of the curé is soon established. There is a melancholic cast to it; he writes of the boredom of his parish, he broods on a dreary November day over its character and fate. The melancholy is traditional, is attended by an intellectualizing habit, an innate conservatism, a criticism of modernity.

While spiritually and intellectually acute, the curé is a fool to the world. He cannot manage his affairs, doesn't understand finance or agriculture, lives poorly, bungles socially. Bernanos creates through the curé a deep tension between the spirit and the world. The tension is enriched on the doctrinal level in that the curé is an exemplification of the Beatitudes, the book a defence of them. He is a figure of the poor, of meekness, of mourning particularly for his lost youth and other's sorrows, of mercy, of purity of heart; he hungers after justice, occasionally with surprising vehemence; he is a peacemaker—that is behind his interview with Mme de Comtesse; and after her death he is persecuted for his righteousness' sake, suffering without attempt at justification unjust accusations, the disappointment of his mentor, the possible loss of his parish. A great deal of the matter of the book—on lust, poverty, justice, maturity, childhood and childlikeness—substantiates its exploration of the meaning of the Beatitudes. As well as illuminating in his being the tension between the spirit and the world and, finally, its resolution, the curé is an embodiment of the conditions of the fallen world that he inhabits. As de Torcy and the doctor Laville point out, he is in his ill health a product of the generations of poverty and drink and despair which preceded him. His own childhood was scorched by evil, informed by it— "To early in life I was forced to see vice as it really is, and though in the very depths of myself I feel compassion for these poor souls, the vision their misfortune evokes in me is almost too horrible to bear" (p. 88). Imbued so deeply with an understanding of evil, ill and truly poor in spirit from generations of waste, the curé stands at the centre of the fallen world. In embodying the effects of the fall he embodies and is qualified to answer the strongest of all charges against God, that he permits the innocent to suffer. Bernanos has created in the curé a matrix of great doctrinal, tragic and strategic power; a personal and richly theodic drama is made possible.

Although the salvation of the Comtesse is the dramatic centre of the novel, with its brilliant narrative techniques and its moving pursuit of a soul almost lost in hate and pride by a shaken servant of God, the most important plot of the book is the sanctification of the curé. Early notice is given that his inner self is to be a concern of the novel; in his second entry about the diary itself, we are led to a sense of an undiscovered self. The curé writes that although what he will record are "the very trivial secrets of a very ordinary kind of life," he has "a sort of unreasoning fear, a kind of instinctive warning" (p. 12). The consciousness his inner examination reveals is not the one he expected but "another conscience, previously unknown to me, a cloudy mirror in which I feared a face might suddenly appear. Whose face? Mine, perhaps. A forgotten, rediscovered face. . . ." Instead of being firm, as he wishes, in meeting his truth, "all inner strength seem[s] to melt away in floods of self-pity and rising tears. . . ." (p. 13). Later, while writing in the diary, he senses a presence "which surely could not be God—rather a friend made in my image, although distinct from me, a separate entity"; towards this "imaginary listener" he turns his head "with a longing cry that shamed me" (p. 26). It is towards a reconciliation in God with this other conscience and friend, his hidden and divine self, that the novel moves.

The first movement of the novel, which extends to the confrontations with Chantal and the Comtesse, is one of increasing despair and pain for the curé. While he learns from de Torcy the true mission of the Church, to bring joy, and while he struggles with the problem of poverty, he expends great energy in various "schemes" attempts to raise the spiritual life of his parish though influence-peddling, self-help services, a sports club, catechism classes. In these attempts he trusts in the world: "I am very preoccupied about my coming visit to the Château. The success of some important schemes very dear to me may depend on this first contact, for the money and influence of M. le Comte would certainly allow me to achieve them." (p. 37). But in this effort, so typical of the Church, he meets divine resistance: "Last night after writing this [concerning the sports club], I knelt at the foot of my bed and prayed that Our Lord might bless my resolutions. Suddenly I was overwhelmed by a sense of destruction, a feeling that all the dreams, hopes and ambitions of my youth had been broken down" (p. 35). As he struggles on his physical suffering increases, he has deep doubts and depressions, finally feels himself abandoned by God, without hope, without the power of prayer, without the capacity to love. It is in this section that the curé most concerns himself about the nature of evil. As he struggles in deep pain with his own and the world's ills he moves, unawares, towards his own good. When he does come to do God's will it is not the succour of the poor or the salvation of the parish but the bearing of the burdens of two wealthy and proud women. When he stands before the Comtesse in her need he can say "I, too, have suffered," for mysteriously his loss of hope and power to love prepare him to bear her loss of hope and power to love. His turning point begins when, in the confessional with Chantal, he has a vision of her face and is willing to accept in himself the suffering she endures: "I could hardly bear such sadness and yet I was anxious to share it, to assume it in its entirety, to let it flood my soul, my heart, my bones, my whole being" (pp. 118-9). As he accepts the burden and presents himself as a living sacrifice, his sense of the presence of God begins to return; he gains back "The old silence . . . wherein the voice of God can be heard" (p. 119). In the midst of his interview with the Comtesse he becomes aware of the presence and guidance of God, and is given back the power of prayer. After she has received hope and peace the curé witnesses joyfully to the mystery of exchange: "Oh, miracle—thus to be able to give what we ourselves do not possess, sweet miracle of our empty hands! Hope which was shrivelling in my heart flowered again in hers; the spirit of prayer which I thought lost in me for ever was given back to her by God and—who can tell—perhaps in *my* name!" (p. 157). The reader has witnessed this miracle, has seen and felt the psychological and moral truth of it through the curé's suffering and wisdom and the dramatization of the Comtesse's sorrow and need. Although he has opened the way for the operation of a transcendence in the world, Bernanos resolutely refuses to admit simplicities or pieties; Chantal has remained unrepentant, although the curé has discerned that the battle has turned, and then the Comtesse, having found peace, unexpectedly dies of a heart attack. On her face is not a smile but a grimace. There is no tender death-bed scene. The curé is thrown into confusion and doubt, he has his scene with her misrepresented and comes under suspicion as the cause of her death, he is taken as an alcoholic, he later collapses from a hemorrhage at night alone.

The curé and the reader come gradually to see that these things are by God's permission and are part of his redemptive work. The curé best states the situation in a prayer: "Lord, I am stripped bare of all things, as You alone can strip us bare, Whose fearful care nothing escapes, nor Your terrible love!" (p. 157). In this new ordeal the curé discovers the freedom to stand unjustified and accused before the world, for the truth is too complex for human extrication and excuse; he is able to free himself from his reliance on de Torcy; and he learns that all agony is not merely of the Spirit but is the Spirit himself, and is the only true form under which fallen man can be perceived. Suddenly, things begin to go better for him; he gains in authority, the sky begins to brighten, his pains decrease, and he meets in the soldier and outcast Olivier, nephew to the Comtesse, a true friend. Through Olivier, and conscious that he is under the guidance of God, the curé discovers the blessed risk of youth and its physical joy, "the carnal form of hope"

(p. 203). The curé's pastoral visits go well, and the world seems to be opening up to him; he has, however, farther to go. In his visit to the doctor, Laville, he learns that he has terminal stomach cancer. With that discovery comes new knowledge, a realization that he truly loves the world: "Alas, I had thought I was crossing the world almost without seeing, as one walks with downcast eyes in a glittering crowd, and sometimes I believed I despised it. But this was because I was ashamed of myself—not of life. I was like an unfortunate lover who loves without daring-to say so, without even admitting it to himself. I know my tears may have been cowardly. But I think, too, they were tears of love. . . ." (p. 237). He goes for the night to the home of the pretentious fool and failed priest, Dufréty, a scene of cramped squalor, and feels that he was unwise; but after an attack there he meets his own image in the person of Dufréty's woman, a little uneducated charwoman, no longer young, who suffers and loves and gives of herself. With, in a sense, her aid, he finds that at the heart of agony is love, "for human agony is beyond all an act of love" (p. 252). He learns in his last hours that he was destined for youth, that he has no age in him, and he learns that he has been a lover of life and of mankind; he is, at the end, wholly reconciled to himself, and understands that "if pride could die in us, the supreme grace would be to love oneself in all simplicity—as one would love any of those who themselves have suffered and loved in Christ" (p. 254). The curé has been increasingly conscious that throughout his life God has been at work. He has been granted faith and has lived faithfully and in love, learning wisdom out of suffering (*Rom.* 5:3-5), bearing the burdens of his fellows, growing to a reconciliation with the world's pain and with himself. He has earned the truth of his last words, "Tout est grâce," grace is everywhere or all is grace. Bernanos has these last words reported in a pretentious letter by Dufréty so that their potential sentimentality will be tempered through irony by the reality of man's fallen state, to which reality he has willed to be faithful.

The character of the curé and the drama of his sanctification are essential methods of incarnating the nature of spiritual innerness and the truth of Christian doctrine. The particular form of the novel enables a sense of authenticity and a realization of the subtleties of spiritual life. These strategies are given great power by the sense of realism Bernanos creates, a sense without which the book cannot thrive as a novel. Not only are physical and psychic details precisely reported, but a very vital psychological realism is attained. Take for instance the scene in which the curé, unable to pray, throws himself down on the floor in a gesture of self-abandonment. From the second his lips touch the floor he is filled with a sense of shame, because he knows the gesture to be a lie. The gesture of despair is undercut by his truthful consciousness, but that in itself creates a more intense sense of despair, for it is a lucid unsentimental realization of futility, witnessed to rather than related; in creating a melodrama internally undercut, Bernanos has reaped the benefits of the gesture by the consciousness of its emptiness. The scene has irony, psychological acuity, it shuns the sentimental and gains insight. The sense of realism in the book is increased by the participation demanded of the reader: the book has many ironies for the reader, and many complexities of experience and perception; the intuitive mind of the curé demands acute attention; and the reader is at times required to intervene to defend the curé against his own unjust accusations of himself. And finally, there are many dramatic scenes movingly reported. The reader's attention throughout is not on the decoding of allegorical references and spiritually significant images and polarities but on a vividly realized life.

The meditative diary form meets many of the difficulties of including the necessary doctrine convincingly. Doctrine is also included dramatically and rhetorically through the mentor-figure the Curé de Torcy. De Torcy is an appealingly manly figure, competent and authoritative. Bernanos artfully manages to reveal both de Torcy's own suffering and his deep concern for and insights into the curé and these things, with his brusque life-loving manliness, establish his believability as a spokesman for the Christian life. His passionate homilies are full of a care for the curé which the reader cannot but share, and so their content is, although often theological, not alienating. The curé's life itself incarnates and demonstrates the truth of the Beatitudes and of several doctrines central to Christian maturity—the offering of oneself as a living sacrifice, the bearing of other's burdens, and the redemptive quality of faithful suffering. Bernanos aids his case immeasurably by refusing sentimentality and false hopes; the novel does not shrink from the evil and pain of the world or from the possible charges against God and against Christian sanctity—rather it directs us to compassion and attracts us with the heroism of men who can face the odds, including the odds of their own pity and pride.

Bernanos manages to include, as well as doctrine, a sense of the real presence of God; this is a difficult task, but it is necessary if a full sense of the inner Christian life is to be realized. The curé has visions, but he does not alienate the reader by claiming them as such; rather they are "peculiar things," not really visions, things that he says he will merely report without attempting to explain, and so the surface fabric of realism necessary to the novel is retained. Similarly his understanding that Chantal has a letter in her purse is a "strange thing" which he merely recounts, perhaps a shot in the dark, "yet I knew I was right" (p. 120). There is no claim that these things are miraculous, the workings of God, yet the contexts and the effects leave no doubt that they are; real moral, psychological, and physical results ac-

crue which help work out the discernible developing spiritual order of the book. In dramatizing God's presence Bernanos follows a certain pattern. He is evidenced first by the suffering of the curé when he thinks that he has lost contact with him; God is so constantly present to the curé's mind and so desperately missed that he begins to gain a reality. In the interview with Chantal various works of the Spirit are manifest but not claimed, and here the curé receives hope of the presence of God in the "old silence." After that interview he feels bereft, a fool and a bungler, and the reader is called to step in to affirm him and, of necessity, the spiritual realities which he feels that he has failed and the reader can affirm that he has not; at the point at which God begins to enter the book positively, Bernanos creates the greatest gap between the curé's understanding of his situation and the reader's wiser one, and the reader is thus forced into an emotional and spiritual leap. The felt presence of God increases in the tense interview with the Comtesse, in the spiritual fabric of which the reader cannot but become involved. Here the curé acknowledges God's direct aid, and this aid is innerly authenticated by the renewal of the power of prayer—another alleviation of his felt absence—and outerly authenticated by the effects on the Comtesse. Throughout the remainder of the book the curé has a sense of God's purposeful direction in his discovery of his true self and the real riches of the world. Despite this pattern the presence of God would probably not be fully convincing were it not for the sense of the authenticity of the curé's sufferings the form provides and the persuasive drama of the crucial scenes in which God emerges from absence. As it is, Bernanos has skilfully involved the reader in a realized world in which the presence of God is inescapable.

Bernanos has achieved through a complex strategy a moving representation of Christian inner life and of the operation of the Christian God in the world. *The Diary* is realistic, it focuses on an individual in a particular historical setting, it does not undermine the novel form's mimetic base with allegory, iconic symbolism or careful intellectualized polarities, and it does not betray its fidelity to felt life with appeals to the sublime or to false emotion. Ordinarily the novel form, with its secular ontological ground, resists attempts to portray transcendent reality whereas Christian life, fusing as it does transcendent and immanent truth, insists upon that reality. I have attempted to show the means whereby Bernanos conquered this problem. Central to those means are the formal affiliations with the spiritual confession and the meditation, and the sense of authentic witness and spiritual consciousness they provide; the anti-bourgeois stance, especially in the idea of evil; the use of a romantic heroism and a tragic sense; the theodic nature of the book; and the person and drama of the Cure d'Ambricourt who, intelligent and intuitive, a true representative of the suffering of the world yet a faithful servant of the Lord, forms a centre of consciousness through which the pain of the world and the triumph of a soul can be dramatized without sentimentality. Bernanos obtains the reader's presence and his accession to the potential truth of the spiritual experience through mystery, drama, pathos and intervention. The work is faithful to sociological, psychological and moral truth, and it faces with integrity the difficult problems of inequity and suffering. Through its power to create an integral interpretation of human experience and through its various fictional and dramatic strategies **The Diary of a Country Priest** succeeds in meeting a difficult and long-standing challenge, the resistance of the novel form to an ancient, traditional, and still common mode of experience, the Christian spiritual life.

Notes

1. Librarie Plon, Paris, 1936. The text used here is the 1937 translation by Pamela Morris; the edition the most available, the MacMillan paperback (New York, 1962).

2. *Dostoevsky* [1923], trans. Donald Attwater, Meridian Books (The World Publishing Company, Cleveland and New York, 1957), p. 36.

3. This term of Henry James's contains the essence of successful realism.

4. On the Ontological Mystery [1933], *The Philosophy of Existentialism*, trans. Manya Harari, Philosophical Library (The Citadel Press, New York, 1956), p. 24.

5. By "mystery" Marcel means a thing or relation considered in its true state, embedded in a complex and value-laden being. Mysteries, when subject to analysis, become "problems," deracinated mysteries which can yield only remnants of the truth or delusions concerning it. The distinction is fundamental to Marcel's thought and is oft repeated; see, for instance, "On the Ontological Mystery."

Stephen Maddux (essay date 1986)

SOURCE: Maddux, Stephen. "Satan with and without a Face in Georges Bernanos." *Claudel Studies* 13, no. 2 (1986): 22-33.

[*In the following essay, Maddux probes the reason why the figure of Satan only physically appears, in all of Bernanos's works, in the novel* Under the Sun of Satan, *concluding that the answer is not because the author's conception of evil changed during his career but because his protagonist-priest in this work is different from those in his other novels. The critic maintains, "It*

is the changing character of his priestly protagonists that determines, more than anything else, why in one case evil puts on a human mask, and in another remains invisible."]

On the very first page of his journal, Bernanos' curé d'Ambricourt remarks on how good and evil always manage to balance each other. An equilibrium between the two invariably establishes itself, he imagines, even in parishes like his. However, as he ruefully admits, it may do so on so low a level that the conflict between them is practically invisible: "le bien et le mal doivent s'y faire équilibre, seulement le centre de gravité est placé bas, très bas."[1] In his own cure, sin or evil manifests itself (at first) principally as lassitude, rather than any flamboyant and energetic devotion to vice. The conflict, or standoff, between good and evil thus remains entirely underground. It takes the hero a considerable amount of time and effort (not to mention extraordinary graces) to pierce below the surface, confront the lurking evil, and force it to acknowledge itself.

Even at that point, that is, even when the priest-hero does uncover what lies hidden beneath the surface of his parish, the evil he must then combat still does not take on a very concrete form. It lies within the sinners he struggles to save, or else surrounds them miasma-like, drawing them together into an infernal communion of undifferentiated sin: never does it take on a shape of its own. How could it? The very essence of sin is its formlessness. It is almost impossible even to conceive of its existence, much less picture it concretely. As the *curé* confides, in one of the meditative passages of his journal:

> Le monde du Mal échappe tellement, en somme, à la prise de notre esprit! D'ailleurs, je ne réussis pas toujours à l'imaginer comme un monde, un univers. Il est, il ne sera toujours qu'une ébauche, l'ébauche d'une création hideuse, avortée, à l'extrême limite de l'être.
>
> (1143)

It is a (formless) world; it is also a consuming force, which devours, or eats away at its victims from within, turning them into something as lifeless and shapeless as itself. The image the diarist uses to describe this process anticipates the end of the decaying Monsieur Ouine: "La personne humaine aura été lentement rongée, comme une poutre par ces champignons invisibles qui, en quelques semaines, font d'une pièce de chêne une matière spongieuse que le doigt crève sans effort" (1143). Sin or evil is thus a formless, impersonal (because depersonalized) force, a powerless power,[2] the effect of which is to destroy personhood and individuality and, joining all together in one indifferent mass, create a hideous imitation of the communion of the saints (v. 1139).

Small wonder, then, that demons make no physical appearances in **Journal d'un curé de campagne**. The hero sees many unusual things, of course, but, of these, the only supernatural being is a heavenly one (the Blessed Virgin); for the rest, what the curé senses or actually sees in his strange visions and intuitions is always, in one sense or another, a double of himself—another human soul with whom he has entered into an extraordinary communion and identification, or else his own childhood, coming to greet him as though it were a separate person. What a contrast with the experience of an Abbé Donissan, who has such a hair-raising encounter with Satan in the central section of *Sous le soleil de Satan.* Like his less spectacular fellow-priest, Donissan too receives the gift of clairvoyance (the ability to read souls), but he is given it only *after* and *because of* his prior meeting with the Evil One and the things that transpire there (v. 180-82, 188). Further, one gathers that the demon will manifest himself to the "futur saint de Lumbres" on many other occasions, even if never in quite the same way as on this first, particularly extraordinary, meeting.

How can we best explain this great contrast in the way Bernanos represents evil in these two novels? In truth, we could just as well phrase the question: why does Satan appear, in the literal meaning of the word, only in *Sous le soleil de Satan?* He has his creatures, of course, in the later works—a Cénabre, a Fiodor, a Simone Alfieri, a Monsieur Ouine; he is frequently named; but he never shows his face again, indeed never plays any direct role in the action, with the single exception of the possession of Abbé Cénabre in *l'Imposture* (the first novel to follow *Soleil de Satan*). The answer does not seem to lie in a radical change in the way Bernanos conceived of evil itself; too many common themes, in this matter, connect his first novel with those that were to come after. Satan is the father of lies, at the outset, and he remains so: he is the one who encourages souls in their self-deceptions and their revolt, leading them on in their illusory ambitions until the point at which every illusion has been destroyed and nothing remains but despair. Likewise, everywhere in Bernanos' fictional *oeuvre,* and especially in these two novels, Satan uses the same tools: an outraged childhood, shame, self-hatred; and everywhere his efforts produce the same effects: *ennui,* despair, and destruction of the person— spiritual and, often enough, physical destruction. To be sure, by the time of *Journal d'un curé de campagne* the theme of *ennui* has grown in importance, but it is by no means absent from *Sous le soleil de Satan.* It is accompanied, there, by the same kind of image the curé d'Ambricourt will later develop at greater length: "Le personnage qu[e Mouchette] affectait d'être détruisait l'autre peu à peu, et les rêves qui l'avaient portée tombaient un par un, rongés par le ver invisible: l'ennui" (94). One may imagine that, though the expression "royaume du Mal" does not appear in his first novel, the idea of a depersonalized and depersonalizing Kingdom of Evil, characterized by *ennui,* is not, even at this point, completely unfamiliar to Bernanos.

Nor does the explanation lie in the mere fact that, in the first novel, the confrontation of good and evil is conceived of as a combat, requiring presumably an identifiable antagonist as well as a protagonist. The problem here is that *Journal d'un curé de campagne* is every bit as much the story of a combat between two forces. Its hero is a fighter, no less than Donissan. He is one of those in the front ranks of the battle, whose loss makes a difference for the outcome (1122). No matter that his heroism is of a special kind (1245); no matter that, unlike Abbé Donissan, he does not seek out despair in order to struggle with it, but rather is thrown to it, like a puppy thrown into the water to be drowned (1144). He does not choose the role of soldier, but, once given it, lives up to it fully, never once flinching when he is called upon to "faire face." This story, too, then, is one of the great conflict, even though the adversary never appears in person.

I think we are likely to find an important reason for the differing representations of evil elsewhere—not so much in Bernanos's conception of evil in itself, which in the final analysis probably remains fairly constant, nor in the mere idea of the cosmic struggle between good and evil, but rather in Bernanos's heroes and the contrasting types of sanctity they embody. It is the changing character of his priestly protagonists that determines, more than anything else, why in one case evil puts on a human mask, and in another remains invisible.

All Bernanos's saintly heroes are singular. They live in limit-situations, and their circumstances and actions cannot, therefore, be taken as exemplary.[3] The curé d'Ambricourt, even as, in last days of life, he becomes reconciled with himself, realizes that, had he been allowed to live longer, he would not have worked out well as a parish priest (1254). The reason for this inadaptability is not far to seek. Saints typically appear, to earthly eyes, an extreme, because in the heavenly scheme something radical is needed to counterbalance the great weight of evil. To maintain the necessary equilibrium, at times remedies are called for that seem excessive to a narrow view of things; the saints are those remedies.

Nevertheless, it is true that some singularities are more singular than others, and, among Bernanos's exceptional, unexemplary heroes, the Abbé Donissan appears particularly exceptional, singular among the singular. Terrifying as the apparition of Satan in the middle portion of the story may be, it is really no more troubling than what we have already learned of this priest's inner life. Endowed with "l'esprit de force" though he may be (133), he surely takes his combat against evil too far when he rejects definitively the offer made to him of joy (141, 145-51). He finds the offer ambiguous, a possible ruse; he is conscious of an apparently friendly presence, but he does not know whose it is (146) and refuses to let down his guard. His rejection, however, is equally or even more ambiguous. On the one hand, as Bernanos lets us know, Donissan is refusing a true grace and, furthermore, allowing Satan to take the place of God as the presence that will haunt his life (147). On the other hand, the hero makes this tremendous choice "with a pure heart." Once he has made it, we do not see him fall immediately into the abyss; if he falls at all, it is from one kind of sainthood into another. More than one kind exists, we are given to understand, and Donissan is simply choosing, as he is apparently allowed to do, the one that suits him best. Nonetheless, the particular choice he makes—or perhaps it is the simple fact that he dares to make a choice, refusing what is offered in favor of something else he likes better—leaves us perplexed and apprehensive. Is a saint supposed to forge his own vocation for himself? Can he refuse God's gifts, and make himself Satan's prey, with impunity?

Ambiguity marks this saint's beginnings; it will be present at every step of his career thenceforth. Has the saint made a good choice or a bad one? Was it even a lawful choice? Has he, or has he not, handed himself over, in an altogether disastrous and inadmissible way, into Satan's hands? The central episode of "la Tentation du désespoir," Donissan's nocturnal encounter with the enemy, amazes and baffles us with its feints and sudden reversals, as well as with what it reveals about Satan's disguises and powers, but above all it troubles us by showing how closely united the devil is to his holy prey and how helpless his prey is to get rid of him. Earlier, it is true, the narrator has spoken as though this unwanted union were the lot of all the saints:

> Il est dans l'oraison du Solitaire, dans son jeûne et sa pénitence, au creux de la plus profonde extase, et dans le silence du coeur . . . Il empoisonne l'eau lustrale, il brule dans la cire consacrée, respire dans l'haleine des vierges, déchire avec la haire et la discipline, corrompt toute voie.
>
> (154)

In the description of this dreadful night, we are given other, similar indications that Satan insinuates himself into every heart. "Je vous baise tous," says the false *maquignon,* meaning all priests (174); likewise, the narrator affirms that the Evil One has entered into the thoughts of each one of us (173). Even so, I for one cannot shake the impression that Satan has singled out Donissan as the special object of his terrible affection and will be present in a special way as an "ignominieux associé" (173) in everything the priest does. How can we believe unreservedly in the goodness and efficacy of Donissan's works, if the Evil One has invaded every one of them?

Moreover, this invasion, this Satanic penetration, will continue as long as Donissan keeps up his efforts; he will never enjoy a definitive victory over Satan. The struggle on this particular night goes first one way, then another; at one point, Donissan seems to have gained the upper hand (175-82). In the end, however, the demon seems to have regained all his power over the priest; his parting words show his assurance that Donissan will never be free of him: "Je t'ai tenu sur ma poitrine; je t'ai bercé dans mes bras. Que de fois encore, tu me dorloteras, croyant presser *l'autre* sur ton coeur! Car tel est ton signe. Tel est sur toi le sceau de ma haine" (184). On this occasion, Satan is telling the truth, for, as we have learned by the end of the novel, in the very last moments of his life, Donissan is still fighting (306), which is to say that Satan has continued as his companion to the very end.

In this uncertainty, we could revert to the principle, "By their fruits ye shall know them." If Donissan's ministry is successful, if he does in fact save souls, then we can say that he does win out over Satan, in spite of Satan's presence and in spite of the fact that he must struggle against Satan every day of his life. Now, Donissan's record is a strong one, and yet curiously unsatisfactory. Conversions and other works the "saint de Lumbres" certainly has performed, but they remain completely marginal to the story. The narrator refers to them in a stilted, distant fashion that does not impress: "Ses oeuvres y sont connues de tous. La gloire, auprès de laquelle toute gloire humaine pâlit, alla chercher dans ce lieu désert le nouveau curé d'Ars" (232). In any event, though no doubt these works are real, we never see them. The one event we do see from the hero's days at Lumbres, related at great length in the last third of the novel, is the account of a failure: it is the attempted miracle that should have served as a seal to Donissan's supernatural vocation and does not quite take place.

One undoubted victory of Donissan's we do almost see, earlier in the novel: Mouchette's repentance. Here, if anywhere, the priest's great struggles bear fruit. Even this victory, however, we do not actually see; it is related by a third party, not a very favorably disposed one, either—a fact which would not be so important in itself (the end of the curé d'Ambricourt is similarly related by a person who has no appreciation of it), but which certainly does not help to emphasize the victorious character of the event. Further, just before it takes place, the Abbé Menou-Segrais, Donissan's spiritually astute superior, is by no means sure how to interpret the vicar's previous dealings with Mouchette:

> J'attendais de jour en jour une confirmation surnaturelle des desseins de Dieu sur votre âme. . . . Et dans votre vie si troublée, si pleine d'orages, le signe a éclaté comme la foudre. [He is referring to Donissan's "reading" of Mouchette's soul.] Il me laisse plus perplexe qu'avant. Car il est sûr désormais que ce signe est équivoque, que le miracle même n'est pas pur!
>
> (229)

In short, a mysterious sense of failure hovers over everything the "saint de Lumbres" does—even, it would seem, over his one undoubted success, and certainly over his life as a whole. Is then the final outcome of the conflict of his life a draw, a victory for good . . . or, indeed, in some sense, a victory for evil?

In one essential regard, indeed, the "saint de Lumbres" does seem to have let himself be vanquished by the Evil One. For Bernanos, Satan is the great liar, and nowhere more so than in this novel. It seems likely that the principal victim of his trickery is none other than Abbé Donissan. "La grâce même de Dieu peut-elle être dupée?" asks the narrator (162). Apparently it can. From the moment of his fateful decision onward, Donissan lives under what must be, from a normal Christian perspective, a delusion: it is the belief that, in his effort to save souls, he may sacrifice everything, incuding his own salvation. So great is his hatred for Satan's works, that he is willing to forget every other consideration, every thought of balance or moderation, every hope for joy, in his struggle to combat them. Hearing the fearful choice his vicar has made, the horrified Abbé Menou-Sergrais attributes it at once to his having been misled by Satan: "Entendez-moi, malheureux! Vous êtes (depuis combien de temps? . . .) la dupe, le jouet, le ridicule instrument de celui que vous redoutez le plus" (224-25). Even in this matter, however, ambiguity reigns. If Donnison had truly chosen despair, he would be a sinner and no saint. If he despaired, and thought himself to be obeying God's will in doing so, he would be greatly in error, not to say a heretic (and is despair not itself a heresy?). What Donissan has in fact done, apparently, is to come as close to despair as is possible without actually embracing it in a culpable way. "Vous avez entretenu le désespoir en vous," cries Menou-Segrais at one point; a little later, however, he qualifies this judgment: "L'espérance est presque morte en vous, à jamais. Il n'en reste que cette dernière lueur sans quoi toute oeuvre deviendrait impossible et tout mérite vain" (228). The "presque" is what saves Donissan and allows him to continue to function as a saint in the impossible context of despair. No less than Mouchette, he has summoned the abyss, but it was with a pure heart (155); necessarily he will remain a paradox and a figure of doubtful interpretation.

What was Bernanos trying to show with this strange portrait? I do not think he intended for us to interpret Donissan in a completely negative way, to the point of actually denying Donissan's sanctity. The hero of this novel is a saint; certainly not the only kind of saint possible, probably not the ideal kind of saint, but still a saint. However, the author may have wanted, through the portrait of this very unusual holy man, whose holiness comes so close to contradicting itself, to make a point about the necessarily strange, unsettling character of any saint. Whether or not an Abbé Donissan could in

fact ever exist, this much, at least, Bernanos might well have insisted on: sainthood, belonging so fully as it does to the supernatural realm, takes us beyond the ordinary and the easily conceivable. By rights it *should* shock us; whatever it is, it should be so extreme as to seem impossible, as well as at the limit or even just beyond the limit of what would have seemed permissible. The war that the saints wage against Satan must likewise be an all but unimaginable one, and not only to the "coeurs sensibles, bouches lyriques" Bernanos apostrophizes so contemptuously (153). Now, in this first novel, his device for suggesting the inconceivable character of the saints' combat was to present us with an undoubted saint performing, or *almost* performing, something even an ordinarily virtuous person could not possibly do, that is, hand himself over to Satan.

Whatever the underlying message, however, and in spite of a few hints that others like him exist (e.g., 308), Donissan appears not as a representative, but as a singular, figure. "Nul autre audacieux n'a fait avant lui ce pacte avec les ténèbres" (159). Indeed, the most characteristic thing about him, aside from his unquenchable hatred for Satan's works, is his solitude. Already cut off from his fellow man by his aspiration to sainthood and his pity for the "bétail humain," he cuts himself off from God as well when he refuses joy. He can make such a choice, because he cares more about the combat against evil than about the peace to come after the combat. Intent on his solitary struggle, Donissan expects nothing from God; entirely given over to the thought of what mankind has lost, he looks forward to no happier life in God's company: "Pour moi, dès l'enfance, j'ai vécu moins dans l'espérance de la gloire que nous posséderons un jour que dans le regret de celle que nous avons perdue" (225). While his anger at Satan drives him into this solitary combat, his enormous strength deceives him into thinking he has no need of help in pursuing it: "Au plein du combat le plus téméraire qu'un homme ait jamais livré contre lui-même, il ne délibère pas de le livrer seul: littéralement, il n'éprouve le besoin d'aucun appui" (157). Only at one point, during his unsuccessful night journey to Etaples, does his attitude vary; here, he at last becomes painfully aware for awhile of his solitude. In this moment of need, the only kindly spirit he encounters is, by a bitter irony, his great enemy. He succeeds in overcoming the momentary weakness that made him desire a friend and takes up his solitary battle once more; however, henceforth he will never be entirely alone again, for, like it or not, he will always be burdened with the presence of Satan as his intimate companion (184). His essential isolation from God and men seems only the more absolute.

Now, the conjunction of Abbé Donissan's isolation from others with the degrading, hateful presence of Satan in his soul is, I believe, no accident. Precisely in the priest's solitariness lies the real explanation for the dramatic, personalized form evil takes in *Sous le soleil de Satan*. Not that Bernanos did not believe in a personal principle of evil; however, one could not imagine it taking on such an individualized, personal shape, were it not in response to a special kind of adversary, a saint-hero who was himself very strongly individualized by being set off from the rest of humanity. It is as though one titanic, isolated supernatural figure called forth another. Donissan, alone, pits himself against the evil of the world, and evil obliges by manifesting itself as a singular being, Donissan's special, elected enemy. So much are they absorbed in each other that, apart from their struggle, little else seems to exist (at least this is true for large portions of the novel, almost the entirety for instance of "la Tentation du désespoir"). God, and sinful humanity, form a very distant backdrop to their encounter, an encounter so exclusive of others that Satan can treat it almost as a kind of marriage.

Such, then, Bernanos may be saying, is the fate of one who would fight evil in isolation. Cut off from God and man by the very fierceness of the *Non serviam* he throws in Satan's face, he places himself at the same moment in a close relationship with his hated enemy. More can be said, however, about the precise mechanism by which this solitary saint thus becomes the intimate of the Evil One. If Satan is able to introduce himself into the elect soul in the frightening way he does with Donissan, this is in large part because he was there to begin with. Every soul, Abbé Menou-Segrais tells his curate, possesses two natures:

> Chacun de nous . . . est tour à tour, de quelque manière, un criminel ou un saint, tantôt porté vers le bien . . . par un élan de tout l'être, . . . tantôt tourmenté du goût mystérieux de l'avilissement, de la délectation au goût de cendre, le vertige de l'animalité, son incompréhensible nostalgie.
>
> (221)

It is an unpleasant truth for Donissan to have to accept: "Sommes-nous vraiment si malheureux?" he asks. I suspect he is thinking primarily about himself at this moment. Is evil, hence Satan, really a part of me (and not just of the poor wretches I must save)? When I defied Satan and summoned him out of the abyss, was I in fact calling him forth from the abyss of my own soul? If so, then in fighting Satan, I must fight myself; in hating Satan, I must hate myself. And it is true: Donissan's wrath is turned as much against his own person as against the Evil One. Hence the narrator can say: "tout en lui et hors de lui porte le signe de la colère" (162).

Lest the claim that Satan springs from Donissan's own soul should seem ill-supported, let me quote what the narrator himself says clearly enough (though in rather convoluted syntax) at the opening of the section in which the hero meets Satan face to face:

> O fous que nous sommes de ne voir dans notre propre pensée, que la parole incorpore pourtant sans cesse à l'univers sensible, qu'un être abstrait dont nous n'avons à craindre aucun péril proche et certain! O l'aveugle qui ne se reconnaît pas dans l'étranger rencontré face à face, tout à coup, déjà ennemi par le regard et le pli haineux de la bouche, ou dans les yeux de l'étrangère!
>
> (163)

In Abbé Donissan's case, thought does not remain abstract, but rather takes shape before him as a friendly-seeming *maquignon*; and, whether he realizes it or not, he is in fact looking at himself when he gazes at the demonic little horse-dealer, "l'étranger rencontré face à face." An important event that occurs toward the end of the encounter, the hero's vision of himself, provides additional (albeit indirect) evidence that Satan is intimately linked to Donissan's soul, and possibly in some sense to be identified with it. It is the Unholy One himself who calls the image forth, as though he were the master of the priest's inner life. Donissan's response to the vision similarly suggests the close link between his inner self and Satan, for he destroys the image, just as he would no doubt like to destroy Satan (180-81).

I should like to forestall two false inferences here. One is, once again, that Bernanos did not really believe in Satan, but only in certain evil tendencies in the human spirit that can be personified as an evil being. His thought in this novel seems to be rather that the mysterious being, the powerless power, the depersonalized person, though it does exist (Mouchette, after all, gives herself to something), has become so closely wedded to the soul that we humans can no longer separate the two, and a saint of Abbé Donissan's type and stature, in attacking the one, cannot avoid attacking the other. Satan strikes at God through man (257); Donissan gets back at Satan, likewise, if not through men in general, at least through one man—himself. Alas for humans, who find themselves in the middle! The point, however, is that the two extremes, though mingled with the human element, nonetheless exist on their own. The second false conclusion is that the hero, since he is fighting with himself, can do no good for other souls. Clearly, the contrary is the case. He is to be the prey of the souls in his charge, Menou-Segrais tells him (134). However, it seems that, with Mouchette, the expiation he accomplishes on her behalf is done apart from her, and apart from the one brief interview they have; it takes place just beforehand, in the terrifying night encounter with Satan. Now, if the way he saves Mouchette is typical of how he will help souls in the future, then we must say that his struggles for souls will take place at some distance from them, in solitude, on a battlefield that includes only Donissan and his Satanic shadow. We can expect that, whenever Satan endangers the souls of his parishioners, the "saint de Lumbres," to protect them, will go after the Satan in himself.

Donissan, then, is the solitary saint, and the form in which evil presents itself to him can be understood in large part as a result of the extreme, almost inconceivable, almost (for a Christian) impossible solitude in which he lives out his vocation to sainthood.

Now, the odd thing about Bernanos's other saints, and especially the curé d'Ambricourt, when we compare them with Donissan, is how *much* they have in common with him. That is, it is surprising they are so like him, when they are clearly so different from him—progressively more retiring, weaker, each one more passive, so it seems, than the last, until we reach the extreme case of Blanche de la Force, who is weakness incarnate. Nevertheless, like Donissan, they expiate the sins of others by their own suffering;[4] Blanche de la Force and the curé d'Ambricourt direct towards themselves just as violent a self-hatred; and these two, likewise, have just as close a brush with despair. In the case of the curé d'Ambricourt we could add the fact I have mentioned above, that he is just as much a fighter as the sturdy Donissan, just as brave, and just as ready to oppose evil and injustice and face unpleasant truths.

An important difference between Donissan and these other saintly figures, however, and it may be the essential difference, is that the later heroes and heroines never elect solitude in the way he does. In the perspective of *Journal d'un curé de campagne,* such a choice would be impossible, because there solitude is seen as the great evil. It is part of the lie Satan tries to involve us in: the belief that we are fatherless, "enfants trouvés," independent but also alone in the world, a belief that at first may bring relief or delight, but leads in the end to despair and devouring *ennui.* In particular, this false belief has the following evil effect: suffering humanity, which may indeed have been deceived into thinking itself abandoned because of its suffering, turns against itself, in an attempt to ease its pain. On the level of society, it would like to take the natural, unavoidable differences of strength and weakness, wealth and poverty, and the like, and use them to introduce an absolute division of the race into two groups, with suffering as much as possible the exclusive reserve of the second one. The Ancient World performed this division in an open fashion, making slavery an institution: "La plus grande somme possible d'ignorance, de révolte, de désespoir réservée à une espèce de peuple sacrifié, un peuple sans nom, sans histoire, sans bien . . ." (1066). With the coming of Christianity, this institutionalization of injustice became impossible, but injustice still exists "éparse dans le monde," continuing its work. In a very similar way, humanity also turns against itself on the level of the individual, when, hating the weakness and suffering he finds in himself, a person rebels against and would destroy himself as sufferer.

One solitude thus produces other solitudes (or: the single condition of solitude has several aspects). Cut off

from communion with its Maker, humanity, frightened by and hating its own weaknesses, ends up destroying communion within itself, both communion among the separate members of the human family, and communion of the individual with himself. Now, the curé d'Ambricourt comes to know all these solitudes very well; he experiences to the fullest extent possible the state of the outraged, humiliated soul, in revolt at its own condition and the condition of other sufferers, and full of self-hatred and despair. However, in great contrast to the "Saint de Lumbres," he does not *choose* to experience this state of abandonment and self-hatred. Even more important, his manner of experiencing it is of a sort to undo it. Even at the farthest reaches of isolation and despair, indeed there most especially, he is communing with other souls. Thanks to his own unwished-for solitude, he can enter into union with all the other sufferers of the novel, both the innocent and (especially) those who have been led by their suffering into a culpable revolt. Everyone (Delbende, Chantal, the countess, Olivier, Laville, the companion of Louis Dufréty, the curé's entire parish [1052]) becomes his double. In addition, in spite of the self-contempt he suffers from through much of the novel, he is in the end reconciled with himself as well (1244) or, as he also puts it, with his childhood (1254), a presence he has been haunted by from the opening pages of the diary (1036) and at last sees clearly when he is about to die. Donissan's double was Satan, the false friend, called out of himself and indeed part of himself and yet forever the implacable enemy, with whom reconciliation is impossible; the curé d'Ambricourt's double is his own youth, his weaker self, long feared, but at length acknowledged as part of himself and loved.

In an important respect, then, the kind of sanctity the curé d'Ambricourt represents is the opposite of what Donissan practices. The one experiences solitude, just as the other does, but he is always moving through solitude toward communion. The logical outcome of the movement is the integration of the person with himself and the restoration of the human family as a communion of selves—these two things necessarily going together. Indeed, the saint is unthinkable apart from the community he helps save; his community is like another Self, another double with whom he must be reconciled and united: "Le visage de ma paroisse! . . . j'imagine qu'il ressemble un peu au mien lorsque je cesse de me débattre, que je me laisse entraîner par ce grand fleuve invisible qui nous porte tous, pêle-mêle, vers la profonde Eternité" (1052). One could go even further and say that, just as, at various points, the saint identifies himself with the suffering and sin of the community, so, at the end of the whole process (not quite reached in *Journal d'un curé de campagne*), the community will take on the qualities of the saint. The curé d'Ambricourt already imagines that the entire Russian people could be a saint (1070). The thing really does happen in *Dialogues des Carmélites.* It is an error, I think, in considering this work, to concentrate too much attention on the character of Blanche de la Force. It is true she is the "faible" of the story and therefore would have to play a central role, in Bernanos's scheme of things; but she is not *the* saint in the sense that Donissan or even the curé d'Ambricourt is. The real saint is the entire community, a network of selves in communion with each other and carrying on constant exchanges from almost the beginning of the drama. To be sure, this community must become reconciled with itself, Mère Marie with Soeur Blanche, much in the way the curé d'Ambricourt must come to accept his own childhood. It is a coming to terms of strength with weakness (1690), unimaginable from the vantage-point of *Sous le soleil de Satan,* but which in a way could be looked on as the synthesis of the spirit of that novel with the spirit of *Journal d'un curé de campagne.*

With the union of person with self and person with community at the center of the later works, it is understandable that in them Satan, the great disintegrator, does not borrow human features. He remains what he is in fact, formless, a void, unpicturable. He simply could not stand up against a curé d'Ambricourt, in whom the power to integrate and restore personhood is so great; there would be no room for him, and the curé would have no time for him. For this priest, the very fact that you can meet with a being means that hope still exists: a soul resides there that can still be saved, drawn out of the shapeless chaos of sin into which it was falling and back into communion; its suffering can still be purified and restored to its original innocence. A creature for whom this cannot be attempted is, he admits, beyond his imagining (1157). A meeting with Satan is, therefore, excluded from the outset: if he could be met with, he would not be what he was. *A fortiori* Satan could not be met with in *Dialogues des Carmélites,* in which the bonds of communion are even stronger, purer, or more joyous than in *Journal d'un curé de campagne.*

The real mystery is that *any* of Bernanos's heroes should have seen the Evil One face to face. I have tried to suggest why it was possible in the case of Abbé Donissan, the only one of the pantheon to have chosen to live fixed in hatred, separated from others and at war with himself, miraculously preserved from dissolution only by the purity of his heart. For him, so divided, so enraged, Satan could indeed take on a human visage—one the priest lent him out of his own substance. Donissan was thus able to meet Satan in single combat; but the price was that he had also to wage a life-long war against himself. It was an abnormal state of affairs, even in Bernanos's adventurous realm of the supernatural; neither the author nor his saints could have been satisfied with it for very long. For them, even as for ordinary humans, it is fitting that Satan should remain invisible.

Notes

1. Georges Bernanos, *Oeuvres romanesques,* "Bibliothèque de la Pléiade," texte établi par Albert Béguin (Paris: Gallimard, c1961), p. 1031. All references to the fictional works of Bernanos are to this edition, and will be given in the body of the article.

2. Cf. Hans Urs von Balthasar, *Le chrétien Bernanos,* tr. Maurice de Gandillac (Paris: Seuil, c1956), pp. 227, 332.

3. See, on this matter, Balthasar, p. 26.

4. I would take issue with what William Bush has to say in this regard about the hero of *Journal d'un curé de campagne.* For Bush, the saint in this novel is no longer the expiator of another's sins, and the lines linking him in this way to the sinners he encounters are not as clear as in the first three novels. See his *Souffrance et expiation dans la pensée de Bernanos,* Thèmes et mythes 8 (Paris: Minard, 1962), p. 27. It seems to me more correct to say that, while this hero certainly unites himself very closely to the other characters in their suffering, his own suffering also has an expiatory (or liberating) value for them.

Malcolm Scott (essay date 1997)

SOURCE: Scott, Malcolm. "The Curé and His World." In *Bernanos*: Journal d'un curé de campagne, pp. 29-46. London: Grant & Cutler Ltd., 1997.

[*In the following essay, Scott delineates the two worlds represented in Bernanos's* The Diary of a Country Priest, *namely the "microcosm" of the parish at Ambricourt and "the macrocosm of the wider world," noting the "thematic connections" between these two worlds and maintaining that social and political issues "form a major part of the novel's interest."*]

(I) A TYPICAL PARISH

The opening words of the novel, 'Ma paroisse est une paroisse comme les autres' (p. 1031/29), identify Ambricourt as a place with nothing to distinguish it from the multitude of France's rural parishes. Its ordinariness reflects the modest character of the priest whose mission is to serve it, for the site of his vocation can hardly inspire delusions of grandeur, let alone aspirations to saintliness. His first words also reinforce the intentions which Bernanos expressed to Vallery-Radot when the novel was in its planning phase: 'Je voudrais aussi que ce petit village fût un "condensé" de notre pays—le châtelain, l'adjoint, l'épicier, les gosses, je les vois tous' ([*Oeuvres romanesques*] 8, II, p. 48). Bernanos espouses here the ambition of a Realist writer: the creation of a world which, while imaginary, holds up a mirror to the real world outside literature. His 'seeing' these details, through the eye of imagination but corroborating that vision by reference to the eyes of the flesh, is also a characteristic of the Realist's aim: what one of Zola's characters, the painter Claude Lantier in *L'Œuvres* [*L'Oeuvres romanesques*], describes as 'tout voir et tout peindre'. And, also like the great Realist novelists, he subscribes, at least provisionally, to an aesthetic of the ordinary and the average. The resemblance of Ambricourt to all other parishes makes it not just ordinary, but also typical—and through its typicality, extraordinary in its power of representation of the French rural world at large. Bernanos illustrates here the paradox of the Realist mode of fiction which by its exemplary completeness achieves the status of the symbolic. What Balzac said of literary characters—'Tout personnage typique devient colossal par ce seul fait'—is true also of places.

Ambricourt represents any parish and all parishes because, the curé remarks in his second sentence, 'Toutes les paroisses se ressemblent', only to add, importantly: 'Les paroisses d'aujourd'hui, naturellement.' This is another early indication of how we should read this text, namely, with a consciousness of historical perspective. Christendom was once different, the curé's afterthought implies; his parish is representative of the modern parish, and of modern Christendom. Other characters in the book may espouse a more static view of the world and of the Church's place within it. Not so the curé, who is aware of change and of the need for institutions, including the Church, to adapt to it.

These social and religious ideas form a major part of the novel's interest. Although the world it reflects existed sixty years ago, the concerns it inspired in Bernanos—the decline in moral and spiritual values, the relationship between rich and poor, the conflicts between the various political responses to these questions—are still of the utmost relevance today. It is true that the options for 1930s France were clearer and starker than the plurality of routes that beckons our world of the 1990s, but the reminder of the moral implications of choosing between them has lost none of its urgency. The Fascist dictatorships established in two of France's neighbour countries, Italy and Germany, and with a Spanish version literally taking shape around Bernanos as he sat writing the novel in Palma, offered one model of social organisation, attractive to many of his former associates within the authoritarian Action Française. The Marxist-Leninist model of Soviet Russia offered another, the strong temptation of which in the eyes of a depressed proletariat is understood by the curé. During the later stages of the novel's composition, a left-wing Popular Front government came to power in France and instituted the most serious programme of social welfare

ever seen in that country; its equivalent and forerunner, the Frente Popular government in Spain, was at the same time in the process of being crushed by Franco's rebellion. Drawn in one direction by political affiliation and in the other by compassion for the poor, Bernanos was acutely aware of a need for fresh thinking and of a lack of leadership and commitment within the Church and in its ranks of traditional supporters.

His novels habitually allude to such political issues, but in indirect ways. He once described *Sous le soleil de Satan* as a response to the demonic slaughter of the Great War, and *Nouvelle histoire de Mouchette* as a novel inspired by the fratricidal conflict in Spain, although war and politics are not specifically mentioned in either but are reflected at the deeper level of moral or theological theme. It is necessary to read the *Journal* [*Journal d'un curé de campagne*] in the same way, with an awareness of background and a sensitivity to thematic connections between its different levels. There are two focal points to consider in studying its social and political dimensions: the microcosm of the particular parish in which these issues are exemplified and the macrocosm of the wider world to which they relate symbolically and through the magnifying glass of their typicality.

(II) THE CURÉ AND HIS PARISH

The *Nouveau Petit Larousse* defines 'paroisse' as 'territoire sur lequel s'étend la juridiction spirituelle d'un curé'; and 'curé' is defined by the *Petit Robert* as 'prêtre placé à la tête d'une paroisse'. A parish is both a geographical and spiritual space, and the curé's leadership of it is inscribed in the constitution of the Church. In the novel's opening lines this relationship is underlined by almost incantatory repetition. In the first three paragraphs, 'paroisse' occurs eight times, and the associated noun 'village' four times. To these twelve verbal signifiers of the territory of Ambricourt, there correspond (ignoring the intercalated conversation with the curé de Norenfontes) thirteen first-person indicators ('je', 'me', 'mon/ma', 'mienne') which identify the diarist as its guardian and protector. This near-perfect lexical balance thrusts priest and parish, together and in equal proportions, to the forefront of the text in a symbiotic relationship grounded in its verbal substance. It is there again in an echoing passage twenty pages later when, on the 'anniversary' (three months, to be precise) of his arrival in Ambricourt, the curé views the village from the same vantage point and confesses that he cannot utter the word 'paroisse' without emotion. The noun is used four more times, each time with the adjective 'ma', again underpinning grammatically his conviction that 'nous sommes l'un à l'autre pour l'éternité' (p. 1052/56).

The village, when first seen, appears passive and indifferent. The curé describes it as a tired cow, steaming in the late autumn rain, then disappearing into the night.

To this image of the wandering beast there corresponds that of the 'petit vacher' (p. 1031/30), whom he imagines coming home from school and leading the herd to its warm stable. The 'maître à suivre' required by the morally lost herd/parish must possess the childlike qualities of the little schoolboy/cowherd. The novelist already prompts the reader to realise that, just as the parish is the archetype of all parishes, the curé is the archetype of the saviour, identified metaphorically as the little cowherd, and symbolically as a Christ figure. A saint, writes the diarist, is required to save this village, but his own fitness for that role remains unformulated.

The second passage refers to the village's 'regard' or way of looking at him, which he describes as the 'regard' of Christendom, or of the entire human race, searching imploringly for a guide. The image bites deep into his imagination; he uses it in a sermon, to his own embarrassment, for nobody understands. And when he tries once more, a few pages later, to catch its 'regard' from his favourite hilltop, the village also fails to respond. Yet he is conscious still of a latent sign of recognition: 'Je ne crois pas d'ailleurs non plus qu'il m'ignore. On dirait qu'il me tourne le dos et m'observe de biais, les yeux mi-clos, à la manière des chats. Que me veut-il? Me veut-il même quelque chose?' (pp. 1060-61/67). Again the novelist's prompting answers the diarist's question—what the village will want of the curé is Christ-like suffering on its behalf. For the young priest, we are told, sometimes imagines himself nailed to a cross by the village and watched, as he dies, by its piercing look.

Such thoughts are alien to the people of Ambricourt. The 'village' does not behave as a 'paroisse' in the spiritual sense, and not once do we see its inhabitants acting together in the practice of their supposed faith. On the contrary: they project a reverse image of a Christian community, a negative that is tantamount to a picture of evil. The curé does not leap immediately into such theological areas of vocabulary, but rather diagnoses the condition of the villagers as one of 'ennui' (pp. 1031-32/30). By this word he obviously means something more profound than its dictionary sense of 'boredom'. Readers of Baudelaire will register Bernanos's probably conscious echo of his use of the word to signify a pervasive world-weariness and self-disgust. The curé defines it as a kind of devouring cancer or leprosy, spreading slowly and contagiously through the world. It is a deep-grained despair, an absence of the Christian virtue of hope, a symbol of the 'christianisme décomposé' (p. 1032/31) which is the essence of our secularised society. The curé regards his parishioners as the passive victims of this corruption. It is part of the air they breathe, coating their bodies and invading their lungs like an invisible dust. Exposure to it is the perpetual condition of life in the modern world.

The curé sees the villagers as victims rather than perpetrators of evil. They include rapacious merchants like M. Pamyre, who dupes him out of his meagre resources (p. 1035/54), or the local schoolmaster who sells patent drugs as a sideline and is offended by the curé's well-meaning free distribution of medicines which he happens to receive from an old seminary friend (p. 1110/127). These may appear trivial examples of the suffering of a socially awkward individual in a hard economic world. Less trivial are the signs of a deep-rooted hostility towards him among the villagers, manifested by attempts to interrupt his sleep, and culminating in anonymous letters advising him to leave (pp. 1111/127-28). Such persecution, accompanied by a reputation for alcoholism created by his growing consumption of wine—the only beverage he can tolerate as his abdominal pains increase—is incomprehensible to the curé; this rejection of God's representative amounts to a hatred of God Himself, so evil that he thinks it must be of diabolical origin: 'La haine de Dieu me fait toujours penser à la possession . . .' (p. 1105/121).

Even the young people of Ambricourt have been contaminated by this all-pervading spiritual sickness. The curé seeks shelter in his catechism classes, hoping they will bring him closer to the children for whom, remembering Christ's words 'Sinite parvulos' ('Except ye [. . .] become as little children . . .', Matthew 18. 3), he feels a special tenderness. But the children too are already versed in the ways of the world, and respond with smutty-minded resistance to his teachings on spiritual love. The peasant girl Séraphita Dumouchel for whom he feels particular compassion shows a talent for precocious sexual teasing. More compromising for the curé is his attempt to befriend the young house-painter Sulpice Mitonnet, in whom he naïvely fails to detect a sexual ambivalence which causes the other youths to boycott him.

These encounters with the economic and sexual realities of the world's corruption are aggravated by evidence of its loss of Christian belief. This is expressed not by an intellectual character but by a simple man in whom the curé had expected to find the old beliefs intact: the gravedigger Arsène, who declares that he does not believe in conversion or even in resurrection: 'Quand on est mort, tout est mort' (p. 1182/216). The curé reassures himself that Arsène, who works for the Church and regards himself as a member of its body, no doubt does believe in eternity, albeit unthinkingly. But he is shaken by this glimpse of the scepticism that lies within an allegedly Christian community.

The family of the count and countess sets no better example, although exemplary behaviour is precisely what the curé expects from these traditional allies of the Church. Bernanos expresses nostalgia here for the ideals of a pre-industrial feudal society, in which the local lord's God-given authority over his peasant tenants was accorded on the condition of his reciprocal care and guidance of them. That such ideals no longer correspond to modern reality is a lesson which the curé learns only gradually. He awaits his first visit to the château in anticipation and is even flattered to be invited, for his simple, passively resigned background has left him with no jealousy or resentment of the rich. The count, he comments, 'ressemble certainement plus à un paysan comme moi qu'à n'importe quel riche industriel', and even the mantilla of the countess 'm'a rappelé celle que ma pauvre maman mettait le dimanche . . .' (p. 1059/65). He is charmed by their naturalness and elegance, and more at ease in their company than in that of the 'anciens minotiers' who have recently bought a neighbouring château. Yet the count's values are later revealed as no less material than theirs. As the chanoine de la Motte-Beuvron tells the curé, 'Il n'y a plus de nobles, mon cher ami, mettez-vous cela dans la tête. [. . .] Les nobles d'aujourd'hui sont des bourgeois honteux' (pp. 1174-75/206-07). Far from leading his community, the count is revealed in all his mediocrity as a man responsible for the fragmentation of his own family through his affair with the governess Mlle Louise, which is pushing his daughter Chantal towards flight or even suicide. 'On devrait beaucoup prier pour les familles,' he tells the curé (p. 1175/208): this great central institution, bulwark of traditional values, is in no less danger of collapse than other ancient institutions of France.

Among these threatened guardians of values is the Church itself, and again the fault lies within. It would be a mistake to imagine that Bernanos, fervent Catholic though he was, assumed an automatically defensive position with regard to his Church. Indeed, in his eyes the modern Church had betrayed the mission confided in it, and his assessment of the attitudes of its hierarchy is so critical that it would not be excessive to define it as a form of anticlericalism. Against the tide of the institution's failure, however, swim various 'bons prêtres'. The first of these, mentioned only once, is the curé de Norenfontes, 'très bienveillant, très paternel', but also, significantly, with a reputation in the archbishop's circle of being 'un esprit fort, un peu dangereux' (p. 1031/29). He seems to be an *alter ego* of the curé de Torcy or, not impossibly, simply an early version of Torcy, introduced and then forgotten during textual redraftings. Torcy too had once been the priest at Norenfontes (p. 1075/85); and like him, this man bears the traces of suffering and fatigue which move the curé almost to tears. Brief though his appearance is, he is the first of the curé's soul-brothers, an early sign of his need for human solidarity and warmth, his capacity for emotional involvement.

His superiors, certainly, provide none of this solace. Individual priests are not encouraged to have their own views, but are advised to emulate the quietude of the monk. This indoctrination is dispensed through lectures which the curé attends, reluctantly and at the command of his *doyen*, but which he finds pointless and irrelevant. One is delivered by the archiprêtre de Bailloeil, '[un] ancien professeur de lettres [qui] soigne sa diction comme ses mains', a typical example of 'le prêtre lettré [qui] m'a toujours fait horreur' (pp. 1033-34/32). The lecture is on 'Ce que j'ai vu à Verchocq', but the curé is sceptical of the interest of what can be seen in that monastery or any other. Whereas earlier Catholic novelists like Huysmans or Léon Bloy had been so moved by the spectacle of monastic life as to situate large sections of their novels in such environments, Bernanos was obviously of the opinion that exemplary piety is easier to achieve in the cloister than in the hurly-burly world of the parish. His novel reflects here the age-long tension within the Church between regular and secular clergy; but it also indicates his own greater interest in a setting where religious and social concerns can be explored in their direct interrelationship.

As for the second lecture attended by the curé, on the schisms of the Church in the sixteenth century, he is sensitive to its relevance to the problematic issue of the Church's twentieth-century survival. The other priests, less imbued with Bernanos's historical sense, are oblivious to this. What they understand are matters of which the curé is wholly ignorant: financial realities into which, as the son of poor peasants, he has never been initiated. The Church's institutional concern with money, and its complicity with the world of commerce, are represented by a further priest, the rebarbative doyen de Blangermont who, reproaching the curé for his unpaid debts to the Pamyres, defends the latter as pillars of a social class 'qui fait encore la richesse et la grandeur de notre cher pays' (p. 1081/92). The Church's alliance with the property-owning 'bourgeoisie travailleuse, épargnante', now threatened by 'les éléments de désordre', has for him a scriptural backing, for 'le droit de propriété n'est-il pas inscrit dans l'Evangile?' Property, wealth and order are clearly superior in this priest's scale of values to pastoral care or even to saintliness—for he protests unconvincingly that his cry 'Dieu nous préserve [. . .] des saints!' was a mere 'boutade' (p. 1082/93).

A second highly ranked clergyman to represent a particular interest against the curé is the chanoine de la Motte-Beuvron, who, as the count's uncle, is concerned to protect the family name after the countess's sudden death. Although he has harsh words to say about his nephew he is careful to distance himself from the curé also. With impeccable correctness, he declares his wish to respect his young colleague's authority in his own parish, and he speaks to him 'sur un ton d'égal à égal, presque de déférence', but at the same time he assures him: '[qu'] il est probable que nous n'avons pas deux idées communes en ce qui touche le gouvernement des paroisses' (pp. 1172-73/204). Thus, siding with no-one and standing back from all, his every sentence cancelling the one before, the unctuous canon shows that he belongs to the category of devious and unscrupulous career priests described by Bernanos in *L'Imposture*. He may feign respect for the curé, but he is also insistent, ecclesiastical civil servant that he is, that his young colleague should write down the details of his last encounter with the countess, to be shown to the bishop and then safely filed away within the bowels of the institution. This cold and efficient man is a telling portrait of the type of priest who sits comfortably aloof in the hierarchy of a Church whose true mission, Bernanos believes, is to involve itself in the everyday world and cure it of its cancer.

(III) THE MACROCOSM: THE CHURCH AND THE WORLD

Collectively, these individual portraits of members of the parish and Church constitute a remarkably complete impression of a traditional society, divided into its classical 'three estates': aristocracy, priests and a multifarious 'tiers état' composed of merchants, artisans and peasant farmers. However, behind this apparent structural stability, old distinctions of class are fragmenting, the aristocracy has surrendered its central place to a commercial middle-class, itself pressurised by the financial crash of 1929, and in the background there are glimpses of a poor and deprived rural community. The role of the Church in this society has become unclear - as unclear, precisely, as the role of the curé in his parish, so that defining the one is the key to elucidating the other. This task of definition is the function of the long passages of discursive dialogue which account for about a fifth of the entire novel, and in which the central figures are the curé de Torcy, doctor Delbende and the countess's nephew Olivier Tréville-Sommerange.

Dialogue in general is a dominant component of all of Bernanos's novels, for most of their important scenes are dramatic two-person confrontations. The central 'countess scene', as well as the curé's conversations with the count, Chantal, Louise and, later, with Doctor Laville, Dufréty and Dufréty's mistress, are all examples of such 'dramatic' dialogues. One can distinguish from them the dialogues which amplify the themes noted above: the curé's five discussions with Torcy, and especially the two great dialogues early in the book (pp. 1036-47/35-48, 1066-80/74-91); the brief but important exchange with Delbende (pp. 1091-96/104-10); the longer one with Olivier near the end of the Ambricourt sequence of the novel (pp. 1209-21/249-64). To label these as 'discursive' dialogues is not to imply that they are abstract essays that might have strayed into the novel from works of non-fiction. On the contrary, in reporting the discourse of his interlocutors, the curé re-

produces the circumlocutions and frequent incoherence of their spontaneous utterances. He does not rephrase them in his own more analytical style, but allows the voices of the various speakers to be heard in their own idiom, as essential elements of their portraits. Bernanos, who makes his curé say: 'Je ne suis pas l'ambassadeur du Dieu des philosophes, je suis le serviteur de Jésus-Christ' (p. 1096/110), is not 'philosophising', but putting into his characters' mouths half-formed thoughts on which the curé, often just listening in virtual silence, reflects and comments later. His meditations on these thoughts (pp. 1047-48/48-50, 1061-66/68-74), linking the dialogues and carrying the chain of ideas forward as an integral part of the narrative, are the final components of a fugue of developing themes, important both as a commentary on the social situation underlying the narrative and as a clarification of the nature and significance of the curé's mission.

No summary in English can do justice to the rich language of the interlocutors, nor capture the teeming complexity of their ideas. Even their personalities are elusive. Henri Giordan argues that the curé de Torcy defies analysis: 'Bernanos y a introduit des éléments difficiles à concilier de prime abord' (*9* (d), p. 98). This is no doubt because this sympathetic priest, described by Robert Speaight as Bernanos's nearest approach to a self-portrait (*42*, p. 147), is caught in different moods in his various appearances. The curé's companion, self-imposed mentor and debating partner, he is sometimes carried away by the resonance of his own eloquence, at other moments moved to tears by his thoughts of human suffering. A man of courage, vigour, mock irreverence and humour—he is indeed the main provider of an attractively humorous dimension in the novel—he represents through his own character his conviction that Christianity exists to bring joy to the world. Yet Torcy's 'gros rire bonhomme' is also an ironic guard against too intimate a relationship with others, a trait which the curé finds disappointing. There is also a vulnerability in him, born of the conflicts with the Church hierarchy related in the second dialogue. The curé realises, observing Torcy's trembling hands as they discuss the Church's social role, the damage incurred in Torcy from the 'luttes terribles où avaient failli sombrer son courage, sa raison, sa foi peut-être' (p. 1071/80). He seems to have emerged from these struggles as a tamer man, at least in public. While passionately declaiming his rebelliousness in the privacy of his room, there is little to suggest a continuing active role. Though far from being the self-seeking careerist priest, establishment flatterer or pretentious intellectual of the type from whom the curé recoils, the fact that Torcy is a possible candidate for the deanship of Heuchin (p. 1036/35) suggests that he has exercised care in recent times not to be seen as a trouble-maker. He has the worldly wisdom which the curé lacks. There is even a suggestion that he leans towards the side of the villagers in their judgment of the curé, believing as they do that he is an alcoholic. Torcy also realises, however, his colleague's qualities and the special calling which awaits him.

Olivier and Delbende also offer the curé a fraternity based on shared values. Both, like him, have known rejection. Olivier's early reputation as 'un garçon très difficile' (p. 1210/250) has made him a semi-outcast from the countess's family. With this soldier in the Foreign Legion, whose everyday life involves the possibility of violent death, the curé enjoys an exhilarating motor-cycle ride that represents a brief experience of physical excitement and risk in a life committed to meditation and prayer. Olivier represents courage and self-sacrifice through his vocation and indeed his very name: Olivier was the companion of Roland in the Old French epic, and Tréville the captain of Musketeers in Dumas's well-known historical novel, so that legendary heroism and the image of the Christian soldier are evoked through him from the outset. Delbende's name is also significant for less literary reasons. He shares his Christian name Maxence with one of Bernanos's closest friends from his days as a royalist militant, Maxence de Colleville, to whom *La Grande Peur des bien-pensants* was dedicated. To which another detail is added by the novelist's son Jean-Loup Bernanos: namely, that his father, in his days in the seminary of Aire-sur-la-Lys, lodged with an Abel Delbende, the local mayor, and his three sons (*22*, p. 59). Henri Giordan records that Bernanos paid tribute to Abel Delbende's sense of honour in a letter to a later member of the family (*9* (d), pp. 119-120). Honour is indeed Delbende's most cherished value—'la question sociale,' he insists, 'est d'abord une question d'honneur' (p. 1095/109)—and its rarity in the society around him has made him too a marginal figure, in whom the curé recognises 'une blessure profonde de l'âme' (p. 1096/110). He is given an immediate human warmth by Bernanos's portrait of a no-nonsense countryman in corduroy trousers, living in the company of an adoring dog. He is brusque and to the point about the curé's emaciated state and failing health, and he too regards his patient as having a hereditary drink problem. But the curé is pleased to be described by Delbende as belonging to 'la même race' as Torcy and himself. A group of kindred spirits is formed here, augmented later when Olivier recognises in the curé 'un hors-la-loi, dans notre genre' (p. 1216/258)—for 'le bon Dieu lui-même aura du mal à distinguer des mauvais garçons les saints de la famille' (p. 1214/255).

What all of these soul-mates share is first of all regret at the passing of a Christian era. It is Torcy who expresses this first, in his homily on the great edifice of Christendom which the early Church had set out to build: 'un empire auprès duquel celui des Césars n'eût été que de la crotte—une paix, la Paix romaine, la vraie' (p. 1044/45). He contrasts the lack of authority of 'vous autres jeunes prêtres' with the sterner leadership of their predecessors in an alleged golden age in which the Church trained its priests as 'des chefs de paroisse, des maîtres, quoi, des hommes de gouvernement' (p. 1037/36). Their task, like that of the *sacristaine* in his parable, who killed herself in the vain attempt to create for her church a perfectly and permanently clean floor, can never be accomplished once and for all. The best tactic in Torcy's view is to concentrate on the simple tasks: bring straw to the ox, groom the ass. Such a practical approach to the priest's mission, eschewing the abstractions of theology, was taught, he insists, to seminarists in the good old days—a notion which leads him back in an expansive circle to his starting-point: to his vision of a militant Church and a Christian people whose common characteristics were joy and youthfulness of spirit.

Delbende, in his allusions to the Church as an army with its corporals (the ordinary members) and its field-marshals (the saints), echoes Torcy's vision of a quasi-military religious order, but whose task is unaccomplished after twenty futile centuries. This disillusionment has turned the doctor into a confirmed atheist. For him the Church is not a spiritual institution, but a bastion of social attitudes and a force for the maintenance of moral tradition. On this level, the curé naturally disagrees with Delbende. 'L'Eglise n'est pas [. . .] ce qu'il imagine,' he writes, 'une espèce d'Etat souverain avec ses lois, ses fonctionnaires, ses armées,—un moment, si glorieux qu'on voudra, de l'histoire des hommes' (pp. 1103-04/119). Such an essentially secular view of the Church as a temporal institution identifies Delbende as a representative of the attitudes of the Action Française. Bernanos's portrait of him expresses both rejection and homage: wrong in their refusal of a religious belief, his former associates were admirable still in their defence of the values of pre-revolutionary France.

As for Olivier, he is literally a member of an army; and his regret is that the spirit which the Church is meant to represent has been allowed to wither in his institution as in others. Ambivalent as to the nature of his religious beliefs, the failure of the Church's social mission also grieves him. The Church, he says, is arguably the accomplice of injustice. It no longer opposes the corrupt attitudes of society, which he identifies as refusal, pleasure and the thirst for money; these only the soldier combats, but even the soldier's status is debased: the last true Christian soldier died on May 30th 1431—Joan of Arc. Modern warfare, says Olivier in words that reveal in Bernanos an uncanny prophet of the destruction of Guernica, to take place within two years of the novel's composition, will become characterised by the actions of morally detached pilots, dropping their bombs on civilian populations from thirty thousand feet. And, he concludes, such mass murderers will be given the absolution of the Church more readily than the poor devil who has succumbed to sexual temptation.

Olivier's nightmare vision of mechanised warfare fore-shadows Bernanos's polemical work, *La France contre le robots* (1944), and his veneration of Joan of Arc also corresponds to Bernanos's own—he had written an essay on this saint in 1934, and had even married Jeanne Talbert d'Arc, a descendant of Joan's brother (*42,* p. 24). Delbende and Torcy also speak for the novelist when they express their lament for a failed Christendom and for a Church which has abdicated its responsibilities. But they represent, however movingly, the pessimistic and in some ways negative faces of Bernanos's thought, because their ideals are ossified in a past world which he knew could not be recaptured. The curé also knows this, and accordingly rises above and beyond the horizons of his companions. He disagrees with Torcy's notion of unchanging remedies for a fundamentally unchangeable society. The social policy of the Church, though its timeless mission is encapsulated in the impressive fifteenth-century church at Ambricourt, must be one of constant reassessment. Torcy by contrast, for all his charm and comic verve, appears in the first dialogue—importantly, he will change later—as a man of the previous generation. The gulf between generations is one of the central concepts in Bernanos's social thinking, identifying him not as a conservative but as a radical thinker, a man whose values are traditional but who insists on the need for each age to reformulate its strategy for relating them to the contemporary world.

Far from merely reacting to change, however, the Church in the curé's eyes is the prime agent of change. He reflects on the demise of the ancient world, based as it was on a system of slavery which the moral force of Christianity had swept away. Slavery, anti-Christian in that it threw the burden of original sin on to the backs of one social class, was the ancient world's version of injustice; but, the curé goes on, the modern world has its own form of this evil. A society 'indifférente au bien ou au mal' has been eradicated, replaced by one with 'une âme à perdre ou à sauver' (p. 1066/74). But having disappeared from our laws, injustice continues to flourish in the relationships between men. Its final elimination, for the curé and for Bernanos, is the great unfinished task of the modern Church. And Bernanos's identification of where modern injustice lies introduces the second great theme of the discursive dialogues: poverty.

(IV) THE ETERNAL POOR

Torcy, on reading this section of the diary, develops the curé's view of injustice to greater political depths. A different face of this complex priest appears in the second dialogue: stirred by suppressed memories, the garrulous sage is retransformed into the fervent militant he once was. No longer dreaming of a mythical Christian past, he now attacks the present-day capitalist system, which has replaced slavery while duplicating its inhumanity, and the state, which assumes in a merely half-hearted way its responsibility to the poor: 'Il torche les gosses, panse les éclopés, lave les chemises, cuit la soupe des clochards, astique le crachoir des gâteux, mais regarde la pendule et se demande si on va lui laisser le temps de s'occuper de ses propres affaires' (p. 1068/76). Torcy, great metaphorist that he is, produces a memorable image here of a modern clock-watching welfare state, devoted to 'nine to five' charity.

He recalls his youth as a priest in the mining area of Norenfontes, when Pope Leo XIII's encyclical *Rerum novarum* of 1891—famous in its day as an appeal to Catholics to involve themselves in social problems—inspired him to protest from the pulpit against the exploitation of workers, thus earning himself the reputation of a 'red' priest and banishment to another parish. His interest in the Soviet Union's social policies is thus no coincidence, although he now rejects them, for in seeking to exterminate poverty the Russians threaten the abolition of the poor: an ambition which serves the anti-Christian goals of communism, for the poor man is 'le témoin de Jésus-Christ, l'héritier du peuple juif' (p. 1069/77). Torcy thus, in the great turning-point of this whole sequence, reorientates the political debate into a spiritual one, and he is followed in this by the curé, in an important parenthesis.

Here we learn of the curé's childhood experience of dire poverty, which enables him to understand the suffering of the Russian people. After his father's death, his mother had gone into hospital for the removal of a cancerous tumour, while he was entrusted to an aunt who ran a sordid bar in the mining town of Lens. The only light in this social darkness came from the books lent to him by his schoolteacher, among them the childhood memoirs of Maxim Gorky. This book, unnamed, but presumably *My Childhood,* the first volume of Gorky's autobiographical trilogy—is clearly an inspiration of his own urge to write. Like his diary, it is, in Gorky's translated words, 'the creation of a sincere artist with a passionate devotion to the truth, however cruel' (Penguin, p. 25). It tells a story similar in outline to his own: that of a poor boy in Tsarist Russia, his father dead, his hapless mother unable to protect him from the brutality of other members of the family into whose charge he is placed; and it had revealed to him the existence of poverty on a vast scale: a whole nation turned, collectively, into a patron saint of *misère.* However, he had come to a very different conclusion from that of Gorky, whose angry defence of the poor had made him the literary spokesman of a Leninist regime committed, at least in theory—for Bernanos in 1936 was as blissfully unaware as most other westerners of collective farms and labour camps—to the removal of social inequalities. For the curé, what is missing from Gorky's great cry of lament is a religious dimension. His book may be a hymn to suffering, but it is not a church hymn, nor does it have any element of prayer. It inspires pity and horror, but fails to point to the one true source of alleviation, which, concludes the curé, is to be found 'sur l'épaule de Jésus-Christ' (p. 1071/79).

Returning to centre-stage, Torcy relates the vulnerability of the poor man to that of the child—thus completing the thematic bridge to the first dialogue—and adds that the rich man can never be taught the virtues of childlikeness. By 'rich man', he means not just one with money and possessions, but a man possessed by the spirit of wealth. Conversely, to be poor is not just to lack material wealth; it is to embrace the spirit of poverty in a childlike trust in God's paternal love. While poverty can never be taught to the rich, the love of poverty has to be taught to the poor, for their special mission in the world is to represent to all eternity 'la pauvreté de Jésus-Christ' (p. 1075/84). This is the message encapsulated in Christ's words to Judas: 'Il y aura toujours des pauvres parmi vous', which Torcy describes as 'la parole la plus triste de l'Evangile, la plus chargée de tristesse' (p. 1078/88). It is nevertheless, he insists, 'la Parole, et nous l'avons reçue'.

This torrent of evangelical poetry is followed immediately by its negative counterpart in the ensuing dialogue with Blangermont, described above. Again the curé's afterthoughts provide a necessary coda to the dialogue. He realises that the *doyen,* well-known for his vigorous opposition to 'les jeunes prêtres démocrates' (p. 1086/97), must put him in that category. But he is no left-wing revolutionary, no socialist priest resentful of the rich for economic reasons. He does not support class revolution, but rather a revolution of values; not the redistribution of wealth, but its relegation below the criterion of true nobility. It would be easier for him to swear allegiance to a prince or a king, deriving his authority from God through the social contract of medieval Christendom, than to a millionaire: 'La notion de richesse et celle de puissance ne peuvent encore se confondre, la première reste abstraite' (p. 1086/98).

The cycle of dialogues on poverty is completed by the encounter with Delbende, who declares that 'il ne devrait plus y avoir de honte à être pauvre' (p. 1095/108), and demands action from the Church to reverse the places of rich and poor within its structures. The curé, however, in a last reflective passage on the theme, argues that the kingdom of God is not of this world. Efforts to eradicate poverty are misguided, for the poor man lives, not on equality, but on the charity due to him by virtue of his poverty. Charity, he muses: 'Quel mot sublime' (p. 1104/120). And he resumes the dilemma thus: 'Problème insoluble: rétablir le Pauvre dans son droit, sans l'établir dans la Puissance' (ibid.).

This formulation has force and poetic beauty as the curé's sharply honed distillation of the tortured and rambling discourse of his companions. But it may well disappoint today's readers of the novel, conscious of mass poverty on a global scale greater even than the Europe-wide concerns of Bernanos, and who still look to the Church for answers to it. Bernanos, for all his fierce onslaught on the economic corruption of our world, offers no political or economical solution to the problems he poses. He substitutes a mystical and supernatural order for that of society's institutions. As Torcy acknowledges, few poor men will find this strategy reassuring, and they might suspect Bernanos of arguing, incoherently and despite his intentions, in favour of a static paternalist state in which the leaders have the fattest pocket books. The role of the novelist, however, is perhaps best seen as to disturb rather than to offer panaceas. And in the context of this novel, the spiritual nature of the curé's conclusions on his great theme acts as a further pointer as to where the true focus of the novel lies: in a parallel world of which the events and characters described so far are merely the visible shadows. Governments, the *Journal* implies, cannot reverse the world's moral decline. What is needed, as the curé argues in his first few pages, are saints. He does not consciously realise that his own status as both poor man and spiritual child identifies him as the 'petit vacher' who can fill the saint's role in the parish and the world. Yet his destiny is a supernatural one, and every one of his relationships has to be re-read and re-examined in this light.

Select Bibliography

Sections A-C are arranged chronologically, the other sections alphabetically by author. Unless otherwise stated, all French books were published in Paris, and all books in English, and editions with English introduction and notes, in London. *Journal d'un curé de campagne* has been abbreviated to *JCC* throughout.

A. Some Editions of JCC

JCC, in *Œuvres romanesques; Dialogues des Carmélites,* préface par Gaëtan Picon, texte et variantes établis par Albert Béguin, notes par Michel Estève, Bibliothèque de la Pléiade, Gallimard, 1980, pp. 1029-1259.

JCC, préface inédite d'André Malraux, notice bibliographique de Jean-Loup Bernanos. Pocket, 1984.

B. Books by Bernanos, Other than Novels, Referred to in this Guide

La Grande Peur des bien-pensants, in *Essais et écrits de combat,* textes présentés et annotés par Yves Bridel, Jacques Chabot et Joseph Jurt sous la direction de Michel Estève, Bibliothèque de la Pléiade. Gallimard. 1971.

Prefatory Note

References to *Journal d'un curé de campagne* are followed by a double set of page numbers. The first number relates to the preferred critical edition: *Œuvres ro-*

manesques, Bibliothèque de la Pléiade (Gallimard, 1980), edited by Albert Béguin, with notes by Michel Estève and preface by Gaëtan Picon; the second to the Pocket edition (1994), which is the most easily available current paperback edition.

References to other novels and sundry writings by Bernanos, unless otherwise indicated, are to the Pléiade edition, and are followed by one single page number.

References to other books are shown by italicised numbers in parentheses which refer to works in the Select Bibliography.

William S. Bush (essay date 2000)

SOURCE: Bush, William S. "Translator's Introduction." In *Monsieur Ouine,* by Georges Bernanos, translated by William S. Bush, pp. vii-xx. Lincoln, Neb.: University of Nebraska Press, 2000.

[*In the following essay, published as his introduction to a new English-language edition of Bernanos's* Monsieur Ouine, *Bush describes the novel, on one level, "as a disturbing allegory of the end of post-Renaissance European civilization," but he also points out that it is "a highly poetic novel with the interplay of human attraction," a detective novel, and a story of initiation.*]

If any title at all springs to mind when the name Georges Bernanos (1888-1948) is mentioned to an English-speaking reader, it is usually that of his *Journal d'un curé de campagne* (*The Diary of a Country Priest*), to which the French Academy awarded the Grand Prix du Roman in 1936. The probing depths of that prize-winning novel seem to have secured Bernanos's reputation among English-speaking readers as "the novelist of the priestly soul."

Nor has the success of Bernanos's one play, *Dialogues des carmélites* (*The Carmelites*), best known in English-speaking countries in its operatic adaptation by Francis Poulenc, contributed to dispelling the too facile dismissal of Bernanos as a mere "French Catholic novelist." Even when placed in that very restrictive category, there is often a certain hesitancy to view Bernanos as equal to his more frequently cited contemporary François Mauriac. Certainly it would be hard to find an English-language critic declaring that the author of *The Diary of a Country Priest* was "the greatest novelist of his time."

André Malraux, who thus spoke almost thirty years after Bernanos's death, had by that time distinguished himself as de Gaulle's minister of culture. Neither a believer, nor inclined to favor Catholic novelists, he was

in his own right a novelist of no mean distinction. In his own time critics referred to his *La Condition humaine* as one of the ten great novels "of all time."

That Malraux's time was the time of Bernanos as well as of novelists such as Gide, Mauriac, Giraudoux, Green, Sartre, Camus, Céline, and Genêt only adds weight to the importance of his assessment. The usual Anglophone dismissal of Bernanos as "nothing more than a Catholic novelist" would seem seriously called into question when a novelist-critic such as Malraux evaluates Bernanos as "the greatest novelist of his time" after thirty years of mature reflection.

From the beginning there were indications that Bernanos was by no means just another Catholic novelist. In 1926, some fifty years before Malraux's remark, when Bernanos's first novel, **Sous le soleil de Satan,** burst on the French literary scene as a bestseller, Léon Daudet, the son of Alphonse Daudet and an acclaimed novelist himself, had compared Bernanos's genius to that of Proust.

Part of the reason the English-speaking world has not taken Bernanos's work more seriously may be that, to date, **Monsieur Ouine,** his greatest novel, has remained virtually unknown. Yet **Monsieur Ouine** is the only one of the author's eight novels that he himself ever dubbed his "GREAT NOVEL." Repeatedly he inscribed these two proud words in bold capital letters on the covers of the copybooks containing his first drafts for this singularly ambiguous, mysterious, and highly paradoxical masterpiece. Indeed, because of its rather startling narrative structure, certain critics have insisted on viewing Bernanos's GREAT NOVEL as a precursor of the "new novel."

The circumstances surrounding the publication of the first edition of **Monsieur Ouine** in Brazil in 1943 (Rio de Janeiro: Atlantica) contributed nothing to assuring the novel's success in English-speaking countries. That highly faulty text was the only one available when Geoffry Dunlop translated it in 1945 under the title of **The Open Mind** (John Lane/The Bodley Head, London). Revealed ten years later to be not only bristling with errors but also missing entire pages, that original French text, reprinted in Paris in 1946, was never proofread by the author, preoccupied as he was with the war, the future of France, and the fate of Christian civilization.

Moreover, Geoffry Dunlop's rather idiosyncratic English rendering of that faulty French text published in Brazil a half century ago, in addition to being long out of print, would seem to do little to make this difficult novel more accessible to today's vast, international English-speaking public or enhance Bernanos's stature among English readers.

It was Bernanos's literary executor, the eminent Swiss critic Albert Béguin, who spotted the problem with both the 1943 Brazilian edition and its Paris reissue in 1946.

Working from Bernanos's final fair copy, he replaced those earlier texts in 1955 with a text published by the Club des Libraires de France, universally regarded today as the only valid one. Prior to the present translation, however, it has never been put into English.

As one of the century's more astute critics, Albert Béguin was fascinated by the extraordinary qualities of *Monsieur Ouine*. He consistently defended it as Bernanos's masterpiece, maintaining that in *Monsieur Ouine* Bernanos had gone the furthest yet in pursuing his creative vision, risking in this attempt at literary grandeur far more than in any of his other seven novels.

Begun in France in February 1931 and completed in May 1940, *Monsieur Ouine* was continually rewritten, revised, and rewritten as Bernanos worked on its composition over almost a decade. *Monsieur Ouine* should have appeared as the author's fourth novel, following *Sous le soleil de Satan* (1926) (*The Star of Satan*), *L'Imposture* (1927) (*The Impostor*), and *La Joie* (*Joy*) (Prix Femina for 1929) but was repeatedly set aside to be taken up again as the author completed four further novels. This accounts for its being completed only in May 1940, in Brazil, a whole ocean away from France and on the very day Hitler launched his forces against France, as Bernanos himself remarked. From Pirapora, deep in the Brazilian interior, the author wrote Charles Ofaire, his Swiss-German publisher in Rio de Janeiro, on 10 May 1940 that he had just completed the last page of his GREAT NOVEL.

Thus Bernanos finally concluded that singular work that he had stubbornly refused to bring to term before the end of its long, nine-year gestation, much to the despair of his publisher, family, and friends. He had asked only to be left in peace, all the way to the end, to "dream out" this, his oneiric masterpiece. Even though it meant financial disaster and almost a decade of largely hand-to-mouth, nomadic existence for his long-suffering wife and six children, he consistently refused to be hounded into finishing it. He thus produced his last four novels, as it were, on the side during those nine years of "dreaming out" *Monsieur Ouine*. These works consisted of a crime novel entitled *A Crime* (1935), dashed off in haste for quick and much needed funds; the justly celebrated *Diary of a Country Priest* (1936); the short stylistic jewel *Nouvelle Histoire de Mouchette* (1937; *Mouchette*); and a posthumously published work, also begun in 1931, then abandoned for *Monsieur Ouine*: *Un Mauvais Rêve* (1950; *Night Is Darkest*). But the long, imposing final chapter of *Monsieur Ouine*, describing the character's enigmatic, dreamlike death, was to come only after he had written all these. In its subtly ambiguous and hauntingly pregnant pages is cloaked Bernanos's definitive vision as a great novelist. *Monsieur Ouine*'s last great scene describes an adolescent boy magnetically drawn to his suspect master's deathbed like a fascinated frog fatally fixed by a snake.

The curious juxtaposition the author made of this final chapter with the fall of France in 1940 serves as a clue to the deeper significance Bernanos attached to *Monsieur Ouine*. Thus *Monsieur Ouine* may perhaps best be read as a disturbing allegory of the end of post-Renaissance European civilization. Bernanos describes, with searing accuracy, what he believed to be the cancer devouring Western civilization. And that civilization, he would undoubtedly still remind us today, is not totally unlike the body of a machine-quickened patient in the terminal ward of a modern hospital, kept alive by forces extraneous to itself. Many European countries, even while prospering materially, are unable today to maintain their population, just as, for centuries now, Europe, with its touted material progress and technological advances, has been unable to raise—let alone conceive—any pinnacle of spiritual beauty to rival the Cathedral of Chartres.

Such were the matters Bernanos was prone to dwell upon, explore, and seek to understand in his many volumes of essays. In *Monsieur Ouine,* however, certain of Bernanos's preoccupations are made flesh. They are incorporated into the novel's intricate fabric as characters conversing and interacting with one another.

The setting for this high allegory is the familiar and humble one the author chose for his best-known novels: a fictitious village in the Pas-de-Calais region of northern France. This was the part of France Bernanos knew best as a boy because his Parisian family had acquired a large country home at Fressin, hard by the battlefield of Agincourt. There the boy, freed from the restrictions of life in a Catholic boarding school, spent his summers and holidays, exploring the woods and lush countryside.

In *Monsieur Ouine* the fictitious village is called "Fenouille" and is mysteriously subject to the troubling presence of the character of Monsieur Ouine, a retired professor of modern languages, now a permanent guest at the neighboring chateau of Wambescourt. The eponymous hero's unusual name conveys to the reader the character's perverse penchant for saying "yes" and "no" (*oui* and *ne*) at the same time. Such indeed had become the raison d'être of this former professor of modern languages, author of a work on pedagogy.

Moreover, saying yes and no simultaneously was a characteristic Bernanos ascribed in particular to his celebrated contemporary André Gide. When he began his GREAT NOVEL he confided to his young disciple, Dr. Jean Bénier, that he was going to write "the strongest thing yet against Gide." Indeed, Bernanos was deeply concerned by his contemporaries' deep-seated inability to distinguish between yes and no, an inability, Bernanos maintained, encouraged by Gide's outlook on life.

Taken into the chateau of Wambescourt by the rather dull local squire, Anthelme de Néréis, Monsieur Ouine soon rules the life of both Anthelme and his eccentric, outlandish wife, Ginette, dubbed "Woolly-Leg" ("Jambe-de-Laine") by the villagers because of her woolen stockings. The subject of dark gossip, Madame de Néréis dashes about country roads at all hours of the day and night in an open carriage drawn by a gigantic, whinnying mare. The great mare seems a sort of elemental life force, displaying an imposing, ungovernable dynamism. Disaster seems to erupt almost inevitably whenever the carriage of the lady of Wambescourt bursts onto the scene.

As mistress of Wambescourt, Ginette de Néréis, no less than her husband, conveys Bernanos's biting, yet melancholy, image of the old aristocracy, ending its days in inglorious decay in forgotten pockets of the provinces. This decline is accentuated by the dilapidated state of the chateau. Rain pours in, cascading down the stairways like a waterfall. The chateau's disintegration is further underlined by the physical decline of both Anthelme and the dying Monsieur Ouine. A representative of European culture, the old professor is figuratively being clutched, one last time, to the paternalistic bosom of a decaying aristocracy.

Within this framework Bernanos situates his chief protagonist, a fourteen-year-old, fatherless boy, Philippe Dorval, born during the First World War and nicknamed "Steeny." Stifled by the hothouse atmosphere of his female-dominated home in Fenouille revolving around his hypersensitive, widowed mother, Michelle, and her enigmatic English friend, Miss, Steeny is in the midst of an adolescent crisis. In the novel's opening chapter we perceive his visceral revolt, first against Miss's attempts to play physical games with him, then against the secretive, cloying tenderness expressed between Miss and his mother. Ostensibly Steeny's tutor, Miss has brought with her to the secluded, peaceful house in Fenouille the dark, uneasy aura of her own bleak childhood in England. An orphan rescued by a Wesleyan pastor from a disabled, aging soldier-uncle who sexually abused her, she had been sent to good schools, qualifying her for her present post.

On impulse, Steeny follows Madame de Néréis to Wambescourt, where his crisis is only exacerbated. There the dying squire assures him that his father is alive and well and that his mother and Miss have been lying in telling him that his father died in the war. Cast into an irreparable solitude as he looks at life, the forsaken fourteen-year-old finds himself on that fatal night at the chateau yielding to desire's dark seduction. There, in the very shadow of death, Steeny, not totally unwillingly, succumbs to Monsieur Ouine's embrace after falling into a drunken sleep in the old professor's bed.

The events of that tempestuous night subsequently provide the motivation for the upheaval seizing the whole village early the next morning. At dawn the naked body of a young farm boy is found floating in the storm-swollen stream in the woods between the chateau and Fenouille. It is the little cowherd Monsieur Ouine had dispatched from Wambescourt to warn Steeny's mother in Fenouille that the boy was sleeping at the chateau. The nude body bears the marks of strangulation. A search for the assassin is launched.

As Bernanos's poetic prose becomes almost hallucinatory in its power of evocation, he weaves into his plot the obscure story of three members of the strange Devandomme family: the old grandfather, who dreams of descent from the old nobility; his orphaned and crippled visionary grandson, Guillaume, Steeny's one friend and confidant, whom he calls his "soul"; and, finally, the old man's headstrong daughter, Hélène, Guillaume's aunt, who has disgraced the family by her passionate union with an untamed outlaw, the poacher Eugène. It is upon this secretive and mysterious son-in-law of Devandomme that falls the accusation of the unexplained murder.

When the rumor begins to circulate that Eugène the poacher is to be arrested since he had been spotted with the victim that night in the woods, old Devandomme, intent upon avoiding public disgrace, precipitates the suicide of his hated son-in-law and thus, inadvertently, also brings about the death of his daughter. The love between Hélène and Eugène shown in the scene of their double suicide affords us a rare example of Bernanos's powerfully erotic prose, chaste though it may seem at a time when readers have grown used to far less noble, but more explicit, literary expression.

Other violent acts quickly follow the double suicide. Indeed, the whole village seems to seethe and ferment around the little farm hand's body, and the public funeral for the victim takes on epic proportions. Bernanos skillfully weaves many strands into his description of this event, producing a panoramic presentation of a whole social unit bent on a course of self-destruction. The priest's startling refusal to give his blessing at the funeral, the empty rhetoric of the French republic's representative in the person of the inspector of education, and, finally, the emotional collapse of the debauched mayor of Fenouille, kneeling in tears by the little coffin, all lead up to the lynching of Madame de Néréis, who, with her great mare, noisily intrudes into the charged atmosphere of the burial.

Bernanos's presentation of the friendless lady of Wambescourt striding across the cemetery, a predestined victim with whitened face soon to be reddened with her own blood, evokes a clownlike image worthy of a Georges Rouault. Instinctively the villagers sense in her not only an image of France's fading aristocracy but, with it, an image of their own destitution. The suspect lady of Wambescourt thus joins the humble cowherd as she too falls victim to the invisible evil devouring the decaying parish as it moves toward its demise. These elements of self-destruction are even more intensely analyzed in the two following chapters where sexual obsession is probed in the person of the mayor of Fenouille.

Though Bernanos's prose may be chaste, he was a reader of Freud and Jung and far from indifferent to the power of sexuality. In contrast to the almost adolescent concupiscence prominent in the novels of Mauriac and Green, Bernanos moves beyond mere empathy with his distraught characters, questioning, analyzing, and at times even elucidating certain subtle, hidden facets of one of mankind's most mysterious imperatives. One of the author's deepest and most fascinating preoccupations was to show how sins of the flesh can finally turn against the very flesh from which they seem to spring. For he understood that sexual obsession can bring about either physical destruction or else an impotence similar to that of a drug-induced state. The author himself seems to be speaking when he has the priest say to the doctor, regarding the source of the mayor's obsessions: "Rather than the obsession with impurity, you'd do better to fear the nostalgia for purity."

In these later chapters Bernanos uses the ineffectual and pathetic young priest to give us his own disturbing prophecies concerning the world's destitution. For the author understood the human race to be not only fallen, but also radically destitute and unable to save itself from death and disintegration. This conviction is evident throughout his drafts and manuscripts. Indeed, has the poverty of the human race ever been revealed as poorer or more threatening than at the end of the twentieth century when the possibility of annihilation has become generally conceivable, whether from man-made sources or from nature itself where lurk as yet unnamed, unimaginable forces of death?

The mysterious and rather startling resolution in the final panel of Bernanos's tapestry is classical in its stark simplicity: a last encounter between the boy and the dying old professor in a dialogue full of nuances, half-truths, and ambiguities, as well as an occasional deep truth. Steeny's last encounter with Monsieur Ouine may well be read as a sort of allegory of Bernanos himself receiving what he believed to be the last gasp of wisdom to be drawn from European civilization—the civilization that had made him what he was. Thus we find Steeny (Bernanos) nihilistically suggesting that perhaps there is nothing, "absolutely nothing." In response, Monsieur Ouine (civilization), for a brief second, seems to drop all usual ambiguity to reply: "Idiot! If there were nothing, then I would be something, good or evil. It is I who am nothing."

Although the author had at one point thought of calling this novel "The Dead Parish," his emphasis in the end

was not religious, but sociological. Moreover, the social disintegration Bernanos emphasized sixty years ago—drug abuse, alcoholism, child abuse, homosexuality, murder, and suicide—seems startlingly contemporary.

The young priest of Fenouille may seem to be unfairly foreordained for failure, thrown as he is into such a "muck heap," as Monsieur Ouine terms it. Yet in this work, as in his vision of the real world, Bernanos did not hesitate to pit Christianity against two uncompromising realities of modern times: blind faith in science (represented by Malépine, the village doctor) and blind faith in human nature (represented by Arsène, the mayor).

Bernanos's highly lyrical construction of a sociological microcosm of rural French society around 1930 illustrates not only the pathetic surviving remnants of France's old pre-Revolutionary regime portrayed by the decaying aristocracy and impotent church (represented, respectively, by Anthelme and Ginette de Néréis and the floundering curé of Fenouille), but also the post-Revolutionary civil order. Civil society is vigorously represented by the inspector of education (a caricature of the republic's civil idealism, reminiscent of Homais in Flaubert's *Madame Bovary*); by the doctor, high priest of the new religion of scientific progress; and by the still potent but pathetically neurotic mayor, who would like to throw off all Christian restraints to return to a pagan religion that, he imagines, would allow sexual freedom. Against these conflicting social forces Bernanos, in a rare tour de force, patiently traces Steeny's searing personal drama of seeking his lost father as he is initiated into the dark mysteries of adulthood.

Particularly striking in this novel for the first-time reader are certain elements of a murder mystery, launched in chapter 3 when the little cowherd is first mentioned and continuing all the way to the end of chapter 17 where Steeny is still asking: "Who killed the little hired boy?" Bernanos himself refuses to give an answer to this irritating question. Originally he appears to have conceived that the assassin was Monsieur Ouine, since, in the first draft, the doctor discovers a tuft of gray hair in the little cadaver's gripped fist—hair that one would assume belonged to Monsieur Ouine, or else to the mayor, Arsène, or even to Woolly-Leg. In any case, this suppressed clue certainly rules out the implied guilt of the virile, young poacher, Eugène.

Nothing was ever really clear-cut, even in the first draft. Early in the morning after the murder, shortly after the naked little body has been laid out in the village hall, the lady of Wambescourt drives her great mare into the village and, with her usual theatricality, officially accuses Monsieur Ouine of being the murderer. She even brings with her a package of clothing and shoes belonging to the victim, saying that she found them in a closet outside Monsieur Ouine's room. This evidence proves false, however. The dead child was wearing other shoes and other clothing the night before, and the clothes brought in by Woolly-Leg had been abandoned at the beginning of November while the boy was working at the chateau. Yet a haunting question remains: how had the lady of Wambescourt learned, so early in the morning, that the little boy had been murdered during the night?

For the reader who insists upon resolving the murder in Bernanos's novel, all these strange and highly contradictory clues are frustrating. A study of the author's drafts and manuscripts confirms that he consciously pushed the elements of the detective story back into a secondary place. His real goal was symbolic; the murder of an innocent child serves as a symbol of the slaughter of innocents in World War I where, Bernanos maintained, youth had been conscripted and sacrificed for the profit of their elders. Moreover, Bernanos associated the end of Western civilization with the defeat of France in 1940. He realized that his homeland, bled white just twenty years earlier by World War I, but still for him the noblest, most glorious, and most brilliant representative of Christian European culture, had shown herself impotent before the enemy and too anemic to resist another onslaught.

Disillusioned with the European situation, Bernanos and his family immigrated to South America in July 1938. It was in the backwoods of Brazil, where, after a year's search, he had just acquired a large cattle ranch beyond Pirapora, that his darkest suspicions were confirmed: the capitulation of France in 1940 and the signing of the armistice with Germany. Moreover, within months of acquiring his property and his herds, Bernanos suddenly found himself deprived of the needed personnel for running his ranch: his two older sons, his nephew, and his young disciple, Dr. Jean Bénier, had answered General de Gaulle's appeal to fight with the Free French and returned to Europe.

Forsaken and alone, the aging Bernanos, crippled since a motorcycle accident in 1933, was obliged to bury his dream of becoming a prosperous rancher. Unable to fight except with his pen, all he wrote in Brazil, apart from the last chapter of *Monsieur Ouine,* and particularly during those dark years of the occupation of France, were essays and articles devoted to sustaining French morale and trying to vindicate French Christian honor.

Underneath his voluminous writings on France there lurked a searing, prophetic insight into the future demise of Europe. Bernanos would probably say of what survives of European civilization today exactly what he has Monsieur Ouine say in describing Fenouille to the curé: "A bazaar, a fair, where everything, be it good or evil, is spread out pell-mell on display, in the most hideous disorder." Could a better description be given of what an ever increasing proportion of the world's inhabitants consumes nightly thanks to that great leveler of late-twentieth-century society, television, and, more recently, that much touted panacea, the Internet?

Already in the 1930s, in *Monsieur Ouine,* Bernanos seems to predict today's refugees and boat people, warning us that the footsteps of the starving and dispossessed would soon make the whole world tremble. In his posthumously published novel *Night Is Darkest,* written during the same period, he also foresaw the time when Christmas stockings would be filled with drugs and hypodermic needles. It is, however, in *Monsieur Ouine* that he makes his most striking prediction. Bernanos foresaw that modern medicine would be powerless to contend with the number of suicides caused by the survival of humanity's inner nostalgia for something for which it shall have forgotten both the concept and the word: purity. For long after the death of the concept, long after the disappearance of the word, the instinct, Bernanos insists, will secretly survive in the depths of the human heart. There, unexpressed and inexpressible, it will fester. "An epidemic of suicides" will result as people, violently driven by an inarticulate self-hatred, shall seek to destroy both themselves and others.

Monsieur Ouine is many things at once. It is a sociological study, yet it is also a highly poetic novel with the interplay of human attraction, as in life itself—be it asexual, heterosexual, or homosexual—potently at work. From its opening pages Bernanos relentlessly traces the impact of child abuse as it is perpetuated into adult life. Above all it may be seen as a novel of initiation, describing an adolescent's rite of passage into adulthood. As a novel of initiation, *Monsieur Ouine* achieves a nobility and diffused subtlety difficult to find in modern literature save in such rare examples as William Faulkner's vintage legacy, *The Reivers.*

Finally, to the extent that George Orwell's *Animal Farm* and *1984,* or even Aldous Huxley's *Brave New World,* may be viewed as prophetic novels, so too *Monsieur Ouine* may be looked upon as prophetic. Yet none of these elements, nor any imagined combination of them, can convey the poetic finesse or innovative delicacy with which Georges Bernanos wove the many dark strands of life into the rich, hallucinatory tapestry he called his GREAT NOVEL.

Bernanos once wrote in a dedication of a copy of *Monsieur Ouine* that he wanted hope to burst forth from this dark, chaotic book, just as light had burst from the chaos of precreation. It is the translator's hope that the presentation of the complete and corrected text of Bernanos's GREAT NOVEL, by elucidating the complexity and richness of the author's rare genius, may also give the English-language reader a better understanding of André Malraux's startling assessment that Bernanos was "the greatest novelist of his time."

Michael R. Tobin (essay date 2007)

SOURCE: Tobin, Michael R. "A Spiritual Testament: The Art (1940-1948)." In *Georges Bernanos: The Theological Source of His Art,* pp. 185-99. Montreal: McGill-Queen's University Press, 2007.

[*In the following essay, Tobin interprets Bernanos's* The Carmelites *in the context of France's "indignity" during the German occupation of World War II, saying that the work "embraces all of the themes of his wartime and postwar essays: liberty, justice, and, most of all, honour."*]

Bernanos's patriotism had a chauvinistic edge. In 1942, for example, he publicly addressed his countrymen with the words: "Europe is you—you are Europe" (**Oe III** [*Essais et écrits de combat Volume II*] 390). Even after the rout of 1940 and the stigma of the Vichy collaboration, he partially exonerated his homeland, as he did in 1947 during a lecture in Switzerland, by declaring that France had been betrayed by her intellectual elite. He felt sure that the singular destiny of the French people was nonetheless intact. France's travails had caused him terrible anguish, of course, but his faith in his country remained steadfast because his patriotism was essentially an article of faith, an unwavering religious conviction: "Oui l'idée de patrie est une idée religieuse, que le christianisme a surnaturalisée tout entière" [Yes, the idea of the motherland is a religious idea that Christianity has completely supernaturalized] (**Oe III** 1275). During the immediate postwar years, this credal patriotism would allow him frequently to declare, however great the evidence to the contrary, that France would stand alone against the culture of technology and "la production sans limite pour la destruction sans mesure" [the infernal cycle of production without limit for destruction without measure] (**Oe III** 1283). French people would never seek their salvation in Robot Heaven.

What was needed, he felt, was a total restoration of honour, to expunge the "spirit of Munich," forever, first from among the French, and then, through them, from Western culture at large. Bernanos knew that such a renaissance was not imminent, and was certain that he would never live to see it (**Oe III** 4), but the seeds would surely be sown, as the painful time of deterioration would then give way to a new harvest in the hearts of Europeans. Such was the ineluctable destiny of France. In his mind, it had been called as a nation to save Christendom: "L'honneur français est un honneur chrétien, notre honneur est un honneur baptisé" [French honour is a Christian honour, our honour is a baptised honour] (**Oe III** 26). But how was all this to come about?

In 1962 the distinguished scholar William Bush mentioned in passing that Bernanos's polemical writings, particularly those that date from later than 1940, must be understood in the light of a close reading of *Dialogues of the Carmelites*[1] (*Souffrance* 199). I would add to this lucid insight that the obverse is also true; that is, the *Dialogues* [*Dialogues of the Carmelites*] only become intelligible after one has pored over the several thousand pages of wartime and postwar journalistic prose. When, for example, the heroine of *Dialogues,* Blanche de la Force, humiliated by her cowardice, avows her proposed bargain with God: "Je lui sacrifie tout, j'abandonne tout, je renonce à tout pour qu'il me rende l'honneur" [I sacrifice everything to him, I renounce everything so that he might restore my honour] (**Oe I** [*Oeuvres romanesques*] 1583), one hears the unmistakable echo of the polemicist's rallying call. The restoration of honour? Again, by what means? Certainly, none that Blanche, privileged daughter of the Marquis de la Force, could imagine as the play's first scenes unfold.

Dialogues is about honour, but, a very Bernanosian kind of honour. The work takes place during the dark days of the Reign of Terror, a mirror image of Bernanos's own world in its mass destruction, violence, and ruthless depreciation of the human person. When the Revolution's "Representative" and his soldiers invade the cloistered sanctum of the Carmelite nuns at Compiègne, the exchange between the revolutionary fanatic and the prioress is reminiscent of Bernanos's attack upon modern systems, whose agents assume a double role as middle-class gentlemen and killing machines:

LE COMMISSAIRE:

> Le peuple n'a pas besoin de servantes.

MÈRE MARIE:

> Mais il a grand besoin de martyrs, et c'est là un sacrifice que nous pouvons assumer.

LE COMMISSAIRE:

> Peuh! En des temps comme celui-ci, mourir n'est rien.

MÈRE MARIE:

> Vivre n'est rien, c'est cela que vous voulez dire. Car il n'est plus que la mort qui compte lorsque la vie est dévaluée jusqu'au ridicule, n'a plus de prix que vos assignats.

> (**Oe I** 1681)

[THE REPRESENTATIVE:

The people don't need servants.

MOTHER MARIE:

But they have a great need of martyrs, and that is one service we can render them.

THE REPRESENTATIVE:

Pah! In times like these, dying is nothing.

MOTHER MARIE:

Living is nothing, that is what you mean. Because only death matters when life has been so thoroughly cheapened that it has no more value than your revolutionary bank notes.]

Life is deprived of its value precisely at a time when such "values" as the Rights of Man, the Social Contract, Equality, Fraternity, and Liberty are acclaimed in ringing tones. It is not difficult to see the correlation between this fictional portrayal and Bernanos's actual world where democracies had emerged from the war sanguine about the prospects for the United Nations, and while socialists and communists waxed lyrical about equality and justice. Bernanos clearly perceived a relationship of inverse proportions between the grounds for optimistic rhetoric and the circumstances that imperilled its ideals. It is during the very periods of history when civilization waxes the most lyrical about high ideals that the killing Machine is most likely to begin operating.

Had Bernanos not pointed out the irony of the democratic allies formulating the ideals of the Atlantic Charter while their planes were obliterating German cities? Now, in **Dialogues,** the revolutionaries arrive at the convent, first to inspect this house of "superstition," and then to expel the nuns and demolish it. Determined to advance the egalitarianism decreed by their political masters, they raise the spectre of the killing Machine. Mother Marie, however, exasperates the government agents:

MÈRE MARIE:

Vous avez le pouvoir de me contraindre au silence, mais non pas celui de m'en faire une obligation. Je représente ici la Révérende Mère Prieure et je ne recevrai pas d'ordre de vous.

UN COMMISSAIRE:

Sacrée mâtine! On ne lui fera pas fermer son bec, citoyen, mais rappelez-lui que la République dispose d'une machine à couper le sifflet.

(**Oe I** 1639)

[MOTHER MARIE:

You have the power to force me to keep silent, but you cannot compel me to be morally obliged to do so. I represent the Reverend Mother Prioress and I take orders from her alone.

A REPRESENTATIVE:

Sly bitch! We won't muzzle her, citizen, but remind her that the Republic has at its disposal a machine for shutting people's traps.]

Since the modern world approves of force, the reference to the guillotine is not surprising. However, the apparent sincerity of the "citizens," their romantic idealism, seems to conflict with such a ready threat of violence. The nuns' chaplain observes: "Dans les affaires de ce monde, vous le savez, lorsque tout espoir de conciliation est perdu, la force est le suprême recours" ["You know that, in the affairs of this world, when all hope of conciliation is lost, force is the ultimate recourse"] (**Oe I** 1643). Bernanos's sketch in **La France contre les robots** of the decent pilot-cum-family man had already touched on this moral schizophrenia, the conclusion of which was that human beings cannot live with such discrepancies; only robots can. And indeed, the revolutionary Representatives seem drawn from Bernanos's non-fiction depictions of creatures of the modern age who are programmed to be obedient and submissive to the collective will. Without a hint of irony, the Representative lays claim to the moral high ground: "Nous ne connaissons d'autre règle que la Loi. Nous sommes représentants de la Loi" ["We know no other rule than Law. We are the representatives of the Law"] (**Oe I** 1636). Like the imbecile robots of Bernanos's postwar essays, they speak in slogans approved either by the state or by the party. One of them, for examle, imagining that young Sister Blanche's terror results from her being held in the convent against her will, poses as her saviour, spouting all the requisite jargon:

"Assez! je réitère d'avoir à observer la contenance d'un véritable représantant du peuple. (*Il se tourne vers Blanche.*) Jeune citoyenne, ne craignez rien de nous qui sommes vos libérateurs. Dites un seul mot, et vous vous trouverez hors du pouvoir de ceux qui pour mieux vous assujettir n'ont pas craint d'offenser la nature en usurpant jusqu'au nom sacré de Mère. Sachez que vous vous trouvez dès maintenant sous la protection de la Loi."

(**Oe I** 1640)

["Enough! I see before me the countenance of a true image of the people. (*He turns toward Blanche.*) Young citizen, you have nothing to fear from us, we are your liberators. Say but the word and you will be delivered from the power of those who, to better constrain you, have dared to offend nature itself by usurping the sacred name of Mother. Know that you are, from this moment on, under the protection of the Law."]

Later, when Blanche appears before the Revolutionary Tribunal to plead for her condemned father's life, a former servant addresses the judges on her behalf, employing the same officially sanctioned language:

"Citoyens juges, la jeune et intéressante personne qui m'accompagne est la fille du ci-devant. La République vient de la tirer de la main des prêtres qui l'avaient arrachée à son vieux père, pour l'enfouir à jamais dans les geôles du fanatisme et de la superstition . . . La petite citoyenne vient remercier ses protecteurs et ses libérateurs."

(Oe I 1697)

["Citizen judges, the young interested party with me is the daughter of the accused. The Republic has just liberated her from the priests who had snatched her from her father in order to bury her forever in the dungeons of fanaticism and superstition. The young citizen has come to thank her liberators and protectors."]

Two principal themes emerge from this authorized jargon; the first is that a "house of prayer," as Mother Marie calls their convent, poses a danger to the state; the second is the mantra of "Liberty." Hostility toward the inner life is incompatible with the championing of freedom, recalling Bernanos's caveat against a civilization that threatens the spiritual life, without which liberty itself is meaningless.

On one level, at least, the Representatives and the nuns enact the conflict between liberty as a mental abstraction and liberty lived as an actual force proceeding from deep within the human spirit. The verbal sparring between Mother Marie and the chief Representative brings this dimension plainly forward:

LE COMMISSAIRE:

Il n'y a pas de liberté pour les ennemis de la Liberté.

MÈRE MARIE:

La nôtre est hors de vos atteintes.

(Oe I 1642)

[THE REPRESENTATIVE:

There is no liberty for the enemies of Liberty.

MOTHER MARIE:

Ours is beyond your reach.]

Later, the prioress assures the imprisoned nuns that their confinement deprives them only of a superficial freedom, which is in any case of little importance: "Nul ne saurait nous ravir une liberté dont nous nous sommes dépouillées depuis longtemps" ["No one could deprive us of a liberty of which we have, long since, stripped ourselves"] (Oe I 1710).

Only a few months before beginning to writing *Dialogues* during the winter of 1947-48, Bernanos had defined the inner life as that deep point of contact with the divine from which true freedom flows. A brief meditation by Sister Marthe, one of the play's characters, resumes this theme:

Au jardin des Oliviers, le Christ n'était plus maître de rien. L'angoisse humaine n'était jamais montée plus haute, elle n'atteindra plus jamais ce niveau. Elle avait tout recouvert en Lui, sauf cette extrême pointe de l'âme où est consommée la divine acceptation.

(Oe I 1668)

[In the Garden of Olives, Christ was no longer master of anything. Anguish had never before risen to such heights, nor will it ever again. It had overtaken his very being, except for that farthest point of the soul where divine acceptance was consummated.]

Bernanos envisages Christ's encounter with his divinity, deep within his own *human* heart, as an experience of the freedom to say "yes" to an expiative death. In larger terms, He fully accepted his weakness, that is, the the full human experience—in short—his own poverty.

Any pretense of invulnerability is stripped away with brutal realism from the very outset of the *Dialogues*. The death of the old Prioress in the second "tableau," for example, is an occasion of scandal for her community. She has been the mother superior for many years, wise, strong, and a model of religious probity; and yet as death approaches, thirty years of mortification and prayer seem to count for little. Her fear of death prompts an almost pouting, desperate appeal for reassurance— had she not eaten all her soup that day, and hadn't the worst passed? (Oe I 1589). Nature is intent on depriving her of her dignity, and yet she clings to her self-image. A pathetic *amour propre* recoils at the prospect of the other sisters seeing her as limp as a drowned man pulled from the water, as she puts it, but even her wish to be seated in a chair when she receives her community is denied. The old woman tries to console herself with religious thoughts, but the articles of faith nurtured over a lifetime seem ineffectual, and God Himself assumes an unfamiliar form: "Dieu s'est fait lui-même une ombre" ["God Himself has become a shadow"] (Oe I 1598). Acutely aware that she is presenting no ideal model of a good death, she expresses her trust that, in the end, God will stand by her: "J'ai confiance que Dieu ne m'abandonnera pas" ["I am confident that God will not abandon me"] (Oe I 1602). Like Jesus Himself, however, she seems forsaken in a lonely darkness. Her final vision of desolation proves to be prophetic for the community as a whole, and, believing that God has renounced her, she dies in fear and humiliation. The consolation of faith, the fruits of a lifetime of self-discipline and prayer, even simple human dignity, are wrested from her. Yet she is granted a moment of spiritual lucidity that pierces the cloud of fear and permits her to see the glory of her abasement: "Je ne puis donner maintenant que ma mort, une très pauvre mort . . . (*Silence.*) Dieu se glorifie dans ses saints, ses héros et ses martyrs. Il se glorifie aussi dans ses pauvres" ["I have nothing left to give now save my death, a very poor death . . . God glorifies himself in his saints, his heroes and his martyrs. He also glorifies himself in his poor"] (Oe I 1601).

The full weight of poverty crushes the play's young heroine, Blanche de la Force, however. Suffering from a pathological fear of the world beyond her privileged enclave, Blanche has entered the Carmel seeking a refuge. She is shamed by a timidity that earns her the disapprobation, for the most part unspoken, of her religious sisters. Like so many of Bernanos's characters, she suffers the temptation to self-hatred, which her superiors warn her against on at least three occasions: "Le malheur, ma fille, n'est pas d'être méprisée, mais seulement de se mépriser soi-même" ["The tragedy, my daughter, is not in being despised, but only in despising oneself"] (**Oe I** 1702).

Despite, or perhaps because of, her fragile emotional state, Blance seeks admittance to the Carmel by telling the old prioress she comes in search of a "heroic life." The prioress seems not to doubt the ultimate success of such an enterprise, but is prescient and wise enough to understand that God's idea of heroism may well be different from the world's, or indeed from Blanche's: "Ce qu'il veut éprouver en vous n'est pas votre force, mais votre faiblesse" ["What he wishes to put to the test is not your stength, but your weakness"] (**Oe I** 1585). Blanche herself views her emotional paralysis not as a form of poverty, but as something to be overcome. Because her understanding of poverty is limited to her acquaintance with the privations and mortifications of Carmelite life, she naively declares to the prioress: "Je n'ai pas peur de la pauvreté" ["I have no fear of poverty"] (**Oe I** 1601). The aged superior responds with a wisdom that Blanche will come to share only in the nick of time: "Oh! il y a bien des sortes de pauvreté, jusqu'à la plus misérable, et c'est de celle-là que vous serez rassasiée ["Oh! there are many kinds of poverty, including the most wretched, and that's the kind you'll have your share of"] (**Oe I** 1601). When the nuns are expelled from their convent by order of the Republic, putting their lives in mortal peril, their chaplain, a fugitive and clandestine visitor, expands on the mystery of poverty in his Good Friday sermon:

> "Le Seigneur a vécu et vit toujours parmi nous comme un pauvre. Le moment vient toujours où Il décide de nous faire pauvres comme Lui, afin d'être reçu et honoré par les pauvres, à la manière des pauvres, de retrouver ainsi ce qu'Il a connu jadis tant de fois sur les routes de Galilée, l'hospitalité des misérables, leur simple accueil. Il a voulu vivre parmi les pauvres, Il a aussi voulu mourir avec eux. Car ce n'est pas comme un Comte à la tête des hommes de sa ménie qu'Il a marché vers la mort, c'est-à-dire vers Jérusalem, le lieu de Son sacrifice, dans ces sinistres jours qui précédèrent la pâque. C'était parmi de pauvres gens qui, bien loin de songer à défier personne, se faisaient tout petits, afin de passer inaperçus le plus longtemps possible . . .

> Faisons-nous donc aussi maintenant tout petits, non pas, comme eux, pour échapper à la mort, mais pour la souffrir, le cas échéant, comme Il l'a soufferte Lui-même."

> (**Oe I 1659**)

["Our Lord lived, and continues to live among us, as one of the poor. The time always comes when He decides to make us poor like Himself, so that He might be received and honoured by the poor as one of them, so that He might thereby rediscover what, long ago, He so often experienced on the roads of Galilee—the hospitality of the destitute, their simple welcome. He wanted to live among the poor, and He wanted to die among them too. For it was not as a nobleman at the head of his troops that He marched toward death, that is toward Jerusalem, the place of His sacrifice, during those sinister days that preceded Easter. He walked with the poor who, far from wanting to stand up to anyone, made themselves little, so as to pass unnoticed for as long as possible . . . Let us now make ourselves very little, not like them, to escape death, but, if necessary, to suffer it as He Himself suffered it."]

The poverty the priest speaks of is not, of course, material, since the Republic could no more deprive the nuns of their riches than of their liberty. He is inviting them to surrender to human weakness by joining it to Christ's own. Even before their expulsion from the Carmel, during the uneasy days when some still dared hope that the state might leave them in peace, the nature of such a mystical union is pondered and clarified. When, for example, the old prioress lies moribund, her words of disconsolation cannot but evoke the image of Jesus in Gethsemane, in the company of his disciples yet all the more alone:

> "Hé bien, ma Mère, il est vrai que je me vois mourir. Rien ne me distrait de cette vue. Certes, je me sens touchée de vos soins, j'y voudrais répondre, mais ils ne m'apportent aucune aide, vous n'êtes pour moi que des ombres, à peine distinctes des images et des souvenirs du passé. Je suis seule, ma Mère, absolument seule, sans aucune consolation."

> (**Oe I 1597**)

["Ah yes, Mother, it is true that I am watching myself die. Nothing can distract me. Of course, I'm touched by your care, and I would like to return it, but it doesn't bring me any solace. You are now nothing more than shadows for me, barely distinct images, like past memories. I am alone, Mother, absolutely alone, without any consolation at all."]

When she expresses her reluctance to let her contorted face be seen by her "daughters," the two solitudes, human and divine, converge in Mother Marie's response: "C'est peut-être celui de notre doux Seigneur à Gethsémani" ["Perhaps it is our gentle Lord's at Gethsemane"] (**Oe I** 1603). A sublime irony is not lost on the dying woman. We learn that she had entered the convent as a young girl with the intention of being consecrated under the name of "Holy Agony." Only the warnings of

her superior had dissuaded her: "Qui entre à Gethsémani n'en sort plus. Vous sentez-vous le courage de
rester jusqu'au but prisonnière de la Très Sainte Ago-
nie?" ["Whoever enters Gethsemane never leaves it.
Do you have the courage to remain a prisoner of the
Most Holy Agony right to the end?"]

(**Oe I** 1598)

The same irony betrays the mark of Providence when,
many years later, Blanche de la Force requests permission of the now mortally ill prioress to take the religious name "Sister Blanche of the Agony of Christ."
For the old prioress, the name signifies a solitary confrontation with death in the dark abandonment of the
Garden of Olives; for Blanche, it is the summation of a
young life's experience, something she reflects upon in
a conversation with her brother, the Chevalier de la
Force, at the beginning of the play:

LE CHEVALIER:

> Puisque vous vous retirez dans votre appartement, de-
> mandez tout de suite des flambeaux, et n'y restez pas
> sans compagnie. Je sais que le crépuscule vous rend
> toujours mélancolique. Vous me disiez quand vous étiez
> petite: "Je meurs chaque nuit pour ressusciter chaque
> matin."

BLANCHE:

> C'est qu'il n'y a jamais eu qu'un seul matin, Monsieur
> le Chevalier: celui de Pâques. Mais chaque nuit où l'on
> entre est celle de la Très Sainte Agonie.

(**Oe I** 1575)

[THE CHEVALIER:

> Since you are retiring to your rooms, ask for some
> torches right away, and don't stay there without com-
> pany. I know that twilight always makes you melan-
> cholie. You used to say to me when you were little: "I
> die each night so as to rise again each morning."

BLANCHE:

> There has only ever been one morning, Monsieur le
> Chevalier: Easter morning. But each night I enter is the
> darkness of the Holy Agony.]

Bernanos allows the inscrutable wisdom of God to lead
this frightened girl to a religious refuge where she is
soon visited by the Terror.

The last recourse of the world is force, but God's last
recourse is the sacrifice of consecrated souls (**Oe I**
1643). When it becomes apparent that all is lost, Mother
Marie leads her community in taking a vow of martyrdom for the salvation of France and the Carmel.
Blanche is especially on her mind, not because she
fears that the youngest member of the community will
fail in her duty, but because she too perceives in
Blanche's religious name the working of Providence:

> "Dans la bataille, c'est aux plus braves que revient
> l'honneur de porter l'étendard. Il semble que Dieu ait

voulu remettre le nôtre entre les mains de la plus faible
et peut-être de la plus misérable. N'est-ce pas là comme
un signe du Ciel?"

(**Oe I** 1648-9)

["In battle, the honour of carrying the standard goes to
the bravest. It seems to me that God has willed that
ours be put in the hands of the weakest and perhaps the
most wretched. Is it not a sign from heaven?"]

God, who chooses the weak, eschews the wisdom of
the world. Of course, Blanche's road to martyrdom is
not smooth. Her terror doubles, and in panic she flees
the convent disguised as a servant girl and hides in her
father's château, while her religious sisters, with the exception of Mother Marie, languish in prison. But in the
last scene, as the nuns file solemnly toward the guillotine chanting a Latin hymn, Blanche suddenly emerges
from the crowd and joins the doomed procession, the
last to die.

When the nuns had taken their vow of martyrdom,
Mother Marie had spoken to them about their poverty:
they were to be under no illusion that their "poor" lives
were of any great price, and it was the giving, not the
gift, that counted (**Oe I** 1684). Because Blanche's life is
the poorest of all, her oblation is the most pleasing to
God. It is another divine irony that when she tries to
hide from her weakness, it cripples her. When she surrenders to it, she encounters, as Bernanos had written in
1946, the "Pauvre des pauvres, en qui toute pauvreté se
divinise" [Poorest of the poor, in whom all poverty is
divinized] (**Cor III** [Correspondœnce. Volume III
(*Lettres retrouvées*)] 430), and discovers the courage to
resume the terrible pilgrimage from Gethsemane to Cal-
vary. The very structure of *Dialogues* carries Blanche
along in this process of divinization which, as the new
prioress affirms, is the play's theological axis:

> "Lorsqu'on les considère de ce jardin de Gethsémani
> où fut divinisée, en le Cœur Adorable du Seigneur,
> toute l'angoisse humaine, la distinction entre la peur et
> le courage ne me paraît pas loin d'être superflue."

(**Oe I** 1653)

["When one reflects upon them from the point of view
of the Garden of Gethsemane, where all human anguish was divinized in the Sacred Heart, the distinction
between fear and courage seems almost superfluous to
me."]

These dialogues are Bernanos's response to the postwar
obsession with justice. By no stretch of the imagination
does the world applaud the execution of the innocent as
just. Yet, as he had written after the war, justice and injustice mean radically different things to the unbeliever
and to the one who places his faith in the Incarnation
and the divinization of humanity upon the Cross. The
nuns' chaplain points out to them the paradoxical nature of the spiritual economy: "Dans les grands troubles

comme celui-ci, le pire risque n'est pas d'être criminel, mais innocent, ou seulement suspect de l'être. L'innocent va payer bientôt pour tout le monde" ["In troubled times like these, the greatest danger is not being guilty, but being innocent, or even suspected of being so. The innocent will soon pay the price for everybody else"] (**Oe I** 1675). Sister Catherine reminds the others that the Christian perception of justice and injustice springs from Christ Himself: "Le plus innocent et le plus criminel, n'ayant commis aucune faute et répondant de toutes, dévoré par la Justice et l'injustice à la fois, comme deux bêtes enragées" ["The most innocent and the most guilty, sinless yet bearing the burden of all sin, devoured both by Justice and injustice, like two enraged beasts"] (**Oe I** 1669). Christ assumed human culpability as a free act of love, and the theological optique of the **Dialogues** presents God's justice and His love as indistinguishable, the latter informing the former. The nuns enter the mystery of the Incarnation by raising justice to the level of sacrifice, a spiritual sublimation that Mother Marie elucidates for Blanche near the play's end: "Il n'est d'horreur que dans le crime, ma fille, et c'est par le sacrifice des vies innocentes que cette horreur est effacée, le crime lui-même restitué à l'ordre de la divine charité" ["The only truly loathsome thing is murder, my daughter, and it is by the sacrifice of innocent lives that this abomination is wiped away, so that even murder is enfolded by the very love of God"] (**Oe I** 1707).

Dialogues was a fictional expression of Bernanos's mourning for his country after the debacle of 1940, a grief that compelled him to leave aside fiction until the eve of his death. It embraces all the themes of his wartime and postwar essays: liberty, justice, and, most of all, honour. Blanche plausibly represents the France of 1940, debased and an object of scorn. Even Mother Marie, who could well be Bernanos contemplating his country's indignity, is filled with contempt and anger at her own cowardice. Nor is it difficult to see in the old prioress a metaphor for the Motherland, humiliated but still called to spiritual greatness. When Blanche had declared, at the beginning of **Dialogues,** that she would sacrifice anything for the sake of honour, Bernanos had allowed her to pronounce a truth the profundity of which escaped her. The essence of honour is sacrifice.

Only months before beginning this last great literary effort, Bernanos had written: "L'amour de la patrie comme l'amour de Dieu est fondé sur le don volontaire de soi" [The love of country, like the love of God, is founded upon the voluntary gift of self] (**Oe III** 1275). Blanche's honour, as the old prioress tells her, is in the care of God (**Oe I** 1601). So too with France, whose glory, Bernanos was sure, lay not in technological triumph, but in sacrifice; not in power, but in an abandon-

ment to its poverty. The Carmelite tragedy enacted in miniature what happened on a larger scale to France as a whole, with both dramas culminating in self-sacrifice.

Note

1. In 1947 Bernanos's Dominican friend, Father Bruckberger, asked him to write the script for a film based upon Gertrude von le Fort's novel *Die Letzte am Shaffot,* which was inspired by an actual historical event, the guillotining of sixteen Carmelite nuns on 17 July 1794. The script that Bernanos produced was not what the producers wanted, and it ended up in the bottom of a trunk, where it was discovered by Albert Béguin after Bernanos's death.

Bibliography

Cor III - Correspondance. Volume III (*Lettres retrouvées*), 1904-1948.

Oe I   - *Œuvres romanesques* (Complete Novels).

Oe III - *Essais et écrits de combat* Volume II.

Bernanos, Georges. *Essais et écrits de combats.* Tome II. Textes établis, présentés et annotés par Yves Bridel, Jacques Chabot, Michel Estève, François Frison, Pierre Gille, Joseph Jurt, et Hubert Sarrazin sous la direction de Michel Estève. Paris: Gallimard, "Bibliothèque de la Pléiade," 1995.

————*La France contre les robots.* Suivi de textes inédits. Présentation et notes de Jean-Loup Bernanos. Paris: Plon, 1988.

————*Œuvres romanesques, suivies de Dialogues des Carmélites.* Préface par Gaëton Picon. Textes et variantes établis par Albert Béguin. Notes par Michel Estève. Paris: Gallimard, "Bibliothèque de la Pléiade," 1961.

Bush, William. *Souffrance et expiation dans la pensée de Bernanos.* Paris: Minard Lettres Modernes, 1962. "Thèmes et Mythes" No. 8.

Ralph McInerny (essay date 2007)

SOURCE: McInerny, Ralph. "Georges Bernanos." In *Some Catholic Writers,* pp. 13-16. South Bend, Ind.: St. Augustine's Press, 2007.

[*In the following essay, McInerny summarizes Bernanos's accomplishments as a fiction writer and essayist, contending that his "novels give us Catholic fiction, not as an interesting sub-genre, but as the only serious viewpoint from which the mystery of human existence can be imaginatively grasped."*]

Only by the recovery of the mystery of the human person, and the sense of the profundity of freedom and human destiny, can the trivialization of human existence be overcome.

Georges Bernanos was 38 years old when his first novel, **Under the Sun of Satan,** was published in 1926. It is a remarkable novel whose power is easily felt by the English reader in the Harry Lorin Binsse translation that appeared in 1949. (An earlier, less effective translation had appeared in 1940.) The prologue is a chilling portrait of evil: The Story of Mouchette.

Mouchette is a sixteen-year-old girl who, when the story opens, is pregnant by a womanizing marquis, a fact she denies to her father, who nonetheless confronts the marquis and is laughed out of the room. That night, Mouchette sneaks out and visits the marquis, anxious to assure him that she did not tell her father. The marquis is puzzled by this. Subtly, subtly, Bernanos opens before us a girl who has chosen to be evil, not simply to act wrongly. She lies, not to save herself or the marquis or her parents but in order to lie. The emotional mutations of this scene with the marquis move plausibly and inexorably to Mouchette's shooting the marquis.

The next set scene presents Mouchette, now three months pregnant, in a doctor's waiting room. We learn that she is now having an affair with the doctor, whom she tries to convince that he is the father of her child. He dismisses this, she doesn't press it, and the scene becomes a cat-and-mouse game, in which the girl toys with a frantic frightened middle-aged man whose wife is upstairs.

No summary can possibly convey the skill with which Bernanos creates this portrait of gratuitous evil. What is the prologue a prologue to? To a portrait of sanctity, of a young country bumpkin priest modeled on the Curé d'Ars.

Moral failure is easier to imagine and to portray than virtue or heroism. Still, many artists have given us convincing, moving, ennobling portraits of heroism. But moral failure is not evil nor is heroism sanctity. Georges Bernanos, from the outset of his literary career, had an almost unique ability to provide his reader with an unforgettable sense of the stakes of life: good or evil, heaven or hell, God or Satan.

This first novel was not a fluke, a unique achievement. **Imposture** (1928), **Joy** (1929), and **Diary of a Country Priest** (1936) continue Bernanos's amazing performance. Hoping to make some money, he tried to write a murder mystery (**A Crime**), but he could not confine himself to the stylization of moral fault, as the genre may seem to require; inevitably, as it seems, the book was transformed into something far more, something profound, something that tapped the very wellsprings of human action.

Who was this man who in his late thirties commenced a literary career of such depth? After service in World War I, Georges Bernanos married and sold insurance in the provinces. Born in Paris, educated by the Jesuits, far right, a member of Action Française and indeed a royalist, he might have seemed an enthusiastic and doctrinaire young man. His war experience and then marriage tilted him in the direction of middle-class respectability. Wife, family, selling insurance—against that background, the novels surprise, even astound.

The truth is that from boyhood, Georges Bernanos's faith permeated his view of life. He was anti-democratic because he felt that modern political life trivialized the human agent, the free, intelligent person whose deeds and decisions in this life are decisive for eternity. His break with Action Française, his subsequent rejection of the Franco cause in Spain (**The Great Cemeteries under the Moon**), display a man who judged politics from a religious point of view, not vice versa.

Looked upon simply as a novelist, Bernanos's work can be seen as a corrective to the banality of much modern fiction. But it is a corrective taken in the name of the importance of the subject of fiction, namely, the responsible human agent with an eternal destiny.

In 1934, aged 46, after suffering an accident that left him lame, Bernanos moved with his family to Majorca in an effort to keep down expenses, and four years later he moved to South America, Paraguay briefly, then Brazil. Thus it was from exile that this quintessential Frenchmen, whose love of his country survived his disgust with and criticism of its moral and political tone, wrote the great non-fiction polemics which, added to his fiction, make him one of the greatest of French authors.

The Spanish Civil War presented many with a crossroads. Doctrinaire leftists and fellow travelers supported the Republic unquestioningly, a certain kind of Catholic blindly supported Franco. There were noble exceptions among French—and American—Catholics, and none more noble than Georges Bernanos. Living in Majorca, he had close-up experience of what was at issue. The late Thirties, the Second World War, swept Bernanos into a new role as a polemicist. Combative, prophetic, angry, Bernanos spoke from the heart to his countrymen throughout the war and the agony of occupation.

Asked by General De Gaulle, he returned to France in 1945, but he remained unclubbable. The Fourth Republic became the new target of his criticism. He was furious when it was proposed that he put himself forward for the French Academy. He avoided being honored by a society he considered corrupt, even after the crucible of its defeat and occupation.

Such a late work as **France against the Robots,** treating the mechanization of human life, can be read today for its perceptiveness. "A world dominated by power is an abominable world, but a world dominated by number is ignoble." In a society governed by polls, where self-knowledge and self-appraisal are sought through surveys and questionnaires, we are painfully aware of the quantification and false-objectification of human existence. Bernanos did not look to politics, now become the manipulation of citizens, for the remedy of modern ills. Only by the recovery of the mystery of the human person, and the sense of the profundity of freedom and human destiny, can the trivialization of human existence be overcome. Is there any wonder that Pope John Paul II came back again and again to the nature of the human person?

Bernanos foresaw what would happen when humans began to see themselves as robots, as machines responsive to extrinsic causes, their actions mere reactions. Nowadays even bishops speak of the misbehavior of the clergy, for example, as corrective by means of counseling, therapy, external causes. The concept of sin, of moral responsibility, has been weakened.

Shortly before he died, in 1948, in a letter to an old friend, Bernanos closed with a remark that sums up his vision of life. "May you feel the sweet presence of Jesus Christ who makes into one reality sorrow and joy, life and death." Bernanos was incapable of an unctuous remark or of pietism. He speaks here—he could not speak otherwise—out of the abundance of his heart. His novels give us Catholic fiction, not as an interesting sub-genre, but as the only serious viewpoint from which the mystery of human existence can be imaginatively grasped.

FURTHER READING

Biography

Speaight, Robert. *Georges Bernanos: A Study of the Man and the Writer.* London: Collins & Harvill Press, 1973, 285 p.

Book-length biographical study of Bernanos that seeks "to situate" his work "in relation to his life, and to introduce him to a public which knows less of him than he deserves."

Criticism

Andrew, Dudley. "Desperation and Meditation: Bresson's *Diary of a Country Priest* (1951), from the Novel by Georges Bernanos." In *Modern European Filmmakers and the Art of Adaptation,* edited by Andrew Horton and Joan Magretta, pp. 20-37. New York: Frederick Ungar Publishing Co., 1981.

Discusses the groundbreaking nature of Robert Bresson's film adaptation of Bernanos's *The Diary of a Country Priest,* noting the steps Bresson took "to challenge the aesthetics of the French filmmaking industry," especially in working counter to the theories of "French quality cinema."

Armus, Seth. "Georges Bernanos, Emmanuel Mounier, and French Catholic Anti-Americanism." In *National Stereotypes in Perspective: Americans in France, Frenchmen in America,* edited by William L. Chew III, pp. 327-50. Amsterdam: Rodopi, 2001.

Compares the "anti-American" writings of the 1930s by Bernanos and fellow French author Emmanuel Mounier, asserting that "the critiques offered by these two writers mirrored the concerns of their generation in that they attacked the spirit of America, rather than the reality, and America came to symbolically represent all that the French had to fear from modernity."

Browne, Nick. "Film Form/Voice-Over: Bresson's *The Diary of a Country Priest.*" *Yale French Studies,* no. 60 (1980): 233-40.

Studies the meaning and effect of director Robert Bresson's use of the "voice-over" device in his film adaptation of Bernanos's *The Diary of a Country Priest.*

Bush, William. *Bernanos' "Dialogues des Carmélites".* Campiègne, France: Carmel de Campiègne, 1987, 23 p.

Identifies Bernanos's departures from historical record in his play *The Carmelites,* claiming that "our admiration for Bernanos' play will only become greater when we understand the essential role it has played in disseminating the story of the Campiègne community's sacrifice and praise of God in the face of the surest destruction."

———. "The Love of God and Human Suffering: Simone Weil and Georges Bernanos." In *The Beauty That Saves: Essays on Aesthetics and Language in Simone Weil,* edited by John M. Dunaway and Eric O. Springsted, pp. 185-96. Macon, Ga.: Mercer University Press, 1996.

Compares Simone Weil's treatment of "the relationship between human suffering and God's love" in her article "The Love of God and Afliction" with Bernanos's consideration of the theme in one of his last lectures, titled "Our Friends the Saints," presented in April 1947.

Céleste, Sister Marie. "Bernanos: A Man of Spirit." *Culture* 21, no. 4 (December 1960): 413-18.

Discusses the development and nature of Bernanos's Christian faith and his decision, early in life, "to give himself entirely to God."

————. "Bernanos and Graham Greene on the Role of the Priest in *The Diary of a Country Priest* and *The Power and the Glory.*" *Culture* 30, no. 4 (December 1969): 287-98.

Compares the portraits of the priest-heroes in Bernanos's *The Diary of a Country Priest* and Graham Greene's *The Power and the Glory,* noting how both men "attain sanctity" through personal suffering and "their devotion to the Church and to souls."

Champigny, Robert. "Spirits in Fiction: The Example of Bernanos." In *The Vision Obscured: Perceptions of Some Twentieth-Century Catholic Novelists,* edited by Melvin J. Friedman, pp. 129-39. New York: Fordham University Press, 1970.

Posits various ways of reading Bernanos's mixture of socio-historical spirits and fictional characters and events in a number of his novels, ultimately ruling out labeling these texts as either parody or sermon, and concluding that it would have been better, for the "coherence and integrity" of his fictional world, if Bernanos had invented his supernatural spirits rather than "rely heavily on socio-historical identification."

Cooke, John E. *Georges Bernanos: A Study of Christian Commitment.* London: Avebury, 1981, 197 p.

Focuses mainly on Bernanos's "polemical works" and assesses the author's Christian ideals, specifically his concept of "*élites,*" those "privileged beings who were specifically chosen by God to assume the task of saving the social organism from spiritual decay," to "give a coherent explanation of his *Weltanschauung,* even though this must remain on the level of a tentative interpretation."

Didier, Pierre. "Bernanos' World." *Yale French Studies* 8 (1951): 101-07.

Outlines Bernanos's treatment of the modern world in his fiction and stresses his "Christian message" as the only cure for the spiritual suffering of modern life.

Dorschell, Mary Frances Catherine. *Georges Bernanos' Debt to Thérèse of Lisieux.* Lewiston, Pa.: Mellen University Press, 1996, 267 p.

Book-length study that attempts to demonstrate the close links between Bernanos's life and thought and the life and acts of the Carmelite nun Saint Thérèse of Lisieux, who died in 1897, when Bernanos was nine years old.

Flower, J. E. *Georges Bernanos:* Journal d'un Curé de Campagne. London: Edward Arnold, 1970, 64 p.

Focuses on Bernanos's handling of the literary elements and "the problems of novel writing" in his masterpiece *The Diary of a Country Priest,* describing the novel as "one of the most complex books to have been written during the first half of this century."

Frohock, W. M. "Georges Bernanos and His Priest-Hero." *Yale French Studies,* no. 12 (fall-winter 1953): 54-61.

Notes the importance of "the priest-hero" in Bernanos's work, claiming that the figure was an "obsessive" focal point of the author, so much so that his interest in the character-type marred the technical artistry of his early novels. Not until he wrote *The Diary of a Country Priest,* Frohock states, did Bernanos successfully integrate the figure into his fiction.

————. "Georges Bernanos (1888-1948)." In *The Politics of Twentieth-Century Novelists,* edited by George A. Panichas, pp. 160-73. New York: Hawthorn Books, Inc., 1971.

Outlines Bernanos's political beliefs revealed in his writings, arguing that while he is often described as "apolitical," he held strong political views throughout his life, many of which, according to Frohock, were "absurd," ill-conceived, reactionary, and even racist.

Gerlach, John. "*The Diary of a Country Priest*: A Total Conversion." *Literature/Film Quarterly* 4, no. 1 (winter 1976): 39-45.

Analyzes filmmaker Robert Bresson's adaptation of Bernanos's *The Diary of a Country Priest,* highlighting especially "the precise nature of Bresson's departure from the techniques of the novel, as well as his paradoxical reproduction of it," to support his claim that the film is "the most successful of all adaptations."

Guers-Villate, Yvonne. "Revolt and Submission in Camus and Bernanos." *Renascence* 24, no. 4 (summer 1972): 189-97.

Compares the central scene of *The Diary of a Country Priest* in which the Countess, being counseled by the priest, rails against God over the death of her son, with that in Albert Camus's *The Plague,* in which the character Rieux "revolts against the idea of a God who would let innocent children die."

Molnar, Thomas. "The Political Thought of Bernanos." *The Review of Politics* 20, no. 2 (April 1958): 225-42.

Traces the development of Bernanos's political thought during his career as a writer, stating that after World War II his fiction and nonfiction "became increasingly preoccupied with the study of three problems": how "to save France from the madness of the modern world"; how "to save the world from the excesses of mechanized civilization"; and how "to save the individual from the pressure of the collectivity and from the state."

Noth, Ernst Erich. "Georges Bernanos 1888-1948." *Books Abroad* 23, no. 1 (winter 1949): 19-24.

Tribute to Bernanos on the occasion of his death in 1948.

————. "The Prophetism of Georges Bernanos." *Yale French Studies* 2, no. 2 (1949): 105-19.
Emphasizes the central role of "prophetism" in Bernanos's work, especially his prose writings, saying that the author is not merely a "visionary" but that he "gives testimony of his own time." Noth adds that Bernanos's "daring lies in his audacity in taking an unyielding stand as a Christian, whatever the consequences."

O'Donnell, Donat. "The Faust of Georges Bernanos." In *Maria Cross: Imaginative Patterns in a Group of Modern Catholic Writers,* pp. 41-60. New York: Oxford University Press, 1952.
Relates Bernanos's depiction of evil and his fascination with satanic characters in his fiction to the Faustian tradition in European literature, stating that his "whole career as a novelist . . . has been a long effort, often hardly coherent, to convey to his readers his own burning conviction of the existence and power of the Devil."

Reinhardt, Kurt F. "Georges Bernanos: *The Diary of a Country Priest.*" In *The Theological Novel of Modern Europe: An Analysis of Masterpieces by Eight Authors,* pp. 93-129. New York: Frederick Ungar Publishing Co., 1969.
Offers a brief biography of Bernanos and discusses what the author himself regarded as his greatest work, *The Diary of a Country Priest,* which Reinhardt says "represents one of those rare instances where a writer finds a fully adequate external form for his inner vision."

Sonnenfeld, Albert. "A Sharing of Darkness: Bernanos and Dostoevsky." *Renascence* 17, no. 2 (winter 1964): 82-8.
Discerns influences of Fyodor Dostoevsky's works and ideas in a number of Bernanos's novels, saying that, in addition to both writers' "predilection for essentially melodramatic plot constructions," there exist "subtler harmonies of intention and execution which may help to explain Bernanos' elective affinity for the Russian master."

Additional coverage of Bernanos's life and career is contained in the following sources published by Gale: *Contemporary Authors,* **Vols. 104, 130;** *Contemporary Authors New Revision Series,* **Vol. 94;** *Dictionary of Literary Biography,* **Vol. 72;** *Encyclopedia of World Literature in the 20th Century,* **Ed. 3;** *Guide to French Literature,* **Vol. 1789 to the Present;** *Literature Resource Center;* *Reference Guide to World Literature,* **Eds. 2, 3; and** *Twentieth-Century Literary Criticism,* **Vol. 3.**

Rebecca Harding Davis
1831-1910

(Born Rebecca Blaine Harding) American novelist, short story writer, essayist, and memoirist.

The following entry provides an overview of Davis's life and works. For additional information on her career, see *TCLC*, Volume 6.

INTRODUCTION

Davis, a pioneer of American realism, is best known for her groundbreaking work, *Life in the Iron Mills,* first published in the *Atlantic Monthly* in 1861. In this novella, which is alternately described as a short story, the author offered a stark depiction of the brutal conditions imposed on factory workers during the Civil War era; in so doing, she became one of the first writers in America to expose the dehumanizing effects of the Industrial Revolution. Throughout her career, Davis anticipated the realistic style, naturalist themes, and social concerns of later American writers, such as William Dean Howells, Kate Chopin, and Stephen Crane. In addition to her indictment of industrial capitalism, she was also one of the first authors to create complex African-American characters and realistically portray racial prejudice and the ramifications of the Civil War. In later writings, she focused on issues pertaining to women's lives, addressing the attitudes and expectations that limited the scope of their freedom and experience. Davis was largely forgotten in the decades following her death, but recent scholarship has affirmed her position as a valuable and revolutionary figure, who broke new aesthetic ground in American literature. Whitney A. Womack, writing in 2005, asserted that "Davis can be understood as participating in an evolving tradition of industrial reform literature," concluding that despite her accomplishments as a writer, she "has too often been dismissed as an anomaly, an oddity in American fiction, left to lurk in the shadows of the canon."

BIOGRAPHICAL INFORMATION

Davis was born June 24, 1831, in Washington, Pennsylvania, to Richard and Rachel Leet Wilson Harding. During the first five years of her life, she lived with her family in Alabama, after which the family moved to Wheeling, Virginia, which is now part of West Virginia. Initially educated at home by her mother and private tutors, the author read avidly, particularly the writings of John Bunyan, Charles Dickens, and Nathaniel Hawthorne. Between 1845 and 1848, Davis completed her formal education at the Washington Female Seminary while living with an aunt in Washington, Pennsylvania. She graduated with highest honors and returned to Wheeling to help her mother manage the Harding household and teach her younger siblings. Over the next twelve years, Davis worked among immigrant laborers and their families in Wheeling and honed her writing skills by working occasionally for the *Wheeling Intelligence.* Her first and best-known work, *Life in the Iron Mills,* appeared in the April 1861 issue of the *Atlantic Monthly.* Following this success, the author produced a second work, *Margret Howth,* which was first serialized in the magazine and then published in book form in 1862. That summer, Davis traveled to Boston, where she was introduced to Oliver Wendell Holmes, Louisa May Alcott, and Ralph Waldo Emerson, as well as her literary idol, Hawthorne. Before returning home, Davis visited Philadelphia to meet an apprentice lawyer, Lemuel Clarke Davis, who had initiated a correspondence after reading her work. They became engaged during the visit and were married on March 5, 1863.

Because Wheeling was situated on the border between the north and the south, Davis had a unique understanding and experience of the Civil War. Her stories, published in the *Atlantic Monthly* during this time, reflect her perspective and awareness of the conflicts and social issues that the war evoked. After marrying, Davis primarily lived in Philadelphia and continued writing. She published the novels *Dallas Galbraith* and *Waiting for the Verdict,* both in 1868, and in 1869 became a contributing editor for the *New York Tribune.* Beginning in the mid-1860s, Davis increasingly produced stories that addressed issues and pressures pertaining to the lives of women, many of which appeared in the *Atlantic Monthly,* as well as *Scribner's Magazine.* After the death of her husband in 1904, Davis began to experience problems with her eyesight, which at times left her unable to read or write, and she moved in with her daughter, Nora. Her autobiography, *Bits of Gossip,* was published the same year as her husband's death, and she produced another seventeen works over the next six years, including essays and short stories. Near the end of her life, Davis moved to Mount Kisco, New York, to live with her son, Richard Harding Davis. On September 29, 1910, the author died of complications due to heart disease.

MAJOR WORKS

In her debut work, *Life in the Iron Mills,* Davis explored naturalist themes ten years before Emile Zola's naturalist writings appeared, and more than thirty years before Stephen Crane's novel *Maggie* marked the rise of naturalism in America. Davis's groundbreaking story describes the harsh environment in which two mill workers struggle for daily survival, without hope for escape. Employing realistic language and authentic vernacular, Davis chronicles the fates of two protagonists in the work: Hugh Wolfe, a sensitive young man with artistic leanings, and his hunchbacked cousin, Deb. While Wolfe hungers for freedom and creative expression, Deb longs for love, but their low wages and poor working conditions determine their descent into a life without hope. Reduced to thievery, Deb is saved from jail by her ties to the Quakers, but Wolfe is eventually imprisoned and commits suicide. In addition to exploring environmental determinist themes in the story, Davis highlights the redemptive power of art, contrasts the moral superiority of the hardworking poor with the self-centered carelessness of the wealthy, and promotes the idea of social reform through the recovery of authentic Christian values. In her second major work, *Margret Howth,* Davis focuses on the working class and their struggle for physical and spiritual nourishment. Some scholars have suggested, however, that to appease her editor at the *Atlantic Monthly,* where the novel was first serialized, the author diluted her original intent for the work, which was to be a harsh critique exposing the harmful effects of industrial capitalism on American democracy. The novel follows the plight of the titular heroine, Margret, who is abandoned by her fiancé, Stephen Holmes, for a wealthier woman and forced to take a job as a bookkeeper in a woolen mill to support her ailing parents. Eventually, Holmes realizes that the pursuit of material wealth is inadequate and returns to marry Margret, an ending that some critics have described as a jarring concession to editorial demands. Regardless, Davis explores significant themes in the work, including issues related to poverty and the horrors of American industrial labor, as well as the beauty and spirituality that can be found in the mundane aspects of life.

In addition to longer works of fiction, Davis produced several notable short stories throughout her career, many of which address the significant social issues of her time. "John Lamar," "David Gaunt," "Blind Tom," and "Paul Blecker," all of which appeared in the *Atlantic Monthly* in 1862 and 1863, focus on the question of slavery. In addition to revealing her abhorrence of the practice and taking issue with the sanctioning of war by some mainstream southern churches, Davis treated African-American characters as complex individuals with multifaceted personalities and experiences in these stories, suggesting that as a result of their lower position in society, American women had an innate understanding of the suffering of slaves. While these tales primarily reflect on the interior lives of characters, they are considered among the first to offer a realistic portrayal of the Civil War. Following these works, Davis also began writing stories that reflected her growing concern for issues pertaining to women in American society. "The Wife's Story," published in the *Atlantic Monthly* in 1864, examines the effects of marriage and domestic duties on the female artist's struggle for autonomy and creative expression. Regarded for its depiction of the female protagonist's navigation of consciousness and mediation of public and private spheres, the story describes the guilt and fear she experiences in her attempt to balance familial responsibility and her commitment to her art. "In the Market," published in *Peterson's* magazine in 1868, also focuses on the ramifications of marriage. The protagonist, a resourceful and independent woman, rejects marriage as "legal prostitution" until she is able to enter a union of equal partnership. Many of the stories collected in *Silhouettes of American Life* (1892) also feature strong female protagonists. A woman's resilience, faith, and generosity are portrayed in "At the Station," while "The Doctor's Wife" depicts an unconventional young woman, who is able to transcend the class-consciousness and narrow-mindedness of those around her. Despite Davis's focus on the complexities of the female perspective and experience, some scholars have argued that she is not a feminist writer, noting that her female characters often possess traditionally feminine traits, such as self-sacrifice, compassion, and a sense of duty, and that many of her stories reinforce the idea that marriage and motherhood are a woman's primary vocation.

CRITICAL RECEPTION

With the publication of her first work, *Life in the Iron Mills,* in 1861, Davis drew considerable popular and critical attention. The author's daring depiction of poor working-class conditions in the narrative had a profound effect on the eastern intellectual community and garnered notice from major literary figures of the time, including Nathaniel Hawthorne, Ralph Waldo Emerson, and Louisa May Alcott. Having also won the admiration of James T. Fields, the editor of the *Atlantic Monthly,* Davis was able to publish her first full-length work of fiction, *Margret Howth,* in the magazine, and then in book form in 1862. While the novel was generally admired, some critics suggested that Fields's influence on Davis, as well as the author's desire to market her work, may have resulted in a dilution of the stark, realistic themes in the novel. Indeed, while some commentators of her time dismissed sentimental turns in Davis's writing, for which Fields may have been responsible, other contemporaries were repelled by the harsh realities that some of these writings conveyed, particularly those pertaining to the Civil War. Over the next several decades, Davis continued to write, producing over five hundred fiction and nonfiction pieces, many of which were published in the most influential journals of the period, such as the *Atlantic Monthly, Harper's, Peterson's* and *Scribner's.* Nevertheless, her reputation waned as the years progressed, and she was increasingly overshadowed by the successful career of her journalist son, Richard Harding Davis. By the time Davis published her memoir *Bits of Gossip* in 1904, she had been largely forgotten. After decades of neglect, Davis and her writings once again gained notice during the 1970s, after the Feminist Press reissued *Life in the Iron Mills* in 1972, along with an essay by author Tillie Olsen, who described the work as a "rediscovered classic."

Since the 1970s, interest in Davis's literary contributions has increased dramatically. The author's seminal work, *Life in the Iron Mills,* has remained a primary focus for many scholars, including John Conron and Jean Pfaelzer, the latter of whom contended that the novella "must be reconsidered as a central text in the origins of American realism, American proletarian literature, and American feminism." Some commentators, however, have examined Davis's often-neglected works, including her fiction and nonfiction produced later in her career. In her 1991 survey, noted Davis scholar Sharon M. Harris challenged dismissals of the author's late novels, stories, and essays, describing them as "well-written, insightful commentaries on the end of the nineteenth century," which "move into the modern period both artistically and thematically." Other critics have focused on the complex formal and thematic elements of Davis's work. While Jane Atteridge Rose and Michele L. Mock studied the author's interaction with feminist issues and the theme of creative expression, Kenneth W. Noe stressed Davis's contributions as a local colorist. In the late 1990s and early 2000s, Pfaelzer, Susan V. Donaldson [see Further Reading], and Sara Britton Goodling explored the tensions between realism and sentimentalism in Davis's writings. In her seminal 1996 book-length study of Davis, Pfaelzer suggested that the author employed sentimental themes and motifs in such works as *Margret Howth* to mitigate the "masculine" realist form and "romantic egoism" prevalent at the time, and to show that "if political hunger is not regulated by family, love, and the female definition of true community, it could degenerate into a destructive and hungry egoism that uses others as it promotes its unful-

filled desire in the name of social progress." Conversely, Donaldson, writing in 1998, demonstrated how Davis treated "the inadequacy of sentimentalism" and promoted the social benefits of realism in her works. As a result of these and other recent studies, Davis's standing in American literary history has been reassessed, such that she is increasingly respected as an innovative writer who offered an authentic and original portrait of the social concerns of her time. Writing in 1999, Janice Milner Lasseter claimed that in "her unprecedented depiction of the grim lives of the working class, Davis inaugurates literary realism twenty years before those usually credited for its advent." Lasseter concluded that from her "insights into the human condition, Rebecca Harding Davis learned to invest the commonplace with an imagination that captured the history, the national character, and the social issues of her own time."

PRINCIPAL WORKS

Margret Howth (novel) 1862
Dallas Galbraith (novel) 1868
Waiting for the Verdict (novel) 1868
John Andross (novel) 1874
A Law Unto Herself (novel) 1878
Kent Hampden (novel) 1892
Silhouettes of American Life (short stories) 1892
Doctor Warrick's Daughters (novel) 1896
Frances Waldeaux (novel) 1897
Bits of Gossip (reminiscences) 1904
Life in the Iron Mills; or, The Korl Woman (novella) 1972
Life in the Iron Mills, and Other Stories (novella and short stories) 1985
A Rebecca Harding Davis Reader (novella, short stories, and essays) 1995
Rebecca Harding Davis's Stories of the Civil War Era (short stories) 2010

*This work was originally published as "Life in the Iron Mills" in the *Atlantic Monthly* in April, 1861.

CRITICISM

John Conron (essay date fall 1980)

SOURCE: Conron, John. "Assailant Landscapes and the Man of Feeling: Rebecca Harding Davis's *Life in the Iron Mills.*" *Journal of American Culture* 3, no. 3 (fall 1980): 487-500.

[*In the following essay, Conron examines Davis's treatment of the effect of "the industrial landscape" on "the man or woman of feeling" in* Life in the Iron Mills,

*contending that in this work, Davis opts for "moral re-
form" of the "failed men of feeling" rather than "for
legislation or revolt to alleviate the assailant-victim relationships of the industrial environment."*]

Less than three decades after Hawthorne's visit in 1839
to the lime kilns of western Massachusetts and little
more than a decade after he published "Ethan Brand" in
1850, Rebecca Harding Davis, an avid reader of Hawthorne, sketched in *Life in the Iron Mills* (1861) her
native city of Wheeling, West Virginia: an industrial
landscape both more extensive and more massive in its
human impact than that of the kiln in the Berkshires.
The "gleam of fierce firelight flicking" through the
chinks and crevices of Hawthorne's stone tower became, in Davis's story, "a city of fires" giving off an
ugly, dark, enervating effluvium. In the figures of Hugh
Wolfe, a furnace-tender, and Deborah, his hunch-backed
cousin and a cotton mill worker, she introduced more
representative social types of the industrial worker than
Ethan Brand. In the figures of Kirby, Doctor May, and
Mitchell ("the pocket," "the heart," and "the mind of
the world"), moreover, she began to formulate the perception of industry as not only a physical, but also a social environment, for these figures appear in the story
as the perpetuators of "a vast machinery of system by
which the bodies of workmen are governed, that goes
on unceasingly from year to year."[1]

The differences between "Ethan Brand" and *Life in the
Iron Mills* suggest not only a quantum leap in the development of industrial technology, but also a transitional moment in the evolution from romantic to realist
perceptions of the industrial landscape. Even the pictorial vocabulary shows signs of this change. Where
"Ethan Brand" is a sequence of painterly portraits and
genre landscapes (or tableaux), *Life in the Iron Mills,*
with its harsh, gritty images and the elaborately senti-
mentalized gestures of its characters, seems more like
an early silent film.

The two fictions nevertheless share a vocabulary of images and sensations with which they enact remarkably
similar dramas of interaction between industrial technology and human identity. In both, industrial technology is to be understood not chiefly from a social or an
historical but from a symbolic perspective—not chiefly,
that is, in terms of power or of the changing relationship between man and machine over time, but in terms
of the relation between human and technological energy.[2] Both testify to the fact that "we invest our machines with our deepest hopes and terrors," mostly our
terrors; that machines "buzz and flash through our
imaginations . . . threaten to destroy us, steal our souls,
trick us into serving them, bewilder and enrage us."[3]
More specifically, Davis's industrial landscape is the
expression of an aesthetic of picturesque sublimity, and
her characters are versions of the man or woman of

feeling. Viewed from a distance, her landscape both
fascinates and horrifies—fascinates because of its sub-
limely mystifying obscurity, vastness and suprahuman
energy; horrifies because its energy deforms both natural and domestic spaces. Experienced up close, this
landscape becomes the relentless assailant of the man
or woman of feeling, who is defined largely as the psychic victim of its assault. With qualifications about the
degree and nature of the assault, the same may be said
of "Ethan Brand."[4]

At the same time, the significant differences between
the two demonstrate that the symbolic is not, finally,
separable from historical or social perspectives. Where
Hawthorne may be said to dramatize the Romantic's
fear that human consciousness is victimized by becoming too much like the industrial energies it serves, Davis
dramatizes the more pervasively modern fear that both
the landscape and the human body are deformed and
drained and the human consciousness repressed,
dwarfed, corrupted by these energies.[5] This evolution in
symbolic meaning, in turn, carries with it potentially
enormous ideological implications. The industrial forces
associated with Brand's degeneration have an air of
tragic and inevitable fatality, and Hawthorne's laissez-
faire individualism makes Brand more clearly their accomplice than their victim. Those associated with
Wolfe's degeneration, on the other hand, are at least in-
termittently related to a system which, controlled by
men, can be changed by men to alleviate the damage
they cause.

On closer reading, however, the central landscape of
Life in the Iron Mills, the mill itself, reveals a diffuseness of imagery suggesting that it had not come into
sharp focus for Davis, perhaps because she did not have
a worker's intimacy with it, perhaps because—ahead of
her time—she could neither find nor fully invent the
new pictorial vocabulary which it demanded. (That she
brought American fiction into landscapes peripheral to
the mill itself is evident in the stunningly evocative
sketches which begin the story.) The diffuseness in turn
engenders an ambiguity which divides the moral from
the ideological significances which she invests in her
industrial landscape, undercutting both. And that ambiguity carries over into the characterization of Hugh
Wolfe and into the plot itself, which dramatizes Wolfe's
final act of resistance against his assaultive industrial
environment as paradoxically both necessary and corrupt. Prophetic as it is of realist perceptions of the industrial environment which emerged in the 1880s and
'90s, *Life in the Iron Mills* is thus a work between eras
aesthetically, morally and ideologically.

Like so many of the reform movements which emerged
in the 1840s and '50s (there are, indeed, traces of abolitionist, nativist, temperance and feminist sentiment in
the story, as well as the more overt concern for the con-

dition of the working class), the reformist impulse underlying *Life in the Iron Mills* is divided between a sense of the need for moral reform of individuals and that of the need for social reform of oppressive human environments, between a kind of laissez faire and a social activist approach to the problems created by industrial technology. Troubled by "the gulf of pain and wrong, . . . the underlife of America,"[6] Davis resolves this dilemma in implicit favor of moral reform.

I

Life in the Iron Mills begins with an elaborative sketch of the industrial landscape (11-26), whose perspective shifts from a house on the outskirts of the "city of fire" to the "hovels" of the workers, to its center, the furnaces of the iron mills. Visually, the effect is that of a zoom lens moving steadily in, at street-level, from panorama to close-up. But Davis adds a typically picturesque complexity to this visual logic with the use of three overlayering points of view. There is, first, the perspective of a narrator who is not unlike Rebecca Davis herself: an inhabitant living on the periphery of the landscape; a window-watcher and *flaneur* more than a participant; a woman of cultivated sensibility who both feels and comprehends what she sees—but from a distance—and who acts, like the maker of a documentary, as observer-narrator and advocate for the victims of the assailant landscape. Then there is the perspective of Deborah, one of the maimed, a character robbed of intellection but endowed with a capacity to feel and to comprehend intuitively what is happening to Hugh Wolfe. (Her love for him is one of the casualties of their environment.) Wolfe is, of course, the focal point of the interaction between technological and human energies, a man of feeling first presented as rendered nearly insensate, then brought to a crisis when his "slumbering" inner life is awakened sufficiently to register both the assaults of his environment and the hope for liberation.

In this interplay of perspectives, the landscape is meant to elaborate from a physical into a psychological and a social environment; the manifoldly violent effects of its industrial energies, to be calibrated by a kind of collective consciousness: a distancing intelligence (the narrator's), a sympathetic sensibility (the narrator's and Deborah's), and a dream-haunted bundle of nerves (Hugh Wolfe's).

The landscape of the iron mills first takes picturesquely sublime shape as an atmosphere vast, obscure and powerful—though its effects are anything but exalting. Viewed from the front window of a respectable parlor, a confluence of pollutions darkens and befouls the air like an obscene and permanent storm. From a cloudy pre-dawn sky, "muddy, flat, immoveable," pour natural, human and industrial effluents: rain, the "clammy . . .

breath of crowded human beings," the odor of tobacco being smoked by drunken Irishmen and most of all—"the idiosyncracy of this town"—the "slow folds" of smoke from the iron mills. The smoke deforms as much as it darkens and sours. It settles down "in black, slimy pools on the muddy streets"; clings "in a coating of greasy soot" to the narrator's house, to "two faded poplars" (the disappearing traces of picturesque beautification in town landscaping), to mules with "a foul vapor hanging to their reeking sides," to human faces. It penetrates even the narrator's parlor sanctuary to deform its ikons of genteel sensibility, turning "clotted and black" the wings of a broken angel on the mantel.

From the narrator's back window, there is a view of more pervasive and permanent deformations of the landscape: a river transformed by industrial use, its banks turned into a brick-yard and strewn with rain butts and tubs. The river water reflects an entropic transfer of energies from the natural landscape to the mills—the dominant theme, as well, of the relation of its human inhabitants to the mill. A series of adjectives describing the river, indeed, superimpose on it the image of a familiar human victim: it is "dull and tawny-colored," sluggish, and there is "a look of weary, dumb appeal" on its "negro-like" face as it "slavishly" bears "the heavy weight of boats and coal-barges." (12)

In picturesque characterization human figures are perceived as a kind of interface between a physical environment and an inner life, the energies of the one mirrored in or counterposed against the energies of the other and both of them evoked in expressive details of physiognomy, dress and motion.[7] The effect of the narrator's shift by association from the river out her back window to "the slow stream of human life" moving past her front window is that of a mirror. Between the two streams manifold correspondences appear:

> Masses of men, with dull, besotted faces bent to the ground, sharpened here and there by pain or cunning; skin and muscle and flesh begrimed with smoke and ashes; stooping all night over boiling caldrons of metal, laired by day in dens of drunkenness and infamy; breathing from infancy to death an air saturated with fog and grease and soot, vileness for soul and body.
>
> (12)

Both the natural landscape and its inhabitants are thus pervaded by a force which dominates, deforms and enervates them.

Here and throughout the story, pastoral images—mostly mere memories—sharpen by contrast the effects of the industrial wasteland. Smoke in the parlor saps the dream, "almost worn out," of "green fields and sunshine" (12). "La belle riviere!," the narrator ejaculates in her description of the stained, burdened river (12).

And having related the disfigured stream of men to the river, she heightens the effect of human squalor and constriction with a contrast between the two:

> What if [the river] be stagnant and slimy here? It knows that beyond there waits for it odorous sunlight,—quaint old gardens, dusky with soft, green foliage of apple-trees, and flushing crimson with roses,—air, and fields, and mountains. The future of the Welsh puddler passing just now is not so pleasant. To be stowed away, after his grimy work is done, in a hole in the muddy graveyard, and after that,—*not* air, nor green fields, nor curious roses.
>
> (13)

Much of Hugh Wolfe's mental activity, when it is awakened, expresses itself in pastoral images, but, as if to suggest that the values imaged in them are no longer tenable for industrial workers, Davis shows them to be, for Wolfe, both self-indulgent and futile. Ironically, Wolfe physically enters a pastoral landscape only when he is stowed away, after *his* grimy work is done, in a Quaker graveyard across the river, where "the light lies warm . . . and the winds of God blow all the day" (62). It is only Deborah who makes it alive to the sanctuary of the Quaker community, which meets in "a homely pine house . . . whose windows overlook broad, wooded slopes and clover-crimsoned meadows,—niched into the very place where the light is warmest, the air freest" (63).

The river triggers yet another play of association when the narrator avers that fragments of the story she wishes to tell "float up before me" (13), as if in "secret underlying sympathy between that story and this day with its impure fog and thwarted sunshine" (atmospheric equivalents of the iron workers' mental lives), and it is at this point that she beckons the reader out into "the fog and mud and foul effluvia" of the city in pursuit of the story.

It is when the narrator enters the street and begins to follow Deborah's movements that her images of this industrial landscape—a cellar hovel, the street and the mill itself—begin to grow increasingly diffuse and her sense of their significances increasingly ambiguous.

The relatively brief sketch of the cellar hovel achieves its suggestive power by a stratum of images evoking a place deformed not so much by pollution as by shelterlessness. This "home" for Deborah, her cousin Hugh Wolfe, Wolfe's sick father, and Janey, an Irish neighbor's child whose father is in jail, is a kind of tomb: a dark, dank, chill, underground place, its "earthen floor covered with a slimy green moss,—a fetid air smothering the breath" (16). Unlike the pastoral cottage shared by Bartram and his son in "Ethan Brand," this heatless, underground hovel seems almost to decompose its exhausted inhabitants, turning them flaccid and shapeless.

Deborah's face, when she enters it, is "ghastly, her lips bluer, her eyes more watery" than those of old Wolfe, who lies sleeping on straw (16). Janey's face is "haggard and sickly; her eyes were heavy with sleep and hunger: real Milesian eyes . . . , dark, delicate, blue, glooming out from black shadows" (17-18).

The brief sketch of rainy black streets, as Deborah sets out on them to bring Wolfe his dinner of cold potatoes and ale, extends these impressions of shelterlessness. "Long rows of houses" stretch out miles before her, flickering gas lamps lighting here and there "an uncertain space of muddy footwalk and gutter," "skulking" mill-hands, "an occasional lager-bier shop" (19)—the latter providing the only apparent means of warmth and stimulation.

While these sketches evoke a strong moral sympathy for the characters' domestic problems, the problems are given no clear ideological significance. Only in retrospect does the reader come to see that, like the mill in this city of fires, the houses, too, create an entropic drain of human energies. That they are also directly related to the new industrial economy is never made overtly clear.

The sketch of the mill itself is meant to evoke both ideological and moral overtones. The mill emerges first as a "vast machinery of system," which couples an abstract social organization (the division of "hands" into "watches" on the basis of a twenty-four hour day) to the ferocious energies of the industrial process: the "groan and shriek" of "unsleeping engines," the "boil and surge" of "fiery pools of metal" (19). It is this coupling, the narrator indicates, which drains the physical energies of the workers "unceasingly from year to year." Significantly, however, the ideological description of the mill appears before the mill itself appears—an abstraction not grounded in the particulars of the sketch. Significantly, too, Deborah is left unaware of this "machinery of system." The din of a thousand unsleeping engines sounds to her only like "far-off thunder."

When the mill does appear, the narrator's first impulse is to describe it as a "picturesque oddity," the language of the curious tourist supplanting the language of the social anatomist.[8] The cinder-covered road, the narrator observes, is flanked on one side by "abrupt and bare" quarried rock, on the other by the "sluggish and black" river. The mills for rolling iron, covering acres of bare ground, have "tent-like roofs" through whose open sides appears "firm in every . . . form." If the flames in Hawthorne's lime kiln give off associations of anarchic power and disorder, the flames in Davis's iron mill give off associations of witchery, hellish punishment and ghostly menace:

> pits of flame waving in the wind; liquid metal-flames writhing in tortuous streams through the sand; wide caldrons filled with boiling fire, over which bent ghastly

wretches stirring the strange brewing; and through all, crowds of half-clad men, looking like revengeful ghosts in the red light, hurried, throwing masses of glittering fire.

(20)

Here Deborah responds in closer concert with the narrator, though less elaborately: "'T looks,' she exclaims, 'like t' Devil's place!'"

The moral implications of these perceptions, though subordinate to a kind of visual 'delight in destruction,' are relatively clear. Like Hawthorne, Davis associates the industrial transformation of raw material into finished goods with alchemy and witchcraft, with the hubristic and perhaps demonic human desire for control over nature. Like Hawthorne, she associates the workers in this process with the victims of hellfire, though unlike Hawthorne she suggests, in the image of "revengeful ghosts," the fearful possibility of their retaliating. Powerful as these moral implications are, however, they undercut Davis's perception of the mill as a social system devised by men and therefore capable of being changed by men to alleviate the human damage they cause. The associations with hellfire, moreover, impart to the mill a sense of inevitable fatality and to the workers an implication of moral complicity.

Later, when Mitchell compares the mill furnaces to Dante's *Inferno* and Kirby, evidently blind to the irony of his association, points out a figure who is "Farinata himself in the burning tomb" (28), the significance of Davis's industrial landscape has clearly become moral rather than ideological.[9] Like the responses of the narrator and of Deborah, those of Mitchell and Kirby tell more about the seer than the scene. The two women perceive in terms of what Hawthorne called the "moral picturesque"—with deep feeling for the human import of the landscape. Kirby does not, and neither does Mitchell: "'This is hot, with a vengeance'," he declares. "'A match, please'?—lighting his cigar."

II

The ambiguities of judgment multiply when Davis turns from the depiction of the landscape to the depiction of her central character. Perhaps because her outrage surpassed her knowledge of life in the iron mills, she does not dramatize the process of physical and psychological degeneration in Hugh Wolfe; details of "the slow, heavy years of constant, hot work" (25) which have wasted him are few. He is first seen simply "heaping coal on a furnace" (20); later, "bent over the furnace with his iron pole" (23); and later still, digging into the furnace of molten iron "with his pole, dully thinking only how many rails the lump would yield" (26). His environment seems to have made him, almost, an object; almost as mechanical as his shovel and his pole; almost

as mentally inert as the coal and the iron; and almost as anonymously obscure as other things in his smoke-clouded, flame-bright landscape.

Davis is nevertheless moved to exposit, if not to dramatize, Wolfe's degeneration, and her exposition has two related strategies. First, she attempts to make Wolfe a representative class and ethnic type of the iron worker; then she makes him an exemplary type of the man of feeling, whose feelings have been repressed by his environment. Here, too, both her strategy and her vocabulary anticipate in several ways those of realist-naturalist fiction. Yet here, too, the ambiguities between moral and social reform tend to undercut each other.

Like Hawthorne with his two lime-burners, Davis recognizes the obscurity of her character as a type in fiction and must explain him as a social phenomenon and defend him as a subject for fiction even as she introduces him dramatically. Like, say, the Zola of *Germinal* (1884) and the Sinclair of *The Jungle* (1906), she defines Wolfe and his co-workers in terms of their work. Unlike Brand, whose work gives him too much time to think, Davis's mill workers are "soul-starved," and "their brains are full of unawakened power" (14), which is kept barely stimulated in the grimy dark of their off-hours by cockfights, terrier fights, drink, visits to "dens of infamy" (the whole catalogue of sins in a 'respectable' society); by the feeling of pain or the assertion of cunning. Brief and melodramatic as it may be, this is an early outline of a familiar case history in American fiction; and, "the soul of his class," "a morbid, gloomy man, untaught, unled, left to feed his soul in grossness and crime, and hard, grinding labor" (24), Hugh Wolfe is an early dramatization of it.

When she tries to render Wolfe as an ethnic type, however, Davis is led unfortunately to explain much of Wolfe's character in terms of a collective personality whose exaggeratedly passive traits seem merely aggravated rather than caused by their environment. Wolfe is a Welshman, and Welshmen, the narrator observes, "are a trifle more filthy" (more slovenly or more tainted by their environment?); "their muscles are not so brawny; they stoop more" than other ethnic groups; and when they are drunk, "they neither yell, nor shout, but skulk along like beaten hounds." They seem to Davis to be without will, to have capitulated to a life of "incessant labor, eating rank pork and molasses, drinking—God and the distillers only know what" (15). Obscuring as it does the question of when and how Wolfe's victimization began, this element of characterization has the effect nearly of turning a study of the interaction of technology and human identity into a stereotype reflecting the biases both of a nativist and a temperancer.

The second way in which Davis attempts to calibrate the effects of industrial violence is to make Wolfe's portrait a record of his personal history. In picturesque terms, the face can be seen—by an observer of sensibility—not only in terms of its physical resemblances to the environment, a human being transformed by a field of forces, but also as an image of the effects of suffering and capitulation or resistance over time. Instinctive movements and gestures, visibly orchestrating the motions of the mind in acquiescence or in resistance to the energies of the environment, become the "dramatic expression of deep and invisible energies within the character."[10]

Like the river landscape and the sociological sketch of the mill workers, the portrait of Hugh Wolfe emphasizes the debilitating transfer of his physical energies into the industrial process and the repression of mental energies to the point of 'dwarfing' his consciousness and reducing him to a state of futility, desperation and (occasionally) to aimless violence: "He had already lost the strength and instinct vigor of a man [the narrator observes], his muscles were thin, his nerves weak, his face . . . haggard, yellow with consumption." (24) Significantly, he has been reduced by this sapping and damming of energies not to an object or a brute but to a state of womanliness. Unmanned by incessant labor and by "countless," "cankering" days, he has been transformed into what his fellow-workers call "one of the girl-men." His face is "a meek, woman's face," with a "weak, uncertain mouth" (he has no "words for his thought" [30]) and "desperate eyes," a face in which the narrator nevertheless discerns "a heavy weight of brain" (35).

Yet if this feminine imagery is the sign of his degeneration through violence, it is also the sign of his exemplary status as a man of feeling, an implicit promise that he can still feel though he might not be able to act out his feelings in acceptable male ways. He shuns dogfights and cockfights and does little drinking (and that desperate rather than social). To his fellow workers, his school-learning (not specified) has ruined him "as a good hand in a fight." Significantly, it is the violence of fights with his fellow-workers rather than the violence of the machine which most reduces him: he is always the one "thrashed, pommelled to jelly." He is not one of them, "though outwardly as filthy and ash-covered." He is "silent, with foreign thoughts and longings breaking out in innumerable ways" (24).

In her delineation of these thoughts and longings, Davis makes Wolfe an exemplary type—an industrial version of the man of feeling. The resolution of the inward disturbances of the man of feeling—the resolution of his story—depends upon the narrator's perceptions of their outward cause. If the world is perceived as by its very nature disturbing, hostile, assaultive (as it is, say, in "Ethan Brand"), the industrial man of feeling can only resolve his dilemma by striking an attitude of resignation and, toward others, of healing commiseration. If,

on the other hand, the world is perceived as a place of human deception and oppression (as it is, say, in Sinclair's *The Jungle*), the industrial man of feeling might be moved toward more active attitudes of outrage, defiance, reform or revolution. This range of possibilities allowed the picturesque aesthetic and its personification, the man of feeling, to survive the evolution from romanticism to realism and naturalism. Hugh Wolfe seems in part to have undergone this evolution, but here again Davis's ambiguities between social and moral reform tend to undercut each other.

Where Ethan Brand's inner life is completely attuned to his kiln fire, Wolfe's—when we first see it—is in desperate resistance to his industrial environment. He is in several ways a nascent protester. His "loving poet's heart" (25) is made manifest not only in his concern for the men and women working by his side (most especially for Deborah and for Janey), but also in his response to the beauty and the kindness which elude and enrage him:

> There are moments when a passing cloud, the sun glinting on the purple thistles, a kindly smile, a child's face, will rouse him to a passion of pain,—when his nature starts up with a mad cry of rage against God, man, whoever it is that has forced this vile, slimy life upon him.
>
> (25)

His "fierce thirst for beauty" breaks out chiefly into his sculptures, fashioned in "off-hours from the furnace," from the korl (the refuse of the ore after the pig-metal is run), into picturesquely "hideous, fantastic . . . but sometimes strangely beautiful" human figures. A sculpted nude, described later in the story, expresses both outrage and compassion:

> There was not one line of beauty or grace in it: a nude woman's form, muscular, grown coarse with labor, the powerful limbs instinct with some one poignant longing. One idea: there it was in the tense, rigid muscles, the clutching hands, the wild, eager face, like that of a starving wolf's.
>
> (32)[11]

His "great blind intellect" expresses itself in an awareness of being, somehow, wronged by the industrial order and the "social riddle" on which it is based; it expresses itself, as well, in his fantasy of raising "these men and women working at his side up with him" (41).

By a paradox typical of American industrial fiction (and typical of documentary expression as well), it is precisely the sensibility that sets him apart from his fellow workers which allows him to be the most powerful case for their situation, the most intense register of their common environment. He is a worker "by habit only" (25). By nature, he is a nascent artist, revolutionary, exemplar of moral benevolence. So too, though less evidently, are the "untaught" men and women around him. To "raise" by teaching them, indeed, seems to be Wolfe's unrealized particular calling.

It is the business of the story's plot to let Wolfe's internal forces break out into more active form. Yet the ultimate expression of Wolfe's "thoughts and longings" makes him, like Brand, a morally deviant rather than an exemplary type; the effect of that expression is to elevate his hopes only briefly and illusorily before pitching him, like Brand, into despair and suicide; and in the process, his identity as a potentially heroic figure in a drama of social reform is displaced by his identity as a victim in a kind of morality play.

III

The "trial day" of Hugh Wolfe's life begins when his consciousness awakens sufficiently to make him feel with renewed anguish what has become of him from the assaults of the industrial environment on his body and his mind and, at the same time, to imagine a way of liberating himself from these assaults. His trial begins as an encounter with the values of an American elite—represented chiefly by Kirby, the son of the mill-owner; by Doctor May; and by Mitchell, an intellectual "spending a couple of months in the borders of a Slave State, to study the institutions of the South" (29).

It is clear from her characterizations of this elite that Wolfe is not the only one whom Davis seeks to try. Mitchell introduces the issue by which each of the visitors is to be judged: the question of their responsibility, as an elite, to lead the workers up from poverty, ignorance and despair. Clearly Davis believes that they have such a responsibility. But encountering the "*De profundis clamavi*" of Wolfe's sculpted korl-woman and "the awful question, 'What shall we do to be saved?'" in Wolfe's eyes, each of the three repeats, in his own way, the response of Pontius Pilate at the trial of Christ: "'I am innocent of the blood of this man. See ye to it!'" (36).

The norm by which each of the judges is judged and found wanting is the moral norm of the man of feeling. Kirby, "the pocket of the world," admits that he is simply drifting "with the stream" of industrial progress because he "cannot dive deep enough to find bottom" (35):

> I do not think, I wash my hands of all social problems,—slavery, caste, white or black. My duty to my operatives has a narrow limit,—the pay-hour on Saturday night. Outside of that, if they cut korl, or cut each other's throats . . . I am not responsible.

Abrogating the responsibility of his conscience, accepting the industrial system as inevitable, he has a perverse emotional response to the misery he encounters.

"What are taste, reason, to creatures who must live such lives as this?" he asks, having already answered: "It would be kindness" to reduce the workers to "machines,—nothing more,—hands" (34).

Doctor May, "the heart of the world," evades responsibility by resorting to the fiction of the self-made man. "Make yourself what you will," he says to Wolfe, "it is your right," but when Wolfe asks, "Will you help me?" he responds: "I have not the means. You know, if I had, it is in my heart to take this boy and educate him"—but then, he asks, "Why should one be raised, when myriads are left?" (37)

Mitchell, "the head" of the world—its "taste, culture, refinement," makes the most serious denial of responsibility. It is he who has raised the question of responsibility in the first place, but when called upon to declare himself, his facial expression betrays the "insufferable disgust" of the aesthete at the "thick, unclean odor" of the mill (38). That is his most telling rejection, but he adds, "it would be of no use. I am not one of them."

> Reform is born of need, not pity. No vital movement of the people's has worked down. . . . Some day, out of bitter need will be thrown up their own light-bringer,— their Jean Paul, their Cromwell, their Messiah.

Davis clearly does not agree. Apparently the most radical of the elite's responses, Mitchell's is dramatically demonstrated to be merely the glib rationale of an *isolato* of acute perception but with a conscience cut off from the impulses of benevolent feeling. Mitchell merely cultivates feeling for its own sake.

Wolfe, too, is tried and found wanting in this encounter, though Davis softens her judgment of him by an appeal to extenuating circumstances. "Suddenly roused from his indifferent stupor" by this "mysterious class that shone down on him . . . with the glamor of another order of being" (26), his resurrection—and his passion—as a man of feeling begin when he tries to grapple with the "social riddle" that makes him different from them. In his struggle, however, his longings for the liberation of his class through social or artistic protest are displaced by a mental image of Mitchell as "a clear, projected figure of himself, as he might become" (41).

Far more than the physical and psychological transformations, the story's dramatic logic implies, it is the moral transformations of the industrial worker which must appall. In Wolfe's transference of values, Davis dramatizes with great power the corruption at the heart of the American dream as it adapted itself to the conditions of industrial society. "I do not plead his cause," says the narrator. "I only wish to show you the mote in my brother's eye" (46).

Placed there primarily by "the mind" of an industrial society, the mote makes Wolfe blind both to the self-indulgence and (for his class) the futility of the dream.

Blind to Mitchell's moral bankruptcy, Wolfe first catches "with quick pleasure . . . every small sign of [Mitchell's] refinement": a white hand, "the blood-glow of a red ring," a voice like music—"low, even, with chording cadences" (29). He represses his old longing "to be able to speak, to know what was best, to raise these men and women working by his side up with him" and gives in to a mere impulse "to escape,—only to escape,—out of the wet, the pain, the ashes, somewhere, anywhere,—only for one moment of free air on a hill-side, to lie down and let his sick soul throb itself out in the sunshine" (41). Aping Mitchell, he begins to gravitate toward the assumption that life is a matter of "full development" rather than self-restraint, "the fullest flow of spontaneous harmony" rather than "voluntary suffering for truth's sake" (46).

Extenuated as it is by his heightened consciousness of the assaults of his industrial environment, Wolfe's moral corruption is compounded by the actions he begins to take in pursuit of his dream. Ironically, however, the moral dilemma which these actions create is at least as painful as the assaults of the environment he wishes to escape. His conscience, until he stills it, adds remorse to his anguish and self-loathing. He is "stung with a sudden remorse" when his cry of self-pity ("Is it my fault that I am no better?") reduces Deborah to "thankless tears" (41). He is "stung" by "some bitterer thought" when he touches "the worn white arm" of Janey, for she no longer has a part in his "plan for the future" (42). When Deborah confronts him with the money she has stolen (ironically, from Mitchell) and with her image of Wolfe able, with the money, to walk like a king in a sunlit pastoral meadow with ladies in silken gowns and men like Mitchell, he guiltily hides his face in his hands and then, "stunned with pain and weariness," retreats into sleep (44).

Awakening on Sunday evening, his conscience is assailed even by words. Deborah has argued his "right" to keep the stolen money, but the word now strikes him, clings to him, becomes "the fierce devil's whisper in his ear" (45). The word "theft" comes to his mind: first it sickens him, then he grapples with it; then, though the thought of being a thief brings "clammy drops of sweat from his forehead," he sees himself with the money "as he might be, strong, helpful, kindly" (46).

It is a cloudscape lit by the setting sun, "a glimpse of another world than this,—of an infinite depth of beauty and of quiet somewhere,—somewhere,—a depth of quiet and rest and love," which completes his metamorphosis into a negative and pathetic image of Mitchell. This landscape becomes the amorphous, conscienceless and unrealizable image of his liberation:

> The sun had sunk quite below the hills, but his last rays struck upward, touching the zenith. The fog had risen, and the town and river were steeped in its thick, gray damp; but overhead, the sun-touched smoke-clouds opened like a cleft ocean,—shifting, rolling seas of crimson mist, waves of billowy silver veined with blood-scarlet, inner depths unfathomable of glancing light. Wolfe's artist-eye grew drunk with color. The gates of that other world! Fading, flashing before him now! What, in that world of Beauty, Content, and Right, were the petty laws, the mine and thine, of mill-owners and mill-hands?

(47)

When darkness erases this dreamscape of beauty, content, and right, "the trial day of this man's life" is over, and what follows is "mere drifting circumstance" (50). Sentenced to nineteen years for theft, the chasm between "what might have been, and now" become unbreachable, he tells Deb: "I cannot bear to be hurted any more" (57). Still compelled by an impulse to escape, he dreams increasingly of a cool, easeful darkness. Then he saws his wrists open with a shard of tin.

What, precisely, are the cautionary lessons being conveyed by this morality play? Davis's delineations of Wolfe, Mitchell, Kirby and Doctor May as failed men of feeling suggests the need for a reform of sensibility rather than for legislation or revolt to alleviate the assailant-victim relationships of the industrial environment. Like the muck-raking journalists of the late 19th century, she seems to believe that exposure of this relationship is sufficient to activate the consciences of a fundamentally benevolent citizenry. Unlike the muckrakers, however, she bases her appeal for redress not on the assumption that people in power will behave badly unless controlled by the power of civil law, but on a self-activated impulse to moral reform in the hearts and minds of the elite, once they are shown the error of their ways. To the extent that Mitchell, Kirby and Doctor May can be helped to become exemplary men of feeling, the story suggests, to that extent can the assaults of the industrial environment begin to be alleviated.

Yet how are these assaults to be alleviated? For the workers, as Hugh Wolfe's case negatively demonstrates, they must be countered, with help, by the education of social conscience and not by escape to the pastoral ease or the asocial refinement of the alienated heart and mind. A reformed elite would, evidently, act as both exemplars and educators of the way "up" from the physical, psychological and moral inferno of industrial slavery. Whether the Hugh Wolfes so ministered to would remain workers or be elevated to the status of an elite (artists, social workers and political leaders with a conscience, if not Jean Pauls, Cromwells, Messiahs) is a problem Davis does not address; nor does she address the problem of who would willingly enter the inferno, and under what conditions, to forge iron. Her negative case for the need to raise the industrial worker, in short, has all the ambiguities and unanswered questions which

Henry Nash Smith long ago located in frontier and agricultural versions of the rise of the common man.[12]

Nevertheless, the story suffers not so much from the lack of a coherent social ideology as from the lack of a resolution between conflicting awarenesses of the interaction between industrial technology and human identity. Even this conflict, however, makes the story a memorable expression of those tenaciously divided attitudes, so characteristically American, toward the ideal of individualism and the realities of a social organization of which technology is but one manifestation. And in the end, the power of **Life in the Iron Mills** emerges not from its divided cautionary concerns, but from the possibilities which Rebecca Harding Davis imparted to an evolving imagination of the assailant industrial landscape and the man of feeling.

Notes

1. Rebecca Harding Davis, *Life in the Iron Mills; or the Korl Woman* (New York: The Feminist Press, 1972), p. 19. All subsequent page numbers refer to this edition and are cited parenthetically in the text.

2. For a fine distinction between social, historical and symbolic perspectives on technology, see David Wright, "Promethean Legacy: Ambivalent Relations Between Man and His Tools," *American Examiner,* V:3 (Spring 1978), pp. 4-13.

3. Harvey Cox, "The Virgin and the Dynamo Revisited: An Essay on the Symbolism of Technology," *Soundings,* 44:2 (Summer 1971). Quoted in Wright, *ibid.,* p. 7.

4. I have argued this in "The Industrial Sublime: Assailant Landscapes and the Man of Feeling," *American Examiner, op. cit.,* pp. 26-49.

5. In this, she anticipates modern fictional versions of 'the landscape of ruin.' See my "Deformations: Twentieth Century Landscapes of Ruin," *The American Landscape* (New York: Oxford University Press, 1974), pp. 3-6.

6. Davis, *Bits of Gossip* (1904). Quoted in Tillie Olsen, "A Biographical Interpretation," the Afterword to *Life in the Iron Mills,* p. 73.

7. See "The Industrial Sublime," *op. cit.,* p. 32.

8. The phrase "picturesque oddity" conventionally suggests an element of landscape valued for its surprise and its novelty, both visually and for the associations it generates in the mind of the cultivated traveler.

9. Farinata degli Uberti led the Ghibelline revolts against the Guelfs in Florence and was condemned for heresy in 1283. He appears, waist-deep in flames, in Canto X of Dante's *Inferno.* Kirby's allusion is one of several indications of his fear of revolt among the iron workers.

10. Martin Price, "The Picturesque Moment," From Sensibility to Romanticism, eds. Frederick W. Hilles and Harold Bloom (New York: Oxford University Press, 1965), p. 285.

11. The play on wolf/Wolfe suggested by Davis's simile invites the perception of the sculpted korl-woman as Wolfe's self-portrait. The sculpture thus powerfully completes the characterization of a man "feminized" by his assaultive environment. If this implies that sexual disorder is one of the psychological effects of life in the iron mills, it also seems to imply that 'female' sensibility is a latent counterforce to those effects.

12. In *Virgin Land* Smith traced the ambiguities inherent in the rise of the common man as a literary theme to two conflicting ideologies. One ideology "assumed that the common man had risen to dominate, or at least to share control of the government without ceasing to be the common man"—"a process whereby power in the state passed from one class to another." The other ideology assumed "not a destruction of the class system but the rise of an individual member of the lower class in a social scale which itself is not changed." In this version, the common man rises "to the rank of a bold and independent yeoman"—and, if merited by his character, eventually to judge, general or some other exemplar (Chapter XII). It is this second version, Smith suggests, which dominated American frontier and agricultural fictions until about the 1890s. Davis, too, gravitates toward this version, though with the important qualifications that for Wolfe and his fellow workers, self-reliance will not suffice; that they must be taught how to reconcile ambition with moral restraint; and that their upper class teachers must first teach themselves the same lesson.

Jean Pfaelzer (essay date May/June 1981)

SOURCE: Pfaelzer, Jean. "Rebecca Harding Davis: Domesticity, Social Order, and the Industrial Novel." *International Journal of Women's Studies* 4, no. 3 (May/June 1981): 234-44.

[*In the following essay, Pfaelzer emphasizes the significance and singularity of Davis's* Life in the Iron Mills *in American literature, contending that the novella "must be reconsidered as a central text in the origins of American realism, American proletarian literature, and American feminism." The critic especially notes Davis's contribution to the unsentimental depiction of industrial life in America through her honest portraits of working-class women.*]

I

The literary structures of *Life in the Iron Mills*[1] provided Davis with a form that in itself reflects the contradiction of a sympathetic middle-class woman describing working-class life. Through observation and projection, Rebecca Harding Davis' experiences as a woman allowed her to understand something of the family and factory experience of the working class. To be sure, because of her own class affiliation Davis distorted working class life, but because of her sex she was able to see oppression where others did not. While the putative synthesis of sexual oppression and class oppression fails, Rebecca Harding Davis managed to introduce into American literary realism the people who made the industrial revolution. Specifically, she portrayed the changed nature of women's role in industrial family life.

Life in the Iron Mills is the story of the Wolfes, a working class Welsh family that rebels against the poverty and dehumanization of factory life through theft and through art. In the narrative tradition of the "frame tale" and contemporary "tall tale," a middle-class persona introduces and concludes the story, "framing" the action and controlling our point of view. What is unique here is that the narrator is a woman and the "folk" being described are not comic local yokels. In fact, where the gentlemanly narrator of the tall tale must distance himself from the folk to maintain the humor of the tale and to contain the plebeian energy of the folk, here the narrator identifies with the emotional suffocation of industrial poverty and the factory worker's rebellion against it, suggesting Davis' own discontent with her arid intellectual and sexual life as a spinster in a booming mid-western town.

She introduces the tale: "A cloudy day: Do you know what that is in a town of iron-works? The sky sank down before dawn, muddy, flat, immovable. The air is thick, clammy with the breath of crowded human beings. It stifles me. I open the window, and looking out, can scarcely see through the rain the grocer's shop opposite, where a crowd of drunken Irishmen are puffing Lynchburg tobacco in their pipes. I can detect the scent through all the foul smells ranging loose in the air." [p. 11] Like the women in the illustrated magazines of the time, the narrator stands alone in a room watching the world of work and activity through a window.[2] She sits removed from the action in a domestic world that is defined and enclosed yet she identifies with the oppression of the "stifling" atmosphere of the life outside.

Rebecca Harding Davis also introduced the double oppression of working-class women into American fiction. Her tale begins late Saturday night when a group of Welsh and Black women leave the cotton mills, drunk, and half-naked. In the nineteenth century mill workers and miners often removed the bulky Victorian clothes which posed a serious danger near machinery and hot furnaces; many reformist demands for the abolition of child labor were based on the visible nudity of women and men who worked in the factories and mines. Here the women have helped each other finish work and they invite Deborah Wolfe, a hunchback Welsh woman, to go drinking. Instead Deborah dutifully returns to her hovel which she shares with her cousin Hugh and his father, and she learns that Hugh must work the night shift at the iron mill. Although Deborah is cold and tired, she makes Hugh a dinner pail of bread and "flitch" (rank salt pork) and includes her own portion of ale. Recurrent images of hunger and inadequate food early in the novel build toward Davis' unifying image of working class "soul starvation." In the dirty rain, Deborah carries the meal to Hugh at the mill. In Deborah, Rebecca Harding Davis shows the life of a woman who works a twelve hour shift in the mill and then tries to feed and maintain a family.

By the 1850s, pressured by the social and psychological tensions of the new industrialism, popular fiction projected the family as a refuge, a mediation from the tensions of the work place. This role of the family was central to the Cult of the True Woman;[3] Davis offers the first literary attack on a central social rationalization. Rebecca Harding Davis confronts the era's romanticization of the family (Louisa May Alcott's best seller *Little Women* appeared in 1869) by portraying the dual character of Deborah's work, as a picker in the cotton mills and the nurturer of her family at home. Clearly working class survival depends on its own women. The family in *Life in the Iron Mills* is the only enclave of support and cooperation in the story. In *Life in the Iron Mills* the family unit is Deborah, the hunchback picker, her cousin Hugh Wolfe, his father, "Old Wolfe," and a young blond girl, Janey, whom Hugh loves. They share a dark cellar in a house rented by six families. Their room "was low, damp—the earthen floor covered with green slimy moss a fetid air smothering the breath." [p. 16] When Deborah comes from the mill Janey and the old man are asleep on heaps of straw, wrapped in torn horse blankets. Hugh is on night shift in the mill; there is not time for family life. Davis does not mystify the family, nor, when she sends Deborah out with Hugh's rank supper after her twelve hour shift in the mill, does she make a distinction between paid work and unpaid or hidden work. Deborah's labor is part of the whole social order, although her source of emotional support comes from the women in the mill. Ironically, Deborah will destroy her family in her desperate attempt to provide for it.

Davis' description of Deborah's nightly visit to the iron works is also one of the first detailed pictures of a factory in American fiction: "The mills for rolling iron are simply immense tent-like roofs, covering acres of ground, open on every side. Beneath these roofs Deborah looked in on a city of fires, that burned hot and fiercely in the night. Fire in every horrible form: pits of flame waving in the wind; liquid metal-flames writhing in tortuous streams through the sand; wide cauldrons filled with boiling fire, over which bent ghastly wretches stirring the strange brew; and through all, crowds of half-clad men, looking like revengeful ghosts in the red light, hurried, throwing masses of glittering fire." [p. 20] Her images of heat and activity take us far beyond Melville's reductive portrayal of work in a paper mill in "The Paradise of Bachelors and the Tartarus of Maids" where an extended sexual metaphor of machinery subsumes his descriptions of female labor.[4] Davis makes clear through the vast panorama of the factory, which employed over one thousand men at one shift, the reduced power and individuality of the mill workers. The "pits of flame," the imagery of fire and brimstone, and the set contrasts of red and black from contemporary melodrama intensify the terror of the scene for a Christian audience. The workers are not only "the ghastly wretches" but also "the revengeful ghosts."

Davis goes beyond a description of the factory to a description of the system which produces it and which governs the bodies of the workmen. Davis was writing at a time when the night shift was just being introduced in American manufacturing, led to a large extent by the iron and steel industry in which Hugh worked, and she recognizes this new arrangement: "Not many even of the inhabitants of a manufacturing town know the vast machinery of a system by which the bodies of workmen are governed, that goes on unceasingly," [p. 19] but she explains the new system of twelve-hour night and day shifts. Davis is describing the new Bessemer process for making steel, invented in 1851, in which it was simply too expensive to cool down and fire up the furnaces of pig iron each day:[5] the individual consciousness of Davis' hero arises within a concrete historical situation.

II

Unique to American literature before such turn-of-the-century naturalists as Theodore Dreiser and Ellen Glasgow, *Life in the Iron Mills* is also a story of working-class rebellion. The rebellion is reflected both in the open defiance of Hugh and Deborah as we shall see, and in "covert rebellion." *Life in the Iron Mills* reveals the signs of "covert rebellion" that Elaine Showalter has discovered in female narratives which, on the surface, portray stoical womanly suffering.[6] These signs include sexual solidarity among female characters, sympathy for the plight of unmarried women, and feminized male heroes. Although we never see the cotton mill, and first meet the women after they leave work, Davis makes it clear that an interracial collective has devel-

oped among the women mill workers. They have covered for one of the women who is "alays behint" in her work; they are sympathetic to the plight and fatigue of the hunchback who has stood twelve hours at the spools, and they are going to celebrate their half day off together. Secondly, Deborah is a hunchback; again the unmarried woman is crippled. Yet Davis is acutely sympathetic to the potential loneliness and isolation of the single woman, isolation which explicitly crosses class lines. The narrator comments, "One sees the dead vacant look steal sometimes over the rarest, finest of women's faces—in the midst, it may be, of their warmest summer's day; and then one can guess at the secret of intolerable solitude that lies hid beneath the delicate laces and brilliant smile." [p. 22] Davis' allegiances are clearly with Deborah. She notes that the men at the iron mill see her as a "limp dirty rag," a "drowned cat" who painfully hides behind the machines, watching Hugh eat, knowing that he is only eating to please her. She accepts his condescension: "It was his nature to be kind, even to the very rats that swarmed in the cellar, kind to her in just the same way." [p. 22] The lonely narrator, confined in her upstairs room, idly tapping the window, suggests that Hugh's rejection "had given Deborah's face its apathy and vacancy more than her low torpid life." [p. 22]

Moreover, Hugh is an archetypical example of the feminized male hero. Hugh "had already lost the strength and instinct vigor of a man, his muscles were thin, his nerves weak, his face (a meek, woman's face) haggard, yellow with consumption. In the mill he was known as one of the girl-men: 'Molly Wolfe' was his sobriquet. He was never seen in the cock pit, did not own a terrier, drank seldom; when he did, desperately. He fought sometimes, but was always thrashed, pommelled to a jelly." [p. 24] Rebecca Harding Davis' hero, Hugh Wolfe, is a feminized projection of the rebel artist.

Rebellion in *Life in the Iron Mills* is also overt and confrontational. Late in the night shift, while Deborah has fallen asleep on a bundle of rags behind a furnace, the mill overseer brings a doctor, a journalist, and an effete aristocrat to tour the mill. Hugh is attracted to the visitors who perhaps, like the readers of *The Atlantic*, are out slumming. The visitors are curious, then disdainful, discussing the millworkers as if they were invisible and deaf. Suddenly, they are startled by "the white figure of a woman . . . of giant proportions, crouching on the ground, her arms flung out in some wild gesture of warning." [p. 31] The woman is a statue which Hugh has carved from "korl," like himself, the pink refuse of the mill. The feminized hero as artist has created Davis' most severe attack, not only on factory life, but on the Cult of The True Woman as well: "There was not one line of beauty or grace in it: a nude woman's form, muscular, grown coarse with labor, the powerful limbs instinct—with some poignant longing. One idea there was in it: the tense, rigid muscles, the clutching hands, the wild eager face, like that of a starving wolf's." [p. 32]

This is a woman whose body is not confined by bustle and bodice, whose existence is not defined by her maternal role, whose morality is not derived through avoiding the outside world. This is a working woman's body, strong, tired, and dissatisfied, totally in contrast to the subservient and genteel ideals expressed by the heroines of the contemporary domestic novel such as Suzanna Warner's *Wide Wide World* (1850) or Maria Cummens' *The Lamplighter* (1854). The Korl Woman is a producer, valued for her activity rather than for her essentialist qualities. Unlike the sentimental heroines popular at the time whose fate (marriage to an eligible hero) was determined by her acceptance of her instinctual subservience,[7] Davis' demanding statue ties women to worldly activity and necessity. In contrast to the goals for women outlined in *Godey's Lady's Book* and other "advice" literature of the time, Davis does not mask economic realities in her depiction of the Korl Woman.[8]

Stunned by the urgency of the Korl Woman the visitors debate the meaning of the statue. At a time when American artists never sculpted or painted middle class women nude, the mill owner is primarily intrigued with the statue's sensuality. The affable but ingenuous doctor John May, is also confounded by her body, for he cannot reconcile Hugh's explanation, "She be hungry" with her palpable muscles and strength. Only Mitchell, the cynical aristocrat and passive intellectual, understands "the awful question" posed by the statue and Hugh's interpretation, "she wants summat to make her live." [p. 33]

As the visitors re-phrase the riddle of the Korl Woman who looks into each of their faces and poses the awful question, "What shall we do to be saved?" Deborah commits the most defiant act in the novel. When she hears the visitors agree that money is the final answer to the riddle, that only money can save Hugh, she steals Mitchell's wallet which contains two gold pieces and very large check.[9] Later that night Deborah gives the money to Hugh to build a home for Janey and himself. She offers to disappear from his life, but insists to him, "it is hur [your] right to keep it." [p. 45] If Deborah represents the material present, Janey is the idealized future, passive, indeed almost always asleep, but typically, a female character who functions for Hugh, in George Eliot's phrase, as "the margin of dreams." Nevertheless, it is only at the moment of rebellion that Hugh acknowledges Deborah's power and beauty in phrases which recall the statue of the Korl Woman. As Deborah describes her theft Hugh saw, "that she was young, in deadly earnest; her faded eyes, and wet, ragged figure caught from their frantic eagerness a power akin to beauty." [p. 43]

Like most nineteenth-century literary rebels, Hugh and Deborah must choose between subservience and death. The next day Hugh is arrested with the money on him. At his trial his own defense was "the money was his by rights . . . all the world had gone wrong." [p. 51] The judge sentenced him to nineteen years' hard labor. After two desperate efforts to escape, suffering from tuberculosis and isolated from the world which he, like the narrator, now views beyond his prison window, Hugh kills himself in his cell. Deborah is sentenced to three years in jail as his accomplice. We hear no more of Janey or Old Wolfe. The family, which is neither filial nor patriarchal, has been destroyed.

Deborah's rebellion and deformity determined her sexual destiny. Like the women in the sentimental novels, Deborah pays for her assertion, in this case with prison and spinsterhood. In the end Deborah goes into the hills to live with the Quakers, "pure and meek . . . more silent than they, more humble, more loving." [p. 63-64] We see her, like the narrator, waiting, looking toward hills "higher and purer than these on which she lives." [p. 64] Ultimately, the religious metaphor subsumes the political metaphor, although Davis believes that rural life is regenerative and possibly still available. The narrator closes the story in her own dark room, one aware that the "dream of green fields and sunshine is a very old dream—almost worn out, I think" [p. 12] She tries to hide the statue behind a curtain, but sometimes she sees in its look "the eyes of dumb brutes—horses dying a curtain under the lash. I know." [p. 64]

III

What, in fact, did the narrator, looking at the world from her window, "know?" Tillie Olsen, in her biographical interpretation of *Life in the Iron Mills* argues that Rebecca Harding Davis wrote in "absolute identification" with "thwarted wasted lives," despised love, imperfect art. A thirty-year-old spinster in a booming Ohio River town, influenced by her father, businessman and City Treasurer who hated "vulgar American life" and read only Shakespeare and believed that the United States was incapable of culture. Olsen traces the themes of Davis' early fiction: young unmarried women devoted to difficult fathers, young men, like Hugh, "hungry to know," young women, like Deborah, penalized for their appearance. The women are sexual but "loathe themselves."[10] Olsen suggests that the more Davis read of Nathaniel Hawthorne, Oliver Wendell Holmes, and James Russell Lowell, the more constricted she felt. She walked. And, in secret, she wrote. After years, she sent *Life in the Iron Mills* to *The Atlantic Monthly*, prestigious, literate, and with a new editor open to women authors as well as articles on women's rights. Also, *The Atlantic Monthly* had announced that it sought materials dealing with "real life." The magazine paid her $50. In a time when Ralph Waldo Emerson had called for a resurgence of literature about the "mass of creatures" Nathaniel Hawthorne recognized *Life in the Iron Mills* as a literary landmark. Nonetheless *Life in the Iron Mills* was out of print until The Feminist Press republished the story in 1972. Literary critics have still virtually ignored the piece.

Life in the Iron Mills, however, must be reconsidered as a central text in the origins of American realism, American proletarian literature, and American feminism. Davis has drawn her hero and heroine directly into the stresses of real history. Her themes are neither remote nor exotic. The historical dynamics of the industrial revolution determine the character of her people. The narrator is static, we never see her leave her room, but her subjects acknowledge the concrete limits and the abstract potentialities of working class life. Davis articulated tendencies whose significance had not previously been recognized or understood, and she refused a facile reconciliation.

Rebecca Harding Davis described American working class life in a period of rapid transition from an artisan or small manufacturing economy to a young industrial economy; perhaps she tried to reverse this process in the end by returning Deborah to a rural community. At first this cycle was a historical fact. Gerda Lerner noted that in the early stages of industrialism rural men were "not available and not willing to enter factories," which appeared first in the textile trades.[11] Spinning and weaving were traditionally women's occupations, which certainly prepared the popular mind to accept women's employment in textile factories. There was, however, little carry over of skills between handi-craft and machine work in the production of cloth and clothing. At first the new mills employed Yankee women who thought factory work was well paid, respectable, and above all temporary; within a decade, the new factories, needing more employees and facing the effects of rural depopulation and native women's organized fight for the ten hour day, hired immigrant women such as Deborah Wolfe. This shared history of Yankee and immigrant women may partially explain why, in the 1850's, lines of allegiance such as that between the narrator and Deb crossed classes more easily for women than for men.[12]

Deborah is a "picker" in a cotton mill, "picker" denoting both the machine which cleaned and fluffed the raw cotton and the person who tended the picker. Like the reductive phrase "hands" for worker which also appears in *Life in the Iron Mills,* the person and the machinery are linguistically one, "picker" defined by specialized function. Meanwhile, as industry took women's labor out of the home, the material value of housework declined.[13]

Life in the Iron Mills was written in a decade of active reform movements. Davis was most likely aware of

contemporary demands for co-operative stores, abolition of slavery, utopian communities, the ten-hour workday, and free access to public lands. Davis is writing from an active reformist tradition when she effectively describes the machinery, the housing, and the work relations of the new factory life. During the decade when Transcendental authors proposed Deist and retrogressive solutions to the problems of American industrialism, Davis must have been aware of mass demands for the ten hour day. In particular, Davis shows us the relentless nature of industrial work through Hugh's and Deborah's monotonous rhythms and long shifts, "The hands of each mill are divided into watches that relieve each other regularly as the sentinels of an army. By night and day the work goes on, the unsleeping engines groan and shriek, the fiery pools of metal boil and surge. Only for a day in the week, in half-courtesy to public censure, the fires are partially veiled; but as soon as the clock strikes midnight, the great furnaces break forth with renewed fury, the clamor begins with fresh, breathless vigor, the engines sob and shriek like 'gods in pain'." [p. 19] While these phenomena were seeping into the political consciousness of the times, this is totally new matter for American literature. Factory heat, noise, repetition, and fatigue. Her setting, characters, and plot represent a total break from the cultural traditions she was raised in and the literary traditions she had to draw upon.

Rebecca Harding Davis, trapped in her room, sex and class in the 1850s, portrays the fatigue and dehumanization of factory life, although not the tenacious opposition it generated. The statue of the Korl Woman allows Davis to break with the cultural dominance of the Cult of the True Woman, but because of the limits of Davis' experience the statue cannot fully represent the political and cultural rebellion of working class people. In the 1850s working class people had not readily succumbed to the statue's bewildered passivity, "Is this the End? . . . Nothing beyond? . . . No more?" [p. 64] The narrator closes the story in her own dark room, where she has tried to hide the statue behind a curtain, but sometimes it "accidentally" faces her, she must see her "rough ungainly thing." [p. 64]

Ultimately Davis would not repress her statue, her image of articulation and defiance. Rebecca Harding Davis faced the major contradictions of a nineteenth century middle-class reformer writing about working-class factory and family life. The physical isolation and economic dependency of her sex, projected through her narrator, helped Davis transcend the inevitable myopia of one class writing about another. Paradoxically, the narrator, the literary structure that helped her transcend the class differences, also created its own problems in perspective and point of view. For example, the narrator repeatedly insists that we "come down and look" and "judge" the millworkers. She addresses the readers of the *Atlantic Monthly* in elevated literary diction, "The river, dull and tawny colored, *la belle riviere*" [p. 12] while the millworkers speak in a Welsh accent, "Begorra. On the spools. Alleys behint, though we helped her we dud. An wid yee." [p. 16] Interestingly, while Hugh speaks in a Welsh accent when addressing the doctor, "She be hungry," he generally speaks in standard literary English to Deborah: "What am I worth, Deb? Is it my fault that I am not better? My fault? My fault?" [p. 41]

Although Rebecca Harding Davis' family traced English origins, the Wolfes were Welsh and Davis did not escape the nativist literary stereotypes of her time in assigning to them debased animal behavior. "The old man was Welsh,—had spent half of his life in the Cornish tin-mines. You may pick the Welsh emigrants, Cornish miners, out of the throng passing the windows, any day. They are trifle more filthy; their muscles are not so brawny, they stoop more. When they are drunk, they neither yell, nor shout, nor stagger, but skulk along like beaten hounds." [p. 15] These images reproduce the literary stereotypes of the time for in fact the Welsh were not totally impoverished immigrants. Because England's industrial revolution pre-dated America's by about thirty years, Britain provided the new American industries with an important supply of skilled labor. The Welsh miners and industrial workers crossed the Atlantic in both directions, consciously responding to the laws of supply and demand. Seeking work in the period between the abolition of indentured labor and the rise of organized recruitment of immigrant workers through bribes, agents, and utopian descriptions of American life, the Welsh were mainly tempted here by letters from other Welsh immigrants. They paid their own fares. [p. 14]

In *Life in the Iron Mills* Davis portrays the monotony of factory life, but her details which antedated the Naturalists do not reflect the continuity and autonomy of working class culture. By exclusively presenting images of fatigue, poverty, and alcoholism, Davis flattens working class life: "The Wolfes lives were like those of their class: incessant labor, sleeping in kennel like rooms, eating rank pork and molasses, drinking—God and distillers only know what; with an occasional night in jail, to atone for some drunken excess. Is that all of their lives? Of the portion given to them and these their duplicates swarming the streets today?" [p. 15] Working people are, in turn "rats" and "spaniels." Through the perspective of the middle class narrator, we do not see the working class capacity for self-protection.

The Welsh however, were not the passive and inert, albeit overworked people Davis describes in *Life in the Iron Mills*, although Davis could not see the powerful continuities of culture which persisted in immigrant populations. While the statue of the Korl Woman is a strong but silent image of resistance, repetition and fatigue, during these decades working people actively fought for the ten-hour day and, as soon as that was institutionalized, they began the long fight for the eight-hour day. To the dismay of American industrialists, immigrant workers maintained their traditional and still recent artisan habits of grog rations, eating at work and week-long religious celebrations. They took seasonal time off for hunting and harvesting. In company-owned towns workers struck for their right to raise pigs and maintain market gardens. Many refused to wear company uniforms.[14]

Although lacking a reform tradition of her own, and inevitably unaware of such labor publications as *The Voice of Industry* (1845-1848)[15] which were written by factory operatives and ignored by literary circles, Davis was deeply critical of the world of wealth and culture which offered no solutions to Hugh and Deborah. Kirby, the overseer of the mill, announces, "I wash my hands of all social problems,—slavery, caste, white or black. My duty to my operatives has a narrow limit,—the payhour on Saturday night." [p. 35] The doctor, while sympathetic is helpless. "Why should one be raised, when myriads are left?—I have not the money, boy." [p. 37] The aristocrat urges patience, and assures Hugh that some day a Cromwell or Messiah will arise from his own class to ferment "the heaving, cloggy mass." [p. 39] In the era of Robert Owen and Francois Fourier, Rebecca Harding Davis was aware of the utopian resolutions. After Deborah leaves jail she goes into the mountains and joins a devout Quaker community, "waiting like them: in her grey dress, her worn face, pure and meek, turned now and then to the sky." [p. 63] Nevertheless, despite the inherent potential for escape in the popular communitarian movements of the time, the Quakers were well known as leaders in the movements for prison reform and the abolition of slavery.

As in the writings of the later Naturalists, the environment dwarfs the characters in *Life in the Iron Mills*. From the first epigram,

> Is this the end?
> O Life, as futile, then, as frail!
> What hope of answer of redress?

the future is determined: "there is no hope that it will ever end," [p. 25] is a refrain in the text. Environment and instinct set the future for Davis' characters. Although each character is defeated, in the process Davis exploded the optimistic beliefs of Jacksonian democracy: the rule of the common man and the possibility of reduced labor and raised standards of living with the new technology. She showed the social consequences of the change from a domestic to an industrial economy, the pollution of the air and water, and most uniquely, the character of women as industrial workers and the dual nature of women's work. She traced the consequences of overwork on the extended family. Through the three central female images, the confined narrator, the hunchback picker, and the Korl Woman, Davis also exposed the aesthetic and sexual repressions of The Cult of the True Woman. Writing at a time when the American industrial revolution was little over a generation old, Davis predicted the effects of technology on character and culture.

As the curtain draws back to reveal the statue, the lonely narrator concludes her tale: "A bare arm stretched out imploringly in the darkness, and an eager, wolfish face watching mine: a wan, woeful face, through which the spirit of the dead korl-cutter looks out, with its thwarted life, its mighty hunger, its unfinished work. Its pale, vague lips seem to tremble with a terrible question. 'Is this the End?' they say,—'nothing beyond?—no more?'" [p. 64]

The final image mirrors the contradictions of Davis' perspective. As an image of working class rebellion, the statue is frightening and must be contained; in *Life in the Iron Mills* Davis confronted and repressed the image of her own fears. As an image of a woman and artist, however, the statue of the Korl Woman assumes the frustrations of Rebecca Harding Davis' own life: unfinished, hungry, and eager to know.

Notes

1. Rebecca Harding Davis, "Life in the Iron Mills," *Atlantic Monthly,* 7 April 1861. In 1972, The Feminist Press issued the first reprint appending "A Biographical Interpretation" by Tillie Olsen. For convenience, page references are to the reprint, and follow quotations in brackets.

2. Linda Morris, "The Image of Women in Magazine Illustrations, 1880-1889," unpublished manuscript, University of California at Berkeley, 1972.

3. Barbara Welter, "The Cult of True Womanhood, 1820-1860," in *Dimity Convictions* (Athens, Ohio: Ohio Univ. Press, 1976), p. 21. See also: Katherine Ellis, "Paradise Lost: The Limits of Domesticity in the Nineteenth Century Novel," *Feminist Studies,* 2, 2/3 (1975).

4. Herman Melville, "The Paradise of Bachelors and the Tartarus of Maids," *Harpers New Monthly Magazine,* April 1855. This story is generally credited with being the first portrait of industrial labor in American fiction.

5. The night shift generally followed the introduction of the Bessemer process. Management wanted to make steel cheaply enough to produce large pieces such as the artillery shell and the long gun barrel. Instead of refining pig iron by placing it directly on a pile of coal, Bessemer invented the process of keeping it molten in a vat and blowing cold air through it. The air, with the oxidized impurities now attached to it, would come out the top. This process required maintaining huge vats of molten pig iron which took a great deal of time to heat up and cool down. In order to minimize labor and coal costs, management introduced the night shift.

6. Elaine Showalter, "Dinah Murlock Craik and the Tactics of Sentiment: A Case Study in Victorian Female Authorship," *Feminist Studies,* 2, 2/3 (1975).

7. Henry Nash Smith, "The Scribbling Women and the Cosmic Success Story," *Critical Inquiry,* (Sept. 1974), 20.

8. William R. Taylor and Christopher Lasch, "Two 'Kindred Spirits': Sorority and Family in New England 1839-1846," *New England Quarterly,* 36, (1963), 23-41, describe the impact of industrialization, immigration, and migration on women's productive and educative roles in the family and the consequent development of the "cult of the home."

9. This reading disagrees with that of Walter Hesford, "Literary Context of *Life in the Iron Mills,*" *American Literature,* 49, 1 (1977), who, in tracing romance elements in the story asserts "the Korl woman's hunger can be honestly and permanently satisfied only with spiritual food," (p. 77).

10. Tillie Olsen, "Biographical Interpretation," pp. 69-78.

11. Gerda Lerner, "The Lady and the Mill Girl: Changes in the Status of Women in the Age of Jackson," *Mid-continent American Studies Journal,* 10 (1969), p. 10.

12. For a lively and detailed, although somewhat out of date history of women's leading role in the fight for the ten-hour day, see Alice Henry, *Women and the Labor Movement* (New York: George Duran and Co., 1923). A useful history of the employment of women and children in the early textile mills is Edith Abbot, *Women in Industry: A Study in American Economic History* (New York: Appleton and Co., 1910) Harriet Robinson's *Loom and Spindle,* recently reprinted, presents an interesting first-hand account of mill life in this period, (1898; rpt. Kailu, Hawaii; Press Pacifica, 1976).

13. Useful evidence for the changing nature of household work can be found in: Gerda Lerner, *The Female Experience: An American Documentary* (Indianapolis: Bobbs-Merrill Company, 1977); Rosalyn Baxandall, Linda Gordon, and Susan Reverby, *America's Working Women; A documentary*

History - 1600 to the Present (New York: Vintage Books, 1976); Nancy Cott, *Roots of Bitterness: Documents of the Social History of American Women* (New York: E.P. Dutton, 1972).

14. Herbert Gutman, *Work Culture and Society in Industrial America: Essays in American Working Class Social History,* (New York: Alfred A. Knopf, 1976).

15. *The Voice of Industry* (Boston: New England Workingman's Association and New England Labor Reform League, 1845-1848). See also, *The Factory Girl* (New Market, New Hampshire, 1841-1843); *The Factory Girls' Album and Operatives Advocate* (Exeter, New Hampshire, 1846); *The Factory Girls Garland* (Exeter, New Hampshire, 1844). Many articles from these and other early working womens journals are collected in Philip Foner, *The Factory Girls* (Urbana: University of Illinois Press, 1977).

Sharon M. Harris (essay date 1991)

SOURCE: Harris, Sharon M. "The Decadence of a Race." In *Rebecca Harding Davis and American Realism*, pp. 242-77. Philadelphia: University of Pennsylvania Press, 1991.

[*In the following essay, Harris surveys Davis's literary work and details aspects of her life during the 1890s and early 1900s, saying that her "nonfiction and fiction alike" of the period should not be dismissed by critics as inferior to her earlier writings; she describes Davis's late novels, stories, and essays as "well-written, insightful commentaries on the end of the nineteenth century, and they move into the modern period both artistically and thematically."*]

The tradition in Davis scholarship has been to assert that Davis's writings of the last two decades of her life were insignificant in terms of her own canon and in relation to American literary history.[1] Yet her renewed vigor of the late 1880s was carried forth into the next decade, and Davis's nonfiction and fiction alike offer well-written, insightful commentaries on the end of the nineteenth century, and they move into the modern period both artistically and thematically. It was not Davis's fin de siècle, and we do her and American literature a disservice by ignoring these later contributions. The themes that had concerned her for the past thirty years—stifled lives, the consequences of speculation and greed, the shameful glorification of war—became topical once again in the 1890s, as the country entered a period of increased progress coupled with high unemployment, insurrections, colonization, and military involvement in other countries.

When Davis was not traveling, she regularly published her social commentary in *The Independent* and continued writing for *Peterson's, Youth's Companion,* and *St. Nicholas.* In addition, she returned to the renowned literary journals of the day, including *Harper's, Century Magazine,* and the *North American Review,* and she expanded her forums for publication to include periodicals such as *The Living Age, The World,* and *Good Housekeeping.* More important, two leading publishing firms, Charles Scribner's Sons and Harper & Brothers, each published two full-length works by Davis in this decade. Thus, as she entered her sixties, she not only saw both of her sons establish themselves in the field of literature but returned to it herself as a commanding presence.

One of her first major works was the 1890 short story, **"An Ignoble Martyr,"** published by *Harper's New Monthly Magazine.* This was the year that saw the publication of William James's *Principles of Psychology*[2] and Jacob A. Riis's *How the Other Half Lives.* Seemingly disparate, the themes of James's and Riis's studies were anticipated in Davis's short story through the psychological realism of her characterization of that "other half." She had chronicled the lives of the working oppressed in **"Life in the Iron Mills,"** but her attention now focused more and more upon the stifled lives of women, as it had in the 1870s. In this fictionalized form, and in a later outspoken essay on New England's abandoned spinsters, Davis was concerned with the psychological damage suffered by women who were deprived of healthy relationships and satisfying careers. But Davis also demanded activism; these women needed to insist upon changes and to accept them when the opportunity arose.

In **"An Ignoble Martyr,"** Priscilla (Prue) Pettit represents the failure of both society and the individual—her social education thwarts her ability to prevail against traditions, and her own reliance upon the safety of tradition forces her to deny herself the route to personal fulfillment that she desires. The people in Prue's hometown of North Leedom have taken an honest virtue and distorted it into a destructive obsession: "they had reduced the economy of their Puritan ancestors to an art so hard and cruel that it dominated them now in body and soul. To save . . . had become the highest of duties."[3] Each generation's niggardliness had increased until their lives are now stripped of all means of enjoyment: "They came at last in their fierce zeal for saving to begrudge smiles and welcomes to each other or kisses and hugs to their children" (96). This excessive frugality leaves them physically and spiritually hungry, so much so that when opportunity enters in the form of M. Rameaux, they deny their own desires for a different way of life. Rameaux, a Mississippian whose community "carried the kindness and pity of their hearts ready for constant use" (99), offers Prue a chance for a new life in his symbolically fertile homeland. But because she has rarely seen anyone courted and more rarely seen love expressed, she has insufficient courage to leave her resolute mother: "it seemed to her, the gates were opened, the kingdoms of the world were laid at her feet. Of her own will she had given them up" (108).

Prue does incorporate some of Rameaux's influence into her barren life after he leaves. She plants a few flowers, reads some novels, and even visits New Bedford, where she rallies her courage enough to step into a retail shop and touch "some crimson silk and black-plumed hats" (109). But Davis discerns no heroism in martyrdom;[4] she presents these touches of finery in an otherwise destitute life as pathetic substitutes for the full life Prue might have lived. Davis had explored this theme in several of her longer works of the 1870s, and Rose Terry Cooke had detailed a similar theme in the late 1850s; but in **"[An] Ignoble Martyr,"** Davis expressly presents the complicity women bear in this process, a position that Mary E. Wilkins Freeman also presented in several of her short stories, including "A Poetess." As the women of the 1890s explored new avenues of personal development, Davis presented in **"An Ignoble Martyr"** a warning against the bleak alternatives to such activism.

This short story also challenges a prominent theme in New England literary traditions. From *The Scarlet Letter* to "A New England Nun," that region's authors had repeatedly suggested that a prolonged courtship or chastity itself enabled "the flowering of man";[5] Davis, however, following Catherine Maria Sedgwick's early if incomplete challenges to the premise, envisioned New England provincialism as a potential arena for women's entrapment. There is no "flowering" for Prue, only a slow death upon the stifling vine of New England custom.

* * *

Davis had been associated with the Boston weekly *The Living Age* for some time when, in May, they reprinted portions of her essay, **"The Plague Spot of America."** *The Living Age* reprinted American fiction, poetry, and essays and was known for its reprints of the best fiction and articles from English periodicals such as *Blackwood's, Macmillan's,* and *The Spectator.* The weekly's motto was, "These publications of the day should from time to time be winnowed, the wheat preserved, and the chaff thrown away," and the editors had discerned that **"The Plague Spot"** and several short stories by Davis warranted preservation. Thus Davis took advantage of this association to tout the talents of her eldest son to Mr. Bridgeman, an editor for *The Living Age.* Bridgeman had commented positively on some of Richard's early work, for which Davis heartily thanked him: "I am glad that you like my boy's work. You would like

him. I have never heard him say an unkind malicious thing of any human being. And I have known him a long time!"[6]

She drew on other literary contacts to encourage Richard's career as well. In April, she wrote to her old friend from Houghton, Mifflin, Horace Elisha Scudder, who had recently accepted the editorship at the *Atlantic Monthly.* "Do you remember a talk we once had about our children and our hopes for them?" she asked Scudder, who, like Davis, had published many works for children. "Now my boy has done something which gives a hint of what manner of man he is and I venture to ask you as an old friend to let the Atlantic pass judgment on it." But she cautioned Scudder that she did not want preferential treatment for Richard: "'Be just and fear not' even a mother's disappointment, if the verdict is not favourable."[7] Scudder took her at her word and declined the manuscript. Davis had not told Richard of her efforts on his behalf, however, so he remained unaware of this rejection. He was, in fact, gaining his own way in the literary world. He had been working for the New York *Evening Sun* as a reporter for almost six months, under the tutelage of managing editor Arthur Brisbane, and in March of 1890 the Van Bibber stories began to appear; they were to make him a household name. Charles published short fiction and essays, but he never gained the recognition of his elder brother. Today, Charles's authorship is known primarily in terms of *The Adventures and Letters of Richard Harding Davis* (1917), his laudatory assessment of his brother's life.

Three Davis authors—Rebecca, Richard, and Charles—soon found themselves congenially competing for space in several literary periodicals. No tensions of competitiveness seem to have marred their relationships; instead, their letters reveal a heartfelt encouragement regarding each other's work. A few years later, when Rebecca and Richard had books published simultaneously, Richard wrote to his mother: "I am so glad to hear about the book. It seems too cosy and nice for us to be coming out together. People will buy both so as to be sure to get the right one and we will get rich and go to Europe *by land.* . . . I am so glad about it and much more interested than if it were my own."[8] He signed the letter with his usual phrase, "Your boy, Dick." Although scholars have since forgotten, the Davises were one of America's most prolific and prominent literary families at the end of the nineteenth century.

In 1891, Davis's sons encouraged her to return to longer fiction. Though *Natasqua* had been reprinted four years earlier, no significant long fiction by Davis had appeared in novel form since the 1870s. She contacted her old friend Richard Watson Gilder, who had been an assistant editor of *Scribner's Monthly* when she was a regular contributor and who now headed *Century Magazine.* "Are you for treating us to a long serial?" Davis asked Gilder. "My boys have been anxious for a long time that I should write one." Davis had the novel well under way and had an offer from another publisher, but, as she told Gilder, "I would rather see it in the Century than anywhere else."

Davis, however, felt a certain trepidation at reentering the field of novel writing. It had been more than fifteen years since she had put her mind to an endeavor of such length and, she cautiously observed, "Whether my hand has lost whatever cunning it once had, I cannot tell."[9] She need not have worried. Her fiction of this decade has the grace of tone and style reflective of an ability to write out of artistic interest rather than financial compunction. The novel was **Kent Hampden,** an excellent story designed for adolescent readers, which draws on the factual history of Wheeling and is reminiscent of Davis's own early family life.

Other factors made *Century Magazine* a logical source for Davis's fiction, since the journal was now devoting much of its space to the new realistic fiction. In this decade the *Century* serialized Howells's *A Modern Instance* and *The Rise of Silas Lapham,* Henry James's *The Bostonians,* Jack London's *The Sea-Wolf,* and Joel Chandler Harris's "Uncle Remus" stories. The periodical also published several essays and works of fiction by established and new women realists, including Elizabeth Stuart Phelps, Mary E. Wilkins (Freeman), and Octave Thanet (Alice French). In a few years, Davis would return to its pages with her own realistic fiction, but she or Gilder, or perhaps both, decided against *Century Magazine* for **Kent Hampden.**

Instead, the novel was serialized in *Youth's Companion* and published in book form by Charles Scribner's Sons in 1892. The novel was dedicated to her brothers, Hugh Wilson Harding and Richard Harris Harding, "who have hunted over every foot of Kent's hills"; it was for them that she "inscribe[d] this little story of our old home." The Hampden family bears many resemblances to the Hardings, especially in terms of its father figure, but the story is a fictionalized retelling of early nineteenth-century life in West Virginia that includes excellent adventure and mystery sequences. The reviewer for *The Critic* especially praised Davis for her attention to "local color" and the "spirit" with which she recreated life in Wheeling at the beginning of the century.[10]

If Davis had learned anything from her self-imposed "retirement" of the 1880s, it was that she needed to balance her highly productive literary career with periods of rest and relative quiet. Thus she informed William Hayes Ward, superintending editor of *The Independent,* that she wished to take a year's leave from her regular contributions to the periodical. She held as closely to this goal as possible, considering the creative energies recently awakened in her: she published four short pieces for him in 1891. Her decision to forego journalism for a time was not made so that she might have more rest; instead, she sought time to complete several long works that she had in mind. In subsequent years, Davis produced some excellent fiction that brought her once again into the arena of contemporary experimental fiction.

Throughout this decade, Davis was also barraged with requests from editors of national dictionaries and literary collections for biographical details, interviews, and photographs. She graciously produced details of her life or referred the inquirer to previously published data. One of the most interesting mentions of Davis in a study of the period was Helen Gray Cone's study of "Woman in American Literature," which appeared in the October 1890 issue of *Century Magazine.* Cone began her study by acknowledging the negative effects of considering women's literary contributions separately from men's, which has allowed "the suave and chivalrous critic, . . . judging all 'female writers' by a special standard," to assess women's works according to a different set of criteria.[11] Thus Cone sought to produce an objective literary history of women's writings that acknowledged the "accessions of force" attained in women's literary contributions in recent years, a force which she felt was gradually increasing (921). Beginning with Anne Bradstreet, Phillis Wheatley, and Mercy Otis Warren, and moving through the nineteenth century, Cone includes Davis as one of the notable women of the mid- to late-nineteenth century, along with Catherine Maria Sedgwick, Lydia Maria Child, Harriet Beecher Stowe, Elizabeth Stuart Phelps, and others.

Such acknowledgments Davis welcomed, but she continued to refuse requests for photographs or interviews. When Charles Wells Moulton requested a portrait to illustrate a sketch of Davis's life that he was preparing, she declined both, asserting, "Nothing ever happened to me which would give point to an item. And I have a dislike to seeing anything about myself (personally) in print. But I quite appreciate your compliment."[12] While Davis's reluctance to promote herself in the literary marketplace was perhaps honorable, it was also detrimental to her lasting fame. But, as she asserted in **"The Temple of Fame,"** honor is always preferable to fame.

What Davis did appreciate was the personal rather than the public gesture. Thus she was delighted when the renowned Philadelphia Shakespeare scholar Horace Howard Furness honored her by sending her a copy of *The Tempest.* The gift recalled to her mind the joy and the strange other-worldliness she had discovered in the bard's pages when, at age eight, she had received copies of *Julius Caesar* and *The Tempest* from her mother. "But if I had been told," she wrote Furness,

> that some time the high priest of Shakespeare for all the world would send the Tempest to me—*me,* it would

have seemed much stranger and more unreal than Ariel or Caliban or any of their spiriting.

So I won't be humble and think that you sent this to Clarke's wife or Dick's mother but to—*me*. And I'm very glad you did it.[13]

Her appreciation of Furness's thoughtful gesture echoed her response when she had heard, so many years earlier, that Nathaniel Hawthorne intended to visit her in Wheeling.

Even more delightful to Davis was her renewed association with Mary Mapes Dodge, editor of *St. Nicholas.* Davis had not published in *St. Nicholas* since the mid-1870s, in large part because *Youth's Companion* paid so much more than Dodge's periodical,[14] but perhaps also because Dodge had, for a short time in the mid-seventies, replaced Annie Fields as Davis's most intimate female correspondent. With her children grown, Davis may have felt the need for renewed contact—this time without the urgency that her strained relations with Fields had added to her earlier contact with Dodge. Thus, in the summer of 1890, Davis decided to submit a short story (**"The Great Tri-Club Tennis Tournament"**) to *St. Nicholas*; Dodge published the story in the September issue. The following spring, Dodge invited Davis to a tea she was hosting in New York. Davis declined, but her letter reveals the pleasure she received from the offer:

My dear Mrs. Dodge

I cannot content myself with sending cards to show how sorry I am not to be able to go to your tea.

How long it is since I saw or heard from you! Do you never come to this quiet corner of the earth? We live in the same old house [at] 230 South 21st Street. *Do* come. I heard you had a boy in town but I suppose he would be bored by an old woman.

If I ever go to New York I shall find the Cordova and claim friendship with you.[15]

Yet Davis and Dodge remained in contact only sporadically over the intervening years. It was not until 1897 that they would renew their literary association and revive a friendship that extended until Dodge's death in 1905.

During this period, Davis also continued her personal activism for women in her community, and she did not hesitate to use her literary connections in these endeavors. For example, she contacted Richard Watson Gilder at the *Century* and urged him to publish two articles that had been sent to her by "a little Scotchwoman here in whom Mr. Davis and I are much interested." Davis described the unnamed woman as bright and sensitive but impoverished and struggling to provide a home for a severely retarded child. Davis asserted that the illustrated articles, "one on Barrie's country and the other

on Gladstone's early life," ought to be of interest to the *Century*'s readership since they were drawn by the pen of a writer who came from the "Thrums" region.[16] Davis also sought Horace Scudder's assistance. This time, Davis and a friend, Mrs. Wells,[17] were attempting to send a sick woman to the country for a much-needed rest. Davis approached Scudder with a translation that Mrs. Wells had prepared and hoped to publish in *Riverside Magazine.* Davis wittingly relied upon Scudder's senses of humor and honor: Mrs. Wells, she observed, "has an idea that you publishers have a sort of Ali-Baba cave—of which one only needs to know the pass-word to go in and pick up gold in bushel measures. I gave her the pass-word now and—*have not undeceived her.* I am sure *you* will not for the honor of the craft."[18] Mrs. Wells remained "undeceived."

* * *

In conjunction with her enthusiasm for returning to full-length works of fiction, Davis aggressively pursued a publisher for her second book of the period. Scribner's had recently published **Kent Hampden,** and she now proposed to them the publication of a collection of her short stories, which they enthusiastically agreed to publish.[19] Davis's collection, drawn from stories she had written over the previous twenty years, is indicative in itself of her pioneering work in the field of realism. In 1891 Hamlin Garland had published his collected study of the decaying countryside, *Main-Travelled Roads,* and Mary Wilkins Freeman had also published her short-story collection, *A New England Nun,* which presents the same images of decay but with a special focus on women's lives. The realism, nostalgia, and at times bitterness of these two authors' works deeply echo the mood of Davis's collection, **Silhouettes of American Life.**

Silhouettes [*Silhouettes of American Life*] is one of those forgotten "gems" in American literature. The writing is superb, the vision Davis gives us of America in the last half of the nineteenth century is invaluable, and the stories entertain as well as educate. The short stories, with one exception, had been previously published in *Scribner's, Harper's, Lippincott's,* and the *Atlantic Monthly.* Many of these stories have been discussed in previous chapters, but a few warrant special attention here. The one new entry, **"The End of the Vendetta,"** follows a literary trend of this period of returning to the early eras of American life. Recent publications that manifested this trend included biographies of Lincoln, John Fiske's study of *The American Revolution,* Thomas Nelson Page's *The Old South,* Stephen Crane's *The Red Badge of Courage,* Moses Coit Tyler's *Literary History of the American Revolution,* and Mary Wilkins Freeman's *Giles Corey, Yeoman,* which focused on the Salem witch trials.

"Vendetta" [**"The End of the Vendetta"**] is set in the days of Reconstruction and follows a young Northern woman, Lucy Coyt, as she journeys into the South, expecting adventures at every turn and "a very different human species" from any she has known (197). Davis delights once again in satirizing the Northerner's preconceived notions about the South and its people. Lucy Coyt believes she is an expert when it comes to analyzing human nature; after all, she "had gone to the Fairview Female Seminary, and had read Carlyle, and the Autocrat in the 'Atlantic,' and 'Beauties of German Authors'" (198). There is an element of self-mockery in this as well, since Lucy's early history closely parallels Davis's own youthful education and reading patterns. But **"Vendetta"** suggests that Lucy has the potential to set aside her romantic perspectives and gain a truer sense of herself and of Southerners. Lucy, however, returns to the North after accepting a marriage proposal, thus ending "her experiment" in the South, and the people she tried to "educate" return to their own "usual quiet routine of life" (217). The final mood is one of enveloping stasis in which Davis questions the effectiveness of Northern influences on the long-held traditions of the South. Prior to writing **"Vendetta,"** Davis had vacationed in Warm Springs, Virginia, during the summer of 1892, and her observations of the region left her with the disquieting realization that, although Reconstruction had ended officially in 1876, little had changed on either side.

One of the most interesting stories in the collection, both in terms of its artistry and its place in American literary history, is **"The Yares of Black Mountain,"** subtitled **"A True Story."** Originally published in *Lippincott's* in 1875, this story chronicles the integrity of an impoverished mountain family that had tried to remain neutral during the war but, in the end, had paid dearly in lives and memories. The realistic detailing of the mountain life and the abject poverty of the Yares' existence is graphically rendered, but the story is most interesting for Davis's attention to the vernacular of the mountain people and to the role that women played in the Underground Railroad during the war. In addition, Davis satirizes the new breed of political writer, in the person of Miss Cook, who converses with a few people for five or ten minutes, assuming that they, and now she, have the "facts" about this region. Miss Cook visits the jail-house at the foot of the mountains where, as she records it, men "are actually secured in iron cages like wild beasts! I shall use that fact effectively in my book on the 'Causes of the Decadence of the South': one chapter shall be given to 'The Social and Moral Condition of North Carolina'" (251). When a local woman protests that Miss Cook will need her entire vacation to gather materials for such a project, the political essayist responds with haughty patronization: "Why, child, I

have them all now—got them this morning. Oh, I can evolve the whole state of society from half a dozen items. I have the faculty of generalizing, you see" (252).

Davis juxtaposes Miss Cook's surface reporting with the reality of the existence and "terrible history" of the Yares (259). The sons who had tried to remain neutral during the war are forced into hiding in order to avoid being drafted into the Union army, but Jonathan Yare is badly wounded. Although their home is occupied by Union soldiers, their sister, Nancy, manages to sneak away at intervals to build a hut in which John is protected from the bitter cold of the winter nights while he recovers from his wounds. She cuts down logs, builds a six-by-ten-foot hut, floors it, and covers it with brush. When the hut is discovered by the soldiers, however, she is jailed and threatened with imprisonment in the Salisbury prisoner-of-war camp or hanging if she refuses to reveal her brother's whereabouts. Nancy remains silent; she and her four brothers are saved only by their tenacity and Lee's surrender two weeks later. All that remains of value in the Yares' lives is their serene if impoverished existence in the mountains and the knowledge that the family is together again.

Davis's story, which was innovative in theme as well as in its attention to North Carolinian vernacular, had influenced several writers of the seventies. Mary Noailles Murfree published at that time a series of stories on the Cumberland Mountain region under the pseudonym of Charles Egbert Craddock; one of these early stories had appeared in the same issue of *Lippincott's* as **"Yares,"** [**"The Yares of Black Mountain"**] and a subsequent story, "The Dancin' Party at Harrison's Cove," is indebted to Davis's **"Yares"** in its assimilation of several themes and scenes from the Davis work.[20] Helen Woodward Shaeffer's early biography of Davis more explicitly acknowledges the importance of **"The Yares"** in American literary history. **"Yares"** also influenced Murfree's *In the Tennessee Mountains* (1884), and Shaeffer recounts the ongoing discussion of the 1940s, when she was completing her biography of Davis, as to whether Murfree or Constance Fenimore Woolson "was first in presenting a picture of the North Carolina mountaineers"; in fact, Shaeffer notes, Murfree's "Dancin' Party" and Woolson's "Crowder's Cove: A Story of the War" both appeared after Davis's story was published in *Lippincott's*. In **"Yares,"** Shaeffer confirms, "Mrs. Davis shows her realistic writing at its best."[21]

Davis is also in top form in **"Marcia,"** another short story collected in **Silhouettes**; it had first appeared in *Harper's* in 1876.[22] In this short story, Davis exposes the limited opportunities that existed for women in the major American periodicals, but she is especially concerned with the prevalence, in contemporary writing, of young authors who refuse to learn their craft. Davis had expressed similar ideas in her essay **"Shop and Coun-**

try Girls" (1889), wherein she observed that often a young rural woman "painted a few plates or had a few months' instruction in crayon drawing, and is looked upon as a genius by her family and neighbors. She comes to town. She fails. 'Art is a drug,' she tells her fellow artist, as they sit in their bare attic making pathetic little sketches in their bedaubed apron."[23] Marcia's writings are sentimental; she tells the established woman writer who acts as narrator of the story that she "had vowed herself to literature . . . resolved to assist in the Progress of humanity" (270). At this juncture in her professional life, Davis reflected current literary trends by moving away from an appreciation of sentimental literature; here, she no longer synthesizes her realism with that perspective nor does she praise those who continue in that mode.

Marcia Barr thinks she needs only to be educated in the ways of Philadelphia publishing, but the narrator notes that the young woman's manuscripts are crude at best: her "spelling was atrocious, the errors of grammar in every line beyond remedy. The lowest pupil in our public schools would have detected her ignorance on the first page" (273). Had this been the sum total of Marcia's talent, the narrator would have sent her away as she had so many other young would-be writers. But, in spite of the crudity of Marcia's writing, the elder woman notes a potential for developing realism in the young woman's style: "there was no trace of imitation"; instead of repeating the locales of the popular fiction, Marcia writes about her home—about what she knows (273). The narrator detects the potential for originality, *if* the young writer is willing to learn her craft, willing to labor for two or three years in order to hone her talents. But Marcia has accepted the "popular belief in the wings of genius, which can carry it over hard work. . . . Work was for commonplace talent, not for those whose veins were full of the divine ichor" (274). Thus Marcia's "fate," not unlike Hugh Wolfe's, is especially tragic because she had the talent necessary for her art. Instead, she struggles to survive in the city and finally is jailed after she succumbs to theft in order to survive. Her persistent lover from home comes to her assistance, but that "salvation" is tragic. Life as Mrs. Biron (certainly an intentionally ironic name) will be little different for Marcia than her residency in the city jail. At the story's conclusion, Marcia knows that she has sold her talent—her entire future—and now must substitute for it this marriage that she abhors. When Marcia asks that her work be destroyed and departs in silence, it is because she knows, at last, this excruciating truth.

Silhouettes was both a critical and popular success. It was reviewed widely and repeatedly praised for its "strong, clear impressions" of American life.[24] *The Independent*'s reviewer was laudatory in his comments, as would be expected from a publication for which Davis

was a regular contributor. But the reviewer also captures the two most significant aspects of Davis's fiction that had made her a lasting figure in American literature for almost three decades: the stories are "strikingly original, and they are all thoroughly and truthfully American."[25] One of the best reviews came, surprisingly, from Davis's old nemesis, *The Nation*. Although the reviewer began with typically lukewarm praise (the sketches are "worth the reading"), he took exception only with **"A Wayside Episode"** (a woman-centered story), and concluded: "Among the rest, where there is such an even range of excellence, it would be hard to pick."[26] It was impressive praise from the usually reticent *Nation*. **Silhouettes** went into three editions, and Richard wrote his mother after the third edition appeared in 1893, "These *young* writers are working me to the wall."[27]

* * *

In 1893, Davis's thirty-two-year association with *Peterson's Magazine* ended—with neither a breach nor a celebration but with a farewell "grumble." *Peterson's* had begun the decade with Davis at the top of its list of notable contributors, and she had published four items during the nineties before ending her career with the magazine. In January 1893, the editors began a new series and retitled the periodical *The New Peterson Magazine*. Several authors new to the magazine appeared in its pages at this time, including Julian Hawthorne, Joseph Kirkland, Agnes Repplier, Thomas Wentworth Higginson, and Octave Thanet. In the first issue of the *New Peterson's,* the editors began a section entitled "By the Fireside," devoted to their better-known authors' contributions.

The new magazine's first issue became Davis's last, since the Davises had finally reached a financial stage wherein she could forego the higher payments made by *Peterson's* and concentrate on writing only those books and articles that interested her. Davis's final essay for the magazine, **"A Grumble,"** was printed in the "Fireside" section. In the essay, she lamented the lack of American individuality at the end of the nineteenth century: no single footstep can be heard, only "the measured tramp of clubs, committees, guilds, and congresses, both day and night."[28] No longer is there time to sit "By the fireside" and have discussions with old friends (a rather ironic lament, since Davis's life had afforded her scant time for such endeavors). You can neither hate nor love the new breed of American, she asserts, using scientific metaphors: "They are molecules in the mass which moves against capital or labor, which lifts the lower classes by university extension lectures or college settlements or Browning clubs. They will not allow you to creep along your own shady path, either—they make a molecule of you too; you must be an atom of a committee or an organization, or you are naught"

(103). She returns to the fears of her first major literary publication when she worries that "we shall all be stifled" by the mass consensus and discipline of modern existence (104). Although she admits her "protest is as vain as is the chirp of the sandpiper against the incoming tides of the ocean," she recalls an ancient parish priest, Reverend Walker, whose personal concern and charitable activism had earned him the nickname of "The Wonderful" (104). He had survived a grueling life by reserving for himself one hour of solitude every day; today, Davis asserts, "he would rush to a club or convention when his soul needed repairs" (104). It is true, she admits, that there is useful work in the modern world; but her final words for *Peterson's* acknowledges her sense of loss: "we have no more Wonderful Walkers" (104).

Her farewell was made easier by the fact that it cost her no personal alienation from old friends, as had occurred so often in the past when she separated with a long-term publisher. Charles Peterson, her long-time friend and editor, had died in 1887. She simply passed the baton without remorse to the next generation of *New Peterson's* authors. That next generation included her second son, Charles, whose fiction appeared in the February issue, and younger metarealists such as Harriet Prescott Spofford and Mary Wilkins Freeman. Indeed, an interesting aspect of the canonization of American literature was visible in *New Peterson's* during late 1896 and early 1897, when the editors ran a five-part series entitled "Pioneers of American Literature." Those pioneers, according to the series' authors, were Irving, Cooper, Hawthorne, Emerson, and Poe. *Peterson's* own loyal pioneer realist was not included nor was any other woman writer. However, if Davis had closed the door on this phase of her literary career, she was about to reopen it to full-length works of fiction. She had no intention of relinquishing her artistic voice.

* * *

While Davis allowed her next two novels to develop in her mind, she returned to her regular contributions for *The Independent* and wrote several other pieces for major periodicals over the next two years. In 1894, however, when it seemed that everyone in the family was basking in the luxury of fame and well-being,[29] a frightening event occurred that caused Davis to set aside her own writing for a period of time. Charles then held a government post in Italy, Nora was in Florence visiting her brother, and Clarke, who had taken over the editorship of the Philadelphia *Public Ledger* the previous year when William V. McKean had retired, was engrossed in the work that would occupy him until his death. Richard, who at age thirty was consulting with his employers at Harper's about the possibility of resigning that post for an opportunity to do more traveling, was suddenly stricken with another of his recurring attacks of sciatica; this time, however, it resulted in a far more serious bout with severe depression, and Richard returned to his family home to be nursed by his mother.

Davis had suffered her own mental travails when she was in her early thirties, and she understood the devastating realities of depression in a way that friends and family could not. Richard had been ordered to bed for a month because of the sciatica, but the emotional disturbance that befell him lasted for more than ten months.[30] It is little wonder that Davis's letters of the period are rife with apologies for failure to attend to her mail. A typical letter reads, "Your letter with many others have been neglected because of serious illness in my family. I hope that you will believe that no discourtesy was intended by the delay."[31]

At the beginning of summer, difficulties also began to arise in Davis's long-term, friendly association with *The Independent*. She had not had to barter with Dr. Ward over payments until H. S. Chandler, the publisher, interceded. The tension is evident in a brief letter Dr. Ward sent to Davis in June: "My dear Madam: I am very sorry to say that I am not now allowed by our publishing department to pay $100 for a story of 3,500 or 4,000 words, such as yours have been. I wish I might do it."[32] On Ward's copy of the letter, there is a handwritten note in the upper right-hand corner: "Copy shown to H.S.C. who said 'That is all right, sir.'" Chandler wished to limit payment to fifty dollars, or one-half of what Davis was accustomed to receiving, and on at least one occasion she was forced to quibble over whether they would pay her twenty-five or thirty dollars for a short article. This occurred at a time when Davis received, on an average, between forty and one hundred dollars for her articles, depending on length. Not surprisingly, she balked, and Ward himself was obviously dismayed at Chandler's tactics. The era of the genteel publisher was nearly over. A revealing letter from Chandler to Susan Hayes Ward, a staff member of *The Independent* who also had argued on Davis's behalf, suggests the publisher's attitude toward literature and authors:

> My dear Miss Ward:
>
> A story is a story and business is business. The idea that writers for newspapers and magazines are not supposed to do business in a business way, it seems to me, ought to be exploded. The only way to treat with R. H. D. or with any other writer is from a business standpoint. If they write for money they enter the business arena and they must treat and be treated accordingly.[33]

The tension grew between Davis and her editor. She became reluctant to write for *The Independent* and returned to the specificity of conditions that she usually reserved for new places of publication:

Dear Sir

I did not understand that I was to send you a story. When you asked me for one, I declined to write it, for the very low price paid by the Independent and asked you if you were willing to pay more, to write to me.

I received no answer of any kind.

I am very busy at other work but if you have counted on my help I will try and send you a short story by Saturday Dec. 14. The price to be $50 *paid on receipt of Ms.* If this will suit you please write by return mail.[34]

The friendship between Davis and Ward was eventually restored, but, ironically, Chandler's concern for proper business methods seemed to operate only in one direction: Davis often had to write *The Independent*'s business manager to remind him that she had not received payment. In September she informed Ward that the manager had not responded "by money nor apology. How blessed the next world will be—where we shall have no use—let us hope, for money or business managers!"[35] She continued to raise the issue of payment before each submission now, insisting that for longer stories she receive full compensation:

Dear Dr. Ward

Sept 20

I have a Thanksgiving story in my mind—do you want it when it is on paper for the Independent? The price will be $100.

I write to you now because you often have asked me for stories so near to Thanksgiving or Christmas that I could do justice neither to you nor myself.

Please let me hear from you soon.[36]

When, in spite of this letter, Ward waited until early November to request a Thanksgiving story, Davis responded with a delightfully cryptic note: "Dear Dr. Ward—I will try. But you *are* an unconscionable man!"[37] She continued to write for *The Independent* during the remainder of her life—and she continued to name her price before submitting an item.

* * *

In addition to writing several topical essays for *The World* during this period,[38] Davis wrote fiction and essays for the *Congregationalist,* a Boston weekly. Harriet Prescott Spofford also contributed to the periodical in the mid-nineties, and Frances E. Willard found in its pages a platform for her temperance petition. Alice Morse Earle, a nineteenth-century chronicler of early American women's lives, also began to publish short articles on the New England Puritans in the *Congregationalist* during this decade. The weekly was conservative and opposed to women's suffrage; and while it advocated women's higher education, its essays on that theme, such as "The College Girl—Her Present Need,

Her Future Possibility," by Mary M. Adams of Wisconsin University, unwittingly reflected the limited inroads women had made in higher education to date. Adams propounds the "clear and untrammeled right" of young women to a college education and the "healthful and . . . stimulating" atmosphere of college life, but she concludes that women should have a curriculum distinguished from men's course of study by its emphasis upon the "true woman" theme.[39] Davis's work for the *Congregationalist* similarly focused on topical themes, such as marriage, charity, and blacks' roles in society, but her presentations were often didactic in style and conservative in their conclusions. That conservatism, always quivering beneath the surface of Davis's less distinguished writings, would emerge periodically in her final years, as it had throughout her life.

In February of 1895, however, Davis returned to the pages of *Century Magazine* with one of her finest essays. That periodical's attention to the new realistic fiction and to social consciousness in its essays had attracted such authors as Joel Chandler Harris, Mary E. Wilkins (Freeman), Elizabeth Stuart Phelps, Octave Thanet, and John Hay. Hamlin Garland published "A Spring Romance" in *Century Magazine* early in the decade, and Mark Twain's *Pudd'nhead Wilson* was serialized the year before Davis's article appeared. Kate Chopin was also beginning to appear in the magazine's pages; she published a few short stories and one poem during the decade. In the following years, Frank Norris found the magazine receptive to his reporting of the Spanish-American War, and Annie Fields published several articles of literary criticism in the pages of the *Century* at the end of the decade. Although the distribution of male authors' works in the *Century* compared to that of female authors remained relatively unchanged from the previous decade, the magazine, instead of relying upon a few women contributors, had expanded its number of female authors significantly.

Davis had last published in the journal in the early 1880s, when it was still *Scribner's Monthly.* Her return was marked by the startling aggressiveness and outspoken realism with which she presented a theme she had been developing over the last two decades: how society perpetuates women's wasted intellectual and emotional lives. It is in this essay, **"In the Gray Cabins of New England,"** that Davis's theme is fully realized.[40] Many New England women writers, including Phelps, Stowe, and later, Jewett, praised the matriarchal isolation of rural New England; but Davis, extending Rose Terry Cooke's lead, recognized that the region was not a utopia. The realities of a desperate impoverishment and sense of abandonment, to Davis's mind, only led women to personal and spiritual deprivation.

In her inimitable spirit of questioning outdated "orthodox formulas," Davis begins her essay by challenging the long-held belief that the greatest intellectual energy in America was to be found in "the gray cabins of New England" (620). True as this idea may have been one hundred or even fifty years earlier, it is, she insists, an arguable assertion in the mid-1890s. While this assertion continues Davis's lifelong rejection of the primacy of Boston literary modes, she had learned over the years to temper her attacks through initial acknowledgment of the values of Boston-centered literature as well. Thus she notes that "nobody who is not made imbecile by prejudice" would deny that Boston, Concord, and a select few other New England cities constitute the most influential literary centers in America. She is also aware that the pattern of questioning the validity of this concentration of influence (which she had begun in the early 1860s) was now the vogue. Momentarily, Davis takes the side of the Boston literati and confirms that they do occasionally acknowledge outsiders' work, and she praises them for their genuine intellectual pursuit of contemporary literature, which they strive for instead of responding only to the classics.

The problem with their widely praised perspective, Davis asserts, is that they have failed to recognize their own region's intellectual decline, and, with this turn in the essay, Davis documents that process of decline. Ten years earlier, she notes, she had visited one of these lonely districts in the very "soul of New England" that are supposed to be harboring the next generation of Hawthornes and Emersons. What she found, however, echoes Hamlin Garland's Border stories: there were only "dull-eyed old men and lean old women"; the young people had gone west or south. Yet even more important was the fact that the remaining New Englanders, who had been well educated, now preferred "the most sensational fiction in a circulating library" and never touched the cover of the best of contemporary fiction (620-21). When the young men left, the vitality of intellectualism went with them. The most pathetic residue of this abandonment were the unmarried women: "These people have not enough food for their bodies, or occupation for their minds. The niggardly economy forced upon their forefathers by the barren soil . . . is honored as the chief of virtues" (621).

This "barren soil" metaphor symbolizes the women both spiritually and sexually. The New Englander's "plain living," Davis asserts, has not "lifted him into high thinking. He is stingy of love, of friendship, of emotion" (621). She had fictionalized the pathos of this tradition of abject economy in **"An Ignoble Martyr"** and in her characterization of Emma Cramer in **"Tirar y Soult,"** but in **"Gray Cabins"** [**"In the Gray Cabins of New England"**] Davis pursues the theme more broadly. The enshrinement of the Puritan faith and temperament, she discerns, has led to increasing numbers of divorces but it has carried a greater price: the New Englander has lost "the secret" of God's election and thinks only of "milk-cans or potatoes," and the "most

hopeless feature in his case is absolute complacency" (62). He has remained since the days of Emerson's reign so assured of himself as "the highest type of man" that, though the soul beneath may be "true and generous," his inherited "iron armor of self-control" will not let it surface. Activism and passion, of the intellect and of the emotions, has been completely stifled.

The lively activities of the New England cities cloud that area's recognition of its own declining country counterpart, Davis asserts. The New England city dweller mistakenly identifies "the eventless drama" of the country dwellers' lives as picturesque and fails to perceive that it is "the symptom of the decadence of a race" (622). The children, having never been educated in the English language and grammar, still speak "with an Irish brogue or a Canadian patois." The community as a whole is no longer interested in religion since they have found spiritualism, faith cures, or theosophy. Davis's ever-present demand for activism comes in her deeply sardonic comparison of the New Englanders' present spiritual condition with that of their forefathers: "Really the whipping of Quakers and the hanging of witches argued a better spiritual condition than this apathy. When Cotton Mather declared that 'the smell of the roasting flesh of the savages was a sweet savor in the nostrils of the Almighty,' he had at least a live faith in—something" (622).

But one segment of the population has the most urgent need for change, Davis avers: the unattached women who, though well educated, have no important work:

> they have sensitive instincts, strong affections, and the capacity to do high work in the world. But from the sheer force of a single circumstance,—the majority of their sex in certain States,—they have neither husbands nor children, and there is no occupation for them but household drudgery. Nervous prostration is an almost universal ailment among them, following, as it always does, long self-repression.
>
> (622)

Wealthy New England women have the power to remove themselves, to live in the region's prosperous cities and to "find an outlet for their strength, if not in marriage, in active work, charitable or literary or social" (622). With revealing modernity and in a significant shift from her own traditional stance of lauding the rural over the urban, Davis adamantly rejects the proposition that contact with the outside world, as it were, is in any way a detriment to these urban women: "Friction with the world has kept them healthy in thought" while their country-bound sisters "for want of work and that friction are overtaken by neurosis, or driven to spiritualism, to Buddhism, or to opium" (622).

While Davis admonishes New Englanders for their ignorance of this situation, she also demands that these village women share in the responsibility for their wasted lives. Though there are many new opportunities for women in turn-of-the-century America, they refuse to leave the security of their homes. Education simply becomes part of the burden: "The intellectual training of these women only makes their cramped existence more intolerable. . . . Education [the New Englander] believes to be the royal road to civilization. But to what does it lead in these villages—in fact, not in theory?" (622) It unfits the woman for village life and allows her no outlet for her intellect. Following the same vein, Davis strongly rejects a sentimental perspective of New England women's lives, observing that "Miss Jewett, Miss Wilkins, and Mrs. Slosson . . . have written the petty tragedy of [these women's] lives with a power which has held the whole country attentive" (623); unfortunately, she asserts, these stories are so powerful that the spectator has forgotten there is no need for these lives to be petty or tragic:

> These genre artists show us the tender, heroic spirit in a famishing woman which makes her boil her last egg for a neighbor nearer starvation than herself. But if the heroic spirit be there, why should it not have a nobler outlet than the boiling of an egg? With the whole big, seething world around us full of God's highest work to do, one grows a little impatient of human souls who make a life-drama out of their hair pictures or muddied kitchen floors.
>
> (623)

Women who have become little more than silent "human machines" should not be praised for what is, in part, self-repression.

What these women do need is our attention, Davis contends. New England villages are not just *materiel* for the artist or author, but a problem of wasted human life and force" (623). Davis demands that New Englanders, known for their generosity with "the freedman, the Indians, the lepers in India, and Nihilists in Siberian mines," do not forget "these starved, coffined lives at home" (623). Do not bathe them in sympathy, she instructs. Give them "practical help": remunerative work at home, and, if that is not available, help them emigrate to the West or South or Middle States, just as their brothers have. Second, once they have found work, encourage them to marry. Davis's insistence that women as well as men needed sexually active lives scandalized some of her "puritanical readers,"[41] much as, in 1862, she had shocked her New England hosts in Boston and Concord by asserting that women's sexual needs were as strong as men's. Still, in **"Gray Cabins,"** Davis emphasizes that the best means of assistance is employment: "Nothing need be done for them after that. Through wholesome work and intercourse with healthy-minded people they will soon find again what they have now entirely lost—their proper relations to their brother-man and to God" (623). At the time of the publication of **"Gray Cabins,"** a young Edith Wharton was beginning to publish her poetry and short stories in many of the same periodicals as Davis. This essay, Davis's next two novels, and several of her earlier short stories, as noted earlier, are precursors to Edith Wharton's distinctive literary themes and style. In the next decade, Wharton would begin to publish her excellent novels of New England that continued the tradition of depicting women's wasted lives.

One amusing response to **"Gray Cabins"** came from Frances E. Willard, the leader of the temperance movement and president of the Women's Christian Temperance Union, who was, like Davis, a contributor to the *Congregationalist.* Willard, however, was more conservative than Davis in her approach to the realms of women's lives. In a conversation, she reportedly asked Davis if New England women's involvement in the temperance movement, which Willard deemed a spiritual movement, did not constitute sufficient activism for ladies. Davis is reported to have simply "smiled in silence."[42]

* * *

The 1890s are often defined by the rise of the leisure class in America, which was most prominently signaled by the increase in European travel by Americans. In Philadelphia during this decade, however, the emergence of numerous and varied clubs—sports clubs, religious societies, the Association of Working Women's Societies—reflected the social stratification and group consciousness that was part of the leisure-class world,[43] that society which Davis had commented upon in **"A Grumble."** It was this underside of the leisure-class nineties that Davis would explore in her fiction and essays of the decade. But she, too, participated in the mobilization of Americans when she traveled to Europe during the summer of 1895.[44]

In spite of a three-decade career in the literary arts, Davis could not afford such a luxury on her own. It was her son, Richard—who became a symbol of the era as the male figure in the Gibson Girl portraits—who funded his mother's vacation from his royalties from *The Rulers of the Mediterranean.*[45] Nora, a distinguished young woman of nineteen who often visited New York and had already traveled in Italy while her brother Charles was residing there, accompanied her mother to Europe. Clarke preferred Grover Cleveland's invitation to do some serious fishing in Marion, Massachusetts.[46] The Davis family had moved its summer home from Point Pleasant to Marion after the summer of 1892, when Clarke had first visited the Massachusetts area with Cleveland and fallen in love with the region. No record remains of Davis's specific travels in Europe, but her final novel of the decade draws heavily upon these locales and critiques the blind nationalism so many traveling Americans projected onto their European experiences.

Whether Richard could actually afford his magnanimous gesture of funding his mother and sister's trip was another question. In the following year, Davis discovered that her son's flamboyant lifestyle was paralleled by his fiscal irresponsibility, and she severely admonished him. Richard had intended to visit his brother Charles in Florence, but Davis insisted that he postpone his plans until he straightened out his finances. As Richard explained to Charles, "she got it fixed in her mind that I must pay off those bills first and . . . that if I went abroad I could not finish my South American stories in time to get the money necessary to pay for them."[47] Clarke at first sided with Richard, who at thirty-one was surprisingly acquiescent to his parents' control, but Davis prevailed. For a writer who had spent her life scrimping and manipulating payment for her work so that it arrived in time to pay the monthly bills and who had often found it necessary to forego her own serious writing in order to produce the quantities of fiction necessary to the family's survival, slack fiscal policies were intolerable at any age, and she would not countenance it in a son who had received the benefits of her own sacrifices.

* * *

With her commentaries continuing to appear in *The Independent* and her return to the pages of the major literary journals, Davis was reaffirmed as a renowned and sought-after author. The unexpected consequences of this, however, were that she was once again confronted with the economics of literature. On the morning of October 17, 1895, she picked up the latest issue of *The Critic,* a literary magazine edited by Jeannette and Joseph Gilder that was especially interesting to Davis for its insightful reviews and openness to innovative works, including the early writings of Whitman and Joel Chandler Harris. But on this morning, Davis was astonished to discover an advertisement for a children's magazine, *Frank Leslie's Pleasant Hours for Boys and Girls,* which announced that Davis was a contributor to their first issue. Upon investigation, Davis learned that a story she had written many years earlier had already been reprinted in the first issue of *Pleasant Hours.* She quickly wrote the Gilders a letter disclaiming association with the Frank Leslie Company and detailing the events of publication, concluding, "The matter is, of course, of no real interest to the general public, but still I think I should feel more comfortable if you would say for me that I never have written and never expect to write a line for the Frank Leslie publications."[48]

Frank Leslie (the pseudonym of Henry Carter) was an English emigrant who began his career as an engraver and became a publisher of several American illustrated journals; the most widely known was *Frank Leslie's*

Popular Monthly. Davis had been a prolific writer of children's stories for the highly reputable *St. Nicholas* and *Youth's Companion* magazines, but she had no desire to extend this aspect of her writing, especially for a publisher who used such tactics. Although the tone of Davis's letter had downplayed the apparently unscrupulous nature of Leslie's use of her fiction, the Gilders published her letter under the heading of "Editorial Ethics." Frank Lee Farnell, editor of *Pleasant Hours,* promptly responded, denying any wrongdoing on the magazine's part. He purported that the inclusion of Davis's manuscript was a last-minute decision that was made because there had been insufficient time to commission a new story. A search of the magazine's inventory had led the editorial staff to Davis's story, which was deemed "appropriate and worthy of reproduction." The story was, Farnell observed, the property of *Pleasant Hours*; it had been purchased at an earlier date from "a publishing firm in Boston." Thus the editors felt "no hesitancy" in reprinting the story. He concluded: "Had Mrs. Davis known that it is a common practice among leading publishers who issue more than one periodical to reprint in one of them matter that has previously appeared in another, she would not, I feel sure, have written as she did, although she was certainly justified in letting the public know that the story did not represent her latest work."[49] All previous reprints of Davis's fiction in other journals or in collections had been published with her explicit permission and with appropriate compensation. Farnell admitted that the success of the first issue in which Davis's story appeared had made the magazine "well known" and that the editorial offices were now "overrun with submitted manuscripts." That the Leslie Company had legitimately purchased another publisher's copyrights did little to appease Davis's sense of misappropriation—not only of her work but of her name, which had helped *Pleasant Hours* establish itself as a reputable children's magazine.

* * *

Davis's last two novels, **Doctor Warrick's Daughters** (1806) and **Frances Waldeaux** (1897), are well written and often modern in theme and style. Both focus on the wealthy upper class, or those who yearn to enter that class, and both novels were published by Harper & Brothers. **Doctor Warrick's Daughters** earned Davis a flat twenty-five-hundred-dollar serial-rights fee and fifteen percent of the retail price of each novel sold; for **Frances Waldeaux,** a shorter novel, Davis was paid seven hundred dollars and the same percentage on copies sold.[50] At the beginning of the decade, she had dedicated her short story collection, **Silhouettes of American Life,** to her eldest son, Richard; now, **Warrick** [**Doctor Warrick's Daughters**] was dedicated to Charles, and **Waldeaux** [**Frances Waldeaux**] to her daughter, Nora, with the inscription: "A Remembrancer of BRITTANY for the Best Fellow-Traveller in the World," recalling their excursion two years earlier to England, which was the locale for most of the novel's action.

Doctor Warrick's Daughters is an astute critique of recent changes in American society: "Even as early as '65, Luxborough [Pennsylvania] was called a city by the contractors who had recently pushed in and built mills."[51] She notes that the builders immediately took control of the business segment of the community by electing themselves to the mayorship and city council. They tried, too, to influence the architectural tastes of the burgeoning city with their homes, mere imitations, Davis notes, of all other styles with interior decors that reeked "of gilt and plush and vases of alabaster" (1). But the descendents of the town's founding families refused to be influenced. They ignored the contractors as they had the rest of the world. While Davis continued to abhor the consequences of seeming progress, she also delightfully captures in *Warrick* that small-town self-satisfaction in the community's belief that they constitute "the final result of the creation" (1). Luxborougheans refuse to lower themselves to participate in trade; thus they "wrapped [their] poverty about [them] as a royal garment and smiled down patronage on the world" (2). New England was not the only region to pride itself on its past while its future slipped away. But the second generation declension, so lamented in New England, is also evident here; this generation is less willing than their parents to ignore the ways of the newcomers and thus has lately converted their ancestors from Swedish peasants and Penn's mechanics into Scotch and English noblemen (recalling a theme Davis had explored in her essay, **"Our National Vanities"**). Old Luxborough asserts its own sense of privilege "most strenuously in the Monthly Whist Club (established A.D. 1767)" (2). No mill owners were allowed admittance, to their barely hidden chagrin.

In this atmosphere, Davis creates the tensions of two worlds that clash socially and economically and are represented through the maturing of Dr. Warrick's two daughters: Anne, the social climber who, as a child, liked to pose in the barn window for passersby, pretending to be "Liberty" or a bride; and Mildred, self-effacing, homely, and so completely acquiescent that no one had ever heard her express an opinion of her own. Davis readdresses in this novel several themes that she had begun in earlier works. Her characterization of the doctor, for instance, presents a wonderful study of the type of individual she had begun to identify in her early fiction of the 1860s: the good-hearted but completely unreliable "provider" who erroneously believes he has a genius for a particular trade. Dr. Warrick believes his innate "genius" will lead him to discover the germ for cholera, though he is not a scientist and much prefers to

read novels than sit in his expensively furnished laboratory. This dreamer, professing all the while to be terribly overworked and burdened by his need to support his daughters, is in fact incapable of supporting anyone, including himself. The financial crisis into which he allows the family to drift precipitates the social and developmental crises that Anne and Mildred must face as they attempt to support their father, assuage his ego, and maintain their honor and dignity in the face of social Old Luxborough. The novel details the moral decline of a local society that represents America at large—"the decadence of a race," as Davis had termed it in **"Gray Cabins,"** that is governed by greed. Only Mildred finds fulfillment and an inner strength to resist the influences of money; Anne discards her passionate love for John Soulé in order to marry a wealthy but repugnant man, David Plunkett.

Although Davis now more explicitly rejected sentimentalism than she had in the past, she also recognized that sentimentalism was not an exclusively female tradition. Thus in this novel she critiques the literary *"poseurs"* of the age "who could take and hold the centre of the stage" with their melodramatic, ultrasentimental prose and verse. John Soulé's essays, published in the *Picayune* (where Davis herself published several articles), are purely sentimental melodramas, resembling the excess of Emmeline Grangerford's poetic creations in Twain's *Huckleberry Finn*; but Anne, deeming herself an astute literary critic, insists that John's work constitutes great poetry. The poems are, Davis notes with wry sarcasm, highly publishable. Davis's own prose in this novel has a newness of style that prefigures the early works of twentieth-century modernists. When Anne experiences her first emotional awakening, "She could not breathe . . . She saw, far off in the bay, a white sail flicker up out of the mist and slowly disappear" (128). For Anne, that brief flickering of the sail symbolizes her own fleeting happiness, captured in the dream-like world of the gulf state bayoux but snuffed out by her submission to the impulse toward greed. Her wealthy spouse, determined as a youth to write great poetry, also forfeits that desire to the power of money. On rare occasions, David "felt the strength that was in him to do wider work in the world; strength that could never be used . . . that struggle in the soul, that choking pant of unspent power" (300). It was, to Davis's mind, the tragedy of contemporary American life.

One ironic aspect of the publication of *Doctor Warrick's Daughters* was that the last pages of the hardbound edition included four pages of advertisements for the novels of William Dean Howells. Though Davis preceded Howells both in the creation of realistic fiction and in the theory of the commonplace by more than twenty years, it is his reputation that remains intact today, while Davis's is relatively forgotten. As James C. Austin has noted concerning *Warrick,* "The revolutionary character of Mrs. Davis's writing was no longer noticeable or objectionable. She had anticipated the taste of the nineties and subsequent decades."[52] In her own day, **Warrick** was widely reviewed and highly praised. The exception, oddly enough, was *The Independent,* whose reviewer was offended by Davis's realism and by the novel's lack of retributive punishment for immoral characters. However, the *Nation*'s reviewer once again expressed nothing but hosannas for her novel:

> 'Dr. Warrick's Daughters' is good reading, for its excellent workmanship were there no other reason. It is a pleasure to miss the crudities of the average novel. . . . [*Warrick*] is full of interest, depicting with practised touch life in an old Pennsylvania town . . . The Gray and the Blue, differentiated with the skill of a minute observer, shimmer through the fabric of her story, and even so blend, light and dark, the weaknesses and virtues of her many characters. The sermon of the book, breathed not preached, is against the great god Mammon, who is made very repulsive, while yet his worshippers are seen to be sometimes men of like passions with ourselves.[53]

Although Harriet Beecher Stowe died the year that **Warrick** was published, one might delight to imagine her amazement at such praise from what she viewed as an old cigar-smoking male bastion!

If numerous earlier texts by Davis call to mind the novels of Henry James and Edith Wharton, **Frances Waldeaux** explicitly does so, especially in its awareness of Americans' attitudes toward their European experiences. In the figure of James Perry, a minor character who is an assistant editor of a literary magazine, Davis satirizes the American who travels to Europe only to criticize the Old World for not being American. Perry, so full of himself and his assistant editorship, scoffs at the history of the ancient buildings, preferring "a clean, new American church."[54] While he professes to be concerned only with the issues of the day—"the negro problem, or Tammany, or the Sugar Trust"—his rejection of history reflects his ignorance of its importance in relation to contemporary events.

Frances Waldeaux is not a heroine either, for this novel is keenly realistic. She is a woman whose wasted life is a result of pretension and excessive self-sacrifice for her child. For years she has posed as a wealthy widow so that her pompous son might pursue an active social life and commit himself to study at Princeton. In fact, Frances Waldeaux has scrimped all her life to provide for George because her husband had been a speculator and had left them completely impoverished upon his death. Frances's earnings come chiefly from her satiric writings for a less-than-reputable periodical. If Frances is merely a poseur, she has ingrained in herself all the values of the upper class. She is without sympathy for lower class women who try to better themselves but

succumb to a life of decadence. This type of woman is represented in Frances's mind by the now-deceased Pauline Felix, and when George unwittingly marries Pauline's daughter, Lisa, Frances cannot forgive the daughter for her mother's sins. Frances is so driven by her controlling love for her son and by her rejection of any sign of taint from his wife that she attempts to murder Lisa. Frances is not punished, but Lisa dies after giving birth to a son. Frances has to live with her crime, but she believes that her newly found faith in God will help her live with the knowledge that "I have it in me still to be worse than a murderer" (204).

Davis's characterization of this woman is so well developed that, while we detest her act, it is impossible not to champion her independence. In her fifties, Frances refuses to be supported by others, "If I live to be seventy, or a hundred, I shall be the same Frances Waldeaux. . . . Even out in that other world I shall not be only a mother. I shall be me. *Me!*" (202, 204). Although Frances's characterization is not autobiographical, this statement resounds with Davis's own self-image. She used the exact phrasing—". . . me. *Me!*"—at least twice when her work was acknowledged by other literary figures whom she admired, most notably Nathaniel Hawthorne and Horace Howard Furness. If she had ended the 1880s with concern over the diminishing role of motherhood in her adult children's lives, she had subsequently grasped the opportunities that newly found freedom afforded her and proudly acknowledged that in "that other world" she had earned a place of recognition.

Ironically, several reviewers interpreted Frances's turning to God as complete salvation. Chicago's *Living Church* reviewer, for instance, praised the novel and declared that it was absolutely "absorbing" and that the characterizations and situations reverberated with "a real vitality."[55] More perceptive as to the novel's ending is the reviewer for *The Critic*: "The concession of a good ending, however, is not made by the author to the reader, but by Providence to Frances Waldeaux's intensity, which is so great that it imposes the fulfillment of her desires even upon the universal order of things. The story of her later life is conceived with power and told with directness." The reviewer is less comfortable with, and yet compelled to admire, the modernity of Davis's prose style:

> If one were to complain of anything in the book, it would be of its excess of lucidity. The style is concise to the point of dryness. We are told only the things which are directly pertinent to the tale, and the result is a certain lack of atmosphere. The characters stand out with the crystalline brilliancy of figures seen through an expanse of plate-glass, and in admiring their clearness we forget now and then that the reader's task is that of sympathy.[56]

If **Warrick** ironically included advertisements for Howells's work, a similar irony is notable in this review of

Waldeaux: directly preceding it is a review of Honoré de Balzac's *Juana and Other Stories* in which the reviewer discusses Balzac's continual "remodelling" of the theme of the revolt of the oppressed class. The reviewer notes that "Zola has attempted the same subject—far less successfully—in 'La Terre,' for in Balzac we have realism drawn from actual experience."[57] As closely aligned as these reviews are, critics of the time failed to recognize the correlations between Davis's work and that of the French realists, just as many of them failed to remember her pioneering work of the 1860s and 1870s. Only at her death would the comparison be made, and then the chronology would be reversed, identifying Davis's work as "Zolaesque."

At age sixty-six, with two novels recently completed and critically acclaimed, Davis decided to return to children's literature and journalism, both of which were less demanding but profitable forms of writing for her since financial demands never completely abandoned her. She also took this opportunity to renew her acquaintance with Mary Mapes Dodge: "It *is* I—," she wrote Dodge in June of 1897, "still in the flesh—although so many years have passed since I have heard from you." Davis wanted to write a story for boys and inquired as to Dodge's interest in the piece for *St. Nicholas*. She enclosed a copy of **Kent Hampden** "to show you what kind of a story-teller for boys I am. I could not do better than 'Kent.'"[58] She insisted that Dodge make the decision herself and not allow an assistant to determine its worth. She closed her letter with reminiscences of their pleasant association "in the old time." No record remains of Dodge's response to this unidentified manuscript, but the overture from Davis acted as stimulus for their renewed interest in each other as literary associates and friends.

* * *

For the remainder of the decade, Davis devoted herself to journalism. Though she wrote for *Harper's* and the *North American Review* during this time, she continued to find her greatest freedom of expression in the pages of *The Independent*, in spite of her financial differences with Chandler. When she decided to return to *The Independent* on a regular basis, she wrote William Hayes Ward, as adamant about the timeliness of her work as she had been as a young novelist in 1861, "It is a long time since I sent you any comments on the world and its ways. So I hope you will welcome this little paper. It is something which I thought somebody ought to say *now*."[59] She knew that while she had traveled to Europe and worked on her novels *The Independent* had maintained its reputation for aggressive commentary on social, economic, and political issues. In these last years before the turn of the century, she was joined in the pages of *The Independent* by socially conscious writers such as Booker T. Washington, president of the Tuske-

gee Institute; the great Russian realist, Leo Tolstoy, who submitted essays on "The Czar's Peace Conference" and a "Letter to the Russian Liberals"; Henry James; Agnes Repplier; Paul Lawrence Dunbar; and W. E. B. DuBois, who had recently joined the faculty of Atlanta University.

At the end of the previous decade, Davis had collaboratively addressed the issue of women and marriage; in this decade, she was again asked to join a select group of notable women to address the question of "The Enlargement of Woman's Sphere," as the headlines to *The Independent*'s series of comments termed it. Subtitled "Views of Distinguished Progressive Women," the series includes essays by Julia Ward Howe, Frances E. Willard, Lucy Stone, Susan Hayes Ward, the Reverend Phoebe Hanaford, and nearly a dozen other women. Each approached the question of woman's sphere from her area of expertise: Howe wrote on "Women in Politics," Grace Dodge concentrated on the New York Association of Working Girls' advances, and Davis discussed **"Women in Literature."**

In addition to the significance of the collaborative element of the series, Davis's essay is also important in terms of understanding her own assessment of American literature at the end of the nineteenth century and, especially, the position women held in that field. She begins with a direct assertion: "There can surely be little doubt that women will occupy a much wider space in American literature during the next thirty years than they have done hitherto."[60] This will be true, Davis asserts, for several reasons, including the fact that increased population will compel greater numbers of women to earn their own living and that literature is a reputable field in which "you can, if you choose, find the best of good company," while other women will seek the "crown" of fame and notoriety. In the final reason Davis lists, however, she defines her sense of herself as an artist: there are a few women, she asserts, who will write "because there is in them a message to be given, and they cannot die until they have spoken it" (1). For whatever reason women enter the field, there will be sufficient numbers who will satisfy their own needs and help the world at the same time through their artistic expressions.

While it is difficult to define what new fields of literature will emerge for women, Davis asserts, genres such as the memoir, the journal, and the autobiography have been greatly overlooked by the American author. On the other hand, there is one facet of literature which she hopes all writers will avoid: the Great American Novel. No canvas would be large enough to do it justice, to capture the various "phases of our national life" or the complexities of groups such as "the red man; the Mafian and Molly Maguire brethren; and the Chicago millionaire!" (2). It is preferable to present "Genre pictures of individual characters in our national drama, each with his own scene and framing" (2); and this is the realm that women authors have already conquered through their natural perception for detail, their concern for the individual, and their powers of dramatic representation.

Not only does Davis suggest that the "distinctively American portraits and landscapes are the work of woman" in our literary history, but she records their achievements, naming those whom she signifies as the major American realists in terms of "genre pictures":

> Marion Harland preserved for us the old Virginia plantation with its men and women. Miss Murfree has made the mountaineer of Tennessee as immortal as his mountains. Mary Dean painted pictures of rural New York with a touch as fine and strong as Meissonier's own. Mrs. Catherwood and Mary Halleck Foote have sketched picturesque poses of the Western man. Miss Woolson on her larger canvas inserts marvelous portraits of gentle lazy, shrewd Southern women, and while Elizabeth Phelps draws the educated Puritan woman from the life, Sara Jewett and Miss Wilkins give us pictures of the race in its decadence, the New England villager, hungry in soul and body, with a fidelity equal to any other photographs of dying men.
>
> (2)

In this succinct summary, Davis canonizes the contributions of late-nineteenth-century American women writers and defines realism itself as "genre pictures," that is, as a literary perspective that incorporates a distinctive style but moves us away from the question of what *is* realism to an enlightened sense in which we should be asking how realism *functions*, how it apportions discourse. It would be almost three-quarters of a century before the contributions of these women whom Davis acknowledges as the instigators of this style of realism would once again be remembered and so accurately assessed.

* * *

Davis's themes in the pages of *The Independent* during the 1890s ranged from the effects of money on morality, to the ongoing question of equality for blacks, to the swindling of the government by ex-soldiers who falsified injuries and service in order to claim pensions while the country was struggling to survive economic depressions; on the other hand, her xenophobic position on immigration is also continued, most notably in "Achill." Several articles from this period deserve special attention.

"The Work Before Us," published in January 1899, is a strong indictment of English and American colonization practices.[61] Commenting on Lord Kitchener's ongoing attempts to Anglicize the Sudanese, Davis asserts the need for each race to retain its own culture and customs. She foresaw the backlash of such Anglicized "education" that has become prevalent in the Third World today, where the English-educated nationals are "no longer at ease" in their old society and never fully accepted into the new.[62] "The plain fact," Davis asserts, at the end of the nineteenth century, is that this plan of Kitchener's "has its root in the complacent self-conceit of the English race" that is shared by Americans: "We are always right; hence all other races must be more or less wrong" (178). Our language, customs, and dress become the criteria for measuring other races; that we presume they are inferior represents a "monstrous content with ourselves" (178). Davis recognizes in this arrogance our own loss as well, since it "blinds us, too, to the possibilities in other races, and unfits us to deal with them intelligently" (178). All of her life Davis had challenged the distorted sense of progress in America, and she raises that challenge again in this new context: "Is civilization after all a matter of railways or even the ballot box?" (179). Relying upon American history, Davis reminds her readers that we chose a policy similar to Kitchener's with our own Native American peoples and have the ever-present record of that failure before us. Public men must be held accountable for their motives, Davis concludes. Are they concerned about their nation or the next election? Is their worship of God or money?

In three other articles for *The Independent* during the 1890s, Davis confronted the tension-filled issue of racism in America at the end of the nineteenth century. In 1892, she published an essay entitled **"Alien Brothers,"** in which she observed that "Every philanthropist and politician has now a pet theory or scheme to hurl at the poor struggling [Negro]."[63] While these advisers are well meaning, their arguments are flawed, Davis asserts, because they continue to view blacks as a type rather than as individuals. In acknowledging the social and educational differences among blacks, she argues that they must cross those gulfs and embrace each other if the race is to advance: "Despite the centuries of savagery and slavery through which they have passed, no race has preserved more noble qualities. Why should they be ashamed of each other?" (7). If the decency of this argument is not sufficient, Davis counters, "A more ignoble reason is that it is the surest and quickest way to win that respect and recognition from the white race which they weakly crave. Douglass, Bruce, Tanner, and Durham have achieved success by *being black*. They were satisfied to be the exponents and representatives of the Negro race" (7). Because of the accomplishments of these men, there is "a sufficiently large class of educated, refined and often wealthy colored people in our cities to form a society among themselves and to exercise an elevating influence upon their less lucky brethren" (7).

Davis continues this theme at the end of the century in two essays, **"Two Points of View"** and **"Two Methods With the Negro."** The first is her reaction to the opposing views of W. E. B. DuBois and Booker T. Washington; as in the past, Davis conservatively preferred Washington's stance. She agrees with DuBois that the oppression of his race has been and continues to be extraordinary: "The prejudice against the Negro in the Northern States has been as unjust and cruel in its effects as was slavery. We opened our schools and universities to him, and when he was ready and eager to earn his living we barred every way before him except those which led to the kitchen and the barber-shop."[64] However, she abhors the tone of despair and lack of hope in his vision, especially as a vehicle for change. The other point of view, she observes, had recently been submitted by the Committee of the General Negro Conference at Hampton; the committee's perspective "is alive with energy and hope and common sense," all of the traits which Davis had admired throughout her life. Davis asserts that this group of blacks has no concerns for the opinions of whites; instead they are building their own communal infrastructure to raise their people out of poverty and hardship.

As always, there is an underlying conservatism to Davis's position on blacks in American society, although she believed she was presenting a radically liberal stance. Thus she cannot forego reminding DuBois and his followers that, while their charges of prejudice are true, "it is to the white man he owes his freedom, his right to vote, the chance of education" (2). She insists that, as strong as prejudice remains, "it is weakening every day. In 1847 it was an offense punishable by law in the South to teach a Negro to read. In 1897 every district has its school or college for black pupils" (2). She discusses amalgamation, but adds, "The Negro should remember, however, that his progress depends, not on his affiliation, political, mercantile or social, with the whites, but on the development of his own people. The time that he spends . . . in denouncing them or upbraiding them, is only so much time wasted" (2). For all of her good intentions, her view remains the perspective of one who was an "outsider."

In the following year, Davis returned to the issue, admonishing the American public for attending so assiduously to the "noise of the 'Maine'" (the U.S. battleship that was sunk in February of 1898, thereby precipitating the Spanish-American War) and ignoring the Negro Conference at Tuskegee and the "plans of these earnest black leaders."[65] Her position was that "a war with Spain is an affair of months, while the progress of this people will concern us for all time. I know of no more important or dramatic action in contemporary history than the slow upgrowth of this nation within the American nation" (1). In that statement, we have the strength and the weakness of Davis's lifelong position: an honorable concern for the well-being and fair treatment of all races, and yet an unwitting reconstitution of separation, revealed in her rhetoric of "this nation within the American nation." Although she insists she wants blacks to be her "neighbor and friend," she fails to understand the depth of prejudice that remained in the country and in herself. In one respect, however, she truthfully captured the extraordinary differences between experiences with slavery and the younger generation's fortunate lack of such experience. It would be easy to brush aside her assertion in **"Two Methods"** [**"Two Methods With the Negro"**]—"I came from a slave State, and the evils that I saw in slavery made me an Abolitionist before these excitable young men probably were born"—as the pontificating of an elderly woman who feels herself at odds with the youth of America. However, the almost inconceivable changes that Davis had confronted in her lifetime are revealed in her son's assertion that it was "momentous" actually to view enslaved people when he traveled in Morocco.[66] Perhaps no two generations were as distinguishable as those of pre- and post-Civil War Americans.

In her most notable essay from these last years of the century, **"The Mean Face of War,"** Davis finds herself, thirty years after her first challenge to the romanticization of war, faced with that issue once again. Disturbed by the American policy of policing the Philippines and recognizing that the present generation had only been exposed to stories about war rather than its realities, she begins her essay by outlining the ways in which wars are made heroic through the intentional use of romantic symbolism: the heroic Mars doing battle for his country, or the noble Christian doing God's work.[67] But she commands her readers to look this "god" in the face and see its true ugliness. In challenging the chivalric view of war that was being perpetuated in the pages of newspapers and in political speeches, Davis insists that genuine history be recorded, not this falsified brand. She recalls living in a border state during the Civil War days of her youth and demands that Americans envision the reality of that experience, not its romanticized history-book version. Certainly, Davis acknowledges, there was truth in the "countless paeans" to the heroism of soldiers in the North and South, "But I never yet have heard a word of the other side of the history of that great campaign, which is equally true, of the debilitating effect upon most men in mind and morals of years in camp, and the habits acquired of idleness, of drunkenness and of immorality" (1933). In her seventieth year, Davis would center her autobiography on her desire to record that genuine history of the Civil War period and the harsh realities of its effects upon American people and the country.

Her sense of the political manipulation of public sentiment for building an American war machine in **"The Mean Face of War"** still carries reverberations for the late twentieth century. Politicians are trying "to induce the American people to make war its regular business," Davis asserts (1933). The people are told we must increase the size of the army and glorify military service and its economic rewards; the persuaders especially include the "talk of glory and heroism and the service of the country," and it is a sure-fire means to entice "gallant immature boys" (1933). But Davis exposes the fact that the motives behind these speeches were not so heroic: "What is really intended, of course, is the establishment of a uniformed guard to police the Philippine Islands in the interests of certain trusts" (1933). Davis concludes her essay with a challenge to Americans to confront the "ugly, mean features" of war before committing themselves to such policies. The implications of these policies remain with us in the twentieth century, of course. As journalist Katherine Ellison recently noted, "the erratic and confused U.S. drift—for reasons at once racist, greedy and idealistic—into an imperial role" in the Philippines remains a noteworthy chronicle.[68] Davis, at the moment of crisis, recognized that "racist, greedy and idealistic" drift and attempted to reveal its insidiousness to the American public.

* * *

As Davis entered the last years of her life, her voice of social consciousness rang as clearly and as truly as it had when she began her critique of American society and literary styles in the comparatively innocent era of antebellum America. When the publisher Paul Reynolds now approached her with his unwittingly ironic offer to republish some of her novels in England, Davis could decline the once-longed-for opportunity. Secure in her reputation and desirous of continuing her commitment to social commentary, she refused his offer with the simple statement, "I have no book which I wish to republish in London now."[69]

Another ironic episode of this period centered on an offer from Albert Bigelow Paine, a dramatist[70] and novelist as well as an editor. He had greatly admired *Kent Hampden* and indicated that if Davis were preparing another novel for children he would be interested in publishing it. She did not want to extend herself at this time to write a full-length work for children, but she did suggest that since she had already written about boys' adventures in *Kent Hampden* she would like to prepare a collection of "short stories for girls—all written of the same village—if you choose. Something like Mrs. Deland's 'Old Chester Tales.' The same town and the same families—."[71] Margaret (Margaretta) Wade Campbell Deland, born in Pennsylvania, also used her native region as the setting for many of her novels and short stories. *Old Chester Tales* had appeared in 1898; the collection centers on the lives of the citizens of Old Chester, which was modeled on Deland's hometown of Manchester. Davis's proposition suggested that her col-

lection of stories for girls would repeat the historical realism and depth of characterization that had made *Kent Hampden* a success, but whether Paine was not interested in stories about girls or for whatever reason, he did not respond to Davis's suggestion. Today Paine's own best-remembered works are his three-volume biography of Mark Twain and his collection of Twain's correspondence, both of which appeared shortly after Davis's death. One can only imagine how different Davis's own literary fate might have been if such immediate attention to preserving her works and thoughts had occurred.

Notes

Letters from and to Rebecca Harding Davis (RHD) are designated with an "L." Permission to quote from the following sources is gratefully acknowledged:

BC   Overbury Collection, Barnard College Library

BE   -G: James Fraser Gluck Collection;

BE   -M: Charles Wells Moulton Collection;
        Buffalo and Erie County Public Library

CU   -G: General Manuscripts Collection;

        -H: Harper Bros. Papers;

        -R: Paul R. Reynolds Papers;

        -W: Theodore F. Wolfe Papers;
        Rare Book and Manuscript Library, Columbia University

HH   The Huntington Library, San Marino, California

HHU   The Houghton Library, Harvard University

NYPL   -A: Alfred W. Anthony Collection;

        -B: Henry W. and Albert A. Berg Collection;

        -C: William Conant Church Papers;

        -CC: Century Company Records;

        -H: Josiah Gilbert Holland Papers;
        Rare Book and Manuscripts Div., New York Public Library, Astor, Lenox and Tilden Foundations

PU   -D: Donald and Robert M. Dodge Collection of Mary Mapes Dodge;

        -M: Mary Mapes Dodge, *St. Nicholas* Correspondence;

        -W: Wilkinson Collection of Mary Mapes Dodge;
        Princeton University Library

UP   Horace Howard Furness Memorial Library, Special Collections, Van Pelt Library, University of Pennsylvania

UV   Richard Harding Davis Collection (#6109), Clifton Waller Barrett Library, Manuscripts Div., Special Collections Dept., University of Virginia Library

1. See, for instance, Langford [Gerald Langford, *The Richard Harding Davis Years: A Biography of a Mother and Son* (New York: Holt, Rinehart and Winston, 1961)] and Olsen [Tillie Olsen, "Bibliographic Interpretation," in *"Life in the Iron Mills"*

and Other Stories (Old Westbury, NY: Feminist Press, 1985)]; a notable earlier exception was Shaeffer [Helen Woodward Shaeffer's unpublished dissertation, "RHD: Pioneer Realist" (University of Pennsylvania, 1947)], RHD's earliest biographer.

2. William James's classic study [*Principles of Psychology*] presented the development of psychological knowledge in America to this time. RHD had used the term "psychologist" as early as 1861 in "Life" and had composed works of psychological realism over the subsequent three decades; she was keenly perceptive about issues of human motivation and free will.

3. Subsequent references to "An Ignoble Martyr" (*Harper's New Monthly* 80 [Mar. 1890]: 604-10) in *Silhouettes* [Rebecca Davis, *Silhouettes of American Life* (New York: Charles Scribner's Sons, 1892; reprint New York: Garrett, 1968); the Garrett Press edition is cited in the text hereafter.], pp. 92-110, are in the text.

4. It was only in her early sentimental fiction for *Peterson's* that RHD suggested a value to martyrdom and then with limitations. In "One of Life's Martyrs" (*Peterson's* 54 [Oct. 1868]: 282-90), for instance, John Lennox's life was devoted to the care of others and thus he is depicted as having a worthwhile purpose in his otherwise tragic martyrdom.

5. The term is Thoreau's. I am indebted to Buell's discussion of this motif [Lawrence Buell, *New England Literary Culture: From Revolution to Renaissance* (New York: Cambridge University Press, 1986)], pp. 345-46. While *The Scarlet Letter* is, as Buell suggests, an anachronism in some ways in the tradition, I intentionally include it to suggest that even within distinctive approaches the theme is pervasive.

6. L, March 10, probably 1890 (BC).

7. L, dated only "April 27" (HHU).

8. Undated L, on Harper & Brothers' letterhead (UV), probably 1892, when RHD published *Silhouettes* and Richard published *Van Bibber and Other Stories*.

9. L, dated on August 5, from Point Pleasant (NYPL-CC).

10. *The Critic,* Feb. 4, 1893, p. 61.

11. Helen Gray Cone, "Woman in American Literature," *Century Magazine* (Oct. 1890): 921; subsequent references are in the text.

12. L, March 15, probably 1890 (BE).

13. L, March 18, 1892 (UP).

14. At one point after the publication of *Kent Hampden,* RHD observed that Ford had offered her "a huge price" for a boy's story for *Youth's Companion* (L, dated only "Jan. 15th" [PU-M]).

15. L, April 2, 1891 (PU-D).

16. L, dated only "Feb. 19" (NYPL-CC).

17. I have been unable to identify this woman further.

18. L, dated only "April 18" (HHU).

19. Subsequent references from the Garrett Press edition are in the text.

20. See Richard Cary, *Mary N. Murfree* (TUSAS 121. New York: Twayne, 1967), 21-22.

21. Shaeffer, pp. 307-8.

22. "Marcia" has recently been reprinted in *Legacy* (Sp 1987), with an introduction by Jean Pfaelzer. Pfaelzer accurately notes that in this story RHD "challenges the rationalization that the family promises women a refuge from economic and worldly tensions" (4). However, Pfaelzer asserts that "Marcia" is a sentimental story; I would argue that *Marcia's* writings are sentimental, not Davis's. Other comments of this decade suggest RHD's move away from sentimentalism at this juncture in her professional life, as detailed below.

23. *The Independent,* Aug. 15, 1889, p. 1.

24. *The Critic,* Feb. 4, 1893, p. 61.

25. *The Independent,* Nov. 3, 1892, p. 23.

26. *The Nation,* Oct. 6, 1892, p. 262.

27. Undated L, [1893] (UV).

28. "A Grumble," *Peterson's* 103 (Jan. 1863): 103; subsequent references are in the text.

29. The exception, of course, is always Nora. RHD refused to "market" her daughter, but she had so long advocated the need for young women to learn a trade for their own self-sufficiency that one can only wonder if Nora was thus educated; no record is extant. She apparently chose not to turn to writing as a vocation, as every other member of her family had. Perhaps this in itself was her act of independence.

30. Langford, pp. 148-49. Langford attempts to downplay Richard's depression, but it was a chronic ailment that plagued him throughout his adult life.

31. L, March 28, 1894 (HH).

32. L, June 16, 1894 (BC).

33. Undated L (BC).

34. L, dated only "Dec 6" (BC).

35. L, September 15, [1894], from Marion, MA (BC).

36. L, dated only "Sept 20" (BC).

37. L, November 3 (BC).

38. RHD's correspondence with her editor at *The World,* Mr. Moffatt, is housed at the Huntington Library.

39. *The Congregationalist,* Apr. 12, 1894, p. 524.

40. Subsequent references to "In the Gray Cabins of New England" (*Century Magazine* 49 [Feb. 1895]: 620-23) are in the text.

41. Langford, p. 163.

42. Downey, p. 309.

43. Burt and Davies [Nathaniel Burt and Wallace E. Davies's essay, "The Iron Age 1876-1905," in *Philadelphia: A 300-Year History,* ed. Russell F. Weigley (New York: Norton, 1982),], pp. 520-23; see also Larzer Ziff, *The American 1890s* (New York: Viking, 1966).

44. Shaeffer dates RHD's vacation in Europe as the summer of 1891; however, I agree with Langford that the correct date is 1895.

45. Langford, p. 149. Tillie Olsen has depicted RHD as a reclusive, humbled writer in her later years, asserting that from the mid-1870s until her death RHD "went almost nowhere" (146-47). In fact, RHD had a wide circle of friends in Philadelphia with whom she socialized, many of whom were in the literary field; and, in addition to the family summers at Point Pleasant, New Jersey, and Marion, Massachusetts, RHD traveled to North Carolina in 1874 and Alabama in 1884 to gather materials for her writing, as well as vacationing in Warm Springs, Virginia—all prior to her trip to Europe in 1895. She also visited Richard in New York City several times during the decade. RHD led an active and full life until her health failed in her final years.

46. RHD and Richard were less enamored of Cleveland than Clarke. RHD was vocal in her criticisms of Cleveland's policies; in "The Death of John Payne" (*The Independent* 50 [Jul. 28, 1898]: 241-49), for instance, one character discusses the tremendous burden of the national debt upon American citizens due to "Cleveland's loans."

47. Quoted in Langford, p. 161.

48. *The Critic,* Oct. 26, 1895, p. 271.

49. *The Critic,* Nov. 2, 1895, p. 285.

50. Rates for comparable works of the period are difficult to ascertain, but it is interesting to compare these rates with Edith Wharton's publication of *The House of Mirth* a few years later. For *Mirth,* Wharton received a flat fee of five thousand dollars and a royalty of fifteen percent of the list price; by the time Wharton published *The Age of Innocence* in 1920, she received eighteen thousand dollars for serial rights alone (R. W. B. Lewis, *Edith Wharton* [New York: Fromm, 1975]).

51. *Doctor Warrick's Daughters* (New York: Harper and Brothers, 1896), 1; subsequent references are in the text.

52. Austin, "Success," [James C. Austin, "Success and Failure of RHD," *Midcontinent American Studies Journal* 3.1 (1962):] pp. 47-48; however, Austin echoes the typical—and, as I have asserted throughout, to my mind, erroneous—claim that RHD "had made her compromise with the sixties, and although she continued to write about as well as she began, she did not progress." If RHD is judged even as having maintained the stature of her writing of the sixties, her reputation will be secure, although much will be lost by ignoring her later work.

53. *Nation,* Jun. 11, 1896, p. 459.

54. *Frances Waldeaux* (New York: Harper and Brothers, 1897), 71; subsequent references are in the text.

55. Review quoted on recto of title page to *Waldeaux.*

56. *The Critic,* Apr. 10, 1897, p. 251.

57. Ibid.

58. L, June 17, [1897] (PU-D).

59. L, dated only "August 16" from Warm Springs (BC).

60. "Women in Literature," *The Independent* 43 (May 7, 1891): 1; subsequent references are in the text.

61. Subsequent references to "The Work Before Us" (*The Independent* 51 [Jan. 19, 1899]: 177-79) are in the text.

62. The phrase is taken from Nigerian author Chinua Achebe's 1960 novel of that title and theme.

63. "Alien Brothers," *The Independent* 44 (Jul. 7, 1892): 7; subsequent references are in the text.

64. "Two Points of View," *The Independent* 49 (Sep. 9, 1897): 2; subsequent references are in the text.

65. "Two Methods With the Negro," *The Independent* 50 (Mar. 31, 1898): 1; subsequent references are in the text.

66. Quoted in Langford, p. 135.

67. Subsequent references to "The Mean Face of War" (*The Independent* 51 [Jul. 20, 1899]: 1931-33) are in the text.

68. Ellison's remarks are part of her review of Stanley Karnow's seminal study of the history of American involvement in the Philippines, *In Our Image* (New York: Random House, 1989); Ellison's review appeared in the *Philadelphia Inquirer,* May 7, 1989, pp. 1G, 4G.

69. Undated L (CU).

70. Paine is probably best remembered today for his play, *The Great White Way* (1901), which became the popular designation for New York City's theater district.

71. L, dated only "January 8th"; handwriting suggests late 1890s (HH).

Jane Atteridge Rose (essay date 1991)

SOURCE: Rose, Jane Atteridge. "The Artist Manqué in the Fiction of Rebecca Harding Davis." In *Writing the Woman Artist: Essays on Poetics, Politics, and Portraiture,* edited by Suzanne W. Jones, pp. 155-74. Philadelphia: University of Pennsylvania Press, 1991.

[*In the following essay, Rose discerns at the center of all of Davis's stories and novels a portrait of the struggles of "the artist manqué," who battles against society's definitions of femininity but ultimately either fails or surrenders to "a life as wife and mother." The critic sees this pattern in the writings of other female authors of the nineteenth century, and she situates Davis's fiction within this feminist tradition.*]

The narrator of Rebecca Harding Davis's **"Life in the Iron-Mills, or The Korl Woman"**[1] concludes the tragic tale of Hugh Wolfe's artistic failure by contemplating the artist's unfinished creation: "Nothing remains to tell that the poor Welsh puddler once lived, but this figure of the mill-woman cut in korl." The "wan, woeful face, through which the spirit of the dead korl-cutter looks out," haunts the narrator, "with its thwarted life, its mighty hunger, its unfinished work."[2]

It is not necessary to know this story of the redemptive death of Hugh Wolfe, the immigrant iron puddler who creates statues in odd moments at the mill, or of his devoted cousin Deb, to appreciate the presence of motifs central to feminist reading suggested by this passage. Wolfe emblemizes his own "reality of soul starvation, of living death" in his statue's "mad, half-despairing gesture of drowning" (23, 33). Like Hugh Wolfe's fictional life, the lives of nineteenth-century female writers are often revealed in their works. And often, like the statue of the korl woman, their texts delineate characters who are frustrated by their "thwarted life," who are unsuccessful in their "unfinished work," or who lack the fulfillment of their "mighty hunger."

"Life in the Iron-Mills," like much of Rebecca Harding Davis's work, illuminates the nineteenth-century female experience. Although the novella usually attracts attention as a landmark in proletarian fiction and in naturalistic realism,[3] this story, along with the rest of Davis's corpus, deserves more attention as a nineteenth-century woman's text.[4] Like a number of her stories, it is a *Künstlerroman* of an artist manqué.[5] Davis is here typical of nineteenth-century writing women, whose fictional female artists all experience various forms of failure.[6]

Because of the autobiographical relationship between the fictional artist and the female writer, the *Künstlerroman* of the artist manqué helps us to understand how female artists were affected by their ideological context.[7] Literary women of the last century were inextricably entangled in a web of beliefs that made their successful development as artists difficult, if not impossible.[8] Their fictions enact a conflict between an individual empowered with the potential for creative autonomy and the ideological restrictions undermining it. The winner in this contest, staged by female writers and waged by their fictive artist doubles, seems always to be domestic ideology. The individual artist fails, or surrenders, or turns traitor to her own cause.[9]

Rebecca Harding Davis's many *Künstlerromane,* written over a period of forty years, show that domestic ideology exerted its force at every stage of women's lives. When plotted chronologically beside her biography, variations in Davis's depiction of the artist and in the form of failure that each of her protagonists experiences reveal changes in her attitude toward her own role as a woman writer as her life progressed.[10] These changes, which mark three specific stages in her life, roughly coincide with the three defining elements of the artist manqué: the young artist, whose socially determined identity prohibits her free artistic expression, is frustrated; the mature artist, who attempts to reconcile her artistic identity with a domestic one in a society that defines the two as antithetical, is unsuccessful; and the older artist, who has long ago renounced art in order to realize a life as wife and mother, lacks fulfillment.

Though she sometimes defied or denied certain social expectations regarding her life and her work, Rebecca Harding Davis was a white, Protestant, middle-class woman of the nineteenth century. As such, she sincerely maintained many received domestic values concerning the role of women even though they conflicted with her artistic desire. Her fiction, like that of other female writers in this milieu, demonstrates that within domestic ideology the role of women was culturally invested with a number of values that determined self-perception.[11] For these women, the egoistic self-assertion necessary for an artist was antithetical to the passive, self-abnegating service that defined femininity. As a result, their texts, like Davis's, are often conflicted, especially when they treat artists striving to retain their integrity without disenfranchising themselves from society.

In her own life, Davis was constantly mediating the conflicting values that marked the nineteenth-century female writer and her texts. For instance, although, like other girls of her class, she returned to her parents' home after graduating as valedictorian from her three-year education at the Washington (Pennsylvania) Female Seminary, she not so typically lived a life of retirement there for the next twelve years—reading her brother's college books and writing, only rarely participating in the precourtship social life of her hometown, Wheeling, West Virginia. The facts of Davis's long life show that she continued, with remarkable success, to mediate between her equally strong antithetical desires to be a good writer and to be a good wife-mother.[12] However, her fictional enactments of this same conflict, which always delineate a failed artist, hint at her concern that in art, at least, compromise is a form of failure. Struggling against compromise leads only to frustration; acquiescing to it brings the pain of being unfulfilled.

Though men, her earliest artists of the 1860s, Hugh Wolfe of **"Life in the Iron-Mills"** (1861) and the Tom of **"Blind Tom"** (1862), articulate the frustration experienced by female artists.[13] Here, political issues that also pertain to gender are played out as problems of class. In both these stories, the protagonist's artistic freedom is prohibited by his socially prescribed role. The capitalists and slave owners, who define and limit, oppress the uneducated laborers and slaves, who have been limited by social definition. Domestic ideology also limited the potential of a class. Although Davis, like most nineteenth-century women, accepted her female definition as God-ordained, she maintained that society had erroneously limited that definition. This was particularly true early in her career when she suffered most from its restrictions.

Davis's Hugh Wolfe is frustrated in life by the inhumane economic forces that determine his inability to fulfill his creative desire, to finish his sculpture. His talent brings anguish, not joy because the korl woman fails to communicate Wolfe's inarticulate longing.[14] She is an insoluble puzzle to the mill officials who discover her—"some terrible problem lay in this woman's face, and troubled these men" (34). Worse, as expression stimulates greater comprehension, her full meaning remains outside her creator's ken also; all Wolfe can say is "She be hungry" (33). Like his statue of the korl woman, Hugh Wolfe fails to satisfy his hunger, to use his power, to find his voice; he kills himself. Davis's first protagonist, like the artist figure in the fiction of most female writers of this period, is both oppressed and repressed.

The anguish of frustrated creative desire voiced by her first artists, who, like Wolfe, cry that "all the world had gone wrong" (51), seems very close to Davis's own frustration as a young woman beginning her writing career. Never overtly defiant, Rebecca Harding—an anomaly in her time as a spinster apparently unconcerned about approaching thirty in the home of her parents, interested only in pursuing her unorthodox literary interests—surely knew frustration. She must have felt it as she exhausted her father's extensive library; as she mastered her brother's college curriculum; as she wrote, rewrote, and discarded innumerable manuscripts. Although at this time she had no name for her frustration, she would later repeatedly show her female protagonists rebelling against "decorative uselessness" and against the notion that purity requires innocence. Her frustrated desire to escape these restrictions at least temporarily is probably what first led her to develop her lifelong fondness for "vagabonding": hours-long walks with no predetermined destination.

Her vagabonding was itself a perhaps unconscious strategy for negotiating between illicit desire and propriety. Aimlessly, yet decorously, walking, she could escape the protective confines of her comfortable home in Wheeling and experience the nearby sights and sounds of its industrial riverfront, considered inappropriate for young ladies. She could know "the fog and mud and foul effluvia" of slums, where people passed "with drunken faces," going to the factories where "unsleeping engines groan and shriek" (**"Iron-Mills"** [**"Life in the Iron-Mills"**] 14, 19).

Not surprisingly, Davis created her greatest number of male protagonists during this early period marked by frustration. Even as she wrote of artists whose freedom was restricted, her own artistic freedom was limited because she was a young woman; vagabonding could not take her everywhere. While her work was appearing in nearly every number of *Atlantic Monthly* and being praised by the Boston literati, family concern for propriety forced Davis to remain isolated at home.[15] In 1862, she lacked an escort and thus could not accept the repeated invitation of her *Atlantic* editor, James T. Fields, and his wife, Annie, to visit their home in Boston. In a letter to Annie Fields, she voiced her irritation over women's restrictions, complaining, "How good it must be to be a man when you want to travel."[16] In her fictive projections of frustrated artistic desire, Davis seems to have transcended her own specific gender oppression, transferring it to male protagonists and issues of class in **"Iron-Mills"** or race in **"Blind Tom."**

In these early stories, Davis created an antagonism between her protagonists and their society, which thwarts artistic development, silences expression, and inhibits self-comprehension. The conflicts of the early fictional artists suggest that anger at restricted artistic freedom composed at least one dimension of her own attitude toward society. Davis's ambivalence toward her frustrated creative desire and her guilt about being a woman with this desire are evident in every narrative strategy from her use of multiple anonymous identities to her ambivalent plots.[17] These strategies are nowhere more evident than in **"Iron-Mills."**

The conclusion to this story illustrates Davis's attempt to detach herself from her artist's tale. Here she amplifies the usual doubling of the *Künstlerroman* writer through her artist protagonist and creates a quadruple relationship between herself, the narrator, the protagonist, and the statue. Davis, the female author, has created a narrator whose sex is not designated and, therefore, particularly in 1861, would be assumed masculine. This fictive narrator—a writer, an artist, and a musician—sits in his library, amid such value-laden objects as "a broken figure of an angel pointing upward," a "dirty canary chirp[ing] desolately in a cage" (12), "a half-moulded child's head," and a rendering of Aphrodite (65). The narrator is pondering the mystery of a female statue, made of refuse korl, with "not one line of grace in it: a nude woman's form, muscular, grown coarse with labor, the powerful limbs instinct with some one poignant longing" (32). In this female image, the narrator comprehends the "spirit of the dead korl-cutter." He tells the story of its creator, Hugh Wolfe, the immigrant iron-foundry worker and repressed artist who committed suicide with his own sculpting knife rather than be confined in a jail, knowing only that "the world had gone all wrong" (51).

The narrator, the protagonist, and the statue are each a projection of spiritual longing. Davis projects her animus through her male narrative voice and her male artist protagonist and then, further, through them into their shared anima projection, the korl woman. It is this object that communicates "something pure and beautiful, which might have been and was not: a hope, a talent, a love, over which the soul mourns, like Esau deprived of his birthright" (64). The narrator ends the tale by looking on this image of desperate soul-starvation and saying simply, "I know" (64), uniting all the identities in sympathy with the repressed artist's "thwarted energy and unused power" (46).

Although Davis's cross-dressing of her protagonist as well as her narrator is extreme in **"Iron-Mills,"** the autobiographical relationship between the artist-writer and her artist-creation asserted in this closing passage illuminates an anxiety of authorship that seems particularly female. The statue of the korl woman, to which the narrator has fallen heir, stands "in a corner of [the] library" in order to "keep it hid behind a curtain." But like any repressed desire, sometimes at night "the curtain is ac-cidentally drawn back," and "its mighty hunger, its unfinished work" are painfully visible (64).

Davis's artists are also frustrated because they are anomalous in a worldview based on rigid gender distinction. In **"Iron-Mills"** Hugh Wolfe, the protagonist, is frustrated not just in his creative desire but also in his social relationships. A frail consumptive with a "meek, woman's face," he is known as one of the "girl-men" at the mill. Because of his atypical sensitivity, the other men call him "Molly Wolfe" (24). Although it is more emphasized in her early works, Davis's artist protagonists are always androgynous, making them larger as artists but painfully less as social beings. This is true for most of the female artists of her later work also: Jane Derby, a professional writer in **Earthen Pitchers,** is typical in that she was aware of her unattractive "hard eyes; and that her lips were thin and her breast flat. 'Even Nature,' she said to herself, 'forgot that I was a woman.'"[18]

In **"Blind Tom,"** published the year after **"Iron-Mills,"** Davis grappled with another frustration for the creative spirit that was common to the experience of many women who, like herself, wanted to write stories unlike the sentimental romances considered appropriate for female authors. This story of an enslaved genius confronts the evil of sanctioned control over individual talent rather than the repression of it. It is basically a true account of a blind slave boy, who was owned by a south Georgia planter.[19] Tom was a musical prodigy of such unexplainable dimension that he was treated as an idiot savant, performing in packed concert halls throughout the slave states and even at the White House. Davis's account apparently results from her having seen his performance at one of these concerts. Although she had no insight into what Tom's soul longed to play, she was most pained by those moments in his concert when it became clear that he could not play what he wanted:

> the moments when Tom was left to himself,—when a weary despair seemed to settle down on the distorted face, and the stubby little black fingers, wandering over the keys, spoke for Tom's own caged soul within.
>
> (585)

Davis, who in the writing of stories like **"Blind Tom"** was trying to break free of restrictions about appropriate subject matter and tone, keenly perceived that, like so many female writers of the period, the slave was not even free to use his gift as he chose. The music of Tom—like the statue of Hugh Wolfe, and the stories of their creator, a minimally educated young woman from West Virginia—proves that the divine spark of talent can appear in socially unacceptable, disenfranchised individuals. It also reminds us that, for the artist who must serve the two masters of self and society, creative desire can bring the gifted as much pain as it does joy.

The frustrated male artists of her early pieces, such as **"Iron-Mills"** and **"Blind Tom,"** are also deformed. Though not physically impaired like Tom, Wolfe is considered by others to be deficient as a man. Also Deb Wolfe—who, though not an artist, shares the role of protagonist with her cousin—is a hunchbacked cripple. These protagonists all bear the physical mark of their anomalous, alienated condition. They suggest an anxiety felt by Davis, at this time a young woman in pursuit of art, that deformity was somehow concomitant with her vocation.

Rebecca Harding Davis's middle period is marked by her becoming a wife and mother. She married L. Clarke Davis and moved to his sister's Philadelphia home in March 1863. There Davis gave birth to her first son Richard on April 18, 1864, and she moved with husband and baby into the first home of her own in September of that year. Her third and last child was born in 1872. After her marriage at the age of thirty-one, Rebecca Harding Davis's personal life became more typical of that known by most wives in middle-class America, except that her domestic situation seems to have been happier than most. In her marriage to L. Clarke Davis, she enjoyed an experience rare in either the nineteenth or the twentieth century: she married a man who had first fallen in love with her mind through her writing. Clarke Davis always championed his wife's career; however, as a crusading journalist, his own literary taste for didactic fiction and the journals that specialized in it served to discourage her pursuit of objective realism. The work of Davis's middle period, primarily written in the late 1860s and 1870s, begins to take a view of the artist that differs from her earlier work. The change in her fiction parallels the great change in her life at this time from anomalous spinster and aspiring author to wife-mother and successful author.

While her earlier stories feature frustrated male artists whose creativity is stifled by their oppressive society, those written during this period, like **"The Wife's Story"** (1864) and **"Marcia"** (1876), feature female artists struggling with more internal conflicts. They also bear a greater resemblance to Davis in their ambivalence toward society and their prescribed role in it. These women must choose between feminine, maternal domesticity and egoistic, artistic ambition.[20] The *Künstlerromane*, written during this time when Davis was herself trying to integrate art with domesticity, reify the idea that the role of wife-mother and the role of artist are mutually exclusive.[21] The protagonists of these stories are unsuccessful because, either by external societal judgment or by their own, their pursuit of art causes them to fail as women or their need to accept their womanhood causes them to fail as artists.[22]

Interestingly, while Davis repeatedly enacted the failure of artistic-domestic resolution in her fiction, in her own

life she was attaining it, though compromising quality to do so. Always writing at home, she never allowed pursuit of her art to take precedence over her role as wife-mother. Writing became, in these years, work of secondary importance. Fragments of a journal, written during this time, talk only about Pet (Clarke), Hardy (Richard), Charlie, and Nolly (Nora); entries rarely mention the writing for publication that was occurring at the same time.[23] However, the constant reiteration of anxiety over failure in her fiction at this time suggests that Davis considered her recent move toward journalistic writing a sign of artistic failure.

The earliest of these tales, **"The Wife's Story,"** marks a transition in Davis's attitude. This story reveals changes in her depiction of the artist and in her own narrative technique. This first appearance of a narrating protagonist is made doubly significant in that it is also one of her first stories in which the protagonist is a woman. Hetty, the wife, begins: "I will tell you the story of my life, since you ask it . . . though the meaning of the life of any woman of my character would be the same" (177). In this story—filled with the need to transfer, act out, and punish guilty desire—Davis's narrating protagonist, Hetty Manning, is an unhappy new wife-mother who longs to be a composer of opera. After she suffers humiliating failure in her one attempt to realize her dream, she renounces her artistic ambition for domesticity. Although the overt theme of this story is the necessary female renunciation of art, the story deconstructs itself with the voice of desire speaking more eloquently than the voice of guilt.[24] Suddenly, in the last pages, the reader is asked to disregard the protagonist's struggle against allowing "this power within me to rot and waste" (204), which has composed the entire story, as merely a hysterical dream. However, the dream has been so powerful that the reality is hard to accept.

Hetty, a New England woman who "had an unquiet brain and moderate power" (181), has been strongly influenced by Margaret Fuller. She is a recurring character type in Davis's fiction, suggestive of anxiety. A mature woman of developed sensibility who has married, rather late, a widower with several children, Hetty finds it impossible to acclimate herself to her new domestic role. She feels no kinship with her new family of exuberant but insensitive Westerners or even with her own new baby daughter, "a weazen-faced little mortal, crying night and day" (192). Having been raised on Fuller's motto, "The only object in life is to grow," she finds herself unable to abandon her dream:

> There had been a time when I had dreams of attaining Margaret's stature, and as I thought of that, some old sublime flame stirred in me with a keen delight. New to me, almost; for, since my baby was born, my soul as well as my body had been weak and nauseated.
>
> (192)

In addition to Fuller's influence, the memory of Hetty's previous acquaintance with Rosa Bonheur haunts the fictional protagonist of this story. She remembers the Parisian artist saying of her art: "Any woman can be a wife or mother, but this is my work alone" (193). A new wife and mother, Hetty sits in the hearth glow of domestic peace, amid "the white bust of Psyche, and a chubby plaster angel" (185), and agonizes over her un-realized talent—her "gift," her "power"—asking, "was I to give it unused back to God? I could sing: not that only; I could compose music,—the highest soul-utterance" (193). She regrets her marriage, realizing, "If I remained with Doctor Manning, my role was outlined plain to the end: years of cooking, stitching, scraping together of cents" (194). Hetty's crime in this story is twofold: the rejection of her domestic role and the as-sertion of artistic egoism. "No poet or artist," she says, "was ever more sincere in the belief that the divine power spoke through him than I" (197).

Hetty does not leave her husband, though, and when events cause the family to move to Newport, Rhode Is-land, she eagerly goes too. There, Hetty meets an im-presario from New York who is willing to produce her opera and to feature her in the leading role. One day, after long and troubled deliberation, she finally decides to do her opera. Her decision occurs during a solitary walk on the beach, in contemplation of the sea's affinity with her own soul: "It [the sea] was no work of God's praising Him continually: it was the eternal protest and outcry against Fate,—chained, helpless, unappealing" (200). When produced, her opera fails; the audience's rejection of her composition and of her performance is described in humiliating detail. This scene illuminates another dimension of the female artist's anxiety. In ad-dition to fearing the consequences that will befall her rejection of the divinely ordained domestic role, there is the very real fear of independence. Independence is fan-tasized as a double-edged sword that is both attractive and frightening. Hetty leaves the theater penniless, homeless, hungry, ashamed, and beaten:

> If the home I had desolated, the man and child I had abandoned, had chosen their revenge, they could not have asked that the woman's flesh and soul should rise in me with a hunger so mad as this, only to discover that [I would fail].
>
> (213)

However, Davis has not yet punished her artist self-projection enough. Hetty soon discovers that her loving husband has been in the audience and has had a heart attack. Racked with grief and guilt, she wanders the Bowery, longing for death, until she awakes to find that the entire attempt at being an artist has all been a dream of her "brain-fever," which has hit her while out by the sea (217). Renouncing art as an enticing false value, she joyfully accepts her regained life as wife and mother.

The brain-fever, by which the dream-state rebellion of the new wife-mother in this story is both explained and excused, was a condition that Davis knew. "The Wife's Story" was written sometime during the first year of Davis's marriage when she was living with her hus-band's family in a strange city. She was also suffering a difficult pregnancy, which in its early stages was marked by a type of nervous breakdown, then called "brain-fever." Interestingly, her physician for this illness was probably S. Weir Mitchell, a family friend, who treated her, as he did Charlotte Perkins Gilman, author of "The Yellow Wallpaper," by restricting her reading and her writing.[25] Although Davis's story reflects a far less indi-viduated response to the experience than Gilman's, it similarly illuminates the tragedy of a female writer's re-pressed, guilty desire.

Other tales of artistic-domestic conflict during this pe-riod—"Clement Moore's Vocation" (1870), *Earthen Pitchers* (1873-74), and "The Poetess of Clap City" (1875)—repeat variations on the theme of failure anxi-ety that appears in "A Wife's Story."[26] In each case the protagonist fails as an artist because she is internally or externally impelled to abandon art for womanhood. Sometimes she is tragically forced to surrender to social forces greater than herself, as in "Marcia," Davis's darkest, most realistic vision of the failed artist.

The story "Marcia," like "The Wife's Story," is typi-cal of Davis's middle period in that it dramatizes an at-tempt to mediate the conflict between art and domestic-ity that ends in failure. Also like Hetty, Marcia Barr, the would-be writer from Yazoo, Mississippi, is a recurring female type in Davis's fiction who reflects another facet of Davis's self-image during this middle period. Marcia is courageous in her determination to break out of the oppressive rural culture that trapped her opium-addicted mother. Marcia describes her mother, a woman with "one of the finest minds in the world," more like a slave than a plantation mistress. She has never been "further than twenty miles from the plantation; she has read nothing, knows nothing" (925). Marcia herself is proud of her refusal to compromise her dream by ac-cepting a protected life of marriage to a man who, like her father, "thinks women are like mares—only useful to bring forth children." But, according to the profes-sional writer who narrates the story, she is tragically in-nocent:

> The popular belief in the wings of genius, which can carry it over hard work and all such obstacles as igno-rance of grammar or even the spelling-book, found in her a marked example.
>
> (926)

Although Marcia resembles Davis's young rebellious artists, her story, told from the perspective of the older narrator reveals a compromised vision that comes with age.

However, the narrator is moved by Marcia's valiant, if ingenuous, battle for independence. Marcia struggles to find work writing, suffering hunger and also frustration because she has "something to say, if people only would hear it" (927). After several years, when she has become a ragged, gaunt writer of social and commercial puffs for the papers, Zack Biron, her father's plantation overseer, comes to find her and take her home. He is "an ignorant, small-minded man" (926), but he is genuinely horrified by Marcia's straits and determined that she be cared for "like a lady" (928). In the narrator's description of the leave-taking of the new Marcia, "magnificent in plumes, the costliest that her owner's [husband's] money could buy," this story voices both sadness at Marcia's failure and horror at her victimization. Without question, defeat is total as Marcia hands the narrator her unpublished manuscripts, asking, "Will you burn them for me? All: do not leave a line, a word" (928).

The voice of the author is totally conflicted in this story. The narrator, a writer and successful publisher whose own sex is fascinatingly indeterminate, voices attitudes that more closely resemble Davis's at this time than does the protagonist.[27] The narrator is ambivalent toward Marcia—admiring her grit and integrity, pitying her victimization, and blaming her innocence. Figures like Marcia, idealists who fail, reappear as admonitions in Davis's fiction and essays of this middle period and later. There is always much of Rebecca Harding, the young woman from West Virginia, in them. But in this story, Davis seems to have split herself into two; there is also much of her in the narrator, who constantly needs to validate the compromises she has made.

Most of Davis's middle-period artists are not as overtly victimized as Marcia Barr. More often, indoctrinated and defined by domestic ideology, their failure results from a subtler self-destruction. Usually, like Hetty Manning, the female artist voluntarily forsakes art in order to fulfill her redemptive role as wife-mother. This is the choice made by Maria Heald, the artist in **"The Poetess of Clap City,"** and it is the true work discovered by the artist protagonist in **"Clement Moore's Vocation."** *Earthen Pitchers,* a serialized novel from Davis's middle period, enacts the title's implications: that the transcendent or autonomous motive of art is antithetical to the corporeal, serving nature of woman's domestic being. In this novel, Audry Swenson, a musician of promise, witnesses the atrophy of her unused talent; her complement, Jane Derby, a successful journalist, also renounces professional achievement for domesticity. The resolutions of all these stories are painfully ambiguous regarding the tragedy or the wisdom of the protagonists' choices. They assert more than anything else a psyche in conflict. Like Maria in **"The Poetess of Clap City,"** the two artists in *Earthen Pitchers* are forced to confront the facts that undeveloped power atrophies and wasted talent is irrevocably lost. Davis's fictional artists of this middle period fail in their attempts to deny their domestic role or to mediate it with their artistic aspirations. Their eventual success as wives and mothers is undermined by awareness of their failure as artists. Interestingly, Davis allows none of these artists the option of mediation through compromise that she herself chose.

These *Künstlerromane* were written by Davis at a time when she was enjoying the fulfilled life of a happily married mother of three children. But they are also the stories of a writer who, though always writing, was forsaking her talent, producing increasingly less of the intense, demanding fiction of which she was capable. Instead of submitting to the respected journals that continued to solicit her work, at this time she was more often submitting easy potboilers for popular children's and women's fashion magazines. These are what she had time and energy for, but the continued occasional appearance of her work in better journals demonstrates that she still knew and valued quality in her own writing. In her artists of this period, we see her ambivalence about the life she had chosen. Unlike the domestic contentment found in much of her fiction of this period, her stories of artists feature women who voice both anxiety about the compromising of their maternal, female role with their egoistic artistic desire and guilt about being unable to renounce that desire successfully.

The transition to the next period in Davis's fiction is marked by her development of an artist manqué in *A Law Unto Herself* (1877), written just a few years after *Earthen Pitchers.*[28] Cornelia Fleming, the female artist in this novel, is a minor character whose primary role is that of the other woman in a love triangle. However, she suggests a change in the nature of Davis's anxiety about her art from guilt to regret, which marks the older female artist. In the creation of this character's unfulfilled life, Davis seems again to be transferring attitudes to her characters; however, this instance seems motivated by the author's insecurity. Cornelia's inability to find fulfillment, which reinforces the idea that domestic desire cannot be repressed or mediated, hints at Davis's need for reassurance about the choice she herself had made. Even though Cornelia's failure at love has permitted her pursuit of art, she still finds herself unable to find satisfaction without domestic definition. In this case, Cornelia's singular pursuit of art results from, rather than causes, her inability to find completion in her womanhood. This scenario differs from those of Davis's previous period, in which the pursuit of art threatens success as a woman, and from those of her later period, in which the pursuit of domesticity causes her lack of fulfillment as an artist.

At the close of this story, Cornelia, who has lost the man of her dreams to the novel's protagonist, finally settles in Rome and brings to its artist colony all her frustrated domestic desire; "she makes her studio one of the pleasantest resorts for the young artists in Rome." There, with "her hair cut short" and "man's collar," she attempts to have both worlds—domestic centrality and artistic autonomy—but she fails to be successfully fulfilled by either. "A good fellow, Corny," the other artists say, "but what a pity that she is not a man" (731). Cornelia's ironic unfulfillment seems to reify Davis's fears about the impossibility of a woman's successful denial of her domestic urges: Cornelia is not only an artist manqué, she is also a male manqué.

When she wrote this story, Davis was the mother of three children, ranging in age from five to thirteen. She was also the wife of the editor of the *Philadelphia Inquirer*. Davis, who always practiced her belief that mothers should not work out of the home unless doing so was financially necessary, chose to subordinate her writing to her domestic commitments. Nevertheless, the prodigious output of her fifty-year career demonstrates that, while she was a wife and mother, Davis was also always a writer.[29] When her eldest son, Richard Harding Davis, was beginning his career, she once responded to a suggestion he had received that an unhappy writer should stop writing by saying, "God forbid. I would almost as soon say stop breathing, for it is the same thing."[30]

Davis's works of the late 1880s through the 1890s are the creations of a more mature woman with grown children, who as a writer was beginning to confront the consequences of her choices. In her treatment of the artist in stories like **"Anne"** (1889) and ***Frances Waldeaux*** (1897), artistic expression is linked with individualism more than with creativity.[31] While these stories are not marked with frustration or with anxiety about failure as thoroughly as the earlier artists' tales, they are tinged with regret and resignation at a lack of fulfillment.[32] Older women whose age and situation often closely resembles Davis's, these protagonists have either rejected the pursuit of art, seeing it as irreconcilable with domesticity, or like Davis, they have compromised their art in order to pursue it. In both cases they are unfulfilled.

The older artists of this period, like the title character of **"Anne,"** mourn the loss of creative fulfillment but conclude eventually that its loss is the inevitable price of maturity. The creative impulse, seen in retrospect by the mature author and by her mature protagonist, is characterized by strength, beauty, and selfishness; these qualities seem to equate it with the shallowness of youth. In **"Anne,"** the discovery of being unfulfilled as a woman is realized first as the discovery of being unfulfilled creatively, and both discoveries are revealed dramatically at a moment of middle-age crisis.

Davis's emphasis on the protagonist's interiority shows the ironic disparity between the female artist as expressive subject and the wife-mother as silenced object. Throughout there are two Anne's. The external Mrs. Anne Palmer, "a stout woman of fifty with grizzled hair and a big nose," tries to sing, but produces only a "discordant yawp." However, always "something within her" cries out, "I am here—Anne! I am beautiful and young. If this old throat were different my voice would ring through earth and heaven" (227).

Anne's mid-life crisis is the crushing discovery of being unfulfilled, common to the mature artist in Davis's later fiction. Anne, a "woman of masculine intellect" who has assumed management of the family peach farm since her husband's death and who, through shrewd stock investments has considerably improved the family estate, is bored with her life. Increasingly her mind wanders to her first love, George Forbes, now a famous author. Unknown to either of her two overly solicitous children, the Anne within is racked with discontent, crying out, "I should have had my true life" (232). This story of an artist whose situation—solicitous adult children, domestic comfort, and economic productivity—strongly resembles Davis's own is actually a rebellion fantasy by a woman who rarely in her own voice uttered discontent with her personal life.

In the story, the Anne within finally even convinces Mrs. Anne Palmer, the widow and mother of grown children, to run away:

> She would go away. Why should she not go away? She had done her full duty to husband, children and property. Why should she not begin somewhere else, live out her own life? Why should she not have her chance for the few years left? Music and art and the companionship of thinkers and scholars, Mrs. Palmer's face grew pale as she named these things so long forbidden to her.
>
> (234)

She does run away, but eventually, like Hetty Manning and many other of Davis's rebellious women, she is led by events to realize that life is best and values are truest at home. Once again, though, Davis's commitment to her "it's-a-wonderful-life" theme is suspect. She first develops her comfortable conclusion in which Anne, who has been welcomed home, enjoys a "quiet, luxurious, happy life." But she adds a final reassertion of Anne's interiority that invites suspicion of the author's surface text:

> Yet sometimes in the midst of all this comfort and sunshine a chance note of music or the sound of the restless wind will bring an expression into her eyes which her children do not understand, as if some creature unknown to them looked out of them.
>
> At such times Mrs. Palmer will say to herself, "Poor Anne!"
>
> (242)

In her last novel, *Frances Waldeaux,* Davis again treats the elderly female artist, this time depicting her fictive double with satiric objectivity as an aging woman hack. This protagonist's discovery of unfulfillment is ironic. Well aware that she has injured her artistic potential in the name of motherhood, the protagonist discovers late in life that, in her attempt to live the domestic ideal of abnegation, she has actually annihilated any sense of herself as an individual.

Frances Waldeaux, widowed at a young age by a sweet but irresponsible wastrel, has made a successful career more like that of Davis's contemporary Fanny Fern than like Davis's. Frances is a successful writer of "comical squibs" that are "not vulgar but coarse and biting" (14). Like Fern, she also uses a pseudonym: "Quigg." Frances, however, maintains her anonymity for reasons slightly different from Fern's and from those that impelled Davis's frequent choice of anonymity. She hides her successful identity in order to delude her grown son into thinking that his support comes from his father's well-planned trust.

In this final treatment of the artist, Davis depicts her protagonist's failure to find fulfillment in her choices of self-abnegation as a writer and as a mother. In the character of Frances Waldeaux, Davis embodies the error of compromised choices and mediated desires, the choices that had directed Davis's own life. Frances's error originates in the sacrifice of her own identity. During an early conversation with her adored son, George, she reveals that she is unfulfilled to the point of hollowness:

> I never think of you as my son, or a man, or anything outside of me—not at all. You are just me, doing the things I should have done if I had not been a woman. . . . when I was a girl it seemed as if there was something in me that I must say, so I tried to write poems. . . . I've been dumb, as you might say, for years. But when I read your article, George—do you know if I had written it I should have used just the phrases you did? . . . I am dumb, but you speak for me now. It is because we are just one.
>
> (9)

But they are not one; he leaves, and Frances is left alone. The novel's plot centers on Frances's gradual and troubled acceptance of George's right to an individual existence—his choice of career, his wife, and his home. It also deals with her discovery that domestic self-abnegation can be harmful. By turning to potboiling journalism, Frances has done what Maria Heald in **"The Poetess of Clap City"** refused to do: sold her "birthright"—her poems and her individual identity— "for a mess of pottage." Though more extreme, Frances's choice is essentially the one that Davis made. In earlier stories of anxiety the artists are frustrated by or fearful of unused talent. Even in later stories like **"Anne,"** the artist regrets unused talent. In this last rendering, however, misuse of talent seems as disastrous as its disuse.

Frances Waldeaux is autobiographical in a number of ways, not the least of which is that the protagonist is a doting mother of a now-grown son in the support of whom she has silently, voluntarily sacrificed her integrity as a writer. This is a novel by a mother who took greater pride in the accomplishments of her son, Richard Harding Davis, than she ever did in her own work. However, this is also the final novel of an aging author who, looking back at her early work like **"Life in the Iron-Mills"** and remembering the indignant passion that had filled her with purpose, might have regretted the atrophy of that power. Finally, this is the work of a sixty-five-year-old widow, who for all her free-thinking individualism, was a product of her culture. No matter what special power she possessed, she also shared possession of her culture's dominant domestic ideology.

Rebecca Harding Davis, like her characters, an artist and a woman in the nineteenth century, was forced in every stage of her life to make choices that placed her in a dilemma, assuring failure—by being either frustrated, unsuccessful, or unfulfilled. She experienced the frustration of her artistic desires because they were incompatible with her role as wife-mother. She was unsuccessful in her attempts to mediate the role of artist with those that defined a woman, and she admitted failure in the necessary rejection of one of the conflicting roles. Finally, she recognized a lack of fulfillment within the narrow limitations of her selected identity; she even had to confront being unfulfilled by the compromises necessary to allow the female pursuit of art. Davis made choices that she knew were right for her as a woman, but choices that she also knew were wrong for her as an artist.

Like many other women writers, Davis often appeased the guilt and frustration inherent in the double-bind of being a female artist by becoming her own worst enemy, creating fictional projections of herself as artist and then negating their power, punishing them, or having them recant their unacceptable artistic desire. The paradigm of the artist manqué allowed women writers in the nineteenth century to exorcise their illicit desires by simultaneously asserting and denying them. It provided a way for a woman like Davis to fantasize her desire, to punish her guilt, to salve her pain, and still to be a writer.

Notes

1. "Life in the Iron-Mills," *Atlantic* 7 (1861), 430-51, did not appear with "The Korl Woman" as a subtitle, although Davis had submitted it as an alternative title to "Iron-Mills"; the reprint *Life in the Iron Mills and Other Stories,* biographical interp. Tillie Olsen, rev. ed. (Old Westbury, N.Y.: Feminist Press, 1985), which is cited, prints the subtitle.

2. P. 64; korl is a pinkish-white, chalky substance left from the Bessemer steel smelting process.

3. This aspect of Davis's writing, which is indeed essential, is enriched, not refuted, by feminist reading. For various genre/tradition arguments, see James C. Austin, "Success and Failure of Rebecca Harding Davis," *Midcontinent American Studies Journal* 3 (1962), 44-49; Walter Hesford, "Literary Contexts of 'Life in the Iron-Mills,'" *American Literature* 49 (1977), 70-85; John Conran, "Assailant Landscapes and the Man of Feeling: Rebecca Harding Davis's *Life in the Iron Mills,*" *Journal of American Culture* 3 (1980), 487-500; and Sharon M. Harris, "Rebecca Harding Davis: From Romanticism to Realism," *American Literary Realism* 21.2 (winter 1989), 4-20.

4. Tillie Olsen's insightful biographical interpretation of "Iron-Mills" gave Davis new literary life. But, while her Feminist Press editions (1972, 1985) have created a sizable readership, they have stimulated surprisingly little critical interest, compared with that in some other rediscovered woman writers. For discussion of Davis's fiction from a feminist perspective, see Margaret M. Culley, "Vain Dreams: The Dream Convention in Some Nineteenth-Century Women's Fiction," *Frontiers* 1.3 (1976), 94-104; Louise Duus, "Neither Saint nor Sinner: Women in Late Nineteenth-Century Fiction," *American Literary Realism* 7 (1974), 276-78; Charlotte Goodman, "Portraits of the *Artiste Manquée* by Three Women Novelists," *Frontiers* 5 (1981), 57-59; Jean Pfaelzer, "Rebecca Harding Davis: Domesticity, Social Order, and the Industrial Novel," *International Journal of Women's Studies* 4 (1981), 234-44, and the introduction to "Marcia," *Legacy* 4 (1987), 3-5; and Jane Atteridge Rose, "Reading 'Life in the Iron-Mills' Contextually: A Key to Rebecca Harding Davis' Fiction," in *Conversations: Contemporary Critical Theory and the Teaching of Literature,* ed. Charles Moran and Elizabeth Penfield (Urbana, Ill.: National Council of Teachers of English, 1990) 187-99. Also see brief references in Susan Gubar, "The Birth of the Artist as Heroine: (Re)production, the *Künstlerroman* Tradition, and the Fiction of Katherine Mansfield," in *The Representation of Women in Fiction,* ed. Carolyn G. Heilbrun and Margaret R. Higonnet (Baltimore: Johns Hopkins University Press, 1983), pp. 19-59; and Rachel Blau DuPlessis, "To 'bear my mother's name': *Künstlerromane* by Women Writers," in *Writing Beyond the Ending: Narrative Strategies of Twentieth-Century Women Writers* (Bloomington: Indiana University Press, 1985), pp. 84-104. For a concise overview, see Judith Fetterley, *Provisions* (Bloomington: Indiana University Press, 1985), pp. 306-14.

5. This French word *manqué* is critically appropriate as an umbrella term because it encompasses the various ways failure can occur: frustration, lack of success, lack of fulfillment.

6. For further discussion of this genre, see Linda Huf, *A Portrait of the Artist as a Young Woman: The Writer as Heroine in American Literature* (New York: Ungar, 1983); also see DuPlessis, Goodman, and Gubar.

7. This discussion is largely premised on two studies: the understanding of duplicity in nineteenth-century women's fiction, provided by Sandra M. Gilbert and Susan Gubar, *The Madwoman in the Attic: The Woman Writer and the Nineteenth-Century Literary Imagination* (New Haven, Conn.: Yale University Press, 1979); and the understanding of values implicitly operating in middle-class nineteenth-century America, provided by Jane Tompkins, *Sensational Designs* (New York: Oxford University Press, 1985). It is also influenced by the understanding that women interpret and thereby reconstruct their particular position in history, provided by Linda Alcoff "Cultural Feminism Versus Post-Structuralism: The Identity Crisis in Feminist Theory," *Signs Journal of Women in Culture and Society* 13.3 (1988), 405-36.

8. For biographical reading of other women writers in consideration of ideological construction of female identity, see Mary Kelley, *Private Woman, Public Stage* (New York: Oxford University Press, 1984).

9. For further discussion of the artist manqué as evidence of women's collusion with patriarchal ideology continuing into the twentieth century, see Linda Dittmar, "When Privilege Is No Protection: The Woman Artist in *Quicksand* and *The House of Mirth,*" in this volume. For a provocative alternative view of Elizabeth Barrett Browning's *Aurora Leigh,* often seen as the epitome of the nineteenth-century *Künstlerroman* of the artist manqué in its conclusion that "Art is much but Love is more," see Holly A. Laird, "*Aurora Leigh*: An Epical *Ars Poetica,*" in this volume.

10. For biography of Davis, see Gerald Langford, *The Richard Harding Davis Years A Biography of a Mother and Son* (New York: Holt, Rinehart and Winston, 1961) and Sharon Harris, *Rebecca Harding Davis and American Realism* (Philadelphia: University of Pennsylvania Press, 1991).

11. For discussion of the socioeconomic aspects of domestic ideology, see Kirk Jeffrey, "The Family as Utopian Retreat from the City," *Soundings* 55 (1972), 22-41; Barbara Epstein, *The Politics of Domesticity* (Middletown, Conn.: Wesleyan Uni-

versity Press, 1981); and Susan Moller Okin, "The Woman and the Making of the Sentimental Family," *Philosophy and Public Affairs* 11 (1982), 65-88; for discussion of the religious aspects of domestic ideology, see Ann Douglas, *The Feminization of American Culture* (New York: Oxford University Press, 1985); and Tompkins, *Sensational Designs.*

12. In similar fashion, she dutifully moved to her husband's home in Philadelphia after her marriage, yet, once there, she spent more time in the library than she did keeping house. Later, when she had children, she always stayed home with them, but she spent the time writing.

13. "Blind Tom," *Atlantic* 10 (1862), 580-85; also as "Blind Black Tom," *All Year Round* 8 (1862), 126-29.

14. Many of Davis's protagonists suffer some form of "dumbness," her term for the silence that Tillie Olsen has shown to be the mark of women's texts in patriarchal culture (*Silences* [New York: Delacorte, 1978]). For another instance of silence, see Linda Hunt, *The Alberta Trilogy*: Cora Sandel's Norwegian *Künstlerroman* and American Feminist Literary Discourse," in this volume.

15. The real dangers of life in a border state during the Civil War only exacerbated the status quo of double standards and dependency.

16. Rebecca Harding [Davis], letter to Annie Fields, May 27, 1862, Richard Harding Davis Collection (#6109), Manuscript Division, Special Collections Department, University of Virginia Library, Charlottesville.

17. Maintaining anonymity long after it had ceased as a convention, Davis established several identities through textual lineage, her two most used being "by the author of 'Margret Howth'" (realism) and "by the author of 'The Second Life'" (sensationalism). Sometimes she published very different stories simultaneously in the same journals.

18. *Earthen Pitchers,* in *Scribner's Monthly* 7 (1873-74), 73-81, 199-207, 274-81, 490-94, 595-600, 714-21.

19. The real enslaved musician was named Tom Cauthen and was the property of a plantation owner by that name in Columbus, Georgia.

20. "The Wife's Story," *Atlantic* 14 (1864), 1-19, rpt. Olsen, *Silences,* pp. 177-221; "Marcia," *Harper's* 53 (1876), 925-28, which is cited, has also been recently reprinted in *Legacy* 4 (1987), 6-10.

21. Although certainly less extreme, the perceived conflict between a life of art and a life of domesticity has not disappeared. Other essays in this volume demonstrate that the destructive power of this tension is not specific to one age or one culture. See Renate Voris, "The Hysteric and the Mimic: A Reading of Christa Wolf's *Quest for Christa T.*," Katherine Kearns, "From Shadow to Substance: The Empowerment of the Artist Figure in Lee Smith's Fiction," and Linda Hunt, "*The Alberta Trilogy,*" all in this volume.

22. These stories, as a group, also show that this subject was an obsession of Davis's at this time of her life and not something tailored to appeal to a particular journal; her stories of failed artists appeared in *Atlantic, Harper's, Scribner's,* and *Peterson's* magazines, covering the total spectrum of fiction presses in the period after the Civil War.

23. Rebecca Harding Davis, Diary (1865-79), University of Virginia, Charlottesville.

24. Asserting that for nineteenth-century women dreams of artistic achievement were "not so much vain, as in vain," Culley argues that ambivalent dreams in fiction like "The Wife's Story" indicate that Davis and others "may have been unable to admit to themselves the full extent and meaning of their fantasies of the married woman in America" (102).

25. Rebecca Harding Davis, letter to Annie Fields (1866), University of Virginia, Charlottesville; on the occasion of Mitchell's first publication in *Atlantic,* Davis made reference to his care of her during her first, emotionally difficult pregnancy: "I owe much to him—life—and what is better than life." For fuller discussion, see Jane Atteridge Rose, "Images of Self: The Example of Rebecca Harding Davis and Charlotte Perkins Gilman," *English Language Notes* 29.1 (1991).

26. "Clement Moore's Vocation," *Peterson's* 57 (1870), 54-59; "The Poetess of Clap City," *Scribner's Monthly* 9 (1975), 612-15.

27. In her introduction to "Marcia," Pfaelzer defines the narrator as male, which the narrator's professional status would certainly indicate. However, comments like the narrator's statement that Biron did not have to be so quick declaring his business, because "any woman would soon have guessed" it, suggest the character is female. The most plausible explanation seems to be that Davis became so aligned with her male character that she let her persona slip.

28. *A Law Unto Herself,* in *Lippincott's* 2 (1877), 39-49, 167-82, 292-308, 464-78, 614-28, 719-31.

29. Davis wrote and published continuously from 1861 until three months before her death in January 1910. During this time she published well over

five hundred stories and essays, in addition to twelve books. For bibliography, see Jane Atteridge Rose, "The Fiction and Non-Fiction of Rebecca Harding Davis," *American Literary Realism* 22.3 (spring 1990) pp. 67-86.

30. *The Adventures and Letters of Richard Harding Davis,* ed. Charles Belmont Davis (New York: Scribner's, 1917), pp. 34-35.

31. "Anne," *Harper's* 78 (1889), 744-50, rpt. in Olsen, *Silences,* 225-42; *Frances Waldeaux* (New York: Harper, 1897).

32. Kearns's reading of Lee Smith's fiction, in this volume, suggests an interesting contrast between nineteenth-century and twentieth-century projections of the woman artist. Davis's artists manqués, which reflect each stage of her life, never conquer or successfully reconcile the tension in their lives. Smith's sequence of artists, however, seem increasingly to have integrated their womanhood with their art.

Jean Pfaelzer (essay date 1996)

SOURCE: Pfaelzer, Jean. "The Common Story of *Margret Howth*." In *Parlor Radical: Rebecca Harding Davis and the Origins of American Social Realism,* pp. 54-75. Pittsburgh: University of Pittsburgh Press, 1996.

[*In the following essay, Pfaelzer addresses the issue of "the tension between realism and sentiment" in Davis's* Margret Howth, *disagreeing with the view of some critics that the novel fails because, in it, the author attempted to graft sentimental themes and motifs on an otherwise starkly realistic narrative in order to appease her editor at the* Atlantic Monthly. *The critic asserts instead that Davis employed the sentimental convention to mitigate the "masculine" form of realism and "romantic egoism" in the novel, and to show that "if political hunger is not regulated by family, love, and the female definition of true community, it could degenerate into a destructive and hungry egoism that uses others as it promotes its unfulfilled desire in the name of social progress."*]

In a role he would play throughout his tenure at the *Atlantic Monthly,* James Fields, Rebecca Harding Davis's literary mentor, attempted to contain her narrative radicalism. In May 1861, one month after the successful publication of **"Life in the Iron-Mills,"** Fields rejected Davis's next piece, "The Deaf and the Dumb,"[1] as too gloomy for the *Atlantic.* Davis wrote back, apparently abject and insecure about the literary direction she was taking:

> I am sorry. I thank you for the kindness with which you veil the disappointment. Whatever holier meaning life or music has for me, has reached me through the "pathetic minor." I fear that I only have the power to echo the pathos without the meaning. When I began the story, I meant to make it end in full sunshine—to show how even "Lois" was not dumb, how even the meanest things in life, were "voices in the world, and none of them *without* its signification." [Lois's] life and death were to be the only dark thread. But . . . in my eagerness . . . I "assembled the gloom" you complain of."

At this early point in her career, Davis seems conciliatory: "[Do] you think I could . . . make it acceptable by returning to my original idea. Let her character and death (I cannot give up all, you see) remain, and the rest of the picture be steeped in warm healthy light. A 'perfect day in June.'"[2] Eight weeks later, she sent Fields a revised manuscript; he accepted it immediately and published it anonymously.

Like the insistent statue of the korl woman, the "rough ungainly thing" that remains hidden behind the curtains at the end of **"Life in the Iron-Mills,"** *Margret Howth* embodies competing tendencies. Jean Fagan Yellin argues that in writing *Margret Howth* Rebecca Harding Davis suffered from a deep self-division, a consequence of her attempts to conform to the expectations of the Brahmin world of the *Atlantic* on the one hand and her ambivalence about her artistic self-assertion on the other. Reading through Davis's letters to Fields, Yellin astutely re-creates Davis's editing process and concludes that throughout the summer and early fall of 1862 Davis reluctantly acceded to many of Fields's editorial suggestions, apparently adding ninety sunny pages to placate him.[3] In my view, however, *Margret Howth,* like the korl woman, both expressed and repressed Davis's own Promethean desires as she struggled to create a literary form that could embody her growing social anger.

I believe that *Margret Howth* burst open the optimistic foundations of American romanticism. Even though Davis wrote Fields that she was "afraid to touch forbidden subjects so only the husk of the thing was left,"[4] powerful images of the degrading effects of slavery, the reactionary arrogance of secessionists, the social myopia of organized religion, the hardships of industrial life, the suppression of women's work, and in particular the transcendental attraction to solipsism waft through the novel—written, as Davis insists, "from the border of the battlefield, and I find in it no theme for shallow argument or flimsy rhymes."[5]

The story of life in a new factory town in Indiana is hardly a portrait of a perfect day in June. Although she promised Fields a summertime story "steeped in warm healthy light," her tale opens with these words: "Men have forgotten to hope, forgotten to pray"; they survive only through "the bitterness of endurance"; in the morning they say, "'Would God it were even!' and in the evening, 'Would God it were morning!'"(3). Throughout the text, the narrator realigns the reader's romantic expectations as she explodes the epic and public themes of the first year of the Civil War: "Let me tell you a story of To-day,—very homely and narrow in its scope and aim. Not of the To-Day whose significance in the history of humanity only those shall read who will live when you and I are dead." Having preemptively killed off her reader (whom I allege to be Fields), she adds, "Neither I nor you have the prophet's vision to see the age as its meaning stands written before God." Further, she goes on, the Civil War did not assure a happy ending for the war-torn nation: "Those who shall live when we are dead may tell their children, perhaps, how, out of anguish and darkness such as the world seldom has borne, the enduring morning evolved of the true world and the true man. It is not clear to us" (4).

Rejecting nationalistic rhetoric, Davis turns to affectional discourse, the language of "mercy and love," to tell her "story of today." The narrator announces that she has renounced the language of "patriotism and chivalry" in order to record "less partial truths . . . that do not speak to us in bayonets and victories." Insistently reiterating, "Do not call me a traitor," she returns to the female vocabulary of sentimentalism to forge a social and realistic rhetoric, and along the way she repudiates the solipsistic and overreaching will of romanticism.

Sentimentalism was a tradition that linked private feeling to public action, moral faculties to social activity, and emotion and ethics to law and economics. As modern readers consider Davis's choice of discourse, it is important to bear in mind that sentimental ethics held a highly political charge. In the mid-nineteenth century, sentimentalism was viewed as unmediated expression of human nature, *socially defined.* As Fred Kaplan observes, "Most Victorians believed that the human community was one of shared moral feelings, and that sentimentality was a desirable way of feeling and of expressing ourselves morally."[6] *Margret Howth* portrays how the new industrialism was challenging visions of a shared national morality by encouraging assertive individualism. In Davis's view, individualism is a political identity that sits rather comfortably with the egoism of literary romanticism. In her first full-length novel, the discourse of feelings confronts both the vocabulary of romantic egoism and the emerging imagery of utilitarianism, invention, and political economy.

Davis believes that male energies—equally necessary to patriotism, narcissism, capitalistic self-advancement, and romantic self-discovery, threaten female drives—gestures toward self-growth through friendship and family bonds. She holds that the greatest danger to the commonweal is ego, which she pictures in the willingness of male characters to buy and sell people through slavery, wages, marriage, and utopian visions of politi-

cal omnipotence; her best hope for social change lies in "harmony," which she sees as "faith in God, faith in her fellow-man, faith in herself" (77). Harmony to Davis is the sine qua non of a better society. In assigning harmony to female characters, Davis suggests that women's right and capacity to express social outrage derives from their social authority *as women.* Only visions of community, whether utopian, socialist, pastoral, or familial, can resist the pressures of industrial capitalism toward atomization, expressed in terms of character as selfishness, loneliness, and greed. Paradoxically in *Margret Howth,* each communal dream is found seriously wanting, contaminated by the system that has spawned it. In *Margret Howth,* the debate over the true course of social change thus emerges as a political expression of the tension Davis finds between the egotistical love of men and the self-denying love of women.

Viewing sentimentalism as a species of mid-nineteenth-century discourse may account for the considerable dissonance between the modern and the contemporary receptions of *Margret Howth.* Nineteenth-century reviewers received the book enthusiastically, specifically praising its social concerns. A reviewer for *Peterson's Magazine,* a popular journal with a mostly female audience, observed,

> On some of the deepest problems that agitate humanity [Davis] has evidently thought much and deeply; and she has come back, from the solemn quest . . . full of heaven-like faith. . . . Such characters as Holmes and Knowles, in their robust strength and originality, exist nowhere in the novels of female writers, except in those of Charlotte Bronte; and we would say that Holmes and Knowles are more powerful creations than even the best of Charlotte Bronte's if we were not afraid of being too eulogistic.

The reviewer goes on to predict that the anonymous author of *Margret Howth* "will eventually be confessed to be the greatest of American novelists."[7] Likewise, the *Continental Monthly,* a new journal with strong abolitionist sentiments and a commitment to early realism, praised *Margret Howth* as a realistic exploration of "a new field, right into the rough of real life, bringing out fresher and more varied forms than had been done before."

Echoing the narrator of **"Life in the Iron-Mills,"** the *Continental'*s reviewer observed that "few, especially in the Atlantic cities, know what becomes of culture among men and women who 'work and weave in endless motion' in the counting-house, or factory, or through daily drudgery and the reverses from wealth to poverty."[8] This review admired Davis's pictures of "incidents" of industrial life and her portrait of the "inner being" of residents of industrial towns, that is, the relationship between the new economic system and subjectivity:

One may believe, in reading it, that the author, wearied of the old cry that the literature of our country is only a continuation of that of Europe, had resolved to prove, by vigorous effort, that it *is* possible to set forth, not merely the incidents of our industrial life in many grades, in its purely idiomatic force, to make the world realize that in it vibrate and struggle outward those aspirations, germs of culture and reforms that we seldom reflect on as forming a part of the inner-being of our very practical fellow-citizens.[9]

The reviewer saw that in Davis's portrait nationalist struggles for reform reside, in part, in consciousness and desire.

By contrast, Sharon Harris finds *Margret Howth* "ultimately a failure in artistic terms precisely because of the incongruous insertions of 'full sunshine' into an otherwise stridently realistic work."[10] Jean Fagan Yellin accounts for this incongruity by suggesting that Davis "trimmed" *Margret Howth* to conform to the requirements of the literary establishment surrounding the *Atlantic Monthly.* In privatizing public problems, ignoring economic hunger, and eradicating spiritual hunger, Yellin argues, Davis made the revisions that would placate Fields and thereby she "feminized" and weakened her tale.[11]

In my view, the tension between realism and sentiment in the novel marks Davis's definition of social responsibility as active participation in a sympathetic community. With the Civil War raging around her, with industrialism polluting both the air and the social fabric of Wheeling, overawed by the abolitionist and secessionist passions that she saw rending her town, in *Margret Howth* Davis launched her lifelong theme of political desire and elevated the Promethean theme of **"Life in the Iron-Mills"** to social debate. Influenced by the ideology of sentiment, she suggested that if political hunger is not regulated by family, love, and the female definition of true community, it could degenerate into a destructive and hungry egoism that uses others as it promotes its unfulfilled desire in the name of social progress. *Margret Howth* confronts the politics of romantic egoism through a literary convention in which the give-and-take of domestic relationships regulates desire.[12]

It is this tension that may have raised Davis's concern about a comparison between herself and Charlotte Brontë. In August, as she was undertaking minor revisions to *Margret Howth,* she wrote to Fields, "You did not think I imitated Charlotte Bronte, did you? I would rather you had sent it back than thought that, but tell me candidly if you did. I may have done it unconsciously."[13] Davis's unease in fact points to the transnational influences of women authors that forged an "imagined community"[14] and suggests that she, along with other nineteenth-century American women authors,

did not write in intellectual isolation. As in *Jane Eyre,* in *Margret Howth* sentimental motifs confront patriarchal assumptions within the reform tendencies of romanticism. Rather than a story of female capitulation (in the tradition of Ann Douglas, who bemoans the "feminization" of American literature), *Margret Howth,* like *Jane Eyre,* should be read as a gendered paradigm of the social tensions embodied in the movement from romanticism to realism, from the "egotistical sublime" to a genre based on the growth of individuals who interact with an expanding industrial society.

Romanticism, Nina Baym reminds us, promises an *idea* of America where individuals can achieve complete self-definition because they can exist in some meaningful sense prior to and apart from history. Romanticism inscribes a confrontation between the American individual, the pure American self divorced from specific social circumstances, and the promise offered by the idea of America:

> This promise is the deeply romantic one that in this new land identity is untrammeled by history and social accident. Behind this promise is the assurance that individuals come before society, that they exist in some meaningful sense outside the societies in which they happen to find themselves. The romantic myth also holds that as something artificial and secondary to human nature, society exerts an unmitigatedly destructive pressure on individuality.[15]

Further, as Mary Poovey suggests, the romantic absence of social regulation and the egotistical drive to assert and extend the self, deny—to use Kant's phrase—the otherness of others.[16] In *Margret Howth,* as in *Jane Eyre,* women's identity is enmeshed within the network of family and community; the Emersonian idealization of autonomy represents a masculine threat to communal sensibility. The power of sentiment can contain egoism, but usually at the price of repressing men's and women's deep hunger for "summat to make them live."

By appending a sentimental resolution to a realist novel, by appending a June ending to her wintry tale, Davis appealed to two democratic literary traditions: the vernacular characterization of farmers and factory workers, and the sentimental discourse of female emotionality, piety, and moral commitment. The sentimental novel, as Jane Tompkins reminds us, saw itself as an "agent of cultural formation," a blueprint for women's survival under a specific set of political, economic, social, and religious conditions.[17] Sentimental authors adopted a familiar idiom, assured that a contemporary audience would know how to respond. In these terms, readers of *Margret Howth* would have recognized that the ending, dissonant though it may be to us, left Margret in a familiar context of common female opportunities and oppressions. Thus, I think that the apparent tension between the sections, voices, and discourses of *Margret*

Howth partakes of what Susan Harris, in Bakhtinian terms, calls the "heteroglossia" of women's fiction of the time, the frequent use of multiple discursive modes within one text to represent a female author's ongoing debate about how to live in the world.[18]

In this way, *Margret Howth* also recalls "The American Scholar," in which Emerson, a great influence on Davis, finds no tension between such discourses when he said that the office of the scholar or "poet" is "to cheer, to raise, to guide men by showing them facts amidst appearances. . . . He is the world's eye. He is the world's heart."[19] *Margret Howth* works through both the eye and the heart, conflating Davis's industrial topic and her realist technique through the metaphor of literary language itself:

> My story is very crude and homely, as I said,—only a rough sketch of one or two of those people whom you see every day, and call "dregs," sometimes,—*a dull, plain bit of prose*, such as you might pick for yourself out of any of these warehouses or back-streets.

Perhaps addressing Fields himself, she notes sardonically,

> I expect you to call it stale and plebeian, for I know the glimpses of life it pleases you best to find; idylls delicately tinted; passion-veined hearts, cut bare for curious eyes; prophetic utterances, concrete and clear.

Responding to Fields's insistent pressure to revise her gloom, Davis persists:

> You want something, in fact, to lift you out of this crowded, tobacco-stained commonplace, to kindle and chafe and glow in you. I want you to dig into this commonplace, this vulgar American life, and see what is in it. Sometimes I think it has a new and awful significance that we do not see.
>
> (6)

She then goes on to summon this reader, whose "manlier nature" has been awakened by the trumpet of the Civil War, to the other great "warfare" going on, a war that also "has its slain. Men and women, lean-jawed, crippled in the slow, silent battle, are in your alleys, sit beside you at your table; its martyrs sleep under every green hill-side." From this class war, she insists, "money will buy you no discharge" (7).[20]

Davis also disagreed with Fields about the title of her novel. Originally she wanted to call it either "The Deaf and the Dumb" or "A Story of Today," either one a more appropriate title than *Margret Howth,* which Fields bestowed on the manuscript.[21] Her preferred title, *A Story of Today,* and her frequent references to "today" also echo Emerson, who said, "I do not ask for the great, the remote, the romantic; what is doing in Italy or Arabia; . . . I embrace the common, I explore and sit at the feet of the familiar, the low. Give me insight into to-day."[22]

Margret Howth is a highly contemporary story about a raw mill town in Indiana. Hunger and poverty have forced Margret, a spinster daughter of a retired and blind schoolmaster, to take a man's job as a bookkeeper in a large woolen mill. The mill is owned by Dr. Knowles, an abolitionist and romantic reformer who is selling the property to Stephen Holmes, one of the new men who will mold the age, like "all men around him . . . thrusting and jostling and struggling, up, up" (121). The penniless but ambitious Holmes, living for "self-salvation, self-elevation," ends his romance with Margret so he can use the dowry of a young heiress to buy the property. But before he can pay for the mill, it burns down, torched by an angry ex-convict, Joe Yare, an African American who works in the mill as a night stoker. Eventually Knowles, Holmes, and Margret redesign their personal and social visions through the humble and self-sacrificing love of Joe's daughter, Lois, a deformed mulatto peddler, who dies from the toxic fumes breathed while rescuing Holmes from the fire. Her death instructs them in the power of sympathy and the values of humility, duty, and family; thus it redeems them all.

Margret Howth is also the story of the breakup of rural social structures in an emerging industrial capitalist economy. The novel begins with an image of one of the most profound changes of industrialization, the painful and repressive adjustment of a young woman who leaves home and enters the workplace for the first time. It explores how new relationships of production surrounding the woolen mill—wages, contracts, and competition—are replacing the rural networks of family, barter, gossip, and charity. Thus Davis contrasts the atomized and defensive personalities spawned by the economy of the mill—Knowles, Holmes, and Joe Yare—to the caring and responsible relationships of dependency sustaining those who work and live in the surrounding countryside, outside the economic aura of the mill—the Howths, local farmers, and, in particular, the peddler Lois. In contrast to the sham utopianism embraced by Knowles, Lois unites the community by trading its garden produce, a role that links her to its preindustrial economy. By comparing the new manufacturing town with the rural life of the farms (the Howth farm is still just a long walk from the mill), Davis exposes the tensions in the early stages of capitalist development. Mercantile and farm ethics of hard work, thrift, attachment, honesty, and community are yielding to individualism, secularity, self-interest, competition, alcoholism, and petty crime.

The novel begins on Margret's first day of work, her twentieth birthday, when she enters the mill as a bookkeeper in order to "support a helpless father and mother; it was a common story" (19). Clearly, her status has worsened. Margret's climb onto her stool on October 20, 1860, in a small "closet," a dark seventh-floor office, is mainstream American literature's first record of a young rural woman leaving home to work in a factory. The floors shake with the incessant thud of the looms, and the office is heavy with the smell of dye and copperas, a sulfate of copper, iron, and zinc used in woolen dyes. Seated uncomfortably on her stool which is, metaphorically, "too high for a small woman," the American heroine is no longer looking out a window, but finds herself fully occupied by the world of work within. As in **"Life in the Iron-Mills,"** images of artistic repression define industrial work. Unwilling to "dramatiz[e] her soul in writing" (8), she has taken up ledger work, the uncreative and monotonous copying from one book to another. With her steel pen "lining out her life, narrow and black," she soon wipes the ink from her pen in a "mechanical fashion" (10)—reified by her task. Through the imagery of writing itself Davis replaces sentimental fiction's metaphoric and literal closet of the house with the realist's enclosed office: female confinement endures.[23]

In contrast to her own anonymous "cramped quiet lines," Margret soon discovers a series of charcoal sketches drawn on the office walls by her predecessor, P. Teagarden, who has boldly emblazoned his name on the ceiling with the smoke of a candle—an interesting literary gesture from a woman novelist who is pleading with her publisher to keep her work anonymous.[24] Teagarden has also left behind a doleful chicken pecking the floor of a wire cage, which, along with the drawings, prompts Margret to recall how, as an aspiring and imaginative young girl, she planned to "dig down into the middle of the world, and find the kingdom of the griffins, or . . . go after Mercy and Christiana in their pilgrimage" (11). As Margret walks past soot-stained warehouses toward her home in the hills after her first day of work, the narrator observes, "One might have fancied her a slave putting on a mask, fearing to meet her master" (17)—an image of alienation and self-disguise that fuses wage slavery, chattel slavery, and the repressions of domestic life. These images of mechanical confinement and artistic inhibition anticipate such images as the caged parrot of Kate Chopin's *The Awakening,* who incessantly chants, "Allez-vous en!" ("Go away!" "Get out!") and the wallpaper in Charlotte Perkins Gilman's "The Yellow Wallpaper," whose design becomes a frightening projection of female repression.

Despite Fields's title for her novel, Davis always saw Dr. Knowles as the center of the story.[25] Influenced by his readings of early European socialists, Knowles, like Hollingsworth in Hawthorne's *Blithedale Romance,* plans to use the profits from the sale of the mill to launch a utopian community made up of the most degraded and impoverished residents of the town—alcoholics, prostitutes, and abandoned women—and he hopes to recruit Margret (suggesting Margaret Fuller, perhaps) as his aide. The relationship between Margret and Knowles, rather like that between Hollingsworth

and Zenobia, distills the tensions between the telos of sentimentalism and the telos of romanticism. Knowles presumes that Margret "had been planned and kept by God for higher uses than daughter or wife or mother. It was his part to put her work into her hands." Like her mother, who thinks that "Margret never had any opinions to express" (29), Knowles presumes that her desire is a species of his own, which he fantasizes as incestuous and repressed intimacy: "Between the two there lay that repellent resemblance which made them like close relations,—closer when they were silent" (19).

While Margret views her office job as a consequence of her father's financial incompetence and of Holmes's rejection—"perhaps life had nothing better for her, so she did not care"—Knowles, who consistently misreads Margret, sees her work as a romantic test. Intending to "make use" (23) of her in his utopian community, "he must know what stuff was in the weapon before he used it. He had been reading the slow, cold thing for years,—had not got into its secret yet. But there was power there, and it was the power he wanted" (19). He is convinced that Margret is an emanation of his best self and that if he can control her it will assign them both significance. To Knowles, Margret is a "Damascus blade which he was going to carry into battle" (23). But only in his phallic projection is she dangerous; in fact, Margret's repression and plainness undercut Knowles's egoistic fantasies: "There were no reflected lights about her; no gloss on her skin, no glitter in her eyes" (22).

In my view, a central problem with Davis's novel comes from a contradiction within transcendentalism itself: how to reconcile egoism with the dissolution of self that allows for political engagement. Like Bronson Alcott, Knowles tries to resolve this profound impasse by linking his ambitious quest to the universal good, a fusion of the personal and the public at the core of utopianism. In assigning political righteousness to his dominating fantasies of Margret, Knowles legitimizes her powerlessness at the same time that he blesses it with historical possibility. Margret's social vision, by contrast, derives from sentimentalism. Fred Kaplan explores how sentimentalism inherited the Enlightenment faith in the redemptive power of emotions over self-calculation. He cites David Hume, for example, who argues that "the ultimate ends of human actions can never . . . be accounted for by *reason,* but recommend themselves entirely to the sentiments and affections of mankind, without any dependence on the intellectual faculties."[26] Kaplan thus distinguishes sentiment, an "access of feeling," from the romantic "excess of feeling," which, almost by definition, must deny the world. Furthermore, he suggests, while sentiment offers an optimistic vision overall, it nonetheless takes its force from a keen awareness of human nature that, paradoxically, jeopardizes its claims to an ideal world.[27] Margret's dilemma is thus to find a way to defend the sentimental woman against the self-sufficient romantic imagination on the one hand, and the post-Calvinist forces of philosophical realism on the other. If sentimentalism sought to atrophy woman in her emotions and traditional social duties, realism sought to limit woman as the dubious product of her social conditions and biology. To Davis, neither race, gender, class, nor region should be prescriptive.

For Davis, the split between preindustrial and industrial values has a gendered valence. She believes that transcendentalism prompts patriarchal self-interest, which fits comfortably with the industrial breakup of rural and familial communities. In Knowles and Holmes, both mill owners, she portrays men who assert their self-reliance while they remain emotionally and financially dependent. The romantic man needs the sentimental woman, typified by Lois, as an enduring sign of the living gospel, and as an apostle of anti-egotistical and anticapitalistic values that can heal the culture as a whole. In *Margret Howth,* it is as the vessel for men's salvation that women's essential nature takes on a transformative role in the ongoing social debate about American industrialism.[28] In this Davis again echoes Emerson, who holds that self-reliance is not a paradigm of freedom from duty, but rather a model of an internalized standard of duty.

Thus, rather than a protonaturalist text, *Margret Howth* belongs to a discursive category that Thomas Laqueur terms the "humanitarian narrative," a hybrid of sentimentalism and early realism in which details of suffering, particularly bodily suffering, prompt compassion—understood in its time as a moral imperative to undertake social change.[29] Sentiment thereby shapes Davis's vision of social goals. For example, Margret, despairing of her plight, agrees to accompany Knowles on a visit to a crowded railroad shack, a "haunt of the lowest vice," where he hopes to recruit members for his celibate community. In this passage Davis recalls the nighttime visit to the mill in **"Life in the Iron-Mills,"** but this time the witness is female, as are the homeless Irish women and fugitive slaves who live in the shack; as an empathic female, the narrator repudiates Knowles's romantic appropriation of suffering.

True to the lineaments of sentimentalism, the suffering of the industrial poor is pictured as an imprisoning and confining female site where gender transcends class. Knowles views poverty as erotically female: "'Come here!' he said, fiercely, clutching [Margret's] hand. 'Women as fair and pure as you have come into dens like this,—and never gone away. Does it make your delicate breath faint?'" (150). Knowles and Margret stand over women who are prostrate and drunk, incompetent as mothers and incapable of taking action on their own behalf: "Women, idle trampers, whisky-bloated, filthy, lay half-asleep, or smoking on the floor,

set up a chorus of whining and begging when they entered. Half-naked children crawled about in rags."

The destitute women are further distinguished by their Catholic faith, which, to Davis, marks them as recent immigrants: "On the damp mildewed walls, there was hung a picture of . . . Pio Nono, crook in hand, with the usual inscription, 'Feed my sheep'" (151). This ironic reference to Pius IX (the pope whose betrayal of the Italian revolution of 1848 was bitterly described by Margaret Fuller)[30] points to Davis's lifelong hostility to Catholicism as well as to Protestant churches that were unwilling to engage in the Social Gospel. Davis conflates the Irish women with runaway slaves, who are mutually eroticized: "In the corner slept a heap of half-clothed blacks. Going on the underground railroad to Canada. Stolid, sensual wretches" (151). The narrator's racial discourse is indistinguishable from that of Knowles, who, while viewing the slave women as his future utopians, is trapped in the rhetoric of human commerce, and who observes, "so much flesh and blood out of the market, unweighed!" (151). When Margret, by contrast, picks up a slave child and kisses her face, Knowles responds, "Would you touch her? . . . Put it down" (151). Locked in their own discursive systems, Margret and Knowles appropriate the poor in different ways.

Eventually Margret agrees to join the community, a reluctant choice that mainly stems from her plight as a lonely single woman who is tired of taking care of her pettish mother and her bigoted father. Margret is repulsed by Mr. Howth's dreams of secession, his admiration for Napoleon, and his tiresome investigations of the Middle Ages when commoners still believed in the "perfected manhood in the conqueror" (31). Unlike Knowles, her father believes that now "the world's a failure. All the great dreams are dead" (34). Even in a novel that prioritizes affectional bonds, Davis, like Susan Warner in *The Wide Wide World,* satirizes a father who is self-interested, unreliable—indeed, "blind." Margret's decision to enter Knowles's "House of Refuge," a parody of the idealized home, reflects the disempowerment of domesticity and frustrations at her parents' house, "in which her life was slowly to be worn out: working for those who did not comprehend her; thanked her little,—that was all" (61).

Davis, herself a single woman taking care of her parents, is unromantic about the trials of housewifery on a meager income, the "white leprosy of poverty" (38). She pictures how Mrs. Howth forages in the harvested fields for late peas or corn, until Margret "could see the swollen circle round the eyes, and hear her [mother's] breath like that of a child which has sobbed itself tired" (37)—a role reversal that exposes the protective covenant of motherhood. Not only is the family vulnerable to economic pressures outside its moral sway; Davis's satiric representations of Margret's family as conflicted and inept—indeed, her very act of ironizing the family—destroys it as sentiment's utopian telos. Thus, Margret's choice to follow Knowles is based not only on her poverty, but also on her own isolation as a woman whose lover has rejected her, whose dog has run away, and whose mother prefers the company of her father. Compared to the House of Refuge, her parents' home offers neither Margret nor her mother female authority, emotional transcendence, or the moral significance of domestic work. Margret also turns to a life of social duty because Jesus (often shaped in sentiment as a consoling figure who protects women from isolation)[31] also "had been alone" (159).

Unlike Margret, but also unlike the romantic figure Mitchell in **"Life in the Iron-Mills,"** Knowles has a political role: "Fanatics must make history for conservative men to learn from" (180). Knowles is a follower of the French utopian socialists Fourier (1772-1827) and Saint-Simon (1760-1825) and of the German romantic and founder of "absolute idealism," Johann Gottlieb Fichte (1762-1814), whose works Davis probably read with her brother, Wilson, a student of European romanticism. From Fourier's design for phalansteries, Knowles planned a community that would work "like leaven through the festering mass under the country he loved so well" (154-55). From Fichte, who was influenced by the "ethical activism" of Jean-Jacques Rousseau and Emmanuel Kant, Knowles inherited the view of a morally empowered ego. Unlike the solipsistic strain found in many transcendentalists, Fichte believed in a socially ethical self that could withstand pressures from the competitive and aggressive world of nature. History, once a prerogative of God, now belonged to the individual, who had a duty to create a rational, moral, egalitarian, and self-sufficient community free from the "anarchy of trade." Organized into guilds, the tightly organized community would provide each member with tools, the value of one's labor, and the right to a full creative life.[32] While Davis never develops Knowles's utopian design, in his plans to "make use" of Margret, however, he also exhibits the authoritarianism of Hawthorne's Hollingsworth and of Saint-Simon, who argued that leadership belongs to the educated elite—scientists, physiologists, historians, and economists—who can best design and supervise a technocratic but providential state on behalf of the poorest and most numerous classes.

Unlike Margret, Knowles identifies with social as well as personal suffering. On the one hand, the details of the humanitarian narrative touch his Fichtean sense of moral empiricism: "All things were real to this man, this uncouth mass of flesh that his companion sneered at; most real of all, the unhelped pain of life, the great seething mire of dumb wretchedness in streets and alleys, the cry for aid from the starved souls of the world" (49-50). On the other hand, still reiterating the word *real*, Davis locates Knowles's political drive in his own racial oppression. In her first reference to the plight of Native Americans, the narrator explains that Knowles's mother was a Creek Indian and notes: "You and I have other work to do than to listen,—pleasanter. But he, coming out of the mire, his veins thick with the blood of a despised race, had carried up their pain and hunger with him: it was the most real thing on earth to him,—more real than his own share in the unseen heaven or hell" (50).

In contrast to the social egoism that compels Knowles is Stephen Holmes's "self-existent soul" (160). Holmes, who has purchased the mill with his fiancée's dowry, is driven by economic self-interest. He has "turned his back on love and kindly happiness and warmth, on all that was weak and useless in the world" (139), that is, everything he identifies with Margret. A representative of the emerging ideology of bourgeois individualism, Holmes views his new fiancée, the mill, its workers, and Margret as his property, which he will try to transform into an aspect of his self. Since purchasing the mill, he has become so mechanized that to Margret his familiar footsteps now sound like an "iron tread, . . . so firm and measured that it sounded like the monotonous beatings of a clock" (87). Now, "in the mill he was of the mill" (117). Eventually he even decides to sleep in the mill, where his hard bed and chairs are made of iron—"here was discipline" (120). Only money, he finds, is erotic: "it made his fingers thrill with pleasure to touch a full pocket-book as well as his mistress's hand" (104).

Fusing his utilitarian belief that "all things were made for man" (105) with a romantic vision of the self, Holmes seeks "a savage freedom, . . . the freedom of the primitive man, the untamed animal man, self-reliant and self-assertant, having conquered Nature" (107). As Margret realizes that she must leave Holmes to his "clear self-reliant life,—with his Self, dearer to him than she had ever been" (62), Davis marks the dangers of romanticism through a character who has chosen solitary wholeness over communal fragmentation. Nonetheless, even in a sentimental narrative that values nurturance and concern, both Margret and Dr. Knowles are attracted to Holmes whose credo is *Ego sum* (112). Margret finds Holmes "a master among men: fit to be a master" (62), and Knowles likewise observes "If there were such a reality as mastership, that man was born to rule" (80).

Holmes rather than Knowles thus inherits the mantle from Mitchell in **"Life in the Iron-Mills."** Pictured, like Mitchell, through images of coolness and ice, Holmes is an exponent of the "great idea of American sociology,—that the object of life is *to grow*" (121). Unlike the korl woman, however, who is "hungry to know," Holmes has a "savage hunger" (137) that drives him to transcend his childhood in the slums and become a "merchant prince." In contrast to the statue, he believes that "endurance is enough" for the slaves and destitute factory workers who work at his mill (113). Images of slavery surround Holmes; he believes that he has been "bought and sold" by his fiancée, who "held him a slave to her fluttering hand." While she is "proud of her slave," he resents the fact that "there were no dark iron bars across her life" (139). It is tempting to think that having promised Fields a perfect day in June, Davis was mocking her publisher when Miss Herne masquerades as June in a tableau vivant. Anticipating the tableaux vivants in Edith Wharton's *House of Mirth*, Miss Herne dresses as a seductive, dangerous, and serpentine figure who, in Holmes's view, glows with a "smothered heat beneath the snaring eyes" and whose "unclean sweetness of jasmine-flowers mixed with the . . . smells of the mill . . . Patchouli or copperas,— what was the difference? The mill and his future wife came to him together" (126-27). Miss Herne's decadent sexuality, a form of promiscuity earlier associated with aristocratic excesses that threatened middle-class virtues,[33] has in *Margret Howth* evolved into a female metaphor for the seductive power of industrial capitalism itself. Margret's chastity, by contrast, emerges as a trope for bourgeois morality, which, in the end, prevails.

In *Margret Howth,* true community arises through the understanding of shared suffering rather than through the design of any single individual. In the figure of Lois Yare, Davis's first African-American character, the politics of pathos bridge the discourses of sentimentalism and realism, mobilizing democratic sentiment through the values of domesticity.[34] Lois embodies the tension between personal pain, inscribed in the language of sentimentality, and industrial oppression, inscribed in the language of vernacular realism. To signify the loss of preindustrial innocence, Davis invokes the racist stereotype of a childlike, physically handicapped, mentally retarded mulatto woman: "Her soul, being lower, it might be, than ours, lay closer to Nature" (65). Nonetheless, when speaking for herself Lois insists that it is the mill (where she had worked from the time she was seven until she turned sixteen), not her nature, that has ruined her mind and her health. Like Stephen Holmes, she was "of" the mill: "I kind o' grew into that place in them years; seemed to me like as I was part o' the' engines, somehow."

Countering the narrator's racist observation that Lois's "tainted blood" had "dragged her down" is Lois's own clear insistence on the erotic force and toxic ecology of the mill:

> Th' air used to be thick in my mouth, black wi' smoke 'n' wool 'n' smells. In them years I got dazed in my head. . . . 'T got so that th' noise o' th' looms went

on in my head night 'n' day,—allus thud, thud . . . th' black wheels 'n' rollers was alive, starin' down at me, 'n' th' shadders o' th' looms was like snakes creepin',— creepin' anear all th' time.

> (69)

Lois's sense of defilement by the mill marks her passage to adulthood and affiliates her narrative with that of other girls in sentimental fiction (such as Ellen Montgomery in Susan Warner's *Wide Wide World,* 1850), who are initiated into a culture that has abused their bodies and repressed their emotions. Lois recalls that before she went to work on the looms she used to play house in the lumberyard at the mill; now she realizes that her "crushed brain and unawakened powers" were caused by the "mass of iron and work and impure smells" of those years (171).

But for Davis, writing from a slave state in 1861, the traditional midcentury fictional ending of marriage and home is historically and imaginatively unavailable for a black woman character—a tension that Davis seems to have understood. Initially Margret identifies with Lois, the disfigured and bitter survivor of years of slavery and brutal child labor, through their common female suffering, acknowledging that her own "higher life" was also "starved, thwarted" (71). As Julie Elison observes, in the nineteenth century pain (which is always gendered) serves as the link between the body and power.[35] However, Margret soon recognizes a crucial distinction: unlike Lois she "was free,—and liberty . . . was the cure for all the soul's diseases" (72). Thus Davis refuses to let slavery and blackness serve as a generic metaphor for many other sorts of pain.

Although permanently deformed, Lois recovers spiritually through her relationship to nature. In the figure of Lois we can trace the profound influence of Emerson on Davis. Lois is indeed a nature scholar who, in Emerson's sense, "can read God directly."[36] In a series of passages that adhere rather closely to the prescriptions of "The American Scholar" and "Nature," Lois reveals what Emerson calls an "original relation to the universe."[37] Emerson argues that a primal contact with nature allows one to experience God first-hand, unmediated by corrupt churches or biblical interpretation; able to be "read" by anyone, nature can replace the Bible as the greatest spiritual text. Further, a nature scholar is unalienated because he is infantile:

> Few adults can see nature. Most persons do not see the sun. At least they have a very superficial seeing. The sun illuminates only the eye of the man, but shines into the eye and heart of the child. The lover of nature is he whose inward and outward sense are still truly adjusted to each other; who has retained the spirit of infancy even into the era of his manhood . . . In the presence of nature a wild delight runs through them, in spite of real sorrows.[38]

In *Margret Howth* Lois is a child-artist who reads nature as a great spiritual text; she becomes the world's eye. For Davis, Lois's primal ability arises from the fact that she is black and female. Even though Lois is clearly a young adult, the narrator and various characters refer to her as a cheerful child. Unlike Knowles and Holmes, Lois has eyes quick to know the other light that "went into the fogs of the fetid dens from which the coarser light was barred" (91). Like the scholar-artist, she has the simplicity of character to become an "interpreter" of nature who understands that nature is (in Emerson's phrase) a "remoter and inferior incarnation of God, a projection of God in the unconscious."[39] Thus Lois, says the narrator, can see glimpses of the "heavenly clearness" of God's light: "Was it weakness and ignorance that made everything she saw or touched nearer, more human to her than to you or me?" (93). Surrounded by Emersonian images of sunlight, Lois "liked clear, vital colours . . . the crimsons and blues. They answered her somehow. They could speak. There were things in the world that like herself were marred,—did not understand—were hungry to know: the gray sky, the mud streets, the tawny lichens" (92).

Emerson's scholar inevitably becomes a realist artist whose unmediated sensibility is shaped not by tradition or imagination but by the eye: "To the human eye that the primary forms, as the sky, the mountain, the tree, give us . . . a pleasure arising from outline, color, motion, and grouping."[40] Lois is such an artist, fulfilling Emerson's requirement that art should become an epitome of the real world, a "result or the expression of nature, in miniature."[41] Lois instinctively composes her cart along such lines: "Patched as it was, [it] had a snug, cosy look; the masses of vegetables, green and crimson and scarlet, were heaped with a certain reference to the glow of color . . . What artist sense had she,—what could she know—this ignorant huckster—of the eternal laws of beauty or grandeur?" (64-65). Davis frequently judges her characters by this transcendent artistic capacity. Like Hugh Wolfe, Lois, an "ignorant huckster," has built her sculpture from the materials of her work. By contrast, despite his humanitarian inclinations Knowles is "blind to the prophecy written on the earth," and, similarly, in his isolated myopia Holmes sees that "the windless gray, the stars, the stone under his feet, stood alone in the universe, each working out its own soul into deed. If there were any all embracing harmony, one soul through all, he did not see it" (161).

While Davis masculinizes society, she feminizes nature which, as such, is vulnerable to male exploitation and definition. Viewed in relation to urban life and industrial control, nature in *Margret Howth* becomes a projection of woman's unconscious and an image of her recurrent need for mothering. Like Emerson, who sees nature as a "beautiful mother,"[42] Lois finds in nature a

new mother who "longs to take her uncouth child home again" (263). Onto this maternal sensibility Davis layers a feminized sense of erotic unity. While Holmes's impetus is toward separation, discontinuity, and self-denial, Lois moves toward a transcendent sense of nature that erases boundaries—"Why, sometimes, out in the hills, in the torrid quiet of summer noons, she had knelt by the shaded pools, and buried her hands in the great slumberous beds of water-lilies, her blood curdling in a feverish languor, a passioned trance, from which she roused herself, weak and tired" (93)—a romantic and erotic erasure of the self and others, subject and object. The surrender to the romantic universal also removes the entranced child-woman from the inevitability of history, represented by the mill. Marianne Hirsch suggests that in female romanticism sleep not only signifies withdrawal into the symbolic landscape of the innermost self; it also suggests the one-dimensional nature of a woman's development. Excluded from social interaction, she is thrown back into herself, where she can explore her spiritual or emotional sides, but only at the expense of other aspects of her selfhood.[43]

For Emerson, Lois's transcendent capacity would have had a social function: "The office of the scholar is to cheer, to raise, to guide men by showing them facts amidst appearances."[44] In contrast to Knowles, who is ineffectually trying to forge a utopian society in his own image, Lois, the peddler, through her "Great Spirit of love and trust" (77) and her romanticized trinity of "a faith in God, faith in her fellow-man, faith in herself," offers the enduring possibility of a true preindustrial community. One morning, for example, as Margret walks alongside Lois into town, they stop and visit at each farmhouse, collecting produce and butter and enjoying several breakfasts. Repudiating the imagery of mechanical time that surrounds Holmes, Lois's leisurely work connects Margret, the isolated bookkeeper, with her neighbors. For the first time "the two women were talking all the way. In all his life Dr. Knowles had never heard from this silent girl words as open and eager as she gave to the huckster about paltry, common things" (72). As she shares "disjointed" womanly talk with Lois, Margret feels "keenly alive" (73) for the first time. Even in the town, where Margret used to see the houses as closed and silent, she discovers through Lois a sisterhood of servants, housemaids, and news vendors.

In the end, rage generated by racism and poverty brings down the industrial house—a danger that Davis believed the North must heed. Lois rescues Holmes from a fire that her angry father, Joe, has started at the mill, and dies after inhaling the fumes of burning copperas. But her death does not represent the Christian martyrdom of Stowe's Uncle Tom or Little Eva. Lois's preoedipal attachments, her allegiance to childhood, her dissolution of boundaries, and her sense of the dangers of industrialism render her death an inevitable effect of the adult world of industrial and chattel slavery. Her death actualizes sentimental rage, reiterating the novel's choice between romance and self, community and ego. As Lois lies dying, the community, black and white, comes together and invests her death with the power of social redemption. In *Margret Howth* Davis revises the theme of much female fiction from the mid-nineteenth century—the endless attempt to achieve self-sacrifice[45]—by viewing women's submission as a tragic consequence of masculine assertion and romantic egoism. Eventually Margret quits the House of Refuge and forgives Stephen Holmes, who has repented of his ambitious romance and returned to Margret, announcing, "I need warmth and freshness and light: my wife shall bring them to me. She shall be no strong-willed reformer, standing alone: a sovereign lady with kind words . . . only to that man whom she trusts" (242). The narrator notes, however, that Margret "paid no heed" to this final comment.

Davis was quite disappointed with Margret, and wrote to James Fields that she did not want the novel named after its heroine because "she is the completest failure in the story, besides not being the nucleus of it." Whether Margret dissatisfied her author as a woman or as a literary achievement is tauntingly unclear.[46] If Margret's betrothal and reentry into her family sanction what Davis took to be available forms of female adulthood for middle-class women, Lois's death from the brutality of child labor and the toxic waste of the mill suggests the sorrowful fate of mill girls and former slaves. Since Fields had vetoed Davis's plan to "kill Dr. Knowles at Manassas,"[47] in the end, she leaves Knowles and Holmes mutually penniless from the fire. Knowles abandons his utopian plan and quietly builds the House of Refuge as a homeless shelter. The impoverished Howth family, however, is ironically rescued by their slave, Joel, who discovers oil on their farm—a portentous omen of industrial inevitability in a book that marks its risks.

Margret Howth critiques transcendentalism's investment of the egotistical imagination with social power. In this early novel Davis challenges literary and philosophical systems that, in their formal structures and social textures, divorce the reader from life in the commonplace. Midway through the novel, as Davis prepares to satisfy Fields and "come to the love part of [her] story," she speaks to her place in literary history: "I am suddenly conscious of dingy colors on the palette with which I have been painting." She compares her ambivalent characters, who must navigate difficult choices in their public and personal lives, to figures in "once upon a time" fiction, when readers "had no fancy for going through the world with half-and-half characters." Nature, she reminds herself, no longer turns out "complete specimens of each class." Refusing to write of a hero-

ine who "glides into life full-charged with rank, virtues, a name three syllabled, and a white dress that never needs washing," she announces that her heroines will never be "ready to sail through dangers dire into a triumphant haven of matrimony." Thus, Davis introduces the reconciliation of Margret and Holmes with a manifesto on realism: "I live in the commonplace. Once or twice I have rashly tried my hand at dark conspiracies, and women rare and radiant in Italian bowers; but I have a friend who is sure to say, 'Try and tell us about the butcher next door, my dear'" (102). This became her lifelong literary charge.

In *Margret Howth* Davis extends her discourse of realism and talks about "the butcher next door," seeking to challenge the restrictive tenets of sentimentalism—its illusion that domestic culture can transcend political culture, that the self can be divorced from social circumstances, and that domestic life can guarantee women status, autonomy, economic security, and moral redemption. Romanticism, she found, severed the individual from history just as the imperatives of slavery and industrialism were threatening the American illusion of community. Indeed, autonomy became a snare that threatened women's identity as social subjects. Exploring subjectivity in the history of slavery and early industrialization, Davis finds that her characters face aesthetic frustration and emotional repression. In fastening the emerging strategies of literary realism onto felt experience, Davis reclaims from sentimentalism its subjectivity and intensity of feeling. In *Margret Howth,* her first novel, the social practices of domesticity, female labor, free black labor, and nascent industrialization authorize emotional appeals, shaping American realism as an indigenous and heartfelt political narrative.

Notes

Unless otherwise specified, citations from Davis's work are from *A Rebecca Harding Davis Reader,* ed. Jean Pfaelzer (Pittsburgh: University of Pittsburgh Press, 1995).

1. See RHD to James Fields, 11 April 1861, U.Va. [in Richard Harding Davis Collection, Clifton Waller Barrett Library, Manuscript Division, Special Collection Department, University of Virginia Library, hereafter "U.Va."], which indicates that "The Deaf and Dumb" was the initial title for this story.

2. RHD to James Fields, 10 May 1861, Huntington Library, [San Marino, California.]

3. Jean Fagan Yellin, "Afterword," in Rebecca Harding Davis, *Margret Howth: A Story of Today* (New York: Feminist Press, 1990), 271-302. RHD received $125 for the book form of her novel, a minimal royalty of about one-half of one percent

(see chap. 9). See Sharon Harris, *Rebecca Harding Davis and American Realism* (Philadelphia: University of Pennsylvania Press, 1991), 82-33.

4. RHD to James Fields, 30 July 1861, U.Va.

5. Rebecca Harding Davis, *Margret Howth: A Story of To-day,* ed. Jean Fagan Yellin (New York: Feminist Press, 1990), 3. All further quotations are from this edition.

6. Fred Kaplan, *Sacred Tears: Sentimentality in Victorian Literature* (Princeton: Princeton University Press, 1987), 3.

7. Review of *Margret Howth, Peterson's Magazine* 41:4 (April 1862): 343-44.

8. Review of *Margret Howth, Continental Monthly* 1 (April 1862): 467.

9. Ibid.

10. Harris, *Rebecca Harding Davis and American Realism,* 63.

11. Yellin, "Afterword."

12. See Mary Poovey, "My Hideous Progeny: Mary Shelley and the Feminization of Romanticism," *PMLA* 95 (January 1980): 333-34, for a discussion of the politics of romantic eroticism, in particular.

13. RHD to James Fields, 9 August 1861, U.Va.

14. I am indebted to Benedict Anderson for this term. See in particular *Imagined Communities: Reflections on the Origin and Spread of Nationalism,* rev. ed. (New York: Verso, 1991), chap. 1.

15. Nina Baym, "Melodramas of Beset Manhood: How Theories of American Fiction Exclude Women Writers," *American Quarterly* 33 (1981): 132.

16. Poovey, "My Hideous Progeny," 334.

17. Jane Tompkins, *Sensational Designs: The Cultural Work of American Fiction, 1790-1860* (New York: Oxford University Press, 1985), xvii ff.

18. Susan Harris, "'But is it any *good*?': Evaluating Nineteenth-Century American Women's Fiction," *American Literature* 63:1 (March 1991): 60.

19. Ralph Waldo Emerson, "The American Scholar," in *Selected Essays, Lectures, and Poems of Ralph Waldo Emerson,* ed. Robert E. Spiller (New York: Washington Square Press, 1965), 73.

20. Davis is referring to the practice whereby draftees into the Union Army could hire a substitute or pay a commutation fee of $300, a privilege that produced the slogan "Rich man's war and poor man's fight." James McPherson, *Battle Cry of Freedom: The Civil War Era* (New York: Oxford University Press, 1988), 603.

21. RHD to James Fields, 11 April 1861, U.Va.

22. Emerson, "The American Scholar," 78.

23. Jane Tompkins observes, "'Sentimental' novels take place, metaphorically and literally, in the 'closet.' Their heroines rarely get beyond the confines of a private space—the kitchen, the parlor, the upstairs chamber—and most of what they do takes place inside the 'closet' of the heart" ("Afterword," in Susan Warner, *The Wide, Wide World* [New York: Feminist Press, 1987], 594).

24. See RHD to James Fields, 17 August [1861], U.Va.; RHD to James Fields, n.d., U.Va.; 16 January [1862], U.Va.; RHD to James Fields, n.d. [probably autumn 1862], U.Va. Harris notes that in the late 1860s Davis, encouraged by her husband Clarke, allowed her name to appear as "Mrs. R. H. Davis." Beginning in the 1870s, with her focus on women's issues, she changed her by-line to "Rebecca Harding Davis" (*Rebecca Harding Davis and American Realism,* 318, n. 38).

25. RHD to James Fields, 17 August [1861], U.Va.

26. Kaplan, *Sacred Tears,* 17-18.

27. Ibid., 16.

28. Leslie Rabine holds that while contemporary critics view essentialism as necessarily conservative, thereby making women complicitous with the ideology of the dominant class and race, the strategy of changing structural relations around an unchanging essence in fact offered the only means available to speak against the ideology of gender ("Essentialism and Its Contexts: St. Simonian and Post-Structuralist Feminisms," *Differences* 1:2 [1990]: 105-23).

29. Thomas Laqueur, "Bodies, Details, and the Humanitarian Narrative," in *New Cultural History,* ed. Lynn Hunt (Berkeley: University of California Press, 1989), 176-204.

30. See, for example, Margaret Fuller's dispatches to the *Tribune* of 7 and 13 May 1848, in Bell Gale Chevigny, *The Woman and the Myth: Margaret Fuller's Life and Writings* (Boston: Northeastern University Press, 1994), 449-53.

31. Nancy Schnog, "Inside the Sentimental: The Psychological Work of *The Wide, Wide World,*" *Genders* 4 (spring 1989): 18.

32. Originally, Davis may have intended Holmes to display the influence of Fichte. As she first considered revising the story, she wrote to Fields,

"Would the character of Holmes be distasteful to your readers? I mean—the development in common vulgar life of the Fichtian philosophy and its effect upon a self made man, as I view it?" (RHD to James Fields, 10 May 1861, Huntington Library).

33. Nancy Cott, "Passionlessness: An Interpretation of Victorian Sexual Ideology, 1790-1850," *Signs* 4 (1978): 223.

34. Suzanne Clark, *Sentimental Modernism: Women Authors and the Revolution of the Word* (Bloomington: Indiana University Press, 1991), 21.

35. Julie Elison, *Delicate Subjects: Romanticism, Gender and the Ethics of Understanding* (Ithaca: Cornell University Press, 1990), 13-14.

36. Emerson, "The American Scholar," 68.

37. Emerson, "Nature," in *Selected Essays,* 179.

38. Ibid., 181.

39. Ibid., 211.

40. Ibid., 185.

41. Ibid., 189.

42. Ibid., 208.

43. Marianne Hirsch, "Spiritual *Bildung*: The Beautiful Soul as Paradigm," in *The Voyage In: Fictions of Female Development* (Hanover, N.H.: University Press of New England, 1983), 23-24.

44. Emerson, "The American Scholar," 73.

45. See Tompkins, "Afterword," 584-607.

46. RHD to James Fields, 17 August 1861, U.Va.

47. See RHD to James Fields, 26 November 1861, U.Va, about revising the serialized story for publication in book form.

Kenneth W. Noe (essay date 1999)

SOURCE: Noe, Kenneth W. "'Deadened Color and Colder Horror': Rebecca Harding Davis and the Myth of Unionist Appalachia." In *Confronting Appalachian Stereotypes: Back Talk from an American Region,* edited by Dwight B. Billings, Gurney Norman, and Katherine Ledford, pp. 67-84. Lexington, Ky.: The University Press of Kentucky, 1999.

[*In the following essay, Noe discusses Davis's contribution to the "myth" of "Unionist Appalachia" and her treatment of the American Civil War in the Appalachian Mountains generally in a number of her wartime and postbellum short stories. While not all of her stories depict the Appalachian people as supporting the Northern cause, according to the critic, in her best-known tale, "The Yares of the Black Mountains," Davis unequivocally portrayed Unionist mountaineers as "the heroes of the mountain war," in order to make a political and social point about the North's abandonment of the region following the conflict.*]

"When the civil war came," Berea College president William Goodell Frost confidently wrote in 1899, "there was a great surprise for both the North and the South. Appalachian America clave to the old flag. It was this old-fashioned loyalty which held Kentucky in the Union, made West Virginia 'secede from Secession,' and performed prodigies of valor in east Tennessee, and even in the western Carolinas."[1]

Most students of Appalachia[2] are aware that one of Frost's great legacies is the mature incarnation of the mountain stereotype. While earlier generations of local colorists and missionaries had publicized and profited from the alleged "strangeness" and "otherness" of southern mountain society, it took Frost's 1899 essay, "Our Contemporary Ancestors in the Southern Mountains," to place firmly and finally in the national imagination, just in time for the twentieth century, the fully developed stereotype of a large, homogeneous, backward, and isolated "other" America he christened "Appalachian America." What largely has been forgotten is that an essential component of Frost's original argument that southern mountaineers were Americans' "contemporary ancestors" was their "Revolutionary patriotism," which allegedly reawoke as Unionism in 1861 after decades of dormancy. To Frost and many of his contemporaries, mountaineers' all-but-universal opposition to slavery and secession was a central component of Appalachian imagery, one of the few positive factors that made an otherwise ignorant and backward population deserving of gratitude, assistance, and uplift.[3]

As with the better-known elements of the Appalachian stereotype, broad descriptions of mountain Unionism such as Frost's have been rejected recently by modern Appalachian historians, although the tradition of a totally Unionist Appalachia survives in the popular mind, even among many mountaineers who disparage the rest of the hillbilly myth.[4] Starting in the late 1970s, historians concerned with the period before mountain industrialization began to put to rest the notion that Appalachia was an antislavery, Unionist monolith that "clave to the old flag" with "old-fashioned loyalty." Some rediscovered the region's slaves and slave-owners, and maintained that the peculiar institution was not only important to mountain masters but also absolutely vital to the psyche of many nonslaveholders. Others began to relate the tragic wartime divisions and escalating violence between fluid groupings of Confederate sympathizers,

Unionists, and those who rejected both ideologies in a futile attempt to avoid the horrors of war. While Unionism certainly was a dominant creed in places such as East Tennessee and West Virginia, they contend, support for secession and the Confederacy reigned supreme elsewhere, as in Southwest Virginia or western North Carolina. The residents of still other mountain sections defy such easy categorization altogether, so confused and volatile was the real situation. The end results of such heterogeneity were localized "inner civil wars" characterized by division, fear, privation, and the violence of guerrilla warfare.[5]

If division rather than Unionist consensus truly characterized the southern mountains during the Civil War, how then did the fictional Unionist monolith propagated by commentators such as Frost, the "Myth of Unionist Appalachia," take root in America's collective memory? In what manner were the southern mountains' slaves and Johnny Rebs swept under the nation's intellectual rug, and why?[6] Henry D. Shapiro came closest to answering those questions in 1978 in his seminal discussion of Appalachian imagery. While largely concentrating on the other degrading aspects of the stereotype, Shapiro did consider the Unionist myth. He explained it as the end result of a two-stage process that largely had to do with attracting northern dollars to the mountains. During the first phase, which lasted from 1865 until 1883, writers downplayed sectionalism and ignored the war as much as possible in hopes of attracting northern investment and Yankee immigrants. In the reunited Union, reminders of the mountains' Confederate past were at best irrelevant and at worst stumbling blocks to industrialization, development, and modernization. In such a climate, accurate memories of wartime divisions and especially mountaineers in gray were liabilities. Thus, of the thirty-nine popular works concerning the region that were published between Appomattox and 1883 and considered by Shapiro, only nine mentioned the Civil War in any way. Moreover, of those nine, essays such as Edward King's "The Great South: Among the Mountains of North Carolina" and Edward A. Pollard's "The Virginia Tourist" dismissed the topic in a few sentences. The Civil War was a theme to be avoided for most chroniclers of Appalachia in the immediate postwar period.[7]

Then in 1883, according to Shapiro, an abrupt about-face occurred. Spearheaded by one of Frost's Berea predecessors, Professor Charles Fairchild, northern-born mountain missionaries enthusiastically embraced war themes. Confronted with the fact that sectional wounds had not healed and that as a result many potential donors still balked at donating to "southern" causes, missionaries like Fairchild manipulated the very real fact of mountain Unionism so as to "desouthernize" the mountains entirely and make them a separate region in the American mind. Heroic depictions of mountain patriots

and martyrs, one piled atop another, cumulatively suggested that all mountaineers had been loyal Unionists and therefore deserved northern financial assistance, preferably funneled through an institution such as Berea, founded before the war by abolitionists.[8] By the time Frost took over the college, Fairchild's 1883 assertion that "this whole section was loyal in the battle for a united country unstained by slavery" was a major fund-raising ploy at Berea and an accepted truth in northern religious and literary circles.[9]

While Shapiro's explanation remains important, more recent scholars interested in Appalachia's Civil War have called for modifications that taken as a whole suggest the need for a reconsideration of the myth's genesis. John C. Inscoe, for example, evaluated a literary genre heretofore ignored—at least by Appalachian scholars—that dealt squarely with the region's Civil War, the memoirs of Union veterans who escaped from Confederate prisons into the mountains. Such memoirs highlighted mountain Unionism and moreover contained a strikingly positive general assessment of mountain society that today provides a refreshing contrast to the all-too-familiar degrading stereotype. Importantly, however, few of the twenty-five writers discussed by Inscoe—including the nine who published before Fairchild's 1883 article—asserted that all mountaineers were Unionists. Indeed, much of the book's drama—or melodrama—grew from the seemingly universal conviction on the part of the authors that no white mountaineer could be trusted at first. A highlander was just as likely to be a dangerous Confederate sympathizer as a Lincolnite, more likely if a white male, hence the danger and excitement inherent in an escape. The overall portrait is of a region in ideological confusion and compassed with danger, rather than an enclave united in its Unionism.[10]

Another student of the region, Shannon H. Wilson, has rejected Shapiro's contention that the founding fathers of Berea College drastically reversed course and took up the bloody shirt only in 1883. Rather, Wilson demonstrates conclusively that before and during the Civil War, the founders of Berea College already had planted in the American mind the notion of loyal, antislavery mountaineers, a concept that at least northerners of abolitionist leanings apparently found reassuring if successful fund-raising serves as a useful guide. Immediately after Appomattox, the Unionist myth went to work as a stock tool of the college's fund-raisers, and from 1865 until 1883 Berea hammered away at the theme for all who would pay attention. Fairchild's assertion that Appalachia was a Unionist monolith "unstained by slavery," then, was no new departure at all, but instead was merely business as usual. Indeed, Fairchild said next to nothing that had not already been printed regularly in the college's own publications and fund-raising literature.[11]

Both Inscoe and Wilson, in other words, call into question parts of Shapiro's explanation. A third difficulty emerges as well. Like other students of Appalachia, Shapiro glanced over at least three authors, writing during and just after the war, who like Inscoe's veterans dealt with the mountain conflict in a manner radically different than that found in the publications of Berea College. In several widely read magazine articles, all but one works of fiction, their dissenting voices addressed the war and its horrors squarely, depicting a tragically divided and often bloody Appalachia in which Confederate sympathizers seemed to either equal or outnumber Unionists. All called American readers' attention to Appalachia's Civil War, and the last of the works clearly provided a needed transitional framework for the myth to follow. That such a counterinterpretation existed in addition to the prison narratives studied by Inscoe means that the myth of Unionist Appalachia did not emerge from a vacuum of avoidance in 1883, but rather in opposition to contrary voices who provided truer descriptions of wartime mountain divisions.

Who were these dissenters? The earliest, and certainly the most important, was Rebecca Harding Davis. Largely forgotten, except as the mother of dashing turn-of-the-century journalist Richard Harding Davis, she recently has been rediscovered by several scholars of women's studies. Far from unimportant in her own right, Rebecca Harding Davis was in fact one of the most popular and prolific writers of fiction and nonfiction in the second half of the nineteenth century. Revolutionary in her realistic depictions of women, she also became one of the most talented local colorists, and many of her stories and essays concerned the southern mountain region. It was an area she knew well. Although born in Pennsylvania in 1831 and for a short time an Alabamian, young Rebecca Harding grew up largely in Wheeling, [West] Virginia. She burst onto the national scene in April 1861—along with the Civil War—with her powerful and acclaimed short story **"Life in the Iron Mills,"** one of the first examples of American realism and today her best-remembered work. A mountain Unionist, a sincere abolitionist, and a friend to federal general John C. Frémont and his talented wife Jessie as well, she nonetheless sympathized with southerners and particularly maintained that the southern states had a constitutional right to secede. With her own loyalties confused and friends serving on both sides, Davis quickly came to view the war as nothing more than a horrible tragedy that had divided homes and communities and unleashed brutal and needless violence. She had little patience for the rhetoric of nobility or causes, a sentiment that came across dramatically in her fiction.[12]

Davis's initial story depicting Appalachia's Civil War—probably the first work of fiction on the war written by anyone—was **"John Lamar,"** a tale published in April 1862 in *Atlantic Monthly*. Set in the author's native western Virginia like all of the wartime stories, **"John Lamar"** is the powerful story of the title character, a Confederate officer; Captain Charley Dorr, Lamar's Unionist kinsman and an old friend; and Lamar's slave, Ben. As the story opens, Dorr is holding Lamar prisoner on their grandfather's farm, now "a strong point for the Federal troops . . . a sort of wedge in the Rebel Cheat counties of Western Virginia." Determined to escape, Lamar has arranged for Ben to saw into his jail, a shed, and aid his flight. Ben, however, begins to have second thoughts. Overhearing a conversation between Dorr and Lamar in which neither advocates black freedom—Dorr in fact insists that "this slavery question must be kept out of the war"—Ben abandons hopes for his own freedom in the North. "He understood enough the talk of the white men," Davis writes, "to know that there was no help for him,—none. Always a slave." Further confused by Dave Hall, an Illinois soldier and ardent abolitionist who delivers a lay sermon calling for vengeance against the South—but then offers no real help—Ben ultimately saws into the shed only to murder Lamar and escape northward into the hills. Left to guard the body, Hall worries that his fiery antislavery rhetoric was responsible for the crime but finally convinces himself that all Americans share guilt for the war and are to be scourged by God for their sins. "The day of the Lord is nigh . . . ," Hall says, "it is at hand; and who can abide it?"[13]

In many respects, **"John Lamar"** could have been set just as easily elsewhere in the occupied Confederacy. Davis's overarching theme of a nation's collective guilt and her specific condemnation of those who sought to use Christianity to justify man enslaving or killing man was hardly confined to Appalachia. Indeed, most of the characters were not even mountaineers: Hall is from the Midwest, Ben is a Georgia field hand in the hills by chance, and Lamar is a western Virginian only in heritage. What makes **"John Lamar"** particularly important to mountain scholars are the accurate details concerning the Federals' West Virginia campaign against Gen. John B. Floyd's Confederates, and more important, the author's depiction of the everyday brutality of Appalachia's Civil War. Crisscrossing in the background throughout the narrative are various bands of Unionist guerrillas, "Snake-hunters," and their Confederate "Bushwhacker" counterparts, killing each other without mercy or seemingly even cause in a region heavy with "stagnation . . . deadened color and . . . colder horror." For Lamar and Dorr, that horror literally comes close to home; their grandfather, as well as a neighbor's young daughter, are killed by "Secesh" bushwhackers and the homestead burned. Cruelly, Lamar's captors even take him to the site, "to the wood-pile to show him where his grandfather had been murdered, (there was a red mark,) and buried, his old hands above the ground." Bitterly, Davis adds that the mountaineers themselves bear relatively little of the responsibility for the bloody mountain war. "Both armies used [mountaineers] in Virginia as tools for rapine and murder," she has Lamar conclude.[14]

A few months later, Davis followed up **"John Lamar"** with another short story set in West Virginia, **"David Gaunt."** Published in *Atlantic Monthly* like the first tale, **"David Gaunt"** also depicts a region where war has tragically divided friends and family, with terrible consequences. The title character is a young, itinerant Methodist minister, originally from the Virginia Tidewater, who at length has decided to join the Union army. Gaunt is convinced that the North's cause "was God's cause, holy: Through its success the golden year of the world would begin on earth." His views run counter, however, to those of his only real friend, Joe Scofield. An older man whose son George died in Confederate service at Manassas, "Scofield was a Rebel in every bitter drop of his heart's blood." One winter night, the two men set out to a meeting of Unionists to be held at a local Methodist church. Neither tells the other his true purpose: Gaunt plans to enlist, while Scofield hopes to confirm rumors of a Federal attack on a party of nearby Rebels and then warn the Confederates.[15]

On the way, the pair encounter Douglas Palmer, the local Unionist captain and a man absolutely convinced of the righteousness of his cause: "he accepted it, in all its horror, as a savage necessity."[16] Palmer had been George Scofield's closest friend, and when encountered, is on the way to Scofield's cabin to woo Scofield's daughter Dode. The chance meeting leaves Gaunt shaken, for he too loves Dode and as a result hates Palmer. The Yankee captain rides on to the cabin, where Dode rejects him, surprisingly not for his ideology but rather because of his religious skepticism. Returning to the church to lead the planned attack, he is surprised to learn that Gaunt has joined his band, but has a friendly chat with Scofield, who for his part has been spying the entire time.

"David Gaunt" ends with expected melodrama. Scofield rides off in the snow to warn the Rebels, but the old man moves slowly enough that the blue column catches him. Lieutenant Jim Dyke, an Ohioan who "had quit the hog-killing for the man-killing business," orders Gaunt to shoot a figure seen moving ahead in the road.[17] The victim turns out to be Scofield; Gaunt has knowingly killed his dearest friend for the sake of an ill-defined ideology. Palmer is wounded in the ensuing melee, but a guilt-ridden Gaunt rescues him, takes him back to Scofield's cabin, and marries the two lovers for good measure before laying down his gun forever and going west to serve as a nurse. Palmer and his new bride also abandon political causes and turn the Scofield farm into a hospital open to all.

Above all, **"David Gaunt"** is an antiwar story. War, in Davis's mind, was an abomination that not only divided friends and family but also perverted the true message of the Prince of Peace, turning ministers into murderers and churches into military headquarters where killing is planned.[18] That the story is something of a religious polemic is made even clearer on the first page, where the author compares her characters to John Bunyan's virtues personified in *Pilgrim's Progress*: Gaunt is "Christian," Scofield "Rebellion," and Dode "Infidelity," and the characters literally encounter "Evil" in an Appalachian "Valley of Humiliation."[19]

Again, however, Davis realistically depicts an Appalachia violently at war with itself in a feeding frenzy of murder and retaliation. Not only is one circle of friends divided, but so is the neighboring community. Both the ambushed Confederates and the attacking Yankees are local men, former friends, and fellow communicants of the same church, while the loafers on the church steps cynically cheer for both the Union and Jefferson Davis. The local war is brutal as well. Danger is everywhere: "rebel guerrillas lurked behind every tree, and every woman in the village-shanties was ready to risk limbs or life as a Rebel spy." Another woman "had found her boy's half-charred body left tied to a tree by Rebel scouts."[20]

Davis saves her greatest criticism for the soldiers who callously burned homes and made war on women and children. Those enemies of domesticity "had work to do on the road back: the Rebels had been sheltered in the farmer's houses near; the 'nest must be cleaned out': every homestead but two from Romney to the Gap was laid in ashes. It was not a pleasant sight for the officers to see women and children flying half-naked and homeless through the snow, nor did they think it would strengthen the Union sentiment; but what could they do? As great atrocities as these were committed by Rebels. The war, as Palmer said, was a savage necessity."[21] That this description of an atrocity so much resembles a real event in January 1862, Col. George Crook's Chapman's Store-Gardinier's Store Raid, suggests that Davis, as often was the case, was spurred by a real incident.[22]

In 1863, Davis married and moved to Philadelphia, where she spent much of the rest of the war years grappling with illness (hers and others'), pregnancy, depression, and financial problems that increasingly forced her to churn out more and more stories of lesser quality. Intellectually, she moved on as well. While she still used West Virginia as a setting for other short stories, the locale and the mountain war itself became more and more incidental after 1862; clearly Davis had said most of what she had to say about the conflict raging in her backyard. Sometimes, as in **"The Promise of Dawn: A Christmas Story"** and **"The Luck of Abel Steadman,"** the region furnished nothing more than familiar scenery for tales that might have been set anywhere. Likewise, West Virginia's Civil War is merely background for the first half of **"Paul Blecker,"** an ambitious and melodramatic love story in three parts in which the title character, a Union doctor, finally gets the girl after her cruel Confederate husband is mortally wounded at Fredericksburg. Ranging from Harpers Ferry to Broadway via the celebrated battlefields of Virginia, **"Paul Blecker"** asserts the primacy of faith, love, and home over the political ideologies that create wars and make "machines" of men.[23]

At other times, West Virginia's Civil War functioned as an abstract, otherworldly symbol. During the second half of the war, Davis curiously published two ambitious versions of **"Ellen,"** based on the true story of a simple young Michigan woman searching for her soldier brother in western Virginia. The second, expanded version is much darker than the first, but in both, the real war ultimately is incidental to an existential plot. Appalachia is Ellen's personal "heart of darkness," the final destination of a terrifying personal journey that takes her deeper and deeper into danger and toward madness. The antithesis of Ellen's quiet fishing village, West Virginia is a sort of domestic version of the stereotype of darkest Africa. In the later version, published in 1865, Davis describes the area as "the border region, where the war was breaking ground, with all its dull, gross reality of horrors, to which the farther South and North were strangers; the broken talk in the cars was . . . of quiet farmers murdered in cold blood, of pillaging and outrage, of anticipated insurrections among the slaves, and vengeance for their wrongs." At least, mountain people (including a thinly disguised author) retain their humanity in both "Ellens" and, like the kindly Yankee civilians encountered north of the Ohio, largely help the bewildered traveler. It is a cruel northern woman, a sutler affiliated with a Federal regiment, who puts Ellen in her greatest peril when the woman dismisses Ellen's tale and accuses her of spying. In the first version, published in 1863, Ellen finally triumphs; she not only finds brother Joe but true love as well with a Yankee lieutenant. The two siblings return to domestic bliss in Michigan. There is no happy ending in the later version, however, as Ellen vanishes into the dark void of West Virginia's Civil War, never to be heard from again. As late as 1863, it seems, Davis had hopes that the American family could survive the war. By 1865 she was no longer sure.[24]

For nearly a decade after the revised publication of **"Ellen,"** Davis largely remained silent on Appalachia's conflict and wrote little in general about the war. So did others. As several scholars have written, most Americans shied away from the Civil War as a literary theme during the first decade after Appomattox. Veterans "hibernated" according to Gerald Linderman and allowed their emotional wounds to heal. Meanwhile, as Nina Silber maintains, noncombatant northerners proclaimed "forgetfulness," or "historical amnesia," to be a virtue that demonstrated one's high-minded character and progressive nature.[25]

Writers interested in the mountain South, such as Davis, were no exception. Thus, the theme of a divided wartime region beset with localized guerrilla violence re-emerged in postwar popular literature in full force only in 1873, in one of the most cited (and damned) early local color depictions of the southern mountains, Will Wallace Harney's short story "A Strange Land and Peculiar People." Henry Shapiro borrowed Harney's title for the entire concept of Appalachian "otherness," and one certainly can find much of the nascent mountain stereotype in Harney's infamous narrative. Yet, ultimately, "Strange Land" is really about the Civil War, and in that respect at least it is decidedly nonstereotypical.[26]

As the unnamed southern narrator and his sickly bride pass through southeastern Kentucky, the former relates two tales of the war. The first concerns the young, noble Lassie, torn between loyalty to her Confederate brother and love for her "Captain Cophetua," an old friend of the brother who has joined the Union army. When Lassie's neighborhood is occupied by Federal troops, her lover returns to marry her. Then, the brother delivers under a flag of truce Mrs. G———, ostensibly a southern lady seeking the body of her late husband. Lassie's simple mountain charms cannot compete with Mrs. G———'s elite refinement, and soon the Federal captain is smitten. It is a near-fatal error. Mrs. G——— turns out to be a Rebel spy, and the lover is arrested for treason. Only the last-minute interdiction of the two women at the captain's Louisville court-martial saves the unfortunate soldier from the gallows.

All ends well for Lassie and her beau—they marry and live happily ever after—but lest the reader view the entire mountain war benignly, Harney appends a second, starker tale, of which the lesson is "War is a bad thing always, but when it gets into a simple neighborhood, and teaches the right and duty of killing one's friends, it becomes demoniac. . . . Up in the poor hills they could only kill and burn, and rob the stable and smokehouse." Shorter and without any recognizable protagonists, the second story describes the deaths of thirty Confederate soldiers ambushed and killed at a dance by six former neighbors turned Unionist guerrillas. Harney's imagery is brutal: "with shrieks and groans, and deep, vehement curses, the rapid reports of pistols fill the chambers. The beds, the floors, the walls, are splashed with blood, and the chambers are cumbered with dead and dying men in dreadful agony."[27]

One year after the publication of "A Strange Land and Peculiar People," journalist Edward King also rediscovered a divided Appalachia. Dispatched by *Scribner's Magazine* president Roswell Smith to play up the South's economic potential and promote sectional reconciliation, King considered the southern mountain region in two installments of a series. Having all but ignored the Civil War in his essay on western North Carolina, the Massachusetts-born journalist makes the conflict a central theme of "The Great South: Southern Mountain Rambles in Tennessee, Georgia, and South Carolina." In the latter essay, King describes in great detail the fighting around Chattanooga. More important, he implies that most mountaineers along the Georgia-Tennessee border supported the Confederacy. Even that celebrated bastion of Unionism, East Tennessee, was politically "difficult to classify," according to King. "There were . . . hosts of uncompromising Union men in Eastern Tennessee," he writes, "so there were, also, many committed to the interests of the Confederacy, and both classes were much broken in fortune." Overall, King asserts that the great themes of Appalachia's Civil War were the bitter divisions between Unionists and secessionists—the now-familiar cliche of "brother against brother"—and the tremendous privation resulting from plundering armies. In other words, King advanced a thesis strikingly similar to that of recent historians, but markedly unlike that of the myth to come.[28] That his observations on widespread mountain support for the Confederacy were made in a series designed to stimulate "good feeling between the lately hostile sections" adds to their import.[29]

More important, Rebecca Harding Davis finally returned to the theme of a divided, war-torn Appalachia at the same time as Harney and King. Curiously, her tentative and somewhat disappointing initial foray was a story for children, **"Our Brothers: A Story of the War,"** which appeared at the end of 1873 in *The Youth's Companion.* More than King's essay, **"Our Brothers"** was a blatant plea for sectional reconciliation. In the story, young Bob, an eager listener to adventure stories of the war, is "discomfited" by a less-than-glorious tale from his usually taciturn grandfather, Charles Hooper. Investigating reports of depredations against local civilians in Virginia's Shenandoah Valley, Hooper had been lured into a trap by Mrs. Vance, the widow of a Rebel soldier, only to be saved by an unlikely, Davisesque coincidence. The woman learns that Hooper not only had befriended her husband while the latter was a prisoner, but finally had buried the unfortunate man in the Hooper family cemetery in Pennsylvania. Shaken, she warns him just in time to escape from a Confederate ambush. Little Bob, who already had taken on the task of caring for Vance's grave, places a flower on it, having learned "the difference between his *brothers* and beasts of prey." Clearly, the other "Bobs" who read *The Youth's Companion* were to come to the same conclusion.[30]

As in her earlier Civil War stories, Davis proclaims the supremacy of Christian love and family ties over the rhetoric of ideological causes. Yet, the most notable attribute of **"Our Brothers,"** at least in terms of Appalachia's Civil War, is Davis's surprising lack of concern for realism. Not only does she have Robert E. Lee's Army of Northern Virginia operating in the Shenandoah Valley, a surprising gaffe that by itself would suggest a story scribbled hastily for a well-paying serial,[31] she also denies the horror of the war described so vividly in her earlier stories. The mountain war has become orderly, bloodless, and benign in **"Our Brothers."** The reported depredations turn out to be largely unfounded, and even the treacherous widow agrees that "The country hadn't had such order kep' up for years"[32] thanks to the gentlemanly Federal occupiers. Conceivably, Davis put sectional reconciliation ahead of her earlier regard for accuracy. Perhaps more likely, the western Virginia of **"John Lamar"** and **"David Gaunt"** remained too ugly for the eyes of young people.

That Davis had lost none of her edge became apparent soon after with a much darker story intended for an adult audience, **"The Rose of Carolina."** A reportorial study of elite mountain women not from West Virginia, but rather Buncombe County, North Carolina, it was published in 1874 and like King's piece appeared in the slightly prosouthern *Scribner's.* **"The Rose of Carolina"** begins with the image of a woodcut of Confederate General P.G.T. Beauregard placed next to a photograph of Rose's eldest brother, apparently killed in battle at Chattanooga, dressed in Confederate uniform. Rose's father, a slave owner identified only as the "Colonel," also served the Confederacy, losing an arm at Appomattox. Davis relates the family's hardships during the war and then, after stimulating sympathy for the family, turns to Rose's older sister, who "used to keep watch . . . upon the house of a poor farmer, whose sons were Union men hiding in the mountains for three years." One night, after seeing the sons return, Rose's sister alerted the home guards. "When she heard the shots an hour after, and the terrified negroes rushed in to tell her that the men, her neighbors all her life, lay dead, outside the very door, she cooly bade them go help to bury them, as though it had been dogs or mountain boomers she spoke of." After the war, the coldly calculating sister hypocritically keeps up appearances by paternalistically doting on the Unionists' widowed mother, "and when the old woman is sick makes her nice little dishes, for she stays with her at night, leaving her baby to the nurse."[33]

Davis's major themes of political division and the horrors of a local war first reemerged in **"The Rose of Carolina."** However, the story ultimately acts only as a prologue for the best and by far the most crucial of Davis's stories of wartime Appalachia, her classic **"The Yares of the Black Mountains."** Published in 1875 in

Lippincott's Magazine, **"The Yares"** [**"The Yares of the Black Mountains"**] also was set in western North Carolina and, like the two tales called **"Ellen,"** concerns a young woman's journey into the unknown represented by Appalachia. It is a journey into light, however, rather than into darkness. **"The Yares"** begins as the young, sad, and simple New York widow Mrs. Denby, her sickly son Charley, and Miss Cook, a condescending writer and dilettante, travel past where "Civilization stops" and on toward Asheville. Mrs. Denby has been advised by her doctor that the only chance of saving the child's life is to "journey to the balsam mountains . . . Charley must have mountain-air." In Asheville, much to Cook's dismay, she hires a seemingly brutish local hunter named Jonathan Yare to take her farther "among the balsams." Before she leaves, Denby is warned by Cook that the Yares have "a terrible history" and "live like wild beasts."[34]

In the mountains, the young northerner finds neither madness nor despair, as Ellen Carrol did, but rather salvation. At the man's home, a simple cabin, the mother and child are taken in immediately by the "peculiar" but "courtly" Yare family and treated with unaccustomed kindness. Despite the dirty squalor, a constant in Davis's mountain stories, Charley recovers in the care of the Yares, "a family born with exceptionally strong intellects and clean, fine instincts." The Yares turn out to be not brutes, but rather untutored saints; the father resembles "some ancient knight." At the end of the tale, Davis concludes: "She lived in their hut all summer. Her baby grew strong and rosy, and the mountains gave to her also their goodwill and comfort."[35]

By that conclusion, however, one cares less about Charley than his knightly benefactors, for it becomes apparent that Davis's real concerns are neither the local colorist Cook nor the mother, but rather the Yares themselves. Like the young widow, the reader is led deeper into the mountains, away from a familiar civilization and along a bewildering path, to discover not only the Yare's Christian virtue, but also their tragic secret. That is revealed one night when Mrs. Denby mentions the warnings of the family's "terrible history," leading the family's matriarch to explain, "It was not their fights with wolves and bears that turned the people at Asheville agen the name of my boys and their father. They were the ony men anigh hyar that stood out for the Union from first to last. They couldn't turn agen the old flag, you see, Mistress Denby."[36]

The family's history indeed had been "terrible." Just after the war began, Federal soldiers brutally killed all the male members of the nearby Granger family, including an eight-year-old boy "with nine bullets in his breast." Sickened, the Yare sons refuse to join Federal regiments despite their support for the Union cause. Instead, the mother explains, "My sons' work in them years was to protect an' guide the rebel deserters home through the mountings . . . an' to bring Union prisoners escaped from Salisbury and Andersonville safe to the Federal lines in Tennessee."[37]

These Unionist activities make the Yares targets of Confederate authorities. Stymied in their attempts to capture the men, Confederates arrest first their sister Nancy, who had been taking food to her brothers in the mountains, and then the aged father. Nancy is locked up in Asheville, and the old man is imprisoned in Richmond's infamous Libby Prison. To save the others, the Yare sons turn themselves in. Refusing a last chance to put on the gray, they are sentenced to die. However, when Jonathan displays "pluck" by crying out, "By God, I am a Union man!" the honorable Rebel captain allows the men to live.[38] Two weeks later, Lee surrenders.

Mrs. Denby trembles with emotion. Her late husband David had escaped from Salisbury Prison during the war. "He might have slept in this very bed where the child lay. These people might have saved him from death." She later pleads with the family "to come out of their solitude to the North. 'There are hundreds of men there,' she said, 'of influence and distinction whose lives your sons have saved at peril of their own. Here they will always pass their days in hard drudgery and surrounded by danger.'"[39] Mother Yare refuses, however, sagely realizing that the family would be lost beyond their beloved hills.

In one sense, **"The Yares"** was not a major departure from Davis's other tales of the Civil War in Appalachia, nor for that matter did it present a starkly different moral than did King or Harney. The mountaineers beyond Asheville were divided in sympathies, and the Unionist Yares remain the exceptions in a region dominated by mountain people loyal to the Confederacy. We are not yet in Unionist Appalachia. There is, however, a crucial shift in emphasis that ultimately makes **"The Yares"** very different from the author's earlier stories. In **"The Rose of Carolina"** Unionists are sketchily described victims of a wealthy slave owner's petty cruelty. In **"John Lamar"** and **"David Gaunt"** Unionists and Secessionists are equals ostensibly, but in truth the latter elicit more sympathy from both the author and the reader. **"Gaunt"**'s Joe Scofield is a brave old man, while Douglas Palmer is an atheist devoid of feeling until the love of a southern woman redeems him.

In contrast, Unionist mountaineers clearly are the heroes of the mountain war in **"The Yares."** Davis, who like many other local colorists that often wrote with political reform and social justice in mind, had a point to make. Northerners had to return to the mountains and provide their noble former comrades with protection, education, and better lives. Unionist mountaineers were the Jonathans to the North's Davids, beloved friends who deserved thanks, and not the animals depicted by the Miss Cooks of American letters. Since they refused for good reason to leave the land—to "come to the North"—the North had to go to them. Here then was the basic, transitional framework for the myth of Unionist Appalachia. Mountain Unionists were no longer deluded cogs in a senseless war machine, as in Davis's earlier stories, "tools" of outsiders, but rather heroes subsequently and shamefully abandoned by a North too willing to forget.[40]

Thus, while Rebecca Harding Davis's greater role in Appalachian myth-making surprisingly remains sadly unappreciated if not ignored by mountain scholars—certainly **"The Yares"** greatly influenced Mary Noailles Murfree's early work, and John Fox Jr. was a family friend—the Yares of the Black Mountains clearly were the archetypal Unionist mountaineers of popular literature. All that remained was for other writers to reassure the northern public that the noble Yares were not representatives of a noble minority, as Davis more realistically maintained, but rather typical mountaineers. At that moment, writers such as the founders of Berea College stepped forward to tell the literate and monied northeast exactly what it now wanted to hear.[41]

Notes

1. William Goodell Frost, "Our Contemporary Ancestors in the Southern Mountains," *Atlantic Monthly* 83 (1899): esp. 313-14. The present essay is a greatly expanded version of my earlier, preliminary exploration of these themes, "Toward the Myth of Unionist Appalachia, 1865-1883," *Journal of the Appalachian Studies Association* 6 (1994): 67-74. I am grateful to Kenneth J. Bindas and John C. Inscoe for their comments on that earlier work, which informed the present study.

2. "Appalachia" clearly is a presentist term that was all but unknown in the period under discussion. Nonetheless, for the sake of clarity, I will use the term interchangeably with "southern mountains" or "southern mountain region" throughout.

3. Frost, "Our Contemporary Ancestors"; Henry D. Shapiro, *Appalachia on Our Mind: The Southern Mountains and Mountaineers in the American Consciousness, 1870-1920* (Chapel Hill: Univ. of North Carolina Press, 1978), 68, 119-32, 275; Allen W. Batteau, *The Invention of Appalachia* (Tucson: Univ. of Arizona Press, 1990), 5, 74-79, 84-85, 195.

4. For an example see James G. Branscome and James Y. Holloway, "Nonviolence and Violence in Appalachia," in *Appalachia Inside Out: A Sequel to Voices from the Hills*, ed. Robert J. Higgs, Ambrose N. Manning, and Jim Wayne Miller, vol. 1, *Conflict and Change* (Knoxville: Univ. of Tennes-

see Press, 1995), 309. For a discussion of various definitions of "myth" and "tradition," see Michael Kammen, *Mystic Chords of Memory: The Transformation of Tradition in American Life* (New York: Alfred A. Knopf, 1991), esp. 17-39.

5. Notable examples include Martin Crawford, "Confederate Volunteering and Enlistment in Ashe County, North Carolina," *Civil War History* 37 (March 1991): 29-50, and "Political Society in a Southern Mountain Community: Ashe County, North Carolina, 1850-1861," *Journal of Southern History* 55 (Aug. 1989): 373-90; Durwood Dunn, *Cades Cove: The Life and Death of a Southern Mountain Community, 1818-1937* (Knoxville: Univ. of Tennessee Press, 1988); several works by John C. Inscoe, notably *Mountain Masters, Slavery, and the Sectional Crisis in Western North Carolina* (Knoxville: Univ. of Tennessee Press, 1989); Ralph Mann, "Family Group, Family Migration, and the Civil War in the Sandy Basin of Virginia," *Appalachian Journal* 19 (summer 1992): 373-93, and "Mountains, Land, and Kin Networks: Burkes Garden, Virginia, in the 1840s and 1850s," *Journal of Southern History* 58 (Aug. 1992): 411-34; James B. Murphy, "Slavery and Freedom in Appalachia: Kentucky as a Demographic Case Study," *Register of the Kentucky Historical Society* 80 (spring 1982): 151-69; Kenneth W. Noe, *Southwest Virginia's Railroad: Modernization and the Sectional Crisis* (Urbana: Univ. of Illinois Press, 1994); Philip Shaw Paludan, *Victims: A True Story of the Civil War* (Knoxville: Univ. of Tennessee Press, 1981); Jonathan D. Sarris, "Anatomy of an Atrocity: The Madden Branch Massacre and Guerrilla Warfare in North Georgia, 1861-1865," *Georgia Historical Quarterly* 77 (winter 1993): 679-710; Peter Wallenstein, "Which Side Are You On? The Social Origins of White Union Troops from East Tennessee," *Journal of East Tennessee History* 63 (1991): 72-103. See also Kenneth W. Noe and Shannon H. Wilson, eds., *The Civil War in Appalachia: Collected Essays* (Knoxville: Univ. of Tennessee Press, 1997).

6. Not all twentieth-century purveyors of popular culture, of course, fully accepted the Unionist myth. Native Kentuckian D.W. Griffith, for example, made a divided Civil War Appalachia the locale of films such as *The Fugitive*, and John Fox Jr. depicted a divided Appalachia in his *Little Shepherd of Kingdom Come* (New York: Scribners, 1903). See Jack Temple Kirby, *Media-Made Dixie: The South in the American Imagination* (Baton Rouge: Louisiana State Univ. Press, 1978), 1-17, 39-43.

7. Edward King, "The Great South: Among the Mountains of North Carolina," *Scribner's Monthly*

7 (March 1874): 513-44; Edward A. Pollard, "The Virginia Tourist," pt. 1, *Lippincott's Magazine* 5 (May 1870): 487-97; Shapiro, *Appalachia on Our Mind,* 311-14.

8. Shapiro, *Appalachia on Our Mind,* 16, 85-91, although the inelegant term "desouthernize" is mine.

9. Charles Fairchild, "Address of Professor C.E. Fairchild," *American Missionary,* n.s., 36 (Dec. 1883): 393.

10. John C. Inscoe, "Moving through Deserter Country: Fugitive Accounts of the Inner Civil War in Southern Appalachia," in Noe and Wilson, *Civil War in Appalachia,* 158-86.

11. Shannon H. Wilson, "Window on the Mountains: Berea's Appalachia, 1870-1930," *Filson Club History Quarterly* 64 (July 1990): 384-400; and "Lincoln's Sons and Daughters: Berea College, Lincoln Memorial University, and the Myth of Unionist Appalachia, 1866-1910," in Noe and Wilson, *Civil War in Appalachia,* 242-64.

12. Rebecca Harding Davis told her own life story in *Bits of Gossip* (Boston: Houghton Mifflin, 1904). Spurred by Tillie Olson, ed., *Life in the Iron Mills and Other Stories* (New York: Feminist Press, 1972; revised and expanded ed., 1985), a Davis renaissance happily has begun. Two notable recent biographies are Sharon M. Harris, *Rebecca Harding Davis and American Realism* (Philadelphia: Univ. of Pennsylvania Press, 1991), esp. 20-166, 208-55; and Jane Atteridge Rose, *Rebecca Harding Davis* (New York: Twayne, 1993), esp. 1-56. Neither approaches Davis from an Appalachian perspective, however. One older work that does stress the mountain connection, albeit briefly, is Arthur Hobson Quinn, *American Fiction: An Historical and Critical Survey* (New York: Appleton-Century-Crofts, 1936), 181-90. The best sources, of course, are Davis's works. See Jane Atteridge Rose, "A Bibliography of Fiction and Non-Fiction by Rebecca Harding Davis," *American Literary Realism* 22 (spring 1990): 67-86.

13. [Rebecca Harding Davis], "John Lamar," *Atlantic Monthly* 9 (April 1862): 411-23; quotes on 411, 417, 419, 421. For the assertion that the story was the first American work of fiction on the Civil War, see Quinn, *American Fiction,* 184; and Rose, *Rebecca Harding Davis,* 52. Olson, *Life in the Iron Mills,* 97, called it "the most chilling and perfectly executed of her stories."

14. [Davis], "John Lamar," 412, 413; Harris, *Rebecca Harding Davis,* 76-81, interprets the story somewhat differently. Focusing on Ben and Hall, she explains it as Davis's radical criticism of those naive abolitionists who refused to see that their pie-in-the-sky abolition rhetoric might (and perhaps should) lead to bloodshed and revolution. Jan Cohn, "The Negro Character in Northern Magazine Fiction of the 1860s," *New England Quarterly* 43 (1970): 582-84, also stresses the importance of Ben, noting that the story was perhaps the first with a black protagonist.

15. [Rebecca Harding Davis], "David Gaunt," parts 1 and 2, *Atlantic Monthly* 10 (Sept./Oct. 1862): 257-71, 403-21, quotes on 261, 259.

16. Ibid., 404.

17. Ibid., 403.

18. In one notable passage, Gaunt purifies the church by removing an American flag, although "he hardly knew why he did it. There were flags on every Methodist chapel, almost: the sect had thrown itself into the war *con amore.*" [Davis], "David Gaunt," 407. For other comments, see Harris, *Rebecca Harding Davis,* 92-94; Olson, *Life in the Iron Mills,* 102; and Rose, *Rebecca Harding Davis,* 53-55.

19. [Davis], "David Gaunt," 257.

20. Ibid., 405, 404.

21. Ibid., 411.

22. For Crook's raid, see Kenneth W. Noe, "'Exterminating Savages': The Union Army and Mountain Guerrillas in Southern West Virginia, 1861-62," in *Civil War in Appalachia,* Noe and Wilson, 116-17. Davis might well have heard details of the incident, for her home was just across the street from Union headquarters. See Olson, *Life in the Iron Mills,* 89.

23. [Rebecca Harding Davis], "The Promise of Dawn: A Christmas Story," *Atlantic Monthly* 11 (Jan. 1863): 10-25; idem, "Paul Blecker," parts 1 and 2, *Atlantic Monthly* 11 (May/June 1863): 580-98, 677-91, quote on 684; part 3, *Atlantic Monthly* 12 (July 1863): 52-69; and idem, "The Luck of Abel Steadman," *Atlantic Monthly* 16 (Sept. 1865): 331-41. For Davis's problems and new interests see Olson, *Life in the Iron Mills,* 114-29; Rose, *Rebecca Harding Davis,* 56-65, as well as Harris, *Rebecca Harding Davis,* 103-27, 143.

24. [Rebecca Harding Davis], "Ellen," *Peterson's Magazine* 44 (July 1863): 38-48; idem., "Ellen," *Atlantic Monthly* 16 (July 1865): 22-34, quote on 29. In the earlier version, Davis again makes a direct connection to *Pilgrim's Progress* to remind readers that her characters—and I believe even the setting—were symbolic. Harris, *Rebecca Harding Davis,* 126-27, and Rose, *Rebecca Harding Davis,* 41-42, 47-48, 89, point out that the two "Ellens" led to charges of plagiarism and a rather weak reply from a pregnant and exhausted Davis.

25. Gerald F. Linderman, *Embattled Courage: The Experience of Combat in the American Civil War* (New York: Free Press, 1987), 266-97; Nina Silber, *The Romance of Reunion: Northerners and the South, 1865-1900* (Chapel Hill: Univ. of North Carolina Press, 1993), 2-12, 61-63. See also Kammen, *Mystic Chords of Memory,* 13, 101-31.

26. Will Wallace Harney, "A Strange Land and Peculiar People," *Lippincott's Magazine* 12 (Oct. 1873): 429-38. For Shapiro's comments, see *Appalachia on Our Mind,* 3-5, 267-68.

27. Harney, "Strange Land," 435, 436-37.

28. Edward King, "The Great South: Southern Mountain Rambles in Tennessee, Georgia, and South Carolina," *Scribner's Monthly* 8 (May 1874): 5-33, quote on 19-20. For information on King, see Robert Underwood Johnson, *Remembered Yesterdays* (Boston: Little, Brown, 1923), 96-97; Silber, *Romance of Reunion,* 45, 73; and Anne Rowe, *The Enchanted Country: Northern Writers in the South, 1865-1910* (Baton Rouge: Louisiana State Univ. Press, 1978), xi-xx.

29. Johnson, *Remembered Yesterdays,* 97.

30. Rebecca Harding Davis, "Our Brothers: A Story of the War," *Youth's Companion,* Dec. 25, 1873, 417-18, quotes on 417, 418. Davis, who had become a regular contributor to the publication, also wrote of the war for young people—but the war beyond the mountains—in stories such as "Hard Tack," *Youth's Companion,* Jan. 5, 1871, 46-47. For Davis and juvenile literature, see Harris, *Rebecca Harding Davis,* 152, 164, 165, 167, 242, 248, 294; and Rose, *Rebecca Harding Davis,* 91, 113, 144. See also an earlier story for adults curiously set in wartime Missouri, "Captain Jean," *Peterson's Magazine* 56 (Nov. 1896): 351-59.

31. Harris, *Rebecca Harding Davis,* 165, 248.

32. Davis, "Our Brothers," 417.

33. Rebecca Harding Davis, "The Rose of Carolina," *Scribner's Monthly* 8 (October 1874): 723-26, quotes on 725-26. While the older sister hardly is an attractive character today, she may have seemed more so to Davis's original audience. As Nina Silber pointed out, the stock character of the hostile, hate-filled southern woman was giving way during the period in question to another stereotype, the "innocent creature" or "sympathetic victim" whose anger could be explained away as irrational feminine emotion or at least contrasted with more admirable qualities, notably her determination to hold her head high through defeat and deprivation. See Silber, *Divided Houses,* 26-29, 49-51.

34. Rebecca Harding Davis, "The Yares of the Black Mountains," *Lippincott's Magazine* 16 (July 1875): 35-41, quotes on 38, 41. Davis reprinted the story in her only contemporary collection, *Silhouettes of American Life* (New York: Scribners, 1892). Silber, *Romance of Reunion,* 66-73, notes that the sickly northerner looking for a healthy climate was very much a stock character for the local colorists. Silber even titles one chapter "Sick Yankees in Paradise."

35. Davis, "Yares," 43, 47.

36. Ibid., 44.

37. Ibid.

38. Ibid., 46.

39. Ibid., 45, 46.

40. For local colorists and reform, see Grace Toney Edwards, "Emma Bell Miles: Feminist Crusader in Appalachia," in *Appalachia Inside Out,* Higgs, Manning, and Miller, vol. 2, *Culture and Custom* 709-10. Harris, *Rebecca Harding Davis,* 250-51, concentrates on Davis's use of vernacular. Rose, *Rebecca Harding Davis,* 114-16, underplays the reform implications of the story and interprets it rather as a "story of spiritual homecoming" in which nature and the domestic bonds of family heal victims of modern society and teach the rejuvenating value of domesticity. To be sure, Davis often used "simple" characters to teach life's "great lessons," notably a brain-damaged and physically deformed former mill worker named Yare in her novel *Margret Howth* (Boston: Ticknor, 1862).

41. Harris, *Rebecca Harding Davis,* 251. Scholars of Appalachia inexplicably have ignored Davis. Batteau, *Invention of Appalachia,* does not mention her at all, while Shapiro, *Appalachia on Our Mind,* 6, only lists her as one of many writers who visited western North Carolina. Much remains to be done.

Janice Milner Lasseter (essay date 1999)

SOURCE: Lasseter, Janice Milner. "Hawthorne's Legacy to Rebecca Harding Davis." In *Hawthorne and Women: Engendering and Expanding the Hawthorne Tradition,* edited by John L. Idol, Jr. and Melinda M. Ponder, pp. 168-78. Amherst, Mass.: University of Massachusetts Press, 1999.

[*In the following essay, Lasseter emphasizes the considerable and lifelong influence Nathaniel Hawthorne exerted on Davis's fiction, most notable in the latter's commitment to the "commonplace subject" as a keystone of her realistic literature, concluding, "From Hawthorne as well as from her own insights into the human condition, Rebecca Harding Davis learned to invest the commonplace with an imagination that captured the history, the national character, and the social issues of her own time."*]

Rebecca Harding Davis, who was born 24 June 1831 and spent her first five years in Huntsville, Alabama, lived until her marriage in Wheeling, Virginia (later West Virginia). She was schooled informally by her mother and various tutors until at age twenty-four she entered Washington Female Seminary where she graduated with honors in 1848. Little is known about the period of her life between 1848 and the 1861 publication of **Life in the Iron-Mills,** her first and most significant work. This startling story about the laboring class began her work as a pioneer of American realism. In addition to fiction, Davis wrote extensively on women's issues and other social issues in newspapers and periodicals. Toward the end of her life, her fame was eclipsed by that of her son Richard Harding Davis, a glamorous celebrity and writer (Langford x). It is quite ironic that her *New York Times* obituary characterizes her as the mother of Richard Harding Davis, an irony repeated more recently in James Mellow's biography of Hawthorne. The book notes that Julian Hawthorne, on a trip as a journalist to Cuba to cover the Spanish-American War, was accompanied by Richard Harding Davis, but makes no mention of the visit of his now more famous mother's visit to the Hawthornes' home at the Wayside in 1862 (587). A prolific fiction writer, essayist, reviewer, and journalist who was well known during her publishing life, Davis virtually disappeared for almost eighty years until Tillie Olsen discovered Davis's first book serialized in musty, coverless copies of the *Atlantic Monthly* in an Omaha junkshop. In her unprecedented depiction of the grim lives of the working class, Davis inaugurates literary realism twenty years before those usually credited for its advent. This novella launched a fifty-year career which yielded a corpus of 500 published works including short stories, novellas, novels, sketches, and social commentary. Late in her life, Davis recalled the young Rebecca's avid reading of books by Bunyan, Maria Edgeworth, and Sir Walter Scott, but to Nathaniel Hawthorne she attributed the commonplace subject matter in her writing, although the Hawthorne effect surfaces variously in her work.

Davis considered herself the literary progeny of Nathaniel Hawthorne. Describing Hawthorne as "the greatest of living romancers," Davis reveals that Hawthorne's classic status was firmly in place as early as the 1860s. In naming him her literary forebear, she linked herself not to his artistic vision of romance but to "the commonplace folk and things which [she] saw every day" when, as a young girl, she read three of his unsigned early sketches.[1] The primary legacy Hawthorne bequeathed to Davis was subject matter. The characters who inhabit realist fiction were the common folk who became the center of her literary theory, a program she announces in her second work of fiction: "I want you to dig into this *commonplace,* this vulgar American life, and see what is in it. Sometimes I think it has a new and awful significance that we do not see." Expounding on this realist aim midway through the book, the author interjects:

> I live in the *commonplace.* Once or twice I have rashly tried my hand at dark conspiracies, and women rare and radiant in Italian bowers; but I have a friend who is sure to say, "Try and tell us about the butcher next door, my dear," . . . I must show men and women as they are in that especial State of the Union where I live.

> (*Margret Howth* 6, 102, 105)

Writing about the here and now, Davis participated in the creation of a national literature. In the "Boston in the Sixties" chapter of her memoir **Bits of Gossip,** she descried the prevailing philosophical discussions in pejorative terms amid an account of an evening spent at the Wayside, the Hawthornes' home in Concord. Arguing that the transcendentalist pawing over and dissecting the eternal verities lack "some back-bone of fact," she associates herself with Hawthorne's skepticism: "Whether Alcott, Emerson, and their disciples discussed pears or the War, their views gave you the same sense of unreality, of having been taken, as Hawthorne said, at too long a range" (36). From her perspective, Hawthorne "was an alien among these men, not of their kind," because they were out of touch with the "real world" and "never would see it as it is" (**Bits of Gossip** [hereafter **BOG**] 32-33). Those whose visions she found more authentic, more real, were credited with the flowering of American literature: "We were in the flush of our triumph in the beginnings of a national literature. We talked much of it. Irving, Prescott, and Longfellow had been English, we said, but these new men—Holmes, Lowell, and Hawthorne—were our own, the indigenous growth of the soil" (**BOG** 47). Her ambition to join this literary pantheon, the influence her early reading of Hawthorne's sketches exerted over her, and their similar attitudes toward the Civil War deepened her awe of Hawthorne.

Respect for other writers was characteristic of Davis, but not reverence. In her memoir, awe characterizes her analysis of Hawthorne. He replied to her youthful letter, "saying that he was then at Washington, and was coming . . . to see coming to see . . . me. *Me.* Well, I suppose Esther felt a little in that way when the king's sceptre touched her" (**BOG** 31). That scepter imbued her, she believed, with a magic touch which issued her into "his enchanted country" (**BOG** 31, 64). Its magical properties did not grant her a place alongside him in the literary canon emerging in the 1860s, but Hawthorne's "touch" did steep her in a literary practice that has earned her, finally, a place in the canon as a pioneer of American realism.

Davis's debut into American letters with *Life in the Iron-Mills* in the *Atlantic Monthly* (1861) almost coincided with her reading of Hawthorne's *Twice-told Tales*. In this his first collection, she learned the name of the author whose literary art had enchanted her as a child. Her memoir recalls her climbing into a tree-house erected in a cherry tree back of her Wheeling (not yet West) Virginia, home with a two-volume set titled *Moral Tales*.

> It was in two volumes; the cover was of yellow paper and the name was "Moral Tales." . . . The publisher of "Moral Tales," whoever he was, had probably stolen these anonymous papers from the annuals in which they appeared. Nobody called him to account. Their author was then, as he tells us somewhere, the "obscurest man of letters in America."
>
> (*BOG* 30-31)

Among the tales were "two or three unsigned stories" she recalled with precision:

> One was a story told by a town-pump, and another the account of the rambles of a little girl like myself, and still another a description of a Sunday morning in a quiet town like our sleepy village . . . in these papers the *commonplace* folk and things which I saw every day took on a sudden mystery and charm.
>
> (*BOG* 30)

The stories mentioned—"Little Annie's Ramble," "A Rill from the Town Pump," and "Sunday at Home"—do not appear in *Moral Tales,* but the specificity in her naming and description of the book leaves no doubt that she did indeed read such a book and recognized some of Hawthorne's work there.

Moral Tales is "a collection of anonymous pieces, probably pirated from annual gift books," as Jane Atteridge Rose plausibly explains (4). Published in 1840 by Littlefield Press under the name of Samuel Griswold Goodrich, *Moral Tales* contains six works by Hawthorne: "The Wedding Knell" and "David Swan" appear in volume 1; "Night Sketches, beneath an Umbrella," "The Canterbury Pilgrims," "The Haunted Mind," and "Sights from a Steeple" in volume 2. But the stories Davis recalled were published elsewhere. Of Hawthorne's stories that did appear in *Moral Tales,* only two seem akin to the three she recalls as having influenced her. "Sights from a Steeple" shares with "Little Annie's Ramble" a narrator surveying town life. But storms, boiling seas, and darkness infuse "Sights from a Steeple" with Gothic undertones. "Night Sketches, beneath an Umbrella" has a lonely narrator noting the people he meets on a stormy night's walk. The spectral quality of "The Wedding Knell," the oneiric ambience in "David Swan" and "The Haunted Mind," and the parabolic elements of "The Canterbury Pilgrims" would have interested Davis. Similar qualities in Edgeworth, Bunyan, and Scott had

engaged her interest (*BOG* 31). Not these Gothic qualities alone but also the authors' knights, pilgrims, and fiends shared the "magic world" of the commonplace folks in the three sketches she recalls as having influenced her (*BOG* 30).

The gloomy tone of Hawthorne's work in *Moral Tales* may account for the specificity of her recall of the book itself. That eerie quality emanating from human doubt and moral gloom as glosses on the commonplace coexists, even complements, her sense of herself as one who tends to see both sides of any issue, a trait she believed she shared with Hawthorne, as we will see later (*BOG* 109). Davis employs Hawthorne's use of the common folk and common places for her stories about people and places not traditionally thought proper subjects for artistic expression in the early 1860s. She wants to convey the underside of conventional precepts and social mores, to lead her readers into "the fog and . . . foul effluvia" as a means of correcting demeaning and destructive social practices. As Howells would say in 1881, realists want "to know and to tell the truth," and the truth of the commonplace in American culture for Davis was all too often fiercely realistic.

The correspondences between those three sketches in which she discovered the magic of the commonplace may be detected in *Life in the Iron-Mills, Margret Howth: A Story of To-Day, Waiting for the Verdict,* and some of her short fiction. *Life in the Iron-Mills'* treatment of the commonplace resonates with the somber mood of her invitation into a new kind of fiction:

> I want you to hide your disgust, take no heed to your clean clothes, and come right down with me,—here, into the thickest of the fog and mud and foul effluvia. I want you to hear this story. This is a secret down here, in this nightmare fog, that has lain dumb for centuries: I want to make it a real thing to you.
>
> (13-14)

The moral gloom resident in much of Hawthorne's work is usually associated with sin, guilt, and doubt, not specifically social reform. Still as Richard Brodhead posits, despite his attempt to detach himself from the social dramas of his time, Hawthorne wound up exploding them into narratives "afflicted with intense unreality" (147-48). The gloom in Davis's work also associates guilt with social issues, but her social dramas are treated with intense reality. What Davis valued in Hawthorne's sketches appears unabashedly in her best-known and first-published story, *Life in the Iron-Mills.* Hawthornesque doubt coexists with grim reality in the pall industrialism casts on Davis's artistic vision. It surfaces in her soliciting her readers' empathy for the lives of factory workers who eke out a meager existence in the dank, dark underside of their lives and in the questions art asks of God. The commonplace lives Davis depicts in **Margret Howth** differ in depth and kind from the more lighthearted characters of the commonplace in "Little Annie," "Sunday," and "Rill." Annie's ramble occurs in the sunshine, her good life assured by a loving father who escorts her. The sequestered narrator of "Sunday at Home" peeps through his window at the parade of commonplace folk entering church—children, elderly women and men, pretty girls, the clergyman, and long lines of others. It too is a primarily lighthearted sketch, a candidate for the kind of writing that may have gotten Hawthorne the reputation as the "man who means no meanings," an interpretation Melville overturned in "Hawthorne and His Mosses." The sketch that has more in common with Davis's commonplace characters is "A Rill from the Town Pump." In it, the pump as narrator is a character who surveys all the town's citizens, both the young and the old, the pauper, the drunkard, Indians, governors, and even the animals, but keeps them all at a distance, never permitting the dust, "the turbulence and manifold disquietudes of the world" to sully what may be called its "soul" (*CE* 9: 147-48). The everyday lives of everyday people in the three sketches were endowed with meaning and mystery for young Rebecca. For her the commonplace folk are usually working-class people, slaves or former slaves, women, and the middle class, the people among whom she lived. Industrialism's dire consequences for the working class and American culture in general, the class warfare pivotal to the slavery issue, the competing claims of domesticity for women which shape much of the social impetus of her work coincide with its realist qualities.

To limn the human condition of lives she could only imagine, she employed a Hawthornesque narrative strategy. As in "Sunday at Home" and "Sights from a Steeple," the narrator of **Life in the Iron-Mills** stands above the folk about whom she writes; the narrator inhabits the third story of the house in which the puddlers occupied the cellar. Looking out the street window at the "slow stream of human life" plodding to the great mills, the narrator pleads for a new subject matter for fiction—"I am going to be honest. This is what I want you to do"—and implores readers to risk identifying with "massed, vile, slimy lives" (13-14). She aims to expose the misconception that the higher, nobler traits do not exist in the common folks. **Life in the Iron-Mills** illustrates the utter waste of human potential when economic plight blights the spirit. The story imagines such waste in artistic terms. The artist's predicament that appears both in *The Marble Faun* and in "The Artist of the Beautiful" lies at the heart of Hugh Wolfe's sculpture of the Korl Woman, the image that grips the men inspecting the mill with unflinching force. Social reform is demanded implicitly by Hugh's interpreting the sculpture's meaning as "She be hungry" and by the question the sculpture asks, "What shall I do to be saved?" One of the onlookers realizes that "money"

would provide not only the requisite spiritual freedom but the economic redemption as well. When people of means exonerate themselves of the guilt they bear for the desperate straits of workers imprisoned by oppressive class structures, as do overseer Clarke, Kirby, the Doctor, and even Mitchell, the whole culture is impoverished and endangered. The Dantean fires form part of the mythic dimensions Judith Fetterley notices in **Life in the Iron-Mills,** the white-hot fire reminiscent of the same in "Ethan Brand." The infernal fires of the mills suggest not only the hell of the puddlers' existence but also the callous hearts of the mill owner, overseers, and their companions; the fiery lime kiln calcifies the heart of one who had hovered, as have the puddlers and their superiors, over a white-hot, richly symbolic fire of mythic magnitude (Fetterley 310). The civil and moral lapse, the inefficacy of the church, and the malaise of the mill workers, which forecast Hugh's death, bespeak hellish proportions.

Hawthorne's sense of history, his historical settings and subjects appear to have inspired another realistic impetus in Davis's work. Sharon Harris links Davis's literary theory of the commonplace to her abiding interest in national and local politics. Davis sought to understand current politics by examining the history that gave it rise. Harris attributes to Hawthorne (and Sedgwick) Davis's "acute interest in historical locales and in how the ideologies of the past informed the present." Furthermore, Harris concludes, Hawthorne influenced "Davis' own belief that to study American history and . . . to expose the mythos of the past were requisite preliminary stages if one was concerned with artistically recording the 'accurate history' of the present" (7). The "unhindered progress" intrinsic to expansion was invested with a grim underside because expansion and economic success relied on slavery. For Davis, this dilemma in American culture arose from "corrupted history" (27). Comparisons may be drawn between Hawthorne and Davis's affinity for writing fictional accounts of historical events with Davis's **"A Faded Leaf of History"** and a number of Hawthorne's stories—the Salem witchcraft trials ("Young Goodman Brown"), pre-revolutionary overthrows of monarchical intervention ("My Kinsman, Major Molineux"), and trials that dramatize the consequences for humanity caught in the interstice of theocratic Puritan rule and individual autonomy ("The May-Pole of Merry Mount" and *The Scarlet Letter*).

Although the history-making Civil War was a rich imaginative historical source, Hawthorne's writings about it were nonfiction prose, such as "Chiefly about War Matters," "Northern Volunteers," and *A Biography of Franklin Pierce*. In Davis's work, repeated explorations of the bitter internecine struggle become recurrent. During her 1862 visit to Concord, she was shocked at the prevailing optimism in the "Areopagites'" philosophizing about everything from the eternal verities to pears to the war. Nothing she heard among most of the inhabitants of the "modern Athens" gripped her more than their wrongheaded analyses of the Civil War.[2] In the parlor at the Wayside, Bronson Alcott described the war as "an armed angel . . . wakening the nation to a lofty life unknown before" with Emerson's "profound submissive attention," while Hawthorne's "laughing, sagacious eyes" watched "full of mockery" (**BOG** 34). Both Davis and Hawthorne had actually seen the war. Hawthorne had recently visited several battle sites and had just composed "Chiefly about War Matters" for the *Atlantic*. Davis, whose home state (Virginia) was about to split over the war issue and whose first five years had been lived in the slave-holding state Alabama, had herself witnessed the war's brutality. Hawthorne responded to Alcott, the man he described as "the Sage of Concord": "We cannot see that thing at so long a range. Let us go to dinner" (**BOG** 35). Davis's reply to Alcott appeared much later, in her memoir: "War may be an armed angel with a mission, but she has the personal habits of the slums" (**BOG** 34). Hawthorne's restrained chiding of his cohort confirmed Davis's private remonstrance. She interpreted Hawthorne's perceptions to be intellectually and politically kin to her own, a melding, a collapsing of identities comparable to that frequently detected in Melville's relationship with Hawthorne. In casting Hawthorne as the "unfortunate man who saw both sides" of the issue, Davis repeats a characterization of herself as one who always "had a perverse inclination to see the other side of the question" (**"Men's Rights"** 212). Not only did Hawthorne and Davis have a penchant for taking the opposing side, or seeing two sides of all questions, they also were the only persons in the Wayside parlor who had seen the War itself. Both were in touch with the gloomier aspects of the war and of life. As was true of the later realists, the war decidedly affected her intent to write about the gloomy, the vulgar in American life. The entire conversation in the Wayside parlor effected in Rebecca the recognition that Hawthorne was here—as he was in Boston—"an alien among these men, not of their kind" (**BOG** 55). The clash of transcendental optimism with Hawthorne's cautious objectivity and Rebecca's pessimism about the waste and destruction of the war is drawn in sharp relief in Rebecca's memoirs. She recalls Bronson Alcott standing before the fireplace in "the little parlor of the Wayside, . . . his long gray hair streaming over his collar, his pale eyes turning quickly from one listener to another to hold them quiet, his hands waving to keep time with the orotund sentences" (34). All the while "Mr. Emerson stood listening, his head sunk on his breast, with profound submissive attention, but Hawthorne sat astride of a chair, his arms folded on the back, his chain dropped on them, and his laughing, sagacious eyes watching us, full of mockery" (34). Appalled by Alcott's rhapsodizing, Rebecca inwardly

fumed: "I had just come up from the border where I had seen the actual war, the filthy spewing of it; the political jobbery in Union and Confederate camps, the malignant personal hatreds wearing patriotic masks, and glutted by burning homes and outraged women. . . . This would-be seer who was talking of [the war], and the real seer who listened, knew no more of war as it was, than I had done in my cherry-tree when I dreamed of bannered legions of crusaders debouching in the misty fields" (34).

For Davis, witnessing partitioning of her own state and dealing all too closely with the war's realities made the Civil War a ripe subject for imaginative examination. The galvanizing effects of her sensing in Hawthorne a kinship with her perception of the war were evident in the subjects of her fiction after her visit to Concord. Among her many writings about the war, **Waiting for the Verdict, David Gaunt,** "John Lamar," "The Yares of Black Mountain," and "Blind Tom" rank among the best. After *Life in the Iron-Mills,* most critics rate **Waiting for the Verdict** second among her writings. The novel's title conveys the dilemma the nation faced after the war. The issue is raised by slave mother Anny: "de black man . . . is waitin' for de whites to say which dey shall be—men or beasts. Waitin' for the verdict" (354). This book exposes the illusory hope at war's end that the nation might fully heal and thus be able to achieve its early ideals. On the subject of the national rupture we call the Civil War, Davis creates a history chronicling the catastrophic consequences to the lives of all Americans in all classes.

Davis's admiration for Hawthorne never waned. His scepter never lost its enchantment for her. It is less certain, though, that Hawthorne would have appreciated her claiming him her literary ancestor. If Sophia Hawthorne's assessment of Davis is, as she claims, Hawthorne's as well, he was unimpressed, especially with **Margret Howth.** Sophia wrote a note to Miss Harding, as she preferred to call Rebecca, shortly after Harding's departure from Concord. A few months later, in November of 1862, Sophia wrote Annie Fields: "Mr. Hawthorne and Julian think [Gail Hamilton] . . . the only good lady-author in America" (Stewart 303). Then in a May 1863 letter to Annie, Sophia castigates "Miss Harding":

> Tell Heart's Ease that he must objurgate Miss Harding (I like to call her so) for her use of that bominable unenglish, affected word "pulsing" and "Pulses" (as a verb) and "pulsates" in her papers. It is unpardonable, Mr. Hawthorne cannot read her productions now, they are so distasteful to him from her bad style and slimy gloom—alas! that I should say so. I always read what she writes, because of the ability she shows but I also tire of the mouldiness, east wind and grime which she will mix in with her pictures of life.
>
> (Stewart 304)

Sophia's credibility is undermined by the pettiness implied in the "I like to call her so" remark. Whether or not Hawthorne did refuse to read Davis's work, it is clear that the distinctions drawn here do distinguish romance from realism in almost definitive terms. This issue needs further examination in Davis's work, for she felt that her freedom to express her own vision was hampered by her publishers. Jean Fagan Yellin's cogent essay on the detrimental effect of Fields's insisting on a sunnier ending to **Margret Howth** leaves no doubt that in her attempt to satisfy her publisher Davis dramatically diminished the artistic achievement of her second novel. Another example of the conflict she experienced in this regard is noted in Harris's discussion of Davis's story **"John Lamar."** When "Fields accepted the story without admonishing its dark vision," Davis remarked that she needn't have written it "with one hand tied behind my back . . . after all" (qtd. in Harris 73). She fought this battle most of her publishing life, especially until the 1870s when she moved into journalism as a commentator on pressing current social issues.

An especially important parallel to Hawthorne is the nineteenth-century concern with domesticity. A muzzled critique of the relations between man and woman so integral to Hawthorne's novels permeates much of Davis's short fiction, such as **"Marcia,"** the powerful **"In the Market,"** **"Doctor Sarah,"** **"The Wife's Story,"** and several other of Davis's stories and essays. Hester of **"The Wife's Story"** decidedly resembles the Hester of *The Scarlet Letter* in her struggle with a self-definition at odds with that her culture expects. The protagonist of most of these stories would have to commit intellectual suicide much as Zenobia committed literal suicide in *The Blithedale Romance* to experience autonomy and definition in a world where female independence wars against domesticity. The young woman writer in **"Marcia"** faced the same fate Hawthorne had implied should happen to "ink-stained Amazons" in his essay "Mrs. Hutchinson." As did Hawthorne, Davis grappled with the inward complexities of women's lives. Her women usually opt for marital happiness, aiming simultaneously to find meaningful work outside that role. It is interesting that Davis's memoirs include her assessment of the Hawthornes' marriage as admirable, and of Sophia as the perfect wife to Hawthorne.

When Davis attributed to Hawthorne her commonplace subject, she is most in line with genre theorists who tend to believe that American realists get from their romanticist ancestors subject matter that the realists then treat more objectively. Although Davis believed that she and Hawthorne were more objective in their view (both were certainly nay-sayers to transcendentalism), still she knew the difference. She knew she was writing an innovatively objective fiction that borders on naturalism at times, but she knew she was no writer of romance. Of him, she concluded in her memoir, "America may

have great poets and novelists, but she never will have more than one necromancer" (**BOG** 59). The nightmarish quality of the inner life of most of Hawthorne's characters is translated in Davis's fiction to the nightmarish quality of a culture tottering on the brink of disaster as industrialism and war wreaked havoc on the lives of the common folk.

It was not the influence of Hawthorne's best fiction that Davis acknowledged as influencing her but the common folk in those three little sketches written about people she believed she might have known, someone potentially like herself. Not only did his writing for children get replicated in her own long career, but primarily the sketches about Annie, the town pump, and the invisible narrator watching the townspeople go to church sparked her youthful and mature imagination immeasurably and interminably. When she left Concord, she reports, Hawthorne "hesitated shyly," held out his hand, and said: "I am sorry you are going away. It seems as if we had known you always." Her final analysis leaves no doubt about the enormous awe she always had for him: "because of the child in the cherry tree, and the touch which the magician laid upon her [his farewell words] seemed to take me, too, for one moment into his enchanted country" (**BOG** 64). Little wonder then that one of her last publications followed Hawthorne's earliest model—a collection of short tales about indigenous American soil entitled *The Silhouettes of American Life.* These tales, which lack the naturalistic cast of Davis's early realism, depict the lives of colonists, slaves, and women of all ages. They delicately nuance the dilemmas of persons seeking autonomy in a subtly menacing social context.

Having abandoned the stark realism which won her acclaim in her own time and canonical stature now in ours, the aging Davis focused on creating a distinctly American literature, writing what she believed was indigenous fiction—far from the interior fiction James perfected. Melville's dictum that Hawthorne "says NO, in thunder" might be said as well of Davis, and not just because she, like Hawthorne, rejected transcendentalism. Her resistance to James's high-culture realism is one reason her work did not fit within the ensuing course of American realism. Despite quibbles among some of Davis's contemporaries and high modernist objections of many twentieth-century readers, a growing number of current scholars find the bulk of her work compelling, as evidenced by *American Literary Scholarship: An Annual 1996*: "Rebecca Harding Davis's literary stock is rising" (Oliver 257). Her elevated stature may be explained by the success with which Davis fulfilled her own goal of leaving behind a story that would "make history live and breathe" (**BOG** i). From Hawthorne as well as from her own insights into the human condition, Rebecca Harding Davis learned to invest the commonplace with an imagination that captured the history, the national character, and the social issues of her own time.

Notes

1. She was in good company in this regard, for Longfellow, who was Hawthorne's Bowdoin classmate and a well-known poet, also noted how his friend invested the "commonplace" with poetry and romance (Hawthorne, *Centenary Edition* 9: 508; hereafter cited as *CE*).

2. Rebecca Harding's visit to the Hawthornes in Concord took place during her visit to her new friends James T. and Annie Fields. Fields, editor of the *Atlantic* and friend, publisher, promoter of Hawthorne, had been responsible for publishing *Life in the Iron-Mills*. At 138 Charles Street, as she did for so many literary figures, Annie Fields introduced Rebecca to prominent people, such as Oliver Wendell Holmes and Louisa May Alcott. At the Wayside on Wednesday, 18 June, Rebecca, as guest of the Hawthornes, because of the discussion with Emerson and Alcott about the war, was disappointed in the "Atlantic coterie" from a realist's perspective: "while they thought they were guiding the real world, they stood quite outside of it, and never would see it as it was" (*BOG* 32-33).

Works Cited

Brodhead, Richard H. *The School of Hawthorne.* New York: Oxford UP, 1986.

Davis, Rebecca Harding. *Bits of Gossip.* New York: Houghton Mifflin, 1904.

———. *Life in the Iron-Mills and Other Stories.* Ed. Tillie Olsen. New York: Feminist, 1972.

———. *Margret Howth: A Story of To-Day.* Ed. Jean Fagan Yellin. New York: Feminist, 1990.

———. "Men's Rights." *Putnam's Magazine* ns 3 (1869): 212-24.

———. *Waiting for the Verdict.* Upper Saddle River, N.J.: Gregg, 1968.

———. "The Wife's Story." *Life in the Iron-Mills and Other Stories.* 177-222.

Fetterley, Judith, ed. *Provisions: A Reader from 19th-Century American Women.* Bloomington: Indiana UP, 1985.

Grayburn, William F. "The Major Fiction of Rebecca Harding Davis." Diss. Pennsylvania State U, 1965.

Harris, Sharon M. *Rebecca Harding Davis and American Realism.* Philadelphia: U of Pennsylvania P, 1991.

Hawthorne, Nathaniel. *The Centenary Edition of the Works of Nathaniel Hawthorne.* Ed. William Charvat et al. Columbus: Ohio State UP, 1984.

Hawthorne, Sophia Peabody. "Sophia Hawthorne's Diary for June 1861." Ed. Thomas Woodson. *Nathaniel Hawthorne Review* 15 (1989): 1-5.

Herbert, Walter T. *Dearest Beloved: The Hawthornes and the Making of the Middle-Class Family.* Berkeley: U of California P, 1993.

Hesford, Walter. "Literary Contexts of *Life in the Iron-Mills.*" *American Literature* 49 (1977-78): 70-85.

Jones, Wayne Allen. "The Hawthorne-Goodrich Relationship." *Nathaniel Hawthorne Journal* 1975: 91-140.

Langford, Gerald. *The Richard Harding Davis Years: A Biography of a Mother and Son.* New York: Holt, 1961.

Mellow, James. *Nathaniel Hawthorne in His Times.* Boston: Houghton Mifflin, 1980.

Oliver, Lawrence J. "Late-19th-Century Literature." *American Literary Scholarship: An Annual* 1996. Ed. David J. Nordloh. Durham: Duke UP, 1998. 215-42.

Pfaelzer, Jean. Introduction. "Marcia." By Rebecca Harding Davis. *Legacy* 4 (1987): 3-10.

Quinn, Arthur Hobson. *American Fiction: An Historical and Critical Survey.* New York: Appleton, 1936.

Rose, Jane Atteridge. *Rebecca Harding Davis.* New York: Twayne, 1993.

Schaeffer, Helen Woodward. "Rebecca Harding Davis, Pioneer Realist." Diss. U of Pennsylvania, 1947.

Smith, Henry Nash. *Popular Culture and Industrialism, 1865-1890.* New York: Doubleday, 1967.

Stewart, Randall. "Hawthorne's Last Illness and Death." *More Books* 19 (1944): 303-13.

Yellin, Jean Fagan. Afterword. *Margret Howth: A Story of To-Day.* By Rebecca Harding Davis. New York: Feminist, 1990.

Michele L. Mock (essay date 2001)

SOURCE: Mock, Michele L. "'An Ardor That Was Human, and a Power That Was Art': Rebecca Harding Davis and the Art of the Periodical." In *"The Only Efficient Instrument": American Women Writers and the Periodical, 1837-1916,* edited by Aleta Feinsod Cane and Susan Alves, pp. 126-46. Iowa City, Iowa: University of Iowa Press, 2001.

[*In the following essay, Mock refers to Davis as a "textual activist," and she highlights the many ways in which the author used the periodical format as an "ideal forum . . . to enact her philosophies of art as an immediate, accessible, and ameliorating force." According to the critic, Davis "understood that her most effective feminist methodology embraced the periodical and the pen."]*

An entry on Rebecca Harding Davis in the 1898 *National Cyclopedia of American Biography* surprisingly cites the author encapsulating her life in the following manner: "I never belonged to a club nor any kind of society; never made a speech and never wanted to do it" (8: 177). While this activist may never have engaged in group affiliations nor joined the lecture circuit popular to many in the women's rights movement, Davis nonetheless tirelessly devoted her life's work to designing a textualized social activism, one that utilized the public gaze as a positive and reformatory force. Accordingly, to meet her agenda, Davis intentionally employed the periodical, a specular form characterized for its ability to make its reader "look" at herself as she "looks" at the magazine, perusing its contents; in turn, this complex and multifarious text reflects and defines not only the reader but the world around her.[1]

Davis, a prolific writer, composed more than five hundred works—the majority of which appeared first in periodical form. Drawing society's averted eyes to critical issues, Davis textually conjoins her artistry and activism in a theoretical and pragmatic practice she consistently referred to as the doctrine of the "good Samaritan" (*Bits* [*Bits of Gossip*] 148). This author's philosophies and critiques of art, manifest in her first short story, **"Life in the Iron-Mills"** (1861), argue that a criteria for art should include a categorization of literature according to its animus of social reform and its efficacy in promoting societal change.[2] A textual activist, Davis perceived art not as an elusive and elitist form but rather as a participative and dialogic expression of social activism. She denounced dominant theories held by bourgeois "art-critics," who could not foresee a communicative and melioristic artistry: "The world is full of these vulgar souls that palter with the eternal Nature and the eternal Arts, blind to the Word who dwells among us" (**"Blind Tom"** 583). The nineteenth-century American periodical, then, was the ideal forum for Davis to enact her philosophies of art as an immediate, accessible, and ameliorating force, one that satisfied her need "for writing of *today,*" rather than the lofty, insular, and transcendent art with its accompanying forms that she so frequently denounced.[3]

Davis firmly believed that writing for the popular culture did not disqualify the work as art, nor did it necessarily entail the creation of an inferior product. One of Davis's rubrics of art mandated that in order for art's animus and efficacy to be realized, the lines between "high" culture and popular culture, demarcations as strict as those between genders, must be abolished. In agreement, Elizabeth Stuart Phelps claimed a "personal indebtedness" to Davis for her textual activism, one written, as Phelps wrote, with "an ardor that was human and a power that was art" (119, 120).[4] Davis's complex philosophies of art and activism, further complicated by the "ephemeral" form of the periodical in which they are housed, to use Margaret Beetham's term, testify that Davis perhaps understood that her most effective feminist methodology embraced the periodical and the pen.[5]

This concentration of art and reform is best exemplified in an exposé Davis published in 1870 to awaken public sentiment to unethical practices implemented in insane asylums, to challenge unjust laws regarding incarceration of those deemed mentally ill, and, ultimately, to incite her audience to action. *Put Out of the Way,* serialized in the widely popular and long-running *Peterson's Ladies' National Magazine* (1842-98), is but one example of Davis's attempt to promulgate her philosophies of an efficacious art. The oscillating masculine and feminine tropes of this narrative not only rupture configurations of "woman," "monsters," and "madness" that attempt to imprison women within their bodies, but more important, her gendered economies challenge inequitable legislation informed by these very configurations that made institutional incarceration an actuality for a number of women. In short, Davis's unstable tropes indict the stability of a legal system predicated upon the pathologizing of women's bodies.

Accordingly, Davis's choice of *Peterson's* was deliberate, and she used her power as a writer to solicit social change. Beetham reminds us that writers for the periodical press vied for power in a delicate balance with editors, publishers, advertisers, and readers and, consequently, needed to exercise their power in order to "make their meanings stick" ("Towards a Theory of the Periodical" 20). Serialization in particular, as Susan Belasco Smith tells us, "offers a special form of communication for a writer, involving a complex negotiation by which a writer acts on as well as reacts to a particular and evolving publishing environment" (76). I suggest that Davis was fully cognizant of the inherent power of the periodical and its concomitant mode of novel serialization. *Put Out of the Way* serves as a significant example of Davis's understanding of art, activism, power, and the periodical. Like many nineteenth-century women writers, Davis was cognizant of the extensive audience she could reach through popular women's magazines.[6] As Sharon M. Harris asserts in "Redefining the Feminine," Davis deliberately selected Charles J. Peterson's magazine to publish *Put Out of the Way* in order to expose the abuses of mental health institutions (118). To be sure, Davis's ability to reach a large audience with her writing satisfied her philosophies regarding the animus and efficacy of art; her individual activism embraced the pen rather than the podium as a call for awareness and reform.

Although Davis had already published sixteen works in the *Atlantic* by 1868, it was her husband's essay on the need for mental health reform, "A Modern Lettre de Cachet" that appeared there, two years prior to the publication of her own serial novel in *Peterson's*. In his work, L. Clarke Davis, a Philadelphia attorney, cites several questionable cases of incarceration in Philadelphia institutions, including the prestigious Pennsylvania Hospital for the Insane; he concludes his essay with a call for "official notice and reform" (602). Notwithstanding, Harris tells us in her study of Davis's canon, *Rebecca Harding Davis and American Realism,* that "Clarke's presentation inevitably suffers in comparison to the fictionalized call for reform that Rebecca presented in [***Put Out of the Way***]" (154).

According to Davis, after publication of her husband's work, a "bitter battle" ensued that delayed publication of ***Put Out of the Way.*** Minimizing her input in their dialogic advocacy, Davis proudly boasted that her husband had fought this battle "single-handed [sic] through press and legislature" in spite of "virulent opposition" (qtd. in Harris, *American Realism* 154). It is important to note here that as a man in the postbellum era, Clarke Davis possessed a greater number of discursive options than Rebecca Harding Davis; moreover, as an attorney, he was able to propose changes in the public, legislative realm that she could solely enact in print. The courtroom provided the forum necessary for Clarke Davis to address legal ramifications of unjust laws; as a politically appointed member of a commission of inquiry, he could recommend the amelioration of sundry laws to the governor. On the other hand, as a woman in postbellum American culture, Davis was not only legally disenfranchised but was also restricted from a variety of professional opportunities to challenge inequitable legal and social practices. Therefore, Davis's letters and her serial novel, ***Put Out of the Way,*** testify to more than the Davises' own dialogism. Davis's work is testament to her concern regarding women's issues and serves as an example of her advocacy in a realm that was open-ended, immediate, and receptive to her voice. The periodical was a site that not only encouraged her voice but rapidly circulated it far and wide. In spite of its range in print culture, the periodical nonetheless remained a site of contingency and complex meaning. Notwithstanding, the periodical became and remained Davis's forum; as a diverse site rife with contradictory and situated meanings, it was the ideal locus for Davis to enact her feminist vision. Perhaps because Davis's participation in a public sphere was so severely limited, her theories of "answerability" to her art, to use Bakhtin's term, were so pronounced.[7]

Davis, cognizant that art is predicated upon communication, employed *Peterson's Magazine* as the forum for initiating dialogue through the text, what she called a "message to be given." In an 1891 essay entitled

"Women in Literature," Davis wrote, "A few women . . . will write . . . simply because there is in them a message to be given, and they cannot die until they have spoken it" (612). To be sure, much of Davis's canon embodies her philosophies of the "good Samaritan" and her "message to be given," predating Bakhtinian theories of answerability.

In spite of the two-year span between publication of the Davises' works, their project was a dialogic one, each clearly interanimating the other. Emphasizing "situated knowledges"—what Donna Haraway calls the "partial, contradictory, permanently unclosed constructions" of knowledge—the Davises textually met their agendas and enacted reform (157). As a result of Clarke Davis's publication, an act of assembly was passed in 1869 that amended inhumane laws of 1836, one of which declared that only one physician was necessary in order to commit. The new Act 54 of 1869 mandated that an individual could be placed in a hospital for the insane by legal guardians, or by friends or relatives in cases of no surviving guardians, but "never without the certificate of two or more reputable physicians." This revised legislation somewhat lessened the possibility of fraudulent committals. It also prohibited interference with inmates' letters addressed to counsel (P.L. Act No. 54: Section 1 and 2, 1869). Prior to the enactment of this law, patients could literally be "put out of the way," with no judicial recourse and no connection to the outside world. As a result of Rebecca Harding Davis's 1870 publication of ***Put Out of the Way*** and the Davises' continued advocacy, Clarke Davis was appointed by the governor in May 1874 to a Pennsylvania state commission for inquiry into the condition of the criminally insane. That very month, another act for protection of the insane was passed. Rebecca Harding Davis's philosophies of an accountable, efficacious art thus became concrete, filtered through a transitory form—the periodical.

Davis enjoyed a long history of publication with *Peterson's* magazine. Initially acquainted with Philadelphia publisher Peterson through correspondence with her future husband, Rebecca Harding began writing for the magazine just several months after **"Life in the Iron-Mills"** appeared in the *Atlantic*. By 1870 *Peterson's* held the largest circulation of women's magazines in the nation; their readership boasted more than 150,000 subscribers, clearly a large audience by nineteenth-century standards. Initially, *Peterson's* was second in circulation only to *Godey's Lady's Book* (1830-98), also based in Philadelphia.[8] During the Civil War, however, *Peterson's* surpassed *Godey's* in subscribers and by 1870 had become the widest-circulating ladies magazine in the nation, less than two decades after its inception (Mott 320). Like *Godey's, Peterson's* targeted a female audience and regularly included the incongruous coupling of colored fashion plates, reifying ideals of "woman," and literary works, which either subverted or reified those ideals.[9]

While Davis may have told *Atlantic* editor James T. Fields in 1862 that "[p]eople do *not* like serial tales," she apparently did not believe it (qtd. in Rose 39). The author's pronouncement was apparently one of subterfuge so that she could more comfortably write serials elsewhere for greater financial remuneration. And write she did.[10] Before **Put Out of the Way** was published, Davis saw seven novels serialized in *Peterson's*; in addition to her serial novels, Davis published thirty-four short stories in the magazine before 1870. Overall, in her more than thirty-years' affiliation with Peterson, Davis published twelve serial novels and eighty-two short stories in *Peterson's*. Given this author's prolific publishing history, even in the context of a thriving nineteenth-century print culture, I am unwilling to state that Davis's astute sense of business conflicted with or negated her artistry. I am suggesting, however, that the relationship Davis shared with her editors was a dynamic one; she refused to be victimized by a publishing world microcosmic of the nineteenth-century's doctrine of separate spheres, which, Susan Coultrap-McQuin has argued, often rendered women writers "invisible" (7).

Traditionally, scholars have alleged that a number of Davis's contributions to *Peterson's*, including **Put Out of the Way,** are "trite" and "melodramatic" fictions. Not surprisingly, these works have met with relative neglect, despite Davis's enduring agenda of women's rights and social melioration, themes that have received critical attention when appearing in more prestigious sites like the *Atlantic*.[11] Such criticism (or lack thereof) reflects in part the "logic of exclusion" that Christine Battersby asserts has historically denied genius and artistry to women. In her study of feminist aesthetics, Battersby argues that the "logic of exclusion," an exclusionary paradigm informed by Greco-Roman tradition, gave priority to works reifying phallocentrism, such as those printed in the elitist *Atlantic,* over intersubjective works produced for mass culture and consumption, such as those published in *Peterson's* (4). Preceding feminist aesthetics and poststructuralist critics, Davis challenges the vision of ethereal art or transcendent existence as an alienation of self and other. Such philosophies, she writes, are "like beautiful bubbles blown from a child's pipe, floating overhead with queer reflections on them of sky and earth and human beings, all in a glow of fairy color and all a little distorted" (**Bits** [**Bits of Gossip**] 36). Rather, Davis stresses what Jean Pfaelzer has identified as "connectedness," the means whereby women writers form "a basis for female sympathy across classes and races" (93). Accordingly, the nature of women's writing reflects an intersubjectivity ideally suited for representation within the context of the periodical, a site Beetham describes as "above all an ephem-

eral form, produced for a particular day, week, or month. Its claims to truth are always contingent, as is clear from the date which is prominently displayed. . . . This affects its material form as well as its meaning" (*A Magazine of Her Own?* 9). The periodical, then, particularly one targeting the female consumer, is the consummate forum to connect and coalesce women's literary representations, one that can enhance our understanding of the situated nature of women's writing. As Battersby notes, "Since a woman in our culture has to construct her self out of fragments, the work that she produces is likely to seem incoherent unless we fit it together into an overarching unity. This unity will not be seamless or monolithic" (151).

Notwithstanding, popular women's periodicals and the literature appearing therein continue to encounter devaluating assessments. In his study *American Literary Magazines,* Edward E. Chielens refuses to consider *Peterson's* "literary." While he notes that the magazine was widely popular and rivaled *Godey's* in circulation (a periodical that is indeed addressed in *American Literary Magazines*), *Peterson's,* despite its success, lived a long but "undistinguished" life, according to Chielens, and does not merit discussion in his study (app. A). Not surprisingly, contributions to such defamed periodicals have suffered similar stigma. Chielens denounces the contents of *Peterson's* as "sentimental and undistinguished" (461). Traditionally, women writing for women have been leveled with allegations of "hack work" and "potboilers" in reference to their literature. It is not surprising, then, to note that Davis's **Put Out of the Way** has largely met with categorizations equally pejorative, or simply, with silence.[12]

Attempting to break the silence surrounding institutional incarceration and asylum care, Davis utilizes **Put Out of the Way** to solicit reform. The editorial column of the June 1870 issue of *Peterson's,* which also carried part 2 of the serial, delivered a message that Davis insisted be printed: "The author wishes us to say that there is no exaggeration in the story for that every leading incident has substantially happened, as can be proved from the records of various courts." Peterson continued, noting that the author's purpose "is not to assail any particular asylum, but rather to assist in awakening public sentiment to the necessity of a reform in the manner in which patients can be committed to such hospitals" (472). Davis deliberately set her narrative in New York as opposed to Philadelphia in order to avoid maligning any particular institution. Relative anonymity was maintained as usual.[13] It is ironic to note that the gendered economies operating in the serial novel interpolated the magazine, for Peterson referred to Davis in the generic masculine form.[14]

In the year *Peterson's* published Davis's exposé, forty-five thousand persons were being treated in insane asylums throughout the country. The field of psychiatry became firmly entrenched in the public consciousness as an increasingly respectable medical, scientific, and legal institution. Along with a growing movement of organized philanthropy, asylum care during the postbellum period also grew extremely politicized. Economics, too, informed institutionalization. In **"Two Methods"** (1893), Davis, always sensitive to her philosophies of art, denounced society's emphasis on aesthetics as opposed to action. "We Americans," she wrote, "are apt to spend our money upon the buildings in which a work is to be done instead of the work itself." Davis argued that insane asylums are generally "huge, magnificent edifices" because the public is more concerned with the aesthetics of "marble and mortar" than with the care of its inmates, subject to attendants who are "cheaply hired" and lack the appropriate training (416).

The politicization of philanthropy caused Davis to repeatedly question its agency. Care of the mentally ill, which was perceived as a familial duty and responsibility in the early nineteenth century, grew to be seen as the state's duty and responsibility in the eyes of the urban middle class by the latter half of the nineteenth century. Once politicized, the status of the insane became increasingly conjoined to women's status as the "weaker vessel"; their care became symbolic of patriarchal protection, despite the fact that care of the ill and infirm at home was predominantly the task of women. For example, noted health-care expert C. H. Hughes was not alone in his assertion that "[j]ust as the weakness of woman secures to her that chivalrous protection in society which her own frail arms could not obtain for her," so too, should the state care for infirm and insane individuals (189).

Not surprisingly, during the 1860s and 1870s, gender-specific methods of treatment flourished as a result of what Michel Foucault has identified as the "hysterization of women's bodies," whereby the female body became pathologized (*History of Sexuality* 1: 104). Psychiatric and medical spheres, informed by socio-idealogues, hypothesized insanity in the form of gynecological functioning. Myths regarding menstruation and women's reproductive system virtually endorsed women's embodiment as the weaker sex in both physical and intellectual realms. Although he certainly was not the first, Sigmund Freud published his theories of hysteria that posited a direct and causal connection between women's reproductive organs and insanity.[15] Also during this time, Silas Weir Mitchell perfected his rest cure, a paternalistic behavior modification designed specifically for women. By now we readily recognize Mitchell's presence in Charlotte Perkins Gilman's "The Yellow Wallpaper" (1892), but we are less acquainted with Davis's own, early chronicle of the rest cure, **"The Wife's Story"** (1864).[16] Historian Ellen Dwyer suggests that the nineteenth-century medical and psychiatric establishment, fearful of the female reproductive system,

believed that women's "susceptibility to endometriosis and cervical ulceration increased women's susceptibility to insanity" (95). Digital massage, subfumigation, hydrotherapy, and electromagnetic charges were applied to stabilize the "deranged" uterine system. Of all procedures, clitoral cauterization remained the most extreme, but practiced, measure.

In 1871 the Association of Medical Superintendents of American Institutions for the Insane declared at its twenty-fifth meeting that the vast majority of insane persons required institutional treatment (Geller and Harris 102). Nonetheless, Davis challenged the steadfast assumption that all who are committed to a lunatic asylum are insane; she perceived the nominalization to inhabit a slippery and unstable slope, particularly involving legal, medical, and social spheres. In her essay **"Paul"** (1884), the author classed the insane as the precariously positioned few "who do not look on life from the stand-point of the great majority" (2). Davis's view predates feminist theorist Phyllis Chesler's work by nearly a century. In *Women and Madness*, Chesler notes that the definition of "woman" in patriarchal society in conjunction with orthodox psychotherapy, is basically a prescription for insanity for women (2).

The Davises' efforts meliorated Pennsylvania's legislation regarding commitment of individuals, but other states were reluctant to follow suit. In addition, the judicial system frequently privileged criminals over patients. Those accused of a crime received due process of the law; those committed to insane asylums were denied their constitutional right of due process. Davis, then, continued to battle for the rights denied those committed to hospitals for the insane and the ease with which male family members could legally commit others there, to literally and legally have another "put out of the way." In *Put Out of the Way*, Davis exposes the following: unjust laws that enable a single physician to issue a certificate that can easily commit any individual to an insane asylum; the despotic position of the asylum's director who is given sole supervision of the institution and answers to no one—yet that same superintendent has no power to discharge an inmate without the consent of those who had placed the patient there; the writ of habeas corpus in which the burden of proof of mental health rests upon the inmate and the incarceration alone of the prisoner, which is regarded as prima facie evidence against him or her; cruel and abusive treatment of prisoners; and economic justifications for incarceration and extended commitment of the inmate, in some cases for periods up to thirty years. Given the range of power afforded to male family members in the nineteenth century, it is not surprising to note that many of those inmates were women.

Davis's own experience as a woman writing in the second half of the nineteenth-century print culture would make her acutely aware of what Foucault has termed the "animality of madness" (78). In *Madness and Civilization,* Foucault argues that once equated with monsters, "madmen remained monsters—that is etymologically, beings or things to be shown" (70). Certainly postbellum demarcations of sex, gender, and desire would have given Davis an acute aversion to threats of bestial, monstrous animality by which creative women were metaphorically embodied.[17] From this standpoint, Davis may have been able to equate the shared matrices of those incarcerated unjustly—either the sane, legally "put out of the way," or the mad, "present on the stage of the world," as Foucault has said—with the specularization of women (69). I am suggesting that Davis, doubly circumscribed as a woman artist, consistently utilized a complex, sophisticated form of gendered economies to typify her literature and her reform, as she does in the feminization of protagonist Richard Wortley in *Put Out of the Way.* Davis employed gendered economies as a critical tool to illustrate the debilitating effects of gender construction in a patriarchal culture; in this manner she effectively deployed binary systems of sexuality and gender. Through oscillating and situated gender inversions, Davis frequently feminized male characters and masculinized female characters in order to demystify nineteenth-century essentialized gender demarcations and to call for a reform of institutional practices predicated upon this doctrine of separate spheres that continued to perpetrate injustices upon those disenfranchised and disempowered. Davis's critical exploration of gender exemplified the unstable and reversible nature of gender constructions and the appropriation of women's essential biology for hegemonic production. In this manner, Davis's technique of gendered economies anticipates Foucault's theoretical paradigm of genealogy and contemporary Foucauldian feminists' use of genealogy of gender in order to demonstrate that categorization of sex, gender, and desire is a specific effect of institutional formations of power in order to decenter that power.

Foucault proposes, "Madness is the purest, most total form of *quid pro quo*; it takes the false for the pure, death for life, man for woman" (*Madness and Civilization* 33). Defined as deviant, incarcerated in a private space, the feminized Wortley is powerless to control his destiny; his plight parallels the imprisonment of the subplot's female protagonist, Lotty Hubbard. Integrating the dilemma faced by both characters, Davis incorporates notions of "madness" and "justice" to promulgate her gendered economies, not only to call attention to illicit but legal practices regarding institutionalization, but also to challenge and unmask iniquitous notions of gender that inform these practices. Davis's novel, loosely based upon the case of Morgan Hinchman,[18] integrates Hinchman's experience with factual accounts found in a number of women's asylum narratives. The product of this integration is a character akin to one of Fanny Fern's characters in *Ruth Hall* (1855),

the intriguing Mary Leon, who is valued solely as a "necessary appendage to Mr. Leon's establishment" (51). Nonetheless, when he tires of her, Mr. Leon commits his wife to an insane asylum because institutionalization offers an easier solution than divorce. There, incarcerated with countless other women, she dies, "forgotten by the world" (109). Like Davis's work, Fern's fiction is informed by fact. Vacationing in New England in the summer of 1862, Fern visited an insane asylum and was aghast at the disproportionate number of women there; later that year she would theorize why in the *New York Ledger,* citing the vast number of outlets provided for men to release emotional pressure, outlets that she claimed were denied to women (Warren 246).

Davis, however, believed that judicial processes were accountable, and she used the Philadelphia-based *Peterson's* to voice her concerns. An 1852 Pennsylvania state act sanctioned the theft of any married woman's real and personal estate, provided the thief was her husband and his chosen committee of three, one of whom needed to be a practicing physician, could issue a certificate claiming her insanity. Once a woman was pronounced insane and institutionalized, her husband possessed full power to dispose of not only his estate but also hers, as "if his said wife was sane and gave her full consent thereto" (P.L. Act No. 433, Sec. 7, 1852). Not surprisingly, many women spent the remainder of their lives incarcerated in institutions, paid for by the proceeds of their own estates. Some were eventually released and wrote about their unjust incarceration in asylum narratives. For example, Tirzah F. Shedd, an inmate of the Illinois State Hospital for the Insane between 7 July and mid-October 1865, wrote about her horror at discovering the inequities that lurked in American democracy. "It may be a land of freedom for the men," she wrote, "but I am sure it is not for the married women!" (qtd. in Geller and Harris 80). Torn from her three children, Shedd found that her personal liberty was placed entirely in the hands of her husband, who was "fully determined to use this legal power to subject my views to his will and wishes" (80). Legally, in many states, men found it a more expedient procedure to find a committee willing to incarcerate one's wife in a lunatic asylum than to obtain a divorce, a far more complicated judicial process which entailed annulling the marriage contract by a legal act.

Reflective of a number of women's asylum narratives, Davis's novel *Put Out of the Way* follows the incarceration of both Lotty Hubbard and the feminized Wortley. Hubbard is a young woman who finds herself, upon the death of her father, taken into the guardianship of Colonel Ned Leeds until she comes of age to receive her inheritance and, thus, economic independence. Imprisoned in a domestic space, Hubbard symbolizes women's economic dependence and restriction from the public sphere, conditions, Davis stresses, that facilitate the false incarceration of women in asylums. In contrast, Colonel Leeds, symbolic of the patriarchal head, exemplifies the social sanctions that deny women full access to the public sphere, imprisoning them within their bodies and their homes. Like the protagonist of Gilman's "The Yellow Wallpaper," Hubbard eventually grows "sickly and morbid in mind and body from her unwonted confinement" (362); her condition is analogous to the increasing powerlessness experienced by her cousin, Dick Wortley.

Employing reversible gendered economies to better epitomize nineteenth-century women's plight, Davis initially presents a masculine Wortley. Each scene enacts power relationships that are microcosmic of the era's doctrine of separate spheres; masculinity is equated with either potency or efficacy while femininity is conflated with impotency or inefficacy. Wortley, a "six-foot young fellow, with his hearty voice, yet polished, man-of-the-world address" (359), is highly masculinized; he is the epitome of a "manly man" (360). When Dick discovers Colonel Leeds's plan to marry Lotty to his son in order to gain her inheritance, he confronts both men, who, in turn, become intent on silencing him. Here, Davis reminds her readers of women's continued legal disenfranchisement that has placed them, as Dawn Keetley has noted, as "involuntary subjects within marriage" (347); Davis returns to tropes of gender and silence to illustrate her women readers' status as femes covert. Moreover, Davis also indicts unjust laws that continue to facilitate false imprisonment in asylums while she denounces the infrastructure's capacity for alienation. Leeds assures his son that with the proper economic means, Dick can be silenced: "It is a quiet, safe means, which a gentleman can use with no fear of punishment. There must be secrecy, . . . Only pay enough, and get up your case right, as the lawyers say, you have science and philanthropy both to assist you" (435). Politically astute, Davis recognized that via the matrices of the "law, and science, and philanthropy" (436), one needed only to obtain a certificate from a physician (who need not see the victim) to certify that individual insane and, thus, literally imprison one "for life" (436).

In this manner, Davis also challenges the judicial system. If Wortley had committed a crime, he would have the privilege of counsel and a trial before his peers prior to incarceration for the crime; his trial (and he) also would be scrutinized by the public gaze. Here Davis inverts notions that equate madness with the gaze; Foucault suggests that, historically, madness has been associated with "pure spectacle" (69). As a woman writer exposed to the public gaze, however, and as an activist cognizant of the art of the periodical, Davis believed the gaze could also be utilized as a positive force,

a lifting of the veil in order to alter unjust practices through awareness. The same public gaze that guaranteed criminals the right to trial by jury was averted for the insane who were confined to institutions, sometimes for life, "without judge or jury, or a chance to escape" (437). Because the practice escaped public scrutiny, Davis argued, it remained perfectly legal—and perfectly immoral.[19]

Davis possessed a vast body of knowledge regarding nineteenth-century jurisprudence; her canon consistently displays her shrewd grasp of legal machinations. In *Put Out of the Way,* she indicates that statutory law does not technically require the certificate, but rather common law or custom demands it (441). To be sure, patients were not subjected to examination or tests to prove insanity; the institution solely relied upon the physician's certification to define madness as prima facie evidence. As Foucault has suggested, once objectified as mad, all behavior of the "madman" is perceived as insane. Through Wortley's character, Davis shows us that societal conventions of "civilized" discourse and practice do not apply in the insane asylum.

Indeed, a number of asylum narratives substantiate Davis's claims of asylum abuse. One leading expert on jurisprudence of insanity in the mid-nineteenth century wrote, "Many of the depots for the captivity of intellectual invalids may be regarded only as nurseries for and manufactories of madness,—magazines or reservoirs of lunacy, from which is issued, from time to time, a sufficient supply for perpetuating and extending this formidable disease" (qtd. in "A Modern Lettre de Cachet" 598). Or as Adeline T. P. Lunt, an inmate of a facility in New England, wrote upon her release, "INSANE ASYLUM. A place where insanity is made" (12). Before Foucault postulated that the nineteenth century's animality of madness could not be ministered to or rectified through medicine or correction, but only "mastered" by "discipline and brutalizing" (75), Davis addressed the bestial, insane-making treatment patients endured in asylums.

Chthonic detail supports the narrative to better depict the "netherworld-liness" of the asylum as a forgotten underworld of society. Wortley remembers reading that "letters from the patients of insane asylums were generally suppressed," and he slowly comes to the realization that he is indeed "buried alive" (443), when the asylum's superintendent, an inhumane, mechanical man ironically named Dr. Harte intercepts Dick's letters to family and counsel calling for help. Again, Davis returns to issues of voice, signifying that the oppressor can find power only in the silencing of the subaltern.

Davis depicts other power relations through one of the hospital's "keepers," a man whose barbarous treatment of the incarcerated exemplifies the image of animality that Foucault suggests "haunted" the asylums of that period (72). Davis inscribes the scene with predatory and violent terms: "[The keeper's] great carcass of muscle was cool and slow. When the time seemed to him to be ripe, he gave a sniff, and leveled Dick with a foul blow, jumping on his chest with his knees. Dick remained quite quiet there. It did not need any blows, the weight was enough" (158). Thus the beast becomes the "keeper" of the man like Wortley, once described as the "manliest of men" (360). Davis's message to her readers is explicitly clear: this man's use of brute force to subjugate another parallels a patriarchal legal system that strong-arms women to silence. The madness of this system, Davis reminds her audience, not only silences the victim, it dehumanizes the oppressor. Indeed, madness embodies the reversible world. "Madness," to quote Foucault again, "takes the false for the true, death for life, man for woman" (33). Davis utilizes the reversible spirit of gendered economies—the feminization of Dick Wortley—not only to unmask false legal claims, nor solely to illustrate the countless women in the nineteenth century who were subject to institutionalization (a number of them her readers), but also, as the narrative's subplot attests, to draw her readers' attention to society's sanction of women imprisoned in the domestic sphere, economically dependent and powerless. In this instance, however, Davis's protagonist is not contained within a domestic abode but in a cell. These cells are precisely the same, she tells us, as the cells convicts inhabit on death row, except that in the asylum the superintendent is "judge, and executioner, and public" (34). Again, Davis enacts the public gaze as a positive force; her details are accurate and hauntingly factual. In a direct address to her readers intended to secure their attention, Davis graphically depicts the inhumanities perpetrated upon inmates: they are frequently left in a state of nudity; their "cells" are infested by vermin; and they are forced to lie in the "dark and heat, surrounded with creeping, nauseous things, whose shapes [you] could guess at, with the air about [you] filled with fiendish yells and forlorn sobbings from the maniacs in the near cells" (37).

At this point in the narrative, Dick's feminization occurs precisely at the same time his body becomes the site for the breaking of his mind. The appropriation of his body by physical violence is Davis's method of conjoining pressing issues of domestic abuse and the torturous methods asylums employed to "cure" women and the mentally ill. Her descriptions are graphic, far removed from sentimental rhetoric. After another beating as a method of sedation, "Dick Wortley's head dropped to one side, grew sickly and livid as when he was a jaundiced baby: then the blood slowly rose to his mouth, and dripped, dripped on the floor" (35). Davis then reveals haunting details about treatments used for both male and female patients, methods such as the

"saddle," the shower-bath, and the "hose" (114), a wooden machine in which victims were strapped on their backs with their head, legs, and arms hanging down in order for the blood to be driven to the brain. Often the procedure lasted until the patient passed out. She also painstakingly details the shower-bath to which Dick is subjected, a tortuous practice in which one slow drop of water after another falls upon a singular spot on the forehead (presumably in order to better reach the brain), "until from the frenzied eyes, and unconscious moans of agony, it seemed as though the tortured soul within was seeking, at eyes and mouth, some means of escape" (85). The only quality attributable to the shower, Foucault notes, is its "violence"; its curative power derived from "destroying even the smallest traces of the extravagant ideas of the insane, which can be done only by obliterating, so to speak, these ideas in a state close to that of death" (172). In other words, the nineteenth century's violent legal methods of "curing" those deemed insane privileged death to difference.[20]

In the femininization of her protagonist, Davis also interpolates recurrent issues of voice and rebellion for her readers. Dick "had learned reticence; he asked no questions, made no comments" (85). Silenced, his feminization is nearly complete; he can no longer rely upon the physical strength he once possessed as a free man; now he looks with "loathing" upon his "trembling hands and legs" (86). He fears that his mind will succumb to the influence of his surroundings, "an insane world, where there was nothing reliable or tangible to grasp by, he began to reason insanely" (37). It is here that Davis finds the scandal of Dick's incarceration. For as Foucault asserts, "The scandal lies only in the fact that the madmen are the brutal truth of confinement, the passive instrument of all that is worst about it. Is this not symbolized by the fact . . . that a sojourn in a house of correction necessarily leads to madness? Having to live in this delirious world, amid the triumph of unreason, how may one avoid joining, by the fatality of the site and the event, the very men who are its living symbol?" (225). Davis's awareness was participatory and political rather than removed and philanthropic, and through Dick's feminization he becomes a tool and object of the patriarchy, a system that was indeed a site of madness. One year prior to the publication of *Put Out of the Way*, Davis wrote, "It is not *women* who have first tainted society and literature; it is not weak, starving, ill-paid women who are to blame for this Gehenna of prostitution that underlies our social fabric" (**"Men's Rights"** 216).

Returning to the narrative, Dick's feminization is complete; yet his escape is certain, a "hot and cold shiver shot through him as though he had been a woman" (109). Disempowered though he may be, he seeks escape, noting, "I am as weak as an hysteric girl! . . .

They've scaled my manhood from me pretty thoroughly" (110). Wortley does escape but unfortunately is captured again on the asylum's grounds. Significantly, once completely feminized, he cannot leave the sanitarium through his own efforts; he can only escape through the active intervention of another. It is crucial to note here that his writing and the *dialogic, volitional act of another* saves him. Davis fuses the climax of the narrative's plot with her philosophies of art's efficacy; her narrative enacts precisely what Davis consistently argues that the art of the periodical should perform. Before his capture on the hospital's grounds, Dick throws a letter across the wall; like Davis's work, her character's epistolary act serves as a call for awareness and a plea for intervention. When Dick is caught and again placed in the hospital among the forgotten souls "who had been kept there for forty, fifty years, whose histories, whose very names, were long ago forgotten," significantly, his letter—his utterance—remains (38). There, it is found by a young girl who symbolizes Davis's interdependent philosophy of the "good Samaritan." A quiet, nondescript girl, Jessy seemingly keeps to herself, yet her act ultimately saves Dick. She quietly pockets the letter, seals it in an envelope, and mails it. In other words, she actively responds to his utterance. The letter reaches the proper channels, and Dick is released. Jessy's private act of charity toward a stranger is the apex of Davis's narrative and the textual embodiment of her philosophies of the active and participatory art of the periodical.

When Dick is released from the asylum, penniless and ill-clothed, Davis attempts to re-"masculinize" him, conjoining freedom with the renewal of his masculinity: "Give me dry clothes . . . and some oysters and I'm a man again" (115). Colonel Leeds and his son continue to worry about Dick's interference with their plans, and even debate the possibilities of murdering Dick, yet they are reminded that until now their immoralities have been sanctioned by law. Davis unequivocally denounces the inanities of an inequitable judicial system by rupturing the narrative with a direct address to her readers: "What a farce" (115).

The novel concludes with Dick and Lotty's marriage, where they live happily in "the Indian Summer of [their] lives." Despite the sentimental rhetoric concluding the story, in which the narrator tells us that the "sun is warm, and God is good" (118), Davis's narrative resists closure: the judicial system remains unchanged, the avarice of institutions continues, and public philanthropy persists as a removed and idealized institution that dismantles the possibility of human relationships. Yet Davis's philosophies of art and reform remain explicitly clear. The character of Jessy, so like Davis herself,[21] reminds readers of the importance of maintaining interdependent relations with others, even those of face-less strangers. Through the narrative and the art of the periodical, Davis exemplifies that the "grasp of the hand" can indeed alter circumstances.[22] Accordingly, Davis's novel did more than serve as the means to question prevailing notions of art, her work utilized a popular women's periodical effectively to draw the nation's averted gaze to this crucial issue in order to reform inequitable legislation. Her choice of *Peterson's* enabled Davis to exemplify doubly her philosophies regarding the animus and efficacy of art in nineteenth-century culture; through a popular women's periodical, she simultaneously enacted her theories of art and activism in both form and content. Representing the art of the periodical, **Put Out of the Way** employs gendered economies to rupture androcentric discourse, thereby unmasking the seemingly stable nature of gender constructs as a highly unstable fortress in which to imprison a sex.

Ten years prior to the formation of the National Association for the Protection of the Insane and the Prevention of Insanity, an association established in 1880 to monitor and reform mental asylums, Davis—a woman who had never joined a committee, association, club, or group—challenged *and altered* inequitable legislation predicated upon an alienation that could render individuals powerless. Legally disenfranchised, this author grasped the dialogic power of the periodical to cast her voice far and wide. This "power," as contemporary Elizabeth Stuart Phelps noted, was "art . . . concentrated upon the passion of humanity and governed thereby in every line she wrote" (119, 120). To be sure, Rebecca Harding Davis recognized that her individual power as an activist required more than passion, it demanded the pen—and the periodical.

Notes

1. In *A Magazine of Her Own?*, Margaret Beetham links Victorian women's periodicals with the bourgeois commodity culture and resulting definitions of femininity. Beetham suggests that the woman consumer "was defined both by the activity of looking—whether through plate-glass windows or at newspaper advertisements—and by how she looked herself" (8). Beetham notes that there was indeed a dynamic relationship between the revisioning and redefining of femininity and the material basis of magazines. Ellen Gruber Garvey also stresses the interrelated web of advertisements, fiction, essays, and editorial material as a coalescing context for nineteenth-century American women consumers. See Garvey, *The Adman in the Parlor: Magazines and the Gendering of Consumer Culture, 1880s to 1910s* (New York: Oxford UP, 1996).

2. My study is informed by Andrew Scheiber, whose work also focuses on the post-structuralist impulses in Davis's fiction that simultaneously en-

gage and subvert. In "An Unknown Infrastructure," Scheiber suggests that Davis's "Life in the Iron-Mills" is a work dedicated "not to the creation of aesthetic values, but to the interrogation and demolition of them" (102).

3. In a letter accompanying the draft of "John Lamar," Davis urgently wrote *Atlantic* editor James T. Fields, "[W]on't you publish John Lamar as soon as you can? I have a fancy for writing of *today* you see" (qtd. in Harris 73). Notwithstanding, Davis's philosophies regarding the power of the periodical involved immediacy as well as immanence. For example, in "Doctor Pajot," published in *Appletons' Journal* in 1877, Davis implements the Pegasus myth as a metaphor to delineate these philosophies and, thus, dismantle paradigms of "high" culture and elitist art. Her protagonist, Mrs. Pajot, a writer, notes that "Pegasus can show the stuff that's in him by pulling a cart as well as in any other way" (553).

4. In her examination of periodical fiction, "Stories That Stay" (1910), Phelps insisted that "the writer of a short story must know how to tell it; but it is more important that [s]he should have something to tell" (123).

5. See Beetham, *A Magazine of Their Own?* 9. Tania Modleski's work illustrates that the very qualities of magazines—their sense of fragmentation and openness—lend credence to theories that the forum is inherently subversive to masculine cultural norms. See Tania Modleski, *Loving With a Vengeance: Mass-Produced Fantasies for Women* (New York: Methuen, 1982). Accordingly, Davis deliberately conjoins gendered economies with discussions of art throughout her periodical fiction not only to question the animus and efficacy of art but also to subvert traditional engendering of art as "male," hence my use of the term "feminist" to describe Davis's methodology.

6. Sharon M. Harris illustrates that while Davis was unable (or unwilling) to join public demonstrations for women's rights, she privately endeavored to help extend women's rights, particularly in terms of helping needy friends find self-reliance through careers (*American Realism* 121-22). I would add that Davis also utilized her writing as a feminist methodology. Despite his unfortunate choice of words, I cite Davis's eldest son, Richard Harding Davis, who praised his mother for her cultural work: "[Y]ou were always year after year making the ways straighter, lifting up people, making them happier and better. No shrieking suffragette will ever understand the influence you wielded, greater than hundreds of thousands of women's votes" (qtd. in Rose, *Rebecca Harding Davis* 165).

7. Mikhail Bakhtin explained for himself in the following way: "I have to answer with my own life for what I have experienced and understood in art" ("Art" xx). In *Toward a Philosophy of the Act*, Bakhtin would refer to the philosophy Davis called the "good Samaritan" as the artistic process of "answerability," the "moral philosophy" by which the artist lives and accounts for her art (56). This accountability is twofold, he explains, "both from within its product and from the standpoint of the author as answerable participant" (54).

8. *Peterson's*, however, sold for two dollars a year—one dollar less than its competitor, thus making the magazine more accessible to a greater number (Mott 320).

9. Beetham suggests that the definition of female beauty proved to be a highly difficult concept to erase. Throughout the century, the "discourse of dress," particularly in the illustrations presented in middle-class women's magazines, continued to define ideals of femininity (*A Magazine of Her Own?* 7). Clearly, the combination of fashion plates and literature that could either subvert or reify the ideals of feminine beauty depicted in the illustrations makes for a fascinating study of the complexities inherent in the periodical press as a genre.

10. Davis was an artist with an astute sense of business and learned by trial and error to navigate through the complex maze of the nineteenth-century publishing world. Harris tells us that *Peterson's* was known to pay Davis as much as a thousand dollars for a serialized novel as early as the 1860s (*American Realism* 73). Clearly this amount was more than she could receive from the *Atlantic*, and the author apparently had no qualms about making this fact known to Fields: "You know I would like to write only for you, partly because we are friends, and partly because I am *in earnest* when I write and I find the audience I like in Atlantic readers. But I'm going to be perfectly honest now. If I wrote stories suitable for other magazines I could make more." Explaining, "as times are, I am not justified in refusing the higher price," she craftily urged Fields to "give as much for future articles as you can legitimately afford so that I can write solely for the A[tlantic] M[onthly]." Davis, however, continued to write for both periodicals, authoring nine works for *Peterson's* to the *Atlantic's* three that year, despite her promise to Fields to write "for the Atlantic exclusively for this year [1862]" (qtd. in Rose 38). See Jane Atteridge Rose, "A Bibliography of Fiction and Non-Fiction by Rebecca Harding Davis" in *American Literary Realism* 22.3:67-86.

11. In addition to Davis's *Put Out of the Way,* the stories "The Story of Christine" (1866), "At Bay" (1867), "In the Market" (1868), and "Clement Moore's Vocation" (1870), all published in *Peterson's,* are merely a few examples of intriguing works that continue to receive scant critical attention but exemplify the active women-centered agenda of Davis's canon. Notwithstanding Harris's critical attention to "In the Market," one can only assume that an integral aspect of their relative neglect derives in part from their periodical placement.

12. Certainly, my statement precludes Davis scholars Sharon M. Harris and Jane Atteridge Rose, who have both addressed *Put Out of the Way* in their perspective studies of Davis and her works, *Rebecca Harding Davis and American Realism* (1991) and *Rebecca Harding Davis* (1993). Clearly, Harris's examination of Davis's novel has greatly informed my own; it was her critical examination of Davis's novel as an exposé that led me to a greater understanding of Davis as an activist. See Harris, *Rebecca Harding Davis and American Realism* 154-60. In addition, Jane Atteridge Rose's exploration of Davis's novel also notes Davis's work as a well-researched and documented exposé. See Rose, *Rebecca Harding Davis* 75-76. Although another leading Davis scholar, Jean Pfaelzer, does not discuss *Put Out of the Way* in great depth, her *Rebecca Harding Davis Reader* (Pittsburgh: U of Pittsburgh P, 1995) and her examination of Davis's social activism in *Parlor Radical: Rebecca Harding Davis and the Origins of American Social Realism* (Pittsburgh: U of Pittsburgh P, 1996) have greatly enhanced my understanding of Davis as a writer. The scholarly work of Harris, Pfaelzer, and Rose has, in true dialogic fashion, incited and informed my own.

13. After 1865 *Peterson's* generally published Davis's work under the pseudonyms that associated her with *Margret Howth* and *A Second Life.* In *Put Out of the Way,* Davis is identified as the author of *A Second Life.*

14. I intentionally refer to Louis Althusser's theoretical term in which one's positioning may be described as ideological, as in an inserting or "interpellating" of individuals and/or their works into constructed social identities that enable the individual to make sense of the world. See Althusser, "Ideology and Ideological State Apparatuses (Notes towards an Investigation)," and "A Letter on Art in Reply to Andre Daspré" in *Lenin and Philosophy and Other Essays,* trans. Ben Brewster (London: New Left, 1971). 121-73, 203-08.

15. See Rachel P. Maines, *The Technology of Orgasm: "Hysteria," the Vibrator, and Women's Sexual Satisfaction* (Baltimore: Johns Hopkins UP, 1999).

16. Although we have no extant documentation in which she specifically names the Philadelphia neurospecialist, in all probability, Mitchell, a friend of the Davis family, prescribed Davis's rest cure. See Davis, "The Wife's Story," *Atlantic* 14 (1864): 1-19.

17. Dominant gender demarcations in postbellum American society doubly configured the woman artist. Defined by their biology and denied the unencumbered existence integral to the male artist, women were denied artistry at the expense of biology. Women who refused to accept a "natural" existence due to biological essence, choosing artistry instead, were perceived as "unnatural" and, at times, monstrously deviant. In "Resisting the Gaze of Embodiment," Sidonie Smith examines the "metaphysical" male self and the female, embodied "self of essences" (75). Also see Mary Kelley, *Private Woman, Public Stage: Literary Domesticity in Nineteenth-Century America* (New York: Oxford UP, 1984).

18. Morgan Hinchman, a Pennsylvania Quaker, was falsely committed to the Frankford Lunatic Asylum by his wife's family following a disagreement with family members regarding finances. The physician who had provided the certificate necessary to commit the young Quaker was not his personal physician, nor had he seen the man for four months prior to its issue. After six months of incarceration, Hinchman escaped the asylum and pressed a civil suit for damages against his in-laws (592-5). This case served a pivotal role in Clarke Davis's "A Modern Lettre de Cachet"; Rebecca Harding Davis's inclusion of the case in her novel substantiates the dialogics occurring between wife and husband. In like fashion, Clarke Davis's descriptions of the legal injustices perpetrated against women in his essay's conclusion point to Rebecca Harding Davis's influence and, ultimately, exemplify the dialogic activity between the Davises.

19. The theme of legal and moral laws is repeated throughout Davis's canon. For a notable example, see *A Law Unto Herself,* serialized in *Lippincott's Magazine* 2 (1877): 39-49, 167-82, 291-308, 464-78, 614-28, 719-31.

20. Davis's active empathy for victims of debilitating "cures" was rooted in experience. In July of 1863, after nearly four months of marriage, Davis suffered brain fever and was forced to endure the rest cure. "The Wife's Story," written shortly after her treatment, is the product of her "cure"; it too de-

tails a psychological breakdown and recovery. However, in Davis's depiction of Dick Wortley's recovery, we glimpse a less domestic but equally enclosed image of hell: "It was late in June before he was himself enough to know that the claw-like fingers, picking at the sheet, were his own" (35).

21. Davis saw herself as an unassuming and unattractive figure. Jean Pfaelzer suggests that because Davis envisioned herself as such, she "identified with a series of [her] homely but artistic characters whose creative and sexual passions are stymied by their bodies—as female, plain, or deformed" (49-50).

22. In *Rebecca Harding Davis and American Realism,* Harris reminds us that Davis's "grasp of the hand" image captures one of her "most prevalent metaphors for personal activism" (23). The artist's complex metaphor adopts additional layers of meaning when we examine Roman law regarding marriage ceremonies and the most sacred type of marriage ceremony; this rite placed a woman in manus: to mean literally "in the hand of" her husband. As wives in manus, women were under the authority of their husbands and their husbands' families who had power over virtually every aspect of these women's lives (Battersby 55). Davis's legal acumen and knowledge of legal discourse are manifest in *Put Out of the Way,* and, in all probability, she was quite familiar with the etiology of in manus and deliberately employed the metaphor to better serve her feminist agenda.

Works Cited

Althusser, Louis. "Ideology and Ideological State Apparatuses (Notes Towards an Investigation)." *Lenin and Philosophy and Other Essays.* Trans. Ben Brewster. New York: Monthly Review Press, 1971.

Bakhtin, Mikhail M. "Art and Answerability." *Art and Answerability: Early Philosophical Essays by M. M. Bakhtin.* Eds. Michael Holquist and Vadim Liapunov. Austin: U of Texas P, 1990. 1-3.

———. *Toward a Philosophy of the Act.* Ed. Vadim Liapunov and Michael Holquist. Trans. Liapunov. Austin: U of Texas P, 1993.

Battersby, Christine. *Gender and Genius: Towards a Feminist Aesthetics.* Bloomington: Indiana UP, 1989.

Beetham, Margaret. *A Magazine of Her Own? Domesticity and Desire in the Woman's Magazine 1800-1914.* London: Routledge, 1996.

———. "Towards a Theory of the Periodical as a Publishing Genre." *Investigating Victorian Journalism.* Eds. Laurel Brake, Aled Jones, and Lionel Madden. London: Macmillan, 1990. 19-32.

Chesler, Phyllis. *Women and Madness.* New York: Avon, 1972.

Chielens, Edward E. *American Literary Magazines: The Eighteenth and Nineteenth Centuries.* Vol. 1. Westport, CT: Greenwood, 1992. 2 vols.

Coultrap-McQuin, Susan. *Doing Literary Business: American Women Writers in the Nineteenth Century.* Chapel Hill: U of North Carolina P, 1990.

Davis, L. Clarke. "A Modern Lettre de Cachet." *Atlantic Monthly* 1868: 588-602.

Davis, Rebecca Harding. *Bits of Gossip.* Boston: Houghton 1904.

———. "Blind Tom." *Atlantic Monthly* 1862: 580-85.

———. "Doctor Pajot." *Appletons' Journal* ns 2 (1877): 551-56.

———. "Men's Rights." *Putnam's Magazine* ns 3 (1869): 212-24.

———. "Paul." *Independent* 3 Jan. 1884: 2.

———. *Put Out of the Way. Peterson's Magazine* 57 (1870): 355-67, 431-43; 58: 30-41, 109-18.

———. "Two Methods." *Independent* 30 Mar. 1893: 416.

———. "Women in Literature." *Independent* 7 May 1891: 612-13.

Dwyer, Ellen. "The Weaker Vessel: Legal Versus Social Reality in Mental Commitments in Nineteenth-Century New York." *Women and the Law: A Social Historical Perspective.* Vol. 1. Ed. D. Kelly Wisberg. Cambridge, MA: Schenkman, 1982. 119-32. 3 vols.

Fern, Fanny [Sara Payson W. E. F. Parton]. *Ruth Hall.* 1855. Ed. Joyce W. Warren. New Brunswick, NJ: Rutgers UP, 1986.

Foucault, Michel. *The History of Sexuality: An Introduction.* Vol. 1. Trans. Robert Hurley. New York: Random House, 1990. 3 vols.

———. *Madness and Civilization: A History of Insanity in the Age of Reason.* Trans. Richard Howard. New York: Random House, 1988.

Geller, Jeffrey L., and Maxine Harris. "Period II: 1866-1890." *Women of the Asylum: Voices from Behind the Walls, 1840-1945.* New York: Doubleday, 1994. 89-107.

Haraway, Donna J. *Simians, Cyborgs, and Women: The Reinvention of Nature.* New York: Routledge, 1991.

Harris, Sharon M. *Rebecca Harding Davis and American Realism.* Philadelphia: U of Pennsylvania P, 1991.

———. "Redefining the Feminine: Women and Work in Rebecca Harding Davis's 'In the Market.'" *Legacy* 8 (1991): 118-21.

Hughes, C. H. "The Rights of the Insane." *Alienist and Neurologist* 4 (1883): 183-89.

Keetley, Dawn. "Victim and Victimizer: Female Fiends and Unease over Marriage in Antebellum Sensational Fiction." *American Quarterly* 51.2 (1999): 344-84.

Kelley, Mary. *Private Woman, Public Stage: Literary Domesticity in Nineteenth-Century America.* New York: Oxford UP, 1984.

Lunt, Adeline T. P. *Behind Bars.* Boston: Lea and Shepard, 1871.

Mott, Frank Luther. *American Journalism: A History, 1690-1960.* 3rd ed. New York: Macmillan, 1962.

———. *A History of American Magazines.* Cambridge, MA.: Harvard UP, 1938-68. 5 vols.

Pfaelzer, Jean. "Domesticity and the Discourse of Slavery: 'John Lamar' and 'Blind Tom' by Rebecca Harding Davis." *ESQ* 38 (1992): 31-56.

———. "Subjectivity as Feminist Utopia." *Utopian and Science Fiction by Women: Worlds of Difference.* Ed. Jane Donawerth and Carol Kolmerten. Syracuse, NY: Syracuse UP, 1994. 93-106.

Phelps, Elizabeth Stuart. "Stories That Stay." *Century* 81 (1910): 118-24.

Rose, Jane Atteridge. *Rebecca Harding Davis.* New York: Twayne, 1993.

Scheiber, Andrew J. "An Unknown Infrastructure: Gender, Production, and Aesthetic Exchange in Rebecca Harding Davis's 'Life in the Iron-Mills.'" *Legacy* 11 (1994): 101-17.

Smith, Sidonie. "Resisting the Gaze of Embodiment." *American Women's Autobiography: Fea(s)ts of Memory.* Ed. and Introd. Margo Culley. Madison: U of Wisconsin P, 1992. 75-110.

Smith, Susan Belasco. "Serialization and the Nature of *Uncle Tom's Cabin.*" *Periodical Literature in Nineteenth-Century America.* Eds. Kenneth M. Price and Susan Belasco Smith. Charlottesville: UP of Virginia, 1995. 69-89.

Warren, Joyce W. "Uncommon Discourse: Fanny Fern and the New York Ledger." *Periodical Literature in Nineteenth-Century America.* Eds. Kenneth M. Price and Susan Belasco Smith. Charlottesville: UP of Virginia, 1995. 51-68.

———. "The Cult of True Womanhood: 1820-1860." *Dimity Convictions: the American Woman in the Nineteenth Century.* Athens: Ohio UP, 1976.

Sara Britton Goodling (essay date 2003)

SOURCE: Goodling, Sara Britton. "The Silent Partnership: Naturalism and Sentimentalism in the Novels of Rebecca Harding Davis and Elizabeth Stuart Phelps." In *Twisted from the Ordinary: Essays on American Literary Naturalism,* edited by Mary E. Papke, pp. 1-22. Knoxville, Tenn.: The University of Tennessee Press, 2003.

[*In the following essay, Goodling provides "close readings" of Davis's* Margret Howth *and Elizabeth Stuart Phelps's* The Silent Partner *to demonstrate the unlikely connection between sentimentalism and naturalism in these two novels, maintaining that both works include "typical sentimental heroines" who enter into naturalistic worlds and "encounter naturalistic characters whose lives are determined by the powerful forces of biology and environment."*]

> Nothing remains to tell that the poor Welsh puddler once lived, but this figure of the mill-woman cut in korl. I have it here in a corner of my library. I keep it hid behind a curtain,—it is such a rough, ungainly thing. Yet there are about it touches, grand sweeps of outline, that show a master's hand. Sometimes,—tonight, for instance,—the curtain is accidentally drawn back, and I see a bare arm stretched out imploringly in the darkness, and an eager, wolfish face watching mine: a wan, woful face, through which the spirit of the dead korl cutter looks out, with its thwarted life, its mighty hunger, its unfinished work. Its pale, vague lips seem to tremble with a terrible question. "Is this the End?" they say,—"nothing beyond?—no more?" Why, you tell me you have seen that look in the eyes of dumb brutes,—horses dying under the lash. I know.
>
> —"Life in the Iron Mills," 1861

At the close of **"Life in the Iron Mills,"** Rebecca Harding Davis's narrator stands at the window of an upper room in the house the Wolfes, a family of factory workers, once occupied. Formerly a collection of "kennel-like rooms" rented to half-a-dozen families (5), the house has been reclaimed by the middle class and transformed into a seemingly secure domestic space. Scattered around the room are "homely fragments" that confirm this transformation: a "half-molded child's head" and a sculpture of Aphrodite suggest love and motherhood; a "bough of forest-leaves" represents the taming and aestheticization of the natural world; an angel statue on the mantel introduces Christianity and moral authority (3, 34). The narrator's own idleness as she tells her story and the artistic tasks that await her are privileges of class that establish her economic security.[1] And her ability to articulate the Wolfes' frustration and oppression, her frequent assertions that "I know," establish her sympathetic but superior relationship to her tale.

The apparently secure position of this privileged sentimental narrator is precarious, however, for her home is located in the midst of the marketplace.[2] Her back window looks out over a "dirty" yard that is hemmed in by a "narrow brick-yard, strewed with rain-butts and tubs." Her front window looks out onto muddy streets through which the laborers "creep" on their way to and from "the great mills." She need not, or perhaps cannot,[3] go down into "the fog and mud and foul effluvia." Her class status protects her from this. But she cannot prevent the masses from entering her home. She hears their voices. She smells their tobacco. The air of her room is "thick, clammy with the breath of [these] crowded human beings." It is polluted as well by the smoke that is the breath of the mills. Even the wings of her angel statue are "covered with smoke, clotted and black." And lurking in the corner, partially concealed by a curtain, is the korl woman. Devoid of beauty or grace, carved from the refuse of the mills, this ugly, naked female body brings the "massed, vile, slimy lives" of the mill workers into the very room the narrator occupies, contaminating her domestic space with their hunger, sexuality, oppression, and exhaustion—contaminating, that is, sentimentalism with naturalism (3-4).

Located in "the borders of a Slave State" in 1861 (13), **"Life in the Iron Mills"** is written in the shadows of a great war, and it tells of the battle that raged between industrialism and domesticity, between the wage slave and his or her masters. The text is also a battlefield on which American literary naturalism and American sentimentalism struggle. Davis's project in **"Life in the Iron Mills"** is clearly sentimental; her text foregrounds female sympathy as it encourages readers to identify with and extend compassion to the industrial poor. It is only through the language of naturalism, however, that the story of the industrial poor can be told, and so naturalism and sentimentalism continually confront each other in this text. Sentimentalism's sympathy and optimism soften the naturalistic brutality of the Wolfes' story, in the same way the narrator's curtain conceals the korl woman. But just as this curtain is sometimes "accidentally drawn back," revealing a bare, imploring arm and a questioning face, naturalism's pessimistic determinism interrogates and challenges sentimentalism's "great hope" (4). This interrogation continues in other sentimental novels of the 1860s and 70s, in particular Davis's own *Margret Howth: A Story of To-day* (1862) and Elizabeth Stuart Phelps's *The Silent Partner* (1871).

How can this be? Naturalism this early in the century? Naturalism in texts written by women? Naturalism alongside sentimentalism? The suggestion will seem strange to those who accept the conventional definition of American literary naturalism—that it is a phenomenon of the 1890s, a European import, and a male genre; that it is sordid and dark, scientific and amoral; that its characters are bestial and its narrators detached. For the sentimental novel, written "by, for, and about women" (Tompkins 125), is set in the middle-class home rather than the tenement, and focuses on the family and domesticity, not the alienation of the individual in an industrial society. While naturalist narrators approach

their tales with irony, distancing themselves and their readers from their texts, sentimental narrators display sympathy, inviting their readers' engagement with their texts. While naturalist authors construct a godless universe controlled by powerful, unfeeling forces, sentimental authors present a world governed by moral laws and a merciful God.

The differences are striking, but sentimental texts are nevertheless peculiarly suited to be the birthplace of American literary naturalism for several reasons. First, sentimentalism's political project of boundary crossing, its desire to "effect connections across gender, race, and class" lines (Samuels 6), allows for the introduction of the kinds of monstrous, racialized, lower-class characters who people the landscape of naturalism. Prostitutes, drunks, disabled "freaks," madmen, and abusive husbands all make their appearance in sentimental texts. Second, sentimentalism's assertion that identity is dependent on the condition of the body introduces naturalism's fear of embodiment and biological determinism. As Karen Sanchez-Eppler states, "sentimental fiction constitutes an intensely bodily genre" (26). As a result, in sentimental fiction, "the recognition of ownership of one's body as essential to claiming personhood is matched by the fear of being imprisoned, silenced, deprived of personhood by that same body" (33). Third, sentimentalism's detailed description of material conditions—its effort to reproduce those conditions so accurately that its readers will be able to understand and experience characters' suffering—not only anticipates naturalism's journalistic style but also introduces naturalism's social and economic determinism. Philip Fisher, for instance, recognizes this in his reading of *Uncle Tom's Cabin*, for he notes that Stowe's portrayal of the material conditions of slavery leads readers to conclude that her characters' lives have been determined by the underlying economic system (122-26).

Finally, and most importantly, sentimentalism's uneasy marriage of reformism and resignation anticipates naturalism's inconsistency, its failure to sustain the pessimistic determinism that allegedly forms its ideological core. For the past fifty years, theorists of American literary naturalism have struggled to understand and account for naturalist authors' inability to produce a work of "pure" naturalism.[4] According to naturalist philosophy, human beings are devoid of free will and are acted upon by powerful forces which they can neither fully understand nor resist. The purpose of a naturalist text is to reveal the workings of these forces by describing, in an unimpassioned, scientific way, their effects upon the novel's characters. But few, if any, novelists actually achieve this ideal. Instead, they invest their characters with too much dignity, tell their stories with too much emotion, and slip into something which, as described by Malcolm Cowley, sounds remarkably like sentimentalism. "[M]ost of the naturalists are tender minded,"

Cowley says. "The sense of moral fitness is strong in them; they believe in their hearts that nature *should* be kind, that virtue *should* be rewarded on earth, that men *should* control their own destinies" (328). Naturalists thus taint their pessimistic determinism with impulses toward reform.

Similarly, sentimentalists seem to taint their reformism with an attitude of resignation. While sentimental narratives present benevolence as a "defining human virtue" (Howard, "Sentimentality" 70) and encourage readers to respond with compassionate action on behalf of the oppressed, they also suggest that submission, *not* an effort to change one's circumstances, is the proper response to suffering. Sentimental heroines rarely move beyond the confines of private, domestic space, and most of the action of sentimental novels takes place in the human heart (Tompkins 150). So while these heroines perform the kind of sympathetic identification with the oppressed that is encouraged in readers (Hendler 686), they, like Davis's narrator in **"Life in the Iron Mills,"** do not take action to bring about change. Justice, these novels suggest, is found only in the next world. The injustice of this world must simply be endured. In its subject matter, its thematics, and its marriage of reformism and determinism, sentimentalism thus anticipates naturalism,[5] a claim I will illustrate with close readings of both Davis's **Margret Howth** and Phelps's *The Silent Partner.*

Margret Howth is a young woman who goes to work as a bookkeeper in a mill in order to support her aging mother and blind, narcissistic father. Realizing that her former lover will soon own the mill, Margret is encouraged by Dr. Knowles, a family friend, to find her true life's calling, something "higher" than marriage, motherhood, or caring for her parents (70). He urges her to join him in establishing a utopian community of social outcasts—immigrants, former slaves, and prostitutes. But an apocalyptic fire in the mill injures her lover, and he recalls his devotion to Margret as he recovers his health. The novel ends with the discovery of oil on the Howths' otherwise barren land, and we are left to assume that the two young lovers will live happily ever after.

In contrast, the heroine of *The Silent Partner,* Perley Kelso, is the daughter of a wealthy manufacturer and, at the novel's opening, is engaged to the son of her father's business partner. But when her father dies, crushed by a train, Perley moves to Five Falls, the fictional New England town where her father's mills are located, and becomes interested in her father's business and employees. There, she befriends Sip Garth, a mill girl, and Sip's deaf-mute sister Catty. Although Perley's request to be named partner in the mills is summarily dismissed by her fiancé and his father, Perley nonetheless finds purposeful work to do in Five Falls. She breaks her engagement, retreats from "Society," and devotes herself to improving the life of the mill people, particularly that of Sip and Catty.

Summarized in this way, neither text seems a likely candidate for the earliest naturalist novel in America. In their subplots, however, we find greater evidence of these texts as naturalism's progenitors. June Howard suggests that in some naturalist texts, characters are constructed according to a variety of generic codes that are determined by the characters' class status: middle-class characters are sentimental, lower-class characters are naturalistic (*Form and History* 175-76).[6] Davis and Phelps anticipate this class/genre dualism. Margret and Perley are for the most part typical sentimental heroines,[7] but both befriend lower-class characters who inhabit worlds far different from their own. As Margret and especially Perley enter these worlds, they encounter naturalistic characters whose lives are determined by the powerful forces of biology and environment.

In **Margret Howth,** one such group of characters is presented to readers in a sort of naturalistic tableau. To reveal the life of the underclass in an industrial society, Dr. Knowles takes Margret to a run-down house on the edge of town. Anticipating Charles Child Walcutt, who saw in naturalism "the jungle at our back door, full of creatures who do not answer to the social norms" (130), Knowles calls this place "a bit of hell: outskirt" (149). Margret finds herself in one dark room

> swarming with human life. Women, idle trampers, whiskey-bloated, filthy, lay half-asleep, or smoking, on the floor, and set up a chorus of whining begging when [Margret and Dr. Knowles] entered. . . . In the corner slept a heap of half-clothed blacks, going on the underground railroad to Canada. Stolid, sensual wretches, with here and there a broad, melancholy brow, and desperate jaws. . . . "So much flesh and blood out of the market, unweighed!"
>
> (150-51)

While Davis assures us that this is "human life," these "creatures" can only whine, beg, and lie prostrate in alcohol or sleep-induced stupor. Their bodies, whether bloated or black, bear the marks of poverty, unemployment, and slavery. The escaped slaves have little hope of reaching freedom. The "swarming," directionless women will drink themselves to death, as has one who already lies dead in their midst.

Anticipating naturalism's objectivity and amorality, Knowles refuses to fault this mob for their condition, saying to Margret, "'Can they help it? Think of the centuries of serfdom and superstition through which their blood has crawled'" (151). In pointing to their helplessness in his attempt to defend them, Knowles also anticipates naturalism's dehumanization of the lower classes. His excusing them of moral responsibility robs them of moral agency. Incapable of making right choices, they are incapable of assuming meaningful social roles. Knowles thus asserts their worthlessness even as he tries to convince Margret to join him in his charitable venture, urging her to a life of reform even as he presents these lives as "unreformable."

If initially Knowles blames the condition of these people on historical determinism—years of poverty and enslavement—eventually he turns to biological explanations. For after failing miserably in his effort to educate the children of the "dregs" he concludes, ". . . there's a good deal of an obstacle in blood. I find difficulty, much difficulty . . . in giving to the youngest child true ideas of absolute freedom, and unselfish heroism" (187). Knowles suggests that for these characters, as Lars Åhnebrink writes of Émile Zola's, "the outcome of life was usually hopeless sorrow, sometimes stolid resignation; often there was no other end than annihilation" (Åhnebrink 28).

This fleeting glimpse Davis gives us into a naturalistic underworld is less significant, however, than the more fully developed naturalistic portrait she provides in the person of Lois, a friend of Margret's whom Walcutt might recognize as one of his "little monsters" (129).[8] Lois's monstrous body is emphasized from the first. She is introduced as "hopelessly crippled" (54), and we are told that "some deformity of her legs," probably caused by a vitamin deficiency, "made her walk with a curiously rolling jerk" (55). Her head is "misshapen" as well, and her face scarred (168). As if to accentuate her crippled body, Davis also gives her a damaged huckster's cart—a cart that "went jolting along in such a careless, jolly way, as if it would not care in the least, should it go to pieces any minute just there in the road"—as well as a disabled donkey who is "bony and blind of one eye" (53). She is a creature whom "Nature had thrown impatiently aside as a failure, so marred, imperfect, that even the dogs were kind to her" (64).

Her damaged body is matched by a damaged brain. Though the nature of her mental disability is unclear, its source is unquestionably the mill. She had worked in the mill for only nine years, but she tells Margret, "''T seemed longer to me 'n 't was. 'T seemed as if I'd been there allus,—jes forever, yoh know'" (68). She goes on to say:

> "I kind o' grew into that place in them years: seemed to me like as I was part o' th' engines, somehow. . . . 'T got so that th' noise o' th' looms went on in my head night 'n' day,—allus thud, thud. 'N' hot days, when th' hands was chaffin' 'n' singin', the black wheels 'n' rollers was alive, starin' down at me, 'n' th' shadders o' th' looms was like snakes creepin',— creepin' anear all th' time."
>
> (68-69)

The sexual imagery of this passage and Lois's suggestion that she had become a part of the machinery of the mill indicates that she is a product of industry. She was forced by her health to leave the mill at age sixteen, but not before the "slow years of ruin" had "eaten into her brain" (69). And so she still fears the mill, recognizing it as a threatening presence in her life:

> The mill,—even now, with the vague dread of some uncertain evil to come, the mill absorbed all fear in its old hated shadow. Whatever danger was coming to them lay in it, came from it, she knew, in her confused, blurred way of thinking. It loomed up now, with the square patch of ashen sky above, black, heavy with years of remembered agony and loss. . . . Her crushed brain, her unwakened powers, resented their wrong dimly to the mass of iron and work and impure smells, unconscious of any remorseless power that wielded it.
>
> (170-71)

In Lois's eyes, the mill is "a monster that kept her wakeful with a dull mysterious terror" (171). This monstrous place in part produced her monstrous body.

While Lois suggests both the destructive power of industry and the restrictive nature of embodiment, it is not only against these forces that she struggles, for as in **"Life in the Iron Mills,"** *Margret Howth* is "written from the border of the battlefield" (3), and so surrounding industry is slavery. As the child of a former slave, Lois struggles against "all the tainted blood in her veins of centuries of slavery and heathenism [that are] trying to drag her down" (69). And just as she has been "ruined" by industry, her father, Joe Yare, has been ruined by slavery. Though he is a thief and an escaped convict, we are warned against judging Joe too harshly. He says in his own defense, "'Who taught me what was right? Who cared? No man cared fur my soul, till I thieved 'n' robbed; 'n' then judge 'n' jury 'n' jailers was glad to pounce on me.'" (166). Davis adds,

> There was not much in the years gone to soften his thought, as it grew desperate and cruel: there was oppression and vice heaped on him, and flung back out of his bitter heart. Nor much in the future; a blank stretch of punishment to the end. . . . What if he were black? what if he were born a thief? what if all the sullen revenge of his nature had made him an outcast from the poorest poor? Was there no latent good in this soul for which Christ died, that a kind hand might not have brought to life?
>
> (167)

Through Joe, naturalism confronts the social gospel of sentimentalism. In keeping with sentimentalism, Davis suggests that Joe is innately good and lays the responsibility for his behavior on the "absence of a kind hand" to bring that goodness to life. Instead, a mysterious "wrong done to his soul in a day long past" rankles in Joe and drives him to add arson and attempted murder to his long list of crimes (168). Davis uses Joe to warn readers about the consequences of their own apathy, but society is not solely to blame, for Davis also points to Joe's race, suggests that he was "born" into vice, and indicates that he had inherited a sullen, revengeful soul. Joe shares Lois's "tainted blood," and, like Knowles's wretches, struggles against both heredity and history.

Though she shares his blood, Lois does not share her father's moral corruption. Like Crane's Maggie, she is able to rise above her surroundings, to recognize and create beauty from filth.[9] To a degree, Lois transcends naturalism, particularly in her redemptive death. Late one night, Joe sets a fire in the mill in an attempt to kill the mill owner, Stephen Holmes, who has threatened to return Joe to prison. Lois sees the fire, realizes her father is responsible, breathes in deadly fumes while rescuing Holmes, and dies as a result. Her sacrificial death inspires Holmes's mercy and secures a second chance for her father. But Davis still insists that the sins committed by and against Lois's father are visited on the daughter. It is Joe who sets the fire that kills Lois, and Davis declares that the wrong done to Joe was "a wrong done to both . . . *irreparable,* and *neuver to be recompensed*" (168; emphasis added). Using the language of naturalism, Davis indicates that both Lois and Joe are shaped and destroyed by biological and environmental forces much more powerful than they.

In *The Silent Partner,* Phelps continues this naturalistic investigation of the effects of "blood" and industry on the lower classes. Like Davis, her conclusions are bleak. Drawing her story from the pages of the Report of the Massachusetts Bureau of the Statistics of Labor,[10] Phelps describes with almost journalistic precision the stifling atmosphere of the mills, the smelly dampness of the tenements, and the inadequacy of the mill workers' food and clothing. This detailed documentation of urban and tenement life will become a standard of literary naturalism. Like Davis, Phelps also portrays the mill machinery as monsters and describes their power not only to silence the mill girls by "crunching" their songs (75-76) but also to crush the body of a young boy whose clothing gets caught in their "teeth" (170). And as in Davis, the monstrous mills produce monstrous people. Phelps suggests this partly through references to the animalism of the lower classes. One child laborer crawls up the stairs on his way to work "on 'all fours,' so much, so very much, like a little puppy!" (212). Another lies "curled up like a skulking dog" on the steps of a building (118). Phelps also points to the disfigured bodies of the mill workers, the "peculiar bleached yellow faces" of many of the mill women (119), the dyed yellow hands of the mill men (166), and the tendency of some workers, in the heat of the mills, to turn "black" as the blood gathers in their faces (232).

Catty, one of the mill women befriended by Perley Kelso, provides the most striking example of monstros-ity. Her body has been destroyed by industry. Deafened by the great wheels of the mills while still in the womb, deformed by her labor, eventually blinded by a disease she contracts while picking cotton, Catty is both senseless and "repulsive" (96). She hears nothing but the noise of the great wheels of the mills which constantly "beat about in her head" (96). Her speech resembles the "snarl" of "an annoyed animal" (150). And she is "[a]n ugly girl,—a very ugly girl," so ugly, in fact, that Phelps describes her to readers as though she were an exhibit in a traveling freak show: "Look at her; it is a very loathsome under lip. Look well at her; they are not pleasant eyes" (88). "Walled up and walled in from that labyrinth of sympathies, that difficult evolution of brain from beast, the gorgeous peril of that play at good and evil which we call life" (86), Catty is hardly human.

Her behavior is as monstrous as her body. She drinks, she runs wild in the streets, and, Sip, Catty's sister, tells Perley, "worse," suggesting sexual promiscuity (84). Sip insists that Catty is not to blame, for she has had no one to teach her right from wrong (197), but Phelps suggests that Catty is nonetheless "corrupt," even beyond redemption. Describing Catty's death scene, Phelps writes:

> It was too late for dear love to touch her. Its piteous call she could not hear. Its wrung face she could not see. Her poor, puzzled lips moved as if to argue with it, but made no sound. Type of the world from which she sprang,—the world of exhausted and corrupted body, of exhausted and corrupted brain, of exhausted and corrupted soul, the world of the laboring poor as man has made it, and as Christ has died for it, of a world *deaf, dumb, blind, doomed,* stepping confidently to its own destruction before our eyes.
>
> (277-78; emphasis added)

Through Catty, Phelps links damnation with disability, conflates both with poverty, and locates their source in industrialization.

Even more powerful than industry, however, is the economic discourse of the mills. Borrowing from Davis's **"Life in the Iron Mills,"** Phelps develops the idea expressed by Kirby, a visitor to the mill, that workers would be better off if they could be reduced to machine-like hands, untroubled by thoughts, ambitions, and emotions. "'If I had the making of these men,'" says Kirby, "'these men who do the lowest part of the world's work should be machines,—nothing more,—hands. It would be kindness. God help them! What are taste, reason, to creatures who must live such lives as that?'" Addressing the mill employees, Phelps echoes Davis's text, saying, "Hayle and Kelso label you. There you are. The world thinks, aspires, creates, enjoys. There you are. You are the fingers of the world. You take your patient place. The world may have need of you, but only that it may think, aspire, create, enjoy" (71). The mill owners, exercising their class privilege, have developed a discourse that assigns physicality to the lower classes and reserves disembodiment for the wealthy.[11] In *The Body in Pain*, Elaine Scarry explains that "to be intensely embodied is the equivalent of being unrepresented" (201) while disembodiment is associated with power, voice, and control. This discourse of "heads" and "hands" thus insures the disempowerment and voicelessness of the mill workers.

Catty provides graphic visual representation of this discourse, for she is all "hands." Her "long, lithe, magnetic fingers" are her defining feature (86). The other mill employees, however, are equally embodied and therefore disempowered. Phelps makes this evident when the workers threaten to strike in response to a wage reduction. She writes:

> There is something noteworthy about this term "strike." A head would think and outwit us. A heart shall beat and move us. The "hands" can only struggle and strike us,—foolishly too, and madly, here and there, and desperately, being ill-trained hands, never at so much as a boxing school, and gashing each other principally in the contest.
>
> (245)

As defined by the ruling economic discourse, the "hands" lack reason, emotion, voice, and discipline. They are violent, foolish, and self-destructive. Like Catty, they are rendered senseless by industry and are powerless to change their situation.

The powerlessness, poverty, and embodiment of Davis's and Phelps's naturalistic characters introduce many of the fears to which later naturalists were said to be responding in their work: fear of physicality and a resulting vulnerability to biology and environment; fear of helplessness in the face of powerful social and economic forces. In order to defuse the fears these characters embody, Phelps and Davis, like later naturalists, deliberately distance them from readers. In later naturalist texts, this distancing is accomplished largely through irony. As Cowley explains, "There is something superior and ultimately tiresome in the attitude of many naturalists toward the events they describe. Irony—like pity, its companion—is a spectator's emotion, and it sets a space between ourselves and the characters in the novel" (332). Phelps and Davis do not employ the same kind of irony. Their narrative stance tends to be sentimental and therefore engaging. But their sentimental appeals for sympathy, forgiveness, or rescue on behalf of their characters place readers in an equally "superior" position.

Later naturalist authors also distance characters from themselves and their readers by conflating brutishness with physical, moral, racial, and economic "deviance." Their characters, who are poor, weak, and unsophisti-

cated to begin with (Pizer 86), are frequently described using such racially charged terms as primitive, slime, savage, brutal, and instinct (Cowley 319). Naturalist authors often project images of violence, sexuality, and drunkenness onto their characters as well (Howard, *Form and History* 79), resulting in the absolute alienation of these characters from naturalism's white, middle-class, able-bodied Christian readers. Phelps and Davis anticipate these distancing techniques in their novels, demonstrating through their portrayals of Catty and Lois how the fears invoked by naturalism could be neutralized.

Davis heaps "deviance" onto Lois. Physically and mentally disabled, part African American, and "wretchedly low in the social scale" (54), Lois is thoroughly debased. Even her soul, Davis tells readers, is "lower, it might be, than ours, lay closer to nature, knew the language of the changing day, of these earnest-faced hills, of the very worms crawling through the brown mould" (65). According to Jean Pfaelzer, this passage demonstrates Emerson's influence on Davis, for Lois is a nature scholar who can "read" God in her surroundings and so know Him directly (71). But Davis may also be demonstrating the influence of Darwinian theory, for even before the American publication of *The Origin of Species* in 1860, people began using Herbert Spencer's evolutionary theory to establish racial hierarchy.[12] Davis's assertion that Lois's soul is "lower" than "ours" certainly engages such a hierarchy and assures readers of their privileged racial position. Her suggestion that Lois "lay" closer to nature invites images of prostration before a higher order of beings. Lois's ability to understand the language of the "worms crawling through the brown mould" implies that she cannot walk erect, that she belongs to a "primitive" species, and that she is mired in dirt. Lois's debasement—social, physical, mental, and racial—arouses in everyone, including readers, "an undefined sense of pride in protecting this wretch whose portion of life was more meagre and low than theirs" (77). She lends readers confidence, making them feel strong, wise, capable, and white.

Catty is even more distanced from readers, for as was mentioned earlier, Phelps compounds Catty's disabilities and poverty with immorality. Phelps also draws more heavily than Davis on Darwinian views of race and class, for as Rosemarie Garland Thomson suggests, Catty is animalistic, even simian in appearance (576).[13] Catty's "low forehead," the "dull stoop" of her head, her "thick, drooping upper lip," and her "long, lithe, magnetic fingers" suggest racial "inferiority" even as they qualify her for display as a "missing link" (86). In fact, she closely resembles the subject of P. T. Barnum's "What Is It?" exhibit put on display in New York in 1860. The subject of this exhibit was a mentally handicapped African American man. Rather than identify him as such, Barnum invited audiences to decide for themselves what "it" was. No viewer, however, seemed to question "its" racial origin; indeed, every newspaper account discussing the exhibit assumed "it" must be African (Cook 152). A major reason for this was the man's low forehead, which was considered distinctly African. In Barnum's words, "The upper part of the head and the forehead in particular, instead of being four or five inches broad, *as it should be, to resemble that of a human being,* is Less Than Two Inches!" (qtd. in Cook 148). Though she is never identified as African American, Catty's low forehead, "ape-like" fingers, and "thick" lips distance her from white readers. "Walled up and walled in" from society by her physical, moral, social, and racial "deviance" (86), Catty, like Lois, assures readers that she is the "monster," not them.

In *Margret Howth* and *The Silent Partner,* however, the effort to distance readers from naturalistic characters such as Lois and Catty is complicated by a sentimental movement toward sympathy, identification, and reform.[14] Philip Fisher explains that the sentimental novel "depends on experimental, even dangerous, extensions of the self of the reader." Sentimental authors extend normalcy and normal states of feeling to people to whom these traits have been denied, and in so doing, they extend full humanity to "others" (98). Readers of these novels are thus encouraged to look beyond the bodies of characters, the outward markers that differentiate us from them, and to identify with people from other social categories. In fact, sentimentalism attempts to transcend the body and biological markers altogether, locating identity elsewhere—in "the (feminized) heart"—thus denying the importance of external differences (Clark 22). As Shirley Samuels says, readers of sentimental novels are asked to make "connections across gender, race, and class boundaries" (6). This sentimental project is achieved in varying degrees in the works of Davis and Phelps, but its influence is always evident, and the result is a movement toward identification with naturalistic characters who are at the same time distanced from readers in all the ways described above.

As noted earlier, however, Davis and Phelps prefigure naturalism even in this sentimental moment. June Howard explains that though brutish characters are clearly represented as "others" in naturalist works, they are always reflections or doubles of the author's white, middle-class self, demonstrating the precariousness and fragility of the secure position that naturalist authors attempt to establish for themselves and their readers (*Form and History* 101). Donald Pizer also notes that distance between the self and other, author and character, is seldom sustained in naturalism:

> *Compassion* for the fallen, *hope* of betterment for the lot of the oppressed, bitterness toward the *remediable* which lies unremedied—all the *emotions* which derive from a writer's sense that he is not a dispassionate ob-

server of a scientific process but instead an imaginative presence infusing dignity and a sense of tragic potential into what he observes—create a living *engagement* between artist and subject matter that results in a fullness and complexity of expression rather than an emotionally sterile portrait of "forces at work."

(20, emphasis added)

Using the vocabulary of sentimentalism, Pizer explains that naturalist authors frequently fail to adhere to the role of objective observer, and as they cease to be spectators, characters cease to be spectacles and become more fully human. As this happens, barriers between self and other are broken down, and the forces that work on "them" are seen as forces that work on "us."

In *Margret Howth,* this movement toward identification arises at the very end of the novel when Lois reveals emotional and sexual desires that tie her to readers, particularly female readers. From her deathbed, Lois observes the interaction of a young neighborhood couple, Jenny and Sam. They are to be married soon, and Jenny has come to show Lois her wedding dress:

> The poor deformed girl lay watching them, as they talked. Very pretty Jenny looked, with her blue eyes and damp pink cheeks; and it was a manly, grave love in Sam's face, when it turned to her. A different love from any she [Lois] had known: better, she thought. It could not be helped; but it *was* better. After they were gone, she lay a long time quiet, with her hand over her eyes. Forgive her! she, too, was a woman.

(258)

Davis's insistence that "she, *too,* was a woman" indicates her belief that in this one emotion, if in no other, readers might find some way to identify with Lois, an otherwise "otherized" character. The absence of a man's love and the loneliness of a spinster can be understood by all women, those with blue eyes and pink cheeks as well as those with "black" blood and "crooked" legs.[15]

In *The Silent Partner,* Phelps also encourages her readers to identify with naturalistic characters through their shared understanding of spinsterhood. Unlike Lois, Sip has opportunity to marry—the night watchman for Hayle and Kelso proposes to her. But Sip refuses him, saying, "I'll never bring children into this world to be factory children, and to be factory boys and girls, and to be factory men and women, and to see the sights I've seen, and to bear the things I've borne. . . . They'd never get out of the mills. It's from generation to generation. It couldn't be helped. I know. It's in the blood" (287-88). Naturalism is evident even in this sentimental moment, for Sip's statement confirms the power of industry, conflates social and biological determinism, and sees no solution to oppression but voluntary extinction. Still, Phelps follows this statement by inviting readers to recognize Sip's humanity: "Sip had

. . . a 'large share of human nature,' and she loved Dirk, and she led a lonely life. She was neither a heroine, nor a saint, nor a fanatic . . ." (290). She was simply a woman, Phelps implies, with emotions, desires, and tears that Phelps's readers can understand.

Perley can understand, and she models the sympathy Phelps desires from her readers. Perley shares Sip's singleness, choosing not to marry a devoted man and a "good" match because he does not share her interest in reform. Sip and Perley share other ties as well, for both women lost their mothers as children, and their fathers were both crushed by machinery. Their shared enslavement to the ruling economic discourse, however, ties them most closely together, for the discourse of "heads" and "hands" that so powerfully determines Sip's and Catty's existence also determines Perley's. As a member of the moneyed classes, Perley is a "head," but the label is far from empowering. It has essentially disabled Perley by denying her the use of her hands. From the first, Phelps draws our attention to Perley's white, creamy, listless hands. She tells us, in fact, that Perley's hand has "—rings" and in doing so, immediately indicates her powerlessness (10). As Judith Fetterley says, "The hand might have had fingers—strong capable ones, or weak listless ones, or nervous restless ones; instead it has '—rings,' and in having '—rings' it is had" (19). Perley's hands are not her own, and they bear the mark of male domination in the form of a ring.

Phelps again indicates the powerlessness of Perley's hands later in the novel when Perley requests to be made a partner. Mr. Hayle treats her request with condescension and quickly dismisses it as foolish, but Perley's fiancé Maverick, junior partner in the mill, drifts away from the conversation, ignoring her request altogether, and studies her hands. He draws the conclusion that "Story,[16] the next time he was in the country, should make a study of a hand upon squares of gray and green" (56). Later in the conversation, he occupies himself by "making little faces on Perley's pink, shell-like nails with the pencil" (60). Through these seemingly idle actions, Maverick demonstrates his conviction that Perley's hands are incapable of employment and her body unfit for the kind of work she desires. Perley's hands are "tied" (141) by a fiancé who, whenever she expresses a desire for an occupation, "fold[s] her two hands like sheets of rice-paper over his own, with an easy smile" (13); and by a discourse that aestheticizes her hands, making them objets d'art rather than useful, powerful parts of her body. This "disability" establishes a bond between Perley, Sip, and Catty that challenges the barriers of race, class, and embodiment.[17]

Phelps and Davis thus encourage the kind of sentimental identification between characters and readers that often complicates naturalism. However, they consummate this impulse toward identification by providing their naturalistic characters with sentimental endings not found in later naturalist texts.[18] In so doing, they seem to lose sight of their naturalistic vision. Like Little Eva's in *Uncle Tom's Cabin,* Lois's death in **Margret Howth** is steeped in Christian symbolism: she dies to save her father from the consequences of his sin (starting a fire in the factory); she runs through hellish flames to rescue a man who does not deserve her mercy, for he has shown no mercy to others; she forgives her father for his sin and begs for forgiveness on his behalf (211). Her Christlike sacrifice is justly rewarded, for as she dies, "a strange calm, unknown before, stole over her face; her eyes flashed open with a living joy." Davis assures us, "The cripple was dead; but *Lois,* free, loving, and beloved, trembled from her prison to her Master's side in the To-Morrow" (262). Lois does not share Little Eva's beauty, but she does share her frailty, her childlike faith, and her triumphant parting.

As noted above, Catty's death scene is more problematic than Lois's, for Phelps implies that Catty may be beyond redemption. At the end of the novel, however, Phelps counters this implication by suggesting that Catty, like Lois, has found freedom and wholeness in death, for somehow she has found a voice:

> Passed into the great world of signs, the deaf-mute, dead, grew grandly eloquent. The ring of the flood was her solemn kiss. The sunshine on the kitchen floor tomorrow would be her dear good-morning. Clouds and shadows and springing green gave her speech forever. The winds of long nights were language for her. Ah, the ways, the ways which Catty could find to speak . . . !
>
> (279-80)

Through death, Catty becomes a "head," a disembodied voice who is "eloquent," "solemn," and "dear." She is purified through her alignment with nature and nature's God (292). She is a character with whom readers might identify after all.

In *Sensational Designs,* Jane Tompkins argues that this sort of sentimental ending enacts a theory of power in which the innocent victim is granted the capacity to change the world through her redemptive death (128-30). In contrast, naturalism's pessimistic determinism does not allow for innocence, redemption, or change, and the naturalist novel generally ends in despair. However, Davis and Phelps give us glimpses of naturalism even in their sentimental endings, for they imply that there is no way out for their naturalistic characters but through death. They offer hope of a great hereafter, but they suggest that the here and now cannot be changed, and in their texts, little does change for their naturalistic characters. **"Life in the Iron Mills"** takes place thirty years after Hugh Wolfe's death, but the ironworkers still creep through muddy streets, and the korl woman's question remains unasked and unanswered. Nothing has changed. At the end of **Margret Howth,** "poor old Knowles" is "bewildered at the inexplicable failure" of his charitable cause. He "doubts everything in the bitterness of wasted effort," and Davis acknowledges the bleakness of her text, saying, "My story is but a mere groping hint? It lacks determined truth, a certain yea and nay? It has no conduit of God's justice running through it, awarding apparent good and ill? I know: it is a story of To-Day" (264). Nothing can change for Knowles's "wretches" until "To-Morrow."

In *The Silent Partner,* Perley tries to take Sip out of the mills by finding her a new occupation, but Sip fails as a cook, a nursemaid, a waitress, a seamstress, a clerk, and a printer, and returns to her loom. "'I told you it was no use,'" Sip says to Perley. "'It's too late. What am I fit for? Nothing. What do I know? Nothing. I weave; that's all. I'm used to that. I'm used to the noise and the running about. I'm used to the dirt and the roughness. . . . It's too late. I'm spoiled. I knew I should come back. My father and mother came back before me. It's in the blood'" (199-200). Perley can establish libraries, relief societies, schools, lectures, and reading rooms for the mill's employees (133), but she cannot counter the forces of history and heredity. So nothing changes for Sip, and nothing changes for the mill hands—not in this world anyway.

Davis and Phelps suggest that reform is desirable, but in the depiction of their lower-class characters, they imply that "it's too late." This tension between reformism and determinism, hope and despair, is the tension of naturalism. In the texts of Davis and Phelps, sentimental hope generally triumphs over naturalistic despair. In later naturalist texts, despair is often the victor. The struggle, however, is the same, and its birthplace is the sentimental novel.

Notes

1. There has been some debate concerning the gender of Davis's narrator. Some critics choose to read the narrator of "Life in the Iron Mills" as male—see, for example, Jane Atteridge Rose. Kirk Curnutt insists that the narrator's gender cannot be determined and that Davis deliberately creates an androgynous storyteller (150). Like the majority of Davis critics, however, I read the narrator as female. Though Davis never refers to the narrator as "she," Davis surrounds her with symbols of domesticity and motherhood—the child's head, the angel on the mantelpiece. Davis's narrator also possesses the peculiarly feminine trait of sympathy, and she demands of her readers that they, too, sympathize with the plight of the Wolfes and temper their judgment of the Wolfes' actions with mercy, another feminine trait. The narrator's identification with Deb, the korl woman, and the femi-

nized Hugh Wolfe provides further evidence of her own femininity. Finally, the narrator tells her story while standing at her window, looking out—a typical pose for a female subject in the paintings and illustrations of the time.

2. See Mark Seltzer's discussion of the marketplace in "Life in the Iron Mills" in "The Still Life."

3. Jean Pfaelzer suggests that Davis's female narrator is trapped in her domestic space, which is as "defined" and "enclosed" as the hovels of the ironworkers. "Unlike a roaming male narrator," Pfaelzer writes, "this woman is physically constrained by her gender. . . . Hence, although the narrator boasts that her 'eyes are free to look deeper' (5), Davis surrounds her with images of containment and repression" (28). Although Pfaelzer argues against a naturalistic reading of "Life in the Iron Mills," her discussion of the narrator acknowledges naturalistic images of entrapment and imprisonment in Davis's text.

4. June Howard notes that for the past fifty years, naturalism has consistently been associated with pessimistic determinism but that the "next most frequently made observation about naturalism must surely be that it is *not* pessimistic determinism" (*Form and History* 36). Critics often find inconsistency in naturalist texts, a failure to follow through with the naturalistic agenda. This failure has been accounted for in many ways. Malcolm Cowley feels that American naturalists were too "tender-minded" and could not conceal their personal grief and anger in their texts (328). Charles Child Walcutt insists that no one could produce a coherent naturalist text, for the act of writing is "an exercise of creative intelligence which in itself denies what [the novelist] may be saying about the futility of life and the folly of man" (29). He also locates the source of naturalism's inconsistency in American transcendentalism. Donald Pizer and Lars Åhnebrink find traces of the romantic spirit in naturalist texts, particularly in the American naturalists' refusal to concede that life is meaningless. "While the naturalist novel does reflect a vast skepticism about the conventional attributes of experience," Pizer writes, "it also affirms the significance and worth of the seeking temperament, of the character who continues to look for meaning in experience even though there is probably no meaning" to be found (24). June Howard, on the other hand, looks not to the literary traditions that preceded American naturalism but to the historical moment that produced it. She identifies the antinomies of "this moment of naturalism"—the 1890s—as "human effort and determining forces," or "the human and the brutal" (*Form and History* 69). According to Howard,

the contemporary philosophical struggle between these concepts is embodied in the pages of naturalist texts, resulting in a form defined by dynamic opposition rather than consistent adherence to a single concept, such as pessimistic determinism.

5. For at least a half-century, readers of Davis have hailed her as a pioneer in the development of American literary realism and naturalism. In 1951, for example, Bernard Bowron claimed that Davis "pioneered in . . . the literature of industrialism, critically concerned with contemporary social problems, which would ultimately give rise to American naturalism" (qtd. in Yellin 274). Sandra Gilbert and Susan Gubar in *The Norton Anthology of Literature by Women* write of "Life in the Iron Mills," "Some six years before the French novelist Émile Zola began publishing what were called 'naturalistic' novels, a thirty-year-old Virginian had brilliantly dramatized the socioeconomic implications of environmental determinism" (903). And Sharon Harris, in *Rebecca Harding Davis and American Realism,* examines in more depth the role Davis played in ushering in the age of realism and naturalism in American letters. (See also Jean Pfaelzer, "Rebecca Harding Davis: Domesticity, Social Order, and the Industrial Novel," *International Journal of Women's Studies* 4 [1981]: 234-44.) These readers do not, however, look beyond Davis to posit a broader relationship between sentimentalism and naturalism. Rather, they view Davis's industrial texts as remarkable anomalies of mid-nineteenth-century American women's literature.

Those scholars who have begun to examine the connections between sentimentalism and naturalism rarely reference Phelps's work. In *Hard Facts,* for example, Philip Fisher discusses the conflation of sentimental and naturalistic motifs in *Uncle Tom's Cabin* and argues that naturalism grows out of both sentimentalism and regionalism—another female literary tradition of the American nineteenth century. Donna Campbell, in *Resisting Regionalism,* offers a more thorough defense of this latter claim, arguing that American male naturalist authors deliberately defined themselves against what they viewed as overly feminine regionalist writing even as they borrowed significantly from the tradition. A lengthy study of the relationship between sentimentalism and naturalism, particularly in the industrial fiction of Davis, Phelps, and their contemporaries, thus remains to be done.

6. In *Form and History in the American Novel,* Howard claims that most naturalist novels contain a variety of competing narrative strategies, including the "domestic formula," or sentimentalism. However, she does not see sentimentalism as a starting point for American naturalism. Rather, she presents sentimentalism as either a crutch that naturalists sometimes "fall back on" (177) or a set of conventions against which naturalists define themselves: "In naturalism the conventionalized image of the domestic space becomes an enclave that can never seem wholly safe, for it is penetrated by the very impulses that are attributed to the wild man outside the campfire and is only tenuously independent of the pitiless economic jungle that looms outside the hearth" (181).

7. The typical sentimental heroine is a genteel, white, liberal, sympathetic orphan. As Glenn Hendler explains, she is also "feminine: other oriented, selfless, and emotionally tied to those who have helped her or who need help" (686). She models for readers the sympathy and identification that sentimental texts encourage. At the end of the novel, she is rewarded for her behavior with marriage or an equally intimate familial relationship.

8. In discussing the characters of Frank Norris's novels, Walcutt writes, "The assemblage of big and little monsters creates a sense of sociological extremes—of people or creatures who have to be in a new dimension of Darwinian thought rather than in the established frames of social conformity and orientation" (129).

9. In *Margret Howth,* Lois is said to possess an artist's sense. She is a "born colourist" who arranges the contents of her cart as though arranging colors on a canvas (110). Like Hugh Wolfe in "Life in the Iron Mills," Lois's artistry allows her to "rise above the level of her daily life" (94). The respite that her art provides, however, is temporary. She, like Hugh, is still mired in drudgery.

10. Phelps's note at the beginning of *The Silent Partner* reads, "I desire it to be understood that every alarming sign and every painful statement which I have given in these pages concerning the condition of the manufacturing districts could be matched with far less cheerful reading, and with far more pungent perplexities, from the pages of the Report of the Massachusetts Bureau of the Statistics of Labor, to which, with other documents of a kindred nature, and to the personal assistance of friends who have 'testified that they have seen,' I am deeply in debt for the ribs of my story."

11. For a discussion of the relationship between class and embodiment in Davis's "Life in the Iron Mills," see Mark Seltzer's *Bodies and Machines.*

12. For a discussion of the influence of theories of evolution on nineteenth-century American literature, see Ronald Martin's *American Literature and the Universe of Force* and Richard Hofstadter's *Social Darwinism in American Thought.*

13. Phelps makes several direct references to Darwinian theory in her 1882 novel *Doctor Zay*. Her heroine both refers to Darwin's theory of natural selection (98) and recommends that another character read one of Darwin's books on plant life (103).

14. In her afterword to *Margret Howth*, Jean Fagin Yellin traces the inconsistencies of the novel to its publishing history and contends that were it not for James Fields's insistence that Davis make her text less "gloomy" (289), *Margret Howth* would have presented a darker, more evenly sustained vision of industrialism and the underclass. Yellin finds the published novel's conclusion "hard to accept," for it attempts an "impossible transformation from scarcity to abundance" and an "equally impossible transformation from a narrative that presents itself as a self-conscious critique of conventional fiction to a narrative that presents itself within fictional convention" (286, 292). One wonders how much more naturalistic *Margret Howth* might have been had Davis not been required to make her text less despairing.

15. Davis makes a similar appeal to readers in "Life in the Iron Mills," suggesting that Deb Wolfe's look of "apathy" and "vacancy," a result of her unreciprocated love for Hugh, should be familiar to all women. Davis writes, "One sees that dead, vacant look steal sometimes over the rarest, finest of women's faces,—in the very midst, it may be, of their warmest summer's day; and then one can guess at the secret of intolerable solitude that lies hid beneath the delicate laces and brilliant smile" (9).

16. The reference is to William Westmore Story, nineteenth-century American sculptor.

17. In *The Silent Partner*, Phelps's use of the body of the wage slave to highlight the oppression of wealthy white women is similar to feminists' and abolitionists' use of the body of the slave woman. For a discussion of the slave body in feminist and abolitionist texts, see Karen Sanchez-Eppler's *Touching Liberty*, pp. 15-48.

18. According to Glenn Hendler, sentimental texts end either in marriage or in the restoration of the family. Often this involves a redefinition of the traditional family unit in which blood ties matter less than truly sympathetic relationships (686-87). Davis ends *Margret Howth* with Margret's marriage. Phelps concludes *The Silent Partner* by establishing a kind of sisterhood between Sip and Perley.

Works Cited

Åhnebrink, Lars. *The Beginnings of Naturalism in American Fiction*. Cambridge: Harvard UP, 1950.

Campbell, Donna M. *Resisting Regionalism: Gender and Naturalism in American Fiction, 1885-1915*. Athens: Ohio UP, 1997.

Clark, Suzanne. *Sentimental Modernism: Women Writers and the Revolution of the Word*. Bloomington: Indiana UP, 1991.

Cook, James W. "Of Men, Missing Links, and Nondescripts: The Strange Career of P. T. Barnum's 'What Is It?' Exhibition." *Freakery: Cultural Spectacles of the Extraordinary Body*. Ed. Rosemarie Garland Thomson. New York: New York UP, 1996. 139-57.

Cowley, Malcolm. "Naturalism in American Literature." *Evolutionary Thought in America*. Ed. Stow Persons. New Haven: Yale UP, 1950. 213-333.

Curnutt, Kirk. "Direct Addresses, Narrative Authority, and Gender in Rebecca Harding Davis's 'Life in the Iron Mills.'" *Style* 28 (1994): 146-68.

Davis, Rebecca Harding. "Life in the Iron Mills." *A Rebecca Harding Davis Reader*. Ed. Jean Pfaelzer. Pittsburgh: U of Pittsburgh P, 1995. 3-34.

———. *Margret Howth: A Story of Today*. New York: Feminist Press, 1990.

Fetterley, Judith. "'Checkmate': Elizabeth Stuart Phelps's *The Silent Partner*." *Legacy* 3.2 (1986): 17-30.

Fisher, Philip. *Hard Facts: Setting and Form in the American Novel*. New York: Oxford UP, 1985.

Gilbert, Sandra, and Susan Gubar. *The Norton Anthology of American Literature: The Tradition in English*. New York: Norton, 1985.

Harris, Sharon. *Rebecca Harding Davis and American Realism*. Philadelphia: U of Pennsylvania P, 1991.

Hendler, Glenn. "The Limits of Sympathy: Louisa May Alcott and the Sentimental Novel." *American Literary History* 3.4 (1991): 685-706.

Hofstadter, Richard. *Social Darwinism in American Thought, 1860-1915*. Philadelphia: U of Pennsylvania P, 1945.

Howard, June. *Form and History in American Literary Naturalism*. Chapel Hill: U of North Carolina P, 1985.

———. "What Is Sentimentality?" *American Literary History* 11.1 (1999): 63-79.

Martin, Ronald. *American Literature and the Universe of Force*. Durham: Duke UP, 1981.

Pfaelzer, Jean. *Parlor Radical: Rebecca Harding Davis and the Origins of American Social Realism*. Pittsburgh: U of Pittsburgh P, 1996.

Phelps, Elizabeth Stuart. *Doctor Zay*. New York: Feminist Press, 1987.

———. *The Silent Partner and "The Tenth of January."* New York: Feminist Press, 1983.

Pizer, Donald. *The Theory and Practice of American Literary Naturalism: Selected Essays and Reviews.* Carbondale: Southern Illinois UP, 1993.

Rose, Jane Atteridge. "Reading 'Life in the Iron Mills' Contextually: A Key to Rebecca Harding Davis's Fiction." *Conversations: Contemporary Critical Theory and the Teaching of Literature.* Ed. Charles Moran and Elizabeth F. Penfield. Urbana: NCTE, 1989. 187-99.

Samuels, Shirley, ed. Introduction. *The Culture of Sentiment: Race, Gender, and Sentimentality in Nineteenth-Century America.* New York: Oxford UP, 1992. 3-8.

Sanchez-Eppler, Karen. *Touching Liberty: Abolition, Feminism, and the Politics of the Body.* Berkley: U of California P, 1993.

Scarry, Elaine. *The Body in Pain: The Making and Unmaking of the World.* New York: Oxford UP, 1985.

Seltzer, Mark. *Bodies and Machines.* New York: Routledge, 1992.

———. "The Still Life." *American Literary History* 3.3 (1991): 455-86

Thomson, Rosemarie Garland. "Benevolent Maternalism and Physically Disabled Figures: Dilemmas of Female Embodiment in Stowe, Davis, and Phelps." *American Literature* 68.3 (196): 555-86.

Tompkins, Jane. *Sensational Designs. The Cultural Work of American Fiction, 1790-1860.* New York: Oxford UP, 1985.

Walcutt, Charles Child. *American Literary Naturalism: A Divided Stream.* Minneapolis: U of Minnesota P, 1956.

Yellin, Jean Fagin. Afterword. *Margret Howth: A Story of Today.* New York: Feminist Press, 1990. 271-302.

Whitney A. Womack (essay date 2005)

SOURCE: Womack, Whitney A. "Reforming Women's Reform Literature: Rebecca Harding Davis's Rewriting of the Industrial Novel." In *Our Sisters' Keepers: Nineteenth-Century Benevolence Literature by American Women,* edited by Jill Bergman and Debra Bernardi, pp. 105-31. Tuscaloosa, Ala.: The University of Alabama Press, 2005.

[*In the following essay, Womack interprets Davis's* Margret Howth *as the author's "direct response to and critique of" the British industrial reform novel, specifically as represented by Elizabeth Gaskell's* North and South, *stating that in both the original draft of the novel, titled "The Deaf and the Dumb," and in her published version, Davis "consciously set out to rewrite Gaskell's novel" by breaking with "the typical plot-line" and complicating the genre's "often simplistic notions of reform and easy solutions to complex social and economic problems."*]

> Met Miss Harding, author of **Margret Howth,** which has made a stir and is very good. A handsome, quiet woman, who says she never had any troubles, though she writes of woes. I told her I had lots of troubles; so I write jolly tales; and we wondered why we each did so.
>
> —Louisa May Alcott, 1862

Rebecca Harding Davis was never fully satisfied with her first novel **Margret Howth: A Story of To-Day** (1862), a view shared by many contemporary readers and literary critics.[1] When Davis first submitted the manuscript—then titled "The Deaf and the Dumb"—to the *Atlantic Monthly* in May 1861, editor James T. Fields rejected it. Just the month before, Davis had burst onto the national literary scene with the *Atlantic Monthly*'s publication of her short story **"Life in the Iron-Mills,"** the story of the physical and spiritual starvation of factory workers in an anonymous industrial town. As a long-time resident of Wheeling, Virginia (later West Virginia), Davis was a firsthand witness to America's exploding Industrial Revolution, a phenomenon that had not yet entered the nation's literary imagination.[2] Her habit of taking "vagabond tramps" allowed the middle-class Davis to observe Wheeling's iron works, coal mines, cotton mills, and nail factories as well as the lives, habits, and dialects of their employees, which she incorporated into her short story. **"Life in the Iron-Mills"** was well received and heralded by critics for its realism, its industrial subject matter, and its raw, unpolished prose style. Its success brought the obscure thirty-one-year-old writer to the attention of America's literati, including Nathaniel Hawthorne, Bronson and Louisa May Alcott, Ralph Waldo Emerson, and Oliver Wendell Holmes.[3] Indeed, Fields was so impressed with Davis's story that he encouraged her literary efforts and offered her the substantial sum of one hundred dollars for another submission (Rose, *Rebecca Harding Davis* 22).

Considering Fields's unbridled enthusiasm for her fiction the month before, his negative response to "The Deaf and the Dumb" must have come as a great shock to Davis, who clearly had been at work on her first novel for some time. Davis later destroyed the original manuscript, but we know the plot of this draft, as well as Fields's objections to it, from what exists of their correspondence. Fields asserted that the text was written in a "pathetic minor" and that the "assembled gloom" of its conclusion—ending with the suicide of factory owner Stephen Holmes on Christmas Eve and the dedication of heroine Margret Howth to a quiet life of social reform work—was altogether too pessimistic for the *Atlantic*'s readers (qtd. in Yellin 287-88). While Davis provided an eloquent defense of her manuscript in her reply to Fields's rejection letter, she was clearly shaken by his criticism, asking "do you care to have me as a contributor?" In order to appease the powerful and influential editor, Davis promised, perhaps a bit sarcastically, that she would replace the novel's gloom with "a warm healthy light," transforming the "gloom" into a "perfect day in June" (288). Fields accepted the revised manuscript, delivered a mere eight weeks later, and retitled it *Margret Howth: A Story of To-Day*—a decidedly more optimistic title, one perhaps intended to be more appealing to a female readership. Although few readers would claim that this grim story of life in an industrial town is truly a "perfect day in June," Davis did weave in a marriage plot and more conventional happy ending. *Margret Howth* ran serially in the *Atlantic* from October 1861 to March 1862 and received several positive reviews, including one in *Peterson's* that favorably compares the novel to the works of Charlotte Brontë (Pfaelzer 57). It was popular enough to merit republication in book form later that year, selling a respectable, if not record-setting, 2,500 copies in three editions (Harris 82).

While Fields was disappointed with "The Deaf and the Dumb," Davis was disappointed with *Margret Howth,* which she felt failed to convey the "true history of To-Day" that she intended to write. In an 1861 letter, she claimed the revised novel was "like giving people broken bits of apple-rind to chew"—in other words, not at all satisfying or fulfilling (qtd. in Yellin 289). She urged Fields to allow her the opportunity to revise the novel again before its publication in book form, a request he denied. Most Davis critics agree with the author's assessment of the novel. Tillie Olsen, who resurrected Davis's fiction in the 1970s after decades of critical neglect, pronounces the novel "sometimes embarrassingly bad" (95).[4] Sharon M. Harris laments Davis's compromises and declares that *Margret Howth* is "ultimately a failure in artistic terms precisely because of the insertions of 'full sunshine' into an otherwise stridently realistic work" (63). Many critics accuse Fields, the quintessential "Gentleman-Publisher,"[5] of undermining the "integrity of [Davis's] hard-hitting fiction" (Tichi 10) and containing her "narrative radicalism" (Pfaelzer 54) as well as attempting to feminize Davis's discussion of industrial capitalism by urging her to expel the "gloom" and add elements more typical of sentimental "woman's fiction."[6]

Fields, as well as contemporary critics, may have misunderstood Davis's intentions in both the early draft and final version of *Margret Howth.* I read Davis's novel as a direct response to and critique of the conventions and assumptions of the industrial reform novels that were commercially and critically popular in England during the mid-nineteenth century.[7] Like both **"Life in the Iron-Mills"** and *Margret Howth,* British industrial reform novels, a widely popular form of benevolence literature, sought to give a human face to the suffering of industrial workers and expose the injustices of industrial capitalism and laissez-faire policies. Today we tend to associate such male writers as Benjamin Disraeli, Charles Kingsley, and Charles Dickens with the industrial novel, yet it was in fact women writers like Frances Trollope, Charlotte Elizabeth Tonna, Elizabeth Gaskell, Charlotte Brontë (among Rebecca Harding Davis's favorite writers), and George Eliot who pioneered and sustained this subgenre throughout the mid-nineteenth century. As Joseph Kestner explains in *Protest and Reform: The British Social Narrative by Women,* "[n]ot only were many women part of this tradition; they also entered it far earlier than their male counterparts" (3). In industrial reform novels by both male and female novelists, so-called women's values—benevolence, empathy, compassion—are prescribed as the antidotes to the ills of industrial capitalism and utilitarianism. In almost every industrial reform novel, idealized women characters are empowered to act as moral guides, class mediators, and saviors of the industrial world. Industrial reform novels inevitably imagine middle-class women bringing about peaceful resolutions to England's industrial crisis and diffusing the very real threat of class revolution during the turbulent Chartist period of the 1840s and 1850s, in spite of the limited social and political positions of women in this era. Feminist literary critics—notably, Constance Harsh, Catherine Gallagher, Rosemarie Bodenheimer, and Barbara Leah Harman—have reshaped our vision of industrial reform novels, which had long been dismissed as heavy-handed and overly didactic, by exploring the radical possibilities embedded in the representations of middle-class women reformers and the novels' implicit critiques of separate spheres ideology.

Davis was undoubtedly familiar with the tradition of British industrial reform fiction.[8] These texts were widely available in authorized and "pirated" editions throughout the United States in the 1850s, making it very likely that the well-read Davis came into contact with them before or during the composition of *Margret Howth.*[9] Davis's Anglo-Irish father had instilled a love of British literature in his daughter, and her writing reveals a considerable knowledge of British authors. In *Margret Howth* alone there are allusions to William Shakespeare, Samuel Johnson, Fanny Burney, Maria Edgeworth, Percy Bysshe Shelley, Thomas Carlyle, Charles Dickens, and Charles Darwin. When Davis sat down to write about the United States' new industrial landscape, it is likely that she looked to British industrial reform novels as examples. Indeed, Davis recognized potential comparisons between herself and Brontë, author of the industrial reform novel *Shirley.* She expressed a concern about the association in a letter to Fields regarding **Margret Howth**: "You did not think I imitated Charlotte Bronte [*sic*], did you? I would rather you sent it back than thought that, but tell me candidly if you did. I may have done it unconsciously" (qtd. in Pfaelzer 59). Davis also had a strong desire to be published in England, where, according to Harris, she "felt she could have the political freedom to write as realistically as she desired" and was disappointed when Fields failed to locate a British publisher for **Margret Howth** (96-97).[10]

While American literary critics have hailed Davis as the pioneer of such American literary movements as realism and naturalism,[11] they have largely overlooked the fact that she was working within a well-established British literary tradition. Considering the longstanding, institutional resistance to transatlanticism in literary studies, this omission is perhaps not surprising. In the last decade, however, many scholars have argued for a dismantling of the traditional national canons and for a new focus on the complex and multiple cultural conditions in which texts have been produced, distributed, read, and critiqued.[12] In his recent study *Romantic Dialogues: Anglo-American Continuities,* Richard Gravil asserts that critics who continue to ignore the impact of transatlanticism on both American and British literature in the nineteenth century are guilty of "offering a bowdlerized literary history" (xx). It should come as no surprise that British and American writers engaged in dialogues about industrialization, especially given the significant transatlantic literary discussions regarding the abolition of slavery, the other major social reform movement of the early and mid-nineteenth century. Indeed, such recent studies of abolitionist literature as Audrey Fisch's *American Slaves in Victorian England: Abolitionist Politics in Popular Literature and Culture* and Helen Thomas's *Romanticism and Slave Narratives: Transatlantic Testimonies* document the fluid circulation of texts and cross-fertilization of abolitionist texts and rhetoric across the Atlantic.[13] Placing **Margret Howth** in the context of the British industrial novel compels us to rethink earlier critiques of the novel and helps to dismiss the mistaken, but all too common, notion that Davis was a literary enigma "without precedent or predecessor," writing about industrial issues in a vacuum (Olsen 10). In fact, we can see her as part of a larger "imagined community," to borrow Benedict Anderson's term.

I argue that Davis sought specifically to challenge and subvert Elizabeth Gaskell's novel *North and South,* published serially in 1854-55 in Dickens's journal *Household Words,* popular in both nations. There are striking, even uncanny similarities between the characters, settings, and plots of *North and South* and **Margret Howth,** which strongly suggest that Davis consciously set out to rewrite Gaskell's novel. From the

Davis-Fields correspondence, it appears that in "The Deaf and the Dumb" Davis attempted to break with the typical plotline of industrial novels and complicate their often simplistic notions of reform and easy solutions to complex social and economic problems.

In particular, Davis initially refused to include a romance plot, which is used in *North and South* (and other industrial reform novels) to symbolize the union of opposites and suggest a reconciliation of masters and men. Even in the revised **Margret Howth,** with its reluctant romance plot, Davis still manifests a critique, evidenced by the narrator's frequent disruptions and metafictional commentaries. These narrative asides serve to subvert the very romance plot that Fields requested Davis include. As Lisa Long notes in her article "Imprisoned in/at Home: Criminal Culture in Rebecca Harding Davis' **Margret Howth,**" Davis may have in fact "duped Fields" by "adding rather than subtracting narrative complexity" when she revised the text (83). Although Davis was clearly critical of many tropes and traditions of the industrial reform novel, I do not believe she set out to write an anti-industrial reform novel. With **Margret Howth** Davis sought not to destroy but to reform the industrial novel by exposing its fundamental flaws and fallacies and participating in ongoing, transnational conversations about women's roles in benevolent and reform work and the shape of industrial reform narratives.

Readers can recognize links between *North and South* and **Margret Howth** almost immediately, beginning with the remarkably parallel lives of the novels' protagonists. The heroines share the initials "M. H." and similar names: Margaret Hale and Margret Howth. Davis's clipped, two-syllable spelling of the name "Margaret" is significant, marking Margret Howth as different from a sentimental heroine who, the narrator claims, would have a "name *three-syllabled,* and a white dress that never needs washing, ready to sail through dangers dire into a triumphant haven of matrimony" (Davis 102, emphasis mine). In addition, the two women are almost exactly the same age—Margaret Hale is nineteen, while Margret Howth turns twenty on the opening day of the novel. Davis does provide a pointed contrast in the characters' social situations. At the beginning of *North and South,* Margaret Hale lives in her aunt's fashionable London home, in fact leading the sentimental heroine's charmed life, and seems destined to find her way into the "triumphant haven of matrimony." Davis, however, immediately saddles Margret, "a quiet, dark girl, coarsely dressed in brown," with real-life problems and practical concerns (9).

Both the Hale and the Howth families find themselves geographically and economically displaced, forcing Margaret and Margret to enter and negotiate the public sphere and forsake their own dreams for the future.

Their ineffectual fathers are unable to deal with the new industrial world and yearn for the past: Reverend Hale is teacher of dead languages and literatures, while Mr. Howth, a former teacher himself, hungers for the age of feudalism and chivalry, a sentiment that echoes the ideals of British politician and reform writer Benjamin Disraeli and other members of the Young England movement (33).[14] Margaret Hale ventures out into the dirty streets of Milton-Northern (a thinly disguised version of Manchester, Gaskell's home) to make housekeeping arrangements for her family. She travels "up and down to butchers and grocers" in an effort to hire a suitable servant girl, a difficult task in a mill town where girls can earn better wages working in factories (109). At one point Margaret jokes that she has become more like "Peggy the laundry-maid" than "Margaret Hale the lady," but she never truly loses her middle-class, entitled position (115).

Middle-class Margret Howth, however, falls much further down the social ladder when she is forced to take a job as a bookkeeper at Knowles & Co., a monstrous, seven-story textile mill, a world away from the Howths' rural Indiana farm. This is also a much bolder step into the public sphere; while Margaret Hale makes only a few trips alone into public spaces, Margret is forced to travel alone each day to the factory, where she is subject to the gaze of male workers. Margret's experience working at the mill is described in sensory terms: her office is a cramped closet on the seventh floor; her one small window provides only a view of the wool-dyeing vats; she is inundated with the smell of sickening dyes; and the floor shakes with "the incessant thud of the great looms" (15). Margret soon learns the mind-numbing effects of the factory, for after just one day of monotonous copying work, she already handles herself in a "mechanical fashion" (10). Later Margret is described as having "dead, dull eyes" (59), and after several months in the mill she is like an "automaton" (225). Davis makes a point of showing how the factory system strips workers, even white-collar workers like Margret, of their identities, transforming them into anonymous "hands." In the happy endings of both novels, the protagonists are able to escape their reduced economic circumstances and finally marry, fulfilling a woman's proper destiny, due to unexpected cash windfalls. Margaret Hale is made an heiress after the death of her godfather, the ivory tower Oxford don Mr. Bell. Davis mocks Gaskell's deus ex machina conclusion with the timely but rather improbable discovery of oil on the Howths' central Indiana farm, which presumably will grant them a comfortable income and stable future.

Davis's resistance to Gaskell's narrative is also made clear in her representations of the domestic sphere. Despite their reduced circumstances, the Hales have a cozy home, which is more comfortable and inviting, in fact, than factory owner John Thornton's grand but sterile house. The majority of Gaskell's novel takes place in domestic spaces, with only a few forays into the public world of work and industry. Certainly Margaret's appearance before a mob of striking workers at Marlborough Mills is a significant moment in the history of female public appearance, but she quickly retreats to the domestic sphere. In contrast, very little of *Margret Howth* takes place in domestic spaces. Instead, Davis takes Margret and her readers into the bowels of a factory and on a tour of the "under-life of America," a world populated by society's "dregs":

> The room was swarming with human life. Women, idle trampers, whiskey-bloated, filthy, lay half-asleep, or smoking, on the floor, and set up a chorus of whining begging when they [Knowles and Margret] entered. Half-naked children crawled about in rags. . . .
>
> A girl of fifteen, almost a child, lay underneath [a sheet], dead,—her lithe, delicate figure decked out in a dirty plaid skirt, and stained velvet bodice,—her neck and arms were bare. . . . Margret leaned over her, shuddering, pinning her handkerchief around the child's dead neck.
>
> (150-53)

Even when we do enter the Howth household, Davis highlights the fact that the domestic, private sphere is not an idealized safe haven, immune from the effects of the public world and marketplace. As Jean Pfaelzer explains, Davis purposefully "blurs the public-private distinction from which the very notion of gender arises" (17). The slow dismantling of the Howth household, as the family pawns their most valuable possessions in order to keep from starvation, manifests this critique of the idealization of the domestic. Mrs. Howth and Margret cannot bring themselves to tell the blind Mr. Howth what they have done, and the old man continues to insist that Margret dust paintings and bric-a-brac the family no longer owns: "You can clean the pictures today, Margret. Be careful, my Child" (39). This "white leprosy of poverty" even leads the once domestic and genteel Mrs. Howth to forage for food in the fields around their house (38).

Davis also subverts Gaskell's idealized vision of the reformer-heroine, exemplified by Margaret Hale, who is an eager, benevolent social activist. In creating Margaret Hale, Gaskell herself was rewriting the longstanding stereotype of Lady Bountiful, a term describing those upper- and middle-class women who would condescendingly visit and dispense charity—along with a heaping dose of moral instruction as well as lessons in proper domesticity—to the "worthy" poor.[15] These benevolent women would work zealously on behalf of philanthropic societies but would never actually venture into factories, slums, or red-light districts to interact with the "objects" of their good works. Both Gaskell and Davis would have appreciated Dickens's caricature of such

Lady Bountifuls in *Bleak House*: "They took a multitude of titles. They were the Women of England, the Daughters of Britain, the Sisters of all the Cardinal Virtues separately, the Females of America, the Ladies of a hundred denominations. . . . It made our heads ache to think, on the whole, what feverish lives they must lead" (93-94).

In contrast, Gaskell presents a very different image of the type of the benevolent work women ought to do. She grants Margaret Hale publicity, voice, and agency—transforming Lady Bountiful into a woman reformer. This reform work enables Margaret to maintain her class position, despite the Hale family's loss of status and income after her father resigns his position as a clergyman due to a crisis of faith. As Mary Templin notes in her study of "panic fiction," in this volume, such "charitable acts protect middle-class women's social identity" and "emphasize the moral and intellectual superiority of the female philanthropist" (82-83). Margaret feels entitled to do this work, considering it her right, even her moral duty to step into the fray and act as translator and mediator between the "masters" and "men" of Milton-Northern, represented by factory "hand" Nicholas Higgins and mill owner John Thornton. When she discovers that the root of class antagonism is a lack of communication, she easily and successfully forges a personal connection between the men. Because of Margaret, Thornton is brought face-to-face, man-to-man with Higgins, which enables him to see past the "mere cash nexus" (525). He decides to soften his policies and provide a communal dining room, where he can share an occasional "hot-pot" with his workers (446). This is an interesting example of instituting women's domestic values in the public sphere, yet ultimately it acts as a bandage on the gaping wound of class oppression. Gaskell imagines Margaret's benevolent work ameliorating her own life far more than it affects the conditions of Milton's industrial workers. Margaret becomes an active participant in the public world, continuing her reform work when she moves back to London after the deaths of her parents, and later gaining economic agency by becoming a factory owner when she purchases Thornton's financially troubled Marlborough Mills with her unexpected inheritance.[16]

Davis upsets readers' expectation that Margret Howth, like the female protagonists of other industrial novels, will stand up and lead the charge against the injustices of the factory system by easily slipping into the role of woman reformer. Unlike Margaret Hale, who has the time and the ability to argue with "masters and men" and mediate strikes, Margret Howth is exhausted from her long hours at the mill and shy about expressing her opinions (29). She feels "stifled" in her new position, and her "higher life" is "starved, thwarted" (71). Indeed, Davis compares Margret with the pathetic caged chicken kept in the mill office (11). In order to endure

her current situation, Margret in effect buries herself: "She thrust out of sight all possible life that might have called her true self into being, and clung to this present shallow duty and shallow reward" (44). Although she clearly believes that "[s]omething is wrong everywhere," she does not believe she has the inherent power or strength to right this wrong (68).

Davis provides Margret with the opportunity to take on the role of social reformer when Dr. Knowles, a former factory owner turned socialist and philanthropist, asks her to serve as a benevolent worker in his planned "communist fraternity" for the poor (83). Throughout her life Davis was skeptical of organized and institutionalized forms of benevolence, particularly, as Pfaelzer explains, of "any formula whereby the dreams of a single man would shape a community" (20).[17] Davis objected to the nineteenth-century movement toward what Monika Elbert in this volume terms "scientific charity" or "philanthropology" (160). Davis was writing during America's great age of organized reform work; by the midcentury, there were literally thousands of local and national associations, societies, commissions, and institutions devoted to benevolence and philanthropy. As noted elsewhere in this volume, due to women's "peculiar influence," many of these organizations were led by, managed by, and composed of public-spirited, middle-class women. In *Women and the Work of Benevolence,* Lori Ginzberg chronicles the history and influence of such women's organizations as the American Female Anti-Slavery Society, the New York Moral Reform Society, and the Women's Central Association of Relief. A strong advocate of the abolition of slavery, Davis certainly could not have been blind to the political good that could come from organized agitation, but she also saw in these associations the potential for misuse and hypocrisy. Davis instead advocated concrete, immediate acts of charity, encouraging individual over collective activism. Davis exposes the difference between these two approaches to reform in an anecdote in her memoirs *Bits of Gossip*:

> One of our good friends, years ago, was Dr. J. G. Holland. . . . He had incessant disputes with me about almsgiving, I upholding the ancient lax methods of the good Samaritan, who, out of his own pocket, helped the man fallen by the wayside, not inquiring too closely as to his character. The Doctor maintained vehemently that all alms should be given through the agents of the Organized Charity Boards, and then only after close examination, to those whom they found worthy.
>
> (148-49)

Davis similarly blasts those people who would substitute institutionalized charity for individual benevolence and social responsibility in her editorial "Indiscriminate Charity": ". . . when a man shifts his personal responsibility for the poor wholly to legal action or organized associations, does he not rob his needy brother and himself of that reality of human brotherhood . . . ?" (qtd. in Harris 54).

By definition a "communitarian fraternity" should be a place of brotherhood/sisterhood and equality, but Davis makes it clear that Knowles envisions his role as the head of the commune, as the great paternalist leader of his own flock. His plans for the commune seem to come more out of his own desire for self-aggrandizement than any concern about the poor and marginalized whom he describes as mere "atoms," a swarming mass rather than as individuals (89). Knowles is reminiscent of the utopian visionary Hollingsworth in Hawthorne's *The Blithedale Romance,* whose "godlike benevolence has been debased into all-devouring egotism" (71) and has rendered him "not altogether human" (70). When Knowles takes Margret to the slums, he is shocked when she easily and unthinkingly picks up and kisses a little "pickaninny," admonishing her to "[p]ut *it* down, and come on" (151, emphasis mine). Margret refuses his offer of work, which in fact reads more like a command: "I want you to do your work. It is hard; it will wear out your strength and brain and heart. Give yourself to these people. God calls you to it. There is none to help them. Give up love and the petty hopes of women" (154). She refuses Knowles not because she doesn't care about the poor—indeed she seems to feel far more compassion for them than Knowles does—but because she is not convinced that benevolent work is her calling, because she already has a paid position, and because she is not willing to sacrifice herself completely, which is what Knowles demands of her. The clergyman Van Dyke astutely points out that Knowles sees Margret as a machine to do his work, claiming that "It is the way with modern reformers. Men are so ploughs and harrows to work on the 'classes'" (216).

Ironically, Davis offers up Lois Yare, the most abject figure in the narrative, as her model of a true social reformer, not Dr. Knowles or Margret Howth. As an African American, disabled, working-class woman, Lois is at the bottom of America's social hierarchy, one of the "dumb" Davis refers to in her original title "The Deaf and the Dumb." Like Bessy Higgins in *North and South,* Lois's health has been ruined by her work as a child laborer. Lois, symbolically nicknamed "Lo," recalls her factory work: "I kind o' grew into that place in them years, seemed to me like I was part o' the engines, somehow" (69). She is left with "some deformity of her legs [that] made her walk with a curious rolling jerk" (55) as well as "an injured brain" (93). Using Elizabeth Grosz's theory of the human body as text, an inscriptive surface on which messages can be written, we can read both Bessy's and Lois's scarred and battered bodies as indictments of industrial capitalism, their bodily suffering representing class oppression (117). In her article "Benevolent Maternalism and Physically Disabled Figures," Rosemarie Garland Thomson argues that such disabled characters are an essential rhetorical element in benevolent literature, noting that these narratives inevitably are based on,

> mutually defining relationships between foregrounded, idealized versions of white maternal benefactresses and muted, marginalized female figures who require spiritual and material redemption. Distinguishing each of these subordinate figures is a visible physical disability. This mark of Otherness operates as a badge of innocence, suffering, displacement, and powerlessness that renders the disabled women sympathetic and alarming figures of vulnerability who cry out for rescue.

(557)

Thomson also claims that these narratives are designed to showcase the able-bodied benefactresses, who "boldly enact voice, agency, and self-determination [while] the vulnerable figures languish on the narrative margins, ensnared by the limitations of their own bodies" (569).

Margaret Hale and Bessy clearly embody these roles, with Margaret providing spiritual and material comfort to the bedridden Bessy as she dies of "fluff," a disease caused by inhaling cotton fibers in textile mills. But in Davis's novel it is Margret Howth who suffers from soul starvation and Lois who is granted the power to save and redeem, emerging as the novel's unlikely "benefactress." Margret curses her life of sacrifice and work, which has left her with a "hopeless thirst" for "every woman's right—to love and be loved," and doesn't see how she could possibly help or encourage others (61). Lois, however, inspires people, for "some subtle [*sic*] power lay in the coarse, distorted body, in the pleading child's face, to rouse, wherever they went, the same curious, kindly smile. . . . No human soul refused to answer its summons" (76-77). After spending a day with Lois as she makes her rounds, Margret comes away spiritually nourished and transformed: "her morbid fancies were gone; she was keenly alive; the coarse real life of this huckster fired her, touched her blood with a more vital stimulus than any tale of crusader" (78). Her reference to the "crusader" alludes both to her father's medieval fancies and to the philanthropist Dr. Knowles, who fashions himself as a modern-day crusader. But neither Mr. Howth nor Dr. Knowles are able to combat what Davis sees as the true "enemy, Self"— their self-interested desires for money or position or self-fulfillment (7). It is only Lois Yare, with her focus on human interaction and her simple, optimistic message—"things allus do come right"—who can reform the crisis of soul starvation that Davis believes afflicted people of all social classes in an industrial world, not just the poor (68).

Davis further complicates representations of reform and benevolence by introducing the issue of race. While *North and South* focuses almost exclusively on issues of social class, with a brief allusion to ethnic tensions between British and Irish laborers, *Margret Howth* addresses the overlapping, and at times competing, issues of class and race in America. Davis's novel opens with explicit references to the conflict on every American's mind in 1861: the Civil War. In fact, it initially appears the novel will be about the war and the question of slavery from Davis's opening remarks:

> I write on the border of the battlefield. I find in it no theme for shallow arguments or flimsy rhymes. . . . Hands wet with a brother's blood for the Right, a slavery of intolerance, the hackneyed cant of men, or the blood-thirstiness of women, utter no prophecy to us of the great To-Morrow of content and right that holds the world.
>
> (3-4)

Davis literally was writing the novel from the "border of the battlefield"—Virginia was a slaveholding state, though Davis's region was a Union stronghold and seceded in 1862 to form West Virginia. However, Davis makes it clear that she will be addressing a different war, a war she has also witnessed firsthand: "the life-long battle for butter and bread" (20). Yet with the creation of Lois Yare and her father Joe Yare, Davis constantly reminds us of the nation's simmering issue of racial conflict, showing how intertwined racial and economic oppression are in the United States.[18] Davis makes Lois the most exemplary character in the novel, the one person not working solely for his or her own self-interest. We can read Lois as Davis's indictment of a racist society that would likely be blinded to the power of a figure like Lois due to prejudice. Pfaelzer, however, objects to Davis's depiction of Lois, claiming that Davis invokes a "racist stereotype of a childlike, physically handicapped, mentally retarded mulatto woman" (70). By making Lois an object of sympathy, she argues, Davis ultimately undercuts Lois's power.

Yet Davis grants Lois the ability to unite people, allowing her to transcend borders and barriers and mediate between different races and classes, between the rural and urban worlds: "everybody along the road knew Lois, and she knew everybody, and there was a mutual liking and perpetual joking, not very refined, perhaps, but hearty and kind" (73). Lois stops at houses even if there is no produce to pick or drop off, bringing mail, news, small gifts, or "'jes' to inquire fur th' fam'ly," and is inevitably urged to stay and share a meal with the family—with food serving as an antidote to both emotional and physical hunger (74). Lois, who has little to spare, helps feed the poor by selling them food at prices below those in the capitalist, male-dominated marketplace (76). Davis represents her belief in the reciprocal nature of charity, for in return for her good deeds Lois is showered with love and affection from all people in the community. Unlike Knowles's institution-

alized approach to reform, Lois's reform efforts are personal, immediate, hands-on, and spiritual. Her relational bonds with the community, as well as her Emersonian connection to Nature (which is somehow "alive to her"), enable her to reform a heartless, mechanical society (93). Jean Fagan Yellin argues that Lois's "faith, hope, and charity (as well as the Christian suffering and transcendence)" are what will "save the nation" (282).

Christ-like Lois sacrifices her own body, rushing into the burning mill to rescue factory owner Stephen Holmes. The fire had been deliberately set by Lois's father Joe Yare, a former slave and ex-convict who has only recently returned to town and taken a job as a stoker in the mill's furnace room (162). Although Yare is desperately "tryin' to be a different man" (165), Holmes decides to reveal a forgery Yare committed years before. Despite Yare's pleas for mercy—"It'll kill my girl,—it'll kill her. Gev me a chance, Marster"—Holmes plans to turn him over to the authorities, who will inevitably return him to prison (166). Rather than leave Lois again, Yare sets the mill on fire, knowing that Holmes sleeps there and will be killed in the blaze. Pfaelzer claims that in this scene Davis is demonstrating her fear that "the rage of racism and poverty" could bring down "the industrial house" and that the factory system could literally implode (73). Davis surely meant to evoke images of violent slave revolts, in which slaves would rise up and burn down the master's house. Yare's plan goes awry, though, when selfless Lois awakens to see the fire; realizing that Holmes is within and remembering that he had always been "so kind to her," she rushes in (172). Despite her physical limitations and her desperate fear of the mill (which she envisions as "a live monster"), Lois manages to bring Holmes to safety (171). She pays the ultimate price for this selfless act of heroism; the fumes she inhales in the fire lead to her death on New Year's Eve. The narrator dwells on Lois's body, imagining her afterlife: "I like to think of her poor body lying there: I like to believe that the great mother . . . took her uncouth child home again, that had been so fully wronged,—folded it in her warm bosom with tender, palpitating love" (263).

Harris condemns Davis's decision to kill off Lois, claiming that the novel's "placebic happy ending" is "ironically accomplished at the expense of the single potentially redeeming figure in the novel" (67). Pfaelzer, however, acknowledges that Davis had few options, for "the traditional mid-century fictional ending of marriage and home is historically and imaginatively unavailable for a black woman character" (71). Lois has helped to reform the current social system by bringing people of all races and classes together, yet narrow-minded, racist American society is not ready to embrace her or allow her to lead a full and fulfilled life. It is the middle-class Margret, then, who is left at the novel's end to carry on Lois's mission. While Gaskell sets up the middle-class

Margaret Hale as industrial society's savior from the beginning, Davis only reluctantly appoints Margret Howth to this role, and even then leaves us with real doubts about her ability to transform society.

The scene of Lois's bodily sacrifice provides an interesting parallel to the strike scene in *North and South* in which Margaret Hale uses her body to shield Thornton from a mob of striking workers. Margaret shames Thornton into facing these men, who have surrounded Marlborough Mills to protest being "turned out" and replaced with Irish scab labor:

> "Mr Thornton," said Margaret, shaking all over with her passion, "go down this instant, if you are not a coward. Go down and face them *like a man*. Save these poor strangers [the Irish], whom you have decoyed here. Speak to your workmen as if they were human beings. Speak to them kindly. Don't let the soldiers come in and cut down poor creatures who are driven mad. I see one there who already is. If you have any courage or noble quality in you, go out and speak to them, man to man!"
>
> (232, emphasis mine)

In a novel so intensely concerned with gender roles, it is interesting that Margaret urges Thornton to "act like a man," not to hide in the house like a coward—or a woman. As we soon see, Margaret decides she can embody this "man's role" herself. She watches as Thornton reluctantly stands, statue-like, in front of the rioters, then tears off her bonnet, throws open a window, and leans out—positioning herself half in and half out of the domestic sphere. But when she sees that the "infuriated men and reckless boys" (233) are armed with rocks and clogs and ready to explode into violence, she decides she must step onto the public stage, enacting what Elaine Hadley has termed "theatricalized dissent" (2). Margaret acts because something must be done, reminding us of British writer and reformer Harriet Martineau's observation, "when women are able to do they will do, with or without leave from men" (qtd. in Poovey 165). Using her body to shield Thornton from the angry workers, Margaret takes on the typically masculine role of protector:[19]

> The hootings rose and filled the air,—but Margaret did not hear them. Her eye was on the group of lads who had armed themselves with their clogs some time before. She saw their gesture—she knew its meaning,—she read their aim. Another moment, and Mr. Thornton might be smitten down,—he whom she had urged and goaded to come to this perilous place. She only thought of how she could save him. She threw her arms around him; she made her body into a shield from the fierce people beyond. Still, with his arms folded, he shook her off.
>
> "Go away," said he, in his deep voice. "This is no place for you."
>
> "It is!" said she.
>
> (234)

Bodenheimer reads this scene as the enactment of the "fantasy of female social rescue," in which women, by virtue of their womanhood, are able to save society: "[Margaret's] imperious maternal instincts, a proof of Margaret's special courage, demand that we redefine women as strong protectors . . ." (65). But Gaskell does show the inherent dangers of the public sphere; a stone clearly intended for Thornton strikes Margaret: "A sharp pebble flew by her, grazing forehead and cheek, and drawing a blinding sheet of light before her eyes" (235). While Margaret walks away relatively unscathed save for a scratch on the forehead, Lois dies as a result of her injuries at the mill—yet another example of the way that Davis seeks to replace idealized or romanticized moments in *North and South* with examples of harsh reality and suffering for workers and reformers.

In *North and South,* Gaskell employs what Lyde Cullen Sizer, in her book on Civil War-era women writers, terms a "rhetoric of unity," bringing together opposing factions and ideologies: North and South, public and private, industrial and domestic, masters and workers, capitalism and compassion. The novel's marriage plot, culminating in the engagement of Margaret and Thornton in the final chapter, symbolizes this union of opposites. Ruth Bernard Yeazell argues that industrial novelists like Gaskell invoke the sentimental novel's convention of the marriage plot to contain "social and political anxieties" (127). In *North and South,* the marriage plot redirects our attention, often at key moments in the narrative, away from the public sphere of industrialization and class strife to the private sphere of love, romance, and sexual politics. For instance, after the riot, Gaskell focuses on Margaret's relationship with Thornton, not on the conditions and demands of the workers, who are largely forgotten. Margaret's actions in front of the mob are read by virtually everyone as a sign of her love for Thornton, leading him to propose to her. Margaret, however, insists that love or personal feelings had nothing to do with her decision to join him on the public stage: "It was only a natural instinct; any woman would have done just the same. . . . [A]ny woman, worthy of the name of woman, would come forward to shield, with her reverenced helplessness, a man in danger from the violence of numbers" (252-53). Margaret refuses this first proposal, and the second half of the novel is more about their "pride and prejudice" relationship than about the very real threats of violence and class revolution that are simmering beneath the surface in Milton.

From what we know of "The Deaf and the Dumb," it appears that Davis abandoned Gaskell's rhetoric of unity and marriage plot. Although in **Margret Howth** Davis does bring Margret and Holmes together, to appease Fields and perhaps to fulfill readers' expectations, she constantly undermines their romance through commentaries by the novel's confrontational narrator, the alter ego of the engaging narrator found in such reform texts as *Mary Barton* and *Uncle Tom's Cabin.*[20] This narrator confronts and challenges readers, who may want to escape reality through fiction: "You want something . . . to lift you out of this crowded, tobacco-stained commonplace, to kindle and chafe and glow in you. I want you to dig into this commonplace, this vulgar American life, and see what is in it. Sometimes I think it has a new and awful significance that we do not see" (6). Davis critics cite these frequent narrative intrusions in their discussions of the novel's aesthetic failures, largely overlooking the important and subversive role they play in this text. While Gaskell seamlessly weaves together reform and romance in *North and South,* Davis intentionally allows her seams and gaps to show, as the confrontational narrator comments repeatedly on the difficulty—and perhaps the futility—of combining these two story lines. Chapter five, for example, opens with the narrator wondering whether a traditional romance narrative even belongs in this novel:

> Now that I have come to the love plot of my story, I am suddenly conscious of dingy common colors on the palette with which I have been painting. I wish I had some brilliant dyes. I wish, with all my heart, I could take you back to that "Once upon a time" in which the souls of our grandmothers delighted. . . . How can I help it, if the people in my story seem coarse to you,—if the hero, unlike all other heroes, stopped to count the cost before he fell in love. . . . Of course, if I could, I would have blotted out every meanness before I showed him to you; I would have told you Margret was an impetuous, whole-souled woman, . . . but what can I do? I must show you men and women as they are in that especial State of the Union where I live.

(101-5)

Davis recognizes, and even sympathizes, with her readers' desires for romance, but she argues that they nonetheless need to be instructed in the reality of the industrial world, despite its dingy colors. She notes that if she were to write a fairy tale about dashing heroes and radiant heroines, her readers would surely recognize the dishonesty of her story and insist on the commonplace, asking her to "tell us about the butcher next door, my dear" (102). *Margret Howth* concludes with more metafictional commentary that destabilizes the seemingly happy union of Margret and Holmes: "My story is but a mere groping hint? It lacks determined truth, a certain yea or nay? I know: it is a story of To-Day" (264). This coda leaves the novel intentionally indeterminate. We are left without assurance that the social, economic, and political crises the novel describes will be resolved with Margret and Holmes's marriage, just the opposite of the effect of Margaret and Thornton's

marriage plans in *North and South.* This ending is more optimistic and conciliatory than it was in "The Deaf and The Dumb," but it is not the promised "perfect day in June."

Margret Howth is a perfect example of a text that truly benefits from a transatlantic reading. Davis has too often been dismissed as an anomaly, an oddity in American fiction, left to lurk in the shadows of the canon. *Margret Howth* has long suffered from a lack of critical context and, according to the sales department of the Feminist Press, their 1993 reprint of the novel has sold poorly, making it likely that the novel will again be out of print and inaccessible. But when read in the context of Gaskell and other British writers, Davis can be understood as participating in an evolving tradition of industrial reform literature and a critical dialogue about the effectiveness of benevolent work in nineteenth-century England and the United States. Davis's novel critiques both the traditional Lady Bountiful figure and the idealized middle-class woman reformer figure common in British industrial reform fiction. Ultimately, Davis forces her readers to confront and question simplified images of women's benevolent work.

Notes

1. The epigraph is taken from an 1862 entry from Alcott's diary and is published in *Louisa May Alcott: Her Life, Letters, and Journals* (131).

2. There are certainly examples of American fiction that address the social injustices brought about by the Industrial Revolution before Davis's "Life in the Iron-Mills," most notably Herman Melville's diptych "The Paradise of Bachelors and the Tartarus of Maids" and stories by factory workers themselves that appeared in such journals as the *Lowell Offering* and the *Voice of Industry.* But industrial fiction in the United States did not yet have the wide readership and significant cultural impact that it did in England. I agree with Cecilia Tichi's recent claim that Davis "established the genre of industrial fiction in the United States," a genre Tichi traces from Davis through the works of such naturalist writers as Frank Norris and Upton Sinclair (21).

3. After repeated urgings by Fields and his wife Annie to visit Boston and repeated delays caused by the Civil War and her father's ill health, Davis was finally able to travel North in June 1862. She was introduced to her literary idol Hawthorne (and even given a rare invitation to stay at his home), and to Emerson, Holmes, Bronson Alcott, and Louisa May Alcott (whom Davis very much admired; Alcott's impression of this meeting is quoted in the essay's epigraph). Davis's memories of this two-week stay in Boston and Concord are recorded in the chapter "Boston in the Sixties" from her memoirs *Bits of Gossip* (28-64).

4. Tillie Olsen first discovered Davis's "Life in the Iron-Mills" when, at age fifteen, she read "three water-stained, coverless volumes of bound *Atlantic Monthlys* bought for ten cents each in an Omaha junkshop" (Olsen 157). Olsen looked to the anonymous author of "Life in the Iron-Mills" (whose name she did not learn until some years later) for inspiration, for a sign that "[l]iterature can be made out of the lives of despised people" (158). Olsen's interest in Davis led to the republication of "Life in the Iron-Mills" by the Feminist Press in 1972, which prompted the movement to recover and republish other forgotten nineteenth-century women writers. The Feminist Press edition and the more recent Bedford Cultural Series edition of "Life" (edited by Cecilia Tichi) have made this story a fixture in American literature anthologies and syllabi, and given Davis at least a marginal position in the literary canon. The recovery of the rest of Davis's extensive corpus—which includes twelve novels, 275 short stories and pieces of serialized fiction, 125 juvenile stories, and over 200 journalistic essays—has been slow (Rose, "A Bibliography" 67). The Feminist Press reprinted *Margret Howth* in 1990, the New College and University Press reprinted *Waiting for the Verdict* in 1995, and the University of Pittsburgh Press published a Davis anthology (*A Rebecca Harding Davis Reader*) with fifteen short stories and sixteen essays in 1995. In 2001, Vanderbilt Press released *Rebecca Harding Davis: Writing Cultural Biography,* edited by Janice Milner Lasseter and Sharon M. Harris, which contains Davis's autobiography *Bits of Gossip* plus a previously unpublished family history by Davis.

5. In *Doing Literary Business: American Women Writers in the Nineteenth Century,* Coultrap-McQuinn describes the uneasy relationship between nineteenth-century women writers and their "Gentleman-Publishers," male publishers like Fields who positioned themselves as literary guides, moral guardians, and father-figures to their female charges, the writing "ladies." Their paternalism sought to replicate and reinforce the notion of separate spheres by keeping women away from the business side of publishing, and, in many cases, underpaying them (38). Davis suffered financially from this relationship; while it was common for writers to receive at least 10% of the profits for their publications, Davis was paid just one-half of 1% of the profits of *Margret Howth* (Harris 82). The *Atlantic*'s poor compensation led Davis to publish her work in more popular journals, especially *Peterson's, Harper's, Youth's Companion,* and later, the *Saturday Evening Post.* In *Rebecca Harding Davis and American Realism,* Sharon M. Harris provides a more detailed history of Davis's relationship with Fields, which lasted for well over a decade.

6. In *Woman's Fiction: A Guide to Novels by and about Women in America, 1820-70,* Nina Baym introduced her theory of midcentury "woman's fiction": novels that "are written by women, are addressed to women and tell one particular story about women, . . . the 'trials and triumph' . . . of a heroine who, beset with hardships, finds within herself the qualities of intelligence, will, resourcefulness, and courage sufficient to overcome them" (22). Such sentimental midcentury bestsellers as Susan Warner's *The Wide, Wide World* (1850) and Maria Susanna Cummins's *The Lamplighter* (1854) fit this model of female triumph over adversity. Davis's rejection of sentimentality can be read as a backlash against this type of popular woman's fiction.

7. The industrial novel—alternately referred to as the reform novel, the social problem novel, the Condition-of-England novel, the humanitarian novel, the political novel, and the novel with a purpose—thrived in England from the 1830s to the 1860s, gaining particular popularity during the "Hungry Forties" and the rise of the Chartist movement. Industrial novelists, most of whom were middle class, imagined peaceful solutions to the nation's class crisis and prompted middle-class readers to social action. Certainly earlier novels had addressed social issues and injustices, but, according to Constance Harsh, "for the first time fiction felt it could compete with non-fictional genres such as essays and sociological documentation; it claimed to have as much authority as they did in representation as well as the analysis of social reality" (6). The best recent studies of the industrial novel are Catherine Gallagher's *The Industrial Reformation of English Fiction,* Barbara Leah Harman's *The Feminine Political Novel,* and Harsh's *Subversive Heroines: Feminist Resolutions of Social Crisis in the Condition-of-England Novel.*

8. A few critics have mentioned Davis's possible links to British literature in general and the industrial novel tradition in particular, though none have pursued these connections further. For example, in his article "Success and Failure in Rebecca Harding Davis" (1963), James Austin asserts that "Miss Harding's strong, crusading spirit suggests the influence of Elizabeth Gaskell" (45). In his biography *The Richard Harding Davis Years: A Biography of Mother and Son* (1961), Gerald Langford observes that "Rebecca was influenced by the humanitarian fiction of English writers like Charles Kingsley and Charles Reade, and especially Gaskell's *Mary Barton*" (17). More recently, Jean

Pfaelzer has noted common motifs in Brontë's *Jane Eyre* and *Margret Howth*, suggesting that nineteenth-century American women writers "did not write in intellectual isolation" from their British counterparts (59).

9. Most British industrial novels were reprinted—in authorized as well as "pirated" editions, since authors were not yet protected by international copyright laws—by American publishers and were advertised and reviewed in American periodicals. Harriet Beecher Stowe wrote an introduction for a three-volume American edition of *The Works of Charlotte Elizabeth* in 1845, which included two early industrial novels (*The Wrongs of Woman* and *Helen Fleetwood*) and went through multiple editions in the United States in the 1840s and 1850s. *Harper's* published an authorized edition of Elizabeth Gaskell's industrial novel *Mary Barton;* Gaskell's works were popular enough in the United States that the *Nation* published a moving obituary after her death in 1865, claiming that her "novels [are] in book-stalls all over the union" (qtd. in Easson 518). As is clear from the immense popularity of his reading tours in the United States, Dickens was a favorite of American readers as well.

10. Davis did publish a story in England later in 1862, the only British publication of her work during her lifetime. Fields sent Dickens a copy of Davis's "Blind Tom," a biting and timely indictment of slavery. The story is based on the real life of a slave boy who was mentally incapacitated but possessed amazing musical talent, an idiot savant. Tom was displayed by his master and forced to play concerts throughout the South, one of which Davis attended. Dickens responded, "I have read that affecting paper . . . with strong interest and emotion. You may readily suppose that I have been most glad and ready to avail myself of your permission to print it" (qtd. in Harris 97). The story was simultaneously published in the *Atlantic* in the United States and in *All the Year Round* in England. Clearly Davis was familiar with Dickens's journals, in which he published many British industrial stories and serialized novels, including Gaskell's *North and South* in 1854-55.

11. Ever since Olsen's recovery of "Life in the Iron-Mills," critics have debated where to position Davis within the existing American literary canon. Most Davis critics have championed her as a significant figure in the transition from romanticism to realism in American fiction. Previously, critics held up William Dean Howells, Frank Norris, and other male writers of the 1880s and 1890s as the forerunners of the realist aesthetic, largely ignoring the contributions of women writers. In *Rebecca Harding Davis and American Realism,* Sharon M. Harris notes that "Davis had a well-developed theory of the 'commonplace' nearly two decades before Howells shaped his own version of the concept," and was undoubtedly an influence on Howells, who worked as an assistant editor for the *Atlantic Monthly* during Davis's association with the journal (9-10). Focusing on Davis as perhaps the first American realist helps to give her, and women writers in general, a higher profile in the canon. While Harris, Pfaelzer, and others do recognize Davis's generic hybridity (particularly the ways she blends elements of romanticism, sentimentalism, and regionalism with realism), they do not look beyond the borders of the United States for literary traditions to which Davis may have been contributing.

12. There have been major strides in the field of transatlanticism in recent years. The journal *Symbiosis: A Journal of Anglo-American Literary Relations,* created in the mid-1990s, is dedicated to the growing field of transatlanticism, and its editors proclaim that their mission is to address "the artificial divide between literatures in English on either side of the Atlantic, a divide recognized by few creative writers but enshrined in the modern academic community." More recently, Heidi Macpherson and Will Kaufman's collection *Transatlantic Studies* seeks to define this interdisciplinary field of inquiry. Further, the January 2003 issue of *PMLA* devoted to the special topic "America: The Idea, the Literature" includes several articles on transatlanticism and transnationalism (Julia Ortega's "Transatlantic Translations," Paul Giles's "Transnationalism and Classic American Literature," and John Carlos Rowe's "Nineteenth-Century United States Literary Culture and Transnationality"), a sign of the field's mainstream acceptance.

13. One of the clearest examples of a transatlantic abolitionist text is Harriet Beecher Stowe's *Uncle Tom's Cabin,* which was an unprecedented bestseller in England, selling an astounding 1.5 million copies and leading to the cultural phenomenon the *Spectator* dubbed "Tom-mania" (Fisch 13). Interestingly, both Gaskell and Davis have ties to Stowe, perhaps the best-known reform writer of the nineteenth century. Stowe and Gaskell met during the London stop of Stowe's first European tour. In an 1853 letter, Gaskell notes, "Oh! and I saw Mrs Stowe after all; I saw her twice; but only once to have a good long talk to her; then I was 4 or 5 hours with her, and liked her very much indeed" (*Letters of Mrs. Gaskell* 237). The two women writers corresponded until at least 1860, and at one point Stowe even proposed that they collaborate on a travel narrative

about their trips to Italy (Stowe, "Letter"). Stowe, who, like Davis, worked closely with James T. Fields, sent Davis a supportive letter in 1869 after Henry James published a scathing review of Davis's *Waiting for the Verdict* in the *Nation.* Works by Stowe, Elizabeth Stuart Phelps, and other women writers had been similarly attacked in the *Nation,* and Stowe exposed this fact in Boston press, calling James "brutal" and "unmannerly" (Pfaelzer 156). In her letter to Davis, Stowe noted that the *Nation* had "no sympathy with any deep & high moral movement" (qtd. in Hedrick 345).

14. Before he became Prime Minister in 1868, Benjamin Disraeli published a trilogy of industrial reform novels: *Coningsby* (1844), *Sybil, or The Two Nations* (1845), and *Tancred* (1847). In the 1840s, Disraeli was part of the Young England movement, a loosely organized group of young conservatives in Parliament who split from Sir Robert Peel and the traditional Tory party. The Young Englanders held a romantic view of the Middle Ages and envisioned the creation of a neo-feudal hierarchy, in which paternal noblemen would take care of industrial "peasants," as the antidote to the dehumanizing system of industrial capitalism. Middle-class industrialists are figured as the true enemy, and the Young Englanders sought to strip them of their growing political, social, and economic power. See chapter three of Edgar Feuchtwanger's *Disraeli* for a more complete history of the movement.

15. As Jill Bergman and Debra Bernardi note in the introduction to this volume, American benevolent societies and workers often distinguished between the "worthy" and "unworthy" poor, a practice shared by their British counterparts (3). Worthiness was based on many factors, including the individual's "perceived morality," with sympathy and charity denied to those viewed as immoral or responsible for their own poverty (3).

16. When Margaret Hale learns of Thornton's business failures, she arranges with an attorney to lend him the money to reopen the mill. Significantly, Margaret demonstrates her business savvy by ensuring that "the principal advantage would be on her side" in this arrangement (529). With the loan, Margaret rescues Thornton, recreating her role as rescuer and savior at the workers riot, and allows him to continue his "experiments" with the workers at Marlborough Mills. Pamela Corpron Parker correctly points out that according to Victorian laws "Margaret's marriage vows will transfer all legal control of her property and capital to Thorn-

ton" (330). But the legal contract protects Margaret's interests (at least the £18,057 she lends him) and serves as a sort of "prenuptial agreement" (330).

17. Knowles sees it as his right to intrude on the lives of the poor and gaze upon them, almost as if they are animals in a zoo rather than human beings with basic rights. In "'The Right to Be Let Alone': Mary Wilkins Freeman and the Right to a 'Private Share,'" Debra Bernardi notes that "for poor people in want of the aid of charity organization societies, there was no fundamental right to domestic privacy" (137). Knowles seeks to erode this privacy further by having the poor move into his communist fraternity, where they will undoubtedly be under constant surveillance, scrutiny, and control.

18. Davis also introduces race with the character of Dr. Knowles, who is a quarter Creek Indian. We are told that he has the "blood of a despised race" and carries in his veins "their pain and hunger" (50).

19. While I see Margaret as assuming a masculine role, thus blurring the lines between feminine and masculine, I do not agree with Felicia Bonaparte's rather far-fetched argument that this scene renders Margaret "a man" (192). Bonaparte goes on to claim that the business partnership at the end of the novel is the only way that Margaret can "maintain her identity as an independent, male, woman" (193). Like Harman, I believe that "[t]o assign male status to Margaret is to diminish rather than to highlight the transgressive quality of her activity" (195).

20. In her study *Gendered Interventions: Narrative Discourse in the Victorian Novel,* Robyn Warhol discusses the rhetorical value of the "engaging narrator" prevalent in many nineteenth-century novels, especially reform novels. For instance, in *Uncle Tom's Cabin,* Stowe employs a narrator who directly addresses the audience, pulling at their heartstrings and revealing the common humanity of whites and enslaved blacks. The last chapter of the novel contains her most passionate entreaty, directed specifically at mothers:

> And you, mothers of America—you who have learned, by the cradles of your own children, to love and feel for all mankind . . .—I beseech you, pity the mother who has all your affections, and not one legal right to protect, guide, or educate the child of her bosom! By the sick hour of your child; by those dying eyes, which you can never forget; by those last cries, that wrung your heart when you could neither help nor salve; by the desolation of that empty cradle, that silent nursery,—I beseech you, pity those mothers that

are constantly made childless by the American slave-trade! And say, mothers of America, is this a thing to be defended, sympathized with, passed over in silence?

(384)

Works Cited

Alcott, Louisa May. *Louisa May Alcott: Her Life, Letters, and Journals.* Ed. Ednah D. Cheney. Boston: Little, Brown, 1898.

Anderson, Benedict. *Imagined Communities: Reflections on the Origin and Spread of Nationalism.* London: Verso, 1991.

Austin, James C. "Success and Failure of Rebecca Harding Davis." *Midcontinent American Studies Journal* 3 (1962): 44-49.

Baym, Nina. *Woman's Fiction: A Guide to Novels by and about Women in America, 1820-70.* 2nd ed. Urbana: U of Illinois P, 1993.

Bodenheimer, Rosemarie. *The Politics of Story in Victorian Social Fiction.* Ithaca: Cornell UP, 1988.

Bonaparte, Felicia. *The Gypsy-Bachelor of Manchester: The Life of Mrs. Gaskell's Demon.* Charlottesville: U of Virginia P, 1992.

Coultrap-McQuinn, Susan. *Doing Literary Business: American Women Writers in the Nineteenth Century.* Chapel Hill: U of North Carolina P, 1990.

Davis, Rebecca Harding. *Bits of Gossip.* Boston: Houghton, Mifflin, 1904.

———. "Life in the Iron-Mills." 1861. New York: Feminist Press, 1982.

———. *Margret Howth: A Story of To-Day.* 1861-62. New York: Feminist Press, 1990.

Dickens, Charles. *Bleak House.* 1853. New York: Bantam, 1985.

Easson, Angus, ed. *Elizabeth Gaskell: The Critical Heritage.* London: Routledge, 1991.

Feuchtwanger, Edgar. *Disraeli.* New York: Oxford UP, 2000.

Fisch, Audrey. *American Slaves in Victorian England: Abolitionist Politics in American Popular Literature and Culture.* Cambridge: Cambridge UP, 2000.

Gallagher, Catherine. *The Industrial Reformation of English Fiction: Social Discourse and Narrative Form, 1832-1867.* Chicago: U of Chicago P, 1985.

Gaskell, Elizabeth. *Mary Barton: A Tale of Manchester Life.* 1848. New York: Penguin, 1970.

———. *North and South.* 1854-55. London: Penguin, 1986.

Ginzberg, Lori D. *Women and the Work of Benevolence: Morality, Politics, and Class in the Nineteenth-Century United States.* New Haven: Yale UP, 1990.

Gravil, Richard. *Romantic Dialogues: Anglo-American Continuities, 1776-1862.* New York: St. Martin's, 2000.

Grosz, Elizabeth A. *Volatile Bodies: Toward a Corporeal Feminism.* Bloomington: Indiana UP, 1994.

Hadley, Elaine. *Melodramatic Tactics: Theatricalized Dissent in England's Marketplace, 1800-1885.* Stanford: Stanford UP, 1995.

Harman, Barbara Leah. *The Feminine Political Novel in Victorian England.* Charlottesville: U of Virginia P, 1998.

Harris, Sharon M. *Rebecca Harding Davis and American Realism.* Philadelphia: U of Pennsylvania P, 1991.

Harsh, Constance D. *Subversive Heroines: Feminist Resolutions of Social Crisis in the Condition-of-England Novel.* Ann Arbor: U of Michigan P, 1994.

Hawthorne, Nathaniel. *The Blithedale Romance.* 1852. New York: Penguin, 1986.

Hedrick, Joan D. *Harriet Beecher Stowe: A Life.* New York: Oxford UP, 1994.

Kaufman, Will, and Heidi Macpherson. *Transatlantic Studies.* Lanham: UP of America, 2000.

Kestner, Joseph. *Protest and Reform: The British Social Narrative by Women, 1827-1862.* Madison: U of Wisconsin P, 1985.

Langford, Gerald. *The Richard Harding Davis Years: A Biography of Mother and Son.* New York: Holt, Rinehart, and Winston, 1961.

Lasseter, Janice Milner, and Sharon M. Harris, eds. *Rebecca Harding Davis: Writing Cultural Autobiography.* Nashville: Vanderbilt UP, 2001.

Long, Lisa A. "Imprisoned in/at Home: Criminal Culture in Rebecca Harding Davis' *Margret Howth: A Story of To-day.*" *Arizona Quarterly* 54.2 (1998): 65-98.

Olsen, Tillie. "Biographical Interpretation." *Life in the Iron Mills and Other Stories.* New York: Feminist Press, 1972. 69-174.

Parker, Pamela Corpron. "Fictional Philanthropy in Elizabeth Gaskell's *Mary Barton* and *North and South.*" *Victorian Literature and Culture* 25 (1997): 321-31.

Pfaelzer, Jean. *Parlor Radical: Rebecca Harding Davis and the Origins of American Social Realism.* Pittsburgh: U of Pittsburgh P, 1996.

Poovey, Mary. *Uneven Developments: The Ideological Work of Gender in Mid-Victorian England.* Chicago: U of Chicago P, 1988.

Rose, Jane Atteridge. "A Bibliography of Fiction and Non-Fiction by Rebecca Harding Davis." *American Literary Realism* 22 (1990): 67-86.

———. *Rebecca Harding Davis.* New York: Twayne, 1993.

Sizer, Lyde Cullen. *The Political Work of Northern Women Writers and the Civil War, 1850-1872.* Chapel Hill: U of North Carolina P, 2000.

Stowe, Harriet Beecher. Introduction. *The Works of Charlotte Elizabeth.* 2nd ed. New York: M. W. Todd, 1845.

———. Letter to Elizabeth Gaskell. July 10, 1860. Hartford: The Harriet Beecher Stowe Center and Library.

———. *Uncle Tom's Cabin.* 1851-52. New York: Norton, 1994.

Thomas, Helen. *Romanticism and Slave Narratives: Transatlantic Testimonies.* Cambridge: Cambridge UP, 2000.

Thomson, Rosemarie Garland. "Benevolent Maternalism and Physically Disabled Figures: Dilemmas and Female Embodiment in Stowe, Davis, and Phelps." *American Literature* 68 (1996): 555-86.

Tichi, Cecelia, ed. *Life in the Iron-Mills.* Boston: Bedford Cultural Editions, 1998.

Warhol, Robyn. *Gendered Interventions: Narrative Discourse in the Victorian Novel.* New Brunswick: Rutgers UP, 1989.

Yellin, Jean Fagan. Afterword. *Margret Howth: A Story of To-Day.* New York: Feminist Press, 1990. 271-302.

Yeazell, Ruth Bernard. "Why Political Novels Have Heroines: *Sybil, Mary Barton,* and *Felix Holt.*" *Novel* 18.2 (1985): 126-44.

David Dowling (essay date 2009)

SOURCE: Dowling, David. "Dollarish All Over: Rebecca Harding Davis's Market Success and the Economic Perils of Transcendentalism." In *Capital Letters: Authorship in the Antebellum Literary Market,* pp. 109-26. Iowa City, Iowa: University of Iowa Press, 2009.

[*In the following essay, Dowling counters the view, derived from the anti-materialist and social reform themes in Davis's fiction, that the author was naïve and idealistic as a professional writer, claiming just the opposite—that she was shrewd and knowledgeable about the changing nature of the American literary market, and that she embraced the realist aesthetic in her life and work—and just as strongly opposed Emersonian transcendentalism—because it suited "the practical demands of the increasingly economic and competitive country America was rapidly becoming."*]

For Fern and Whitman, the antebellum market revolution inspired innovations in aesthetics to fit the leading-edge business practices of arguably the greatest self-promoters in the history of American literature. As they adapted the genre conventions of the domestic novel and the romantic poet to fit their radical marriage of art and laissez-faire capitalism, they reimagined gender roles in the business world. It was precisely those new gender roles in the new economy to which Davis and Melville reacted. This chapter examines their reactions to the market revolution in terms of its impact on women—not as victims caught in a wildfire of economic change, but as free agents at the precipice of tremendous social and material advancement. Would such opportunity be squandered? What was the future of women's roles in society and the workforce given the profound changes brought by the market revolution? Was there hope in factory work? Could maternal demands survive women's movement into the public sphere? Were women encroaching on male territory, according to Victorian values, that could somehow be deemed justifiable and not "unladylike" or over-ambitious? As women moved into the professional art world, the question arose as to how their presence would engage and de-center romantic male notions of creativity. What promise did the market hold for women artists, and was its master narrative of self-reliant talent transcending the material reality of the publishing industry setting women up for exploitation, underpayment, or rejection from the cruel masses?

Davis and Melville worry the woman question in the next two chapters of this book: Davis imagines the future of women artists in the market, warning that idealized, romantic notions of self-as-artist are particularly vulnerable at the dawn of the Gilded Age. Melville worries the woman question in terms of what he sees as an almost inevitable breakdown of separate-spheres ideologies, yielding futures of freedom at the cost of exploitation for women, as he playfully de-centers notions of male authorship.

The pulse of Rebecca Harding Davis's professional life was strong, steady, and undeniably robust. **"Life in the Iron-Mills,"** the first publication for the thirty-year-old woman from Wheeling, Virginia, appeared in the *Atlantic Monthly* in April 1861, initiating a long and prolific literary career for Davis. In the next fifty years, she would publish at least 292 stories and serials in over twenty-five different journals. As a writer of magazine fiction and essays, Davis contributed to prestigious periodicals such as *Scribner's, Harper's,* and the *Atlantic Monthly* as well as to popular presses such as *Peterson's,* the journal with the largest circulation in the country. She also took positions writing for the *New York Tribune,* the *New York Independent,* and the *Saturday Evening Post.* Of her serialized writings, twelve were published as books. She was a savvy businessperson, particularly wise in her negotiations with editors such as James T. Fields.

Davis's authorial persona of the anti-"money-getting" realist reformer complements rather than contradicts her role as literary entrepreneur. Her anti-Emersonian view of artistic production did not make her a rabid materialist in the literary market either. Instead she was aware of the fashionability of an antimaterialist stance toward the production of art, and utilized it in her best financial interest. Two different perspectives of authorship popular in the nineteenth century emerge: Davis's anti-greed tales and her own clever capitalism appear to contradict each other but share a strong refutation of the divinely inspired artist. What obscures this connection is the misconception that Davis possessed weak business skills and the underestimation of the depth and breadth of her fictional refutation of idealized conceptions of artistic creation. The paradox at the heart of these competing images of authorship for Davis is her varying use of Emerson to justify each. **"Marcia," "Ellen," "The Wife's Story," "Anne,"** and **"Life in the Iron-Mills"** showcase characters who suffer the perils of transcendentalist views of authorship, especially when they try to conjoin them with the market. Aesthetic ambition becomes perverted into economic ambition in each of these cases; their transcendental leanings make them too capitalistic. Interestingly, in Davis's own career, her ethic could not have been more capitalistic, as she regarded any divine sense of her own vocation with the guarded skepticism of a wily seasoned professional: she employed such romantic notions of authorship in her dealings with publishers and editors only calculatingly and fully aware that the market was never so flush with sympathetic wealthy patrons as the Horatio Alger novels would lead us to believe. How can we reconcile these opposites then? Was Davis hypocritically mastering the free-market game of producing and selling fiction she so sharply moralized against as "dollarish all over" (Harris, *Realism* 58), scorning the "mere shopman of literature" (Davis, **"Anne"** 241)—phrases that might have come from Emerson himself, a man famous for lines like "things, not men, ride in the saddle of the nation" and "out of doors all seems a market" (qtd. in Gilmore 114)?

Common to these competing models of authorship is Davis's distaste for the transcendental artist. If her pro-capitalist career seems irreconcilable with her anticapitalist fiction, one need only look to Davis's own deep respect of the market's cruelty for answers. She was acutely aware of its coldness, anonymity, and ability to turn self-reliant aesthetes with stars in their eyes into paupers. In both her fiction and her career, Davis possessed a heightened sensitivity toward the prospect of professional failure, measurable as both humiliation—particularly in **"The Wife's Tale"**—for the artist who bears his or her soul in the public eye, and financial ruin. In both, she believed transcendental notions of artistry could do no favors, functioning only as a blinding agent that could potentially transform artists into buffoons, whose failure becomes in itself entertainment to an audience she knew could swiftly turn savage. The key to these opposite notions of authorship, then, springs directly from Davis's belief in realism as an aesthetic and work ethic preferable to transcendentalism, which not only produces bad art but also encourages bad business. Indeed, the biggest threat to Davis's aspiring women (or heavily feminized male) artists and inept self-promoters (alternately conned and exploited by its tradesmen, or rejected by mocking audiences) in her fiction is the punishment of failing in the market, much as it was in her own career. Davis's ethos was clear: the merciless punishment the market unleashes on its failed artists is elicited by a chain beginning with bad aesthetics and incorporating an egocentric sense of self, a bankrupt set of guiding career principles, incompetent business practices, and eventual ruin. Her cautionary tales embrace realism precisely as a tonic for misguided professional ambition and a corrective for aesthetically reaching beyond the material and social realities of one's grasp.[1]

While Davis rejects the transcendental poet for an artist grounded in material and cultural realities in both her anti-greed tales and the clever capitalism of her career, what problematizes her materialist, business-savvy situation in the nonidealist camp is her use of antimaterialist sentiment in her fiction. I want to move beyond the rather obvious explanation that she chose anticapitalist moralizing in her fiction because crass materialism did not sell (although it most certainly did when it was heavily moralized in sentimental rags-to-riches tales, particularly in the Gilded Age fiction of Horatio Alger). Instead, I argue that Davis's rejection of romantic notions of artistry also signals her embrace of realism, both literary and as a guiding set of professional principles. She faults the transcendental artist figure in the fiction for displaced and inappropriately acted-upon ambition, the sin of aesthetic idealism that becomes greed, while she denounces the romantic model of literary production in her own career precisely because it hampers efficiency and limits profits by blinding the author to the social exigencies of readers and publishers: the transcendental poet conflates aesthetics with economics in both cases, neglecting the imperatives of labor for the family unit in the fiction and overlooking the reality of the literary market in her career. Realism, rather than hypocrisy, is at the core of this paradoxical advocacy of Davis's contrasting views of authorship. The savvy and guile she exercised in her own career reflects this ethos, which was a perfect match for the zeitgeist of the emergent Gilded Age, one worried about the perils of venture capitalism as much as its economic impact on art and the roles of women.

My argument makes a connection that has not yet been demonstrated in Davis scholarship. My sense of Davis's rejection of Emerson and embrace of a realistic ethos that guided her career and ultimately led to her success springs from my reading of her letters to her son, her publishers, and her editors. Davis possessed an uncanny business sense that informed her shrewd negotiations with editors and her use of conventional sentimental plots, often featuring antimaterialistic themes and marriage endings. As her long and successful career showed, the domestic role and the artistic role were not in the debilitating conflict that one might have assumed.[2]

Maternal advice and sage literary wisdom are perfectly consonant, for example, in a letter Davis wrote to her son, Richard. Under Davis's tutelage, Richard would establish himself as a famous public figure; he had his mother to thank for his literary work ethic. The recipe for success is quintessential Davis in its foregrounding of the importance of human sympathy, humor, and the sharpening of skills through real practice, all packaged with a pragmatic punch aimed at disabusing the young man of any pretensions to romantic notions of authorship: "It is not inspiration—it never was that—without practice, with any writer from Shakespeare down . . . real success takes time and patient, steady work," she advised, signing off unsentimentally to roll up her sleeves and return to work: "I had to stop my work to say all this, so goodbye dear old chum" (qtd. in Harris, *Realism* 68). In this chapter, I reclaim Davis's business expertise—predicated on her particularly pragmatic approach to the authorial vocation—at several key junctures in her career. I then examine how her understanding of the writer's role that guided those business relations directly shaped her attacks on Emersonian notions of the self as foils to her grounded, politically engaged perspective, which Jean Pfalezer usefully describes as "deriving from her belief in human agency" and yielding prose with the ability "to refer, to typify, to depict . . . to connote, if not denote, material reality" (21).

Davis's first negotiations as an author appear on the surface to be the antithesis of the savvy author who would provide her son thirty years later with the hard truth that getting published "depends on the article's suiting the present needs of the magazine, and also"—less nobly, yet true to the often arbitrary power editors hold over authors—"on the mood of the editor when he reads it" (qtd. in Olsen 149). The arbiter of culture who helped launch Davis's career was James T. Fields, the editor of the *Atlantic Monthly.* At the age of twenty-nine, Davis sent **"Life in the Iron-Mills"** in 1860 to the *Atlantic Monthly,* and in January 1861 she received

a response. Years later she described in a letter to her son how she "carried the letter half a day before opening it, being so sure it was a refusal" (C. Davis 40). Instead, she discovered Fields's eager acceptance and a check for $50. (This check echoes the one Mitchell writes for Hugh in **"Life in the Iron-Mills,"** as Hugh also carries it around until finally deciding upon his relation to it in a way that dictates his fate.) Davis replied in a letter that **"Life in the Iron-Mills"** was perhaps too dull a title and could be "more 'taking.'" She suggested, "[H]ow would **"The Korl Woman"** do? . . . However, I shall be satisfied with your choice—whatever it may be" (qtd. in Harris, *Realism* 57).

Davis's response to Fields's request for another story following the publication of **"Iron-Mills"** [**"Life in the Iron-Mills"**] makes her appear, on the surface, to care little about money. Although noting its playfulness, Harris takes Davis's antimaterialistic pose at face value, suggesting that the economics of authorship were not a major concern for Davis. But at a closer look, Davis shrewdly employs an attitude that was highly salable among writers of the day: the author's purpose was "higher" than merely commercial values might dictate. The persona that voices her extended metaphor of the shallowness of money is ethically opposed to monetary incentives, much in the way her anticapitalist reformer narrator is in **"Iron-Mills."** Instead of bad business sense, I find the following stance consonant with the **"Iron-Mills"** narrator's—an anti-greed position highly sensitive to the power of money to ruin artists or at least "cheapen" their art. Davis knew the paradoxical salability of this stance as it commanded $50 from the *Atlantic Monthly* for **"Iron-Mills."** She wrote,

> I receive the offer as frankly as you made it but you must pardon me if I decline it. Money is enough a 'needful commodity' with me to make me accept with a complacent smile whatever you think the articles are worth. But if I were writing with a hundred dollar bill before me in order to write on it 'I have paid him' I am afraid the article would be broad and deep just $100 and no more—dollarish all over.
>
> (qtd. in Harris, *Realism* 58)

Davis goes on in the letter to ask for constructive criticism of her writing rather than money, suggesting that she valued artistic integrity over monetary compensation: "I will ask a favor of you instead of money. If any of your exchanges notice the story will you send them to me? That is a trouble, is it not? I would like to see them, partly from selfish notions and partly because it would please my father and mother—I trust your kindness, to give me the pleasure—provided any one likes the article as you do" (Harris, *Kindred* 62). Her insistence that she cares more about constructive criticism than money is the humble pose of a fledgling writer, a convention used in many of Emily Dickinson's letters to Thomas Wentworth Higginson.[3]

Such a humble pose, further, simultaneously expresses that she values her work more than any one short cash advance, refusing to allow the carrot of a $100 bill before her to function as incentive. It would not only predetermine the scope and depth of her writing, but would suggest that it was a one-time freelance job without the dignity of a more permanent and ongoing material reward. The phrase "dollarish all over" is not a complete renunciation of capital so much as it is a rejection of definitions of her writing and career as ephemeral, which she appraised at a far higher value than the hypothetical $100 bill; she envisioned her writing career lasting well beyond the single job it would take to earn it. This position not only lends her more dignity than a single advance can reflect, but also appeals to the *Atlantic Monthly*'s association with literary rather than popular fiction and its sense of great literature as immortal, as opposed to the so-called ephemera of popular tales, like those Henry David Thoreau denigrates in the chapter "Reading" in *Walden*.

Davis's correspondence with Fields, furthermore, took place at a crucial juncture in the life of the *Atlantic Monthly*. Fields had recently taken over as editor in 1861, "eager to bolster the magazine's subscription rate," so he began including more fiction by women. His aim dramatically shifted by the middle of the decade, however, "to distinguish between high and low fiction, favoring work by Henry James and John W. De-Forest to the stories of romance and domestic concerns by women," as Anne Boyd observes (211). Davis nonetheless seemed a perfect fit, as she was a woman writer who could entertain, yet with a gritty realism that fit the new direction of the magazine. Davis knew she was an exception to the rule that "as literary tastes tended more toward realism, the kind of stories that many women were contributing were deemed less important" (Boyd 211).[4]

Davis displays strength in the letter given the vagaries of trade courtesy (publishers' first rights to authors) then very much in flux. Refusing the advance kept her a free agent to market her wares to the highest bidder; acceptance of Fields would have been like a professional marriage vow of loyalty to him only, an unnecessary constraint to her future growth. Indeed, she wanted him to value her voice and vision above capital to establish the *Atlantic Monthly* as a continuing outlet for her work, yet she wished to remain free to accept higher bids should they arise.[5] Thus she could avoid breaking a promise to him she did not want to keep. Davis consistently wrote for *Peterson's* throughout her career, especially when she needed the money most. Her "dedication" to the *Atlantic Monthly* was anything but loyal as she continued to market her writing to the highest bidder in a free market of self-interested professional authors. In fact, Davis received a tantalizing offer of $300 from *Peterson's* for a story she had written in two

weeks in 1862, just one short year after her $50 debut publication of **"Iron-Mills"** in the *Atlantic Monthly*. She wrote her *Atlantic Monthly* editor to inform him that he had been outbid by the popular ladies' magazine. In a bold business maneuver, she went on to explain that she had little respect for pieces commonly published in *Peterson's,* urging Fields to increase his payments because "[i]f I wrote stories suitable for other magazines I could make more" (qtd. in Rose 168). He responded by offering her $8 per page, to which she replied, "I accept your offer to write solely for the A. M."—a promise she happily broke on more than one occasion shortly thereafter (within the following year) and throughout her career.

Davis knew she could literally afford to employ antimaterialistic rhetoric in her initial negotiations with Fields because, at the time, she was living with her parents free from financial pressures. After she married and had children, however, her husband could not support her with two low-paying part-time jobs as a legal assistant and postal clerk the way her father had as a substantial businessman and city official. But while at home, there was no real need for her to extract money from Fields immediately because Davis's economic situation in her father's household was comfortable enough for her not to work for money in any capacity during the thirteen years she lived there after graduating from the three-year Female Seminary in Philadelphia in 1848.

Davis's letters to Fields also appear deferential because they support the concept of the gentleman publisher, as Sharon Harris notes (*Kindred* 61). Yet it is equally important to remember that this is her first relationship with a publisher, and therefore she lacks the experience and accomplishments in the trade to force her will. Nonetheless, the core import of the March 1861 letter to Fields asserts her judgment over his, as she says "you over estimate" **"Life in the Iron-Mills"** because of "the novelty of the scene of the story" (Harris, *Kindred* 62). The realist in her would take over as her career progressed and her successes mounted. She gradually dropped any early deference to the code of the gentleman publisher. In these letters to her editors and publishers, Davis exhibits similar crafty maneuvering, yet with a decidedly different tone and tropes. This is particularly evident when reading her letters to publishers chronologically throughout her career. She becomes more assertive and powerful with her demands by the late 1860s, as the early coquettishness, so calculatingly employed as to call attention to its own artifice—"[I] accept with a complacent smile whatever you think these articles are worth"—all but vanishes (qtd. in Harris, *Realism* 58). In its place, we see the businesswoman take over, selecting her metaphors with the no-nonsense clarity and bluntness of a CEO directing an urgent deal. Witness the swift and severe way in which she dispatches F. P. Church and William Conant Church in her

April 1868 letter addressing their demands that she abridge *Waiting for the Verdict* to fit the reduced page size of their journal after originally promising no limits on length: "It would be the equivalent of asking Mr. Hennessy to cut off the heads of his figures because you wanted to alter the size of your page" (Harris, *Kindred* 66). The analogy of decapitating figures in fine art sets the tone for her demand, thinly veiled as a threat, to finish the story only under the condition "that you give me not less than 35 pages in each number after May 1st" (Harris, *Kindred* 67).

The pragmatic focus on fundamentals of length and spelling, particularly with regard to silent edits of the slang in *Margret Howth* and length, combines with a self-effacing sense of her own craft that is more humor and swagger than it is meek, naïve, or fearful. She makes no pretentions to literary timelessness, reflecting on the contemporary relevance of her earlier writing in a letter to Charles Scribner written late in her career. He had asked her for a collection of her stories, eventually published in 1892 as *Silhouettes of American Life.* "I know that these stories are not at all modern nor at all 'up to date,'" she confessed, "[b]ut are there not a few people still living who prefer a musty tang in their books as in their Madeira?" (Harris, *Kindred* 68). One cannot picture any of the transcendentalists, for example, Margaret Fuller, characterizing their life's work as growing a funky "musty tang" to appeal to heartier readers.

Davis's business expertise was on display later in her career as she again successfully capitalized upon the erosion of the gentleman publisher's code, the mutual recognition of editors and publishers of first rights to an author's work. Using her pseudonymous authorship to her advantage, Davis published the same story for two different journals, generating double returns from her work. Of course, this raises ethical questions of professional integrity today, but the rules of the writer's trade were not yet firmly established in the 1860s during the early commercialization of letters. Business ethics were in flux during this transitional period toward professionalized authorship, as the patron system gave way to a literary market in which writers worked as entrepreneurs with no loyal ties. This is especially true in Davis's willingness to submit the same weird-but-true story to two journals. "Ellen" first appeared in *Peterson's* by the author of **"The Second Life"** in 1863. Davis sent the *Atlantic Monthly* the same story two years later in 1865 when they solicited a true story about the war. The *Atlantic Monthly* published **"Ellen"** by the author of **"Life in the Iron-Mills."** The two manuscripts are almost identical, as Helen Woodward Shaeffer discovered. *Peterson's* defended Davis by claiming that their story was fiction based on real-life events, while the *Atlantic Monthly*'s was "the bald facts" of **"Ellen's"** history (Shaeffer 117). The cover-up

worked and Davis profited. Ironically, Davis would publish an essay at the end of her career in 1902 for the *Independent* called **"The Disease of Money-Getting"**: apparently her own entrepreneurial guile was not part of this hampering illness.[6]

The double publication of **"Ellen"** blurs the boundaries between popular fiction and "serious" literature in the Davis canon. Tillie Olsen's suggestion that Davis abandoned artistry for money and acquiesced to financial pressures by writing popular trash as a "professional workhorse" (135) becomes dubious when an identical story was suitable to both the highbrow conservative tastes of the *Atlantic Monthly* editors and the pulpy sensationalism of the *Peterson's* editors. Davis's "serious" writing, such as **"Iron-Mills,"** employed the sensationalized "realism" of popular literary modes. **"Ellen"** typifies how Davis's fiction straddled high and low literary tastes. Like **"Iron-Mills,"** **"Ellen"** is based on social realities, especially human suffering in a historically specific contemporary cultural context. Hugh Wolfe's tale in **"Iron-Mills"** also might have been very suitable for *Peterson's* given its sensationalism and the spectacle it makes of Hugh's tragic suicide as well as the deformity and vile repulsiveness of the freak-show character Deborah. *Peterson's* often published gothic and mystery stories, with which the rhetoric of **"Iron-Mills"** is consonant. The generic division between high and low, serious and potboiler is not so clear when we look at **"Iron-Mills"** in the context of popular writing. If one were to excise the philosophizing of Mitchell and the men on their tour of the mills, the story would have been extremely suitable for the popular ladies' magazine given the presumed absence of the "intellectual" component for the educated, mostly male, elite *Atlantic Monthly* audience.

Writing for money was always part of Davis's conception of authorship, part of her realistic ethos that spread to other dimensions of her life. The promise of long-term financial stability from writing, I suggest, pulled her out of the biggest emotional and professional breakdown of her life. In 1863, she married Clarke Davis in Wheeling, Virginia, and moved to his sister's home in Philadelphia. Clarke's income was not enough for them to live on their own, so the new couple was forced to share living space with relatives. The lack of money, in fact, precluded any honeymoon. The living situation with Clarke's sister, Carrie Cooper, and her husband and small children was not amenable to Rebecca's plans for writing and/or caring for a domestic sphere of her own. All accounts show that there was no outwardly expressed animosity between the Davises and the Coopers. Davis responded by escaping the demands of the domestic sphere, of helping Carrie with what amounted to tasks for the betterment of the Cooper household. This situation had made domestic labor all the more alienating, since the children and the home itself were not Davis's own. She sought refuge in the Philadelphia Public Library, where she could write in order to provide a much needed supplement to Clarke's meager income.

The struggle to produce profitable literature and have a baby in a home not truly her own contributed to a nervous breakdown in June 1863. Throughout the winter of her pregnancy, Davis's physical and mental health fluctuated, sometimes incapacitating her. She spent much of her time bedridden, which she said was "like the valley of the shadow of death," feeling "afraid of the end" (qtd. in Rose 158). Significantly, Davis's physician advised her not to engage in "the least reading or writing for fear of bringing back the trouble in her head" (qtd. in Rose 158). This was part of the treatment prescribed for "hysteria" by writer/physician S. Weir Mitchell, whose prohibition of Charlotte Perkins Gilman's reading and writing inspired the horrifying story "The Yellow Wall-Paper." Mitchell was a close family friend of the Davises in Philadelphia and commonly treated the mysterious female "hysteria" by severely isolating the patient and abruptly cutting off all literary activities.

Of course, Davis was not rehabilitated by such therapy. What most likely returned her to health was the fact that she *did* write during this period despite her doctor's orders. Unbeknownst to her doctor, she wrote during her pregnancy an extremely self-reflexive piece, **"The Wife's Story,"** which was published shortly after the birth of Richard Harding Davis in April 1864. Her literary production, plus Clarke's promise (which she reported to her close friend Annie Fields, wife of publisher James T.: "If I get well we are going directly to live by ourselves—it is all clear now. *You* know what that means to me"), were tokens of future economic autonomy that buoyed her (qtd. in Olsen 128). Her sense of success both as a mother with the healthy birth of her child and as a writer with the completion of a publishable manuscript coincided with the end of her illness. By fall of 1864, the family of three moved out of the Coopers' residence into a home of their own, bringing Davis full reign over her domestic sphere as well as a less crowded writing environment for the first time since her marriage.

After the move, Davis was still actively interested in gaining as much capital from her writing as possible, as finances continued to be tight. So she more vigorously cultivated her relationship with the editors at the popular magazine *Peterson's,* for whom she had written a sensational murder mystery called **"Murder of the Glen Ross."** *Peterson's,* unlike the *Atlantic Monthly,* did not target the relatively small readership of the educated elite, but instead was designed for the masses, boasting "the largest circulation of any ladies' periodical in the United States, or even in the world" with 140,000 subscribers (*Peterson's* January-June 1863 350). Davis's interest in publishing for the magazine was driven by its larger economic base than the *Atlantic Monthly*'s, promising to pay writers "more for all its original stories than all other ladies' magazines put together" (*Peterson's* July-December 1865 291).

Such unprecedented financial rewards now available to women set up the ethical dilemma Davis placed at the center of **"The Wife's Story."** Davis knew this was a philosophical and cultural problem of immense importance to readers interested in the market's impact on the domestic sphere. The subject was not only timely, it was worthy of producing passionate prose, since the issue had recently touched her life. The protagonist of the story, written during Davis's pregnancy, dreams of becoming an artist. In the dream, the character Hetty writes an opera, only to watch its first production fail miserably, much to her public humiliation. At the low point of the dream, after having lost it all in the cultural market (including her husband to a heart attack during the performance!), she wakes up to embrace the security of motherhood with new zest. What looks like a rejection of public, professional writing for the safety and security of motherhood is more emphatically a rejection of the Emersonian myth of the divinely inspired artist, as her worst sin is the assertion of artistic egotism: "No poet or artist," she says, "was ever more sincere in the belief that the divine spoke through him than I" (**"Wife's Story"** 14). Hetty's attempt to isolate herself from her immediate social network of her husband and child represents exactly the kind of disaffiliation and self-reliance in the name of artistry that Davis disapproves of. Like **"Life in the Iron-Mills,"** **"The Wife's Story"** critiques this sort of blind, radical individualism that overtakes the character with artistic propensities: the delusions of absolute transcendence above the imperatives of economic and social relations are projected as deadly. This is not a conservative, antifeminist promotion of fawning female dependence so much as it is a warning against transcendental notions of artistic production.[7] Davis herself showed that one could both meet the domestic responsibilities of antebellum motherhood and produce appealing literary merchandise as a professional because **"The Wife's Story"** appeared in the June issue of the *Atlantic Monthly* following the birth of her son in April 1864. Davis showed by her own example that the production of art does not necessarily sever the writer's social and familial ties.

Davis's 1876 story **"Marcia"** depicts yet another female writer protagonist who decides to reject marriage to fulfill her professional ambitions. The story's dark conclusion advocates independence from male possession more so than **"The Wife's Story."** Marcia's failed career sends her back under the command of her "owner" (that is, husband) who takes her back "in plumes, the costliest that her owner's money could buy"

(928). The narrator voices both sadness at Marcia's failure and horror at her exploitation. What is important for our purposes is that Marcia's writing career fails for the same reason Hetty's attempt at professional writing does: both are tainted by idealizations of artistic production. While Hetty's artistic egotism and conceit of divine inspiration are her downfall, Marcia's flaw is her tragic naïveté about the work of writing: "The popular belief in the wings of genius, which can carry it over hard work and all such obstacles as ignorance of grammar or even the spelling book, found in her a marked example" (926). Just as Marcia overlooks the necessity of hard work and the fundamentals of spelling and grammar in her idealized view of writing, Hetty lacks the humility to see the power of the mass audience to turn an author out into the streets, failed and hungry. Both characters are reflections of the danger in the Emersonian divinely inspired poet of neglecting the basics of audience awareness and the skills of the craft, aspects of authorship on which Davis prided herself. In a letter to her son, she employs the language of the skilled trades—"You are a journeyman, not a master workman"—to define his current phase of authorial development, noting that he must diligently practice the basics, such as the expression of "mood," "tone," and character through the descriptive detail of "looks" and "dress" (qtd. in Olsen 149). Her advice is to keep his dream from becoming a transcendental nightmare.

Gothic horror conventions express the nightmarish consequences of such delusional aspirations in **"Life in the Iron-Mills."** Within the context of abusive labor conditions, the narrator assures us that the realism that describes Hugh's working class will read like a gothic thriller, for "no Ghost horror would terrify you more."[8] Hugh's story, like any shocking horror tale, promises the ghoulish details of "living death" and "soul starvation" (Davis, **"Iron-Mills"** 23). The realism of Davis, according to Sharon M. Harris's useful definition, "insists upon reporting quotidian American life, abandoning the 'rose tinted' and homogeneous perspective of that life and rendering her material so as to give her readers an illusion of actual experience. . . . Davis was acutely interested in historical locales . . . and concerned with artistically recording the 'accurate history' of the present" (*Realism* 6-7). Davis registers the effect of the environment on Hugh through violent, grotesque imagery, which makes a spectacle of him and his sculpture; her aim is to reflect the artist in his economically oppressive condition in a way that draws attention to its superlative and sensational horror. His sculpture, for example, bears a "mad, half-despairing gesture of drowning" (Davis, **"Iron-Mills"** 23). Death, torture, and madness are the hallmarks of this artist figure; the "dirty canary desolately chirp[ing] in its cage" at the beginning of the story symbolizes Hugh's longing for artistic expression in liberating conditions (Davis, **"Iron-Mills"** 12). The well-documented nineteenth-century practice of keeping caged birds in mines to indicate air toxicity evokes a sense of degradation and sullied dreams of freedom.

Such gothic tropes actively work against what Jean Pfaelzer calls the "pastoral nostalgia of sentimentalism" to foreground the "class consciousness" of Davis's social realist agenda (21). America inherited that pastoral sentimentalism's attendant romantic myth of authorship from the late English romantic poets[9] Shelley, Wordsworth, Keats, and Byron, in whose tradition artists are economically detached. The created dramatic identity of the romantic poet has little concern for labor and the poet's ability to earn a material reward. Indeed, the problems of the economic world are represented by the American romantics,[10] especially the transcendentalists, as mutually exclusive to the production of art. In writing primarily against romanticism, Davis makes Hugh the opposite of Emerson's idealized poet in that she situates him within the social realities of the industrial world. The networks of economic relations shape Hugh Wolfe because he directly participates in them. This is the opposite of a transcendentalist literary persona, like Emerson's,[11] whose identity is formed in part by a negative relation to the economic world: in Thoreau we find catalogs of what socioeconomic factors do *not* affect him, while Emerson proclaims the supremacy of the ideal poet by how little money matters to him. Quite the contrary, Hugh, the writer figure, is a construct of industrial culture just as surely as his iron ore sculptures are. His demise occurs precisely when his vision of capital passes into a diseased version of pastoral transcendental idealism.

Transcendental images of nature function in **"Life in the Iron-Mills"** to heighten by contrast the palpably oppressive mood of immediacy in the story. The narrator's description of the scene outside his window—smoke from "the iron-foundries . . . settles down in black, slimy pools on the muddy streets . . . clinging in a coating of greasy soot to the house-front, the two faded poplars, the faces of the passers-by"—draws on the thwarted romantic vision of natural purity to enhance the incarcerating atmosphere (**"Iron-Mills"** 12). Both the soiled bird and the angel in the narrator's quarters evoke the symbolic resonance of romance, especially the pastoral ideal that informs their "dream of green fields and sunshine [that] is a very old dream,—almost worn out" (**"Iron-Mills"** 12). Hugh actively cultivates the "almost worn-out" romantic dreams[12] of freedom from his oppressive working-class conditions. He constantly envisions a better life that Deborah endorses and pins all of her hopes on: "a pure life, a good-hearted life, full of beauty and kind words" and the pastoral "moment of free air on a hill-side" splashed in golden sunshine (**"Iron-Mills"** 41). The central conflict arises when Deborah conflates her dream of success, the very real need for money to transcend her class, with the pastoral romantic vision. Her conception of money marks the generic collision between realism and romanticism in the story, because "money" enables the oppressed workers "to go out,—*out,* I say,—out, lad, where t' sun shines, and t' heath grows, and t' ladies walk in silken gownds, and God stays all t' time" (**"Iron-Mills"** 43). Material prosperity ("silken gownds"), pastoral purity ("where t' sun shines"), and religious sanctity ("God stays all t' time") are all possible through the acquisition of money in Deborah's view. So, understandably, she picks Mr. Mitchell's pocket, for it contains not just money, but the stuff of transcendence, in a sympathetic version of Eve's transgression in the Garden of Eden—only the sin in Davis clearly lies in the economic environment and not in the individual.

In **"Iron-Mills,"** the good hearts of the poor, such as Hugh, become spoiled and ruined by the introduction of capital into their world. Hugh's art is presented as a longing for freedom from economic oppression; it is clear that this freedom, as Deborah assumes, cannot be attained without money. But the moment he appropriates Mitchell's capitalist ideology's dream of prosperity, Hugh begins his spiritual decline. The fusion of money and art, Davis tells us, is lethal because of the severity of Hugh's economic oppression. He is starving for the cultivation of his art just as surely as he is starving for financial justice. But the desire to quench both his economic and artistic thirst all at once translates into greed in Davis's lexicon. Once he trains his artistic imagination on colorful visions of plenitude and success with Mitchell's stolen money clenched in his palm, he becomes intoxicated, and in the spirit of temperance reform literature, his death follows soon after. The drunken reverie the greed throws him into is a dangerous concoction of the imagination and unfettered, radically idealistic material ambition:

> There were times when soft floods of color in the crimson and purple flames, or the clear depth of amber in the water below the bridge, had somehow given him a glimpse of another world than this,—of infinite beauty and quiet somewhere. . . . *Wolfe's artist-eye grew drunk with color.* . . . A man . . . free to work, to live, to love! Free! His right! He folded the scrap of paper in his hand.
>
> (**"Iron-Mills"** 47; emphasis mine)

The artistic vision, when drawn into the cycle of greed perpetuated by the factory owners, corrupts Hugh. The heavenly bliss of the floods of color in the "other world" quickly sinks into the vice of greed and immoral criminality, as Hugh decides to keep Mitchell's stolen money. Davis uses a temperance reform trope (his "artist-eye grew drunk with color") to describe Hugh's deluded visions of class mobility (as he glimpses "another world . . . of infinite beauty") (**"Iron-Mills"** 47). The religious and artistic allusions become a dangerous drunken

reverie not because of some intrinsically bad quality in each, but because they become evil in the context of the temptation of greed reflected in the "folded scrap of paper" Hugh clutches in his hand (**"Iron-Mills"** 47).

Hugh's surrender to the deadly sin of avarice turns him into a radical individualist, drunk on his own power to reinvent himself through delusions of autonomy. Davis severely criticizes the myth of self-creation and the fulfillment of success via capital accumulation, portraying Hugh's ambition as leading to inevitable doom. The social irresponsibility of Hugh's decision to keep the money, and therefore commit a crime, is not covered up by Davis; his decision is wrong and she shows it. But what prompts his sin is the money he grips in his hand, the essential source of his fall into evil. The language of reform, especially temperance writing, echoes through the description of Hugh drinking the money into his soul, giving way to false dreams of socioeconomic success: his "nervous fingers took it in, limp and blotted, so his soul took in the mean temptation, lapped it in fancied rights, in dreams of improved existences, drifting and endless as the cloud seas of color" (**"Iron-Mills"** 48).

A starving artist imbued with transcendental reckless romanticism is set up to fail according to Davis. The two cultural forces she calls into question are the egocentric, socially irresponsible Emersonian aesthetic fueling that romantic recklessness and the industrial capitalism and class inequality responsible for that neediness. Herein lies Davis's confirmation that art is an economically driven endeavor that requires an audience of consumers or a wealthy patron (which Mitchell would have been, ironically, as a check for Hugh was in the billfold that Deborah pilfered). Because the tragic victim of the story is an artist, the sadness and sense of waste in the lives of the working class become enhanced to make reform a more urgent necessity. Artists live here, the narrator tells us, within conditions where one would have never expected art to be produced, and feed their souls by producing art out of the most unlikely rubbish. Yet Hugh's discontent—like the soul ache of Frederick Douglass shortly after his newly acquired literacy enlightens him to the true horrors of his condition—escalates upon his realization that money is the root of his artistic frustration, driving him to the madness of a drunkard thirsty for capital. Severe economic disenfranchisement combines with romantic notions of the self and ambition, especially artistic, to lead to social disarray, discord, jail, and suicide in the story. Hugh is not just an anonymous laborer, but an artist, making his death all the more painful for middle-class eyes to watch.

Hugh, Hetty, and Marcia all embrace distorted illusions of their craft riding on the "popular belief in the wings of genius" (**"Marcia"** 926). Davis was acutely aware of the dangers in carrying this sort of transcendental mythology into the professional era of authorship. Just as rosy visions of green hills doom Hugh, the impractical conceptions of artistry held by Hetty and Marcia are warnings about the work of writing in the Gilded Age. Her fiction urged idealized conceptions of creativity to adapt to the practical demands of the increasingly economic and competitive country America was rapidly becoming. Davis countered Emersonian romanticism because she believed in the social responsibility of the authorial vocation, rooted in the ethos of sympathy she instructed her son, Richard, to cultivate. An entrepreneur with moral vision, she shared Cynthia Ozick's sense of how in romanticism "'the will becomes supernatural, and only consupiscence remains. . . . [S]omething more diametrically opposed to ethics than Romanticism would be hard to find': what did it lead to? The self. What did it mean? Self-pride. What did it achieve? Self-delusion and delium" ("Youthful" 35). Transcendentalism was not inherently corrupt to Davis; it failed precisely because it was so ill suited, impractical, and potentially dangerous (especially in the hearts and minds of the working class and women) within the context of the increasingly capitalistic era. Davis's pragmatic sense of authorship as practiced in her career, by contrast, was well adapted to the financial condition in which she wrote. Her professional poise gave her the insight to dramatize in her fiction the precise moment when healthy ambition transforms into self-destruction. To assume from her fiction that Davis did not believe women should harbor professional aspirations is to overlook her own ability to realize those very aspirations. The result lies in some of the most popular and incisive assessments of capitalism and the limitations of individualism of the entire era, an era ever more industrial, leaving the pastoral "dream of green fields and sunshine [that] is a very old dream,—almost worn out" (**"Iron-Mills"** 12).

Notes

1. The exception is Ruth Stoner, who recently reclaims not only the financial savvy of Davis that made her "one of the most popular writers of the nineteenth century," but also thirty-three years of what critics have habitually dismissed as potboiler writing for *Peterson's,* which she presents as "works of art" rather than cultural artifacts of interest to "social historians" (44). Although such tales were "embedded within very conventional imagery and sentimental plots," Stoner argues, they contained subversive thinking about women's sexual repression (44). I further her findings by suggesting that Davis's use of such mainstream conventions, especially marriage endings and her antimaterialist sentiment, were designed to sell not only her popular fiction, but her didactic reform tales as well.

2. Sharon M. Harris claims in *Rebecca Harding Davis and American Realism* that many of Davis's stories, "perhaps unwittingly," leave their heroines "rooted in a highly patriarchal world," especially in "The Wife's Story," which ultimately "is a very dissatisfying ending for twentieth-century [as well as twenty-first-century] audiences" (114). I argue later that such stories intentionally supported domestic work, for the alternative was not the realistic sort of authorship/artistry that Davis herself practiced, but transcendentalism. Further, Harris tends to overemphasize how after the birth of her son, "she now found balancing her marriage and career even more exhausting with the addition of motherhood" and how "the inequities of responsibilities" were a common complaint, for she had "little time for celebrations and none to think of her own career" (115-6). The evidence shows that Davis was still engaged in a political and literary sense, albeit mostly through letters to Annie Fields, indicating growth if not publications. Such engagement is not so much evidence of literary paralysis, a sort of professional death by domesticity, but a testament to her resourcefulness and grit. Such attributes are underestimated by Rose in "The Artist Manque in the Fiction of Rebecca Harding Davis," whose focus on Davis's victimization and unfulfilled, frustrated vision at the hands of S. Weir Mitchell's rest cure, which I discuss later, misses how her production in spite of it is nothing short of inspirational.

3. See, for example, Dickinson's letters to Higginson dated 15 April 1862, 25 April 1862, and 7 June 1862 (Dickinson, *Letters* 171-5). Sharon M. Harris also connects Davis's pose with those of the Dickinson/Higginson correspondence (*Kindred* 57), but her implication is that Davis was merely minding her manners, as indeed she was. She was honoring the cultural expectation of deference to a potential employer and thus social superior. Etiquette books from the era "continued to devise a number of ways to demonstrate respect for class superiors" (Hemphill 138); to not defer would be to display "coarse familiarity confounding traditional notions of rank" (Kasson 138). Yet she is doing more than showing deference, especially in light of the business tactics visible later in her career. I submit that Davis was angling for a full and ongoing commitment from Fields through a show of seriousness to obtain more than a temporary cash advance. I do not mean to imply that Davis was insincere here; her motivation was not only for a bigger payoff in the future, but for a chance at social change through a highly respected venue, both aims very much sincere and not in

conflict to Davis whatsoever. My discussion of her double publication of "Ellen" points more obviously to Davis operating according to a profit motive.

4. Jean Pfaelzer's insight qualifies this point. She argues that much of Davis's "portraits of daily life and domestic power" attributed to realism really derived from the domestic sentimental novels (Pfaelzer 17). Realism, and its association with literary fiction, was nonetheless coded male, as it remained the driving force behind "the percentage of contributions by women [which] dropped significantly from 90-100 percent of the total fiction featured in the first seven years of the magazine to only 30-40 percent," as Anne Boyd notes (210). Such a precipitous drop, Boyd rightly concludes, unmasked the editorial agenda of the *Atlantic Monthly* to return to its original identity as a men's magazine, a fact that is crushingly obvious in light of Fields's willingness to drop Davis from the list of contributors in 1868, right as her star was rising as the new face of realism. He did not want that face to be female, as the writing staff by 1871 was mostly male. Such critics as Richard Brodhead have been blind to the institutional sexism of such editorial business practices. His assumption that Fields was operating a meritocracy as the magazine "underwent a palpable stiffening of its selection criteria" is painfully wrong (along with his unfortunate phallocentric imagery to express it) (qtd. in Boyd 209). Fields did not raise the bar of his selection criteria so much as he shut out women.

5. Melissa Homestead has convincingly argued that "weak copyright laws" were not a disincentive for women to write, but an incentive to "wholeheartedly exploit, and even help invent, the structures of commodity capitalism" while also "maintaining an emotional detachment from the market," one that she says was not so much an affective decision as a legal fact since "the law effectively created a distance by refusing to grant most women the legal status of proprietors" (3). Yet women writers still made huge profits by literally transforming business practices, particularly the gentleman publisher's code, with their tremendous consumer demand and profit potential. The trade courtesy of the early national period was one of the structures of capitalism that was destabilized by women writers like Davis and Fanny Fern of the 1850s, whose popularity gave publishers a disincentive to recognize one another's prior claims on authors, transforming the market into a free-market scramble of competitive open bidding.

6. Such a display of Davis's business skill shows a full engagement with and manipulation of the market, a dynamic at odds with the predominant pattern of emotional and psychological detachment from the market described in Ann Douglas, *The Feminization of American Culture*; Lori Merish, *Sentimental Materialism: Gender, Commodity Culture, and Nineteenth-Century American Literature*; and Mary Kelley, *Private Woman, Public Stage: Literary Domesticity in Nineteenth-Century America*. My perspective derives from Susan Coultrap-McQuin, who demonstrates that antebellum gender codes of conduct governing the publication industry were not always in conflict with but in many ways supported professional women writers.

7. Kristin Bordeau has noted that "The Wife's Story" is a "powerful working class critique of Emerson," arguing that Hetty rejects self-reliance not only for domesticity, but for the family and, significantly, the body, which the disembodied aesthetics of transcendentalism so denies (132). Her focus on the maternal and physical aspects of identity complements my emphasis on realistic images of authorship; Davis embraced motherhood and writing equally with the same realistic ethos. (Her advice to her son is a beautiful confluence of the maternal and authorial roles, not at odds, but mutually reinforcing in their own toughminded, rooted way.) I would suggest that the binary is a false one in Davis's own life, and that its presence in the story functions as a narrative tool to create a polarized, intense philosophical debate about professions and women that would help sell the article, in this case, especially to *Atlantic Monthly* readers of significantly more conservative gender politics than the women who read *Peterson's*. By contrast, the latter relished her veiled subversive commentary about repressed female sexuality that Ruth Stoner has so convincingly explained in "Rebecca Harding Davis's 'Second Life'; or 'Her Hands Could Be Trained as Well as His.'"

8. Mixed-genre narratives were common during this era, among which "Iron-Mills" is a sterling example. The interior of an average antebellum American bookstore is indicative of the lack of clear-cut divisions between literary genres. Ronald Zboray in *A Fictive People: Antebellum Economic Development and the American Reading Public* has shown that generic divisions of literary categories were in radical flux at the time. His examination of evidence from Homer Franklin's 1841 New England bookstore brought him to the conclusion that "relatively few books had a chance of appearing next to one of the same genre. Combined with high incidence of adjacency of books with wildly different genres, the inventories demonstrate the disarray of Franklin's bookstore" (154). The larger implications for this finding,

Zboray says, point up "the fragmented state of knowledge" and the "boundlessness of antebellum intellectual life" (154). The generic mixing in Davis is symptomatic of this kaleidoscope of kinds of books and authors "old and new of every stripe" that "stood side by side as the antebellum book purchaser browsed the shelves. . . . People would grasp for religion, advice, essays, history, biography, novels, poetry, educational material, anything to help them make sense out of the unprecedented complexity they faced" (154-5).

9. Wordsworth conceived of the process of literary production not as actively crafted, methodical labor, but as the "spontaneous overflow of powerful feelings" (Abrams 8). Coleridge's organic view equally evades realistic economic contexts and relations, isolating the creative process in the self and describing "a great work of literature to be a self-originating and self-organizing process that begins with a seedlike idea in the poet's imagination . . . and evolves into an organic whole in which the parts are integrally related to each other and to the whole" (Abrams 8). Hazlitt underlines the romantic concept of authorship as a passive activity in the same spirit of Wordsworth's "spontaneous overflow" and Coleridge's "organic growth" when he claims that "the definition of genius is that it acts unconsciously" (Abrams 8).

10. One could certainly include Washington Irving's economically disinterested authorial figures here as examples of American romantics who are not transcendentalists writing in this mode. R. Jackson Wilson's *Figures of Speech: American Writers and the Literary Marketplace, from Benjamin Franklin to Emily Dickinson* treats Irving in chapter 2 as a writer who crafted various nonprofit authorial personae in his career for sale on the literary marketplace. One of these artist figures is especially drawn from the romantic tradition, as he casts himself as a suffering romantic whose lifelong love had perished. Wilson shows that Irving barely knew the woman, but wove a semifictional devotion to her that conformed to the self-effacing romantic author figure that was very marketable in the 1820s.

11. J. F. Buckley adds the important qualification that "the realism of 'Iron-Mills' rejects the notion implicit in transcendentalism of the divinely inspired artist as a self-reliant force for cultural improvement at the very time that its romanticism supports the transcendental notion that such an artist is of fundamental importance to society. Davis places the poet within the everyday society of industrialized nineteenth-century America" (73). The story read in isolation from Davis's career appears to simultaneously reject and support transcenden-

talism. But her career indicates an alternative model of artistic creativity, one fully adapted to the market, economically grounded, balanced, and realistically engaged with demand. There was never a delusional pursuit of capital in her career as with Hugh. His sacrifice to industrialization is a function of the incompatibility of his conception of artistry with his economic surroundings, a kind of perverse amalgamation of capitalism and Emersonian aesthetic idealism, with a fatal consequence that brings out the worst in both systems: an individualistic egotism that has Hugh behaving like a hallucinating drug addict and a compulsive gambler at various moments in the story. Thus Davis mourns the passing of the "divinely inspired artist" but easily sees how ill suited it is to the current economic climate. Such mourning is indeed the source of much of the story's sentimentality, yet as her realistic conception of authorship in her career shows, a viable socially engaged and profitable alternative vision indeed existed.

12. For more on Davis's use of romanticism, see Walter Hesford, "Literary Contexts of *Life in the Iron-Mills*." Hesford examines the function of a variety of genres in the story but does not treat the economic consequences of those literary contexts the way I do here.

Works Cited

Abrams, M. H. "Introduction." *The Norton Anthology of English Literature: The Romantic Period*. Vol. 2. Ed. M. H. Abrams, et al. New York: W. W. Norton, 1986. 1-15.

Bordeau, Kristin. "'The Woman's Flesh of Me': Rebecca Harding Davis's Response to Self-Reliance." *American Transcendentalism Quarterly* 6.2 (1992): 132-40.

Boyd, Anne E. *Writing for Immortality: Women and the Emergence of High Literary Culture in America*. Baltimore: Johns Hopkins University Press, 2004.

Brodhead, Richard. *Cultures of Letters: Scenes of Reading and Writing in Nineteenth-Century America*. Chicago: University of Chicago Press, 1993.

Buckley, J. F. "Living in the Iron Mills: A Tempering of Nineteenth-Century America's Orphic Poet." *Journal of American Culture* 16.1 (1993): 62-73.

Coultrap-McQuin, Susan. *doing Literary Business: American Women Writers in the Nineteenth Century*. Chapel Hill: University of North Carolina Press, 1990.

Davis, Charles Belmont, ed. *The Adventures and Letters of Rebecca Harding Davis*. New York: Scribner's Sons, 1917.

Davis, Rebecca Harding. "Anne." *Life in the Iron Mills and Other Stories*. Ed. Tillie Olsen. New York: The Feminist Press at the City University of New York, 1985. 223-42.

———. "Life in the Iron-Mills, or The Korl Woman." *Life in the Iron Mills and Other Stories*. Ed. Tillie Olsen. New York: The Feminist Press at the City University of New York, 1985. 9-65.

———. "Marcia." *Harper's Monthly* 53 (1876): 925-8.

———. "The Wife's Story." *Atlantic Monthly Magazine* 14 (July 1864): 1-19.

Dickinson, Emily. *Selected Letters*. Ed. Thomas H. Johnson. Cambridge, MA: Belknap Press, 1986.

Douglas, Ann. *The Feminization of American Culture*. New York: Farrar, Strauss and Giroux, 1998.

Gilmore, Michael T. *American Romanticism and the Marketplace*. Chicago: University of Chicago Press, 1985.

Harris, Sharon M. *Rebecca Harding Davis and American Realism*. Philadelphia: University of Pennsylvania Press, 1991.

———. "Rebecca Harding Davis (1831-1910)." *Kindred Hands: Letters on Writing by British and American Women Authors, 1865-1935*. Ed. Jennifer Cognard-Black and Elizabeth MacLeod Walls. Iowa City: University of Iowa Press, 2006.

Hemphill, C. Dallett. *Bowing to Necessities: A History of Manners in America, 1620-1860*. New York: Oxford University Press, 1999.

Hesford, Walter. "Literary Contexts of *Life in the Iron-Mills*." *American Literature* 49 (1977): 70-85.

Homestead, Melissa. *American Women Authors and Literary Property, 1822-1869*. Cambridge: Cambridge University Press 2005.

Kasson, John F. *Rudeness and Civility: Manners in Nineteenth-Century Urban America*. New York: Hill and Wang, 1990.

Kelley, Mary. *Private Woman, Public Stage: Literary Domesticity in Nineteenth-Century America*. New York: Oxford University Press, 1984; rpt. University of North Carolina Press, 2003.

Merish, Lori. *Sentimental Materialism: Gender, Commodity Culture, and Nineteenth-Century American Literature*. Durham, NC: Duke University Press, 2000.

Olsen, Tillie. "A Biographical Interpretation." *Life in the Iron Mills and Other Stories*. Ed. Tillie Olsen. New York: The Feminist Press at the City University of New York, 1985. 69-174.

Ozick, Cynthia. "A Youthful Intoxication." *New York Times Book Review*, 10 December 2006, 35.

Peterson's Magazine. Advertisement. January-June 1863, 350.

Peterson's Magazine. Advertisement. July-December 1865, 291.

Pfaelzer, Jean. *Parlor Radical: Rebecca Harding Davis and the Origins of American Social Realism*. Pittsburgh: University of Pittsburgh Press, 1997.

Rose, Jane Atteridge. "The Artist Manque in the Fiction of Rebecca Harding Davis." *Writing the Woman Artist*. Ed. Suzanne W. Jones. Philadelphia: University of Pennsylvania Press, 1991. 155-74.

Shaeffer, Helen Woodward. "Rebecca Harding Davis: Pioneer Realist." Ph.D. dissertation, University of Pennsylvania, 1947.

Stoner, Ruth. "Rebecca Harding Davis's 'Second Life'; or 'Her Hands Could Be Trained as Well as His.'" *Legacy* 19.1 (2002): 44-52.

Thoreau, Henry David. *Walden*. Ed. J. Lyndon Shanley. Princeton: Princeton University Press, 1971.

Wilson, R. Jackson. *Figures of Speech: American Writers and the Literary Marketplace, from Benjamin Franklin to Emily Dickinson*. Baltimore: Johns Hopkins University Press, 1989.

Zboray, Ronald J. *A Fictive People: Antebellum Economic Development and the American Reading Public*. Oxford: Oxford University Press, 1993.

FURTHER READING

Bibliography

Rose, Jane Atteridge. "A Bibliography of Fiction and Non-Fiction by Rebecca Harding Davis." *American Literary Realism 1870-1910* 22, no. 3 (spring 1990): 67-86.

> Bibliography of Davis's writings that "attempts to be as complete as possible" and lists all of her published work, with the exception of her unsigned essays written for the *New York Tribune* between 1869 and 1889.

Criticism

Benesch, Klaus. "The Author in Pain: Technology and Fragmentation in Rebecca Harding Davis and Walt Whitman." In *Romantic Cyborgs: Authorship and Technology in the American Renaissance*, pp. 157-81. Amherst, Mass.: University of Massachusetts Press, 2002.

Studies Davis's *Life in the Iron Mills* and Walt Whitman's poem collection *Drum-Taps* within a broader discussion of the response of American antebellum writers to "the forces of mechanization" in mid-nineteenth-century society, asserting that whereas earlier authors, such as Edgar Allan Poe and Nathaniel Hawthorne, sought "to realign the forces of material and artistic production," the "besieged artist" in Davis's and Whitman's texts "is rendered as mute and paralyzed as the wasted scrivener when confronted with modern technology."

Curnutt, Kirk. "Direct Address, Narrative Authority, and Gender in Rebecca Harding Davis's 'Life in the Iron Mills'." *Style* 28, no. 2 (summer 1994): 146-68.

Maintains that Davis's blending of realistic and sentimental narrative devices in *Life in the Iron Mills* is not a sign of "artistic immaturity" but is a concerted effort to construct what the critic calls a "cross-gendered" narrative "to accommodate a range of potential response" from her reading public, and to prevent "gendered assumptions about plot or genre from allowing the story to be categorized solely as addressing one sex or the other."

Dingledine, Don. "Romances of Reconstruction: The Postwar Marriage Plot in Rebecca Harding Davis and John William De Forest." In *Back to Peace: Reconciliation and Retribution in the Postwar Period,* edited by Aránzazu Usandizaga and Andrew Monnickendam, pp. 146-59. Notre Dame, Ind.: University of Notre Dame Press, 2007.

Compares and contrasts Davis's handling of the post-Civil War marriage plot, which typically features the marriage of a white Northern man to a white Southern woman, in her novel *Waiting for the Verdict* with that put forth by John William De Forest in his *Miss Ravenel's Conversion from Secession to Loyalty.*

Donaldson, Susan V. "Contending Versions of Realism: Rebecca Harding Davis and William Dean Howells." In *Competing Voices: The American Novel, 1865-1914,* pp. 20-42. New York: Twayne Publishers, 1998.

Compares how both Davis and William Dean Howells treat "the inadequacy of sentimentalism" and champion the social benefits of realism in their novels *Waiting for the Verdict* and *The Rise of Silas Lapham,* respectively, noting that while both writers shared the perspective of the dangers of sentimentalism in postbellum, urbanized America, they offered different definitions of realism and the real in their works.

Dow, William. "Class and the Performative in Rebecca Harding Davis's *Life in the Iron Mills* and Stephen Crane's *Maggie.*" In *Narrating Class in American Fiction,* pp. 45-73. New York: Palgrave Macmillan, 2009.

Stresses what he calls the "performative" nature of the techniques of naturalism that both Davis and Stephen Crane employed in their works *Life in the Iron Mills* and *Maggie,* respectively, arguing that "Davis and Crane place their readers uncomfortably close to the live melodramas of the classes and class conflicts they portray," and in so doing "go far beyond the realistic and naturalistic labels so commonly attached to them."

Harris, Sharon M. "Rebecca Harding Davis: From Romanticism to Realism." *American Literary Realism 1870-1910* 21, no. 2 (winter 1989): 4-20.

Explores "the complex narrative structure" of Davis's *Life in the Iron Mills* "in terms of its movement from romanticism to realism" and argues that "at its core" the novel "is indeed a work of pure naturalism."

Lasseter, Janice Milner and Sharon M. Harris. Introduction to *Rebecca Harding Davis: Writing Cultural Autobiography,* by Rebecca Harding Davis, edited by Janice Milner Lasseter and Sharon M. Harris, pp. 1-19. Nashville, Tenn.: Vanderbilt University Press, 2001.

Introduction to a collection of Davis's autobiographical writings that includes a portrait of the author and emphasizes the cultural and historical nature of her autobiographical text.

Long, Lisa A. "Rebecca Harding Davis (1831-1910)." In *Nineteenth-Century American Women Writers: A Bio-Bibliographical Critical Sourcebook,* edited by Denise D. Knight, pp. 88-98. Westport, Conn.: Greenwood Press, 1997.

General reference essay that recounts Davis's life, traces the major themes in her work, summarizes her critical reception, and provides a selected primary and secondary bibliography.

———. "Imprisoned In/At Home: Criminal Culture in Rebecca Harding Davis' *Margret Howth: A Story of Today.*" *Arizona Quarterly* 54, no. 2 (summer 1998): 65-98.

Studies the close link between the home and the prison, and between domesticity and criminality, in Davis's *Margret Howth,* stating that, in this early work, "Davis shows how the domestic ideology of the home conspires with that of the criminal to contain individual desire and maintain social stasis rather than enable social mobility."

———. "The Postbellum Reform Writings of Rebecca Harding Davis and Elizabeth Stuart Phelps." In *The Cambridge Companion to Nineteenth-Century American Women's Writing,* edited by Dale M. Bauer and Philip Gould, pp. 262-83. Cambridge, England: Cambridge University Press, 2001.

Links the literary careers and styles of Davis and Elizabeth Stuart Phelps and maintains that both writers have been marginalized and misunderstood because they each created an individual type of "reform fiction" that stood apart from the realistic and sentimental conventions of the late nineteenth century.

Pfaelzer, Jean. "The Common Stories of Rebecca Harding Davis: An Introduction." In *A Rebecca Harding Davis Reader,* by Rebecca Harding Davis, edited by Jean Pfaelzer, pp. xi-li. Pittsburgh: University of Pittsburgh Press, 1995.

Biographical and critical survey included as her introduction to a new edition of Davis's most important stories and essays that claims that the author's writings provide "an ongoing critique of the literary and philosophical systems of romanticism and transcendentalism, which, in their formal structures and social textures, remove us from life in the commonplace, both its inner life and history of the time."

———. "Engendered Nature/Denatured History: 'The Yares of Black Mountain' by Rebecca Harding Davis." In *Speaking the Other Self: American Women Writers,* edited by Jeanne Campbell Reesman, pp. 229-45. Athens, Ga.: The University of Georgia Press, 1997.

Maintains that in her story "The Yares of Black Mountain," Davis devised new narrative strategies that repudiated the conventions of the picturesque and the masculine perception of nature as either a space of romantic isolation or an untamed wilderness that must be harnessed to the "demands of industrial capitalism," offering instead, through her female community of Black Mountain, a picture of nature "as a space of female interdependence, communication, and balanced reciprocity rather than a site of man's dominion over all living things."

Rose, Jane Atteridge. *Rebecca Harding Davis.* New York: Twayne Publishers, 1993, 191 p.

Biographical and critical study of Davis that describes the bulk of her fiction as "critical realism" that was intended "to inform and reform," and maintains that "the most distinctive feature of [her] writing is its juxtaposition of antithetical values."

Stoner, Ruth. "Sexing the Narrator: Gender in Rebecca Harding Davis's 'Life in the Iron Mills'." In *Scribbling Women & the Short Story Form: Approaches by American & British Women Writers,* edited by Ellen Burton Harrington, pp. 28-36. New York: Peter Lang, 2008.

Traces some of the critical readings of the gender and identity of the unnamed narrator in Davis's *Life in the Iron Mills* and argues that the figure's sexual ambiguity precisely fits the author's purpose in the story and, more specifically, reflects her own desire to remain anonymous and sexless as the author of the work.

Additional coverage of Davis's life and career is contained in the following sources published by Gale: *American Writers Supplement,* **Vol. 16;** *Contemporary Authors,* **Vols. 104, 179;** *Dictionary of Literary Biography,* **Vols. 74, 239;** *Feminist Writers; Gale Contextual Encyclopedia of American Literature; Literature Resource Center; Novels for Students,* **Vol. 14;** *Reference Guide to American Literature,* **Ed. 4;** *Short Stories for Students,* **Vol. 26;** *Short Story Criticism,* **Vols. 38, 109;** *Twayne's United States Authors;* **and** *Twentieth-Century Literary Criticism,* **Vol. 6.**

Robert Walser
1878-1956

Swiss novelist, short story writer, poet, playwright, and essayist.

The following entry provides an overview of Walser's life and works. For additional information on his career, see *TCLC*, Volume 18.

INTRODUCTION

Walser is considered one of the leading German-Swiss authors of the early twentieth century. In addition to volumes of short prose, he is remembered for producing such impressionistic novels as *Geschwister Tanner* (1907; *The Tanners*), *Der Gehülfe* (1908; *The Assistant*), and his best-known work, *Jakob von Gunten* (1909). In these writings, Walser defied literary conventions and redefined linguistic boundaries through his experiments with rhythm, syntax, tone, and meaning. The author also explored modernist themes, including the absurdities and contradictions of modern existence, the disparity between art and reality, and the tensions between the individual and society. Often misunderstood during his lifetime, Walser nevertheless won the admiration of several notable contemporaries, including Franz Kafka, Herman Hesse, and Walter Benjamin. In recent decades, he has been increasingly recognized for his prescient themes and innovative formal style, and today numerous critics view him as a master stylist and a major figure of modern Swiss literature. In praise of Walser's prose, Christopher Middleton suggested that his writing "might be viewed as a subtle record of the mastery—and the lapses—with which a great artist of the word patrols the hairline fractures, the delicate intervals, also the dizzyingly gulfs, between segments into which human beings categorically carve the world of their experience—individual and social."

BIOGRAPHICAL INFORMATION

Walser was born April 15, 1878, in Biel, Switzerland, to Elisa and Adolf Walser, a merchant. The author attended a secondary school with a limited classical curriculum but was removed in 1892 due to strained finances in his family; he was then apprenticed as a clerk in a local bank. Walser's mother, who suffered from a severe nervous disorder, died in 1894. The following year, after completing his training, the author left home and worked at a bank in Basel before taking a position in Stuttgart, Germany, as a clerk for two large publishers. In Stuttgart, Walser began to pursue a career in theater but eventually turned to literature. During the fall of 1896, the author returned to Switzerland and settled in Zurich, where he began writing while working a variety of jobs to support himself. Beginning in 1898, Walser's poems and short prose works appeared in influential literary journals, such as *Der Bund* and *Die Insel*. Over the next few years, the author worked in various locations, including Thun, Solothurn, and Winterthur, and performed military service in Bern in 1903. His first book, *Fritz Kochers Aufsätze*, a collection of prose pieces initially published in *Der Bund*, appeared in 1904.

In 1905, Walser traveled to Berlin, where he joined his brother, Karl Walser, a successful visual artist, and met several influential artists, writers, publishers, and thinkers as a result of his brother's connections. In Berlin, Walser continued writing short prose pieces, some of which appeared in *Die Schaubühne*, but he was anxious to produce longer works of fiction; he subsequently produced three novels: *The Tanners, The Assistant,* and *Jakob von Gunten*. His publisher, Bruno Cassirer, also issued a collection of Walser's poetry in 1909, titled *Gedichte*. Cassirer was not particularly supportive of Walser's work, however, and the author's financial situation deteriorated. He returned to Switzerland in 1913 and lived with family before finally settling into an austere garret room at the Hotel Blaues Kreuz in Biel. Over the next two decades, ten more volumes of Walser's work were published, including *Aufsätze* (1913), *Geschichten* (1914), and *Die Rose* (1925). In 1921, Walser moved to Bern. While the author continued to write and generate ideas for new projects, most of his efforts were rejected by publishers. An unfinished novel from this period, *Der Räuber,* was included in his collected works, *Das Gesamtwerk* (1966-78), and later published in English as *The Robber* (2000). In 1929, Walser committed himself to a mental health clinic outside of Bern, after attempting suicide. After a few months, he resumed writing, but in 1933 he was forcibly removed to another institution in Herisau, in eastern Switzerland, after he refused to live in a halfway house in the countryside. The author stopped writing and lived out the rest of his life as a patient, performing simple manual labor. On December 25, 1956, Walser died of a heart attack while on a solitary walk in the hills around Herisau.

MAJOR WORKS

Walser's experimental novels are considered among his most important literary contributions. Notable for their characterizations and narrative forms, these works share several common features, including minimal plot and a youthful protagonist in an urban or suburban setting. Walser's first novel, *The Tanners,* centers on Simon Tanner, a young man who quits his job in protest over society's demands for conformity and material success. Throughout the episodic narrative, Tanner drifts through the city streets, takes odd jobs, and maintains relationships with friends and siblings. While much of the novel focuses on the internal life of the self-critical protagonist, the work also explores the intricacies of a society in flux. Walser's next novel, *The Assistant,* features protagonist Joseph Marti, a young man hired to assist Carl Tobler, an inventor. Financial problems threaten the stability of the Tobler family, and Marti goes unpaid while trying to secure funding and help Tobler avoid his creditors. Initially, Marti is tempted to believe that he can bridge the social distance between himself and his employers, but eventually he recognizes the futility of his situation and leaves. In constructing the novel, Walser alternated narration with Marti's interior monologues, rather than dividing his prose into chapters. His next novel, *Jakob von Gunten,* was inspired by Walser's month-long experience at a school for servants in Berlin. In this work, the eponymous hero is the last scion of an aristocratic family, who enrolls in the Institute Benjamenta, where he is taught how to be a good servant. The novel, written as Jakob's diary, chronicles the protagonist's intentional descent from a position of privilege to one of ordinary status, and describes his dreamlike and grotesque experiences, as he seeks to discover dignity in anonymity and poverty. Overlooked during Walser's lifetime, *Jakob von Gunten* is now considered one of his greatest works. Scholars have noted the bleak, introspective tone of the novel, as well as its parodic treatment of the nineteenth-century *Bildungsroman* genre, prompting some critics to describe Walser as an early postmodernist. Attention was brought to the work in 1995, when British directors, the Brothers Quay, adapted it for the award-winning film, *Institute Benjamenta; or, This Dream That One Calls Human Life.*

In addition to three significant novels, Walser produced numerous short prose works throughout his literary career. His first published book, *Fritz Kochers Aufsätze,* comprises essays written from the perspective of a fictional schoolboy named Kochers. Presented as school assignments, the essays cover a range of topics, including courtesy, poverty, friendship, and nature. The titular persona at the center of the essays is a precocious youth, who through naive commentary explores fundamental social issues. *Fritz Kochers Aufsätze* also introduces several recurring themes from Walser oeuvre, such as

the dissatisfaction of the office employee, the primacy of nature, and issues pertaining to the artist's calling. Published later in Walser's career, *Aufsätze* and *Geschichten* are comprised of short prose pieces, written primarily during the author's time in Berlin, many of which are focused on the theater. Among the pieces collected in these works are arguments for and against the theater, a defense for anti-realistic drama, a surreal stage phantasmagoria, a fairy tale performed by cats, and prose versions of scenes from classic plays. The volumes also contain numerous portraits of artistic personalities, including painters, draftsman, and German authors of the eighteenth and nineteenth centuries. *Der Spaziergang,* originally published separately in 1917, and later translated and published in *The Walk, and Other Stories* (1957), is considered one of Walser's most successful works of short fiction. On the surface, the narrative describes the experience of a man's day-long wandering through a small Swiss city. The story also charts the mind and interior life of the protagonist, however, as he considers his own eccentricities and isolation from society. Some scholars have interpreted the tale as Walser's apologia for himself as a writer-artist. One of the author's later collections, *Die Rose,* includes short texts that explore such topics as self-transformation, love, adoration, rejection, and isolation, as well as fictive letters, literary studies, and the montage, "Eine Ohrfeige und Sonstiges," or "A Slap in the Face and So Forth."

CRITICAL RECEPTION

Walser first drew attention during the late 1890s when he began publishing his poems, essays, and plays in the magazines *Der Bund* and *Die Insel*. Championed by such critics as J. V. Widmann and Franz Blei, and by the Czech writer Max Brod, Walser's reputation continued to grow over the next few years, and with the publication of his early prose collection, *Fritz Kochers Aufsätze,* he achieved some notoriety in the elite literary circles of Zurich, Munich, and Berlin. Many of these efforts alienated members of the broader reading public, however, who found his prose demanding and difficult, and his writings were increasingly disregarded as the years progressed. His novels also met with limited success, and even supporters such as Widmann dismissed *Jakob von Gunten,* claiming that the work exhibited too many "excesses." Although Walser published roughly fifteen hundred works of short prose between 1902 and 1933, literary acclaim and financial security continued to elude him. Walter Benjamin, one of the only scholars to consider Walser's literary achievements during this time, argued in 1929 that in "any contemplation of Walser's pieces what is most crucial is the insight that this nothingness is weighty, this letting go a form of perseverance," and he described his writing as "a total merging of extreme lack of intention with the highest form of intention." Finding it difficult to get his work published in later years, and becoming more and more alienated from the world around him, Walser committed himself to a mental institution in 1929; shortly thereafter, he ceased writing, living the remainder of his life in obscurity. Following the author's death in 1956, however, academic interest in his writing grew, reaching a peak after the twelve volumes of his collected works, *Das Gesamtwerk,* began to appear in 1966. Since the 1960s, Walser's canon has continued to draw critical attention, and many works have found a broader audience, particularly among German-language readers.

In recent years, commentators have addressed a number of issues with regard to Walser's innovative formal style and thematic focus, with many revisiting previous assumptions about his work. Writing in 1978, Martin Walser countered the idea that Walser was a "charming genius living entirely off soulful spontaneity," as some earlier critics had claimed, arguing instead that the author worked hard to develop an "unrelenting style" based on "self-restraint" and an intimate awareness that "happiness and suffering are the closest of friends." Several scholars, such as Agnes Cardinal [see Further Reading], have noted the contradictory nature of Walser's work, particularly with regard to language, art, and truth. Describing his writing as a "paradoxical art" that tends "toward tentative circumscriptions," Cardinal asserted that his prose "turns into a maze of signs and formulae constructed around a truth that must remain too complex and too delicate ever to be caught by words." Both Christopher Middleton and Valerie Heffernan emphasized the importance of Walser's role as a marginal figure in German-Swiss literature, who used his art to subvert literary traditions and navigate the intricacies of human experience, while John Pizer and Susan Bernofsky highlighted the modernist aspects of the author's work, including his thematic exploration of the complex role of art in society and use of self-conscious metafictional techniques. Walser's original formal style has attracted notice from several scholars, including Middleton, Bernofsky, and Samuel Frederick. Middleton and Bernofsky both noted Walser's innovative use of syntax, while Frederick identified "digressivity" as a characteristic of the author's work, studying the ways in which he tested the limits of "plotless narration." What is common to recent assessments of Walser's oeuvre is the view that his art is much more complex than previous critics perceived. As a result, his position within German-Swiss literature has undergone considerable revision. Once marginalized, the author is now regarded as an innovator and a major modernist figure, who challenged literary conventions and expanded the boundaries of Swiss writing. Heffernan, writing in 2007, asserted that through "Walser's original writing style, we are compelled to read beyond the confines of a literature ruled by convention and tradition and appreciate the value of the borderline."

PRINCIPAL WORKS

Fritz Kochers Aufsätze (prose) 1904
Geschwister Tanner [*The Tanners*] (novel) 1907
Der Gehülfe [*The Assistant*] (novel) 1908
Gedichte (poetry) 1909
Jakob von Gunten (novel) 1909
Aufsätze (essays) 1913
Geschichten (short stories) 1914
*Der Spaziergang (short story) 1917
Die Rose (short stories) 1925
Große kleine Welt (short stories) 1937
The Walk, and Other Stories (short stories) 1957
Unbekannte Gedichte (poetry) 1958
†*Das Gesamtwerk.* 12 vols. (novels, short stories, prose, poetry, plays, and essays) 1966-78
Selected Stories (short stories) 1982
Masquerade and Other Stories (short stories) 1990
The Robber (unfinished novel) 2000
Speaking to the Rose: Writings, 1912-1932 (short stories) 2005
Microscripts (short stories) 2010
Berlin Stories (short stories) 2011

*This work was translated as "The Walk" and published in *The Walk, and Other Stories* in 1957.

†This edition of Walser's collected works includes the unfinished novel *Der Räuber,* which was translated and published in English as *The Robber* in 2000.

CRITICISM

Walter Benjamin (essay date September 1929)

SOURCE: Benjamin, Walter. "Robert Walser." In *Robert Walser Rediscovered: Stories, Fairy-Tale Plays, and Critical Responses,* by Robert Walser, edited and translated by Mark Harman, pp. 144-47. Hanover, N.H.: University Press of New England, 1985.

[*In the following essay, originally published in German in the journal* Das Tagebuch *in September 1929, Benjamin stresses the central importance of the "how" rather than the "what" and "the significance of the actual writing itself" in Walser's work, describing his style, in an often-quoted remark, as "a total merging of extreme lack of intention with the highest form of intention."*]

There is a lot of Robert Walser to read, but there is nothing written about him. What can those who know how to take these marketplace glosses in the right spirit tell us: those, that is, who, unlike the schmuck trying to exalt them as he "elevates" them to his level, can glean purifying vigor from Walser's insolently unassuming availability. Few, indeed, realize what this "short form," as Alfred Polgar called it, is all about; how many hopeful butterflies find refuge in its modest chalices from the cliff face of so-called great literature. And the others have no idea how much, amid the sterile jungle of the newspapers, they owe the gentle or prickly blossoms of a Polgar, a Hessel, a Walser.[1] They would even think of Robert Walser last. For the first stirrings of their miserably bookish education, which is all they have in literary matters, prompts them to emphasize "cultivated" and "noble" forms as a means of recouping what they call the nothingness of the content. And just then in Walser they notice a going to seed which is very unusual and difficult to describe. In any contemplation of Walser's pieces what is most crucial is the insight that this nothingness is weighty, this letting go a form of perseverance.

It is not easy. While we are used to seeing the mysteries of style emerge out of more or less fully developed and purposeful works of art, here we are faced with language running wild in a manner that is totally unintentional, or at least seems so, and yet that we find attractive and compelling. A letting go, moreover, that ranges through all forms from the graceful to the bitter. Seemingly unintentional, we have just said. Occasionally there have been arguments over whether that is really so. But, the moment we recall Walser's admission that he never corrected a line of his things, we realize that it is a mute argument. There is no need to take him at his word, but it would be worthwhile to do so. For then the following thought can put us at ease: to write and never to correct what one has written amounts certainly to a total merging of extreme lack of intention with the highest form of intention. So far, so good. It need after all hardly prevent us from getting to the bottom of this running wild which, as we have already said, takes every form. To which we now add: with a single exception. Precisely that of the most common form for which only content is crucial, and nothing else. Since the how of his work is of such moment to Walser, everything he wishes to say takes second place behind the significance of the actual writing itself. We are almost tempted to say that the what dissipates in the writing. This needs some explanation. And here we stumble across something very Swiss in this poet: reticence. There is a story about Arnold Böcklin, his son Carlo, and Gottfried Keller:[2] One day they were sitting in an inn as was their wont. The reserved and taciturn ways of the drinking partners had made their table famous. Once again the company was sitting together in silence. After a long time had elapsed, the young Böcklin observed: "It's hot"; then, a quarter of an hour later, the elder one added: "And absolutely calm." Keller for his part waited some time, then got up saying: "I'm not drinking with such babblers." This peasant reticence with words, captured here by a witty bon mot, is Walser's turf. No

sooner has he taken up his pen than he is overpowered by the urges of a desperado. Everything seems lost; a surge of words gushes forth in which each sentence only has the task of obliterating the previous one. In a virtuoso piece he turns the following [Schiller] monologue into prose: "Through this sunken path must he come." He begins with the classical words: "Through this sunken path," but then anxiety catches hold of his Tell, and seeing himself already defenseless, small, and lost, he continues: "Through this sunken path, I believe, he must come."

There have certainly been precedents. This chaste and artful clumsiness in all spheres of language is a legacy of the fool. If Polonius, that archetype of babblers, is a juggler, Walser wreathes himself Bacchus-like with garlands of language which keep tripping him up. The garland is indeed a figure for his sentences. But, like the heroes of Walser's prose, the thought staggering about in them is a thief, a vagabond, a genius. Indeed he can only portray "heroes," cannot get away from his main figures, and letting matters rest with his three early novels, has henceforth devoted himself solely and uniquely to the brotherhood of his hundred favorite vagabonds.

It is well known that in Germanic literatures there are above all some great exemplars of the windbag, lazybones, and petty thief of a hero who has gone to the dogs. A master of such figures, Knut Hamsun, has just recently been celebrated.[3] Eichendorff,[4] with his *Taugenichts* (Good for Nothing), and Hebel,[5] who created Zundelfrieder, are others. How do Walser's figures make out in this company? And where do they come from? We know where the *Taugenichts* comes from. From the forests and valleys of Romantic Germany. Zundelfrieder, from the rebellious, enlightened lower-middle class of Rhenish towns at the turn of the century. Hamsun's figures from the primeval world of the fjords—they are people whose homesickness draws them to the trolls. Walser's? Perhaps from the Glarn Mountains? Or from his native Alpine meadows at Appenzell? Not in the least. They come out of the night, where it is darkest, a Venetian night, one might say, lit by skimpy lanterns of hope, with some festive cheer in the eyes, but troubled and sad to the point of tears. What they cry is prose. For sobbing is the melody of Walser's loquacity. It divulges where his loves come from. From madness, that is, and from nowhere else. These are figures who have put madness behind them and can thus remain so laceratingly, inhumanly, and unfailingly superficial. If we wish to find one word to describe what is pleasing and uncanny about them, we may say: *they are all cured.* We, of course, never find out about this process of healing, unless, that is, we dare approach his *Snowwhite*—one of the most profound compositions in recent literature—which itself alone would suffice to explain why this seemingly most playful of all writers was a favorite author of the unrelenting Franz Kafka.

The wholly exceptional gentleness of these stories is apparent to all. But not everyone sees that the life they contain is not the nervous tension of decadence, but the pure and lively atmosphere of convalescence. "What horrifies me is the thought that I might be successful in this world," as Walser puts it in a paraphrase of Franz Moor's dialogue. All his heroes share this horror. But why? Certainly not out of any aversion to the world, nor out of moralistic resentment or pathos, but for purely epicurean reasons. They want to be able to take pleasure in themselves. And they are quite exceptionally adept at that. They also display an unusual nobility in this regard. And have an unusually strong right to do so. For nobody enjoys as does the convalescent. Everything orgiastic is alien to him: he hears in brooks the flowing of his replenished blood and, blowing from the tree tops, the purer breath on his lips. Walser's people share this childlike nobility with the figures of fairy tales who, of course, also arise from night and madness, in other words from myth. It is usually assumed that this awakening took place in the established religions. If this is the case, then the form it took was at least not simple and clear cut. To find that form one has to explore the great secular confrontation with myth which the fairy tale represents. Of course its figures do not simply resemble Walser's. They still struggle to free themselves from suffering. Walser begins where the fairy tales leave off. "And if they have not died, then they live to this day." Walser shows *how* they live. His pieces, and here I wish to end as he begins, are called: stories, essays, poems, short prose, and the like.

Notes

1. Alfred Polgar (1873-1955) was considered a master of polished short prose; Franz Hessel (1880-1941) was a novelist and author of impressionistic sketches.

2. Arnold Böcklin (1827-1901) was a Swiss painter; Gottfried Keller (1819-90) was an influential nineteenth-century Swiss novelist.

3. Knut Hamsun (1859-1952) is the pseudonym of Knut Pedersen, the Norwegian novelist.

4. Josef Freiherr von Eichendorff (1788-1857) was a Romantic poet and author of *Aus dem Leben eines Taugenichts* (1826), a lyrical novella describing the wanderings of the child-hero and celebrating the joys of nature. In its time the novella was one of the most widely read works of German Romanticism.

5. Johann Peter Hebel (1760-1826) was a pastor and poet of whom Goethe said that "he makes a peasant of the universe in the most naïve and charming way." Hebel collected a group of his unassertively didactic stories in *Schatzkästlein des rheinischen Hausfreundes* (1811).

George C. Avery (essay date 1968)

SOURCE: Avery, George C. "Simon Tanner." In *Inquiry and Testament: A Study of the Novels and Short Prose of Robert Walser,* pp. 36-60. Philadelphia: University of Pennsylvania Press, 1968.

[*In the following essay, Avery provides a close analysis of the protagonist Simon Tanner in Walser's first published novel,* The Tanners, *focusing specifically on the character's "search for relation to and integration in the world," and concluding that "the definition and attempted actualization" of the hero's relation to the world "never leave Simon's conscious or unconscious mind and explain what was to remain among all of Walser's work the unique breadth of canvas of this first novel."*]

Simon Tanner, a young man in his early twenties, is the first of Walser's three self-seekers. He moves through the three segments of the plot (the first stay in the city, dominated by the relationship to Klara Agappaia; the sojourn in the country with his sister Hedwig; and his aimless life after his return to the city) with so strong an appearance of resiliency and insouciance that he might be mistaken for a lighthearted drifter, an eternally blissful "Sonntagskind." Such a view would overlook the fact that Simon's joy is a precariously held island threatened by a tide of unhappiness often hinted at as the rootlessness of a marginal existence, but rigorously disregarded. The Simon we see as a carefree human being represents the freedom implicit in his still-unrealized possibilities of life. Seen against the background of the search for relation to and integration in the world he faces—a search that parallels his search for identity through the book—his failure to utilize his talents becomes as insistent a threat of psychological extinction as that experienced by the artist-journal writer in Rilke's *The Notebooks of Malte Laurids Brigge.*

If we seek to understand Simon as a human being and as a literary creation symptomatic for a particular historical perception of reality, we are confronted with contradictions and inconsistencies.[1] He is brash, daring, and unperturbedly outspoken in the many, frequently lengthy "speeches" in which he presents himself to the exterior world and which are his principal medium for seeking a relation to it.[2] As public utterances they establish an initial ambivalence in Simon's personality in the "childish" contradiction between their opinionated, forceful expression and Simon's aversion to the display of emotion, which he holds to be a weakness (cf. *T* [*Geschwister Tanner*], 38, 130-133). The tone and the substance of these speeches varies with what occasions them, but they all exhibit a pathos of rhetoric, a high degree of self-awareness, and an unmistakable irony reflecting the uncertainty of Simon's situation.

The book begins abruptly with such a speech, the volubility of which takes the reader by surprise. Yet the image Simon creates of himself, with the successful intention of persuading a book dealer to employ him on the spot, is misleading. In a turnabout after eight days, during which a "quiet, shy" Simon had worked "so very reliably" (*T,* 17), he quits the job, scolds his employer in a long pronouncement on the meanness of the employment, and appends a gratuitous threat "to sell his freedom for good" by going into the army rather than continue to deny his talents their full development behind the bookdealer's "old, scroungy, narrow" desk.

The opening scene typifies Simon's resistance to the institutionalization of his life. His ambition to utilize his talents is correspondingly directed more at relationships with individuals than toward his own advancement. Simon's most meaningful encounters in the book are with women, but his relationship to them is ambiguous and there is no easy identification of them with his ambitions. When he once fancies himself married, his imagined behavior toward his wife is alternately maudlin or sadistic (*T,* 126f.). During his brief employment as a servant in the home of a rich lady, he senses the failure of his service to effect a human contact, and insult is substituted for reverence (*T,* 204-205). More often, his wish is to revere and idealize women, as is the case with Klara Agappaia. The book never treats of Simon's sexual impulses; they are dormant or are consumed in the idealized gift of himself to Klara.

Behind Simon's personal ambition is a desire to function as a part of a larger whole. His opportunity to do so in the first segment of the novel is the various employment he takes. He departs from each position as precipitously as he did from the bookdealer's. A short time later, when he is seeking work at an employment office, he defends the frequency of his job changes by insisting that a marginal existence such as his demands the courage needed to discover where he can serve his fellowman (*T,* 19-20). This same speech ends with an initial, exaggerated instance of Simon's desire to equate employment with service and divorce it from livelihood in his ironic refusal to take a job with a vacation.

> I won't have anything to do with vacations. I absolutely hate vacations. Just don't get me a position with a vacation. That doesn't attract me in the least; as a matter of fact, I would die if I were to get a vacation. I want to do battle with life, I don't care if I collapse, I don't want to experience either freedom or comfort, I hate freedom if it's just tossed at me, the way you throw a bone to a dog.

> Ich will mit Ferien nichts zu tun haben. Ich hasse die Ferien geradezu. Verschaffen Sie mir nur nicht einen Posten mit Ferien. Das hat nicht den geringsten Reiz für mich, ja ich würde sterben, wenn ich Ferien bekäme. Ich will mit dem Leben kämpfen, bis ich meinetwegen umsinke, will weder Freiheit noch Bequemlichkeit kosten, ich hasse die Freiheit, wenn ich sie so hingeworfen bekomme, wie man einem Hund einen Knochen hinwirft.

(*T,* 20)

The above quotation concludes a speech in which a tone of humility provides a counterweight to the more obvious irony. We come closer to Simon, however, if we recognize behind the irony a criticism of a bourgeois ethos which makes it impossible—other than through the indirection of this irony—to plead for a morality no longer existent.

The social criticism of the mercantile world representing the society Simon seeks to enter becomes more explicit in Simon's speech to the director of a large bank (*T,* 42-44). He denounces bank employment as too costly in terms of its damage to the human spirit. Simon assures the director of his willingness to do any work that demands all his abilities, but he brusquely rejects the director's offer of a letter of recommendation. As a fictional hero, Simon enters the novel unburdened by, and not identifiable with a conventional view of social reality. In the context of society, he starts morally from scratch so as to better justify an absolute claim on reality.

> A testimonial? No, don't write one out for me. . . . From now on I'll make up my testimonials myself. All I will do from now on if anybody asks me for references is give them my own name. . . . I don't want a future, I want to have a present. That seems more valuable to me. You only have a future when you don't have any present and if you do have a present you forget to even think about a future.

> Ein Zeugnis? Nein, stellen Sie mir keines aus. . . . Ich selbst stelle mir von jetzt an meine Zeugnisse aus. Ich will mich von nun an nur noch auf mich selbst berufen, wenn jemand nach meinen Zeugnissen fragt. . . . Ich will keine Zukunft, ich will eine Gegenwart haben. Das erscheint mir wertvoller. Eine Zukunft hat man nur, wenn man keine Gegenwart hat, und hat man eine Gegenwart, so vergißt man, an eine Zukunft überhaupt nur zu denken.

(*T,* 44)

Simon's conversation in Chapter Four with Klaus, his scholar brother, gives the first overt indication of a discrepancy between Simon's outer and inner person and cautions against too complete a reliance on the appearance Simon creates. The conversation is one of those held during the nocturnal lakeside scenes when the single meeting of all the Tanners occurs. This chapter represents a first climax; all of the characters have been introduced, most of the themes have been touched on, and, consistent with the compositionally lyric nature of this work, these themes are repeated in much greater proximity to one another during this single meeting of the Tanner siblings. The conversations in this chapter and the next, during the "glorious evening" climaxed by the speech in which Simon makes the spiritual gift of himself to Klara Agappaia (*T,* 83-86), terminate the first segment of the novel. The speech adds a new perspective to his person since the fate of lovelessness he foresees is spoken of with a passionate certainty that precludes irony.

The conversation with Klaus attempts to answer his older brother's concern about the goallessness of Simon's life. Simon's concept of the role he may be destined to fill considers the possibility a unilateral accommodation to life in which the world does not participate. This gives Simon's irony a more humane cast. It reveals much of Simon's previous and subsequent aggressiveness as more than the provocation it clearly intends to be; Simon is indeed "the *eiron* of Greek comedy . . . the ironic outsider" (*Middleton,* 410), but his irony also comprehends a special plea for communication and contact. Simon's words are the first articulation in the novels of the *primus agens* for all three heroes, the incontrovertible reality of individual existence.

> I'm not in the habit of showing that I feel respect for many things. That's the sort of thing I keep to myself, for I tell myself, what use is it to put on an earnest air if one is destined by fate, I mean maybe chosen, to play the fool. There are lots and lots of fates and it's before these that I want first and foremost to curb my pride. There's no choice in the matter.

> Es ist nicht meine Gewohnheit, zu zeigen, daß ich Ehrfurcht vor vielen Dingen besitze. So etwas pflege ich für mich zu behalten, denn ich denke, was nützt es, eine ernste Miene aufzusetzen, wenn man vom Schicksal dazu bestimmt, ich meine vielleicht dazu erwählt ist, den Narren zu spielen. Es gibt viele, viele Schicksale, und vor ihnen will ich in allererster Linie meinen Nacken beugen. Es bleibt nichts anderes zu tun übrig.

(*T,* 71)

The subsequent change of locale from city to country brings with it a change in Simon's character. Until he returns to the city from the country at the beginning of Chapter Eleven, he is, by comparison, strangely mute and incommunicative. The speeches subside; he takes comfort from the thought "of being a forgotten person" (*T,* 115); the world of the first phase of the novel silently recedes. Kaspar devotes himself to his painting, Klara Agappaia's husband leaves on an expedition in search of a lost Greek city, and Klara herself unaccountably vanishes from the scene of the novel after the transitional sixth chapter. Simon lives secluded and withdrawn until he sets out to visit his sister. There is no external reason to explain why the verbal and emotional energies of the first part subside; there is only the decisiveness of this elliptical transition at the beginning of Chapter Seven: "Winter came" (*T,* 115). The new rhythm that asserts itself thereafter is marked by a reestablished intimacy between Simon and his sister Hedwig based on their mutual respect and their shared childhood, by the fantasies sparked in Simon by the placidity of rural life, and the expository essay "Country Life" which he writes to earn money. Life proceeds in this new rhythm with a "presentness" and immediacy that leaves no room new rhythm with a "presentness" and immediacy that leaves no room for retrospection or commentary on what transpired through Chapter Five.

From the time of Simon's return to the city until the end of the book still another tonality predominates. The final phase of the novel is a modulation of the first phase, dealing with the phenomenon of an urban society increasingly subject to the dictates of a modern economy. Simon's figure as an unabsorbed individual is in no way diminished in this setting, but Simon is missing the foil of society. His confrontations are now with individuals and with himself; his vociferousness of statement is unimpaired, but it is uttered in markedly greater isolation. Simon wouldn't now be able to muster the *sang-froid* and indulgent self-importance such as are found in the restaurant scene, where he reflects gratefully that he can enjoy modest pleasures "more impetuously and more sensually" than others do greater ones (*T,* 65). He can still be vain, opportunistic, and relentless in his imagination, but it is now his tolerance, sensitivity, and respect for the denizens of the world between the urban anonymity of respectability and the anonymity of the uprooted and the rootless where he himself dwells that stand out in sharpened relief.

In contrast to the first phase of the book, the portrayal of Simon is gradually shifted to the interior person, preparatory to the open end of the final chapter. Simon's long defense of unhappiness in Chapter Fourteen is a step toward this. The impassioned tone of this speech is comparable to and implicitly adds to the significance of Simon's remarkable declaration of enduring love to Klara on the lake shore—a gift of love given on the premise that it not be requited. Simon delivers this speech after overhearing two men discuss the decline into madness of a young man who is revealed as a heretofore unmentioned Tanner sibling.

As with the speech to Klara, Simon's words here attest to the balance struck between strong emotion and reflection. To Klara he had projected a vision of human relations based on his acceptance of a fate of lovelessness. Now Simon carries his tactic of definition in a new direction, radically postulating the origin of the soul and describing a metaphysics for it that is free of the categories of formalized or intellectual religion. Underlying Simon's inquiry and statement is the antithesis between the implicit belief that the affirmation of life's plurality is grace and the absence or remoteness of God (cf. the snow-child fairy tale below and *Greven,* 99). In Simon's own thinking the antithesis is bridged here by a spiritualization of the body in terms impossible in German literature before the advent of Modernism. The sensualist orientation of Simon's idealism in itself reveals a shift in the cognitive role of perception. Of equal historical significance is the linguistic form of the will to encounter a new age with an appropriate moral commitment. Whereas the fragileness of post-Goethean idealism can be seen in the increasing reliance in literature on the themes of renunciation and resignation to shore it up, here an individual moral impulse is articulated in a verbally flamboyant, "public" statement. Simon has "forgotten" his brother because of the completeness of his struggle for moral and personal identity. "You see," he says, "I never get around to thinking about him, for I am a person who has to fight with his hands and feet to be able to stand up in the world. I won't give in until it's impossible to think of getting up off the floor again" (*T*, 239). Consistent with the derivation of Simon's knowledge from the alogical level of dream, misfortune is perceived as an inevitable, transcendental force, unrelated to Idealism (or poetry [*T*, 242f.]) but based rather in a vitalistic concept of nature that replaces idealized nature with reverence for the manifestations of life. The completeness of identification Simon seeks with all things underlies the unsparing breadth of a view of reality in which suffering and misfortune, as integral parts of reality, are given the same consciousness of experience as their more courted opposites.

> Misfortune is formative. . . . Misfortune is the friend in our lives who is all the more honest for being rather morose. It would be quite impudent and dishonorable of us to overlook that. We never comprehend misfortune in the first moment, that's why we hate it at the moment of its coming. . . . Yes; fate, misfortune is beautiful. It is good, for it also includes happiness, its opposite. . . . It awakens new life when it destroys old life it didn't like. It's an incitement to live better. All beauty—if we still hope to experience beauty—we owe to it. . . . Most people don't have the courage to greet misfortune as something in which you can bathe the soul, like limbs in water. . . . Misfortune has to be added to this abundance of splendor and happiness—if one is really ready to regard the naked, taut, mobile, warm member that came with our life on earth as such an abundance. It keeps us from frothing over, it gifts us with soul. It develops our ears to hear the sound made when the soul and the body, blended into one, having crossed over into one another, respire together. It makes something corporeal-soulful of our bodies, and the soul settles down in our very middle, so that we can, if we like, feel our entire body as a soul. . . . It lets us love, for where would there be love without some unhappiness? Dreams are more beautiful than reality, for when we dream, we suddenly understand the sensuality and the rapturous goodness of misfortune.

> Das Unglück bildet . . . Das Unglück ist der etwas mürrische, aber desto ehrlichere Freund unseres Lebens. Es wäre ziemlich frech und ehrlos von uns, das zu übersehen. Im ersten Augenblick verstehen wir das Unglück nie, deshalb hassen wir es im Moment seines Kommens. . . . Ja, das Schicksal, das Unglück ist schön. Es ist gut; denn es enthält auch das Glück, sein Gegenteil . . . Es weckt neues Leben, wenn es altes erschlagen hat, das ihm nicht gefallen hat. Es reizt zum Besser-Leben. Alle Schönheit, wenn wir noch hoffen, Schönes zu erleben, verdanken wir ihm . . . Den meisten mangelt der Mut, das Unglück zu begrüßen als etwas, worin man die Seele baden kann, wie Glieder im Wasser . . . Zu dieser Fülle von Pracht und Glück, wenn man wirklich geneigt ist, das nackte, straffe, bewegliche, warme, mit auf das Erdenleben bekommene

> Glied als eine solche Fülle zu betrachten, muss eine Art Gegengewicht treten: das Unglück! Es kann uns hindern überzuschäumen, es schenkt uns die Seele. Es bildet unsere Ohren dafür aus, den schönen Klang zu vernehmen, der tönt, wenn Seele und Körper, ineinandervermischt, ineinanderübergetreten, zusammen atmen. Es macht aus unserem Körper etwas Köperlich-Seelenvolles und die Seele bringt es zu einem festen Dasein mitten in uns, daß wir, wenn wir wollen, unseren ganzen Körper als eine Seele empfinden . . . Es macht uns erst lieben, denn wo liebte man, mit nicht auch ein wenig Unglück? In den Träumen ist es noch schöner als in der Wirklichkeit, denn wenn wir träumen, verstehen wir auf einmal die Wollust und entzückende Güte des Unglücks.

> (*T*, 240-242)

In the unbroken rhythm of physical isolation and transient human encounters characteristic of the final phase of the novel, Simon's temporary association with the homosexual male nurse (*T*, 253-268) actualizes the sharpening anomaly between his insistence on absolutes and provisional and ephemeral existence. This emerges both in his conduct with the nurse during their association and in his lengthy and unusually fair self-appraisal at the beginning of their acquaintanceship (*T*, 254-258). Implicit throughout the speech to the nurse is Simon's determination to give meaning to his existence by insisting on man's responsibility to fulfill his own fate, thus placing him near to the development towards a *homo dei* which Emrich sees climaxing, in Hans Castorp in *The Magic Mountain* the development of Thomas Mann's heroes (*Emrich*, 174). But the primacy of experience that Simon posits ("I am always afraid that a single experience of life might escape me. To this end I am as ambitious as ten Napoleons" [*T*, 258].) sees a uniqueness in experience that determines its quality of individual inevitability. The measured, almost defensive tone of his remarks to the nurse bespeaks Simon's readiness to accept poverty as the price for freedom and the opportunity to remain a human being. Seeking an undefined absolute and as yet unwilling to acknowledge any norm or law as binding, he is ready to pay any price in personal terms for a fiat for his unlimited, but arbitrary commitment.

> ". . . why don't they let me try to wrest from life its excitment in my own way, everyone tries that, everyone; they just don't all do it in the same way. . . . You see, I don't want any wreaths on my grave, that's the whole difference. I don't care what my end will be. They keep telling me, the others do, that I am going to have to atone for my high spirits. Good enough, then I'll atone and then I'll know what it means to atone."

> . . . sie mögen mich auf meine Weise dem Leben seinen Reiz abzureißen versuchen lassen, das versuchen alle, alle, nur nicht alle auf die gleiche Art . . . Sehen Sie, ich will keine Kränze auf mein Grab bekommen, das ist der ganze Unterschied. Mein Ende ist mir gle-

ichgültig. Sie sagen mir immer, jene andern, ich werde meinen Übermut noch büßen müssen. Nun wohl, dann büße ich und erfahre dann doch, was büßen heißt.

(*T,* 257f.)

Before their relationship collapses under the single-mindedness of the nurse's interest, Simon exhibits a disquieting tolerance toward the nurse's advances, even restraining his own instinctive repugnance by telling himself: "One has to get to know everything, and you only get acquainted with everything if you contact it without flinching" (*T,* 266). This instance of Simon's "absolute 'lack of prejudice'" (*Greven,* 54) is one of many affronts to accepted social mores, which, since they are motivated in Simon by momentary, wholly subjective impulses, only cumulatively achieve the force of criticism.

The remainder of Simon's portraiture and his increasingly real exile within the homeland he refuses to leave can be easily summarized. Unemployed and without the ambiguous solace of his siblings, he copies addresses to stave off starvation and inveigles his landlady into lending him money. Even the coincidental meeting with Klara, to whom he is lead through a subconscious divination, is unable to brake the momentum of his descent. Immediately after his return to the city he had accepted an offer to care for a sickly child in a wealthy home in the belief that his individualism was less valuable than the chance to serve others. The life he had "frittered away" because it had seemed "quite without value" would, he said, merge into other's needs and he would live for their "purposes, interests and intentions" (*T,* 187). By contrast, the absence of a grantee after his descent into an emotional and social "lower depths" seems to mock the donor. In the final scene of the novel Simon wanders back to the site of what used to be the Agappaias' *Waldhaus,* where the club manageress who befriends him listens to the last and longest of Simon's speeches. As a climactic résumé placed where the conventional novel resolves plot, Simon's final public statement merits our attention. This unparagraphed twelve-page outpouring begins with a chronicle of the Tanner parents and their children, after which Simon relates his own school life, his unsuccessful bank apprenticeship, his hypersensitivity, and his subsequent removal to another town. Throughout the book Simon had foresworn the promise of a "smooth future" (*T,* 258) in his search for a vital present. Now he adduces recollection and memory not as nostalgia but as the definition of a past from which he seeks release, knowing that youth is often "more difficult and more pensive than the life of many an old man" (*T,* 328). His estimate of his present situation is in two parts. On the one hand he stresses the human irrelevancy of his encounters with the mercantile world when he denies a failure due to having

followed the wrong road: "I would have been just as far along as I am now, in any profession" (*T,* 329). Then he employs a critical image of himself as beggar and dreamer vainly awaiting admission at the door of life. We shall refer to this image in the following section. We should note here that the reappearance of a dream at the conclusion of an individual segment of emotional discourse, such as found in the following quotation, establishes an interrelation between inner and outer reality as well as a connecting road of unimpeded access between them.

> As for myself, up until now I've remained the most incompetent of men. . . . I still stand before the door of life, knocking, to be sure not too impetuously, and I just listen intently, whether someone might come to push back the bolt for me. A bolt of this sort is a little heavy, and if someone has the feeling that it's a beggar standing outside and knocking, he doesn't like to come. I am nothing but a listener and a waiter, but as such absolutely perfected, for I have learned how to dream while I wait . . .

> . . . Was mich betrifft, so bin ich bis jetzt der untüchtigste aller Menschen geblieben . . . Ich stehe noch immer vor der Türe des Lebens, klopfe, allerdings mit wenig Ungestüm, und horche nur gespannt, ob jemand komme, der mir den Riegel zurückschieben möchte. So ein Riegel ist etwas schwer, und es kommt nicht gern jemand, wenn er die Empfindung hat, daß es ein Bettler ist, der draußen steht und anklopft. Ich bin nichts als ein Horchender und Wartender, als solcher allerdings vollendet, denn ich habe es gelernt, zu träumen, während ich warte . . .

(*T,* 329)

In the climax and conclusion of the speech Simon acknowledges an indebtedness to the world which he promises to satisfy; he expresses a love for human beings coming from his realization of his dependence on them. He renews and strengthens his offer of service to people, "to be used by them" (*T,* 330). In this climactic situation Simon makes his first admission to others of what is at least a guilt of omission. He also repudiates the longings that previously occasioned indifference and scorn of mankind; these have been dissolved in the knowledge that the repayment of his debt will call on all his energies and faculties.

Simon's final speech poses a problem of interpretation. The reader may be puzzled by Simon's sudden abdication of a sense of absolute individual responsibility. Recognizing the figure he cuts in the world, or being, as he says, "aware of my virtues and my weaknesses" (*T,* 329) seems insufficient to enable Simon to sidestep the burden of his own person and its inwardness. The discrepancy of Simon's apparent surrender, the abandonment of principle in one whose existence was given shape—if not meaning—by principle, and the abrupt termination of the novel with no apparent esthetic logic raise questions which neither the plot nor the author answer. Even if we allow for the critical juncture of this "speech," note the absence of nearly all vestiges of mimicry, pose, self-intoxication, and irony, and acknowledge its sincerity and judiciousness, we still question the claim of this new promise for greater credibility than the earlier resolves to undertake a "useful" life (*T,* 101, 105, 248, 299). Is it the truncation of the narrative one short paragraph after the end of the "speech" that accounts for the undeniable sense of skimpiness of statement? Or is it the contrast between the final scene and the richness and suggestiveness of the rest of the novel, which an early critic sensed when he characterized the novel as a *Weltgedicht* (Benn, 133)? More than our concentration on Simon's public life has been able to indicate, **Geschwister Tanner** succeeds in giving substance to a complex, richly modulated existence at whose isolated center stands Simon. This richness is in part due to the depiction of this existence as one revolving about his vital concern that he maintain an equilibrium between his inner and outer life and that the primacy of this existence, if not absolutely based on the inner life, at least not be abrogated by rationally derived dicta. For another part it is due to the insight and human wisdom of his reflections on his encounters (*i.a. T,* 36f., 183f., 256, 271), on the death of the poet Sebastian, and on religion (*T,* 263-265), even where the human contact is not permanent and reflections do not advance the plot (cf. *Greven,* 53-54).

The symbolic expansion given his presentiment of this existence in his self-appointed role as fool makes the conclusion of the novel seem an esthetic and logical *lapsus memoriae.* Two passages, one a rare intrusion by the author as omniscient observer to comment on Simon, immediately before the final scene, the other Simon's definition of his debt from the final "speech," shed further light on the ending of the novel. In the first passage Simon is seen exercising in his unheated room, his courage bolstered by the knowledge that he had after all been able to live into the winter whose advent he so feared. The author says of his spiritual and physical exertions that "at the time he resembled a person who has lost money and who sets all his willpower on gaining it back, but who does nothing more to regain it than merely to set his will to it and does nothing beyond that" (*T,* 309). Simon thus enters the final scene under the shadow of the author's doubt about the effectiveness of an act of will divorced from the context of human relations. What is noteworthy about the world, as Simon defines it in his subsequent promise to accommodate himself to it, is that it is not the world of social and commercial enterprises, at whose extremity Simon

had ventured to live, but a "maternal earth" closer to the isolated center Simon occupies, a world he can only articulate as an opposite.

> ". . . [the world] stands facing me like an angered, offended mother; wondrous visage that infatuates me: the countenance of maternal earth demanding expiation! I am going to pay off what I've neglected, what I've transgressed, and what I've lost in playing and dreaming."[3]

> ". . . [die Welt] steht mir gegenüber wie eine erzürnte, beleidigte Mutter: wundervolles Antlitz, in das ich vernarrt bin: das Antlitz der Sühne fordernden, mütterlichen Erde! Ich zahle ab, was ich vernachlässigt, verspielt, verträumt und verbrochen habe".

(*T,* 332)

The second section of this chapter attempts to relate interior action in the hero to what has been summarized above. The purpose of the contrast of the two will be to indicate the possibility of reading Simon's final speech as an unintentional but nonetheless real admission of defeat in a spirit whose sensitivity and difficulty bridled pride permitted only a promise of an accommodation whose fulfillment lies in an unknown future, but which is more appropriately read as the questions concerning the nature of existence to which his society provides no answers. Simon's failure to achieve personal form outweighs the protestations of sanguineness in his monolog, his reversion to the interior realm symbolized by the image of the earth (in contrast to "the world") gives a meaning of poetic statement to a conclusion which is not a conclusion as much as a structural *fermata.*

Before proceeding to characteristic interior episodes we shall deal with the commentaries on Simon's character by his brother Klaus and by the novel's principal female figures as a further perspective on Simon from the expository level of the novel. These will, it is hoped, provide a balance to the confinement of our discussion so far to Simon's own actions and utterances.

Klaus' analysis of Simon occurs during his brief reappearance in the novel's second autumn. In contrast to the uniformly sympathetic commentary on Simon by the women in the book, Klaus' well-meaning pedantry and his antipodal bourgeois role to Simon fault his brother's "immaturity." He complains that Simon has "something too wild" about him which "in the twinkling of an eye" can be a tenderness, "which for its part demands much too much tenderness of people, to be able to abide" (*T,* 305). Klaus also imputes to his brother an imbalance of values, saying that he senses offence "from entirely self-evident things that emerge from life and the world" (*ibid.*) while he is insensitive to things that should hurt him. Neither Klaus' recitation of Simon's capabilities nor the charge that Simon's longings are unworthy of a "citizen, a human being and above all a man" (*T,* 305) elicit a response from Simon. Although the curt termination of the scene leaves it without commentary, its juxtaposition to the two remaining scenes of the final chapter effectively achieves implicit commentary.

Hedwig is the only other Tanner to comment on Simon. She speaks of him in a long monolog at the end of his stay in the country (*T,* 176-180). Characteristically frank in its insights, the monolog shares with the comments of other women in the novel the quality of idealizing and somewhat abstract interpolation. The fate of lovelessness in one who claims to love all of life's manifestations elicits a reaction in Hedwig compounded of superiority towards the selflessness that she feels would allow Simon to commit "much that is indecent" if it were asked of him and the knowledge that behind the unprepossessing impression of love he makes on people the same selflessness is capable of an act of heroism. Behind Simon's lack of concern for his prospects, Hedwig finds a person who can elicit unconstrained self-expression in his opposite number. Hedwig too asks him to try to change, since "for most people you will be an uninteresting phenomenon, for you'll seem dull to girls, insignificant to women, and to men untrustworthy and lethargic" (*T,* 177), but her long list of contradictions between outward appearances and inner resources is not her last word. As the alternating emotions of scorn, gratitude, and the resolutely unemotional leave-taking at the end of Chapter Ten make clear (*T,* 180-181), her discursive analysis of her brother leaves unarticulated the significance of her brother's presence for Hedwig, namely the fullness of human response and communication they shared.

Whereas the figure of Hedwig achieves esthetic integrality through the creation of an area of emotional resonance between her words and her being, the rich lady who temporarily employs Simon is too sketchily traced to warrant reading her thoughts on Simon as anything but a projection of the author on the hero. She too intuits a contrast in Simon between a special gift of accommodation and "a slight addition of shamelessness and defiance" (*T,* 196). Like Klaus, with whom she shares bourgeois ideals, her personal association with Simon is based on a wish to reform his character. She is no more successful than Klaus, despite the sensitivity she brings to the undertaking. "He has soul, this young man" she thinks, "and for that reason one has to approach him soulfully, with an awareness of the soul, in order to accomplish anything with him" (*T,* 197).

Simon's attitude toward this woman (*T,* 204f.) might be described as gingerly submissiveness; it complements the uncritical idealization that characterizes his relation to Klara. The two attitudes coalesce in Walser's later writing, principally in the prose of the twenties, into adoration of a beloved who retains this position only if she remains separated from her "troubador." This development is not yet discernible in the relation between Simon and Klara. Her few remarks on Simon are spoken in emotion (following the revelation of her love for Kaspar and at the time of Simon's gift of himself to her) and are restricted to the enigma of Simon's personality. "One can't describe you" she says. "Your heart is what is beautiful about you. I understand that one doesn't understand you. You understand everything" (*T,* 58).

The club manageress who listens to Simon's final speech is a more significant figure than the briefness of her appearance and the artistic incongruity of her role as spokesman for the author would indicate. She establishes her credentials for this role by immediately recognizing Simon as "an exceptionally lonely young man" who desires "to come into contact with human beings" (*T,* 311). She reveals herself as the Egeria of Walser's first novel through her capacity for divining the composition of Simon's personality. The curiosity and fascination she feels in Simon's presence are a mirror image of the persuasion in Simon that the insignificant and the unobtrusive partake of an uncharted profundity and ineffable complexity. In speaking to him she realizes that one easily misjudges Simon and fails to sense his inner resources "because one has been dealing with a completely composed person who simply disdained assuming an attitude and who wouldn't want to appear better and more dangerous than he is . . ." (*T,* 319).

The manageress succeeds in touching Simon as no other figure in the novel has done because she speaks assuredly of a utopian human society still bound to the "maternal earth" which Simon finally acknowledges as his mistress. She spells out her hopes for the "brothers and sisters," for the "human beings on this lonely, forlorn planet" (*T,* 312) in views that coincide with Simon's own liberal Christianity. As reluctant as Simon is to evade the present, she hesitates to shift her gaze to a future she characterizes as "this bold arch across a dark water . . . this forest full of trees . . . this child with radiant eyes" (*T,* 315), believing, as does Simon, that "the present is the future" (*T,* 315). That she herself is not deluded by Simon's assuaging promise of a different future for himself is manifest in the final paragraph of the book. There, as Simon's "poor, happy captive" she leads him not into the world but into the adjoining forest, thus returning Simon to the realm of nature.

INTERIOR SEARCH

The search undertaken by Simon in his public life ends abortively with his untenable equation of the world into which he, as a non-committed participant seeks entrance, to the sub-cognitive world of nature, drawn together in the image of the "maternal earth." This situation, accurately conveyed by Simon's depiction of himself as a beggar at the door of life, a "listener and a waiting man," consummates as he says, "I have learned to dream while I wait" (*T*, 329). An interior search paralleling the outer one takes shape in the monologs during Simon's extended periods of solitary life, in his experience of nature, and in the statements found in Simon's two pieces of writing (the essay "Landleben" and the reminiscences of his youth); this fragmented search culminates in Simon's dream of Paris and his final fantasy before he visits the *Waldhaus*. A separate treatment of the exterior and the interior person suggests itself in seeking to define the emotional integer that contrasts with the failure of Simon's public life. Such a treatment, too, is dictated by the style and form of the novel. In a novel of which Walser himself said he had disdained esthetic conventions "in order to simply make music" (*Wdgg*, 14), the cadences that unify a superficially discursive work have their source in the tension between these two modes of experience.

Simon's search for clarification and identity proceeds at two levels, corresponding to the two esthetic levels of discourse in the novel. The esthetic rationale for these two levels of Simon's life parallels the symbolic irreconcilability of the two. As a public figure Simon is astonishingly voluble, yet in explaining his decision not to answer a letter from Klaus he touches on a crucial impediment to the transferral of the interior search into conscious, specifically intellectual modes of expression. "I don't know how to depict my situation," he says, "it is not even worth describing. I have no reason to complain, just as little as to leap for joy, but every reason for being silent" (*T*, 18).

Using a more abstract approach than that utilized by the novel, a bridge can be made between Simon's public and private life by seeking to find his ideals, since ideals may signify a public designation for a segment of personal commitment. The characterizations of Simon by other figures in the book all implicitly pose the question of the nature of such ideals. As Simon admitted to Klaus (*T*, 71) and as the manageress correctly intuits (*T*, 319), he does not bare his ideals. He expressly rejects the suggestion of the two men before whom he defended unhappiness that he is motivated by ideals: "I am in the habit of making rules for myself and in general am hardly inclined to be swept off my feet by fantasies and ideals, since I regard that as extremely unwise and presumtuous" (*T*, 242f.).

Simon's single consciously creative act in the novel, the essay "Landleben" (*T*, 146-153), is written during the restorative interlude in the country. It aims to do no more than describe and document the presumptuousness of ideals in their disengagement from the conduct of life. Paralleling this reform ethos is the intentional transparency of a creative effort that presumes to be no more than description and documentation based on a reflective appraisal of the visible present. As such Simon's essay develops the form used in *Fritz Kochers Aufsätze* and parallels the short prose Walser wrote during his Berlin period. As a personal document the moral probity and balanced linguistic vigor of the essay contrast to the "wild talk" (*T*, 258) and the aggressiveness of some of Simon's "speeches." The thematic antithesis inherent in the essay contrasts city and country. Simon describes his own situation when he writes of the dignity one can maintain in rural poverty against the degradation and ostracism it means in the city: ". . . for there everything is judged by what people say and do, while here grief grieves on silently and pain subsides naturally in pain" (*T*, 148). His most incisive insight is based on his knowledge of the loss of contact between rich and poor in modern urban life. He perceives a human dilemma so acute that he pleads for a relationship even at the price of sustaining it through cruelty and self-advantage rather than have the propertied ignore the poor.

> Better to torment them, to force them into bondage, to let them feel hardship and blows, then a relationship ensues at least; rage, an agitation of the heart, and that's a kind of communication too. But to keep oneself holed up behind gold garden gates, in elegant homes, and to be afraid of sensing the warm breath of human beings, not to dare to live lavishly any more for fear the embittered oppressed might notice it, to oppress and yet not have the courage to show that one is an oppressor, to fear even the people one oppresses, neither to feel comfortable with one's wealth nor to afford others comfort, to use ugly weapons which don't presume any real defiance or manly courage, to have money, just money, and not any splendor along with it. This is the present image of the cities and it seems to me an unbeautiful image, one in need of improvement.[4]

> Besser, man peinige sie, zwinge sie zu fronen, lasse sie Druck und Schläge fühlen, so entsteht doch eine Zusammenhang, eine Wut, ein Herzklopfen und das ist auch eine Art Verbindung. Aber sich in eleganten Häusern, hinter goldenen Gartengittern verkrochen zu halten und sich zu fürchten, den Hauch warmer Menschen zu spüren, keinen Aufwand mehr treiben zu dürfen, aus Furcht, er könnte von den erbitterten Gedrückten wahrgenommen werden, drücken und doch den Mut nicht besitzen, zu zeigen, daß man ein Unterdrücker ist, seine Unterdrückten noch zu fürchten, sich in seinem Reichtum weder wohl zu fühlen, noch andere wohl sein zu lassen, unschöne Waffen zu gebrauchen, die keinen echten Trotz und Mannesmut voraussetzen, Geld zu haben, nur Geld, und doch damit keine Pracht. Das ist gegenwärtig das Bild der Städte, und es scheint mir ein unschönes, der Verbesserung bedürftiges Bild zu sein.

(*T*, 149f.)

Simon's disavowal of ideals follows from his obstinate insistence that "it is a question of this world" (*T,* 255). In this sense his brother Klaus is correct when he says that Simon asks too much of the world (*T,* 305), for what Klaus sees as Simon's omissions, his lethargy, fatuousness, and the insouciance of his public life, are a disquieted renunciation of a world that shares neither his hierarchy of values nor the tolerance he brings to their definition. The vitality of Simon's encounter with the world cannot be mistaken either for estheticism or *fin-de-siècle* lassitude since his actions reveal his endeavor to guide his life according to intuitive convictions and aspirations. When, in the context of his final speech, he says "I should like to take definitive form as late as possible" (*T,* 330) his freedom of spiritual movement not only expresses his concern that many of his contemporaries have incontrovertibly abdicated their claim to a unified life while still professing ideals, and thereby falsifying them, but he becomes the medium for what should have been their own continuing awareness and inquiry.

An earlier instance of interior definition are Simon's reminiscences of his youth, written after the disappearance of the figures who had so compellingly enlivened the first segment of the novel (*T,* 115-124). The creativity of the essay "Landleben" lies in its attempt to fuse the present with Simon's imagination. The reminiscences, on the other hand, successfully form an essay in self-knowledge undertaken at the realized risk of re-experiencing the grief and the traumatizing brutality (*T,* 119-120) as well as the love that constituted the original experiences. The author is careful to dissociate what Simon writes from even the suggestion of literary creativity by having him say that he started to write "unintentionally without thinking" (*T,* 115), simply to document "what I still know from those days" (*T,* 119). That Simon's reminiscences are intended to fill no other function than to help him define an emotional locale from which he can do battle with life is unmistakable when Simon immediately destroys what he has written: "Then he tore up what he had written, without ill-humor and without deliberating much, simply because it had no further value for him" (*T,* 124).

The area of paradox between Simon's public appearance—with the disdain and denial of fantasy appropriate to this figure (*i.a. T,* 242f.)—and the dreamer and daydreamer is enlarged in monologs and fantasies. Many of these are highly discursive and lack formal integration. The principal monologs are those dealing with resolutions to lead a more socially purposeful life (*T,* 99-102; 248-249) and Simon's fear of the approaching winter (*T,* 281-283). A fantasy about the possibility of a settled life in the country (*T,* 125-129) points to Simon's awareness of the lack of resolution at the end of the first section of the novel. A crude, tasteless fantasy concerning Hedwig (*T,* 139-143) is a literarily honest indication of Simon's willingness to approach his sister in her new role as a mature woman, while it in itself is a tangle of unbridled associative fancy (cf. also *T,* 215f.; 248).

Both in his defense of unhappiness and in his remarks to the club manageress, Simon refers to dreams as the vehicles of insight. The most determinative dream in the novel, Simon's dream of Paris (*T,* 218-227), providing a conjunction of the creativity of imagination and the self-restriction demanded by the exterior world, successfully integrates into the structure of the book a revelation of Simon's inner life and an anticipation of plot. The narrative isolation of this dream within the novel is accentuated by the complete absence of any commentary on the dream by the author. No further indication is given that Simon ponders the dream he himself characterizes as "melancholy" (*T,* 228) after awakening, despite the remark introducing the dream: "He had a strange dream that occupied him for a long time afterwards" (*T,* 218). The remainder of the novel makes clear that Simon in fact does occupy himself with the dream, but at a cognitive level beneath, albeit parallel to that of the narrative of his public life.

The first of the dream's three sections is a street scene that heightens and synthesizes other street scenes in the novel (*i.a. T,* 183-184; 197f.; 245-246) and anticipates passages in the two later novels where the transient heroes encounter humanity. The description of Parisian streets captures an atmosphere at once graceful and elegantly light to the point of almost tangible mobility, yet invested with the illogical, piercing beauty of a nocturnal paradise. This scene contrasts to the street scenes in the last six chapters of the book, where they are dominated by the meanness and hopelessness of an existence that drives men to degrading acts (*T,* 300f.). It focuses and heightens the "glorious evening" on the lakeshore and the dissolution of that evening into motion, thereby transforming this dream street into a royal road for humanity. The figures in the dream belong to Simon's world, just as many of the elements in it can be recognized as a pot-pourri from the events of Simon's waking life, but he stares at them with the awe of a stranger and non-participant. In contrast to the demonic energy of the street scenes in *Jakob von Gunten* the precision of detail in this synesthaesia of sound, color, music, and motion is Simon's projection of a *theatrum mundi* beyond the reality of life.

The second section of the dream adds to its irreality. Simon finds himself on a dark staircase. He enters a room where Klara had been sleeping on a divan. She awakens and they are sumptuously served by a Negro "while a soft, muffled music rustled down from the ceiling of the room, like the gurgling of a rare ingenious fountain, which now sounded far away and then next to his ear" (*T,* 222). Klara identifies herself as a sorceress and, taking her wand, successively opens three doors to show Simon visions of his siblings. Klaus is hard at work, but anxious about Simon. Hedwig's corpse lies under a white linen, a victim of the sorrow she had expatiated on to Simon (*T,* 171 *passim*). Her death is presented in terms stressing the separateness of all the Tanners: "She leaves without having answered the question the world asked her: 'why don't you come?'" (*T,* 223). The third of these magic chambers or dreams within a dream, shows Kaspar at work painting. This vision is the most important of the three, permitting Klara to appear both as an idealized selfless lover and as an advocate of art, and suffering only from its disproportionate length in the dream.

A "wondrous, incomprehensible music" (*T,* 226) begins the final section of the dream. The apparitions have dissolved; now Klara opens a window to show Simon a summer snowfall that will eventually cover the houses and imprison the inhabitants of the city for an entire month. During this time Klara will sleep. Then spring will return, trees will blossom overnight, the heavens will descend into the Paris streets and even the poor will have money. "Then you'll see," Klara prophesies, "how people will embrace right out on the streets after the long confinement and weep for joy at seeing one another again" (*T,* 227). Shortly thereafter Klara falls asleep and Simon awakens.

The climax of the dream, the chiliastic re-birth of humanity following the purity of the snowfall and the fruition of spring,[5] uses metaphors drawn from nature to express Simon's utopian hopes more expansively than he expresses them in his final "speech." But Simon is neither the agent of his own vision nor even its prophet. It is clear from the two street scenes in the dream—the first "real" within the dream, the second a promise in the future of the dream—as well as from the pertinency of the release "after the long confinement," that the direction and the details of the dream stem from Simon. The prophet of Simon's ideals is a Klara whose past he distorts in the dream to make of her a sorceress and near vestal virgin. The remoteness of the synthesis in the dream of art and self-restriction is apparent in the setting of this vision in a future within the dream and in the suspension of time at the scene of the vision ("There aren't any definite seasons of the year here," Klara says in explaining the summer snow [*T,* 226]). Two factors account for the transferral to Klara of Simon's own latent ideals: the stringency with which the author separates Simon's imaginative life from art and Simon's inability to articulate or even dream of a relation between

nature and society. Thus Klara has to "explain" the disordered chronology in terms of gracious behavior, cautioning Simon not to show his surprise at the summer snowfall (*T,* 226).

The thematically most integrated fantasy and the one most revelatory of the symbolism of Simon's inner life occurs after Klaus' visit in the final chapter (*T,* 306-308). Besides circumscribing Simon's isolation it indicates, in contrast to Simon's passivity in the Paris dream, the extent and area in which the author sanctions creativity in Simon. The passage begins as a presentation of Simon's thoughts during the first snowfall. He is exulting in the transformation the snow works on the city scene, while he is ridiculing his recurrent fears that he would not live to see the winter. Relying solely on the associative force of the metaphoric purity of snow, a transition is made to Simon's inner life using as a threshold between his thoughts about the winter scene and the following tale no more than the remark that the scene seemed like a fairy tale to him (*T,* 306).

> Once upon a time there was a man. He was completely black. He wanted to wash himself, but he had no soap and water. When he saw that now it was snowing, he went out to the street and washed himself with snow water and this made his face as white as snow. Now he could show it off and he did. But he started to cough and now he was always coughing; the poor man had to cough for a whole year, until the next winter. Then he ran up the mountain until he began to sweat, but he still had the cough. The coughing just wouldn't stop any more. Then a little child came up to him, it was a beggar child. In its hand it had a snowflake. The flake looked like a delicate little flower. "Eat the snowflake," the child said. And now the big man ate the snowflake and the cough was gone. Then the sun went down and all was dark. The beggar child was sitting in the snow and yet it wasn't cold. It had gotten a beating at home; why, it didn't really know. You see, it was a little child and didn't know anything yet. Its little feet weren't cold either and yet they were naked. A tear gleamed in the child's eye, but it wasn't yet clever enough to know it was weeping. Perhaps the child froze in in the night, but it felt nothing at all, it was too small to feel anything. God saw the child, but it didn't move Him. He was too great to feel anything.

> Es war einmal ein Mann, der war ganz schwarz, da wollte er sich waschen, aber er hatte kein Seifenwasser. Als er nun sah, daß es schneite, ging er auf die Straße und wusch sich mit Schneewasser und davon wurde sein Gesicht weiß wie Schnee. Da konnte er prahlen damit, und das tat er. Aber er bekam den Husten, und nun hustete er immer, ein ganzes Jahr lang mußte der arme Mann husten, bis zum nächsten Winter. Da lief er den Berg hinauf, bis er schwitzte, und noch immer hustete er. Das Husten wollte gar nicht mehr aufhören. Da kam ein kleines Kind zu ihm, es war ein Bettelkind, das hatte einen Schneeflocken in der Hand, der Flocken sah aus wie eine kleine zarte Blume. "Iß den Schneeflocken" sprach das Kind. Und nun aß der große Mann den Schneeflocken, und weg war der Husten. Da gang die Sonne unter, und alles war dunkel. Das Bettelkind

saß im Schnee und fror doch nicht. Es hatte zu Hause
Schläge bekommen, warum, das wußte es selber nicht.
Es war eben ein klein Kind und wußte noch nichts.
Seine Füßchen froren ihm auch nicht, und doch waren
sie nackt. In des Kindes Auge glänzte eine Träne, aber
es war noch nicht gescheit genug, um zu wissen, daß
es weinte. Vielleicht erfror das Kind in der Nacht, aber
es spürte gar nichts, es war zu klein, um etwas zu
spüren. Gott sah das Kind, aber es rührte ihn nicht, er
war zu groß, um etwas zu spüren.

(T, 307f.)

Taken together with the dream of Paris this brief scene
helps reduce the "querying and astonishment" (*T,* 318)
the manageress feels before Simon. Permitting us to see
Simon without the public mask of rhetoric he assumes
in his long speeches, it suggests why, in the Paris dream,
the prophecy is attributed to Klara. The dream thus enables us to understand more clearly the implications of
the final scene of the book, where a compositional termination of the narrative sequence is lacking and the
intimation of a new direction in Simon's life is so presented as to be ambiguous both by the logic of human
nature and that of literature.

The syntactical parataxis in the narrative style, the
nearly exclusive concentration on the "action," the di-
minutives and the archaizing vocabulary, all identify the
story of the snow-child as a fairy tale. The first, fable-
like half deals with the man "who was completely
black," the second section, following the sharp transition made at the fall of night, with the beggar child.
This second section utilizes restricted, parabolic analysis, the submerged rhetoric and implied question of poetry. The dominant structural element in both halves is
contrast: black and white, large and small, perspiration
and cold, the man's energetic activity and the child's
impassiveness, pain and insentience, the timelessness of
the flower-snowflake.

Here a child appears as a servant-redeemer. It cures
mankind of an inner estrangement from nature through
the spiritual gift of the flower-snowflake (cf. Klara's
prophecy of the summer snowfall). After the performance of the redemptive mission the child is abandoned to an unpeopled and loveless night. The child's
insentience to the beating and the frost establish its gen-
derless purity and validate its sacrificial fate. The tragedy and the resolution of the fairy tale have one and the
same source: the child's gift. Too untutored to know the
world, it is too small and insignificant to be cared for
by the world, while God, Who is remote and intractable, has discharged His responsibility by leaving the
child in the hands of man. The parable of the snow
child ends less conclusively than this resumé indicates
because of the intermingling of contrast with aural associations in the anaphoric use of the verb *spüren* relating both to the child, and, in the last sentence, to God.
The near zeugma thereby created intimates a relationship between them expressly denied in the tale.[6]

Superficially only an episodic connection exists between the three scenes of the final chapter (the meeting
with Klaus, the fairy-tale scene, and the return to the
Waldhaus). Actually, the fairy tale links the other two
by commenting on them thematically. The fairy tale is,
first of all, Simon's answer to Klaus' admonitions to
conform to the society around him. It reiterates at a less
conscious level their inability to communicate with one
another. More importantly the fairy tale depicts Simon's
own situation at a more intimate level than his conscious temporizing does, since it irrevocably separates
the elements of the equation Simon has made to the
manageress between the world and the spontaneous affirmation of life as part of nature.

Very shortly after this scene, taking up the image found
in the fairy tale, Simon characterizes himself as a beggar at the door of life. If he is not clever enough to
know that his long speech is a lament and an admission
of his failure to combine the freedom of nature with the
self-restriction of society, the manageress is. She responds to the plea implicit in his speech and allegori-
cally anticipated in the passivity and the willingness to
serve that Simon shares with the fairy-tale figure.
Whereas the principal figures in Walser's earliest work,
Komödie, consciously renounce the world as a threat to
their self-sufficient inwardness (*Greven*: "reine Innerli-
chkeit," 29 *passim*), Simon's share of the world is the
freedom of isolation, much as the snow-child is left to
the care of the world.

The presence in the first part of the Paris dream of the
mysterious fleet-footed, blue-frocked linkboys called
"Teufelsjungen" (*T,* 220) is an earlier variant within the
novel of the snow-child's minority life. Seeing them Simon wonders: "Where did they live; did they too have
parents, brothers, sisters; did they too go to school;
could they grow up, marry, procreate children, get old
and die?" (*op. cit.*). Like the fairy-tale child they stand
outside the course of normal life and are unaffected by
the demands implicit in the symbiosis an idealized Klara
embodies. Like the fairy-tale child they represent an an-
thropological, and therefore moral problem because
their freedom lacks any integration with the world
which they illuminate with "a magical, white light" (*op.
cit.*). Only in *Jakob von Gunten,* and after, does Walser
raise such figures from the realm of dream and fantasy
and provide them with the mixture of playfulness and
earnestness that Thomas Mann associated with mythic
existence and creativity when he discussed his Joseph
figure.[7] In Simon Tanner they are still part of the silent
subterranean stream of life within, where the knowledge of isolation and the experience of sorrow live on
despite its public suppression by the will. The evidences
of this life dictate the depth of Simon's awareness of
himself as beggar and dreamer. The greater esthetic per-
suasiveness of the interior life and the failure of the attempt to subsume the interior life to a commitment to

society points to their ultimate opposition in this book. From *Geschwister Tanner* on the tension between irreconcilable opposites remains a thematic constant through all of Walser's formal and stylistic variations.

Taken as a whole *Geschwister Tanner* derives its vitality from the presentation in a solitary figure of the infinite quality of one human life. Simon's commitment to his fellow man is encompassed by his vision of a love whose completeness of sacrifice provides for its own sufficiency. On the acceptance or rejection of this love rests the answer to whether his contact with society and the implementation of his nominal acceptance of its demands will prove viable or ineffectual. To the manageress he says: "I offer any person my knowledge, my strength, my thoughts, my achievements, and my love, if he can make use of them. If he points his finger and motions to me, in that event someone else might hobble up, but I run, you see, . . . bowl over and tread carelessly on all my memories just to be able to run all the more freely" (*T,* 330). At the base of his keenness of receptivity are the moral compassion of his celebration of misfortune, the knowledge of the intricacies of the heart in the sense of communion he feels with the underprivileged (*T,* 68-69; 272-275), and the vision of humanity in the Paris dream. It would thus be misleading to regard this sensitivity as solipsistic or as the "complete sentience" associated with Neo-Romanticism. The restriction of Simon's creativity within the realm of nature or its sublimation in Klara illustrates the role this novel played in Walser's attempt to counteract the post-1900 sentiment of esthetic resignation. Early in the novel Klaus accurately judges Simon's intemperate outbursts less as disaffection with the world, than "as a certain search in his younger brother's soul for clarification of his own condition in relation to the world" (*T,* 72). The definition and the attempted actualization of this relation define the quality and the point of view of the novel; they never leave Simon's conscious or unconscious mind and explain what was to remain among all of Walser's work the unique breadth of canvas of this first novel.[8] The statement of the novel is the paradigmatic function of this search through its variations in the denunciation of a mercantile society, the objectivation of boredom and vacuity outside this society, the courage to sacrifice his identity in service, and in the fact and the metaphor of his wanderings punctuated by human encounters.

Notes

1. Greven (*Greven,* 225) has noted as essentially one-sided the attempts to characterize Simon or the novel by speaking, on the one hand, of "seeing the world as an unabating miracle" (Christian Morgenstern), or as the "unique personalization of the given reality" (*Middleton,* 411), as well as views, which in contrast, speak of Simon's "ster-

ile individualism" (Jean Moser, *Le roman contemporain en Suisse allemande de Carl Spitteler à Jakob Schaffner* [Lausanne, 1934], p. 73) or of his "disrupted" relation to the world (*Bänziger,* 73).

The quotation from the poet Christian Morgenstern comes from an "aphorism" Morgenstern probably wrote after reading the manuscript of *Geschwister Tanner.* He appended it to a letter written to Cassirer on January 22, 1907, when he was reporting on what we must assume was the manuscript of a novel Walser subsequently destroyed. Despite Morgenstern's tendency to read Walser from the vantage point of his own spiritualizing proclivities, his remarks deserve mention as the earliest attempt to describe the quality of Walser's art. Morgenstern correctly emphasizes Walser's loquaciousness, the relation between nature and freedom, the naïveté, and the aimlessness of his wandering, all critical aspects of Walser's work.

Morgenstern's remarks on the "new novel" begin as follows:

> . . . was Walsers neuen Roman betrifft, so kann ich nur wiederholen, was ich schon früher gesagt habe, nur daß es mir jetzt noch viel berechtigter erscheint. Ich glaube nicht zu große Worte zu gebrauchen, wenn ich meine, daß diese neue Arbeit eine der größten Versprechungen bedeutet, die je von jungen Dichtern gegeben worden sind. Sie enthält Partien von so reiner und rührender Schönheit, daß kein reifer Leser unbewegt davon bleiben kann und daß keiner den Glauben wird unterdrücken können, daß hier jemand auf dem Wege zum schlechtweg Außerordentlichen begriffen ist.
>
> (*Ein Leben in Briefen,* ed. Margarete Morgenstern [Insel, 1952], p. 242-243)

2. Friedman speaks of the prevalence of such "rites of identification" in the heroes of stream-of-consciousness novels from Proust through Joyce (*Friedman,* 158).

3. Thomas Mann's nearly contemporaneous *Tonio Kröger* (1903) undertakes an analogous search for identity following from a failure of acceptance. Kröger turns his back on society from the time of his departure from his birthplace until the revelatory visions on the island of Aalsgard. Yet Simon, despite his isolation, never wittingly follows this path. Tonio Kröger explicitly anticipates Simon's belief that every man must follow his own path, no matter how aberrant it may seem, but whereas Tonio takes solace in a career as an artist, the trenchancy of Simon's encounters and his determination to comprehend them comes from his acceptance of the limitless variety of life as personally pertinent. In the more drastic terms of the Nietzschean dichotomy between life and art as

found in Walser, the denial to art of even a stop-gap efficacy is indeed more reminiscent of Hofmannsthal's substitution of an adventurer for the artist in the comedies following the "Letter of Lord Chandos" (cf. Martin Stern's Afterword to his edition of Hofmannsthal's *Florindo*: Bibliothek Suhrkamp, Bd. 112 [Frankfurt a. M., 1963]).

4. The praise of the unnoticed and unsung formative aspects of the country upon its people and the timeless, ritualist, and near-religious significance of the land in contrast to the atrophying city ("Who wants to own a house in the city? . . . The houses are filled with the greatest variety of human beings, all of whom pass one another by without knowing one another, without expressing the desire to be able to get to know each other" [*T*, 150]) is thematically related to the work of the poet Georg Trakl. The central presence of a speaker as against Trakl's receding narrator, however, and the absence of the mute, self-enclosed images that create the ghostly beauty in Trakl's earliest poems ("Die schöne Stadt" and "Kleines Konzert") create an incomparably different tone.

5. In his usually impressive dissertation, Greven interprets Walser's extensive use of a snow image as the symbol of a death wish, principally on the basis of the poems and dramolets written before the novels. He assigns this meaning to the snow image in a discussion of the early works as responses to the question of how to live (See *Greven*, 38f.; 41-43; and Notes 45 and 46), while recognizing that the same image—often simultaneously—also stands for purity. By emphasizing the philosophical implications of the early work, both its artistic statement and its stylistic relation to later work are neglected. As a consequence, the snow image is too narrowly defined. As a death symbol the image fits neither Simon's dream of Paris nor the beggar child in the fairy tale who "was sitting in the snow and still wasn't cold" (*T*, 307). Nor does it fit Jakob von Gunten's transformation of the garden behind the Institute Benjamenta when he imagines snow falling on it. After the early work the snow image is just as often the medium for transition—a tangible, transitory mask for transformation that offers respite and attests to endurance and to the ability to out-last vicissitudes. Even Greven's quotations can as easily be read in their contexts as literary manifestations of Nietzsche's "eternal return" as of the desire for death.

6. The pathos and the disspiriting tone of the fairy tale parallel the bleak fairy tale told by the grandmother in the final scenes of Georg Büchner's *Woyzeck* (according to Seelig, Walser read Büchner intensively early in the Zurich period [*KGS*,

351]). The eight negatives in seven sentences underlining the unbridged separation between man and God that exists despite man's longings is a stylistic device found in Kafka's crystalline, inexorable parables.

7.   Und ist nicht vor allem der Held dieses Romanes ein solcher Zelebrant des Lebens: Joseph selbst, der mit einer anmutigen Art von religiöser Hochstapelei den Tammuz-Osiris-Mythos in seiner Person vergegenwärtigt, sich das Leben des Zerrissenen, Begrabenen und Auferstehenden "geschehen läßt" und sein festliches Spiel treibt mit dem, was gemeinhin nur aus Tiefe heimlich das Leben bestimmt und formt: dem Unbewußten? Das Geheimnis des Metaphysikers und des Psychologen, da die Geberin alles Gegebenen die Seele ist,—dies Geheimnis wird leicht, spielhaft, künstlerisch und eulenspiegelhaft in Joseph; es offenbart in ihm seine *infantile* Natur . . .

    (Thomas Mann, "Freud und die Zukunft," *Adel des Geistes* [Stockholm, 1948], pp. 583-84)

8. The publisher Bruno Cassirer's decision to excise material from the original manuscript because it seemed boring to him was a mistake of judgment, since Simon is only comprehensible if his portrayal includes the counterweights to his insight and emotional and intellectual energies.

The novelist's personal relation to this novel was, however, greater than to his two other novels. When Walser thought of himself as a novelist, it was generally with *Geschwister Tanner* in mind (cf. "'Geschwister Tanner'" (*FKR*); "Walser über Walser" (*Prager Presse*, July 27, 1925). The determinative role Simon's figure occupies in Walser's imagination can be seen in a forerunner of the novel hero in "Simon, eine Liebesgeschichte" (*KGS*).

Bibliographical Note

The varied sources of the texts used for this study due to the lack of a complete edition of Walser's prose works at the present, make necessary a prefatory note on the book publications of his writings.

Fritz Kochers Aufsätze (Leipzig: Insel, 1904).

Geschwister Tanner (Berlin: Cassirer, 1907).

Jakob von Gunten (Berlin: Cassirer, 1909).

Komödie (Berlin: Cassirer, 1919).

All of these titles have long since been out of print; if available, they are sold as collector's items. Even the reprintings of Walser's novels (*Geschwister Tanner* [Zurich: Rascher, 1933]; *Der Gehülfe* [St. Gallen: Schweizer Bücherfreunde, 1936]; *Jakob von Gunten* [Zurich: Steinberg, 1950]) are difficult to find.

In 1953 a projected ten-volume edition of Walser's prose works, entitled *Dichtungen in Prosa*, began to appear under the editorship of Carl Seelig. At the time of Seelig's accidental death in 1962, the five volumes listed below had appeared, the first two published by Holle Verlag (Geneva), the others by Verlag Helmut Kossodo (Geneva):

Vol. I (1953): *Aufsätze / Kleine Dichtungen.*

[This volume contains all of the prose pieces originally published under the first title and more than half of those originally included in *Kleine Dichtungen.*]

Vol. II (1954): *Unveröffentlichte Prosadichtungen.*

[This volume contains only a small portion of the prose writings not previously collected in book form.]

Vol. III (1955): *Der Gehülfe.*

Vol. IV (1959): *Fritz Kochers Aufsätze / Die Rose / Kleine Dichtungen.*

[In addition to the first two titles, this volume contains the thirty-one pieces from *Kleine Dichtungen* not included in Vol. I.]

Vol. V (1961): *Komödie / Geschichten / Der Spaziergang.*

KEY TO ABBREVIATIONS

WORKS BY WALSER:

GW IV = *Das Gesamtwerk.* Herausgegeben von Jochen Greven, Band IV (1967): *Geschwister Tanner; Jakob von Gunten.*

DICHTUNGEN IN PROSA. HERAUSGEGEBEN VON CARL SEELIG [1953-1961].

FKR = Vol. IV (*Fritz Kochers Aufsätze / Die Rose / Kleine Dichtungen*).

KGS = Vol. V (*Komödie / Geschichten / Der Spaziergang*).

T = *Geschwister Tanner* (in *GW, IV*).

OTHER WORKS AND STUDIES:

Benn = Joachim Benn, "Robert Walser," *Die Rheinlande,* 24. Bd. (1914), 131-134.

Emrich = Wilhelm Emrich, *Protest und Verheißung. Studien zur klassischen und modernen Dichtung* (Frankfurt am Main/Bonn: Athenäum, 1960).

Friedman = Melvin Friedman, *Stream of Consciousness: A Study in Literary Method* (New Haven: Yale University Press, 1955).

Greven = K. J. W. Greven, *Existenz, Welt und reines Sein im Werk Robert Walsers. Versuch zur Bestimmung von Grundstrukturen* (Cologne: W. Kleikamp, 1960 [photomechanic reproduction of dissertation typescript]).

Middleton = J. C. Middleton, "The Picture of Nobody. Some Remarks on Robert Walser, with a Note on Walser and Kafka," *RLV,* XXIV (1958), 5, 404-428.

MLB = Rainer Maria Rilke, *The Notebooks of Malte Laurids Brigge,* tr. M. D. Herter Norton (New York: W. W. Norton, 1949).

Wdgg = Carl Seelig, *Wanderungen mit Robert Walser* (St. Gallen, Tschudy, n.d. [1957]).

Martin Walser (essay date 1978)

SOURCE: Walser, Martin. "Unrelenting Style." In *Robert Walser Rediscovered: Stories, Fairy-Tale Plays, and Critical Responses,* by Robert Walser, edited by Mark Harman and translated by Joseph McClinton, pp. 153-68. Hanover, N.H.: University Press of New England, 1985.

[*In the following essay, originally published in German in 1978, Walser attempts to define Robert Walser's "unrelenting style" as a writer, countering the view put forth by a number of critics that he was nothing more than "the gifted dilettante" and "the charming genius living entirely off soulful spontaneity." Instead, the critic asserts, Walser worked hard to develop his literary style, which he says is based on "self-restraint" and an intimate awareness that "happiness and suffering are the closest of friends."*]

Shall we enroll our author forever among the ranks of the so-called controversials? We know that is no longer necessary. Those who understand have compared him with Shakespeare, Mozart, Schubert. That he is a classic is admitted today even by those who do not much care for him. Especially by them, perhaps. So they can be rid of him. Apparently there is no need to fear that anyone will actually read him. From the man who did the very fine translation of *Jakob von Gunten* into English, I learned in 1973 that in the previous year sixteen copies had been sold in the United States of America. Ten years ago I would have said zealously: And how many hundreds of thousands of Hesse! But I don't say that any more. Years of associating with Robert Walser's books have developed in me a sensation that might be captured like this: There are books that spread like brush fire, and books that sink gradually into us; they never cease sinking into us, and we never cease wondering that books can have such an endless, gentle weight or that there are in us such depths to be awakened. The accompanying feeling is something like happiness. I have now had this experience three times: with Hölderlin, with Kafka, and with Robert Walser. For an author who offers such a degree of inexhaustibility, there is no need to fear, for all eternity. So one is free to just talk about him. If one can.

I would like to talk about the tone of Robert Walser. Who would not be glad to help free this author from the scented cloud, still with us, of the gifted dilettante, that of the charming genius living entirely off soulful spontaneity? The big-shot critics and colleagues, those especially, recognized in him the most charming of all authors. Since they believed him nothing more than that, they were only too glad to consider him a kind of exquisitely lyrical poet-simpleton, who had staggered out of the competitive arena and whom they might readily grant a grain or two of their superior attention. I would like to mention the manufacturedness of Walser's tone—his attempt to treat life ever more exclusively as if it were writing. With the counterbalancing smile that for him had to accompany every big word, he himself designates what he has thus achieved as his "unrelenting style."[1]

When his first book, *Fritz Kochers Aufsätze,* appeared in November 1904, one reviewer believed the author to be an overrefined offshoot of some extremely refined house; possibly even of Mann's *Tonio Kröger,* which had appeared the year before. But even if one did not take the contents to be pure realism—"Papa has carriages and horses," and such like—the Fritz Kocher tone sounded over-delicate and graceful. And naïve. Incredibly naïve. Well, at least Tonio Kröger had never been that, not for one second. How haughtily Tonio Kröger despises everything that is not up to his current standards! And with what naïve vehemence Fritz Kocher adores everything that happens to come before his scent-addicted nose! That is how literary society perceived and maintained the author: as the Paragon of Sincerity, the poet who walks about on dreamed legs, and who, to his good fortune, does not quite know what is happening when yet another pretty line springs forth from him. In brief appearances in the Wedekind salon in Munich, involving dreamily sudden passes at girls' legs and chitchat as easily confiding as it was productively uninhibited, Robert Walser was only too glad to play the role of boy-page-cherub-poet against a completely provincial Alemannic backdrop. Even more so from 1905 to 1912, amongst the twining *Jugendstil* tendrils in the western suburbs of Berlin, which seemed as though prepared for him alone. For a time, he played the shepherd boy, the Beardsley figure from Biel, so well apparently that for years afterwards he was forced to hear that he was really much better in person than on the page. The split began when they all thought him nothing more than his role. In the eleven or twelve or thirteen hundred prose pieces that he wrote because he considered himself "bottomlessly unsuccessful" as a novelist, he was forced to react again and again to the period from 1895 to 1913. In 1928, when even his prose piece writing had been soured for him by the general lack of recognition, he described his debut in literary society with *Fritz Kocher* [*Fritz Kochers Aufsätze*] in the prose piece "The First Step" ("Der erste Schritt"):

"So-and-so-many years ago I sped, not unlike a traveling journeyman, through brownish green forests and over shimmering, yellowish blue flowered, unforeboding plains, and arrived in all innocence at a place where important contemporaries, standing one and all on a terrace, received me with a friendly smile, crying out with unmistakable amusement: Behold, here marches and dances our way one who still seems completely unassailed, unspoiled."[2] He says that fellow writers to whom he himself had told his life story would then thunder at him regularly: "How gloriously embarrassed you then stood there, so magnificently sweet natured, with such a wonderful shepherd-boyishness?"[3] And in 1932, shortly before he had to quit, he wrote in the prose piece **"The Midget"** (**"Der Knirps"**), this too is one of his roles: "Now and then, his facility, arising as it were from a kind of sleep, bore the stamp of calculated naïveté or artificial artlessness."[4]

The grotesque thing is that his cleverest contemporaries—including even Kafka and Walter Benjamin—were unable to see through the shepherd boy, whereas he himself, the naïve child, was able to formulate grandiose diagnoses of this misunderstanding in terms as clear and hard as a diamond. As well intentioned as Kafka and Benjamin were towards Robert Walser, I nevertheless believe that Kafka's much-cited love for him is a creation of Max Brod, who, in his capacity as editor, published Robert Walser's prose pieces for years, and also, by a stroke of intellectual luck, attempted just about the only analysis of his poetic method we have. Walter Benjamin, with his admiring murmurs about the enigmatic qualities of Robert Walser's "language returned to the wild" and his "letting himself go," did more to nourish the cultural rumor of the naïve poet than to make his poetics comprehensible.[5]

There is a fine touch of lunacy to Robert Walser's finding himself surrounded by "younger intellectualizers" in the late twenties who urge him, as he himself puts it, to "free [himself] from his novice ways," while also making him "most respectfully, i.e., painstakingly, aware of the jewel of still being absolutely unaccomplished."[6]

So who is naïve? Those who took him (and still take him) to be a *Jugendstil* version of the Romantic *Taugenichts,* or the Walser who could describe his role so accurately:

> They laugh at me primarily because I seem in earnest. They think it happens unwittingly, whereas in fact it's by design. But my vocation, my mission, consists mainly in making every effort to keep my audience believing that I am truly simple. I give them the illusion that unspoiledness and naïveté still exist.[7]

If he shows himself at his "full height, carefully gone to seed from head to toes," then, he says, "this sloppiness [is] a product of art."[8] Even Walter Benjamin was unequal to this sophistication from the town of Biel. Possibly he got his impressions from reading magazines now and again. The reader who can survey the *Collected Works* has an easier time recognizing the author as an author.

Today anyone can see, for example, that the *Kocher* [*Fritz Kochers Aufsätze*] prose piece about poverty cannot have been written either by a scion of affluence or by somebody who is totally naïve. In one of his favorite roles, that of the servant Tobold, Walser reworked his stay at Dambrau Castle in Silesia in the fall of 1905; in the guise of Tobold he lets himself say that he wants to take part always in the battle of good against evil, of the "movable ones against the hard boiled . . . , of the diligent toilers against those who do nothing and nevertheless still stay on top, in the battle of the innocent against the shrewd and the sly."[9] In this Robert Walser battle plan, the front which pits the movable against the hard boiled tells us most about the struggles of his life. Mobility, getting carried away, instability are his wealth and his poverty, his happiness and his distress, the sine qua non of his existence, which he assumes and develops as his profession. He wants to become an author immediately, of course. And famous, with all his heart. Fritz Kocher is already the fundamental figure for his life: The child, a poet; or, the poet as child. And he enters with just as great a thirst for great enterprises as Hölderlin at his youngest. "I am frightfully ambitious," says Fritz Kocher.[10] Like the earliest Hölderlin, he feels almost naked with ambition. He has no theme, he just wants to write. But was he really so themeless, so pointlessly and emptily ambitious as he, the scruple-struck lad from the petite bourgeoisie, accuses himself of being? The manner in which this child Fritz Kocher turned away from the industry of his home town! He does not concern himself, he says, with what is made in the factories. "I only know that all the poor people work in the factory, perhaps as a punishment for being so poor."[11]

The poor are punished for being poor "by having to work in the factory"; in other words, it serves them right. Since Swift made his famous "modest proposal" that the poor should sell their extra children to the rich for the Sunday dinner table, thus simultaneously solving the problems of a surplus of children and a shortage of suckling pigs, probably no ironic author has gone as far as our young naïf, who declares poverty a crime properly punishable with work in a factory. I find it astonishing how soon he completely masters the art of pronouncing an evil reasonable. And in the next few years, this becomes the task through which he develops his style. Personal distress, far from being represented or lamented as such, is to be answered experimentally in the affirmative, and this yeasaying to want and distress is to be developed ever more reasonably, ever more richly. He dispatches Fritz Kocher off into the forest to this end. Subsequent Robert Walser characters

also find in nature an otherness which has at least the advantage of not being a society intent upon doing harm. It is as with Hölderlin. Thus nature is not a fixed opposite, but is itself a process. "The forest flows," we read in *Kocher,* "it is a green, deep flowing away, a running away, its branches are its waves."[12] In this movement, which of course proceeded from the ego and was amplified by the forest, the ego itself is caught up, unstable as it is. Whoever flees society and comes suffering into the forest, will experience, in this region of amplification, a back and forth with nature that finally makes him able to say his happiness kisses his suffering, indeed his suffering is his happiness; he has learned that from the forest. Happiness and suffering are the closest of friends. Here it sounds precocious, cheeky, preposterous: At the end of the forest piece, which is the end of the *Kocher* book, the author can already demonstrate his kind of tone and procedure—that is, his method—applied to his own writing. He would really have preferred to pour out his feelings in front of the beauties of nature, he says, but there he learned that "pouring out in the art of writing demands a perpetual self-restraint."[13] What this colorfully spoken but still very green poet-youth formulates here might readily remind one of Jean Paul at his most mature—who would not become one of our young man's favorite authors until years later. Irony, said Jean Paul, requires "a perpetual keeping to oneself or objectification . . . [a] countering frost in the language."[14] A fellow wants to pour out his feeling, but notes it would carry him away too far, so he restrains himself and instead formulates a completely different tone so as not to lose himself; when he hears how the countertone sounds, compared to the spontaneous one, he is pleased. We can see that the countertone stems from a countersteering. Instead of letting go, a person has oppressed himself a little. And lo and behold, he has a much clearer sense of himself as his own oppressor than he would have as one who gets carried away and loses himself. That too is an achievement; it reminds one of the rewards for good behavior in a petit bourgeois childhood and adolescence. Instead of biting into the chocolate, one makes a face as if one had bitten into it. And this becomes a method. It is decisive that no blows from the world around him—and these blows, as we know, get lower and lower—could make this author give up writing.

Goethe, I believe, once advised his colleague Eckermann that young writers should be careful not to get caught up in projects that would more or less tie them up for a long time. He himself, said Goethe, could have achieved still more if he had been less intent on long-term projects and had thus been even more alive to the stimulus of the moment. It took the crashing failure of Walser's three novels, written and published in Berlin, and the know-it-all advisors drawn like bluebottles to this failure, to drive Walser away from the novel and make him a writer of short prose, at the mercy of everyday events. That is, he had to be driven in a great fall from his planned course, in which he competed with Cervantes, Stendhal, Dostoyevsky, and Keller, down to the chicken-run of the manufacturer of prose pieces, who could answer to his experiences only with the kind of complaisance and limited scope grimly prescribed by the fine arts page. In 1907 he could still write, rather breezily, to Christian Morgenstern that he would rather join the army than become a supplier to magazines. Yet that is exactly what he became. He put up with it until 1933. But by then, in the prose piece form allotted him, he had truly carried out his project. Even if one wants to gnash one's teeth a little in rage, reading his **Robber** novel, at the thought that more of the kind has been lost to us, Walser's enforced concentration on the prose piece bore an uncanny fruit: a life-novel, consisting of a thousand and several hundred segments. In the late twenties he himself wrote that in his opinion his prose pieces formed "nothing more nor less than parts of a long, plotless, realistic story. For me the sketches are . . . shorter or lengthier chapters of a novel. The novel, on which I am constantly writing, is still the same one, and it might be described as a variously sliced-up or torn-apart book of myself."[15]

He had his ego appear in this book in the roles of the youths Fritz, Wenzel, Simon, Kasimir, Fridolin, Felix; in the bookkeepers Tanner, Helbling, and Josef Marti; in the servants Tobold and Jakob; in those eerie celebrities named Mehlmann, Oskar, Wladimir, and Schwendimann; he was also fond of letting himself be guessed or even easily discovered as Kleist or Brentano; naturally he also wrote about Kleist, Lenau, Lenz, Cézanne, Watteau, Mozart, Beardsley, Voltaire, and so on, without bringing in himself every time as the main character. But he liked to dress up as [Schiller's] Karl and Franz Moor; even more, in the garb of the Prodigal Son. And best of all, and more and more frequently, with no name at all. To him, names were things that tied up, pasted down, shut in. He was much fonder of appearing under labels signifying a function, an activity, a relationship; most preferably as a child; then as a page; as a servant. In a prose piece from the late twenties about a lackey, his gift for mobility dictated the following to him: "He lacked the desire to be what he was."[16]

If one wants to get any real sense of Walser's style—without getting lost in a merry-go-round of aesthetic ghosts—then at some point one must also take into account that possibly no poet has ever wanted to make a friendlier entrance into the world. Whenever he recalls it, one senses this. "Certainly I was beautiful then, I know that now," he says.[17] Everything made him glad, he said. He loved everything, welcomed everything without exception. "Yes, I used to stand and go about like a person entitled to say he was carousing." "The wind flew in blue waves across the field, and bells chimed, and everything was namelessly beautiful . . . ,

I was free as never before . . . , each thought a part of life, and each living apparition immediately a thought." And he needed no objects for his rapture. "The simple awareness of existence, enchanting me, dug down deep within me in search of love, which was flying through screens and walls all about into the Measureless and whatever came next. Outside, amid the echoes and the noise, a stillness embraced me as though I could never again fail. Everything around me was blue as fluttering flags and red as blossoming lips and young as the eyes and cheeks of children. Then seriousness was alongside laughter, and dying was alongside living. So it went, back and forth in constant movement; the flashing days were like shimmering fruit." Naturally, he then took a man on the road at night to be Jesus Christ. Naturally, for him writing and praying were one. But the seraphic tone of the man from Biel produced a dissonant echo in his time and world. And he does not reject this echo, but absorbs it and makes it his own. He says, quite right. Not immediately. Not all at once. It's not that easy to say yes to the world's saying no. After the fall, being the fallen one, he first had to feel himself all over. When he fell in Berlin with his novels, he wrote his first Brentano prose piece.[18] It says: "He saw no more future before him . . . , the past was like . . . something incomprehensible. All justifications scattered like dust. Voyages and journeys . . . had become oddly repulsive to him: he was afraid to take a step, and at the idea of changing his abode he shuddered as at something monstrous." First he begins to reproach mankind, then himself: he was "the most unreliable, most lascivious, and least faithful thing on earth." At this point one sees directly how it is possible for the world, for society, to arouse someone dangerously against himself. He would like to separate himself from the person who put him in this situation. He still believes in a better self within him. "O, his person," he cries, "he would have liked to rip it away from his essence, which was still good. To kill one half of himself so as to save the other from destruction, to save the man from destruction, to keep the God within him from being completely lost." Then he returns to Biel. Beaten, but sheltered again. His prose piece **"The Entrance"** (**"Die Einfahrt"**) may very possibly be the most insuperably beautiful piece ever bestowed upon a country by a returning Prodigal Son.[19] "Slowly, as if it were prey to a profound reflectiveness, and as if it had a need to advance hesitantly, the train moved along; it was a workman's train." "The homeland, and the high, golden thought of it, soared around my heart . . . O what beautiful train riding among mild-mannered, sensible, serious fellow countrymen, all the way into embracedness." By virtue of the powerful gratitude of one who has been saved—or who considers himself saved—all the prose pieces about the return home are simply magnificent. In Biel, to be sure, he was not forced to perform the self-alienating salon tricks of Berlin; for here he remained from the outset at his own level; but the lack of confirmation and recognition, the not being perceived or understood, broke him down again over the years until, in the end, he was worse off than after the Berlin fiasco. Now there was no longer any Switzerland to shelter him. At this point something occurred that he, who had called himself "a man of development,"[20] had feared—life itself threatened to grind to a halt. A prose piece that bears witness to this after six years of Biel is called **"The Street"** (**"Die Strasse"**) (1919):[21] "I had taken steps that had proved useless, and now I went into the street, upset, numbed. First I was as if blind, and thought no one saw anyone any more, that all had gone blind, and that life had come to a standstill because everything was groping about madly." This is also the night he goes up to a figure standing in the dark. But it is no longer Jesus Christ, as in bygone days. Now he says: "This heaped-up collectivity wants and does nothing. They are tangled in one another; they do not move, are as if locked in; surrender themselves to indistinct force, and yet are themselves the power that weights them down and fetters their minds and limbs." He escapes to Bern. Wants to stay in motion. But by failing utterly to perceive his movements, the world around him intensifies its negation of them. He must not only cope with this. He must—unrelentingly—approve it. To sanctify the misery by lamenting it in the tone it had itself set, that was out of the question. A professional does not permit himself such directness. He could not allow himself to be an unjustly unrecognized writer and complain of it into the bargain. No, he cries: Nothing does a writer such good as a hefty portion of nonrecognition. Nothing is as good as misery, because from the vantage point of the worst you can only look ahead to better. "Stendhal was well off because he was badly off."[22] That's how the unrelenting style puts it. It is a movement of existence that allows not a single second of peace or safety. Recognition is, after all, as the story **"The Negro"** (**"Der Neger"**) puts it, "a soft shattering of something that, supported by unconsciousness, has been building within us." That is unrelentingly petit bourgeois realistic. Every one of Walser's readers knows his racing fugues of modesty, those orgies of belittlement that eliminate all imitators as surely as do Kafka's subjunctive snares. Yet in Robert Walser, as in Kafka, there is nothing that expresses solely the author and not his fellow citizen just as well. Not for one second did Walser feel justified as an author. No experience can extinguish his passionate desire to be the good neighbor. Nor can experience diminish the strength of his love. But as a result of all that experience, love gradually begins to consider itself comic. He has his "Robber" go to a doctor and say: "maybe my illness, if I can call my condition that, is that of loving too much. I have a horrifyingly large fund of love in me, and each time I go out on the street I start to love something, someone, and everywhere as a result they call me a man of no character: I would like

to request you to laugh a little at that."[23] Max Rychner, who could not have known this passage, compared him to Shakespeare; after which Walser—in his own tone—called himself the Shakespeare of the "wee prose piece." So the blissful early tone has evidently attended the school of hard knocks that inclines one to comedy. After the "midsummer night's dream," the person in question knows that under certain conditions love is comic; indeed—if it does not behave correctly—it can even be called a sickness.

In other words, the blissful tone, which has never been at all naïve, produces a terrible echo, which the author does not bewail, but instead prefers to amplify to the shrillest. "If dying must be done anyway, I'd sooner die willingly than unwillingly"—that is what his style dictates.[24] Anyone who still takes the passage in the **"Negro"** story about recognition as demolition to be the product of a genius feigning modesty can be directed to passages of the same tendency that have no aesthetic horizons, but only moral ones. For instance in 1926: "Admiration, after all, begets arrogance, hardness."[25] Or, both morally and aesthetically, in 1915-16: "Isn't defeat better than the wan smile of triumph?"[26] And again from the twenties, in a section in which he again represents himself as a forty-year-old child: "Mockery and lovelessness made him happy."[27] And in the Wladimir role: "Seemingly peculiar that he admits having often been joyous as a down-and-out and morose as a success story."[28] The worst is really and truly the best—that is the thrust in the development of his unrelenting tone; it is to be demonstrated again and again until calm plausibility sets in. In a prose piece written after 1930, he still allows himself to be questioned about his failure; letting himself respond, we read, "reluctantly and at the same time openheartedly." So, just as in Kocher's days, self-restraint and pouring out belong together. And that is how the answer turns out: "Bad writers [he said] are sometimes more entitled than good ones. . . . Anyway, all recognition has forever tended to turn into a trap or a ditch, and lying within rejection are all kinds of encouragement."[29] In the prose role of the adventurer, he uttered the same with shrill pride: "I would wither away, lose myself, if everyone with reason to do so were to respect me."[30] Here he ascribes to contempt rights that are downright fabulous. One must often recall as the source of energy the petit bourgeois Christian treasure chest of morality; otherwise this radical cultivation simply evaporates into aesthetics. In one of his finest roles, that of the servant Tobold, he says: "if, of my own free will, borne by courage and compassion into higher frames of mind, I renounce heaven: then will I not, sooner or later, as a reward for upright behavior, fly to a heaven many times more beautiful?"[31] One should also place the instability of his ego, and thus his mobility and preference for change, within their real context, which he himself names often enough—poverty: "only the poor man is able to walk away contemptuously from the narrow self, so as to lose himself in something better, . . . in movement that does not come to a halt, . . . in the vibrating generality, in the inextinguishable mutuality that bears us" (1919).[32] Or: "There was a cheerful mobility and freedom in poverty. The cold provided scorching heat."[33] A poor man, we read somewhere else, respects everything except himself. "Where would he have gotten respect for himself?"[34] Indeed, perhaps he even began writing, he says, because he had been poor and needed to start a sideline to make himself feel richer.

I have spent too long showing his method only as it applies to himself; it is really one-sided to demonstrate the elaboration of his unrelenting irony only through the ever-more-successful touting and justification of his own failure. His dialectical art, derived from the most personal experience of deprivation, can also solve problems. He proves this as early as *Jakob von Gunten* when, in a crazy passage of dialectic, we are led to concede that only the suppression of freedom makes it possible to experience freedom, that only a life not being lived is really a life.[35] Twenty years after *Gunten* [*Jakob von Gunten*] he still calls his "never having lived" a "gigantic, magnificent, radiantly green tree."[36] The cunning of reason which Hegel discerned in world history is not for one second alien to this author's perception of reality. "The bad are of use to the good,"[37] he says. "The Swiss," he writes twenty years after *Gunten,* "perhaps owe their freedom not only to William Tell, the fighter for freedom, but also to Governor Gessler, who considered freedom out of place, and who provided the former with the occasion to set himself in motion. . . . The shover and the shovee, the one who exerts pressure and the one who shakes it off, somehow complement each other; and as for freedom, it desperately needs governors, etc., in order to grow."[38] Later on, he presents Tell and Gessler as "a single contradictory personality."[39] What interests him is solely the "circumstance of the giving-cause-for-movement."[40] Tell and Gessler are an "inseparable unity;"[41] for him movement becomes the highest value, as for Hölderlin, Fichte, Hegel, and Kierkegaard it had become the highest value, the only absolute. "The movable is always the most just," he writes.[42] One can now look back differently on his preference for misfortune, on his serious attempt to praise his failure, on his preference for the negative, on his ability, developed to the point of virtuosity, to experience, represent, and acclaim as the most pleasant that which is least pleasant: Nothing should remain, absolutely nothing. Thus whoever spent a moment among the elect would the very next moment have to face becoming one of the disadvantaged. The orderly, the diligent, the much approved, the good, the successful, the ruling, the fortunate, the living: because time continually pulls all things down, everything will be thrust next moment into its opposite. That is all they have to look forward to now. "Because things cannot be

otherwise than that they become otherwise, they became otherwise," says he in jest, in a truly Hegelian mood.[43] On the other hand, whoever exists only in the negated moment is constantly looking forward to existence. Maturity was always alien to him. Spring engendered autumn in him, and autumn spring. There was no summer. Absolutely not to be in the present moment, or perhaps to be absolutely not in the present moment—therein lies the countertone that he developed against time as well as world.

Once we have followed Walser all the way into these frequencies of his realistic sense of history, we can finally get beyond compassion for the author as one who was and still is misunderstood. Otherwise it would be like feeling sorry for Jesus because he was crucified. Some people are simply able to transform what has been inflicted upon them into their work. They become objective. That is the highest goal. Robert Walser achieved it. And formulated it thus: "My activity is stronger than I."[44] There is—one must say this with all due awe—no one whom Robert Walser approached more often or more boldly than Jesus, whom he simply called his favorite. As early as 1913 the man who had returned completely beaten from Berlin to Biel allowed himself the perspectival luxury of calling himself a "vanquisher," whereupon he of course immediately had "an attack of laughter."[45] If one entrusts Jesus' message of love to the unrelenting style of this terrible, gentle man from Biel, it comes out like this: "There is something almost malicious in not hating anything."[46] Or: "With modesty you can practically do in somebody."[47] And can any author formulate more like Jesus than one who writes that his best lines are those that "make the reader consider himself superior to the author?"[48] People have restricted themselves too emphatically to extolling this author's funny-masochistic lapdog antics as the droll achievement of his charm. Someday we must realize that he mediates himself into Jesus just as exactly and uninhibitedly as he did into Kleist, Brentano, Schwendimann, or Knirps. He has the scribes thus confront his favorite role, Jesus: "Your modesty is all artfulness."[49] As with the Negro role, this applies at least as much to the Bieler as to the Nazarene. He can now express everything, even the greatest bliss, in the form of a negation. He can also express the worst in the form of a completely perceptible, magnificent affirmation. At times one can even get the impression that the style has reached these turning points all by itself. It has become that highly developed; an author's existence has become that professionalized. But however monstrous its achieved phrasings, this stylistic movement borrows not a gram of weight from any traditional workshop for making impressions. While playing, he achieves sentences such as the following: "It will sound exquisite if I say I know, with enviable precision, that the present essay contains errors, and that this certainty is something beautiful."[50] Such a sentence has an effect on me like news from a better world. Just when, by dint of interference, scolding, disdain, and rejection, they have almost wholly deprived a man of his sense of self, he manages to make the bundle of impositions his own and uses it to produce phrases of Mozartian lightness. That his most extreme gestures should still be light as a feather is probably due to the way his Alemannic mother tongue watches over these unrelenting movements. This linguistic womb pursues her child, who wants to become pathetically independent in standard German, with all kinds of ridicule. Often enough one watches Robert Walser hammer the most intractable raw materials of the thing-addicted Alemannic dialect into a lyrical sketch that is fine to the point of making one faint.

If I now go on to point out that agglomerated contradictions begin to proliferate almost frighteningly in his works, I should add—as stridently as possible—that these knots of contradictions, through which he practically allows his prose to decompose itself, have nothing in common with the mania for opposites that led a different "literary often-mentioned" of the age to set up mechanically opposing rows of dummy concepts, between which the author dashes back and forth for a while, only to betray them cheerfully to one another, while raising himself above them to hover on high, untouchable, most eminent, and incontestably himself. It does make a difference whether one descends from Friedrich von Schlegel or from Hegel. Schlegel prided himself on his ability always to top one heaven with yet another. Robert Walser wanted to learn to renounce heaven completely, so as to become worthy of an even higher heaven, which he would then, of course, also renounce for a still higher one. In reality, that meant renunciation of heaven, absolutely; but not as a single act—rather, as a lifelong movement in the work. Hence the conspicuous increase in his style of compound contradictions: He would have preferred most of all to hyphenate each adjective with the opposite that language holds in store. And he does that, too, more and more frequently. Just as Kafka, with his chains of speculations, gradually throttles all movement by his characters so that absolute indeterminacy can assume its dominion in prose, Robert Walser takes each point wanting to pin itself down and jams it headlong into its counterpoint, thus yielding a knot of words that shivers with the tension of contradiction; or perhaps a patch of bright darkness such as one finds in Rembrandt—one can no longer dwell anywhere. Gradually one does grasp that the language arisen from our story of pain always arose through a tearing apart of something whole. Because of its origins, language is always a specialized deprivation. It is language because of its ability to distinguish life from death. In reality, faith and skepticism, life and death, and so on are unstoppable points along paths of movement; it is only when the various verbal labels are superimposed that they are transformed into opposites, in a way that annihilates their movement, and therefore

their sense. The last step of this prose restores the real contradictions as inducements to movement. Nothing is separated from anything any more. Everything is linked by its negation to everything else. In a century in which authors have adopted the oddly unprofessional notion of considering themselves the representatives and vicars of all that is possible, we would be almost morally endangered if this genius of change had not arisen among us as a corrective. His countertext earns us a future: "To a great degree, one possesses only what one lacks, for then one must seek it."[51] Has the negative ever been as beautiful in anyone else's writing? To me, some of his sentences seem suitable as an elegiac apocalypse of the bourgeois age.

Having failed to reach their goal, the benefactors could no longer sleep in peace.[52] If *everything* can be expressed as deprivation, then language has for once exhausted its possibilities. After all, that is the purpose for which language arose in the first place. Robert Walser makes no reproaches—he loves, and loves, and loves again. So he arrives as if by himself at his unrelenting mildness: "The vouchsafers are out in search of supplicants."[53] This is Jesus, despecialized. The last days of a class that set out alongside the declaration of human rights. But something must have then gone wrong. Maybe domination. Once again, domination. Once again, humanity—well not quite. But the apocalyptic mildness of that sentence stores and preserves completely the splendid first steps of this class: "The vouchsafers are out in search of supplicants." I want to bring one final sentence of his into play; I have already marveled at it a hundred times, and each time it has rewarded me. It arose out of the author's experience, out of his utterly clear recognition that he was born to mediate and that mediation is work that does not survive the second in which it is accomplished. The sentence comes from his prose piece **"Sketch" ("Skizze")**:[54] "The garden somewhat resembled a thought fortunately never thought to a conclusion; and my sketch I compare—although I have no idea where I get the effrontery to do so—to a swan, singing with unheard-of ardor, who gives voice screechingly to unmediated things." So, with the simplicity of a Hölderlin and the beauty of a Robert Walser, he expresses his work as a writer. The fact that he compares his activity, which is stronger than he, to a swan giving voice screechingly to unmediated things tells me how wrong it was earlier to suggest that there are those who can simply fashion what has been inflicted upon them into their own work. I wanted to redeem our author from the fate of having to be pitied. But that emphasis underlines the notion that the prose piece just completed can affect his consciousness retroactively and stabilize it for what is to come. This is precisely not the case. The distress, which individual prose pieces mediate, passed away with them. The author then had to confront the next imposition without any particular stability. If I say that, through his assent, he succeeded in conquering all adversities, then, just like those who thought the Kocher boy merely naïve, I have been taken in by his irony. Perhaps, at times, even the author himself fell for his own unrelenting, stronger-than-he-was form of writing. True irony always wants to be involuntary.

The sketch that screeches about unmediated things makes me realize that with this author one can never reach solid ground. He himself never reached it. The sketch screeches out loudly and beautifully that the poet's business of mediation never achieves permanent success. Writing means to make necessities look like freedom. But the *like* remains a *like,* and needs to be sung and screeched with ardor. Let us briefly recall that Robert Walser by no means undertook to mediate everything. He had a deadly serious precondition for creativity: Freedom from other work. His being dismissed so often as a clerk in Zurich attests that, in order to write, he always first had to make his "out-of-the-way thoughts" come true.[55] Only when "occupied to the highest degree" at "being unoccupied" could he write.[56] At such moments he had the heat turned off, "for I didn't want to have it easy, I wanted to freeze."[57] Here we find him already in the midst of mediation. To be free, however, in the sense of unoccupied, was his axiom, so to speak. All distress occurring thereafter he accepted as a task, and began to rewrite it unrelentingly into something beautiful, something right, something welcome. If I'm to die, then better willingly. But mediating, after all, means to create not another condition, but only a different consciousness about the same condition. For Robert Walser the situation is no different than for Fichte, who was, as it were, unable to derive a single second of truly stable self-awareness from his lifelong "I-not I" billiards—and thus had to keep on playing a lifelong game with the theory of science. For Robert Walser it is no different than for Kierkegaard, who could not for a single day call off the dialectical hunt in which skepticism roused faith out of the bushes and faith in turn roused skepticism; otherwise his existence would grind to a halt and become undetectable. So too it may have been with the other saints of movement: Saint Hegel, Saint Marx. So it was, as has been noted often enough, with Kafka, the only ironist in the German language comparable to Robert Walser.

Irony leads to nothing. The unrelenting hunt itself is the only bearable situation, a situation comprised of nothing but movement. And this movement supplies the sensibility with a sound that can be experienced—an almost perceptible rustle of identity. If the unrelenting dialectical hunt were to come to a stop, so would life; one would get lost in the disequilibrium of distress. So long as it is possible to rewrite every incoming grain of distress into a grain of freedom—that is, to mediate it for consciousness as the sweetest, most welcome of experiences—then the movement may continue; one can

believe in equilibrium, can almost hear the yearned-for rustle of identity. But if one is then put against one's will into an asylum, the mediation, the writing itself, is no longer possible. There is no irony that could transform this asylum into a freely chosen home. Freedom, the precondition for writing, is totally absent.

Don Quixote has to surrender. His only name now, it turns out, is Cervantes, or Robert Walser. He is no longer a boy, or a page, or a servant, or a lackey, or Jesus, or a child—in other words not an author, either. Only a quite healthy man of fifty-five, one who can defend himself no longer and, from now on, for another twenty-three years, will make no attempt to defend himself—i.e., to write. Truly, to welcome this inmate's existence, with unrelenting irony, as a fate imbued with freedom—to do that, a person would really have to be sick. But since he is healthy, he lets the asylum be an asylum, lets himself be a patient. The swan becomes an inmate, and screeches about unmediated things no more, enduring them instead, silently, it seems, and probably also patiently. His twenty-three-year-long silence denies us any right to speculate. But if you please—we can be truly happy with what the swan from Biel gave us, while still a swan.

Notes

1. *Je t'adore,* in Robert Walser, *Das Gesamtwerk* (Frankfurt, 1978), 10: 430f.

2. Ibid. 11: 212.

3. Ibid.

4. Ibid. 12: 278.

5. "Robert Walser," in *Über Robert Walser,* ibid., 126ff.

6. Ibid. 11: 212.

7. Ibid. 10: 538.

8. Ibid.

9. Ibid. 2: 346.

10. Ibid. 1: 19.

11. Ibid., 36.

12. Ibid., 100.

13. Ibid., 106.

14. Jean Paul, *Werke* (Munich, 1963), 5: 471.

15. *Das Gesamtwerk* 12: 323.

16. Ibid. 11: 359.

17. Ibid. 9: 64f.

18. Ibid. 1: 319ff.

19. Ibid. 2: 165ff.

20. Ibid. 11: 215.

21. Ibid. 9: 22ff.

22. Ibid., 358.

23. Ibid. 6: 304.

24. Ibid. 10: 188.

25. Ibid., 9.

26. Ibid. 3: 204.

27. Ibid., 403.

28. Ibid., 335.

29. Ibid., 12: 283.

30. Ibid. 10: 132.

31. Ibid. 2: 346.

32. Ibid. 9: 92.

33. Ibid. 8: 282.

34. Ibid., 158.

35. Ibid. 6: 103ff.

36. Ibid. 10: 534.

37. Ibid., 202.

38. Ibid. 11: 185f.

39. Ibid., 262.

40. Ibid.

41. Ibid.

42. Ibid. 1: 294.

43. Ibid. 9: 298.

44. Ibid. 12: 74.

45. Ibid. 8: 318.

46. Ibid. 10: 124.

47. Ibid. 3: 406.

48. Ibid. 10: 202.

49. Ibid., 524.

50. Ibid. 11: 225.

51. Ibid. 10: 409.

52. Ibid., 382f.

53. Ibid., 489.

54. Ibid. 12: 110.

55. Ibid. 2: 315.

56. Ibid., 316.

57. Ibid.

Select Bibliography

GERMAN EDITIONS

Das Gesamtwerk. 13 vols. Ed. Jochen Greven. Geneva/Hamburg: Kossodo, 1966-75; Frankfurt: Suhrkamp, 1978.

ENGLISH TRANSLATIONS

Jakob von Gunten. Trans. and with an introduction by Christopher Middleton. Austin: University of Texas Press, 1969; New York: Vintage Books, 1983.

CRITICAL WRITINGS (ENGLISH)

CRITICAL WRITINGS (GERMAN)

Kerr, Katharina, ed. *Über Robert Walser.* 3 vols. Frankfurt: Suhrkamp, 1978-79. A comprehensive collection of essays with an extensive bibliography.

Christopher Middleton (essay date 1985)

SOURCE: Middleton, Christopher. "A Parenthesis to the Discussion of Robert Walser's Schizophrenia." In *Robert Walser Rediscovered: Stories, Fairy-Tale Plays, and Critical Responses,* by Robert Walser, edited by Mark Harman, pp. 190-94. Hanover, N.H.: University Press of New England, 1985.

[*In the following essay, Middleton describes Walser as "a paradigmatic liminoid personality," saying that his prose "might be viewed as a subtle record of the mastery—and the lapses—with which a great artist of the word patrols the hairline fractures" and "the dizzying gulfs" between his experience of the internal and external worlds.*]

It occurs to me that we might risk taking a categorical leap away from the notion of schizophrenia. The term blankets a malaise that is in any case a clinical enigma—and the blanket is somewhat moth eaten, too. I suggest that Walser presents us with the spectacle, purely and simply, or in aspects variously displaced, of a liminoid personality in action.

To be more precise: he represents to us strikingly liminoid traits in bursts of idiosyncratic prose. By *liminoid* I mean that a particular vein of imaginative energy, with which certain artists are endowed, tends to undulate or oscillate back and forth across regions of the mind, provinces of expression that are normally marked by heavy distinctions, barriers, borders, boundaries, and thresholds (*limes* being Latin for threshold). The supposedly less nervous, less peculiarly imaginative person tends to stand foursquare enough on one side or another of any threshold. Of Walser's madness, one might say that it became apparent only after he had slipped, or graduated, from the liminoid to the lunatic. Or else one might say that he was progressively victimized into lunacy ("suicided by society," perhaps, in Artaud's ugly phrase). Either way, the "humble servant" outdid himself.

Walser's prose, then, might be viewed as a subtle record of the mastery—and the lapses—with which a great artist of the word patrols the hairline fractures, the delicate intervals, also the dizzying gulfs, between segments into which human beings categorically carve the world of their experience—individual and social. Does this not happen more often than we might think? Rilke's poetry matures the moment he lights on intervals, interstices, fugitive threshold situations, as the proper leverage for imaginative work, as volatile nowheres in which reality is to be most singularly sensed. That is the reality that Wallace Stevens conceived of as not external or solid or even immediate, but "a shade that traverses / A dust, a force that traverses a shade."

Or consider the improbable fusion in the singing voice of Kiri Te Kanawa, of freedom and power, grace and force, ecstasy and control. In Walser's case, one might think of the acrobat and his wobble, or of the bicyclist's inconspicuous, near-miraculous recoveries of balance by means of which he propels his vehicle. Walser was able to sustain his own exhilarating kinetic wobble through self-doubt, despair, nightmare, and spates of stubborn work, not to mention poverty and rejection, until about 1929. Then the wobble began to catch up with him and to shake him. Could that be because, given such a liminoid imagination, nothing in life is ever quite resolved?

So, on one hand we might have before us a paradigmatic liminoid personality. At large in that paradigm, on the other hand, there seems also to be what Jungians (notably Marie von Franz) have called a *puer aeternus*: an individual or innocent imagination, who has so much "eternity" lodged in his nature that he hardly ever does what ordinary folks resolve to do—grow up. The *puer aeternus*, for all his radiance and vitality, for all his courage and tormenting self-insistence, often gets into trouble at about the age of fifty. (The "midlife crisis" is less troubling for him because he knows he is not getting old.) Briefly, before we opt for any standard clinical description of Walser in 1929, we might recognize this liminoid elfin Walser who stubbornly declines to grow up, to accommodate himself to society, who refuses to be *tamed*.

In addition, I suggest that the *puer aeternus* Walser might be contrasted with another one: Goethe. Once in a blue moon a *puer aeternus* remains intact and reaches an advanced age with his creative powers not much diminished. Goethe did so. The grand maturity of his mind, tested and seasoned by a multitude of external interests and profound experiences, including responsiveness to the radiance of the erotic (which does not seem to have figured in the script of Walser's fortune), trained and transformed, and was not impeded by, his unquenchable gusto, his ability to be almost constantly emergent, variously to refresh himself.

Even then, we should not forget how problematic Goethe was, as a *puer aeternus* of the passions: how scatty he could be, how angry he could get, how biased, how despairing, how unkind. The contrast I am suggesting becomes clearer if one pictures a reading at which the young Weimarian Goethe and the Berliner Walser are billed to perform, before a mixed German and Swiss public. Goethe carries it off with splendor, improvising, parodying, serious, mysterious, entertaining, and generally confident, clad in his green huntsman's mantle and with his dark Italianate eyes aglow. But Walser? His voice does not carry, he cannot externalize the supple vocality intrinsic to his text, he cannot mask his unliterary accent, and his enunciation is as drab as his threadbare clothes.

This resistance, the defiance that consorts with the liminoid personality, prohibits or inhibits even simulation of concern for proprieties. Sometimes, too, the defiance mushrooms into self-love or "inflated consciousness," which even when craving for alterity renders all other subjectivities opaque and schematic. (Here a nihilism lends a hand.) But when a crisis does come, or when that which was always in a condition of crisis is no longer sustained by fabulous gyrations and fascinating volatility, then breakdown can occur. No longer can one oscillate and undulate fruitfully from one side of a threshold to another. Even so, was not Walser still writing at his best in 1932? The Cézanne essay is not just ironically charming, it is glowing, balanced, incisive. Perhaps Walser was only mad in flashes, only mad to the extent that he resolved to accept, with a shrug of the shoulders, wryly, as is the way with a *puer aeternus,* the designation "mad" that flowed as naturally from doctors and decorum as his own prose had flowed from him. (Yet there can be no doubt: he was crushed by suffering.)

To that extent he had been flirting with madness for a long time. Consider certain strange sentences in the earlier Walser (around 1910), sentences of a kind that Kafka probably noticed—later modulating and intensifying what Walser had hit on, and inflecting that kind of structure with what he took from Kleist. I mean the kind of sentence that begins with an assertion, then qualifies it, then modifies the qualification, then soon is unraveling itself through (typically) interstitial details, and eventually it cancels itself out in a labyrinth of negative/positive qualifications. (The cancellation may resemble the portrayal of hidden and hollow spaces in Cubism.) This appears, at all events, to be the general structure of Kafka's "sliding paradox"—first identified as such by Gerhart Neumann. The initial positive modulates into a negative, to expose, bit by bit, the shimmer of uncertainty that overlays the threshold of so much verbal representation. The sentence so structured vibrates with volatile personality, and it has a distinct voice. It carries signatures of incalculable interior shiftings and foldings, graspings and lettings-go of the volatile liminoid imagination—its makeshifts, its dubiety, its permanent condition of emergence—Piaget's "standing wave" structure. Liminoid personalities, I suspect, have an exceptionally and sometimes painfully keen sense of these things, of the variable differentials that contrive language, contrive the undulant psychodrome in which language does its act or clowns around.

There is another problem here. You might say that Thomas Mann, too, is liminoid, with his antitheses and tensions, and his antagonisms—thematic or formal contrast effects. Yet with Mann there is an immensely intricate intellectual superstructure to the narrative; a massive culture is enshrined there. Perhaps that mass serves to cushion the authorial imagination. With Walser it is obviously otherwise. He is footloose and barefoot, and he dances rather than plods. His dance is that of an autodidact (albeit he read widely), exposed, boyish, defenseless, wholly dependent on a spontaneity that eludes, as much as it challenges, the sequential determinacy of ideas. It is amazing that he held out as long as he did against the loneliness, horror, disappointments, and maybe against a cruel death-wish that he fended off with all the zest and crispness of sensibility at his command.

As for the term *liminoid,* I must mention two books by Victor Turner: *The Ritual Process,* about African rites, and *Image and Pilgrimage,* on pilgrimage rites in Mexico, Spain, and Ireland. Victor Turner reserves the word *liminal* for properly religious festive events, like Carnival, where norms and values are overthrown for a measure of time so that individuals and groups alike may be ventilated, purged of grievance, ennui, repressed urges, and so forth. In liminal rites, people traverse thresholds in consciousness, they cross a *limes* and arrive, momentarily, or maybe for a week, through the mediation of sundry colorful or ascetic disciplines, in an alternative reality (as long as all goes well). Under those changed conditions, in the alterity contrived by the rites in which all who are present participate imaginatively, the undersides and othersides of things and selves are glimpsed; a reversed image of reality is brought to blossom in the mind. The liminal may shade into the liminoid: the latter term is reserved by Turner for enterprise in learning and the arts, artisanal concerns, and so forth. In the liminoid category of experience we may reach peaks of imaginative and intellectual clarity at which, creatively enough, we again penetrate the miasmas of normative codes, arrive at an unpremeditated insight, behold the world afresh, even fall in love again with the look and spirit of the world—but all this from beyond delusion (as long as deliverance from it lasts).

Yet the liminoid imagination is dangerous. It is dangerous to others and to the personality that is its vehicle. Rites, as everyone knows, are wonderful mechanisms for releasing dangerous energy and for insulating it. Practice in the arts is rather less wonderful, and besides, the poet stands naked and alone in the lightning storm. He does not only witness the carnival, he creates it, and for it he invents a language that can extend from the commonplace to the monstrous, from the familiar to the unknown.

One certainly burrows into such matters while trying to translate Walser. Repeatedly observed in his short prose, for instance, is an extension of the picaresque tradition (*carnivalization* in Bakhtin's terms) into a province where lyrical subjectivity, mysterious as ever, not narrative mass, is the measure of things. Liminoid and picaresque, this prose has a mobility rare enough in itself, although it distinguishes other German-language writers, who, in whatever mood, are masters of *brio*—Büchner, Heine, Nietzsche. The mystery in Walser cannot be "boiled down" to anything, but it can be sought in his rhythm. His rhythm is unlike that of his avatars. Indeed, he makes the most of that inaudible, nonapparent function of language that we call syntax. Mallarmé regarded syntax as the principle of motion, creative motion, in language. A radiant spirit dances in the body of the vocables. That spirit, did it eventually dance Walser clean off the map of words? Had society suicided him, at last? No. He just decided, let us say, that he had had enough, done enough. It was time to be mad, a duller carnival perhaps, but one that might diminish the agony of a future, of uncertain survival through a future. So then, he might as well try it.

William H. Gass (essay date 1990)

SOURCE: Gass, William H. "Robert Walser, an Introduction." In *Masquerade and Other Stories,* by Robert Walser, translated by Susan Bernofsky, pp. ix-xix. Baltimore: The Johns Hopkins University Press, 1990.

[*In the following essay, included as his introduction to a 1990 English edition of some of Walser's short stories, Gass calls the author's short prose pieces "meditations," which offer "a response to the moves and meanings of both human life and nature," and which achieve, "like the purest poetry, an understanding mix of longing, appreciation, and despair."*]

They found Robert Walser's body in the middle of a snowy field. It was Christmas Day, so the timing of his death was perhaps excessively symbolic. I like to think the field he fell in was as smoothly white as writing paper. There his figure, hand held to its failed heart, could pretend to be a word—not a statement, not a query, not an exclamation—but a word, unassertive and nearly illegible, squeezed into smallness by a cramped hand. It would be a word, if it *were* a word (such doubtful hesitations were characteristic of Walser), which would bring to an end a life of observant idling, city strolling, mountain hikes, and woodland walks, a life lived on the edges of lakes, on the margins of meadows, on the verges of things, a life in slow but constant motion, at a gawker's pace: sad, removed, amused, ironic, obsessively reflexive.

At least three of Walser's seven siblings were successful. Success was something Walser studied, weighed, admired, mocked, refused. He had a grandfather who was a journalist, a father who bound books. He would write for periodicals himself, and author novels. He was born in Biel, by Bieler See, in northwest Switzerland, but left school at fourteen, worked briefly in a bank; with the desire to be an actor went to Stuttgart where he found employment in a publishing house, turned up in Zurich in 1896 to begin his odd jobs life in earnest; and managed, by the time he was twenty, to get his first poems in a Berne newspaper.

He was a kind of columnist before the time of columns. So many of his pieces are brief, reflective, simple enough in their syntax and diction to be columns, deceptively ordinary in their observations, a little like those cozy nature notes that prop up editorial pages still, a little like some letters to the editor, too: the signature, HARMLESS CRANK, could be appended to quite a few without discordance or much malice. And yet reading them one is astonished that any were ever put in print, because Walser matches trivial thoughts to trivial subjects—as rug to drape—with relentless insistence, so that about ladies' shoes, for instance, he dares to believe that they are either brown or black in color; moreover, his transitions are abrupt as table edges; non sequiturs flock his pages like starlings to their evening trees; the pieces turn, often savagely, against themselves, or they dwindle away in apparent weariness and, unable to find a reason to cease, cease for want of a reason for going on.

Walser passes nine quiet years in Zurich, eight in Berlin, where he lives for a time in his brother's apartment and cares for the cat, eight more back in Biel, near his sister this time, twelve in Berne (eight go by there before he has himself institutionalized after several possibly suicidal episodes and his sister's insistence); then, finally, the remaining removed and silent twenty-three in the asylum at Herisau, taking his walks, busy about the idle business of being mad, waiting for the blank which would blanket his attendant blankness (such word play was characteristic of Walser), and finding it, we might say, when his heart failed in a field full of snow.

Throughout this time, he's been an inventor's assistant, worked in banks and insurance offices, as an archivist or the secretary of an art dealer, attended a school for servants, and become a butler for a bit, before he accepts insanity as his true profession.

Lightly attached to people, to the formalities of society, to any work which lies beneath another's will like a leg beneath a log, and more in love with localities and their regularities (like the seasons) which do not require him, Walser draws a borderline near poverty for himself and lives his increasingly frugal life in little rooms, in donated leftover spaces, in otherwise unoccupied attics, in circumstances straightened to the shape of his thin frame, shrunk to the size of his microscopic script, a miniaturization perhaps too suitable to his status (such patterned repetitions are characteristic). Walser is always the dog beneath the dogs, a ne'er-do-well and a nobody. He pens lines for which he receives small recognition and less pay. He composes novels which get lost or are so artfully mislaid, they might have been murdered. He stays out of other people's way, posting his innumerable ruminations to publications which not infrequently publish them—surprising even themselves. Most float back, leaf after leaf, to pile up eventually into books.

His is the perfect stroller's psychology. To his eye, everything is equal; to his heart, everything is fresh and astonishing; to his mind, everything presents a pleasant puzzle. Diversion is his principal direction, whim his master, the serendipitous the substance of his daily routine. I think that Walser most loved his lovely walks in the woods, and in particular that moment when a clearing came into view like sunshine between clouds, or a lake rose from its labor of duplicating mountains to drench the spaces between trees. In any case, his characters run away to the woods as often as creatures in fairy tales, and more often than not with similar results.

Walser's prose frequently reads as if it had been lifted from a tourist brochure because his narrators almost never see things with Kafka's scrupulously realistic and coolly dispassionate gaze: they look upon a commonplace world in terms of conventional values and received opinions. Things are therefore said to be "lovely," "dear," "sweet," "charming," "little," "clever," "perfect," or "enchanting." Things are tritely characterized as beautiful and good, deliciously tempting, absolutely true to their type; they are as pleasing as can be imagined, as delightful as anywhere can be found. Things are meant to be presented to us exactly as they appear to smug, assured, accepted, and acceptable estimation. Walser paints a postcard world.

> A farmer's market is bright, lively, sumptuous, and gay . . . Sun-splashed sausages have a splendid appearance. The meat shows off in all its glory, proud and

purple, from the hooks on which it hangs. Vegetables laughing verdantly, oranges jesting in gorgeous yellow heaps, fish swimming about in wide tubs of water . . . This joyful, simple life, it's so unpretentiously attractive, it laughs at you with its homey, petit-bourgeois laugh. And then the sky with its topnotch, first-rate blue.

His narrators consequently split their point of view, merging their removed and alienated angles of vision with the way the observed believe and wish themselves to feel: at weddings, happy as all git-out, at funerals, sad as Niobe or Job, enjoying their gluttonies without anxiety or future pangs, exercising their tyrannies without guilt or fear of overthrow. His narrator's noses are pressed to the window: surely those are goodies there, beyond the fogged glass. The young servant thinks: look at the family eat—how delicious the food must be; listen to their laughter—how happy they are; how nice it must be to be beautifully dressed, to own a fine carriage, to live in this house I work so hard and helplessly to keep clean.

And the food *is* no doubt delicious. It *is* pleasant to be well got up and possess a closet of consequence. It *is* certainly lovely to look down on the soiled hats of passers-by when wheeling through the park. It doesn't take a tired proverb to tell us that, between high life and low, high is higher. But it is also true that the wide sky is the property of rich and poor alike; that the broad lake will not refuse the body of any bather, even one cockeyed with care; that the massive range of mountains will stare indifferently at good and evil equally, at fortune or misfortune, at noble and knave; that each—sky, lake, peak—that surrounds and shelters us is honestly serene, and cool and blue—first rate in every way.

If Kafka's neutrality widens our eyes with horror and surprise, Walser's depictions, always working within what is socially given, are equally revealing. The effect is complex, and almost wholly his own. No writer I know employs the adjectives and adverbs of value so repeatedly, with such real appreciation and conviction, with such relentless resentment. Standing alongside the lunching patrons of a Berlin bar, his word-making voice can genuinely claim that "it's a sincere pleasure to watch people fishing for frankfurters and Italian salad."

If his narrators sometimes seem to be ninnies, it is because they are beguiled by surface, by the comfort of commonplace persiflage. Falsefaces frighten them, yet they entrust themselves to strangers whose smiles are matched by the ninny's own grins and good feelings. They fall for any startling detail like those who are fated to stub their toes on the beach's single stone. Watch the "the good," "the true," and "the beautiful" dance hand in hand while a reassuring lie unfolds, a jolt gets delivered, in the following characteristically shrewd sentence: "Carefree and cheerful as only a true pauper

can be, a good youth with a ridiculous nose wandered one day through the beautiful green countryside." Yet the ohs and ahs of these innocent souls cynically amuse the very mouths which make them, because the extent of every narrator's self-deprecation is at the same time a measure of the congratulations they will shower on themselves—superior in the form and fullness of their inferiority like a simple paperclip or tack or pin beside the welder's torch or the rivet gun.

The effect of such writing is complex and contradictory. It is as if, holding in one's hand a postcard picturing, let us say, a pretty Swiss scene—perhaps an inn at the edge of a snowy village with the Alps (as they ought to be) above, blue lake below—one were in the same look to sense behind the little window with its painted pot the shadow of a weeping woman, while in another room of the inn there was loneliness cold as the window glass, cruelty in the severely scraped and shoveled walk, death in the depths of the lake, a cloud of callousness about the mountain peaks; and then, with nary a word about what one had seen—about bitterness, sadness, deprivation, boredom, defeat, failure added to failure—it is as if, having seen these things, sensed these things, felt them like a cinder in the shoe, one were nevertheless to write (and Walser is the writer to do it) an apparently pleasant description of the pretty Swiss inn on its pretty site, colors as bright as printed paint, surfaces as shiny and slick as ice, smoke as fixed and frozen in its coils as on the quarter-a-copy card, with its space for any message, provided the message is trite and true, gay and brief.

So the prose strolls, and what it reports primarily qualifies the character and color of its concerns, not the character and color of things. As it strolls, observing what it wishes to observe, it dreams: so that about the figure of a young woman, who is cutting roses in her garden, it may place its usually decorous yet desirous arms; it selects: so that an overheard remark will be passed around like a snack on a plate; it ponders: and in the face of some innocuous scene, it can nevertheless hem and haw itself into revelations. If Walser is a descriptive writer, and he is surely that, what he is describing, always, is a state of mind . . . and mostly the same mind, it would seem.

To say that the prose strolls is to suggest that it follows the contours of its subject. There is no narrative because there is no thread. The text stops before this item, ruminates a bit, then it stops before that; it thinks one thing (who knows why?), then another; but there is no continuity, for the cat will not be followed in its flight up a tree, only caught with its back bowed and its fur erect. A shade is pulled, a pitcher sits upon a table, someone is met, the narrator is addressed, he gives banal advice, but each of these is a moment only in the arc of a life quite accidentally intersected. Nor is a thought, which might have been provoked by the drawn shade or the scared cat, allowed to grow others, to flower so far as theory, or to link up and chuff-chuff as a train. Nor will the narrator act on anything, however violent and effective he has been in his fantasies. If he says he has kissed, doubt it; if he says he is drunk, don't believe. Not even nothing does he do.

The formless look of many of these pieces, then, is only a look, because the prose does imitate the shape of its subject. If the narrator takes a walk, so does the tale; if the narrator is nervous, so is the prose. An early piece, **"Lake Greifen,"** for instance, is already characteristic of Walser's art. Here, a very self-conscious description of a lake is set in the text the way the lake lies in its language. The doubling up of the language reflects the doubling images of trees and sky in the bright light.

> But let's give the description itself, in its traditional effusiveness, a chance to speak: a wide, white stillness it is, ringed in turn by an ethereal, green stillness; it is lake and encircling forest; it is sky, such a light blue, half overcast sky; it is water, water so like the sky it can only be sky, and the sky only blue water; sweet, blue, warm stillness it is, and morning; a lovely, lovely morning.

The narrator, who has left a large city lake to seek out this small hidden one, swims far out with the greatest joy, but perhaps he has swum too far, for now he must struggle back to shore where he lies panting and happy on the beach. What will such a swim be like, he wonders, when the lake is dark and the sky is full of stars? The story says no more (the story is over), but we can guess the rest, including the prose for the missing part: calm as slate, composed of starlight, water, and death.

Walser is no ordinary voyeur, consumed by the secrets he feels have enraptured his eye, because quite prominent in any of his observations is the observer himself, and that person, too, Walser is watching. He follows each thought, each feeling, from the time one arrives on the scene to the moment it leaves, with a fond but skeptical regard, so that it is the seeing of the thing seen, he sees; and then, since he is also an author, composing a page, in addition to everything else he must take into account, he watches the writing of the writing itself (both the walk through the woods and the corresponding walk of the words), until a person who has been simply encountered in *this* world becomes a person perceived in *his,* and until, in turn, this complex, pale, increasingly imaginary figure is further transformed by words into words; words which talk about themselves, moreover, which smile at their own quirks and frills, and wave farewell while a substantial and often painful world dwindles away into this detached, multi-phenomenal, pleasantly impotent, verbal object.

How absurdly philosophical we have become, Walser might exclaim at this point, and threaten (it would be characteristic) to drop our entire subject, lift my pen and his abruptly from the page.

The world he views should not become a view to be framed and hung in his attic room, or exposed to the morning amusement of casual people. He feels guilty when he turns a lovely woman into words; when a longed-for caress becomes a sentence perhaps shaped by that yearning. Walser's lyricism, which is intense, attempts to revivify his verbal world, often with images which burst like bullets from the text. In his extraordinary novel, *Jakob von Gunten,* which exploits the author's experiences as a butler-in-training, he has his narrator remark about Fuchs, a fellow student, that he "speaks like a flopped somersault," a metaphor which would turn anybody's head. In this collection's piece called **"Comedy Evening,"** he writes: "In the mezzanine beneath me, an elderly lady blew her nose with a ferociously lacy handkerchief. I found everything beautiful, enormously bewitching." In **"Tobold,"** an important story, he tells us that "With both swiftness and, understandably, great ceremoniousness, I bore the beverage to the beautiful woman, who appeared constructed and constituted entirely of fresh milk." Had there been a woman whose soft pale lucent skin had given rise to this witticism, would it be fitting that all that is now anonymously remembered of her is the milk a fictional servant felt she was made of?

In this same significant story, there is a small speech which I call a "blurt," because the author's usual reticence is lifted, and Walser speaks directly about one of the contradictions which troubles him: that between the surface of the well-off world (to which he has devoted so many flattering phrases) and the interior gloom beneath—a gloom resembling the gloom of the poor and the ugly—a resemblance which is deeply troubling.

> Can princesses cry too? I've always thought it impossible. Such high-placed women, I always thought, would never insult and sully their pure, clear eyes, the pure and sparkling sky of their vision, with soiling, defiling tears, which disfigure the unchanging expression of their faces. Why are you crying? If even princesses cry, if wealthy, powerful people can lose their balance and their proud, imperious bearings, can be depressed and overcome by a profound weariness: then what can one say and how can one be surprised to see beggars and beggar-women bent over in suffering and misery, if one sees the poor and the humble wringing their piteous hands in despair, at a loss as to what more they can do than bathe themselves in unending, miserable signs and moans and in torrents of tears. Nothing, then, is certain in this world shaken by storms and afflictions. Everything, then, everything is weak. Well, if this is so, I'll be glad to die some day, I'll gladly take leave of this hopeless, sick, weak, troubled world to rest in my relaxing, dear, good grave from all my uncertainties and hardships.

The page is the dear good grave where everything which lasts will finally rest. For Walser, this conclusion was never quite comforting enough.

Thomas Hobbes described the State of Nature as a state of war with every man's hand against every man's, and argued that only the mutual relinquishment of rights and their implementing means could guarantee peace. He furthermore wrote of the paradox of power, which meant that as any man obtained power, he would need still more power to protect it, because envy of him would increase along with the fear, since in the customary State it is the sovereign who is most perilously placed. If you were, however, a nobody, a nebbish; if you had nothing which could be desired; if you were dismally undistinguished; then perhaps you would be ignored and could go about the little business of your life unnoticed, invisible as a servant is supposed to be, performing small services quietly, unthreatened and serene.

To hold a priceless vase in your hands may be pleasing, but you are at the same time in danger of dropping it. If you possess any authority over others, you are in a position—through indolence, incompetence, or spitefulness—to injure them. Success survives on success; the higher you rise, the dizzier you become, obligations weigh, moment by moment, more heavily upon you, others begin to rest their limbs, their lives, upon your limbs and life, which the postures of sex not even secretly symbolize. Thus what Robert Walser fears, and flees from, is power when he feels it in his own hands. The power others possess is something that, like a great outcropping of rock, may fall upon you; but it is also a shade under which you may find shelter.

His mind pleads incompetence. Asylums *are* asylums. There he can guiltlessly surrender his fate and pass his days at the behest of others. He will no longer need to write in such a way that its public obscurity is assured. He will no longer need to write. The daily walk will suffice.

Among Immanuel Kant's many important distinctions is the one he made between willing something to happen and wishing for it to occur. When we will an end, he said, we must also necessarily will some means which will be effective in obtaining it. If you hear me speaking of my love of boating and the sea, of my dream one day of owning my own yacht and sailing the Chesapeake as if it were my private lake, you will be quite properly disabused of your belief in my desire when you notice that I subscribe to not a single boating magazine; that I do not follow the Cup races in the papers; that I have not set aside any sums toward the purchase of so much as a jaunty cap; that, in fact, I spend my vacations with my family in the desert Southwest. In short, I may wish for such a luxury, but I have never willed it. When I wish, my means are dreams. Each evening, before sleep and in place of love, I imagine my vessel parting the waves: I cry to the sky the salty orders of a shipmaster and eat heartily without any fear of sickness from the sea that lies around me like my cool, uncohabited sheets. As a people, as a race, Kant observed, we always will War; we only wish for Peace.

Walser's narrators (and we can presume, in this case, Walser himself) have become will-less wanderers, impotent observers of life, passive perceivers of action and passion. Only on the page, will the Will risk the expression and exercise of its considerable means.

And when the circumstances of life—my six children and my fruitful but frigid wife, perhaps, my boringly repetitive work as an insurance adjuster, my rascally relatives and a harsh climate, the painfully pushed-forward designs of those who would exploit me—when these force me (as I think) to give up my own aims altogether, then I shall find myself in a classical state of powerless resentment, aggrieved because existence has become a broken promise; and my head shall fill with willing woman, my yacht will always find the best breeze, I shall dream of flames while I stir my ashes, and my soul will swell like a balloon to float over the world, touching it only as a shadow.

The details of the disappointment will differ; the site of the defeat will shift; the resistance to one's fate or one's readiness to accept it will vary in their strength; but the pattern is plain enough, its commonness is common, indeed, its dangers real. Switzerland is a prison. Consequently the world is one.

If I were then to try to save myself through writing, how difficult it would be for me to maintain the posture of a realist, for I should have had little acquaintance with the real (indeed, less and less), rather more with the subjects of my wishes than the objects of my will. In order to confer the blessings of Being upon the small, hollow dreams of my soul, these harmlessly private elaborations will have to somehow achieve the heartless powers of the page; yet my characters must be inventions, and how quickly these inventions will feel my disdain. What value could they have if they remain so utterly in my power? So much for the story, too, which can be pushed and pulled this way and that, or dropped, suddenly, like a weighted sack into the lake.

Through a course of such "thinking," if I read him aright, Walser became a post-modernist well before the fashion. The painfully beautiful, brief "essay," **"A Flaubert Prose Piece,"** deals with the way a successful fiction fictionalizes its author, so that both his invented woman, and the author's *moi* she was, eventually "glided and passed among the people gliding and passing by, like a dream vision within the vision of a dream."

As Walser's final confinement nears, his writing seems increasingly made of dissociated sentences. To turn time, like an hourglass, abruptly over, so that its many days fall the other way, his *feuilletons* resemble the work of Donald Barthelme, almost collage-like in their structural juxtapositions. Not a few, like the brutally disturbing **"Salon Episode,"** have a genuinely surreal surface. The detached, desperate "inhumanity" of his work remains. It has been many years since a figure in one of his fictions has had a real name. And if one had a name, it would be generic, like Pierrot. But it is easier now to follow the inner flow beneath these scraps of language, to appreciate the simple clarity of the sentences he has constructed, to recognize that these meditations (for they have never been anything else) move not in the manner of events or in the manner of a river or in the manner, either, of thought, or in the "happy hour" fashion of the told tale (each brought so beautifully together in "Boat Trip," one of the triumphs of Walser's art), but in the way of an almost inarticulate metaphysical feeling; a response to the moves and meanings of both human life and nature, which is purged of every local note and self-interested particularity and which achieves, like the purest poetry, an understanding mix of longing, appreciation, and despair, as if they were the pigments composing a color to lay down upon the surface of something passing—sweetly regretful—like the fall of light upon a bit of lost water, or a brief gleam caught in a fold of twilit snow, as if it were going to remain there forever.

John Pizer (essay date 1993)

SOURCE: Pizer, John. "'Man schaffe ihn auf eine sanfte Manier fort': Robert Walser's *Lenz* as a Cipher for the Dark Side of Modernity." In *Space to Act: The Theater of J. M. R. Lenz,* edited by Alan C. Leidner and Helga S. Madland, pp. 141-49. Columbia, S.C.: Camden House, 1993.

[*In the following essay, Pizer treats Walser's dramatic sketch* Lenz, *and more specifically the sketch's namesake protagonist, within "a modernist context," maintaining that while the figure reflects the modernist concept of the restorative power of art and the creative imagination, he also "shows the dark side of modernism," in which "the passion of the artist, far from enacting redemption, condemns him to a painful sense of exteriority."*]

Robert Walser's brief dramatic sketch *Lenz* (1912) has received scant critical treatment. It is generally examined from either a biographical angle, as a work where Walser utilizes the figure of Lenz to give vent to his own sense of loneliness and alienation,[1] or as, in principle, a slightly redirected extension of Büchner's much better-known tale.[2] Though these approaches are quite legitimate, a somewhat different reading is possible when we consider Walser's sketch in the context of literary modernism. Walser has emerged as one of the most important writers associated with the modernist movement.[3] Some of Walser's works—his anti-fairy tale *Schneewittchen* (1901) for example—are modernist in their positive vision of the redemptive power of art, art's ability (or near ability) to bring about familial reconciliation and spiritual harmony. Alan Wilde has spoken of a "consolation in the thought of other, more perfect worlds—those heterocosms that haunt the modernist imagination,"[4] and Walser's works are capable of evoking such utopian realms, realms generally absent in more contemporary, postmodern fiction. But Walser's *Lenz* shows the dark side of modernism, modernism's sense that the artist's efficacy and power have become subtly diminished in society. Outside the fairy tale realm, confronted with life in its often alienating normativeness (as Lenz was in Weimar and Sesenheim, two of the sites in Walser's dramatic sketch), the passion of the artist, far from enacting redemption, condemns him to a painful sense of exteriority.

Büchner's treatment of Lenz also brings out Lenz's marginality, as both artist and lover, in eighteenth-century German social circles. But while Büchner's "Lenz" (circa 1836) was an undoubted influence, Walser's *Lenz* belongs to the dramatic genre, and this allows Lenz's warmth and passion a less restrictively modulated expression, quite distinct from Büchner's almost clinically described figure. Büchner's tale is based on the diary of the Waldersbach pastor Johann Friedrich Oberlin (1740-1826), at whose residence Lenz sought solace and refuge over a year after he had left Weimar for good, and when he was already deep in the throes of insanity. The last episodes of Walser's dramatic sketch take place *in* Weimar. Though he already senses the onset of insanity in this work, Lenz emerges as an artist in control of his faculties, whose powerful argument for art's restorative possibilities contrasts sharply with the fictive Goethe's tepid formalism and desire for order. The choice of the dramatic genre allows Walser to represent Lenz's passion with an immediacy lacking in Büchner's prose account, the detachment of which is enhanced by the use of an objective, third-person narrative perspective. The passion of Walser's Lenz is especially evident in his encounter with the beautiful *Gräfin*; he cannot channel his feelings for her in a socially acceptable manner, and the Duke of Weimar decides, in conversation with Goethe, to have him "gently" removed from court. Lenz thus becomes a cipher for Walser's characteristically modernist fear that the artist is the victim of a process of marginalization more discreet but thereby more ominous than that sensed by writers of earlier periods. The historical Lenz's miseries in Weimar symptomize the failure of many premodern writers to find love or professional support—the aid of a court or individual Maecenas—in a highly structured feudal society. The similarly tragic fate of artistic outsiders such as Walser took on new contours in the modern age. For while Walser experienced interpersonal and professional frustrations like those of Lenz, they resulted in his case from an inability to find an entry point into both the more amorphous social network which characterizes modernity and into the elusive, more impersonal network of literary mass marketing. Perhaps because he was a writer who stood throughout his life outside the gateways to these networks, partly through necessity and partly through choice, Walser makes Lenz into the victim of such an anonymous fate by turning his exile from Weimar into a (for Lenz) invisible conspiracy. The bulk of this paper will examine Walser's treatment of Lenz in this modernist context.

Of course, Walser's representation of the consequences of Lenz's mysterious Weimar "Eselei" is consistent with much unfounded speculation on the part of literary historians, who assume Goethe and the Duke of Weimar acted in concert to arrange for Lenz's banishment from the duchy.[5] But Walser's decision to base the conclusion to his sketch on this speculation is consistent with his treatment of writers in general as victims of a subtle, opaque process of marginalization. In his story **"Kleist in Thun"** (1907), for example, Heinrich von Kleist is portrayed as a brooding, childish creator living in virtual isolation, whose manuscripts lie on the floor of his room "wie von Vater und Mutter scheußlich verlassene Kinder" when he develops a writer's block near the end of the story ([***Das Gesamtwerk***] 1:182-183).[6] As Kleist departs Thun in the company of his sister, the narrator refers to the marble tablet attached to the front of the Thun residence where he had lived. After noting that all who visit Thun can read this plate, the narrator elides Kleist from the story's conclusion. For the story ends with this narrator giving a brief description of the region, the accuracy of which he casts into doubt by stating that he *used* to be employed there by a beer firm, and that he *believes* it once had an industrial exhibition four years ago (1:184-185). Kleist's exteriorization is thus threefold: he was marginalized as a writer during his lifetime, he is forgotten by the masses in the modern age except when they stop to glance at the marble tablet, and he is finally obliterated from the text by a contemporary narrator who, in thrusting himself center-stage into the text, shows his own powers of recollection to be unreliable. Martin Walser has said of his cousin by name: "Was es mit sich brachte, so alleinstehend zu bleiben, hat ihn weniger geschert als die Furcht vor stabilen Verhältnissen."[7] This is also true of Walser's Kleist and Walser's Lenz, who are shown to have caring acquaintances or relatives. But their ostracism is also colored by Walser's own modernist social perspective, his fear that the writer was being elided from modern consciousness.

Walser's dramatic sketch *Lenz* consists of eight brief scenes or episodes. Characters and locales shift from one scene to another without any sense of transition or thematic continuity. While it is true that the presence of Lenz in the first seven scenes does serve to connect them, he is excluded from the final episode, much as Kleist was in the final lines of **"Kleist in Thun."** Again, this is consistent with Walser's wish to evoke the marginalization of the writer from a modernist perspective. And the fragmentary, episodic character of Walser's brief sketch has a modernist resonance as well. As David Frisby has noted, one of the essential features of modernity "was the discontinuous experience of time, space and causality as transitory, fleeting and fortuitous or arbitrary." The exploration of these fundamental elements of modernist experience links three of its most significant investigators, according to Frisby: Georg Simmel, Siegfried Kracauer, and Walter Benjamin.[8] Frisby also cites Baudelaire's seminal definition of modernity, in which he announces that "'by modernity I mean the ephemeral, the fugitive, the contingent, the half of art whose other half is the eternal and the immutable.'"[9] The structure of Walser's *Lenz* is thus consistent with both the aesthetics and the temporal/spatial experience of modernism. The fragmentary, discontinuous quality of the different scenes lends them a discrete, mutable, fugitive character, and this circumstance establishes on a formal level Lenz's complete isolation and alienation throughout Walser's brief sketch. For Walser, this isolation of the artist, and the misunderstandings resulting from it, are quite natural. As he puts it in his essay **"Über den Charakter des Künstlers"** (1911): "So sehen wir ihn fort und fort einzig nur auf sich selbst angewiesen und verstehen daher zuweilen seine Fröhlichkeit, aber auch seinen Gram nicht; und wir brauchen ihn ja auch nicht zu verstehen" (6:57-58). But Walser does find it necessary to understand such things, and he attributes them in his speculative treatment of such figures as Kleist and Lenz to the selfsame isolation and self-reliance of the artist, conditions heightened by the impersonality, discontinuity and exteriority faced by artists such as himself in the modern age.

At this point, a summary of the episodes which constitute Walser's dramatic sketch is in order. In the opening scene, Lenz is in a room in Sesenheim together with "Friederike." Of course, it is well-known that the historical Lenz was infatuated with Friederike Brion, who was one of Goethe's lovers. Walser's Friederike opens the sketch by attempting to talk Lenz out of his sadness. She asks him whether he takes it amiss that she is in a cheerful mood. He responds by expressing his ardor for her, but realizes she doesn't share his passion. This makes him even more miserable. After scolding him for this, she spies the approaching Goethe, for whom she expresses her passion as the scene concludes: "Weiß Gott, es nimmt mich, es reißt mich, wie ich diesen lieben Menschen sehe" (1:331). With the clarity, precision and terseness characteristic of another great modernist to whom he is often compared, Franz Kafka,[10] Walser thus evokes the classic lovers' triangle. The next scene finds Lenz alone in Friederike's chamber, bemoaning his fate, expressing his passion, kissing her stockings, shivering and declaring his insanity (1:332).

One might expect the continuation of the development of the Goethe-Friederike-Lenz triangle. But, consistent with Walser's modernist employment of a discontinuous narrative line, the matter is dropped without any further references to it subsequent to this second scene. Instead, the third scene finds Goethe and Lenz together atop the Strasbourg Cathedral, discussing unrelated matters. Goethe praises the panoramic view from the cathedral's spire, grasped and released by the human eye, which is "eine seltsame Maschine." He is pleased by the orderly sight of the dream-trapped but industrious procession of humanity below, and concludes: "Ist nicht Ordnung immer wieder das Schöne?" (1:332-333). Lenz counters this commendation of orderliness by a prematurely classicized Goethe with the passionate call for the destruction of the old, decaying house of German literature; a storm must pass through this house and tear it down, leaving a natural language and literature in its place. In tones one recognizes as endemic to the Sturm und Drang, he presents a view of beauty diametrically opposed to the one expressed by Goethe: "Was: schön. Schön ist nur das Wogende, das Frische. Ah, ich wollte Hämmer nehmen und drauflos hämmern. Der Funke, Goethe, der Funke. Die 'Soldaten,' bilde ich mir ein, müssen so etwas wie ein Blitz werden, daß es zündet" (1:333).

It is clear that Walser did not attempt to approximate a sense of historical accuracy in creating this scene. Indeed, the very notion of holding onto a faithful, reliable, historical memory was anathema to much of modernity in general and to Walser in particular, as Tamara Evans has indicated.[11] John Osborne has noted that Lenz's relationship to Goethe was quite friendly and harmonious in Strasbourg; a falling out did not take place until Lenz and Goethe were together in Weimar.[12] Together in Strasbourg, Lenz and Goethe held far from conflicting views on the questions of art, revolution and order. Indeed, when Walser's Lenz admonishes Goethe: "Man muß klettern. Man muß wagen" (1:333), one recalls the opening scenes of Lenz's *Pandämonium Germanicum,* written in 1775, at the time of his closest friendship with Goethe in Strasbourg. Lenz's portrayal of Goethe in this work presents an antithetical image to the Goethe confronted in Strasbourg by Walser's Lenz. For it is precisely Lenz's Goethe who dares boldly (and literally) to climb to the heights in this satire, leaving the mass of conventional, stultified contemporary critics and poets beneath him, and forcing the timid, dazed Lenz to scramble in his footsteps, exclaiming: "Mir ist

vom Klettern das Blut in den Kopf geschossen."[13] Walser himself was an admirer of Goethe; he describes him in a 1918 letter as "ein herrlicher Weltkenner" (12/2:129). However, his fictive Goethe valorizes order, the panoramic harmony of nature glimpsed by the machine-like eye, and the pleasing spectacle of regularity in space and time afforded by the sight of the working masses milling about below him. Walser, on the other hand, consistent with one of modernism's fundamental impulses, championed discontinuity, a surrealistic blending of spatial and temporal elements, and the creation of dissonant modes of perception at odds with the consonant, rational form of cognition tacitly embraced by his Goethe.[14] This does not mean Walser was opposed to realism; it is precisely the powerful naturalness and actuality of Lenz's *Die Soldaten* (1776) which he singles out for praise in a 1907 article on this work. He imagines it would have a gripping impact on the stage (6:22-23), a belief shared by his fictional Lenz (1:333).

When Lenz claims this play must become inflammatory like lightning, Goethe remains silent; he simply looks at Lenz and smiles (1:333). This gesture constitutes the concluding moment of the scene. Goethe will appear but once more, at the sketch's conclusion, to denounce Lenz as an "Esel" in the brief meeting with the duke that will lead to Lenz's banishment from court (1:336). Examined retroactively from this final moment of the sketch, Goethe's gaze and his smile are transformed into an exteriorizing act, a condescending glance through which Lenz is made to feel his own marginality and insignificance. This is confirmed by the following scene, where Lenz is alone in an alley on a rainy day, and all the positive expectations he expressed with regard to *Der Hofmeister* and *Die Soldaten* have vanished: "Es wird mir hier alles barbarisch. Ich verkomme. Kein Fingerzeig. Die Illusionen schwinden. Kein Traum mehr. Und wie tot, wie schwül ist alles" (1:333). Consistent with the sketch's ultimate elision of Lenz in an absence which will lead to Lenz's *permanent* absence from Weimar, Goethe's gesture of exclusion occurs in a space of silence for Lenz. His ostracism is essentially that suffered by Walser: the unobtrusive marginalization of the artist in modernity.

The fifth scene finds Lenz in a room in the castle at Weimar. He is addressed by the well-disposed duchess. She urges Lenz to moderate both his savageness and his shyness. She expresses her pleasure at Lenz's presence in Weimar, extols the virtues of the town, and (as she admits) pedantically attempts to get him to be more sociable. She feels his face shows the promise of more refined, polite behavior and a gratitude for her words of wisdom, which Lenz cannot express verbally: "Es hat alle Artigkeiten und Höflichkeiten schon längst ausgesprochen" (1:334). She thus shapes Lenz's silence into an appropriate courtly discourse. In her presence, Lenz blushes and is unable to speak. When she finally leaves, he feels as if he has lost his bearings (1:334). The following scene finds him alone and again in despair; he cannot write, he detests the empty formality of court life, wonders whether things were better for him in Strasbourg, and agonizes over his inability to establish himself, to take root somewhere (1:335). His sense of isolation and loneliness is as profound following his encounter with the duchess as it was following his encounter with Goethe. But the shift from one meeting to the other represents an oscillation between two extremes. For while Goethe was cold and distant towards him, the duchess overwhelms him with her warm extroversion. In connection with the story **"Der Spaziergang"** (1917), Evans has spoken of Walser's evocation of an "Angst vor dem Ersticktwerden durch weibliche Fürsorge,"[15] and we also see this fear in Lenz's embarrassed silence and awkwardness following the duchess's warm, energetic speech (1:334). Evans indicates that Walser's wavering between desire for and aversion towards domesticity is symptomatic both of his liminoid personality and of the abrupt oscillations of modernist art. Modernists such as Walser produce art where there is little or no transition between states of dreaming and waking, yearning and repulsion, loneliness, and an intense dread of the other. In this sense, Walser's Lenz, like Walser himself and many fellow modernists, are "Bewohner der Zwischenwelt," as Evans puts it.[16] It is thus no coincidence that the dialogues with Friederike, Goethe and the duchess are followed by very brief monologues which portray Lenz as lonely and in despair. For Friederike's indifference, the condescending, distancing smile of Walser's Goethe, and the duchess's warm eagerness to socialize Lenz all devastate his sense of integrity and worth. He needs love, the recognition of his fellow writer, and a respect for his alterity by a woman of wealth and influence. Receiving none of these, his sense of marginalization becomes all-pervasive. Nevertheless, given Walser's tendency to invest his characters with his own liminoid personality[17] and modernist sensibility, one imagines his Lenz would have been equally miserable had Walser defied historical facts even more boldly and granted his character some kind of social, artistic and/or interpersonal fulfillment.

The penultimate scene of Walser's dramatic sketch represents his vision of Lenz's mysterious, much discussed "Eselei." There is virtually no concrete indication of what happened to inspire Goethe to enter the terse remark "Lenzens Eseley" in his diary on November 26, 1776. Apparently, he had been deeply insulted by Lenz, and his sense of insult may have been generated by Lenz's relationship to Frau von Stein.[18] But Walser's portrayal of Lenz's nocturnal visit to the boudoir of the "Hofdame Gräfin so und so" is purely the product of fantasy. Most of the scene consists of Lenz's plea to the countess to take pity on him, to rescue him. He rhetorically asks whether his passionate love for the beautiful

countess would not excuse his breach of etiquette, and declares that he will be destroyed if she has no feeling for him. He senses this is the case, and that his sweet, heavenly dreaming is at an end. Modernist movements such as surrealism tended to valorize dreams as both a liberating force and the locus of the artistic imagination, and in works such as his famous novel *Jakob von Gunten* (1909), Walser anticipates this emphasis on the connection between dreams and aesthetically creative fantasy. When Walser's Lenz senses his dreams are at an end, we are thus made to understand that he will no longer be able to function as an artist. Indeed, Lenz feels life is at an end, that he is effectively silenced: "Ich soll schweigen, ich soll jetzt wohl einsehen, daß ich die höchste aller Unziemlichkeiten begangen habe, ich soll fühlen, daß alles kalt ist, und daß alles zu Ende ist" (1:336). Lenz has indeed committed an absurd indiscretion, but as Bernhard Böschenstein has indicated, the silencing of the doubtful, absurd and questionable represents for Walser a death blow to the artist's necessarily subversive perspective.[19] Though it is the countess who exclaims "Ich bin sprachlos" at the end of Lenz's declamation (1:336), it is therefore Lenz himself whose language is effectively at an end. His final words simply express his inability to comprehend how the beauty of the countess can generate anything but a gentle demeanor. The scene concludes with the countess ordering Lenz from her room, declaring that his behavior must lead her to believe him insane (1:336).

The last scene of Walser's dramatic sketch, which takes place in the duke's study, is very brief. Goethe declares that Lenz is an "Esel." The duke is more sympathetic; he views Lenz as nothing so much as an unhappy child, but feels he must nevertheless be banished from court: "Man schaffe ihn auf eine sanfte Manier fort. Mein Hof kann dergleichen nicht dulden" (1:336). Of course, this scene is as speculative as the representation of Lenz's "Eselei." But Walser's use of artistic license in his brief portrayals of well-known writers represents one of his most significant contributions to modern literature. For as Max Brod noted, Walser's literary portraits are inscribed more by premonition, indeed even by pure fancy, than by whatever biographical knowledge Walser might have possessed in connection with the figures he depicts, and precisely Walser's freedom in this regard justifiably leads Brod to credit him with the creation of a brand new poetic genre, "eine neue Art kleiner literarischer Gemälde."[20] George Avery makes the claim that "the most manifest expression of Walser's modernity" is "his symbolic concentration on the consciousness of single protagonists."[21] This tendency of Walser to focus his works on the exploration of one individual perhaps explains the brevity of the final, conspiratorial scene in *Lenz* following the removal of the eponymous protagonist from the sketch. If Walser's exploration of Lenz's psyche paradigmatizes both one of his most innovative formal contributions to modern literature and the clearest expression of his modernity, his ultimate elision of Lenz can be said to reveal his darkest fear of modernity, the fear that the artist is being "gently" banished to its fringes.

Notes

1. Timm Menke, *Lenz-Erzählungen in der deutschen Literatur* (Hildesheim: Olms, 1984) 91.

2. Inge Stephan and Hans-Gerd Winter, *'Ein vorübergehendes Meteor?' J. M. R. Lenz und seine Rezeption in Deutschland* (Stuttgart: Metzler, 1984) 116-117.

3. See esp. Tamara Evans, *Robert Walsers Moderne* (Berne: Francke, 1989).

4. Alan Wilde, "Barthelme Unfair to Kierkegaard: Some Thoughts on Modern and Postmodern Irony," *boundary* 2/5 (Fall, 1976): 45-70.

5. See Egon Menz, "Lenzens Weimarer Eselei," *Goethe Jahrbuch* 106 (1989):91-105. "Daß Goethe den Herzog zur Vertreibung überredete, ist allgemein angenommen worden, jedoch nicht beweisbar; der Herzog kann aus eigenem Antrieb gehandelt haben" (94).

6. All references to Robert Walser's oeuvre are taken from *Das Gesamtwerk,* ed. Jochen Greven, 13 vols. (Geneva: Kossodo, 1966-1975), and are cited in the text by volume and page number.

7. Martin Walser, "Alleinstehender Dichter. Über Robert Walser," in *Über Robert Walser II,* ed. Katharina Kerr (Frankfurt: Suhrkamp, 1978) 18.

8. David Frisby, *Fragments of Modernity: Theories of Modernity in the Work of Simmel, Kracauer and Benjamin* (Cambridge: MIT Press, 1986) 4.

9. Charles Baudelaire, cited in Frisby (16).

10. See esp. Nicole Pelletier, *Franz Kafka et Robert Walser: Étude d'une relation littéraire* (Stuttgart: Hans-Dieter Heinz, 1985), and Hans Dieter Zimmermann, *Der babylonische Dolmetscher: Zu Franz Kafka und Robert Walser* (Frankfurt/Main: Suhrkamp, 1985). Kafka apparently had a high regard for Walser's *Lenz.* On this point, see George C. Avery, *Inquiry and Testament: A Study of the Novels and Short Prose of Robert Walser* (Philadelphia: U of Pennsylvania P, 1968) 252.

11. See Evans's chapter "Ausstieg aus der Geschichte," 45-80.

12. John Osborne, *J. M. R. Lenz: The Renunciation of Heroism* (Göttingen: Vanden-hoeck & Ruprecht, 1975) 10.

13. Jakob Michael Reinhold Lenz, *Werke und Briefe in drei Bänden,* ed. Sigrid Damm (Munich: Hanser, 1987) 1: 249.

14. On this element of Walser's modernism, see Evans, 93-107.

15. Evans, 25.

16. This is the title of one of the chapters in Evans's book (24-44).

17. A brief discussion of Walser's liminoid personality, and of how his schizophrenia is resonant in the style and structure of his writing, can be found in Christopher Middelton, "A Parenthesis to the Discussion of Robert Walser's Schizophrenia" in *Robert Walser Rediscovered: Stories, Fairy-Tale Plays, and Critical Responses,* ed. Mark Harman (Hanover: U P of New England, 1985) 190-194. On this topic see also Timm Menke's essay in this volume.—eds.

18. See Menz, 92-95.

19. Bernhard Böschenstein, "Theatralische Miniaturen. Zur frühen Prosa Robert Walsers," in *Probleme der Moderne: Festschrift für Walter Sokel,* ed. Benjamin Bennett, Anton Kaes and William J. Lillyman (Tübingen: Niemeyer, 1983) 71-72.

20. Max Brod, "Kleine Prosa," *Neue Rundschau,* 24/2 (1913): 1043-1044.

21. Avery, viii.

Bibliography

EDITIONS OF LENZ'S WORKS

Lenz, Jakob Michael Reinhold. *Werke und Briefe in drei Bänden.* Ed. Sigrid Damm. Leipzig: Insel, 1987 and Munich & Vienna: Hanser, 1987.

SECONDARY LITERATURE

Böschenstein, Bernhard. "Theatralische Miniaturen. Zur frühen Prosa Robert Walsers." In *Probleme der Moderne: Festschrift für Walter Sokel.* Ed. Benjamin Bennett, Anton Kaes and William J. Lillyman. Tübingen: Niemeyer, 1983.

Büchner, Georg. *Sämtliche Werke und Briefe: Historisch-Kritische Ausgabe mit Kommentar.* Ed. Werner R. Lehmann. Hamburg & Munich: 1967.

Menke, Timm. *Lenz-Erzählungen in der deutschen Literatur.* Hildesheim: Olms, 1984.

Osborne, John. *J. M. R. Lenz: The Renunciation of Heroism.* Göttingen: Vandenhoeck & Ruprecht, 1975.

Stephan, Inge and Hans-Gerd Winter. *"Ein vorübergehendes Meteor?" J. M. R. Lenz und seine Rezeption in Deutschland.* Stuttgart: Metzler, 1984.

Susan Bernofsky (essay date 2000)

SOURCE: Bernofsky, Susan. Introduction to *The Robber,* by Robert Walser, translated by Susan Bernofsky, pp. v-xiii. Lincoln, Neb.: University of Nebraska Press, 2000.

[*In the following essay, published as the introduction to her English translation of Walser's unfinished novel,* The Robber, *Bernofsky describes the work as "a quirky masterpiece of high modernism" and claims that its central purpose is not about events in the life of its protagonist but to tell "a story about the impossibility of its own telling."*]

Robert Walser's 1925 novel *The Robber* is a quirky masterpiece of high modernism, a love story that unravels as it goes along. Its opening sentences—"Edith loves him. More on this later"—set the stage for a game of narrative hide-and-seek that will continue throughout the novel, affecting not only the storyline but phrasings, characterizations, and mise-en-scène as well. Consider this sketch of Edith, the protagonist's beloved:

> She sat right in front and was dressed all in snow-white, and her cheeks, down these cheeks plunged a red like a dauntless knight plunging over a cliff into an abyss in order to break the spell over the countryside with his sacrifice.

Here a sentence that begins with straightforward description is suddenly seized by a runaway simile that carries us off into an apparently unrelated scenario. One blush, and we find ourselves astray in the world of fairy tale, where spells are cast on countrysides and knights in shining armor come charging down hillsides to rescue—whom? Blushing maidens? Is this headlong metaphor merely the daydream of the character Edith, whose description we are reading? Possibly; but how odd, then, that it is triggered by a color that she herself does not see. It is more likely the narrator himself, susceptible as he is to flights of fancy, who has swooned his way into yet another digression, which nonetheless reflects and comments on the "real" story in progress. Edith, preparing to listen to her lover's public lecture on his love for her, really is a romantic heroine, and has not the landscape of the novel shown itself to be subject to the protagonist's love-besotted imagination? A release from this spell appears to be in sight, but at what cost to the knight himself, who is valiantly urging his steed not up a mountain made of glass but into the depths of an abyss?

The Robber was written and set in Berne, Switzerland, where Walser spent his last professionally active years, and it belongs to the phase of his artistic development that most clearly justifies his inclusion among the ranks of the great modernists. The novel showcases many of the idiosyncrasies of Walser's late prose: sudden shifts and leaps of perspective, interruptions of the narrative line, comically extended metaphors, and mutually exclusive or excessively relativized statements. These are techniques that challenge literature's mimetic function, its ability to correspond to and represent the world. Like his contemporaries Gertrude Stein, Virginia Woolf, and James Joyce, Walser (1878-1956) understood the extent to which language creates its own reality. His mutations of standard German syntax often climax in breathtakingly multiclaused sentences that by a sort of linguistic hopscotch enter a rarefied, metaphysical space where, in the words of one Walser persona, "the true truths" lie. His use of language to point beyond the realm of the readily sayable won him the admiration of Robert Musil, Hermann Hesse, Franz Hessel, Walter Benjamin, and Franz Kafka.

The 1920s marked not only the pinnacle but also the end of Walser's thirty-year public career as a writer. While the previous decade had seen the appearance of nine of his fourteen books, by 1920 publishers' interest in his work had waned, and in the years that followed he was able to publish only a single volume, *Die Rose* (*The Rose,* 1925), a collection of stories. The newspapers and magazines in whose feuilleton pages his work had frequently appeared began to send rejections. Walser's editor at the *Berliner Tagblatt* even reported having received letters from angry readers threatening to cancel their subscriptions if the "nonsense" didn't stop. Walser's work had become too perplexing, his sentences too playfully convoluted, for the tastes of a reading public schooled on naturalism and the Literature of Ideas à la Thomas Mann. Still, he remained as productive as ever: his work of the 1920s includes a good two thousand pages of short prose, as well as poems, "dramolettes," and the lost novel "Theodor."

The Robber remained unpublished until 1972. It is the last of Walser's nine novels by his own count (all but four were destroyed or lost) and was written in a period of great deprivation and disillusionment. Too poor to rent his own apartment, Walser had been living the life of an urban nomad, moving up to a dozen times a year from one furnished room to the next. His writing brought in relatively little money, and he was distressed by the lack of public recognition of his work. When Walser wrote *The Robber,* he must have been fully aware, at least after the first few pages, that he would never be able to publish it. This would explain why he never prepared a clean copy of the manuscript for submission to publishers.

Even a cursory glance into the pages of the novel makes it easy to see why Walser's prose came as such a challenge to his readers. Like most of his short fiction of the period, the novel flirts with plotlessness, foregrounding not so much the adventures of the protagonist as the daredevil manner of their telling. The narrative skips from theme to theme, returning to pick up a thread here and reprise a detail there, and after several sections an elaborate web of interwoven tales surrounds the puzzled reader. Seemingly hard facts shimmer and disappear. The Robber comes across "a house that was no longer present, or, to say it better, to an old house that had been demolished on account of its age and now no longer stood there, inasmuch as it had ceased to make itself noticed." But Walser's skillful and stylish unravelling of the world he describes is, at the same time, its reconstitution as a strange and beautiful object that dazzles with its contradictions but also with its truth.

The sleight-of-hand of Walser's narration often conjures away the ground beneath our feet, but each loss of orientation brings us back—after a detour or two—to terra firma, though generally not the one we had in mind. "Aimlessness leads to the aim," Walser tells us in his story **"Energetic,"** "while firm intentions often miss." If the narrator of *The Robber* seems to beat around the bush, it is because he is trying to get at a mystery so mercurial it might dematerialize if named outright. That which is to be expressed resists identification with that which can be said. The novel is in some sense a story about the impossibility of its own telling. And in fact the title character is himself a writer, a "robber" who "steals" from reality by writing about it. His adventures as a romantic hero constitute a series of encounters with the muse. And the muse herself, being a modern woman, cannot be expected to take kindly to finding herself the victim of such theft.

The novel itself is full of borrowings, not only from other authors (Stendhal, Dante, Dostoevsky, Gotthelf), but from painters as well. Henri Rousseau's 1886 *A la lisière du bois* [At the edge of the forest]—which perhaps Walser saw in the Kunsthaus Zurich—is the source of the "Henri Rousseau woman," and the long description of the Robber early on in the novel is inspired by a watercolor portrait of the sixteen-year-old Robert Walser dressed up as the hero of Schiller's play *The Robbers* (painted by his brother Karl, then seventeen). From real life Walser purloins the politician Walther Rathenau, Weimar Germany's famously melancholy foreign minister (and an acquaintance of Walser's), whose assassination allows us to put a date to the events of the novel: 1922.

In continental Europe, Walser is acknowledged along with Musil, Döblin, and Thomas Mann as one of the foremost German-language modernists. His reputation among English-language readers has lagged somewhat behind, a circumstance due only in part to a shortage of translations. The first Walser translations into any language were into English. Christopher Middleton's *The Walk and Other Stories* (London: Calder, 1957), was

followed by the novel *Jakob von Gunten* (also trans. Middleton; Austin: Univ. of Texas Press, 1969), *Selected Stories* (trans. Middleton and others; New York: Farrar, Straus & Giroux, 1982) and *Masquerade and Other Stories* (translated by myself with Tom Whalen; Baltimore: Johns Hopkins Univ. Press, 1990). All of the above volumes have been reprinted. Yet for us Walser still inhabits the fringes of the European canon. Perhaps this is because of his habit of thumbing his nose at Great Books and stubbornly embracing the inconspicuous—or perhaps simply because the modernist canon was established at a time when Walser's work was all but forgotten even in Germany.

In the English-speaking world, the most widely known fact about Robert Walser—even among those who have not read him—is that he spent the last twenty-six years of his life in mental institutions. This biographical circumstance is sometimes invoked, foolishly, as an explanation of his style. Never mind that the radical decentering of ostensibly stable reality is a constitutive feature of high modernist literature. Walser is firmly established in the minds of many as a writer whose every page demonstrates that he teetered on the brink. This misconception can only be strengthened, it seems, by the evidence of *The Robber,* in which Walser writes explicitly of mental illness. The Robber, his narrator tells us, "was surely ill 'in those days,' when he arrived in our city, filled with a curious disequilibrium, agitation. Certain inner voices, so to speak, tormented him. Had he come here to recover, to transform himself into a cheerful, contented member of society?" Indeed, many of the pranks and acts of exuberant rudeness in which the Robber indulges suggest profound instability. Also, we can discern a curious Jekyll-and-Hyde relationship between narrator and protagonist: the further the novel progresses, the more likely it seems that the two are in fact one and the same figure who is only playing at duality. And so the reader may be tempted to take this at least partly autobiographical novel as a record of the author's own deterioration.

Against this all too easy interpretation, I wish to present two cautionary notes. First, to argue from within the narrative, Walser makes protracted writer's block one of the symptoms of the Robber's unspecified malaise. It is only at the end of the book, when he undergoes a sort of redemption, that he recovers his ability to write. (In fact, Walser himself was immensely productive during the 1920s.) Second, it is crucial to remember the obvious but sometimes elusive difference between portrayals of madness and its expression. Nothing in the novel would force the reader ignorant of Walser's biography to conclude that its author was mentally unsound. Madness is the subject of *The Robber,* not its form.

We will never know precisely how bad, or bad in precisely what way, Robert Walser's mental health was. He checked himself into the Waldau mental clinic outside Berne in 1929, complaining of sleeplessness, depression, and an inability to concentrate, and there is little evidence that the diagnosis finally attached to his record—schizophrenia—was justified. Certainly his behavior during the 1920s was markedly odd (he made marriage offers to various women in rapid succession, greeted at least one guest by pretending to be his own butler, and leaped from his chair in a hotel restaurant to shout insults at fellow diners whose conversation annoyed him), but it does not now seem obvious that his confinement to the clinic was necessary. Visitors to Walser during his twenty-three years in the closed asylum at Herisau—to which he was transferred against his will in 1933—reported him to be perfectly lucid and ready to converse on a wide variety of literary and political topics.

The assumption that Walser gave up writing at Herisau has recently been discredited in an interview with Josef Wehrle, a former attendant. Wehrle told Walser's French biographer Catherine Sauvat that in fact Walser wrote a great deal in the asylum, on scraps of paper that he kept in his vest pocket and refused to show to anyone. He wrote standing up at a windowsill after meals, using a small pencil also kept stowed in a pocket. Wehrle was unable to say what became of these scraps of paper; he assumed Walser either gave them to his guardian, Carl Seelig, or destroyed them. Since it was Seelig who reported Walser's ostensible refusal to write in confinement, we must assume that Walser's final work was destroyed, like many of his earlier texts, by its author.

What might Walser have written during these final years? His prose pieces from the time of his stay at Waldau appear unexpectedly poised and calm after the rambunctious chaos of his 1920s work. One story from 1932/33, **"The Girl,"** concludes:

> *Small birds were trilling in the treetops, the sun shone down the avenue, people strolled to and fro, and water swam past the girl.*
>
> *She was grateful to the sun, the twittering she found delightful and the people she compared to the water that came and went.*

Here the apparent simplicity of observation compresses, in a manner far more artful than antic, precisely that same destabilization of reference we see in *The Robber*. It seems that to each of the stimuli mentioned in the first sentence there is a corresponding reaction in the second. But after the pleased mention of sun and birds there follows a curious reversal of what has come before. "People strolled to and fro, and water swam past the girl." The water is not flowing but swimming, itself displaying animal if not anthropomorphic behavior. And yet the girl, viewing the scene, compares the people with this water, which has been presented as being like the people. We are left with a knot of language in our hands that leads us around and around its own braid but never outside it. Walser's own hunger for written language—he had a reputation at Herisau for reticence and taciturnity—was apparently not sated by the stories he wrote there. Wehrle tells us he worked his way through the many volumes of bound newspapers in the asylum's library, one by one solving all the crossword puzzles.

Since Walser never prepared a fair copy of *The Robber,* the novel comes down to us in microscript form. The microscripts, now housed in the Robert Walser-Archiv in Zurich, were tiny, densely pencil-jotted manuscripts in which Walser composed the rough drafts of his texts starting as early as 1917. The paper he used for this was an assortment of small sheets of art-print paper, halved calendar pages, envelopes, correspondence cards (often he wrote between the lines of notes he'd received), and even single-sided advertisements cut from magazines and books. The microscript texts are so difficult to read that when this collection of 526 diminutive pages was first discovered after Walser's death, they were thought to be written in a sort of secret code. In fact the microscripts were written in *Sütterlin* script, then the standard style of German handwriting, but in a script that varied in height from one to two millimeters, executed with an often none-too-sharp pencil. These drafts seem to have been primarily an aid to composition: Walser generally recopied his texts within a few days of having written them, and it is not clear whether he himself would have been able to read his own writing had he waited too long.

The microscripts in Walser's literary estate, which were painstakingly deciphered in over a decade of labor by Bernhard Echte and Werner Morlang after the first transcriptions by Jochen Greven appeared in 1972, proved to contain a full six volumes of previously unknown texts (as well as drafts of various pieces published elsewhere). Since Walser left a number of his late prose works uncopied—being largely unable to get them published—the microscripts are a rich source of new material for hungry readers of Walser's work. *The Robber* in manuscript occupies a mere twenty-four pages of octavo-sized sheets.

My work on the translation was supported by a grant from the National Endowment for the Arts. To Werner Morlang and Bernhard Echte I am grateful, as ever, for their patience, generosity, and advice on the translation.

Heartfelt thanks are due as well to the denizens of the *Europäisches Übersetzer-Kollegium* in Straelen where most of the translation took shape.

Valerie Heffernan (essay date 2007)

SOURCE: Heffernan, Valerie. "Replaying the Pretexts." In *Provocation from the Periphery: Robert Walser Re-examined*, pp. 29-64. Würzburg, Germany: Königshausen & Neumann, 2007.

[*In the following essay, Heffernan analyzes Walser's early* Märchen, *or fairy tale, adaptations and the so-called* feuilletons *he wrote for various newspapers during his career, proposing that these, as well as all of the author's texts, are fundamentally influenced by his status as a marginal and borderline writer in German-Swiss literature, and by his desire to subvert all forms of "cultural authority" in his work.*]

Walser's peculiar mode of representing and challenging social, cultural and literary norms in his texts is motivated by a desire to expose the power structures and authority that underlie all social and cultural institutions. This chapter will shed light on Walser's ambivalent position à propos his literary and cultural environment by considering the characteristic way in which the writer reacts to the authority inherent in the cultural canon and established literary forms. It seems that very early in his literary career, Walser was already devising new endings for established narratives and new approaches to standard forms of literature. Walser's distinctive way of dealing with these 'pre-texts' is intimately linked to his subtle subversion of cultural norms and cultural authority.

This chapter will consider three aspects of literary authority and how they are represented in Walser's work. The focus here will be on the notion of mimicry, on the way in which Walser, through imitating an earlier text, manages at the same time to reveal its inappropriateness as a vessel for expression. Imitation is the sincerest form of flattery, or so the saying goes, and mimicry is often considered to be similar to imitation. However, as Bhabha points out, mimicry can never be equated with imitation, since it inevitably discloses both similarity and difference; it produces an exaggerated copy of the original which disavows that original as it reflects it.

The forms and genres that Walser has chosen for his work provide him with a framework for reflecting on the political and social context. As recent studies have shown, Walser was very much in tune with the concerns and interests of his era.[1] However, it cannot be denied that this writer has a very original and radically different way of looking at these questions. The ideas and ideologies that are manifest in the world around him are articulated and negotiated in his texts; however, through an ambivalent process of mimicry, he also questions their authority and exposes the power structures that drive them. Nothing is unassailable, Walser would argue; everything should be questioned, probed, examined, queried.

Of course, this can be somewhat disconcerting for the reader who expects Walser's *Märchen* to follow the tradition of the Grimm tales, or who expects his *Feuilletons* to provide an interesting but ultimately forgettable commentary on society. Walser uses the reader's expectations against him and exploits his naïve anticipation of what is to come. The reader soon finds that it is not just power-structures and institutions of authority that are being challenged here, but also his own ideas of what constitutes a literary text—ideas which are rooted in a certain tradition and ruled by literary convention. It is this approach that is under constant attack throughout Walser's work, indeed it drives his work. It is only when we throw off the shackles of literary convention and adopt a new attitude towards his writing that we can appreciate the subtlety, the confusion, and the game that is the Walser text.

WALSER'S MÄRCHEN

The *Märchen* or fairy tale could be considered one of literature's most fixed and inflexible narrative forms. Although the genre has come to be associated with the Grimm brothers through their famous *Kinder- und Hausmärchen*, versions of these tales, with similar characters and plots, have been told through the ages all over the world.[2] It is no wonder, then, that so many writers have attempted to get to grips with this particular narrative form to tell their own versions of the time-honoured stories. The Grimm brothers' *Märchen* or fairy tales are re-evaluated in Walser's earlier writings, and indeed, Walser will come back to these narratives at many times in his literary career. Walser's short dramas and prose pieces play with the motifs, characteristics and features of this form and re-cast them in a modern light. In his work, Walser uses the framework of this genre to challenge notions of identity and subjectivity in the modern era.

Walser's peculiar *Märchen-Dramolette* or fairy tale dramas have already gained some attention in the secondary literature, and indeed, this is not without some justification.[3] As early as 1899, Walser was using the genre of the fairy tale, with its conservative values and fixed narrative forms, to question the accepted norms and institutions of society. Walser's distinctive versions of the Grimm pre-texts challenge the unified, consistent totality presented in the Grimm narratives and draw attention to its artificiality. Thus, his whimsical *Märchen-*

Dramolette demonstrate that the resistance to authority that is an integral stance in Walser's later work is already apparent in his earlier pieces.

On a formal level too, Walser's fairy tale plays question traditional notions of genre. His decision to translate the prose texts of the brothers Grimm into drama suggests his scepticism towards the formulaic character of this narrative structure. Such a fixed literary form, with a clearly delineated beginning, middle and end, is plainly at odds with Walser's vision and his methods of literary production, and thus it is no surprise that his renderings of the Grimm texts break with convention to offer new perspectives on the familiar model. In effect, the rendering of prose in drama produces a hybrid genre, neither prose nor drama, and yet both at once.[4] In a letter to his publishers Ernst Rowohlt and Kurt Wolff in December 1912, Walser explains how he views his fairy tale plays:

> Sie sind ganz Poesie, und durchaus nur für künstlerisch genießende Erwachsene. [. . .] Sie sind auf den Stil und auf die Schönheit angelegt, und der Genuß des *Buches* ist daran die Hauptsache. Ob sie je aufgeführt werden könnten, etwa mit Musik, ist ganz und gar fraglich und erscheint vorläufig völlig nebensächlich. Sie sind auf Rede und Sprache gestimmt, auf Takt und rhythmischen Genuß.[5]
>
> ([*Briefe*])

Evidently, Walser is less concerned with the question of how these short dramatic pieces can be categorized than what his playful blending of genres can yield.

Walser's first flirtation with the genre of the *Märchen* is his dramatic rendering of the Grimm fairy tale of Snow White, '**Schneewittchen**' (GW [*Das Gesamtwerk in 12 Bänden*] VII, 104-145). This piece, first published in *Die Insel* in September 1901, was rated by Walter Benjamin as "eines der tiefsinnigsten Gebilde unserer neuen Dichtung".[6] Walser's '**Schneewittchen**', however, is not a simple reproduction of the Grimm pretext. The drama opens at what could be considered the end of the Grimm fairy tale: Snow White has been revived by the Prince, but has returned to live at her father's castle, with the beautiful Queen who gave her the poisoned apple that caused her death. Action in the piece centres on the conflict between Snow White and her stepmother, and all other characters, including the prince, play only secondary roles.[7] Thus, Walser's dramatic version of the fairy tale does not re-enact the main events of the story, but rather, portrays the characters' reactions to the course of events and to their own roles in the action. Interestingly, however, Walser's '**Schneewittchen**' adheres to the conventional finale of the Grimm fairy tale; the drama ends as Snow White agrees to overlook her stepmother's past misdeeds and live happily ever after.

Walser's dramatic version of the Cinderella fairy tale ('**Aschenbrödel**' GW VII, 59-103) was written around the same time as his '**Schneewittchen**' and published in *Die Insel* in June 1902. This drama, too, is rooted in the tradition of the Grimm *Märchen*, but like the Snow White play, it too breaks away from the storyline of that version. Cinderella declares her love for the Prince, but when the latter offers her his kingdom, she refuses, protesting that if she were to give up her servant girl's clothes in favour of a more regal costume, she would no longer be Cinderella. The Prince, however, objects to this resolution, insisting that this is not how the *Märchen* goes. It is only when he insists to his beloved that they have no choice in their fate that she agrees to marry him; "Das Märchen will's. Das Märchen ist's / gerad', das uns verlobt will sehn." (**GW** VII, 101) Faced with an inevitable denouement, the two characters accept their fate and are united at the end of the drama.

Walser's dramatic adaptation of the Sleeping Beauty story, published in December 1920 in *Pro Helvetia,* comes much later than his other two *Märchen-Dramolette*; it is also significantly shorter and linguistically somewhat less sophisticated than the earlier plays. The '**Dornröschen**' drama (**GW** VII, 209-218) consists of one short act, which opens at the end of the fairy tale, when the handsome stranger wakes Sleeping Beauty with a kiss. In the Grimm version of the tale, this act brings about the happy resolution of the story; in the Walser version, as one might expect, the happy ending is not a foregone conclusion. The visitor to the castle has woken Sleeping Beauty out of her hundred-year slumber with his kiss, but neither she nor the rest of the court are particularly pleased at being woken up. More importantly for the storyline of the fairy tale, Sleeping Beauty sees no reason why the kiss entitles the stranger to her hand in marriage. However, when the newcomer explains to Sleeping Beauty how he came to find her in her tower, Sleeping Beauty is moved by his story and particularly by those candidates who were unsuccessful in their plight. Persuaded by the fairy story, she begins to waver; "Doch fang' ich langsam an zu glauben, / du hab'st ein Recht auf mich, und es sei billig, / daß ich nun dir gehöre" (**GW** VII, 216), she pronounces. Thus convinced that this is the inevitable end of the story, the play closes as the characters chorus in unison, "So wär' die Sache angenehm / beendet mit 'ner frohen Hochzeit." (**GW** VII, 218)

It is not surprising that Walser's fairy tale plays have gained so much attention from the secondary literature, since they enact a peculiar type of mimicry of the well-known Grimm tales. There is no doubt that the basis for his dramas are the stories penned by the brothers Grimm. All of the stock characters appear, and although the characters seem at times to step outside of the parameters of the dramas to comment on the action, the storylines are at least based on the Grimm originals. Indeed, Walser's imitation of the Grimm narrative is a very deliberate gesture. His dramatic rewritings of these time-honoured tales work within the parameters of the well-known stories and use their familiar figures and narrative structures to allow for a subtle criticism of the genre. Thus, through his mimicry of the Grimms' *Märchen* and its inevitable slippage, Walser manages simultaneously to expose the restrictions of the genre and to question its appropriateness as a vehicle for expression. Walser's comic renderings of these tales raise some fundamental questions regarding the norms and conventions of the genre. They enact a subtle reversal of the power relationships inherent in society and they introduce novel modes of subjectivity that challenge traditional notions of the subject in narrative.

Critics have suggested that Walser's fairy tale plays can be seen as a sort of "Metatheater" that reflects on the possibilities, and more importantly, on the limitations of the genre of the fairy tale.[8] His mimicry of the conventions of the *Märchen* reveals the rigidity of its boundaries, the one-dimensionality of its characters and the inflexibility of its conclusions. Through his *Märchen-Dramolette*, Walser exposes the power play that drives the whole notion of genre. Innocuous as these models may appear, it seems that Walser perceives their rigid structures and predetermined order as representative of a power that seeks to shape and limit his writing.[9] In order to represent his resistance to that authority, Walser cannot merely follow the conventions of the genre; however, if he also wishes to expose the inherent authority of this genre, neither can he completely ignore its norms and traditions. Thus Walser "bedient sich zunächst aus dem Spracharsenal und Personal des konventionellen Märchens" in order to disrupt the rigid world of the *Märchen* from within.[10] Through his distinctive reconstructions of the Grimm tales, Walser exposes the limitations of the genre of the *Märchen* and compels the reader to reflect on the rigidity and inflexibility of its dictates.

Accordingly, Walser's *Märchen* abide by the formulaic happy ending that we have come to expect of the genre.[11] Nevertheless, there are strong hints in his dramas that the characters are unhappy with the contrived harmony that the genre demands. In **'Schneewittchen'**, for example, the characters agree on a version of reality, but it seems clear that Snow White's submission to the dictates of the fairy tale involves significant compromises and even denial of the truth; thus, a happy-ever-after ending is only possible when a new *Märchen* is invented to replace the old one. In Walser's **'Aschenbrödel'**, Cinderella and the prince give in to the predetermined conclusion of their story, so that ultimately, the *Märchen* does triumph; however, once again, this is only in modified form, as Cinderella makes explicit her unwillingness to give up her role as servant. Finally, one might be forgiven for taking the happy ending of Walser's **'Dornröschen'** and its corny closing lines with a pinch of salt. The outcome of this drama is certainly consonant with the ending of the familiar

fairy tale, but once again, we have the distinct impression that it is only through compromise and considered acceptance of the predetermined order of the *Märchen* that this plan can be achieved. As the prince remarks, "es ginge ja nicht anders" (**GW** VII, 217). Thus, Walser's fairy tale plays do adhere to the formulaic happy ending prescribed by the fairy tale, but in undermining that harmonious conclusion, they emphasize that it is one which is imposed by the norms of the genre.

If Walser's dramatic versions of the Grimm fairy tales serve to expose the power and authority that underlie this genre, they are equally concerned with revealing the authority that is manifest in culture and society. Walser is clearly playing on the notion that the textual world created in the famous Grimm tales, a realm anchored in simplistic values and rigid hierarchies, is a paradigm for human society on a larger scale.[12] Within Walser's fictional realms, power structures are challenged and even inverted. In particular, the assumption in the fairy tale that happiness must be equated with marriage and riches comes under attack in his dramas.[13] The master/servant dialectic, a recurring motif in his work, makes an appearance in the **'Aschenbrödel'** drama in the form of the relationship between Cinderella and her Ugly Sisters; however, it is unclear where the power lies in this constellation. Cinderella seems to enjoy her role as slave, indeed, seems to take pleasure from being dominated, to the extent that she claims to love this role and is unwilling to give it up for the prince. Also, as Peter Utz observes, the King makes a cursory appearance in this drama, only to be told by his son, "Du hast hier weder Wort noch Macht" (**GW** VII, 88).[14] Within his fairy tale plays, Walser imagines a realm in which the power structures on which society is based are questioned and destabilized.

Critics who have dealt with Walser's fairy tale plays have also pointed to the unusual and at times provocative notion of subjectivity engendered within their borders.[15] The characters object to the rigid confines of the roles allocated to them by the norms of the genre and underline their difference from this imposed identity. Thus, the Queen in **'Schneewittchen'** complains that she has been cast in the role of the evil stepmother, a role which she seems unable to shake; she begs Snow White, "Ach glaub doch / solch aberwitzigem Märchen nicht, / das in der Welt begierig Ohr / die Nachricht schüttet, ich sei toll / aus Eifersucht, bös von Natur, / was alles ein Geschwätz nur ist" (**GW** VII, 108). In **'Aschenbrödel'**, Cinderella articulates her difference from her ascribed role by refusing to be unhappy about her lamentable position as servant to her sisters; as Utz comments, "ihre Nicht-Identität mit der von der Gattung und der Märchenvorlage verlangten Identität ist [. . .] die Bedingung ihrer Identität."[16] Insofar as Sleeping Beauty is unwilling to internalize the fate ascribed her by the *Märchen*, she too expresses an identity that is split and at variance with itself. Even the minor characters in the '**Dornröschen**' drama question the parameters of the roles attributed to them by the fairy tale model and object to their limitations. The meta-consciousness of the characters in Walser's *Märchen-Dramolette* thus lifts them out of the one-dimensional world of the fairy tale and suggests a form of identity that is both elusive and fractured.

The '**Dornröschen**'-*Dramolett* is the last of Walser's dramatic renderings of the *Märchen* form; however, it is plain from his prose texts that the form and content of the famous Grimm tales continued to preoccupy him in his later writings. In particular, one short text, which appears on the 457th page of Walser's **Mikrogramme,** clearly represents a rewriting of the Rapunzel fairy tale by the brothers Grimm. This **Mikrogramm** from 1929 opens with the telling line, 'Lange wohnte sie nun schon im Turm der Geduld'. It is evident from this text that although Walser may have moved away from the dramatic form as a means of revitalizing the genre in this **Mikrogramm,** his way of exploiting the material and form of the *Märchen* is similar. However, as we shall see, this **Mikrogramm** presents a more radical revision of the Grimm original.

> Lange wohnte sie nun schon im Turm der Geduld,
> indem sie oft ihr Haar
> zu ihrem Vergnügen aus dem Fenster herunter-
> fließen und -gleiten ließ, das
> der Retter, der noch immer nicht mit Bestimmtheit
> zu wissen schien, ob er
> zur Arbeit des Rettens zu schreiten habe oder nicht,
> leise zum Mund zog,
> 5   einem aus dem Ungefähren herbeieilenden und
> -wehenden Windchen
> erlaubend, mit den kostbaren Fäden, die sich in
> wundervollen
> Krümmungen um ihre eigene Feinheit wanden, zu
> spielen. Im Vergleich
> zum Turm kam sich der unten auf einer blümeligen
> Wiese Stehende
> geringfügig vor, und in Anbetracht, daß er sich die
> Hände derjenigen, die
> 10 er eigentlich längst gerettet haben sollte, als überaus
> schön vorstellte und
> ihr in seiner Phantasie ein Gesicht schenkte, das alle
> anderen Gesichter in
> Bezug auf Lieblichkeit übertraf, erschien sie ihm
> mitunter wie eine
> Retterin, die den Retter rettete. Im Raum ringsum-
> her sah es aus, als
> existiere irgendwie und -wo ein rätselhaftes Läch-
> eln, das die Lippen der

> 15 Unverstandenheit selbst verziere, die ein Symbol ist.
> Aber auch die
> Rettungherbeisehnende, in und an sich Gerettete
> lächelte bei der Idee in
> ihrem Turmgemach, daß der Retter sie nach wie vor
> retten zu müssen
> meinte. Letzterem kam amüsant vor, daß sich ihm
> die Wiese zum
> Aufentha[l]tsplatz trefflich eigne, daß ihn die Höhe
> und die romantische
> 20 Gestalt des Turmes auf's Lebhafteste interessiere,
> die Haare der
> rettungslos Entschwundenen für ihn keineswegs auf
> Nimmer-wiedersehen
> entflohen seien und der somit sich die Freiheit
> nahm, sie zu küssen, die ihn
> gerettet hatten, indem sie ihn vor eine schwierige
> Aufgabe stellten, die
> beides sein kann, ein Retten und ein Gerettetwer-
> den. Das Leben zog am
> 25 unerschütterlich seinen Standpunkt einnehmenden,
> *bestän[d]igkeit*-
> vergegenwärtigenden Turm mit den buntesten und
> unerwartetsten Bildern
> vorbei. Der Retter sowohl wie diejenige, die gerettet
> werden sollte, hatten
> reichlich zum Verglichenwerden Zeit gefunden und
> schienen sich in
> diesem angenehmen Zustand auf's denkbar Trefflic-
> hste zu spiegeln, indem
> 30 eine Menge begreiflicher Eitelkeiten sich in ihren
> Seelen einnistete.
> Solange ihn der Wunsch zu retten belebte, blieb er
> Retter, und inwiefern
> gerettet zu werden hoffen *läßt*, blieb sie der in jeder
> Weise interessante
> und anziehende Gegenstand des Rettungseifers, we-
> shal[b] ich mich
> auszusprechen bewogen fühlen muß: "Laßt sie so!"

(BG ([*Aus dem Bleistiftgebiet. Mikrograme au den Jahren 1924-1932***]) V, 160-1)**

It is clear from the opening lines of this **Mikrogramm** that the central image of the Grimm fairy tale will also be the point of departure for Walser's piece. Long-haired Rapunzel—though she is not named in the **Mikrogramm**—is trapped in her tower, while her rescuer below contemplates how best to save her. However, the similarity between the **Mikrogramm** and its Grimm original ends there, as Walser's text makes a definitive break with the norms of the genre.

In terms of language, Walser's **Mikrogramm** signifies a move away from the highly stylized verse form of the earlier fairy tale plays. Although this is already evident in the **'Dornröschen'** drama, in which Walser forgoes the lyrical verse employed in **'Schneewittchen'** and **'Aschenbrödel',** the shift from dramatic dialogue into prose represents a complete *volte-face* in terms of the form of the piece. In some respects, this could be seen as a move back to the narrative form and an attempt to realign his prose pieces with the Grimm tales. However, the incongruity between the Grimm stories and Walser's radical rewritings of those tales becomes all the more apparent when the discrepancy in form is less noticeable. Walser's language gives the impression of being far more open, more fluid and more playful than the formulaic prose of the Grimm brothers' texts. With its inventive word compounds such as *"bestän- [d]ig*keitvergegenwärtigend" (lines 25-26), and with its consistent questioning of apparently unambiguous terms such as 'Retter' and 'Gerettete', Walser's language proves much more self-reflexive than the Grimm tale that it emulates. We are presented here with an intricate web of sentences that, like Rapunzel's beautiful curls, "sich in wundervollen Krümmungen um ihre eigene Feinheit [wenden]" (lines 6-7).

The inherent power structures in human interaction, which are reflected in a subtle way in Walser's fairy tale dramas, are expressed here in unambiguous form. Nowhere is this more evident than in Walser's play on the clichéd image of the tower that separates Rapunzel from her prince. At the centre of this text, the tower presides as an obvious symbol of power. It reflects the hierarchy between Rapunzel and her rescuer, but it presents that hierarchy in a much more ambivalent way than suggested in the Grimm version of the tale. The fact that Rapunzel is high up in the tower suggests that she is the more powerful partner in this hierarchy. Even the prince, standing on the meadow below, is forced to consider the inequality of this situation. As he views the colossal tower that separates him from Rapunzel, he himself feels rather inadequate: "Im Vergleich zum Turm kam sich der unten auf einer blümeligen Wiese Stehende geringfügig vor" (lines 7-9).

Walser's text challenges the simplicity of the hierarchy between rescuer and rescued, and suggests that it is not as straightforward as might initially seem. The prince is presented as far less confident than his Grimm predecessor, and he begins to question his role as 'Retter' (rescuer) within this dynamic. Rather, it seems more plausible to him that Rapunzel is the more active party within their relationship; "sie [erschien] ihm mitunter wie eine Retterin, die den Retter rettete." (lines 12-13) Rapunzel is equally sceptical about her role as 'Gerettete' (rescued), and in fact, seems to find the idea quite amusing; "die Rettungherbeisehnende, in und an sich Gerettete lächelte bei der Idee in ihrem Turmgemach, daß der Retter sie nach wie vor retten zu müssen meinte." (lines 15-18) Thus, Walser's **Mikrogramm**

presents us with a 'Retter' who is obviously not able to fulfil that duty and a 'Gerettete' who does not exhibit the characteristics traditionally associated with that role. This questioning of the fixity of hierarchies is obviously connected to Walser's attempt to query power structures within culture and society. However, it also continues the interrogation of identity that is going on in the earlier *Märchen-Dramolette*. The view of subjectivity expressed in this **Mikrogramm** envisions a fluid subject, one that cannot be pinned down or expressed in simplistic terms.

This juxtaposition of the prince and the tower can be read as an exaggerated representation of the type of hierarchy in human society that Walser hints at in his earlier versions of the fairy tales. The reversal of the hierarchy between Rapunzel and the prince also calls into question the conventional version of the story, which depends very much on the passive woman being saved by the active man. As such, Walser's rewriting represents a challenge to traditional gender roles. Critics have often considered Walser's fairy tale dramas from a feminist perspective, in that in his rewritings, the women figures play a more active role in their fate.[17] When we consider that Walser's Cinderella is at first unwilling to give up her position as servant girl to marry the prince, and his Sleeping Beauty refuses to go along with the Grimm brothers' version of events, which offers her to the prince as a reward for his valour, we can see how the female protagonists in Walser's dramas put their Grimm ancestors in the shade. In this respect also, Walser's **Mikrogramm** goes one step further, since Rapunzel could be seen as one of the most passive of the Grimm brothers' heroines. Locked away in her tower, she is the epitome of submissiveness, introversion and modesty. In their account, she is objectified as the focus of the prince's desire and she provides the means for him to attain that goal. Walser's narrative, on the other hand, breaks with that mould quite significantly; he plays on this image of her as "der in jeder Weise interessante und anziehende Gegenstand des Rettungseifers" (lines 32-33) and yet provides her with her own sense of agency. She too is a rescuer in this situation; she too is presented as energetic and dynamic.

Given the blatant phallic connotations of the tower, it is interesting to note how this icon is used within the **Mikrogramm** to destabilize patriarchal authority within the fairy tale world. According to the tradition of the fairy tale, the tower is a male-dominated domain. The innocent maiden is forced against her will to live in isolation within its walls; she can only be liberated from this helpless situation through the intervention of her knight in shining armour. In Walser's rewriting of the *Märchen*, Rapunzel has taken control of the tower and thus appropriated the power with which it is associated.

She rejects the possible intervention of a male suitor, opting instead to continue to live in seclusion. Thus, both literally and metaphorically, she looks down on her bewildered prince from a position of power that he would usually occupy.

The prince, for his part, seems confused by this state of affairs; Rapunzel's occupation of the tower has left him emasculated, disempowered and unsure of his place within the fairytale realm. He begins to question his role as rescuer; "der Retter [schien] noch immer nicht mit Bestimmtheit zu wissen [. . .], ob er zur Arbeit des Rettens zu schreiten habe oder nicht" (lines 3-4). The interrogation of the fairytale hero that was begun in the fairy tale plays is thus taken to a higher level in the *Mikrogramm,* as the more general issue of masculine identity is challenged. The emasculated prince is depicted now in an overtly feminine setting, "unten auf einer blümeligen Wiese" (line 8). His power to rescue Rapunzel, and indeed her desire to be rescued, are rejected out of hand in this prose text; rather, we are presented with an image of Rapunzel—the apparent victim in this scenario—laughing up her sleeve at her supposed saviour. If Walser's fairy tale dramas are concerned with challenging accepted hierarchies, then this original perspective on the relationship between rescuer and rescued shows that the *Mikrogramm* is involved in the same kind of deconstruction.

Walser's emancipation of the fairytale heroines must also be seen in the context of a more general attempt to animate a genre that has lost any form of spontaneity. In this respect, the tower serves as an interesting metaphor. The tower is most notable for its constancy; it remains unchanging in a changing world. The *Mikrogramm* informs us: "Das Leben zog am unerschütterlich seinen Standpunkt einnehmenden, *bestän[d]ig*keitvergegenwärtigenden Turm mit den buntesten und unerwartetsten Bildern vorbei." (lines 24-27) This could be seen as emblematic of the position of the *Märchen* in the modern world. It refuses to change with the times, but remains fixed and inert. Walser's earlier dalliances with the genre reveal an attempt to vitalize the genre by tying it to the genre of the "lyrische Komödie" (lyrical comedy).[18] Here, he uses the image of the tower, the focus of the Grimm fairy tale, to present an image of the genre of the *Märchen* as rigid and static.

In Walser's *Mikrogramm,* the potential love-relationship between Rapunzel and the prince undergoes a radical revision, and Rapunzel's' hair takes on new connotations. Within this narrative Rapunzel's show of letting down her hair is not so much gesture of reaching out to her would-be rescuer, as something she does for her own pleasure. Thus, where in the original fairy tale, Rapunzel's hair functions as a metonym for the young woman, allowing the prince access to her, it loses that associative quality in Walser's rewriting. The fact that

she does not want to be saved by the prince makes her an unattainable object of desire, an elusive figure that is always just out of his reach. Rapunzel's hair is all that is left for the prince, and thus it becomes a fetishized object of desire for him, as the following lines illustrate:

> Lange wohnte sie nun schon im Turm der Geduld, indem sie oft ihr Haar zu ihrem Vergnügen aus dem Fenster herunterfließen und -gleiten ließ, das der Retter [. . .] leise zum Mund zog, einem aus dem Ungefähren herbeieilenden und -wehenden Windchen erlaubend, mit den kostbaren Fäden, die sich in wundervollen Krümmungen um ihre eigene Feinheit wanden, zu spielen.

> (lines 1-7)

Rapunzel's lovely tresses no longer point to the real girl, but rather, offer the prince a rather less complicated outlet for his unfulfilled desire.

Homi Bhabha's ideas on the role of the fetish in the relationship between self and other may be of some interest in this context.[19] Bhabha points out that this relationship is highly complex, built as it is on a peculiar combination of anxiety and desire. In addition, the fetish functions by replacing the object that it is supposed to point to so that it disavows the object in the process. In this *Mikrogramm,* the prince's fetishization of Rapunzel's hair enables him to control his conflicting thoughts and feelings about the woman; it allows him to express his desire without the having to deal with the anxiety aroused by her powerful position in this relationship. In effect, the woman is rejected in favour of the fetishized object. However, as Bhabha has pointed out, the fetish is "an arrested, fixated form of representation" which denies the ambivalence of the precarious relationship between self and other.[20] Any possibility of an encounter between the prince and Rapunzel is excluded by the prince's unwillingness or inability to deal with his inconsistent feelings for the woman.

However, what makes this revision of the fairy tale Walser's most radical is the fact that the standard happy ending is rejected altogether in favour of a more original resolution. In the final sentence of the piece, the narrator steps in to distance himself from the lovely image he has created. He is so affected by the picturesque scenario that he will make a definitive break with the *Märchen* original. Moved by the beauty of the *Märchen,* he decides not to disturb this beautiful image, but to arrest it in the moment before the prince saves the maiden; he is compelled to call out, "Laßt sie so!" (line 34).[21] The general feeling in this fairy tale seems to be that it is better not to disturb the order of things, since the reality could never really be as perfect as the fantasy. Rapunzel's rescuer is somewhat hesitant about saving this maiden, "in Anbetracht, daß er [. . .] ihr in seiner Phantasie ein Gesicht schenkte, das alle anderen Gesichter in

Bezug auf Lieblichkeit übertraf" (lines 9-12), and has no idea what she will really look like. For this reason, it is better to hang onto the intact ideal, even if it means that the relationship between Rapunzel and her suitor can never be fulfilled, rather than risk destroying it altogether.

The implications of this radical revision of the happy ending for the genre of the *Märchen* are twofold. On the one hand, it is clear that Walser does appreciate the beauty and perfection of the *Märchen* and depicts it in his prose as an ideal. On the other hand, he makes it clear that such beauty can only ever be static and lifeless, and can be easily shattered if it is disturbed. We can infer that for Walser, the genre of *Märchen* is unparalleled when it comes to representing beauty and harmony, but equally, that the cliché can never transcend the fantasy, so that the genre has little relevance in the modern world. By making a definitive break with the happy ending that is the preordained conclusion of the fairy tale, Walser's mimicry of the Rapunzel *Märchen* goes a step further in challenging the limitations of the genre.

WALSER'S MODERN MÄRCHEN

It is clear that Walser's *Märchen* imitate the motifs and dictates of the Grimm pre-text, whilst at the same time raising fundamental questions as to the validity of this model for contemporary literature. The act of writing a *Märchen* can be see as an attempt to conform, at least on the surface. However, it is only a superficial attempt to be seen to play the game, and the real motive of his camouflage becomes clear; he is using the very structures and formulations of this genre to expose its inappropriateness for modern times. Walser's crafty mimicry of the traditions and conventions of the Grimms' *Märchen* questions the authority of the genre from within that genre and offers a voice of resistance from the margins.

A 1910 prose text entitled **"Märchen I"** (GW [*Das Gesamtwerk in 12 Bänden,*] VI, 122-123) may offer some further insights into the motives behind Walser's mimicry of the genre. The text begins conventionally: "Es war einmal ein Kaiser". The traditional opening sentence attests to a deliberate attempt to remain within the parameters of the *Märchen,* but as Jens Tismar remarks, 'Die vertraute Floskel "es war einmal" steht wie ein umgedrehter Wegweiser da'.[22] The rest of the fairy tale serves to emphasize this point: "aber der Kaiser war krank, und zwar, wie wir gar nicht zweifeln, deshalb, weil der Raum der Zeit, in der er lebte und regierte, krank war. Nichts war den Leuten mehr heilig; das Volk besaß keinerlei Ideale mehr." This is no longer the era of fairy tales; the infirmity of the Kaiser points to a world in which kings and queens have lost their power and must learn to adapt in order to survive. The Kaiser

must accept that the ideals have changed with the times; where once, nobleness, virtue and honour were paramount, nowadays, more practical considerations reign supreme. In such a world, the Kaiser can only dream of what could have been, and his longing for times past is clear: "In des Kaisers Augen blitzte oftmals der Zorn auf über das Verhängnis, dem er mehr und mehr verfiel und das ihn nötigte, sich wie ein Geschäftemacher zu benehmen, wo er hätte mögen ein Ritter und Fechter sein." (**GW** VI, 123)

This text is more than just a sad story about a disillusioned Kaiser—though there is no question that it is also that; it bears witness to loss, the loss of an age in which fairy tales are possible, in which honour reigns and good triumphs. The narrator's candid declaration that "auch im Leben gab es nichts Schönes mehr" makes it clear that this is not the fault of a Kaiser who cannot move with the times, but of an era which makes no room for beauty, simplicity and truth. What is left is desolation and barrenness; "das Land, so sehr auch der Handel gedeihen mochte, glich einer Wüste." (**GW** VI, 123) This text is clearly more of a testimony to the state of the modern world than a fairy tale. The world has changed, society has changed, and the time of kingdoms and fairy tales is over. The twentieth century is not a time for fairy tales, for the idealized and harmonious image or the world that they create and nurture. Like the Kaiser, the *Märchen* has lost its power in the modern era. That is not to say that Walser is necessarily glad that this is so. If anything, the desolate final image of 'Märchen (I)', that is the world as a desert, would seem to indicate that the loss of the harmonious world of the *Märchen* is very much a loss to humanity.

TELLING THE NATION: WALSER'S RETELLINGS OF THE TELLSAGE

Walser's prose text **'Märchen I'** was written in 1910, at a time when the great powers of Europe were gathering force and preparing for war, therefore it is not surprising that such issues as national sovereignty, industrial development and the changing face of Europe, which would have preoccupied any writer or cultural commentator of the era, feature in his prose pieces of this time. The writer's aversion to all institutions and notions of power and authority—great leaders, great nations, great men—mean that he is equally sceptical towards the forms and genres associated with such powerful concepts.[23] However, the connection between form and content also allows the writer an appropriate space to challenge the authority of cultural norms and cultural authority.

The folk tale of the Swiss national hero, Wilhelm Tell plays a very particular role within the concept of Swiss nationhood. The *Tellsage,* as it is known in German, is supposed to have taken place in the Swiss canton of

Uri, at the beginning of the fourteenth century. Tell's revolt against the local *Landvogt* Gessler is said to have sparked an uprising of the Swiss against their despotic Austrian rulers, which ultimately resulted in the unification and independence of the Swiss nation. The tale is thus ascribed to a specific historical, geographical and political context; the story of Wilhelm Tell has become historically embedded, to the extent that it was mentioned in early Swiss history books, most notably Ägidius Tschudi's *Chronikon Helveticum* of 1570 and Johannes Müller's *History of the Swiss Federation* of 1786.[24] However, it should be noted that its content reflects similar tales told in Scandinavia in the twelfth and thirteenth centuries and even in Persia in the twelfth century.[25]

However, it was Friedrich Schiller's play *Wilhelm Tell,* first staged in 1804, which launched Wilhelm Tell onto the European stage.[26] Schiller's drama is based on two main plot lines, which run parallel. On the one hand, the drama depicts the popular revolt of the Swiss people against the tyrannical Austrian invaders, represented most visibly in Schiller's re-enactment of the legendary scene at the Rütli meadow, where the Swiss gather to pledge support to each other and allegiance to a united Switzerland. Alongside the drama of the collective, Schiller portrays on the other hand Wilhelm Tell's individual battle with the ruthless *Landvogt* Gessler, who punishes him for his disobedience by forcing him to shoot an apple placed on his son's head, and then has him arrested for treason when he reveals that he would have killed the *Landvogt* if he had hurt his son. This second plot line culminates in Tell's famous soliloquy at the narrow pass near Küßnacht, as he lies in wait for Gessler. Tell's meeting with Johannes Parracida in the final act of the drama unites the two plot lines, as the brutal murder of Gessler is interpreted as a heroic act of nationalism.[27] The drama concludes with the Swiss people celebrating Tell as their saviour: "Es lebe Tell! Der Schütz und der Erretter!"[28]

Schiller's play has been read and understood as a drama that celebrates the triumph of the small man against the evil tyrant, and Schiller's Tell is fêted as a Swiss national hero. Schiller's dramatic rendering of the *Tellsage* has had such an impact that it has come to represent and even supplant all previous versions of the story of the Swiss hero—despite the fact that it was penned by a German playwright who had never even been to Switzerland.[29] This play is the source of most Swiss people's knowledge of the Wilhelm Tell story today, and popular pageants around Switzerland often recreate the story of the folk tale through re-enactments of Schiller's play. In addition, many nineteenth and twentieth century writers who engage with the story of Wilhelm Tell do so by means of Schiller's version of his story.[30]

Interestingly, Matthias Luserke-Jaqui suggests that the impact of Schiller's drama has less to do with the play's content than the turbulent times in which it was written and performed. He considers the drama against a backdrop of revolution and civil unrest in the nineteenth and twentieth centuries:

> Nach den Befreiungskriegen von 1813 bis 1815 wird der Tell mit Bezug auf das Stickwort 'Freiheit' geschätzt. Und auch noch in der Zeit der Märzrevolution von 1848 sind es politische Gründe, um derentwillen das Stück hochgeschätzt wird. [. . .] In der zweiten Hälfte des 19. Jahrhunderts gelangt das Stück dann in den Kanon der Schullektüre und wird nicht zuletzt dadurch zu einem Teil des Bildungsguts. Die Wertschätzung Schillers und des *Wilhelm Tell* halt sich—natürlich mit unterschiedlichen Akzentsetzungen—bis in die Zeit des Nationalsozialismus, der in dem Rütlischwur 'Wir wollen sein ein einzig Volk von Brüdern' (V.1448) geradezu den Sinn der 'nationalen Erhebung' zum Ausdruck gebracht sieht.[31]

Luserke-Jaqui's comments imply that the content and significance of Schiller's play is less important for the audience than the function it serves as a space onto which the aspirations of the nation are projected. In its reception and re-enactment in the last two hundred years, Schiller's *Wilhelm Tell* has been employed to celebrate Switzerland's heroic past. As such, it plays a fundamental role in the development of Swiss nationalism in the last two centuries.

WALSER AFTER SCHILLER

Robert Walser has some rather quirky perspectives on the Swiss folk hero Wilhelm Tell and on the heroic Swiss past that he signifies. Interestingly, the Tell that Walser takes in hand is always Schiller's Tell, that troubled individual who, through numerous productions and performances, has become an icon of Swiss nationalism.[32] Walser's re-tellings of the *Tellsage* do not focus on Tell's skill as an archer, his heroism in the face of adversity, his independent spirit, or, indeed, his morality in killing the tyrant Gessler. Rather, Walser's retellings of Schiller's rendition of folk tale offer a sly civility of their pre-text; while seeming to conform to the tradition, they exploit its authority to question a heroic past and offer a new position on the Swiss national hero.

The figure of Wilhelm Tell is one who seems to have preoccupied Walser throughout his literary career; he produced no less than four prose texts that purport to re-tell the story of Tell, though each departs from Schiller's drama in its own way. Two of these prose texts were published during Walser's lifetime—'**Tell in Prosa**' (**GW** I, 258-60) was published in October 1907 in *Die Schaubühne,* and '**Tell**' (**GW** VIII, 23-28) was printed in *Die Zukunft* in July 1909. Two other prose pieces were copied out in ink and prepared for publication, but were not submitted—'**Wilhelm Tell**' (**GW** XI,

261-62), a text which was penned in 1928/29 and finally, another piece entitled **'Tell'**, written around 1919/20 but only published recently.[33] The first three of these texts have gained considerable attention from the secondary literature, and thus require only brief discussion here.[34] The fourth text, which has only come to light in recent years, will be analysed in a little more detail.

It is interesting to note that all four of Walser's texts are written in prose, unlike Schiller's authoritative pre-text. As discussed earlier, Walser did also produce dramatic scenes and short theatre pieces, and thus his decision here to present his rewriting in prose undoubtedly reveals the writer's dissatisfaction withbthe way in which Schiller's leading man has been recast as a Swiss hero. Thus, in contrast to his dramatic mimicry of the Grimm prose tales, Walser opts here to present a drama in prose, once again opening up the concept of genre to include hybrid forms. Walser's prose texts seek to present a different Tell from the hero of Schiller's drama, who has been reduced to an inert icon to be exploited to further nationalistic aims.

Walser's first encounter with Tell already reveals disillusionment with the accepted significance of the Schiller's play. It is noteworthy that this piece is entitled **"Tell in Prosa"** (**GW** I, 258-60), warning us from the outset that this Tell will not speak in poetry and metaphor, as the Tell of the Schiller play. However, by deliberately distancing itself from Schiller's famous drama, the title of the piece also makes clear to us that Schiller's Tell is the point of reference for Walser's departure from tradition. Walser's Tell is a modern-day version of Schiller's hero, filled with apprehension, uncertainty and scepticism about his own role in the creation of a nation.[35] This particular re-telling chooses to ignore completely the apple-scene, which is the highlight of most tellings of the story and the centre of the Schiller play. Instead, Walser moves directly to the narrow pass near Küßnacht, as he waits for Gessler to fall into his trap, and presents a provocative rewriting of Tell's famous soliloquy from Schiller's drama:

Hohlweg bei Küßnacht

TELL (TRITT ZWISCHEN DEN BÜSCHEN HERVOR):

> Durch diese hohle Gasse, glaube ich, muß er kommen. Wenn ich es recht überlege, führt kein andrer Weg nach Küßnacht. Hier muß es sein. Es ist vielleicht ein Wahnsinn zu sagen: Hier muß es sein, aber die Tat, die ich vorhabe, bedarf des Wahnsinns.

> (**GW** I, 258-59)

The decisiveness and virtue of the legendary Tell are destabilized here, as Tell's continuous references to his own lack of conviction about what he is about to do undermine the boldness of the act. Phrases such as "glaube

ich", "wenn ich es recht überlege" and "vielleicht" call into question the authority of Tell's ostensibly moral undertaking. Furthermore, the action of murdering Gessler and freeing the Swiss nation from tyranny is no longer presented as the virtuous, upright feat of a time-honoured hero, but an act of madness.[36] The self-questioning and hesitancy of Walser's leading man has led Peter Utz to remark, "Mit diesem Tell ist kein Staat zu machen".[37] Certainly, Walser's prose rendition of Schiller's Tell reveals an ambivalent attitude towards a heroic Tell and a heroic past.

Walser returns to the figure of Wilhelm Tell just two years later, in a text published under the title 'Tell' (**GW** VIII, 23-28). In this text, Walser focuses instead on the moment when Tell jumps out of Gessler's boat onto the rocks. This first instance of resistance, when Tell refuses to submit to Gessler's authority, is seen here as the primary moment of Tell's struggle for freedom; "er hat schon hier den Drachen getötet, hier schon ist das feige Tyrannen-Ungeheuer erschossen worden" (**GW** VIII, 24). It is not the action of killing the tyrant that is most threatening to authority, but the initial moment of resistance. Walser now relocates this fissure even further back, to the place where resistance is first expressed:

> Ein Knecht seines Herrn, ein Untertan seines Gebieters war er, ein Sohn seines Landes war er, ein hutabziehendes, gehorsames, demütiges Geschöpf war er. War er? Er hat ja aber eines Tages seinen Hut nicht mehr abziehen und den Gewohnheitsknix nicht mehr machen wollen; und hier vielleicht schon, bei der urplötzlichen Verweigerung des erniedrigenden Alltagsgehorsams ist der Tyrann erschossen worden.

> (**GW** VIII, 26)

Tell is not a hero because he shot Gessler and freed the Swiss people from tyranny; rather, he is a hero because he does not conform to the conventions of the ruling power, because he resists authority, pushes back the borders of his own role within this system and turns the tables on the agency that seeks to control him. As the narrator asserts, "Er ist nicht mehr geplagt, sondern er verfügt, bestimmt und regiert jetzt". (**GW** VIII, 26) Walser rejects here the idea of Wilhelm Tell as an exceptional individual, an example for all Swiss people to emulate; instead, he is the same as everyone else, a hero only because he refuses to accede to authority. Walser stresses this issue: "Tell ist kein dichtender und trachtender, kein denkender und spekulierender, sondern ein einfacher, ein tragischer Mensch, ein Mensch der Tat, ein Held ist er, geboten, sich unsterblich zu machen." (**GW** VIII, 26) In insisting here that Tell is "ein tragischer Mensch", Walser also implicitly questions Schiller's depiction of Tell, since Schiller's play is not a tragedy.

What is particularly interesting in this prose text is that Walser, in a complex word-play, juxtaposes Tell's gesture of resistance with the situation of the writer; "er, Tell, er springt, er macht Sätze von Fels zu Fels" (**GW VIII**, 25). The German construction 'Sätze machen' of course also signifies to make sentences, to write; Tell is the writer, skipping across rocky territory. The writer or re-writer of a canonical text such as Schiller's *Wilhelm Tell* finds himself facing a double-edged sword; he must choose between staying within the parameters of the authoritative pre-text or rebelling against its cultural authority, deconstructing its claims and undermining its validity for the modern world—a gesture which may itself be perceived as provocative or threatening. Walser's answer to this dilemma seems unambiguous: "Was nützen dem Vaterland gefesselte, an Mastbäume gebundene energische Männer? Was hat die Allgemeinheit davon, daß ein großer Mann in der Gefangenschaft schmachtet? Tell mußte frei werden; er wurde aber auch frei: er ist es jetzt." (**GW VIII**, 24)

The kitschiness of the Tell story is the point of departure for another flirtation with the Tell motif, a text entitled '**Wilhelm Tell**' (**GW XI**, 261-62). The prose text opens with a seemingly off-the-cuff observation about literature: "Ich leite diesen Essay mit dem einsichtsreichen Geständnis ein, mir schiene, es gebe in der Literatur Kitsch, der entzückend, und anderseits komme manches Nichtkitschige vor, das befremdend sein könne." (**GW XI**, 261) The immediate allusion to the figure of Wilhelm Tell after this remark, and of course the title of the text, would seem to indicate that this remark is directed at literary interpretations of the *Tellsage*. Is this a subtle criticism of Schiller's dramatic representation of Tell, which has universal appeal for an avid Swiss public? Or does Schiller's drama fall into the category of the non-kitschy that can be alienating—perhaps because it presents immoral acts as moral ones and murderers as national heroes?

From this opening remark, the narrator moves into his interpretation of Tell's story. Walser avoids alluding to a heroic Tell in this reversion of the *Tellsage*, and focuses instead on the dynamics of the power-relationship between Tell and Gessler. He rejects out of hand the traditional black and white version of the tale that has been passed on through the years and replicated in its literary representations; he states quite unambiguously, "Bezüglich der Tellsage interessiert mich die Frage nicht so sehr, ob Tell ein guter, der Landvogt aber ein böser Mensch war" (**GW XI**, 262). Rather, he suggests that the bond that connects Gessler and Tell is one based on mutual dependence: "Ich bin z.B. überzeugt, daß, um auf Wilhelm Tell zurückzukommen, der Schweizer, der die Freiheit liebt, dem [. . .] Landvogt viel zu verdanken hat, indem letzterer erstern zu Taten usw. anspornte." (**GW XI**, 261-62) The relationship between the two men is presented as much more complex, much more dynamic than a simple good guy / bad guy scenario. The conventional depiction of the two characters

is revised, and Walser suggests that to look at the power-relationship as purely one-sided is too simplistic. Rather, he declares: "Mir scheint bedeutend zu sein, daß beide ein Unzertrennliches, Einheitliches bilden: um einen Tell hervorzubringen, bedurfte die Geschichte eines Landvogts. Einer ist ohne den andern undenkbar." (**GW XI**, 262) This break with traditional interpretations of the Tell-Gessler relationship is developed further, into a blurring of the line between the two characters: "Sollte man nicht beinahe mit der Idee einiggehen dürfen, Landvogt und Tell seien eine einzige widerspruchsvolle Persönlichkeit?" (**GW XI**, 262) This suggestion that Tell and Gessler are one and the same represents a definitive break with Schiller's play and the myth of Wilhelm Tell, and indeed, on a more general level, with the moral message with which both have become imbued.

This retelling departs most radically from the pre-text, in that Walser makes no attempt at all to keep within the bounds of Schiller's drama. Instead, he focuses on apparently marginal issues: "Was den Wilhelm Tell betrifft, so hat mich von jeher, d.h. vor etlicher Zeit, die Frage beschäftigt, ob etwa der Herr Landvogt eine hübsche Frau gehabt habe." (**GW XI**, 261) In fact, Walser's unpublished text '**Tell**' (**F** [*Feuer*], 53-54) does make reference to a *Landvögtin,* who watches the shooting of the apple from horseback and who seems more than a little interested in Tell's fate. This seemingly trivial question seems to point towards an urge to break with the exemplary heroism and moral message of Schiller's play. Walser undermines the patriarchal authority of the national hero by subverting the gender-coding of his story.

The unpublished piece '**Tell**' (**F**, 53-54) deals exclusively with the Wilhelm Tell from Schiller's play and with Tell as a literary construct. From the outset, Walser calls into question the cliché he has become, and the very process of myth making:

> Im Lande Uri, das an der Straße liegt, die nach Italien führt, wo die Orangen wachsen, lebte einst ein Mensch, der sich dadurch wichtig machte, daß er einen federgeschmückten Hut nicht grüßen wollte, weshalb er von einer Anzahl trivialer Leute umzingelt und abgefaßt und fortgeführt wurde.
>
> (**F**, 53)

Tell's heroic act of resistance, applauded in Walser's earlier prose texts, is here put down to an attempt to draw attention to himself, 'sich wichtig machen'. Myths are made, it seems, not through heroic acts, but through the individual's success in presenting himself as an example to be followed. Furthermore, if the legend had any value as a folk tale, this has been overshadowed by the countless clichéd portrayals of Schiller's drama. The apple scene, in particular, is presented as a frivolous, theatrical gesture: "hierauf kam es zum Apfelschuß, der unzählige Male über die Bretter ging. Das Stück ist meisterhaft wie alles, was Schiller geschrieben hat." (**F**, 53) This is not heroism, but staged heroism; any meaning the legend may once have had has been lost through numerous representations. What claims to embody Swiss integrity and independence reveals itself as a kitschy caricature of Swissness.

In this retelling of the Wilhelm Tell story, Walser revises Schiller's text and the story of Wilhelm Tell through the eyes of the present, pointing to its unsuitability as a vessel for expression. After Tell's arrest, the narrator tells us:

> Die Gesellschaft segelte nach Luzern, wo der Freiheitsheld derart untergebracht werden sollte, daß er weder Sonne noch Mond je wieder zu sehen bekäme. Doch es kam anders. Tell hatte wenig Lust, lebendig begraben zu werden. Lieber ging er in den Schützengraben oder trat zu Lenin und Trotzki in Beziehung.
>
> (**F**, 53)

The references to the trenches, and to Lenin and Trotsky are certainly out of place in the context of a tale that is supposed to date back to the end of the thirteenth century, and would seem to indicate Walser's dissatisfaction with the suitability of the legend of Tell to express the modern condition. These contemporary references to World War I and the Russian Revolution hint at the negative consequences of nationalism and raise some interesting questions about the way in which the figure of Wilhelm Tell and Schiller's drama have been instrumentalized to further nationalist causes. Walser's remarks thus serve to disrupt the connection between the Swiss hero and the ideals that he is supposed to represent.

Equally, the narrator's frequent references to himself in the process of his retelling also represent a disruptive force in the narrative. The mention of the city of Lucerne, for example, offers a space for divergence from the story:

> Luzern war sicher schon dazumal ein lieblicher und wohnlicher Ort. Heute ist's eine berühmte Fremdenstadt, die alle erdenklichen Annehmlichkeiten bietet. Ich selbst war einmal vor Jahren dort. Leider regnete es, doch bekam ich immerhin den Pilatusberg zu sehen, der fabelhaft aus Nebelwolken tauchte.
>
> (**F**, 53)

It is surely no coincidence that this romantic description of Lucerne is reminiscent of the idyllic image of the _Vierwaldstättersee_ described at the opening of Schiller's play. Walser's depiction of Lucerne as a modern tourist destination points to the clichéd romanticism of Schiller's image of Switzerland, and thereby undermines the authority of that image. It also implies that Schiller's depiction of the Swiss national hero is just as idealistic and unoriginal.

As in the earlier versions of the folk tale, Tell's heroism is revised and rationalized in this retelling. When depicting Tell's escape from Gessler's boat, for example, the narrator remarks that this accomplishment demonstrates that Tell was "nicht nur ein Meisterschütze, sondern auch noch ein guter Turner"! (**F**, 54) The obvious irony of this remark reveals a fundamentally sceptical attitude towards the portrayal of Wilhelm Tell as a hero. The Küßnacht scene is again revisited; again, it is no longer the purely virtuous deed of a gallant hero, but a somewhat brutal resolution of the story. The narrator remarks, "Zweifellos ging es etwas schroff zu, und die Art, wie Tell für Garantie sorgte, wird kaum nach jedermanns Geschmack sein." (**F**, 54)

In all cases, Walser's prose rewritings of the Tell saga attempt to deconstruct the Schiller pre-text and the heroic nationalism that it represents. His texts revisit the main locations of Tell's ostensibly heroic actions. However, the notion of Tell as a hero, an example to be emulated, is rejected; rather, the blatantly ironic depiction of Tell's virtue and skilfulness, and his portrayal as a literary construct undermine any attempts to align the folk tale with the formation of a national identity. By the same token, the killing of Gessler, far from being depicted as a moral deed, is revealed for what it is—a brutal murder that apparently lies at the root of Swiss independence. The folk tale of Wilhelm Tell is exposed as being outdated, hackneyed and above all, just a story. The national identity it portrays and generates is only ever a cliché of Swissness, and a community based on such an image can only ever be a parody of itself.

FROM MIKROGRAMM TO FEUILLETON: MIMICRY IN ACTION

The genre of the _Feuilleton_ is the one that is perhaps most obviously connected with cultural commentary, since this is the space where the events, issues and problems of society and culture are articulated and negotiated. From as early as 1907, Walser was a regular contributor to the _Feuilleton_ section of prominent newspapers such as the _Berliner Tagblatt_ and the _Frankfurter Zeitung,_ and in reviews such as _Die Schaubühne_ and the _Neue Schweizer Rundschau._[38] The newspapers paid well for short poems, dialogues and prose pieces, and Walser, along with many of his contemporaries, saw this as an easy way of earning enough money to keep him going until he could finish another novel.[39]

The _Feuilleton_ as a distinct genre first emerged in the German-speaking countries in the early part of the 19th century and gained ground in the years following the 1848 revolution, when changing censorship laws allowed writers to deal with political issues in a more playful way.[40] The poet and journalist Heinrich Heine is usually considered to be the father of the modern _Feuilleton_ in Germany.[41] His _Briefe aus Paris,_ published in the *Augsburger Allgemeine Zeitung* in the 1830s, offered a sort of commentary on the times; the personal tone of a letter allowed him to offer a subjective impression of society and culture. In Heine's love of form in his journalistic texts, and in his unique way of introducing an element of social criticism so subtle that it managed to escape the German censor's watchful eye, there emerged that distinct style which defines the *Feuilleton* of today.

That the earliest *Feuilletons* were actually letters, addressed to a particular readership, is crucial in terms of the development of the style of the genre. The *Feuilleton* is defined by its personal and chatty tone, similar in character to a letter. It is as if the writer were directly addressing his reader; thus the strong presence of a writer, who writes in the first person, and the implicit presence of a reader are already woven into in the fabric of these texts. The practice of separating the more factual news reports from *Feuilleton* section of the newspaper with a black line across the page also had consequences for the perception of those contributions that were printed below this dividing line. The *Feuilleton* is generally seen as being less serious, less important and more whimsical than factual journalism.

In terms of content, the scope of the *Feuilleton* is very broad, ranging from film, theatre and literary reviews to political and social commentary.[42] The diversity of this field is so great that Wolfgang Preisendanz questions the validity of using the unifying term *Feuilleton* to define the genre.[43] The *Feuilleton* can be considered a hybrid genre because it crosses several boundaries—between realism and entertainment, reportage and fiction, journalism and literature. In some ways, it can be seen a sort of in-between space of writing, separate from more lofty interests such as politics or current affairs and yet intimately connected to society and culture. For this reason, the *Feuilletonist* has always been seen as a borderline figure, a *flâneur* between life and literature.

At the same time, the field of the *Feuilleton* is one that, perhaps more than any other literary genre, is ruled by the demands of the market. The reader is the consumer; in the simplest terms, if he does not like what he reads, he will not buy the newspaper the next day.[44] Thus, the necessity of appealing to a wider public is crucial, and every *Feuilletonist* is compelled to conform, at least on the surface, to the expectations of the reading public.

This is of course very much at odds with the aspirations of a writer to achieve lasting recognition, to produce something that will endure beyond his death. The conflict between the transitory nature of the medium and the writer's desire to become immortal through his work was such that many writers did not want to write for the newspapers. Others went on to publish some of their better journalistic pieces in anthologies, hoping to achieve in a bound volume the enduring recognition

that seemed to be excluded by the medium. A few writers found this tension between the temporary and the everlasting to be productive. As Hugo Wittmann claims, the best *Feuilletonisten* wrote "für den Tag, wie man für die Ewigkeit schreibt, für die Zeitung, als ob ein Morgenblatt ein Jahrhundert währte".[45]

The mélange of divergent features makes the *Feuilleton* a terrain that is, on the one hand, freer and more open, and on the other, more treacherous than any other literary field. If a writer succeeds in tapping into the mood of the day, in offering an interesting and quirky perspective on the issues that preoccupy his society; if his text is written in a language and a style that goes beyond the realms of a daily newspaper, then he may find himself the darling of the day. If, however, his contribution offends the sensitivities of some of his readers; if its content proves just a little too polemical for the political times; or if its style is just a little too self-conscious, a little too different, then he may find himself confronted with the suspicion and mistrust of his editors. Thus, with the genre of the *Feuilleton,* as perhaps with no other, it is vitally important that that writer find the delicate balance between conformity and distinction that will ensure continued publication of his work.

'Ein Unsterblicher'

The 269th page of Walser's **Mikrogramme** contains the first drafts of four *Feuilletons*.[46] In February 1926, Walser sent the final versions of three of these texts to Otto Pick, at that time the literary editor of the *Prager Presse*.[47] All three were published in April of the same year. Only one text, **'Ein Unsterblicher'**, was not sent to the paper, although there are indications in the text that it was revised and redrafted at the same time as the others. This *Feuilleton* was eventually published by the *Prager Presse,* however, not until 1932. This raises a question as to why this particular text was not selected for inclusion with Walser's 1926 submission. Obviously, there is something unusual about this text which distinguishes it from the others on the same **Mikrogramm** and which would seem to indicate that this text deserves closer analysis.

Indeed, if we compare the **Mikrogramm** with the published version, it soon becomes clear that the method of revision undertaken deviates to some extent from the author's standard procedure.[48] As we know, Walser's peculiar method of producing meant that he sketched the first drafts of his literary texts in pencil, in his tiny, enigmatic script, and then revised and copied them out in ink in his impeccable handwriting. As a rule, he made only slight modifications to his drafts in the process of revision, cutting out certain episodes or condensing his text a little. However, there are a number of more substantial adjustments in this particular piece that go beyond of simple editing. A comparison of the two versions of this text thus casts doubt on Walter Benjamin's claim that Walser had "in seinen Sachen nie eine Zeile verbessert".[49] The *Feuilleton* **'Ein Unsterblicher'** therefore offers an interesting insight into the process of textual revision and the motivation for certain changes.

Let us first consider the published version of the text:

> "Ein Unsterblicher"
> Es gab einmal einen sehr begabten Dichter, der die zartesten Verse schrieb,
> und der dies inmitten des hauptstädtischen Lebens tat, während vielleicht
> in der Provinz hauptsächlich Romane gelesen wurden. Dort, im Schimmer
> der Metropole, mag er für angezeigt gehalten haben, sich sozusagen
> 5 mitunter, o, was für Umstände ich da mache, zu betrinken, und er führte
> tatsächlich aus, was ihm als überaus passend vorschwebte. In der
> Betrunkenheit, die man unter solcher Voraussetzung beinah heilig erklären
> muß, gelangen ihm die denkbar schönsten dichterischen Produkte.
> Natürlich nenne ich ihn nicht, die Namensnennung gliche doch wohl
> 10 beinahe bereits einer Entweihung. Man soll meiner Ansicht nach mit
> Sündern vorsichtig umgehen. Gewiß kann Lasterhaftigkeit nicht nur im
> höchsten Grad rührend, sondern sogar großartig sein. Ich besitze übrigens
> gegenwärtig viel gesellschaftlichen Schliff, was ich speziell für diejenigen
> sage, die es nicht für möglich zu halten vermögen. Welch einen
> 15 wundervollen, frühlingsblütenhaft sich entwickelnden Kampf ich kämpfe!
> Nun kam aber plötzlich der genannte bedeutende Dichter auf die drollige
> Idee, anständig zu werden, fein, nett, artig, lieb, brav und unschuldig wie
> ein neugeborenes Kind. So etwas fiel noch nie einem Menschen ein,
> solange die Welt steht. 'Mir beliebt, zu denen zu gehen, bei denen meine
> 20 Gedichte auf den tischtuchbedeckten Tischen liegen', glaubte er für
> gegeben erachten zu können, wo er doch schon mit dem Äußern eines
> nachdrücklich Gesunkenen einherlief, obschon von Laufen usw. bei ihm

nicht gut gesprochen werden kann. Da begegnete ihm eine merklich hohe,
> für gewöhnlich Sterbliche total unsichtbare Gestalt, die zu ihm sprach:
> 25 'Mach dich nicht lächerlich. Hast du vergessen, daß Größe etwas Unfeines
> ist, und daß bei den Feinen alles, was nicht als fein empfunden werden
> kann, unmöglich ist? Du gehörst mir!' Die dies sprach, hieß die
> Unsterblichkeit.

(**GW** X, 388-89)

The *Mikrogramm* draft of **'Ein Unsterblicher'** deals with the same subject matter; however, any similarity between the two texts stops there. From the outset, the tone of the *Mikrogramm*-version differs radically from that of the published *Feuilleton*:

> Es gab einmal ein großes Schwein in Form eines sehr begabten Dichters.
> Schwälbchen umflogen seine Schaffenswerkstatt, und er schrieb die
> zartesten Verse voll Wahrheit und Erleb[t]heit, während auf ihren
> Landsitzen in der Provinz Gebieterinnen, auf Bequemlichkeit gebettet,
> 5 Romane lasen. Das hochbedeutsame Schwein bewohnte die Hauptstadt.
> Es fand für angezeigt, sich sauber zu betrinken, und führte auch aus, was
> ihm passend schien, und nun trug er also die formidabe[l]sten Räusche
> nach Hause, um in der Besoffenheit oder Benebeltheit die denkbar
> schönsten lyrischen Produkte hervorzubringen. Wir reden demnach von
> 10 einem Genie. Ein junger Gutsverwalter hielt nichtsdestoweniger eines
> schönen Tages um die Hand seiner Prinzipalin an, die ihm um seiner
> hervorragenden Qualitäten willen bewilligt wurde. 'Waren Sie einsam',
> sprach er in der Tonart der Aufrichtigkeit zu ihr, 'so ist's schön für mich
> zu glauben, daß mir gegeben wäre zu sorgen, Sie könnten aufhören, es zu
> 15 sein.' Während der junge Romanheld dies sagte, wälzte sich das Schwein,
> von dem wir zu sprechen wagen, im sittlichen Dreck. Man gestatte uns,
> unumwunden zu reden. Es ist für mich und meine Leser besser so. Es liegt

ja auch etwas Amüsantes darin. Die Verse des Schweins erschienen in

Buchform, und gerade die kultiviertesten Leute
schafften sich die Edition

20 an und lasen sie mit Vergnügen. Hundert Luxuse[x-
]emplare bezahlten sich

enorm hoch. Verlage und Buchhändler schienen mit
der Existenz des

Schweins einverstanden. Da kam aber das Monstrum auf die Idee,

anständig zu werden. Was für ein lachhafter Einfall.
Das Schwein zog sich

nett an, aber auf dem Weg in die Honettheit hinein
genehmigte es [sich]

25 ein Dutzend Schnäpse. Es gehörte dies eben einmal
so zu seinen

Gewohnheiten. Natürlich langte es nun nicht in
sonderlich emfehlendem

Zustand vor den Türe an, die sich ihm dann nun
doch öffnete. 'Was beliebt

Ihnen?' wurde gefragt. Vor dem größten Schwein,
das je die Zivilisation

schmückte, stand das niedlichste Dienstmädchen.
'Mir beliebt denen einen

30 Besuch abzustatten, auf deren Tisch meine Gedichte
liegen', wurde

gesprochen, nein, eher gedacht. 'Lernen Sie erst
ordentlich sprechen',

wurde abfertigend erwidert. Die Tür flog zu, und
der große Dichter,

der zugleich ein großes Schwein war, sah sich
genötigt, vom Vorhaben

abzustehen, sich ein gutbürgerliches Aussehen zu
verleihen. Er machte

35 begreiflicherweise Anstrengungen, nicht über sich
zu erstaunen. Da

begegnete ihm in der Wirrnis, in die er aus eigener
Verschuldung

hineingeraten war, eine Gestalt, die ihn göttlich leicht anrührte und mit

einer Sorte von Liebe und Güte zu ihm sprach:
'*Lieber* überirdisch *Schöner.*

Du kommst zu mir. Ich bin die Unsterblichkeit.'

(**BG** VI, 548-49)

Both versions of this piece offer a criticism of a lyrical
poet whose rather decadent lifestyle casts doubt on his
character. Indications from similar texts on the same
Mikrogramm suggest that the writer depicted in this
text is actually Heinrich Heine, a circumstance which
must be considered significant, given Heine's promi-
nence for this genre.[50] Where the revised version describes Heine as "einen sehr begabten Dichter"

(*Feuilleton,* line 1), the **Mikrogramm** depicts "ein
großes Schwein in Form eines sehr begabten Dichters"
(**Mikrogramm,** line 1). Thus, although each text deals
essentially with the same subject matter, it is clear from
the beginning that the tone in which it is presented differs fundamentally. The tone in the **Mikrogramm** is
much more scornful, more irreverent and more contemptuous than in the amended version. It seems clear
that the *Feuilleton* is more than just a simple reworking
of the **Mikrogramm,** but re-presents the subject matter
from a very different perspective.

In the **Mikrogramm,** the poet is presented as being not
only immoral, but quite revolting, a "Monstrum"
(**Mikrogramm,** line 22) or a "Schwein" (**Mikrogramm,**
line 5), who rolls in the dirt and drinks too much. The
revised text, by contrast, plays down this facet of the
poet's character and instead, concentrates on the beauty
of his poetry. His drunkenness, for example, is justifiable if it allows him to produce "die denkbar schönsten
lyrischen Produkte" (*Feuilleton,* line 8); indeed, under
the circumstances, it should be considered "beinahe
heilig"! (*Feuilleton,* line 7) The narrator is here playing
on an image of the Dionysian creativity of the artist,
which is a well-known topos in literature; however, the
allusion rings somewhat hollow in this context, and the
irony is not lost on the reader. Thus, the published
Feuilleton is not entirely uncritical of this drunken bard.
The criticism that is unambiguous in the **Mikrogramm**
is still very much present in the published text, albeit in
a more subtle form.

The movement from **Mikrogramm** to *Feuilleton* reflects
a movement from an explicit to an implicit criticism,
and the reader must read between the lines to discern
the extent to which the narrator is mocking the poet he
depicts. For example, since the corruption of the artist
is played down quite significantly in the revised version
of the text, his decision to become "anständig"
(*Feuilleton,* line 17), or respectable, does not have the
same effect as in the **Mikrogramm,** where it marks a
sharp contrast to his former behaviour. The narrator
opts to emphasize the absurdity of the poet's sudden
urge to be good by expanding on it; the poet aspires to
become not only "anständig", but also "fein, nett, artig,
lieb, brav und unschuldig wie ein neugeborenes Kind"
(*Feuilleton,* lines 17-18). The irony inherent in this long
list of adjectives suggests, of course, that the poet is, in
fact, none of these.

Some comments Walser made regarding his distinctive
method of writing offer some clues as to his motives
for making certain revisions in preparing a text for publication. In Walser's oft-cited letter to Max Rychner, in
which he makes reference to his "Bleistiftsystem", he
also makes the following remarks about the process of
revision of one particular *Feuilleton*:

Die Sache mit diesem Brief an ein Mitglied der Gesellschaft ist die, daß er ursprünglich, d.h. auf dem Brouillon, an eine hiesige Dame gerichtet wurde, daß ich aber diskretionshalber fand, dieser besondere Umstand, weil er als zu pikant empfunden werden könnte, müsse verschleiert, verallgemeinert, vermännlicht, d.h. ganz einfach zu einer *kulturellen Angelegenheit* umgestempelt werden.[51]

Walser shows himself here to be aware of the importance of the *Feuilleton* as a "kulturelle Angelegenheit" and of its intimate connection to society and culture. This also suggests that the process of revising a text for publication implies a shift from the private sphere into a public arena, with its standards and its canons. Walser's **'Bleistiftskizze'**, which describes his unique two-stage writing process, highlights that the author is well aware that the move from pencil to ink involves a move "in die Bestimmtheit" (**GW XI**, 122). The product of this reworking, namely the *Feuilleton*, is quite clearly directed at a reading public, and consequently, it is of great importance that it appeals to its readership. Under these circumstances, Walser must try to ensure that his text conforms to the conventions of this type of literature, at least to the extent that it will be published. The first issue we are faced with in this analysis, therefore, is that Walser quite deliberately modifies his text in the process of revision so that it corresponds to the implicit norms of this genre.

REVISION AS CONFORMISM

While on the whole, it is true to say that the genre of the *Feuilleton* is not as institutionalized as other literary forms, it does have certain norms and conventions. As Peter Utz suggests, the genre is usually characterized by its personal, almost chatty tone, which gives rise to a type of dialogue between reader and text.[52] To achieve this dialogue, two entities are necessary: a strong narratorial function and a rhetorical address of the reader.

With this in mind, it is useful to look at the roles of the narrator in the two versions of **'Ein Unsterblicher'**. In the first draft, the figure of the narrator is not very obvious. Here, the narrator tends not to speak of himself in the first person; not once does he use "ich", the subject form of the pronoun, in relation to himself and his function in the text. On one occasion, the object form "mich" appears, but even this is diluted in the formulation "für mich und meine Leser" (**Mikrogramm,** line 17). Instead, a more general "wir" is favoured. However, even this pronoun appears in rather vague verbal constructions, such as "von dem wir zu sprechen wagen" (**Mikrogramm,** line 16) or "man gestatte uns [. . .] zu reden" (lines 16-17).

On the other hand, the figure of the narrator in the *Feuilleton* plays a much stronger and more active role in the text. As early as the fourth line, he begins to comment on the narrative, with his "o, was für Umstände ich da mache" (*Feuilleton,* line 5). Walser frequently uses the "ich" form in the revised text, and more often than not, in combination with very concrete verbs, such as "ich mache" (line 54), "ich nenne" (line 9), "ich besitze" (line 12), "ich sage" (line 13-14) and even "ich kämpfe" (line 15). The narratorial function in this version is active and dynamic. It is clearly the narrator who is producing the narrative and directing the action. It is also noteworthy that it is he who has the last word in the final version of the text.[53]

Just as a strong narrator figure is integral to the dialogical structure of the *Feuilleton,* so too is a strong sense of an implicit reader. Interestingly, there is already a sense of an implied rhetoric in the **Mikrogramm,** since the formulation "für mich und meine Leser" (*Mikrogramm,* line 17) makes a direct reference to this implied reader. The implicit inclusion of the reader in the writing, even at the level of the **Mikrogramm,** emphasizes that the influence of the outside world plays a role within Walser's *Bleistiftgebiet*; thus, this area must be considered not as a separate sphere, entirely cut off from the influence of the literary establishment, but rather as a space of resistance which lies within the broader realm of society and culture. In the **Mikrogramm,** the dialogue with the reader is played out on the level of the text, and the narrator is already anticipating a negative reaction on the part of the reader. However, in the same way that we cannot assume that the narrator represents Walser himself, neither can we assume the rhetorical reader of the **Mikrogramm** to represent the real Walser reader. Rather, the text is playing on the potential *Feuilleton's* attempt to realize a dialogue with the reader.

A further attribute of the *Feuilleton* can be seen in the deliberate attempt to introduce an element of textual linearity in the process of revision. Whilst this is not necessarily a defining characteristic of the genre, it is clear that some sense of a "roter Faden" is necessary in order to ensure that the text holds the reader's attention. Much of what appears in the first draft of the text is left out in the revised version, as is obvious from the length of each text. For example, the monster's encounter with the *Dienstmädchen,* an episode that takes up thirteen lines of the **Mikrogramm,** is simply left out in the published version of the piece. This revision does not really represent a serious loss in terms of criticism of the poet; rather, it can be seen as a deliberate attempt to conform to the formal requirements of the *Feuilleton* and strengthen the linearity of the finished product.

FEUILLETON AS METATEXT

It has already been mentioned that in the transition from **Mikrogramm** to *Feuilleton,* there is a shift from an explicit criticism to a more subtle, implied critique. Indeed, on the whole, the *Feuilleton* is much more meditative and reflective than its first draft. In fact, if we compare the two versions of this text, it is clear that it is not only the content of the **Mikrogramm** that is reflected in the process of the revision, but also the very act of revision itself. Thus, on many levels, the *Feuilleton* can also be understood as a sort of meta-text, a text that reflects on the process of writing a text, and it is the narrator who takes on the role of the editor in this process.

In this way, the correction process is not something that Walser undertakes privately, but rather, it is carried out on the level of the text itself. Indeed, Walser's manuscripts are unique, in that conventional corrections such as crossed-out words, alternative formulations or additions do not appear very often.[54] Rather, the narrator undertakes these corrections, making them part of the body of the text. Other texts of Walser's provide richer and more powerful examples of this explicit process of correction. However, this piece too contains some evidence of the narrator's reflection on the words of the text; the word "einherlief" (*Feuilleton*, line 22), for example, seems inappropriate to the narrator, who adds that "von Laufen usw. bei ihm nicht gut gesprochen werden kann" (line 22-23). This peculiar method of correction lends the text a sense of a being a work-in-progress and allows the reader an unparalleled insight into its conception and evolution.

In this context, the self-reflexive comments of the narrator also offer some interesting insights into the writing process. In the first draft of the piece, the narrator makes the following remark: "Man gestatte uns, unumwunden zu reden. Es ist für mich und meine Leser besser so. Es liegt ja auch etwas Amüsantes darin." (*Mikrogramm*, lines 16-18) These lines express quite clearly the advantages of Walser's *Bleistiftgebiet*. Within the parameters of this first draft, the narrator can speak quite openly and freely. Nevertheless, the reference to a reader already at this stage in the writing process indicates that the transition from pencil to ink is not a simple shift from a private to a public forum. Still, when rewriting his text in ink, Walser is even more aware of the import of this change. His allusions to a type of auto-censorship in the aforementioned letter to Rychner are thus equally relevant for **'Ein Unsterblicher'**. Conscious that his *Feuilleton* must be understood as "eine kulturelle Angelegenheit", Walser, to use his words, *veils, generalizes,* and *masculinizes* his text so that it is not perceived as being "zu pikant" for public consumption.[55]

In the *Feuilleton* **'Ein Unsterblicher'**, it is the narrator who undertakes this task. He censors and modifies the text to make it more appropriate for publication, and he does this before our eyes. With reference to the immoral poet who is the object of so much criticism, the narrator makes the following concession: "Natürlich nenne ich ihn nicht, die Namensnennung gliche doch wohl beinahe bereits einer Entweihung. Man soll meiner Ansicht nach mit Sündern vorsichtig umgehen." (*Feuilleton,* lines 9-11) The poet's name will not be mentioned, because this would be inappropriate—even blasphemous!—in the context of a *Feuilleton*. When we take into account that this critique is directed at Heine, who is generally considered to be the father of the *Feuilleton,* then the criticism seems all the more sacrilegious. However, the fact that in this text, Heine appears only as a lyrical poet, and not as a social commentator or *Feuilletonist,* suggests that the censure is more aimed at the poet than the genre.[56] Either way, the narrator makes it clear to us here that he is being extremely careful in his criticism.

A couple of lines later, the narrator refers directly to his role as editor and its implications: "Ich besitze übrigens gegenwärtig viel gesellschaftlichen Schliff, was ich speziell für diejenigen sage, die es nicht für möglich zu halten vermögen. Welch einen wundervollen, frühlingsblütenhaft sich entwickelnden Kampf ich kämpfe!". (*Feuilleton,* lines 12-15)[57] In order to produce a publishable *Feuilleton,* it is clear that the narrator must indeed prove his "gesellschaftlichen Schliff" or social refinement, in that he is attempting to please a reading public. The narrator's tongue-in-cheek comments seem also to be directed at a certain readership, who might elsewhere have suggested that this writer did not possess much "gesellschaftlichen Schliff".

There are clearly ironic undertones running through these lines, and so we take the narrator's assertion that this stage of artistic production represents a type of "Kampf" (line 15) or struggle for the author with a pinch of salt. However, this process of revision is clearly a tension of sorts, a confrontation between two literary domains that are becoming blurred in this instance. This struggle is not necessarily negative, however, since there is something productive emerging from this overlap. The development of the writing from the initial pencil sketch into its subsequent composition in ink has something wonderful, something "frühlingsblütenhaft" about it (line 15). The metaphor of the spring bloom thus represents quite appropriately the blossoming of the **Mikrogramm** into the *Feuilleton*; the final version of the text stems from the **Mikrogramm** but grows into something new and original.

Thus, as can be seen from the above analysis, **Mikrogramm** and *Feuilleton* are not so much variants of the one prose piece, but two independent texts. The basic content of these texts may be the same, but it is represented here from an entirely different perspective, in a completely different tone and within wholly different parameters.[58]

In his letter to Rychner, Walser makes explicit that in writing—or rewriting—the *Feuilleton,* he marks it as a "kulturelle Angelegenheit". From the above analysis, we can clearly see that Walser recognizes the inherent rules of the literary institution and plays upon them. Thus, his confrontation with his cultural milieu is carried out on the level of the text. In this representation (or re-presentation) of the ***Mikrogramm,*** the pressure to adhere to literary and cultural norms and the very act of conforming are written into the fabric of this text. However, the fact that Walser also emphasizes the internal "Kampf" which this causes for him means that he simultaneously underlines his own difference from the system to which he must conform. Thus, we can conclude that Walser does, to some extent, write into a literary system that is foreign to his writing, but he rewrites it from the margins.

WALSER'S MIMICRY OF THE FEUILLETON

The ambivalent position that Walser occupies as a *Feuilletonist* can be compared with the peculiar situation of Homi Bhabha's mimic man who, in conforming to the authority of the foreign power, inevitably draws attention to his own difference from that authority. It is clear that Walser resents any attempt to control and shape his writing, yet it is equally clear that he must be seen to adhere to the norms of the genre if he is to succeed in placing his text with a publisher. He must, in effect, learn to speak the language of the foreign power, in order to obtain the stamp of approval of that power. Walser's rationalization in his letter to Max Rychner that his text "müsse [. . .] zu einer kulturellen Angelegenheit umgestempelt werden" makes it clear that he was well aware of this.[59] Equally, however, he must find some way of expressing his own dissatisfaction with the bounds of the literary institution if his text is to be anything more than a mere replica of every other *Feuilleton.* In preparing **"Ein Unsterblicher"** for publication, Walser takes advantage of this ambivalence inherent in mimicry to reveal that subversive potential of his apparent conformity.[60] This is certainly imitation, but it is an imitation that compromises the ***Mikrogramm.*** In Walser's feigned mimicry of the *Feuilleton* form, his imitation of the genre is thematized in the *Feuilleton,* so the ironic undertones of this act of conformity are laid bare. Thus, Walser's *Feuilletons* go beyond the bounds of this genre and ultimately call into question the authority of the literary institution.

When we look closely at the two "versions" of this text, we can see that the process of revision produces something new, something quite distinct from the ***Mikro-gramm.*** A new and dynamic text is produced in the process of revision, in this overlap of two literary spaces. On a broader level, this raises questions as to the status of Walser's ***Mikrogramme*** in relation to his published work. Traditionally, the ***Mikrogramm*** 'originals' have always been seen as mere forerunners to the 'actual' texts; the first draft is considered to be cruder and less refined than the published version, which is generally taken to be the definitive text-variant.[61] However, if we compare the two versions of a text, it becomes clear that the relationship between ***Mikrogramm*** and *Feuilleton* is not so simple. The first drafts of Walser's texts often prove to be more radical and provocative than his published work. The freedom of the *Bleistiftgebiet* allows the author to play on the limitations of the genre, as the first draft of **'Ein Unsterblicher'** shows. Thus, rather than viewing the ***Mikrogramm*** and *Feuilleton* as two versions of the same text, it may be more appropriate to consider them as two autonomous texts, produced in different circumstances, within different parameters and with a different intent.

It is clear that the *Feuilleton* arises from the ***Mikro-gramm.*** However, it is equally true that the potential *Feuilleton* serves as a frame for the ***Mikrogramm,*** even at the point where it is being produced. The ***Mikro-gramm*** already contains many of the characteristics of *Feuilleton,* in its subjective style and in the rhetorical address of a reader. Thus, each is produced in the shadow of the other - and both texts develop in the overlap of two literary spaces. Both reveal symptoms of the hybridity that is usually associated with the post-colonial text. It is only when we begin to recognize the autonomy of each text that we truly appreciate the heteronomy of both.

CONCLUSION: WALSER'S 'SLY CIVILITY' OF
CULTURAL AUTHORITY

Walser's texts take a peculiar stance towards cultural norms and cultural authority. His adaptations of the Grimm fairy tales reveal a fundamental doubt in the plausibility of a happy ending which is anything other than an artificially imposed compromise. His rewritings of Schiller's iconic *Wilhelm Tell* call into question the notions of heroism and nationalism and challenge which the play has come to represent. Finally, his *Feuilletons* emphasize their own conception and construction, ensuring that the reader is aware that any attempt to fit in with the norms and conventions of the genre is only ever a feigned conformity, in Homi Bhabha's terms, "sly civility". It should however be emphasized that in all cases, Walser does represent the pre-texts which he is implicitly criticizing, albeit to excess. Walser works *from within* the system to question the system, and it is this ambivalent stance that makes Walser's mimicry all the more potent.

Homi Bhabha conceives the image of the mimic man the milieu of a colonial society. The forms of cultural authority that surround him and dominate his daily life are very real and tangible. Bhabha has used the concept of colonial mimicry with specific reference to cultures with a colonial past, and it is certainly applicable in this context. However, Bhabha's concept of mimicry is equally appropriate to represent the situation of an artist who attempts to move within a cultural institution that is at odds with his way of writing. What is at issue here is the way in which Walser perceives the notion of genre and what he sees as outside attempts to govern and shape his writing, for example, from the literary and cultural institution which decides whether or not his work is to receive the stamp of approval. In effect, it is arbitrary whether these forms of control are real or imaginary, since, as the investigations above have shown, Walser's work is permeated by the writer's perception of authority in his literary environment.

Walser manages through a process of mimicry to call into question the power structures and institutions of authority that pervade his literary milieu. His methods may confuse and challenge the readers, and may often go against their expectations, but through this ambivalent way of writing, Walser provokes us to rethink our own expectations as readers, to question the authority which shapes and controls our role as readers and which governs our definitions of what constitutes literature. Through Walser's original writing style, we are compelled to read beyond the confines of a literature ruled by convention and tradition and appreciate the value of the borderline.

Notes

1. Peter Utz, in his very comprehensive examination of the writer's work in terms of its "Jetztzeitsstil", emphasizes that Walser should be read as a poet of his era. In order to situate the writer's work within this broader cultural context, he attempts to reconstruct the backdrop of themes and discourses that preoccupied his literary and cultural milieu. Thus, amongst other issues, he discusses Walser's take on the discourse around the concept of "Nervosität", his play on Nietzschean ideas, his erosion of the alpine motif and the ideology it represents and his unique rendering of the *Feuilleton* genre. Utz, *Tanz auf den Rändern. Robert Walsers "Jetztzeitsstil"* (Frankfurt am Main, Suhrkamp, 1998).

   Tamara Evans attempts to show that Walser is not merely an outsider of literature, as he has often been dismissed, but rather that his writing is in constant dialogue with the main themes and techniques of the modernist époque. Evans, *Robert Walsers Moderne* (Berne: Francke, 1989). Dominik Müller also addresses this problem in a short essay, 'Robert Walser. Außenseiter der literarischen Tradition?', in: *Probleme und Methoden*

der Literaturgeschichtsschreibung in Österreich und in der Schweiz, ed. by Wendelin Schmidt-Dengler, (Vienna: Praesens, 1997) pp. 69-76. Müller is reacting to Elizabeth Pulver's categorization of Walser as an outcast of literature in *Kindlers Literaturgeschichte der Gegenwart. Die zeitgenössischen Literaturen der Schweiz*, ed. by Manfred Gsteiger, (Zurich: Kindler, 1974), pp. 8-89.

2. Jakob & Wilhelm Grimm, *Kinder- und Hausmärchen*. Vols. I-III, (Berlin: Nicolai, 1812-22). These volumes were also translated and distributed across Europe and the rest of the world.

3. Andrea Hübner's analysis is the most comprehensive treatment of these elaborate and yet highly amusing dramas. Hübner focuses on the recurrent motifs of the fairy tale in Walser's work, and shows how the writer uses material from these categories to deconstruct the significance that is bound to these forms. Hübner, *Ei', welcher Sinn liegt im Unsinn? Robert Walsers Umgang mit Märchen und Trivialliteratur* (Tübingen: Stauffenberg, 1995). Martina Schaak also deals with the fairy tale plays in connection with the motif of the theatre in Walser's work and the theatricality of the world imagined in his texts: Martina Schaak, '*Das Theater, ein Traum'. Robert Walsers Welt als gestaltete Bühne*, (Berlin: Wissenschaftlicher Verlag Berlin, 2000), pp. 175-201. Peter Utz analyses Walser's *Aschenbrödel* against the backdrop of the concerns of the time in which it was written: Utz, 'Das Spiel mit Märchenmelodie und Märchenkleid.' Walsers 'Aschenbrödel' im Zeitkontext', in: *Tanz auf den Rändern*, pp. 23-52. Mark Harman's foreword to the English translation of the fairy tale plays provides a useful starting-point for the English-speaking reader: Harman, 'Introduction: A reluctant modern', in: *Robert Walser Rediscovered: Short Stories, Fairy tale Plays, and Critical Responses*, ed. by Mark Harman, (Hanover: New England UP, 1985), pp. 1-14.

4. Susanne Andres points to Walser's tendency to mix genres in the prose of the Berne era; often, a prose text will contain a few lines of poetry. Andres, *Robert Walsers arabeskes Schreiben*, (Göttingen: Cuvillier, 1998), p. 80.

5. Walser, *Briefe*, p. 59.

6. Benjamin, 'Robert Walser', first published 1929, reprinted in *Über Robert Walser*, ed. by Katharina Kerr, Vol. I, pp. 126-29, p. 128.

7. Cf. Urs Herzog, *Robert Walsers Poetik. Literatur und soziale Entfremdung*. (Tübingen: Niemeyer, 1974), p. 13.

8. See Dieter Borchmeyer, 'Robert Walsers Metatheater. Über die Dramolette und szenischen Prosastücke' in *"Immer dicht vor dem Sturze"*. *Zum Werk Robert Walsers*, ed. by Paolo Chiarini and Hans Dieter Zimmermann, (Frankfurt: athanäum, 1987), pp. 129-143, 129. Cf. also Andrea Hübner, *Ei', welcher Unsinn liegt im Sinn?*, p. 66.

9. Cf. Peter Utz: "Gattungsnormen [. . .] werden *als* Herrschaftsnormen bestimmt und subvertiert." *Tanz auf den Rändern*, p. 46.

10. Ulf Bleckmann, '"Das Märchen will's." Robert Walsers produktive Märchenrezeption', in *Märchen und Moderne: Fallbeispiele einer intertextuellen Relation*, ed. by Thomas Eicher, (Münster: Lit, 1996), pp. 21-47, p. 24.

11. Therese Poser makes the valid point that not all of the fairy tales penned by the Grimm brothers end on a positive note; however, the happy ending has come to represent a crucial feature of the genre *Märchen*. Therese Poser, *Das Volksmärchen. Theorie—Analyse—Didaktik*, (Munich: Oldenbourg, 1980), p. 18. See also Lutz Röhrich, 'Märchen mit schlechtem Ausgang', in *Handbuch der deutschen Volkskunde*, Vol. 2, ed. by W. Peßler, (Potsdam, 1938), p. 316f.

12. Cf. Max Lüthi, *Märchen*, Realien zur Literatur Vol. 16, 9th edition, (Stuttgart/Weimar: Metzler, 1996), p. 27-28. See also Lutz Röhrich, *Märchen und Wirklichkeit*, 4th edition, (Wiesbaden: Steiner, 1979).

13. Therese Poser, *Das Volksmärchen*, p. 19.

14. Utz, *Tanz auf den Rändern*, p. 28.

15. See in particular Hübner, *Ei', welcher Unsinn liegt im Sinn?*, pp. 133-63, and Utz, *Tanz auf den Rändern*, p. 25-52.

16. Utz, *Tanz auf den Rändern*, p. 45.

17. See for example Urs Herzog, *Robert Walsers Poetik*, p. 12, and Andrea Hübner, *Ei', welcher Unsinn liegt im Sinn?*, p. 67.

18. Cf. Peter Utz's treatment of the genre of the *lyrische Komödie* in his analysis of the *Aschenbrödel-Dramolett* in *Tanz auf den Rändern*, pp. 37-46.

19. See the analysis of Bhabha's 'The Other Question' in the Introduction to this analysis.

20. Bhabha, *The Location of Culture*, p. 75.

21. It is interesting to note here that the words of the *Retter*, "Laßt sie so!", refer implicitly to the reading public and thus to the norms of the literary sphere into which Walser is writing. Thus, although this *Mikrogramm* is not being prepared for publication yet, the influence of the readership is already perceptible at this early stage in the writing process. The ambiguous question of the influence of the outside world on the *Mikrogramme* will be the subject of later discussions.

22. Tismar, *Das deutsche Kunstmärchen des zwanzigsten Jahrhunderts*. (Stuttgart, 1981).

23. In the much discussed the Berne prose piece 'Minotauros', Walser's narrator depicts his distaste for all such conceptions of national sovereignty and supremacy: "Gestern aß ich Speck mit Bohnen und dachte dabei an die Zukunft der Nationen, welches Denken mir nach kurzer Zeit deshalb mißfiel, weil es mir den Appetit beeinträchtigte" (GW XI, 192).

24. See John Prudhoe, *Schiller's William Tell*, (Manchester: Manchester UP, 1973), p. (x). Although Tschudi's volume represents the first historical account of Tell's revolt, Tell was feted as a national hero in the *Bundeslied* of 1477 and in the *Weiße Buch von Sarnen* (1470-2). See on this point Matthias Luserke-Jaqui, *Schiller-Handbuch*, (Stuttgart: Metzler, 2005), p. 216.

25. Lutz Röhrich, *Sage*, (Stuttgart: Metzler, 1966), p. 50.

26. Friedrich Schiller, *Wilhelm Tell*, in: *Sämtliche Werke*, ed. by Peter-André Alt, (Munich: Carl Hanser, 2004), Vol. II 'Dramen 2', pp. 913-1029.

27. Some critics argue that Schiller never meant his play to contribute to a nationalist cause. Ernest Stahl puts the case thus: "When he [Tell] kills Gessler the national idea is far from his mind. Schiller made it quite clear that the assassination was not inspired by patriotic motives and he stressed the point in a letter to Iffland." E.L. Stahl, *Friedrich Schiller's Drama. Theory and Practice*, (Oxford: Clarendon, 1954), p. 141.

28. Schiller, *Wilhelm Tell*, v.3281.

29. Henry Garland notes that in a letter dated 5th December 1803, Schiller professed a desire to see Switzerland for himself before completing his play. However, he never actually visited there. *Schiller the Dramatic Writer*, (Oxford: Clarendon, 1969), p. 262.

30. Peter Utz' examination, *Die ausgehöhlte Gasse*, is particularly enlightening on this point. Utz discusses the influence that Schiller's drama has had on the work of prominent writers such as Gottfried Keller, Jeremias Gotthelf, Wilhelm Raabe, Theodor Fontane, Robert Walser and Karl Kraus. Utz, *Die ausgehöhlte Gasse. Stationen der*

Wirkungsgeschichte von Schillers "Wilhelm Tell" Hochschulschriften Literaturwissenschaft 60, (Königstein: Forum Academicum, 1984).

31. *Schiller-Handbuch*, p. 226.

32. On Walser's preoccupation with Schiller and on the numerous renditions of Schiller's dramas in his work, see Martina Schaak, 'Das Theater, ein Traum', pp. 224-251.

33. Bernhard Echte describes how the manuscript containing a handwritten version of this piece was discovered by a Swiss book-dealer in America in the mid 1990s. Echte, 'Tell im Unterseeboot,' in *Du*, 10/1994, p. 6. This newly discovered Walser text was included in the recently published volume *Feuer. Unbekannte Prosa und Gedichte*, ed. by Bernhard Echte, (Frankfurt: Suhrkamp, 2003), pp. 53-54. All further references to this edition are given in parentheses after the quotation with the symbol "F" in the form (F, Page number).

34. For a comprehensive discussion of *Tell in Prosa* (1907), *Tell* (1909) and *Wilhelm Tell* (1928/29), see Peter Utz, *Die ausgehöhlte Gasse*, pp. 201-219. See also Martina Schaak, 'Das Theater, ein Traum', pp. 229-38 and Tamara Evans, *Robert Walsers Moderne*, (Berne: Francke, 1989), pp. 185-92.

35. Cf. Tamara Evans, *Robert Walsers Moderne*, p. 189.

36. Martina Schaak underlines the destabilizing effect of this modification as follows: "das Unabänderliche in Tells Entscheidung und damit der bevorstehende Tat, das gerade seine Charakerfestigkeit ausmacht, [wird] hier dem Irrationalen des Wahnsinns gleichgesetzt." 'Das Theater, ein Traum', pp. 231.

37. Peter Utz, *Die ausgehöhlte Gasse*, p. 207.

38. Fritz Hackert was the first critic to examine Walser's short prose texts as representative of the genre of the *Feuilleton*: Hackert, 'Robert Walser. Feuilletonist', in *Provokation und Idylle. Über Robert Walsers Prosa, Der Deutschunterricht* 23/1971, Beiheft I, pp. 7-27. More recently, Peter Utz's analysis of Walser's feuilletonistic texts reveal the writer's productive engagement with this genre. Utz, 'In den Feuilletonpantoffeln tanzen', in: *Tanz auf den Rändern*, pp. 295-368.

39. In February 1907, Walser wrote to Alfred Walter Heymel: "Ich fabriziere kleine Sachen für Zeitungen und Zeitschriften. Solches tut man ja eigentlich nur, um Luft zu gewinnen, die nötig ist, größeres anzufangen." Robert Walser, *Briefe*, p. 51.

40. Hans Bender, *Klassiker des Feuilletons*, (Stuttgart: Reclam, 1967), pp. 240-41.

41. Ibid., p. 222.

42. Kai Kauffmann and Erhard Schütz's recent volume emphasizes this point. Their work takes as its starting point Georg Jäger's call for a renewed investigation of the *Feuilleton* (1988) and seeks to offer an overview of the status of research into the genre. The diversity of the contributions included in the volume underlines the multiplicity of approaches to the *Feuilleton*. Kauffmann/ Schütz, *Die lange Geschichte der Kleinen Form. Beiträge zur Feuilletonforschung*, (Berlin: Weidler, 2000).

43. Preisendanz, quoted in Kai Kauffmann, 'Zur derzeitigen Situation der Feuilleton-Forschung,' in: Kauffmann/Schütz, *Die lange Geschichte der Kleinen Form*, pp. 10-24, 12.

44. Bodo Rollka emphasizes this consumer aspect of the *Feuilleton* by positing it between entertainment and advertising. Rollka, 'Feuilleton, Unterhaltung und Werbung. Frühes Berliner Feuilleton', in: Kauffmann/Schütz, *Die lange Geschichte der Kleinen Form*, pp. 81-101.

45. Wittmann, cited in Bender, *Klassiker des Feuilletons*, p. 235.

46. See Jochen Greven's note on the text 'Ein Unsterblicher' in: Robert Walser, *Sämtliche Werke in Einzelausgaben*, ed. by Jochen Greven, Vols. I-XX, (Frankfurt: Suhrkamp, 1985-86), Vol. 18, 348. All further references to this edition are given in parentheses after the quotation with the symbol "SW" in the form (SW Volume number, Page number).

47. Walser's letter to Otto Pick (8th February 1926) refers only to three texts, and makes no mention of "Ein Unsterblicher". Robert Walser, *Briefe*, p. 262.

48. There have been few such comparisons carried out in the secondary literature. The following are worthy of note: Wolfram Groddeck, '"Weiß das Blatt, wie schön es ist?" Prosastück, Schriftbild und Poesie bei Robert Walser', in *Text. Kritische Beiträge*, Vol. 3 (1997) 'Entzifferung', pp. 25-43; Stephan Kammer, '(Ab)Schreiben.' Zur Genese von 'Autorschaft' in Robert Walsers 'Mondscheingeschichte'", in *Text. Kritische Beiträge*, Vol. 5 (1999) 'Textgenese', pp. 83-103; Elke Siegel, *Aufträge aus dem Bleistiftgebiet. Zur Dichtung Robert Walsers*, (Würzburg: Königshausen & Neumann, 2001).

49. Benjamin, 'Robert Walser', p. 126. Cf. Bernhard Echte, 'Nie eine Zeile verbessert? Beobachtungen an Robert Walsers Manuscripte', in *Wärmende Fremde. Robert Walser und seine Übersetzer im Gespräch*, Akten des Kolloquiums an der Universität Lausanne, ed. by Peter Utz, (Berne: Lang, 1994), pp. 61-70.

50. The *Mikrogramm* on which the draft of 'Ein Unsterblicher' appears also contains a draft of the *Feuilleton* 'Diskussion', which was published in the *Prager Presse* in April 1926. The published version of that text contains the following lines: "Dieser Heinrich Heine ist von einer grünenden Immortalität, und doch dichtete er die unmoralischsten Sachen, aber sein Schicksal stempelte ihn zum Unvergeßlichen." (GW X, 228) Cf. Bernhard Echte's introduction to the *Mikrogramm* (BG VI, 548).

51. Robert Walser. *Briefe*, p. 300. (My emphasis)

52. Utz, *Tanz auf den Rändern*, p. 309.

53. Stephan Kammer notes a similar shift in the published version of Walser's 'Mondscheingeschichte'. He sees this movement as reflecting the genesis of authorship in the revision process; "Die Figur des Erzählers wird durch die Abschrift in eine Instanz der Autorschaft transformiert." Kammer, '(Ab)Schreiben', p. 89.

54. For a more detailed analysis of the type of changes which Walser undertakes in preparing a text for publication, see Echte, 'Nie eine Zeile verbessert?,' in particular pp. 67-69. Cf. also Stephan ammer, *Figurationen und Gesten des Schreibens. Zur Ästhetik der Produktion in Robert Walsers Prosa der Berner Zeit*, (Tübingen: Niemeyer, 2003), pp. 134-36.

55. The idea that Walser renders his text more masculine in preparing it for publication will be explored in Chapter 5.

56. Bender, *Klassiker des Feuilletons*, p. 222.

57. These two sentences are repeated almost word for word in 'Geschichte von den beiden Reisenden', the first draft of which appears on the same *Mikrogramm* as 'Ein Unsterblicher'. In that text, the narrator remarks, "Ich besitze gegenwärtig viel gesellschaftlichen Schliff" and then about ten lines later, "Welch einen wundervollen inneren Kampf ich kämpfte!" (GW X, 404)

58. It is clear to see that in some cases, a comparison of so-called text-variants reveals more difference than similarity, due to the distinctive circumstances under which each text is produced. This type of analysis bears witness to the need for a critical edition of Walser's work, which would examine in greater detail the process of textual production and offer a context-based analysis of some of Walser's more radical texts.

59. Robert Walser, *Briefe*, p. 300.

60. See my discussion of Bhabha's notion of colonial mimicry in the Introduction to this analysis.

61. Jochen Greven states quite clearly in the 'Vorwort des Herausgebers' of Vol. XII of Walser's *Gesamtwerk* that the *Mikrogramme* are not of the same quality as his published work. (GW XII, 9) This view is also undoubtedly the reason behind Bernhard Echte and Werner Morlang's decision to exclude from their transcription work those *Mikrogramme* that had been revised and prepared for publication by Walser. By contrast, Stephan Kammer points to the "Unangemessenheit der Gegenüberstellung von 'Konzept' oder 'Entwurf' und Reinschrift". *Figurationen und Gesten des Schreibens*, p. 114. Cf. also Werner Morlang, 'Trascrittore—Traditore? Zur Kennzeichnung einer zwielichtigen Tätigkeit', in Peter Utz, *Wärmende Fremde*, pp. 71-80, 74.

Bibliography

PRIMARY LITERATURE

Robert Walser, *Das Gesamtwerk in 12 Bänden*, edited by Jochen Greven (Zurich: Suhrkamp, 1978).

———, *Sämtliche Werke in Einzelausgaben*, ed. by Jochen Greven, 20 volumes (Frankfurt: Suhrkamp, 1985-86).

———, *Aus dem Bleistiftgebiet. Mikrogramme aus den Jahren 1924-1932*, transcribed and ed. by Bernhard Echte and Werner Morlang, 6 volumes (Frankfurt: Suhrkamp, 1985-2000).

———, *Briefe*, ed. by Jörg Schäfer, (Geneva: Kossodo, 1975).

———, *Feuer. Unbekannte Prosa und Gedichte*, ed. by Bernhard Echte, (Frankfurt: Suhrkamp, 2003).

SECONDARY LITERATURE

Andres, Susanne, *Robert Walsers arabeskes Schreiben*, (Göttingen: Cuvillier, 1998)

Baur, Wolfgang, *Sprache und Existenz*, (Göppingen: Kümmerle, 1974).

Benjamin, Walter, 'Robert Walser', in *Über Robert Walser*, ed. by Katharina Kerr, 2 vols (Frankfurt: Suhrkamp, 1978), I, pp. 126-29.

Bleckmann, Ulf, '"Das Märchen will's." Robert Walsers produktive Märchenrezeption', in *Märchen und Moderne: Fallbeispiele einer intertextuellen Relation*, ed. by Thomas Eicher, (Münster: Lit, 1996), pp. 21-47.

Borchmeyer, Dieter, 'Robert Walsers Metatheater. Über die Dramolette und szenischen Prosastücke', in *"Immer dicht vor dem Sturze". Zum Werk Robert Walsers*, ed. by Paolo Chiarini and Hans Dieter Zimmermann, (Frankfurt: athanäum, 1987), pp. 129-43.

Chiarini, Paolo, and Hans Dieter Zimmermann, *"Immer dicht vor dem Sturze". Zum Werk Robert Walsers*, (Frankfurt: athanäum, 1987).

Echte, Bernhard, '"Ich verdanke dem Bleistiftsystem wahre Qualen [. . .]". Bemerkungen zur Edition von Robert Walsers "Mikrogrammen"', in *Text: kritische Beiträge*, Vol. 3 (1997), 'Entzifferung', pp. 1-21.

————, 'Nie eine Zeile verbessert? Beobachtungen an Robert Walsers Manuscripte', in *Wärmende Fremde. Robert Walser und seine Übersetzer im Gespräch*, Akten des Kolloquiums an der Universität Lausanne, ed. by Peter Utz, (Berne: Lang, 1994), pp. 61-70.

Evans, Tamara, *Robert Walsers Moderne*, (Berne: Francke, 1989).

Groddeck, Wolfraum, '"Weiß das Blatt, wie schön es ist?" Prosastück, Schriftbild und Poesie bei Robert Walser', in *Text: Kritische Beiträge*, Vol. 3 (1997) 'Entzifferung', pp. 25-43.

Gsteiger, Manfred, ed., *Kindlers Literaturgeschichte der Gegenwart. Die zeitgenössischen Literaturen der Schweiz*, (Zurich: Kindler, 1974).

Hackert, Fritz, 'Robert Walser. Feuilletonist', in *Provokation und Idylle. Über Robert Walsers Prosa, Der Deutschunterricht*, 23/1 (1971), pp. 7-27.

Harman, Mark, ed., *Robert Walser Rediscovered: Short Stories, Fairy tale Plays, and Critical Responses*, (Hanover: New England UP, 1985).

Herzog, Urs, *Robert Walsers Poetik. Literatur und soziale Entfremdung*, (Tübingen: Niemeyer, 1974).

Hübner, Andrea, *Ei', welcher Sinn liegt im Unsinn? Robert Walsers Umgang mit Märchen und Trivialliteratur*, (Tübingen: Stauffenberg, 1995).

Kammer, Stephan, '(Ab)Schreiben. Zur Genese von "Autorschaft"' in Robert Walsers 'Mondscheingeschichte', in *Text. Kritische Beiträge*, Vol. 5 (1999) 'Textgenese', pp. 83-103.

————, *Figurationen und Gesten des Schreibens. Zur Ästhetik der Produktion in Robert Walsers Prosa der Berner Zeit*, (Tübingen: Niemeyer, 2003).

Kerr, Katharina ed., *Über Robert Walser*, 2 vols (Frankfurt: Suhrkamp, 1978).

Morlang, Werner, 'Trascrittore—Traditore? Zur Kennzeichnung einer zwielichtigen Tätigkeit', in *Wärmende Fremde. Robert Walser und seine Übersetzer im Gespräch*, Akten des Kolloquiums an der Universität Lausanne, ed. by Peter Utz, (Berne: Lang, 1994), pp. 71-80.

Müller, Dominik, 'Robert Walser. Außenseiter der literarischen Tradition?', in *Probleme und Methoden der Literaturgeschichtsschreibung in Österreich und in der Schweiz*, ed. by Wendelin Schmidt-Dengler, (Vienna: Praesens, 1997), pp. 69-76.

Schaak, Martina, *'Das Theater, ein Traum'. Robert Walsers Welt als gestaltete Bühne*, (Berlin: Wissenschaftlicher Verlag Berlin, 2000).

Siegel, Elke, *Aufträge aus dem Bleistiftgebiet. Zur Dichtung Robert Walsers*, (Würzburg: Königshausen & Neumann, 2001).

Utz, Peter, *Die ausgehöhlte Gasse. Stationen der Wirkungsgeschichte von Schillers "Wilhelm Tell"*. Hochschulschriften Literaturwissenschaft 60, (Königstein: Forum Academicum, 1984).

————, *Tanz auf den Rändern. Robert Walsers "Jetztzeitsstil"*, (Frankfurt, Suhrkamp, 1998).

————, (ed.) *Wärmende Fremde. Robert Walser und seine Übersetzer im Gespräch*, Akten des Kolloquiums an der Universität Lausanne, (Berne: Lang, 1994).

OTHER LITERATURE

Bender, Hans, ed., *Klassiker des Feuilletons*, (Stuttgart: Reclam, 1967).

Bhabha, Homi K., *The Location of Culture*, (London: Routledge, 1994).

Eicher, Thomas, *Märchen und Moderne: Fallbeispiele einer intertextuellen Relation*, (Münster: Lit, 1996).

Garland, Henry, *Schiller the Dramatic Writer*, (Oxford: Clarendon, 1969).

Grimm, Jakob & Wilhelm, *Kinder- und Hausmärchen*, 3 vols (Berlin: Nicolai, 1812-22).

Kauffmann, Kai, 'Zur derzeitigen Situation der Feuilleton-Forschung,' in: *Die lange Geschichte der Kleinen Form. Beiträge zur Feuielletonforschung*, ed. By Kai Kauffmann and Erhard Schütz, pp. 10-24.

————, and Erhard Schütz, *Die lange Geschichte der Kleinen Form. Beiträge zur Feuielletonforschung*, (Berlin: Weidler, 2000).

Klose, Werner, *Didaktik des Hörspiels*, (Stuttgart: Reclam, 1974)

Luserke-Jaqui, Matthias, *Schiller-Handbuch*, (Stuttgart: Metzler, 2005).

Lüthi, Max, *Märchen*, Realien zur Literatur Vol. 16, 9th edn (Stuttgart/Weimar: Metzler, 1996).

Peßler, W., ed., *Handbuch der deutschen Volkskunde*, 2nd Vol. (Potsdam, 1938).

Poser, Therese, *Das Volksmärchen. Theorie—Analyse—Didaktik*, (Munich: Oldenbourg, 1980).

Prudhoe, John, *Schiller's William Tell*, (Manchester: Manchester UP, 1973).

Röhrich, Lutz, 'Märchen mit schlechtem Ausgang', in *Handbuch der deutschen Volkskunde*, Vol. 2, ed. by W. Peßler, (Potsdam, 1938).

————, *Märchen und Wirklichkeit*, 4th edn (Wiesbaden: Steiner, 1979).

————, *Sage*, (Stuttgart: Metzler, 1966).

Rollka, Bodo, 'Feuilleton, Unterhaltung und Werbung. Frühes Berliner Feuilleton', in *Die lange Geschichte der Kleinen Form*, ed. by Kai Kauffmann and Erhard Schütz, pp. 81-101.

Schiller, Friedrich, *Wilhelm Tell,* in: *Sämtliche Werke,* ed. by Peter-André Alt, (Munich: Carl Hanser, 2004), Vol. II 'Dramen 2', pp. 913-1029.

Schmidt-Dengler, Wendelin, *Probleme und Methoden der Literaturgeschichtsschreibung in Österreich und in der Schweiz,* (Vienna: Praesens, 1997).

Stahl, E.L., *Friedrich Schiller's Drama. Theory and Practice,* (Oxford: Clarendon, 1954).

Tismar, Jens, *Das deutsche Kunstmärchen des zwanzigsten Jahrhunderts,* (Stuttgart, 1981).

Samuel Frederick (essay date 2011)

SOURCE: Frederick, Samuel. "Stealing the Story: Robert Walser's *Robber*-Novel." In *Digressions in European Literature: From Cervantes to Sebald,* edited by Alexis Grohmann and Caragh Wells, pp. 130-42. Houndmills, England: Palgrave Macmillan, 2011.

[*In the following essay, Frederick addresses the issue of the "Walserian digressivity" and the "plotless narration" of his fiction by focusing on his posthumously published novel,* The Robber, *stating that this work "becomes for Walser the site of some of his most extreme digressivity, an occasion for him to test to what degree and to what length plotlessness can be maintained without a collapse into non-narrative."*]

The Swiss writer Robert Walser (1878-1956), known mostly for his eccentric novels and short stories, insisted that his prolific output in the genre of his choice, the short prose piece, ultimately amounted to nothing more than 'one long, plotless, realistic story' ([*Sämtliche Werke in Einzelausgaben*] 1986b: 322). This statement is in its seeming contradictoriness extremely revealing. For, on the one hand, most of Walser's prose work is indeed conspicuously lacking the dynamics and determinations of plot. Even those pieces that at least initially or ostensibly conform to the expectations of narrative—and a good portion of them simply do *not*—end up preoccupied with something *other than* the story, and in the process undermine or neutralize the mechanisms of plot progression. The apparent story in Walser's work is either lost in a barrage of excessive narratorial reflection or abandoned as a result of the narrator's thematic promiscuity.[1] Walser's self-characterization is in this regard felicitous: his is a genuinely 'plotless' prose. And yet he maintains that what he is writing is *not* simply prose, but *narrative*: a 'realistic story'. This paradox—that his works are at once 'stories', though they contain no plots—describes the governing logic of Walserian narrative. His 'stories' are only ever told by a process of deferral, digression, dismissal, or denial of the story. Walser's narratives come to be *despite* but also *by virtue of* the narratorial

impulses that appear to prevent them from being, those that want to dispense with plot or at least render its teleological tendencies null and void.

But isn't the 'plotless story' an oxymoron? How can we speak of a story in the absence of plot? What else is a story if not its progression towards the end that defines its dynamic and grants it design, if not purpose?[2] Walser's work as a whole can be read as a series of implicit, experimental answers to these questions, his storyless stories as alternatives to the plot-centred narrative. Instead of reading selections from his large corpus of short prose—a form that lends itself more easily to the jettisoning of plot—the following analysis of Walserian digressivity and its resulting plotless narration will focus on one of his novels, a form even more beholden to the strictures and expectations of plot progression. Perhaps as a challenge to its prevailing form, to its all-too-familiar reliance on narrative necessity, the novel becomes for Walser the site of some of his most extreme digressivity, an occasion for him to test to what degree and to what length plotlessness can be maintained without a collapse into non-narrative. The novel becomes the critical space where Walser most rigorously demonstrates that only in suspending plot is he able to forge anything like narrative at all.

The only novel-length incarnation of Walser's late period experimentation, *The Robber,* is one of the most outrageously eccentric and utterly aberrant artifacts of modernism, a cultural phenomenon already famous for its celebration of the new, the unusual and the unconventional. And it is, importantly, an *artifact,* no mere book; a work that is anomalous both as a linguistic and narrative construct, and as a textual object, as a manuscript comprised of the material and materiality of paper and writing itself. **The Robber** was written in the summer of 1925, a time during which Walser wrote on scraps of paper, backs of letters, used calendar pages, envelopes, even business cards, in a penciled cursive averaging 1 millimetre in height. These texts (which, along with this novel, consisted of poetry, short prose and dramatic scenes) took over 17 years to decipher, though they fill only six volumes. The so-called **Robber**-Novel (it bears no title in Walser's hand) was found among these 'microscripts', spread across merely 24 pages of finely penciled script, appearing more like pages awash with grey: murky, enigmatic, impenetrable.[3] (The novel, of course, is not nearly as short as its manuscript suggests: transcribed and placed in standard typeface, Walser's two dozen microgrammed pages multiply nearly sixfold to fill out over 140 pages.)

As if this minuscule materiality could only give birth to a novel that mirrored its grapho-formicating paper landscape, an apparent restlessness that is in fact static, a blur of ashen alphabet in strings of nearly formless, leaden inscriptions, Walser's last novel skirts the boundaries of its own form, moving forward without ever really progressing, almost succumbing to its own digressive mania. For *The Robber* is a work of nearly unrelenting asides, a novel that sacrifices story in its onslaught of hesitations, prolepses, deliberations, non sequiturs, meta-commentary, retractions, contradictions, exhausting inattentiveness, apologies and a seemingly limitless supply of other dilatory tactics. The announced intention of telling a story (which has nothing whatever to do with an adventurer or criminal, as the title might suggest) is, nonetheless, its apparent backbone, even if it is an infirm, scoliotic support. This serpentine, even labyrinthine, structure is repeatedly shown to be feeble and fragmentary, by no means sufficient for holding the text together *as* narrative, in the conventional sense. The story elements found here among an inchoate concatenation of narrative material are simply not allowed to assume the shape of a plot. For this reason the novel defies summary: the events contained in it (and yes, there are events recounted here) are not provided the necessary causal or even temporal interconnections and determinations that would result in any familiar narrative design, however crude or confusing. Therefore even events that might constitute the building-blocks of a plot become digressions themselves by virtue of the fact that they contribute nothing to any story structure or intention.

An example of how Walser treats such potentially plot-productive material can be gleaned in the following excerpt:

> And while two such schoolmates were scaling these so formidable bourgeois rungs, the Robber now paid a visit to Fräulein Selma so as to inquire courteously as to whether or not she might, for example, be in any way in need of him. 'What can I do for you?' she asked. She was drinking her coffee over the newspaper. One must add that Fräulein Selma lived largely without meat, that is, consumed a skimpy, delicate diet, in other words voluntarily submitted, in culinary matters, to the most well-thought-out limitations. She also, incidentally, let a room to a Russian girl who was a student.
>
> (2000: 94-5)

Coming in at the tail end of a two-page-long digression about two of the Robber's schoolmates (who appear to have no bearing on his life, except that they became respectable members of the bourgeoisie, while he did not), the narrator shifts mid-sentence to the Robber's visit with Fräulein Selma. Instead of making this visit the occasion for character development or for attempting to establish the relationship between these two figures (a relationship that elsewhere has explicit romantic overtones, which however remain unexploited), Walser isolates the encounter, providing neither context nor motivation. The pivotal question addressed to our eponymous 'hero', one that has all the potential for setting a series of plotted events in motion, is given tantalizingly in direct discourse, but then abruptly suspended. It does not, as far as we know, remain unanswered; it

is, however, left unnarrated while we shift from what might be a meaningful interaction to a banal description of what Fräulein Selma was doing at the moment she asked her question. This description, however, does not serve as a transition back to the conversation, but rather compels the narrator ('One must add [. . .]') to stray further from the narrative situation by mentioning Selma's vegetarianism. Not only is this dietary fact inconsequential, the narrator insists on repeating it in three different, increasingly verbose variations: Selma lived 'largely without meat' becomes 'consumed a skimpy, delicate diet' and, lastly, in a baroque version of the first, rather succinct, expression: 'voluntarily submitted, in culinary matters, to the most well-thought-out limitations'. Each restatement is not only increasingly wordy, but also increasingly imprecise (neither mentions a specifically meatless diet), so that each protracted iteration is further removed from the content of the original digression. And as if these unnecessary reformulations were not sufficiently dilatory or off-topic, the narrator proceeds by adding—'incidentally'—that a Russian student boards with Selma. We have up to this point not heard of this student, and will only encounter her once again, in passing. The Robber's visit, then, is not just cut off and diverted to trivialities, these trivialities are proliferated by narratorial discursiveness. Neither does our storyteller's circuitousness simply trail off before he returns us to the narrative situation already introduced. Instead, after his remark about the Russian lodger, his excursus abruptly ends, and with it ends the entire section (the novel is separated into 35 chapter-like divisions). This sharp caesura, furthermore, is not followed in the next section by information about what had transpired between the Robber and Selma while the narrator was unsuccessfully meandering through variations on vegetarianism. Rather, the situation—itself only a *possible* plot seed—is fully abandoned, left to fall between the fallow cracks of the novel's disconnected digressions.

If there is one candidate that might be said to have out-shandied *Tristram Shandy,* this is it. For despite its slim size, in particular next to *Shandy*'s impressive girth, Walser's novel is even more radically digressive and dilatory. Moreover, it is lacking that which makes Sterne's masterpiece more than just an ingenious display of the *fabula interrupta.* Simply put: *The Robber* has no Uncle Toby. We are, therefore, denied those master strokes of characterization that are central to Sterne's achievement and that contribute to his novel's greatness and renown as palpably as its famed digressiveness. Walser's is a novel of utterly empty characters. Even its titular hero is a cipher, neither presented with an inner life (let alone a complex one), nor shown to perform any heroic acts. As one of the novel's figures remarks to him, 'you are entirely lacking in character' (Walser 2000: 87), by which she does not just mean he lacks moral grounding. Neither is he empty of qualities but brimming with ideas, like the figure of

Ulrich whom Robert Musil—incidentally a great admirer of Walser—thought best suited for the modern novel. When Walser's narrator is not stealing his stage time in circumlocutionary excess, the Robber (who is not even given a name) can only be glimpsed stealing across the page like a spectre, as fleeting and insubstantial as the story to which he is supposed to belong. Without plot, without character what are we left with? Nothing, really. And it is upon this nothing that Walser appears to erect his novel. Indeed, nothing is there from the very start:

> Edith loves him. More on this later. Perhaps she *never* [*nie*] should have initiated relations with this good-for-*nothing* who has *no* money. It appears she's been sending him emissaries, or—how shall we put it—ambassadresses. He has lady friends everywhere, but *nothing* ever comes of them, and what a *nothing* has come of this famous, as it were, hundred francs! Once, out of *nothing* but affability, benevolence, he left one hundred thousand marks in the hands of others. Laugh at him, and he'll laugh as well. This alone might make a dubious impression. And *not* [**Nicht** *einmal*] one friend to show for himself. In 'all this time' he's spent here among us, he's failed [*nicht gelungen*]—which delights him—to gain the esteem of gentlemen. Can you imagine [*Ist das* **nicht**] a more flagrant *lack* of talent?
>
> (Walser 2000: 1 and [*Aus dem Bleistiftgebiet*] 1986a: 11)[4]

As if responding to a challenge, Walser digresses from the novel's story not just after its first sentence, but after the novel's first three words. Though betraying the necessity for the semblance of plot in order to instantiate his digressive gesture, Walser reduces this plot to its barest minimum: subject, verb, object. And he promptly dismisses it in just as many words, at least in the original German: 'Hiervon nachher mehr' ('More on this later').[5] With the most extreme economy, these opening two sentences of the novel enact a limit-case of digressive storytelling in announcing and performing in its first six words the novel's governing principle. And as if to acknowledge and even to celebrate this nearly absurd narrative reduction, which leaves the reader with next to *nothing* by way of a story, Walser's narrator sprinkles the following few sentences with a series of 'nothings' (*nichts*), 'nots' (*nicht*), a 'never' (*nie*), as well as 'no money' (*kein Geld*) and a final 'lack of talent' that we are to assume will contribute to the stuff of the story. Unable to orient ourselves in this breathless opening, we are left instead with the repetition of *nichts, nichts, nichts, nichts* in close succession, followed—after a short, two-sentence breather—by *nicht, nicht, nicht,* in only slightly larger intervals, which together appear to be parsing out the novel's structural principle, subliminally intoning its aesthetic of negation.

When we turn to the actual content of the novel we do not find *nothing,* of course, but we do find *nothing* in the way of novelistic material, which is to say: there is no coherent story here. Or rather, there is just enough story to make palpable how unimportant that story is. On the one hand, Walser is parodying plot.[6] In the novel's fifth sentence (quoted above), the reader is introduced to a 'famous [. . .] hundred francs', without further explanation. It is as if the public and readerly attraction of this plot point about 100 francs has by the very start of the novel already run its course. They *were* famous, but now they have 'come to nothing', like so much else ostensibly important to the story the narrator intends to tell. We find out later that the Robber inherited these 100 francs from his uncle, and that this seemingly generous act in fact led to the series of events that the narrator attempts to—but ultimately wishes he did not have to—relate: 'Ah, how clear it is to me now that this entire story is the fault of no one other than the mediocrity of this Batavian uncle' (Walser 2000: 120). The giving of 100 francs—itself a trivial act—thus sets into motion one event after the other, each of which is shown to be arbitrary, not teleologically motivated and therefore (for any pretence of plot) uninteresting. Cause may lead to effect, but each chain of causal relations does not necessarily make a plot; in fact, as the novel makes abundantly clear, causes will always lead to effects, to endless effects, but these are also endlessly *ordinary*. They will only ever 'come to nothing'.

And therefore Walser's novel not only tells us 'nothing' by way of a story, it also lacks any edifying content: 'I am constructing here a commonsensical book from which nothing at all can be learned' (2000: 4-5). Though the story of this novel has been overgrown by rampant, seemingly uncontrollable digressivity, the narrator tells us here that we should not even be looking for that which is frequently to be found in a novel's digressive passages, namely, didactic or instructive discourses. If 'nothing' is to be learned from the book, and, as the narrator admits, the story itself 'will come to nothing', what impulse hides behind the narrator's insistence to keep on writing? And, more importantly, why do we bother to keep on reading? The answer (to both questions) lies in Walser's particular means of exploiting that *nothing* for narrative ends. 'Nothing', the novel's very lack both of story and edifying discourse, becomes part of its marshalling of negation for the means of narrativization. It is the very absence of story that proliferates the text that, despite and by virtue of its plotlessness, takes on a different kind of narrativity altogether.

We can begin to better grasp the logic of this deviant narrativity by turning to some of the numerous self-reflexive moments in which Walser allows his narrator to speculate on writing itself:

> You've no idea what a pile of things I have to tell you. A stalwart friend might perhaps be necessary, that is, important for me, though I consider friendship unfeasible: it seems too difficult a task. On this specific point various reflections might be made, but my little finger

cautions me to avoid verbosity. Today I gazed into a marvelous thunderstorm whose tumultuous strength delighted me. Enough, enough. Already I'm afraid I've bored the reader atrociously.

(2000: 5)

In this passage the narrator acknowledges his dilatory mania, except that in doing so he also perpetuates it—one of the supreme ironies of Walserian digression. Our storyteller not only introduces a digression to comment on his digressivity, he also digresses within the digression that itself only exists by virtue of his excessive digressions. Since that 'pile of things' he has to tell us itself consists mostly in digressions that delay the story of the Robber, the narrator is effectively delaying his further delays of the story in reflecting on his propensity to delay. In this way the novel's proliferation of nothings feeds back into itself. 'We'll do well to add nothing more to this sentence' (2000: 121), the narrator later notes, only dimly aware, it seems, that in saying he will add 'nothing more' to the sentence, he is in fact *adding* more to the sentence. Except that what he is adding is really only 'nothing'—or rather, nothing except to comment that nothing will be added. Similarly the narrator remarks after a brief description of a pretty woman: 'This woman's significance for us is absolutely nothing' (2000: 49).' She means 'nothing' to the narrator and to his story, and yet he writes about her, again suggesting that in some way 'nothing' itself is that which is mysteriously and productively significant for the novel.

Even though he claims the Robber's story is a priority, the narrator insists that he is doing the right thing by continuing to relate trivial nothings:

> Once, in that other restaurant, he dined on chicken while sipping Dôle. We say this only because, at the moment, nothing of more weight occurs to us. A pen would rather say something improper than lie idle even for an instant. This is perhaps a secret of quality literature, in other words, the writing process must work on impulse.

(2000: 54)

For the narrator, therefore, it is perfectly proper to 'say something improper' (that is, something irrelevant and with no bearing on the story) because the ultimate narratorial impropriety is to 'lie idle even for an instant'. Silence—saying nothing—is to be avoided at all cost, even if that means filling the page with nothing, that is, trivialities. 'It's best we say nothing' (2000: 64), the narrator writes several pages later, acknowledging that 'saying nothing', paradoxically, does not equate with pure silence or the blank page. To say nothing—to *tell* nothing—manifests itself as loquaciousness, the narrator's unceasing digressivity. Walter Benjamin referred to this quality of Walser's prose as its 'Geschwätzigkeit' (1991: 327), its garrulousness. It is indeed the performance of narrative voice that permeates so much of

Walser's prose. Here the narrator reminds us he is writing ('the pen'), and yet that this process is and ought to be driven by 'impulse'. We need to ask, however: towards what is that impulse directed? Or is it only directed back at itself? Is the narrator of **The Robber** only writing for the sake of writing, or does he mean to sustain our interest in something like a story? And, most decisively: is there, for him, a difference?

To begin answering these questions we should consider one of the narrator's favourite techniques: the anticipatory prolepsis. We already saw this mode of the introduction and delay of a plot point in the first two sentences of the novel, where the space between that introduction and its postponement was brought to an extreme minimum: 'Edith loves him. More on this later.' The novel abounds in such prolepses: 'More will be said of this at some later point' (2000: 20); 'I'll elucidate later the reason for this' (2000: 28); 'We'll want to return, by and by, to this' (2000: 49). Scores of examples could be provided; the anticipatory prolepsis appears on almost every other page. It is an essential part of the novel's logic of narrative proliferation through plot negation, of the narrator's proclivity for 'saying nothing' through excess verbiage. Characteristically, the narrator reflects on his need to delay and, unsurprisingly, provides conflicting reasons for his compulsive dilatoriness. On the one hand, he has his readers in mind:

> On some later occasion we shall elucidate, illuminate this. Much in these pages may strike the reader as mysterious, which we, so to speak, hope, for if everything lay spread wide open to the understanding, the contents of these lines would make you yawn.

(2000: 41)

The narrator here claims to be delaying the details and explanations of his story strategically so as to assure sustained interest on the part of the reader. He is cognizant of the reader's expectations, and does not want us to be bored. This strategy would seem to make sense in terms of the conventional dynamics and desires of reading narrative, except that the narrator rarely fulfils his proleptic promises (that is, much of what he promises to reveal later is never returned to) and elsewhere claims to be simply 'filling time':

> The Robber now came to a house that was no longer present, or, to say it better, to an old house that had been demolished on account of its age and now no longer stood there, inasmuch as it had ceased to make itself noticed. He came, then, in short, to a place where, in former days, a house had stood. These detours I'm making serve the end of filling time, for I really must pull off a book of considerable length, otherwise I'll be even more deeply despised than I am now. Things can't possibly go on like this. Local men of the world call me a simpleton because novels don't tumble out of my pockets.

(2000: 74-5)

The Robber's perambulations—a central motif in Walser's work as a whole, and one intimately related to his digressivity—manifest themselves on this page as the ramblings of the narrator who traces and retraces his steps in his seemingly futile attempt to express the *absence* of a particular architectural structure. This passage again displays one of the structural paradoxes of the novel: its narrator is occupied with relating that which is really nothing (here quite literally: the space where a house had once stood), and in doing so ends up unfurling sentence after sentence *in the service of* that nothing. To what end? That of 'filling time', the narrator freely admits, appealing to his reputation as a less-than-prolific writer. But if 'filling time' is really his motive, why doesn't he fill time with those shards of story that he so liberally tosses aside for the supposed purpose of keeping his readers interested? On the very same page he rejects such a story—'the Robber once treated an unemployed person to a sausage. Perhaps we'll return to this later' (2000: 75)—in favour of further reflection on the Robber's meanderings.

Ultimately it becomes clear that there is little difference between the narrator's notion of 'filling time' with 'detours' and those repeated suspensions of story elements inaugurated by the anticipatory prolepsis. To suspend a story does not and really cannot come down to any true cessation of the novel's progress, which is why narrative digression always brings us closer to the end of the book, even if it moves us further from the end of the story. Suspensions of story in **The Robber** coincide with those 'detours' that only *fill time* because, as the narrator frequently demonstrates, to narrate suspension—the discontinuance of narration—is to keep on narrating something, anything, or (as he would like it) nothing. And this nothing that fills both the time and space of the novel does not simply delay plot development and the fulfilment of proleptic promises for a later time, it does so almost perpetually. For even those plot points to which the narrator *does* in fact return (and these are few) are revealed to be of little importance, primarily because Walser has managed to shift this novel's narrative weight from the centre to its periphery so that it moves by constantly circling around the centre towards which it always points, even though this centre is shown to be empty. To delay plot 'in the interest of sustaining interest' (2000: 31), as the narrator of **The Robber** claims to be doing, becomes for Walser a kind of pleasurable deferral that exposes the tautology of narrative suspense, and then neuters it. Interest leads to interest, which generates more interest, ultimately leading nowhere. Without the end to give meaning to the sequence, without the fulfilment of that which is postponed, narrative teleology is short-circuited and sent into a self-perpetuating loop. In **The Robber** this circular movement appears as a dynamic circuitousness that generates the paradoxical narrative logic of the novel, one in which nothing itself is repeatedly covered up and simultaneously perpetuated.

This perpetual, pleasurable (and productive) circling points to Walser's alternative notion of narrative desire. Typically digression grants us those crucial moments of 'satisfaction and reassurance', as Derek Attridge notes, in returning and importantly ceding to the main narrative. Digressions maintain the 'order and wholeness of the text' in being temporary, in always ultimately bringing the reader back to the story they had abandoned in a manner that grants us 'the sweet pleasure of relevance' (Attridge 1988: 222). That Walser denies the readers of **The Robber** this crucial satisfaction by no means undermines the novel's pleasurability. In fact, he claims it makes the pleasure of the text possible in the first place. Walser is seeking to redefine our relation to narrative by insisting on the satisfaction that can be had from perpetually postponing plot, not in order to maintain suspense, but in order to heighten and take pleasure in the unfulfilled desires of narrative. The narrator of **The Robber** equates narrating nothing (or trivialities) with filling time *and* sustaining interest because for Walser the unfulfilled desires in fact *fulfil* in remaining unfulfilled. In this novel and in much of his prose Walser insists that we take pleasure in being denied pleasures, just as the Robber 'take[s] pleasure in robbing [himself] of pleasure' (2000: 95), in part because if our desires were to be fulfilled, they would also be annihilated.

In this way, Walser's digressivity is importantly not destructive of narrative. It does not, for example, neutralize the generic markers of narrativity, reversing the centre-periphery relation of plot to excursus so that the text 'can be read for something *other* than the narrative', as Attridge suggests of the radically digressive work (1988: 228). Neither do Walser's digressions lose their quality of digressivity in diminishing the influence of the plot against which they must define themselves. Walser maintains a productive tension between digression and plot that affirms the former's subversiveness while insisting on the narrativity generated from its restless process of plot-negation. This activity of subversion is—within the text—a *perpetual* movement (circular, tracing out the shape of the nought), one that cannot come to a halt or reach completion lest it merely accede to the usurped position of plot whose dynamic it is seeking to annul.[8] In insisting on telling stories freed from the influences of plot, as he does in **The Robber** and in much of his narrative work, Walser gestures towards relocating narrative dynamics from plotting to the active efforts to thwart that plotting. Plot is therefore necessarily always present in his work as that which is being deferred or playfully deconstructed, that which must be suspended to inaugurate a new mode of (plotless) narrativity. The inverted logic of negation underlying these narrative movements is not only structurally pivotal to Walser's work, it is also one of its principal thematic preoccupations. In **The Robber,** in particular, we find one of the most apt formulations of this governing paradox: 'To be able to fall asleep, then, one should make the effort to remain awake. One shouldn't make an effort to sleep. To be able to love, one should make an effort not to love' (2000: 119-20). To be able to tell a story, we might add, one should make the effort not to tell a story. And this is precisely what Walser has done. Except that *not telling a story* is for him no mere privation of activity; it is an 'effort'. In **The Robber** the story has therefore not so much been left untold as it has been actively stolen. The novel has been forged not out of the absence, but out of the *absenting,* of story. Thus, in stealing the story Walser succeeds in negating normative narrativity, thereby setting in motion an elusive new mode of narrativity whose locus is neither in plot nor in digression, but in their dialectical interaction.

Notes

1. Throughout the chapter I use 'story' not only in a somewhat untechnical, descriptive sense—following Walser's usage—as roughly synonymous with narrative itself (in whatever guise), but also, normatively, as the content readers typically expect from a narrative, its plotted events and characters. The slippage between these two notions of story is—as we will see—itself a product of Walser's idiosyncratic narrative mode. I therefore do not mean by 'story' the structuralist-narratological or Russian Formalist notion of the raw material of 'plot'. This raw material I call the 'story elements' or 'events'.

2. See Peter Brooks's famous theory of plot (1984).

3. On Walser's writing as *process* and its visuality, see Siegel (2001: 103-25).

4. Emphasis mine; Bernofsky's translation slightly altered to reflect repetition of 'nichts'.

5. This first digression is also importantly a verbless sentence. The syntactical unit of progression has been excised, action itself suspended.

6. On Walser's parodying of trivial literature, see Fuchs (1993: 103-32).

7. Bernofsky's translation altered slightly.

8. The literature on Walser's digressivity (which is surprisingly small) tends to fall into the trap of supplementarity by positing exactly such a reversal of the story—digression dichotomy that would ultimately only recentre the marginal digression in the former position of the central story. See, for example, Annette Fuchs (1993: 89ff.), or Susanne Andres, who insists on the collapse of primary and peripheral narrative strands—to claim that everything in *The Robber* is digression—without acknowledging that this collapse would result in our inability to recognize digression *as* digression, let alone identify the text as narrative (1997: 154). A more sophisticated reading of Walser's digressivity is explored by Peter Utz (1998: 369-423).

Bibliography

Andres, Susanne. 1997. *Robert Walsers arabeskes Schreiben* (Göttingen: Cuvillier Verlag)

Attridge, Derek. 1988. *Literature as Difference from the Renaissance to James Joyce* (Ithaca, NY: Cornell University Press)

Benjamin, Walter. 1991. *Gesammelte Schriften,* ed. Rolf Tiedemann and Hermann Schweppenhäuser, II: *Aufsätze Essays Vorträge* (Frankfurt a.M.: Suhrkamp)

Brooks, Peter. 1984. *Reading for the Plot: Design and Intention in Narrative* (Cambridge, Mass.: Harvard University Press)

Fuchs, Annette. 1993. *Dramaturgie des Narrentums. Das Komische in der Prosa Robert Walsers* (Munich: Wilhelm Fink Verlag)

Siegel, Elke. 2001. *Aufträge aus dem Bleistiftgebiet. Zur Dichtung Robert Walsers* (Würzburg: Königshausen und Neumann)

Utz, Peter. 1998. *Tanz auf den Rändern. Robert Walsers 'Jetztzeitstil'* (Frankfurt a.M.: Suhrkamp)

Walser, Robert. 1986a. *Aus dem Bleistiftgebiet,* ed. Bernhard Echte and Werner Morlang, III: *'Räuber'-Roman, 'Felix'-Szenen* (Frankfurt a.M.: Suhrkamp)

————1986b. *Sämtliche Werke in Einzelausgaben,* ed. Jochen Greven, XX: *Für die Katz: Prosa aus der Berner Zeit 1928-1933* (Frankfurt a.M.: Suhrkamp)

————2000. *The Robber,* trans. Susan Bernofsky (Lincoln and London: University of Nebraska Press)

FURTHER READING

Bibliography

Wilbert-Collins, Elly. "Robert Walser." In *A Bibliography of Four Contemporary German-Swiss Authors: Friedrich Dürrenmatt, Max Frisch, Robert Walser, Albin Zollinger,* pp. 53-63. Bern, Switzerland: Francke Verlag, 1967.

    Bibliography devoted to Walser and three other German-Swiss writers that contains both primary and secondary sources, including criticism of the author and his works published in books, journals, newspapers, "and various other media."

Criticism

Bernofsky, Susan. "Secrets, Not Code: On Robert Walser's Microscripts." In *Microscripts,* by Robert Walser, translated by Susan Bernofsky, pp. 9-18. New York: New Directions, 2009.

Discusses the purpose and possible evolution of Walser's "pencil system" of writing and his production of "microtexts"—small scraps of paper containing tiny handwritten texts—as the basis of his work late in his career, most of which went unpublished and has only recently been deciphered.

Cardinal, Agnes. *The Figure of Paradox in the Work of Robert Walser.* Stuttgart, Germany: Hans-Dieter Heinz, 1982, 115 p.

Studies the essential role of paradox in Walser's life and art, maintaining that "the paradoxical stance which manifests itself so unmistakably in Walser's life-style is even more salient in his art, where paradox is elevated into an all-embracing mode of approach to every intellectual and emotional problem."

Coetzee, J. M. "Robert Walser." In *Inner Workings: Literary Essays 2000-2005,* pp. 15-29. New York: Viking, 2007.

Summarizes Walser's life and accomplishments as a writer, commenting, in particular, on the novels *Jakob von Gunten* and *The Robber.* Coetzee states that Walser's texts "proceed neither by logic nor by narrative but by moods, fancies, and associations," and that "he was less a thinker following an argument or even a storyteller following a narrative line than a belletrist."

Gleber, Anke. "The Secret Cities of Modernity: Topographies of Perception in Georges Rodenbach, Robert Walser, and Franz Hessel." In *The Turn of the Century: Modernism and Modernity in Literature and the Arts,* edited by Christian Berg, Frank Durieux, and Geert Lernout, pp. 363-79. Berlin: Walter de Gruyter, 1995.

Studies what she calls "flâneur texts" by Walser, Georges Rodenbach, and Franz Hessel within their historical and cultural environments, asserting that "flânerie," in its "intoxication with images as icons of modern mythology," interprets the world as "a modern text" and an aesthetics "redolent of many aesthetic constructions of modernity."

Harman, Mark. "Stream of Consciousness and the Boundaries of Self-Conscious Fiction: The Works of Robert Walser." *Comparative Criticism* 6 (1984): 119-34.

Emphasizes Walser's "self-consciousness" as a writer and notes the ongoing conflict within the author's "autobiographical project" between "the confessional urge" and his self-irony, asserting that "his desire for a form of self-revelation which would capture the flux of his consciousness makes Walser one of the earliest and most radical practitioners of stream of consciousness writing."

Kaufman, Herbert L. "Robert Walser: Church and Religion." *Modern Languages* 54, no. 1 (March 1973): 22-6.

Investigates Walser's attitude towards the church and religion by studying passages from his novels and stories, concluding that the author regarded the institution of the church negatively and favored instead a direct relationship with God through nature and "love of one's fellow man."

Pizer, John. "The Disenchantment of Snow White: Robert Walser, Donald Barthelme and the Modern/Postmodern Anti-Fairy Tale." *Canadian Review of Comparative Literature* 17, no. 3-4 (September-December 1990): 330-47.

Compares and contrasts the "anti-fairy tales" based on Grimm's Snow White by Walser and the American postmodern writer Donald Barthelme, maintaining that both of these works "invest" the original tale "with a sense of moral entropy and flawed communication" and "call into question the very transmissibility of an ordered, traditional system of values."

Sebald, W. G. "Le Promeneur Solitaire: A Remembrance of Robert Walser." In *The Tanners,* by Robert Walser, translated by Susan Bernofsky, pp. 1-36. New York: New Directions, 2009.

Hommage to Walser that stresses the "precariousness" of his life and the "indefinability" of his writings, which, despite their "tendency to vanish into thin air," often "conceal the profoundest depths of meaning."

Additional coverage of Walser's life and career is contained in the following sources published by Gale: *Contemporary Authors,* Vols. 118, 165; *Contemporary Authors New Revision Series,* Vols. 100, 194; *Dictionary of Literary Biography,* Vol. 66; *Encyclopedia of World Literature in the 20th Century,* Ed. 3; *Literature Resource Center*; *Short Story Criticism,* Vol. 20; and *Twentieth-Century Literary Criticism,* Vol. 18.

How to Use This Index

The main references

> **Calvino, Italo**
> 1923-1985 .... CLC **5, 8, 11, 22, 33, 39,**
> **73; SSC 3, 48**

list all author entries in the following Gale Literary Criticism series:

AAL = *Asian American Literature*
BG = *The Beat Generation: A Gale Critical Companion*
BLC = *Black Literature Criticism*
BLCS = *Black Literature Criticism Supplement*
CLC = *Contemporary Literary Criticism*
CLR = *Children's Literature Review*
CMLC = *Classical and Medieval Literature Criticism*
DC = *Drama Criticism*
FL = *Feminism in Literature: A Gale Critical Companion*
GL = *Gothic Literature: A Gale Critical Companion*
HLC = *Hispanic Literature Criticism*
HLCS = *Hispanic Literature Criticism Supplement*
HR = *Harlem Renaissance: A Gale Critical Companion*
LC = *Literature Criticism from 1400 to 1800*
NCLC = *Nineteenth-Century Literature Criticism*
NNAL = *Native North American Literature*
PC = *Poetry Criticism*
SSC = *Short Story Criticism*
TCLC = *Twentieth-Century Literary Criticism*
WLC = *World Literature Criticism, 1500 to the Present*
WLCS = *World Literature Criticism Supplement*

The cross-references

> See also CA 85-88, 116; CANR 23, 61;
> DAM NOV; DLB 196; EW 13; MTCW 1, 2;
> RGSF 2; RGWL 2; SFW 4; SSFS 12

list all author entries in the following Gale biographical and literary sources:

AAYA = *Authors & Artists for Young Adults*
AFAW = *African American Writers*
AFW = *African Writers*
AITN = *Authors in the News*
AMW = *American Writers*
AMWR = *American Writers Retrospective Supplement*
AMWS = *American Writers Supplement*
ANW = *American Nature Writers*
AW = *Ancient Writers*
BEST = *Bestsellers*
BPFB = *Beacham's Encyclopedia of Popular Fiction: Biography and Resources*
BRW = *British Writers*
BRWS = *British Writers Supplement*
BW = *Black Writers*
BYA = *Beacham's Guide to Literature for Young Adults*
CA = *Contemporary Authors*
CAAS = *Contemporary Authors Autobiography Series*
CABS = *Contemporary Authors Bibliographical Series*
CAD = *Contemporary American Dramatists*
CANR = *Contemporary Authors New Revision Series*
CAP = *Contemporary Authors Permanent Series*
CBD = *Contemporary British Dramatists*
CCA = *Contemporary Canadian Authors*
CD = *Contemporary Dramatists*
CDALB = *Concise Dictionary of American Literary Biography*

CDALBS = *Concise Dictionary of American Literary Biography Supplement*
CDBLB = *Concise Dictionary of British Literary Biography*
CMW = *St. James Guide to Crime & Mystery Writers*
CN = *Contemporary Novelists*
CP = *Contemporary Poets*
CPW = *Contemporary Popular Writers*
CSW = *Contemporary Southern Writers*
CWD = *Contemporary Women Dramatists*
CWP = *Contemporary Women Poets*
CWRI = *St. James Guide to Children's Writers*
CWW = *Contemporary World Writers*
DA = *DISCovering Authors*
DA3 = *DISCovering Authors 3.0*
DAB = *DISCovering Authors: British Edition*
DAC = *DISCovering Authors: Canadian Edition*
DAM = *DISCovering Authors: Modules*
   DRAM: *Dramatists Module;* **MST**: *Most-studied Authors Module;*
   MULT: *Multicultural Authors Module;* **NOV**: *Novelists Module;*
   POET: *Poets Module;* **POP**: *Popular Fiction and Genre Authors Module*
DFS = *Drama for Students*
DLB = *Dictionary of Literary Biography*
DLBD = *Dictionary of Literary Biography Documentary Series*
DLBY = *Dictionary of Literary Biography Yearbook*
DNFS = *Literature of Developing Nations for Students*
EFS = *Epics for Students*
EW = *European Writers*
EWL = *Encyclopedia of World Literature in the 20th Century*
EXPN = *Exploring Novels*
EXPP = *Exploring Poetry*
EXPS = *Exploring Short Stories*
FANT = *St. James Guide to Fantasy Writers*
FW = *Feminist Writers*
GFL = *Guide to French Literature,* Beginnings to 1789, 1798 to the Present
GLL = *Gay and Lesbian Literature*
HGG = *St. James Guide to Horror, Ghost & Gothic Writers*
HW = *Hispanic Writers*
IDFW = *International Dictionary of Films and Filmmakers: Writers and Production Artists*
IDTP = *International Dictionary of Theatre: Playwrights*
LAIT = *Literature and Its Times*
LAW = *Latin American Writers*
JRDA = *Junior DISCovering Authors*
MAICYA = *Major Authors and Illustrators for Children and Young Adults*
MAICYAS = *Major Authors and Illustrators for Children and Young Adults Supplement*
MAWW = *Modern American Women Writers*
MJW = *Modern Japanese Writers*
MTCW = *Major 20th-Century Writers*
NCFS = *Nonfiction Classics for Students*
NFS = *Novels for Students*
PAB = *Poets: American and British*
PFS = *Poetry for Students*
RGAL = *Reference Guide to American Literature*
RGEL = *Reference Guide to English Literature*
RGSF = *Reference Guide to Short Fiction*
RGWL = *Reference Guide to World Literature*
RHW = *Twentieth-Century Romance and Historical Writers*
SAAS = *Something about the Author Autobiography Series*
SATA = *Something about the Author*
SFW = *St. James Guide to Science Fiction Writers*
SSFS = *Short Stories for Students*
TCWW = *Twentieth-Century Western Writers*
WLIT = *World Literature and Its Times*
WP = *World Poets*
YABC = *Yesterday's Authors of Books for Children*
YAW = *St. James Guide to Young Adult Writers*

Literary Criticism Series
Cumulative Author Index

Adler, Carole Schwerdtfeger
See Adler, C. S.

Adler, Renata 1938- .... **CLC 8, 31**
See also CA 49-52; CANR 95; CN 4, 5, 6;
MTCW 1

Adorno, Theodor W(iesengrund)
1903-1969 .... **TCLC 111**
See also CA 89-92; 25-28R; CANR 89;
DLB 242; EWL 3

Ady, Endre 1877-1919 .... **TCLC 11, 253**
See also CA 107; CDWLB 4; DLB 215;
EW 9; EWL 3

A.E.
See Russell, George William

Aelfric c. 955-c. 1010 .... **CMLC 46, 128**
See also DLB 146

Aelred of Rievaulx 1110-1167 .... **CMLC 123**

Aeschines c. 390B.C.-c. 320B.C. .. **CMLC 47**
See also DLB 176

Aeschylus 525(?)B.C.-456(?)B.C. . **CMLC 11,
51, 94; DC 8; WLCS**
See also AW 1; CDWLB 1; DA; DAB;
DAC; DAM DRAM, MST; DFS 5, 10,
26; DLB 176; LMFS 1; RGWL 2, 3;
TWA; WLIT 8

Aesop 620(?)B.C.-560(?)B.C. .... **CMLC 24;
SSC 164**
See also CLR 14; MAICYA 1, 2; SATA 64

Affable Hawk
See MacCarthy, Sir (Charles Otto) Desmond

Africa, Ben
See Bosman, Herman Charles

Afrika, Jan
See Breytenbach, Breyten

Afton, Effie
See Harper, Frances Ellen Watkins

Agapida, Fray Antonio
See Irving, Washington

Agar, Emile
See Kacew, Romain

Agee, James 1909-1955 ..... **TCLC 1, 19, 180**
See also AAYA 44; AITN 1; AMW; CA 108;
148; CANR 131; CDALB 1941-1968;
DAM NOV; DLB 2, 26, 152; DLBY
1989; EWL 3; LAIT 3; LATS 1:2; MAL
5; MTCW 2; MTFW 2005; NFS 22;
RGAL 4; TUS

Agee, James Rufus
See Agee, James

A Gentlewoman in New England
See Bradstreet, Anne

A Gentlewoman in Those Parts
See Bradstreet, Anne

Aghill, Gordon
See Silverberg, Robert

Agnon, S. Y. 1888-1970 . **CLC 4, 8, 14; SSC
30, 120; TCLC 151**
See also CA 17-18; 25-28R; CANR 60, 102,
211; CAP 2; DLB 329; EWL 3; MTCW
1, 2; RGHL; RGSF 2; RGWL 2, 3; WLIT
6

Agnon, Shmuel Yosef Halevi
See Agnon, S. Y.

Agrippa von Nettesheim, Henry Cornelius
1486-1535 .... **LC 27**

Aguilera Malta, Demetrio 1909-1981 . **HLCS
1**
See also CA 111; 124; CANR 87; DAM
MULT, NOV; DLB 145; EWL 3; HW 1;
RGWL 3

Agustini, Delmira 1886-1914 .... **HLCS 1**
See also CA 166; DLB 290; HW 1, 2; LAW

Aherne, Owen
See Cassill, R(onald) V(erlin)

Ai 1947-2010 .... **CLC 4, 14, 69; PC 72**
See also CA 85-88; CAAS 13; CANR 70;
CP 6, 7; DLB 120; PFS 16

Aickman, Robert (Fordyce) 1914-1981 . **CLC
57**
See also CA 5-8R; CANR 3, 72, 100; DLB
261; HGG; SUFW 1, 2

Aidoo, (Christina) Ama Ata 1942- .... **BLCS;
CLC 177, 314**
See also AFW; BRWS 15; BW 1; CA 101;
CANR 62, 144; CD 5, 6; CDWLB 3; CN
6, 7; CWD; CWP; DLB 117; DNFS 1, 2;
EWL 3; FW; WLIT 2

Aiken, Conrad 1889-1973 .. **CLC 1, 3, 5, 10,
52; PC 26; SSC 9, 166**
See also AMW; CA 5-8R; 45-48; CANR 4,
60; CDALB 1929-1941; CN 1; CP 1;
DAM NOV, POET; DLB 9, 45, 102; EWL
3; EXPS; HGG; MAL 5; MTCW 1, 2;
MTFW 2005; PFS 24; RGAL 4; RGSF 2;
SATA 3, 30; SSFS 8, 34; TUS

Aiken, Conrad Potter
See Aiken, Conrad

Aiken, Joan (Delano) 1924-2004 ..... **CLC 35**
See also AAYA 1, 25; CA 9-12R, 182; 223;
CAAE 182; CANR 4, 23, 34, 64, 121;
CLR 1, 19, 90; DLB 161; FANT; HGG;
JRDA; MAICYA 1, 2; MTCW 1; RHW;
SAAS 1; SATA 2, 30, 73; SATA-Essay
109; SATA-Obit 152; SSFS 33; SUFW 2;
WYA; YAW

Ainsworth, William Harrison 1805-1882 .....
NCLC 13
See also DLB 21; HGG; RGEL 2; SATA
24; SUFW 1

Aitmatov, Chingiz 1928-2008 . **CLC 71; SSC
131**
See also CA 103; CANR 38; CWW 2; DLB
302; EWL 3; MTCW 1; RGSF 2; SATA
56

Aitmatov, Chingiz Torekulovich
See Aitmatov, Chingiz

Ajar, Emile
See Kacew, Romain

Akers, Floyd
See Baum, L. Frank

Akhmadulina, Bella 1937-2010 ...... **CLC 53;
PC 43**
See also CA 65-68; CWP; CWW 2; DAM
POET; DLB 359; EWL 3

Akhmadulina, Bella Akhatovna
See Akhmadulina, Bella

Akhmatova, Anna 1888-1966 ... **CLC 11, 25,
64, 126; PC 2, 55**
See also CA 19-20; 25-28R; CANR 35;
CAP 1; DA3; DAM POET; DLB 295; EW
10; EWL 3; FL 1:5; MTCW 1, 2; PFS 18,
27, 32, 36; RGWL 2, 3

Aksakov, Sergei Timofeevich 1791-1859 ......
NCLC 2, 181
See also DLB 198

Aksenov, Vasilii
See Aksyonov, Vassily

Aksenov, Vasilii Pavlovich
See Aksyonov, Vassily

Aksenov, Vassily
See Aksyonov, Vassily

Akst, Daniel 1956- .... **CLC 109**
See also CA 161; CANR 110

Aksyonov, Vassily 1932-2009 .... **CLC 22, 37,
101**
See also CA 53-56; CANR 12, 48, 77;
CWW 2; DLB 302; EWL 3

Aksyonov, Vassily Pavlovich
See Aksyonov, Vassily

Akutagawa Ryunosuke 1892-1927 .. **SSC 44;
TCLC 16, 259**
See also CA 117; 154; DLB 180; EWL 3;
MJW; RGSF 2; RGWL 2, 3; SSFS 35

Alabaster, William 1568-1640 .... **LC 90**
See also DLB 132; RGEL 2

Alain 1868-1951 .... **TCLC 41**
See also CA 163; EWL 3; GFL 1789 to the
Present

Alain de Lille c. 1116-c. 1203 ..... **CMLC 53,
138**
See also DLB 208

Alain-Fournier
See Fournier, Henri-Alban

Al-Amin, Jamil Abdullah 1943- ..... **BLC 1:1**
See also BW 1, 3; CA 112; 125; CANR 82;
DAM MULT

Alan of Lille
See Alain de Lille

Alanus de Insluis
See Alain de Lille

Alarcon, Pedro Antonio de 1833-1891 ....
NCLC 1, 219; SSC 64

Alas (y Urena), Leopoldo (Enrique Garcia)
1852-1901 .... **TCLC 29**
See also CA 113; 131; HW 1; RGSF 2

Albee, Edward (III) 1928- ... **CLC 1, 2, 3, 5,
9, 11, 13, 25, 53, 86, 113; DC 11; WLC
1**
See also AAYA 51; AITN 1; AMW; CA
5-8R; CABS 3; CAD; CANR 8, 54, 74,
124; CD 5, 6; CDALB 1941-1968; DA;
DA3; DAB; DAC; DAM DRAM, MST;
DFS 25; DLB 7, 266; EWL 3; INT
CANR-8; LAIT 4; LMFS 2; MAL 5;
MTCW 1, 2; MTFW 2005; RGAL 4; TUS

Albee, Edward Franklin
See Albee, Edward (III)

Alberti, Leon Battista 1404-1472 ..... **LC 173**

Alberti, Rafael 1902-1999 .... **CLC 7**
See also CA 85-88; 185; CANR 81; CWW
2; DLB 108; EWL 3; HW 2; RGWL 2, 3

Alberti Merello, Rafael
See Alberti, Rafael

Albert of Saxony c. 1316-1390 ... **CMLC 110**

Albert the Great 1193(?)-1280 ..... **CMLC 16**
See also DLB 115

Alcaeus c. 620B.C.- .... **CMLC 65**
See also DLB 176

Alcala-Galiano, Juan Valera y
See Valera y Alcala-Galiano, Juan

Alcayaga, Lucila Godoy
See Mistral, Gabriela

Alciato, Andrea 1492-1550 .... **LC 116**

Alcott, Amos Bronson 1799-1888 .. **NCLC 1,
167**
See also DLB 1, 223

Alcott, Louisa May 1832-1888 . **NCLC 6, 58,
83, 218; SSC 27, 98, 164; WLC 1**
See also AAYA 20; AMWS 1; BPFB 1;
BYA 2; CDALB 1865-1917; CLR 1, 38,
109; DA; DA3; DAB; DAC; DAM MST,
NOV; DLB 1, 42, 79, 223, 239, 242;
DLBD 14; FL 1:2; FW; JRDA; LAIT 2;
MAICYA 1, 2; NFS 12; RGAL 4; SATA
100; TUS; WCH; WYA; YABC 1; YAW

Alcuin c. 730-804 .... **CMLC 69, 139**
See also DLB 148

Aldanov, M. A.
See Aldanov, Mark (Alexandrovich)

Aldanov, Mark (Alexandrovich)
1886-1957 .... **TCLC 23**
See also CA 118; 181; DLB 317

Aldhelm c. 639-709 .... **CMLC 90**

Aldington, Richard 1892-1962 .... **CLC 49**
See also CA 85-88; CANR 45; DLB 20, 36,
100, 149; LMFS 2; RGEL 2

Aldiss, Brian W. 1925- . **CLC 5, 14, 40, 290;
SSC 36**
See also AAYA 42; CA 5-8R, 190; CAAE
190; CAAS 2; CANR 5, 28, 64, 121, 168;
CN 1, 2, 3, 4, 5, 6, 7; DAM NOV; DLB
14, 261, 271; MTCW 1, 2; MTFW 2005;
SATA 34; SCFW 1, 2; SFW 4

Aldiss, Brian Wilson
See Aldiss, Brian W.
Aldrich, Ann
See Meaker, Marijane
Aldrich, Bess Streeter 1881-1954 ...... **TCLC 125**
See also CLR 70; TCWW 2
Alegria, Claribel
See Alegria, Claribel
Alegria, Claribel 1924- ... **CLC 75; HLCS 1; PC 26**
See also CA 131; CAAS 15; CANR 66, 94, 134; CWW 2; DAM MULT; DLB 145, 283; EWL 3; HW 1; MTCW 2; MTFW 2005; PFS 21
Alegria, Claribel Joy
See Alegria, Claribel
Alegria, Fernando 1918-2005 .... **CLC 57**
See also CA 9-12R; CANR 5, 32, 72; EWL 3; HW 1, 2
Aleixandre, Vicente 1898-1984 ...... **HLCS 1; TCLC 113**
See also CANR 81; DLB 108, 329; EWL 3; HW 2; MTCW 1, 2; RGWL 2, 3
Alekseev, Konstantin Sergeivich
See Stanislavsky, Constantin
Alekseyer, Konstantin Sergeyevich
See Stanislavsky, Constantin
Aleman, Mateo 1547-1615(?) .... **LC 81**
Alencar, Jose de 1829-1877 .... **NCLC 157**
See also DLB 307; LAW; WLIT 1
Alencon, Marguerite d'
See de Navarre, Marguerite
Alepoudelis, Odysseus
See Elytis, Odysseus
Aleshkovsky, Joseph 1929- .... **CLC 44**
See also CA 121; 128; DLB 317
Aleshkovsky, Yuz
See Aleshkovsky, Joseph
Alexander, Barbara
See Ehrenreich, Barbara
Alexander, Lloyd 1924-2007 .... **CLC 35**
See also AAYA 1, 27; BPFB 1; BYA 5, 6, 7, 9, 10, 11; CA 1-4R; 260; CANR 1, 24, 38, 55, 113; CLR 1, 5, 48; CWRI 5; DLB 52; FANT; JRDA; MAICYA 1, 2; MAIC-YAS 1; MTCW 1; SAAS 19; SATA 3, 49, 81, 129, 135; SATA-Obit 182; SUFW; TUS; WYA; YAW
Alexander, Lloyd Chudley
See Alexander, Lloyd
Alexander, Meena 1951- .... **CLC 121**
See also CA 115; CANR 38, 70, 146; CP 5, 6, 7; CWP; DLB 323; FW
Alexander, Rae Pace
See Alexander, Raymond Pace
Alexander, Raymond Pace 1898-1974 .. **SSC 62**
See also CA 97-100; SATA 22; SSFS 4
Alexander, Samuel 1859-1938 .... **TCLC 77**
Alexander of Hales c. 1185-1245 ...... **CMLC 128**
Alexeiev, Konstantin
See Stanislavsky, Constantin
Alexeyev, Constantin Sergeivich
See Stanislavsky, Constantin
Alexeyev, Konstantin Sergeyevich
See Stanislavsky, Constantin
Alexie, Sherman 1966- ... **CLC 96, 154, 312; NNAL; PC 53; SSC 107**
See also AAYA 28, 85; BYA 15; CA 138; CANR 65, 95, 133, 174; CN 7; DA3; DAM MULT; DLB 175, 206, 278; LATS 1:2; MTCW 2; MTFW 2005; NFS 17, 31, 38; PFS 39; SSFS 18

Alexie, Sherman Joseph, Jr.
See Alexie, Sherman
al-Farabi 870(?)-950 .... **CMLC 58**
See also DLB 115
Alfau, Felipe 1902-1999 .... **CLC 66**
See also CA 137
Alfieri, Vittorio 1749-1803 .... **NCLC 101**
See also EW 4; RGWL 2, 3; WLIT 7
Alfonso X 1221-1284 .... **CMLC 78**
Alfred, Jean Gaston
See Ponge, Francis
Alger, Horatio, Jr. 1832-1899 ... **NCLC 8, 83**
See also CLR 87, 170; DLB 42; LAIT 2; RGAL 4; SATA 16; TUS
Al-Ghazali, Muhammad ibn Muhammad 1058-1111 .... **CMLC 50**
See also DLB 115
Algren, Nelson 1909-1981 .... **CLC 4, 10, 33; SSC 33**
See also AMWS 9; BPFB 1; CA 13-16R; 103; CANR 20, 61; CDALB 1941-1968; CN 1, 2; DLB 9; DLBY 1981, 1982, 2000; EWL 3; MAL 5; MTCW 1, 2; MTFW 2005; RGAL 4; RGSF 2
al-Hamadhani 967-1007 .... **CMLC 93**
See also WLIT 6
al-Hariri, al-Qasim ibn 'Ali Abu Muhammad al-Basri 1054-1122 .... **CMLC 63**
See also RGWL 3
Ali, Ahmed 1908-1998 .... **CLC 69**
See also CA 25-28R; CANR 15, 34; CN 1, 2, 3, 4, 5; DLB 323; EWL 3
Ali, Monica 1967- .... **CLC 304**
See also AAYA 67; BRWS 13; CA 219; CANR 158, 205; DLB 323
Ali, Tariq 1943- .... **CLC 173**
See also CA 25-28R; CANR 10, 99, 161, 196
Alighieri, Dante
See Dante
al-Kindi, Abu Yusuf Ya'qub ibn Ishaq c. 801-c. 873 .... **CMLC 80**
Allan, John B.
See Westlake, Donald E.
Allan, Sidney
See Hartmann, Sadakichi
Allan, Sydney
See Hartmann, Sadakichi
Allard, Janet CLC 59
Allen, Betsy
See Harrison, Elizabeth (Allen) Cavanna
Allen, Edward 1948- .... **CLC 59**
Allen, Fred 1894-1956 .... **TCLC 87**
Allen, Paula Gunn 1939-2008 . **CLC 84, 202, 280; NNAL**
See also AMWS 4; CA 112; 143; 272; CANR 63, 130; CWP; DA3; DAM MULT; DLB 175; FW; MTCW 2; MTFW 2005; RGAL 4; TCWW 2
Allen, Roland
See Ayckbourn, Alan
Allen, Sarah A.
See Hopkins, Pauline Elizabeth
Allen, Sidney H.
See Hartmann, Sadakichi
Allen, Woody 1935- ... **CLC 16, 52, 195, 288**
See also AAYA 10, 51; AMWS 15; CA 33-36R; CANR 27, 38, 63, 128, 172; DAM POP; DLB 44; MTCW 1; SSFS 21
Allende, Isabel 1942- .. **CLC 39, 57, 97, 170, 264; HLC 1; SSC 65; WLCS**
See also AAYA 18, 70; CA 125; 130; CANR 51, 74, 129, 165, 208; CDWLB 3; CLR 99, 171; CWW 2; DA3; DAM MULT, NOV; DLB 145; DNFS 1; EWL 3; FL 1:5; FW; HW 1, 2; INT CA-130; LAIT 5;

LAWS 1; LMFS 2; MTCW 1, 2; MTFW 2005; NCFS 1; NFS 6, 18, 29; RGSF 2; RGWL 3; SATA 163; SSFS 11, 16; WLIT 1
Alleyn, Ellen
See Rossetti, Christina
Alleyne, Carla D. CLC 65
Allingham, Margery (Louise) 1904-1966 ..... **CLC 19**
See also CA 5-8R; 25-28R; CANR 4, 58; CMW 4; DLB 77; MSW; MTCW 1, 2
Allingham, William 1824-1889 ..... **NCLC 25**
See also DLB 35; RGEL 2
Allison, Dorothy E. 1949- . **CLC 78, 153, 290**
See also AAYA 53; CA 140; CANR 66, 107; CN 7; CSW; DA3; DLB 350; FW; MTCW 2; MTFW 2005; NFS 11; RGAL 4
Alloula, Malek CLC 65
Allston, Washington 1779-1843 ...... **NCLC 2**
See also DLB 1, 235
Almedingen, E. M.
See Almedingen, Martha Edith von
Almedingen, Martha Edith von 1898-1971 . **CLC 12**
See also CA 1-4R; CANR 1; SATA 3
Almodovar, Pedro 1949(?)- .. **CLC 114, 229; HLCS 1**
See also CA 133; CANR 72, 151; HW 2
Almqvist, Carl Jonas Love 1793-1866 .... **NCLC 42**
al-Mutanabbi, Ahmad ibn al-Husayn Abu al-Tayyib al-Jufi al-Kindi 915-965 .... **CMLC 66**
See also RGWL 3; WLIT 6
Alonso, Damaso 1898-1990 . **CLC 14; TCLC 245**
See also CA 110; 131; 130; CANR 72; DLB 108; EWL 3; HW 1, 2
Alov
See Gogol, Nikolai
al'Sadaawi, Nawal
See El Saadawi, Nawal
al-Shaykh, Hanan
See Shaykh, Hanan al-
Al Siddik
See Rolfe, Frederick (William Serafino Austin Lewis Mary)
Alta 1942- .... **CLC 19**
See also CA 57-60
Alter, Robert B. 1935- .... **CLC 34**
See also CA 49-52; CANR 1, 47, 100, 160, 201
Alter, Robert Bernard
See Alter, Robert B.
Alther, Lisa 1944- .... **CLC 7, 41**
See also BPFB 1; CA 65-68; CAAS 30; CANR 12, 30, 51, 180; CN 4, 5, 6, 7; CSW; GLL 2; MTCW 1
Althusser, L.
See Althusser, Louis
Althusser, Louis 1918-1990 .... **CLC 106**
See also CA 131; 132; CANR 102; DLB 242
Altman, Robert 1925-2006 ..... **CLC 16, 116, 242**
See also CA 73-76; 254; CANR 43
Alurista
See Urista, Alberto
Alvarez, A. 1929- .... **CLC 5, 13**
See also CA 1-4R; CANR 3, 33, 63, 101, 134; CN 3, 4, 5, 6; CP 1, 2, 3, 4, 5, 6, 7; DLB 14, 40; MTFW 2005
Alvarez, Alejandro Rodriguez 1903-1965 .... **CLC 49; DC 32; TCLC 199**
See also CA 131; 93-96; EWL 3; HW 1

Alvarez, Julia 1950- . **CLC 93, 274; HLCS 1**
See also AAYA 25, 85; AMWS 7; CA 147; CANR 69, 101, 133, 166; DA3; DLB 282; LATS 1:2; LLW; MTCW 2; MTFW 2005; NFS 5, 9; PFS 39; SATA 129; SSFS 27, 31; WLIT 1

Alvaro, Corrado 1896-1956 .... **TCLC 60**
See also CA 163; DLB 264; EWL 3

Amado, Jorge 1912-2001 .. **CLC 13, 40, 106, 232; HLC 1**
See also CA 77-80; 201; CANR 35, 74, 135; CWW 2; DAM MULT, NOV; DLB 113, 307; EWL 3; HW 2; LAW; LAWS 1; MTCW 1, 2; MTFW 2005; RGWL 2, 3; TWA; WLIT 1

Ambler, Eric 1909-1998 .... **CLC 4, 6, 9**
See also BRWS 4; CA 9-12R; 171; CANR 7, 38, 74; CMW 4; CN 1, 2, 3, 4, 5, 6; DLB 77; MSW; MTCW 1, 2; TEA

Ambrose c. 339-c. 397 .... **CMLC 103**

Ambrose, Stephen E. 1936-2002 ... **CLC 145**
See also AAYA 44; CA 1-4R; 209; CANR 3, 43, 57, 83, 105; MTFW 2005; NCFS 2; SATA 40, 138

Amichai, Yehuda 1924-2000 . **CLC 9, 22, 57, 116; PC 38**
See also CA 85-88; 189; CANR 46, 60, 99, 132; CWW 2; EWL 3; MTCW 1, 2; MTFW 2005; PFS 24, 39; RGHL; WLIT 6

Amichai, Yehudah
See Amichai, Yehuda

Amiel, Henri Frederic 1821-1881 .. **NCLC 4**
See also DLB 217

Amis, Kingsley 1922-1995 .... **CLC 1, 2, 3, 5, 8, 13, 40, 44, 129**
See also AAYA 77; AITN 2; BPFB 1; BRWS 2; CA 9-12R; 150; CANR 8, 28, 54; CDBLB 1945-1960; CN 1, 2, 3, 4, 5, 6; CP 1, 2, 3, 4; DA; DA3; DAB; DAC; DAM MST, NOV; DLB 15, 27, 100, 139, 326, 352; DLBY 1996; EWL 3; HGG; INT CANR-8; MTCW 1, 2; MTFW 2005; RGEL 2; RGSF 2; SFW 4

Amis, Martin 1949- .. **CLC 4, 9, 38, 62, 101, 213; SSC 112**
See also BEST 90:3; BRWS 4; CA 65-68; CANR 8, 27, 54, 73, 95, 132, 166, 208; CN 5, 6, 7; DA3; DLB 14, 194; EWL 3; INT CANR-27; MTCW 2; MTFW 2005

Amis, Martin Louis
See Amis, Martin

Ammianus Marcellinus c. 330-c. 395 .... **CMLC 60**
See also AW 2; DLB 211

Ammons, A.R. 1926-2001 . **CLC 2, 3, 5, 8, 9, 25, 57, 108; PC 16**
See also AITN 1; AMWS 7; CA 9-12R; 193; CANR 6, 36, 51, 73, 107, 156; CP 1, 2, 3, 4, 5, 6, 7; CSW; DAM POET; DLB 5, 165, 342; EWL 3; MAL 5; MTCW 1, 2; PFS 19; RGAL 4; TCLE 1:1

Ammons, Archie Randolph
See Ammons, A.R.

Amo, Tauraatua i
See Adams, Henry

Amory, Thomas 1691(?)-1788 .... **LC 48**
See also DLB 39

Anand, Mulk Raj 1905-2004 .... **CLC 23, 93, 237**
See also CA 65-68; 231; CANR 32, 64; CN 1, 2, 3, 4, 5, 6, 7; DAM NOV; DLB 323; EWL 3; MTCW 1, 2; MTFW 2005; RGSF 2

Anatol
See Schnitzler, Arthur

Anaximander c. 611B.C.-c. 546B.C. . **CMLC 22**

Anaya, Rudolfo 1937- ..... **CLC 23, 148, 255; HLC 1**
See also AAYA 20; BYA 13; CA 45-48; CAAS 4; CANR 1, 32, 51, 124, 169; CLR 129; CN 4, 5, 6, 7; DAM MULT, NOV; DLB 82, 206, 278; HW 1; LAIT 4; LLW; MAL 5; MTCW 1, 2; MTFW 2005; NFS 12; RGAL 4; RGSF 2; TCWW 2; WLIT 1

Anaya, Rudolfo A.
See Anaya, Rudolfo

Anaya, Rudolpho Alfonso
See Anaya, Rudolfo

Andersen, Hans Christian 1805-1875 .... **NCLC 7, 79, 214; SSC 6, 56; WLC 1**
See also AAYA 57; CLR 6, 113; DA; DA3; DAB; DAC; DAM MST, POP; EW 6; MAICYA 1, 2; RGSF 2; RGWL 2, 3; SATA 100; TWA; WCH; YABC 1

Anderson, C. Farley
See Mencken, H. L.; Nathan, George Jean

Anderson, Jessica (Margaret) Queale 1916- .... **CLC 37**
See also CA 9-12R; CANR 4, 62; CN 4, 5, 6, 7; DLB 325

Anderson, Jon (Victor) 1940- .... **CLC 9**
See also CA 25-28R; CANR 20; CP 1, 3, 4, 5; DAM POET

Anderson, Lindsay (Gordon) 1923-1994 ..... **CLC 20**
See also CA 125; 128; 146; CANR 77

Anderson, Maxwell 1888-1959 .... **DC 43; TCLC 2, 144**
See also CA 105; 152; DAM DRAM; DFS 16, 20; DLB 7, 228; MAL 5; MTCW 2; MTFW 2005; RGAL 4

Anderson, Poul 1926-2001 .... **CLC 15**
See also AAYA 5, 34; BPFB 1; BYA 6, 8, 9; CA 1-4R, 181; 199; CAAE 181; CAAS 2; CANR 2, 15, 34, 64, 110; CLR 58; DLB 8; FANT; INT CANR-15; MTCW 1, 2; MTFW 2005; SATA 90; SATA-Brief 39; SATA-Essay 106; SCFW 1, 2; SFW 4; SUFW 1, 2

Anderson, R. W.
See Anderson, Robert

Anderson, Robert 1917-2009 .... **CLC 23**
See also AITN 1; CA 21-24R; 283; CANR 32; CD 6; DAM DRAM; DLB 7; LAIT 5

Anderson, Robert W.
See Anderson, Robert

Anderson, Robert Woodruff
See Anderson, Robert

Anderson, Roberta Joan
See Mitchell, Joni

Anderson, Sherwood 1876-1941 . **SSC 1, 46, 91, 142; TCLC 1, 10, 24, 123; WLC 1**
See also AAYA 30; AMW; AMWC 2; BPFB 1; CA 104; 121; CANR 61; CDALB 1917-1929; DA; DA3; DAB; DAC; DAM MST, NOV; DLB 4, 9, 86; DLBD 1; EWL 3; EXPS; GLL 2; MAL 5; MTCW 1, 2; MTFW 2005; NFS 4; RGAL 4; RGSF 2; SSFS 4, 10, 11; TUS

Anderson, Wes 1969- .... **CLC 227**
See also CA 214

Andier, Pierre
See Desnos, Robert

Andouard
See Giraudoux, Jean

Andrade, Carlos Drummond de
See Drummond de Andrade, Carlos

Andrade, Mario de
See de Andrade, Mario

Andreae, Johann V(alentin) 1586-1654 .. **LC 32**
See also DLB 164

Andreas Capellanus fl. c. 1185- .. **CMLC 45, 135**
See also DLB 208

Andreas-Salome, Lou 1861-1937 .. **TCLC 56**
See also CA 178; DLB 66

Andreev, Leonid
See Andreyev, Leonid

Andress, Lesley
See Sanders, Lawrence

Andrew, Joseph Maree
See Occomy, Marita (Odette) Bonner

Andrewes, Lancelot 1555-1626 .... **LC 5**
See also DLB 151, 172

Andrews, Cicily Fairfield
See West, Rebecca

Andrews, Elton V.
See Pohl, Frederik

Andrews, Peter
See Soderbergh, Steven

Andrews, Raymond 1934-1991 ...... **BLC 2:1**
See also BW 2; CA 81-84; 136; CANR 15, 42

Andreyev, Leonid 1871-1919 .. **TCLC 3, 221**
See also CA 104; 185; DLB 295; EWL 3

Andreyev, Leonid Nikolaevich
See Andreyev, Leonid

Andrezel, Pierre
See Blixen, Karen

Andric, Ivo 1892-1975 .... **CLC 8; SSC 36; TCLC 135**
See also CA 81-84; 57-60; CANR 43, 60; CDWLB 4; DLB 147, 329; EW 11; EWL 3; MTCW 1; RGSF 2; RGWL 2, 3

Androvar
See Prado (Calvo), Pedro

Angela of Foligno 1248(?)-1309 ... **CMLC 76**

Angelique, Pierre
See Bataille, Georges

Angell, Judie
See Angell, Judie

Angell, Judie 1937- .... **CLC 30**
See also AAYA 11, 71; BYA 6; CA 77-80; CANR 49; CLR 33; JRDA; SATA 22, 78; WYA; YAW

Angell, Roger 1920- .... **CLC 26**
See also CA 57-60; CANR 13, 44, 70, 144; DLB 171, 185

Angelou, Maya 1928- ..... **BLC 1:1; CLC 12, 35, 64, 77, 155; PC 32; WLCS**
See also AAYA 7, 20; AMWS 4; BPFB 1; BW 2, 3; BYA 2; CA 65-68; CANR 19, 42, 65, 111, 133, 204; CDALBS; CLR 53; CP 4, 5, 6, 7; CPW; CSW; CWP; DA; DA3; DAB; DAC; DAM MST, MULT, POET, POP; DLB 38; EWL 3; EXPN; EXPP; FL 1:5; LAIT 4; MAICYA 2; MAICYAS 1; MAL 5; MBL; MTCW 1, 2; MTFW 2005; NCFS 2; NFS 2; PFS 2, 3, 33, 38; RGAL 4; SATA 49, 136; TCLE 1:1; WYA; YAW

Angouleme, Marguerite d'
See de Navarre, Marguerite

Anna Comnena 1083-1153 .... **CMLC 25**

Annensky, Innokentii Fedorovich
See Annensky, Innokenty (Fyodorovich)

Annensky, Innokenty (Fyodorovich) 1856-1909 .... **TCLC 14**
See also CA 110; 155; DLB 295; EWL 3

Annunzio, Gabriele d'
See D'Annunzio, Gabriele

Anodos
See Coleridge, Mary E(lizabeth)

Anon, Charles Robert
See Pessoa, Fernando

Anouilh, Jean 1910-1987 .... **CLC 1, 3, 8, 13, 40, 50; DC 8, 21; TCLC 195**
See also AAYA 67; CA 17-20R; 123; CANR 32; DAM DRAM; DFS 9, 10, 19; DLB 321; EW 13; EWL 3; GFL 1789 to the Present; MTCW 1, 2; MTFW 2005; RGWL 2, 3; TWA

Anouilh, Jean Marie Lucien Pierre
See Anouilh, Jean

Ansa, Tina McElroy 1949- .... **BLC 2:1**
See also BW 2; CA 142; CANR 143; CSW

Anselm of Canterbury 1033(?)-1109 . **CMLC 67**
See also DLB 115

Anthony, Florence
See Ai

Anthony, John
See Ciardi, John (Anthony)

Anthony, Peter
See Shaffer, Anthony; Shaffer, Peter

Anthony, Piers 1934- .... **CLC 35**
See also AAYA 11, 48; BYA 7; CA 200; CAAE 200; CANR 28, 56, 73, 102, 133, 202; CLR 118; CPW; DAM POP; DLB 8; FANT; MAICYA 2; MAICYAS 1; MTCW 1, 2; MTFW 2005; SAAS 22; SATA 84, 129; SATA-Essay 129; SFW 4; SUFW 1, 2; YAW

Anthony, Susan B(rownell) 1820-1906 ....
TCLC 84
See also CA 211; FW

Antin, David 1932- .... **PC 124**
See also CA 73-76; CP 1, 3, 4, 5, 6, 7; DLB 169

Antin, Mary 1881-1949 .... **TCLC 247**
See also AMWS 20; CA 118; 181; DLB 221; DLBY 1984

Antiphon c. 480B.C.-c. 411B.C. ... **CMLC 55**

Antoine, Marc
See Proust, Marcel

Antoninus, Brother
See Everson, William

Antonioni, Michelangelo 1912-2007 ..... **CLC 20, 144, 259**
See also CA 73-76; 262; CANR 45, 77

Antschel, Paul
See Celan, Paul

Anwar, Chairil 1922-1949 .... **TCLC 22**
See also CA 121; 219; EWL 3; RGWL 3

Anyidoho, Kofi 1947- .... **BLC 2:1**
See also BW 3; CA 178; CP 5, 6, 7; DLB 157; EWL 3

Anzaldua, Gloria (Evanjelina) 1942-2004 ...
CLC 200; HLCS 1
See also CA 175; 227; CSW; CWP; DLB 122; FW; LLW; RGAL 4; SATA-Obit 154

Apess, William 1798-1839(?) .... **NCLC 73; NNAL**
See also DAM MULT; DLB 175, 243

Apollinaire, Guillaume 1880-1918 ...... **PC 7; TCLC 3, 8, 51**
See also CA 104; 152; DAM POET; DLB 258, 321; EW 9; EWL 3; GFL 1789 to the Present; MTCW 2; PFS 24; RGWL 2, 3; TWA; WP

Apollonius of Rhodes
See Apollonius Rhodius

Apollonius Rhodius c. 300B.C.-c. 220B.C. ...
CMLC 28
See also AW 1; DLB 176; RGWL 2, 3

Appelfeld, Aharon 1932- .. **CLC 23, 47, 317; SSC 42**
See also CA 112; 133; CANR 86, 160, 207; CWW 2; DLB 299; EWL 3; RGHL; RGSF 2; WLIT 6

Appelfeld, Aron
See Appelfeld, Aharon

Apple, Max 1941- .... **CLC 9, 33; SSC 50**
See also AMWS 17; CA 81-84; CANR 19, 54, 214; DLB 130

Apple, Max Isaac
See Apple, Max

Appleman, Philip (Dean) 1926- .... **CLC 51**
See also CA 13-16R; CAAS 18; CANR 6, 29, 56

Appleton, Lawrence
See Lovecraft, H. P.

Apteryx
See Eliot, T. S.

Apuleius, (Lucius Madaurensis) c. 125-c. 164 .... **CMLC 1, 84**
See also AW 2; CDWLB 1; DLB 211; RGWL 2, 3; SUFW; WLIT 8

Aquin, Hubert 1929-1977 .... **CLC 15**
See also CA 105; DLB 53; EWL 3

Aquinas, Thomas 1224(?)-1274 .. **CMLC 33, 137**
See also DLB 115; EW 1; TWA

Aragon, Louis 1897-1982 . **CLC 3, 22; TCLC 123**
See also CA 69-72; 108; CANR 28, 71; DAM NOV, POET; DLB 72, 258; EW 11; EWL 3; GFL 1789 to the Present; GLL 2; LMFS 2; MTCW 1, 2; RGWL 2, 3

Arany, Janos 1817-1882 .... **NCLC 34**

Aranyos, Kakay 1847-1910 ....
See Mikszath, Kalman

Aratus of Soli c. 315B.C.-c. 240B.C. . **CMLC 64, 114**
See also DLB 176

Arbuthnot, John 1667-1735 .... **LC 1**
See also BRWS 16; DLB 101

Archer, Herbert Winslow
See Mencken, H. L.

Archer, Jeffrey 1940- .... **CLC 28**
See also AAYA 16; BEST 89:3; BPFB 1; CA 77-80; CANR 22, 52, 95, 136, 209; CPW; DA3; DAM POP; INT CANR-22; MTFW 2005

Archer, Jeffrey Howard
See Archer, Jeffrey

Archer, Jules 1915- .... **CLC 12**
See also CA 9-12R; CANR 6, 69; SAAS 5; SATA 4, 85

Archer, Lee
See Ellison, Harlan

Archilochus c. 7th cent. B.C.- ...... **CMLC 44**
See also DLB 176

Ard, William
See Jakes, John

Arden, John 1930- .... **CLC 6, 13, 15**
See also BRWS 2; CA 13-16R; CAAS 4; CANR 31, 65, 67, 124; CBD; CD 5, 6; DAM DRAM; DFS 9; DLB 13, 245; EWL 3; MTCW 1

Arenas, Reinaldo 1943-1990 . **CLC 41; HLC 1; TCLC 191**
See also CA 124; 128; 133; CANR 73, 106; DAM MULT; DLB 145; EWL 3; GLL 2; HW 1; LAW; LAWS 1; MTCW 2; MTFW 2005; RGSF 2; RGWL 3; WLIT 1

Arendt, Hannah 1906-1975 ...... **CLC 66, 98; TCLC 193**
See also CA 17-20R; 61-64; CANR 26, 60, 172; DLB 242; MTCW 1, 2

Aretino, Pietro 1492-1556 .... **LC 12, 165**
See also RGWL 2, 3

Arghezi, Tudor
See Theodorescu, Ion N.

Arguedas, Jose Maria 1911-1969 ... **CLC 10, 18; HLCS 1; TCLC 147**
See also CA 89-92; CANR 73; DLB 113; EWL 3; HW 1; LAW; RGWL 2, 3; WLIT 1

Argueta, Manlio 1936- .... **CLC 31**
See also CA 131; CANR 73; CWW 2; DLB 145; EWL 3; HW 1; RGWL 3

Arias, Ron 1941- .... **HLC 1**
See also CA 131; CANR 81, 136; DAM MULT; DLB 82; HW 1, 2; MTCW 2; MTFW 2005

Ariosto, Lodovico
See Ariosto, Ludovico

Ariosto, Ludovico 1474-1533 . **LC 6, 87; PC 42**
See also EW 2; RGWL 2, 3; WLIT 7

Aristides
See Epstein, Joseph

Aristides Quintilianus fl. c. 100-fl. c. 400 ....
CMLC 122

Aristophanes 450B.C.-385B.C. ...... **CMLC 4, 51, 138; DC 2; WLCS**
See also AW 1; CDWLB 1; DA; DA3; DAB; DAC; DAM DRAM, MST; DFS 10; DLB 176; LMFS 1; RGWL 2, 3; TWA; WLIT 8

Aristotle 384B.C.-322B.C. ... **CMLC 31, 123; WLCS**
See also AW 1; CDWLB 1; DA; DA3; DAB; DAC; DAM MST; DLB 176; RGWL 2, 3; TWA; WLIT 8

Arlt, Roberto 1900-1942 . **HLC 1; TCLC 29, 255**
See also CA 123; 131; CANR 67; DAM MULT; DLB 305; EWL 3; HW 1, 2; IDTP; LAW

Arlt, Roberto Godofredo Christophersen
See Arlt, Roberto

Armah, Ayi Kwei 1939- . **BLC 1:1, 2:1; CLC 5, 33, 136**
See also AFW; BRWS 10; BW 1; CA 61-64; CANR 21, 64; CDWLB 3; CN 1, 2, 3, 4, 5, 6, 7; DAM MULT, POET; DLB 117; EWL 3; MTCW 1; WLIT 2

Armatrading, Joan 1950- .... **CLC 17**
See also CA 114; 186

Armin, Robert 1568(?)-1615(?) .... **LC 120**

Armitage, Frank
See Carpenter, John

Armstrong, Jeannette (C.) 1948- .... **NNAL**
See also CA 149; CCA 1; CN 6, 7; DAC; DLB 334; SATA 102

Armytage, R.
See Watson, Rosamund Marriott

Arnauld, Antoine 1612-1694 .... **LC 169**
See also DLB 268

Arnette, Robert
See Silverberg, Robert

Arnim, Achim von (Ludwig Joachim von Arnim) 1781-1831 . **NCLC 5, 159; SSC 29**
See also DLB 90

Arnim, Bettina von 1785-1859 .... **NCLC 38, 123**
See also DLB 90; RGWL 2, 3

Arnold, Matthew 1822-1888 .... **NCLC 6, 29, 89, 126, 218; PC 5, 94; WLC 1**
See also BRW 5; CDBLB 1832-1890; DA; DAB; DAC; DAM MST, POET; DLB 32, 57; EXPP; PAB; PFS 2; TEA; WP

Arnold, Thomas 1795-1842 .... **NCLC 18**
See also DLB 55

Arnow, Harriette (Louisa) Simpson 1908-1986 .... **CLC 2, 7, 18; TCLC 196**
See also BPFB 1; CA 9-12R; 118; CANR 14; CN 2, 3, 4; DLB 6; FW; MTCW 1, 2; RHW; SATA 42; SATA-Obit 47

Arouet, Francois-Marie
See Voltaire

Arp, Hans
See Arp, Jean

Arp, Jean 1887-1966 ...... **CLC 5; TCLC 115**
See also CA 81-84; 25-28R; CANR 42, 77; EW 10

Arrabal
See Arrabal, Fernando

Arrabal, Fernando 1932- . **CLC 2, 9, 18, 58; DC 35**
See also CA 9-12R; CANR 15; CWW 2; DLB 321; EWL 3; LMFS 2

Arrabal Teran, Fernando
See Arrabal, Fernando

Arreola, Juan Jose 1918-2001 ...... **CLC 147; HLC 1; SSC 38**
See also CA 113; 131; 200; CANR 81; CWW 2; DAM MULT; DLB 113; DNFS 2; EWL 3; HW 1, 2; LAW; RGSF 2

Arrian c. 89(?)-c. 155(?) .... **CMLC 43**
See also DLB 176

Arrick, Fran
See Angell, Judie

Arrley, Richmond
See Delany, Samuel R., Jr.

Artaud, Antonin 1896-1948 .. **DC 14; TCLC 3, 36**
See also CA 104; 149; DA3; DAM DRAM; DFS 22; DLB 258, 321; EW 11; EWL 3; GFL 1789 to the Present; MTCW 2; MTFW 2005; RGWL 2, 3

Artaud, Antonin Marie Joseph
See Artaud, Antonin

Artemidorus fl. 2nd cent. - .... **CMLC 129**

Arthur, Ruth M(abel) 1905-1979 .... **CLC 12**
See also CA 9-12R; 85-88; CANR 4; CWRI 5; SATA 7, 26

Artsybashev, Mikhail (Petrovich)
1878-1927 .... **TCLC 31**
See also CA 170; DLB 295

Arundel, Honor (Morfydd) 1919-1973 . **CLC 17**
See also CA 21-22; 41-44R; CAP 2; CLR 35; CWRI 5; SATA 4; SATA-Obit 24

Arzner, Dorothy 1900-1979 .... **CLC 98**

Asch, Sholem 1880-1957 .... **TCLC 3, 251**
See also CA 105; DLB 333; EWL 3; GLL 2; RGHL

Ascham, Roger 1516(?)-1568 .... **LC 101**
See also DLB 236

Ash, Shalom
See Asch, Sholem

Ashbery, John 1927- .. **CLC 2, 3, 4, 6, 9, 13, 15, 25, 41, 77, 125, 221; PC 26**
See also AMWS 3; CA 5-8R; CANR 9, 37, 66, 102, 132, 170, 230; CP 1, 2, 3, 4, 5, 6, 7; DA3; DAM POET; DLB 5, 165; DLBY 1981; EWL 3; GLL 1; INT CANR-9; MAL 5; MTCW 1, 2; MTFW 2005; PAB; PFS 11, 28; RGAL 4; TCLE 1:1; WP

Ashbery, John Lawrence
See Ashbery, John

Ashbridge, Elizabeth 1713-1755 ...... **LC 147**
See also DLB 200

Ashdown, Clifford
See Freeman, R(ichard) Austin

Ashe, Gordon
See Creasey, John

Ashton-Warner, Sylvia (Constance)
1908-1984 .... **CLC 19**
See also CA 69-72; 112; CANR 29; CN 1, 2, 3; MTCW 1, 2

Asimov, Isaac 1920-1992 .... **CLC 1, 3, 9, 19, 26, 76, 92; SSC 148**
See also AAYA 13; BEST 90:2; BPFB 1; BYA 4, 6, 7, 9; CA 1-4R; 137; CANR 2, 19, 36, 60, 125; CLR 12, 79; CMW 4; CN 1, 2, 3, 4, 5; CPW; DA3; DAM POP; DLB 8; DLBY 1992; INT CANR-19; JRDA; LAIT 5; LMFS 2; MAICYA 1, 2; MAL 5; MTCW 1, 2; MTFW 2005; NFS 29; RGAL 4; SATA 1, 26, 74; SCFW 1, 2; SFW 4; SSFS 17, 33; TUS; YAW

Askew, Anne 1521(?)-1546 .... **LC 81**
See also DLB 136

Asser -c. 909 .... **CMLC 117**

Assis, Joaquim Maria Machado de
See Machado de Assis, Joaquim Maria

Astell, Mary 1666-1731 .... **LC 68, 183**
See also DLB 252, 336; FW

Astley, Thea (Beatrice May) 1925-2004 .... **CLC 41**
See also CA 65-68; 229; CANR 11, 43, 78; CN 1, 2, 3, 4, 5, 6, 7; DLB 289; EWL 3

Astley, William 1855-1911 .... **TCLC 45**
See also DLB 230; RGEL 2

Aston, James
See White, T(erence) H(anbury)

Asturias, Miguel Angel 1899-1974 ... **CLC 3, 8, 13; HLC 1; TCLC 184**
See also CA 25-28; 49-52; CANR 32; CAP 2; CDWLB 3; DA3; DAM MULT, NOV; DLB 113, 290, 329; EWL 3; HW 1; LAW; LMFS 2; MTCW 1, 2; RGWL 2, 3; WLIT 1

Atares, Carlos Saura
See Saura (Atares), Carlos

Athanasius c. 295-c. 373 .... **CMLC 48**

Atheling, William
See Pound, Ezra

Atheling, William, Jr.
See Blish, James

Atherton, Gertrude (Franklin Horn)
1857-1948 .... **TCLC 2**
See also CA 104; 155; DLB 9, 78, 186; HGG; RGAL 4; SUFW 1; TCWW 1, 2

Atherton, Lucius
See Masters, Edgar Lee

Atkins, Jack
See Harris, Mark

Atkinson, Kate 1951- .... **CLC 99**
See also CA 166; CANR 101, 153, 198, 231; DLB 267

Attaway, William (Alexander) 1911-1986 .... **BLC 1:1; CLC 92**
See also BW 2, 3; CA 143; CANR 82; DAM MULT; DLB 76; MAL 5

Atticus
See Fleming, Ian; Wilson, (Thomas) Woodrow

Atwood, Margaret 1939- ...... **CLC 2, 3, 4, 8, 13, 15, 25, 44, 84, 135, 232, 239, 246; PC 8, 123; SSC 2, 46, 142; WLC 1**
See also AAYA 12, 47; AMWS 13; BEST 89:2; BPFB 1; CA 49-52; CANR 3, 24, 33, 59, 95, 133; CN 2, 3, 4, 5, 6, 7; CP 1, 2, 3, 4, 5, 6, 7; CPW; CWP; DA; DA3; DAB; DAC; DAM MST, NOV, POET; DLB 53, 251, 326; EWL 3; EXPN; FL 1:5; FW; GL 2; INT CANR-24; LAIT 5; MTCW 1, 2; MTFW 2005; NFS 4, 12, 13, 14, 19, 39; PFS 7, 37; RGSF 2; SATA 50, 170; SSFS 3, 13; TCLE 1:1; TWA; WWE 1; YAW

Atwood, Margaret Eleanor
See Atwood, Margaret

Aubigny, Pierre d'
See Mencken, H. L.

Aubin, Penelope 1685-1731(?) .... **LC 9**
See also DLB 39

Auchincloss, Louis 1917-2010 .. **CLC 4, 6, 9, 18, 45, 318; SSC 22**
See also AMWS 4; CA 1-4R; CANR 6, 29, 55, 87, 130, 168, 202; CN 1, 2, 3, 4, 5, 6, 7; DAM NOV; DLB 2, 244; DLBY 1980; EWL 3; INT CANR-29; MAL 5; MTCW 1; RGAL 4

Auchincloss, Louis Stanton
See Auchincloss, Louis

Auden, W. H. 1907-1973 .. **CLC 1, 2, 3, 4, 6, 9, 11, 14, 43, 123; PC 1, 92; TCLC 223; WLC 1**
See also AAYA 18; AMWS 2; BRW 7; BRWR 1; CA 9-12R; 45-48; CANR 5, 61, 105; CDBLB 1914-1945; CP 1, 2; DA;

DA3; DAB; DAC; DAM DRAM, MST, POET; DLB 10, 20; EWL 3; EXPP; MAL 5; MTCW 1, 2; MTFW 2005; PAB; PFS 1, 3, 4, 10, 27; TUS; WP

Auden, Wystan Hugh
See Auden, W. H.

Audiberti, Jacques 1899-1965 .... **CLC 38**
See also CA 252; 25-28R; DAM DRAM; DLB 321; EWL 3

Audubon, John James 1785-1851 . **NCLC 47**
See also AAYA 76; AMWS 16; ANW; DLB 248

Auel, Jean
See Auel, Jean M.

Auel, Jean M. 1936- .... **CLC 31, 107**
See also AAYA 7, 51; BEST 90:4; BPFB 1; CA 103; CANR 21, 64, 115, 233; CPW; DA3; DAM POP; INT CANR-21; NFS 11; RHW; SATA 91

Auel, Jean Marie
See Auel, Jean M.

Auerbach, Berthold 1812-1882 ... **NCLC 171**
See also DLB 133

Auerbach, Erich 1892-1957 .... **TCLC 43**
See also CA 118; 155; EWL 3

Augier, Emile 1820-1889 .... **NCLC 31**
See also DLB 192; GFL 1789 to the Present

August, John
See De Voto, Bernard (Augustine)

Augustine, St. 354-430 . **CMLC 6, 95; WLCS**
See also DA; DA3; DAB; DAC; DAM MST; DLB 115; EW 1; RGWL 2, 3; WLIT 8

Aunt Belinda
See Braddon, Mary Elizabeth

Aunt Weedy
See Alcott, Louisa May

Aurelius
See Bourne, Randolph S(illiman)

Aurelius, Marcus 121-180 .... **CMLC 45**
See also AW 2; RGWL 2, 3

Aurobindo, Sri
See Ghose, Aurabinda

Aurobindo Ghose
See Ghose, Aurabinda

Ausonius, Decimus Magnus c. 310-c. 394 ... **CMLC 88**
See also RGWL 2, 3

Austen, Jane 1775-1817 ..... **NCLC 1, 13, 19, 33, 51, 81, 95, 119, 150, 207, 210, 222, 242; WLC 1**
See also AAYA 19; BRW 4; BRWC 1; BRWR 2; BYA 3; CDBLB 1789-1832; DA; DA3; DAB; DAC; DAM MST, NOV; DLB 116, 363, 365, 366; EXPN; FL 1:2; GL 2; LAIT 2; LATS 1:1; LMFS 1; NFS 1, 14, 18, 20, 21, 28, 29, 33; TEA; WLIT 3; WYAS 1

Auster, Paul 1947- .... **CLC 47, 131, 227**
See also AMWS 12; CA 69-72; CANR 23, 52, 75, 129, 165; CMW 4; CN 5, 6, 7; DA3; DLB 227; MAL 5; MTCW 2; MTFW 2005; SUFW 2; TCLE 1:1

Austin, Frank
See Faust, Frederick

Austin, Mary Hunter 1868-1934 ... **SSC 104; TCLC 25, 249**
See also ANW; CA 109; 178; DLB 9, 78, 206, 221, 275; FW; TCWW 1, 2

Averroes 1126-1198 .... **CMLC 7, 104**
See also DLB 115

Avicenna 980-1037 .... **CMLC 16, 110**
See also DLB 115

Avison, Margaret 1918-2007 ... **CLC 2, 4, 97**
See also CA 17-20R; CANR 134; CP 1, 2, 3, 4, 5, 6, 7; DAC; DAM POET; DLB 53; MTCW 1

Avison, Margaret Kirkland
See Avison, Margaret

Axton, David
See Koontz, Dean
Ayala, Francisco 1906-2009 .... **SSC 119**
See also CA 208; CWW 2; DLB 322; EWL 3; RGSF 2
Ayala, Francisco de Paula y Garcia Duarte
See Ayala, Francisco
Ayckbourn, Alan 1939- .... **CLC 5, 8, 18, 33, 74; DC 13**
See also BRWS 5; CA 21-24R; CANR 31, 59, 118; CBD; CD 5, 6; DAM DRAM; DFS 7; DLB 13, 245; EWL 3; MTCW 1, 2; MTFW 2005
Aydy, Catherine
See Tennant, Emma
Ayme, Marcel (Andre) 1902-1967 .. **CLC 11; SSC 41**
See also CA 89-92; CANR 67, 137; CLR 25; DLB 72; EW 12; EWL 3; GFL 1789 to the Present; RGSF 2; RGWL 2, 3; SATA 91
Ayrton, Michael 1921-1975 .... **CLC 7**
See also CA 5-8R; 61-64; CANR 9, 21
Aytmatov, Chingiz
See Aitmatov, Chingiz
Azorin
See Martinez Ruiz, Jose
Azuela, Mariano 1873-1952 . **HLC 1; TCLC 3, 145, 217**
See also CA 104; 131; CANR 81; DAM MULT; EWL 3; HW 1, 2; LAW; MTCW 1, 2; MTFW 2005
Ba, Mariama 1929-1981 ..... **BLC 2:1; BLCS**
See also AFW; BW 2; CA 141; CANR 87; DLB 360; DNFS 2; WLIT 2
Baastad, Babbis Friis
See Friis-Baastad, Babbis Ellinor
Bab
See Gilbert, W(illiam) S(chwenck)
Babbis, Eleanor
See Friis-Baastad, Babbis Ellinor
Babel, Isaac
See Babel, Isaak (Emmanuilovich)
Babel, Isaak (Emmanuilovich)
1894-1941(?) .. **SSC 16, 78, 161; TCLC 2, 13, 171**
See also CA 104; 155; CANR 113; DLB 272; EW 11; EWL 3; MTCW 2; MTFW 2005; RGSF 2; RGWL 2, 3; SSFS 10; TWA
Babits, Mihaly 1883-1941 .... **TCLC 14**
See also CA 114; CDWLB 4; DLB 215; EWL 3
Babur 1483-1530 .... **LC 18**
Babylas
See Ghelderode, Michel de
Baca, Jimmy Santiago 1952- ..... **HLC 1; PC 41**
See also CA 131; CANR 81, 90, 146, 220; CP 6, 7; DAM MULT; DLB 122; HW 1, 2; LLW; MAL 5; PFS 40
Baca, Jose Santiago
See Baca, Jimmy Santiago
Bacchelli, Riccardo 1891-1985 .... **CLC 19**
See also CA 29-32R; 117; DLB 264; EWL 3
Bacchylides c. 520B.C.-c. 452B.C. .... **CMLC 119**
Bach, Richard 1936- .... **CLC 14**
See also AITN 1; BEST 89:2; BPFB 1; BYA 5; CA 9-12R; CANR 18, 93, 151; CPW; DAM NOV, POP; FANT; MTCW 1; SATA 13
Bach, Richard David
See Bach, Richard
Bache, Benjamin Franklin 1769-1798 .... **LC 74**
See also DLB 43

Bachelard, Gaston 1884-1962 ..... **TCLC 128**
See also CA 97-100; 89-92; DLB 296; GFL 1789 to the Present
Bachman, Richard
See King, Stephen
Bachmann, Ingeborg 1926-1973 .... **CLC 69; TCLC 192**
See also CA 93-96; 45-48; CANR 69; DLB 85; EWL 3; RGHL; RGWL 2, 3
Bacigalupi, Paolo 1973- .... **CLC 309**
See also AAYA 86; CA 317; SATA 230
Bacon, Francis 1561-1626 .... **LC 18, 32, 131**
See also BRW 1; CDBLB Before 1660; DLB 151, 236, 252; RGEL 2; TEA
Bacon, Roger 1214(?)-1294 .. **CMLC 14, 108**
See also DLB 115
Bacovia, G.
See Bacovia, George
Bacovia, George 1881-1957 .... **TCLC 24**
See Bacovia, George
See also CA 123; 189; CDWLB 4; DLB 220; EWL 3
Badanes, Jerome 1937-1995 .... **CLC 59**
See also CA 234
Bage, Robert 1728-1801 .... **NCLC 182**
See also DLB 39; RGEL 2
Bagehot, Walter 1826-1877 .... **NCLC 10**
See also DLB 55
Bagnold, Enid 1889-1981 .... **CLC 25**
See also AAYA 75; BYA 2; CA 5-8R; 103; CANR 5, 40; CBD; CN 2; CWD; CWRI 5; DAM DRAM; DLB 13, 160, 191, 245; FW; MAICYA 1, 2; RGEL 2; SATA 1, 25
Bagritsky, Eduard
See Dzyubin, Eduard Georgievich
Bagritsky, Edvard
See Dzyubin, Eduard Georgievich
Bagrjana, Elisaveta
See Belcheva, Elisaveta Lyubomirova
Bagryana, Elisaveta
See Belcheva, Elisaveta Lyubomirova
Bailey, Paul 1937- .... **CLC 45**
See also CA 21-24R; CANR 16, 62, 124; CN 1, 2, 3, 4, 5, 6, 7; DLB 14, 271; GLL 2
Baillie, Joanna 1762-1851 ..... **NCLC 71, 151**
See also DLB 93, 344; GL 2; RGEL 2
Bainbridge, Beryl 1934-2010 ... **CLC 4, 5, 8, 10, 14, 18, 22, 62, 130, 292**
See also BRWS 6; CA 21-24R; CANR 24, 55, 75, 88, 128; CN 2, 3, 4, 5, 6, 7; DAM NOV; DLB 14, 231; EWL 3; MTCW 1, 2; MTFW 2005
Baker, Carlos (Heard) 1909-1987 ...... **TCLC 119**
See also CA 5-8R; 122; CANR 3, 63; DLB 103
Baker, Elliott 1922-2007 .... **CLC 8**
See also CA 45-48; 257; CANR 2, 63; CN 1, 2, 3, 4, 5, 6, 7
Baker, Elliott Joseph
See Baker, Elliott
Baker, Jean H.
See Russell, George William
Baker, Nicholson 1957- .... **CLC 61, 165**
See also AMWS 13; CA 135; CANR 63, 120, 138, 190; CN 6; CPW; DA3; DAM POP; DLB 227; MTFW 2005
Baker, Ray Stannard 1870-1946 .. **TCLC 47**
See also CA 118; DLB 345
Baker, Russell 1925- .... **CLC 31**
See also BEST 89:4; CA 57-60; CANR 11, 41, 59, 137; MTCW 1, 2; MTFW 2005
Baker, Russell Wayne
See Baker, Russell
Bakhtin, M.
See Bakhtin, Mikhail Mikhailovich
Bakhtin, M. M.
See Bakhtin, Mikhail Mikhailovich

Bakhtin, Mikhail
See Bakhtin, Mikhail Mikhailovich
Bakhtin, Mikhail Mikhailovich 1895-1975 .. **CLC 83; TCLC 160**
See Bakhtin, Mikhail Mikhailovich
See also CA 128; 113; DLB 242; EWL 3
Bakshi, Ralph 1938(?)- .... **CLC 26**
See also CA 112; 138; IDFW 3
Bakunin, Mikhail (Alexandrovich)
1814-1876 .... **NCLC 25, 58**
See also DLB 277
Bal, Mieke 1946- .... **CLC 252**
See also CA 156; CANR 99
Bal, Mieke Maria Gertrudis
See Bal, Mieke
Baldwin, James 1924-1987 .... **BLC 1:1, 2:1; CLC 1, 2, 3, 4, 5, 8, 13, 15, 17, 42, 50, 67, 90, 127; DC 1; SSC 10, 33, 98, 134; TCLC 229; WLC 1**
See also AAYA 4, 34; AFAW 1, 2; AMWR 2; AMWS 1; BPFB 1; BW 1; CA 1-4R; 124; CABS 1; CAD; CANR 3, 24; CDALB 1941-1968; CN 1, 2, 3, 4; CPW; DA; DA3; DAB; DAC; DAM MST, MULT, NOV, POP; DFS 11, 15; DLB 2, 7, 33, 249, 278; DLBY 1987; EWL 3; EXPS; LAIT 5; MAL 5; MTCW 1, 2; MTFW 2005; NCFS 4; NFS 4; RGAL 4; RGSF 2; SATA 9; SATA-Obit 54; SSFS 2, 18; TUS
Baldwin, William c. 1515-1563 .... **LC 113**
See also DLB 132
Bale, John 1495-1563 .... **LC 62**
See also DLB 132; RGEL 2; TEA
Ball, Hugo 1886-1927 .... **TCLC 104**
Ballard, James G.
See Ballard, J.G.
Ballard, James Graham
See Ballard, J.G.
Ballard, J.G. 1930-2009 ... **CLC 3, 6, 14, 36, 137, 299; SSC 1, 53, 146**
See also AAYA 3, 52; BRWS 5; CA 5-8R; 285; CANR 15, 39, 65, 107, 133, 198; CN 1, 2, 3, 4, 5, 6, 7; DA3; DAM NOV, POP; DLB 14, 207, 261, 319; EWL 3; HGG; MTCW 1, 2; MTFW 2005; NFS 8; RGEL 2; RGSF 2; SATA 93; SATA-Obit 203; SCFW 1, 2; SFW 4
Ballard, Jim G.
See Ballard, J.G.
Balmont, Konstantin (Dmitriyevich)
1867-1943 .... **TCLC 11**
See also CA 109; 155; DLB 295; EWL 3
Baltausis, Vincas 1847-1910 ....
See Mikszath, Kalman
Balzac, Guez de (?)- ....
See Balzac, Jean-Louis Guez de
Balzac, Honore de 1799-1850 .. **NCLC 5, 35, 53, 153; SSC 5, 59, 102, 153; WLC 1**
See also DA; DA3; DAB; DAC; DAM MST, NOV; DLB 119; EW 5; GFL 1789 to the Present; LMFS 1; NFS 33; RGSF 2; RGWL 2, 3; SSFS 10; SUFW; TWA
Balzac, Jean-Louis Guez de 1597-1654 .. **LC 162**
See also DLB 268; GFL Beginnings to 1789
Bambara, Toni Cade 1939-1995 .... **BLC 1:1, 2:1; CLC 19, 88; SSC 35, 107; TCLC 116; WLCS**
See also AAYA 5, 49; AFAW 2; AMWS 11; BW 2, 3; BYA 12, 14; CA 29-32R; 150; CANR 24, 49, 81; CDALBS; DA; DA3; DAC; DAM MST, MULT; DLB 38, 218; EXPS; MAL 5; MTCW 1, 2; MTFW 2005; RGAL 4; RGSF 2; SATA 112; SSFS 4, 7, 12, 21
Bamdad, A.
See Shamlu, Ahmad

Bamdad, Alef
See Shamlu, Ahmad

Banat, D. R.
See Bradbury, Ray

Bancroft, Laura
See Baum, L. Frank

Bandello, Matteo 1485-1561 .... **SSC 143**

Banim, John 1798-1842 .... **NCLC 13**
See also DLB 116, 158, 159; RGEL 2

Banim, Michael 1796-1874 .... **NCLC 13**
See also DLB 158, 159

Banjo, The
See Paterson, A(ndrew) B(arton)

Banks, Iain 1954- .... **CLC 34**
See also BRWS 11; CA 123; 128; CANR 61, 106, 180; DLB 194, 261; EWL 3; HGG; INT CA-128; MTFW 2005; SFW 4

Banks, Iain M.
See Banks, Iain

Banks, Iain Menzies
See Banks, Iain

Banks, Lynne Reid
See Reid Banks, Lynne

Banks, Russell 1940- . **CLC 37, 72, 187; SSC 42**
See also AAYA 45; AMWS 5; CA 65-68; CAAS 15; CANR 19, 52, 73, 118, 195; CN 4, 5, 6, 7; DLB 130, 278; EWL 3; MAL 5; MTCW 2; MTFW 2005; NFS 13

Banks, Russell Earl
See Banks, Russell

Banville, John 1945- . **CLC 46, 118, 224, 315**
See also CA 117; 128; CANR 104, 150, 176, 225; CN 4, 5, 6, 7; DLB 14, 271, 326; INT CA-128

Banville, Theodore (Faullain) de
1832-1891 .... **NCLC 9**
See also DLB 217; GFL 1789 to the Present

Baraka, Amiri 1934- . **BLC 1:1, 2:1; CLC 1, 2, 3, 5, 10, 14, 33, 115, 213; DC 6; PC 4, 113; WLCS**
See also AAYA 63; AFAW 1, 2; AMWS 2; BW 2, 3; CA 21-24R; CABS 3; CAD; CANR 27, 38, 61, 133, 172; CD 3, 5, 6; CDALB 1941-1968; CN 1, 2; CP 1, 2, 3, 4, 5, 6, 7; CPW; DA; DA3; DAC; DAM MST, MULT, POET, POP; DFS 3, 11, 16; DLB 5, 7, 16, 38; DLBD 8; EWL 3; MAL 5; MTCW 1, 2; MTFW 2005; PFS 9; RGAL 4; TCLE 1:1; TUS; WP

Baratynsky, Evgenii Abramovich
1800-1844 .... **NCLC 103**
See also DLB 205

Barbauld, Anna Laetitia 1743-1825 .. **NCLC 50, 185**
See also CLR 160; DLB 107, 109, 142, 158, 336; RGEL 2

Barbellion, W. N. P.
See Cummings, Bruce F.

Barber, Benjamin R. 1939- .... **CLC 141**
See also CA 29-32R; CANR 12, 32, 64, 119

Barbera, Jack 1945- .... **CLC 44**
See also CA 110; CANR 45

Barbera, Jack Vincent
See Barbera, Jack

Barbey d'Aurevilly, Jules-Amedee
1808-1889 .... **NCLC 1, 213; SSC 17**
See also DLB 119; GFL 1789 to the Present

Barbour, John c. 1316-1395 .... **CMLC 33**
See also DLB 146

Barbusse, Henri 1873-1935 .... **TCLC 5**
See also CA 105; 154; DLB 65; EWL 3; RGWL 2, 3

Barclay, Alexander c. 1475-1552 ...... **LC 109**
See also DLB 132

Barclay, Bill
See Moorcock, Michael

Barclay, William Ewert
See Moorcock, Michael

Barclay, William Ewert
See Moorcock, Michael

Barea, Arturo 1897-1957 .... **TCLC 14**
See also CA 111; 201

Barfoot, Joan 1946- .... **CLC 18**
See also CA 105; CANR 141, 179

Barham, Richard Harris 1788-1845 . **NCLC 77**
See also DLB 159

Baring, Maurice 1874-1945 .... **TCLC 8**
See also CA 105; 168; DLB 34; HGG

Baring-Gould, Sabine 1834-1924 . **TCLC 88**
See also DLB 156, 190

Barker, Clive 1952- ... **CLC 52, 205; SSC 53**
See also AAYA 10, 54; BEST 90:3; BPFB 1; CA 121; 129; CANR 71, 111, 133, 187; CPW; DA3; DAM POP; DLB 261; HGG; INT CA-129; MTCW 1, 2; MTFW 2005; SUFW 2

Barker, George Granville 1913-1991 ... **CLC 8, 48; PC 77**
See also CA 9-12R; 135; CANR 7, 38; CP 1, 2, 3, 4, 5; DAM POET; DLB 20; EWL 3; MTCW 1

Barker, Harley Granville
See Granville-Barker, Harley

Barker, Howard 1946- .... **CLC 37**
See also CA 102; CBD; CD 5, 6; DLB 13, 233

Barker, Jane 1652-1732 ... **LC 42, 82; PC 91**
See also DLB 39, 131

Barker, Pat 1943- .... **CLC 32, 94, 146**
See also BRWS 4; CA 117; 122; CANR 50, 101, 148, 195; CN 6, 7; DLB 271, 326; INT CA-122

Barker, Patricia
See Barker, Pat

Barlach, Ernst (Heinrich) 1870-1938 . **TCLC 84**
See also CA 178; DLB 56, 118; EWL 3

Barlow, Joel 1754-1812 .... **NCLC 23, 223**
See also AMWS 2; DLB 37; RGAL 4

Barnard, Mary (Ethel) 1909- .... **CLC 48**
See also CA 21-22; CAP 2; CP 1

Barnes, Djuna 1892-1982 ... **CLC 3, 4, 8, 11, 29, 127; SSC 3, 163; TCLC 212**
See also AMWS 3; CA 9-12R; 107; CAD; CANR 16, 55; CN 1, 2, 3; CWD; DLB 4, 9, 45; EWL 3; GLL 1; MAL 5; MTCW 1, 2; MTFW 2005; RGAL 4; TCLE 1:1; TUS

Barnes, Jim 1933- .... **NNAL**
See also CA 108, 175; 272; CAAE 175, 272; CAAS 28; DLB 175

Barnes, Julian 1946- .... **CLC 42, 141, 315**
See also BRWS 4; CA 102; CANR 19, 54, 115, 137, 195; CN 4, 5, 6, 7; DAB; DLB 194; DLBY 1993; EWL 3; MTCW 2; MTFW 2005; SSFS 24

Barnes, Julian Patrick
See Barnes, Julian

Barnes, Peter 1931-2004 .... **CLC 5, 56**
See also CA 65-68; 230; CAAS 12; CANR 33, 34, 64, 113; CBD; CD 5, 6; DFS 6; DLB 13, 233; MTCW 1

Barnes, William 1801-1886 .... **NCLC 75**
See also DLB 32

Barnfield, Richard 1574-1627 .... **LC 192**
See also DLB 172

Baroja, Pio 1872-1956 ..... **HLC 1; SSC 112; TCLC 8, 240**
See also CA 104; 247; EW 9

Baroja y Nessi, Pio
See Baroja, Pio

Baron, David
See Pinter, Harold

Baron Corvo
See Rolfe, Frederick (William Serafino Austin Lewis Mary)

Barondess, Sue K. 1926-1977 .... **CLC 3, 8**
See also CA 1-4R; 69-72; CANR 1

Barondess, Sue Kaufman
See Barondess, Sue K.

Baron de Teive
See Pessoa, Fernando

Baroness Von S.
See Zangwill, Israel

Barres, (Auguste-)Maurice 1862-1923 .... **TCLC 47**
See also CA 164; DLB 123; GFL 1789 to the Present

Barreto, Afonso Henrique de Lima
See Lima Barreto, Afonso Henrique de

Barrett, Andrea 1954- .... **CLC 150**
See also CA 156; CANR 92, 186; CN 7; DLB 335; SSFS 24

Barrett, Michele
See Barrett, Michele

Barrett, Michele 1949- .... **CLC 65**
See also CA 280

Barrett, Roger Syd
See Barrett, Syd

Barrett, Syd 1946-2006 .... **CLC 35**

Barrett, William (Christopher) 1913-1992 .. **CLC 27**
See also CA 13-16R; 139; CANR 11, 67; INT CANR-11

Barrett Browning, Elizabeth 1806-1861 ...... **NCLC 1, 16, 61, 66, 170; PC 6, 62; WLC 1**
See also AAYA 63; BRW 4; CDBLB 1832-1890; DA; DA3; DAB; DAC; DAM MST, POET; DLB 32, 199; EXPP; FL 1:2; PAB; PFS 2, 16, 23; TEA; WLIT 4; WP

Barrie, Baronet
See Barrie, J. M.

Barrie, J. M. 1860-1937 .... **TCLC 2, 164**
See also BRWS 3; BYA 4, 5; CA 104; 136; CANR 77; CDBLB 1890-1914; CLR 16, 124; CWRI 5; DA3; DAB; DAM DRAM; DFS 7; DLB 10, 141, 156, 352; EWL 3; FANT; MAICYA 1, 2; MTCW 2; MTFW 2005; SATA 100; SUFW; WCH; WLIT 4; YABC 1

Barrie, James Matthew
See Barrie, J. M.

Barrington, Michael
See Moorcock, Michael

Barrol, Grady
See Bograd, Larry

Barry, Mike
See Malzberg, Barry N(athaniel)

Barry, Philip 1896-1949 .... **TCLC 11**
See also CA 109; 199; DFS 9; DLB 7, 228; MAL 5; RGAL 4

Barry, Sebastian 1955- .... **CLC 282**
See also CA 117; CANR 122, 193; CD 5, 6; DLB 245

Bart, Andre Schwarz
See Schwarz-Bart, Andre

Barth, John 1930- .. **CLC 1, 2, 3, 5, 7, 9, 10, 14, 27, 51, 89, 214; SSC 10, 89**
See also AITN 1, 2; AMW; BPFB 1; CA 1-4R; CABS 1; CANR 5, 23, 49, 64, 113, 204; CN 1, 2, 3, 4, 5, 6, 7; DAM NOV; DLB 2, 227; EWL 3; FANT; MAL 5; MTCW 1; RGAL 4; RGSF 2; RHW; SSFS 6; TUS

Barth, John Simmons
See Barth, John

Barthelme, Donald 1931-1989 . **CLC 1, 2, 3, 5, 6, 8, 13, 23, 46, 59, 115; SSC 2, 55, 142**
See also AMWS 4; BPFB 1; CA 21-24R; 129; CANR 20, 58, 188; CN 1, 2, 3, 4; DA3; DAM NOV; DLB 2, 234; DLBY

1980, 1989; EWL 3; FANT; LMFS 2; MAL 5; MTCW 1, 2; MTFW 2005; RGAL 4; RGSF 2; SATA 7; SATA-Obit 62; SSFS 17

Barthelme, Frederick 1943- .... **CLC 36, 117**
See also AMWS 11; CA 114; 122; CANR 77, 209; CN 4, 5, 6, 7; CSW; DLB 244; DLBY 1985; EWL 3; INT CA-122

Barthes, Roland (Gerard) 1915-1980 .. **CLC 24, 83; TCLC 135**
See also CA 130; 97-100; CANR 66; DLB 296; EW 13; EWL 3; GFL 1789 to the Present; MTCW 1, 2; TWA

Bartram, William 1739-1823 ...... **NCLC 145**
See also ANW; DLB 37

Barzun, Jacques 1907- .... **CLC 51, 145**
See also CA 61-64; CANR 22, 95

Barzun, Jacques Martin
See Barzun, Jacques

Bashevis, Isaac
See Singer, Isaac Bashevis

Bashevis, Yitskhok
See Singer, Isaac Bashevis

Bashkirtseff, Marie 1859-1884 ..... **NCLC 27**

Basho, Matsuo
See Matsuo Basho

Basil of Caesaria c. 330-379 .... **CMLC 35**

Basket, Raney
See Edgerton, Clyde

Bass, Kingsley B., Jr.
See Bullins, Ed

Bass, Rick 1958- . **CLC 79, 143, 286; SSC 60**
See also AMWS 16; ANW; CA 126; CANR 53, 93, 145, 183; CSW; DLB 212, 275

Bassani, Giorgio 1916-2000 .... **CLC 9**
See also CA 65-68; 190; CANR 33; CWW 2; DLB 128, 177, 299; EWL 3; MTCW 1; RGHL; RGWL 2, 3

Bassine, Helen
See Yglesias, Helen

Bastian, Ann CLC 70

Bastos, Augusto Roa
See Roa Bastos, Augusto

Bataille, Georges 1897-1962 .... **CLC 29; TCLC 155**
See also CA 101; 89-92; EWL 3

Bates, H(erbert) E(rnest) 1905-1974 .... **CLC 46; SSC 10**
See also CA 93-96; 45-48; CANR 34; CN 1; DA3; DAB; DAM POP; DLB 162, 191; EWL 3; EXPS; MTCW 1, 2; RGSF 2; SSFS 7

Batiushkov, Konstantin Nikolaevich 1787-1855 .... **NCLC 254**
See also DLB 205

Bauchart
See Camus, Albert

Baudelaire, Charles 1821-1867 ...... **NCLC 6, 29, 55, 155; PC 1, 106; SSC 18; WLC 1**
See also DA; DA3; DAB; DAC; DAM MST, POET; DLB 217; EW 7; GFL 1789 to the Present; LMFS 2; PFS 21, 38; RGWL 2, 3; TWA

Baudouin, Marcel
See Peguy, Charles (Pierre)

Baudouin, Pierre
See Peguy, Charles (Pierre)

Baudrillard, Jean 1929-2007 .... **CLC 60**
See also CA 252; 258; DLB 296

Baum, L. Frank 1856-1919 ..... **TCLC 7, 132**
See also AAYA 46; BYA 16; CA 108; 133; CLR 15, 107; CWRI 5; DLB 22; FANT; JRDA; MAICYA 1, 2; MTCW 1, 2; NFS 13; RGAL 4; SATA 18, 100; WCH

Baum, Louis F.
See Baum, L. Frank

Baum, Lyman Frank
See Baum, L. Frank

Bauman, Zygmunt 1925- .... **CLC 314**
See also CA 127; CANR 205

Baumbach, Jonathan 1933- .... **CLC 6, 23**
See also CA 13-16R, 284; CAAE 284; CAAS 5; CANR 12, 66, 140; CN 3, 4, 5, 6, 7; DLBY 1980; INT CANR-12; MTCW 1

Baumgarten, Alexander Gottlieb 1714-1762 .... **LC 199**

Bausch, Richard 1945- .... **CLC 51**
See also AMWS 7; CA 101; CAAS 14; CANR 43, 61, 87, 164, 200; CN 7; CSW; DLB 130; MAL 5

Bausch, Richard Carl
See Bausch, Richard

Baxter, Charles 1947- .... **CLC 45, 78**
See also AMWS 17; CA 57-60; CANR 40, 64, 104, 133, 188; CPW; DAM POP; DLB 130; MAL 5; MTCW 2; MTFW 2005; TCLE 1:1

Baxter, Charles Morley
See Baxter, Charles

Baxter, George Owen
See Faust, Frederick

Baxter, James K(eir) 1926-1972 .... **CLC 14; TCLC 249**
See also CA 77-80; CP 1; EWL 3

Baxter, John
See Hunt, E. Howard

Bayer, Sylvia
See Glassco, John

Bayle, Pierre 1647-1706 .... **LC 126**
See also DLB 268, 313; GFL Beginnings to 1789

Baynton, Barbara 1857-1929 . **TCLC 57, 211**
See also DLB 230; RGSF 2

Beagle, Peter S. 1939- .... **CLC 7, 104**
See also AAYA 47; BPFB 1; BYA 9, 10, 16; CA 9-12R; CANR 4, 51, 73, 110, 213; DA3; DLBY 1980; FANT; INT CANR-4; MTCW 2; MTFW 2005; SATA 60, 130; SUFW 1, 2; YAW

Beagle, Peter Soyer
See Beagle, Peter S.

Bean, Normal
See Burroughs, Edgar Rice

Beard, Charles A(ustin) 1874-1948 ... **TCLC 15**
See also CA 115; 189; DLB 17; SATA 18

Beardsley, Aubrey 1872-1898 .... **NCLC 6**

Beatrice of Nazareth 1200-1268 . **CMLC 124**

Beattie, Ann 1947- .... **CLC 8, 13, 18, 40, 63, 146, 293; SSC 11, 130**
See also AMWS 5; BEST 90:2; BPFB 1; CA 81-84; CANR 53, 73, 128, 225; CN 4, 5, 6, 7; CPW; DA3; DAM NOV, POP; DLB 218, 278; DLBY 1982; EWL 3; MAL 5; MTCW 1, 2; MTFW 2005; RGAL 4; RGSF 2; SSFS 9; TUS

Beattie, James 1735-1803 .... **NCLC 25**
See also DLB 109

Beauchamp, Katherine Mansfield
See Mansfield, Katherine

Beaumarchais, Pierre-Augustin Caron de 1732-1799 .... **DC 4; LC 61, 192**
See also DAM DRAM; DFS 14, 16; DLB 313; EW 4; GFL Beginnings to 1789; RGWL 2, 3

Beaumont, Francis 1584(?)-1616 . **DC 6; LC 33**
See also BRW 2; CDBLB Before 1660; DLB 58; TEA

Beauvoir, Simone de 1908-1986 ... **CLC 1, 2, 4, 8, 14, 31, 44, 50, 71, 124; SSC 35; TCLC 221; WLC 1**
See also BPFB 1; CA 9-12R; 118; CANR 28, 61; DA; DA3; DAB; DAC; DAM MST, NOV; DLB 72; DLBY 1986; EW 12; EWL 3; FL 1:5; FW; GFL 1789 to the Present; LMFS 2; MTCW 1, 2; MTFW 2005; RGSF 2; RGWL 2, 3; TWA

Beauvoir, Simone Lucie Ernestine Marie Bertrand de
See Beauvoir, Simone de

Becker, Carl (Lotus) 1873-1945 .... **TCLC 63**
See also CA 157; DLB 17

Becker, Jurek 1937-1997 .... **CLC 7, 19**
See also CA 85-88; 157; CANR 60, 117; CWW 2; DLB 75, 299; EWL 3; RGHL

Becker, Walter 1950- .... **CLC 26**

Becket, Thomas a 1118(?)-1170 ... **CMLC 83**

Beckett, Samuel 1906-1989 .. **CLC 1, 2, 3, 4, 6, 9, 10, 11, 14, 18, 29, 57, 59, 83; DC 22; SSC 16, 74, 161; TCLC 145; WLC 1**
See also BRWC 2; BRWR 1; BRWS 1; CA 5-8R; 130; CANR 33, 61; CBD; CDBLB 1945-1960; CN 1, 2, 3, 4; CP 1, 2, 3, 4; DA; DA3; DAB; DAC; DAM DRAM, MST, NOV; DFS 2, 7, 18; DLB 13, 15, 233, 319, 321, 329; DLBY 1990; EWL 3; GFL 1789 to the Present; LATS 1:2; LMFS 2; MTCW 1, 2; MTFW 2005; RGSF 2; RGWL 2, 3; SSFS 15; TEA; WLIT 4

Beckett, Samuel Barclay
See Beckett, Samuel

Beckford, William 1760-1844 ...... **NCLC 16, 214**
See also BRW 3; DLB 39, 213; GL 2; HGG; LMFS 1; SUFW

Beckham, Barry 1944- .... **BLC 1:1**
See also BW 1; CA 29-32R; CANR 26, 62; CN 1, 2, 3, 4, 5, 6; DAM MULT; DLB 33

Beckman, Gunnel 1910- .... **CLC 26**
See also CA 33-36R; CANR 15, 114; CLR 25; MAICYA 1, 2; SAAS 9; SATA 6

Becque, Henri 1837-1899 .. **DC 21; NCLC 3**
See also DLB 192; GFL 1789 to the Present

Becquer, Gustavo Adolfo 1836-1870 .. **HLCS 1; NCLC 106; PC 113**
See also DAM MULT

Beddoes, Thomas Lovell 1803-1849 . **DC 15; NCLC 3, 154**
See also BRWS 11; DLB 96

Bede c. 673-735 .... **CMLC 20, 130**
See also DLB 146; TEA

Bedford, Denton R. 1907-(?) .... **NNAL**

Bedford, Donald F.
See Fearing, Kenneth

Beecher, Catharine Esther 1800-1878 .... **NCLC 30**
See also DLB 1, 243

Beecher, John 1904-1980 .... **CLC 6**
See also AITN 1; CA 5-8R; 105; CANR 8; CP 1, 2, 3

Beer, Johann 1655-1700 .... **LC 5**
See also DLB 168

Beer, Patricia 1924- .... **CLC 58**
See also BRWS 14; CA 61-64; 183; CANR 13, 46; CP 1, 2, 3, 4, 5, 6; CWP; DLB 40; FW

Beerbohm, Max
See Beerbohm, (Henry) Max(imilian)

Beerbohm, (Henry) Max(imilian) 1872-1956 .... **TCLC 1, 24**
See also BRWS 2; CA 104; 154; CANR 79; DLB 34, 100; FANT; MTCW 2

Beer-Hofmann, Richard 1866-1945 ... **TCLC 60**
See also CA 160; DLB 81

Beethoven, Ludwig van 1770(?)-1827 .... **NCLC 227**

Beg, Shemus
See Stephens, James

Begiebing, Robert J(ohn) 1946- ...... **CLC 70**
See also CA 122; CANR 40, 88

Begley, Louis 1933- .... **CLC 197**
See also CA 140; CANR 98, 176, 210; DLB
299; RGHL; TCLE 1:1

Behan, Brendan 1923-1964 .... **CLC 1, 8, 11,
15, 79**
See also BRWS 2; CA 73-76; CANR 33,
121; CBD; CDBLB 1945-1960; DAM
DRAM; DFS 7; DLB 13, 233; EWL 3;
MTCW 1, 2

Behan, Brendan Francis
See Behan, Brendan

Behn, Aphra 1640(?)-1689 . **DC 4; LC 1, 30,
42, 135; PC 13, 88; WLC 1**
See also BRWR 3; BRWS 3; DA; DA3;
DAB; DAC; DAM DRAM, MST, NOV,
POET; DFS 16, 24; DLB 39, 80, 131; FW;
NFS 35; TEA; WLIT 3

Behrman, S(amuel) N(athaniel) 1893-1973 .
CLC 40
See also CA 13-16; 45-48; CAD; CAP 1;
DLB 7, 44; IDFW 3; MAL 5; RGAL 4

Bekederemo, J. P. Clark
See Clark-Bekederemo, J. P.

Belasco, David 1853-1931 .... **TCLC 3**
See also CA 104; 168; DLB 7; MAL 5;
RGAL 4

Belben, Rosalind 1941- .... **CLC 280**
See also CA 291

Belben, Rosalind Loveday
See Belben, Rosalind

Belcheva, Elisaveta Lyubomirova
1893-1991 .... **CLC 10**
See also CA 178; CDWLB 4; DLB 147;
EWL 3

Beldone, Phil "Cheech"
See Ellison, Harlan

Beleno
See Azuela, Mariano

Belinski, Vissarion Grigoryevich
1811-1848 .... **NCLC 5**
See also DLB 198

Belitt, Ben 1911- .... **CLC 22**
See also CA 13-16R; CAAS 4; CANR 7,
77; CP 1, 2, 3, 4, 5, 6; DLB 5

Belknap, Jeremy 1744-1798 .... **LC 115**
See also DLB 30, 37

Bell, Gertrude (Margaret Lowthian)
1868-1926 .... **TCLC 67**
See also CA 167; CANR 110; DLB 174,
366

Bell, J. Freeman
See Zangwill, Israel

Bell, James Madison 1826-1902 ... **BLC 1:1;
TCLC 43**
See also BW 1; CA 122; 124; DAM MULT;
DLB 50

Bell, Madison Smartt 1957- ... **CLC 41, 102,
223**
See also AMWS 10; BPFB 1; CA 111, 183;
CAAE 183; CANR 28, 54, 73, 134, 176,
223; CN 5, 6, 7; CSW; DLB 218, 278;
MTCW 2; MTFW 2005

Bell, Marvin 1937- .... **CLC 8, 31; PC 79**
See also CA 21-24R; CAAS 14; CANR 59,
102, 206; CP 1, 2, 3, 4, 5, 6, 7; DAM
POET; DLB 5; MAL 5; MTCW 1; PFS
25

Bell, Marvin Hartley
See Bell, Marvin

Bell, W. L. D.
See Mencken, H. L.

Bellamy, Atwood C.
See Mencken, H. L.

Bellamy, Edward 1850-1898 .... **NCLC 4, 86,
147**
See also DLB 12; NFS 15; RGAL 4; SFW
4

Belli, Gioconda 1949- .... **HLCS 1**
See also CA 152; CANR 143, 209; CWW
2; DLB 290; EWL 3; RGWL 3

Bellin, Edward J.
See Kuttner, Henry

Bello, Andres 1781-1865 .... **NCLC 131**
See also LAW

Belloc, Hilaire 1870-1953 .. **PC 24; TCLC 7,
18**
See also CA 106; 152; CLR 102; CWRI 5;
DAM POET; DLB 19, 100, 141, 174;
EWL 3; MTCW 2; MTFW 2005; SATA
112; WCH; YABC 1

Belloc, Joseph Hilaire Pierre Sebastien Rene
Swanton
See Belloc, Hilaire

Belloc, Joseph Peter Rene Hilaire
See Belloc, Hilaire

Belloc, Joseph Pierre Hilaire
See Belloc, Hilaire

Belloc, M. A.
See Lowndes, Marie Adelaide (Belloc)

Belloc-Lowndes, Mrs.
See Lowndes, Marie Adelaide (Belloc)

Bellow, Saul 1915-2005 .... **CLC 1, 2, 3, 6, 8,
10, 13, 15, 25, 33, 34, 63, 79, 190, 200;
SSC 14, 101; WLC 1**
See also AITN 2; AMW; AMWC 2; AMWR
2; BEST 89:3; BPFB 1; CA 5-8R; 238;
CABS 1; CANR 29, 53, 95, 132; CDALB
1941-1968; CN 1, 2, 3, 4, 5, 6, 7; DA;
DA3; DAB; DAC; DAM MST, NOV,
POP; DLB 2, 28, 299, 329; DLBD 3;
DLBY 1982; EWL 3; MAL 5; MTCW 1,
2; MTFW 2005; NFS 4, 14, 26, 33; RGAL
4; RGHL; RGSF 2; SSFS 12, 22; TUS

Belser, Reimond Karel Maria de 1929- . **CLC
14**
See also CA 152

Bely, Andrey
See Bugayev, Boris Nikolayevich

Belyi, Andrei
See Bugayev, Boris Nikolayevich

Bembo, Pietro 1470-1547 .... **LC 79**
See also RGWL 2, 3

Benary, Margot
See Benary-Isbert, Margot

Benary-Isbert, Margot 1889-1979 ... **CLC 12**
See also CA 5-8R; 89-92; CANR 4, 72;
CLR 12; MAICYA 1, 2; SATA 2; SATA-
Obit 21

Benavente, Jacinto 1866-1954 .... **DC 26;
HLCS 1; TCLC 3**
See also CA 106; 131; CANR 81; DAM
DRAM, MULT; DLB 329; EWL 3; GLL
2; HW 1, 2; MTCW 1, 2

Benavente y Martinez, Jacinto
See Benavente, Jacinto

Benchley, Peter 1940-2006 .... **CLC 4, 8**
See also AAYA 14; AITN 2; BPFB 1; CA
17-20R; 248; CANR 12, 35, 66, 115;
CPW; DAM NOV, POP; HGG; MTCW 1,
2; MTFW 2005; SATA 3, 89, 164

Benchley, Peter Bradford
See Benchley, Peter

Benchley, Robert (Charles) 1889-1945 ....
TCLC 1, 55
See also CA 105; 153; DLB 11; MAL 5;
RGAL 4

Benda, Julien 1867-1956 .... **TCLC 60**
See also CA 120; 154; GFL 1789 to the
Present

Benedetti, Mario 1920-2009 . **CLC 299; SSC
135**
See also CA 152; 286; DAM MULT; DLB
113; EWL 3; HW 1, 2; LAW

Benedetti, Mario Orlando Hardy Hamlet
Brenno
See Benedetti, Mario

Benedetti Farrugia, Mario
See Benedetti, Mario

Benedetti Farrugia, Mario Orlando Hardy
Hamlet Brenno
See Benedetti, Mario

Benedict, Ruth 1887-1948 .... **TCLC 60**
See also CA 158; CANR 146; DLB 246

Benedict, Ruth Fulton
See Benedict, Ruth

Benedikt, Michael 1935- .... **CLC 4, 14**
See also CA 13-16R; CANR 7; CP 1, 2, 3,
4, 5, 6, 7; DLB 5

Benet, Juan 1927-1993 .... **CLC 28**
See also CA 143; EWL 3

Benet, Stephen Vincent 1898-1943 ... **PC 64;
SSC 10, 86; TCLC 7**
See also AMWS 11; CA 104; 152; DA3;
DAM POET; DLB 4, 48, 102, 249, 284;
DLBY 1997; EWL 3; HGG; MAL 5;
MTCW 2; MTFW 2005; RGAL 4; RGSF
2; SSFS 22, 31; SUFW; WP; YABC 1

Benet, William Rose 1886-1950 .... **TCLC 28**
See also CA 118; 152; DAM POET; DLB
45; RGAL 4

Benford, Gregory 1941- .... **CLC 52**
See also BPFB 1; CA 69-72, 175, 268;
CAAE 175, 268; CAAS 27; CANR 12,
24, 49, 95, 134; CN 7; CSW; DLBY 1982;
MTFW 2005; SCFW 2; SFW 4

Benford, Gregory Albert
See Benford, Gregory

Bengtsson, Frans (Gunnar) 1894-1954 ....
TCLC 48
See also CA 170; EWL 3

Benjamin, David
See Slavitt, David R.

Benjamin, Lois
See Gould, Lois

Benjamin, Walter 1892-1940 .... **TCLC 39**
See also CA 164; CANR 181; DLB 242;
EW 11; EWL 3

Ben Jelloun, Tahar 1944- .... **CLC 180, 311**
See also CA 135; 162; CANR 100, 166,
217; CWW 2; EWL 3; RGWL 3; WLIT 2

Benn, Gottfried 1886-1956 ... **PC 35; TCLC
3, 256**
See also CA 106; 153; DLB 56; EWL 3;
RGWL 2, 3

Bennett, Alan 1934- .... **CLC 45, 77, 292**
See also BRWS 8; CA 103; CANR 35, 55,
106, 157, 197, 227; CBD; CD 5, 6; DAB;
DAM MST; DLB 310; MTCW 1, 2;
MTFW 2005

Bennett, (Enoch) Arnold 1867-1931 .. **TCLC
5, 20, 197**
See also BRW 6; CA 106; 155; CDBLB
1890-1914; DLB 10, 34, 98, 135; EWL 3;
MTCW 2

Bennett, Elizabeth
See Mitchell, Margaret

Bennett, George Harold 1930- .... **CLC 5**
See also BW 1; CA 97-100; CAAS 13;
CANR 87; DLB 33

Bennett, Gwendolyn B. 1902-1981 ... **HR 1:2**
See also BW 1; CA 125; DLB 51; WP

Bennett, Hal
See Bennett, George Harold

Bennett, Jay 1912- .... **CLC 35**
See also AAYA 10, 73; CA 69-72; CANR
11, 42, 79; JRDA; SAAS 4; SATA 41, 87;
SATA-Brief 27; WYA; YAW

Bennett, Louise 1919-2006 ... **BLC 1:1; CLC
28**
See also BW 2, 3; CA 151; 252; CDWLB
3; CP 1, 2, 3, 4, 5, 6, 7; DAM MULT;
DLB 117; EWL 3

Bennett, Louise Simone
See Bennett, Louise

Bennett-Coverley, Louise
See Bennett, Louise

Benoit de Sainte-Maure fl. 12th cent. - .... **CMLC 90**

Benson, A. C. 1862-1925 .... **TCLC 123**
See also DLB 98

Benson, E(dward) F(rederic) 1867-1940 ...... **TCLC 27**
See also CA 114; 157; DLB 135, 153; HGG; SUFW 1

Benson, Jackson J. 1930- .... **CLC 34**
See also CA 25-28R; CANR 214; DLB 111

Benson, Sally 1900-1972 .... **CLC 17**
See also CA 19-20; 37-40R; CAP 1; SATA 1, 35; SATA-Obit 27

Benson, Stella 1892-1933 .... **TCLC 17**
See also CA 117; 154, 155; DLB 36, 162; FANT; TEA

Bentham, Jeremy 1748-1832 . **NCLC 38, 237**
See also DLB 107, 158, 252

Bentley, E(dmund) C(lerihew) 1875-1956 ... **TCLC 12**
See also CA 108; 232; DLB 70; MSW

Bentley, Eric 1916- .... **CLC 24**
See also CA 5-8R; CAD; CANR 6, 67; CBD; CD 5, 6; INT CANR-6

Bentley, Eric Russell
See Bentley, Eric

ben Uzair, Salem
See Horne, Richard Henry Hengist

Beolco, Angelo 1496-1542 .... **LC 139**

Beranger, Pierre Jean de 1780-1857 . **NCLC 34; PC 112**

Berdyaev, Nicolas
See Berdyaev, Nikolai (Aleksandrovich)

Berdyaev, Nikolai (Aleksandrovich) 1874-1948 .... **TCLC 67**
See also CA 120; 157

Berdyayev, Nikolai (Aleksandrovich)
See Berdyaev, Nikolai (Aleksandrovich)

Berendt, John 1939- .... **CLC 86**
See also CA 146; CANR 75, 83, 151

Berendt, John Lawrence
See Berendt, John

Berengar of Tours c. 1000-1088 . **CMLC 124**

Beresford, J(ohn) D(avys) 1873-1947 . **TCLC 81**
See also CA 112; 155; DLB 162, 178, 197; SFW 4; SUFW 1

Bergelson, David (Rafailovich) 1884-1952 ... **TCLC 81**
See also CA 220; DLB 333; EWL 3

Bergelson, Dovid
See Bergelson, David (Rafailovich)

Berger, Colonel
See Malraux, Andre

Berger, John 1926- .... **CLC 2, 19**
See also BRWS 4; CA 81-84; CANR 51, 78, 117, 163, 200; CN 1, 2, 3, 4, 5, 6, 7; DLB 14, 207, 319, 326

Berger, John Peter
See Berger, John

Berger, Melvin H. 1927- .... **CLC 12**
See also CA 5-8R; CANR 4, 142; CLR 32; SAAS 2; SATA 5, 88, 158; SATA-Essay 124

Berger, Thomas 1924- .. **CLC 3, 5, 8, 11, 18, 38, 259**
See also BPFB 1; CA 1-4R; CANR 5, 28, 51, 128; CN 1, 2, 3, 4, 5, 6, 7; DAM NOV; DLB 2; DLBY 1980; EWL 3; FANT; INT CANR-28; MAL 5; MTCW 1, 2; MTFW 2005; RHW; TCLE 1:1; TCWW 1, 2

Bergman, Ernst Ingmar
See Bergman, Ingmar

Bergman, Ingmar 1918-2007 ... **CLC 16, 72, 210**
See also AAYA 61; CA 81-84; 262; CANR 33, 70; CWW 2; DLB 257; MTCW 2; MTFW 2005

Bergson, Henri(-Louis) 1859-1941 ..... **TCLC 32**
See also CA 164; DLB 329; EW 8; EWL 3; GFL 1789 to the Present

Bergstein, Eleanor 1938- .... **CLC 4**
See also CA 53-56; CANR 5

Berkeley, George 1685-1753 .... **LC 65**
See also DLB 31, 101, 252

Berkoff, Steven 1937- .... **CLC 56**
See also CA 104; CANR 72; CBD; CD 5, 6

Berlin, Isaiah 1909-1997 .... **TCLC 105**
See also CA 85-88; 162

Bermant, Chaim (Icyk) 1929-1998 . **CLC 40**
See also CA 57-60; CANR 6, 31, 57, 105; CN 2, 3, 4, 5, 6

Bern, Victoria
See Fisher, M(ary) F(rances) K(ennedy)

Bernanos, (Paul Louis) Georges 1888-1948 .... **TCLC 3, 267**
See also CA 104; 130; CANR 94; DLB 72; EWL 3; GFL 1789 to the Present; RGWL 2, 3

Bernard, April 1956- .... **CLC 59**
See also CA 131; CANR 144, 230

Bernard, Mary Ann
See Soderbergh, Steven

Bernard of Clairvaux 1090-1153 . **CMLC 71**
See also DLB 208

Bernard Silvestris fl. c. 1130-fl. c. 1160 .... **CMLC 87**
See also DLB 208

Bernart de Ventadorn c. 1130-c. 1190 .... **CMLC 98**

Berne, Victoria
See Fisher, M(ary) F(rances) K(ennedy)

Bernhard, Thomas 1931-1989 .... **CLC 3, 32, 61; DC 14; TCLC 165**
See also CA 85-88; 127; CANR 32, 57; CD-WLB 2; DLB 85, 124; EWL 3; MTCW 1; RGHL; RGWL 2, 3

Bernhardt, Sarah (Henriette Rosine) 1844-1923 .... **TCLC 75**
See also CA 157

Bernstein, Charles 1950- .... **CLC 142,**
See also CA 129; CAAS 24; CANR 90; CP 4, 5, 6, 7; DLB 169

Bernstein, Ingrid
See Kirsch, Sarah

Beroul fl. c. 12th cent. - .... **CMLC 75**

Berriault, Gina 1926-1999 ...... **CLC 54, 109; SSC 30**
See also CA 116; 129; 185; CANR 66; DLB 130; SSFS 7,11

Berrigan, Daniel 1921- .... **CLC 4**
See also CA 33-36R, 187; CAAE 187; CAAS 1; CANR 11, 43, 78, 219; CP 1, 2, 3, 4, 5, 6, 7; DLB 5

Berrigan, Edmund Joseph Michael, Jr. 1934-1983 .... **CLC 37; PC 103**
See also CA 61-64; 110; CANR 14, 102; CP 1, 2, 3; DLB 5, 169; WP

Berrigan, Ted
See Berrigan, Edmund Joseph Michael, Jr.

Berry, Charles Edward Anderson 1931- ..... **CLC 17**
See also CA 115

Berry, Chuck
See Berry, Charles Edward Anderson

Berry, Jonas
See Ashbery, John

Berry, Wendell 1934- ... **CLC 4, 6, 8, 27, 46, 279; PC 28**
See also AITN 1; AMWS 10; ANW; CA 73-76; CANR 50, 73, 101, 132, 174, 228; CP 1, 2, 3, 4, 5, 6, 7; CSW; DAM POET; DLB 5, 6, 234, 275, 342; MTCW 2; MTFW 2005; PFS 30; TCLE 1:1

Berry, Wendell Erdman
See Berry, Wendell

Berryman, John 1914-1972 . **CLC 1, 2, 3, 4, 6, 8, 10, 13, 25, 62; PC 64**
See also AMW; CA 13-16; 33-36R; CABS 2; CANR 35; CAP 1; CDALB 1941-1968; CP 1; DAM POET; DLB 48; EWL 3; MAL 5; MTCW 1, 2; MTFW 2005; PAB; PFS 27; RGAL 4; WP

Berssenbrugge, Mei-mei 1947- .... **PC 115**
See also CA 104; DLB 312

Bertolucci, Bernardo 1940- ..... **CLC 16, 157**
See also CA 106; CANR 125

Berton, Pierre (Francis de Marigny) 1920-2004 .... **CLC 104**
See also CA 1-4R; 233; CANR 2, 56, 144; CPW; DLB 68; SATA 99; SATA-Obit 158

Bertrand, Aloysius 1807-1841 .... **NCLC 31**
See also DLB 217

Bertrand, Louis oAloysiusc
See Bertrand, Aloysius

Bertran de Born c. 1140-1215 .... **CMLC 5**

Besant, Annie (Wood) 1847-1933 ... **TCLC 9**
See also CA 105; 185

Bessie, Alvah 1904-1985 .... **CLC 23**
See also CA 5-8R; 116; CANR 2, 80; DLB 26

Bestuzhev, Aleksandr Aleksandrovich 1797-1837 .... **NCLC 131**
See also DLB 198

Bethlen, T.D.
See Silverberg, Robert

Beti, Mongo 1932-2001 ... **BLC 1:1; CLC 27**
See also AFW; BW 1, 3; CA 114; 124; CANR 81; DA3; DAM MULT; DLB 360; EWL 3; MTCW 1, 2

Betjeman, John 1906-1984 ..... **CLC 2, 6, 10, 34, 43; PC 75**
See also BRW 7; CA 9-12R; 112; CANR 33, 56; CDBLB 1945-1960; CP 1, 2, 3; DA3; DAB; DAM MST, POET; DLB 20; DLBY 1984; EWL 3; MTCW 1, 2

Bettelheim, Bruno 1903-1990 .... **CLC 79; TCLC 143**
See also CA 81-84; 131; CANR 23, 61; DA3; MTCW 1, 2; RGHL

Betti, Ugo 1892-1953 .... **TCLC 5**
See also CA 104; 155; EWL 3; RGWL 2, 3

Betts, Doris (Waugh) 1932- .... **CLC 3, 6, 28, 275; SSC 45**
See also CA 13-16R; CANR 9, 66, 77; CN 6, 7; CSW; DLB 218; DLBY 1982; INT CANR-9; RGAL 4

Bevan, Alistair
See Roberts, Keith (John Kingston)

Bey, Pilaff
See Douglas, (George) Norman

Beyala, Calixthe 1961- .... **BLC 2:1**
See also EWL 3

Beynon, John
See Harris, John (Wyndham Parkes Lucas) Beynon

Bhabha, Homi K. 1949- .... **CLC 285**

Bialik, Chaim Nachman 1873-1934 ... **TCLC 25, 201**
See also CA 170; EWL 3; WLIT 6

Bialik, Hayyim Nahman
See Bialik, Chaim Nachman

Bickerstaff, Isaac
See Swift, Jonathan

Bidart, Frank 1939- .... **CLC 33**
See also AMWS 15; CA 140; CANR 106, 215; CP 5, 6, 7; PFS 26

Bienek, Horst 1930- .... **CLC 7, 11**
See also CA 73-76; DLB 75

Bierce, Ambrose 1842-1914(?) ..... **SSC 9, 72, 124; TCLC 1, 7, 44; WLC 1**
See also AAYA 55; AMW; BYA 11; CA 104; 139; CANR 78; CDALB 1865-1917; DA; DA3; DAC; DAM MST; DLB 11, 12, 23, 71, 74, 186; EWL 3; EXPS; HGG; LAIT 2; MAL 5; RGAL 4; RGSF 2; SSFS 9, 27; SUFW 1

Bierce, Ambrose Gwinett
See Bierce, Ambrose

Biggers, Earl Derr 1884-1933 .... **TCLC 65**
See also CA 108; 153; DLB 306

Bilek, Anton F. 1919- ....
See Rankin, Ian
See also CA 304

Billiken, Bud
See Motley, Willard (Francis)

Billings, Josh
See Shaw, Henry Wheeler

Billington, Lady Rachel Mary
See Billington, Rachel

Billington, Rachel 1942- .... **CLC 43**
See also AITN 2; CA 33-36R; CANR 44, 196; CN 4, 5, 6, 7

Binchy, Maeve 1940- .... **CLC 153**
See also BEST 90:1; BPFB 1; CA 127; 134; CANR 50, 96, 134, 208; CN 5, 6, 7; CPW; DA3; DAM POP; DLB 319; INT CA-134; MTCW 2; MTFW 2005; RHW

Binyon, T(imothy) J(ohn) 1936-2004 ... **CLC 34**
See also CA 111; 232; CANR 28, 140

Bion 335B.C.-245B.C. .... **CMLC 39**

Bioy Casares, Adolfo 1914-1999 .. **CLC 4, 8, 13, 88; HLC 1; SSC 17, 102**
See also CA 29-32R; 177; CANR 19, 43, 66; CWW 2; DAM MULT; DLB 113; EWL 3; HW 1, 2; LAW; MTCW 1, 2; MTFW 2005; RGSF 2

Birch, Allison CLC 65

Bird, Cordwainer
See Ellison, Harlan

Bird, Robert Montgomery 1806-1854 ....
NCLC 1, 197
See also DLB 202; RGAL 4

Birdwell, Cleo
See DeLillo, Don

Birkerts, Sven 1951- .... **CLC 116**
See also CA 128; 133, 176; CAAE 176; CAAS 29; CANR 151; INT CA-133

Birney, (Alfred) Earle 1904-1995 . **CLC 1, 4, 6, 11; PC 52**
See also CA 1-4R; CANR 5, 20; CN 1, 2, 3, 4; CP 1, 2, 3, 4, 5, 6; DAC; DAM MST, POET; DLB 88; MTCW 1; PFS 8; RGEL 2

Biruni, al 973-1048(?) .... **CMLC 28**

Bishop, Elizabeth 1911-1979 .... **CLC 1, 4, 9, 13, 15, 32; PC 3, 34; SSC 151; TCLC 121**
See also AMWR 2; AMWS 1; CA 5-8R; 89-92; CABS 2; CANR 26, 61, 108; CDALB 1968-1988; CP 1, 2, 3; DA; DA3; DAC; DAM MST, POET; DLB 5, 169; EWL 3; GLL 2; MAL 5; MBL; MTCW 1, 2; PAB; PFS 6, 12, 27, 31; RGAL 4; SATA-Obit 24; TUS; WP

Bishop, George Archibald
See Crowley, Edward Alexander

Bishop, John 1935- .... **CLC 10**
See also CA 105

Bishop, John Peale 1892-1944 .... **TCLC 103**
See also CA 107; 155; DLB 4, 9, 45; MAL 5; RGAL 4

Bissett, Bill 1939- .... **CLC 18; PC 14**
See also CA 69-72; CAAS 19; CANR 15; CCA 1; CP 1, 2, 3, 4, 5, 6, 7; DLB 53; MTCW 1

Bissoondath, Neil 1955- .... **CLC 120, 285**
See also CA 136; CANR 123, 165; CN 6, 7; DAC

Bissoondath, Neil Devindra
See Bissoondath, Neil

Bitov, Andrei (Georgievich) 1937- .. **CLC 57**
See also CA 142; DLB 302

Biyidi, Alexandre
See Beti, Mongo

Bjarme, Brynjolf
See Ibsen, Henrik

Bjoernson, Bjoernstjerne (Martinius)
1832-1910 .... **TCLC 7, 37**
See also CA 104

Black, Benjamin
See Banville, John

Black, Robert
See Holdstock, Robert

Blackburn, Paul 1926-1971 .... **CLC 9, 43**
See also BG 1:2; CA 81-84; 33-36R; CANR 34; CP 1; DLB 16; DLBY 1981

Black Elk 1863-1950 .... **NNAL; TCLC 33**
See also CA 144; DAM MULT; MTCW 2; MTFW 2005; WP

Black Hawk 1767-1838 .... **NNAL**

Black Hobart
See Sanders, Ed

Blacklin, Malcolm
See Chambers, Aidan

Blackmore, R(ichard) D(oddridge)
1825-1900 .... **TCLC 27**
See also CA 120; DLB 18; RGEL 2

Blackmur, R(ichard) P(almer) 1904-1965 ...
CLC 2, 24
See also AMWS 2; CA 11-12; 25-28R; CANR 71; CAP 1; DLB 63; EWL 3; MAL 5

Black Tarantula
See Acker, Kathy

Blackwood, Algernon 1869-1951 ... **SSC 107; TCLC 5**
See also AAYA 78; CA 105; 150; CANR 169; DLB 153, 156, 178; HGG; SUFW 1

Blackwood, Algernon Henry
See Blackwood, Algernon

Blackwood, Caroline (Maureen)
1931-1996 .... **CLC 6, 9, 100**
See also BRWS 9; CA 85-88; 151; CANR 32, 61, 65; CN 3, 4, 5, 6; DLB 14, 207; HGG; MTCW 1

Blade, Alexander
See Hamilton, Edmond; Silverberg, Robert

Blaga, Lucian 1895-1961 .... **CLC 75**
See also CA 157; DLB 220; EWL 3

Blair, Eric
See Orwell, George

Blair, Eric Arthur
See Orwell, George

Blair, Hugh 1718-1800 .... **NCLC 75**
See also DLB 356

Blais, Marie-Claire 1939- ... **CLC 2, 4, 6, 13, 22**
See also CA 21-24R; CAAS 4; CANR 38, 75, 93; CWW 2; DAC; DAM MST; DLB 53; EWL 3; FW; MTCW 1, 2; MTFW 2005; TWA

Blaise, Clark 1940- .... **CLC 29, 261**
See also AITN 2; CA 53-56; 231; CAAE 231; CAAS 3; CANR 5, 66, 106; CN 4, 5, 6, 7; DLB 53; RGSF 2

Blake, Fairley
See De Voto, Bernard (Augustine)

Blake, Nicholas
See Day Lewis, C.

Blake, Sterling
See Benford, Gregory

Blake, William 1757-1827 ...... **NCLC 13, 37, 57, 127, 173, 190, 201; PC 12, 63; WLC 1**
See also AAYA 47; BRW 3; BRWR 1; CD-BLB 1789-1832; CLR 52; DA; DA3; DAB; DAC; DAM MST, POET; DLB 93, 154, 163; EXPP; LATS 1:1; LMFS 1; MAICYA 1, 2; PAB; PFS 2, 12, 24, 34, 40; SATA 30; TEA; WCH; WLIT 3; WP

Blanchot, Maurice 1907-2003 .... **CLC 135**
See also CA 117; 144; 213; CANR 138; DLB 72, 296; EWL 3

Blasco Ibanez, Vicente 1867-1928 . **TCLC 12**
See also BPFB 1; CA 110; 131; CANR 81; DA3; DAM NOV; DLB 322; EW 8; EWL 3; HW 1, 2; MTCW 1

Blatty, William Peter 1928- .... **CLC 2**
See also CA 5-8R; CANR 9, 124, 226; DAM POP; HGG

Bleeck, Oliver
See Thomas, Ross (Elmore)

Bleecker, Ann Eliza 1752-1783 .... **LC 161**
See also DLB 200

Blessing, Lee 1949- .... **CLC 54**
See also CA 236; CAD; CD 5, 6; DFS 23, 26

Blessing, Lee Knowlton
See Blessing, Lee

Blight, Rose
See Greer, Germaine

Blind, Mathilde 1841-1896 .... **NCLC 202**
See also DLB 199

Blish, James 1921-1975 .... **CLC 14**
See also BPFB 1; CA 1-4R; 57-60; CANR 3; CN 2; DLB 8; MTCW 1; SATA 66; SCFW 1, 2; SFW 4

Blish, James Benjamin
See Blish, James

Bliss, Frederick
See Card, Orson Scott

Bliss, Gillian
See Paton Walsh, Jill

Bliss, Reginald
See Wells, H. G.

Blixen, Karen 1885-1962 .... **CLC 10, 29, 95; SSC 7, 75; TCLC 255**
See also CA 25-28; CANR 22, 50; CAP 2; DA3; DLB 214; EW 10; EWL 3; EXPS; FW; GL 2; HGG; LAIT 3; LMFS 1; MTCW 1; NCFS 2; NFS 9; RGSF 2; RGWL 2, 3; SATA 44; SSFS 3, 6, 13; WLIT 2

Blixen, Karen Christentze Dinesen
See Blixen, Karen

Bloch, Robert (Albert) 1917-1994 ... **CLC 33**
See also AAYA 29; CA 5-8R; 179; 146; CAAE 179; CAAS 20; CANR 5, 78; DA3; DLB 44; HGG; INT CANR-5; MTCW 2; SATA 12; SATA-Obit 82; SFW 4; SUFW 1, 2

Blok, Alexander (Alexandrovich)
1880-1921 .... **PC 21; TCLC 5**
See also CA 104; 183; DLB 295; EW 9; EWL 3; LMFS 2; RGWL 2, 3

Blom, Jan
See Breytenbach, Breyten

Bloom, Harold 1930- .... **CLC 24, 103, 221**
See also CA 13-16R; CANR 39, 75, 92, 133, 181; DLB 67; EWL 3; MTCW 2; MTFW 2005; RGAL 4

Bloomfield, Aurelius
See Bourne, Randolph S(illiman)

Bloomfield, Robert 1766-1823 .... **NCLC 145**
See also DLB 93

Blount, Roy, Jr. 1941- .... **CLC 38**
See also CA 53-56; CANR 10, 28, 61, 125, 176; CSW; INT CANR-28; MTCW 1, 2; MTFW 2005

Blount, Roy Alton
See Blount, Roy, Jr.

Blowsnake, Sam 1875-(?) .... **NNAL**

Bloy, Leon 1846-1917 .... **TCLC 22**
See also CA 121; 183; DLB 123; GFL 1789 to the Present

Blue Cloud, Peter (Aroniawenrate) 1933- ... **NNAL**
See also CA 117; CANR 40; DAM MULT; DLB 342

Bluggage, Oranthy
See Alcott, Louisa May

Blume, Judy 1938- .... **CLC 12, 30**
See also AAYA 3, 26; BYA 1, 8, 12; CA 29-32R; CANR 13, 37, 66, 124, 186; CLR 2, 15, 69; CPW; DA3; DAM NOV, POP; DLB 52; JRDA; MAICYA 1, 2; MAIC-YAS 1; MTCW 1, 2; MTFW 2005; NFS 24; SATA 2, 31, 79, 142, 195; WYA; YAW

Blume, Judy Sussman
See Blume, Judy

Blunden, Edmund (Charles) 1896-1974 .... **CLC 2, 56; PC 66**
See also BRW 6; BRWS 11; CA 17-18; 45-48; CANR 54; CAP 2; CP 1, 2; DLB 20, 100, 155; MTCW 1; PAB

Bly, Robert 1926- ... **CLC 1, 2, 5, 10, 15, 38, 128; PC 39**
See also AMWS 4; CA 5-8R; CANR 41, 73, 125; CP 1, 2, 3, 4, 5, 6, 7; DA3; DAM POET; DLB 5, 342; EWL 3; MAL 5; MTCW 1, 2; MTFW 2005; PFS 6, 17; RGAL 4

Bly, Robert Elwood
See Bly, Robert

Boas, Franz 1858-1942 .... **TCLC 56**
See also CA 115; 181

Bobette
See Simenon, Georges

Boccaccio, Giovanni 1313-1375 .. **CMLC 13, 57, 140; SSC 10, 87, 167**
See also EW 2; RGSF 2; RGWL 2, 3; SSFS 28; TWA; WLIT 7

Bochco, Steven 1943- .... **CLC 35**
See also AAYA 11, 71; CA 124; 138

Bock, Charles 1970- .... **CLC 299**
See also CA 274

Bode, Sigmund
See O'Doherty, Brian

Bodel, Jean 1167(?)-1210 .... **CMLC 28**

Bodenheim, Maxwell 1892-1954 ... **TCLC 44**
See also CA 110; 187; DLB 9, 45; MAL 5; RGAL 4

Bodenheimer, Maxwell
See Bodenheim, Maxwell

Bodker, Cecil
See Bodker, Cecil

Bodker, Cecil 1927- .... **CLC 21**
See also CA 73-76; CANR 13, 44, 111; CLR 23; MAICYA 1, 2; SATA 14, 133

Boell, Heinrich 1917-1985 .... **CLC 2, 3, 6, 9, 11, 15, 27, 32, 72; SSC 23; TCLC 185; WLC 1**
See also BPFB 1; CA 21-24R; 116; CANR 24; CDWLB 2; DA; DA3; DAB; DAC; DAM MST, NOV; DLB 69; 329; DLBY 1985; EW 13; EWL 3; MTCW 1, 2; MTFW 2005; RGHL; RGSF 2; RGWL 2, 3; SSFS 20; TWA

Boell, Heinrich Theodor
See Boell, Heinrich

Boerne, Alfred
See Doeblin, Alfred

Boethius c. 480-c. 524 .... **CMLC 15, 136**
See also DLB 115; RGWL 2, 3; WLIT 8

Boff, Leonardo (Genezio Darci) 1938- . **CLC 70; HLC 1**
See also CA 150; DAM MULT; HW 2

Bogan, Louise 1897-1970 ...... **CLC 4, 39, 46, 93; PC 12**
See also AMWS 3; CA 73-76; 25-28R; CANR 33, 82; CP 1; DAM POET; DLB 45, 169; EWL 3; MAL 5; MBL; MTCW 1, 2; PFS 21, 39; RGAL 4

Bogarde, Dirk
See Van Den Bogarde, Derek Jules Gaspard Ulric Niven

Bogat, Shatan
See Kacew, Romain

Bogomolny, Robert L. 1938- .... **SSC 41; TCLC 11**
See also CA 121, 164; DLB 182; EWL 3; MJW; RGSF 2; RGWL 2, 3; TWA

Bogomolny, Robert Lee
See Bogomolny, Robert L.

Bogosian, Eric 1953- .... **CLC 45, 141**
See also CA 138; CAD; CANR 102, 148, 217; CD 5, 6; DLB 341

Bograd, Larry 1953- .... **CLC 35**
See also CA 93-96; CANR 57; SAAS 21; SATA 33, 89; WYA

Bohme, Jakob 1575-1624 .... **LC 178**
See also DLB 164

Boiardo, Matteo Maria 1441-1494 ..... **LC 6, 168**

Boileau-Despreaux, Nicolas 1636-1711 ... **LC 3, 164**
See also DLB 268; EW 3; GFL Beginnings to 1789; RGWL 2, 3

Boissard, Maurice
See Leautaud, Paul

Bojer, Johan 1872-1959 .... **TCLC 64**
See also CA 189; EWL 3

Bok, Edward W(illiam) 1863-1930 .... **TCLC 101**
See also CA 217; DLB 91; DLBD 16

Boker, George Henry 1823-1890 . **NCLC 125**
See also RGAL 4

Boland, Eavan 1944- .. **CLC 40, 67, 113; PC 58**
See also BRWS 5; CA 143, 207; CAAE 207; CANR 61, 180; CP 1, 6, 7; CWP; DAM POET; DLB 40; FW; MTCW 2; MTFW 2005; PFS 12, 22, 31, 39

Boland, Eavan Aisling
See Boland, Eavan

Bolano, Roberto 1953-2003 .... **CLC 294**
See also CA 229; CANR 175

Bolingbroke, Viscount
See St. John, Henry

Boll, Heinrich
See Boell, Heinrich

Bolt, Lee
See Faust, Frederick

Bolt, Robert (Oxton) 1924-1995 .... **CLC 14; TCLC 175**
See also CA 17-20R; 147; CANR 35, 67; CBD; DAM DRAM; DFS 2; DLB 13, 233; EWL 3; LAIT 1; MTCW 1

Bombal, Maria Luisa 1910-1980 ... **HLCS 1; SSC 37**
See also CA 127; CANR 72; EWL 3; HW 1; LAW; RGSF 2

Bombet, Louis-Alexandre-Cesar
See Stendhal

Bomkauf
See Kaufman, Bob (Garnell)

Bonaventura **NCLC 35, 252**
See also DLB 90

Bonaventure 1217(?)-1274 .... **CMLC 79**
See also DLB 115; LMFS 1

Bond, Edward 1934- . **CLC 4, 6, 13, 23; DC 45**
See also AAYA 50; BRWS 1; CA 25-28R; CANR 38, 67, 106; CBD; CD 5, 6; DAM DRAM; DFS 3, 8; DLB 13, 310; EWL 3; MTCW 1

Bonham, Frank 1914-1989 .... **CLC 12**
See also AAYA 1, 70; BYA 1, 3; CA 9-12R; CANR 4, 36; JRDA; MAICYA 1, 2; SAAS 3; SATA 1, 49; SATA-Obit 62; TCWW 1, 2; YAW

Bonnefoy, Yves 1923- . **CLC 9, 15, 58; PC 58**
See also CA 85-88; CANR 33, 75, 97, 136; CWW 2; DAM MST, POET; DLB 258; EWL 3; GFL 1789 to the Present; MTCW 1, 2; MTFW 2005

Bonner, Marita
See Occomy, Marita (Odette) Bonner

Bonnin, Gertrude 1876-1938 .... **NNAL**
See also CA 150; DAM MULT; DLB 175

Bontemps, Arna 1902-1973 . **BLC 1:1; CLC 1, 18; HR 1:2**
See also BW 1; CA 1-4R; 41-44R; CANR 4, 35; CLR 6; CP 1; CWRI 5; DA3; DAM MULT, NOV, POET; DLB 48, 51; JRDA; MAICYA 1, 2; MAL 5; MTCW 1, 2; PFS 32; SATA 2, 44; SATA-Obit 24; WCH; WP

Bontemps, Arnaud Wendell
See Bontemps, Arna

Boot, William
See Stoppard, Tom

Booth, Irwin
See Hoch, Edward D.

Booth, Martin 1944-2004 .... **CLC 13**
See also CA 93-96; 188; 223; CAAE 188; CAAS 2; CANR 92; CP 1, 2, 3, 4

Booth, Philip 1925-2007 .... **CLC 23**
See also CA 5-8R; 262; CANR 5, 88; CP 1, 2, 3, 4, 5, 6, 7; DLBY 1982

Booth, Philip Edmund
See Booth, Philip

Booth, Wayne C. 1921-2005 .... **CLC 24**
See also CA 1-4R; 244; CAAS 5; CANR 3, 43, 117; DLB 67

Booth, Wayne Clayson
See Booth, Wayne C.

Borchert, Wolfgang 1921-1947 .... **DC 42; TCLC 5**
See also CA 104; 188; DLB 69, 124; EWL 3

Borel, Petrus 1809-1859 .... **NCLC 41**
See also DLB 119; GFL 1789 to the Present

Borges, Jorge Luis 1899-1986 .. **CLC 1, 2, 3, 4, 6, 8, 9, 10, 13, 19, 44, 48, 83; HLC 1; PC 22, 32; SSC 4, 41, 100, 159; TCLC 109; WLC 1**
See also AAYA 26; BPFB 1; CA 21-24R; CANR 19, 33, 75, 105, 133; CDWLB 3; DA; DA3; DAB; DAC; DAM MST, MULT; DLB 113, 283; DLBY 1986; DNFS 1, 2; EWL 3; HW 1, 2; LAW; LMFS 2; MSW; MTCW 1, 2; MTFW 2005; PFS 27; RGHL; RGSF 2; RGWL 2, 3; SFW 4; SSFS 17; TWA; WLIT 1

Borne, Ludwig 1786-1837 .... **NCLC 193**
See also DLB 90

Borowski, Tadeusz 1922-1951 .... **SSC 48; TCLC 9**
See also CA 106; 154; CDWLB 4; DLB 215; EWL 3; RGHL; RGSF 2; RGWL 3; SSFS 13

Borrow, George (Henry) 1803-1881 .. **NCLC 9**
See also BRWS 12; DLB 21, 55, 166

Bosch (Gavino), Juan 1909-2001 .... **HLCS 1**
See also CA 151; 204; DAM MST, MULT; DLB 145; HW 1, 2

Bosman, Herman Charles 1905-1951 . **TCLC 49**
See also CA 160; DLB 225; RGSF 2

Bosschere, Jean de 1878(?)-1953 .. **TCLC 19**
See also CA 115; 186

Boswell, James 1740-1795 ..... **LC 4, 50, 182; WLC 1**
See also BRW 3; CDBLB 1660-1789; DA; DAB; DAC; DAM MST; DLB 104, 142; TEA; WLIT 3

Boto, Eza
See Beti, Mongo

Bottomley, Gordon 1874-1948 .... **TCLC 107**
See also CA 120; 192; DLB 10

Bottoms, David 1949- .... **CLC 53**
See also CA 105; CANR 22; CSW; DLB 120; DLBY 1983

Boucicault, Dion 1820-1890 .... **NCLC 41**
See also DLB 344

Boucolon, Maryse
See Conde, Maryse

Bourcicault, Dion
See Boucicault, Dion

Bourdieu, Pierre 1930-2002 .. **CLC 198, 296**
See also CA 130; 204

Bourget, Paul (Charles Joseph) 1852-1935 . **TCLC 12**
See also CA 107; 196; DLB 123; GFL 1789 to the Present

Bourjaily, Vance 1922-2010 .... **CLC 8, 62**
See also CA 1-4R; CAAS 1; CANR 2, 72; CN 1, 2, 3, 4, 5, 6, 7; DLB 2, 143; MAL 5

Bourjaily, Vance Nye
See Bourjaily, Vance

Bourne, Randolph S(illiman) 1886-1918 ..... **TCLC 16**
See also AMW; CA 117; 155; DLB 63; MAL 5

Boursiquot, Dionysius
See Boucicault, Dion

Bova, Ben 1932- .... **CLC 45**
See also AAYA 16; CA 5-8R; CAAS 18; CANR 11, 56, 94, 111, 157, 219; CLR 3, 96; DLBY 1981; INT CANR-11; MAICYA 1, 2; MTCW 1; SATA 6, 68, 133; SFW 4

Bova, Benjamin William
See Bova, Ben

Bowen, Elizabeth 1899-1973 .... **CLC 1, 3, 6, 11, 15, 22, 118; SSC 3, 28, 66; TCLC 148**
See also BRWS 2; CA 17-18; 41-44R; CANR 35, 105; CAP 2; CDBLB 1945-1960; CN 1; DA3; DAM NOV; DLB 15, 162; EWL 3; EXPS; FW; HGG; MTCW 1, 2; MTFW 2005; NFS 13; RGSF 2; SSFS 5, 22; SUFW 1; TEA; WLIT 4

Bowen, Elizabeth Dorothea Cole
See Bowen, Elizabeth

Bowering, George 1935- .... **CLC 15, 47**
See also CA 21-24R; CAAS 16; CANR 10; CN 7; CP 1, 2, 3, 4, 5, 6, 7; DLB 53

Bowering, Marilyn R(uthe) 1949- ... **CLC 32**
See also CA 101; CANR 49; CP 4, 5, 6, 7; CWP; DLB 334

Bowers, Edgar 1924-2000 .... **CLC 9**
See also CA 5-8R; 188; CANR 24; CP 1, 2, 3, 4, 5, 6, 7; CSW; DLB 5

Bowers, Mrs. J. Milton
See Bierce, Ambrose

Bowie, David
See Jones, David Robert

Bowles, Jane (Sydney) 1917-1973 .... **CLC 3, 68**
See also CA 19-20; 41-44R; CAP 2; CN 1; EWL 3; MAL 5

Bowles, Jane Auer
See Bowles, Jane (Sydney)

Bowles, Paul 1910-1999 ... **CLC 1, 2, 19, 53; SSC 3, 98; TCLC 209**
See also AMWS 4; CA 1-4R; 186; CAAS 1; CANR 1, 19, 50, 75; CN 1, 2, 3, 4, 5, 6; DA3; DLB 5, 6, 218; EWL 3; MAL 5; MTCW 1, 2; MTFW 2005; RGAL 4; SSFS 17

Bowles, William Lisle 1762-1850 . **NCLC 103**
See also DLB 93

Box, Edgar
See Vidal, Gore

Boyd, James 1888-1944 .... **TCLC 115**
See also CA 186; DLB 9; DLBD 16; RGAL 4; RHW

Boyd, Nancy
See Millay, Edna St. Vincent

Boyd, Thomas (Alexander) 1898-1935 .... **TCLC 111**
See also CA 111; 183; DLB 9; DLBD 16, 316

Boyd, William 1952- .... **CLC 28, 53, 70**
See also BRWS 16; CA 114; 120; CANR 51, 71, 131, 174; CN 4, 5, 6, 7; DLB 231

Boyesen, Hjalmar Hjorth 1848-1895 . **NCLC 135**
See also DLB 12, 71; DLBD 13; RGAL 4

Boyle, Kay 1902-1992 .... **CLC 1, 5, 19, 58, 121; SSC 5, 102**
See also CA 13-16R; 140; CAAS 1; CANR 29, 61, 110; CN 1, 2, 3, 4, 5; DLB 4, 9, 48, 86; DLBY 1993; EWL 3; MAL 5; MTCW 1, 2; MTFW 2005; RGAL 4; RGSF 2; SSFS 10, 13, 14

Boyle, Mark
See Kienzle, William X.

Boyle, Patrick 1905-1982 .... **CLC 19**
See also CA 127

Boyle, Roger 1621-1679 .... **LC 198**
See also DLB 80; RGEL 2

Boyle, T.C. 1948- . **CLC 36, 55, 90, 284; SSC 16, 127**
See also AAYA 47; AMWS 8, 20; BEST 90:4; BPFB 1; CA 120; CANR 44, 76, 89, 132, 224; CN 6, 7; CPW; DA3; DAM POP; DLB 218, 278; DLBY 1986; EWL 3; MAL 5; MTCW 2; MTFW 2005; SSFS 13, 19, 34

Boyle, T.Coraghessan
See Boyle, T.C.

Boyle, Thomas Coraghessan
See Boyle, T.C.

Boz
See Dickens, Charles

Brackenridge, Hugh Henry 1748-1816 .... **NCLC 7, 227**
See also DLB 11, 37; RGAL 4

Bradbury, Edward P.
See Moorcock, Michael

Bradbury, Malcolm 1932-2000 . **CLC 32, 61**
See also BRWS 17; CA 1-4R; CANR 1, 33, 91, 98, 137; CN 1, 2, 3, 4, 5, 6, 7; CP 1; DA3; DAM NOV; DLB 14, 207; EWL 3; MTCW 1, 2; MTFW 2005

Bradbury, Ray 1920- .. **CLC 1, 3, 10, 15, 42, 98, 235; SSC 29, 53, 157; WLC 1**
See also AAYA 15, 84; AITN 1, 2; AMWS 4; BPFB 1; BYA 4, 5, 11; CA 1-4R; CANR 2, 30, 75, 125, 186; CDALB 1968-1988; CN 1, 2, 3, 4, 5, 6, 7; CPW; DA; DA3; DAB; DAC; DAM MST, NOV, POP; DLB 2, 8; EXPN; EXPS; HGG; LAIT 3, 5; LATS 1:2; LMFS 2; MAL 5; MTCW 1, 2; MTFW 2005; NFS 1, 22, 29; RGAL 4; RGSF 2; SATA 11, 64, 123; SCFW 1, 2; SFW 4; SSFS 1, 20, 28; SUFW 1, 2; TUS; YAW

Bradbury, Ray Douglas
See Bradbury, Ray

Braddon, Mary Elizabeth 1837-1915 . **TCLC 111**
See also BRWS 8; CA 108; 179; CMW 4; DLB 18, 70, 156; HGG

Bradfield, Scott 1955- .... **SSC 65**
See also CA 147; CANR 90; HGG; SUFW 2

Bradfield, Scott Michael
See Bradfield, Scott

Bradford, Gamaliel 1863-1932 ..... **TCLC 36**
See also CA 160; DLB 17

Bradford, William 1590-1657 .... **LC 64**
See also DLB 24, 30; RGAL 4

Bradley, David, Jr. 1950- ..... **BLC 1:1; CLC 23, 118**
See also BW 1, 3; CA 104; CANR 26, 81; CN 4, 5, 6, 7; DAM MULT; DLB 33

Bradley, David Henry, Jr.
See Bradley, David, Jr.

Bradley, John Ed 1958- .... **CLC 55**
See also CA 139; CANR 99; CN 6, 7; CSW

Bradley, John Edmund, Jr.
See Bradley, John Ed

Bradley, Marion Zimmer 1930-1999 ... **CLC 30**
See also AAYA 40; BPFB 1; CA 57-60; 185; CAAS 10; CANR 7, 31, 51, 75, 107; CLR 158; CPW; DA3; DAM POP; DLB 8; FANT; FW; GLL 1; MTCW 1, 2; MTFW 2005; NFS 40; SATA 90, 139; SATA-Obit 116; SFW 4; SUFW 2; YAW

Bradshaw, John 1933- .... **CLC 70**
See also CA 138; CANR 61, 216

Bradshaw, John Elliot
See Bradshaw, John

Bradstreet, Anne 1612(?)-1672 ..... **LC 4, 30, 130; PC 10**
See also AMWS 1; CDALB 1640-1865; DA; DA3; DAC; DAM MST, POET; DLB 24; EXPP; FW; PFS 6, 33; RGAL 4; TUS; WP

Brady, Joan 1939- .... **CLC 86**
See also CA 141

Bragg, Melvyn 1939- .... **CLC 10**
See also BEST 89:3; CA 57-60; CANR 10, 48, 89, 158; CN 1, 2, 3, 4, 5, 6, 7; DLB 14, 271; RHW

Bragg, Rick 1959- .... **CLC 296**
See also CA 165; CANR 112, 137, 194; MTFW 2005

Bragg, Ricky Edward
See Bragg, Rick

Brahe, Tycho 1546-1601 .... **LC 45**
See also DLB 300

Braine, John (Gerard) 1922-1986 .... **CLC 1, 3, 41**
See also CA 1-4R; 120; CANR 1, 33; CDBLB 1945-1960; CN 1, 2, 3, 4; DLB 15; DLBY 1986; EWL 3; MTCW 1

Braithwaite, William Stanley (Beaumont) 1878-1962 .... **BLC 1:1; HR 1:2; PC 52**
See also BW 1; CA 125; DAM MULT; DLB 50, 54; MAL 5

Bramah, Ernest 1868-1942 .... **TCLC 72**
See also CA 156; CMW 4; DLB 70; FANT

Brammer, Billy Lee
See Brammer, William

Brammer, William 1929-1978 .... **CLC 31**
See also CA 235; 77-80

Brancati, Vitaliano 1907-1954 ...... **TCLC 12**
See also CA 109; DLB 264; EWL 3

Brancato, Robin F. 1936- .... **CLC 35**
See also AAYA 9, 68; BYA 6; CA 69-72; CANR 11, 45; CLR 32; JRDA; MAICYA 2; MAICYAS 1; SAAS 9; SATA 97; WYA; YAW

Brancato, Robin Fidler
See Brancato, Robin F.
Brand, Dionne 1953- .... **CLC 192**
See also BW 2; CA 143; CANR 143, 216;
CWP; DLB 334
Brand, Max
See Faust, Frederick
Brand, Millen 1906-1980 .... **CLC 7**
See also CA 21-24R; 97-100; CANR 72
Branden, Barbara 1929- .... **CLC 44**
See also CA 148
Brandes, Georg (Morris Cohen)
1842-1927 .... **TCLC 10, 264**
See also CA 105; 189; DLB 300
Brandys, Kazimierz 1916-2000 .... **CLC 62**
See also CA 239; EWL 3
Branley, Franklyn M(ansfield) 1915-2002 ...
CLC 21
See also CA 33-36R; 207; CANR 14, 39;
CLR 13; MAICYA 1, 2; SAAS 16; SATA
4, 68, 136
Brant, Beth (E.) 1941- .... **NNAL**
See also CA 144; FW
Brant, Sebastian 1457-1521 .... **LC 112**
See also DLB 179; RGWL 2, 3
Brathwaite, Edward Kamau 1930- ...... **BLC**
2:1; BLCS; CLC 11, 305; PC 56
See also BRWS 12; BW 2, 3; CA 25-28R;
CANR 11, 26, 47, 107; CDWLB 3; CP 1,
2, 3, 4, 5, 6, 7; DAM POET; DLB 125;
EWL 3
Brathwaite, Kamau
See Brathwaite, Edward Kamau
Brautigan, Richard 1935-1984 . **CLC 1, 3, 5,**
9, 12, 34, 42; PC 94; TCLC 133
See also BPFB 1; CA 53-56; 113; CANR
34; CN 1, 2, 3; CP 1, 2, 3, 4; DA3; DAM
NOV; DLB 2, 5, 206; DLBY 1980, 1984;
FANT; MAL 5; MTCW 1; RGAL 4;
SATA 56
Brautigan, Richard Gary
See Brautigan, Richard
Brave Bird, Mary
See Crow Dog, Mary
Braverman, Kate 1950- .... **CLC 67**
See also CA 89-92; CANR 141; DLB 335
Brecht, Bertolt 1898-1956 ... **DC 3; TCLC 1,**
6, 13, 35, 169; WLC 1
See also CA 104; 133; CANR 62; CDWLB
2; DA; DA3; DAB; DAC; DAM DRAM,
MST; DFS 4, 5, 9; DLB 56, 124; EW 11;
EWL 3; IDTP; MTCW 1, 2; MTFW 2005;
RGHL; RGWL 2, 3; TWA
Brecht, Eugen Berthold Friedrich
See Brecht, Bertolt
Brecht, Eugen Bertolt Friedrich
See Brecht, Bertolt
Bremer, Fredrika 1801-1865 .... **NCLC 11**
See also DLB 254
Brennan, Christopher John 1870-1932 ....
TCLC 17
See also CA 117; 188; DLB 230; EWL 3
Brennan, Maeve 1917-1993 .. **CLC 5; TCLC**
124
See also CA 81-84; CANR 72, 100
Brenner, Jozef 1887-1919 .... **TCLC 13**
See also CA 111; 240
Brent, Linda
See Jacobs, Harriet A.
Brentano, Clemens (Maria) 1778-1842 ....
NCLC 1, 191; SSC 115
See also DLB 90; RGWL 2, 3
Brent of Bin Bin
See Franklin, (Stella Maria Sarah) Miles
(Lampe)
Brenton, Howard 1942- .... **CLC 31**
See also CA 69-72; CANR 33, 67; CBD;
CD 5, 6; DLB 13; MTCW 1

Breslin, James
See Breslin, Jimmy
Breslin, Jimmy 1930- .... **CLC 4, 43**
See also CA 73-76; CANR 31, 75, 139, 187;
DAM NOV; DLB 185; MTCW 2; MTFW
2005
Bresson, Robert 1901(?)-1999 .... **CLC 16**
See also CA 110; 187; CANR 49
Breton, Andre 1896-1966 . **CLC 2, 9, 15, 54;**
PC 15; TCLC 247
See also CA 19-20; 25-28R; CANR 40, 60;
CAP 2; DLB 65, 258; EW 11; EWL 3;
GFL 1789 to the Present; LMFS 2;
MTCW 1, 2; MTFW 2005; RGWL 2, 3;
TWA; WP
Breton, Nicholas c. 1554-c. 1626 ...... **LC 133**
See also DLB 136
Breytenbach, Breyten 1939(?)- . **CLC 23, 37,**
126
See also CA 113; 129; CANR 61, 122, 202;
CWW 2; DAM POET; DLB 225; EWL 3
Bridgers, Sue Ellen 1942- .... **CLC 26**
See also AAYA 8, 49; BYA 7, 8; CA 65-68;
CANR 11, 36; CLR 18; DLB 52; JRDA;
MAICYA 1, 2; SAAS 1; SATA 22, 90;
SATA-Essay 109; WYA; YAW
Bridges, Robert (Seymour) 1844-1930 ... **PC**
28; TCLC 1
See also BRW 6; CA 104; 152; CDBLB
1890-1914; DAM POET; DLB 19, 98
Bridie, James
See Mavor, Osborne Henry
Brin, David 1950- .... **CLC 34**
See also AAYA 21; CA 102; CANR 24, 70,
125, 127; INT CANR-24; SATA 65;
SCFW 2; SFW 4
Brink, Andre 1935- .... **CLC 18, 36, 106**
See also AFW; BRWS 6; CA 104; CANR
39, 62, 109, 133, 182; CN 4, 5, 6, 7; DLB
225; EWL 3; INT CA-103; LATS 1:2;
MTCW 1, 2; MTFW 2005; WLIT 2
Brink, Andre Philippus
See Brink, Andre
Brinsmead, H. F.
See Brinsmead, H(esba) F(ay)
Brinsmead, H. F(ay)
See Brinsmead, H(esba) F(ay)
Brinsmead, H(esba) F(ay) 1922- ..... **CLC 21**
See also CA 21-24R; CANR 10; CLR 47;
CWRI 5; MAICYA 1, 2; SAAS 5; SATA
18, 78
Brittain, Vera (Mary) 1893(?)-1970 ..... **CLC**
23; TCLC 228
See also BRWS 10; CA 13-16; 25-28R;
CANR 58; CAP 1; DLB 191; FW; MTCW
1, 2
Broch, Hermann 1886-1951 .. **TCLC 20, 204**
See also CA 117; 211; CDWLB 2; DLB 85,
124; EW 10; EWL 3; RGWL 2, 3
Brock, Rose
See Hansen, Joseph
Brod, Max 1884-1968 .... **TCLC 115**
See also CA 5-8R; 25-28R; CANR 7; DLB
81; EWL 3
Brodkey, Harold (Roy) 1930-1996 . **CLC 56;**
TCLC 123
See also CA 111; 151; CANR 71; CN 4, 5,
6; DLB 130
Brodskii, Iosif
See Brodsky, Joseph
Brodskii, Iosif Alexandrovich
See Brodsky, Joseph
Brodsky, Iosif Alexandrovich
See Brodsky, Joseph
Brodsky, Joseph 1940-1996 .... **CLC 4, 6, 13,**
36, 100; PC 9; TCLC 219
See also AAYA 71; AITN 1; AMWS 8; CA
41-44R; 151; CANR 37, 106; CWW 2;

DA3; DAM POET; DLB 285, 329; EWL
3; MTCW 1, 2; MTFW 2005; PFS 35;
RGWL 2, 3
Brodsky, Michael 1948- .... **CLC 19**
See also CA 102; CANR 18, 41, 58, 147;
DLB 244
Brodsky, Michael Mark
See Brodsky, Michael
Brodzki, Bella **CLC 65**
Brome, Richard 1590(?)-1652 .... **LC 61**
See also BRWS 10; DLB 58
Bromell, Henry 1947- .... **CLC 5**
See also CA 53-56; CANR 9, 115, 116
Bromfield, Louis (Brucker) 1896-1956 ....
TCLC 11
See also CA 107; 155; DLB 4, 9, 86; RGAL
4; RHW
Broner, E. M. 1930-2011 .... **CLC 19**
See also CA 17-20R; CANR 8, 25, 72, 216;
CN 4, 5, 6; DLB 28
Broner, Esther Masserman
See Broner, E. M.
Bronk, William 1918-1999 .... **CLC 10**
See also AMWS 21; CA 89-92; 177; CANR
23; CP 3, 4, 5, 6, 7; DLB 165
Bronstein, Lev Davidovich
See Trotsky, Leon
Bronte, Anne 1820-1849 .. **NCLC 4, 71, 102,**
235
See also BRW 5; BRWR 1; DA3; DLB 21,
199, 340; NFS 26; TEA
Bronte, (Patrick) Branwell 1817-1848 ....
NCLC 109
See also DLB 340
Bronte, Charlotte 1816-1855 ..... **NCLC 3, 8,**
33, 58, 105, 155, 217, 229; SSC 167;
WLC 1
See also AAYA 17; BRW 5; BRWC 2;
BRWR 1; BYA 2; CDBLB 1832-1890;
DA; DA3; DAB; DAC; DAM MST, NOV;
DLB 21, 159, 199, 340; EXPN; FL 1:2;
GL 2; LAIT 2; NFS 4, 36; TEA; WLIT 4
Bronte, Emily 1818-1848 . **NCLC 16, 35, 165,**
244; PC 8; WLC 1
See also AAYA 17; BPFB 1; BRW 5;
BRWC 1; BRWR 1; BYA 3; CDBLB
1832-1890; DA; DA3; DAB; DAC; DAM
MST, NOV, POET; DLB 21, 32, 199, 340;
EXPN; FL 1:2; GL 2; LAIT 1; NFS 2;
PFS 33; TEA; WLIT 3
Bronte, Emily Jane
See Bronte, Emily
Brontes
See Bronte, Anne; Bronte, (Patrick) Bran-
well; Bronte, Charlotte; Bronte, Emily
Brooke, Frances 1724-1789 .... **LC 6, 48**
See also DLB 39, 99
Brooke, Henry 1703(?)-1783 .... **LC 1**
See also DLB 39
Brooke, Rupert 1887-1915 . **PC 24; TCLC 2,**
7; WLC 1
See also BRWS 3; CA 104; 132; CANR 61;
CDBLB 1914-1945; DA; DAB; DAC;
DAM MST, POET; DLB 19, 216; EXPP;
GLL 2; MTCW 1, 2; MTFW 2005; PFS
7; TEA
Brooke, Rupert Chawner
See Brooke, Rupert
Brooke-Haven, P.
See Wodehouse, P. G.
Brooke-Rose, Christine 1923(?)- .... **CLC 40,**
184
See also BRWS 4; CA 13-16R; CANR 58,
118, 183; CN 1, 2, 3, 4, 5, 6, 7; DLB 14,
231; EWL 3; SFW 4
Brookner, Anita 1928- . **CLC 32, 34, 51, 136,**
237
See also BRWS 4; CA 114; 120; CANR 37,
56, 87, 130, 212; CN 4, 5, 6, 7; CPW;

DA3; DAB; DAM POP; DLB 194, 326;
DLBY 1987; EWL 3; MTCW 1, 2; MTFW
2005; NFS 23; TEA

Brooks, Cleanth 1906-1994 ...... **CLC 24, 86,
110**
See also AMWS 14; CA 17-20R; 145;
CANR 33, 35; CSW; DLB 63; DLBY
1994; EWL 3; INT CANR-35; MAL 5;
MTCW 1, 2; MTFW 2005

Brooks, George
See Baum, L. Frank

Brooks, Gwendolyn 1917-2000 ...... **BLC 1:1,
2:1; CLC 1, 2, 4, 5, 15, 49, 125; PC 7;
WLC 1**
See also AAYA 20; AFAW 1, 2; AITN 1;
AMWS 3; BW 2, 3; CA 1-4R; 190; CANR
1, 27, 52, 75, 132; CDALB 1941-1968;
CLR 27; CP 1, 2, 3, 4, 5, 6, 7; CWP; DA;
DA3; DAC; DAM MST, MULT, POET;
DLB 5, 76, 165; EWL 3; EXPP; FL 1:5;
MAL 5; MBL; MTCW 1, 2; MTFW 2005;
PFS 1, 2, 4, 6, 32, 40; RGAL 4; SATA 6;
SATA-Obit 123; TUS; WP

Brooks, Gwendolyn Elizabeth
See Brooks, Gwendolyn

Brooks, Mel 1926- .... **CLC 12, 217**
See also AAYA 13, 48; CA 65-68; CANR
16; DFS 21; DLB 26

Brooks, Peter 1938- .... **CLC 34**
See also CA 45-48; CANR 1, 107, 182

Brooks, Peter Preston
See Brooks, Peter

Brooks, Van Wyck 1886-1963 .... **CLC 29**
See also AMW; CA 1-4R; CANR 6; DLB
45, 63, 103; MAL 5; TUS

Brophy, Brigid 1929-1995 .... **CLC 6, 11, 29,
105**
See also CA 5-8R; 149; CAAS 4; CANR
25, 53; CBD; CN 1, 2, 3, 4, 5, 6; CWD;
DA3; DLB 14, 271; EWL 3; MTCW 1, 2

Brophy, Brigid Antonia
See Brophy, Brigid

Brosman, Catharine Savage 1934- ... **CLC 9**
See also CA 61-64; CANR 21, 46, 149, 222

Brossard, Nicole 1943- ... **CLC 115, 169; PC
80**
See also CA 122; CAAS 16; CANR 140;
CCA 1; CWP; CWW 2; DLB 53; EWL 3;
FW; GLL 2; RGWL 3

Brother Antoninus
See Everson, William

Brothers Grimm
See Grimm, Jacob Ludwig Karl; Grimm,
Wilhelm Karl

The Brothers Quay
See Quay, Stephen; Quay, Timothy

Broughton, T(homas) Alan 1936- ... **CLC 19**
See also CA 45-48; CANR 2, 23, 48, 111

Broumas, Olga 1949- .... **CLC 10, 73**
See also CA 85-88; CANR 20, 69, 110; CP
5, 6, 7; CWP; GLL 2

Broun, Heywood 1888-1939 .... **TCLC 104**
See also DLB 29, 171

Brown, Alan 1950- .... **CLC 99**
See also CA 156

Brown, Charles Brockden 1771-1810 ....
NCLC 22, 74, 122, 246
See also AMWS 1; CDALB 1640-1865;
DLB 37, 59, 73; FW; GL 2; HGG; LMFS
1; RGAL 4; TUS

Brown, Christy 1932-1981 .... **CLC 63**
See also BYA 13; CA 105; 104; CANR 72;
DLB 14

Brown, Claude 1937-2002 ... **BLC 1:1; CLC
30**
See also AAYA 7; BW 1, 3; CA 73-76; 205;
CANR 81; DAM MULT

Brown, Dan 1964- .... **CLC 209**
See also AAYA 55; CA 217; CANR 223;
LNFS 1; MTFW 2005

Brown, Dee 1908-2002 .... **CLC 18, 47**
See also AAYA 30; CA 13-16R; 212; CAAS
6; CANR 11, 45, 60, 150; CPW; CSW;
DA3; DAM POP; DLBY 1980; LAIT 2;
MTCW 1, 2; MTFW 2005; NCFS 5;
SATA 5, 110; SATA-Obit 141; TCWW 1,
2

Brown, Dee Alexander
See Brown, Dee

Brown, George
See Wertmueller, Lina

Brown, George Douglas 1869-1902 ... **TCLC
28**
See also CA 162; RGEL 2

Brown, George Mackay 1921-1996 . **CLC 5,
48, 100**
See also BRWS 6; CA 21-24R; 151; CAAS
6; CANR 12, 37, 67; CN 1, 2, 3, 4, 5, 6;
CP 1, 2, 3, 4, 5, 6; DLB 14, 27, 139, 271;
MTCW 1; RGSF 2; SATA 35

Brown, James Willie
See Komunyakaa, Yusef

Brown, James Willie, Jr.
See Komunyakaa, Yusef

Brown, Larry 1951-2004 .... **CLC 73, 289**
See also AMWS 21; CA 130; 134; 233;
CANR 117, 145; CSW; DLB 234; INT
CA-134

Brown, Moses
See Barrett, William (Christopher)

Brown, Rita Mae 1944- ...... **CLC 18, 43, 79,
259**
See also BPFB 1; CA 45-48; CANR 2, 11,
35, 62, 95, 138, 183, 232; CN 5, 6, 7;
CPW; CSW; DA3; DAM NOV, POP; FW;
INT CANR-11; MAL 5; MTCW 1, 2;
MTFW 2005; NFS 9; RGAL 4; TUS

Brown, Roderick (Langmere) Haig-
See Haig-Brown, Roderick (Langmere)

Brown, Rosellen 1939- .... **CLC 32, 170**
See also CA 77-80; CAAS 10; CANR 14,
44, 98; CN 6, 7; PFS 41

Brown, Sterling Allen 1901-1989 ..... **BLC 1;
CLC 1, 23, 59; HR 1:2; PC 55**
See also AFAW 1, 2; BW 1, 3; CA 85-88;
127; CANR 26; CP 3, 4; DA3; DAM
MULT, POET; DLB 48, 51, 63; MAL 5;
MTCW 1, 2; MTFW 2005; RGAL 4; WP

Brown, Will
See Ainsworth, William Harrison

Brown, William Hill 1765-1793 .... **LC 93**
See also DLB 37

Brown, William Larry
See Brown, Larry

Brown, William Wells 1814(?)-1884 ..... **BLC
1:1; DC 1; NCLC 2, 89, 247**
See also DAM MULT; DLB 3, 50, 183,
248; RGAL 4

Browne, Clyde Jackson
See Browne, Jackson

Browne, Jackson 1948(?)- .... **CLC 21**
See also CA 120

Browne, Sir Thomas 1605-1682 .... **LC 111**
See also BRW 2; DLB 151

Browne of Tavistock, William 1590-1645 ....
LC 192
See also DLB 121

Browning, Robert 1812-1889 . **NCLC 19, 79;
PC 2, 61, 97; WLCS**
See also BRW 4; BRWC 2; BRWR 3; CD-
BLB 1832-1890; CLR 97; DA; DA3;
DAB; DAC; DAM MST, POET; DLB 32,
163; EXPP; LATS 1:1; PAB; PFS 1, 15,
41; RGEL 2; TEA; WLIT 4; WP; YABC
1

Browning, Tod 1882-1962 .... **CLC 16**
See also CA 141; 117

Brownmiller, Susan 1935- .... **CLC 159**
See also CA 103; CANR 35, 75, 137; DAM
NOV; FW; MTCW 1, 2; MTFW 2005

Brownson, Orestes Augustus 1803-1876 ......
NCLC 50
See also DLB 1, 59, 73, 243

Bruccoli, Matthew J. 1931-2008 ..... **CLC 34**
See also CA 9-12R; 274; CANR 7, 87; DLB
103

Bruccoli, Matthew Joseph
See Bruccoli, Matthew J.

Bruce, Lenny
See Schneider, Leonard Alfred

Bruchac, Joseph 1942- .... **NNAL**
See also AAYA 19; CA 33-36R, 256; CAAE
256; CANR 13, 47, 75, 94, 137, 161, 204;
CLR 46; CWRI 5; DAM MULT; DLB
342; JRDA; MAICYA 2; MAICYAS 1;
MTCW 2; MTFW 2005; PFS 36; SATA
42, 89, 131, 176, 228; SATA-Essay 176

Bruin, John
See Brutus, Dennis

Brulard, Henri
See Stendhal

Brulls, Christian
See Simenon, Georges

Brunetto Latini c. 1220-1294 .... **CMLC 73**

Brunner, John (Kilian Houston)
1934-1995 .... **CLC 8, 10**
See also CA 1-4R; 149; CAAS 8; CANR 2,
37; CPW; DAM POP; DLB 261; MTCW
1, 2; SCFW 1, 2; SFW 4

Bruno, Giordano 1548-1600 .... **LC 27, 167**
See also RGWL 2, 3

Brutus, Dennis 1924-2009 .... **BLC 1:1; CLC
43; PC 24**
See also AFW; BW 2, 3; CA 49-52; CAAS
14; CANR 2, 27, 42, 81; CDWLB 3; CP
1, 2, 3, 4, 5, 6, 7; DAM MULT, POET;
DLB 117, 225; EWL 3

Bryan, C.D.B. 1936-2009 .... **CLC 29**
See also CA 73-76; CANR 13, 68; DLB
185; INT CANR-13

Bryan, Courtlandt Dixon Barnes
See Bryan, C.D.B.

Bryan, Michael
See Moore, Brian

Bryan, William Jennings 1860-1925 . **TCLC
99**
See also DLB 303

Bryant, William Cullen 1794-1878 .... **NCLC
6, 46; PC 20**
See also AMWS 1; CDALB 1640-1865;
DA; DAB; DAC; DAM MST, POET;
DLB 3, 43, 59, 189, 250; EXPP; PAB;
PFS 30; RGAL 4; TUS

Bryusov, Valery Yakovlevich 1873-1924 ......
TCLC 10
See also CA 107; 155; EWL 3; SFW 4

Buchan, John 1875-1940 .... **TCLC 41**
See also CA 108; 145; CMW 4; DAB;
DAM POP; DLB 34, 70, 156; HGG;
MSW; MTCW 2; RGEL 2; RHW; YABC
2

Buchanan, George 1506-1582 ...... **LC 4, 179**
See also DLB 132

Buchanan, Robert 1841-1901 .... **TCLC 107**
See also CA 179; DLB 18, 35

Buchheim, Lothar-Guenther 1918-2007 ......
CLC 6
See also CA 85-88; 257

Buchner, (Karl) Georg 1813-1837 .... **DC 35;
NCLC 26, 146; SSC 131**
See also CDWLB 2; DLB 133; EW 6;
RGSF 2; RGWL 2, 3; TWA

Bustos Domecq, Honorio
  See Bioy Casares, Adolfo; Borges, Jorge Luis

Butler, Octavia 1947-2006 . **BLC 2:1; BLCS; CLC 38, 121, 230, 240**
  See also AAYA 18, 48; AFAW 2; AMWS 13; BPFB 1; BW 2, 3; CA 73-76; 248; CANR 12, 24, 38, 73, 145, 240; CLR 65; CN 7; CPW; DA3; DAM MULT, POP; DLB 33; LATS 1:2; MTCW 1, 2; MTFW 2005; NFS 8, 21, 34; SATA 84; SCFW 2; SFW 4; SSFS 6; TCLE 1:1; YAW

Butler, Octavia E.
  See Butler, Octavia

Butler, Octavia Estelle
  See Butler, Octavia

Butler, Robert Olen, Jr.
  See Butler, Robert Olen

Butler, Robert Olen 1945- ...... **CLC 81, 162; SSC 117**
  See also AMWS 12; BPFB 1; CA 112; CANR 66, 138, 194; CN 7; CSW; DAM POP; DLB 173, 335; INT CA-112; MAL 5; MTCW 2; MTFW 2005; SSFS 11, 22

Butler, Samuel 1612-1680 ... **LC 16, 43, 173; PC 94**
  See also DLB 101, 126; RGEL 2

Butler, Samuel 1835-1902 .... **TCLC 1, 33; WLC 1**
  See also BRWS 2; CA 143; CDBLB 1890-1914; DA; DA3; DAB; DAC; DAM MST, NOV; DLB 18, 57, 174; RGEL 2; SFW 4; TEA

Butler, Walter C.
  See Faust, Frederick

Butor, Michel (Marie Francois) 1926- . **CLC 1, 3, 8, 11, 15, 161**
  See also CA 9-12R; CANR 33, 66; CWW 2; DLB 83; EW 13; EWL 3; GFL 1789 to the Present; MTCW 1, 2; MTFW 2005

Butts, Mary 1890(?)-1937 .. **SSC 124; TCLC 77**
  See also CA 148; DLB 240

Buxton, Ralph
  See Silverstein, Alvin; Silverstein, Virginia B.

Buzo, Alex
  See Buzo, Alex

Buzo, Alex 1944- .... **CLC 61**
  See also CA 97-100; CANR 17, 39, 69; CD 5, 6; DLB 289

Buzo, Alexander John
  See Buzo, Alex

Buzzati, Dino 1906-1972 .... **CLC 36**
  See also CA 160; 33-36R; DLB 177; RGWL 2, 3; SFW 4

Byars, Betsy 1928- .... **CLC 35**
  See also AAYA 19; BYA 3; CA 33-36R, 183; CAAE 183; CANR 18, 36, 57, 102, 148; CLR 1, 16, 72; DLB 52; INT CANR-18; JRDA; MAICYA 1, 2; MAICYAS 1; MTCW 1; SAAS 1; SATA 4, 46, 80, 163, 223; SATA-Essay 108; WYA; YAW

Byars, Betsy Cromer
  See Byars, Betsy

Byatt, A. S. 1936- ...... **CLC 19, 65, 136, 223, 312; SSC 91**
  See also BPFB 1; BRWC 2; BRWS 4; CA 13-16R; CANR 13, 33, 50, 75, 96, 133, 205; CN 1, 2, 3, 4, 5, 6; DA3; DAM NOV, POP; DLB 14, 194, 319, 326; EWL 3; MTCW 1, 2; MTFW 2005; RGSF 2; RHW; SSFS 26; TEA

Byatt, Antonia Susan Drabble
  See Byatt, A. S.

Byrd, William II 1674-1744 .... **LC 112**
  See also DLB 24, 140; RGAL 4

Byrne, David 1952- .... **CLC 26**
  See also CA 127; CANR 215

Byrne, John Joseph
  See Leonard, Hugh

Byrne, John Keyes
  See Leonard, Hugh

Byron, George Gordon
  See Lord Byron

Byron, George Gordon Noel
  See Lord Byron

Byron, Robert 1905-1941 .... **TCLC 67**
  See also CA 160; DLB 195

C. 3. 3.
  See Wilde, Oscar

Caballero, Fernan 1796-1877 .... **NCLC 10**

Cabell, Branch
  See Cabell, James Branch

Cabell, James Branch 1879-1958 ... **TCLC 6**
  See also CA 105; 152; DLB 9, 78; FANT; MAL 5; MTCW 2; RGAL 4; SUFW 1

Cabeza de Vaca, Alvar Nunez 1490-1557(?) .... **LC 61**

Cable, George Washington 1844-1925 .. **SSC 4, 155; TCLC 4**
  See also CA 104; 155; DLB 12, 74; DLBD 13; RGAL 4; TUS

Cabral de Melo Neto, Joao 1920-1999 . **CLC 76**
  See also CA 151; CWW 2; DAM MULT; DLB 307; EWL 3; LAW; LAWS 1

Cabrera, Lydia 1900-1991 .... **TCLC 223**
  See also CA 178; DLB 145; EWL 3; HW 1; LAWS 1

Cabrera Infante, G. 1929-2005 .. **CLC 5, 25, 45, 120, 291; HLC 1; SSC 39**
  See also CA 85-88; 236; CANR 29, 65, 110; CDWLB 3; CWW 2; DA3; DAM MULT; DLB 113; EWL 3; HW 1, 2; LAW; LAWS 1; MTCW 1, 2; MTFW 2005; RGSF 2; WLIT 1

Cabrera Infante, Guillermo
  See Cabrera Infante, G.

Cade, Toni
  See Bambara, Toni Cade

Cadmus and Harmonia
  See Buchan, John

Caedmon fl. 658-680 .... **CMLC 7, 133**
  See also DLB 146

Caeiro, Alberto
  See Pessoa, Fernando

Caesar, Julius
  See Julius Caesar

Cage, John (Milton), (Jr.) 1912-1992 ... **CLC 41; PC 58**
  See also CA 13-16R; 169; CANR 9, 78; DLB 193; INT CANR-9; TCLE 1:1

Cahan, Abraham 1860-1951 .... **TCLC 71**
  See also CA 108; 154; DLB 9, 25, 28; MAL 5; RGAL 4

Cain, Christopher
  See Fleming, Thomas

Cain, G.
  See Cabrera Infante, G.

Cain, Guillermo
  See Cabrera Infante, G.

Cain, James M(allahan) 1892-1977 . **CLC 3, 11, 28**
  See also AITN 1; BPFB 1; CA 17-20R; 73-76; CANR 8, 34, 61; CMW 4; CN 1, 2; DLB 226; EWL 3; MAL 5; MSW; MTCW 1; RGAL 4

Caine, Hall 1853-1931 .... **TCLC 97**
  See also RHW

Caine, Mark
  See Raphael, Frederic

Calasso, Roberto 1941- .... **CLC 81**
  See also CA 143; CANR 89, 223

Calderon de la Barca, Pedro 1600-1681 . **DC 3; HLCS 1; LC 23, 136**
  See also DFS 23; EW 2; RGWL 2, 3; TWA

Caldwell, Erskine 1903-1987 . **CLC 1, 8, 14, 50, 60; SSC 19, 147; TCLC 117**
  See also AITN 1; AMW; BPFB 1; CA 1-4R; 121; CAAS 1; CANR 2, 33; CN 1, 2, 3, 4; DA3; DAM NOV; DLB 9, 86; EWL 3; MAL 5; MTCW 1, 2; MTFW 2005; RGAL 4; RGSF 2; TUS

Caldwell, Gail 1951- .... **CLC 309**
  See also CA 313

Caldwell, (Janet Miriam) Taylor (Holland) 1900-1985 .... **CLC 2, 28, 39**
  See also BPFB 1; CA 5-8R; 116; CANR 5; DA3; DAM NOV, POP; DLBD 17; MTCW 2; RHW

Calhoun, John Caldwell 1782-1850 .. **NCLC 15**
  See also DLB 3, 248

Calisher, Hortense 1911-2009 .. **CLC 2, 4, 8, 38, 134; SSC 15**
  See also CA 1-4R; 282; CANR 1, 22, 117; CN 1, 2, 3, 4, 5, 6, 7; DA3; DAM NOV; DLB 2, 218; INT CANR-22; MAL 5; MTCW 1, 2; MTFW 2005; RGAL 4; RGSF 2

Callaghan, Morley 1903-1990 .... **CLC 3, 14, 41, 65; TCLC 145**
  See also CA 9-12R; 132; CANR 33, 73; CN 1, 2, 3, 4; DAC; DAM MST; DLB 68; EWL 3; MTCW 1, 2; MTFW 2005; RGEL 2; RGSF 2; SSFS 19

Callaghan, Morley Edward
  See Callaghan, Morley

Callimachus c. 305B.C.-c. 240B.C. ... **CMLC 18**
  See also AW 1; DLB 176; RGWL 2, 3

Calvin, Jean
  See Calvin, John

Calvin, John 1509-1564 .... **LC 37**
  See also DLB 327; GFL Beginnings to 1789

Calvino, Italo 1923-1985 .... **CLC 5, 8, 11, 22, 33, 39, 73; SSC 3, 48; TCLC 183**
  See also AAYA 58; CA 85-88; 116; CANR 23, 61, 132; DAM NOV; DLB 196; EW 13; EWL 3; MTCW 1, 2; MTFW 2005; RGHL; RGSF 2; RGWL 2, 3; SFW 4; SSFS 12, 31; WLIT 7

Camara Laye
  See Laye, Camara

Cambridge, A Gentleman of the University of
  See Crowley, Edward Alexander

Camden, William 1551-1623 .... **LC 77**
  See also DLB 172

Cameron, Carey 1952- .... **CLC 59**
  See also CA 135

Cameron, Peter 1959- .... **CLC 44**
  See also AMWS 12; CA 125; CANR 50, 117, 188; DLB 234; GLL 2

Camoens, Luis Vaz de 1524(?)-1580 ....
  See Camoes, Luis de

Camoes, Luis de 1524(?)-1580 . **HLCS 1; LC 62, 191; PC 31**
  See also DLB 287; EW 2; RGWL 2, 3

Camp, Madeleine L'Engle
  See L'Engle, Madeleine

Campana, Dino 1885-1932 .... **TCLC 20**
  See also CA 117; 246; DLB 114; EWL 3

Campanella, Tommaso 1568-1639 ..... **LC 32**
  See also RGWL 2, 3

Campbell, Bebe Moore 1950-2006 . **BLC 2:1; CLC 246**
  See also AAYA 26; BW 2, 3; CA 139; 254; CANR 81, 134; DLB 227; MTCW 2; MTFW 2005

Campbell, John Ramsey
  See Campbell, Ramsey

Campbell, John W. 1910-1971 .... **CLC 32**
  See also CA 21-22; 29-32R; CANR 34; CAP 2; DLB 8; MTCW 1; SCFW 1, 2; SFW 4

Campbell, John Wood, Jr.
See Campbell, John W.
Campbell, Joseph 1904-1987 .... **CLC 69;
TCLC 140**
See also AAYA 3, 66; BEST 89:2; CA 1-4R;
124; CANR 3, 28, 61, 107; DA3; MTCW
1, 2
Campbell, Maria 1940- ...... **CLC 85; NNAL**
See also CA 102; CANR 54; CCA 1; DAC
Campbell, Ramsey 1946- .. **CLC 42; SSC 19**
See also AAYA 51; CA 57-60, 228; CAAE
228; CANR 7, 102, 171; DLB 261; HGG;
INT CANR-7; SUFW 1, 2
Campbell, (Ignatius) Roy (Dunnachie)
1901-1957 .... **TCLC 5**
See also AFW; CA 104; 155; DLB 20, 225;
EWL 3; MTCW 2; RGEL 2
Campbell, Thomas 1777-1844 ...... **NCLC 19**
See also DLB 93, 144; RGEL 2
Campbell, Wilfred
See Campbell, William
Campbell, William 1858(?)-1918 .... **TCLC 9**
See also CA 106; DLB 92
Campbell, William Edward March
See March, William
Campion, Jane 1954- .... **CLC 95, 229**
See also AAYA 33; CA 138; CANR 87
Campion, Thomas 1567-1620 ..... **LC 78; PC
87**
See also BRWS 16; CDBLB Before 1660;
DAM POET; DLB 58, 172; RGEL 2
Camus, Albert 1913-1960 ..... **CLC 1, 2, 4, 9,
11, 14, 32, 63, 69, 124; DC 2; SSC 9, 76,
129, 146; WLC 1**
See also AAYA 36; AFW; BPFB 1; CA 89-
92; CANR 131; DA; DA3; DAB; DAC;
DAM DRAM, MST, NOV; DLB 72, 321,
329; EW 13; EWL 3; EXPN; EXPS; GFL
1789 to the Present; LATS 1:2; LMFS 2;
MTCW 1, 2; MTFW 2005; NFS 6, 16;
RGHL; RGSF 2; RGWL 2, 3; SSFS 4;
TWA
Canby, Vincent 1924-2000 .... **CLC 13**
See also CA 81-84; 191
Cancale
See Desnos, Robert
Canetti, Elias 1905-1994 . **CLC 3, 14, 25, 75,
86; TCLC 157**
See also CA 21-24R; 146; CANR 23, 61,
79; CDWLB 2; CWW 2; DA3; DLB 85,
124, 329; EW 12; EWL 3; MTCW 1, 2;
MTFW 2005; RGWL 2, 3; TWA
Canfield, Dorothea F.
See Fisher, Dorothy (Frances) Canfield
Canfield, Dorothea Frances
See Fisher, Dorothy (Frances) Canfield
Canfield, Dorothy
See Fisher, Dorothy (Frances) Canfield
Canin, Ethan 1960- .... **CLC 55; SSC 70**
See also CA 131; 135; CANR 193; DLB
335, 350; MAL 5
Cankar, Ivan 1876-1918 .... **TCLC 105**
See also CDWLB 4; DLB 147; EWL 3
Cannon, Curt
See Hunter, Evan
Cao, Lan 1961- .... **CLC 109**
See also CA 165
Cape, Judith
See Page, P.K.
Capek, Karel 1890-1938 .... **DC 1; SSC 36;
TCLC 6, 37, 192; WLC 1**
See also CA 104; 140; CDWLB 4; DA;
DA3; DAB; DAC; DAM DRAM, MST,
NOV; DFS 7, 11; DLB 215; EW 10; EWL
3; MTCW 2; MTFW 2005; RGSF 2;
RGWL 2, 3; SCFW 1, 2; SFW 4
Capella, Martianus fl. 4th cent. - . **CMLC 84**

Capote, Truman 1924-1984 ...... **CLC 1, 3, 8,
13, 19, 34, 38, 58; SSC 2, 47, 93; TCLC
164; WLC 1**
See also AAYA 61; AMWS 3; BPFB 1; CA
5-8R; 113; CANR 18, 62, 201; CDALB
1941-1968; CN 1, 2, 3; CPW; DA; DA3;
DAB; DAC; DAM MST, NOV, POP;
DLB 2, 185, 227; DLBY 1980, 1984;
EWL 3; EXPS; GLL 1; LAIT 3; MAL 5;
MTCW 1, 2; MTFW 2005; NCFS 2;
RGAL 4; RGSF 2; SATA 91; SSFS 2;
TUS
Capra, Frank 1897-1991 .... **CLC 16**
See also AAYA 52; CA 61-64; 135
Caputo, Philip 1941- .... **CLC 32**
See also AAYA 60; CA 73-76; CANR 40,
135; YAW
Caragiale, Ion Luca 1852-1912 .... **TCLC 76**
See also CA 157
Card, Orson Scott 1951- .... **CLC 44, 47, 50,
279**
See also AAYA 11, 42; BPFB 1; BYA 5, 8;
CA 102; CANR 27, 47, 73, 102, 106, 133,
184; CLR 116; CPW; DA3; DAM POP;
FANT; INT CANR-27; MTCW 1, 2;
MTFW 2005; NFS 5; SATA 83, 127;
SCFW 2; SFW 4; SUFW 2; YAW
Cardenal, Ernesto 1925- .... **CLC 31, 161;
HLC 1; PC 22**
See also CA 49-52; CANR 2, 32, 66, 138,
217; CWW 2; DAM MULT, POET; DLB
290; EWL 3; HW 1, 2; LAWS 1; MTCW
1, 2; MTFW 2005; RGWL 2, 3
Cardinal, Marie 1929-2001 .... **CLC 189**
See also CA 177; CWW 2; DLB 83; FW
Cardozo, Benjamin N(athan) 1870-1938 .....
TCLC 65
See also CA 117; 164
Carducci, Giosue (Alessandro Giuseppe)
1835-1907 .... **PC 46; TCLC 32**
See also CA 163; DLB 329; EW 7; RGWL
2, 3
Carew, Thomas 1595(?)-1640 ... **LC 13, 159;
PC 29**
See also BRW 2; DLB 126; PAB; RGEL 2
Carey, Ernestine Gilbreth 1908-2006 .. **CLC
17**
See also CA 5-8R; 254; CANR 71; SATA
2; SATA-Obit 177
Carey, Peter 1943- ...... **CLC 40, 55, 96, 183,
294; SSC 133**
See also BRWS 12; CA 123; 127; CANR
53, 76, 117, 157, 185, 213; CN 4, 5, 6, 7;
DLB 289, 326; EWL 3; INT CA-127;
LNFS 1; MTCW 1, 2; MTFW 2005;
RGSF 2; SATA 94
Carey, Peter Philip
See Carey, Peter
Carleton, William 1794-1869 . **NCLC 3, 199**
See also DLB 159; RGEL 2; RGSF 2
Carlisle, Henry 1926-2011 .... **CLC 33**
See also CA 13-16R; CANR 15, 85
Carlisle, Henry Coffin
See Carlisle, Henry
Carlsen, Chris
See Holdstock, Robert
Carlson, Ron 1947- .... **CLC 54**
See also CA 105, 189; CAAE 189; CANR
27, 155, 197; DLB 244
Carlson, Ronald F.
See Carlson, Ron
Carlyle, Jane Welsh 1801-1866 .. **NCLC 181**
See also DLB 55
Carlyle, Thomas 1795-1881 ... **NCLC 22, 70,
248**
See also BRW 4; CDBLB 1789-1832; DA;
DAB; DAC; DAM MST; DLB 55, 144,
254, 338, 366; RGEL 2; TEA

Carman, (William) Bliss 1861-1929 . **PC 34;
TCLC 7**
See also CA 104; 152; DAC; DLB 92;
RGEL 2
Carnegie, Dale 1888-1955 .... **TCLC 53**
See also CA 218
Caro Mallén de Soto, Ana c. 1590-c. 1650 ..
LC 175
Carossa, Hans 1878-1956 .... **TCLC 48**
See also CA 170; DLB 66; EWL 3
Carpenter, Don(ald Richard) 1931-1995 .....
CLC 41
See also CA 45-48; 149; CANR 1, 71
Carpenter, Edward 1844-1929 ...... **TCLC 88**
See also BRWS 13; CA 163; GLL 1
Carpenter, John 1948- .... **CLC 161**
See also AAYA 2, 73; CA 134; SATA 58
Carpenter, John Howard
See Carpenter, John
Carpenter, Johnny
See Carpenter, John
Carpentier, Alejo 1904-1980 . **CLC 8, 11, 38,
110; HLC 1; SSC 35; TCLC 201**
See also CA 65-68; 97-100; CANR 11, 70;
CDWLB 3; DAM MULT; DLB 113; EWL
3; HW 1, 2; LAW; LMFS 2; RGSF 2;
RGWL 2, 3; WLIT 1
Carpentier y Valmont, Alejo
See Carpentier, Alejo
Carr, Caleb 1955- .... **CLC 86**
See also CA 147; CANR 73, 134; DA3;
DLB 350
Carr, Emily 1871-1945 .... **TCLC 32, 260**
See also CA 159; DLB 68; FW; GLL 2
Carr, H. D.
See Crowley, Edward Alexander
Carr, John Dickson 1906-1977 .... **CLC 3**
See also CA 49-52; 69-72; CANR 3, 33,
60; CMW 4; DLB 306; MSW; MTCW 1,
2
Carr, Philippa
See Hibbert, Eleanor Alice Burford
Carr, Virginia Spencer 1929- .... **CLC 34**
See also CA 61-64; CANR 175; DLB 111
Carrere, Emmanuel 1957- .... **CLC 89**
See also CA 200
Carrier, Roch 1937- .... **CLC 13, 78**
See also CA 130; CANR 61, 152; CCA 1;
DAC; DAM MST; DLB 53; SATA 105,
166
Carroll, James Dennis
See Carroll, Jim
Carroll, James P. 1943(?)- .... **CLC 38**
See also CA 81-84; CANR 73, 139, 209;
MTCW 2; MTFW 2005
Carroll, Jim 1949-2009 .... **CLC 35, 143**
See also AAYA 17; CA 45-48; 290; CANR
42, 115, 233; NCFS 5
Carroll, Lewis 1832-1898 . **NCLC 2, 53, 139,
258; PC 18, 74; WLC 1**
See also AAYA 39; BRW 5; BYA 5, 13; CD-
BLB 1832-1890; CLR 18, 108; DA; DA3;
DAB; DAC; DAM MST, NOV, POET;
DLB 18, 163, 178; DLBY 1998; EXPN;
EXPP; FANT; JRDA; LAIT 1; MAICYA
1, 2; NFS 27; PFS 11, 30; RGEL 2; SATA
100; SUFW 1; TEA; WCH; YABC 2
Carroll, Paul Vincent 1900-1968 ..... **CLC 10**
See also CA 9-12R; 25-28R; DLB 10; EWL
3; RGEL 2
Carruth, Hayden 1921-2008 .. **CLC 4, 7, 10,
18, 84, 287; PC 10**
See also AMWS 16; CA 9-12R; 277; CANR
4, 38, 59, 110, 174; CP 1, 2, 3, 4, 5, 6, 7;
DLB 5, 165; INT CANR-4; MTCW 1, 2;
MTFW 2005; PFS 26; SATA 47; SATA-
Obit 197

Cisneros, Sandra 1954- ... **CLC 69, 118, 193, 305; HLC 1; PC 52; SSC 32, 72, 143**
See also AAYA 9, 53; AMWS 7; CA 131; CANR 64, 118; CLR 123; CN 7; CWP; DA3; DAM MULT; DLB 122, 152; EWL 3; EXPN; FL 1:5; FW; HW 1, 2; LAIT 5; LATS 1:2; LLW; MAICYA 2; MAL 5; MTCW 2; MTFW 2005; NFS 2; PFS 19; RGAL 4; RGSF 2; SSFS 3, 13, 27, 32; WLIT 1; YAW

Cixous, Helene 1937- .... **CLC 92, 253**
See also CA 126; CANR 55, 123; CWW 2; DLB 83, 242; EWL 3; FL 1:5; FW; GLL 2; MTCW 1, 2; MTFW 2005; TWA

Clair, Rene
See Chomette, Rene Lucien

Clampitt, Amy 1920-1994 ... **CLC 32; PC 19**
See also AMWS 9; CA 110; 146; CANR 29, 79; CP 4, 5; DLB 105; MAL 5; PFS 27, 39

Clancy, Thomas L., Jr.
See Clancy, Tom

Clancy, Tom 1947- .... **CLC 45, 112**
See also AAYA 9, 51; BEST 89:1, 90:1; BPFB 1; BYA 10, 11; CA 125; 131; CANR 62, 105, 132; CMW 4; CPW; DA3; DAM NOV, POP; DLB 227; INT CA-131; MTCW 1, 2; MTFW 2005

Clare, John 1793-1864 . **NCLC 9, 86; PC 23**
See also BRWS 11; DAB; DAM POET; DLB 55, 96; RGEL 2

Clarin
See Alas (y Urena), Leopoldo (Enrique Garcia)

Clark, Al C.
See Goines, Donald

Clark, Brian (Robert)
See Clark, (Robert) Brian

Clark, (Robert) Brian 1932- .... **CLC 29**
See also CA 41-44R; CANR 67; CBD; CD 5, 6

Clark, Curt
See Westlake, Donald E.

Clark, Eleanor 1913-1996 .... **CLC 5, 19**
See also CA 9-12R; 151; CANR 41; CN 1, 2, 3, 4, 5, 6; DLB 6

Clark, J. P.
See Clark-Bekederemo, J. P.

Clark, John Pepper
See Clark-Bekederemo, J. P.

Clark, Kenneth (Mackenzie) 1903-1983 ...... **TCLC 147**
See also CA 93-96; 109; CANR 36; MTCW 1, 2; MTFW 2005

Clark, M. R.
See Clark, Mavis Thorpe

Clark, Mavis Thorpe 1909-1999 ..... **CLC 12**
See also CA 57-60; CANR 8, 37, 107; CLR 30; CWRI 5; MAICYA 1, 2; SAAS 5; SATA 8, 74

Clark, Walter Van Tilburg 1909-1971 . **CLC 28**
See also CA 9-12R; 33-36R; CANR 63, 113; CN 1; DLB 9, 206; LAIT 2; MAL 5; NFS 40; RGAL 4; SATA 8; TCWW 1, 2

Clark-Bekederemo, J. P. 1935- ..... **BLC 1:1; CLC 38; DC 5**
See also AAYA 79; AFW; BW 1; CA 65-68; CANR 16, 72; CD 5, 6; CDWLB 3; CP 1, 2, 3, 4, 5, 6, 7; DAM DRAM, MULT; DFS 13; DLB 117; EWL 3; MTCW 2; MTFW 2005; RGEL 2

Clark-Bekederemo, John Pepper
See Clark-Bekederemo, J. P.

Clark Bekederemo, Johnson Pepper
See Clark-Bekederemo, J. P.

Clarke, Arthur
See Clarke, Arthur C.

Clarke, Arthur C. 1917-2008 . **CLC 1, 4, 13, 18, 35, 136; SSC 3**
See also AAYA 4, 33; BPFB 1; BYA 13; CA 1-4R; 270; CANR 2, 28, 55, 74, 130, 196; CLR 119; CN 1, 2, 3, 4, 5, 6, 7; CPW; DA3; DAM POP; DLB 261; JRDA; LAIT 5; MAICYA 1, 2; MTCW 1, 2; MTFW 2005; SATA 13, 70, 115; SATA-Obit 191; SCFW 1, 2; SFW 4; SSFS 4, 18, 29; TCLE 1:1; YAW

Clarke, Arthur Charles
See Clarke, Arthur C.

Clarke, Austin 1896-1974 ...... **CLC 6, 9; PC 112**
See also BRWS 15; CA 29-32; 49-52; CAP 2; CP 1, 2; DAM POET; DLB 10, 20; EWL 3; RGEL 2

Clarke, Austin 1934- . **BLC 1:1; CLC 8, 53; SSC 45, 116**
See also BW 1; CA 25-28R; CAAS 16; CANR 14, 32, 68, 140, 220; CN 1, 2, 3, 4, 5, 6, 7; DAC; DAM MULT; DLB 53, 125; DNFS 2; MTCW 2; MTFW 2005; RGSF 2

Clarke, Gillian 1937- .... **CLC 61**
See also CA 106; CP 3, 4, 5, 6, 7; CWP; DLB 40

Clarke, Marcus (Andrew Hislop) 1846-1881 .... **NCLC 19, 258; SSC 94**
See also DLB 230; RGEL 2; RGSF 2

Clarke, Shirley 1925-1997 .... **CLC 16**
See also CA 189

Clash, The
See Headon, (Nicky) Topper; Jones, Mick; Simonon, Paul; Strummer, Joe

Claudel, Paul (Louis Charles Marie) 1868-1955 .... **TCLC 2, 10, 268**
See also CA 104; 165; DLB 192, 258, 321; EW 8; EWL 3; GFL 1789 to the Present; RGWL 2, 3; TWA

Claudian 370(?)-404(?) .... **CMLC 46**
See also RGWL 2, 3

Claudius, Matthias 1740-1815 ...... **NCLC 75**
See also DLB 97

Clavell, James 1925-1994 ...... **CLC 6, 25, 87**
See also BPFB 1; CA 25-28R; 146; CANR 26, 48; CN 5; CPW; DA3; DAM NOV, POP; MTCW 1, 2; MTFW 2005; NFS 10; RHW

Clayman, Gregory **CLC 65**

Cleage, Pearl 1948- .... **DC 32**
See also BW 2; CA 41-44R; CANR 27, 148, 177, 226; DFS 14, 16; DLB 228; NFS 17

Cleage, Pearl Michelle
See Cleage, Pearl

Cleaver, (Leroy) Eldridge 1935-1998 ... **BLC 1:1; CLC 30, 119**
See also BW 1, 3; CA 21-24R; 167; CANR 16, 75; DA3; DAM MULT; MTCW 2; YAW

Cleese, John (Marwood) 1939- .... **CLC 21**
See also CA 112; 116; CANR 35; MTCW 1

Cleishbotham, Jebediah
See Scott, Sir Walter

Cleland, John 1710-1789 .... **LC 2, 48**
See also DLB 39; RGEL 2

Clemens, Samuel
See Twain, Mark

Clemens, Samuel Langhorne
See Twain, Mark

Clement of Alexandria 150(?)-215(?) .... **CMLC 41**

Cleophil
See Congreve, William

Clerihew, E.
See Bentley, E(dmund) C(lerihew)

Clerk, N. W.
See Lewis, C. S.

Cleveland, John 1613-1658 .... **LC 106**
See also DLB 126; RGEL 2

Cliff, Jimmy
See Chambers, James

Cliff, Michelle 1946- .... **BLCS; CLC 120**
See also BW 2; CA 116; CANR 39, 72; CD-WLB 3; DLB 157; FW; GLL 2

Clifford, Lady Anne 1590-1676 .... **LC 76**
See also DLB 151

Clifton, Lucille 1936-2010 ...... **BLC 1:1, 2:1; CLC 19, 66, 162, 283; PC 17**
See also AFAW 2; BW 2, 3; CA 49-52; CANR 2, 24, 42, 76, 97, 138; CLR 5; CP 2, 3, 4, 5, 6, 7; CSW; CWP; CWRI 5; DA3; DAM MULT, POET; DLB 5, 41; EXPP; MAICYA 1, 2; MTCW 1, 2; MTFW 2005; PFS 1, 14, 29, 41; SATA 20, 69, 128; SSFS 34; WP

Clifton, Thelma Lucille
See Clifton, Lucille

Clinton, Dirk
See Silverberg, Robert

Clough, Arthur Hugh 1819-1861 . **NCLC 27, 163; PC 103**
See also BRW 5; DLB 32; RGEL 2

Clutha, Janet
See Frame, Janet

Clutha, Janet Paterson Frame
See Frame, Janet

Clyne, Terence
See Blatty, William Peter

Cobalt, Martin
See Mayne, William

Cobb, Irvin S(hrewsbury) 1876-1944 . **TCLC 77**
See also CA 175; DLB 11, 25, 86

Cobbett, William 1763-1835 .... **NCLC 49**
See also DLB 43, 107, 158; RGEL 2

Coben, Harlan 1962- .... **CLC 269**
See also AAYA 83; CA 164; CANR 162, 199

Coburn, D(onald) L(ee) 1938- .... **CLC 10**
See also CA 89-92; DFS 23

Cockburn, Catharine Trotter
See Trotter, Catharine

Cocteau, Jean 1889-1963 . **CLC 1, 8, 15, 16, 43; DC 17; TCLC 119; WLC 2**
See also AAYA 74; CA 25-28; CANR 40; CAP 2; DA; DA3; DAB; DAC; DAM DRAM, MST, NOV; DFS 24; DLB 65, 258, 321; EW 10; EWL 3; GFL 1789 to the Present; MTCW 1, 2; RGWL 2, 3; TWA

Cocteau, Jean Maurice Eugene Clement
See Cocteau, Jean

Codrescu, Andrei 1946- .... **CLC 46, 121**
See also CA 33-36R; CAAS 19; CANR 13, 34, 53, 76, 125, 223; CN 7; DA3; DAM POET; MAL 5; MTCW 2; MTFW 2005

Coe, Max
See Bourne, Randolph S(illiman)

Coe, Tucker
See Westlake, Donald E.

Coelho, Paulo 1947- .... **CLC 258**
See also CA 152; CANR 80, 93, 155, 194; NFS 29

Coen, Ethan 1957- .... **CLC 108, 267**
See also AAYA 54; CA 126; CANR 85

Coen, Joel 1954- .... **CLC 108, 267**
See also AAYA 54; CA 126; CANR 119

The Coen Brothers
See Coen, Ethan; Coen, Joel

Coetzee, J. M. 1940- ... **CLC 23, 33, 66, 117, 161, 162, 305**
See also AAYA 37; AFW; BRWS 6; CA 77-80; CANR 41, 54, 74, 114, 133, 180; CN 4, 5, 6, 7; DA3; DAM NOV; DLB 225,

326, 329; EWL 3; LMFS 2; MTCW 1, 2; MTFW 2005; NFS 21; WLIT 2; WWE 1

Coetzee, John Maxwell
See Coetzee, J. M.

Coffey, Brian
See Koontz, Dean

Coffin, Robert P. Tristram 1892-1955 .... **TCLC 95**
See also CA 123; 169; DLB 45

Coffin, Robert Peter Tristram
See Coffin, Robert P. Tristram

Cohan, George M. 1878-1942 .... **TCLC 60**
See also CA 157; DLB 249; RGAL 4

Cohan, George Michael
See Cohan, George M.

Cohen, Arthur A(llen) 1928-1986 .... **CLC 7, 31**
See also CA 1-4R; 120; CANR 1, 17, 42; DLB 28; RGHL

Cohen, Leonard 1934- . **CLC 3, 38, 260; PC 109**
See also CA 21-24R; CANR 14, 69; CN 1, 2, 3, 4, 5, 6; CP 1, 2, 3, 4, 5, 6, 7; DAC; DAM MST; DLB 53; EWL 3; MTCW 1

Cohen, Leonard Norman
See Cohen, Leonard

Cohen, Matt(hew) 1942-1999 .... **CLC 19**
See also CA 61-64; 187; CAAS 18; CANR 40; CN 1, 2, 3, 4, 5, 6; DAC; DLB 53

Cohen-Solal, Annie 1948- .... **CLC 50**
See also CA 239

Colegate, Isabel 1931- .... **CLC 36**
See also CA 17-20R; CANR 8, 22, 74; CN 4, 5, 6, 7; DLB 14, 231; INT CANR-22; MTCW 1

Coleman, Emmett
See Reed, Ishmael

Coleridge, Hartley 1796-1849 .... **NCLC 90**
See also DLB 96

Coleridge, M. E.
See Coleridge, Mary E(lizabeth)

Coleridge, Mary E(lizabeth) 1861-1907 .... **TCLC 73**
See also CA 116; 166; DLB 19, 98

Coleridge, Samuel Taylor 1772-1834 . **NCLC 9, 54, 99, 111, 177, 197, 231; PC 11, 39, 67, 100; WLC 2**
See also AAYA 66; BRW 4; BRWR 2; BYA 4; CDBLB 1789-1832; DA; DA3; DAB; DAC; DAM MST, POET; DLB 93, 107; EXPP; LATS 1:1; LMFS 1; PAB; PFS 4, 5, 39; RGEL 2; TEA; WLIT 3; WP

Coleridge, Sara 1802-1852 .... **NCLC 31**
See also DLB 199

Coles, Don 1928- .... **CLC 46**
See also CA 115; CANR 38; CP 5, 6, 7

Coles, Robert 1929- .... **CLC 108**
See also CA 45-48; CANR 3, 32, 66, 70, 135, 225; INT CANR-32; SATA 23

Coles, Robert Martin
See Coles, Robert

Colette 1873-1954 .. **SSC 10, 93; TCLC 1, 5, 16**
See also CA 104; 131; DA3; DAM NOV; DLB 65; EW 9; EWL 3; GFL 1789 to the Present; GLL 1; MTCW 1, 2; MTFW 2005; RGWL 2, 3; TWA

Colette, Sidonie-Gabrielle
See Colette

Collett, (Jacobine) Camilla (Wergeland) 1813-1895 .... **NCLC 22**
See also DLB 354

Collier, Christopher 1930- .... **CLC 30**
See also AAYA 13; BYA 2; CA 33-36R; CANR 13, 33, 102; CLR 126; JRDA; MAICYA 1, 2; NFS 38; SATA 16, 70; WYA; YAW 1

Collier, James Lincoln 1928- .... **CLC 30**
See also AAYA 13; BYA 2; CA 9-12R; CANR 4, 33, 60, 102, 208; CLR 3, 126; DAM POP; JRDA; MAICYA 1, 2; NFS 38; SAAS 21; SATA 8, 70, 166; WYA; YAW 1

Collier, Jeremy 1650-1726 .... **LC 6, 157**
See also DLB 336

Collier, John 1901-1980 . **SSC 19; TCLC 127**
See also CA 65-68; 97-100; CANR 10; CN 1, 2; DLB 77, 255; FANT; SUFW 1

Collier, Mary 1690-1762 .... **LC 86**
See also DLB 95

Collingwood, R(obin) G(eorge) 1889(?)-1943 .... **TCLC 67**
See also CA 117; 155; DLB 262

Collins, Billy 1941- .... **PC 68**
See also AAYA 64; AMWS 21; CA 151; CANR 92, 211; CP 7; MTFW 2005; PFS 18

Collins, Hunt
See Hunter, Evan

Collins, Linda 1931- .... **CLC 44**
See also CA 125

Collins, Merle 1950- .... **BLC 2:1**
See also BW 3; CA 175; DLB 157

Collins, Tom
See Furphy, Joseph

Collins, Wilkie 1824-1889 .. **NCLC 1, 18, 93, 255; SSC 93**
See also BRWS 6; CDBLB 1832-1890; CMW 4; DFS 28; DLB 18, 70, 159; GL 2; MSW; NFS 39; RGEL 2; RGSF 2; SUFW 1; WLIT 4

Collins, William 1721-1759 .... **LC 4, 40; PC 72**
See also BRW 3; DAM POET; DLB 109; RGEL 2

Collins, William Wilkie
See Collins, Wilkie

Collodi, Carlo 1826-1890 .... **NCLC 54**
See also CLR 5, 120; MAICYA 1,2; SATA 29, 100; WCH; WLIT 7

Colman, George
See Glassco, John

Colman, George, the Elder 1732-1794 ... **LC 98**
See also RGEL 2

Colonna, Vittoria 1492-1547 .... **LC 71**
See also RGWL 2, 3

Colt, Winchester Remington
See Hubbard, L. Ron

Colter, Cyrus J. 1910-2002 .... **CLC 58**
See also BW 1; CA 65-68; 205; CANR 10, 66; CN 2, 3, 4, 5, 6; DLB 33

Colton, James
See Hansen, Joseph

Colum, Padraic 1881-1972 .... **CLC 28**
See also BYA 4; CA 73-76; 33-36R; CANR 35; CLR 36; CP 1; CWRI 5; DLB 19; MAICYA 1, 2; MTCW 1; RGEL 2; SATA 15; WCH

Colvin, James
See Moorcock, Michael

Colwin, Laurie (E.) 1944-1992 ... **CLC 5, 13, 23, 84**
See also CA 89-92; 139; CANR 20, 46; DLB 218; DLBY 1980; MTCW 1

Comfort, Alex(ander) 1920-2000 .... **CLC 7**
See also CA 1-4R; 190; CANR 1, 45; CN 1, 2, 3, 4; CP 1, 2, 3, 4, 5, 6, 7; DAM POP; MTCW 2

Comfort, Montgomery
See Campbell, Ramsey

Compton-Burnett, I. 1892(?)-1969 ... **CLC 1, 3, 10, 15, 34; TCLC 180**
See also BRW 7; CA 1-4R; 25-28R; CANR 4; DAM NOV; DLB 36; EWL 3; MTCW 1, 2; RGEL 2

Compton-Burnett, Ivy
See Compton-Burnett, I.

Comstock, Anthony 1844-1915 ..... **TCLC 13**
See also CA 110; 169

Comte, Auguste 1798-1857 .... **NCLC 54**

Conan Doyle, Arthur
See Doyle, Sir Arthur Conan

Conde (Abellan), Carmen 1901-1996 . **HLCS 1**
See also CA 177; CWW 2; DLB 108; EWL 3; HW 2

Conde, Maryse 1937- .... **BLC 2:1; BLCS; CLC 52, 92, 247**
See also BW 2, 3; CA 110, 190; CAAE 190; CANR 30, 53, 76, 171; CWW 2; DAM MULT; EWL 3; MTCW 2; MTFW 2005

Condillac, Etienne Bonnot de 1714-1780 ..... **LC 26**
See also DLB 313

Condon, Richard 1915-1996 .... **CLC 4, 6, 8, 10, 45, 100**
See also BEST 90:3; BPFB 1; CA 1-4R; 151; CAAS 1; CANR 2, 23, 164; CMW 4; CN 1, 2, 3, 4, 5, 6; DAM NOV; INT CANR-23; MAL 5; MTCW 1, 2

Condon, Richard Thomas
See Condon, Richard

Condorcet
See Condorcet, marquis de Marie-Jean-Antoine-Nicolas Caritat

Condorcet, marquis de Marie-Jean-Antoine-Nicolas Caritat 1743-1794 .... **LC 104**
See also DLB 313; GFL Beginnings to 1789

Confucius 551B.C.-479B.C. .. **CMLC 19, 65; WLCS**
See also DA; DA3; DAB; DAC; DAM MST

Congreve, William 1670-1729 .. **DC 2; LC 5, 21, 170; WLC 2**
See also BRW 2; CDBLB 1660-1789; DA; DAB; DAC; DAM DRAM, MST, POET; DFS 15; DLB 39, 84; RGEL 2; WLIT 3

Conley, Robert J. 1940- .... **NNAL**
See also CA 41-44R; 295; CAAE 295; CANR 15, 34, 45, 96, 186; DAM MULT; TCWW 2

Connell, Evan S. 1924- .... **CLC 4, 6, 45**
See also AAYA 7; AMWS 14; CA 1-4R; CAAS 2; CANR 2, 39, 76, 97, 140, 195; CN 1, 2, 3, 4, 5, 6; DAM NOV; DLB 2, 335; DLBY 1981; MAL 5; MTCW 1, 2; MTFW 2005

Connell, Evan Shelby, Jr.
See Connell, Evan S.

Connelly, Marc(us Cook) 1890-1980 . **CLC 7**
See also CA 85-88; 102; CAD; CANR 30; DFS 12; DLB 7; DLBY 1980; MAL 5; RGAL 4; SATA-Obit 25

Connelly, Michael 1956- .... **CLC 293**
See also AMWS 21; CA 158; CANR 91, 180; CMW 4; LNFS 2

Connolly, Paul
See Wicker, Tom

Connor, Ralph
See Gordon, Charles William

Conrad, Joseph 1857-1924 .... **SSC 9, 67, 69, 71, 153; TCLC 1, 6, 13, 25, 43, 57; WLC 2**
See also AAYA 26; BPFB 1; BRW 6; BRWC 1; BRWR 2; BYA 2; CA 104; 131; CANR 60; CDBLB 1890-1914; DA; DA3; DAB; DAC; DAM MST, NOV; DLB 10, 34, 98, 156; EWL 3; EXPN; EXPS; LAIT 2; LATS 1:1; LMFS 1; MTCW 1, 2; MTFW 2005; NFS 2, 16; RGEL 2; RGSF 2; SATA 27; SSFS 1, 12, 31; TEA; WLIT 4

Conrad, Robert Arnold
See Hart, Moss
Conroy, Donald Patrick
See Conroy, Pat
Conroy, Pat 1945- .... **CLC 30, 74**
See also AAYA 8, 52; AITN 1; BPFB 1;
CA 85-88; CANR 24, 53, 129, 233; CN
7; CPW; CSW; DA3; DAM NOV, POP;
DLB 6; LAIT 5; MAL 5; MTCW 1, 2;
MTFW 2005
Constant (de Rebecque), (Henri) Benjamin
1767-1830 .... **NCLC 6, 182**
See also DLB 119; EW 4; GFL 1789 to the
Present
Conway, Jill K. 1934- .... **CLC 152**
See also CA 130; CANR 94
Conway, Jill Ker
See Conway, Jill K.
Conybeare, Charles Augustus
See Eliot, T. S.
Cook, Michael 1933-1994 .... **CLC 58**
See also CA 93-96; CANR 68; DLB 53
Cook, Robin 1940- .... **CLC 14**
See also AAYA 32; BEST 90:2; BPFB 1;
CA 108; 111; CANR 41, 90, 109, 181,
219; CPW; DA3; DAM POP; HGG; INT
CA-111
Cook, Roy
See Silverberg, Robert
Cooke, Elizabeth 1948- .... **CLC 55**
See also CA 129
Cooke, John Esten 1830-1886 .... **NCLC 5**
See also DLB 3, 248; RGAL 4
Cooke, John Estes
See Baum, L. Frank
Cooke, M. E.
See Creasey, John
Cooke, Margaret
See Creasey, John
Cooke, Rose Terry 1827-1892 ... **NCLC 110;
SSC 149**
See also DLB 12, 74
Cook-Lynn, Elizabeth 1930- .... **CLC 93;
NNAL**
See also CA 133; DAM MULT; DLB 175
Cooney, Ray CLC 62
See also CBD
Cooper, Anthony Ashley 1671-1713 . **LC 107**
See also DLB 101, 336
Cooper, Dennis 1953- .... **CLC 203**
See also CA 133; CANR 72, 86, 204; GLL
1; HGG
Cooper, Douglas 1960- .... **CLC 86**
Cooper, Henry St. John
See Creasey, John
Cooper, J. California (?)- .... **CLC 56**
See also AAYA 12; BW 1; CA 125; CANR
55, 207; DAM MULT; DLB 212
Cooper, James Fenimore 1789-1851 . **NCLC
1, 27, 54, 203**
See also AAYA 22; AMW; BPFB 1;
CDALB 1640-1865; CLR 105; DA3;
DLB 3, 183, 250, 254; LAIT 1; NFS 25;
RGAL 4; SATA 19; TUS; WCH
Cooper, Joan California
See Cooper, J. California
Cooper, Susan Fenimore 1813-1894 .. **NCLC
129**
See also ANW; DLB 239, 254
Coover, Robert 1932- . **CLC 3, 7, 15, 32, 46,
87, 161, 306; SSC 15, 101**
See also AMWS 5; BPFB 1; CA 45-48;
CANR 3, 37, 58, 115, 228; CN 1, 2, 3, 4,
5, 6, 7; DAM NOV; DLB 2, 227; DLBY
1981; EWL 3; MAL 5; MTCW 1, 2;
MTFW 2005; RGAL 4; RGSF 2
Copeland, Stewart 1952- .... **CLC 26**
See also CA 305

Copeland, Stewart Armstrong
See Copeland, Stewart
Copernicus, Nicolaus 1473-1543 .... **LC 45**
Coppard, A(lfred) E(dgar) 1878-1957 .. **SSC
21; TCLC 5**
See also BRWS 8; CA 114; 167; DLB 162;
EWL 3; HGG; RGEL 2; RGSF 2; SUFW
1; YABC 1
Coppee, Francois 1842-1908 .... **TCLC 25**
See also CA 170; DLB 217
Coppola, Francis Ford 1939- .. **CLC 16, 126**
See also AAYA 39; CA 77-80; CANR 40,
78; DLB 44
Copway, George 1818-1869 .... **NNAL**
See also DAM MULT; DLB 175, 183
Corbiere, Tristan 1845-1875 .... **NCLC 43**
See also DLB 217; GFL 1789 to the Present
Corcoran, Barbara (Asenath) 1911-2003 .....
CLC 17
See also AAYA 14; CA 21-24R, 191; CAAE
191; CAAS 2; CANR 11, 28, 48; CLR
50; DLB 52; JRDA; MAICYA 2; MAIC-
YAS 1; RHW; SAAS 20; SATA 3, 77;
SATA-Essay 125
Cordelier, Maurice
See Giraudoux, Jean
Cordier, Gilbert
See Rohmer, Eric
Corelli, Marie
See Mackay, Mary
Corinna c. 225B.C.-c. 305B.C. ..... **CMLC 72**
Corman, Cid 1924-2004 .... **CLC 9**
See also CA 85-88; 225; CAAS 2; CANR
44; CP 1, 2, 3, 4, 5, 6, 7; DAM POET;
DLB 5, 193
Corman, Sidney
See Corman, Cid
Cormier, Robert 1925-2000 .... **CLC 12, 30**
See also AAYA 3, 19; BYA 1, 2, 6, 8, 9;
CA 1-4R; CANR 5, 23, 76, 93; CDALB
1968-1988; CLR 12, 55, 167; DA; DAB;
DAC; DAM MST, NOV; DLB 52; EXPN;
INT CANR-23; JRDA; LAIT 5; MAICYA
1, 2; MTCW 1, 2; MTFW 2005; NFS 2,
18; SATA 10, 45, 83; SATA-Obit 122;
WYA; YAW
Cormier, Robert Edmund
See Cormier, Robert
Corn, Alfred (DeWitt III) 1943- ..... **CLC 33**
See also CA 179; CAAE 179; CAAS 25;
CANR 44; CP 3, 4, 5, 6, 7; CSW; DLB
120, 282; DLBY 1980
Corneille, Pierre 1606-1684 . **DC 21; LC 28,
135**
See also DAB; DAM MST; DFS 21; DLB
268; EW 3; GFL Beginnings to 1789;
RGWL 2, 3; TWA
Cornwell, David
See le Carre, John
Cornwell, David John Moore
See le Carre, John
Cornwell, Patricia 1956- .... **CLC 155**
See also AAYA 16, 56; BPFB 1; CA 134;
CANR 53, 131, 195; CMW 4; CPW;
CSW; DAM POP; DLB 306; MSW;
MTCW 2; MTFW 2005
Cornwell, Patricia Daniels
See Cornwell, Patricia
Cornwell, Smith
See Smith, David (Jeddie)
Corso, Gregory 1930-2001 ... **CLC 1, 11; PC
33, 108**
See also AMWS 12; BG 1:2; CA 5-8R; 193;
CANR 41, 76, 132; CP 1, 2, 3, 4, 5, 6, 7;
DA3; DLB 5, 16, 237; LMFS 2; MAL 5;
MTCW 1, 2; MTFW 2005; WP

Cortazar, Julio 1914-1984 .. **CLC 2, 3, 5, 10,
13, 15, 33, 34, 92; HLC 1; SSC 7, 76,
156; TCLC 252**
See also AAYA 85; BPFB 1; CA 21-24R;
CANR 12, 32, 81; CDWLB 3; DA3;
DAM MULT, NOV; DLB 113; EWL 3;
EXPS; HW 1, 2; LAW; MTCW 1, 2;
MTFW 2005; RGSF 2; RGWL 2, 3; SSFS
3, 20, 28, 31, 34; TWA; WLIT 1
Cortes, Hernan 1485-1547 .... **LC 31**
Cortez, Jayne 1936- .... **BLC 2:1**
See also BW 2, 3; CA 73-76; CANR 13,
31, 68, 126; CWP; DLB 41; EWL 3
Corvinus, Jakob
See Raabe, Wilhelm (Karl)
Corwin, Cecil
See Kornbluth, C(yril) M.
Cosic, Dobrica 1921- .... **CLC 14**
See also CA 122; 138; CDWLB 4; CWW
2; DLB 181; EWL 3
Costain, Thomas B(ertram) 1885-1965 . **CLC
30**
See also BYA 3; CA 5-8R; 25-28R; DLB 9;
RHW
Costantini, Humberto 1924(?)-1987 ..... **CLC
49**
See also CA 131; 122; EWL 3; HW 1
Costello, Elvis 1954(?)- .... **CLC 21**
See also CA 204
Costenoble, Philostene
See Ghelderode, Michel de
Cotes, Cecil V.
See Duncan, Sara Jeannette
Cotter, Joseph Seamon Sr. 1861-1949 .. **BLC
1:1; TCLC 28**
See also BW 1; CA 124; DAM MULT; DLB
50
Cotton, John 1584-1652 .... **LC 176**
See also DLB 24; TUS
Couch, Arthur Thomas Quiller
See Quiller-Couch, Sir Arthur (Thomas)
Coulton, James
See Hansen, Joseph
Couperus, Louis (Marie Anne) 1863-1923 ..
TCLC 15
See also CA 115; EWL 3; RGWL 2, 3
Coupland, Douglas 1961- .... **CLC 85, 133**
See also AAYA 34; CA 142; CANR 57, 90,
130, 172, 213; CCA 1; CN 7; CPW; DAC;
DAM POP; DLB 334
Coupland, Douglas Campbell
See Coupland, Douglas
Court, Wesli
See Turco, Lewis
Courtenay, Bryce 1933- .... **CLC 59**
See also CA 138; CPW; NFS 32
Courtney, Robert
See Ellison, Harlan
Cousteau, Jacques 1910-1997 .... **CLC 30**
See also CA 65-68; 159; CANR 15, 67, 201;
MTCW 1; SATA 38, 98
Cousteau, Jacques-Yves
See Cousteau, Jacques
Coventry, Francis 1725-1754 .... **LC 46**
See also DLB 39
Coverdale, Miles c. 1487-1569 .... **LC 77**
See also DLB 167
Cowan, Peter (Walkinshaw) 1914-2002 . **SSC
28**
See also CA 21-24R; CANR 9, 25, 50, 83;
CN 1, 2, 3, 4, 5, 6, 7; DLB 260; RGSF 2
Coward, Noel 1899-1973 .. **CLC 1, 9, 29, 51;
DC 45**
See also AITN 1; BRWS 2; CA 17-18; 41-
44R; CANR 35, 132, 190; CAP 2; CBD;
CDBLB 1914-1945; DA3; DAM DRAM;
DFS 3, 6; DLB 10, 245; EWL 3; IDFW
3, 4; MTCW 1, 2; MTFW 2005; RGEL 2;
TEA

Coward, Noel Peirce
See Coward, Noel

Cowley, Abraham 1618-1667 . LC 43; PC 90
See also BRW 2; DLB 131, 151; PAB;
RGEL 2

Cowley, Malcolm 1898-1989 .... CLC 39
See also AMWS 2; CA 5-8R; 128; CANR
3, 55; CP 1, 2, 3, 4; DLB 4, 48; DLBY
1981, 1989; EWL 3; MAL 5; MTCW 1,
2; MTFW 2005

Cowper, William 1731-1800 .... NCLC 8, 94;
PC 40
See also BRW 3; BRWR 3; DA3; DAM
POET; DLB 104, 109; RGEL 2

Cox, William Trevor
See Trevor, William

Coyle, William
See Keneally, Thomas

Coyne, P. J.
See Masters, Hilary

Cozzens, James Gould 1903-1978 .... CLC 1,
4, 11, 92
See also AMW; BPFB 1; CA 9-12R; 81-84;
CANR 19; CDALB 1941-1968; CN 1, 2;
DLB 9, 294; DLBD 2; DLBY 1984, 1997;
EWL 3; MAL 5; MTCW 1, 2; MTFW
2005; RGAL 4

Crabbe, George 1754-1832 .. NCLC 26, 121;
PC 97
See also BRW 3; DLB 93; RGEL 2

Crace, Jim 1946- .... CLC 157; SSC 61
See also BRWS 14; CA 128; 135; CANR
55, 70, 123, 180; CN 5, 6, 7; DLB 231;
INT CA-135

Craddock, Charles Egbert
See Murfree, Mary Noailles

Craig, A. A.
See Anderson, Poul

Craik, Mrs.
See Craik, Dinah Maria (Mulock)

Craik, Dinah Maria (Mulock) 1826-1887 ....
NCLC 38
See also DLB 35, 163; MAICYA 1, 2;
RGEL 2; SATA 34

Cram, Ralph Adams 1863-1942 ... TCLC 45
See also CA 160

Cranch, Christopher Pearse 1813-1892 ....
NCLC 115
See also DLB 1, 42, 243

Crane, Harold Hart
See Crane, Hart

Crane, Hart 1899-1932 . PC 3, 99; TCLC 2,
5, 80; WLC 2
See also AAYA 81; AMW; AMWR 2; CA
104; CDALB 1917-1929; DA; DA3;
DAB; DAC; DAM MST, POET; DLB 4,
48; EWL 3; MAL 5; MTCW 1, 2; MTFW
2005; RGAL 4; TUS

Crane, R(onald) S(almon) 1886-1967 .. CLC
27
See also CA 85-88; DLB 63

Crane, Stephen 1871-1900 .... PC 80; SSC 7,
56, 70, 129; TCLC 11, 17, 32, 216; WLC
2
See also AAYA 21; AMW; AMWC 1; BPFB
1; BYA 3; CA 109; 140; CANR 84;
CDALB 1865-1917; CLR 132; DA; DA3;
DAB; DAC; DAM MST, POET; DLB 12, 54, 78, 357; EXPN; EXPS;
LAIT 2; LMFS 2; MAL 5; NFS 4, 20;
PFS 9; RGAL 4; RGSF 2; SSFS 4, 28,
34; TUS; WYA; YABC 2

Crane, Stephen Townley
See Crane, Stephen

Cranmer, Thomas 1489-1556 .... LC 95
See also DLB 132, 213

Cranshaw, Stanley
See Fisher, Dorothy (Frances) Canfield

Crase, Douglas 1944- .... CLC 58
See also CA 106; CANR 204

Crashaw, Richard 1612(?)-1649 .... LC 24,
200; PC 84
See also BRW 2; DLB 126; PAB; RGEL 2

Cratinus c. 519B.C.-c. 422B.C. .... CMLC 54
See also LMFS 1

Craven, Margaret 1901-1980 .... CLC 17
See also BYA 2; CA 103; CCA 1; DAC;
LAIT 5

Crawford, F(rancis) Marion 1854-1909 ....
TCLC 10
See also CA 107; 168; DLB 71; HGG;
RGAL 4; SUFW 1

Crawford, Isabella Valancy 1850-1887 ....
NCLC 12, 127
See also DLB 92; RGEL 2

Crayon, Geoffrey
See Irving, Washington

Creasey, John 1908-1973 .... CLC 11
See also CA 5-8R; 41-44R; CANR 8, 59;
CMW 4; DLB 77; MTCW 1

Crebillon, Claude Prosper Jolyot de (fils)
1707-1777 .... LC 1, 28
See also DLB 313; GFL Beginnings to 1789

Credo
See Creasey, John

Credo, Alvaro J. de
See Prado (Calvo), Pedro

Creeley, Robert 1926-2005 ... CLC 1, 2, 4, 8,
11, 15, 36, 78, 266; PC 73
See also AMWS 4; CA 1-4R; 237; CAAS
10; CANR 23, 43, 89, 137; CP 1, 2, 3, 4,
5, 6, 7; DA3; DAM POET; DLB 5, 16,
169; DLBD 17; EWL 3; MAL 5; MTCW
1, 2; MTFW 2005; PFS 21; RGAL 4; WP

Creeley, Robert White
See Creeley, Robert

Crenne, Helisenne de 1510-1560 ...... LC 113
See also DLB 327

Crevecoeur, J. Hector St. John de
1735-1813 .... NCLC 105
See also AMWS 1; ANW; DLB 37

Crevecoeur, Michel Guillaume Jean de
See Crevecoeur, J. Hector St. John de

Crevel, Rene 1900-1935 .... TCLC 112
See also GLL 2

Crews, Harry 1935- .... CLC 6, 23, 49, 277
See also AITN 1; AMWS 11; BPFB 1; CA
25-28R; CANR 20, 57; CN 3, 4, 5, 6, 7;
CSW; DA3; DLB 6, 143, 185; MTCW 1,
2; MTFW 2005; RGAL 4

Crichton, John Michael
See Crichton, Michael

Crichton, Michael 1942-2008 . CLC 2, 6, 54,
90, 242
See also AAYA 10, 49; AITN 2; BPFB 1;
CA 25-28R; 279; CANR 13, 40, 54, 76,
127, 179; CMW 4; CN 2, 3, 6, 7; CPW;
DA3; DAM NOV, POP; DLB 292; DLBY
1981; INT CANR-13; JRDA; LNFS 1;
MTCW 1, 2; MTFW 2005; NFS 34;
SATA 9, 88; SATA-Obit 199; SFW 4;
YAW

Crispin, Edmund
See Montgomery, Bruce

Cristina of Sweden 1626-1689 .... LC 124

Cristofer, Michael 1945(?)- .... CLC 28
See also CA 110; 152; CAD; CANR 150;
CD 5, 6; DAM DRAM; DFS 15; DLB 7

Cristofer, Michael Ivan
See Cristofer, Michael

Criton
See Alain

Croce, Benedetto 1866-1952 .... TCLC 37
See also CA 120; 155; EW 8; EWL 3;
WLIT 7

Crockett, David
See Crockett, Davy

Crockett, Davy 1786-1836 .... NCLC 8
See also DLB 3, 11, 183, 248

Crofts, Freeman Wills 1879-1957 . TCLC 55
See also CA 115; 195; CMW 4; DLB 77;
MSW

Croker, John Wilson 1780-1857 ... NCLC 10
See also DLB 110

Crommelynck, Fernand 1885-1970 . CLC 75
See also CA 189; 89-92; EWL 3

Cromwell, Oliver 1599-1658 .... LC 43

Cronenberg, David 1943- .... CLC 143
See also CA 138; CCA 1

Cronin, A(rchibald) J(oseph) 1896-1981 ......
CLC 32
See also BPFB 1; CA 1-4R; 102; CANR 5;
CN 2; DLB 191; SATA 47; SATA-Obit 25

Cross, Amanda
See Heilbrun, Carolyn G.

Crothers, Rachel 1878-1958 .... TCLC 19
See also CA 113; 194; CAD; CWD; DLB
7, 266; RGAL 4

Croves, Hal
See Traven, B.

Crow Dog, Mary (?)- .... CLC 93; NNAL
See also CA 154

Crowfield, Christopher
See Stowe, Harriet Beecher

Crowley, Aleister
See Crowley, Edward Alexander

Crowley, Edward Alexander 1875-1947 ......
TCLC 7
See also CA 104; GLL 1; HGG

Crowley, John 1942- .... CLC 57
See also AAYA 57; BPFB 1; CA 61-64;
CANR 43, 98, 138, 177; DLBY 1982;
FANT; MTFW 2005; SATA 65, 140; SFW
4; SUFW 2

Crowne, John 1641-1712 .... LC 104
See also DLB 80; RGEL 2

Crud
See Crumb, R.

Crumarums
See Crumb, R.

Crumb, R. 1943- .... CLC 17
See also CA 106; CANR 107, 150, 218

Crumb, Robert
See Crumb, R.

Crumbum
See Crumb, R.

Crumski
See Crumb, R.

Crum the Bum
See Crumb, R.

Crunk
See Crumb, R.

Crustt
See Crumb, R.

Crutchfield, Les
See Trumbo, Dalton

Cruz, Victor Hernandez 1949- .. HLC 1; PC
37
See also BW 2; CA 65-68; 271; CAAE 271;
CAAS 17; CANR 14, 32, 74, 132; CP 1,
2, 3, 4, 5, 6, 7; DAM MULT, POET; DLB
41; DNFS 1; EXPP; HW 1, 2; LLW;
MTCW 2; MTFW 2005; PFS 16; WP

Cryer, Gretchen (Kiger) 1935- .... CLC 21
See also CA 114; 123

Csath, Geza
See Brenner, Jozef

Cudlip, David R(ockwell) 1933- ...... CLC 34
See also CA 177

Cuervo, Talia
See Vega, Ana Lydia

Cullen, Countee 1903-1946 .... **BLC 1:1; HR 1:2; PC 20; TCLC 4, 37, 220; WLCS**
See also AAYA 78; AFAW 2; AMWS 4; BW 1; CA 108; 124; CDALB 1917-1929; DA; DA3; DAC; DAM MST, MULT, POET; DLB 4, 48, 51; EWL 3; LMFS 2; MAL 5; MTCW 1, 2; MTFW 2005; PFS 3; RGAL 4; SATA 18; WP

Culleton, Beatrice 1949- .... **NNAL**
See also CA 120; CANR 83; DAC

Culver, Timothy J.
See Westlake, Donald E.

Cum, R.
See Crumb, R.

Cumberland, Richard 1732-1811 ...... **NCLC 167**
See also DLB 89; RGEL 2

Cummings, Bruce F. 1889-1919 ... **TCLC 24**
See also CA 123

Cummings, Bruce Frederick
See Cummings, Bruce F.

Cummings, E. E. 1894-1962 .... **CLC 1, 3, 8, 12, 15, 68; PC 5; TCLC 137; WLC 2**
See also AAYA 41; AMW; CA 73-76; CANR 31; CDALB 1929-1941; DA; DA3; DAB; DAC; DAM MST, POET; DLB 4, 48; EWL 3; EXPP; MAL 5; MTCW 1, 2; MTFW 2005; PAB; PFS 1, 3, 12, 13, 19, 30, 34, 40; RGAL 4; TUS; WP

Cummings, Edward Estlin
See Cummings, E. E.

Cummins, Maria Susanna 1827-1866 ....
NCLC 139
See also DLB 42; YABC 1

Cunha, Euclides (Rodrigues Pimenta) da
1866-1909 .... **TCLC 24**
See also CA 123; 219; DLB 307; LAW; WLIT 1

Cunningham, E. V.
See Fast, Howard

Cunningham, J. Morgan
See Westlake, Donald E.

Cunningham, J(ames) V(incent)
1911-1985 .... **CLC 3, 31; PC 92**
See also CA 1-4R; 115; CANR 1, 72; CP 1, 2, 3, 4; DLB 5

Cunningham, Julia (Woolfolk) 1916- .. **CLC 12**
See also CA 9-12R; CANR 4, 19, 36; CWRI 5; JRDA; MAICYA 1, 2; SAAS 2; SATA 1, 26, 132

Cunningham, Michael 1952- ... **CLC 34, 243**
See also AMWS 15; CA 136; CANR 96, 160, 227; CN 7; DLB 292; GLL 2; MTFW 2005; NFS 23

Cunninghame Graham, R. B.
See Cunninghame Graham, Robert Bontine

Cunninghame Graham, Robert Bontine
1852-1936 .... **TCLC 19**
See also CA 119; 184; DLB 98, 135, 174; RGEL 2; RGSF 2

Cunninghame Graham, Robert Gallnigad Bontine
See Cunninghame Graham, Robert Bontine

Curnow, (Thomas) Allen (Monro)
1911-2001 .... **PC 48**
See also CA 69-72; 202; CANR 48, 99; CP 1, 2, 3, 4, 5, 6, 7; EWL 3; RGEL 2

Currie, Ellen 19(?)- .... **CLC 44**

Curtin, Philip
See Lowndes, Marie Adelaide (Belloc)

Curtin, Phillip
See Lowndes, Marie Adelaide (Belloc)

Curtis, Price
See Ellison, Harlan

Cusanus, Nicolaus 1401-1464 ....
See Nicholas of Cusa

Cutrate, Joe
See Spiegelman, Art

Cynewulf fl. 9th cent. - .... **CMLC 23, 117**
See also DLB 146; RGEL 2

Cyprian, St. c. 200-258 .... **CMLC 127**

Cyrano de Bergerac, Savinien de
1619-1655 .... **LC 65**
See also DLB 268; GFL Beginnings to 1789; RGWL 2, 3

Cyril of Alexandria c. 375-c. 430 . **CMLC 59**

Czaczkes, Shmuel Yosef Halevi
See Agnon, S. Y.

Dabrowska, Maria (Szumska) 1889-1965 ....
CLC 15
See also CA 106; CDWLB 4; DLB 215; EWL 3

Dabydeen, David 1955- .... **CLC 34**
See also BW 1; CA 125; CANR 56, 92; CN 6, 7; CP 5, 6, 7; DLB 347

Dacey, Philip 1939- .... **CLC 51**
See also CA 37-40R, 231; CAAE 231; CAAS 17; CANR 14, 32, 64; CP 4, 5, 6, 7; DLB 105

Dacre, Charlotte c. 1772-1825(?) . **NCLC 151**

Dafydd ap Gwilym c. 1320-c. 1380 .... **PC 56**

Dagerman, Stig (Halvard) 1923-1954 . **TCLC 17**
See also CA 117; 155; DLB 259; EWL 3

D'Aguiar, Fred 1960- .... **BLC 2:1; CLC 145**
See also CA 148; CANR 83, 101; CN 7; CP 5, 6, 7; DLB 157; EWL 3

Dahl, Roald 1916-1990 ..... **CLC 1, 6, 18, 79; TCLC 173**
See also AAYA 15; BPFB 1; BRWS 4; BYA 5; CA 1-4R; 133; CANR 6, 32, 37, 62; CLR 1, 7, 41, 111; CN 1, 2, 3, 4; CPW; DA3; DAB; DAC; DAM MST, NOV, POP; DLB 139, 255; HGG; JRDA; MAICYA 1, 2; MTCW 1, 2; MTFW 2005; RGSF 2; SATA 1, 26, 73; SATA-Obit 65; SSFS 4, 30; TEA; YAW

Dahlberg, Edward 1900-1977 ...... **CLC 1, 7, 14; TCLC 208**
See also CA 9-12R; 69-72; CANR 31, 62; CN 1, 2; DLB 48; MAL 5; MTCW 1; RGAL 4

Dahlie, Michael 1970(?)- .... **CLC 299**
See also CA 283

Daitch, Susan 1954- .... **CLC 103**
See also CA 161

Dale, Colin
See Lawrence, T. E.

Dale, George E.
See Asimov, Isaac

d'Alembert, Jean Le Rond 1717-1783 ... **LC 126**

Dalton, Roque 1935-1975(?) .... **HLCS 1; PC 36**
See also CA 176; DLB 283; HW 2

Daly, Elizabeth 1878-1967 .... **CLC 52**
See also CA 23-24; 25-28R; CANR 60; CAP 2; CMW 4

Daly, Mary 1928-2010 .... **CLC 173**
See also CA 25-28R; CANR 30, 62, 166; FW; GLL 1; MTCW 1

Daly, Maureen 1921-2006 .... **CLC 17**
See also AAYA 5, 58; BYA 6; CA 253; CANR 37, 83, 108; CLR 96; JRDA; MAICYA 1, 2; SAAS 1; SATA 2, 129; SATA-Obit 176; WYA; YAW

Damas, Leon-Gontran 1912-1978 .. **CLC 84; TCLC 204**
See also BW 1; CA 125; 73-76; EWL 3

Damocles
See Benedetti, Mario

Dana, Richard Henry Sr. 1787-1879 . **NCLC 53**

Dangarembga, Tsitsi 1959- .... **BLC 2:1**
See also BW 3; CA 163; DLB 360; NFS 28; WLIT 2

Daniel, Samuel 1562(?)-1619 ...... **LC 24, 171**
See also DLB 62; RGEL 2

Daniels, Brett
See Adler, Renata

Dannay, Frederic 1905-1982 .... **CLC 3, 11**
See also BPFB 3; CA 1-4R; 107; CANR 1, 39; CMW 4; DAM POP; DLB 137; MSW; MTCW 1; RGAL 4

D'Annunzio, Gabriele 1863-1938 .. **TCLC 6, 40, 215**
See also CA 104; 155; EW 8; EWL 3; RGWL 2, 3; TWA; WLIT 7

Danois, N. le
See Gourmont, Remy(-Marie-Charles) de

Dante 1265-1321 ... **CMLC 3, 18, 39, 70; PC 21, 108; WLCS**
See also DA; DA3; DAB; DAC; DAM MST, POET; EFS 1:1, 2:1; EW 1; LAIT 1; RGWL 2, 3; TWA; WLIT 7; WP

d'Antibes, Germain
See Simenon, Georges

Danticat, Edwidge 1969- ...... **BLC 2:1; CLC 94, 139, 228; SSC 100**
See also AAYA 29, 85; CA 152, 192; CAAE 192; CANR 73, 129, 179; CN 7; DLB 350; DNFS 1; EXPS; LATS 1:2; LNFS 3; MTCW 2; MTFW 2005; NFS 28, 37; SSFS 1, 25; YAW

Danvers, Dennis 1947- .... **CLC 70**

Danziger, Paula 1944-2004 .... **CLC 21**
See also AAYA 4, 36; BYA 6, 7, 14; CA 112; 115; 229; CANR 37, 132; CLR 20; JRDA; MAICYA 1, 2; MTFW 2005; SATA 36, 63, 102, 149; SATA-Brief 30; SATA-Obit 155; WYA; YAW

Da Ponte, Lorenzo 1749-1838 ...... **NCLC 50**

d'Aragona, Tullia 1510(?)-1556 .... **LC 121**

Dario, Ruben 1867-1916 ..... **HLC 1; PC 15; TCLC 4, 265**
See also CA 131; CANR 81; DAM MULT; DLB 290; EWL 3; HW 1, 2; LAW; MTCW 1, 2; MTFW 2005; RGWL 2, 3

Darko, Amma 1956- .... **BLC 2:1**

Darley, George 1795-1846 . **NCLC 2; PC 125**
See also DLB 96; RGEL 2

Darrow, Clarence (Seward) 1857-1938 ....
TCLC 81
See also CA 164; DLB 303

Darwin, Charles 1809-1882 .... **NCLC 57**
See also BRWS 7; DLB 57, 166; LATS 1:1; RGEL 2; TEA; WLIT 4

Darwin, Erasmus 1731-1802 .... **NCLC 106**
See also BRWS 16; DLB 93; RGEL 2

Darwish, Mahmoud 1941-2008 .... **PC 86**
See also CA 164; CANR 133; CWW 2; EWL 3; MTCW 2; MTFW 2005

Darwish, Mahmud -2008 ....
See Darwish, Mahmoud

Daryush, Elizabeth 1887-1977 .... **CLC 6, 19**
See also CA 49-52; CANR 3, 81; DLB 20

Das, Kamala 1934-2009 .... **CLC 191; PC 43**
See also CA 101; 287; CANR 27, 59; CP 1, 2, 3, 4, 5, 6, 7; CWP; DLB 323; FW

Dasgupta, Surendranath 1887-1952 .. **TCLC 81**
See also CA 157

Dashwood, Edmee Elizabeth Monica de la
Pasture 1890-1943 .... **TCLC 61**
See also CA 119; 154; DLB 34; RHW

da Silva, Antonio Jose 1705-1739 ...... **NCLC 114**

Daudet, (Louis Marie) Alphonse
1840-1897 .... **NCLC 1**
See also DLB 123; GFL 1789 to the Present; RGSF 2

Delany, Samuel R., Jr. 1942- . **BLC 1:1; CLC 8, 14, 38, 141, 313**
See also AAYA 24; AFAW 2; BPFB 1; BW 2, 3; CA 81-84; CANR 27, 43, 116, 172; CN 2, 3, 4, 5, 6, 7; DAM MULT; DLB 8, 33; FANT; MAL 5; MTCW 1, 2; RGAL 4; SATA 92; SCFW 1, 2; SFW 4; SUFW 2

Delany, Samuel Ray
See Delany, Samuel R., Jr.

de la Parra, Ana Teresa Sonojo
See de la Parra, Teresa

de la Parra, Teresa 1890(?)-1936 .. **HLCS 2; TCLC 185**
See also CA 178; HW 2; LAW

Delaporte, Theophile
See Green, Julien

De La Ramee, Marie Louise 1839-1908 ...... **TCLC 43**
See also CA 204; DLB 18, 156; RGEL 2; SATA 20

de la Roche, Mazo 1879-1961 .... **CLC 14**
See also CA 85-88; CANR 30; DLB 68; RGEL 2; RHW; SATA 64

De La Salle, Innocent
See Hartmann, Sadakichi

de Laureamont, Comte
See Lautreamont

Delbanco, Nicholas 1942- .... **CLC 6, 13, 167**
See also CA 17-20R, 189; CAAE 189; CAAS 2; CANR 29, 55, 116, 150, 204; CN 7; DLB 6, 234

Delbanco, Nicholas Franklin
See Delbanco, Nicholas

del Castillo, Michel 1933- .... **CLC 38**
See also CA 109; CANR 77

Deledda, Grazia (Cosima) 1875(?)-1936 ...... **TCLC 23**
See also CA 123; 205; DLB 264, 329; EWL 3; RGWL 2, 3; WLIT 7

Deleuze, Gilles 1925-1995 .... **TCLC 116**
See also DLB 296

Delgado, Abelardo (Lalo) B(arrientos) 1930-2004 .... **HLC 1**
See also CA 131; 230; CAAS 15; CANR 90; DAM MST, MULT; DLB 82; HW 1, 2

Delibes, Miguel
See Delibes Setien, Miguel

Delibes Setien, Miguel 1920-2010 .... **CLC 8, 18**
See also CA 45-48; CANR 1, 32; CWW 2; DLB 322; EWL 3; HW 1; MTCW 1

DeLillo, Don 1936- ... **CLC 8, 10, 13, 27, 39, 54, 76, 143, 210, 213**
See also AMWC 2; AMWS 6; BEST 89:1; BPFB 1; CA 81-84; CANR 21, 76, 92, 133, 173; CN 3, 4, 5, 6, 7; CPW; DA3; DAM NOV, POP; DLB 6, 173; EWL 3; MAL 5; MTCW 1, 2; MTFW 2005; NFS 28; RGAL 4; TUS

de Lisser, H. G.
See De Lisser, H(erbert) G(eorge)

De Lisser, H(erbert) G(eorge) 1878-1944 .... **TCLC 12**
See also BW 2; CA 109; 152; DLB 117

Deloire, Pierre
See Peguy, Charles (Pierre)

Deloney, Thomas 1543(?)-1600 ... **LC 41; PC 79**
See also DLB 167; RGEL 2

Deloria, Ella (Cara) 1889-1971(?) ..... **NNAL**
See also CA 152; DAM MULT; DLB 175

Deloria, Vine, Jr. 1933-2005 ... **CLC 21, 122; NNAL**
See also CA 53-56; 245; CANR 5, 20, 48, 98; DAM MULT; DLB 175; MTCW 1; SATA 21; SATA-Obit 171

Deloria, Vine Victor, Jr.
See Deloria, Vine, Jr.

del Valle-Inclan, Ramon
See Valle-Inclan, Ramon del

Del Vecchio, John M(ichael) 1947- . **CLC 29**
See also CA 110; DLBD 9

de Man, Paul (Adolph Michel) 1919-1983 .. **CLC 55**
See also CA 128; 111; CANR 61; DLB 67; MTCW 1, 2

de Mandiargues, Andre Pieyre
See Pieyre de Mandiargues, Andre

DeMarinis, Rick 1934- .... **CLC 54**
See also CA 57-60, 184; CAAE 184; CAAS 24; CANR 9, 25, 50, 160; DLB 218; TCWW 2

de Maupassant, Guy
See Maupassant, Guy de

Dembry, R. Emmet
See Murfree, Mary Noailles

Demby, William 1922- .... **BLC 1:1; CLC 53**
See also BW 1, 3; CA 81-84; CANR 81; DAM MULT; DLB 33

de Menton, Francisco
See Chin, Frank

Demetrius of Phalerum c. 307B.C.- . **CMLC 34**

Demijohn, Thom
See Disch, Thomas M.

De Mille, James 1833-1880 .... **NCLC 123**
See also DLB 99, 251

Democritus c. 460B.C.-c. 370B.C. ..... **CMLC 47, 136**

de Montaigne, Michel
See Montaigne, Michel de

de Montherlant, Henry
See Montherlant, Henry de

Demosthenes 384B.C.-322B.C. ..... **CMLC 13**
See also AW 1; DLB 176; RGWL 2, 3; WLIT 8

de Musset, (Louis Charles) Alfred
See Musset, Alfred de

de Natale, Francine
See Malzberg, Barry N(athaniel)

de Navarre, Marguerite 1492-1549 .. **LC 61, 167; SSC 85**
See also DLB 327; GFL Beginnings to 1789; RGWL 2, 3

Denby, Edwin (Orr) 1903-1983 .... **CLC 48**
See also CA 138; 110; CP 1

de Nerval, Gerard
See Nerval, Gerard de

Denham, John 1615-1669 .... **LC 73**
See also DLB 58, 126; RGEL 2

Denis, Claire 1948- .... **CLC 286**
See also CA 249

Denis, Julio
See Cortazar, Julio

Denmark, Harrison
See Zelazny, Roger

Dennie, Joseph 1768-1812 .... **NCLC 249**
See also DLB 37, 43, 59, 73

Dennis, John 1658-1734 .... **LC 11, 154**
See also DLB 101; RGEL 2

Dennis, Nigel (Forbes) 1912-1989 ..... **CLC 8**
See also CA 25-28R; 129; CN 1, 2, 3, 4; DLB 13, 15, 233; EWL 3; MTCW 1

Dent, Lester 1904-1959 .... **TCLC 72**
See also CA 112; 161; CMW 4; DLB 306; SFW 4

Dentinger, Stephen
See Hoch, Edward D.

De Palma, Brian 1940- .... **CLC 20, 247**
See also CA 109

De Palma, Brian Russell
See De Palma, Brian

de Pizan, Christine
See Christine de Pizan

De Quincey, Thomas 1785-1859 .... **NCLC 4, 87, 198**
See also BRW 4; CDBLB 1789-1832; DLB 110, 144; RGEL 2

De Ray, Jill
See Moore, Alan

Deren, Eleanora 1908(?)-1961 . **CLC 16, 102**
See also CA 192; 111

Deren, Maya
See Deren, Eleanora

Derleth, August (William) 1909-1971 .. **CLC 31**
See also BPFB 1; BYA 9, 10; CA 1-4R; 29-32R; CANR 4; CMW 4; CN 1; DLB 9; DLBD 17; HGG; SATA 5; SUFW 1

Der Nister 1884-1950 .... **TCLC 56**
See also DLB 333; EWL 3

de Routisie, Albert
See Aragon, Louis

Derrida, Jacques 1930-2004 ..... **CLC 24, 87, 225**
See also CA 124; 127; 232; CANR 76, 98, 133; DLB 242; EWL 3; LMFS 2; MTCW 2; TWA

Derry Down Derry
See Lear, Edward

Dershowitz, Alan 1938- .... **CLC 298**
See also CA 25-28R; CANR 11, 44, 79, 159, 227

Dershowitz, Alan Morton
See Dershowitz, Alan

Dersonnes, Jacques
See Simenon, Georges

Der Stricker c. 1190-c. 1250 .... **CMLC 75**
See also DLB 138

Derzhavin, Gavriil Romanovich 1743-1816 .... **NCLC 215**
See also DLB 150

Desai, Anita 1937- .... **CLC 19, 37, 97, 175, 271**
See also AAYA 85; BRWS 5; CA 81-84; CANR 33, 53, 95, 133; CN 1, 2, 3, 4, 5, 6, 7; CWRI 5; DA3; DAB; DAM NOV; DLB 271, 323; DNFS 2; EWL 3; FW; MTCW 1, 2; MTFW 2005; SATA 63, 126; SSFS 28, 31

Desai, Kiran 1971- .... **CLC 119**
See also BRWS 15; BYA 16; CA 171; CANR 127; NFS 28

de Saint-Luc, Jean
See Glassco, John

de Saint Roman, Arnaud
See Aragon, Louis

Desbordes-Valmore, Marceline 1786-1859 .. **NCLC 97**
See also DLB 217

Descartes, Rene 1596-1650 .. **LC 20, 35, 150, 202**
See also DLB 268; EW 3; GFL Beginnings to 1789

Deschamps, Eustache 1340(?)-1404 . **LC 103**
See also DLB 208

De Sica, Vittorio 1901(?)-1974 .... **CLC 20**
See also CA 117

Desnos, Robert 1900-1945 .... **TCLC 22, 241**
See also CA 121; 151; CANR 107; DLB 258; EWL 3; LMFS 2

Destouches, Louis-Ferdinand
See Celine, Louis-Ferdinand

De Teran, Lisa St. Aubin
See St. Aubin de Teran, Lisa

de Teran, Lisa St. Aubin
See St. Aubin de Teran, Lisa

de Tolignac, Gaston
See Griffith, D.W.

Deutsch, Babette 1895-1982 .... **CLC 18**
See also BYA 3; CA 1-4R; 108; CANR 4, 79; CP 1, 2, 3; DLB 45; SATA 1; SATA-Obit 33

Doeblin, Alfred 1878-1957 .... **TCLC 13**
See also CA 110; 141; CDWLB 2; DLB 66; EWL 3; RGWL 2, 3

Doerr, Harriet 1910-2002 .... **CLC 34**
See also CA 117; 122; 213; CANR 47; INT CA-122; LATS 1:2

Domecq, Honorio Bustos
See Bioy Casares, Adolfo; Borges, Jorge Luis

Domini, Rey
See Lorde, Audre

Dominic, R. B.
See Hennissart, Martha

Dominique
See Proust, Marcel

Don, A
See Stephen, Sir Leslie

Donaldson, Stephen R. 1947- .. **CLC 46, 138**
See also AAYA 36; BPFB 1; CA 89-92; CANR 13, 55, 99, 228; CPW; DAM POP; FANT; INT CANR-13; SATA 121; SFW 4; SUFW 1, 2

Donleavy, J(ames) P(atrick) 1926- ... **CLC 1, 4, 6, 10, 45**
See also AITN 2; BPFB 1; CA 9-12R; CANR 24, 49, 62, 80, 124; CBD; CD 5, 6; CN 1, 2, 3, 4, 5, 6, 7; DLB 6, 173; INT CANR-24; MAL 5; MTCW 1, 2; MTFW 2005; RGAL 4

Donnadieu, Marguerite
See Duras, Marguerite

Donne, John 1572-1631 .. **LC 10, 24, 91; PC 1, 43; WLC 2**
See also AAYA 67; BRW 1; BRWC 1; BRWR 2; CDBLB Before 1660; DA; DAB; DAC; DAM MST; DLB 121, 151; EXPP; PAB; PFS 2, 11, 35, 41; RGEL 3; TEA; WLIT 3; WP

Donnell, David 1939(?)- .... **CLC 34**
See also CA 197

Donoghue, Denis 1928- .... **CLC 209**
See also CA 17-20R; CANR 16, 102, 206

Donoghue, Emma 1969- .... **CLC 239**
See also CA 155; CANR 103, 152, 196; DLB 267; GLL 2; SATA 101

Donoghue, P.S.
See Hunt, E. Howard

Donoso, Jose 1924-1996 .... **CLC 4, 8, 11, 32, 99; HLC 1; SSC 34; TCLC 133**
See also CA 81-84; 155; CANR 32, 73; CDWLB 3; CWW 2; DAM MULT; DLB 113; EWL 3; HW 1, 2; LAW; LAWS 1; MTCW 1, 2; MTFW 2005; RGSF 2; WLIT 1

Donoso Yanez, Jose
See Donoso, Jose

Donovan, John 1928-1992 .... **CLC 35**
See also AAYA 20; CA 97-100; 137; CLR 3; MAICYA 1, 2; SATA 72; SATA-Brief 29; YAW

Don Roberto
See Cunninghame Graham, Robert Bontine

Doolittle, Hilda 1886-1961 ...... **CLC 3, 8, 14, 31, 34, 73; PC 5, 127; WLC 3**
See also AAYA 66; AMWS 1; CA 97-100; CANR 35, 131; DA; DAC; DAM MST, POET; DLB 4, 45; EWL 3; FL 1:5; FW; GLL 1; LMFS 2; MAL 5; MBL; MTCW 1, 2; MTFW 2005; PFS 6, 28; RGAL 4

Doppo
See Kunikida Doppo

Doppo, Kunikida
See Kunikida Doppo

Dorfman, Ariel 1942- .... **CLC 48, 77, 189; HLC 1**
See also CA 124; 130; CANR 67, 70, 135; CWW 2; DAM MULT; DFS 4; EWL 3; HW 1, 2; INT CA-130; WLIT 1

Dorn, Edward 1929-1999 .. **CLC 10, 18; PC 115**
See also CA 93-96; 187; CANR 42, 79; CP 1, 2, 3, 4, 5, 6, 7; DLB 5; INT CA-93-96; WP

Dorn, Edward Merton
See Dorn, Edward

Dor-Ner, Zvi CLC 70

Dorris, Michael 1945-1997 .... **CLC 109; NNAL**
See also AAYA 20; BEST 90:1; BYA 12; CA 102; 157; CANR 19, 46, 75; CLR 58; DA3; DAM MULT, NOV; DLB 175; LAIT 5; MTCW 2; MTFW 2005; NFS 3; RGAL 4; SATA 75; SATA-Obit 94; TCWW 2; YAW

Dorris, Michael A.
See Dorris, Michael

Dorris, Michael Anthony
See Dorris, Michael

Dorsan, Luc
See Simenon, Georges

Dorsange, Jean
See Simenon, Georges

Dorset
See Sackville, Thomas

Dos Passos, John 1896-1970 .... **CLC 1, 4, 8, 11, 15, 25, 34, 82; TCLC 268; WLC 2**
See also AMW; BPFB 1; CA 1-4R; 29-32R; CANR 3; CDALB 1929-1941; DA; DA3; DAB; DAC; DAM MST, NOV; DLB 4, 9, 274, 316; DLBD 1, 15; DLBY 1996; EWL 3; MAL 5; MTCW 1, 2; MTFW 2005; NFS 14; RGAL 4; TUS

Dos Passos, John Roderigo
See Dos Passos, John

Dossage, Jean
See Simenon, Georges

Dostoevsky, Fedor
See Dostoevsky, Fyodor

Dostoevsky, Fedor Mikhailovich
See Dostoevsky, Fyodor

Dostoevsky, Fyodor 1821-1881 .. **NCLC 2, 7, 21, 33, 43, 119, 167, 202, 238; SSC 2, 33, 44, 134; WLC 2**
See also AAYA 40; DA; DA3; DAB; DAC; DAM MST, NOV; DLB 238; EW 7; EXPN; LATS 1:1; LMFS 1, 2; NFS 28; RGSF 2; RGWL 2, 3; SSFS 8, 30; TWA

Doty, Mark 1953(?)- .... **CLC 176; PC 53**
See also AMWS 11; CA 161, 183; CAAE 183; CANR 110, 173; CP 7; PFS 28, 40

Doty, Mark A.
See Doty, Mark

Doty, Mark Alan
See Doty, Mark

Doty, M.R.
See Doty, Mark

Doughty, Charles M(ontagu) 1843-1926 ...... **TCLC 27**
See also CA 115; 178; DLB 19, 57, 174, 366

Douglas, Ellen 1921- .... **CLC 73**
See also CA 115; CANR 41, 83; CN 5, 6, 7; CSW; DLB 292

Douglas, Gavin 1475(?)-1522 .... **LC 20**
See also DLB 132; RGEL 2

Douglas, George
See Brown, George Douglas

Douglas, Keith (Castellain) 1920-1944 ... **PC 106; TCLC 40**
See also BRW 7; CA 160; DLB 27; EWL 3; PAB; RGEL 2

Douglas, Leonard
See Bradbury, Ray

Douglas, Michael
See Crichton, Michael

Douglas, (George) Norman 1868-1952 .... **TCLC 68**
See also BRW 6; CA 119; 157; DLB 34, 195; RGEL 2

Douglas, William
See Brown, George Douglas

Douglass, Frederick 1817(?)-1895 . **BLC 1:1; NCLC 7, 55, 141, 235; WLC 2**
See also AAYA 48; AFAW 1, 2; AMWC 1; AMWS 3; CDALB 1640-1865; DA; DA3; DAC; DAM MST, MULT; DLB 1, 43, 50, 79, 243; FW; LAIT 2; NCFS 2; RGAL 4; SATA 29

Dourado, (Waldomiro Freitas) Autran 1926- .... **CLC 23, 60**
See also CA 25-28R; 179; CANR 34, 81; DLB 145, 307; HW 2

Dourado, Waldomiro Freitas Autran
See Dourado, (Waldomiro Freitas) Autran

Dove, Rita 1952- . **BLC 2:1; BLCS; CLC 50, 81; PC 6**
See also AAYA 46; AMWS 4; BW 2; CA 109; CAAS 19; CANR 27, 42, 68, 76, 97, 132, 217; CDALBS; CP 5, 6, 7; CSW; CWP; DA3; DAM MULT, POET; DLB 120; EWL 3; EXPP; MAL 5; MTCW 2; MTFW 2005; PFS 1, 15, 37; RGAL 4

Dove, Rita Frances
See Dove, Rita

Doveglion
See Villa, Jose Garcia

Dowell, Coleman 1925-1985 .... **CLC 60**
See also CA 25-28R; 117; CANR 10; DLB 130; GLL 2

Downing, Major Jack
See Smith, Seba

Dowson, Ernest (Christopher) 1867-1900 ... **TCLC 4**
See also CA 105; 150; DLB 19, 135; RGEL 2

Doyle, A. Conan
See Doyle, Sir Arthur Conan

Doyle, Sir Arthur Conan 1859-1930 ..... **SSC 12, 83, 95; TCLC 7; WLC 2**
See also AAYA 14; BPFB 1; BRWS 2; BYA 4, 5, 11; CA 104; 122; CANR 131; CDBLB 1890-1914; CLR 106; CMW 4; DA; DA3; DAB; DAC; DAM MST, NOV; DLB 18, 70, 156, 178; EXPS; HGG; LAIT 2; MSW; MTCW 1, 2; MTFW 2005; NFS 28; RGEL 2; RGSF 2; RHW; SATA 24; SCFW 1, 2; SFW 4; SSFS 2; TEA; WCH; WLIT 4; WYA; YAW

Doyle, Conan
See Doyle, Sir Arthur Conan

Doyle, John
See Graves, Robert

Doyle, Roddy 1958- .... **CLC 81, 178**
See also AAYA 14; BRWS 5; CA 143; CANR 73, 128, 168, 200; CN 6, 7; DA3; DLB 194; 326; MTCW 2; MTFW 2005

Doyle, Sir A. Conan
See Doyle, Sir Arthur Conan

Dr. A
See Asimov, Isaac; Silverstein, Alvin; Silverstein, Virginia B.

Drabble, Margaret 1939- ..... **CLC 2, 3, 5, 8, 10, 22, 53, 129**
See also BRWS 4; CA 13-16R; CANR 18, 35, 63, 112, 131, 174, 218; CDBLB 1960 to Present; CN 1, 2, 3, 4, 5, 6, 7; CPW; DA3; DAB; DAC; DAM MST, NOV, POP; DLB 14, 155, 231; EWL 3; FW; MTCW 1, 2; MTFW 2005; RGEL 2; SATA 48; TEA

Drakulic, Slavenka
See Drakulic, Slavenka

Drakulic, Slavenka 1949- .... **CLC 173**
See also CA 144; CANR 92, 198, 229; DLB 353

Drakulic-Ilic, Slavenka
See Drakulic, Slavenka

Drakulic-Ilic, Slavenka
See Drakulic, Slavenka

Drapier, M. B.
See Swift, Jonathan

Drayham, James
See Mencken, H. L.

Drayton, Michael 1563-1631 . **LC 8, 161; PC 98**
See also DAM POET; DLB 121; RGEL 2

Dreadstone, Carl
See Campbell, Ramsey

Dreiser, Theodore 1871-1945 ... **SSC 30, 114; TCLC 10, 18, 35, 83; WLC 2**
See also AMW; AMWC 2; AMWR 2; BYA 15, 16; CA 106; 132; CDALB 1865-1917; DA; DA3; DAC; DAM MST, NOV; DLB 9, 12, 102, 137, 361; DLBD 1; EWL 3; LAIT 2; LMFS 2; MAL 5; MTCW 1, 2; MTFW 2005; NFS 8, 17; RGAL 4; TUS

Dreiser, Theodore Herman Albert
See Dreiser, Theodore

Drexler, Rosalyn 1926- .... **CLC 2, 6**
See also CA 81-84; CAD; CANR 68, 124; CD 5, 6; CWD; MAL 5

Dreyer, Carl Theodor 1889-1968 .... **CLC 16**
See also CA 116

Drieu la Rochelle, Pierre 1893-1945 . **TCLC 21**
See also CA 117; 250; DLB 72; EWL 3; GFL 1789 to the Present

Drieu la Rochelle, Pierre-Eugene 1893-1945 ....
See Drieu la Rochelle, Pierre

Drinkwater, John 1882-1937 .... **TCLC 57**
See also CA 109; 149; DLB 10, 19, 149; RGEL 2

Drop Shot
See Cable, George Washington

Droste-Hulshoff, Annette Freiin von 1797-1848 .... **NCLC 3, 133**
See also CDWLB 2; DLB 133; RGSF 2; RGWL 2, 3

Drummond, Walter
See Silverberg, Robert

Drummond, William Henry 1854-1907 .... **TCLC 25**
See also CA 160; DLB 92

Drummond de Andrade, Carlos 1902-1987 .... **CLC 18; TCLC 139**
See also CA 132; 123; DLB 307; EWL 3; LAW; RGWL 2, 3

Drummond of Hawthornden, William 1585-1649 .... **LC 83**
See also DLB 121, 213; RGEL 2

Drury, Allen (Stuart) 1918-1998 ..... **CLC 37**
See also CA 57-60; 170; CANR 18, 52; CN 1, 2, 3, 4, 5, 6; INT CANR-18

Druse, Eleanor
See King, Stephen

Dryden, John 1631-1700 .... **DC 3; LC 3, 21, 115, 188; PC 25; WLC 2**
See also BRW 2; BRWR 3; CDBLB 1660-1789; DA; DAB; DAC; DAM DRAM, MST, POET; DLB 80, 101, 131; EXPP; IDTP; LMFS 1; RGEL 2; TEA; WLIT 3

du Aime, Albert
See Wharton, William

du Aime, Albert William
See Wharton, William

du Bellay, Joachim 1524-1560 .... **LC 92**
See also DLB 327; GFL Beginnings to 1789; RGWL 2, 3

Duberman, Martin 1930- .... **CLC 8**
See also CA 1-4R; CAD; CANR 2, 63, 137, 174; CD 5, 6

Dubie, Norman (Evans) 1945- .... **CLC 36**
See also CA 69-72; CANR 12, 115; CP 3, 4, 5, 6, 7; DLB 120; PFS 12

Du Bois, W. E. B. 1868-1963 . **BLC 1:1; CLC 1, 2, 13, 64, 96; HR 1:2; TCLC 169; WLC 2**
See also AAYA 40; AFAW 1, 2; AMWC 1; AMWS 2; BW 1, 3; CA 85-88; CANR 34, 82, 132; CDALB 1865-1917; DA; DA3; DAC; DAM MST, MULT, NOV; DLB 47, 50, 91, 246, 284; EWL 3; EXPP; LAIT 2; LMFS 2; MAL 5; MTCW 1, 2; MTFW 2005; NCFS 1; PFS 13; RGAL 4; SATA 42

Du Bois, William Edward Burghardt
See Du Bois, W. E. B.

Dubos, Jean-Baptiste 1670-1742 ...... **LC 197**

Dubus, Andre 1936-1999 .... **CLC 13, 36, 97; SSC 15, 118**
See also AMWS 7; CA 21-24R; 177; CANR 17; CN 5, 6; CSW; DLB 130; INT CANR-17; RGAL 4; SSFS 10; TCLE 1:1

Duca Minimo
See D'Annunzio, Gabriele

Ducharme, Rejean 1941- .... **CLC 74**
See also CA 165; DLB 60

du Chatelet, Emilie 1706-1749 .... **LC 96**
See also DLB 313

Duchen, Claire CLC 65

Duck, Stephen 1705(?)-1756 .... **PC 89**
See also DLB 95; RGEL 2

Duclos, Charles Pinot- 1704-1772 .... **LC 1**
See also GFL Beginnings to 1789

Ducornet, Erica 1943- .... **CLC 232**
See also CA 37-40R; CANR 14, 34, 54, 82; SATA 7

Ducornet, Rikki
See Ducornet, Erica

Dudek, Louis 1918-2001 .... **CLC 11, 19**
See also CA 45-48; 215; CAAS 14; CANR 1; CP 1, 2, 3, 4, 5, 6, 7; DLB 88

Duerrematt, Friedrich
See Durrenmatt, Friedrich

Duffy, Bruce 1953(?)- .... **CLC 50**
See also CA 172

Duffy, Maureen 1933- .... **CLC 37**
See also CA 25-28R; CANR 33, 68; CBD; CN 1, 2, 3, 4, 5, 6, 7; CP 5, 6, 7; CWD; CWP; DFS 15; DLB 14, 310; FW; MTCW 1

Duffy, Maureen Patricia
See Duffy, Maureen

Du Fu
See Tu Fu

Dugan, Alan 1923-2003 .... **CLC 2, 6**
See also CA 81-84; 220; CANR 119; CP 1, 2, 3, 4, 5, 6, 7; DLB 5; MAL 5; PFS 10

du Gard, Roger Martin
See Martin du Gard, Roger

du Guillet, Pernette 1520(?)-1545 .... **LC 190**
See also DLB 327

Duhamel, Georges 1884-1966 .... **CLC 8**
See also CA 81-84; 25-28R; CANR 35; DLB 65; EWL 3; GFL 1789 to the Present; MTCW 1

du Hault, Jean
See Grindel, Eugene

Dujardin, Edouard (Emile Louis) 1861-1949 .... **TCLC 13**
See also CA 109; DLB 123

Duke, Raoul
See Thompson, Hunter S.

Dulles, John Foster 1888-1959 ..... **TCLC 72**
See also CA 115; 149

Dumas, Alexandre (pere) 1802-1870 . **NCLC 11, 71; WLC 2**
See also AAYA 22; BYA 3; CLR 134; DA; DA3; DAB; DAC; DAM MST, NOV; DLB 119, 192; EW 6; GFL 1789 to the Present; LAIT 1, 2; NFS 14, 19; RGWL 2, 3; SATA 18; TWA; WCH

Dumas, Alexandre (fils) 1824-1895 .... **DC 1; NCLC 9**
See also DLB 192; GFL 1789 to the Present; RGWL 2, 3

Dumas, Claudine
See Malzberg, Barry N(athaniel)

Dumas, Henry L. 1934-1968 . **BLC 2:1; CLC 6, 62; SSC 107**
See also BW 1; CA 85-88; DLB 41; RGAL 4

du Maurier, Daphne 1907-1989 . **CLC 6, 11, 59; SSC 18, 129; TCLC 209**
See also AAYA 37; BPFB 1; BRWS 3; CA 5-8R; 128; CANR 6, 55; CMW 4; CN 1, 2, 3, 4; CPW; DA3; DAB; DAC; DAM MST, POP; DLB 191; GL 2; HGG; LAIT 3; MSW; MTCW 1, 2; NFS 12; RGEL 2; RGSF 2; RHW; SATA 27; SATA-Obit 60; SSFS 14, 16; TEA

Du Maurier, George 1834-1896 .... **NCLC 86**
See also DLB 153, 178; RGEL 2

Dunbar, Alice
See Nelson, Alice Ruth Moore Dunbar

Dunbar, Alice Moore
See Nelson, Alice Ruth Moore Dunbar

Dunbar, Paul Laurence 1872-1906 .... **BLC 1:1; PC 5; SSC 8; TCLC 2, 12; WLC 2**
See also AAYA 75; AFAW 1, 2; AMWS 2; BW 1, 3; CA 104; 124; CANR 79; CDALB 1865-1917; DA; DA3; DAC; DAM MST, MULT, POET; DLB 50, 54, 78; EXPP; MAL 5; PFS 33, 40; RGAL 4; SATA 34

Dunbar, William 1460(?)-1520(?) ..... **LC 20; PC 67**
See also BRWS 8; DLB 132, 146; RGEL 2

Dunbar-Nelson, Alice
See Nelson, Alice Ruth Moore Dunbar

Dunbar-Nelson, Alice Moore
See Nelson, Alice Ruth Moore Dunbar

Duncan, Dora Angela
See Duncan, Isadora

Duncan, Isadora 1877(?)-1927 ...... **TCLC 68**
See also CA 118; 149

Duncan, Lois 1934- .... **CLC 26**
See also AAYA 4, 34; BYA 6, 8; CA 1-4R; CANR 2, 23, 36, 111; CLR 29, 129; JRDA; MAICYA 1, 2; MAICYAS 1; MTFW 2005; SAAS 2; SATA 1, 36, 75, 133, 141, 219; SATA-Essay 141; WYA; YAW

Duncan, Robert 1919-1988 .. **CLC 1, 2, 4, 7, 15, 41, 55; PC 2, 75**
See also BG 1:2; CA 9-12R; 124; CANR 28, 62; CP 1, 2, 3, 4; DAM POET; DLB 5, 16, 193; EWL 3; MAL 5; MTCW 1, 2; MTFW 2005; PFS 13; RGAL 4; WP

Duncan, Sara Jeannette 1861-1922 ... **TCLC 60**
See also CA 157; DLB 92

Dunlap, William 1766-1839 ... **NCLC 2, 244**
See also DLB 30, 37, 59; RGAL 4

Dunn, Douglas (Eaglesham) 1942- .. **CLC 6, 40**
See also BRWS 10; CA 45-48; CANR 2, 33, 126; CP 1, 2, 3, 4, 5, 6, 7; DLB 40; MTCW 1

Dunn, Katherine 1945- .... **CLC 71**
See also CA 33-36R; CANR 72; HGG; MTCW 2; MTFW 2005

Dunn, Stephen 1939- .... **CLC 36, 206**
See also AMWS 11; CA 33-36R; CANR 12, 48, 53, 105; CP 3, 4, 5, 6, 7; DLB 105; PFS 21

Efron, Marina Ivanovna Tsvetaeva
See Tsvetaeva, Marina

Egeria fl. 4th cent. - .... **CMLC 70**

Eggers, Dave 1970- .... **CLC 241, 318**
See also AAYA 56; CA 198; CANR 138;
MTFW 2005

Egoyan, Atom 1960- .... **CLC 151, 291**
See also AAYA 63; CA 157; CANR 151

Ehle, John (Marsden, Jr.) 1925- ..... **CLC 27**
See also CA 9-12R; CSW

Ehrenbourg, Ilya
See Ehrenbourg, Ilya

Ehrenbourg, Ilya Grigoryevich
See Ehrenbourg, Ilya

Ehrenburg, Ilya 1891-1967 . **CLC 18, 34, 62**
See also CA 102; 25-28R; DLB 272; EWL
3

Ehrenburg, Ilya Grigoryevich
See Ehrenbourg, Ilya

Ehrenburg, Ilyo
See Ehrenbourg, Ilya

Ehrenburg, Ilyo Grigoryevich
See Ehrenbourg, Ilya

Ehrenreich, Barbara 1941- .... **CLC 110, 267**
See also BEST 90:4; CA 73-76; CANR 16,
37, 62, 117, 167, 208; DLB 246; FW;
LNFS 1; MTCW 1, 2; MTFW 2005

Ehrlich, Gretel 1946- .... **CLC 249**
See also ANW; CA 140; CANR 74, 146;
DLB 212, 275; TCWW 2

Eich, Gunter
See Eich, Gunter

Eich, Gunter 1907-1972 .... **CLC 15**
See also CA 111; 93-96; DLB 69, 124;
EWL 3; RGWL 2, 3

Eichendorff, Joseph 1788-1857 ...... **NCLC 8,
225, 246**
See also DLB 90; RGWL 2, 3

Eigner, Larry
See Eigner, Laurence (Joel)

Eigner, Laurence (Joel) 1927-1996 ... **CLC 9**
See also CA 9-12R; 151; CAAS 23; CANR
6, 84; CP 1, 2, 3, 4, 5, 6, 7; DLB 5; WP

Eilhart von Oberge c. 1140-c. 1195 .. **CMLC
67**
See also DLB 148

Einhard c. 770-840 .... **CMLC 50**
See also DLB 148

Einstein, Albert 1879-1955 .... **TCLC 65**
See also CA 121; 133; MTCW 1, 2

Eiseley, Loren
See Eiseley, Loren Corey

Eiseley, Loren Corey 1907-1977 .... **CLC 7**
See also AAYA 5; ANW; CA 1-4R; 73-76;
CANR 6; DLB 275; DLBD 17

Eisenstadt, Jill 1963- .... **CLC 50**
See also CA 140

Eisenstein, Sergei (Mikhailovich)
1898-1948 .... **TCLC 57**
See also CA 114; 149

Eisler, Steve
See Holdstock, Robert

Eisner, Simon
See Kornbluth, C(yril) M.

Eisner, Will 1917-2005 .... **CLC 237**
See also AAYA 52; CA 108; 235; CANR
114, 140, 179; MTFW 2005; SATA 31,
165

Eisner, William Erwin
See Eisner, Will

Ekeloef, Bengt Gunnar
See Ekelof, Gunnar

Ekeloof, Gunnar
See Ekelof, Gunnar

Ekelof, Gunnar 1907-1968 . **CLC 27; PC 23**
See also CA 123; 25-28R; DAM POET;
DLB 259; EW 12; EWL 3

Ekelund, Vilhelm 1880-1949 .... **TCLC 75**
See also CA 189; EWL 3

Ekman, Kerstin 1933- .... **CLC 279**
See also CA 154; CANR 124, 214; DLB
257; EWL 3

Ekman, Kerstin Lillemor
See Ekman, Kerstin

Ekwensi, C. O. D.
See Ekwensi, Cyprian

Ekwensi, Cyprian 1921-2007 .... **BLC 1:1;
CLC 4**
See also AFW; BW 2, 3; CA 29-32R;
CANR 18, 42, 74, 125; CDWLB 3; CN 1,
2, 3, 4, 5, 6; CWRI 5; DAM MULT; DLB
117; EWL 3; MTCW 1, 2; RGEL 2; SATA
66; WLIT 2

Ekwensi, Cyprian Odiatu Duaka
See Ekwensi, Cyprian

Elaine
See Leverson, Ada Esther

El Conde de Pepe
See Mihura, Miguel

El Crummo
See Crumb, R.

Elder, Lonne III 1931-1996 . **BLC 1:1; DC 8**
See also BW 1, 3; CA 81-84; 152; CAD;
CANR 25; DAM MULT; DLB 7, 38, 44;
MAL 5

Eleanor of Aquitaine 1122-1204 .. **CMLC 39**

Elia
See Lamb, Charles

Eliade, Mircea 1907-1986 ... **CLC 19; TCLC
243**
See also CA 65-68; 119; CANR 30, 62; CD-
WLB 4; DLB 220; EWL 3; MTCW 1;
RGWL 3; SFW 4

Eliot, A. D.
See Jewett, Sarah Orne

Eliot, Alice
See Jewett, Sarah Orne

Eliot, Dan
See Silverberg, Robert

Eliot, George 1819-1880 .... **NCLC 4, 13, 23,
41, 49, 89, 118, 183, 199, 209, 233; PC
20; SSC 72, 139; WLC 2**
See also BRW 5; BRWC 1, 2; BRWR 2;
CDBLB 1832-1890; CN 7; CPW; DA;
DA3; DAB; DAC; DAM MST, NOV;
DLB 21, 35, 55, 366; FL 1:3; LATS 1:1;
LMFS 1; NFS 17, 20, 34; RGEL 2; RGSF
2; SSFS 8; TEA; WLIT 3

Eliot, John 1604-1690 .... **LC 5**
See also DLB 24

Eliot, T. S. 1888-1965 . **CLC 1, 2, 3, 6, 9, 10,
13, 15, 24, 34, 41, 55, 57, 113; DC 28;
PC 5, 31, 90; TCLC 236; WLC 2**
See also AAYA 28; AMW; AMWC 1;
AMWR 1; BRW 7; BRWR 2; CA 5-8R;
25-28R; CANR 41; CBD; CDALB 1929-
1941; DA; DA3; DAB; DAC; DAM
DRAM, MST, POET; DFS 4, 13, 28; DLB
7, 10, 45, 63, 245, 329; DLBY 1988;
EWL 3; EXPP; LAIT 3; LATS 1:1; LMFS
2; MAL 5; MTCW 1, 2; MTFW 2005;
NCFS 5; PAB; PFS 1, 7, 20, 33; RGAL
4; RGEL 2; TUS; WLIT 4; WP

Eliot, Thomas Stearns
See Eliot, T. S.

Elisabeth of Schonau c. 1129-1165 ... **CMLC
82**

Elizabeth 1866-1941 .... **TCLC 41**

Elizabeth I, Queen of England 1533-1603 ...
LC 118
See also BRWS 16; DLB 136

Elkin, Stanley L. 1930-1995 ..... **CLC 4, 6, 9,
14, 27, 51, 91; SSC 12**
See also AMWS 6; BPFB 1; CA 9-12R;
148; CANR 8, 46; CN 1, 2, 3, 4, 5, 6;
CPW; DAM NOV, POP; DLB 2, 28, 218,

278; DLBY 1980; EWL 3; INT CANR-8;
MAL 5; MTCW 1, 2; MTFW 2005;
RGAL 4; TCLE 1:1

Elledge, Scott CLC 34

Eller, Scott
See Shepard, Jim

Elliott, Don
See Silverberg, Robert

Elliott, Ebenezer 1781-1849 .... **PC 96**
See also DLB 96, 190; RGEL 2

Elliott, George P(aul) 1918-1980 .... **CLC 2**
See also CA 1-4R; 97-100; CANR 2; CN 1,
2; CP 3; DLB 244; MAL 5

Elliott, Janice 1931-1995 .... **CLC 47**
See also CA 13-16R; CANR 8, 29, 84; CN
5, 6, 7; DLB 14; SATA 119

Elliott, Sumner Locke 1917-1991 ... **CLC 38**
See also CA 5-8R; 134; CANR 2, 21; DLB
289

Elliott, William
See Bradbury, Ray

Ellis, A. E. CLC 7

Ellis, Alice Thomas
See Haycraft, Anna

Ellis, Bret Easton 1964- .... **CLC 39, 71, 117,
229**
See also AAYA 2, 43; CA 118; 123; CANR
51, 74, 126, 226; CN 6, 7; CPW; DA3;
DAM POP; DLB 292; HGG; INT CA-
123; MTCW 2; MTFW 2005; NFS 11

Ellis, (Henry) Havelock 1859-1939 .... **TCLC
14**
See also CA 109; 169; DLB 190

Ellis, Landon
See Ellison, Harlan

Ellis, Trey 1962- .... **CLC 55**
See also CA 146; CANR 92; CN 7

Ellison, Harlan 1934- ... **CLC 1, 13, 42, 139;
SSC 14**
See also AAYA 29; BPFB 1; BYA 14; CA
5-8R; CANR 5, 46, 115; CPW; DAM
POP; DLB 8, 335; HGG; INT CANR-5;
MTCW 1, 2; MTFW 2005; SCFW 2;
SFW 4; SSFS 13, 14, 15, 21; SUFW 1, 2

Ellison, Ralph 1914-1994 .... **BLC 1:1, 2:2;
CLC 1, 3, 11, 54, 86, 114; SSC 26, 79;
WLC 2**
See also AAYA 19; AFAW 1, 2; AMWC 2;
AMWR 2; AMWS 2; BPFB 1; BW 1, 3;
BYA 2; CA 9-12R; 145; CANR 24, 53;
CDALB 1941-1968; CN 1, 2, 3, 4, 5;
CSW; DA; DA3; DAB; DAC; DAM MST,
MULT, NOV; DLB 2, 76, 227; DLBY
1994; EWL 3; EXPN; EXPS; LAIT 4;
MAL 5; MTCW 1, 2; MTFW 2005; NCFS
3; NFS 2, 21; RGAL 4; RGSF 2; SSFS 1,
11; YAW

Ellison, Ralph Waldo
See Ellison, Ralph

Ellmann, Lucy 1956- .... **CLC 61**
See also CA 128; CANR 154

Ellmann, Lucy Elizabeth
See Ellmann, Lucy

Ellmann, Richard (David) 1918-1987 .. **CLC
50**
See also BEST 89:2; CA 1-4R; 122; CANR
2, 28, 61; DLB 103; DLBY 1987; MTCW
1, 2; MTFW 2005

Ellroy, James 1948- .... **CLC 215**
See also BEST 90:4; CA 138; CANR 74,
133, 219; CMW 4; CN 6, 7; DA3; DLB
226; MTCW 2; MTFW 2005

Ellroy, Lee Earle
See Ellroy, James

Elman, Richard (Martin) 1934-1997 ... **CLC
19**
See also CA 17-20R; 163; CAAS 3; CANR
47; TCLE 1:1

Elron
See Hubbard, L. Ron
El Saadawi, Nawal 1931- ..... **BLC 2:2; CLC 196, 284**
See also AFW; CA 118; CAAS 11; CANR 44, 92; CWW 2; DLB 360; EWL 3; FW; WLIT 2
El-Shabazz, El-Hajj Malik
See Malcolm X
Elstob, Elizabeth 1683-1756 .... **LC 205**
Eltit, Diamela 1949- .... **CLC 294**
See also CA 253
Eluard, Paul
See Grindel, Eugene
Eluard, Paul
See Grindel, Eugene
Elyot, Thomas 1490(?)-1546 .... **LC 11, 139**
See also DLB 136; RGEL 2
Elytis, Odysseus 1911-1996 ...... **CLC 15, 49, 100; PC 21**
See also CA 102; 151; CANR 94; CWW 2; DAM POET; DLB 329; EW 13; EWL 3; MTCW 1, 2; RGWL 2, 3
Emecheta, Buchi 1944- .. **BLC 1:2; CLC 14, 48, 128, 214**
See also AAYA 67; AFW; BW 2, 3; CA 81-84; CANR 27, 81, 126; CDWLB 3; CLR 158; CN 4, 5, 6, 7; CWRI 5; DA3; DAM MULT; DLB 117; EWL 3; FL 1:5; FW; MTCW 1, 2; MTFW 2005; NFS 12, 14; SATA 66; WLIT 2
Emecheta, Florence Onye Buchi
See Emecheta, Buchi
Emerson, Mary Moody 1774-1863 .... **NCLC 66**
Emerson, Ralph Waldo 1803-1882 .... **NCLC 1, 38, 98, 252; PC 18; WLC 2**
See also AAYA 60; AMW; ANW; CDALB 1640-1865; DA; DA3; DAB; DAC; DAM MST, POET; DLB 1, 59, 73, 183, 223, 270, 351, 366; EXPP; LAIT 2; LMFS 1; NCFS 3; PFS 4, 17, 34; RGAL 4; TUS; WP
Eminem 1972- .... **CLC 226**
See also CA 245
Eminescu, Mihail 1850-1889 . **NCLC 33, 131**
Empedocles 5th cent. B.C.- .... **CMLC 50**
See also DLB 176
Empson, William 1906-1984 .. **CLC 3, 8, 19, 33, 34; PC 104**
See also BRWS 2; CA 17-20R; 112; CANR 31, 61; CP 1, 2, 3; DLB 20; EWL 3; MTCW 1, 2; RGEL 2
Enchi, Fumiko 1905-1986 .... **CLC 31**
See also CA 129; 121; DLB 182; EWL 3; FW; MJW
Enchi, Fumiko Ueda
See Enchi, Fumiko
Enchi Fumiko
See Enchi, Fumiko
Ende, Michael (Andreas Helmuth) 1929-1995 .... **CLC 31**
See also BYA 5; CA 118; 124; 149; CANR 36, 110; CLR 14, 138; DLB 75; MAICYA 1, 2; MAICYAS 1; SATA 61, 130; SATA-Brief 42; SATA-Obit 86
Endo, Shusaku 1923-1996 .... **CLC 7, 14, 19, 54, 99; SSC 48; TCLC 152**
See also CA 29-32R; 153; CANR 21, 54, 131; CWW 2; DA3; DAM NOV; DLB 182; EWL 3; MTCW 1, 2; MTFW 2005; RGSF 2; RGWL 2, 3
Endo Shusaku
See Endo, Shusaku
Engel, Marian 1933-1985 ... **CLC 36; TCLC 137**
See also CA 25-28R; CANR 12; CN 2, 3; DLB 53; FW; INT CANR-12

Engelhardt, Frederick
See Hubbard, L. Ron
Engels, Friedrich 1820-1895 . **NCLC 85, 114**
See also DLB 129; LATS 1:1
Enquist, Per Olov 1934- .... **CLC 257**
See also CA 109; 193; CANR 155; CWW 2; DLB 257; EWL 3
Enright, D(ennis) J(oseph) 1920-2002 . **CLC 4, 8, 31; PC 93**
See also CA 1-4R; 211; CANR 1, 42, 83; CN 1, 2; CP 1, 2, 3, 4, 5, 6, 7; DLB 27; EWL 3; SATA 25; SATA-Obit 140
Ensler, Eve 1953- .... **CLC 212**
See also CA 172; CANR 126, 163; DFS 23
Enzensberger, Hans Magnus 1929- ...... **CLC 43; PC 28**
See also CA 116; 119; CANR 103; CWW 2; EWL 3
Ephron, Nora 1941- .... **CLC 17, 31**
See also AAYA 35; AITN 2; CA 65-68; CANR 12, 39, 83, 161; DFS 22
Epictetus c. 55-c. 135 .... **CMLC 126**
See also AW 2; DLB 176
Epicurus 341B.C.-270B.C. .... **CMLC 21**
See also DLB 176
Epinay, Louise d' 1726-1783 .... **LC 138**
See also DLB 313
Epsilon
See Betjeman, John
Epstein, Daniel Mark 1948- .... **CLC 7**
See also CA 49-52; CANR 2, 53, 90, 193
Epstein, Jacob 1956- .... **CLC 19**
See also CA 114
Epstein, Jean 1897-1953 .... **TCLC 92**
Epstein, Joseph 1937- .... **CLC 39, 204**
See also AMWS 14; CA 112; 119; CANR 50, 65, 117, 164, 190, 225
Epstein, Leslie 1938- .... **CLC 27**
See also AMWS 12; CA 73-76; 215; CAAE 215; CAAS 12; CANR 23, 69, 162; DLB 299; RGHL
Equiano, Olaudah 1745(?)-1797 ... **BLC 1:2; LC 16, 143**
See also AFAW 1, 2; AMWS 17; CDWLB 3; DAM MULT; DLB 37, 50; WLIT 2
Erasmus, Desiderius 1469(?)-1536 .... **LC 16, 93**
See also DLB 136; EW 2; LMFS 1; RGWL 2, 3; TWA
Ercilla y Zuniga, Don Alonso de 1533-1594 .... **LC 190**
See also LAW
Erdman, Paul E. 1932-2007 .... **CLC 25**
See also AITN 1; CA 61-64; 259; CANR 13, 43, 84
Erdman, Paul Emil
See Erdman, Paul E.
Erdrich, Karen Louise
See Erdrich, Louise
Erdrich, Louise 1954- .... **CLC 39, 54, 120, 176; NNAL; PC 52; SSC 121**
See also AAYA 10, 47; AMWS 4; BEST 89:1; BPFB 1; CA 114; CANR 41, 62, 118, 138, 190; CDALBS; CN 5, 6, 7; CP 6, 7; CPW; CWP; DA3; DAM MULT, NOV, POP; DLB 152, 175, 206; EWL 3; EXPP; FL 1:5; LAIT 5; LATS 1:2; MAL 5; MTCW 1, 2; MTFW 2005; NFS 5, 37, 40; PFS 14; RGAL 4; SATA 94, 141; SSFS 14, 22, 30; TCWW 2
Erenburg, Ilya
See Ehrenburg, Ilya
Erenburg, Ilya Grigoryevich
See Ehrenburg, Ilya
Erickson, Stephen Michael
See Erickson, Steve
Erickson, Steve 1950- .... **CLC 64**
See also CA 129; CANR 60, 68, 136, 195; MTFW 2005; SFW 4; SUFW 2

Erickson, Walter
See Fast, Howard
Ericson, Walter
See Fast, Howard
Eriksson, Buntel
See Bergman, Ingmar
Eriugena, John Scottus c. 810-877 ... **CMLC 65**
See also DLB 115
Ernaux, Annie 1940- .... **CLC 88, 184**
See also CA 147; CANR 93, 208; MTFW 2005; NCFS 3, 5
Erskine, John 1879-1951 .... **TCLC 84**
See also CA 112; 159; DLB 9, 102; FANT
Erwin, Will
See Eisner, Will
Eschenbach, Wolfram von
See von Eschenbach, Wolfram
Eseki, Bruno
See Mphahlele, Es'kia
Esekie, Bruno
See Mphahlele, Es'kia
Esenin, S.A.
See Esenin, Sergei
Esenin, Sergei 1895-1925 .... **TCLC 4**
See also CA 104; EWL 3; RGWL 2, 3
Esenin, Sergei Aleksandrovich
See Esenin, Sergei
Eshleman, Clayton 1935- .... **CLC 7**
See also CA 33-36R; 212; CAAE 212; CAAS 6; CANR 93; CP 1, 2, 3, 4, 5, 6, 7; DLB 5
Espada, Martin 1957- .... **PC 74**
See also CA 159; CANR 80; CP 7; EXPP; LLW; MAL 5; PFS 13, 16
Espriella, Don Manuel Alvarez
See Southey, Robert
Espriu, Salvador 1913-1985 .... **CLC 9**
See also CA 154; 115; DLB 134; EWL 3
Espronceda, Jose de 1808-1842 .... **NCLC 39**
Esquivel, Laura 1950- ... **CLC 141; HLCS 1**
See also AAYA 29; CA 143; CANR 68, 113, 161; DA3; DNFS 2; LAIT 3; LMFS 2; MTCW 2; MTFW 2005; NFS 5; WLIT 1
Esse, James
See Stephens, James
Esterbrook, Tom
See Hubbard, L. Ron
Esterhazy, Peter 1950- .... **CLC 251**
See also CA 140; CANR 137, 223; CDWLB 4; CWW 2; DLB 232; EWL 3; RGWL 3
Estleman, Loren D. 1952- .... **CLC 48**
See also AAYA 27; CA 85-88; CANR 27, 74, 139, 177; CMW 4; CPW; DA3; DAM NOV, POP; DLB 226; INT CANR-27; MTCW 1, 2; MTFW 2005; TCWW 1, 2
Etherege, Sir George 1636-1692 . **DC 23; LC 78**
See also BRW 2; DAM DRAM; DLB 80; PAB; RGEL 2
Euclid 306B.C.-283B.C. .... **CMLC 25**
Eugenides, Jeffrey 1960- .. **CLC 81, 212, 312**
See also AAYA 51; CA 144; CANR 120; DLB 350; MTFW 2005; NFS 24
Euripides c. 484B.C.-406B.C. ...... **CMLC 23, 51; DC 4; WLCS**
See also AW 1; CDWLB 1; DA; DA3; DAB; DAC; DAM DRAM, MST; DFS 1, 4, 6, 25, 27; DLB 176; LAIT 1; LMFS 1; RGWL 2, 3; WLIT 8
Eusebius c. 263-c. 339 .... **CMLC 103**
Evan, Evin
See Faust, Frederick
Evans, Caradoc 1878-1945 .. **SSC 43; TCLC 85**
See also DLB 162
Evans, Evan
See Faust, Frederick

Feldman, Irving (Mordecai) 1928- ... **CLC 7**
See also CA 1-4R; CANR 1; CP 1, 2, 3, 4, 5, 6, 7; DLB 169; TCLE 1:1

Felix-Tchicaya, Gerald
See Tchicaya, Gerald Felix

Fellini, Federico 1920-1993 .... **CLC 16, 85**
See also CA 65-68; 143; CANR 33

Felltham, Owen 1602(?)-1668 .... **LC 92**
See also DLB 126, 151

Felsen, Henry Gregor 1916-1995 .... **CLC 17**
See also CA 1-4R; 180; CANR 1; SAAS 2; SATA 1

Felski, Rita CLC 65

Fenelon, Francois de Pons de Salignac de la Mothe- 1651-1715 .... **LC 134**
See also DLB 268; EW 3; GFL Beginnings to 1789

Fenno, Jack
See Calisher, Hortense

Fenollosa, Ernest (Francisco) 1853-1908 .....
TCLC 91

Fenton, James 1949- .... **CLC 32, 209**
See also CA 102; CANR 108, 160; CP 2, 3, 4, 5, 6, 7; DLB 40; PFS 11

Fenton, James Martin
See Fenton, James

Ferber, Edna 1887-1968 .... **CLC 18, 93**
See also AITN 1; CA 5-8R; 25-28R; CANR 68, 105; DLB 9, 28, 86, 266; MAL 5; MTCW 1, 2; MTFW 2005; RGAL 4; RHW; SATA 7; TCWW 1, 2

Ferdousi
See Ferdowsi, Abu'l Qasem

Ferdovsi
See Ferdowsi, Abu'l Qasem

Ferdowsi
See Ferdowsi, Abu'l Qasem

Ferdowsi, Abolghasem Mansour
See Ferdowsi, Abu'l Qasem

Ferdowsi, Abolqasem
See Ferdowsi, Abu'l Qasem

Ferdowsi, Abol-Qasem
See Ferdowsi, Abu'l Qasem

Ferdowsi, Abu'l Qasem 940-1020(?) . **CMLC 43**
See also CA 276; RGWL 2, 3; WLIT 6

Ferdowsi, A.M.
See Ferdowsi, Abu'l Qasem

Ferdowsi, Hakim Abolghasem
See Ferdowsi, Abu'l Qasem

Ferguson, Helen
See Kavan, Anna

Ferguson, Niall 1964- .... **CLC 134, 250**
See also CA 190; CANR 154, 200

Ferguson, Niall Campbell
See Ferguson, Niall

Ferguson, Samuel 1810-1886 .... **NCLC 33**
See also DLB 32; RGEL 2

Fergusson, Robert 1750-1774 .... **LC 29**
See also DLB 109; RGEL 2

Ferling, Lawrence
See Ferlinghetti, Lawrence

Ferlinghetti, Lawrence 1919(?)- ... **CLC 2, 6, 10, 27, 111; PC 1**
See also AAYA 74; BG 1:2; CA 5-8R; CAD; CANR 3, 41, 73, 125, 172; CDALB 1941-1968; CP 1, 2, 3, 4, 5, 6, 7; DA3; DAM POET; DLB 5, 16; MAL 5; MTCW 1, 2; MTFW 2005; PFS 28, 41; RGAL 4; WP

Ferlinghetti, Lawrence Monsanto
See Ferlinghetti, Lawrence

Fern, Fanny
See Parton, Sara Payson Willis

Fernandez, Vicente Garcia Huidobro
See Huidobro Fernandez, Vicente Garcia

Fernandez-Armesto, Felipe 1950- ... **CLC 70**
See also CA 142; CANR 93, 153, 189

Fernandez-Armesto, Felipe Fermin Ricardo
See Fernandez-Armesto, Felipe

Fernandez de Lizardi, Jose Joaquin
See Lizardi, Jose Joaquin Fernandez de

Ferre, Rosario 1938- .... **CLC 139; HLCS 1; SSC 36, 106**
See also CA 131; CANR 55, 81, 134; CWW 2; DLB 145; EWL 3; HW 1, 2; LAWS 1; MTCW 2; MTFW 2005; WLIT 1

Ferrer, Gabriel (Francisco Victor) Miro
See Miro (Ferrer), Gabriel (Francisco Victor)

Ferrier, Susan (Edmonstone) 1782-1854 ......
NCLC 8
See also DLB 116; RGEL 2

Ferrigno, Robert 1947- .... **CLC 65**
See also CA 140; CANR 125, 161

Ferris, Joshua 1974- .... **CLC 280**
See also CA 262

Ferron, Jacques 1921-1985 .... **CLC 94**
See also CA 117; 129; CCA 1; DAC; DLB 60; EWL 3

Feuchtwanger, Lion 1884-1958 .... **TCLC 3**
See also CA 104; 187; DLB 66; EWL 3; RGHL

Feuerbach, Ludwig 1804-1872 ... **NCLC 139**
See also DLB 133

Feuillet, Octave 1821-1890 .... **NCLC 45**
See also DLB 192

Feydeau, Georges 1862-1921 .... **TCLC 22**
See also CA 113; 152; CANR 84; DAM DRAM; DLB 192; EWL 3; GFL 1789 to the Present; RGWL 2, 3

Feydeau, Georges Leon JulesMarie
See Feydeau, Georges

Fichte, Johann Gottlieb 1762-1814 ... **NCLC 62**
See also DLB 90

Ficino, Marsilio 1433-1499 .... **LC 12, 152**
See also LMFS 1

Fiedeler, Hans
See Doeblin, Alfred

Fiedler, Leslie A(aron) 1917-2003 .... **CLC 4, 13, 24**
See also AMWS 13; CA 9-12R; 212; CANR 7, 63; CN 1, 2, 3, 4, 5, 6; DLB 28, 67; EWL 3; MAL 5; MTCW 1, 2; RGAL 4; TUS

Field, Andrew 1938- .... **CLC 44**
See also CA 97-100; CANR 25

Field, Eugene 1850-1895 .... **NCLC 3**
See also DLB 23, 42, 140; DLBD 13; MAICYA 1, 2; RGAL 4; SATA 16

Field, Gans T.
See Wellman, Manly Wade

Field, Michael 1915-1971 .... **TCLC 43**
See also CA 29-32R

Fielding, Helen 1958- .... **CLC 146, 217**
See also AAYA 65; CA 172; CANR 127; DLB 231; MTFW 2005

Fielding, Henry 1707-1754 ...... **LC 1, 46, 85, 151, 154; WLC 2**
See also BRW 3; BRWR 1; CDBLB 1660-1789; DA; DA3; DAB; DAC; DAM DRAM, MST, NOV; DFS 28; DLB 39, 84, 101; NFS 18, 32; RGEL 2; TEA; WLIT 3

Fielding, Sarah 1710-1768 .... **LC 1, 44**
See also DLB 39; RGEL 2; TEA

Fields, W. C. 1880-1946 .... **TCLC 80**
See also DLB 44

Fierstein, Harvey 1954- .... **CLC 33**
See also CA 123; 129; CAD; CD 5, 6; CPW; DA3; DAM DRAM, POP; DFS 6; DLB 266; GLL; MAL 5

Fierstein, Harvey Forbes
See Fierstein, Harvey

Figes, Eva 1932- .... **CLC 31**
See also CA 53-56; CANR 4, 44, 83, 207; CN 2, 3, 4, 5, 6, 7; DLB 14, 271; FW; RGHL

Filippo, Eduardo de
See de Filippo, Eduardo

Finch, Anne 1661-1720 .... **LC 3, 137; PC 21**
See also BRWS 9; DLB 95; PFS 30; RGEL 2

Finch, Robert (Duer Claydon) 1900-1995 ...
CLC 18
See also CA 57-60; CANR 9, 24, 49; CP 1, 2, 3, 4, 5, 6; DLB 88

Findley, Timothy 1930-2002 ... **CLC 27, 102; SSC 145**
See also AMWS 20; CA 25-28R; 206; CANR 12, 42, 69, 109; CCA 1; CN 4, 5, 6, 7; DAC; DAM MST; DLB 53; FANT; RHW

Fink, William
See Mencken, H. L.

Firbank, Louis 1942- .... **CLC 21**
See also CA 117

Firbank, (Arthur Annesley) Ronald 1886-1926 .... **TCLC 1**
See also BRWS 2; CA 104; 177; DLB 36; EWL 3; RGEL 2

Firdaosi
See Ferdowsi, Abu'l Qasem

Firdausi
See Ferdowsi, Abu'l Qasem

Firdavsi, Abulqosimi
See Ferdowsi, Abu'l Qasem

Firdavsii, Abulqosim
See Ferdowsi, Abu'l Qasem

Firdawsi, Abu al-Qasim
See Ferdowsi, Abu'l Qasem

Firdosi
See Ferdowsi, Abu'l Qasem

Firdousi
See Ferdowsi, Abu'l Qasem

Firdousi, Abu'l-Qasim
See Ferdowsi, Abu'l Qasem

Firdovsi, A.
See Ferdowsi, Abu'l Qasem

Firdovsi, Abulgasim
See Ferdowsi, Abu'l Qasem

Firdusi
See Ferdowsi, Abu'l Qasem

Fish, Stanley 1938- .... **CLC 142**
See also CA 112; 132; CANR 90; DLB 67

Fish, Stanley E.
See Fish, Stanley

Fish, Stanley Eugene
See Fish, Stanley

Fisher, Dorothy (Frances) Canfield 1879-1958 .... **TCLC 87**
See also CA 114; 136; CANR 80; CLR 71; CWRI 5; DLB 9, 102, 284; MAICYA 1, 2; MAL 5; YABC 1

Fisher, M(ary) F(rances) K(ennedy) 1908-1992 .... **CLC 76, 87**
See also AMWS 17; CA 77-80; 138; CANR 44; MTCW 2

Fisher, Roy 1930- .... **CLC 25; PC 121**
See also CA 81-84; CAAS 10; CANR 16; CP 1, 2, 3, 4, 5, 6, 7; DLB 40

Fisher, Rudolph 1897-1934 .... **BLC 1:2; HR 1:2; SSC 25; TCLC 11, 255**
See also BW 1, 3; CA 107; 124; CANR 80; DAM MULT; DLB 51, 102

Fisher, Vardis (Alvero) 1895-1968 ... **CLC 7; TCLC 140**
See also CA 5-8R; 25-28R; CANR 68; DLB 9, 206; MAL 5; RGAL 4; TCWW 1, 2

Fiske, Tarleton
See Bloch, Robert (Albert)

Freneau, Philip Morin 1752-1832 . **NCLC 1, 111, 253**
See also AMWS 2; DLB 37, 43; RGAL 4

Freud, Sigmund 1856-1939 .... **TCLC 52**
See also CA 115; 133; CANR 69; DLB 296; EW 8; EWL 3; LATS 1:1; MTCW 1, 2; MTFW 2005; NCFS 3; TWA

Freytag, Gustav 1816-1895 .... **NCLC 109**
See also DLB 129

Friedan, Betty 1921-2006 .... **CLC 74**
See also CA 65-68; 248; CANR 18, 45, 74; DLB 246; FW; MTCW 1, 2; MTFW 2005; NCFS 5

Friedan, Betty Naomi
See Friedan, Betty

Friedlander, Saul
See Friedlander, Saul

Friedlander, Saul 1932- .... **CLC 90**
See also CA 117; 130; CANR 72, 214; RGHL

Friedman, Bernard Harper
See Friedman, B.H.

Friedman, B.H. 1926-2011 .... **CLC 7**
See also CA 1-4R; CANR 3, 48

Friedman, Bruce Jay 1930- .... **CLC 3, 5, 56**
See also CA 9-12R; CAD; CANR 25, 52, 101, 212; CD 5, 6; CN 1, 2, 3, 4, 5, 6, 7; DLB 2, 28, 244; INT CANR-25; MAL 5; SSFS 18

Friel, Brian 1929- . **CLC 5, 42, 59, 115, 253; DC 8; SSC 76**
See also BRWS 5; CA 21-24R; CANR 33, 69, 131; CBD; CD 5, 6; DFS 11; DLB 13, 319; EWL 3; MTCW 1; RGEL 2; TEA

Friis-Baastad, Babbis Ellinor 1921-1970 ..... **CLC 12**
See also CA 17-20R; 134; SATA 7

Frisch, Max 1911-1991 ..... **CLC 3, 9, 14, 18, 32, 44; TCLC 121**
See also CA 85-88; 134; CANR 32, 74; CD-WLB 2; DAM DRAM, NOV; DFS 25; DLB 69, 124; EW 13; EWL 3; MTCW 1, 2; MTFW 2005; RGHL; RGWL 2, 3

Froehlich, Peter
See Gay, Peter

Fromentin, Eugene (Samuel Auguste) 1820-1876 .... **NCLC 10, 125**
See also DLB 123, 366; GFL 1789 to the Present

Frost, Frederick
See Faust, Frederick

Frost, Robert 1874-1963 . **CLC 1, 3, 4, 9, 10, 13, 15, 26, 34, 44; PC 1, 39, 71; TCLC 236; WLC 2**
See also AAYA 21; AMW; AMWR 1; CA 89-92; CANR 33; CDALB 1917-1929; CLR 67; DA; DA3; DAB; DAC; DAM MST, POET; DLB 54, 284, 342; DLBD 7; EWL 3; EXPP; MAL 5; MTCW 1, 2; MTFW 2005; PAB; PFS 1, 2, 3, 4, 5, 6, 7, 10, 13, 32, 35, 41; RGAL 4; SATA 14; TUS; WP; WYA

Frost, Robert Lee
See Frost, Robert

Froude, James Anthony 1818-1894 ... **NCLC 43**
See also DLB 18, 57, 144

Froy, Herald
See Waterhouse, Keith

Fry, Christopher 1907-2005 . **CLC 2, 10, 14; DC 36**
See also BRWS 3; CA 17-20R; 240; CAAS 23; CANR 9, 30, 74, 132; CBD; CD 5, 6; CP 1, 2, 3, 4, 5, 6, 7; DAM DRAM; DLB 13; EWL 3; MTCW 1, 2; MTFW 2005; RGEL 2; SATA 66; TEA

Frye, (Herman) Northrop 1912-1991 .. **CLC 24, 70; TCLC 165**
See also CA 5-8R; 133; CANR 8, 37; DLB 67, 68, 246; EWL 3; MTCW 1, 2; MTFW 2005; RGAL 4; TWA

Fuchs, Daniel 1909-1993 .... **CLC 8, 22**
See also CA 81-84; 142; CAAS 5; CANR 40; CN 1, 2, 3, 4, 5; DLB 9, 26, 28; DLBY 1993; MAL 5

Fuchs, Daniel 1934- .... **CLC 34**
See also CA 37-40R; CANR 14, 48

Fuentes, Carlos 1928- . **CLC 3, 8, 10, 13, 22, 41, 60, 113, 288; HLC 1; SSC 24, 125; WLC 2**
See also AAYA 4, 45; AITN 2; BPFB 1; CA 69-72; CANR 10, 32, 68, 104, 138, 197; CDWLB 3; CWW 2; DA; DA3; DAB; DAC; DAM MST, MULT, NOV; DLB 113; DNFS 2; EWL 3; HW 1, 2; LAIT 3; LATS 1:2; LAW; LAWS 1; LMFS 2; MTCW 1, 2; MTFW 2005; NFS 8; RGSF 2; RGWL 2, 3; TWA; WLIT 1

Fuentes, Gregorio Lopez y
See Lopez y Fuentes, Gregorio

Fuentes Macias, Carlos Manuel
See Fuentes, Carlos

Fuertes, Gloria 1918-1998 .... **PC 27**
See also CA 178, 180; DLB 108; HW 2; SATA 115

Fugard, Athol 1932- ... **CLC 5, 9, 14, 25, 40, 80, 211; DC 3**
See also AAYA 17; AFW; BRWS 15; CA 85-88; CANR 32, 54, 118; CD 5, 6; DAM DRAM; DFS 3, 6, 10, 24; DLB 225; DNFS 1, 2; EWL 3; LATS 1:2; MTCW 1; MTFW 2005; RGEL 2; WLIT 2

Fugard, Harold Athol
See Fugard, Athol

Fugard, Sheila 1932- .... **CLC 48**
See also CA 125

Fuguet, Alberto 1964- .... **CLC 308**
See also CA 170; CANR 144

Fujiwara no Teika 1162-1241 ...... **CMLC 73**
See also DLB 203

Fukuyama, Francis 1952- ...... **CLC 131, 320**
See also CA 140; CANR 72, 125, 170

Fuller, Charles (H.), (Jr.) 1939- .... **BLC 1:2; CLC 25; DC 1**
See also BW 2; CA 108; 112; CAD; CANR 87; CD 5, 6; DAM DRAM, MULT; DFS 8; DLB 38, 266; EWL 3; INT CA-112; MAL 5; MTCW 1

Fuller, Henry Blake 1857-1929 ... **TCLC 103**
See also CA 108; 177; DLB 12; RGAL 4

Fuller, John (Leopold) 1937- .... **CLC 62**
See also CA 21-24R; CANR 9, 44; CP 1, 2, 3, 4, 5, 6, 7; DLB 40

Fuller, Margaret 1810-1850 ..... **NCLC 5, 50, 211**
See also AMWS 2; CDALB 1640-1865; DLB 1, 59, 73, 183, 223, 239; FW; LMFS 1; SATA 25

Fuller, Roy (Broadbent) 1912-1991 . **CLC 4, 28**
See also BRWS 7; CA 5-8R; 135; CAAS 10; CANR 53, 83; CN 1, 2, 3, 4, 5; CP 1, 2, 3, 4, 5; CWRI 5; DLB 15, 20; EWL 3; RGEL 2; SATA 87

Fuller, Sarah Margaret
See Fuller, Margaret

Fuller, Thomas 1608-1661 .... **LC 111**
See also DLB 151

Fulton, Alice 1952- .... **CLC 52**
See also CA 116; CANR 57, 88, 200; CP 5, 6, 7; CWP; DLB 193; PFS 25

Fundi
See Baraka, Amiri

Furey, Michael
See Ward, Arthur Henry Sarsfield

Furphy, Joseph 1843-1912 .... **TCLC 25**
See also CA 163; DLB 230; EWL 3; RGEL 2

Furst, Alan 1941- .... **CLC 255**
See also CA 69-72; CANR 12, 34, 59, 102, 159, 193; DLB 350; DLBY 01

Fuson, Robert H(enderson) 1927- .. **CLC 70**
See also CA 89-92; CANR 103

Fussell, Paul 1924- .... **CLC 74**
See also BEST 90:1; CA 17-20R; CANR 8, 21, 35, 69, 135; INT CANR-21; MTCW 1, 2; MTFW 2005

Futabatei, Shimei 1864-1909 .... **TCLC 44**
See also CA 162; DLB 180; EWL 3; MJW

Futabatei Shimei
See Futabatei, Shimei

Futrelle, Jacques 1875-1912 .... **TCLC 19**
See also CA 113; 155; CMW 4

GAB
See Russell, George William

Gaberman, Judie Angell
See Angell, Judie

Gaboriau, Emile 1835-1873 .... **NCLC 14**
See also CMW 4; MSW

Gadda, Carlo Emilio 1893-1973 .... **CLC 11; TCLC 144**
See also CA 89-92; DLB 177; EWL 3; WLIT 7

Gaddis, William 1922-1998 .. **CLC 1, 3, 6, 8, 10, 19, 43, 86**
See also AMWS 4; BPFB 1; CA 17-20R; 172; CANR 21, 48, 148; CN 1, 2, 3, 4, 5, 6; DLB 2, 278; EWL 3; MAL 5; MTCW 1, 2; MTFW 2005; RGAL 4

Gage, Walter
See Inge, William (Motter)

Gaiman, Neil 1960- .... **CLC 319**
See also AAYA 19, 42, 82; CA 133; CANR 81, 129, 188; CLR 109; DLB 261; HGG; MTFW 2005; SATA 85, 146, 197, 228; SFW 4; SUFW 2

Gaiman, Neil Richard
See Gaiman, Neil

Gaines, Ernest J. 1933- ... **BLC 1:2; CLC 3, 11, 18, 86, 181, 300; SSC 68, 137**
See also AAYA 18; AFAW 1, 2; AITN 1; BPFB 2; BW 2, 3; BYA 6; CA 9-12R; CANR 6, 24, 42, 75, 126; CDALB 1968-1988; CLR 62; CN 1, 2, 3, 4, 5, 6, 7; CSW; DA3; DAM MULT; DLB 2, 33, 152; DLBY 1980; EWL 3; EXPN; LAIT 5; LATS 1:2; MAL 5; MTCW 1, 2; MTFW 2005; NFS 5, 7, 16; RGAL 4; RGSF 2; RHW; SATA 86; SSFS 5; YAW

Gaines, Ernest James
See Gaines, Ernest J.

Gaitskill, Mary 1954- .... **CLC 69, 300**
See also CA 128; CANR 61, 152, 208; DLB 244; TCLE 1:1

Gaitskill, Mary Lawrence
See Gaitskill, Mary

Gaius Suetonius Tranquillus
See Suetonius

Galdos, Benito Perez
See Perez Galdos, Benito

Gale, Zona 1874-1938 .... **DC 30; SSC 159; TCLC 7**
See also CA 105; 153; CANR 84; DAM DRAM; DFS 17; DLB 9, 78, 228; RGAL 4

Galeano, Eduardo 1940- . **CLC 72; HLCS 1**
See also CA 29-32R; CANR 13, 32, 100, 163, 211; HW 1

Galeano, Eduardo Hughes
See Galeano, Eduardo

Galiano, Juan Valera y Alcala
See Valera y Alcala-Galiano, Juan
Galilei, Galileo 1564-1642 .... **LC 45, 188**
Gallagher, Tess 1943- ...... **CLC 18, 63; PC 9**
See also CA 106; CP 3, 4, 5, 6, 7; CWP;
DAM POET; DLB 120, 212, 244; PFS 16
Gallant, Mavis 1922- .... **CLC 7, 18, 38, 172,
288; SSC 5, 78**
See also CA 69-72; CANR 29, 69, 117;
CCA 1; CN 1, 2, 3, 4, 5, 6, 7; DAC; DAM
MST; DLB 53; EWL 3; MTCW 1, 2;
MTFW 2005; RGEL 2; RGSF 2
Gallant, Roy A(rthur) 1924- .... **CLC 17**
See also CA 5-8R; CANR 4, 29, 54, 117;
CLR 30; MAICYA 1, 2; SATA 4, 68, 110
Gallico, Paul 1897-1976 .... **CLC 2**
See also AITN 1; CA 5-8R; 69-72; CANR
23; CN 1, 2; DLB 9, 171; FANT; MAI-
CYA 1, 2; SATA 13
Gallico, Paul William
See Gallico, Paul
Gallo, Max Louis 1932- .... **CLC 95**
See also CA 85-88
Gallois, Lucien
See Desnos, Robert
Gallup, Ralph
See Whitemore, Hugh (John)
Galsworthy, John 1867-1933 .... **SSC 22;
TCLC 1, 45; WLC 2**
See also BRW 6; CA 104; 141; CANR 75;
CDBLB 1890-1914; DA; DA3; DAB;
DAC; DAM DRAM, MST, NOV; DLB
10, 34, 98, 162, 330; DLBD 16; EWL 3;
MTCW 2; RGEL 2; SSFS 3; TEA
Galt, John 1779-1839 .... **NCLC 1, 110**
See also DLB 99, 116, 159; RGEL 2; RGSF
2
Galvin, James 1951- .... **CLC 38**
See also CA 108; CANR 26
Gamboa, Federico 1864-1939 .... **TCLC 36**
See also CA 167; HW 2; LAW
Gandhi, M. K.
See Gandhi, Mohandas Karamchand
Gandhi, Mahatma
See Gandhi, Mohandas Karamchand
Gandhi, Mohandas Karamchand
1869-1948 .... **TCLC 59**
See also CA 121; 132; DA3; DAM MULT;
DLB 323; MTCW 1, 2
Gann, Ernest Kellogg 1910-1991 .... **CLC 23**
See also AITN 1; BPFB 2; CA 1-4R; 136;
CANR 1, 83; RHW
Gao Xingjian
See Xingjian, Gao
Garber, Eric
See Holleran, Andrew
Garber, Esther
See Lee, Tanith
Garcia, Cristina 1958- .... **CLC 76**
See also AMWS 11; CA 141; CANR 73,
130, 172; CN 7; DLB 292; DNFS 1; EWL
3; HW 2; LLW; MTFW 2005; NFS 38;
SATA 208
Garcia Lorca, Federico 1898-1936 ..... **DC 2;
HLC 2; PC 3; TCLC 1, 7, 49, 181, 197;
WLC 2**
See also AAYA 46; CA 104; 131; CANR
81; DA; DA3; DAB; DAC; DAM DRAM,
MST, MULT, POET; DFS 4; DLB 108;
EW 11; EWL 3; HW 1, 2; LATS 1:2;
MTCW 1, 2; MTFW 2005; PFS 20, 31,
38; RGWL 2, 3; TWA; WP
Garcia Marquez, Gabriel 1928- .. **CLC 2, 3,
8, 10, 15, 27, 47, 55, 68, 170, 254; HLC
1; SSC 8, 83, 162; WLC 3**
See also AAYA 3, 33; BEST 89:1, 90:4;
BPFB 2; BYA 12, 16; CA 33-36R; CANR
10, 28, 50, 75, 82, 128, 204; CDWLB 3;
CPW; CWW 2; DA; DA3; DAB; DAC;

DAM MST, MULT, NOV, POP; DLB 113,
330; DNFS 1, 2; EWL 3; EXPN; EXPS;
HW 1, 2; LAIT 2; LATS 1:2; LAW;
LAWS 1; LMFS 2; MTCW 1, 2; MTFW
2005; NCFS 3; NFS 1, 5, 10; RGSF 2;
RGWL 2, 3; SSFS 1, 6, 16, 21; TWA;
WLIT 1
Garcia Marquez, Gabriel Jose
See Garcia Marquez, Gabriel
Garcia Marquez, Gabriel Jose
See Garcia Marquez, Gabriel
Garcilaso de la Vega, El Inca 1539-1616 .....
HLCS 1; LC 127
See also DLB 318; LAW
Gard, Janice
See Latham, Jean Lee
Gard, Roger Martin du
See Martin du Gard, Roger
Gardam, Jane 1928- .... **CLC 43**
See also CA 49-52; CANR 2, 18, 33, 54,
106, 167, 206; CLR 12; DLB 14, 161,
231; MAICYA 1, 2; MTCW 1; SAAS 9;
SATA 39, 76, 130; SATA-Brief 28; YAW
Gardam, Jane Mary
See Gardam, Jane
Gardens, S. S.
See Snodgrass, W. D.
Gardner, Herb(ert George) 1934-2003 . **CLC
44**
See also CA 149; 220; CAD; CANR 119;
CD 5, 6; DFS 18, 20
Gardner, John, Jr. 1933-1982 .. **CLC 2, 3, 5,
7, 8, 10, 18, 28, 34; SSC 7; TCLC 195**
See also AAYA 45; AITN 1; AMWS 6;
BPFB 2; CA 65-68; 107; CANR 33, 73;
CDALBS; CN 2, 3; CPW; DA3; DAM
NOV, POP; DLB 2; DLBY 1982; EWL 3;
FANT; LATS 1:2; MAL 5; MTCW 1, 2;
MTFW 2005; NFS 3; RGAL 4; RGSF 2;
SATA 40; SATA-Obit 31; SSFS 8
Gardner, John 1926-2007 .... **CLC 30**
See also CA 103; 263; CANR 15, 69, 127,
183; CMW 4; CPW; DAM POP; MTCW
1
Gardner, John Champlin, Jr.
See Gardner, John, Jr.
Gardner, John Edmund
See Gardner, John
Gardner, Miriam
See Bradley, Marion Zimmer
Gardner, Noel
See Kuttner, Henry
Gardons, S.S.
See Snodgrass, W. D.
Garfield, Leon 1921-1996 .... **CLC 12**
See also AAYA 8, 69; BYA 1, 3; CA 17-
20R; 152; CANR 38, 41, 78; CLR 21,
166; DLB 161; JRDA; MAICYA 1, 2;
MAICYAS 1; SATA 1, 32, 76; SATA-Obit
90; TEA; WYA; YAW
Garland, (Hannibal) Hamlin 1860-1940 ......
SSC 18, 117; TCLC 3, 256
See also CA 104; DLB 12, 71, 78, 186;
MAL 5; RGAL 4; RGSF 2; TCWW 1, 2
Garneau, (Hector de) Saint-Denys
1912-1943 .... **TCLC 13**
See also CA 111; DLB 88
Garner, Alan 1934- .... **CLC 17**
See also AAYA 18; BYA 3, 5; CA 73-76,
178; CAAE 178; CANR 15, 64, 134; CLR
20, 130; CPW; DAB; DAM POP; DLB
161, 261; FANT; MAICYA 1, 2; MTCW
1, 2; MTFW 2005; SATA 18, 69; SATA-
Essay 108; SUFW 1, 2; YAW
Garner, Helen 1942- .... **SSC 135**
See also CA 124; 127; CANR 71, 206; CN
4, 5, 6, 7; DLB 325; GLL 2; RGSF 2

Garner, Hugh 1913-1979 .... **CLC 13**
See also CA 69-72; CANR 31; CCA 1; CN
1, 2; DLB 68
Garnett, David 1892-1981 .... **CLC 3**
See also CA 5-8R; 103; CANR 17, 79; CN
1, 2; DLB 34; FANT; MTCW 2; RGEL 2;
SFW 4; SUFW 1
Garnier, Robert c. 1545-1590 .... **LC 119**
See also DLB 327; GFL Beginnings to 1789
Garrett, George 1929-2008 .. **CLC 3, 11, 51;
SSC 30**
See also AMWS 7; BPFB 2; CA 1-4R, 202;
272; CAAE 202; CAAS 5; CANR 1, 42,
67, 109, 199; CN 1, 2, 3, 4, 5, 6, 7; CP 1,
2, 3, 4, 5, 6, 7; CSW; DLB 2, 5, 130, 152;
DLBY 1983
Garrett, George P.
See Garrett, George
Garrett, George Palmer
See Garrett, George
Garrett, George Palmer, Jr.
See Garrett, George
Garrick, David 1717-1779 .... **LC 15, 156**
See also DAM DRAM; DLB 84, 213;
RGEL 2
Garrigue, Jean 1914-1972 .... **CLC 2, 8**
See also CA 5-8R; 37-40R; CANR 20; CP
1; MAL 5
Garrison, Frederick
See Sinclair, Upton
Garrison, William Lloyd 1805-1879 . **NCLC
149**
See also CDALB 1640-1865; DLB 1, 43,
235
Garro, Elena 1920(?)-1998 .. **HLCS 1; TCLC
153**
See also CA 131; 169; CWW 2; DLB 145;
EWL 3; HW 1; LAWS 1; WLIT 1
Garshin, Vsevolod Mikhailovich
1855-1888 .... **NCLC 257**
See also DLB 277
Garth, Will
See Hamilton, Edmond; Kuttner, Henry
Garvey, Marcus (Moziah, Jr.) 1887-1940 ....
BLC 1:2; HR 1:2; TCLC 41
See also BW 1; CA 120; 124; CANR 79;
DAM MULT; DLB 345
Gary, Romain
See Kacew, Romain
Gascar, Pierre
See Fournier, Pierre
Gascoigne, George 1539-1577 .... **LC 108**
See also DLB 136; RGEL 2
Gascoyne, David (Emery) 1916-2001 ... **CLC
45**
See also CA 65-68; 200; CANR 10, 28, 54;
CP 1, 2, 3, 4, 5, 6, 7; DLB 20; MTCW 1;
RGEL 2
Gaskell, Elizabeth 1810-1865 .. **NCLC 5, 70,
97, 137, 214; SSC 25, 97**
See also AAYA 80; BRW 5; BRWR 3; CD-
BLB 1832-1890; DAB; DAM MST; DLB
21, 144, 159; RGEL 2; RGSF 2; TEA
Gass, William H. 1924- . **CLC 1, 2, 8, 11, 15,
39, 132; SSC 12**
See also AMWS 6; CA 17-20R; CANR 30,
71, 100; CN 1, 2, 3, 4, 5, 6, 7; DLB 2,
227; EWL 3; MAL 5; MTCW 1, 2;
MTFW 2005; RGAL 4
Gassendi, Pierre 1592-1655 .... **LC 54**
See also GFL Beginnings to 1789
Gasset, Jose Ortega y
See Ortega y Gasset, Jose
Gates, Henry Louis, Jr. 1950- . **BLCS; CLC
65**
See also AMWS 20; BW 2, 3; CA 109;
CANR 25, 53, 75, 125, 203; CSW; DA3;
DAM MULT; DLB 67; EWL 3; MAL 5;
MTCW 2; MTFW 2005; RGAL 4

Gilman, Charlotte Perkins 1860-1935 .. **SSC 13, 62; TCLC 9, 37, 117, 201**
See also AAYA 75; AMWS 11; BYA 11; CA 106; 150; DLB 221; EXPS; FL 1:5; FW; HGG; LAIT 2; MBL; MTCW 2; MTFW 2005; NFS 36; RGAL 4; RGSF 2; SFW 4; SSFS 1, 18

Gilmore, Mary (Jean Cameron) 1865-1962 .... **PC 87**
See also CA 114; DLB 260; RGEL 2; SATA 49

Gilmour, David 1946- .... **CLC 35**

Gilpin, William 1724-1804 .... **NCLC 30**

Gilray, J. D.
See Mencken, H. L.

Gilroy, Frank D(aniel) 1925- .... **CLC 2**
See also CA 81-84; CAD; CANR 32, 64, 86; CD 5, 6; DFS 17; DLB 7

Gilstrap, John 1957(?)- .... **CLC 99**
See also AAYA 67; CA 160; CANR 101, 229

Ginsberg, Allen 1926-1997 ... **CLC 1, 2, 3, 4, 6, 13, 36, 69, 109; PC 4, 47; TCLC 120; WLC 3**
See also AAYA 33; AITN 1; AMWC 1; AMWS 2; BG 1:2; CA 1-4R; 157; CANR 2, 41, 63, 95; CDALB 1941-1968; CP 1, 2, 3, 4, 5, 6; DA; DA3; DAB; DAC; DAM MST, POET; DLB 5, 16, 169, 237; EWL 3; GLL 1; LMFS 2; MAL 5; MTCW 1, 2; MTFW 2005; PAB; PFS 29; RGAL 4; TUS; WP

Ginzburg, Eugenia
See Ginzburg, Evgeniia

Ginzburg, Evgeniia 1904-1977 .... **CLC 59**
See also DLB 302

Ginzburg, Natalia 1916-1991 ..... **CLC 5, 11, 54, 70; SSC 65; TCLC 156**
See also CA 85-88; 135; CANR 33; DFS 14; DLB 177; EW 13; EWL 3; MTCW 1, 2; MTFW 2005; RGHL; RGWL 2, 3

Gioia, (Michael) Dana 1950- .... **CLC 251**
See also AMWS 15; CA 130; CANR 70, 88; CP 6, 7; DLB 120, 282; PFS 24

Giono, Jean 1895-1970 ... **CLC 4, 11; TCLC 124**
See also CA 45-48; 29-32R; CANR 2, 35; DLB 72, 321; EWL 3; GFL 1789 to the Present; MTCW 1; RGWL 2, 3

Giovanni, Nikki 1943- . **BLC 1:2; CLC 2, 4, 19, 64, 117; PC 19; WLCS**
See also AAYA 22, 85; AITN 1; BW 2, 3; CA 29-32R; CAAS 6; CANR 18, 41, 60, 91, 130, 175; CDALBS; CLR 6, 73; CP 2, 3, 4, 5, 6, 7; CSW; CWP; CWRI 5; DA; DA3; DAB; DAC; DAM MST, MULT, POET; DLB 5, 41; EWL 3; EXPP; INT CANR-18; MAICYA 1, 2; MAL 5; MTCW 1, 2; MTFW 2005; PFS 17, 28, 35; RGAL 4; SATA 24, 107, 208; TUS; YAW

Giovanni, Yolanda Cornelia
See Giovanni, Nikki

Giovanni, Yolande Cornelia
See Giovanni, Nikki

Giovanni, Yolande Cornelia, Jr.
See Giovanni, Nikki

Giovene, Andrea 1904-1998 .... **CLC 7**
See also CA 85-88

Gippius, Zinaida 1869-1945 .... **TCLC 9**
See also CA 106; 212; DLB 295; EWL 3

Gippius, Zinaida Nikolaevna
See Gippius, Zinaida

Giraudoux, Jean 1882-1944 .. **DC 36; TCLC 2, 7**
See also CA 104; 196; DAM DRAM; DFS 28; DLB 65, 321; EW 9; EWL 3; GFL 1789 to the Present; RGWL 2, 3; TWA

Giraudoux, Jean-Hippolyte
See Giraudoux, Jean

Gironella, Jose Maria (Pous) 1917-2003 ..... **CLC 11**
See also CA 101; 212; EWL 3; RGWL 2, 3

Gissing, George (Robert) 1857-1903 ..... **SSC 37, 113; TCLC 3, 24, 47**
See also BRW 5; CA 105; 167; DLB 18, 135, 184; RGEL 2; TEA

Gitlin, Todd 1943- .... **CLC 201**
See also CA 29-32R; CANR 25, 50, 88, 179, 227

Giurlani, Aldo
See Palazzeschi, Aldo

Gladkov, Fedor Vasil'evich
See Gladkov, Fyodor (Vasilyevich)

Gladkov, Fyodor (Vasilyevich) 1883-1958 ... **TCLC 27**
See also CA 170; DLB 272; EWL 3

Gladstone, William Ewart 1809-1898 .... **NCLC 213**
See also DLB 57, 184

Glancy, Diane 1941- .... **CLC 210; NNAL**
See also CA 136, 225; CAAE 225; CAAS 24; CANR 87, 162, 217; DLB 175

Glanville, Brian (Lester) 1931- .... **CLC 6**
See also CA 5-8R; CAAS 9; CANR 3, 70; CN 1, 2, 3, 4, 5, 6, 7; DLB 15, 139; SATA 42

Glasgow, Ellen 1873-1945 .... **SSC 34, 130; TCLC 2, 7, 239**
See also AMW; CA 104; 164; DLB 9, 12; MAL 5; MBL; MTCW 2; MTFW 2005; RGAL 4; RHW; SSFS 9; TUS

Glasgow, Ellen Anderson Gholson
See Glasgow, Ellen

Glaspell, Susan 1882(?)-1948 ... **DC 10; SSC 41, 132; TCLC 55, 175**
See also AMWS 3; CA 110; 154; DFS 8, 18, 24; DLB 7, 9, 78, 228; MBL; RGAL 4; SSFS 3; TCWW 2; TUS; YABC 2

Glassco, John 1909-1981 .... **CLC 9**
See also CA 13-16R; 102; CANR 15; CN 1, 2; CP 1, 2, 3; DLB 68

Glasscock, Amnesia
See Steinbeck, John

Glasser, Ronald J. 1940(?)- .... **CLC 37**
See also CA 209

Glassman, Joyce
See Johnson, Joyce

Gleick, James 1954- .... **CLC 147**
See also CA 131; 137; CANR 97; INT CA-137

Gleick, James W.
See Gleick, James

Glendinning, Victoria 1937- .... **CLC 50**
See also CA 120; 127; CANR 59, 89, 166; DLB 155

Glissant, Edouard 1928-2011 .... **CLC 10, 68**
See also CA 153; CANR 111; CWW 2; DAM MULT; EWL 3; RGWL 3

Glissant, Edouard Mathieu
See Glissant, Edouard

Gloag, Julian 1930- .... **CLC 40**
See also AITN 1; CA 65-68; CANR 10, 70; CN 1, 2, 3, 4, 5, 6

Glowacki, Aleksander
See Prus, Boleslaw

Gluck, Louise 1943- . **CLC 7, 22, 44, 81, 160, 280; PC 16**
See also AMWS 5; CA 33-36R; CANR 40, 69, 108, 133, 182; CP 1, 2, 3, 4, 5, 6, 7; CWP; DA3; DAM POET; DLB 5; MAL 5; MTCW 2; MTFW 2005; PFS 5, 15; RGAL 4; TCLE 1:1

Gluck, Louise Elisabeth
See Gluck, Louise

Glyn, Elinor 1864-1943 .... **TCLC 72**
See also DLB 153; RHW

Gobineau, Joseph-Arthur 1816-1882 . **NCLC 17**
See also DLB 123; GFL 1789 to the Present

Godard, Jean-Luc 1930- .... **CLC 20**
See also CA 93-96

Godden, (Margaret) Rumer 1907-1998 .... **CLC 53**
See also AAYA 6; BPFB 2; BYA 2, 5; CA 5-8R; 172; CANR 4, 27, 36, 55, 80; CLR 20; CN 1, 2, 3, 4, 5, 6; CWRI 5; DLB 161; MAICYA 1, 2; RHW; SAAS 12; SATA 3, 36; SATA-Obit 109; TEA

Godoy Alcayaga, Lucila
See Mistral, Gabriela

Godwin, Gail 1937- .... **CLC 5, 8, 22, 31, 69, 125**
See also BPFB 2; CA 29-32R; CANR 15, 43, 69, 132, 218; CN 3, 4, 5, 6, 7; CPW; CSW; DA3; DAM POP; DLB 6, 234, 350; INT CANR-15; MAL 5; MTCW 1, 2; MTFW 2005

Godwin, Gail Kathleen
See Godwin, Gail

Godwin, William 1756-1836 . **NCLC 14, 130**
See also BRWS 15; CDBLB 1789-1832; CMW 4; DLB 39, 104, 142, 158, 163, 262, 336; GL 2; HGG; RGEL 2

Goebbels, Josef
See Goebbels, (Paul) Joseph

Goebbels, (Paul) Joseph 1897-1945 ... **TCLC 68**
See also CA 115; 148

Goebbels, Joseph Paul
See Goebbels, (Paul) Joseph

Goethe, Johann Wolfgang von 1749-1832 ... **DC 20; NCLC 4, 22, 34, 90, 154, 247; PC 5; SSC 38, 141; WLC 3**
See also CDWLB 2; DA; DA3; DAB; DAC; DAM DRAM, MST, POET; DLB 94; EW 5; GL 2; LATS 1; LMFS 1:1; RGWL 2, 3; TWA

Gogarty, Oliver St. John 1878-1957 .... **PC 121; TCLC 15**
See also CA 109; 150; DLB 15, 19; RGEL 2

Gogol, Nikolai 1809-1852 ... **DC 1; NCLC 5, 15, 31, 162; SSC 4, 29, 52, 145; WLC 3**
See also DA; DAB; DAC; DAM DRAM, MST; DFS 12; DLB 198; EW 6; EXPS; RGSF 2; RGWL 2, 3; SSFS 7, 32; TWA

Gogol, Nikolai Vasilyevich
See Gogol, Nikolai

Goines, Donald 1937(?)-1974 .... **BLC 1:2; CLC 80**
See also AITN 1; BW 1, 3; CA 124; 114; CANR 82; CMW 4; DA3; DAM MULT, POP; DLB 33

Gold, Herbert 1924- .. **CLC 4, 7, 14, 42, 152**
See also CA 9-12R; CANR 17, 45, 125, 194; CN 1, 2, 3, 4, 5, 6, 7; DLB 2; DLBY 1981; MAL 5

Goldbarth, Albert 1948- .... **CLC 5, 38**
See also AMWS 12; CA 53-56; CANR 6, 40, 206; CP 3, 4, 5, 6, 7; DLB 120

Goldberg, Anatol 1910-1982 .... **CLC 34**
See also CA 131; 117

Goldemberg, Isaac 1945- .... **CLC 52**
See also CA 69-72; CAAS 12; CANR 11, 32; EWL 3; HW 1; WLIT 1

Golding, Arthur 1536-1606 .... **LC 101**
See also DLB 136

Golding, William 1911-1993 . **CLC 1, 2, 3, 8, 10, 17, 27, 58, 81; WLC 3**
See also AAYA 5, 44; BPFB 2; BRWR 1; BRWS 1; BYA 2; CA 5-8R; 141; CANR 13, 33, 54; CD 5; CDBLB 1945-1960; CLR 94, 130; CN 1, 2, 3, 4; DA; DA3; DAB; DAC; DAM MST, NOV; DLB 15,

100, 255, 326, 330; EWL 3; EXPN; HGG; LAIT 4; MTCW 1, 2; MTFW 2005; NFS 2, 36; RGEL 2; RHW; SFW 4; TEA; WLIT 4; YAW

Golding, William Gerald
See Golding, William

Goldman, Emma 1869-1940 .... **TCLC 13**
See also CA 110; 150; DLB 221; FW; RGAL 4; TUS

Goldman, Francisco 1954- ...... **CLC 76, 298**
See also CA 162; CANR 185

Goldman, William 1931- .... **CLC 1, 48**
See also BPFB 2; CA 9-12R; CANR 29, 69, 106; CN 1, 2, 3, 4, 5, 6, 7; DLB 44; FANT; IDFW 3, 4; NFS 31

Goldman, William W.
See Goldman, William

Goldmann, Lucien 1913-1970 .... **CLC 24**
See also CA 25-28; CAP 2

Goldoni, Carlo 1707-1793 .... **LC 4, 152**
See also DAM DRAM; DFS 27; EW 4; RGWL 2, 3; WLIT 7

Goldsberry, Steven 1949- .... **CLC 34**
See also CA 131

Goldsmith, Oliver 1730(?)-1774 ... **DC 8; LC 2, 48, 122; PC 77; WLC 3**
See also BRW 3; CDBLB 1660-1789; DA; DAB; DAC; DAM DRAM, MST, NOV, POET; DFS 1; DLB 39, 89, 104, 109, 142, 336; IDTP; RGEL 2; SATA 26; TEA; WLIT 3

Goldsmith, Peter
See Priestley, J(ohn) B(oynton)

Goldstein, Rebecca 1950- .... **CLC 239**
See also CA 144; CANR 99, 165, 214; TCLE 1:1

Goldstein, Rebecca Newberger
See Goldstein, Rebecca

Gombrowicz, Witold 1904-1969 ... **CLC 4, 7, 11, 49; TCLC 247**
See also CA 19-20; 25-28R; CANR 105; CAP 2; CDWLB 4; DAM DRAM; DLB 215; EW 12; EWL 3; RGWL 2, 3; TWA

Gomez de Avellaneda, Gertrudis 1814-1873 .... **NCLC 111**
See also LAW

Gomez de la Serna, Ramon 1888-1963 . **CLC 9**
See also CA 153; 116; CANR 79; EWL 3; HW 1, 2

Gomez-Pena, Guillermo 1955- ...... **CLC 310**
See also CA 147; CANR 117

Goncharov, Ivan Alexandrovich 1812-1891 .... **NCLC 1, 63**
See also DLB 238; EW 6; RGWL 2, 3

Goncourt, Edmond de 1822-1896 .. **NCLC 7**
See also DLB 123; EW 7; GFL 1789 to the Present; RGWL 2, 3

Goncourt, Edmond Louis Antoine Huot de
See Goncourt, Edmond de

Goncourt, Jules Alfred Huot de
See Goncourt, Jules de

Goncourt, Jules de 1830-1870 .... **NCLC 7**
See Goncourt, Jules de
See also DLB 123; EW 7; GFL 1789 to the Present; RGWL 2, 3

Gongora (y Argote), Luis de 1561-1627 . **LC 72**
See also RGWL 2, 3

Gontier, Fernande 19(?)- .... **CLC 50**

Gonzalez Martinez, Enrique
See Gonzalez Martinez, Enrique

Gonzalez Martinez, Enrique 1871-1952 ...... **TCLC 72**
See also CA 166; CANR 81; DLB 290; EWL 3; HW 1, 2

Goodison, Lorna 1947- ...... **BLC 2:2; PC 36**
See also CA 142; CANR 88, 189; CP 5, 6, 7; CWP; DLB 157; EWL 3; PFS 25

Goodman, Allegra 1967- .... **CLC 241**
See also CA 204; CANR 162, 204; DLB 244, 350

Goodman, Paul 1911-1972 .... **CLC 1, 2, 4, 7**
See also CA 19-20; 37-40R; CAD; CANR 34; CAP 2; CN 1; DLB 130, 246; MAL 5; MTCW 1; RGAL 4

Goodweather, Hartley
See King, Thomas

GoodWeather, Hartley
See King, Thomas

Googe, Barnabe 1540-1594 .... **LC 94**
See also DLB 132; RGEL 2

Gordimer, Nadine 1923- .... **CLC 3, 5, 7, 10, 18, 33, 51, 70, 123, 160, 161, 263; SSC 17, 80, 154; WLCS**
See also AAYA 39; AFW; BRWS 2; CA 5-8R; CANR 3, 28, 56, 88, 131, 195, 219; CN 1, 2, 3, 4, 5, 6, 7; DA; DA3; DAB; DAC; DAM MST, NOV; DLB 225, 326, 330; EWL 3; EXPS; INT CANR-28; LATS 1:2; MTCW 1, 2; MTFW 2005; NFS 4; RGEL 2; RGSF 2; SSFS 2, 14, 19, 28, 31; TWA; WLIT 2; YAW

Gordon, Adam Lindsay 1833-1870 ... **NCLC 21**
See also DLB 230

Gordon, Caroline 1895-1981 ...... **CLC 6, 13, 29, 83; SSC 15; TCLC 241**
See also AMW; CA 11-12; 103; CANR 36; CAP 1; CN 1, 2; DLB 4, 9, 102; DLBD 17; DLBY 1981; EWL 3; MAL 5; MTCW 1, 2; MTFW 2005; RGAL 4; RGSF 2

Gordon, Charles William 1860-1937 . **TCLC 31**
See also CA 109; DLB 92; TCWW 1, 2

Gordon, Mary 1949- . **CLC 13, 22, 128, 216; SSC 59**
See also AMWS 4; BPFB 2; CA 102; CANR 44, 92, 154, 179, 222; CN 4, 5, 6, 7; DLB 6; DLBY 1981; FW; INT CA-102; MAL 5; MTCW 1

Gordon, Mary Catherine
See Gordon, Mary

Gordon, N. J.
See Bosman, Herman Charles

Gordon, Sol 1923- .... **CLC 26**
See also CA 53-56; CANR 4; SATA 11

Gordone, Charles 1925-1995 .... **BLC 2:2; CLC 1, 4; DC 8**
See also BW 1, 3; CA 93-96; 180; 150; CAAE 180; CAD; CANR 55; DAM DRAM; DLB 7; INT CA-93-96; MTCW 1

Gore, Catherine 1800-1861 .... **NCLC 65**
See also DLB 116, 344; RGEL 2

Gorenko, Anna Andreevna
See Akhmatova, Anna

Gor'kii, Maksim
See Gorky, Maxim

Gorky, Maxim 1868-1936 .... **SSC 28; TCLC 8; WLC 3**
See also CA 105; 141; CANR 83; DA; DAB; DAC; DAM DRAM, MST, NOV; DFS 9; DLB 295; EW 8; EWL 3; MTCW 2; MTFW 2005; RGSF 2; RGWL 2, 3; TWA

Goryan, Sirak
See Saroyan, William

Gosse, Edmund (William) 1849-1928 . **TCLC 28**
See also CA 117; DLB 57, 144, 184; RGEL 2

Gotlieb, Phyllis 1926-2009 .... **CLC 18**
See also CA 13-16R; CANR 7, 135; CN 7; CP 1, 2, 3, 4; DLB 88, 251; SFW 4

Gotlieb, Phyllis Fay Bloom
See Gotlieb, Phyllis

Gottesman, S. D.
See Kornbluth, C(yril) M.; Pohl, Frederik

Gottfried von Strassburg fl. c. 1170-1215 ... **CMLC 10, 96, 132**
See also CDWLB 2; DLB 138; EW 1; RGWL 2, 3

Gotthelf, Jeremias 1797-1854 ..... **NCLC 117**
See also DLB 133; RGWL 2, 3

Gottschalk c. 804-c. 866 .... **CMLC 130**
See also DLB 148

Gottschalk, Laura Riding
See Jackson, Laura

Gould, Lois 1932(?)-2002 .... **CLC 4, 10**
See also CA 77-80; 208; CANR 29; MTCW 1

Gould, Stephen Jay 1941-2002 ...... **CLC 163**
See also AAYA 26; BEST 90:2; CA 77-80; 205; CANR 10, 27, 56, 75, 125; CPW; INT CANR-27; MTCW 1, 2; MTFW 2005

Gourmont, Remy(-Marie-Charles) de 1858-1915 .... **TCLC 17**
See also CA 109; 150; GFL 1789 to the Present; MTCW 2

Gournay, Marie le Jars de
See de Gournay, Marie le Jars

Govier, Katherine 1948- .... **CLC 51**
See also CA 101; CANR 18, 40, 128; CCA 1

Gower, John c. 1330-1408 ..... **LC 76; PC 59**
See also BRW 1; DLB 146; RGEL 2

Goyen, (Charles) William 1915-1983 ... **CLC 5, 8, 14, 40**
See also AITN 2; CA 5-8R; 110; CANR 6, 71; CN 1, 2, 3; DLB 2, 218; DLBY 1983; EWL 3; INT CANR-6; MAL 5

Goytisolo, Juan 1931- .. **CLC 5, 10, 23, 133; HLC 1**
See also CA 85-88; CANR 32, 61, 131, 182; CWW 2; DAM MULT; DLB 322; EWL 3; GLL 2; HW 1, 2; MTCW 1, 2; MTFW 2005

Gozzano, Guido 1883-1916 .... **PC 10**
See also CA 154; DLB 114; EWL 3

Gozzi, (Conte) Carlo 1720-1806 ... **NCLC 23**

Grabbe, Christian Dietrich 1801-1836 .... **NCLC 2**
See also DLB 133; RGWL 2, 3

Grace, Patricia 1937- .... **CLC 56**
See also CA 176; CANR 118; CN 4, 5, 6, 7; EWL 3; RGSF 2; SSFS 33

Grace, Patricia Frances
See Grace, Patricia

Gracian, Baltasar 1601-1658 ...... **LC 15, 160**

Gracian y Morales, Baltasar
See Gracian, Baltasar

Gracq, Julien 1910-2007 .... **CLC 11, 48, 259**
See also CA 122; 126; 267; CANR 141; CWW 2; DLB 83; GFL 1789 to the present

Grade, Chaim 1910-1982 .... **CLC 10**
See also CA 93-96; 107; DLB 333; EWL 3; RGHL

Grade, Khayim
See Grade, Chaim

Graduate of Oxford, A
See Ruskin, John

Grafton, Garth
See Duncan, Sara Jeannette

Grafton, Sue 1940- .... **CLC 163, 299**
See also AAYA 11, 49; BEST 90:3; CA 108; CANR 31, 55, 111, 134, 195; CMW 4; CPW; CSW; DA3; DAM POP; DLB 226; FW; MSW; MTFW 2005

Graham, John
See Phillips, David Graham

Graham, Jorie 1950- ... **CLC 48, 118; PC 59**
See also AAYA 67; CA 111; CANR 63, 118, 205; CP 4, 5, 6, 7; CWP; DLB 120; EWL 3; MTFW 2005; PFS 10, 17; TCLE 1:1

Graham, R. B. Cunninghame
See Cunninghame Graham, Robert Bontine
Graham, Robert
See Haldeman, Joe
Graham, Robert Bontine Cunninghame
See Cunninghame Graham, Robert Bontine
Graham, Tom
See Lewis, Sinclair
Graham, W(illiam) S(ydney) 1918-1986 ...... **CLC 29; PC 127**
See also BRWS 7; CA 73-76; 118; CP 1, 2, 3, 4; DLB 20; RGEL 2
Graham, Winston (Mawdsley) 1910-2003 ... **CLC 23**
See also CA 49-52; 218; CANR 2, 22, 45, 66; CMW 4; CN 1, 2, 3, 4, 5, 6, 7; DLB 77; RHW
Grahame, Kenneth 1859-1932 ..... **TCLC 64, 136**
See also BYA 5; CA 108; 136; CANR 80; CLR 5, 135; CWRI 5; DA3; DLB 34, 141, 178; FANT; MAICYA 1, 2; MTCW 2; NFS 20; RGEL 2; SATA 100; TEA; WCH; YABC 1
Granger, Darius John
See Marlowe, Stephen
Granin, Daniil 1918- .... **CLC 59**
See also DLB 302
Granovsky, Timofei Nikolaevich 1813-1855 .... **NCLC 75**
See also DLB 198
Grant, Skeeter
See Spiegelman, Art
Granville-Barker, Harley 1877-1946 . **TCLC 2**
See also CA 104; 204; DAM DRAM; DLB 10; RGEL 2
Granzotto, Gianni
See Granzotto, Giovanni Battista
Granzotto, Giovanni Battista 1914-1985 ..... **CLC 70**
See also CA 166
Grasemann, Ruth Barbara
See Rendell, Ruth
Grass, Guenter
See Grass, Gunter
Grass, Gunter 1927- . **CLC 1, 2, 4, 6, 11, 15, 22, 32, 49, 88, 207; WLC 3**
See also BPFB 2; CA 13-16R; CANR 20, 75, 93, 133, 174, 229; CDWLB 2; CWW 2; DA; DA3; DAB; DAC; DAM MST, NOV; DLB 330; EW 13; EWL 3; MTCW 1, 2; MTFW 2005; RGHL; RGWL 2, 3; TWA
Grass, Gunter Wilhelm
See Grass, Gunter
Gratton, Thomas
See Hulme, T(homas) E(rnest)
Grau, Shirley Ann 1929- ...... **CLC 4, 9, 146; SSC 15**
See also CA 89-92; CANR 22, 69; CN 1, 2, 3, 4, 5, 6, 7; CSW; DLB 2, 218; INT CA-89-92; CANR-22; MTCW 1
Gravel, Fern
See Hall, James Norman
Graver, Elizabeth 1964- .... **CLC 70**
See also CA 135; CANR 71, 129
Graves, Richard Perceval 1895-1985 ... **CLC 44**
See also CA 65-68; CANR 9, 26, 51
Graves, Robert 1895-1985 . **CLC 1, 2, 6, 11, 39, 44, 45; PC 6**
See also BPFB 2; BRW 7; BYA 4; CA 5-8R; 117; CANR 5, 36; CDBLB 1914-1945; CN 1, 2, 3; CP 1, 2, 3, 4; DA3; DAB; DAC; DAM MST, POET; DLB 20, 100,

191; DLBD 18; DLBY 1985; EWL 3; LATS 1:1; MTCW 1, 2; MTFW 2005; NCFS 2; NFS 21; RGEL 2; RHW; SATA 45; TEA
Graves, Robert von Ranke
See Graves, Robert
Graves, Valerie
See Bradley, Marion Zimmer
Gray, Alasdair 1934- .... **CLC 41, 275**
See also BRWS 9; CA 126; CANR 47, 69, 106, 140; CN 4, 5, 6, 7; DLB 194, 261, 319; HGG; INT CA-126; MTCW 1, 2; MTFW 2005; RGSF 2; SUFW 2
Gray, Amlin 1946- .... **CLC 29**
See also CA 138
Gray, Francine du Plessix 1930- .... **CLC 22, 153**
See also BEST 90:3; CA 61-64; CAAS 2; CANR 11, 33, 75, 81, 197; DAM NOV; INT CANR-11; MTCW 1, 2; MTFW 2005
Gray, John (Henry) 1866-1934 ..... **TCLC 19**
See also CA 119; 162; RGEL 2
Gray, John Lee
See Jakes, John
Gray, Simon 1936-2008 .... **CLC 9, 14, 36**
See also AITN 1; CA 21-24R; 275; CAAS 3; CANR 32, 69, 208; CBD; CD 5, 6; CN 1, 2, 3; DLB 13; EWL 3; MTCW 1; RGEL 2
Gray, Simon James Holliday
See Gray, Simon
Gray, Spalding 1941-2004 ...... **CLC 49, 112; DC 7**
See also AAYA 62; CA 128; 225; CAD; CANR 74, 138; CD 5, 6; CPW; DAM POP; MTCW 2; MTFW 2005
Gray, Thomas 1716-1771 ...... **LC 4, 40, 178; PC 2, 80; WLC 3**
See also BRW 3; CDBLB 1660-1789; DA; DA3; DAB; DAC; DAM MST; DLB 109; EXPP; PAB; PFS 9; RGEL 2; TEA; WP
Grayson, David
See Baker, Ray Stannard
Grayson, Richard (A.) 1951- .... **CLC 38**
See also CA 85-88, 210; CAAE 210; CANR 14, 31, 57; DLB 234
Greeley, Andrew M. 1928- .... **CLC 28**
See also BPFB 2; CA 5-8R; CAAS 7; CANR 7, 43, 69, 104, 136, 184; CMW 4; CPW; DA3; DAM POP; MTCW 1, 2; MTFW 2005
Green, Anna Katharine 1846-1935 ... **TCLC 63**
See also CA 112; 159; CMW 4; DLB 202, 221; MSW
Green, Brian
See Card, Orson Scott
Green, Hannah
See Greenberg, Joanne (Goldenberg)
Green, Hannah 1927(?)-1996 .... **CLC 3**
See also CA 73-76; CANR 59, 93; NFS 10
Green, Henry
See Yorke, Henry Vincent
Green, Julian
See Green, Julien
Green, Julien 1900-1998 .... **CLC 3, 11, 77**
See also CA 21-24R; 169; CANR 33, 87; CWW 2; DLB 4, 72; EWL 3; GFL 1789 to the Present; MTCW 2; MTFW 2005
Green, Julien Hartridge
See Green, Julien
Green, Paul (Eliot) 1894-1981 . **CLC 25; DC 37**
See also AITN 1; CA 5-8R; 103; CAD; CANR 3; DAM DRAM; DLB 7, 9, 249; DLBY 1981; MAL 5; RGAL 4
Greenaway, Peter 1942- .... **CLC 159**
See also CA 127

Greenberg, Ivan 1908-1973 .... **CLC 24**
See also CA 85-88; DLB 137; MAL 5
Greenberg, Joanne (Goldenberg) 1932- ...... **CLC 7, 30**
See also AAYA 12, 67; CA 5-8R; CANR 14, 32, 69; CN 6, 7; DLB 335; NFS 23; SATA 25; YAW
Greenberg, Richard 1959(?)- .... **CLC 57**
See also CA 138; CAD; CD 5, 6; DFS 24
Greenblatt, Stephen J. 1943- .... **CLC 70**
See also CA 49-52; CANR 115; LNFS 1
Greenblatt, Stephen Jay
See Greenblatt, Stephen J.
Greene, Bette 1934- .... **CLC 30**
See also AAYA 7, 69; BYA 3; CA 53-56; CANR 4, 146; CLR 2, 140; CWRI 5; JRDA; LAIT 4; MAICYA 1, 2; NFS 10; SAAS 16; SATA 8, 102, 161; WYA; YAW
Greene, Gael CLC **8**
See also CA 13-16R; CANR 10, 166
Greene, Graham 1904-1991 . **CLC 1, 3, 6, 9, 14, 18, 27, 37, 70, 72, 125; DC 41; SSC 29, 121; WLC 3**
See also AAYA 61; AITN 2; BPFB 2; BRWR 2; BRWS 1; BYA 3; CA 13-16R; 133; CANR 35, 61, 131; CBD; CDBLB 1945-1960; CMW 4; CN 1, 2, 3, 4; DA; DA3; DAB; DAC; DAM MST, NOV; DLB 13, 15, 77, 100, 162, 201, 204; DLBY 1991; EWL 3; MSW; MTCW 1, 2; MTFW 2005; NFS 16, 31, 36; RGEL 2; SATA 20; SSFS 14, 35; TEA; WLIT 4
Greene, Graham Henry
See Greene, Graham
Greene, Robert 1558-1592 .... **LC 41, 185**
See also BRWS 8; DLB 62, 167; IDTP; RGEL 2; TEA
Greer, Germaine 1939- .... **CLC 131**
See also AITN 1; CA 81-84; CANR 33, 70, 115, 133, 190; FW; MTCW 1, 2; MTFW 2005
Greer, Richard
See Silverberg, Robert
Gregor, Arthur 1923- .... **CLC 9**
See also CA 25-28R; CAAS 10; CANR 11; CP 1, 2, 3, 4, 5, 6, 7; SATA 36
Gregor, Lee
See Pohl, Frederik
Gregory, Lady Isabella Augusta (Persse) 1852-1932 .... **TCLC 1, 176**
See also BRW 6; CA 104; 184; DLB 10; IDTP; RGEL 2
Gregory, J. Dennis
See Williams, John A(lfred)
Gregory of Nazianzus, St. 329-389 .. **CMLC 82**
Gregory of Nyssa c. 335-c. 394 . **CMLC 126**
Gregory of Rimini 1300(?)-1358 . **CMLC 109**
See also DLB 115
Gregory the Great c. 540-604 .... **CMLC 124**
Grekova, I.
See Ventsel, Elena Sergeevna
Grekova, Irina
See Ventsel, Elena Sergeevna
Grendon, Stephen
See Derleth, August (William)
Grenville, Kate 1950- .... **CLC 61**
See also CA 118; CANR 53, 93, 156, 220; CN 7; DLB 325
Grenville, Pelham
See Wodehouse, P. G.
Greve, Felix Paul (Berthold Friedrich) 1879-1948 .... **TCLC 4, 248**
See also CA 104; 141, 175; CANR 79; DAC; DAM MST; DLB 92; RGEL 2; TCWW 1, 2
Greville, Fulke 1554-1628 .... **LC 79**
See also BRWS 11; DLB 62, 172; RGEL 2

Gunn Allen, Paula
  See Allen, Paula Gunn
Gunnars, Kristjana 1948- .... **CLC 69**
  See also CA 113; CCA 1; CP 6, 7; CWP;
  DLB 60
Gunter, Erich
  See Eich, Gunter
Gurdjieff, G(eorgei) I(vanovich)
  1877(?)-1949 .... **TCLC 71**
  See also CA 157
Gurganus, Allan 1947- .... **CLC 70**
  See also BEST 90:1; CA 135; CANR 114;
  CN 6, 7; CPW; CSW; DAM POP; DLB
  350; GLL 1
Gurney, A. R.
  See Gurney, A(lbert) R(amsdell), Jr.
Gurney, A(lbert) R(amsdell), Jr. 1930- . **CLC
  32, 50, 54**
  See also AMWS 5; CA 77-80; CAD; CANR
  32, 64, 121; CD 5, 6; DAM DRAM; DLB
  266; EWL 3
Gurney, Ivor (Bertie) 1890-1937 .. **TCLC 33**
  See also BRW 6; CA 167; DLBY 2002;
  PAB; RGEL 2
Gurney, Peter
  See Gurney, A(lbert) R(amsdell), Jr.
Guro, Elena (Genrikhovna) 1877-1913 ....
  TCLC 56
  See also DLB 295
Gustafson, James M(oody) 1925- . **CLC 100**
  See also CA 25-28R; CANR 37
Gustafson, Ralph (Barker) 1909-1995 . **CLC
  36**
  See also CA 21-24R; CANR 8, 45, 84; CP
  1, 2, 3, 4, 5, 6; DLB 88; RGEL 2
Gut, Gom
  See Simenon, Georges
Guterson, David 1956- .... **CLC 91**
  See also CA 132; CANR 73, 126, 194; CN
  7; DLB 292; MTCW 2; MTFW 2005;
  NFS 13
Guthrie, A(lfred) B(ertram), Jr. 1901-1991 .
  CLC 23
  See also CA 57-60; 134; CANR 24; CN 1,
  2, 3; DLB 6, 212; MAL 5; SATA 62;
  SATA-Obit 67; TCWW 1, 2
Guthrie, Isobel
  See Grieve, C. M.
Gutierrez Najera, Manuel 1859-1895 . **HLCS
  2; NCLC 133**
  See also DLB 290; LAW
Guy, Rosa 1925- .... **CLC 26**
  See also AAYA 4, 37; BW 2; CA 17-20R;
  CANR 14, 34, 83; CLR 13, 137; DLB 33;
  DNFS 1; JRDA; MAICYA 1, 2; SATA 14,
  62, 122; YAW
Guy, Rosa Cuthbert
  See Guy, Rosa
Gwendolyn
  See Bennett, (Enoch) Arnold
H. D.
  See Doolittle, Hilda
H. de V.
  See Buchan, John
Haavikko, Paavo Juhani 1931- . **CLC 18, 34**
  See also CA 106; CWW 2; EWL 3
Habbema, Koos
  See Heijermans, Herman
Habermas, Juergen 1929- .... **CLC 104**
  See also CA 109; CANR 85, 162; DLB 242
Habermas, Jurgen
  See Habermas, Juergen
Hacker, Marilyn 1942- ..... **CLC 5, 9, 23, 72,
  91; PC 47**
  See also CA 77-80; CANR 68, 129; CP 3,
  4, 5, 6, 7; CWP; DAM POET; DLB 120,
  282; FW; GLL 2; MAL 5; PFS 19
Hadewijch of Antwerp fl. 1250- .. **CMLC 61**
  See also RGWL 3

Hadrian 76-138 .... **CMLC 52**
Haeckel, Ernst Heinrich (Philipp August)
  1834-1919 .... **TCLC 83**
  See also CA 157
Hafiz c. 1326-1389(?) ..... **CMLC 34; PC 116**
  See also RGWL 2, 3; WLIT 6
Hagedorn, Jessica T. 1949- .... **CLC 185**
  See also CA 139; CANR 69, 231; CWP;
  DLB 312; RGAL 4
Hagedorn, Jessica Tarahata
  See Hagedorn, Jessica T.
Haggard, H(enry) Rider 1856-1925 .. **TCLC
  11**
  See also AAYA 81; BRWS 3; BYA 4, 5;
  CA 108; 148; CANR 112; DLB 70, 156,
  174, 178; FANT; LMFS 1; MTCW 2; NFS
  40; RGEL 2; RHW; SATA 16; SCFW 1,
  2; SFW 4; SUFW 1; WLIT 4
Hagiosy, L.
  See Larbaud, Valery (Nicolas)
Hagiwara, Sakutaro 1886-1942 .... **PC 18;
  TCLC 60**
  See also CA 154; EWL 3; RGWL 3
Hagiwara Sakutaro
  See Hagiwara, Sakutaro
Haig, Fenil
  See Ford, Ford Madox
Haig-Brown, Roderick (Langmere)
  1908-1976 .... **CLC 21**
  See also CA 5-8R; 69-72; CANR 4, 38, 83;
  CLR 31; CWRI 5; DLB 88; MAICYA 1,
  2; SATA 12; TCWW 2
Haight, Rip
  See Carpenter, John
Haij, Vera
  See Jansson, Tove (Marika)
Hailey, Arthur 1920-2004 .... **CLC 5**
  See also AITN 2; BEST 90:3; BPFB 2; CA
  1-4R; 233; CANR 2, 36, 75; CCA 1; CN
  1, 2, 3, 4, 5, 6, 7; CPW; DAM NOV, POP;
  DLB 88; DLBY 1982; MTCW 1, 2;
  MTFW 2005
Hailey, Elizabeth Forsythe 1938- .... **CLC 40**
  See also CA 93-96, 188; CAAE 188; CAAS
  1; CANR 15, 48; INT CANR-15
Haines, John 1924-2011 .... **CLC 58**
  See also AMWS 12; CA 17-20R; CANR
  13, 34; CP 1, 2, 3, 4, 5; CSW; DLB 5,
  212; TCLE 1:1
Haines, John Meade
  See Haines, John
Hakluyt, Richard 1552-1616 .... **LC 31**
  See also DLB 136; RGEL 2
Haldeman, Joe 1943- .... **CLC 61**
  See also AAYA 38; CA 53-56, 179; CAAE
  179; CAAS 25; CANR 6, 70, 72, 130,
  171, 224; DLB 8; INT CANR-6; SCFW
  2; SFW 4
Haldeman, Joe William
  See Haldeman, Joe
Hale, Janet Campbell 1947- .... **NNAL**
  See also CA 49-52; CANR 45, 75; DAM
  MULT; DLB 175; MTCW 2; MTFW 2005
Hale, Sarah Josepha (Buell) 1788-1879 ....
  NCLC 75
  See also DLB 1, 42, 73, 243
Halevy, Elie 1870-1937 .... **TCLC 104**
Haley, Alex 1921-1992 ...... **BLC 1:2; CLC 8,
  12, 76; TCLC 147**
  See also AAYA 26; BPFB 2; BW 2, 3; CA
  77-80; 136; CANR 61; CDALBS; CPW;
  CSW; DA; DA3; DAB; DAC; DAM MST,
  MULT, POP; DLB 38; LAIT 5; MTCW
  1, 2; NFS 9
Haley, Alexander Murray Palmer
  See Haley, Alex
Haliburton, Thomas Chandler 1796-1865 ...
  NCLC 15, 149
  See also DLB 11, 99; RGEL 2; RGSF 2

Hall, Donald 1928- . **CLC 1, 13, 37, 59, 151,
  240; PC 70**
  See also AAYA 63; CA 5-8R; CAAS 7;
  CANR 2, 44, 64, 106, 133, 196; CP 1, 2,
  3, 4, 5, 6, 7; DAM POET; DLB 5, 342;
  MAL 5; MTCW 2; MTFW 2005; RGAL
  4; SATA 23, 97
Hall, Donald Andrew, Jr.
  See Hall, Donald
Hall, Frederic Sauser
  See Sauser-Hall, Frederic
Hall, James
  See Kuttner, Henry
Hall, James Norman 1887-1951 ... **TCLC 23**
  See also CA 123; 173; LAIT 1; RHW 1;
  SATA 21
Hall, Joseph 1574-1656 .... **LC 91**
  See also DLB 121, 151; RGEL 2
Hall, Marguerite Radclyffe
  See Hall, Radclyffe
Hall, Radclyffe 1880-1943 ..... **TCLC 12, 215**
  See also BRWS 6; CA 110; 150; CANR 83;
  DLB 191; MTCW 2; MTFW 2005; RGEL
  2; RHW
Hall, Rodney 1935- .... **CLC 51**
  See also CA 109; CANR 69; CN 6, 7; CP
  1, 2, 3, 4, 5, 6, 7; DLB 289
Hallam, Arthur Henry 1811-1833 ..... **NCLC
  110**
  See also DLB 32
Halldor Laxness
  See Gudjonsson, Halldor Kiljan
Halleck, Fitz-Greene 1790-1867 ... **NCLC 47**
  See also DLB 3, 250; RGAL 4
Halliday, Michael
  See Creasey, John
Halpern, Daniel 1945- .... **CLC 14**
  See also CA 33-36R; CANR 93, 174; CP 3,
  4, 5, 6, 7
Hamann, Johann Georg 1730-1788 . **LC 198**
  See also DLB 97
Hamburger, Michael 1924-2007 . **CLC 5, 14**
  See also CA 5-8R, 196; 261; CAAE 196;
  CAAS 4; CANR 2, 47; CP 1, 2, 3, 4, 5, 6,
  7; DLB 27
Hamburger, Michael Peter Leopold
  See Hamburger, Michael
Hamill, Pete 1935- .... **CLC 10, 261**
  See also CA 25-28R; CANR 18, 71, 127,
  180
Hamill, William Peter
  See Hamill, Pete
Hamilton, Alexander 1712-1756 .... **LC 150**
  See also DLB 31
Hamilton, Alexander 1755(?)-1804 .... **NCLC
  49**
  See also DLB 37
Hamilton, Clive
  See Lewis, C. S.
Hamilton, Edmond 1904-1977 .... **CLC 1**
  See also CA 1-4R; CANR 3, 84; DLB 8;
  SATA 118; SFW 4
Hamilton, Elizabeth 1758-1816 .. **NCLC 153**
  See also DLB 116, 158
Hamilton, Eugene (Jacob) Lee
  See Lee-Hamilton, Eugene (Jacob)
Hamilton, Franklin
  See Silverberg, Robert
Hamilton, Gail
  See Corcoran, Barbara (Asenath)
Hamilton, (Robert) Ian 1938-2001 . **CLC 191**
  See also CA 106; 203; CANR 41, 67; CP 1,
  2, 3, 4, 5, 6, 7; DLB 40, 155
Hamilton, Jane 1957- .... **CLC 179**
  See also CA 147; CANR 85, 128, 214; CN
  7; DLB 350; MTFW 2005

Hamilton, Mollie
See Kaye, M.M.

Hamilton, Patrick 1904-1962 .... **CLC 51**
See also BRWS 16; CA 176; 113; DLB 10, 191

Hamilton, Virginia 1936-2002 .... **CLC 26**
See also AAYA 2, 21; BW 2, 3; BYA 1, 2, 8; CA 25-28R; 206; CANR 20, 37, 73, 126; CLR 1, 11, 40, 127; DAM MULT; DLB 33, 52; DLBY 2001; INT CANR-20; JRDA; LAIT 5; MAICYA 1, 2; MAICYAS 1; MTCW 1, 2; MTFW 2005; SATA 4, 56, 79, 123; SATA-Obit 132; WYA; YAW

Hamilton, Virginia Esther
See Hamilton, Virginia

Hammett, Dashiell 1894-1961 . **CLC 3, 5, 10, 19, 47; SSC 17; TCLC 187**
See also AAYA 59; AITN 1; AMWS 4; BPFB 2; CA 81-84; CANR 42; CDALB 1929-1941; CMW 4; DA3; DLB 226, 280; DLBD 6; DLBY 1996; EWL 3; LAIT 3; MAL 5; MSW; MTCW 1, 2; MTFW 2005; NFS 21; RGAL 4; RGSF 2; TUS

Hammett, Samuel Dashiell
See Hammett, Dashiell

Hammon, Jupiter 1720(?)-1800(?) . **BLC 1:2; NCLC 5; PC 16**
See also DAM MULT, POET; DLB 31, 50

Hammond, Keith
See Kuttner, Henry

Hamner, Earl (Henry), Jr. 1923- .... **CLC 12**
See also AITN 2; CA 73-76; DLB 6

Hampton, Christopher 1946- .... **CLC 4**
See also CA 25-28R; CD 5, 6; DLB 13; MTCW 1

Hampton, Christopher James
See Hampton, Christopher

Hamsun, Knut
See Pedersen, Knut

Hamsund, Knut Pedersen
See Pedersen, Knut

Handke, Peter 1942- .. **CLC 5, 8, 10, 15, 38, 134; DC 17**
See also CA 77-80; CANR 33, 75, 104, 133, 180; CWW 2; DAM DRAM, NOV; DLB 85, 124; EWL 3; MTCW 1, 2; MTFW 2005; TWA

Handler, Chelsea 1975(?)- .... **CLC 269**
See also CA 243; CANR 230

Handy, W(illiam) C(hristopher) 1873-1958 . **TCLC 97**
See also BW 3; CA 121; 167

Haneke, Michael 1942- .... **CLC 283**

Hanif, Mohammed 1965- .... **CLC 299**
See also CA 283

Hanley, James 1901-1985 .... **CLC 3, 5, 8, 13**
See also CA 73-76; 117; CANR 36; CBD; CN 1, 2, 3; DLB 191; EWL 3; MTCW 1; RGEL 2

Hannah, Barry 1942-2010 .. **CLC 23, 38, 90, 270, 318; SSC 94**
See also BPFB 2; CA 108; 110; CANR 43, 68, 113; CN 4, 5, 6, 7; CSW; DLB 6, 234; INT CA-110; MTCW 1; RGSF 2

Hannon, Ezra
See Hunter, Evan

Hanrahan, Barbara 1939-1991 ... **TCLC 219**
See also CA 121; 127; CN 4, 5; DLB 289

Hansberry, Lorraine 1930-1965 .... **BLC 1:2, 2:2; CLC 17, 62; DC 2; TCLC 192**
See also AAYA 25; AFAW 1, 2; AMWS 4; BW 1, 3; CA 109; 25-28R; CABS 3; CAD; CANR 58; CDALB 1941-1968; CWD; DA; DA3; DAB; DAC; DAM DRAM, MST, MULT; DFS 2, 29; DLB 7, 38; EWL 3; FL 1:6; FW; LAIT 4; MAL 5; MTCW 1, 2; MTFW 2005; RGAL 4; TUS

Hansberry, Lorraine Vivian
See Hansberry, Lorraine

Hansen, Joseph 1923-2004 .... **CLC 38**
See also BPFB 2; CA 29-32R; 233; CAAS 17; CANR 16, 44, 66, 125; CMW 4; DLB 226; GLL 1; INT CANR-16

Hansen, Karen V. 1955- .... **CLC 65**
See also CA 149; CANR 102

Hansen, Martin A(lfred) 1909-1955 .. **TCLC 32**
See also CA 167; DLB 214; EWL 3

Hanson, Kenneth O. 1922- .... **CLC 13**
See also CA 53-56; CANR 7; CP 1, 2, 3, 4, 5

Hanson, Kenneth Ostlin
See Hanson, Kenneth O.

Han Yu 768-824 .... **CMLC 122**

Hardwick, Elizabeth 1916-2007 ...... **CLC 13**
See also AMWS 3; CA 5-8R; 267; CANR 3, 32, 70, 100, 139; CN 4, 5, 6; CSW; DA3; DAM NOV; DLB 6; MBL; MTCW 1, 2; MTFW 2005; TCLE 1:1

Hardwick, Elizabeth Bruce
See Hardwick, Elizabeth

Hardy, Thomas 1840-1928 .... **PC 8, 92; SSC 2, 60, 113; TCLC 4, 10, 18, 32, 48, 53, 72, 143, 153, 229; WLC 3**
See also AAYA 69; BRW 6; BRWC 1, 2; BRWR 1; CA 104; 123; CDBLB 1890-1914; DA; DA3; DAB; DAC; DAM MST, NOV, POET; DLB 18, 19, 135, 284; EWL 3; EXPN; EXPP; LAIT 2; MTCW 1, 2; MTFW 2005; NFS 3, 11, 15, 19, 30; PFS 3, 4, 18; RGEL 2; RGSF 2; TEA; WLIT 4

Hare, David 1947- . **CLC 29, 58, 136; DC 26**
See also BRWS 4; CA 97-100; CANR 39, 91; CBD; CD 5, 6; DFS 4, 7, 16; DLB 13, 310; MTCW 1; TEA

Harewood, John
See Van Druten, John (William)

Harford, Henry
See Hudson, W(illiam) H(enry)

Hargrave, Leonie
See Disch, Thomas M.

Hariri, Al- al-Qasim ibn 'Ali Abu Muhammad al-Basri
See al-Hariri, al-Qasim ibn 'Ali Abu Muhammad al-Basri

Harjo, Joy 1951- .... **CLC 83; NNAL; PC 27**
See also AMWS 12; CA 114; CANR 35, 67, 91, 129; CP 6, 7; CWP; DAM MULT; DLB 120, 175, 342; EWL 3; MTCW 2; MTFW 2005; PFS 15, 32; RGAL 4

Harlan, Louis R. 1922-2010 .... **CLC 34**
See also CA 21-24R; CANR 25, 55, 80

Harlan, Louis Rudolph
See Harlan, Louis R.

Harlan, Louis Rudolph
See Harlan, Louis R.

Harling, Robert 1951(?)- .... **CLC 53**
See also CA 147

Harmon, William (Ruth) 1938- .... **CLC 38**
See also CA 33-36R; CANR 14, 32, 35; SATA 65

Harper, Edith Alice Mary
See Wickham, Anna

Harper, F. E. W.
See Harper, Frances Ellen Watkins

Harper, Frances E. W.
See Harper, Frances Ellen Watkins

Harper, Frances E. Watkins
See Harper, Frances Ellen Watkins

Harper, Frances Ellen
See Harper, Frances Ellen Watkins

Harper, Frances Ellen Watkins 1825-1911 .. **BLC 1:2; PC 21; TCLC 14, 217**
See also AFAW 1, 2; BW 1, 3; CA 111; 125; CANR 79; DAM MULT, POET; DLB 50, 221; MBL; RGAL 4

Harper, Michael S. 1938- . **BLC 2:2; CLC 7, 22**
See also AFAW 2; BW 1; CA 33-36R, 224; CAAE 224; CANR 24, 108, 212; CP 2, 3, 4, 5, 6, 7; DLB 41; RGAL 4; TCLE 1:1

Harper, Michael Steven
See Harper, Michael S.

Harper, Mrs. F. E. W.
See Harper, Frances Ellen Watkins

Harpur, Charles 1813-1868 .... **NCLC 114**
See also DLB 230; RGEL 2

Harris, Christie
See Harris, Christie (Lucy) Irwin

Harris, Christie (Lucy) Irwin 1907-2002 ..... **CLC 12**
See also CA 5-8R; CANR 6, 83; CLR 47; DLB 88; JRDA; MAICYA 1, 2; SAAS 10; SATA 6, 74; SATA-Essay 116

Harris, E. Lynn 1955-2009 .... **CLC 299**
See also CA 164; 288; CANR 111, 163, 206; MTFW 2005

Harris, Everett Lynn
See Harris, E. Lynn

Harris, Everette Lynn
See Harris, E. Lynn

Harris, Frank 1856-1931 .... **TCLC 24**
See also CA 109; 150; CANR 80; DLB 156, 197; RGEL 2

Harris, George Washington 1814-1869 .... **NCLC 23, 165**
See also DLB 3, 11, 248; RGAL 4

Harris, Joel Chandler 1848-1908 .... **SSC 19, 103; TCLC 2**
See also CA 104; 137; CANR 80; CLR 49, 128; DLB 11, 23, 42, 78, 91; LAIT 2; MAICYA 1, 2; RGSF 2; SATA 100; WCH; YABC 1

Harris, John (Wyndham Parkes Lucas) Beynon 1903-1969 .... **CLC 19**
See also BRWS 13; CA 102; 89-92; CANR 84; DLB 255; SATA 118; SCFW 1, 2; SFW 4

Harris, MacDonald
See Heiney, Donald (William)

Harris, Mark 1922-2007 .... **CLC 19**
See also CA 5-8R; 260; CAAS 3; CANR 2, 55, 83; CN 1, 2, 3, 4, 5, 6, 7; DLB 2; DLBY 1980

Harris, Norman **CLC 65**

Harris, (Theodore) Wilson 1921- . **BLC 2:2; CLC 25, 159, 297**
See also BRWS 5; BW 2, 3; CA 65-68; CAAS 16; CANR 11, 27, 69, 114; CD-WLB 3; CN 1, 2, 3, 4, 5, 6, 7; CP 1, 2, 3, 4, 5, 6, 7; DLB 117; EWL 3; MTCW 1; RGEL 2

Harrison, Barbara Grizzuti 1934-2002 . **CLC 144**
See also CA 77-80; 205; CANR 15, 48; INT CANR-15

Harrison, Elizabeth (Allen) Cavanna 1909-2001 .... **CLC 12**
See also CA 9-12R; 200; CANR 6, 27, 85, 104, 121; JRDA; MAICYA 1; SAAS 4; SATA 1, 30; YAW

Harrison, Harry 1925- .... **CLC 42**
See also CA 1-4R; CANR 5, 21, 84, 225; DLB 8; SATA 4; SCFW 2; SFW 4

Harrison, Harry Max
See Harrison, Harry

Harrison, James
See Harrison, Jim

Harrison, James Thomas
See Harrison, Jim

Harrison, Jim 1937- . **CLC 6, 14, 33, 66, 143; SSC 19**
See also AMWS 8; CA 13-16R; CANR 8, 51, 79, 142, 198, 229; CN 5, 6; CP 1, 2, 3, 4, 5, 6; DLBY 1982; INT CANR-8; RGAL 4; TCWW 2; TUS

Harrison, Kathryn 1961- .... **CLC 70, 151**
See also CA 144; CANR 68, 122, 194

Harrison, Tony 1937- .... **CLC 43, 129**
See also BRWS 5; CA 65-68; CANR 44, 98; CBD; CD 5, 6; CP 2, 3, 4, 5, 6, 7; DLB 40, 245; MTCW 1; RGEL 2

Harriss, Will(ard Irvin) 1922- .... **CLC 34**
See also CA 111

Hart, Ellis
See Ellison, Harlan

Hart, Josephine 1942-2011 .... **CLC 70**
See also CA 138; CANR 70, 149, 220; CPW; DAM POP

Hart, Moss 1904-1961 .... **CLC 66**
See also CA 109; 89-92; CANR 84; DAM DRAM; DFS 1; DLB 7, 266; RGAL 4

Harte, Bret 1836(?)-1902 . **SSC 8, 59; TCLC 1, 25; WLC 3**
See also AMWS 2; CA 104; 140; CANR 80; CDALB 1865-1917; DA; DA3; DAC; DAM MST; DLB 12, 64, 74, 79, 186; EXPS; LAIT 2; RGAL 4; RGSF 2; SATA 26; SSFS 3; TUS

Harte, Francis Brett
See Harte, Bret

Hartley, L(eslie) P(oles) 1895-1972 .. **CLC 2, 22; SSC 125**
See also BRWS 7; CA 45-48; 37-40R; CANR 33; CN 1; DLB 15, 139; EWL 3; HGG; MTCW 1, 2; MTFW 2005; RGEL 2; RGSF 2; SUFW 1

Hartman, Geoffrey H. 1929- .... **CLC 27**
See also CA 117; 125; CANR 79, 214; DLB 67

Hartmann, Sadakichi 1869-1944 .. **TCLC 73**
See also CA 157; DLB 54

Hartmann von Aue c. 1170-c. 1210 .. **CMLC 15, 131**
See also CDWLB 2; DLB 138; RGWL 2, 3

Hartog, Jan de
See de Hartog, Jan

Haruf, Kent 1943- .... **CLC 34**
See also AAYA 44; CA 149; CANR 91, 131

Harvey, Caroline
See Trollope, Joanna

Harvey, Gabriel 1550(?)-1631 .... **LC 88**
See also DLB 167, 213, 281

Harvey, Jack
See Rankin, Ian

Harwood, Ronald 1934- .... **CLC 32**
See also CA 1-4R; CANR 4, 55, 150; CBD; CD 5, 6; DAM DRAM, MST; DLB 13

Hasegawa Tatsunosuke
See Futabatei, Shimei

Hasek, Jaroslav 1883-1923 .. **SSC 69; TCLC 4, 261**
See also CA 104; 129; CDWLB 4; DLB 215; EW 9; EWL 3; MTCW 1, 2; RGSF 2; RGWL 2, 3

Hasek, Jaroslav Matej Frantisek
See Hasek, Jaroslav

Hass, Robert 1941- ..... **CLC 18, 39, 99, 287; PC 16**
See also AMWS 6; CA 111; CANR 30, 50, 71, 187; CP 3, 4, 5, 6, 7; DLB 105, 206; EWL 3; MAL 5; MTFW 2005; PFS 37; RGAL 4; SATA 94; TCLE 1:1

Hassler, Jon 1933-2008 .... **CLC 263**
See also CA 73-76; 270; CANR 21, 80, 161; CN 6, 7; INT CANR-21; SATA 19; SATA-Obit 191

Hassler, Jon Francis
See Hassler, Jon

Hastings, Hudson
See Kuttner, Henry

Hastings, Selina 1945- .... **CLC 44**
See also CA 257; CANR 225

Hastings, Selina Shirley
See Hastings, Selina

Hastings, Lady Selina Shirley
See Hastings, Selina

Hastings, Victor
See Disch, Thomas M.

Hathorne, John 1641-1717 .... **LC 38**

Hatteras, Amelia
See Mencken, H. L.

Hatteras, Owen
See Mencken, H. L.; Nathan, George Jean

Hauff, Wilhelm 1802-1827 .... **NCLC 185**
See also CLR 155; DLB 90; SUFW 1

Hauptmann, Gerhart 1862-1946 ...... **DC 34; SSC 37; TCLC 4**
See also CA 104; 153; CDWLB 2; DAM DRAM; DLB 66, 118, 330; EW 8; EWL 3; RGSF 2; RGWL 2, 3; TWA

Hauptmann, Gerhart Johann Robert
See Hauptmann, Gerhart

Havel, Vaclav 1936- .... **CLC 25, 58, 65, 123, 314; DC 6**
See also CA 104; CANR 36, 63, 124, 175; CDWLB 4; CWW 2; DA3; DAM DRAM; DFS 10; DLB 232; EWL 3; LMFS 2; MTCW 1, 2; MTFW 2005; RGWL 3

Haviaras, Stratis
See Chaviaras, Strates

Hawes, Stephen 1475(?)-1529(?) .... **LC 17**
See also DLB 132; RGEL 2

Hawk, Alex
See Kelton, Elmer

Hawkes, John 1925-1998 . **CLC 1, 2, 3, 4, 7, 9, 14, 15, 27, 49**
See also BPFB 2; CA 1-4R; 167; CANR 2, 47, 64; CN 1, 2, 3, 4, 5, 6; DLB 2, 7, 227; DLBY 1980, 1998; EWL 3; MAL 5; MTCW 1, 2; MTFW 2005; RGAL 4

Hawking, S. W.
See Hawking, Stephen W.

Hawking, Stephen W. 1942- .... **CLC 63, 105**
See also AAYA 13; BEST 89:1; CA 126; 129; CANR 48, 115; CPW; DA3; MTCW 2; MTFW 2005

Hawking, Stephen William
See Hawking, Stephen W.

Hawkins, Anthony Hope
See Hope, Anthony

Hawthorne, Julian 1846-1934 .... **TCLC 25**
See also CA 165; HGG

Hawthorne, Nathaniel 1804-1864 .. **NCLC 2, 10, 17, 23, 39, 79, 95, 158, 171, 191, 226; SSC 3, 29, 39, 89, 130, 166; WLC 3**
See also AAYA 18; AMW; AMWC 1; AMWR 1; BPFB 2; BYA 3; CDALB 1640-1865; CLR 103, 163; DA; DA3; DAB; DAC; DAM MST, NOV; DLB 1, 74, 183, 223, 269; EXPN; EXPS; GL 2; HGG; LAIT 1; NFS 1, 20; RGAL 4; RGSF 2; SSFS 1, 7, 11, 15, 30, 35; SUFW 1; TUS; WCH; YABC 2

Hawthorne, Sophia Peabody 1809-1871 ...... **NCLC 150**
See also DLB 183, 239

Haxton, Josephine Ayres 1921- ....
See Douglas, Ellen

Hayaseca y Eizaguirre, Jorge
See Echegaray (y Eizaguirre), Jose (Maria Waldo)

Hayashi, Fumiko 1904-1951 .... **TCLC 27**
See also CA 161; DLB 180; EWL 3

Hayashi Fumiko
See Hayashi, Fumiko

Haycraft, Anna 1932-2005 .... **CLC 40**
See also CA 122; 237; CANR 90, 141; CN 4, 5, 6; DLB 194; MTCW 2; MTFW 2005

Haycraft, Anna Margaret
See Haycraft, Anna

Hayden, Robert
See Hayden, Robert Earl

Hayden, Robert E.
See Hayden, Robert Earl

Hayden, Robert Earl 1913-1980 ... **BLC 1:2; CLC 5, 9, 14, 37; PC 6, 123**
See also AFAW 1, 2; AMWS 2; BW 1, 3; CA 69-72; 97-100; CABS 2; CANR 24, 75, 82; CDALB 1941-1968; CP 1, 2, 3; DA; DAC; DAM MST, MULT, POET; DLB 5, 76; EWL 3; EXPP; MAL 5; MTCW 1, 2; PFS 1, 31; RGAL 4; SATA 19; SATA-Obit 26; WP

Haydon, Benjamin Robert 1786-1846 .... **NCLC 146**
See also DLB 110

Hayek, F(riedrich) A(ugust von) 1899-1992 .... **TCLC 109**
See also CA 93-96; 137; CANR 20; MTCW 1, 2

Hayford, J(oseph) E(phraim) Casely
See Casely-Hayford, J(oseph) E(phraim)

Hayman, Ronald 1932- .... **CLC 44**
See also CA 25-28R; CANR 18, 50, 88; CD 5, 6; DLB 155

Hayne, Paul Hamilton 1830-1886 . **NCLC 94**
See also DLB 3, 64, 79, 248; RGAL 4

Haynes, Todd 1961- .... **CLC 313**
See also CA 220

Hays, Mary 1760-1843 .... **NCLC 114**
See also DLB 142, 158; RGEL 2

Haywood, Eliza (Fowler) 1693(?)-1756 .. **LC 1, 44, 177**
See also BRWS 12; DLB 39; RGEL 2

Hazlitt, William 1778-1830 ..... **NCLC 29, 82**
See also BRW 4; DLB 110, 158; RGEL 2; TEA

Hazzard, Shirley 1931- .... **CLC 18, 218**
See also CA 9-12R; CANR 4, 70, 127, 212; CN 1, 2, 3, 4, 5, 6, 7; DLB 289; DLBY 1982; MTCW 1

Head, Bessie 1937-1986 . **BLC 1:2, 2:2; CLC 25, 67; SSC 52**
See also AFW; BW 2, 3; CA 29-32R; 119; CANR 25, 82; CDWLB 3; CN 1, 2, 3, 4; DA3; DAM MULT; DLB 117, 225; EWL 3; EXPS; FL 1:6; FW; MTCW 1, 2; MTFW 2005; NFS 31; RGSF 2; SSFS 5, 13, 30, 33; WLIT 2; WWE 1

Headley, Elizabeth
See Harrison, Elizabeth (Allen) Cavanna

Headon, (Nicky) Topper 1956(?)- ... **CLC 30**

Heaney, Seamus 1939- ...... **CLC 5, 7, 14, 25, 37, 74, 91, 171, 225, 309; PC 18, 100; WLCS**
See also AAYA 61; BRWR 1; BRWS 2; CA 85-88; CANR 25, 48, 75, 91, 128, 184; CDBLB 1960 to Present; CP 1, 2, 3, 4, 5, 6, 7; DA3; DAB; DAM POET; DLB 40, 330; DLBY 1995; EWL 3; EXPP; MTCW 1, 2; MTFW 2005; PAB; PFS 2, 5, 8, 17, 30, 41; RGEL 2; TEA; WLIT 4

Heaney, Seamus Justin
See Heaney, Seamus

Hearn, Lafcadio 1850-1904 .... **SSC 158; TCLC 9, 263**
See also AAYA 79; CA 105; 166; DLB 12, 78, 189; HGG; MAL 5; RGAL 4

Hearn, Patricio Lafcadio Tessima Carlos
See Hearn, Lafcadio

Hearne, Samuel 1745-1792 .... **LC 95**
See also DLB 99

Herder, Johann Gottfried von 1744-1803 ....
NCLC 8, 186
See also DLB 97; EW 4; TWA

Heredia, Jose Maria 1803-1839 ..... **HLCS 2;**
NCLC 209
See also LAW

Hergesheimer, Joseph 1880-1954 .. **TCLC 11**
See also CA 109; 194; DLB 102, 9; RGAL
4

Herlihy, James Leo 1927-1993 .... **CLC 6**
See also CA 1-4R; 143; CAD; CANR 2;
CN 1, 2, 3, 4, 5

Herman, William
See Bierce, Ambrose

Hermogenes fl. c. 175- .... **CMLC 6**

Hernandez, Felisberto 1902-1964 ... **SSC 152**
See also CA 213; EWL 3; LAWS 1

Hernandez, Jose 1834-1886 .... **NCLC 17**
See also LAW; RGWL 2, 3; WLIT 1

Herodotus c. 484B.C.-c. 420B.C. . **CMLC 17**
See also AW 1; CDWLB 1; DLB 176;
RGWL 2, 3; TWA; WLIT 8

Herr, Michael 1940(?)- .... **CLC 231**
See also CA 89-92; CANR 68, 142; DLB
185; MTCW 1

Herrick, Robert 1591-1674 . **LC 13, 145; PC**
9
See also BRW 2; BRWC 2; DA; DAB;
DAC; DAM MST, POP; DLB 126; EXPP;
PFS 13, 29, 39; RGAL 4; RGEL 2; TEA;
WP

Herring, Guilles
See Somerville, Edith Oenone

Herriot, James 1916-1995 .... **CLC 12**
See also AAYA 1, 54; BPFB 2; CA 77-80;
148; CANR 40; CLR 80; CPW; DAM
POP; LAIT 3; MAICYA 2; MAICYAS 1;
MTCW 2; SATA 86, 135; SATA-Brief 44;
TEA; YAW

Herris, Violet
See Hunt, Violet

Herrmann, Dorothy 1941- .... **CLC 44**
See also CA 107

Herrmann, Taffy
See Herrmann, Dorothy

Hersey, John 1914-1993 . **CLC 1, 2, 7, 9, 40,**
81, 97
See also AAYA 29; BPFB 2; CA 17-20R;
140; CANR 33; CDALBS; CN 1, 2, 3, 4,
5; CPW; DAM POP; DLB 6, 185, 278,
299, 364; MAL 5; MTCW 1, 2; MTFW
2005; RGHL; SATA 25; SATA-Obit 76;
TUS

Hersey, John Richard
See Hersey, John

Hervent, Maurice
See Grindel, Eugene

Herzen, Aleksandr Ivanovich 1812-1870 .....
NCLC 10, 61
See also DLB 277

Herzen, Alexander
See Herzen, Aleksandr Ivanovich

Herzl, Theodor 1860-1904 .... **TCLC 36**
See also CA 168

Herzog, Werner 1942- .... **CLC 16, 236**
See also AAYA 85; CA 89-92; CANR 215

Hesiod fl. 8th cent. B.C.- .... **CMLC 5, 102**
See also AW 1; DLB 176; RGWL 2, 3;
WLIT 8

Hesse, Hermann 1877-1962 . **CLC 1, 2, 3, 6,**
11, 17, 25, 69; SSC 9, 49; TCLC 148,
196; WLC 3
See also AAYA 43; BPFB 2; CA 17-18;
CAP 2; CDWLB 2; DA; DA3; DAB;
DAC; DAM MST, NOV; DLB 66, 330;
EW 9; EWL 3; EXPN; LAIT 1; MTCW
1, 2; MTFW 2005; NFS 6, 15, 24; RGWL
2, 3; SATA 50; TWA

Hewes, Cady
See De Voto, Bernard (Augustine)

Heyen, William 1940- .... **CLC 13, 18**
See also CA 33-36R, 220; CAAE 220;
CAAS 9; CANR 98, 188; CP 3, 4, 5, 6, 7;
DLB 5; RGHL

Heyerdahl, Thor 1914-2002 .... **CLC 26**
See also CA 5-8R; 207; CANR 5, 22, 66,
73; LAIT 4; MTCW 1, 2; MTFW 2005;
SATA 2, 52

Heym, Georg (Theodor Franz Arthur)
1887-1912 .... **TCLC 9**
See also CA 106; 181

Heym, Stefan 1913-2001 .... **CLC 41**
See also CA 9-12R; 203; CANR 4; CWW
2; DLB 69; EWL 3

Heyse, Paul (Johann Ludwig von)
1830-1914 .... **TCLC 8**
See also CA 104; 209; DLB 129, 330

Heyward, (Edwin) DuBose 1885-1940 ... **HR**
1:2; TCLC 59
See also CA 108; 157; DLB 7, 9, 45, 249;
MAL 5; SATA 21

Heywood, John 1497(?)-1580(?) .... **LC 65**
See also DLB 136; RGEL 2

Heywood, Thomas 1573(?)-1641 . **DC 29; LC**
111
See also DAM DRAM; DLB 62; LMFS 1;
RGEL 2; TEA

Hiaasen, Carl 1953- .... **CLC 238**
See also CA 105; CANR 22, 45, 65, 113,
133, 168; CMW 4; CPW; CSW; DA3;
DLB 292; LNFS 2, 3; MTCW 2; MTFW
2005; SATA 208

Hibbert, Eleanor Alice Burford 1906-1993 .
CLC 7
See also BEST 90:4; BPFB 2; CA 17-20R;
140; CANR 9, 28, 59; CMW 4; CPW;
DAM POP; MTCW 2; MTFW 2005;
RHW; SATA 2; SATA-Obit 74

Hichens, Robert (Smythe) 1864-1950 . **TCLC**
64
See also CA 162; DLB 153; HGG; RHW;
SUFW

Higgins, Aidan 1927- .... **SSC 68**
See also CA 9-12R; CANR 70, 115, 148;
CN 1, 2, 3, 4, 5, 6, 7; DLB 14

Higgins, George V(incent) 1939-1999 .. **CLC**
4, 7, 10, 18
See also BPFB 2; CA 77-80; 186; CAAS 5;
CANR 17, 51, 89, 96; CMW 4; CN 2, 3,
4, 5, 6; DLB 2; DLBY 1981, 1998; INT
CANR-17; MSW; MTCW 1

Higginson, Thomas Wentworth 1823-1911 ..
TCLC 36
See also CA 162; DLB 1, 64, 243

Higgonet, Margaret CLC 65

Highet, Helen
See MacInnes, Helen (Clark)

Highsmith, Mary Patricia
See Highsmith, Patricia

Highsmith, Patricia 1921-1995 ..... **CLC 2, 4,**
14, 42, 102
See also AAYA 48; BRWS 5; CA 1-4R; 147;
CANR 1, 20, 48, 62, 108; CMW 4; CN 1,
2, 3, 4, 5; CPW; DA3; DAM NOV, POP;
DLB 306; GLL 1; MSW; MTCW 1, 2;
MTFW 2005; NFS 27; SSFS 25

Highwater, Jamake (Mamake)
1942(?)-2001 .... **CLC 12**
See also AAYA 7, 69; BPFB 2; BYA 4; CA
65-68; 199; CAAS 7; CANR 10, 34, 84;
CLR 17; CWRI 5; DLB 52; DLBY 1985;
JRDA; MAICYA 1, 2; SATA 32, 69;
SATA-Brief 30

Highway, Tomson 1951- .... **CLC 92; DC 33;**
NNAL
See also CA 151; CANR 75; CCA 1; CD 5,
6; CN 7; DAC; DAM MULT; DFS 2;
DLB 334; MTCW 2

Hijuelos, Oscar 1951- .... **CLC 65; HLC 1**
See also AAYA 25; AMWS 8; BEST 90:1;
CA 123; CANR 50, 75, 125, 205; CPW;
DA3; DAM MULT, POP; DLB 145; HW
1, 2; LLW; MAL 5; MTCW 2; MTFW
2005; NFS 17; RGAL 4; WLIT 1

Hikmet, Nazim 1902-1963 .... **CLC 40**
See also CA 141; 93-96; EWL 3; PFS 38,
41; WLIT 6

Hildegard von Bingen 1098-1179 ..... **CMLC**
20, 118
See also DLB 148

Hildesheimer, Wolfgang 1916-1991 . **CLC 49**
See also CA 101; 135; DLB 69, 124; EWL
3; RGHL

Hill, Aaron 1685-1750 .... **LC 148**
See also DLB 84; RGEL 2

Hill, Geoffrey 1932- .. **CLC 5, 8, 18, 45, 251;**
PC 125
See also BRWR 3; BRWS 5; CA 81-84;
CANR 21, 89; CDBLB 1960 to Present;
CP 1, 2, 3, 4, 5, 6, 7; DAM POET; DLB
40; EWL 3; MTCW 1; RGEL 2; RGHL

Hill, George Roy 1921-2002 .... **CLC 26**
See also CA 110; 122; 213

Hill, John
See Koontz, Dean

Hill, Susan 1942- .... **CLC 4, 113**
See also BRWS 14; CA 33-36R; CANR 29,
69, 129, 172, 201; CN 2, 3, 4, 5, 6, 7;
DAB; DAM MST, NOV; DLB 14, 139;
HGG; MTCW 1; RHW; SATA 183

Hill, Susan Elizabeth
See Hill, Susan

Hillard, Asa G. III CLC 70

Hillerman, Anthony Grove
See Hillerman, Tony

Hillerman, Tony 1925-2008 ..... **CLC 62, 170**
See also AAYA 40; BEST 89:1; BPFB 2;
CA 29-32R; 278; CANR 21, 42, 65, 97,
134; CMW 4; CPW; DA3; DAM POP;
DLB 206, 306; MAL 5; MSW; MTCW 2;
MTFW 2005; RGAL 4; SATA 6; SATA-
Obit 198; TCWW 2; YAW

Hillesum, Etty 1914-1943 .... **TCLC 49**
See also CA 137; RGHL

Hilliard, Noel (Harvey) 1929-1996 . **CLC 15**
See also CA 9-12R; CANR 7, 69; CN 1, 2,
3, 4, 5, 6

Hillis, Rick 1956- .... **CLC 66**
See also CA 134

Hilton, James 1900-1954 .... **TCLC 21**
See also AAYA 76; CA 108; 169; DLB 34,
77; FANT; SATA 34

Hilton, Walter 1343-1396(?) . **CMLC 58, 141**
See also DLB 146; RGEL 2

Himes, Chester (Bomar) 1909-1984 ..... **BLC**
1:2; CLC 2, 4, 7, 18, 58, 108; TCLC 139
See also AFAW 2; AMWS 16; BPFB 2; BW
2; CA 25-28R; 114; CANR 22, 89; CMW
4; CN 1, 2, 3; DAM MULT; DLB 2, 76,
143, 226; EWL 3; MAL 5; MSW; MTCW
1, 2; MTFW 2005; RGAL 4

Himmelfarb, Gertrude 1922- .... **CLC 202**
See also CA 49-52; CANR 28, 66, 102, 166

Hinde, Thomas 1926- .... **CLC 6, 11**
See also CA 5-8R; CN 1, 2, 3, 4, 5, 6; EWL
3

Hine, (William) Daryl 1936- .... **CLC 15**
See also CA 1-4R; CAAS 15; CANR 1, 20;
CP 1, 2, 3, 4, 5, 6, 7; DLB 60

Hinkson, Katharine Tynan
See Tynan, Katharine

Hinojosa, Rolando 1929- .... **HLC 1**
See also CA 131; CAAS 16; CANR 62;
DAM MULT; DLB 82; EWL 3; HW 1, 2;
LLW; MTCW 2; MTFW 2005; RGAL 4

Honig, Edwin 1919-2011 .... **CLC 33**
See also CA 5-8R; CAAS 8; CANR 4, 45, 144; CP 1, 2, 3, 4, 5, 6, 7; DLB 5

Hood, Hugh (John Blagdon) 1928- ...... **CLC 15, 28, 273; SSC 42**
See also CA 49-52; CAAS 17; CANR 1, 33, 87; CN 1, 2, 3, 4, 5, 6, 7; DLB 53; RGSF 2

Hood, Thomas 1799-1845 .... **NCLC 16, 242; PC 93**
See also BRW 4; DLB 96; RGEL 2

Hooker, (Peter) Jeremy 1941- .... **CLC 43**
See also CA 77-80; CANR 22; CP 2, 3, 4, 5, 6, 7; DLB 40

Hooker, Richard 1554-1600 .... **LC 95**
See also BRW 1; DLB 132; RGEL 2

Hooker, Thomas 1586-1647 .... **LC 137**
See also DLB 24

hooks, bell 1952(?)- .... **BLCS; CLC 94**
See also BW 2; CA 143; CANR 87, 126, 211; DLB 246; MTCW 2; MTFW 2005; SATA 115, 170

Hooper, Johnson Jones 1815-1862 .... **NCLC 177**
See also DLB 3, 11, 248; RGAL 4

Hope, A(lec) D(erwent) 1907-2000 ... **CLC 3, 51; PC 56**
See also BRWS 7; CA 21-24R; 188; CANR 33, 74; CP 1, 2, 3, 4, 5; DLB 289; EWL 3; MTCW 1, 2; MTFW 2005; PFS 8; RGEL 2

Hope, Anthony 1863-1933 .... **TCLC 83**
See also CA 157; DLB 153, 156; RGEL 2; RHW

Hope, Brian
See Creasey, John

Hope, Christopher 1944- .... **CLC 52**
See also AFW; CA 106; CANR 47, 101, 177; CN 4, 5, 6, 7; DLB 225; SATA 62

Hope, Christopher David Tully
See Hope, Christopher

Hopkins, Gerard Manley 1844-1889 . **NCLC 17, 189; PC 15; WLC 3**
See also BRW 5; BRWR 2; CDBLB 1890-1914; DA; DA3; DAB; DAC; DAM MST, POET; DLB 35, 57; EXPP; PAB; PFS 26, 40; RGEL 2; TEA; WP

Hopkins, John (Richard) 1931-1998 . **CLC 4**
See also CA 85-88; 169; CBD; CD 5, 6

Hopkins, Pauline Elizabeth 1859-1930 . **BLC 1:2; TCLC 28, 251**
See also AFAW 2; BW 2, 3; CA 141; CANR 82; DAM MULT; DLB 50

Hopkinson, Francis 1737-1791 .... **LC 25**
See also DLB 31; RGAL 4

Hopkinson, Nalo 1960- .... **CLC 316**
See also AAYA 40; CA 196, 219; CAAE 219; CANR 173; DLB 251

Hopley, George
See Hopley-Woolrich, Cornell George

Hopley-Woolrich, Cornell George 1903-1968 .... **CLC 77**
See also CA 13-14; CANR 58, 156; CAP 1; CMW 4; DLB 226; MSW; MTCW 2

Horace 65B.C.-8B.C. ..... **CMLC 39, 125; PC 46**
See also AW 2; CDWLB 1; DLB 211; RGWL 2, 3; WLIT 8

Horatio
See Proust, Marcel

Horgan, Paul (George Vincent O'Shaughnessy) 1903-1995 . **CLC 9, 53**
See also BPFB 2; CA 13-16R; 147; CANR 9, 35; CN 1, 2, 3, 4, 5; DAM NOV; DLB 102, 212; DLBY 1985; INT CANR-9; MTCW 1, 2; MTFW 2005; SATA 13; SATA-Obit 84; TCWW 1, 2

Horkheimer, Max 1895-1973 ...... **TCLC 132**
See also CA 216; 41-44R; DLB 296

Horn, Peter
See Kuttner, Henry

Hornby, Nicholas Peter John
See Hornby, Nick

Hornby, Nick 1957(?)- .... **CLC 243**
See also AAYA 74; BRWS 15; CA 151; CANR 104, 151, 191; CN 7; DLB 207, 352

Horne, Frank 1899-1974 .... **HR 1:2**
See also BW 1; CA 125; 53-56; DLB 51; WP

Horne, Richard Henry Hengist 1802(?)-1884 .... **NCLC 127**
See also DLB 32; SATA 29

Hornem, Horace Esq.
See Lord Byron

Horne Tooke, John 1736-1812 .... **NCLC 195**

Horney, Karen (Clementine Theodore Danielsen) 1885-1952 .... **TCLC 71**
See also CA 114; 165; DLB 246; FW

Hornung, E(rnest) W(illiam) 1866-1921 ...... **TCLC 59**
See also CA 108; 160; CMW 4; DLB 70

Horovitz, Israel 1939- .... **CLC 56**
See also CA 33-36R; CAD; CANR 46, 59; CD 5, 6; DAM DRAM; DLB 7, 341; MAL 5

Horton, George Moses 1797(?)-1883(?) .... **NCLC 87**
See also DLB 50

Horvath, odon von 1901-1938
See von Horvath, Odon
See also EWL 3

Horvath, Oedoen von -1938 ....
See von Horvath, Odon

Horwitz, Julius 1920-1986 .... **CLC 14**
See also CA 9-12R; 119; CANR 12

Horwitz, Ronald
See Harwood, Ronald

Hospital, Janette Turner 1942- ...... **CLC 42, 145, 321**
See also CA 108; CANR 48, 166, 200; CN 5, 6, 7; DLB 325; DLBY 2002; RGSF 2

Hosseini, Khaled 1965- .... **CLC 254**
See also CA 225; LNFS 1, 3; SATA 156

Hostos, E. M. de
See Hostos (y Bonilla), Eugenio Maria de

Hostos, Eugenio M. de
See Hostos (y Bonilla), Eugenio Maria de

Hostos, Eugenio Maria
See Hostos (y Bonilla), Eugenio Maria de

Hostos (y Bonilla), Eugenio Maria de 1839-1903 .... **TCLC 24**
See also CA 123; 131; HW 1

Houdini
See Lovecraft, H. P.

Houellebecq, Michel 1958- .... **CLC 179, 311**
See also CA 185; CANR 140, 231; MTFW 2005

Hougan, Carolyn 1943-2007 .... **CLC 34**
See also CA 139; 257

Household, Geoffrey 1900-1988 .... **CLC 11**
See also BRWS 17; CA 77-80; 126; CANR 58; CMW 4; CN 1, 2, 3, 4; DLB 87; SATA 14; SATA-Obit 59

Housman, A. E. 1859-1936 .. **PC 2, 43; TCLC 1, 10; WLCS**
See also AAYA 66; BRW 6; CA 104; 125; DA; DA3; DAB; DAC; DAM MST, POET; DLB 19, 284; EWL 3; EXPP; MTCW 1, 2; MTFW 2005; PAB; PFS 4, 7, 40; RGEL 2; TEA; WP

Housman, Alfred Edward
See Housman, A. E.

Housman, Laurence 1865-1959 ...... **TCLC 7**
See also CA 106; 155; DLB 10; FANT; RGEL 2; SATA 25

Houston, Jeanne Wakatsuki 1934- .... **AAL**
See also AAYA 49; CA 103, 232; CAAE 232; CAAS 16; CANR 29, 123, 167; LAIT 4; SATA 78, 168; SATA-Essay 168

Hove, Chenjerai 1956- .... **BLC 2:2**
See also CP 7; DLB 360

Howard, E. J.
See Howard, Elizabeth Jane

Howard, Elizabeth Jane 1923- .... **CLC 7, 29**
See also BRWS 11; CA 5-8R; CANR 8, 62, 146, 210; CN 1, 2, 3, 4, 5, 6, 7

Howard, Maureen 1930- ...... **CLC 5, 14, 46, 151**
See also CA 53-56; CANR 31, 75, 140, 221; CN 4, 5, 6, 7; DLBY 1983; INT CANR-31; MTCW 1, 2; MTFW 2005

Howard, Richard 1929- .... **CLC 7, 10, 47**
See also AITN 1; CA 85-88; CANR 25, 80, 154, 217; CP 1, 2, 3, 4, 5, 6, 7; DLB 5; INT CANR-25; MAL 5

Howard, Robert E 1906-1936 .... **TCLC 8**
See also AAYA 80; BPFB 2; BYA 5; CA 105; 157; CANR 155; FANT; SUFW 1; TCWW 1, 2

Howard, Robert Ervin
See Howard, Robert E

Howard, Sidney (Coe) 1891-1939 ...... **DC 42**
See also CA 198; DFS 29; DLB 7, 26, 249; IDFW 3, 4; MAL 5; RGAL 4

Howard, Warren F.
See Pohl, Frederik

Howe, Fanny 1940- .... **CLC 47**
See also CA 117, 187; CAAE 187; CAAS 27; CANR 70, 116, 184; CP 6, 7; CWP; SATA-Brief 52

Howe, Fanny Quincy
See Howe, Fanny

Howe, Irving 1920-1993 .... **CLC 85**
See also AMWS 6; CA 9-12R; 141; CANR 21, 50; DLB 67; EWL 3; MAL 5; MTCW 1, 2; MTFW 2005

Howe, Julia Ward 1819-1910 . **PC 81; TCLC 21**
See also CA 117; 191; DLB 1, 189, 235; FW

Howe, Susan 1937- ...... **CLC 72, 152; PC 54**
See also AMWS 4; CA 160; CANR 209; CP 5, 6, 7; CWP; DLB 120; FW; RGAL 4

Howe, Tina 1937- .... **CLC 48; DC 43**
See also CA 109; CAD; CANR 125; CD 5, 6; CWD; DLB 341

Howell, James 1594(?)-1666 .... **LC 13**
See also DLB 151

Howells, W. D.
See Howells, William Dean

Howells, William D.
See Howells, William Dean

Howells, William Dean 1837-1920 .. **SSC 36; TCLC 7, 17, 41**
See also AMW; CA 104; 134; CDALB 1865-1917; DLB 12, 64, 74, 79, 189; LMFS 1; MAL 5; MTCW 2; RGAL 4; TUS

Howes, Barbara 1914-1996 .... **CLC 15**
See also CA 9-12R; 151; CAAS 3; CANR 53; CP 1, 2, 3, 4, 5, 6; SATA 5; TCLE 1:1

Hrabal, Bohumil 1914-1997 ..... **CLC 13, 67; TCLC 155**
See also CA 106; 156; CAAS 12; CANR 57; CWW 2; DLB 232; EWL 3; RGSF 2

Hrabanus Maurus 776(?)-856 ...... **CMLC 78**
See also DLB 148

Hroswitha of Gandersheim
See Hrotsvit of Gandersheim

Hrotsvit of Gandersheim c. 935-c. 1000 ...... **CMLC 29, 123**
See also DLB 148

Hsi, Chu 1130-1200 .... **CMLC 42**

Hsun, Lu
See Shu-Jen, Chou

Hubbard, L. Ron 1911-1986 .... **CLC 43**
See also AAYA 64; CA 77-80; 118; CANR 52; CPW; DA3; DAM POP; FANT; MTCW 2; MTFW 2005; SFW 4

Hubbard, Lafayette Ronald
See Hubbard, L. Ron

Huch, Ricarda (Octavia) 1864-1947 .. **TCLC 13**
See also CA 111; 189; DLB 66; EWL 3

Huddle, David 1942- .... **CLC 49**
See also CA 57-60, 261; CAAS 20; CANR 89; DLB 130

Hudson, Jeffery
See Crichton, Michael

Hudson, Jeffrey
See Crichton, Michael

Hudson, W(illiam) H(enry) 1841-1922 ....
TCLC 29
See also CA 115; 190; DLB 98, 153, 174; RGEL 2; SATA 35

Hueffer, Ford Madox
See Ford, Ford Madox

Hughart, Barry 1934- .... **CLC 39**
See also CA 137; FANT; SFW 4; SUFW 2

Hughes, Colin
See Creasey, John

Hughes, David (John) 1930-2005 .... **CLC 48**
See also CA 116; 129; 238; CN 4, 5, 6, 7; DLB 14

Hughes, Edward James
See Hughes, Ted

Hughes, James Langston
See Hughes, Langston

Hughes, Langston 1902-1967 .... **BLC 1:2; CLC 1, 5, 10, 15, 35, 44, 108; DC 3; HR 1:2; PC 1, 53; SSC 6, 90; WLC 3**
See also AAYA 12; AFAW 1, 2; AMWR 1; AMWS 1; BW 1, 3; CA 1-4R; 25-28R; CANR 1, 34, 82; CDALB 1929-1941; CLR 17; DA; DA3; DAB; DAC; DAM DRAM, MST, MULT, POET; DFS 6, 18; DLB 4, 7, 48, 51, 86, 228, 315; EWL 3; EXPP; EXPS; JRDA; LAIT 3; LMFS 2; MAICYA 1, 2; MAL 5; MTCW 1, 2; MTFW 2005; NFS 21; PAB; PFS 1, 3, 6, 10, 15, 30, 38; RGAL 4; RGSF 2; SATA 4, 33; SSFS 4, 7, 29; TUS; WCH; WP; YAW

Hughes, Richard (Arthur Warren)
1900-1976 .... **CLC 1, 11; TCLC 204**
See also CA 5-8R; 65-68; CANR 4; CN 1, 2; DAM NOV; DLB 15, 161; EWL 3; MTCW 1; RGEL 2; SATA 8; SATA-Obit 25

Hughes, Ted 1930-1998 . **CLC 2, 4, 9, 14, 37, 119; PC 7, 89**
See also BRWC 2; BRWR 2; BRWS 1; CA 1-4R; 171; CANR 1, 33, 66, 108; CLR 3, 131; CP 1, 2, 3, 4, 5, 6; DA3; DAB; DAC; DAM MST, POET; DLB 40, 161; EWL 3; EXPP; MAICYA 1, 2; MTCW 1, 2; MTFW 2005; PAB; PFS 4, 19, 32; RGEL 2; SATA 49; SATA-Brief 27; SATA-Obit 107; TEA; YAW

Hughes, Thomas 1822-1896 .... **NCLC 207**
See also BYA 3; CLR 160; DLB 18, 163; LAIT 2; RGEL 2; SATA 31

Hugo, Richard
See Huch, Ricarda (Octavia)

Hugo, Richard F(ranklin) 1923-1982 .. **CLC 6, 18, 32; PC 68**
See also AMWS 6; CA 49-52; 108; CANR 3; CP 1, 2, 3; DAM POET; DLB 5, 206; EWL 3; MAL 5; PFS 17; RGAL 4

Hugo, Victor 1802-1885 .... **DC 38; NCLC 3, 10, 21, 161, 189; PC 17; WLC 3**
See also AAYA 28; DA; DA3; DAB; DAC; DAM DRAM, MST, NOV, POET; DLB

119, 192, 217; EFS 1:2, 2:1; EW 6; EXPN; GFL 1789 to the Present; LAIT 1, 2; NFS 5, 20; RGWL 2, 3; SATA 47; TWA

Hugo, Victor Marie
See Hugo, Victor

Huidobro, Vicente
See Huidobro Fernandez, Vicente Garcia

Huidobro Fernandez, Vicente Garcia
1893-1948 .... **TCLC 31**
See also CA 131; DLB 283; EWL 3; HW 1; LAW

Hulme, Keri 1947- .... **CLC 39, 130**
See also CA 125; CANR 69; CN 4, 5, 6, 7; CP 6, 7; CWP; DLB 326; EWL 3; FW; INT CA-125; NFS 24

Hulme, T(homas) E(rnest) 1883-1917 ....
TCLC 21
See also BRWS 6; CA 117; 203; DLB 19

Humboldt, Alexander von 1769-1859 . **NCLC 170**
See also DLB 90

Humboldt, Wilhelm von 1767-1835 .. **NCLC 134, 256**
See also DLB 90, 366

Hume, David 1711-1776 . **LC 7, 56, 156, 157, 197**
See also BRWS 3; DLB 104, 252, 336; LMFS 1; TEA

Humphrey, William 1924-1997 .... **CLC 45**
See also AMWS 9; CA 77-80; 160; CANR 68; CN 1, 2, 3, 4, 5, 6; CSW; DLB 6, 212, 234, 278; TCWW 1, 2

Humphreys, Emyr Owen 1919- ...... **CLC 47**
See also CA 5-8R; CANR 3, 24; CN 1, 2, 3, 4, 5, 6, 7; DLB 15

Humphreys, Josephine 1945- .... **CLC 34, 57**
See also CA 121; 127; CANR 97; CSW; DLB 292; INT CA-127

Huneker, James Gibbons 1860-1921 . **TCLC 65**
See also CA 193; DLB 71; RGAL 4

Hungerford, Hesba Fay
See Brinsmead, H(esba) F(ay)

Hungerford, Pixie
See Brinsmead, H(esba) F(ay)

Hunt, E. Howard 1918-2007 .... **CLC 3**
See also AITN 1; CA 45-48; 256; CANR 2, 47, 103, 160; CMW 4

Hunt, Everette Howard, Jr.
See Hunt, E. Howard

Hunt, Francesca
See Holland, Isabelle (Christian)

Hunt, Howard
See Hunt, E. Howard

Hunt, Kyle
See Creasey, John

Hunt, (James Henry) Leigh 1784-1859 ....
NCLC 1, 70; PC 73
See also DAM POET; DLB 96, 110, 144; RGEL 2; TEA

Hunt, Marsha 1946- .... **CLC 70**
See also BW 2, 3; CA 143; CANR 79

Hunt, Violet 1866(?)-1942 .... **TCLC 53**
See also CA 184; DLB 162, 197

Hunter, E. Waldo
See Sturgeon, Theodore (Hamilton)

Hunter, Evan 1926-2005 .... **CLC 11, 31**
See also AAYA 39; BPFB 2; CA 5-8R; 241; CANR 5, 38, 62, 97, 149; CMW 4; CN 1, 2, 3, 4, 5, 6, 7; CPW; DAM POP; DLB 306; DLBY 1982; INT CANR-5; MSW; MTCW 1; SATA 25; SATA-Obit 167; SFW 4

Hunter, Kristin
See Lattany, Kristin Hunter

Hunter, Mary
See Austin, Mary Hunter

Hunter, Mollie 1922- .... **CLC 21**
See also AAYA 13, 71; BYA 6; CANR 37, 78; CLR 25; DLB 161; JRDA; MAICYA 1, 2; SAAS 7; SATA 2, 54, 106, 139; SATA-Essay 139; WYA; YAW

Hunter, Robert (?)-1734 .... **LC 7**

Hurston, Zora Neale 1891-1960 ... **BLC 1:2; CLC 7, 30, 61; DC 12; HR 1:2; SSC 4, 80; TCLC 121, 131; WLCS**
See also AAYA 15, 71; AFAW 1, 2; AMWS 6; BW 1, 3; BYA 12; CA 85-88; CANR 61; CDALBS; DA; DA3; DAC; DAM MST, MULT, NOV; DFS 6; DLB 51, 86; EWL 3; EXPN; EXPS; FL 1:6; FW; LAIT 3; LATS 1:1; LMFS 2; MAL 5; MBL; MTCW 1, 2; MTFW 2005; NFS 3; RGAL 4; RGSF 2; SSFS 1, 6, 11, 19, 21; TUS; YAW

Husserl, E. G.
See Husserl, Edmund (Gustav Albrecht)

Husserl, Edmund (Gustav Albrecht)
1859-1938 .... **TCLC 100**
See also CA 116; 133; DLB 296

Huston, John (Marcellus) 1906-1987 ... **CLC 20**
See also CA 73-76; 123; CANR 34; DLB 26

Hustvedt, Siri 1955- .... **CLC 76**
See also CA 137; CANR 149, 191, 223

Hutcheson, Francis 1694-1746 .... **LC 157**
See also DLB 252

Hutchinson, Lucy 1620-1675 .... **LC 149**

Hutten, Ulrich von 1488-1523 .... **LC 16**
See also DLB 179

Huxley, Aldous 1894-1963 .... **CLC 1, 3, 4, 5, 8, 11, 18, 35, 79; SSC 39; WLC 3**
See also AAYA 11; BPFB 2; BRW 7; CA 85-88; CANR 44, 99; CDBLB 1914-1945; CLR 151; DA; DA3; DAB; DAC; DAM MST, NOV; DLB 36, 100, 162, 195, 255; EWL 3; EXPN; LAIT 5; LMFS 2; MTCW 1, 2; MTFW 2005; NFS 6; RGEL 2; SATA 63; SCFW 1, 2; SFW 4; TEA; YAW

Huxley, Aldous Leonard
See Huxley, Aldous

Huxley, T(homas) H(enry) 1825-1895 ....
NCLC 67
See also DLB 57; TEA

Huygens, Constantijn 1596-1687 ..... **LC 114**
See also RGWL 2, 3

Huysmans, Charles Marie Georges
See Huysmans, Joris-Karl

Huysmans, Joris-Karl 1848-1907 .. **TCLC 7, 69, 212**
See also CA 104; 165; DLB 123; EW 7; GFL 1789 to the Present; LMFS 2; RGWL 2, 3

Hwang, David Henry 1957- ... **CLC 55, 196; DC 4, 23**
See also AMWS 21; CA 127; 132; CAD; CANR 76, 124; CD 5, 6; DA3; DAM DRAM; DFS 11, 18, 29; DLB 212, 228, 312; INT CA-132; MAL 5; MTCW 2; MTFW 2005; RGAL 4

Hyatt, Daniel
See James, Daniel (Lewis)

Hyde, Anthony 1946- .... **CLC 42**
See also CA 136; CCA 1

Hyde, Margaret O. 1917- .... **CLC 21**
See also CA 1-4R; CANR 1, 36, 137, 181; CLR 23; JRDA; MAICYA 1, 2; SAAS 8; SATA 1, 42, 76, 139

Hyde, Margaret Oldroyd
See Hyde, Margaret O.

Hynes, James 1956(?)- .... **CLC 65**
See also CA 164; CANR 105

Hypatia c. 370-415 .... **CMLC 35**

Jackson, Shirley 1919-1965 ...... **CLC 11, 60, 87; SSC 9, 39; TCLC 187; WLC 3**
See also AAYA 9; AMWS 9; BPFB 2; CA 1-4R; 25-28R; CANR 4, 52; CDALB 1941-1968; DA; DA3; DAC; DAM MST; DLB 6, 234; EXPS; HGG; LAIT 4; MAL 5; MTCW 2; MTFW 2005; NFS 37; RGAL 4; RGSF 2; SATA 2; SSFS 1, 27, 30; SUFW 1, 2

Jacob, (Cyprien-)Max 1876-1944 ... **TCLC 6**
See also CA 104; 193; DLB 258; EWL 3; GFL 1789 to the Present; GLL 2; RGWL 2, 3

Jacobs, Harriet A. 1813(?)-1897 .. **NCLC 67, 162**
See also AFAW 1, 2; DLB 239; FL 1:3; FW; LAIT 2; RGAL 4

Jacobs, Harriet Ann
See Jacobs, Harriet A.

Jacobs, Jim 1942- .... **CLC 12**
See also CA 97-100; INT CA-97-100

Jacobs, W(illiam) W(ymark) 1863-1943 ......
SSC 73; TCLC 22
See also CA 121; 167; DLB 135; EXPS; HGG; RGEL 2; RGSF 2; SSFS 2; SUFW 1

Jacobsen, Jens Peter 1847-1885 .. **NCLC 34, 237**

Jacobsen, Josephine (Winder) 1908-2003 ....
CLC 48, 102; PC 62
See also CA 33-36R; 218; CAAS 18; CANR 23, 48; CCA 1; CP 2, 3, 4, 5, 6, 7; DLB 244; PFS 23; TCLE 1:1

Jacobson, Dan 1929- ..... **CLC 4, 14; SSC 91**
See also AFW; CA 1-4R; CANR 2, 25, 66, 170; CN 1, 2, 3, 4, 5, 6, 7; DLB 14, 207, 225, 319; EWL 3; MTCW 1; RGSF 2

Jacopone da Todi 1236-1306 .... **CMLC 95**

Jacqueline
See Carpentier, Alejo

Jacques de Vitry c. 1160-1240 ..... **CMLC 63**
See also DLB 208

Jagger, Michael Philip
See Jagger, Mick

Jagger, Mick 1943- .... **CLC 17**
See also CA 239

Jahiz, al- c. 780-c. 869 .... **CMLC 25**
See also DLB 311

Jakes, John 1932- .... **CLC 29**
See also AAYA 32; BEST 89:4; BPFB 2; CA 57-60, 214; CAAE 214; CANR 10, 43, 66, 111, 142, 171; CPW; CSW; DA3; DAM NOV, POP; DLB 278; DLBY 1983; FANT; INT CANR-10; MTCW 1, 2; MTFW 2005; RHW; SATA 62; SFW 4; TCWW 1, 2

Jakes, John William
See Jakes, John

James I 1394-1437 .... **LC 20**
See also RGEL 2

James, Alice 1848-1892 .... **NCLC 206**
See also DLB 221

James, Andrew
See Kirkup, James

James, C.L.R. 1901-1989 .... **BLCS; CLC 33**
See also AMWS 21; BW 2; CA 117; 125; 128; CANR 62; CN 1, 2, 3, 4; DLB 125; MTCW 1

James, Daniel (Lewis) 1911-1988 .... **CLC 33**
See also CA 174; 125; DLB 122

James, Dynely
See Mayne, William

James, Henry Sr. 1811-1882 .... **NCLC 53**

James, Henry 1843-1916 . **DC 41; SSC 8, 32, 47, 108, 150; TCLC 2, 11, 24, 40, 47, 64, 171; WLC 3**
See also AAYA 84; AMW; AMWC 1; AMWR 1; BPFB 2; BRW 6; CA 104; 132; CDALB 1865-1917; DA; DA3; DAB; DAC; DAM MST, NOV; DLB 12, 71, 74, 189; DLBD 13; EWL 3; EXPS; GL 2; HGG; LAIT 2; MAL 5; MTCW 1, 2; MTFW 2005; NFS 12, 16, 19, 32, 37; RGAL 4; RGEL 2; RGSF 2; SSFS 9; SUFW 1; TUS

James, M. R.
See James, Montague

James, Mary
See Meaker, Marijane

James, Montague 1862-1936 ..... **SSC 16, 93; TCLC 6**
See also CA 104; 203; DLB 156, 201; HGG; RGEL 2; RGSF 2; SUFW 1

James, Montague Rhodes
See James, Montague

James, P.D. 1920- .... **CLC 18, 46, 122, 226**
See also BEST 90:2; BPFB 2; BRWS 4; CA 21-24R; CANR 17, 43, 65, 112, 201, 231; CDBLB 1960 to Present; CMW 4; CN 4, 5, 6, 7; CPW; DA3; DAM POP; DLB 87, 276; DLBD 17; MSW; MTCW 1, 2; MTFW 2005; TEA

James, Philip
See Moorcock, Michael

James, Samuel
See Stephens, James

James, Seumas
See Stephens, James

James, Stephen
See Stephens, James

James, T. F.
See Fleming, Thomas

James, William 1842-1910 ...... **TCLC 15, 32**
See also AMW; CA 109; 193; DLB 270, 284; MAL 5; NCFS 5; RGAL 4

Jameson, Anna 1794-1860 .... **NCLC 43**
See also DLB 99, 166

Jameson, Fredric 1934- .... **CLC 142**
See also CA 196; CANR 169; DLB 67; LMFS 2

Jameson, Fredric R.
See Jameson, Fredric

James VI of Scotland 1566-1625 ..... **LC 109**
See also DLB 151, 172

Jami, Nur al-Din 'Abd al-Rahman 1414-1492 .... **LC 9**

Jammes, Francis 1868-1938 .... **TCLC 75**
See also CA 198; EWL 3; GFL 1789 to the Present

Jandl, Ernst 1925-2000 .... **CLC 34**
See also CA 200; EWL 3

Janowitz, Tama 1957- .... **CLC 43, 145**
See also CA 106; CANR 52, 89, 129; CN 5, 6, 7; CPW; DAM POP; DLB 292; MTFW 2005

Jansson, Tove (Marika) 1914-2001 .. **SSC 96**
See also CA 17-20R; 196; CANR 38, 118; CLR 2, 125; CWW 2; DLB 257; EWL 3; MAICYA 1, 2; RGSF 2; SATA 3, 41

Japrisot, Sebastien 1931- ....
See Rossi, Jean-Baptiste

Jarrell, Randall 1914-1965 .. **CLC 1, 2, 6, 9, 13, 49; PC 41; TCLC 177**
See also AMW; BYA 5; CA 5-8R; 25-28R; CABS 2; CANR 6, 34; CDALB 1941-1968; CLR 6, 111; CWRI 5; DAM POET; DLB 48, 52; EWL 3; EXPP; MAICYA 1, 2; MAL 5; MTCW 1, 2; PAB; PFS 2, 31; RGAL 4; SATA 7

Jarry, Alfred 1873-1907 .. **SSC 20; TCLC 2, 14, 147**
See also CA 104; 153; DA3; DAM DRAM; DFS 8; DLB 192, 258; EW 9; EWL 3; GFL 1789 to the Present; RGWL 2, 3; TWA

Jarvis, E.K.
See Ellison, Harlan; Silverberg, Robert

Jawien, Andrzej
See John Paul II, Pope

Jaynes, Roderick
See Coen, Ethan

Jeake, Samuel, Jr.
See Aiken, Conrad

Jean-Louis
See Kerouac, Jack

Jean Paul 1763-1825 .... **NCLC 7**

Jefferies, (John) Richard 1848-1887 . **NCLC 47**
See also BRWS 15; DLB 98, 141; RGEL 2; SATA 16; SFW 4

Jeffers, John Robinson
See Jeffers, Robinson

Jeffers, Robinson 1887-1962 .. **CLC 2, 3, 11, 15, 54; PC 17; WLC 3**
See also AMWS 2; CA 85-88; CANR 35; CDALB 1917-1929; DA; DAC; DAM MST, POET; DLB 45, 212, 342; EWL 3; MAL 5; MTCW 1, 2; MTFW 2005; PAB; PFS 3, 4; RGAL 4

Jefferson, Janet
See Mencken, H. L.

Jefferson, Thomas 1743-1826 . **NCLC 11, 103**
See also AAYA 54; ANW; CDALB 1640-1865; DA3; DLB 31, 183; LAIT 1; RGAL 4

Jeffrey, Francis 1773-1850 .... **NCLC 33**
See also DLB 107

Jelakowitch, Ivan
See Heijermans, Herman

Jelinek, Elfriede 1946- .... **CLC 169, 303**
See also AAYA 68; CA 154; CANR 169; DLB 85, 330; FW

Jellicoe, (Patricia) Ann 1927- .... **CLC 27**
See also CA 85-88; CBD; CD 5, 6; CWD; CWRI 5; DLB 13, 233; FW

Jelloun, Tahar ben
See Ben Jelloun, Tahar

Jemyma
See Holley, Marietta

Jen, Gish 1955- ...... **AAL; CLC 70, 198, 260**
See also AAYA 85; AMWC 2; CA 135; CANR 89, 130, 231; CN 7; DLB 312; NFS 30; SSFS 34

Jen, Lillian
See Jen, Gish

Jenkins, (John) Robin 1912- .... **CLC 52**
See also CA 1-4R; CANR 1, 135; CN 1, 2, 3, 4, 5, 6, 7; DLB 14, 271

Jennings, Elizabeth (Joan) 1926-2001 . **CLC 5, 14, 131**
See also BRWS 5; CA 61-64; 200; CAAS 5; CANR 8, 39, 66, 127; CP 1, 2, 3, 4, 5, 6, 7; CWP; DLB 27; EWL 3; MTCW 1; SATA 66

Jennings, Waylon 1937-2002 .... **CLC 21**

Jensen, Johannes V(ilhelm) 1873-1950 ....
TCLC 41
See also CA 170; DLB 214, 330; EWL 3; RGWL 3

Jensen, Laura 1948- .... **CLC 37**
See also CA 103

Jensen, Laura Linnea
See Jensen, Laura

Jensen, Wilhelm 1837-1911 .... **SSC 140**

Jerome, Saint 345-420 .... **CMLC 30**
See also RGWL 3

Jerome, Jerome K(lapka) 1859-1927 . **TCLC 23**
See also CA 119; 177; DLB 10, 34, 135; RGEL 2

Jerrold, Douglas William 1803-1857 . **NCLC 2**
See also DLB 158, 159, 344; RGEL 2

Jewett, Sarah Orne 1849-1909 .... **SSC 6, 44, 110, 138; TCLC 1, 22, 253**
See also AAYA 76; AMW; AMWC 2; AMWR 2; CA 108; 127; CANR 71; DLB 12, 74, 221; EXPS; FL 1:3; FW; MAL 5; MBL; NFS 15; RGAL 4; RGSF 2; SATA 15; SSFS 4

Jewett, Theodora Sarah Orne
See Jewett, Sarah Orne

Jewsbury, Geraldine (Endsor) 1812-1880 ... **NCLC 22**
See also DLB 21

Jhabvala, Ruth Prawer 1927- . **CLC 4, 8, 29, 94, 138, 284; SSC 91**
See also BRWS 5; CA 1-4R; CANR 2, 29, 51, 74, 91, 128; CN 1, 2, 3, 4, 5, 6, 7; DAB; DAM NOV; DLB 139, 194, 323, 326; EWL 3; IDFW 3, 4; INT CANR-29; MTCW 1, 2; MTFW 2005; RGSF 2; RGWL 2; RHW; TEA

Jibran, Kahlil
See Gibran, Kahlil

Jibran, Khalil
See Gibran, Kahlil

Jiles, Paulette 1943- .... **CLC 13, 58**
See also CA 101; CANR 70, 124, 170; CP 5; CWP

Jimenez, Juan Ramon 1881-1958 .... **HLC 1; PC 7; TCLC 4, 183**
See also CA 104; 131; CANR 74; DAM MULT, POET; DLB 134, 330; EW 9; EWL 3; HW 1; MTCW 1, 2; MTFW 2005; NFS 36; RGWL 2, 3

Jimenez, Ramon
See Jimenez, Juan Ramon

Jimenez Mantecon, Juan
See Jimenez, Juan Ramon

Jimenez Mantecon, Juan Ramon
See Jimenez, Juan Ramon

Jin, Ba 1904-2005 .... **CLC 18**
See Cantu, Robert Clark
See also CA 105; 244; CWW 2; DLB 328; EWL 3

Jin, Ha 1956- .... **CLC 109, 262**
See also AMWS 18; CA 152; CANR 91, 130, 184, 223; DLB 244, 292; MTFW 2005; NFS 25; SSFS 17, 32

Jin, Xuefei
See Jin, Ha

Jin Ha
See Jin, Ha

Jodelle, Etienne 1532-1573 .... **LC 119**
See also DLB 327; GFL Beginnings to 1789

Joel, Billy
See Joel, William Martin

Joel, William Martin 1949- .... **CLC 26**
See also CA 108

John, St.
See John of Damascus, St.

John of Damascus, St. c. 675-749 ..... **CMLC 27, 95**

John of Salisbury c. 1120-1180 .. **CMLC 63, 128**

John of the Cross, St. 1542-1591 ...... **LC 18, 146**
See also RGWL 2, 3

John Paul II, Pope 1920-2005 .... **CLC 128**
See also CA 106; 133; 238

Johnson, B(ryan) S(tanley William) 1933-1973 .... **CLC 6, 9**
See also CA 9-12R; 53-56; CANR 9; CN 1; CP 1, 2; DLB 14, 40; EWL 3; RGEL 2

Johnson, Benjamin F., of Boone
See Riley, James Whitcomb

Johnson, Charles (Richard) 1948- . **BLC 1:2, 2:2; CLC 7, 51, 65, 163; SSC 160**
See also AFAW 2; AMWS 6; BW 2, 3; CA 116; CAAS 18; CANR 42, 66, 82, 129;

CN 5, 6, 7; DAM MULT; DLB 33, 278; MAL 5; MTCW 2; MTFW 2005; RGAL 4; SSFS 16

Johnson, Charles S(urgeon) 1893-1956 ..... **HR 1:3**
See also BW 1, 3; CA 125; CANR 82; DLB 51, 91

Johnson, Denis 1949- . **CLC 52, 160; SSC 56**
See also CA 117; 121; CANR 71, 99, 178; CN 4, 5, 6, 7; DLB 120

Johnson, Diane 1934- .... **CLC 5, 13, 48, 244**
See also BPFB 2; CA 41-44R; CANR 17, 40, 62, 95, 155, 198; CN 4, 5, 6, 7; DLB 350; DLBY 1980; INT CANR-17; MTCW 1

Johnson, E(mily) Pauline 1861-1913 . **NNAL**
See also CA 150; CCA 1; DAC; DAM MULT; DLB 92, 175; TCWW 2

Johnson, Eyvind (Olof Verner) 1900-1976 .. **CLC 14**
See also CA 73-76; 69-72; CANR 34, 101; DLB 259, 330; EW 12; EWL 3

Johnson, Fenton 1888-1958 .... **BLC 1:2**
See also BW 1; CA 118; 124; DAM MULT; DLB 45, 50

Johnson, Georgia Douglas (Camp) 1880-1966 .... **HR 1:3**
See also BW 1; CA 125; DLB 51, 249; WP

Johnson, Helene 1907-1995 .... **HR 1:3**
See also CA 181; DLB 51; WP

Johnson, J. R.
See James, C.L.R.

Johnson, James Weldon 1871-1938 ...... **BLC 1:2; HR 1:3; PC 24; TCLC 3, 19, 175**
See also AAYA 73; AFAW 1, 2; BW 1, 3; CA 104; 125; CANR 82; CDALB 1917-1929; CLR 32; DA3; DAM MULT, POET; DLB 51; EWL 3; EXPP; LMFS 2; MAL 5; MTCW 1, 2; MTFW 2005; NFS 22; PFS 1; RGAL 4; SATA 31; TUS

Johnson, Joyce 1935- .... **CLC 58**
See also BG 1:3; CA 125; 129; CANR 102

Johnson, Judith 1936- .... **CLC 7, 15**
See also CA 25-28R, 153; CANR 34, 85; CP 2, 3, 4, 5, 6, 7; CWP

Johnson, Judith Emlyn
See Johnson, Judith

Johnson, Lionel (Pigot) 1867-1902 .... **TCLC 19**
See also CA 117; 209; DLB 19; RGEL 2

Johnson, Marguerite Annie
See Angelou, Maya

Johnson, Mel
See Malzberg, Barry N(athaniel)

Johnson, Pamela Hansford 1912-1981 . **CLC 1, 7, 27**
See also CA 1-4R; 104; CANR 2, 28; CN 1, 2, 3; DLB 15; MTCW 1, 2; MTFW 2005; RGEL 2

Johnson, Paul 1928- .... **CLC 147**
See also BEST 89:4; CA 17-20R; CANR 34, 62, 100, 155, 197

Johnson, Paul Bede
See Johnson, Paul

Johnson, Robert **CLC 70**

Johnson, Robert 1911(?)-1938 ...... **TCLC 69**
See also BW 3; CA 174

Johnson, Samuel 1709-1784 . **LC 15, 52, 128; PC 81; WLC 3**
See also BRW 3; BRWR 1; CDBLB 1660-1789; DA; DAB; DAC; DAM MST; DLB 39, 95, 104, 142, 213; LMFS 1; RGEL 2; TEA

Johnson, Stacie
See Myers, Walter Dean

Johnson, Uwe 1934-1984 ...... **CLC 5, 10, 15, 40; TCLC 249**
See also CA 1-4R; 112; CANR 1, 39; CD-WLB 2; DLB 75; EWL 3; MTCW 1; RGWL 2, 3

Johnston, Basil H. 1929- .... **NNAL**
See also CA 69-72; CANR 11, 28, 66; DAC; DAM MULT; DLB 60

Johnston, George (Benson) 1913- ... **CLC 51**
See also CA 1-4R; CANR 5, 20; CP 1, 2, 3, 4, 5, 6, 7; DLB 88

Johnston, Jennifer (Prudence) 1930- ... **CLC 7, 150, 228**
See also CA 85-88; CANR 92; CN 4, 5, 6, 7; DLB 14

Joinville, Jean de 1224(?)-1317 ... **CMLC 38**

Jolley, Elizabeth 1923-2007 .... **CLC 46, 256, 260; SSC 19**
See also CA 127; 257; CAAS 13; CANR 59; CN 4, 5, 6, 7; DLB 325; EWL 3; RGSF 2

Jolley, Monica Elizabeth
See Jolley, Elizabeth

Jones, Arthur Llewellyn 1863-1947 . **SSC 20; TCLC 4**
See also CA 104; 179; DLB 36; HGG; RGEL 2; SUFW 1

Jones, D(ouglas) G(ordon) 1929- .... **CLC 10**
See also CA 29-32R; CANR 13, 90; CP 1, 2, 3, 4, 5, 6, 7; DLB 53

Jones, David (Michael) 1895-1974 ... **CLC 2, 4, 7, 13, 42; PC 116**
See also BRW 6; BRWS 7; CA 9-12R; 53-56; CANR 28; CDBLB 1945-1960; CP 1, 2; DLB 20, 100; EWL 3; MTCW 1; PAB; RGEL 2

Jones, David Robert 1947- .... **CLC 17**
See also CA 103; CANR 104

Jones, Diana Wynne 1934-2011 ...... **CLC 26**
See also AAYA 12; BYA 6, 7, 9, 11, 13, 16; CA 49-52; CANR 4, 26, 56, 120, 167; CLR 23, 120; DLB 161; FANT; JRDA; MAICYA 1, 2; MTFW 2005; SAAS 7; SATA 9, 70, 108, 160, 234; SFW 4; SUFW 2; YAW

Jones, Edward P. 1950- . **BLC 2:2; CLC 76, 223**
See also AAYA 71; BW 2, 3; CA 142; CANR 79, 134, 190; CSW; LNFS 2; MTFW 2005; NFS 26

Jones, Edward Paul
See Jones, Edward P.

Jones, Ernest Charles 1819-1869 ...... **NCLC 222**
See also DLB 32

Jones, Everett LeRoi
See Baraka, Amiri

Jones, Gayl 1949- . **BLC 1:2; CLC 6, 9, 131, 270**
See also AFAW 1, 2; BW 2, 3; CA 77-80; CANR 27, 66, 122; CN 4, 5, 6, 7; CSW; DA3; DAM MULT; DLB 33, 278; MAL 5; MTCW 1, 2; MTFW 2005; RGAL 4

Jones, James 1921-1977 .... **CLC 1, 3, 10, 39**
See also AITN 1, 2; AMWS 11; BPFB 2; CA 1-4R; 69-72; CANR 6; CN 1, 2; DLB 2, 143; DLBD 17; DLBY 1998; EWL 3; MAL 5; MTCW 1; RGAL 4

Jones, John J.
See Lovecraft, H. P.

Jones, LeRoi
See Baraka, Amiri

Jones, Louis B. 1953- .... **CLC 65**
See also CA 141; CANR 73

Jones, Madison 1925- .... **CLC 4**
See also CA 13-16R; CAAS 11; CANR 7, 54, 83, 158; CN 1, 2, 3, 4, 5, 6, 7; CSW; DLB 152

Jones, Madison Percy, Jr.
See Jones, Madison

Jones, Mervyn 1922-2010 .... **CLC 10, 52**
See also CA 45-48; CAAS 5; CANR 1, 91; CN 1, 2, 3, 4, 5, 6, 7; MTCW 1

Jones, Mick 1956(?)- .... **CLC 30**

5, 6, 7; DA3; DAM NOV; DLB 143; DLBY 1985; EWL 3; INT CANR-31; MAL 5; MTCW 1, 2; MTFW 2005; SATA 57

Kennedy, William Joseph
See Kennedy, William

Kennedy, X. J. 1929- ...... **CLC 8, 42; PC 93**
See also AMWS 15; CA 1-4R, 201; CAAE 201; CAAS 9; CANR 4, 30, 40, 214; CLR 27; CP 1, 2, 3, 4, 5, 6, 7; CWRI 5; DLB 5; MAICYA 2; MAICYAS 1; SAAS 22; SATA 14, 86, 130; SATA-Essay 130

Kenny, Maurice (Francis) 1929- .... **CLC 87; NNAL**
See also CA 144; CAAS 22; CANR 143; DAM MULT; DLB 175

Kent, Kathleen CLC 280
See also CA 288

Kent, Kelvin
See Kuttner, Henry

Kent, Klark
See Copeland, Stewart

Kenton, Maxwell
See Southern, Terry

Kenyon, Jane 1947-1995 .... **PC 57**
See also AAYA 63; AMWS 7; CA 118; 148; CANR 44, 69, 172; CP 6, 7; CWP; DLB 120; PFS 9, 17, 39; RGAL 4

Kenyon, Robert O.
See Kuttner, Henry

Kepler, Johannes 1571-1630 .... **LC 45**

Ker, Jill
See Conway, Jill K.

Kerkow, H. C.
See Lewton, Val

Kerouac, Jack 1922-1969 ..... **CLC 1, 2, 3, 5, 14, 61; TCLC 117; WLC**
See also AAYA 25; AITN 1; AMWC 1; AMWS 3; BG 3; BPFB 2; CA 5-8R; 25-28R; CANR 26, 54, 95, 184; CDALB 1941-1968; CP 1; CPW; DA; DA3; DAB; DAC; DAM MST, NOV, POET, POP; DLB 2, 16, 237; DLBY 1995; EWL 3; GLL 1; LAIT 1:2; LMFS 2; MAL 5; MTCW 1, 2; MTFW 2005; NFS 8; RGAL 4; TUS; WP

Kerouac, Jean-Louis le Brisde
See Kerouac, Jack

Kerouac, John
See Kerouac, Jack

Kerr, (Bridget) Jean (Collins)
1923(?)-2003 .... **CLC 22**
See also CA 5-8R; 212; CANR 7; INT CANR-7

Kerr, M. E.
See Meaker, Marijane

Kerr, Robert CLC 55

Kerrigan, (Thomas) Anthony 1918- . **CLC 4, 6**
See also CA 49-52; CAAS 11; CANR 4

Kerry, Lois
See Duncan, Lois

Kesey, Ken 1935-2001 .. **CLC 1, 3, 6, 11, 46, 64, 184; WLC 3**
See also AAYA 25; BG 1:3; BPFB 2; CA 1-4R; 204; CANR 22, 38, 66, 124; CDALB 1968-1988; CLR 170; CN 1, 2, 3, 4, 5, 6, 7; CPW; DA; DA3; DAB; DAC; DAM MST, NOV, POP; DLB 2, 16, 206; EWL 3; EXPN; LAIT 4; MAL 5; MTCW 1, 2; MTFW 2005; NFS 2; RGAL 4; SATA 66; SATA-Obit 131; TUS; YAW

Kesselring, Joseph (Otto) 1902-1967 ... **CLC 45**
See also CA 150; DAM DRAM, MST; DFS 20

Kessler, Jascha (Frederick) 1929- ..... **CLC 4**
See also CA 17-20R; CANR 8, 48, 111; CP 1

Kettelkamp, Larry (Dale) 1933- ..... **CLC 12**
See also CA 29-32R; CANR 16; SAAS 3; SATA 2

Key, Ellen (Karolina Sofia) 1849-1926 .... **TCLC 65**
See also DLB 259

Keyber, Conny
See Fielding, Henry

Keyes, Daniel 1927- .... **CLC 80**
See also AAYA 23; BYA 11; CA 17-20R, 181; CAAE 181; CANR 10, 26, 54, 74; DA; DA3; DAC; DAM MST, NOV; EXPN; LAIT 4; MTCW 2; MTFW 2005; NFS 2; SATA 37; SFW 4

Keynes, John Maynard 1883-1946 .... **TCLC 64**
See also CA 114; 162, 163; DLBD 10; MTCW 2; MTFW 2005

Khanshendel, Chiron
See Rose, Wendy

Khayyam, Omar 1048-1131 . **CMLC 11, 137; PC 8**
See also DA3; DAM POET; RGWL 2, 3; WLIT 6

Kherdian, David 1931- .... **CLC 6, 9**
See also AAYA 42; CA 21-24R, 192; CAAE 192; CAAS 2; CANR 39, 78; CLR 24; JRDA; LAIT 3; MAICYA 1, 2; SATA 16, 74; SATA-Essay 125

Khlebnikov, Velimir
See Khlebnikov, Viktor Vladimirovich

Khlebnikov, Viktor Vladimirovich
1885-1922 .... **TCLC 20**
See also CA 117; 217; DLB 295; EW 10; EWL 3; RGWL 2, 3

Khodasevich, V.F.
See Khodasevich, Vladislav

Khodasevich, Vladislav 1886-1939 .... **TCLC 15**
See also CA 115; DLB 317; EWL 3

Khodasevich, Vladislav Felitsianovich
See Khodasevich, Vladislav

Kiarostami, Abbas 1940- .... **CLC 295**
See also CA 204

Kidd, Sue Monk 1948- .... **CLC 267**
See also AAYA 72; CA 202; LNFS 1; MTFW 2005; NFS 27

Kielland, Alexander Lange 1849-1906 .... **TCLC 5**
See also CA 104; DLB 354

Kiely, Benedict 1919-2007 . **CLC 23, 43; SSC 58**
See also CA 1-4R; 257; CANR 2, 84; CN 1, 2, 3, 4, 5, 6, 7; DLB 15, 319; TCLE 1:1

Kienzle, William X. 1928-2001 .... **CLC 25**
See also CA 93-96; 203; CAAS 1; CANR 9, 31, 59, 111; CMW 4; DA3; DAM POP; INT CANR-31; MSW; MTCW 1, 2; MTFW 2005

Kierkegaard, Soren 1813-1855 .... **NCLC 34, 78, 125**
See also DLB 300; EW 6; LMFS 2; RGWL 3; TWA

Kieslowski, Krzysztof 1941-1996 .. **CLC 120**
See also CA 147; 151

Killens, John Oliver 1916-1987 .... **BLC 2:2; CLC 10**
See also BW 2; CA 77-80; 123; CAAS 2; CANR 26; CN 1, 2, 3, 4; DLB 33; EWL 3

Killigrew, Anne 1660-1685 .... **LC 4, 73**
See also DLB 131

Killigrew, Thomas 1612-1683 .... **LC 57**
See also DLB 58; RGEL 2

Kim
See Simenon, Georges

Kincaid, Jamaica 1949- . **BLC 1:2, 2:2; CLC 43, 68, 137, 234; SSC 72**
See also AAYA 13, 56; AFAW 2; AMWS 7; BRWS 7; BW 2, 3; CA 125; CANR 47, 59, 95, 133; CDALBS; CDWLB 3; CLR 63; CN 4, 5, 6, 7; DA3; DAM MULT, NOV; DLB 157, 227; DNFS 1; EWL 3; EXPS; FW; LATS 1:2; LMFS 2; MAL 5; MTCW 2; MTFW 2005; NCFS 1; NFS 3; SSFS 5, 7; TUS; WWE 1; YAW

King, Francis 1923-2011 ...... **CLC 8, 53, 145**
See also CA 1-4R; CANR 1, 33, 86; CN 1, 2, 3, 4, 5, 6, 7; DAM NOV; DLB 15, 139; MTCW 1

King, Francis Henry
See King, Francis

King, Kennedy
See Brown, George Douglas

King, Martin Luther, Jr. 1929-1968 ..... **BLC 1:2; CLC 83; WLCS**
See also BW 2, 3; CA 25-28; CANR 27, 44; CAP 2; DA; DA3; DAB; DAC; DAM MST, MULT; LAIT 3; LATS 1:2; MTCW 1, 2; MTFW 2005; SATA 14

King, Stephen 1947- ..... **CLC 12, 26, 37, 61, 113, 228, 244; SSC 17, 55**
See also AAYA 1, 17, 82; AMWS 5; BEST 90:1; BPFB 2; CA 61-64; CANR 1, 30, 52, 76, 119, 134, 168, 227; CLR 124; CN 7; CPW; DA3; DAM NOV, POP; DLB 143, 350; DLBY 1980; HGG; JRDA; LAIT 5; LNFS 1; MTCW 1, 2; MTFW 2005; RGAL 4; SATA 9, 55, 161; SSFS 30; SUFW 1, 2; WYAS 1; YAW

King, Stephen Edwin
See King, Stephen

King, Steve
See King, Stephen

King, Thomas 1943- .... **CLC 89, 171, 276; NNAL**
See also CA 144; CANR 95, 175; CCA 1; CN 6, 7; DAC; DAM MULT; DLB 175, 334; SATA 96

King, Thomas Hunt
See King, Thomas

Kingman, Lee
See Natti, Lee

Kingsley, Charles 1819-1875 .... **NCLC 35**
See also BRWS 16; CLR 77, 167; DLB 21, 32, 163, 178, 190; FANT; MAICYA 2; MAICYAS 1; RGEL 2; WCH; YABC 2

Kingsley, Henry 1830-1876 .... **NCLC 107**
See also DLB 21, 230; RGEL 2

Kingsley, Sidney 1906-1995 .... **CLC 44**
See also CA 85-88; 147; CAD; DFS 14, 19; DLB 7; MAL 5; RGAL 4

Kingsolver, Barbara 1955- . **CLC 55, 81, 130, 216, 269**
See also AAYA 15; AMWS 7; CA 129; 134; CANR 60, 96, 133, 179; CDALBS; CN 7; CPW; CSW; DA3; DAM POP; DLB 206; INT CA-134; LAIT 5; MTCW 2; MTFW 2005; NFS 5, 10, 12, 24; RGAL 4; TCLE 1:1

Kingston, Maxine Hong 1940- ... **AAL; CLC 12, 19, 58, 121, 271; SSC 136; WLCS**
See also AAYA 8, 55; AMWS 5; BPFB 2; CA 69-72; CANR 13, 38, 74, 87, 128; CDALBS; CN 6, 7; DA3; DAM MULT, NOV; DLB 173, 212, 312; DLBY 1980; EWL 3; FL 1:6; FW; INT CANR-13; LAIT 5; MAL 5; MBL; MTCW 1, 2; MTFW 2005; NFS 6; RGAL 4; SATA 53; SSFS 3; TCWW 2

Kingston, Maxine Ting Ting Hong
See Kingston, Maxine Hong

Kinnell, Galway 1927- ... **CLC 1, 2, 3, 5, 13, 29, 129; PC 26**
See also AMWS 3; CA 9-12R; CANR 10, 34, 66, 116, 138, 175; CP 1, 2, 3, 4, 5, 6,

7; DLB 5, 342; DLBY 1987; EWL 3; INT
CANR-34; MAL 5; MTCW 1, 2; MTFW
2005; PAB; PFS 9, 26, 35; RGAL 4;
TCLE 1:1; WP

Kinsella, Thomas 1928- ...... **CLC 4, 19, 138,
274; PC 69**
See also BRWS 5; CA 17-20R; CANR 15,
122; CP 1, 2, 3, 4, 5, 6, 7; DLB 27; EWL
3; MTCW 1, 2; MTFW 2005; RGEL 2;
TEA

Kinsella, William Patrick
See Kinsella, W.P.

Kinsella, W.P. 1935- .... **CLC 27, 43, 166**
See also AAYA 7, 60; BPFB 2; CA 97-100,
222; CAAE 222; CAAS 7; CANR 21, 35,
66, 75, 129; CN 4, 5, 6, 7; CPW; DAC;
DAM NOV, POP; DLB 362; FANT; INT
CANR-21; LAIT 5; MTCW 1, 2; MTFW
2005; NFS 15; RGSF 2; SSFS 30

Kinsey, Alfred C(harles) 1894-1956 .. **TCLC
91**
See also CA 115; 170; MTCW 2

Kipling, Joseph Rudyard
See Kipling, Rudyard

Kipling, Rudyard 1865-1936 . **PC 3, 91; SSC
5, 54, 110; TCLC 8, 17, 167; WLC 3**
See also AAYA 32; BRW 6; BRWC 1, 2;
BRWR 3; BYA 4; CA 105; 120; CANR
33; CDBLB 1890-1914; CLR 39, 65;
CWRI 5; DA; DA3; DAB; DAC; DAM
MST, POET; DLB 19, 34, 141, 156, 330;
EWL 3; EXPS; FANT; LAIT 3; LMFS 1;
MAICYA 1, 2; MTCW 1, 2; MTFW 2005;
NFS 21; PFS 22; RGEL 2; RGSF 2; SATA
100; SFW 4; SSFS 8, 21, 22, 32; SUFW
1; TEA; WCH; WLIT 4; YABC 2

Kircher, Athanasius 1602-1680 .... **LC 121**
See also DLB 164

Kirk, Richard
See Holdstock, Robert

Kirk, Russell (Amos) 1918-1994 . **TCLC 119**
See also AITN 1; CA 1-4R; 145; CAAS 9;
CANR 1, 20, 60; HGG; INT CANR-20;
MTCW 1, 2

Kirkham, Dinah
See Card, Orson Scott

Kirkland, Caroline M. 1801-1864 ..... **NCLC
85**
See also DLB 3, 73, 74, 250, 254; DLBD
13

Kirkup, James 1918-2009 .... **CLC 1**
See also CA 1-4R; CAAS 4; CANR 2; CP
1, 2, 3, 4, 5, 6, 7; DLB 27; SATA 12

Kirkwood, James 1930(?)-1989 .... **CLC 9**
See also AITN 2; CA 1-4R; 128; CANR 6,
40; GLL 2

Kirsch, Sarah 1935- .... **CLC 176**
See also CA 178; CWW 2; DLB 75; EWL
3

Kirshner, Sidney
See Kingsley, Sidney

Kis, Danilo 1935-1989 .... **CLC 57**
See also CA 109; 118; 129; CANR 61; CD-
WLB 4; DLB 181; EWL 3; MTCW 1;
RGSF 2; RGWL 2, 3

Kissinger, Henry A. 1923- .... **CLC 137**
See also CA 1-4R; CANR 2, 33, 66, 109;
MTCW 1

Kissinger, Henry Alfred
See Kissinger, Henry A.

Kittel, Frederick August
See Wilson, August

Kivi, Aleksis 1834-1872 .... **NCLC 30**

Kizer, Carolyn 1925- .... **CLC 15, 39, 80; PC
66**
See also CA 65-68; CAAS 5; CANR 24,
70, 134; CP 1, 2, 3, 4, 5, 6, 7; CWP; DAM
POET; DLB 5, 169; EWL 3; MAL 5;
MTCW 2; MTFW 2005; PFS 18; TCLE
1:1

Klabund 1890-1928 .... **TCLC 44**
See also CA 162; DLB 66

Klappert, Peter 1942- .... **CLC 57**
See also CA 33-36R; CSW; DLB 5

Klausner, Amos
See Oz, Amos

Klein, A. M. 1909-1972 .... **CLC 19**
See also CA 101; 37-40R; CP 1; DAB;
DAC; DAM MST; DLB 68; EWL 3;
RGEL 2; RGHL

Klein, Abraham Moses
See Klein, A. M.

Klein, Joe
See Klein, Joseph

Klein, Joseph 1946- .... **CLC 154**
See also CA 85-88; CANR 55, 164

Klein, Norma 1938-1989 .... **CLC 30**
See also AAYA 2, 35; BPFB 2; BYA 6, 7,
8; CA 41-44R; 128; CANR 15, 37; CLR
2, 19, 162; INT CANR-15; JRDA; MAI-
CYA 1, 2; SAAS 1; SATA 7, 57; WYA;
YAW

Klein, T.E.D. 1947- .... **CLC 34**
See also CA 119; CANR 44, 75, 167; HGG

Klein, Theodore Eibon Donald
See Klein, T.E.D.

Kleinzahler, August 1949- .... **CLC 320**
See also CA 125; CANR 51, 101, 153, 210

Kleist, Heinrich von 1777-1811 .... **DC 29;
NCLC 2, 37, 222; SSC 22**
See also CDWLB 2; DAM DRAM; DLB
90; EW 5; RGSF 2; RGWL 2, 3

Klima, Ivan 1931- .... **CLC 56, 172**
See also CA 25-28R; CANR 17, 50, 91;
CDWLB 4; CWW 2; DAM NOV; DLB
232; EWL 3; RGWL 3

Klimentev, Andrei Platonovich
See Klimentov, Andrei Platonovich

Klimentov, Andrei Platonovich 1899-1951 ..
SSC 42; TCLC 14
See also CA 108; 232; DLB 272; EWL 3

Klinger, Friedrich Maximilian von
1752-1831 .... **NCLC 1**
See also DLB 94

Klingsor the Magician
See Hartmann, Sadakichi

Klopstock, Friedrich Gottlieb 1724-1803 ....
NCLC 11, 225
See also DLB 97; EW 4; RGWL 2, 3

Kluge, Alexander 1932- .... **SSC 61**
See also CA 81-84; CANR 163; DLB 75

Knapp, Caroline 1959-2002 .... **CLC 99, 309**
See also CA 154; 207

Knebel, Fletcher 1911-1993 .... **CLC 14**
See also AITN 1; CA 1-4R; 140; CAAS 3;
CANR 1, 36; CN 1, 2, 3, 4, 5; SATA 36;
SATA-Obit 75

Knickerbocker, Diedrich
See Irving, Washington

Knight, Etheridge 1931-1991 .... **BLC 1:2;
CLC 40; PC 14**
See also BW 1, 3; CA 21-24R; 133; CANR
23, 82; CP 1, 2, 3, 4, 5; DAM POET; DLB
41; MTCW 2005; PFS 36;
RGAL 4; TCLE 1:1

Knight, Sarah Kemble 1666-1727 .... **LC 7**
See also DLB 24, 200

Knister, Raymond 1899-1932 .... **TCLC 56**
See also CA 186; DLB 68; RGEL 2

Knowles, John 1926-2001 . **CLC 1, 4, 10, 26**
See also AAYA 10, 72; AMWS 12; BPFB
2; BYA 3; CA 17-20R; 203; CANR 40,
74, 76, 132; CDALB 1968-1988; CLR 98;
CN 1, 2, 3, 4, 5, 6, 7; DA; DAC; DAM
MST, NOV; DLB 6; EXPN; MTCW 1, 2;
MTFW 2005; NFS 2; RGAL 4; SATA 8,
89; SATA-Obit 134; YAW

Knox, Calvin M.
See Silverberg, Robert

Knox, John c. 1505-1572 .... **LC 37**
See also DLB 132

Knye, Cassandra
See Disch, Thomas M.

Koch, C(hristopher) J(ohn) 1932- .. **CLC 42**
See also CA 127; CANR 84; CN 3, 4, 5, 6,
7; DLB 289

Koch, Christopher
See Koch, C(hristopher) J(ohn)

Koch, Kenneth 1925-2002 ...... **CLC 5, 8, 44;
PC 80**
See also AMWS 15; CA 1-4R; 207; CAD;
CANR 6, 36, 57, 97, 131; CD 5, 6; CP 1,
2, 3, 4, 5, 6, 7; DAM POET; DLB 5; INT
CANR-36; MAL 5; MTCW 2; MTFW
2005; PFS 20; SATA 65; WP

Kochanowski, Jan 1530-1584 .... **LC 10**
See also RGWL 2, 3

Kock, Charles Paul de 1794-1871 ..... **NCLC
16**

Koda Rohan
See Koda Shigeyuki

Koda Rohan
See Koda Shigeyuki

Koda Shigeyuki 1867-1947 .... **TCLC 22**
See also CA 121; 183; DLB 180

Koestler, Arthur 1905-1983 . **CLC 1, 3, 6, 8,
15, 33**
See also BRWS 1; CA 1-4R; 109; CANR 1,
33; CDBLB 1945-1960; CN 1, 2, 3;
DLBY 1983; EWL 3; MTCW 1, 2; MTFW
2005; NFS 19; RGEL 2

Kogawa, Joy 1935- .. **CLC 78, 129, 262, 268**
See also AAYA 47; CA 101; CANR 19, 62,
126; CN 6, 7; CP 1; CWP; DAC; DAM
MST, MULT; DLB 334; FW; MTCW 2;
MTFW 2005; NFS 3; SATA 99

Kogawa, Joy Nozomi
See Kogawa, Joy

Kohout, Pavel 1928- .... **CLC 13**
See also CA 45-48; CANR 3

Koizumi, Yakumo
See Hearn, Lafcadio

Kolmar, Gertrud 1894-1943 .... **TCLC 40**
See also CA 167; EWL 3; RGHL

Komunyakaa, Yusef 1947- . **BLC 2:2; BLCS;
CLC 86, 94, 207, 299; PC 51**
See also AFAW 2; AMWS 13; CA 147;
CANR 83, 164, 211; CP 6, 7; CSW; DLB
120; EWL 3; PFS 5, 20, 30, 37; RGAL 4

Konigsberg, Alan Stewart
See Allen, Woody

Konrad, George
See Konrad, Gyorgy

Konrad, George
See Konrad, Gyorgy

Konrad, Gyorgy 1933- .... **CLC 4, 10, 73**
See also CA 85-88; CANR 97, 171; CD-
WLB 4; CWW 2; DLB 232; EWL 3

Konwicki, Tadeusz 1926- ...... **CLC 8, 28, 54,
117**
See also CA 101; CAAS 9; CANR 39, 59;
CWW 2; DLB 232; EWL 3; IDFW 3;
MTCW 1

Koontz, Dean 1945- .... **CLC 78, 206**
See Koontz, Dean R.
See also AAYA 9, 31; BEST 89:3, 90:2; CA
108; CANR 19, 36, 52, 95, 138, 176;
CMW 4; CPW; DA3; DAM NOV, POP;
DLB 292; HGG; MTCW 1; MTFW 2005;
SATA 92, 165; SFW 4; SUFW 2; YAW

Koontz, Dean R.
See Koontz, Dean
See also SATA 225

Koontz, Dean Ray
See Koontz, Dean

Kopernik, Mikolaj
See Copernicus, Nicolaus
Kopit, Arthur 1937- . **CLC 1, 18, 33; DC 37**
See also AITN 1; CA 81-84; CABS 3;
CAD; CD 5, 6; DAM DRAM; DFS 7, 14,
24; DLB 7; MAL 5; MTCW 1; RGAL 4
Kopit, Arthur Lee
See Kopit, Arthur
Kopitar, Jernej (Bartholomaus) 1780-1844 .
NCLC 117
Kops, Bernard 1926- .... **CLC 4**
See also CA 5-8R; CANR 84, 159; CBD;
CN 1, 2, 3, 4, 5, 6, 7; CP 1, 2, 3, 4, 5, 6,
7; DLB 13; RGHL
Kornbluth, C(yril) M. 1923-1958 ... **TCLC 8**
See also CA 105; 160; DLB 8; SCFW 1, 2;
SFW 4
Korolenko, V.G.
See Korolenko, Vladimir G.
Korolenko, Vladimir
See Korolenko, Vladimir G.
Korolenko, Vladimir G. 1853-1921 ... **TCLC 22**
See also CA 121; DLB 277
Korolenko, Vladimir Galaktionovich
See Korolenko, Vladimir G.
Korzybski, Alfred (Habdank Skarbek)
1879-1950 .... **TCLC 61**
See also CA 123; 160
Kosinski, Jerzy 1933-1991 ... **CLC 1, 2, 3, 6, 10, 15, 53, 70**
See also AMWS 7; BPFB 2; CA 17-20R;
134; CANR 9, 46; CN 1, 2, 3, 4; DA3;
DAM NOV; DLB 2, 299; DLBY 1982;
EWL 3; HGG; MAL 5; MTCW 1, 2;
MTFW 2005; NFS 12; RGAL 4; RGHL;
TUS
Kostelanetz, Richard 1940- .... **CLC 28**
See also CA 13-16R; CAAS 8; CANR 38,
77; CN 4, 5, 6; CP 2, 3, 4, 5, 6, 7
Kostelanetz, Richard Cory
See Kostelanetz, Richard
Kostrowitzki, Wilhelm Apollinaris de
1880-1918 ....
See Apollinaire, Guillaume
Kotlowitz, Robert 1924- .... **CLC 4**
See also CA 33-36R; CANR 36
Kotzebue, August (Friedrich Ferdinand) von
1761-1819 .... **NCLC 25**
See also DLB 94
Kotzwinkle, William 1938- .... **CLC 5, 14, 35**
See also BPFB 2; CA 45-48; CANR 3, 44,
84, 129; CLR 6; CN 7; DLB 173; FANT;
MAICYA 1, 2; SATA 24, 70, 146; SFW
4; SUFW 2; YAW
Kowna, Stancy
See Szymborska, Wislawa
Kozol, Jonathan 1936- .... **CLC 17**
See also AAYA 46; CA 61-64; CANR 16,
45, 96, 178; MTFW 2005
Kozoll, Michael 1940(?)- .... **CLC 35**
Krakauer, Jon 1954- .... **CLC 248**
See also AAYA 24; AMWS 18; BYA 9; CA
153; CANR 131, 212; MTFW 2005;
SATA 108
Kramer, Kathryn 19(?)- .... **CLC 34**
Kramer, Larry 1935- .... **CLC 42; DC 8**
See also CA 124; 126; CANR 60, 132;
DAM POP; DLB 249; GLL 1
Krasicki, Ignacy 1735-1801 .... **NCLC 8**
Krasinski, Zygmunt 1812-1859 ...... **NCLC 4**
See also RGWL 2, 3
Kraus, Karl 1874-1936 .... **TCLC 5, 263**
See also CA 104; 216; DLB 118; EWL 3
Kraynay, Anton
See Gippius, Zinaida
Kreve (Mickevicius), Vincas 1882-1954 ....
TCLC 27
See also CA 170; DLB 220; EWL 3

Kristeva, Julia 1941- .... **CLC 77, 140**
See also CA 154; CANR 99, 173; DLB 242;
EWL 3; FW; LMFS 2
Kristofferson, Kris 1936- .... **CLC 26**
See also CA 104
Krizanc, John 1956- .... **CLC 57**
See also CA 187
Krleza, Miroslav 1893-1981 ...... **CLC 8, 114**
See also CA 97-100; 105; CANR 50; CD-
WLB 4; DLB 147; EW 11; RGWL 2, 3
Kroetsch, Robert 1927-2011 . **CLC 5, 23, 57, 132, 286**
See also CA 17-20R; CANR 8, 38; CCA 1;
CN 2, 3, 4, 5, 6, 7; CP 6, 7; DAC; DAM
POET; DLB 53; MTCW 1
Kroetsch, Robert Paul
See Kroetsch, Robert
Kroetz, Franz
See Kroetz, Franz Xaver
Kroetz, Franz Xaver 1946- .... **CLC 41**
See also CA 130; CANR 142; CWW 2;
EWL 3
Kroker, Arthur (W.) 1945- .... **CLC 77**
See also CA 161
Kroniuk, Lisa
See Berton, Pierre (Francis de Marigny)
Kropotkin, Peter 1842-1921 .... **TCLC 36**
See also CA 119; 219; DLB 277
Kropotkin, Peter Alekseievich
See Kropotkin, Peter
Kropotkin, Petr Alekseevich
See Kropotkin, Peter
Krotkov, Yuri 1917-1981 .... **CLC 19**
See also CA 102
Krumb
See Crumb, R.
Krumgold, Joseph (Quincy) 1908-1980 ....
CLC 12
See also BYA 1, 2; CA 9-12R; 101; CANR
7; MAICYA 1, 2; SATA 1, 48; SATA-Obit
23; YAW
Krumwitz
See Crumb, R.
Krutch, Joseph Wood 1893-1970 .... **CLC 24**
See also ANW; CA 1-4R; 25-28R; CANR
4; DLB 63, 206, 275
Krutzch, Gus
See Eliot, T. S.
Krylov, Ivan Andreevich 1768(?)-1844 ....
NCLC 1
See also DLB 150
Kubin, Alfred (Leopold Isidor) 1877-1959 ..
TCLC 23
See also CA 112; 149; CANR 104; DLB 81
Kubrick, Stanley 1928-1999 .... **CLC 16; TCLC 112**
See also AAYA 30; CA 81-84; 177; CANR
33; DLB 26
Kueng, Hans
See Kung, Hans
Kumin, Maxine 1925- .. **CLC 5, 13, 28, 164; PC 15**
See also AITN 2; AMWS 4; ANW; CA
1-4R, 271; CAAE 271; CAAS 8; CANR
1, 21, 69, 115, 140; CP 2, 3, 4, 5, 6, 7;
CWP; DA3; DAM POET; DLB 5; EWL
3; EXPP; MTCW 1, 2; MTFW 2005;
PAB; PFS 18, 38; SATA 12
Kumin, Maxine Winokur
See Kumin, Maxine
Kundera, Milan 1929- . **CLC 4, 9, 19, 32, 68, 115, 135, 234; SSC 24**
See also AAYA 2, 62; BPFB 2; CA 85-88;
CANR 19, 52, 74, 144, 223; CDWLB 4;
CWW 2; DA3; DAM NOV; DLB 232;
EW 13; EWL 3; MTCW 1, 2; MTFW
2005; NFS 18, 27; RGSF 2; RGWL 3;
SSFS 10

Kunene, Mazisi 1930-2006 .... **CLC 85**
See also BW 1, 3; CA 125; 252; CANR 81;
CP 1, 6, 7; DLB 117
Kunene, Mazisi Raymond
See Kunene, Mazisi
Kunene, Mazisi Raymond Fakazi Mngoni
See Kunene, Mazisi
Kung, Hans
See Kung, Hans
Kung, Hans 1928- .... **CLC 130**
See also CA 53-56; CANR 66, 134; MTCW
1, 2; MTFW 2005
Kunikida, Tetsuo
See Kunikida Doppo
Kunikida Doppo 1869(?)-1908 ...... **TCLC 99**
See also DLB 180; EWL 3
Kunikida Tetsuo
See Kunikida Doppo
Kunitz, Stanley 1905-2006 .... **CLC 6, 11, 14, 148, 293; PC 19**
See also AMWS 3; CA 41-44R; 250; CANR
26, 57, 98; CP 1, 2, 3, 4, 5, 6, 7; DA3;
DLB 48; INT CANR-26; MAL 5; MTCW
1, 2; MTFW 2005; PFS 11; RGAL 4
Kunitz, Stanley Jasspon
See Kunitz, Stanley
Kunt, Klerk
See Copeland, Stewart
Kunze, Reiner 1933- .... **CLC 10**
See also CA 93-96; CWW 2; DLB 75; EWL
3
Kuprin, Aleksander Ivanovich 1870-1938 ...
TCLC 5
See also CA 104; 182; DLB 295; EWL 3
Kuprin, Aleksandr Ivanovich
See Kuprin, Aleksander Ivanovich
Kuprin, Alexandr Ivanovich
See Kuprin, Aleksander Ivanovich
Kureishi, Hanif 1954- ..... **CLC 64, 135, 284; DC 26**
See also BRWS 11; CA 139; CANR 113,
197; CBD; CD 5, 6; CN 6, 7; DLB 194,
245, 352; GLL 2; IDFW 4; WLIT 4;
WWE 1
Kurosawa, Akira 1910-1998 .... **CLC 16, 119**
See also AAYA 11, 64; CA 101; 170; CANR
46; DAM MULT
Kushner, Tony 1956- ...... **CLC 81, 203, 297; DC 10**
See also AAYA 61; AMWS 9; CA 144;
CAD; CANR 74, 130; CD 5, 6; DA3;
DAM DRAM; DFS 5; DLB 228; EWL 3;
GLL 1; LAIT 5; MAL 5; MTCW 2;
MTFW 2005; RGAL 4; RGHL; SATA 160
Kuttner, Henry 1915-1958 .... **TCLC 10**
See also CA 107; 157; DLB 8; FANT;
SCFW 1, 2; SFW 4
Kutty, Madhavi
See Das, Kamala
Kuzma, Greg 1944- .... **CLC 7**
See also CA 33-36R; CANR 70
Kuzmin, Mikhail (Alekseevich)
1872(?)-1936 .... **TCLC 40**
See also CA 170; DLB 295; EWL 3
Kyd, Thomas 1558-1594 . **DC 3; LC 22, 125**
See also BRW 1; DAM DRAM; DFS 21;
DLB 62; IDTP; LMFS 1; RGEL 2; TEA;
WLIT 3
Kyprianos, Iossif
See Samarakis, Antonis
L. S.
See Stephen, Sir Leslie
Labe, Louise 1521-1566 .... **LC 120**
See also DLB 327
Labrunie, Gerard
See Nerval, Gerard de
La Bruyere, Jean de 1645-1696 . **LC 17, 168**
See also DLB 268; EW 3; GFL Beginnings
to 1789

Larsen, Nella 1893(?)-1963 .. **BLC 1:2; CLC 37; HR 1:3; TCLC 200**
See also AFAW 1, 2; AMWS 18; BW 1; CA 125; CANR 83; DAM MULT; DLB 51; FW; LATS 1:1; LMFS 2

Larson, Charles R(aymond) 1938- . **CLC 31**
See also CA 53-56; CANR 4, 121

Larson, Jonathan 1960-1996 .... **CLC 99**
See also AAYA 28; CA 156; DFS 23; MTFW 2005

La Sale, Antoine de c. 1386-1460(?) . **LC 104**
See also DLB 208

Lasarus, B. B.
See Breytenbach, Breyten

Las Casas, Bartolome de 1474-1566 . **HLCS; LC 31, 203**
See also DLB 318; LAW; WLIT 1

Lasch, Christopher 1932-1994 ...... **CLC 102**
See also CA 73-76; 144; CANR 25, 118; DLB 246; MTCW 1, 2; MTFW 2005

Lasker-Schueler, Else 1869-1945 .. **TCLC 57**
See also CA 183; DLB 66, 124; EWL 3

Lasker-Schuler, Else
See Lasker-Schueler, Else

Laski, Harold J(oseph) 1893-1950 ..... **TCLC 79**
See also CA 188

Latham, Jean Lee 1902-1995 .... **CLC 12**
See also AITN 1; BYA 1; CA 5-8R; CANR 7, 84; CLR 50; MAICYA 1, 2; SATA 2, 68; YAW

Latham, Mavis
See Clark, Mavis Thorpe

Lathen, Emma
See Hennissart, Martha

Lathrop, Francis
See Leiber, Fritz (Reuter, Jr.)

Lattany, Kristin
See Lattany, Kristin Hunter

Lattany, Kristin Elaine Eggleston Hunter
See Lattany, Kristin Hunter

Lattany, Kristin Hunter 1931-2008 . **CLC 35**
See also AITN 1; BW 1; BYA 3; CA 13-16R; CANR 13, 108; CLR 3; CN 1, 2, 3, 4, 5, 6; DLB 33; INT CANR-13; MAICYA 1, 2; SAAS 10; SATA 12, 132; YAW

Lattimore, Richmond (Alexander) 1906-1984 .... **CLC 3**
See also CA 1-4R; 112; CANR 1; CP 1, 2, 3; MAL 5

Laughlin, James 1914-1997 .... **CLC 49**
See also CA 21-24R; 162; CAAS 22; CANR 9, 47; CP 1, 2, 3, 4, 5, 6; DLB 48; DLBY 1996, 1997

Launko, Okinba
See Osofisan, Femi

Laurence, Jean Margaret Wemyss
See Laurence, Margaret

Laurence, Margaret 1926-1987 .... **CLC 3, 6, 13, 50, 62; SSC 7**
See also BYA 13; CA 5-8R; 121; CANR 33; CN 1, 2, 3, 4; DAC; DAM MST; DLB 53; EWL 3; FW; MTCW 1, 2; MTFW 2005; NFS 11; RGEL 2; RGSF 2; SATA-Obit 50; TCWW 2

Laurent, Antoine 1952- .... **CLC 50**

Lauscher, Hermann
See Hesse, Hermann

Lautreamont 1846-1870 .... **NCLC 12, 194; SSC 14**
See also DLB 217; GFL 1789 to the Present; RGWL 2, 3

Lautreamont, Isidore Lucien Ducasse
See Lautreamont

Lavater, Johann Kaspar 1741-1801 .. **NCLC 142**
See also DLB 97

Laverty, Donald
See Blish, James

Lavin, Mary 1912-1996 . **CLC 4, 18, 99; SSC 4, 67, 137**
See also CA 9-12R; 151; CANR 33; CN 1, 2, 3, 4, 5, 6; DLB 15, 319; FW; MTCW 1; RGEL 2; RGSF 2; SSFS 23

Lavond, Paul Dennis
See Kornbluth, C(yril) M.; Pohl, Frederik

Lawes, Henry 1596-1662 .... **LC 113**
See also DLB 126

Lawler, Ray
See Lawler, Raymond Evenor

Lawler, Raymond Evenor 1922- ..... **CLC 58**
See also CA 103; CD 5, 6; DLB 289; RGEL 2

Lawrence, D. H. 1885-1930 . **DC 44; PC 54; SSC 4, 19, 73, 149; TCLC 2, 9, 16, 33, 48, 61, 93; WLC 3**
See also BPFB 2; BRW 7; BRWR 2; CA 104; 121; CANR 131; CDBLB 1914-1945; DA; DA3; DAB; DAC; DAM MST, NOV, POET; DLB 10, 19, 36, 98, 162, 195; EWL 3; EXPP; EXPS; GLL 1; LAIT 2, 3; MTCW 1, 2; MTFW 2005; NFS 18, 26; PFS 6; RGEL 2; RGSF 2; SSFS 2, 6; TEA; WLIT 4; WP

Lawrence, David Herbert Richards
See Lawrence, D. H.

Lawrence, T. E. 1888-1935 ... **TCLC 18, 204**
See also BRWS 2; CA 115; 167; DLB 195, 366

Lawrence, Thomas Edward
See Lawrence, T. E.

Lawrence of Arabia
See Lawrence, T. E.

Lawson, Henry (Archibald Hertzberg) 1867-1922 .... **SSC 18; TCLC 27**
See also CA 120; 181; DLB 230; RGEL 2; RGSF 2

Lawton, Dennis
See Faust, Frederick

Laxness, Halldor (Kiljan)
See Gudjonsson, Halldor Kiljan

Layamon fl. c. 1200- .... **CMLC 10, 105**
See also DLB 146; RGEL 2

Laye, Camara 1928-1980 . **BLC 1:2; CLC 4, 38**
See also AFW; BW 1; CA 85-88; 97-100; CANR 25; DAM MULT; DLB 360; EWL 3; MTCW 1, 2; WLIT 2

Layton, Irving 1912-2006 .... **CLC 2, 15, 164**
See also CA 1-4R; 247; CANR 2, 33, 43, 66, 129; CP 1, 2, 3, 4, 5, 6, 7; DAC; DAM MST, POET; DLB 88; EWL 3; MTCW 1, 2; PFS 12; RGEL 2

Layton, Irving Peter
See Layton, Irving

Lazarus, Emma 1849-1887 ..... **NCLC 8, 109**
See also PFS 37

Lazarus, Felix
See Cable, George Washington

Lazarus, Henry
See Slavitt, David R.

Lea, Joan
See Neufeld, John (Arthur)

Leacock, Stephen (Butler) 1869-1944 ... **SSC 39; TCLC 2, 263**
See also CA 104; 141; CANR 80; DAC; DAM MST; DLB 92; EWL 3; MTCW 2; MTFW 2005; RGEL 2; RGSF 2

Lead, Jane Ward 1623-1704 .... **LC 72**
See also DLB 131

Leapor, Mary 1722-1746 .... **LC 80; PC 85**
See also DLB 109

Lear, Edward 1812-1888 .... **NCLC 3; PC 65**
See also AAYA 48; BRW 5; CLR 1, 75, 169; DLB 32, 163, 166; MAICYA 1, 2; RGEL 2; SATA 18, 100; WCH; WP

Lear, Norman (Milton) 1922- .... **CLC 12**
See also CA 73-76

Least Heat-Moon, William
See Heat-Moon, William Least

Leautaud, Paul 1872-1956 .... **TCLC 83**
See also CA 203; DLB 65; GFL 1789 to the Present

Leavis, F(rank) R(aymond) 1895-1978 . **CLC 24**
See also BRW 7; CA 21-24R; 77-80; CANR 44; DLB 242; EWL 3; MTCW 1, 2; RGEL 2

Leavitt, David 1961- .... **CLC 34**
See also CA 116; 122; CANR 50, 62, 101, 134, 177; CPW; DA3; DAM POP; DLB 130, 350; GLL 1; INT CA-122; MAL 5; MTCW 2; MTFW 2005

Leblanc, Maurice (Marie Emile) 1864-1941 .... **TCLC 49**
See also CA 110; CMW 4

Lebowitz, Fran 1951(?)- .... **CLC 11, 36**
See also CA 81-84; CANR 14, 60, 70; INT CANR-14; MTCW 1

Lebowitz, Frances Ann
See Lebowitz, Fran

Lebrecht, Peter
See Tieck, (Johann) Ludwig

le Cagat, Benat
See Whitaker, Rod

le Carre, John
See le Carre, John

le Carre, John 1931- .... **CLC 9, 15**
See also AAYA 42; BEST 89:4; BPFB 2; BRWR 3; BRWS 2; CA 5-8R; CANR 13, 33, 59, 107, 132, 172; CDBLB 1960 to Present; CMW 4; CN 1, 2, 3, 4, 5, 6, 7; CPW; DA3; DAM POP; DLB 87; EWL 3; MSW; MTCW 1, 2; MTFW 2005; RGEL 2; TEA

Le Clezio, J. M.G. 1940- . **CLC 31, 155, 280; SSC 122**
See also CA 116; 128; CANR 147; CWW 2; DLB 83; EWL 3; GFL 1789 to the Present; RGSF 2

Le Clezio, Jean Marie Gustave
See Le Clezio, J. M.G.

Leconte de Lisle, Charles-Marie-Rene 1818-1894 .... **NCLC 29**
See also DLB 217; EW 6; GFL 1789 to the Present

Le Coq, Monsieur
See Simenon, Georges

Leduc, Violette 1907-1972 .... **CLC 22**
See also CA 13-14; 33-36R; CANR 69; CAP 1; EWL 3; GFL 1789 to the Present; GLL 1

Ledwidge, Francis 1887(?)-1917 ... **TCLC 23**
See also CA 123; 203; DLB 20

Lee, Andrea 1953- .... **BLC 1:2; CLC 36**
See also BW 1, 3; CA 125; CANR 82, 190; DAM MULT

Lee, Andrew
See Auchincloss, Louis

Lee, Chang-rae 1965- ...... **CLC 91, 268, 274**
See also CA 148; CANR 89; CN 7; DLB 312; LATS 1:2

Lee, Don L.
See Madhubuti, Haki R.

Lee, George W(ashington) 1894-1976 .. **BLC 1:2; CLC 52**
See also BW 1; CA 125; CANR 83; DAM MULT; DLB 51

Lee, Harper 1926- .. **CLC 12, 60, 194; WLC 4**
See also AAYA 13; AMWS 8; BPFB 2; BYA 3; CA 13-16R; CANR 51, 128; CDALB 1941-1968; CLR 169; CSW; DA; DA3; DAB; DAC; DAM MST, NOV; DLB 6; EXPN; LAIT 3; MAL 5; MTCW 1, 2; MTFW 2005; NFS 2, 32; SATA 11; WYA; YAW

Lee, Helen Elaine 1959(?)- .... **CLC 86**
   See also CA 148
Lee, John CLC 70
Lee, Julian
   See Latham, Jean Lee
Lee, Larry
   See Lee, Lawrence
Lee, Laurie 1914-1997 .... **CLC 90**
   See also CA 77-80; 158; CANR 33, 73; CP
   1, 2, 3, 4, 5, 6; CPW; DAB; DAM POP;
   DLB 27; MTCW 1; RGEL 2
Lee, Lawrence 1941-1990 .... **CLC 34**
   See also CA 131; CANR 43
Lee, Li-Young 1957- .... **CLC 164; PC 24**
   See also AMWS 15; CA 153; CANR 118,
   206; CP 6, 7; DLB 165, 312; LMFS 2;
   PFS 11, 15, 17, 37
Lee, Manfred B. 1905-1971 .... **CLC 11**
   See also CA 1-4R; 29-32R; CANR 2, 150;
   CMW 4; DLB 137
Lee, Manfred Bennington
   See Lee, Manfred B.
Lee, Nathaniel 1645(?)-1692 .... **LC 103**
   See also DLB 80; RGEL 2
Lee, Nelle Harper
   See Lee, Harper
Lee, Shelton Jackson
   See Lee, Spike
Lee, Sophia 1750-1824 .... **NCLC 191**
   See also DLB 39
Lee, Spike 1957(?)- .... **BLCS; CLC 105, 281**
   See also AAYA 4, 29; BW 2, 3; CA 125;
   CANR 42, 164; DAM MULT
Lee, Stan 1922- .... **CLC 17**
   See also AAYA 5, 49; CA 108; 111; CANR
   129; INT CA-111; MTFW 2005
Lee, Tanith 1947- .... **CLC 46**
   See also AAYA 15; CA 37-40R; CANR 53,
   102, 145, 170; DLB 261; FANT; SATA 8,
   88, 134, 185; SFW 4; SUFW 1, 2; YAW
Lee, Vernon
   See Paget, Violet
Lee, William
   See Burroughs, William S.
Lee, Willy
   See Burroughs, William S.
Lee-Hamilton, Eugene (Jacob) 1845-1907 ...
   TCLC 22
   See also CA 117; 234
Leet, Judith 1935- .... **CLC 11**
   See also CA 187
Le Fanu, Joseph Sheridan 1814-1873 ....
   NCLC 9, 58; SSC 14, 84
   See also CMW 4; DA3; DAM POP; DLB
   21, 70, 159, 178; GL 3; HGG; RGEL 2;
   RGSF 2; SUFW 1
Leffland, Ella 1931- .... **CLC 19**
   See also CA 29-32R; CANR 35, 78, 82;
   DLBY 1984; INT CANR-35; SATA 65;
   SSFS 24
Leger, Alexis
   See Leger, Alexis Saint-Leger
Leger, Alexis Saint-Leger 1887-1975 ... **CLC
   4, 11, 46; PC 23**
   See also CA 13-16R; 61-64; CANR 43;
   DAM POET; DLB 258, 331; EW 10;
   EWL 3; GFL 1789 to the Present; MTCW
   1; RGWL 2, 3
Leger, Marie-Rene Auguste Alexis
   Saint-Leger
   See Leger, Alexis Saint-Leger
Leger, Saintleger
   See Leger, Alexis Saint-Leger
Le Guin, Ursula K. 1929- .... **CLC 8, 13, 22,
   45, 71, 136, 310; SSC 12, 69**
   See also AAYA 9, 27, 84; AITN 1; BPFB 2;
   BYA 5, 8, 11, 14; CA 21-24R; CANR 9,
   32, 52, 74, 132, 192; CDALB 1968-1988;
   CLR 3, 28, 91, 173; CN 2, 3, 4, 5, 6, 7;

CPW; DA3; DAB; DAC; DAM MST,
POP; DLB 8, 52, 256, 275; EXPS; FANT;
FW; INT CANR-32; JRDA; LAIT 5;
MAICYA 1, 2; MAL 5; MTCW 1, 2;
MTFW 2005; NFS 6, 9; SATA 4, 52, 99,
149, 194; SCFW 1, 2; SFW 4; SSFS 2;
SUFW 1, 2; WYA; YAW
Le Guin, Ursula Kroeber
   See Le Guin, Ursula K.
Lehane, Dennis 1965- .... **CLC 320**
   See also AAYA 56; CA 154; CANR 72, 112,
   136, 168, 219; LNFS 1; MTFW 2005
Lehmann, Rosamond (Nina) 1901-1990 ......
   CLC 5
   See also CA 77-80; 131; CANR 8, 73; CN
   1, 2, 3, 4; DLB 15; MTCW 2; RGEL 2;
   RHW
Leiber, Fritz (Reuter, Jr.) 1910-1992 ... **CLC
   25**
   See also AAYA 65; BPFB 2; CA 45-48; 139;
   CANR 2, 40, 86; CN 2, 3, 4, 5; DLB 8;
   FANT; HGG; MTCW 1, 2; MTFW 2005;
   SATA 45; SATA-Obit 73; SCFW 1, 2;
   SFW 4; SUFW 1, 2
Leibniz, Gottfried Wilhelm von 1646-1716 .
   LC 35, 196
   See also DLB 168
Leino, Eino
   See Lonnbohm, Armas Eino Leopold
Leiris, Michel (Julien) 1901-1990 ... **CLC 61**
   See also CA 119; 128; 132; EWL 3; GFL
   1789 to the Present
Leithauser, Brad 1953- .... **CLC 27**
   See also CA 107; CANR 27, 81, 171; CP 5,
   6, 7; DLB 120, 282
le Jars de Gournay, Marie
   See de Gournay, Marie le Jars
Lelchuk, Alan 1938- .... **CLC 5**
   See also CA 45-48; CAAS 20; CANR 1,
   70, 152; CN 3, 4, 5, 6, 7
Lem, Stanislaw 1921-2006 .... **CLC 8, 15, 40,
   149**
   See also AAYA 75; CA 105; 249; CAAS 1;
   CANR 32; CWW 2; MTCW 1; SCFW 1,
   2; SFW 4
Lemann, Nancy (Elise) 1956- .... **CLC 39**
   See also CA 118; 136; CANR 121
Lemonnier, (Antoine Louis) Camille
   1844-1913 .... **TCLC 22**
   See also CA 121
Lenau, Nikolaus 1802-1850 .... **NCLC 16**
L'Engle, Madeleine 1918-2007 .... **CLC 12**
   See also AAYA 28; AITN 2; BPFB 2; BYA
   2, 4, 5, 7; CA 1-4R; 264; CANR 3, 21,
   39, 66, 107, 207; CLR 1, 14, 57, 172;
   CPW; CWRI 5; DA3; DAM POP; DLB
   52; JRDA; MAICYA 1, 2; MTCW 1, 2;
   MTFW 2005; NFS 32; SAAS 15; SATA
   1, 27, 75, 128; SATA-Obit 186; SFW 4;
   WYA; YAW
L'Engle, Madeleine Camp Franklin
   See L'Engle, Madeleine
Lengyel, Jozsef 1896-1975 .... **CLC 7**
   See also CA 85-88; 57-60; CANR 71;
   RGSF 2
Lenin 1870-1924 .... **TCLC 67**
   See also CA 121; 168
Lenin, N.
   See Lenin
Lenin, Nikolai
   See Lenin
Lenin, V. I.
   See Lenin
Lenin, Vladimir I.
   See Lenin
Lenin, Vladimir Ilyich
   See Lenin
Lennon, John 1940-1980 .... **CLC 12, 35**
   See also CA 102; SATA 114

Lennon, John Ono
   See Lennon, John
Lennox, Charlotte 1729(?)-1804 .. **NCLC 23,
   134**
   See also BRWS 17; DLB 39; RGEL 2
Lentricchia, Frank, Jr.
   See Lentricchia, Frank
Lentricchia, Frank 1940- .... **CLC 34**
   See also CA 25-28R; CANR 19, 106, 148;
   DLB 246
Lenz, Gunter CLC 65
Lenz, Jakob Michael Reinhold 1751-1792 ..
   LC 100
   See also DLB 94; RGWL 2, 3
Lenz, Siegfried 1926- .... **CLC 27; SSC 33**
   See also CA 89-92; CANR 80, 149; CWW
   2; DLB 75; EWL 3; RGSF 2; RGWL 2, 3
Leon, David
   See Jacob, (Cyprien-)Max
Leon, Luis de 1527-1591 .... **LC 182**
   See also DLB 318
Leonard, Dutch
   See Leonard, Elmore
Leonard, Elmore 1925- ...... **CLC 28, 34, 71,
   120, 222**
   See also AAYA 22, 59; AITN 1; BEST 89:1,
   90:4; BPFB 2; CA 81-84; CANR 12, 28,
   53, 76, 96, 133, 176, 219; CMW 4; CN 5,
   6, 7; CPW; DA3; DAM POP; DLB 173,
   226; INT CANR-28; MSW; MTCW 1, 2;
   MTFW 2005; RGAL 4; SATA 163;
   TCWW 1, 2
Leonard, Elmore John, Jr.
   See Leonard, Elmore
Leonard, Hugh 1926-2009 .... **CLC 19**
   See also CA 102; 283; CANR 78, 140;
   CBD; CD 5, 6; DFS 13, 24; DLB 13; INT
   CA-102
Leonard, Tom 1944- .... **CLC 289**
   See also CA 77-80; CANR 13, 31; CP 2, 3,
   4, 5, 6, 7
Leonov, Leonid 1899-1994 .... **CLC 92**
   See also CA 129; CANR 76; DAM NOV;
   DLB 272; EWL 3; MTCW 1, 2; MTFW
   2005
Leonov, Leonid Maksimovich
   See Leonov, Leonid
Leonov, Leonid Maximovich
   See Leonov, Leonid
Leopardi, (Conte) Giacomo 1798-1837 ....
   NCLC 22, 129; PC 37
   See also EW 5; RGWL 2, 3; WLIT 7; WP
Le Reveler
   See Artaud, Antonin
Lerman, Eleanor 1952- .... **CLC 9**
   See also CA 85-88; CANR 69, 124, 184
Lerman, Rhoda 1936- .... **CLC 56**
   See also CA 49-52; CANR 70
Lermontov, Mikhail Iur'evich
   See Lermontov, Mikhail Yuryevich
Lermontov, Mikhail Yuryevich 1814-1841 ..
   NCLC 5, 47, 126; PC 18
   See also DLB 205; EW 6; RGWL 2, 3;
   TWA
Leroux, Gaston 1868-1927 .... **TCLC 25**
   See also CA 108; 136; CANR 69; CMW 4;
   MTFW 2005; NFS 20; SATA 65
Lesage, Alain-Rene 1668-1747 .... **LC 2, 28**
   See also DLB 313; EW 3; GFL Beginnings
   to 1789; RGWL 2, 3
Leskov, N(ikolai) S(emenovich) 1831-1895 ..
   See Leskov, Nikolai (Semyonovich)
Leskov, Nikolai (Semyonovich) 1831-1895 ..
   NCLC 25, 174; SSC 34, 96
   See also DLB 238
Leskov, Nikolai Semenovich
   See Leskov, Nikolai (Semyonovich)
Lesser, Milton
   See Marlowe, Stephen

Lessing, Doris 1919- . **CLC 1, 2, 3, 6, 10, 15, 22, 40, 94, 170, 254; SSC 6, 61, 160; WLCS**
See also AAYA 57; AFW; BRWS 1; CA 9-12R; CAAS 14; CANR 33, 54, 76, 122, 179; CBD; CD 5, 6; CDBLB 1960 to Present; CN 1, 2, 3, 4, 5, 6, 7; CWD; DA; DA3; DAB; DAC; DAM MST, NOV; DFS 20; DLB 15, 139; DLBY 1985; EWL 3; EXPS; FL 1:6; FW; LAIT 4; MTCW 1, 2; MTFW 2005; NFS 27, 38; RGEL 2; RGSF 2; SFW 4; SSFS 1, 12, 20, 26, 30, 35; TEA; WLIT 2, 4

Lessing, Doris May
See Lessing, Doris

Lessing, Gotthold Ephraim 1729-1781 ... **DC 26; LC 8, 124, 162**
See also CDWLB 2; DLB 97; EW 4; RGWL 2, 3

Lester, Julius 1939- .... **BLC 2:2**
See also AAYA 12, 51; BW 2; BYA 3, 9, 11, 12; CA 17-20R; CANR 8, 23, 43, 129, 174; CLR 2, 41, 143; JRDA; MAICYA 1, 2; MAICYAS 1; MTFW 2005; SATA 12, 74, 112, 157; YAW

Lester, Richard 1932- .... **CLC 20**

Lethem, Jonathan 1964- .... **CLC 295**
See also AAYA 43; AMWS 18; CA 150; CANR 80, 138, 165; CN 7; MTFW 2005; SFW 4

Lethem, Jonathan Allen
See Lethem, Jonathan

Letts, Tracy 1965- .... **CLC 280**
See also CA 223; CANR 209

Levenson, Jay CLC 70

Lever, Charles (James) 1806-1872 .... **NCLC 23**
See also DLB 21; RGEL 2

Leverson, Ada Esther 1862(?)-1933(?) .... **TCLC 18**
See also CA 117; 202; DLB 153; RGEL 2

Levertov, Denise 1923-1997 . **CLC 1, 2, 3, 5, 8, 15, 28, 66; PC 11**
See also AMWS 3; CA 1-4R, 178; 163; CAAE 178; CAAS 19; CANR 3, 29, 50, 108; CDALBS; CP 1, 2, 3, 4, 5, 6; CWP; DAM POET; DLB 5, 165, 342; EWL 3; EXPP; FW; INT CANR-29; MAL 5; MTCW 1, 2; PAB; PFS 7, 17, 31; RGAL 4; RGHL; TUS; WP

Levi, Carlo 1902-1975 .... **TCLC 125**
See also CA 65-68; 53-56; CANR 10; EWL 3; RGWL 2, 3

Levi, Jonathan CLC 76
See also CA 197

Levi, Peter (Chad Tigar) 1931-2000 .... **CLC 41**
See also CA 5-8R; 187; CANR 34, 80; CP 1, 2, 3, 4, 5, 6, 7; DLB 40

Levi, Primo 1919-1987 ..... **CLC 37, 50; SSC 12, 122; TCLC 109**
See also CA 13-16R; 122; CANR 12, 33, 61, 70, 132, 171; DLB 177, 299; EWL 3; MTCW 1, 2; MTFW 2005; RGHL; RGWL 2, 3; WLIT 7

Levin, Ira 1929-2007 .... **CLC 3, 6**
See also CA 21-24R; 266; CANR 17, 44, 74, 139; CMW 4; CN 1, 2, 3, 4, 5, 6, 7; CPW; DA3; DAM POP; HGG; MTCW 1, 2; MTFW 2005; SATA 66; SATA-Obit 187; SFW 4

Levin, Ira Marvin
See Levin, Ira

Levin, Meyer 1905-1981 .... **CLC 7**
See also AITN 1; CA 9-12R; 104; CANR 15; CN 1, 2, 3; DAM POP; DLB 9, 28; DLBY 1981; MAL 5; RGHL; SATA 21; SATA-Obit 27

Levine, Albert Norman
See Levine, Norman

Levine, Norman 1923-2005 .... **CLC 54**
See also CA 73-76; 240; CAAS 23; CANR 14, 70; CN 1, 2, 3, 4, 5, 6, 7; CP 1; DLB 88

Levine, Norman Albert
See Levine, Norman

Levine, Philip 1928- . **CLC 2, 4, 5, 9, 14, 33, 118; PC 22**
See also AMWS 5; CA 9-12R; CANR 9, 37, 52, 116, 156; CP 1, 2, 3, 4, 5, 6, 7; DAM POET; DLB 5; EWL 3; MAL 5; PFS 8

Levinson, Deirdre 1931- .... **CLC 49**
See also CA 73-76; CANR 70

Levi-Strauss, Claude 1908-2008 ..... **CLC 38, 302**
See also CA 1-4R; CANR 6, 32, 57; DLB 242; EWL 3; GFL 1789 to the Present; MTCW 1, 2; TWA

Levitin, Sonia 1934- .... **CLC 17**
See also AAYA 13, 48; CA 29-32R; CANR 14, 32, 79, 182; CLR 53; JRDA; MAICYA 1, 2; SAAS 2; SATA 4, 68, 119, 131, 192; SATA-Essay 131; YAW

Levon, O. U.
See Kesey, Ken

Levy, Amy 1861-1889 .... **NCLC 59, 203; PC 126**
See also DLB 156, 240

Lewees, John
See Stockton, Francis Richard

Lewes, George Henry 1817-1878 . **NCLC 25, 215**
See also DLB 55, 144

Lewis, Alun 1915-1944 ..... **SSC 40; TCLC 3**
See also BRW 7; CA 104; 188; DLB 20, 162; PAB; RGEL 2

Lewis, C. S. 1898-1963 . **CLC 1, 3, 6, 14, 27, 124; WLC 4**
See also AAYA 3, 39; BPFB 2; BRWS 3; BYA 15, 16; CA 81-84; CANR 33, 71, 132; CDBLB 1945-1960; CLR 3, 27, 109, 173; CWRI 5; DA; DA3; DAB; DAC; DAM MST, NOV, POP; DLB 15, 100, 160, 255; EWL 3; FANT; JRDA; LMFS 2; MAICYA 1, 2; MTCW 1, 2; MTFW 2005; NFS 24; RGEL 2; SATA 13, 100; SCFW 1, 2; SFW 4; SUFW 1; TEA; WCH; WYA; YAW

Lewis, Clive Staples
See Lewis, C. S.

Lewis, Harry Sinclair
See Lewis, Sinclair

Lewis, Janet 1899-1998 .... **CLC 41**
See also CA 9-12R; 172; CANR 29, 63; CAP 1; CN 1, 2, 3, 4, 5, 6; DLBY 1987; RHW; TCWW 2

Lewis, Matthew Gregory 1775-1818 . **NCLC 11, 62**
See also DLB 39, 158, 178; GL 3; HGG; LMFS 1; RGEL 2; SUFW

Lewis, Sinclair 1885-1951 .. **TCLC 4, 13, 23, 39, 215; WLC 4**
See also AMW; AMWC 1; BPFB 2; CA 104; 133; CANR 132; CDALB 1917-1929; DA; DA3; DAB; DAC; DAM MST, NOV; DLB 9, 102, 284, 331; DLBD 1; EWL 3; LAIT 3; MAL 5; MTCW 1, 2; MTFW 2005; NFS 15, 19, 22, 34; RGAL 4; TUS

Lewis, (Percy) Wyndham 1884(?)-1957 . **SSC 34; TCLC 2, 9, 104, 216**
See also AAYA 77; BRW 7; CA 104; 157; DLB 15; EWL 3; FANT; MTCW 2; MTFW 2005; RGEL 2

Lewisohn, Ludwig 1883-1955 .... **TCLC 19**
See also CA 107; 203; DLB 4, 9, 28, 102; MAL 5

Lewton, Val 1904-1951 .... **TCLC 76**
See also CA 199; IDFW 3, 4

Leyner, Mark 1956- .... **CLC 92**
See also CA 110; CANR 28, 53; DA3; DLB 292; MTCW 2; MTFW 2005

Leyton, E.K.
See Campbell, Ramsey

Lezama Lima, Jose 1910-1976 ... **CLC 4, 10, 101; HLCS 2**
See also CA 77-80; CANR 71; DAM MULT; DLB 113, 283; EWL 3; HW 1, 2; LAW; RGWL 2, 3

L'Heureux, John (Clarke) 1934- .... **CLC 52**
See also CA 13-16R; CANR 23, 45, 88; CP 1, 2, 3, 4; DLB 244

Li, Fei-kan
See Jin, Ba

Li Ch'ing-chao 1081(?)-1141(?) ... **CMLC 71**

Lichtenberg, Georg Christoph 1742-1799 ... **LC 162**
See also DLB 94

Liddell, C. H.
See Kuttner, Henry

Lie, Jonas (Lauritz Idemil) 1833-1908(?) .... **TCLC 5**
See also CA 115

Lieber, Joel 1937-1971 .... **CLC 6**
See also CA 73-76; 29-32R

Lieber, Stanley Martin
See Lee, Stan

Lieberman, Laurence (James) 1935- ... **CLC 4, 36**
See also CA 17-20R; CANR 8, 36, 89; CP 1, 2, 3, 4, 5, 6, 7

Lieh Tzu fl. 7th cent. B.C.-5th cent. B.C. ...... **CMLC 27**

Lieksman, Anders
See Haavikko, Paavo Juhani

Lifton, Robert Jay 1926- .... **CLC 67**
See also CA 17-20R; CANR 27, 78, 161; INT CANR-27; SATA 66

Lightfoot, Gordon 1938- .... **CLC 26**
See also CA 109; 242

Lightfoot, Gordon Meredith
See Lightfoot, Gordon

Lightman, Alan P. 1948- .... **CLC 81**
See also CA 141; CANR 63, 105, 138, 178; MTFW 2005; NFS 29

Lightman, Alan Paige
See Lightman, Alan P.

Ligotti, Thomas 1953- .... **CLC 44; SSC 16**
See also CA 123; CANR 49, 135; HGG; SUFW 2

Ligotti, Thomas Robert
See Ligotti, Thomas

Li Ho 791-817 .... **PC 13**

Li Ju-chen c. 1763-c. 1830 .... **NCLC 137**

Liking, Werewere 1950- .... **BLC 2:2**
See also CA 293; DLB 360; EWL 3

Lilar, Francoise
See Mallet-Joris, Francoise

Liliencron, Detlev
See Liliencron, Detlev von

Liliencron, Detlev von 1844-1909 . **TCLC 18**
See also CA 117

Liliencron, Friedrich Adolf Axel Detlev von
See Liliencron, Detlev von

Liliencron, Friedrich Detlev von
See Liliencron, Detlev von

Lille, Alain de
See Alain de Lille

Lillo, George 1691-1739 .... **LC 131**
See also DLB 84; RGEL 2

Lilly, William 1602-1681 .... **LC 27**

Lima, Jose Lezama
See Lezama Lima, Jose

Lima Barreto, Afonso Henrique de
1881-1922 .... **TCLC 23**
See also CA 117; 181; DLB 307; LAW
Lima Barreto, Afonso Henriques de
See Lima Barreto, Afonso Henrique de
Limonov, Eduard
See Limonov, Edward
Limonov, Edward 1944- .... **CLC 67**
See also CA 137; DLB 317
Lin, Frank
See Atherton, Gertrude (Franklin Horn)
Lin, Yutang 1895-1976 .... **TCLC 149**
See also CA 45-48; 65-68; CANR 2; RGAL
4
Lincoln, Abraham 1809-1865 ...... **NCLC 18,
201**
See also LAIT 2
Lincoln, Geoffrey
See Mortimer, John
Lind, Jakov 1927-2007 .. **CLC 1, 2, 4, 27, 82**
See also CA 9-12R; 257; CAAS 4; CANR
7; DLB 299; EWL 3; RGHL
Lindbergh, Anne Morrow 1906-2001 .. **CLC
82**
See also BPFB 2; CA 17-20R; 193; CANR
16, 73; DAM NOV; MTCW 1, 2; MTFW
2005; SATA 33; SATA-Obit 125; TUS
Lindbergh, Anne Spencer Morrow
See Lindbergh, Anne Morrow
Lindholm, Anna Margaret
See Haycraft, Anna
Lindsay, David 1878(?)-1945 .... **TCLC 15**
See also CA 113; 187; DLB 255; FANT;
SFW 4; SUFW 1
Lindsay, Nicholas Vachel
See Lindsay, Vachel
Lindsay, Vachel 1879-1931 .... **PC 23; TCLC
17; WLC 4**
See also AMWS 1; CA 114; 135; CANR
79; CDALB 1865-1917; DA; DA3; DAC;
DAM MST, POET; DLB 54; EWL 3;
EXPP; MAL 5; RGAL 4; SATA 40; WP
Linke-Poot
See Doeblin, Alfred
Linney, Romulus 1930-2011 .... **CLC 51**
See also CA 1-4R; CAD; CANR 40, 44,
79; CD 5, 6; CSW; RGAL 4
Linton, Eliza Lynn 1822-1898 ...... **NCLC 41**
See also DLB 18
Li Po 701-763 .... **CMLC 2, 86; PC 29**
See also PFS 20, 40; WP
Lippard, George 1822-1854 .... **NCLC 198**
See also DLB 202
Lipsius, Justus 1547-1606 .... **LC 16**
Lipsyte, Robert 1938- .... **CLC 21**
See also AAYA 7, 45; CA 17-20R; CANR
8, 57, 146, 189; CLR 23, 76; DA; DAC;
DAM MST, NOV; JRDA; LAIT 5; MAI-
CYA 1, 2; NFS 35; SATA 5, 68, 113, 161,
198; WYA; YAW
Lipsyte, Robert Michael
See Lipsyte, Robert
Lish, Gordon 1934- .... **CLC 45; SSC 18**
See also CA 113; 117; CANR 79, 151; DLB
130; INT CA-117
Lish, Gordon Jay
See Lish, Gordon
Lispector, Clarice 1925(?)-1977 ..... **CLC 43;
HLCS 2; SSC 34, 96**
See also CA 139; 116; CANR 71; CDWLB
3; DLB 113, 307; DNFS 1; EWL 3; FW;
HW 2; LAW; RGSF 2; RGWL 2, 3; WLIT
1
Liszt, Franz 1811-1886 .... **NCLC 199**
Littell, Robert 1935(?)- .... **CLC 42**
See also CA 109; 112; CANR 64, 115, 162,
217; CMW 4
Little, Malcolm
See Malcolm X

Littlewit, Humphrey Gent.
See Lovecraft, H. P.
Litwos
See Sienkiewicz, Henryk (Adam Alexander
Pius)
Liu, E. 1857-1909 .... **TCLC 15**
See also CA 115; 190; DLB 328
Lively, Penelope 1933- .... **CLC 32, 50, 306**
See also BPFB 2; CA 41-44R; CANR 29,
67, 79, 131, 172, 222; CLR 7, 159; CN 5,
6, 7; CWRI 5; DAM NOV; DLB 14, 161,
207, 326; FANT; JRDA; MAICYA 1, 2;
MTCW 1, 2; MTFW 2005; SATA 7, 60,
101, 164; TEA
Lively, Penelope Margaret
See Lively, Penelope
Livesay, Dorothy (Kathleen) 1909-1996 ....
CLC 4, 15, 79
See also AITN 2; CA 25-28R; CAAS 8;
CANR 36, 67; CP 1, 2, 3, 4, 5; DAC;
DAM MST, POET; DLB 68; FW; MTCW
1; RGEL 2; TWA
Livius Andronicus c. 284B.C.-c. 204B.C. .....
CMLC 102
Livy c. 59B.C.-c. 12 .... **CMLC 11**
See also AW 2; CDWLB 1; DLB 211;
RGWL 2, 3; WLIT 8
Li Yaotang
See Jin, Ba
Li-Young, Lee
See Lee, Li-Young
Lizardi, Jose Joaquin Fernandez de
1776-1827 .... **NCLC 30**
See also LAW
Llewellyn, Richard
See Llewellyn Lloyd, Richard Dafydd Viv-
ian
Llewellyn Lloyd, Richard Dafydd Vivian
1906-1983 .... **CLC 7, 80**
See also CA 53-56; 111; CANR 7, 71; DLB
15; NFS 30; SATA 11; SATA-Obit 37
Llosa, Jorge Mario Pedro Vargas
See Vargas Llosa, Mario
Llosa, Mario Vargas
See Vargas Llosa, Mario
Lloyd, Manda
See Mander, (Mary) Jane
Lloyd Webber, Andrew 1948- .... **CLC 21**
See also AAYA 1, 38; CA 116; 149; DAM
DRAM; DFS 7; SATA 56
Llull, Ramon c. 1235-c. 1316 ...... **CMLC 12,
114**
Lobb, Ebenezer
See Upward, Allen
Lochhead, Liz 1947- .... **CLC 286**
See also BRWS 17; CA 81-84; CANR 79;
CBD; CD 5, 6; CP 2, 3, 4, 5, 6, 7; CWD;
CWP; DLB 310
Locke, Alain Leroy 1885-1954 ... **BLCS; HR
1:3; TCLC 43**
See also AMWS 14; BW 1, 3; CA 106; 124;
CANR 79; DLB 51; LMFS 2; MAL 5;
RGAL 4
Locke, John 1632-1704 .... **LC 7, 35, 135**
See also DLB 31, 101, 213, 252; RGEL 2;
WLIT 3
Locke-Elliott, Sumner
See Elliott, Sumner Locke
Lockhart, John Gibson 1794-1854 . **NCLC 6**
See also DLB 110, 116, 144
Lockridge, Ross (Franklin), Jr. 1914-1948 ..
TCLC 111
See also CA 108; 145; CANR 79; DLB 143;
DLBY 1980; MAL 5; RGAL 4; RHW
Lockwood, Robert
See Johnson, Robert
Lodge, David 1935- .... **CLC 36, 141, 293**
See also BEST 90:1; BRWS 4; CA 17-20R;
CANR 19, 53, 92, 139, 197; CN 1, 2, 3,

4, 5, 6, 7; CPW; DAM POP; DLB 14,
194; EWL 3; INT CANR-19; MTCW 1,
2; MTFW 2005
Lodge, David John
See Lodge, David
Lodge, Thomas 1558-1625 .... **LC 41**
See also DLB 172; RGEL 2
Loewinsohn, Ron(ald William) 1937- .. **CLC
52**
See also CA 25-28R; CANR 71; CP 1, 2, 3,
4
Logan, Jake
See Smith, Martin Cruz
Logan, John (Burton) 1923-1987 ...... **CLC 5**
See also CA 77-80; 124; CANR 45; CP 1,
2, 3, 4; DLB 5
Lo-Johansson, (Karl) Ivar 1901-1990 ....
TCLC 216
See also CA 102; 131; CANR 20, 79, 137;
DLB 259; EWL 3; RGWL 2, 3
Lo Kuan-chung 1330(?)-1400(?) .... **LC 12**
Lomax, Pearl
See Cleage, Pearl
Lomax, Pearl Cleage
See Cleage, Pearl
Lombard, Nap
See Johnson, Pamela Hansford
Lombard, Peter 1100(?)-1160(?) .. **CMLC 72**
Lombino, Salvatore
See Hunter, Evan
London, Jack 1876-1916 ..... **SSC 4, 49, 133;
TCLC 9, 15, 39; WLC 4**
See also AAYA 13, 75; AITN 2; AMW;
BPFB 2; BYA 4, 13; CA 110; 119; CANR
73; CDALB 1865-1917; CLR 108; DA;
DA3; DAB; DAC; DAM MST, NOV;
DLB 8, 12, 78, 212; EWL 3; EXPS;
JRDA; LAIT 3; MAICYA 1, 2,; MAL 5;
MTCW 1, 2; MTFW 2005; NFS 8, 19,
35; RGAL 4; RGSF 2; SATA 18; SFW 4;
SSFS 7, 35; TCWW 1, 2; TUS; WYA;
YAW
London, John Griffith
See London, Jack
Long, Emmett
See Leonard, Elmore
Longbaugh, Harry
See Goldman, William
Longfellow, Henry Wadsworth 1807-1882 ..
**NCLC 2, 45, 101, 103, 235; PC 30;
WLCS**
See also AMW; AMWR 2; CDALB 1640-
1865; CLR 99; DA; DA3; DAB; DAC;
DAM MST, POET; DLB 1, 59, 235;
EXPP; PAB; PFS 2, 7, 17, 31, 39; RGAL
4; SATA 19; TUS; WP
Longinus c. 1st cent. - .... **CMLC 27**
See also AW 2; DLB 176
Longley, Michael 1939- ..... **CLC 29; PC 118**
See also BRWS 8; CA 102; CP 1, 2, 3, 4, 5,
6, 7; DLB 40
Longstreet, Augustus Baldwin 1790-1870 ...
NCLC 159
See also DLB 3, 11, 74, 248; RGAL 4
Longus fl. c. 2nd cent. - .... **CMLC 7**
Longway, A. Hugh
See Lang, Andrew
Lonnbohm, Armas Eino Leopold
See Lonnbohm, Armas Eino Leopold
Lonnbohm, Armas Eino Leopold
1878-1926 .... **TCLC 24**
See also CA 123; EWL 3
Lonnrot, Elias 1802-1884 .... **NCLC 53**
See also EFS 1:1, 2:1
Lonsdale, Roger CLC 65
Lopate, Phillip 1943- .... **CLC 29**
See also CA 97-100; CANR 88, 157, 196;
DLBY 1980; INT CA-97-100

Lopez, Barry 1945- .... **CLC 70**
See also AAYA 9, 63; ANW; CA 65-68;
CANR 7, 23, 47, 68, 92; DLB 256, 275,
335; INT CANR-7, CANR-23; MTCW 1;
RGAL 4; SATA 67

Lopez, Barry Holstun
See Lopez, Barry

Lopez de Mendoza, Inigo
See Santillana, Inigo Lopez de Mendoza,
Marques de

Lopez Portillo (y Pacheco), Jose
1920-2004 .... **CLC 46**
See also CA 129; 224; HW 1

Lopez y Fuentes, Gregorio 1897(?)-1966 .....
CLC 32
See also CA 131; EWL 3; HW 1

Lorca, Federico Garcia
See Garcia Lorca, Federico

Lord, Audre
See Lorde, Audre

Lord, Bette Bao 1938- .... **AAL; CLC 23**
See also BEST 90:3; BPFB 2; CA 107;
CANR 41, 79; CLR 151; INT CA-107;
SATA 58

Lord Auch
See Bataille, Georges

Lord Brooke
See Greville, Fulke

Lord Byron 1788-1824 ..... **DC 24; NCLC 2,
12, 109, 149, 256; PC 16, 95; WLC 1**
See also AAYA 64; BRW 4; BRWC 2; CD-
BLB 1789-1832; DA; DA3; DAB; DAC;
DAM MST, POET; DLB 96, 110; EXPP;
LMFS 1; PAB; PFS 1, 14, 29, 35; RGEL
2; TEA; WLIT 3; WP

Lord Dunsany
See Dunsany, Edward John Moreton Drax
Plunkett

Lorde, Audre 1934-1992 .... **BLC 1:2, 2:2;
CLC 18, 71; PC 12; TCLC 173**
See also AFAW 1, 2; BW 1, 3; CA 25-28R;
142; CANR 16, 26, 46, 82; CP 2, 3, 4, 5;
DA3; DAM MULT, POET; DLB 41; EWL
3; FW; GLL 1; MAL 5; MTCW 1, 2;
MTFW 2005; PFS 16, 32; RGAL 4

Lorde, Audre Geraldine
See Lorde, Audre

Lord Houghton
See Milnes, Richard Monckton

Lord Jeffrey
See Jeffrey, Francis

Loreaux, Nichol CLC 65

Lorenzo, Heberto Padilla
See Padilla (Lorenzo), Heberto

Loris
See Hofmannsthal, Hugo von

Loti, Pierre
See Viaud, Julien

Lottie
See Grimke, Charlotte L. Forten

Lou, Henri
See Andreas-Salome, Lou

Louie, David Wong 1954- .... **CLC 70**
See also CA 139; CANR 120

Louis, Adrian C. NNAL
See also CA 223

Louis, Father M.
See Merton, Thomas

Louise, Heidi
See Erdrich, Louise

Lounsbury, Ruth Ozeki
See Ozeki, Ruth L.

Lovecraft, H. P. 1890-1937 . **SSC 3, 52, 165;
TCLC 4, 22**
See also AAYA 14; BPFB 2; CA 104; 133;
CANR 106; DA3; DAM POP; HGG;
MTCW 1, 2; MTFW 2005; RGAL 4;
SCFW 1, 2; SFW 4; SUFW

Lovecraft, Howard Phillips
See Lovecraft, H. P.

Lovelace, Earl 1935- .... **CLC 51; SSC 141**
See also BW 2; CA 77-80; CANR 41, 72,
114; CD 5, 6; CDWLB 3; CN 1, 2, 3, 4,
5, 6, 7; DLB 125; EWL 3; MTCW 1

Lovelace, Richard 1618-1658 .... **LC 24, 158;
PC 69**
See also BRW 2; DLB 131; EXPP; PAB;
PFS 32, 34; RGEL 2

Low, Penelope Margaret
See Lively, Penelope

Lowe, Pardee 1904- .... **AAL**

Lowell, Amy 1874-1925 . **PC 13; TCLC 1, 8,
259**
See also AAYA 57; AMW; CA 104; 151;
DAM POET; DLB 54, 140; EWL 3;
EXPP; LMFS 2; MAL 5; MBL; MTCW
2; MTFW 2005; PFS 30; RGAL 4; TUS

Lowell, James Russell 1819-1891 .. **NCLC 2,
90**
See also AMWS 1; CDALB 1640-1865;
DLB 1, 11, 64, 79, 189, 235; RGAL 4

Lowell, Robert 1917-1977 . **CLC 1, 2, 3, 4, 5,
8, 9, 11, 15, 37, 124; PC 3; WLC 4**
See also AMW; AMWC 2; AMWR 2; CA
9-12R; 73-76; CABS 2; CAD; CANR 26,
60; CDALBS; CP 1, 2; DA; DA3; DAB;
DAC; DAM MST, NOV; DLB 5, 169;
EWL 3; MAL 5; MTCW 1, 2; MTFW
2005; PAB; PFS 6, 7, 36; RGAL 4; WP

Lowell, Robert Trail Spence, Jr.
See Lowell, Robert

Lowenthal, Michael 1969- .... **CLC 119**
See also CA 150; CANR 115, 164

Lowenthal, Michael Francis
See Lowenthal, Michael

Lowndes, Marie Adelaide (Belloc)
1868-1947 .... **TCLC 12**
See also CA 107; CMW 4; DLB 70; RHW

Lowry, (Clarence) Malcolm 1909-1957 .
SSC 31; TCLC 6, 40
See also BPFB 2; BRWS 3; CA 105; 131;
CANR 62, 105; CDBLB 1945-1960; DLB
15; EWL 3; MTCW 1, 2; MTFW 2005;
RGEL 2

Lowry, Mina Gertrude 1882-1966 . **CLC 28;
PC 16**
See also CA 113; DAM POET; DLB 4, 54;
PFS 20

Lowry, Sam
See Soderbergh, Steven

Loxsmith, John
See Brunner, John (Kilian Houston)

Loy, Mina
See Lowry, Mina Gertrude

Loyson-Bridet
See Schwob, Marcel (Mayer Andre)

Lucan 39-65 .... **CMLC 33, 112**
See also AW 2; DLB 211; EFS 1:2, 2:2;
RGWL 2, 3

Lucas, Craig 1951- .... **CLC 64**
See also CA 137; CAD; CANR 71, 109,
142; CD 5, 6; GLL 2; MTFW 2005

Lucas, E(dward) V(errall) 1868-1938 ....
TCLC 73
See also CA 176; DLB 98, 149, 153; SATA
20

Lucas, George 1944- .... **CLC 16, 252**
See also AAYA 1, 23; CA 77-80; CANR
30; SATA 56

Lucas, Hans
See Godard, Jean-Luc

Lucas, Victoria
See Plath, Sylvia

Lucian c. 125-c. 180 .... **CMLC 32**
See also AW 2; DLB 176; RGWL 2, 3

Lucilius c. 180B.C.-102B.C. .... **CMLC 82**
See also DLB 211

Lucretius c. 94B.C.-c. 49B.C. .... **CMLC 48**
See also AW 2; CDWLB 1; DLB 211; EFS
1:2, 2:2; RGWL 2, 3; WLIT 8

Ludlam, Charles 1943-1987 ...... **CLC 46, 50**
See also CA 85-88; 122; CAD; CANR 72,
86; DLB 266

Ludlum, Robert 1927-2001 .... **CLC 22, 43**
See also AAYA 10, 59; BEST 89:1, 90:3;
BPFB 2; CA 33-36R; 195; CANR 25, 41,
68, 105, 131; CMW 4; CPW; DA3; DAM
NOV, POP; DLBY 1982; MSW; MTCW
1, 2; MTFW 2005

Ludwig, Ken 1950- .... **CLC 60**
See also CA 195; CAD; CD 6

Ludwig, Otto 1813-1865 .... **NCLC 4**
See also DLB 129

Lugones, Leopoldo 1874-1938 .... **HLCS 2;
TCLC 15**
See also CA 116; 131; CANR 104; DLB
283; EWL 3; HW 1; LAW

Lu Hsun
See Shu-Jen, Chou

Lu Hsun
See Lu Xun

Lukacs, George
See Lukacs, Gyorgy

Lukacs, Gyorgy 1885-1971 .... **CLC 24**
See also CA 101; 29-32R; CANR 62; CD-
WLB 4; DLB 215, 242; EW 10; EWL 3;
MTCW 1, 2

Lukacs, Gyorgy Szegeny von
See Lukacs, Gyorgy

Luke, Peter (Ambrose Cyprian)
1919-1995 .... **CLC 38**
See also CA 81-84; 147; CANR 72; CBD;
CD 5, 6; DLB 13

Lunar, Dennis
See Mungo, Raymond

Lurie, Alison 1926- .... **CLC 4, 5, 18, 39, 175**
See also BPFB 2; CA 1-4R; CANR 2, 17,
50, 88; CN 1, 2, 3, 4, 5, 6, 7; DLB 2, 350;
MAL 5; MTCW 1; NFS 24; SATA 46,
112; TCLE 1:1

Lustig, Arnost 1926-2011 .... **CLC 56**
See also AAYA 3; CA 69-72; CANR 47,
102; CWW 2; DLB 232, 299; EWL 3;
RGHL; SATA 56

Luther, Martin 1483-1546 ...... **LC 9, 37, 150**
See also CDWLB 2; DLB 179; EW 2;
RGWL 2, 3

Luxemburg, Rosa 1870(?)-1919 .... **TCLC 63**
See also CA 118

Lu Xun 1881-1936 .... **SSC 158**
See also CA 243; DLB 328; RGSF 2;
RGWL 2, 3

Luzi, Mario (Egidio Vincenzo) 1914-2005 ...
CLC 13
See also CA 61-64; 236; CANR 9, 70;
CWW 2; DLB 128; EWL 3

L'vov, Arkady CLC 59

Lydgate, John c. 1370-1450(?) ... **LC 81, 175**
See also BRW 1; DLB 146; RGEL 2

Lyly, John 1554(?)-1606 .. **DC 7; LC 41, 187**
See also BRW 1; DAM DRAM; DLB 62,
167; RGEL 2

L'Ymagier
See Gourmont, Remy(-Marie-Charles) de

Lynch, B. Suarez
See Borges, Jorge Luis

Lynch, David 1946- .... **CLC 66, 162**
See also AAYA 55; CA 124; 129; CANR
111

Lynch, David Keith
See Lynch, David

Lynch, James
See Andreyev, Leonid

Lyndsay, Sir David 1485-1555 .... **LC 20**
See also RGEL 2

Lynn, Kenneth S(chuyler) 1923-2001 .. **CLC 50**
   See also CA 1-4R; 196; CANR 3, 27, 65

Lynx
   See West, Rebecca

Lyons, Marcus
   See Blish, James

Lyotard, Jean-Francois 1924-1998 .... **TCLC 103**
   See also DLB 242; EWL 3

Lyre, Pinchbeck
   See Sassoon, Siegfried

Lytle, Andrew (Nelson) 1902-1995 .. **CLC 22**
   See also CA 9-12R; 150; CANR 70; CN 1, 2, 3, 4, 5, 6; CSW; DLB 6; DLBY 1995; RGAL 4; RHW

Lyttelton, George 1709-1773 .... **LC 10**
   See also RGEL 2

Lytton, Edward G.E.L. Bulwer-Lytton Baron
   See Bulwer-Lytton, Edward

Lytton of Knebworth, Baron
   See Bulwer-Lytton, Edward

Maalouf, Amin 1949- .... **CLC 248**
   See also CA 212; CANR 194; DLB 346

Maas, Peter 1929-2001 .... **CLC 29**
   See also CA 93-96; 201; INT CA-93-96; MTCW 2; MTFW 2005

Mac A'Ghobhainn, Iain
   See Smith, Iain Crichton

Macaulay, Catharine 1731-1791 .... **LC 64**
   See also BRWS 17; DLB 104, 336

Macaulay, (Emilie) Rose 1881(?)-1958 ....
   .... **TCLC 7, 44**
   See also CA 104; DLB 36; EWL 3; RGEL 2; RHW

Macaulay, Thomas Babington 1800-1859 ....
   .... **NCLC 42, 231**
   See also BRW 4; CDBLB 1832-1890; DLB 32, 55; RGEL 2

MacBeth, George (Mann) 1932-1992 ... **CLC 2, 5, 9**
   See also CA 25-28R; 136; CANR 61, 66; CP 1, 2, 3, 4, 5; DLB 40; MTCW 1; PFS 8; SATA 4; SATA-Obit 70

MacCaig, Norman (Alexander) 1910-1996 ..
   CLC 36
   See also BRWS 6; CA 9-12R; CANR 3, 34; CP 1, 2, 3, 4, 5, 6; DAB; DAM POET; DLB 27; EWL 3; RGEL 2

MacCarthy, Sir (Charles Otto) Desmond 1877-1952 .... **TCLC 36**
   See also CA 167

MacDiarmid, Hugh
   See Grieve, C. M.

MacDonald, Anson
   See Heinlein, Robert A.

Macdonald, Cynthia 1928- .... **CLC 13, 19**
   See also CA 49-52; CANR 4, 44, 146; DLB 105

MacDonald, George 1824-1905 ..... **TCLC 9, 113, 207**
   See also AAYA 57; BYA 5; CA 106; 137; CANR 80; CLR 67; DLB 18, 163, 178; FANT; MAICYA 1, 2; RGEL 2; SATA 33, 100; SFW 4; SUFW; WCH

Macdonald, John
   See Millar, Kenneth

MacDonald, John D. 1916-1986 . **CLC 3, 27, 44**
   See also BPFB 2; CA 1-4R; 121; CANR 1, 19, 60; CMW 4; CPW; DAM NOV, POP; DLB 8, 306; DLBY 1986; MSW; MTCW 1, 2; MTFW 2005; SFW 4

Macdonald, John Ross
   See Millar, Kenneth

Macdonald, Ross
   See Millar, Kenneth

MacDonald Fraser, George
   See Fraser, George MacDonald

MacDougal, John
   See Blish, James

MacDowell, John
   See Parks, Tim

MacEwen, Gwendolyn (Margaret) 1941-1987 .... **CLC 13, 55**
   See also CA 9-12R; 124; CANR 7, 22; CP 1, 2, 3, 4; DLB 53, 251; SATA 50; SATA-Obit 55

MacGreevy, Thomas 1893-1967 .... **PC 82**
   See also CA 262

Macha, Karel Hynek 1810-1846 .. **NCLC 46**

Machado (y Ruiz), Antonio 1875-1939 ....
   TCLC 3
   See also CA 104; 174; DLB 108; EW 9; EWL 3; HW 2; PFS 23; RGWL 2, 3

Machado de Assis, Joaquim Maria 1839-1908 . **BLC 1:2; HLCS 2; SSC 24, 118; TCLC 10**
   See also CA 107; 153; CANR 91; DLB 307; LAW; RGSF 2; RGWL 2, 3; TWA; WLIT 1

Machaut, Guillaume de c. 1300-1377 ....
   CMLC 64
   See also DLB 208

Machen, Arthur
   See Jones, Arthur Llewellyn

Machen, Arthur Llewelyn Jones
   See Jones, Arthur Llewellyn

Machiavelli, Niccolo 1469-1527 . **DC 16; LC 8, 36, 140; WLCS**
   See also AAYA 58; DA; DAB; DAC; DAM MST; EW 2; LAIT 1; LMFS 1; NFS 9; RGWL 2, 3; TWA; WLIT 7

MacInnes, Colin 1914-1976 .... **CLC 4, 23**
   See also CA 69-72; 65-68; CANR 21; CN 1, 2; DLB 14; MTCW 1, 2; RGEL 2; RHW

MacInnes, Helen (Clark) 1907-1985 .... **CLC 27, 39**
   See also BPFB 2; CA 1-4R; 117; CANR 1, 28, 58; CMW 4; CN 1, 2; CPW; DAM POP; DLB 87; MSW; MTCW 1, 2; MTFW 2005; SATA 22; SATA-Obit 44

Mackay, Mary 1855-1924 .... **TCLC 51**
   See also CA 118; 177; DLB 34, 156; FANT; RGEL 2; RHW; SUFW 1

Mackay, Shena 1944- .... **CLC 195**
   See also CA 104; CANR 88, 139, 207; DLB 231, 319; MTFW 2005

Mackenzie, Compton (Edward Montague) 1883-1972 .... **CLC 18; TCLC 116**
   See also CA 21-22; 37-40R; CAP 2; CN 1; DLB 34, 100; RGEL 2

Mackenzie, Henry 1745-1831 .... **NCLC 41**
   See also DLB 39; RGEL 2

Mackey, Nathaniel 1947- ... **BLC 2:3; PC 49**
   See also CA 153; CANR 114; CP 6, 7; DLB 169

Mackey, Nathaniel Ernest
   See Mackey, Nathaniel

MacKinnon, Catharine
   See MacKinnon, Catharine A.

MacKinnon, Catharine A. 1946- ... **CLC 181**
   See also CA 128; 132; CANR 73, 140, 189; FW; MTCW 2; MTFW 2005

Mackintosh, Elizabeth 1896(?)-1952 . **TCLC 14**
   See also CA 110; CMW 4; DLB 10, 77; MSW

Macklin, Charles 1699-1797 .... **LC 132**
   See also DLB 89; RGEL 2

MacLaren, James
   See Grieve, C. M.

MacLaverty, Bernard 1942- .... **CLC 31, 243**
   See also CA 116; 118; CANR 43, 88, 168; CN 5, 6, 7; DLB 267; INT CA-118; RGSF 2

MacLean, Alistair 1922(?)-1987 . **CLC 3, 13, 50, 63**
   See also CA 57-60; 121; CANR 28, 61; CMW 4; CP 2, 3, 4, 5, 6, 7; CPW; DAM POP; DLB 276; MTCW 1; SATA 23; SATA-Obit 50; TCWW 2

MacLean, Alistair Stuart
   See MacLean, Alistair

Maclean, Norman (Fitzroy) 1902-1990 . **CLC 78; SSC 13, 136**
   See also AMWS 14; CA 102; 132; CANR 49; CPW; DAM POP; DLB 206; TCWW 2

MacLeish, Archibald 1892-1982 .. **CLC 3, 8, 14, 68; DC 43; PC 47**
   See also AMW; CA 9-12R; 106; CAD; CANR 33, 63; CDALBS; CP 1, 2; DAM POET; DFS 15; DLB 4, 7, 45; DLBY 1982; EWL 3; EXPP; MAL 5; MTCW 1, 2; MTFW 2005; PAB; PFS 5; RGAL 4; TUS

MacLennan, (John) Hugh 1907-1990 .. **CLC 2, 14, 92**
   See also CA 5-8R; 142; CANR 33; CN 1, 2, 3, 4; DAC; DAM MST; DLB 68; EWL 3; MTCW 1, 2; MTFW 2005; RGEL 2; TWA

MacLeod, Alistair 1936- . **CLC 56, 165; SSC 90**
   See also CA 123; CCA 1; DAC; DAM MST; DLB 60; MTCW 2; MTFW 2005; RGSF 2; TCLE 1:2

Macleod, Fiona
   See Sharp, William

MacNeice, (Frederick) Louis 1907-1963 ......
   CLC 1, 4, 10, 53; PC 61
   See also BRW 7; CA 85-88; CANR 61; DAB; DAM POET; DLB 10, 20; EWL 3; MTCW 1, 2; MTFW 2005; RGEL 2

MacNeill, Dand
   See Fraser, George MacDonald

Macpherson, James 1736-1796 .. **CMLC 28; LC 29, 196; PC 97**
   See also BRWS 8; DLB 109, 336; RGEL 2

Macpherson, (Jean) Jay 1931- .... **CLC 14**
   See also CA 5-8R; CANR 90; CP 1, 2, 3, 4, 6, 7; CWP; DLB 53

Macrobius fl. 430- .... **CMLC 48**

MacShane, Frank 1927-1999 .... **CLC 39**
   See also CA 9-12R; 186; CANR 3, 33; DLB 111

Macumber, Mari
   See Sandoz, Mari(e Susette)

Madach, Imre 1823-1864 .... **NCLC 19**

Madden, (Jerry) David 1933- ..... **CLC 5, 15**
   See also CA 1-4R; CAAS 3; CANR 4, 45; CN 3, 4, 5, 6, 7; CSW; DLB 6; MTCW 1

Maddern, Al(an)
   See Ellison, Harlan

Madhubuti, Haki R. 1942- .. **BLC 1:2; CLC 2; PC 5**
   See also BW 2, 3; CA 73-76; CANR 24, 51, 73, 139; CP 2, 3, 4, 5, 6, 7; CSW; DAM MULT, POET; DLB 5, 41; DLBD 8; EWL 3; MAL 5; MTCW 2; MTFW 2005; RGAL 4

Madison, James 1751-1836 .... **NCLC 126**
   See also DLB 37

Maepenn, Hugh
   See Kuttner, Henry

Maepenn, K. H.
   See Kuttner, Henry

Maeterlinck, Maurice 1862-1949 ..... **DC 32; TCLC 3, 251**
   See also CA 104; 136; CANR 80; DAM DRAM; DLB 192, 331; EW 8; EWL 3; GFL 1789 to the Present; LMFS 2; RGWL 2, 3; SATA 66; TWA

Maginn, William 1794-1842 .... **NCLC 8**
See also DLB 110, 159

Mahapatra, Jayanta 1928- .... **CLC 33**
See also CA 73-76; CAAS 9; CANR 15, 33, 66, 87; CP 4, 5, 6, 7; DAM MULT; DLB 323

Mahfouz, Nagib
See Mahfouz, Naguib

Mahfouz, Naguib 1911(?)-2006 . **CLC 52, 55, 153; SSC 66**
See also AAYA 49; AFW; BEST 89:2; CA 128; 253; CANR 55, 101; DA3; DAM NOV; DLB 346; DLBY 1988; MTCW 1, 2; MTFW 2005; RGSF 2; RGWL 2, 3; SSFS 9, 33; WLIT 2

Mahfouz, Naguib Abdel Aziz Al-Sabilgi
See Mahfouz, Naguib

Mahfouz, Najib
See Mahfouz, Naguib

Mahfuz, Najib
See Mahfouz, Naguib

Mahon, Derek 1941- .... **CLC 27; PC 60**
See also BRWS 6; CA 113; 128; CANR 88; CP 1, 2, 3, 4, 5, 6, 7; DLB 40; EWL 3

Maiakovskii, Vladimir
See Mayakovski, Vladimir

Mailer, Norman 1923-2007 .. **CLC 1, 2, 3, 4, 5, 8, 11, 14, 28, 39, 74, 111, 234**
See also AAYA 31; AITN 2; AMW; AMWC 2; AMWR 2; BPFB 2; CA 9-12R; 266; CABS 1; CANR 28, 74, 77, 130, 196; CDALB 1968-1988; CN 1, 2, 3, 4, 5, 6, 7; CPW; DA; DA3; DAB; DAC; DAM MST, NOV, POP; DLB 2, 16, 28, 185, 278; DLBD 3; DLBY 1980, 1983; EWL 3; MAL 5; MTCW 1, 2; MTFW 2005; NFS 10; RGAL 4; TUS

Mailer, Norman Kingsley
See Mailer, Norman

Maillet, Antonine 1929- .... **CLC 54, 118**
See also CA 115; 120; CANR 46, 74, 77, 134; CCA 1; CWW 2; DAC; DLB 60; INT CA-120; MTCW 2; MTFW 2005

Maimonides, Moses 1135-1204 .... **CMLC 76**
See also DLB 115

Mais, Roger 1905-1955 .... **TCLC 8**
See also BW 1, 3; CA 105; 124; CANR 82; CDWLB 3; DLB 125; EWL 3; MTCW 1; RGEL 2

Maistre, Joseph 1753-1821 .... **NCLC 37**
See also GFL 1789 to the Present

Maitland, Frederic William 1850-1906 .... **TCLC 65**

Maitland, Sara 1950- .... **CLC 49**
See also BRWS 11; CA 69-72; CANR 13, 59, 221; DLB 271; FW

Maitland, Sara Louise
See Maitland, Sara

Major, Clarence 1936- ..... **BLC 1:2; CLC 3, 19, 48**
See also AFAW 2; BW 2, 3; CA 21-24R; CAAS 6; CANR 13, 25, 53, 82; CN 3, 4, 5, 6, 7; CP 2, 3, 4, 5, 6, 7; CSW; DAM MULT; DLB 33; EWL 3; MAL 5; MSW

Major, Kevin (Gerald) 1949- .... **CLC 26**
See also AAYA 16; CA 97-100; CANR 21, 38, 112; CLR 11; DAC; DLB 60; INT CANR-21; JRDA; MAICYA 1, 2; MAICYAS 1; SATA 32, 82, 134; WYA; YAW

Maki, James
See Ozu, Yasujiro

Makin, Bathsua 1600-1675(?) .... **LC 137**

Makine, Andrei
See Makine, Andrei

Makine, Andrei 1957- .... **CLC 198**
See also CA 176; CANR 103, 162; MTFW 2005

Malabaila, Damiano
See Levi, Primo

Malamud, Bernard 1914-1986 . **CLC 1, 2, 3, 5, 8, 9, 11, 18, 27, 44, 78, 85; SSC 15, 147; TCLC 129, 184; WLC 4**
See also AAYA 16; AMWS 1; BPFB 2; BYA 15; CA 5-8R; 118; CABS 1; CANR 28, 62, 114; CDALB 1941-1968; CN 1, 2, 3, 4; CPW; DA; DA3; DAB; DAC; DAM MST, NOV, POP; DLB 2, 28, 152; DLBY 1980, 1986; EWL 3; EXPS; LAIT 4; LATS 1:1; MAL 5; MTCW 1, 2; MTFW 2005; NFS 27; RGAL 4; RGHL; RGSF 2; SSFS 8, 13, 16; TUS

Malan, Herman
See Bosman, Herman Charles; Bosman, Herman Charles

Malaparte, Curzio 1898-1957 .... **TCLC 52**
See also DLB 264

Malcolm, Dan
See Silverberg, Robert

Malcolm, Janet 1934- .... **CLC 201**
See also CA 123; CANR 89, 199; NCFS 1

Malcolm X 1925-1965 .... **BLC 1:2; CLC 82, 117; WLCS**
See also BW 1, 3; CA 125; 111; CANR 82; DA; DA3; DAB; DAC; DAM MST, MULT; LAIT 5; MTCW 1, 2; MTFW 2005; NCFS 3

Malebranche, Nicolas 1638-1715 ..... **LC 133**
See also GFL Beginnings to 1789

Malherbe, Francois de 1555-1628 .... **LC 5**
See also DLB 327; GFL Beginnings to 1789

Mallarme, Stephane 1842-1898 ..... **NCLC 4, 41, 210; PC 4, 102**
See also DAM POET; DLB 217; EW 7; GFL 1789 to the Present; LMFS 2; RGWL 2, 3; TWA

Mallet-Joris, Francoise 1930- .... **CLC 11**
See also CA 65-68; CANR 17; CWW 2; DLB 83; EWL 3; GFL 1789 to the Present

Malley, Ern
See McAuley, James Phillip

Mallon, Thomas 1951- .... **CLC 172**
See also CA 110; CANR 29, 57, 92, 196; DLB 350

Mallowan, Agatha Christie
See Christie, Agatha

Maloff, Saul 1922- .... **CLC 5**
See also CA 33-36R

Malone, Louis
See MacNeice, (Frederick) Louis

Malone, Michael 1942- .... **CLC 43**
See also CA 77-80; CANR 14, 32, 57, 114; 214

Malone, Michael Christopher
See Malone, Michael

Malory, Sir Thomas 1410(?)-1471(?) . **LC 11, 88; WLCS**
See also BRW 1; BRWR 2; CDBLB Before 1660; DA; DAB; DAC; DAM MST; DLB 146; EFS 1:2, 2:2; RGEL 2; SATA 59; SATA-Brief 33; TEA; WLIT 3

Malouf, David 1934- .... **CLC 28, 86, 245**
See also BRWS 12; CA 124; CANR 50, 76, 180, 224; CN 3, 4, 5, 6, 7; CP 1, 3, 4, 5, 6, 7; DLB 289; EWL 3; MTCW 2; MTFW 2005; SSFS 24

Malouf, George Joseph David
See Malouf, David

Malraux, Andre 1901-1976 . **CLC 1, 4, 9, 13, 15, 57; TCLC 209**
See also BPFB 2; CA 21-22; 69-72; CANR 34, 58; CAP 2; DA3; DAM NOV; DLB 72; EW 12; EWL 3; GFL 1789 to the Present; MTCW 1, 2; MTFW 2005; RGWL 2, 3; TWA

Malraux, Georges-Andre
See Malraux, Andre

Malthus, Thomas Robert 1766-1834 . **NCLC 145**
See also DLB 107, 158; RGEL 2

Malzberg, Barry N(athaniel) 1939- .. **CLC 7**
See also CA 61-64; CAAS 4; CANR 16; CMW 4; DLB 8; SFW 4

Mamet, David 1947- . **CLC 9, 15, 34, 46, 91, 166; DC 4, 24**
See also AAYA 3, 60; AMWS 14; CA 81-84; CABS 3; CAD; CANR 15, 41, 67, 72, 129, 172; CD 5, 6; DA3; DAM DRAM; DFS 2, 3, 6, 12, 15; DLB 7; EWL 3; IDFW 4; MAL 5; MTCW 1, 2; MTFW 2005; RGAL 4

Mamet, David Alan
See Mamet, David

Mamoulian, Rouben (Zachary) 1897-1987 .. **CLC 16**
See also CA 25-28R; 124; CANR 85

Mandelshtam, Osip
See Mandelstam, Osip

Mandel'shtam, Osip Emil'evich
See Mandelstam, Osip

Mandelstam, Osip 1891(?)-1943(?) ... **PC 14; TCLC 2, 6, 225**
See also CA 104; 150; DLB 295; EW 10; EWL 3; MTCW 2; RGWL 2, 3; TWA

Mandelstam, Osip Emilievich
See Mandelstam, Osip

Mander, (Mary) Jane 1877-1949 .. **TCLC 31**
See also CA 162; RGEL 2

Mandeville, Bernard 1670-1733 .... **LC 82**
See also DLB 101

Mandeville, Sir John fl. 1350- ..... **CMLC 19**
See also DLB 146

Mandiargues, Andre Pieyre de
See Pieyre de Mandiargues, Andre

Mandrake, Ethel Belle
See Thurman, Wallace (Henry)

Mangan, James Clarence 1803-1849 . **NCLC 27**
See also BRWS 13; RGEL 2

Maniere, J. E.
See Giraudoux, Jean

Mankell, Henning 1948- .... **CLC 292**
See also CA 187; CANR 163, 200

Mankiewicz, Herman (Jacob) 1897-1953 .... **TCLC 85**
See also CA 120; 169; DLB 26; IDFW 3, 4

Manley, (Mary) Delariviere 1672(?)-1724 ... **LC 1, 42**
See also DLB 39, 80; RGEL 2

Mann, Abel
See Creasey, John

Mann, Emily 1952- .... **DC 7**
See also CA 130; CAD; CANR 55; CD 5, 6; CWD; DFS 28; DLB 266

Mann, Erica
See Jong, Erica

Mann, (Luiz) Heinrich 1871-1950 .. **TCLC 9**
See also CA 106; 164, 181; DLB 66, 118; EW 8; EWL 3; RGWL 2, 3

Mann, Paul Thomas
See Mann, Thomas

Mann, Thomas 1875-1955 ..... **SSC 5, 80, 82; TCLC 2, 8, 14, 21, 35, 44, 60, 168, 236; WLC 4**
See also BPFB 2; CA 104; 128; CANR 133; CDWLB 2; DA; DA3; DAB; DAC; DAM MST, NOV; DLB 66, 331; EW 9; EWL 3; GLL 1; LATS 1:1; LMFS 1; MTCW 1, 2; MTFW 2005; NFS 17; RGSF 2; RGWL 2, 3; SSFS 4, 9; TWA

Mannheim, Karl 1893-1947 .... **TCLC 65**
See also CA 204

Manning, David
See Faust, Frederick

Manning, Frederic 1882-1935 .... **TCLC 25**
See also CA 124; 216; DLB 260

Manning, Olivia 1915-1980 .... **CLC 5, 19**
   See also CA 5-8R; 101; CANR 29; CN 1,
   2; EWL 3; FW; MTCW 1; RGEL 2
Mannyng, Robert c. 1264-c. 1340 .... **CMLC 83**
   See also DLB 146
Mano, D. Keith 1942- .... **CLC 2, 10**
   See also CA 25-28R; CAAS 6; CANR 26,
   57; DLB 6
Mansfield, Katherine 1888-1923 . **SSC 9, 23, 38, 81; TCLC 2, 8, 39, 164; WLC 4**
   See also BPFB 2; BRW 7; CA 104; 134;
   DA; DA3; DAB; DAC; DAM MST; DLB
   162; EWL 3; EXPS; FW; GLL 1; MTCW
   2; RGEL 2; RGSF 2; SSFS 2, 8, 10, 11,
   29; TEA; WWE 1
Mansfield, Kathleen
   See Mansfield, Katherine
Manso, Peter 1940- .... **CLC 39**
   See also CA 29-32R; CANR 44, 156
Mantecon, Juan Jimenez
   See Jimenez, Juan Ramon
Mantel, Hilary 1952- .... **CLC 144, 309**
   See also CA 125; CANR 54, 101, 161, 207;
   CN 5, 6, 7; DLB 271; RHW
Mantel, Hilary Mary
   See Mantel, Hilary
Manton, Peter
   See Creasey, John
Man Without a Spleen, A
   See Chekhov, Anton
Manzano, Juan Franciso 1797(?)-1854 .... **NCLC 155**
Manzoni, Alessandro 1785-1873 .. **NCLC 29, 98**
   See also EW 5; RGWL 2, 3; TWA; WLIT 7
Map, Walter 1140-1209 .... **CMLC 32**
Mapu, Abraham (ben Jekutiel) 1808-1867 .. **NCLC 18**
Mara, Sally
   See Queneau, Raymond
Maracle, Lee 1950- .... **NNAL**
   See also CA 149
Marat, Jean Paul 1743-1793 .... **LC 10**
Marcel, Gabriel Honore 1889-1973 . **CLC 15**
   See also CA 102; 45-48; EWL 3; MTCW 1,
   2
March, William 1893-1954 .... **TCLC 96**
   See also CA 108; 216; DLB 9, 86, 316;
   MAL 5
Marchbanks, Samuel
   See Davies, Robertson
Marchi, Giacomo
   See Bassani, Giorgio
Marcus Aurelius
   See Aurelius, Marcus
Marcuse, Herbert 1898-1979 ...... **TCLC 207**
   See also CA 188; 89-92; DLB 242
Marguerite
   See de Navarre, Marguerite
Marguerite d'Angouleme
   See de Navarre, Marguerite
Marguerite de Navarre
   See de Navarre, Marguerite
Margulies, Donald 1954- .... **CLC 76**
   See also AAYA 57; CA 200; CD 6; DFS 13;
   DLB 228
Marias, Javier 1951- .... **CLC 239**
   See also CA 167; CANR 109, 139, 232;
   DLB 322; HW 2; MTFW 2005
Marie de France c. 12th cent. - .... **CMLC 8, 111; PC 22**
   See also DLB 208; FW; RGWL 2, 3
Marie de l'Incarnation 1599-1672 .... **LC 10, 168**
Marier, Captain Victor
   See Griffith, D.W.

Mariner, Scott
   See Pohl, Frederik
Marinetti, Filippo Tommaso 1876-1944 .... **TCLC 10**
   See also CA 107; DLB 114, 264; EW 9;
   EWL 3; WLIT 7
Marino, Giambattista 1569-1625 ..... **LC 181**
   See also DLB 339; WLIT 7
Marivaux, Pierre Carlet de Chamblain de 1688-1763 .... **DC 7; LC 4, 123**
   See also DLB 314; GFL Beginnings to
   1789; RGWL 2, 3; TWA
Markandaya, Kamala 1924-2004 ..... **CLC 8, 38, 290**
   See also BYA 13; CA 77-80; 227; CN 1, 2,
   3, 4, 5, 6, 7; DLB 323; EWL 3; MTFW
   2005; NFS 13
Markfield, Wallace (Arthur) 1926-2002 ...... **CLC 8**
   See also CA 69-72; 208; CAAS 3; CN 1, 2,
   3, 4, 5, 6, 7; DLB 2, 28; DLBY 2002
Markham, Edwin 1852-1940 .... **TCLC 47**
   See also CA 160; DLB 54, 186; MAL 5;
   RGAL 4
Markham, Robert
   See Amis, Kingsley
Marks, J.
   See Highwater, Jamake (Mamake)
Marks-Highwater, J.
   See Highwater, Jamake (Mamake)
Markson, David M. 1927-2010 .... **CLC 67**
   See also AMWS 17; CA 49-52; CANR 1,
   91, 158; CN 5, 6
Markson, David Merrill
   See Markson, David M.
Marlatt, Daphne (Buckle) 1942- ... **CLC 168**
   See also CA 25-28R; CANR 17, 39; CN 6,
   7; CP 4, 5, 6, 7; CWP; DLB 60; FW
Marley, Bob
   See Marley, Robert Nesta
Marley, Robert Nesta 1945-1981 .... **CLC 17**
   See also CA 107; 103
Marlowe, Christopher 1564-1593 . **DC 1; LC 22, 47, 117, 201; PC 57; WLC 4**
   See also BRW 1; BRWR 1; CDBLB Before
   1660; DA; DA3; DAB; DAC; DAM
   DRAM, MST; DFS 1, 5, 13, 21; DLB 62;
   EXPP; LMFS 1; PFS 22; RGEL 2; TEA;
   WLIT 3
Marlowe, Stephen 1928-2008 .... **CLC 70**
   See also CA 13-16R; 269; CANR 6, 55;
   CMW 4; SFW 4
Marmion, Shakerley 1603-1639 .... **LC 89**
   See also DLB 58; RGEL 2
Marmontel, Jean-Francois 1723-1799 . **LC 2**
   See also DLB 314
Maron, Monika 1941- .... **CLC 165**
   See also CA 201
Marot, Clement c. 1496-1544 .... **LC 133**
   See also DLB 327; GFL Beginnings to 1789
Marquand, John P(hillips) 1893-1960 . **CLC 2, 10**
   See also AMW; BPFB 2; CA 85-88; CANR
   73; CMW 4; DLB 9, 102; EWL 3; MAL
   5; MTCW 2; RGAL 4
Marques, Rene 1919-1979 . **CLC 96; HLC 2**
   See also CA 97-100; 85-88; CANR 78;
   DAM MULT; DLB 305; EWL 3; HW 1,
   2; LAW; RGSF 2
Marquez, Gabriel Garcia
   See Garcia Marquez, Gabriel
Marquez, Gabriel Garcia
   See Garcia Marquez, Gabriel
Marquis, Don(ald Robert Perry) 1878-1937 .... **TCLC 7**
   See also CA 104; 166; DLB 11, 25; MAL
   5; RGAL 4
Marquis de Sade
   See Sade, Donatien Alphonse Francois

Marric, J. J.
   See Creasey, John
Marryat, Frederick 1792-1848 .... **NCLC 3**
   See also DLB 21, 163; RGEL 2; WCH
Marsden, James
   See Creasey, John
Marse, Juan 1933- .... **CLC 302**
   See also CA 254; DLB 322
Marsh, Edith Ngaio
   See Marsh, Ngaio
Marsh, Edward 1872-1953 .... **TCLC 99**
Marsh, Ngaio 1895-1982 .... **CLC 7, 53**
   See also CA 9-12R; CANR 6, 58; CMW 4;
   CN 1, 2, 3; CPW; DAM POP; DLB 77;
   MSW; MTCW 1, 2; RGEL 2; TEA
Marshall, Alan
   See Westlake, Donald E.
Marshall, Allen
   See Westlake, Donald E.
Marshall, Garry 1934- .... **CLC 17**
   See also AAYA 3; CA 111; SATA 60
Marshall, Paule 1929- .. **BLC 1:3, 2:3; CLC 27, 72, 253; SSC 3**
   See also AFAW 1, 2; AMWS 11; BPFB 2;
   BW 2, 3; CA 77-80; CANR 25, 73, 129,
   209; CN 1, 2, 3, 4, 5, 6, 7; DA3; DAM
   MULT; DLB 33, 157, 227; EWL 3; LATS
   1:2; MAL 5; MTCW 1, 2; MTFW 2005;
   NFS 36; RGAL 4; SSFS 15
Marshallik
   See Zangwill, Israel
Marsilius of Inghen c. 1340-1396 ..... **CMLC 106**
Marsten, Richard
   See Hunter, Evan
Marston, John 1576-1634 .... **DC 37; LC 33, 172**
   See also BRW 2; DAM DRAM; DLB 58,
   172; RGEL 2
Martel, Yann 1963- .... **CLC 192, 315**
   See also AAYA 67; CA 146; CANR 114,
   226; DLB 326, 334; LNFS 2; MTFW
   2005; NFS 27
Martens, Adolphe-Adhemar
   See Ghelderode, Michel de
Martha, Henry
   See Harris, Mark
Marti, Jose 1853-1895 ... **HLC 2; NCLC 63; PC 76**
   See also DAM MULT; DLB 290; HW 2;
   LAW; RGWL 2, 3; WLIT 1
Martial c. 40-c. 104 .... **CMLC 35; PC 10**
   See also AW 2; CDWLB 1; DLB 211;
   RGWL 2, 3
Martin, Ken
   See Hubbard, L. Ron
Martin, Richard
   See Creasey, John
Martin, Steve 1945- .... **CLC 30, 217**
   See also AAYA 53; CA 97-100; CANR 30,
   100, 140, 195, 227; DFS 19; MTCW 1;
   MTFW 2005
Martin, Valerie 1948- .... **CLC 89**
   See also BEST 90:2; CA 85-88; CANR 49,
   89, 165, 200
Martin, Violet Florence 1862-1915 . **SSC 56; TCLC 51**
Martin, Webber
   See Silverberg, Robert
Martindale, Patrick Victor
   See White, Patrick
Martin du Gard, Roger 1881-1958 ... **TCLC 24**
   See also CA 118; CANR 94; DLB 65, 331;
   EWL 3; GFL 1789 to the Present; RGWL
   2, 3

Martineau, Harriet 1802-1876 .... **NCLC 26, 137**
   See also BRWS 15; DLB 21, 55, 159, 163, 166, 190; FW; RGEL 2; YABC 2

Martines, Julia
   See O'Faolain, Julia

Martinez, Enrique Gonzalez
   See Gonzalez Martinez, Enrique

Martinez, Jacinto Benavente y
   See Benavente, Jacinto

Martinez de la Rosa, Francisco de Paula 1787-1862 .... **NCLC 102**
   See also TWA

Martinez Ruiz, Jose 1873-1967 .... **CLC 11**
   See also CA 93-96; DLB 322; EW 3; EWL 3; HW 1

Martinez Sierra, Gregorio
   See Martinez Sierra, Maria

Martinez Sierra, Gregorio 1881-1947 ....
   TCLC 6
   See also CA 115; EWL 3

Martinez Sierra, Maria 1874-1974 . **TCLC 6**
   See also CA 250; 115; EWL 3

Martinez Sierra, Maria de la O'LeJarraga
   See Martinez Sierra, Maria

Martinsen, Martin
   See Follett, Ken

Martinson, Harry (Edmund) 1904-1978 ......
   CLC 14
   See also CA 77-80; CANR 34, 130; DLB 259, 331; EWL 3

Marti y Perez, Jose Julian
   See Marti, Jose

Martyn, Edward 1859-1923 .... **TCLC 131**
   See also CA 179; DLB 10; RGEL 2

Marut, Ret
   See Traven, B.

Marut, Robert
   See Traven, B.

Marvell, Andrew 1621-1678 . **LC 4, 43, 179; PC 10, 86; WLC 4**
   See also BRW 2; BRWR 2; CDBLB 1660-1789; DA; DAB; DAC; DAM MST, POET; DLB 131; EXPP; PFS 5; RGEL 2; TEA; WP

Marx, Karl 1818-1883 .... **NCLC 17, 114**
   See also DLB 129; LATS 1:1; TWA

Marx, Karl Heinrich
   See Marx, Karl

Masaoka, Shiki -1902 ....
   See Masaoka, Tsunenori

Masaoka, Tsunenori 1867-1902 .... **TCLC 18**
   See also CA 117; 191; EWL 3; RGWL 3; TWA

Masaoka Shiki
   See Masaoka, Tsunenori

Masefield, John (Edward) 1878-1967 .. **CLC 11, 47; PC 78**
   See also CA 19-20; 25-28R; CANR 33; CAP 2; CDBLB 1890-1914; CLR 164; DAM POET; DLB 10, 19, 153, 160; EWL 3; EXPP; FANT; MTCW 1, 2; PFS 5; RGEL 2; SATA 19

Maso, Carole 1955(?)- .... **CLC 44**
   See also CA 170; CANR 148; CN 7; GLL 2; RGAL 4

Mason, Bobbie Ann 1940- .. **CLC 28, 43, 82, 154, 303; SSC 4, 101**
   See also AAYA 5, 42; AMWS 8; BPFB 2; CA 53-56; CANR 11, 31, 58, 83, 125, 169; CDALBS; CN 5, 6, 7; CSW; DA3; DLB 173; DLBY 1987; EWL 3; EXPS; INT CANR-31; MAL 5; MTCW 1, 2; MTFW 2005; NFS 4; RGAL 4; RGSF 2; SSFS 3, 8, 20; TCLE 1:2; YAW

Mason, Ernst
   See Pohl, Frederik

Mason, Hunni B.
   See Sternheim, (William Adolf) Carl

Mason, Lee W.
   See Malzberg, Barry N(athaniel)

Mason, Nick 1945- .... **CLC 35**

Mason, Tally
   See Derleth, August (William)

Mass, Anna CLC 59

Mass, William
   See Gibson, William

Massinger, Philip 1583-1640 . **DC 39; LC 70**
   See also BRWS 11; DLB 58; RGEL 2

Master Lao
   See Lao Tzu

Masters, Edgar Lee 1868-1950 ..... **PC 1, 36; TCLC 2, 25; WLCS**
   See also AMWS 1; CA 104; 133; CDALB 1865-1917; DA; DAC; DAM MST, POET; DLB 54; EWL 3; EXPP; MAL 5; MTCW 1, 2; MTFW 2005; PFS 37; RGAL 4; TUS; WP

Masters, Hilary 1928- .... **CLC 48**
   See also CA 25-28R, 217; CAAE 217; CANR 13, 47, 97, 171, 221; CN 6, 7; DLB 244

Masters, Hilary Thomas
   See Masters, Hilary

Mastrosimone, William 1947- .... **CLC 36**
   See also CA 186; CAD; CD 5, 6

Mathe, Albert
   See Camus, Albert

Mather, Cotton 1663-1728 .... **LC 38**
   See also AMWS 2; CDALB 1640-1865; DLB 24, 30, 140; RGAL 4; TUS

Mather, Increase 1639-1723 .... **LC 38, 161**
   See also DLB 24

Mathers, Marshall
   See Eminem

Mathers, Marshall Bruce
   See Eminem

Matheson, Richard 1926- .... **CLC 37, 267**
   See also AAYA 31; CA 97-100; CANR 88, 99; DLB 8, 44; HGG; INT CA-97-100; SCFW 1, 2; SFW 4; SUFW 2

Matheson, Richard Burton
   See Matheson, Richard

Mathews, Harry 1930- .... **CLC 6, 52**
   See also CA 21-24R; CAAS 6; CANR 18, 40, 98, 160; CN 5, 6, 7

Mathews, John Joseph 1894-1979 . **CLC 84; NNAL**
   See also CA 19-20; 142; CANR 45; CAP 2; DAM MULT; DLB 175; TCWW 1, 2

Mathias, Roland 1915-2007 .... **CLC 45**
   See also CA 97-100; 263; CANR 19, 41; CP 1, 2, 3, 4, 5, 6, 7; DLB 27

Mathias, Roland Glyn
   See Mathias, Roland

Matsuo Basho 1644(?)-1694 ... **LC 62; PC 3, 125**
   See also DAM POET; PFS 2, 7, 18; RGWL 2, 3; WP

Mattheson, Rodney
   See Creasey, John

Matthew, James
   See Barrie, J. M.

Matthew of Vendome c. 1130-c. 1200 .... **CMLC 99**
   See also DLB 208

Matthews, (James) Brander 1852-1929 ....
   TCLC 95
   See also CA 181; DLB 71, 78; DLBD 13

Matthews, Greg 1949- .... **CLC 45**
   See also CA 135

Matthews, William (Procter III) 1942-1997 .... **CLC 40**
   See also AMWS 9; CA 29-32R; 162; CAAS 18; CANR 12, 57; CP 2, 3, 4, 5, 6; DLB 5

Matthias, John (Edward) 1941- .... **CLC 9**
   See also CA 33-36R; CANR 56; CP 4, 5, 6, 7

Matthiessen, F(rancis) O(tto) 1902-1950 .....
   TCLC 100
   See also CA 185; DLB 63; MAL 5

Matthiessen, Francis Otto
   See Matthiessen, F(rancis) O(tto)

Matthiessen, Peter 1927- .. **CLC 5, 7, 11, 32, 64, 245**
   See also AAYA 6, 40; AMWS 5; ANW; BEST 90:4; BPFB 2; CA 9-12R; CANR 21, 50, 73, 100, 138; CN 1, 2, 3, 4, 5, 6, 7; DA3; DAM NOV; DLB 6, 173, 275; MAL 5; MTCW 1, 2; MTFW 2005; SATA 27

Maturin, Charles Robert 1780(?)-1824 ....
   NCLC 6, 169
   See also BRWS 8; DLB 178; GL 3; HGG; LMFS 1; RGEL 2; SUFW

Matute (Ausejo), Ana Maria 1925- . **CLC 11**
   See also CA 89-92; CANR 129; CWW 2; DLB 322; EWL 3; MTCW 1; RGSF 2

Maugham, W. S.
   See Maugham, W. Somerset

Maugham, W. Somerset 1874-1965 . **CLC 1, 11, 15, 67, 93; SSC 8, 94, 164; TCLC 208; WLC 4**
   See also AAYA 55; BPFB 2; BRW 6; CA 5-8R; 25-28R; CANR 40, 127; CDBLB 1914-1945; CMW 4; DA; DA3; DAB; DAC; DAM DRAM, MST, NOV; DFS 22; DLB 10, 36, 77, 100, 162, 195; EWL 3; LAIT 3; MTCW 1, 2; MTFW 2005; NFS 23, 35; RGEL 2; RGSF 2; SATA 54; SSFS 17

Maugham, William S.
   See Maugham, W. Somerset

Maugham, William Somerset
   See Maugham, W. Somerset

Maupassant, Guy de 1850-1893 .... **NCLC 1, 42, 83, 234; SSC 1, 64, 132; WLC 4**
   See also BYA 14; DA; DA3; DAB; DAC; DAM MST; DLB 123; EW 7; EXPS; GFL 1789 to the Present; LAIT 2; LMFS 1; RGSF 2; RGWL 2, 3; SSFS 4, 21, 28, 31; SUFW; TWA

Maupassant, Henri Rene Albert Guy de
   See Maupassant, Guy de

Maupin, Armistead 1944- .... **CLC 95**
   See also CA 125; 130; CANR 58, 101, 183; CPW; DA3; DAM POP; DLB 278; GLL 1; INT CA-130; MTCW 2; MTFW 2005

Maupin, Armistead Jones, Jr.
   See Maupin, Armistead

Maurhut, Richard
   See Traven, B.

Mauriac, Claude 1914-1996 .... **CLC 9**
   See also CA 89-92; 152; CWW 2; DLB 83; EWL 3; GFL 1789 to the Present

Mauriac, Francois (Charles) 1885-1970 ......
   CLC 4, 9, 56; SSC 24
   See also CA 25-28; CAP 2; DLB 65, 331; EW 10; EWL 3; GFL 1789 to the Present; MTCW 1, 2; MTFW 2005; RGWL 2, 3; TWA

Mavor, Osborne Henry 1888-1951 . **TCLC 3**
   See also CA 104; DLB 10; EWL 3

Maxwell, Glyn 1962- .... **CLC 238**
   See also CA 154; CANR 88, 183; CP 6, 7; PFS 23

Maxwell, William (Keepers, Jr.) 1908-2000 .... **CLC 19**
   See also AMWS 8; CA 93-96; 189; CANR 54, 95; CN 1, 2, 3, 4, 5, 6, 7; DLB 218, 278; DLBY 1980; INT CA-93-96; MAL 5; SATA-Obit 128

May, Elaine 1932- .... **CLC 16**
   See also CA 124; 142; CAD; CWD; DLB 44

Mayakovski, Vladimir 1893-1930 . **TCLC 4, 18**
See also CA 104; 158; EW 11; EWL 3; IDTP; MTCW 2; MTFW 2005; RGWL 2, 3; SFW 4; TWA; WP

Mayakovski, Vladimir Vladimirovich
See Mayakovski, Vladimir

Mayakovsky, Vladimir
See Mayakovski, Vladimir

Mayhew, Henry 1812-1887 .... **NCLC 31**
See also BRWS 16; DLB 18, 55, 190

Mayle, Peter 1939(?)- .... **CLC 89**
See also CA 139; CANR 64, 109, 168, 218

Maynard, Joyce 1953- .... **CLC 23**
See also CA 111; 129; CANR 64, 169, 220

Mayne, William 1928-2010 .... **CLC 12**
See also AAYA 20; CA 9-12R; CANR 37, 80, 100; CLR 25, 123; FANT; JRDA; MAICYA 1, 2; MAICYAS 1; SAAS 11; SATA 6, 68, 122; SUFW 2; YAW

Mayne, William James Carter
See Mayne, William

Mayo, Jim
See L'Amour, Louis

Maysles, Albert 1926- .... **CLC 16**
See also CA 29-32R

Maysles, David 1932-1987 .... **CLC 16**
See also CA 191

Mazer, Norma Fox 1931-2009 .... **CLC 26**
See also AAYA 5, 36; BYA 1, 8; CA 69-72; 292; CANR 12, 32, 66, 129, 189; CLR 23; JRDA; MAICYA 1, 2; SAAS 1; SATA 24, 67, 105, 168, 198; WYA; YAW

Mazzini, Guiseppe 1805-1872 .... **NCLC 34**

McAlmon, Robert (Menzies) 1895-1956 ......
TCLC 97
See also CA 107; 168; DLB 4, 45; DLBD 15; GLL 1

McAuley, James Phillip 1917-1976 . **CLC 45**
See also CA 97-100; CP 1, 2; DLB 260; RGEL 2

McBain, Ed
See Hunter, Evan

McBrien, William 1930- .... **CLC 44**
See also CA 107; CANR 90

McBrien, William Augustine
See McBrien, William

McCabe, Pat
See McCabe, Patrick

McCabe, Patrick 1955- .... **CLC 133**
See also BRWS 9; CA 130; CANR 50, 90, 168, 202; CN 6, 7; DLB 194

McCaffrey, Anne 1926- .... **CLC 17**
See also AAYA 6, 34; AITN 2; BEST 89:2; BPFB 2; BYA 5; CA 25-28R; 227; CAAE 227; CANR 15, 35, 55, 96, 169; CLR 49, 130; CPW; DA3; DAM NOV, POP; DLB 8; JRDA; MAICYA 1, 2; MTCW 1, 2; MTFW 2005; SAAS 11; SATA 8, 70, 116, 152; SATA-Essay 152; SFW 4; SUFW 2; WYA; YAW

McCaffrey, Anne Inez
See McCaffrey, Anne

McCall, Nathan 1955(?)- .... **CLC 86**
See also AAYA 59; BW 3; CA 146; CANR 88, 186

McCall Smith, Alexander
See Smith, Alexander McCall

McCann, Arthur
See Campbell, John W.

McCann, Colum 1965- .... **CLC 299**
See also CA 152; CANR 99, 149; DLB 267

McCann, Edson
See Pohl, Frederik

McCarthy, Charles
See McCarthy, Cormac

McCarthy, Charles, Jr.
See McCarthy, Cormac

McCarthy, Cormac 1933- .. **CLC 4, 57, 101, 204, 295, 310**
See also AAYA 41; AMWS 8; BPFB 2; CA 13-16R; CANR 10, 42, 69, 101, 161, 171; CN 6, 7; CPW; CSW; DA3; DAM POP; DLB 6, 143, 256; EWL 3; LATS 1:2; LNFS 3; MAL 5; MTCW 2; MTFW 2005; NFS 36, 40; TCLE 1:2; TCWW 2

McCarthy, Mary 1912-1989 ..... **CLC 1, 3, 5, 14, 24, 39, 59; SSC 24**
See also AMW; BPFB 2; CA 5-8R; 129; CANR 16, 50, 64; CN 1, 2, 3, 4; DA3; DLB 2; DLBY 1981; EWL 3; FW; INT CANR-16; MAL 5; MBL; MTCW 1, 2; MTFW 2005; RGAL 4; TUS

McCarthy, Mary Therese
See McCarthy, Mary

McCartney, James Paul
See McCartney, Paul

McCartney, Paul 1942- .... **CLC 12, 35**
See also CA 146; CANR 111

McCauley, Stephen 1955- .... **CLC 50**
See also CA 141

McClaren, Peter CLC 70

McClure, Michael 1932- .... **CLC 6, 10**
See also BG 1:3; CA 21-24R; CAD; CANR 17, 46, 77, 131, 231; CD 5, 6; CP 1, 2, 3, 4, 5, 6, 7; DLB 16; WP

McClure, Michael Thomas
See McClure, Michael

McCorkle, Jill 1958- .... **CLC 51**
See also CA 121; CANR 113, 218; CSW; DLB 234; DLBY 1987; SSFS 24

McCorkle, Jill Collins
See McCorkle, Jill

McCourt, Francis
See McCourt, Frank

McCourt, Frank 1930-2009 ... **CLC 109, 299**
See also AAYA 61; AMWS 12; CA 157; 288; CANR 97, 138; MTFW 2005; NCFS 1

McCourt, James 1941- .... **CLC 5**
See also CA 57-60; CANR 98, 152, 186

McCourt, Malachy 1931- .... **CLC 119**
See also SATA 126

McCoy, Edmund
See Gardner, John

McCoy, Horace (Stanley) 1897-1955 . **TCLC 28**
See also AMWS 13; CA 108; 155; CMW 4; DLB 9

McCrae, John 1872-1918 .... **TCLC 12**
See also CA 109; DLB 92; PFS 5

McCreigh, James
See Pohl, Frederik

McCullers, Carson 1917-1967 ...... **CLC 1, 4, 10, 12, 48, 100; DC 35; SSC 9, 24, 99; TCLC 155; WLC 4**
See also AAYA 21; AMW; AMWC 2; BPFB 2; CA 5-8R; 25-28R; CABS 1, 3; CANR 18, 132; CDALB 1941-1968; DA; DA3; DAB; DAC; DAM MST, NOV; DFS 5, 18; DLB 2, 7, 173, 228; EWL 3; EXPS; FW; GLL 1; LAIT 3, 4; MAL 5; MBL; MTCW 1, 2; MTFW 2005; NFS 6, 13; RGAL 4; RGSF 2; SATA 27; SSFS 5, 32; TUS; YAW

McCullers, Lula Carson Smith
See McCullers, Carson

McCulloch, John Tyler
See Burroughs, Edgar Rice

McCullough, Colleen 1937- ..... **CLC 27, 107**
See also AAYA 36; BPFB 2; CA 81-84; CANR 17, 46, 67, 98, 139, 203; CPW; DA3; DAM NOV, POP; MTCW 1, 2; MTFW 2005; RHW

McCunn, Ruthanne Lum 1946- .... **AAL**
See also CA 119; CANR 43, 96; DLB 312; LAIT 2; SATA 63

McDermott, Alice 1953- .... **CLC 90**
See also AMWS 18; CA 109; CANR 40, 90, 126, 181; CN 7; DLB 292; MTFW 2005; NFS 23

McDonagh, Martin 1970(?)- .... **CLC 304**
See also AAYA 71; BRWS 12; CA 171; CANR 141; CD 6

McElroy, Joseph 1930- .... **CLC 5, 47**
See also CA 17-20R; CANR 149; CN 3, 4, 5, 6, 7

McElroy, Joseph Prince
See McElroy, Joseph

McElroy, Lee
See Kelton, Elmer

McEwan, Ian 1948- .. **CLC 13, 66, 169, 269; SSC 106**
See also AAYA 84; BEST 90:4; BRWS 4; CA 61-64; CANR 14, 41, 69, 87, 132, 179, 232; CN 3, 4, 5, 6, 7; DAM NOV; DLB 14, 194, 319, 326; HGG; MTCW 1, 2; MTFW 2005; NFS 32; RGSF 2; SUFW 2; TEA

McEwan, Ian Russell
See McEwan, Ian

McFadden, David 1940- .... **CLC 48**
See also CA 104; CP 1, 2, 3, 4, 5, 6, 7; DLB 60; INT CA-104

McFarland, Dennis 1950- .... **CLC 65**
See also CA 165; CANR 110, 179

McGahern, John 1934-2006 ... **CLC 5, 9, 48, 156; SSC 17**
See also CA 17-20R; 249; CANR 29, 68, 113, 204; CN 1, 2, 3, 4, 5, 6, 7; DLB 14, 231, 319; MTCW 1

McGinley, Patrick (Anthony) 1937- ..... **CLC 41**
See also CA 120; 127; CANR 56; INT CA-127

McGinley, Phyllis 1905-1978 .... **CLC 14**
See also CA 9-12R; 77-80; CANR 19; CP 1, 2; CWRI 5; DLB 11, 48; MAL 5; PFS 9, 13; SATA 2, 44; SATA-Obit 24

McGinniss, Joe 1942- .... **CLC 32**
See also AITN 2; BEST 89:2; CA 25-28R; CANR 26, 70, 152; CPW; DLB 185; INT CANR-26

McGivern, Maureen Daly
See Daly, Maureen

McGivern, Maureen Patricia Daly
See Daly, Maureen

McGrath, Patrick 1950- .... **CLC 55**
See also CA 136; CANR 65, 148, 190; CN 5, 6, 7; DLB 231; HGG; SUFW 2

McGrath, Thomas (Matthew) 1916-1990 ....
CLC 28, 59
See also AMWS 10; CA 9-12R; 132; CANR 6, 33, 95; CP 1, 2, 3, 4, 5; DAM POET; MAL 5; MTCW 1; SATA 41; SATA-Obit 66

McGuane, Thomas 1939- . **CLC 3, 7, 18, 45, 127**
See also AITN 2; BPFB 2; CA 49-52; CANR 5, 24, 49, 94, 164, 229; CN 2, 3, 4, 5, 6, 7; DLB 2, 212; DLBY 1980; EWL 3; INT CANR-24; MAL 5; MTCW 1; MTFW 2005; TCWW 1, 2

McGuane, Thomas Francis III
See McGuane, Thomas

McGuckian, Medbh 1950- ..... **CLC 48, 174; PC 27**
See also BRWS 5; CA 143; CANR 206; CP 4, 5, 6, 7; CWP; DAM POET; DLB 40

McHale, Tom 1942(?)-1982 .... **CLC 3, 5**
See also AITN 1; CA 77-80; 106; CN 1, 2, 3

McHugh, Heather 1948- .... **PC 61**
See also CA 69-72; CANR 11, 28, 55, 92; CP 4, 5, 6, 7; CWP; PFS 24

Meredith, William Morris
  See Meredith, William
Merezhkovsky, Dmitrii Sergeevich
  See Merezhkovsky, Dmitry Sergeyevich
Merezhkovsky, Dmitry Sergeevich
  See Merezhkovsky, Dmitry Sergeyevich
Merezhkovsky, Dmitry Sergeyevich
  1865-1941 .... **TCLC 29**
  See also CA 169; DLB 295; EWL 3
Merezhkovsky, Zinaida
  See Gippius, Zinaida
Merimee, Prosper 1803-1870 . **DC 33; NCLC
  6, 65; SSC 7, 77**
  See also DLB 119, 192; EW 6; EXPS; GFL
  1789 to the Present; RGSF 2; RGWL 2,
  3; SSFS 8; SUFW
Merkin, Daphne 1954- .... **CLC 44**
  See also CA 123
Merleau-Ponty, Maurice 1908-1961 .. **TCLC
  156**
  See also CA 114; 89-92; DLB 296; GFL
  1789 to the Present
Merlin, Arthur
  See Blish, James
Mernissi, Fatima 1940- .... **CLC 171**
  See also CA 152; DLB 346; FW
Merrill, James 1926-1995 .... **CLC 2, 3, 6, 8,
  13, 18, 34, 91; PC 28; TCLC 173**
  See also AMWS 3; CA 13-16R; 147; CANR
  10, 49, 63, 108; CP 1, 2, 3, 4; DA3; DAM
  POET; DLB 5, 165; DLBY 1985; EWL 3;
  INT CANR-10; MAL 5; MTCW 1, 2;
  MTFW 2005; PAB; PFS 23; RGAL 4
Merrill, James Ingram
  See Merrill, James
Merriman, Alex
  See Silverberg, Robert
Merriman, Brian 1747-1805 .... **NCLC 70**
Merritt, E. B.
  See Waddington, Miriam
Merton, Thomas 1915-1968 ... **CLC 1, 3, 11,
  34, 83; PC 10**
  See also AAYA 61; AMWS 8; CA 5-8R;
  25-28R; CANR 22, 53, 111, 131; DA3;
  DLB 48; DLBY 1981; MAL 5; MTCW 1,
  2; MTFW 2005
Merton, Thomas James
  See Merton, Thomas
Merwin, W. S. 1927- .. **CLC 1, 2, 3, 5, 8, 13,
  18, 45, 88; PC 45**
  See also AMWS 3; CA 13-16R; CANR 15,
  51, 112, 140, 209; CP 1, 2, 3, 4, 5, 6, 7;
  DA3; DAM POET; DLB 5, 169, 342;
  EWL 3; INT CANR-15; MAL 5; MTCW
  1, 2; MTFW 2005; PAB; PFS 5, 15;
  RGAL 4
Merwin, William Stanley
  See Merwin, W. S.
Metastasio, Pietro 1698-1782 .... **LC 115**
  See also RGWL 2, 3
Metcalf, John 1938- .... **CLC 37; SSC 43**
  See also CA 113; CN 4, 5, 6, 7; DLB 60;
  RGSF 2; TWA
Metcalf, Suzanne
  See Baum, L. Frank
Mew, Charlotte (Mary) 1870-1928 . **PC 107;
  TCLC 8**
  See also CA 105; 189; DLB 19, 135; RGEL
  2
Mewshaw, Michael 1943- .... **CLC 9**
  See also CA 53-56; CANR 7, 47, 147, 213;
  DLBY 1980
Meyer, Conrad Ferdinand 1825-1898 ....
  NCLC 81, 249; SSC 30
  See also DLB 129; EW; RGWL 2, 3
Meyer, Gustav 1868-1932 .... **TCLC 21**
  See also CA 117; 190; DLB 81; EWL 3
Meyer, June
  See Jordan, June

Meyer, Lynn
  See Slavitt, David R.
Meyer, Stephenie 1973- .... **CLC 280**
  See also AAYA 77; CA 253; CANR 192;
  CLR 142; SATA 193
Meyer-Meyrink, Gustav
  See Meyer, Gustav
Meyers, Jeffrey 1939- .... **CLC 39**
  See also CA 73-76, 186; CAAE 186; CANR
  54, 102, 159; DLB 111
**Meynell, Alice (Christina Gertrude
  Thompson)** 1847-1922 . **PC 112; TCLC
  6**
  See also CA 104; 177; DLB 19, 98; RGEL
  2
Meyrink, Gustav
  See Meyer, Gustav
Mhlophe, Gcina 1960- .... **BLC 2:3**
Michaels, Leonard 1933-2003 .... **CLC 6, 25;
  SSC 16**
  See also AMWS 16; CA 61-64; 216; CANR
  21, 62, 119, 179; CN 3, 45, 6, 7; DLB
  130; MTCW 1; TCLE 1:2
Michaux, Henri 1899-1984 .... **CLC 8, 19**
  See also CA 85-88; 114; DLB 258; EWL 3;
  GFL 1789 to the Present; RGWL 2, 3
Micheaux, Oscar (Devereaux) 1884-1951 ....
  TCLC 76
  See also BW 3; CA 174; DLB 50; TCWW
  2
Michelangelo 1475-1564 .... **LC 12**
  See also AAYA 43
Michelet, Jules 1798-1874 ..... **NCLC 31, 218**
  See also EW 5; GFL 1789 to the Present
Michels, Robert 1876-1936 .... **TCLC 88**
  See also CA 212
Michener, James A. 1907(?)-1997 . **CLC 1, 5,
  11, 29, 60, 109**
  See also AAYA 27; AITN 1; BEST 90:1;
  BPFB 2; CA 5-8R; 161; CANR 21, 45,
  68; CN 1, 2, 3, 4, 5, 6; CPW; DA3; DAM
  NOV, POP; DLB 6; MAL 5; MTCW 1, 2;
  MTFW 2005; RHW; TCWW 1, 2
Michener, James Albert
  See Michener, James A.
Mickiewicz, Adam 1798-1855 . **NCLC 3, 101;
  PC 38**
  See also EW 5; RGWL 2, 3
Middleton, (John) Christopher 1926- .. **CLC
  13**
  See also CA 13-16R; CANR 29, 54, 117;
  CP 1, 2, 3, 4, 5, 6, 7; DLB 40
Middleton, Richard (Barham) 1882-1911 ....
  TCLC 56
  See also CA 187; DLB 156; HGG
Middleton, Stanley 1919-2009 ..... **CLC 7, 38**
  See also CA 25-28R; 288; CAAS 23; CANR
  21, 46, 81, 157; CN 1, 2, 3, 4, 5, 6, 7;
  DLB 14, 326
Middleton, Thomas 1580-1627 ..... **DC 5, 40;
  LC 33, 123**
  See also BRW 2; DAM DRAM, MST; DFS
  18, 22; DLB 58; RGEL 2
Mieville, China 1972(?)- .... **CLC 235**
  See also AAYA 52; CA 196; CANR 138,
  214; MTFW 2005
Migueis, Jose Rodrigues 1901-1980 ..... **CLC
  10**
  See also DLB 287
Mihura, Miguel 1905-1977 .... **DC 34**
  See also CA 214
Mikszath, Kalman 1847-1910 .... **TCLC 31**
  See also CA 170
Miles, Jack CLC 100
  See also CA 200
Miles, John Russiano
  See Miles, Jack

Miles, Josephine (Louise) 1911-1985 ... **CLC
  1, 2, 14, 34, 39**
  See also CA 1-4R; 116; CANR 2, 55; CP 1,
  2, 3, 4; DAM POET; DLB 48; MAL 5;
  TCLE 1:2
Militant
  See Sandburg, Carl
Mill, Harriet (Hardy) Taylor 1807-1858 ......
  NCLC 102
  See also FW
Mill, John Stuart 1806-1873 .. **NCLC 11, 58,
  179, 223**
  See also CDBLB 1832-1890; DLB 55, 190,
  262, 366; FW 1; RGEL 2; TEA
Millar, Kenneth 1915-1983 . **CLC 1, 2, 3, 14,
  34, 41**
  See also AAYA 81; AMWS 4; BPFB 2; CA
  9-12R; 110; CANR 16, 63, 107; CMW 4;
  CN 1, 2, 3; CPW; DA3; DAM POP; DLB
  2, 226; DLBD 6; DLBY 1983; MAL 5;
  MSW; MTCW 1, 2; MTFW 2005; RGAL
  4
Millay, E. Vincent
  See Millay, Edna St. Vincent
Millay, Edna St. Vincent 1892-1950 ... **PC 6,
  61; TCLC 4, 49, 169; WLCS**
  See also AMW; CA 104; 130; CDALB
  1917-1929; DA; DA3; DAB; DAC; DAM
  MST, POET; DFS 27; DLB 45, 249; EWL
  3; EXPP; FL 1:6; GLL 1; MAL 5; MBL;
  MTCW 1, 2; MTFW 2005; PAB; PFS 3,
  17, 31, 34, 41; RGAL 4; TUS; WP
Miller, Arthur 1915-2005 ... **CLC 1, 2, 6, 10,
  15, 26, 47, 78, 179; DC 1, 31; WLC 4**
  See also AAYA 15; AITN 1; AMW; AMWC
  1; CA 1-4R; 236; CABS 3; CAD; CANR
  2, 30, 54, 76, 132; CD 5, 6; CDALB
  1941-1968; DA; DA3; DAB; DAC; DAM
  DRAM, MST; DFS 1, 3, 8, 27; DLB 7,
  266; EWL 3; LAIT 1, 4; LATS 1:2; MAL
  5; MTCW 1, 2; MTFW 2005; RGAL 4;
  RGHL; TUS; WYAS 1
Miller, Frank 1957- .... **CLC 278**
  See also AAYA 45; CA 224
Miller, Henry (Valentine) 1891-1980 ... **CLC
  1, 2, 4, 9, 14, 43, 84; TCLC 213; WLC
  4**
  See also AMW; BPFB 2; CA 9-12R; 97-
  100; CANR 33, 64; CDALB 1929-1941;
  CN 1, 2; DA; DA3; DAB; DAC; DAM
  MST, NOV; DLB 4, 9; DLBY 1980; EWL
  3; MAL 5; MTCW 1, 2; MTFW 2005;
  RGAL 4; TUS
Miller, Hugh 1802-1856 .... **NCLC 143**
  See also DLB 190
Miller, Jason 1939(?)-2001 .... **CLC 2**
  See also AITN 1; CA 73-76; 197; CAD;
  CANR 130; DFS 12; DLB 7
Miller, Sue 1943- .... **CLC 44**
  See also AMWS 12; BEST 90:3; CA 139;
  CANR 59, 91, 128, 194, 231; DA3; DAM
  POP; DLB 143
Miller, Walter M(ichael, Jr.) 1923-1996 ....
  CLC 4, 30
  See also BPFB 2; CA 85-88; CANR 108;
  DLB 8; SCFW 1, 2; SFW 4
Millett, Kate 1934- .... **CLC 67**
  See also AITN 1; CA 73-76; CANR 32, 53,
  76, 110; DA3; DLB 246; FW; GLL 1;
  MTCW 1, 2; MTFW 2005
Millhauser, Steven 1943- .. **CLC 21, 54, 109,
  300; SSC 57**
  See also AAYA 76; CA 110; 111; CANR
  63, 114, 133, 189; CN 6, 7; DA3; DLB 2,
  350; FANT; INT CA-111; MAL 5; MTCW
  2; MTFW 2005
Millhauser, Steven Lewis
  See Millhauser, Steven
Millin, Sarah Gertrude 1889-1968 . **CLC 49**
  See also CA 102; 93-96; DLB 225; EWL 3

Murasaki Shikibu 978(?)-1026(?) . **CMLC 1, 79**
See also EFS 1:2, 2:2; LATS 1:1; RGWL 2, 3

Murdoch, Iris 1919-1999 . **CLC 1, 2, 3, 4, 6, 8, 11, 15, 22, 31, 51; TCLC 171**
See also BRWS 1; CA 13-16R; 179; CANR 8, 43, 68, 103, 142; CBD; CDBLB 1960 to Present; CN 1, 2, 3, 4, 5, 6; CWD; DA3; DAB; DAC; DAM MST, NOV; DLB 14, 194, 233, 326; EWL 3; INT CANR-8; MTCW 1, 2; MTFW 2005; NFS 18; RGEL 2; TCLE 1:2; TEA; WLIT 4

Murdoch, Jean Iris
See Murdoch, Iris

Murfree, Mary Noailles 1850-1922 . **SSC 22; TCLC 135**
See also CA 122; 176; DLB 12, 74; RGAL 4

Murglie
See Murnau, F.W.

Murnau, Friedrich Wilhelm
See Murnau, F.W.

Murnau, F.W. 1888-1931 .... **TCLC 53**
See also CA 112

Murphy, Arthur 1727-1805 .... **NCLC 229**
See also DLB 89, 142; RGEL 2

Murphy, Richard 1927- .... **CLC 41**
See also BRWS 5; CA 29-32R; CP 1, 2, 3, 4, 5, 6, 7; DLB 40; EWL 3

Murphy, Sylvia 1937- .... **CLC 34**
See also CA 121

Murphy, Thomas 1935- .... **CLC 51**
See also CA 101; DLB 310

Murphy, Thomas Bernard
See Murphy, Thomas

Murphy, Tom
See Murphy, Thomas

Murray, Albert 1916- ...... **BLC 2:3; CLC 73**
See also BW 2; CA 49-52; CANR 26, 52, 78, 160; CN 7; CSW; DLB 38; MTFW 2005

Murray, Albert L.
See Murray, Albert

Murray, Diane Lain Johnson
See Johnson, Diane

Murray, James Augustus Henry 1837-1915 .... **TCLC 117**

Murray, Judith Sargent 1751-1820 ... **NCLC 63, 243**
See also DLB 37, 200

Murray, Les 1938- .... **CLC 40**
See also BRWS 7; CA 21-24R; CANR 11, 27, 56, 103, 199; CP 1, 2, 3, 4, 5, 6, 7; DAM POET; DLB 289; DLBY 2001; EWL 3; RGEL 2

Murray, Leslie Allan
See Murray, Les

Murry, J. Middleton
See Murry, John Middleton

Murry, John Middleton 1889-1957 ... **TCLC 16**
See also CA 118; 217; DLB 149

Musgrave, Susan 1951- .... **CLC 13, 54**
See also CA 69-72; CANR 45, 84, 181; CCA 1; CP 2, 3, 4, 5, 6, 7; CWP

Musil, Robert (Edler von) 1880-1942 ... **SSC 18; TCLC 12, 68, 213**
See also CA 109; CANR 55, 84; CDWLB 2; DLB 81, 124; EW 9; EWL 3; MTCW 2; RGSF 2; RGWL 2, 3

Muske, Carol
See Muske-Dukes, Carol

Muske, Carol Anne
See Muske-Dukes, Carol

Muske-Dukes, Carol 1945- .... **CLC 90**
See also CA 65-68, 203; CAAE 203; CANR 32, 70, 181; CWP; PFS 24

Muske-Dukes, Carol Ann
See Muske-Dukes, Carol

Muske-Dukes, Carol Anne
See Muske-Dukes, Carol

Musset, Alfred de 1810-1857 . **DC 27; NCLC 7, 150**
See also DLB 192, 217; EW 6; GFL 1789 to the Present; RGWL 2, 3; TWA

Musset, Louis Charles Alfred de
See Musset, Alfred de

Mussolini, Benito (Amilcare Andrea) 1883-1945 .... **TCLC 96**
See also CA 116

Mutanabbi, Al-
See al-Mutanabbi, Ahmad ibn al-Husayn Abu al-Tayyib al-Jufi al-Kindi

Mutis, Alvaro 1923- .... **CLC 283**
See also CA 149; CANR 118; DLB 283; EWL 3; HW 1; LAWS 1

My Brother's Brother
See Chekhov, Anton

Myers, L(eopold) H(amilton) 1881-1944 ..... **TCLC 59**
See also CA 157; DLB 15; EWL 3; RGEL 2

Myers, Walter Dean 1937- ..... **BLC 1:3, 2:3; CLC 35**
See also AAYA 4, 23; BW 2; BYA 6, 8, 11; CA 33-36R; CANR 20, 42, 67, 108, 184; CLR 4, 16, 35, 110; DAM MULT, NOV; DLB 33; INT CANR-20; JRDA; LAIT 5; LNFS 1; MAICYA 1; MAICYAS 1; MTCW 2; MTFW 2005; NFS 30, 33, 40; SAAS 2; SATA 41, 71, 109, 157, 193, 229; SATA-Brief 27; SSFS 31; WYA; YAW

Myers, Walter M.
See Myers, Walter Dean

Myles, Symon
See Follett, Ken

Nabokov, Vladimir 1899-1977 . **CLC 1, 2, 3, 6, 8, 11, 15, 23, 44, 46, 64; SSC 11, 86, 163; TCLC 108, 189; WLC 4**
See also AAYA 45; AMW; AMWC 1; AMWR 1; BPFB 2; CA 5-8R; 69-72; CANR 20, 102; CDALB 1941-1968; CN 1, 2; CP 2; DA; DA3; DAB; DAC; DAM MST, NOV; DLB 2, 244, 278, 317; DLBD 3; DLBY 1980, 1991; EWL 3; EXPS; LATS 1:2; MAL 5; MTCW 1, 2; MTFW 2005; NCFS 4; NFS 9; RGAL 4; RGSF 2; SSFS 6, 15; TUS

Nabokov, Vladimir Vladimirovich
See Nabokov, Vladimir

Naevius c. 265B.C.-201B.C. .... **CMLC 37**
See also DLB 211

Nafisi, Azar 1955- .... **CLC 313**
See also CA 222; CANR 203; DLB 366; LNFS 2

Nagai, Kafu 1879-1959 .... **TCLC 51**
See also CA 117; 276; DLB 180; EWL 3; MJW

Nagai, Sokichi
See Nagai, Kafu

Nagai Kafu
See Nagai, Kafu

na gCopaleen, Myles
See O Nuallain, Brian

na Gopaleen, Myles
See O Nuallain, Brian

Nagy, Laszlo 1925-1978 .... **CLC 7**
See also CA 129; 112

Naidu, Sarojini 1879-1949 .... **TCLC 80**
See also EWL 3; RGEL 2

Naipaul, Shiva 1945-1985 .... **CLC 32, 39; TCLC 153**
See also CA 110; 112; 116; CANR 33; CN 2, 3; DA3; DAM NOV; DLB 157; DLBY 1985; EWL 3; MTCW 1, 2; MTFW 2005

Naipaul, Shivadhar Srinivasa
See Naipaul, Shiva

Naipaul, Vidiahar Surajprasad
See Naipaul, V.S.

Naipaul, V.S. 1932- . **CLC 4, 7, 9, 13, 18, 37, 105, 199; SSC 38, 121**
See also BPFB 2; BRWS 1; CA 1-4R; CANR 1, 33, 51, 91, 126, 191, 225; CDBLB 1960 to Present; CDWLB 3; CN 1, 2, 3, 4, 5, 6, 7; DA3; DAB; DAC; DAM MST, NOV; DLB 125, 204, 207, 326, 331; DLBY 1985, 2001; EWL 3; LATS 1:2; MTCW 1, 2; MTFW 2005; NFS 37, 39; RGEL 2; RGSF 2; SSFS 29; TWA; WLIT 4; WWE 1

Nair, Kamala
See Das, Kamala

Nakos, Lilika 1903-1989 .... **CLC 29**
See also CA 217

Nalapat, Kamala
See Das, Kamala

Napoleon
See Yamamoto, Hisaye

Narayan, R. K. 1906-2001 .... **CLC 7, 28, 47, 121, 211; SSC 25, 154**
See also BPFB 2; CA 81-84; 196; CANR 33, 61, 112; CN 1, 2, 3, 4, 5, 6, 7; DA3; DAM NOV; DLB 323; DNFS 1; EWL 3; MTCW 1, 2; MTFW 2005; RGEL 2; RGSF 2; SATA 62; SSFS 5, 29; WWE 1

Narayan, Rasipuram Krishnaswami
See Narayan, R. K.

Nash, Frediric Ogden
See Nash, Ogden

Nash, Ogden 1902-1971 ..... **CLC 23; PC 21; TCLC 109**
See also CA 13-14; 29-32R; CANR 34, 61, 185; CAP 1; CP 1; DAM POET; DLB 11; MAICYA 1, 2; MAL 5; MTCW 1, 2; PFS 31; RGAL 4; SATA 2, 46; WP

Nashe, Thomas 1567-1601(?) ...... **LC 41, 89, 184; PC 82**
See also DLB 167; RGEL 2

Nathan, Daniel
See Dannay, Frederic

Nathan, George Jean 1882-1958 .. **TCLC 18**
See also CA 114; 169; DLB 137; MAL 5

Natsume, Kinnosuke
See Natsume, Soseki

Natsume, Soseki 1867-1916 ...... **TCLC 2, 10**
See also CA 104; 195; DLB 180; EWL 3; MJW; RGWL 2, 3; TWA

Natsume Soseki
See Natsume, Soseki

Natti, Lee 1919- .... **CLC 17**
See also CA 5-8R; CANR 2; CWRI 5; SAAS 3; SATA 1, 67

Natti, Mary Lee
See Natti, Lee

Navarre, Marguerite de
See de Navarre, Marguerite

Naylor, Gloria 1950- . **BLC 1:3; CLC 28, 52, 156, 261; WLCS**
See also AAYA 6, 39; AFAW 1, 2; AMWS 8; BW 2, 3; CA 107; CANR 27, 51, 74, 130; CN 4, 5, 6, 7; CPW; DA; DA3; DAC; DAM MST, MULT, NOV, POP; DLB 173; EWL 3; FW; MAL 5; MTCW 1, 2; MTFW 2005; NFS 4, 7; RGAL 4; TCLE 1:2; TUS

Ndebele, Njabulo (Simakahle) 1948- .... **SSC 135**
See also CA 184; DLB 157, 225; EWL 3

Neal, John 1793-1876 .... **NCLC 161**
See also DLB 1, 59, 243; FW; RGAL 4

Neff, Debra CLC 59

Osborne, David
See Silverberg, Robert

Osborne, Dorothy 1627-1695 .... **LC 141**

Osborne, George
See Silverberg, Robert

Osborne, John 1929-1994 ... **CLC 1, 2, 5, 11, 45; DC 38; TCLC 153; WLC 4**
See also BRWS 1; CA 13-16R; 147; CANR 21, 56; CBD; CDBLB 1945-1960; DA; DAB; DAC; DAM DRAM, MST; DFS 4, 19, 24; DLB 13; EWL 3; MTCW 1, 2; MTFW 2005; RGEL 2

Osborne, Lawrence 1958- .... **CLC 50**
See also CA 189; CANR 152

Osbourne, Lloyd 1868-1947 .... **TCLC 93**

Osceola
See Blixen, Karen

Osgood, Frances Sargent 1811-1850 . **NCLC 141**
See also DLB 250

Oshima, Nagisa 1932- .... **CLC 20**
See also CA 116; 121; CANR 78

Oskison, John Milton 1874-1947 ..... **NNAL; TCLC 35**
See also CA 144; CANR 84; DAM MULT; DLB 175

Osofisan, Femi 1946- .... **CLC 307**
See also AFW; BW 2; CA 142; CANR 84; CD 5, 6; CDWLB 3; DLB 125; EWL 3

Ossian c. 3rd cent. - ....
See Macpherson, James

Ossoli, Sarah Margaret
See Fuller, Margaret

Ossoli, Sarah Margaret Fuller
See Fuller, Margaret

Ostriker, Alicia 1937- .... **CLC 132**
See also CA 25-28R; CAAS 24; CANR 10, 30, 62, 99, 167; CWP; DLB 120; EXPP; PFS 19, 26

Ostriker, Alicia Suskin
See Ostriker, Alicia

Ostrovsky, Aleksandr Nikolaevich
See Ostrovsky, Alexander

Ostrovsky, Alexander 1823-1886 . **NCLC 30, 57**
See also DLB 277

Osundare, Niyi 1947- .... **BLC 2:3**
See also AFW; BW 3; CA 176; CDWLB 3; CP 7; DLB 157

Otero, Blas de 1916-1979 .... **CLC 11**
See also CA 89-92; DLB 134; EWL 3

O'Trigger, Sir Lucius
See Horne, Richard Henry Hengist

Otto, Rudolf 1869-1937 .... **TCLC 85**

Otto, Whitney 1955- .... **CLC 70**
See also CA 140; CANR 120

Otway, Thomas 1652-1685 . **DC 24; LC 106, 170**
See also DAM DRAM; DLB 80; RGEL 2

Ouida
See De La Ramee, Marie Louise

Ouologuem, Yambo 1940- ..... **CLC 146, 293**
See also CA 111; 176

Ousmane, Sembene 1923-2007 ...... **BLC 1:3, 2:3; CLC 66**
See also AFW; BW 1, 3; CA 117; 125; 261; CANR 81; CWW 2; DLB 360; EWL 3; MTCW 1; WLIT 2

Ovid 43B.C.-17 .... **CMLC 7, 108; PC 2**
See also AW 2; CDWLB 1; DA3; DAM POET; DLB 211; PFS 22; RGWL 2, 3; WLIT 8; WP

Owen, Hugh
See Faust, Frederick

Owen, Wilfred (Edward Salter) 1893-1918 . **PC 19, 102; TCLC 5, 27; WLC 4**
See also BRW 6; CA 104; 141; CDBLB 1914-1945; DA; DAB; DAC; DAM MST,

POET; DLB 20; EWL 3; EXPP; MTCW 2; MTFW 2005; PFS 10, 37; RGEL 2; WLIT 4

Owens, Louis (Dean) 1948-2002 .. **CLC 321; NNAL**
See also CA 137, 179; 207; CAAE 179; CAAS 24; CANR 71

Owens, Rochelle 1936- .... **CLC 8**
See also CA 17-20R; CAAS 2; CAD; CANR 39; CD 5, 6; CP 1, 2, 3, 4, 5, 6, 7; CWD; CWP

Oz, Amos 1939- .... **CLC 5, 8, 11, 27, 33, 54; SSC 66**
See also AAYA 84; CA 53-56; CANR 27, 47, 65, 113, 138, 175, 219; CWW 2; DAM NOV; EWL 3; MTCW 1, 2; MTFW 2005; RGHL; RGSF 2; RGWL 3; WLIT 6

Ozeki, Ruth L. 1956- .... **CLC 307**
See also CA 181

Ozick, Cynthia 1928- . **CLC 3, 7, 28, 62, 155, 262; SSC 15, 60, 123**
See also AMWS 5; BEST 90:1; CA 17-20R; CANR 23, 58, 116, 160, 187; CN 3, 4, 5, 6, 7; CPW; DA3; DAM NOV, POP; DLB 28, 152, 299; DLBY 1982; EWL 3; EXPS; INT CANR-23; MAL 5; MTCW 1, 2; MTFW 2005; RGAL 4; RGHL; RGSF 2; SSFS 3, 12, 22

Ozu, Yasujiro 1903-1963 .... **CLC 16**
See also CA 112

Pabst, G. W. 1885-1967 .... **TCLC 127**

Pacheco, C.
See Pessoa, Fernando

Pacheco, Jose Emilio 1939- .... **HLC 2**
See also CA 111; 131; CANR 65; CWW 2; DAM MULT; DLB 290; EWL 3; HW 1, 2; RGSF 2

Pa Chin
See Jin, Ba

Pack, Robert 1929- .... **CLC 13**
See also CA 1-4R; CANR 3, 44, 82; CP 1, 2, 3, 4, 5, 6, 7; DLB 5; SATA 118

Packer, Vin
See Meaker, Marijane

Padgett, Lewis
See Kuttner, Henry

Padilla (Lorenzo), Heberto 1932-2000 . **CLC 38**
See also AITN 1; CA 123; 131; 189; CWW 2; EWL 3; HW 1

Paerdurabo, Frater
See Crowley, Edward Alexander

Page, James Patrick 1944- .... **CLC 12**
See also CA 204

Page, Jimmy 1944- ....
See Page, James Patrick

Page, Louise 1955- .... **CLC 40**
See also CA 140; CANR 76; CBD; CD 5, 6; CWD; DLB 233

Page, Patricia Kathleen
See Page, P.K.

Page, P.K. 1916-2010 ...... **CLC 7, 18; PC 12**
See also CA 53-56; CANR 4, 22, 65; CCA 1; CP 1, 2, 3, 4, 5, 6, 7; DAC; DAM MST; DLB 68; MTCW 1; RGEL 2

Page, Stanton
See Fuller, Henry Blake

Page, Thomas Nelson 1853-1922 ...... **SSC 23**
See also CA 118; 177; DLB 12, 78; DLBD 13; RGAL 4

Pagels, Elaine
See Pagels, Elaine Hiesey

Pagels, Elaine Hiesey 1943- .... **CLC 104**
See also CA 45-48; CANR 2, 24, 51, 151; FW; NCFS 4

Paget, Violet 1856-1935 . **SSC 33, 98; TCLC 5**
See also CA 104; 166; DLB 57, 153, 156, 174, 178; GLL 1; HGG; SUFW 1

Paget-Lowe, Henry
See Lovecraft, H. P.

Paglia, Camille 1947- .... **CLC 68**
See also CA 140; CANR 72, 139; CPW; FW; GLL 2; MTCW 2; MTFW 2005

Pagnol, Marcel (Paul) 1895-1974 ...... **TCLC 208**
See also CA 128; 49-52; DLB 321; EWL 3; GFL 1789 to the Present; MTCW 1; RGWL 2, 3

Paige, Richard
See Koontz, Dean

Paine, Thomas 1737-1809 ..... **NCLC 62, 248**
See also AMWS 1; CDALB 1640-1865; DLB 31, 43, 73, 158; LAIT 1; RGAL 4; RGEL 2; TUS

Pakenham, Antonia
See Fraser, Antonia

Palamas, Costis
See Palamas, Kostes

Palamas, Kostes 1859-1943 .... **TCLC 5**
See also CA 105; 190; EWL 3; RGWL 2, 3

Palamas, Kostis
See Palamas, Kostes

Palazzeschi, Aldo 1885-1974 .... **CLC 11**
See also CA 89-92; 53-56; DLB 114, 264; EWL 3

Pales Matos, Luis 1898-1959 .... **HLCS 2**
See Pales Matos, Luis
See also DLB 290; HW 1; LAW

Paley, Grace 1922-2007 .. **CLC 4, 6, 37, 140, 272; SSC 8, 165**
See also AMWS 6; CA 25-28R; 263; CANR 13, 46, 74, 118; CN 2, 3, 4, 5, 6, 7; CPW; DA3; DAM POP; DLB 28, 218; EWL 3; EXPS; FW; INT CANR-13; MAL 5; MBL; MTCW 1, 2; MTFW 2005; RGAL 4; RGSF 2; SSFS 3, 20, 27

Paley, Grace Goodside
See Paley, Grace

Palin, Michael 1943- .... **CLC 21**
See also CA 107; CANR 35, 109, 179, 229; DLB 352; SATA 67

Palin, Michael Edward
See Palin, Michael

Palliser, Charles 1947- .... **CLC 65**
See also CA 136; CANR 76; CN 5, 6, 7

Palma, Ricardo 1833-1919 .... **TCLC 29**
See also CA 168; LAW

Pamuk, Orhan 1952- .... **CLC 185, 288**
See also AAYA 82; CA 142; CANR 75, 127, 172, 208; CWW 2; NFS 27; WLIT 6

Pancake, Breece Dexter 1952-1979 ...... **CLC 29; SSC 61**
See also CA 123; 109; DLB 130

Pancake, Breece D'J
See Pancake, Breece Dexter

Panchenko, Nikolai CLC 59

Pankhurst, Emmeline (Goulden) 1858-1928 .... **TCLC 100**
See also CA 116; FW

Panko, Rudy
See Gogol, Nikolai

Papadiamantis, Alexandros 1851-1911 .... **TCLC 29**
See also CA 168; EWL 3

Papadiamantopoulos, Johannes 1856-1910 . **TCLC 18**
See also CA 117; 242; GFL 1789 to the Present

Papadiamantopoulos, Yannis
See Papadiamantopoulos, Johannes

Papini, Giovanni 1881-1956 .... **TCLC 22**
See also CA 121; 180; DLB 264

p'Bitek, Okot 1931-1982 ...... **BLC 1:3; CLC 96; TCLC 149**
See also AFW; BW 2, 3; CA 124; 107; CANR 82; CP 1, 2, 3; DAM MULT; DLB 125; EWL 3; MTCW 1, 2; MTFW 2005; RGEL 2; WLIT 2

Peabody, Elizabeth Palmer 1804-1894 .... **NCLC 169**
See also DLB 1, 223

Peacham, Henry 1578-1644(?) .... **LC 119**
See also DLB 151

Peacock, Molly 1947- .... **CLC 60**
See also CA 103, 262; CAAE 262; CAAS 21; CANR 52, 84; CP 5, 6, 7; CWP; DLB 120, 282

Peacock, Thomas Love 1785-1866 .... **NCLC 22; PC 87**
See also BRW 4; DLB 96, 116; RGEL 2; RGSF 2

Peake, Mervyn 1911-1968 .... **CLC 7, 54**
See also CA 5-8R; 25-28R; CANR 3; DLB 15, 160, 255; FANT; MTCW 1; RGEL 2; SATA 23; SFW 4

Pearce, Ann Philippa
See Pearce, Philippa

Pearce, Philippa 1920-2006 .... **CLC 21**
See also BYA 5; CA 5-8R; 255; CANR 4, 109; CLR 9; CWRI 5; DLB 161; FANT; MAICYA 1; SATA 1, 67, 129; SATA-Obit 179

Pearl, Eric
See Elman, Richard (Martin)

Pearson, Jean Mary
See Gardam, Jane

Pearson, Thomas Reid
See Pearson, T.R.

Pearson, T.R. 1956- .... **CLC 39**
See also CA 120; 130; CANR 97, 147, 185; CSW; INT CA-130

Peck, Dale 1967- .... **CLC 81**
See also CA 146; CANR 72, 127, 180; GLL 2

Peck, John (Frederick) 1941- .... **CLC 3**
See also CA 49-52; CANR 3, 100; CP 4, 5, 6, 7

Peck, Richard 1934- .... **CLC 21**
See also AAYA 1, 24; BYA 1, 6, 8, 11; CA 85-88; CANR 19, 38, 129, 178; CLR 15, 142; INT CANR-19; JRDA; MAICYA 1, 2; SAAS 2; SATA 18, 55, 97, 110, 158, 190, 228; SATA-Essay 110; WYA; YAW

Peck, Richard Wayne
See Peck, Richard

Peck, Robert Newton 1928- .... **CLC 17**
See also AAYA 3, 43; BYA 1, 6; CA 81-84, 182; CAAE 182; CANR 31, 63, 127; CLR 45, 163; DA; DAC; DAM MST; JRDA; LAIT 3; MAICYA 1, 2; NFS 29; SAAS 1; SATA 21, 62, 111, 156; SATA-Essay 108; WYA; YAW

Peckinpah, David Samuel
See Peckinpah, Sam

Peckinpah, Sam 1925-1984 .... **CLC 20**
See also CA 109; 114; CANR 82

Pedersen, Knut 1859-1952 . **TCLC 2, 14, 49, 151, 203**
See also AAYA 79; CA 104; 119; CANR 63; DLB 297, 330; EW 8; EWL 8; MTCW 1, 2; RGWL 2, 3

Peele, George 1556-1596 ..... **DC 27; LC 115**
See also BRW 1; DLB 62, 167; RGEL 2

Peeslake, Gaffer
See Durrell, Lawrence

Peguy, Charles (Pierre) 1873-1914 .... **TCLC 10**
See also CA 107; 193; DLB 258; EWL 3; GFL 1789 to the Present

Peirce, Charles Sanders 1839-1914 ... **TCLC 81**
See also CA 194; DLB 270

Pelagius c. 350-c. 418 .... **CMLC 118**

Pelecanos, George P. 1957- .... **CLC 236**
See also CA 138; CANR 122, 165, 194; DLB 306

Pelevin, Victor 1962- .... **CLC 238**
See also CA 154; CANR 88, 159, 197; DLB 285

Pelevin, Viktor Olegovich
See Pelevin, Victor

Pellicer, Carlos 1897(?)-1977 .... **HLCS 2**
See also CA 153; 69-72; DLB 290; EWL 3; HW 1

Pena, Ramon del Valle y
See Valle-Inclan, Ramon del

Pendennis, Arthur Esquir
See Thackeray, William Makepeace

Penn, Arthur
See Matthews, (James) Brander

Penn, William 1644-1718 .... **LC 25**
See also DLB 24

Penny, Carolyn
See Chute, Carolyn

PEPECE
See Prado (Calvo), Pedro

Pepys, Samuel 1633-1703 . **LC 11, 58; WLC 4**
See also BRW 2; CDBLB 1660-1789; DA; DA3; DAB; DAC; DAM MST; DLB 101, 213; NCFS 4; RGEL 2; TEA; WLIT 3

Percy, Thomas 1729-1811 .... **NCLC 95**
See also DLB 104

Percy, Walker 1916-1990 ..... **CLC 2, 3, 6, 8, 14, 18, 47, 65**
See also AMWS 3; BPFB 3; CA 1-4R; 131; CANR 1, 23, 64; CN 1, 2, 3, 4; CPW; CSW; DA3; DAM NOV, POP; DLB 2; DLBY 1980, 1990; EWL 3; MAL 5; MTCW 1, 2; MTFW 2005; RGAL 4; TUS

Percy, William Alexander 1885-1942 . **TCLC 84**
See also CA 163; MTCW 2

Perdurabo, Frater
See Crowley, Edward Alexander

Perec, Georges 1936-1982 .... **CLC 56, 116**
See also CA 141; DLB 83, 299; EWL 3; GFL 1789 to the Present; RGHL; RGWL 3

Pereda (y Sanchez de Porrua), Jose Maria de 1833-1906 .... **TCLC 16**
See also CA 117

Pereda y Porrua, Jose Maria de
See Pereda (y Sanchez de Porrua), Jose Maria de

Peregoy, George Weems
See Mencken, H. L.

Perelman, S(idney) J(oseph) 1904-1979 .... **CLC 3, 5, 9, 15, 23, 44, 49; SSC 32**
See also AAYA 79; AITN 1, 2; BPFB 3; CA 73-76; 89-92; CANR 18; DAM DRAM; DLB 11, 44; MTCW 1, 2; MTFW 2005; RGAL 4

Peret, Benjamin 1899-1959 ... **PC 33; TCLC 20**
See also CA 117; 186; GFL 1789 to the Present

Perets, Yitskhok Leybush
See Peretz, Isaac Loeb

Peretz, Isaac Leib (?)- ....
See Peretz, Isaac Loeb

Peretz, Isaac Loeb 1851-1915 .... **SSC 26; TCLC 16**
See Peretz, Isaac Leib
See also CA 109; 201; DLB 333

Peretz, Yitzkhok Leibush
See Peretz, Isaac Loeb

Perez Galdos, Benito 1843-1920 .... **HLCS 2; TCLC 27**
See also CA 125; 153; EW 7; EWL 3; HW 1; RGWL 2, 3

Peri Rossi, Cristina 1941- . **CLC 156; HLCS 2**
See also CA 131; CANR 59, 81; CWW 2; DLB 145, 290; EWL 3; HW 1, 2

Perlata
See Peret, Benjamin

Perloff, Marjorie G(abrielle) 1931- ...... **CLC 137**
See also CA 57-60; CANR 7, 22, 49, 104

Perrault, Charles 1628-1703 . **LC 2, 56; SSC 144**
See also BYA 4; CLR 79, 134; DLB 268; GFL Beginnings to 1789; MAICYA 1, 2; RGWL 2, 3; SATA 25; WCH

Perrotta, Tom 1961- .... **CLC 266**
See also CA 162; CANR 99, 155, 197

Perry, Anne 1938- .... **CLC 126**
See also CA 101; CANR 22, 50, 84, 150, 177; CMW 4; CN 6, 7; CPW; DLB 276

Perry, Brighton
See Sherwood, Robert E(mmet)

Perse, St.-John
See Leger, Alexis Saint-Leger

Perse, Saint-John
See Leger, Alexis Saint-Leger

Persius 34-62 .... **CMLC 74**
See also AW 2; DLB 211; RGWL 2, 3

Perutz, Leo(pold) 1882-1957 .... **TCLC 60**
See also CA 147; DLB 81

Peseenz, Tulio F.
See Lopez y Fuentes, Gregorio

Pesetsky, Bette 1932- .... **CLC 28**
See also CA 133; DLB 130

Peshkov, Alexei Maximovich
See Gorky, Maxim

Pessoa, Fernando 1888-1935 ..... **HLC 2; PC 20; TCLC 27, 257**
See also CA 125; 183; CANR 182; DAM MULT; DLB 287; EW 10; EWL 3; RGWL 2, 3; WP

Pessoa, Fernando Antonio Nogueira
See Pessoa, Fernando

Peterkin, Julia Mood 1880-1961 ..... **CLC 31**
See also CA 102; DLB 9

Peter of Blois c. 1135-c. 1212 .... **CMLC 127**

Peters, Joan K(aren) 1945- .... **CLC 39**
See also CA 158; CANR 109

Peters, Robert L(ouis) 1924- .... **CLC 7**
See also CA 13-16R; CAAS 8; CP 1, 5, 6, 7; DLB 105

Peters, S. H.
See Henry, O.

Petofi, Sandor 1823-1849 .... **NCLC 21**
See also RGWL 2, 3

Petrakis, Harry Mark 1923- .... **CLC 3**
See also CA 9-12R; CANR 4, 30, 85, 155; CN 1, 2, 3, 4, 5, 6, 7

Petrarch 1304-1374 .... **CMLC 20; PC 8**
See also DA3; DAM POET; EW 2; LMFS 1; RGWL 2, 3; WLIT 7

Petrarch, Francesco
See Petrarch

Petronius c. 20-66 .... **CMLC 34**
See also AW 2; CDWLB 1; DLB 211; RGWL 2, 3; WLIT 8

Petrov, Eugene
See Kataev, Evgeny Petrovich

Petrov, Evgenii
See Kataev, Evgeny Petrovich

Petrov, Evgeny
See Kataev, Evgeny Petrovich

Petrovsky, Boris
See Mansfield, Katherine

Plautus c. 254B.C.-c. 184B.C. ..... **CMLC 24, 92; DC 6**
See also AW 1; CDWLB 1; DLB 211; RGWL 2, 3; WLIT 8

Plick et Plock
See Simenon, Georges

Plieksans, Janis
See Rainis, Janis

Plimpton, George 1927-2003 .... **CLC 36**
See also AITN 1; AMWS 16; CA 21-24R; 224; CANR 32, 70, 103, 133; DLB 185, 241; MTCW 1, 2; MTFW 2005; SATA 10; SATA-Obit 150

Plimpton, George Ames
See Plimpton, George

Pliny the Elder c. 23-79 .... **CMLC 23**
See also DLB 211

Pliny the Younger c. 61-c. 112 ..... **CMLC 62**
See also AW 2; DLB 211

Plomer, William Charles Franklin 1903-1973 .... **CLC 4, 8**
See also AFW; BRWS 11; CA 21-22; CANR 34; CAP 2; CN 1; CP 1, 2; DLB 20, 162, 191, 225; EWL 3; MTCW 1; RGEL 2; RGSF 2; SATA 24

Plotinus 204-270 .... **CMLC 46**
See also CDWLB 1; DLB 176

Plowman, Piers
See Kavanagh, Patrick (Joseph)

Plum, J.
See Wodehouse, P. G.

Plumly, Stanley 1939- .... **CLC 33**
See also CA 108; 110; CANR 97, 185; CP 3, 4, 5, 6, 7; DLB 5, 193; INT CA-110

Plumly, Stanley Ross
See Plumly, Stanley

Plumpe, Friedrich Wilhelm
See Murnau, F.W.

Plutarch c. 46-c. 120 .... **CMLC 60**
See also AW 2; CDWLB 1; DLB 176; RGWL 2, 3; TWA; WLIT 8

Po Chu-i 772-846 .... **CMLC 24**

Podhoretz, Norman 1930- .... **CLC 189**
See also AMWS 8; CA 9-12R; CANR 7, 78, 135, 179

Poe, Edgar Allan 1809-1849 .... **NCLC 1, 16, 55, 78, 94, 97, 117, 211; PC 1, 54; SSC 1, 22, 34, 35, 54, 88, 111, 156; WLC 4**
See also AAYA 14; AMW; AMWC 1; AMWR 2; BPFB 3; BYA 5, 11; CDALB 1640-1865; CMW 4; DA; DA3; DAB; DAC; DAM MST, POET; DLB 3, 59, 73, 74, 248, 254; EXPP; EXPS; GL 3; HGG; LAIT 2; LATS 1:1; LMFS 1; MSW; PAB; PFS 1, 3, 9; RGAL 4; RGSF 2; SATA 23; SCFW 1, 2; SFW 4; SSFS 2, 4, 7, 8, 16, 26, 29, 34; SUFW; TUS; WP; WYA

Poet of Titchfield Street, The
See Pound, Ezra

Poggio Bracciolini, Gian Francesco 1380-1459 .... **LC 125**

Pohl, Frederik 1919- .... **CLC 18; SSC 25**
See also AAYA 24; CA 61-64, 188; CAAE 188; CAAS 1; CANR 11, 37, 81, 140; CN 1, 2, 3, 4, 5, 6; DLB 8; INT CANR-11; MTCW 1, 2; MTFW 2005; SATA 24; SCFW 1, 2; SFW 4

Poirier, Louis
See Gracq, Julien

Poitier, Sidney 1927- .... **CLC 26**
See also AAYA 60; BW 1; CA 117; CANR 94

Pokagon, Simon 1830-1899 .... **NNAL**
See also DAM MULT

Polanski, Roman 1933- .... **CLC 16, 178**
See also CA 77-80

Poliakoff, Stephen 1952- .... **CLC 38**
See also CA 106; CANR 116; CBD; CD 5, 6; DLB 13

Police, The
See Copeland, Stewart; Sting; Summers, Andy

Polidori, John William 1795-1821 ..... **NCLC 51; SSC 97**
See also DLB 116; HGG

Poliziano, Angelo 1454-1494 .... **LC 120**
See also WLIT 7

Pollitt, Katha 1949- .... **CLC 28, 122**
See also CA 120; 122; CANR 66, 108, 164, 200, 229; MTCW 1, 2; MTFW 2005

Pollock, (Mary) Sharon 1936- .... **CLC 50**
See also CA 141; CANR 132; CD 5; CWD; DAC; DAM DRAM, MST; DFS 3; DLB 60; FW

Pollock, Sharon 1936- .... **DC 20**
See also CD 6

Polo, Marco 1254-1324 .... **CMLC 15**
See also WLIT 7

Polonsky, Abraham (Lincoln) 1910-1999 ..... **CLC 92**
See also CA 104; 187; DLB 26; INT CA-104

Polybius c. 200B.C.-c. 118B.C. ..... **CMLC 17**
See also AW 1; DLB 176; RGWL 2, 3

Pomerance, Bernard 1940- .... **CLC 13**
See also CA 101; CAD; CANR 49, 134; CD 5, 6; DAM DRAM; DFS 9; LAIT 2

Ponge, Francis 1899-1988 .... **CLC 6, 18; PC 107**
See also CA 85-88; 126; CANR 40, 86; DAM POET; DLBY 2002; EWL 3; GFL 1789 to the Present; RGWL 2, 3

Poniatowska, Elena 1932- ... **CLC 140; HLC 2**
See also CA 101; CANR 32, 66, 107, 156; CDWLB 3; CWW 2; DAM MULT; DLB 113; EWL 3; HW 1, 2; LAWS 1; WLIT 1

Pontoppidan, Henrik 1857-1943 ... **TCLC 29**
See also CA 170; DLB 300, 331

Ponty, Maurice Merleau
See Merleau-Ponty, Maurice

Poole, (Jane Penelope) Josephine
See Helyar, Jane Penelope Josephine

Poole, Josephine
See Helyar, Jane Penelope Josephine

Popa, Vasko 1922-1991 . **CLC 19; TCLC 167**
See also CA 112; 148; CDWLB 4; DLB 181; EWL 3; RGWL 2, 3

Pope, Alexander 1688-1744 ..... **LC 3, 58, 60, 64, 164; PC 26; WLC 5**
See also BRW 3; BRWC 1; BRWR 1; CD-BLB 1660-1789; DA; DA3; DAB; DAC; DAM MST, POET; DLB 95, 101, 213; EXPP; PAB; PFS 12; RGEL 2; WLIT 3; WP

Popov, Evgenii Anatol'evich
See Popov, Yevgeny

Popov, Yevgeny **CLC 59**
See also DLB 285

Poquelin, Jean-Baptiste
See Moliere

Porete, Marguerite (?)-1310 .... **CMLC 73**
See also DLB 208

Porphyry c. 233-c. 305 .... **CMLC 71**

Porter, Connie (Rose) 1959(?)- .... **CLC 70**
See also AAYA 65; BW 2, 3; CA 142; CANR 90, 109; SATA 81, 129

Porter, Gene Stratton
See Stratton-Porter, Gene

Porter, Geneva Grace
See Stratton-Porter, Gene

Porter, Katherine Anne 1890-1980 .. **CLC 1, 3, 7, 10, 13, 15, 27, 101; SSC 4, 31, 43, 108; TCLC 233**
See also AAYA 42; AITN 2; AMW; BPFB 3; CA 1-4R; 101; CANR 1, 65; CDALBS; CN 1, 2; DA; DA3; DAB; DAC; DAM MST, NOV; DLB 4, 9, 102; DLBD 12; DLBY 1980; EWL 3; EXPS; LAIT 3; MAL 5; MBL; MTCW 1, 2; MTFW 2005; NFS 14; RGAL 4; RGSF 2; SATA 39; SATA-Obit 23; SSFS 1, 8, 11, 16, 23; TCWW 2; TUS

Porter, Peter 1929-2010 .... **CLC 5, 13, 33**
See also CA 85-88; CP 1, 2, 3, 4, 5, 6, 7; DLB 40, 289; WWE 1

Porter, Peter Neville Frederick
See Porter, Peter

Porter, R. E.
See Hoch, Edward D.

Porter, William Sydney
See Henry, O.

Portillo (y Pacheco), Jose Lopez
See Lopez Portillo (y Pacheco), Jose

Portillo Trambley, Estela 1927-1998 .... **HLC 2; TCLC 163**
See also CA 77-80; CANR 32; DAM MULT; DLB 209; HW 1; RGAL 4

Posey, Alexander (Lawrence) 1873-1908 ..... **NNAL**
See also CA 144; CANR 80; DAM MULT; DLB 175

Posse, Abel **CLC 70, 273**
See also CA 252

Post, Melville Davisson 1869-1930 .... **TCLC 39**
See also CA 110; 202; CMW 4

Postl, Carl
See Sealsfield, Charles

Postman, Neil 1931(?)-2003 .... **CLC 244**
See also CA 102; 221

Potocki, Jan 1761-1815 .... **NCLC 229**

Potok, Chaim 1929-2002 .. **CLC 2, 7, 14, 26, 112**
See also AAYA 15, 50; AITN 1, 2; BPFB 3; BYA 1; CA 17-20R; 208; CANR 19, 35, 64, 98; CLR 92; CN 4, 5, 6; DA3; DAM NOV; DLB 28, 152; EXPN; INT CANR-19; LAIT 4; MTCW 1, 2; MTFW 2005; NFS 4, 34, 38; RGHL; SATA 33, 106; SATA-Obit 134; TUS; YAW

Potok, Herbert Harold
See Potok, Chaim

Potok, Herman Harold
See Potok, Chaim

Potter, Dennis (Christopher George) 1935-1994 .... **CLC 58, 86, 123**
See also BRWS 10; CA 107; 145; CANR 33, 61; CBD; DLB 233; MTCW 1

Pound, Ezra 1885-1972 . **CLC 1, 2, 3, 4, 5, 7, 10, 13, 18, 34, 48, 50, 112; PC 4, 95; WLC 5**
See also AAYA 47; AMW; AMWR 1; CA 5-8R; 37-40R; CANR 40; CDALB 1917-1929; CP 1; DA; DA3; DAB; DAC; DAM MST, POET; DLB 4, 45, 63; DLBD 15; EFS 1:2, 2:1; EWL 3; EXPP; LMFS 2; MAL 5; MTCW 1, 2; MTFW 2005; PAB; PFS 2, 8, 16; RGAL 4; TUS; WP

Pound, Ezra Weston Loomis
See Pound, Ezra

Povod, Reinaldo 1959-1994 .... **CLC 44**
See also CA 136; 146; CANR 83

Powell, Adam Clayton, Jr. 1908-1972 .. **BLC 1:3; CLC 89**
See also BW 1, 3; CA 102; 33-36R; CANR 86; DAM MULT; DLB 345

Powell, Anthony 1905-2000 . **CLC 1, 3, 7, 9, 10, 31**
See also BRW 7; CA 1-4R; 189; CANR 1, 32, 62, 107; CDBLB 1945-1960; CN 1, 2, 3, 4, 5, 6; DLB 15; EWL 3; MTCW 1, 2; MTFW 2005; RGEL 2; TEA

Powell, Dawn 1896(?)-1965 .... **CLC 66**
See also CA 5-8R; CANR 121; DLBY 1997

Purdy, James Amos
See Purdy, James
Purdy, James Otis
See Purdy, James
Pure, Simon
See Swinnerton, Frank Arthur
Pushkin, Aleksandr Sergeevich
See Pushkin, Alexander
Pushkin, Alexander 1799-1837 ...... **NCLC 3, 27, 83; PC 10; SSC 27, 55, 99; WLC 5**
See also DA; DA3; DAB; DAC; DAM DRAM, MST, POET; DLB 205; EW 5; EXPS; PFS 28, 34; RGSF 2; RGWL 2, 3; SATA 61; SSFS 9; TWA
Pushkin, Alexander Sergeyevich
See Pushkin, Alexander
P'u Sung-ling 1640-1715 ...... **LC 49; SSC 31**
Putnam, Arthur Lee
See Alger, Horatio, Jr.
Puttenham, George 1529(?)-1590 ..... **LC 116**
See also DLB 281
Puzo, Mario 1920-1999 ...... **CLC 1, 2, 6, 36, 107**
See also BPFB 3; CA 65-68; 185; CANR 4, 42, 65, 99, 131; CN 1, 2, 3, 4, 5, 6; CPW; DA3; DAM NOV, POP; DLB 6; MTCW 1, 2; MTFW 2005; NFS 16; RGAL 4
Pygge, Edward
See Barnes, Julian
Pyle, Ernest Taylor
See Pyle, Ernie
Pyle, Ernie 1900-1945 .... **TCLC 75**
See also CA 115; 160; DLB 29, 364; MTCW 2
Pyle, Howard 1853-1911 .... **TCLC 81**
See also AAYA 57; BYA 2, 4; CA 109; 137; CLR 22, 117; DLB 42, 188; DLBD 13; LAIT 1; MAICYA 1, 2; SATA 16, 100; WCH; YAW
Pym, Barbara (Mary Crampton) 1913-1980 .... **CLC 13, 19, 37, 111**
See also BPFB 3; BRWS 3; CA 13-14; 97-100; CANR 13, 34; CAP 1; DLB 14, 207; DLBY 1987; EWL 3; MTCW 1, 2; MTFW 2005; RGEL 2; TEA
Pynchon, Thomas 1937- . **CLC 2, 3, 6, 9, 11, 18, 33, 62, 72, 123, 192, 213; SSC 14, 84; WLC 5**
See also AMWS 2; BEST 90:2; BPFB 3; CA 17-20R; CANR 22, 46, 73, 142, 198; CN 1, 2, 3, 4, 5, 6, 7; CPW 1; DA; DA3; DAB; DAC; DAM MST, NOV, POP; DLB 2, 173; EWL 3; MAL 5; MTCW 1, 2; MTFW 2005; NFS 23, 36; RGAL 4; SFW 4; TCLE 1:2; TUS
Pynchon, Thomas Ruggels, Jr.
See Pynchon, Thomas
Pynchon, Thomas Ruggles
See Pynchon, Thomas
Pythagoras c. 582B.C.-c. 507B.C. ..... **CMLC 22**
See also DLB 176

Q
See Quiller-Couch, Sir Arthur (Thomas)
Qian, Chongzhu
See Qian, Zhongshu
Qian, Sima 145B.C.-c. 89B.C. ...... **CMLC 72**
See also DLB 358
Qian, Zhongshu 1910-1998 .... **CLC 22**
See also CA 130; CANR 73, 216; CWW 2; DLB 328; MTCW 1, 2
Qroll
See Dagerman, Stig (Halvard)
Quarles, Francis 1592-1644 .... **LC 117**
See also DLB 126; RGEL 2
Quarrington, Paul 1953-2010 .... **CLC 65**
See also CA 129; CANR 62, 95, 228
Quarrington, Paul Lewis
See Quarrington, Paul

Quasimodo, Salvatore 1901-1968 .. **CLC 10; PC 47**
See also CA 13-16; 25-28R; CAP 1; DLB 114, 332; EW 12; EWL 3; MTCW 1; RGWL 2, 3
Quatermass, Martin
See Carpenter, John
Quay, Stephen 1947- .... **CLC 95**
See also CA 189
Quay, Timothy 1947- .... **CLC 95**
See also CA 189
Queen, Ellery
See Dannay, Frederic; Hoch, Edward D.; Lee, Manfred B.; Marlowe, Stephen; Sturgeon, Theodore (Hamilton); Vance, Jack
Queneau, Raymond 1903-1976 .... **CLC 2, 5, 10, 42; TCLC 233**
See also CA 77-80; 69-72; CANR 32; DLB 72, 258; EW 12; EWL 3; GFL 1789 to the Present; MTCW 1, 2; RGWL 2, 3
Quevedo, Francisco de 1580-1645 .... **LC 23, 160**
Quiller-Couch, Sir Arthur (Thomas) 1863-1944 .... **TCLC 53**
See also CA 118; 166; DLB 135, 153, 190; HGG; RGEL 2; SUFW 1
Quin, Ann 1936-1973 .... **CLC 6**
See also CA 9-12R; 45-48; CANR 148; CN 1; DLB 14, 231
Quin, Ann Marie
See Quin, Ann
Quincey, Thomas de
See De Quincey, Thomas
Quindlen, Anna 1953- .... **CLC 191**
See also AAYA 35; AMWS 17; CA 138; CANR 73, 126; DA3; DLB 292; MTCW 2; MTFW 2005
Quinn, Martin
See Smith, Martin Cruz
Quinn, Peter 1947- .... **CLC 91**
See also CA 197; CANR 147
Quinn, Peter A.
See Quinn, Peter
Quinn, Simon
See Smith, Martin Cruz
Quintana, Leroy V. 1944- ..... **HLC 2; PC 36**
See also CA 131; CANR 65, 139; DAM MULT; DLB 82; HW 1, 2
Quintilian c. 40-c. 100 .... **CMLC 77**
See also AW 2; DLB 211; RGWL 2, 3
Quiroga, Horacio (Sylvestre) 1878-1937 ...... **HLC 2; SSC 89; TCLC 20**
See also CA 117; 131; DAM MULT; EWL 3; HW 1; LAW; MTCW 1; RGSF 2; WLIT 1
Quoirez, Francoise
See Sagan, Francoise
Raabe, Wilhelm (Karl) 1831-1910 ..... **TCLC 45**
See also CA 167; DLB 129
Rabe, David 1940- ... **CLC 4, 8, 33, 200; DC 16**
See also CA 85-88; CABS 3; CAD; CANR 59, 129, 218; CD 5, 6; DAM DRAM; DFS 3, 8, 13; DLB 7, 228; EWL 3; MAL 5
Rabe, David William
See Rabe, David
Rabelais, Francois 1494-1553 .... **LC 5, 60, 186; WLC 5**
See also DA; DAB; DAC; DAM MST; DLB 327; EW 2; GFL Beginnings to 1789; LMFS 1; RGWL 2, 3; TWA
Rabi'a al-'Adawiyya c. 717-c. 801 ... **CMLC 83**
See also DLB 311
Rabinovitch, Sholem 1859-1916 ...... **SSC 33, 125; TCLC 1, 35**
See also CA 104; DLB 333; TWA

Rabinovitsh, Sholem Yankev
See Rabinovitch, Sholem
Rabinowitz, Sholem Yakov
See Rabinovitch, Sholem
Rabinowitz, Solomon
See Rabinovitch, Sholem
Rabinyan, Dorit 1972- .... **CLC 119**
See also CA 170; CANR 147
Rachilde
See Vallette, Marguerite Eymery; Vallette, Marguerite Eymery
Racine, Jean 1639-1699 . **DC 32; LC 28, 113**
See also DA3; DAB; DAM MST; DFS 28; DLB 268; EW 3; GFL Beginnings to 1789; LMFS 1; RGWL 2, 3; TWA
Radcliffe, Ann 1764-1823 . **NCLC 6, 55, 106, 223**
See also BRWR 3; DLB 39, 178; GL 3; HGG; LMFS 1; RGEL 2; SUFW; WLIT 3
Radclyffe-Hall, Marguerite
See Hall, Radclyffe
Radiguet, Raymond 1903-1923 ..... **TCLC 29**
See also CA 162; DLB 65; EWL 3; GFL 1789 to the Present; RGWL 2, 3
Radishchev, Aleksandr Nikolaevich 1749-1802 .... **NCLC 190**
See also DLB 150
Radishchev, Alexander
See Radishchev, Aleksandr Nikolaevich
Radnoti, Miklos 1909-1944 .... **TCLC 16**
See also CA 118; 212; CDWLB 4; DLB 215; EWL 3; RGHL; RGWL 2, 3
Rado, James 1939- .... **CLC 17**
See also CA 105
Radvanyi, Netty 1900-1983 .... **CLC 7**
See also CA 85-88; 110; CANR 82; CDWLB 2; DLB 69; EWL 3
Rae, Ben
See Griffiths, Trevor
Raeburn, John (Hay) 1941- .... **CLC 34**
See also CA 57-60
Ragni, Gerome 1942-1991 .... **CLC 17**
See also CA 105; 134
Rahv, Philip
See Greenberg, Ivan
Rai, Navab
See Srivastava, Dhanpat Rai
Raimund, Ferdinand Jakob 1790-1836 .... **NCLC 69**
See also DLB 90
Raine, Craig 1944- .... **CLC 32, 103**
See also BRWS 13; CA 108; CANR 29, 51, 103, 117; CP 3, 4, 5, 6, 7; DLB 40; PFS 7
Raine, Craig Anthony
See Raine, Craig
Raine, Kathleen (Jessie) 1908-2003 . **CLC 7, 45**
See also CA 85-88; 218; CANR 46, 109; CP 1, 2, 3, 4, 5, 6, 7; DLB 20; EWL 3; MTCW 1; RGEL 2
Rainis, Janis 1865-1929 .... **TCLC 29**
See also CA 170; CDWLB 4; DLB 220; EWL 3
Rakosi, Carl
See Rawley, Callman
Ralegh, Sir Walter
See Raleigh, Sir Walter
Raleigh, Richard
See Lovecraft, H. P.
Raleigh, Sir Walter 1554(?)-1618 ...... **LC 31, 39; PC 31**
See also BRW 1; CDBLB Before 1660; DLB 172; EXPP; PFS 14; RGEL 2; TEA; WP
Rallentando, H. P.
See Sayers, Dorothy L(eigh)

Ramal, Walter
  See de la Mare, Walter (John)
Ramana Maharshi 1879-1950 .... **TCLC 84**
Ramoacn y Cajal, Santiago 1852-1934 ....
  TCLC 93
Ramon, Juan
  See Jimenez, Juan Ramon
Ramos, Graciliano 1892-1953 .... **TCLC 32**
  See also CA 167; DLB 307; EWL 3; HW 2;
  LAW; WLIT 1
Rampersad, Arnold 1941- .... **CLC 44**
  See also BW 2, 3; CA 127; 133; CANR 81;
  DLB 111; INT CA-133
Rampling, Anne
  See Rice, Anne
Ramsay, Allan 1686(?)-1758 .... **LC 29**
  See also DLB 95; RGEL 2
Ramsay, Jay
  See Campbell, Ramsey
Ramus, Peter
  See La Ramee, Pierre de
Ramus, Petrus
  See La Ramee, Pierre de
Ramuz, Charles-Ferdinand 1878-1947 ....
  TCLC 33
  See also CA 165; EWL 3
Rand, Ayn 1905-1982 ..... **CLC 3, 30, 44, 79;**
  SSC 116; TCLC 261; WLC 5
  See also AAYA 10; AMWS 4; BPFB 3;
  BYA 12; CA 13-16R; 105; CANR 27, 73;
  CDALBS; CN 1, 2, 3; CPW; DA; DA3;
  DAC; DAM MST, NOV, POP; DLB 227,
  279; MTCW 1, 2; MTFW 2005; NFS 10,
  16, 29; RGAL 4; SFW 4; TUS; YAW
Randall, Dudley 1914-2000 . **BLC 1:3; CLC**
  1, 135; PC 86
  See also BW 1, 3; CA 25-28R; 189; CANR
  23, 82; CP 1, 2, 3, 4, 5; DAM MULT;
  DLB 41; PFS 5
Randall, Dudley Felker
  See Randall, Dudley
Randall, Robert
  See Silverberg, Robert
Randolph, Thomas 1605-1635 .... **LC 195**
  See also DLB 58, 126; RGEL 2
Ranger, Ken
  See Creasey, John
Rank, Otto 1884-1939 .... **TCLC 115**
Rankin, Ian 1960- .... **CLC 257**
  See also BRWS 10; CA 148; CANR 81,
  137, 171, 210; DLB 267; MTFW 2005
Rankin, Ian James
  See Rankin, Ian
Ransom, John Crowe 1888-1974 . **CLC 2, 4,**
  5, 11, 24; PC 61
  See also AMW; CA 5-8R; 49-52; CANR 6,
  34; CDALBS; CP 1, 2; DA3; DAM POET;
  DLB 45, 63; EWL 3; EXPP; MAL 5;
  MTCW 1, 2; MTFW 2005; RGAL 4; TUS
Rao, Raja 1908-2006 . **CLC 25, 56, 255; SSC**
  99
  See also CA 73-76; 252; CANR 51; CN 1,
  2, 3, 4, 5, 6; DAM NOV; DLB 323; EWL
  3; MTCW 1, 2; MTFW 2005; RGEL 2;
  RGSF 2
Raphael, Frederic 1931- .... **CLC 2, 14**
  See also CA 1-4R; CANR 1, 86, 223; CN
  1, 2, 3, 4, 5, 6, 7; DLB 14, 319; TCLE
  1:2
Raphael, Frederic Michael
  See Raphael, Frederic
Raphael, Lev 1954- .... **CLC 232**
  See also CA 134; CANR 72, 145, 217; GLL
  1
Rastell, John c. 1475(?)-1536(?) .... **LC 183**
  See also DLB 136, 170; RGEL 2

Ratcliffe, James P.
  See Mencken, H. L.
Rathbone, Julian 1935-2008 .... **CLC 41**
  See also CA 101; 269; CANR 34, 73, 152,
  221
Rathbone, Julian Christopher
  See Rathbone, Julian
Rattigan, Terence 1911-1977 ..... **CLC 7; DC**
  18
  See also BRWS 7; CA 85-88; 73-76; CBD;
  CDBLB 1945-1960; DAM DRAM; DFS
  8; DLB 13; IDFW 3, 4; MTCW 1, 2;
  MTFW 2005; RGEL 2
Rattigan, Terence Mervyn
  See Rattigan, Terence
Ratushinskaya, Irina 1954- .... **CLC 54**
  See also CA 129; CANR 68; CWW 2
Raven, Simon (Arthur Noel) 1927-2001 ......
  CLC 14
  See also CA 81-84; 197; CANR 86; CN 1,
  2, 3, 4, 5, 6; DLB 271
Ravenna, Michael
  See Welty, Eudora
Rawley, Callman 1903-2004 .... **CLC 47; PC**
  126
  See also CA 21-24R; 228; CAAS 5; CANR
  12, 32, 91; CP 1, 2, 3, 4, 5, 6, 7; DLB
  193
Rawlings, Marjorie Kinnan 1896-1953 ....
  TCLC 4, 248
  See also AAYA 20; AMWS 10; ANW;
  BPFB 3; BYA 3; CA 104; 137; CANR 74;
  CLR 63; DLB 9, 22, 102; DLBD 17;
  JRDA; MAICYA 1, 2; MAL 5; MTCW 2;
  MTFW 2005; RGAL 4; SATA 100; WCH;
  YABC 1; YAW
Raworth, Thomas Moore 1938- .... **PC 107**
  See also CA 29-32R; CAAS 11; CANR 46;
  CP 1, 2, 3, 4, 5, 7; DLB 40
Raworth, Tom
  See Raworth, Thomas Moore
Ray, Satyajit 1921-1992 .... **CLC 16, 76**
  See also CA 114; 137; DAM MULT
Read, Herbert Edward 1893-1968 .... **CLC 4**
  See also BRW 6; CA 85-88; 25-28R; DLB
  20, 149; EWL 3; PAB; RGEL 2
Read, Piers Paul 1941- .... **CLC 4, 10, 25**
  See also CA 21-24R; CANR 38, 86, 150;
  CN 2, 3, 4, 5, 6, 7; DLB 14; SATA 21
Reade, Charles 1814-1884 .... **NCLC 2, 74**
  See also DLB 21; RGEL 2
Reade, Hamish
  See Gray, Simon
Reading, Peter 1946- .... **CLC 47**
  See also BRWS 8; CA 103; CANR 46, 96;
  CP 5, 6, 7; DLB 40
Reaney, James 1926-2008 .... **CLC 13**
  See also CA 41-44R; CANR 42; CAAS 15;
  CD 5, 6; CP 1, 2, 3, 4, 5, 6, 7; DAC;
  DAM MST; DLB 68; RGEL 2; SATA 43
Reaney, James Crerar
  See Reaney, James
Rebreanu, Liviu 1885-1944 .... **TCLC 28**
  See also CA 165; DLB 220; EWL 3
Rechy, John 1934- .... **CLC 1, 7, 14, 18, 107;**
  HLC 2
  See also CA 5-8R; 195; CAAE 195; CAAS
  4; CANR 6, 32, 64, 152, 188; CN 1, 2, 3,
  4, 5, 6, 7; DAM MULT; DLB 122, 278;
  DLBY 1982; HW 1, 2; INT CANR-6;
  LLW; MAL 5; RGAL 4
Rechy, John Francisco
  See Rechy, John
Redcam, Tom 1870-1933 .... **TCLC 25**
Reddin, Keith 1956- .... **CLC 67**
  See also CAD; CD 6

Redgrove, Peter (William) 1932-2003 .. **CLC**
  6, 41
  See also BRWS 6; CA 1-4R; 217; CANR 3,
  39, 77; CP 1, 2, 3, 4, 5, 6, 7; DLB 40;
  TCLE 1:2
Redmon, Anne
  See Nightingale, Anne Redmon
Reed, Eliot
  See Ambler, Eric
Reed, Ishmael 1938- . **BLC 1:3; CLC 2, 3, 5,**
  6, 13, 32, 60, 174; PC 68
  See also AFAW 1, 2; AMWS 10; BPFB 3;
  BW 2, 3; CA 21-24R; CANR 25, 48, 74,
  128, 195; CN 1, 2, 3, 4, 5, 6, 7; CP 1, 2,
  3, 4, 5, 6, 7; CSW; DA3; DAM MULT;
  DLB 2, 5, 33, 169, 227; DLBD 8; EWL
  3; LMFS 2; MAL 5; MSW; MTCW 1, 2;
  MTFW 2005; PFS 6; RGAL 4; TCWW 2
Reed, Ishmael Scott
  See Reed, Ishmael
Reed, John (Silas) 1887-1920 .... **TCLC 9**
  See also CA 106; 195; MAL 5; TUS
Reed, Lou
  See Firbank, Louis
Reese, Lizette Woodworth 1856-1935 ..... **PC**
  29; TCLC 181
  See also CA 180; DLB 54
Reeve, Clara 1729-1807 .... **NCLC 19**
  See also DLB 39; RGEL 2
Reich, Wilhelm 1897-1957 .... **TCLC 57**
  See also CA 199
Reid, Christopher 1949- .... **CLC 33**
  See also CA 140; CANR 89; CP 4, 5, 6, 7;
  DLB 40; EWL 3
Reid, Christopher John
  See Reid, Christopher
Reid, Desmond
  See Moorcock, Michael
Reid, Thomas 1710-1796 .... **LC 201**
  See also DLB 31, 252
Reid Banks, Lynne 1929- .... **CLC 23**
  See also AAYA 6; BYA 7; CA 1-4R; CANR
  6, 22, 38, 87; CLR 24, 86; CN 4, 5, 6;
  JRDA; MAICYA 1, 2; SATA 22, 75, 111,
  165; YAW
Reilly, William K.
  See Creasey, John
Reiner, Max
  See Caldwell, (Janet Miriam) Taylor
  (Holland)
Reis, Ricardo
  See Pessoa, Fernando
Reizenstein, Elmer Leopold
  See Rice, Elmer (Leopold)
Remark, Erich Paul
  See Remarque, Erich Maria
Remarque, Erich Maria 1898-1970 . **CLC 21**
  See also AAYA 27; BPFB 3; CA 77-80; 29-
  32R; CDWLB 2; CLR 159; DA; DA3;
  DAB; DAC; DAM MST, NOV; DLB 56;
  EWL 3; EXPN; LAIT 3; MTCW 1, 2;
  MTFW 2005; NFS 4, 36; RGHL; RGWL
  2, 3
Remington, Frederic S(ackrider)
  1861-1909 .... **TCLC 89**
  See also CA 108; 169; DLB 12, 186, 188;
  SATA 41; TCWW 2
Remizov, A.
  See Remizov, Aleksei (Mikhailovich)
Remizov, A. M.
  See Remizov, Aleksei (Mikhailovich)
Remizov, Aleksei (Mikhailovich)
  1877-1957 .... **TCLC 27**
  See also CA 125; 133; DLB 295; EWL 3
Remizov, Alexey Mikhaylovich
  See Remizov, Aleksei (Mikhailovich)
Renan, Joseph Ernest 1823-1892 . **NCLC 26,**
  145
  See also GFL 1789 to the Present

Renard, Jules(-Pierre) 1864-1910 . **TCLC 17**
See also CA 117; 202; GFL 1789 to the Present

Renart, Jean fl. 13th cent. - .... **CMLC 83**

Renault, Mary 1905-1983 ...... **CLC 3, 11, 17**
See also BPFB 3; BYA 2; CA 81-84; 111; CANR 74; CN 1, 2, 3; DA3; DLBY 1983; EWL 3; GLL 1; LAIT 1; MTCW 2; MTFW 2005; RGEL 2; RHW; SATA 23; SATA-Obit 36; TEA

Rendell, Ruth
See Rendell, Ruth

Rendell, Ruth 1930- ..... **CLC 28, 48, 50, 295**
See also BEST 90:4; BPFB 3; BRWS 9; CA 109; CANR 32, 52, 74, 127, 162, 190, 227; CN 5, 6, 7; CPW; DAM POP; DLB 87, 276; INT CANR-32; MSW; MTCW 1, 2; MTFW 2005

Rendell, Ruth Barbara
See Rendell, Ruth

Renoir, Jean 1894-1979 .... **CLC 20**
See also CA 129; 85-88

Rensie, Willis
See Eisner, Will

Resnais, Alain 1922- .... **CLC 16**

Restif de la Bretonne, Nicolas-Anne-Edme
1734-1806 .... **NCLC 257**
See also DLB 314; GFL Beginnings to 1789

Revard, Carter 1931- .... **NNAL**
See also CA 144; CANR 81, 153; PFS 5

Reverdy, Pierre 1889-1960 .... **CLC 53**
See also CA 97-100; 89-92; DLB 258; EWL 3; GFL 1789 to the Present

Reverend Mandju
See Su, Chien

Rexroth, Kenneth 1905-1982 ... **CLC 1, 2, 6, 11, 22, 49, 112; PC 20, 95**
See also BG 1:3; CA 5-8R; 107; CANR 14, 34, 63; CDALB 1941-1968; CP 1, 2, 3; DAM POET; DLB 16, 48, 165, 212; DLBY 1982; EWL 3; INT CANR-14; MAL 5; MTCW 1, 2; MTFW 2005; RGAL 4

Reyes, Alfonso 1889-1959 .. **HLCS 2; TCLC 33**
See also CA 131; EWL 3; HW 1; LAW

Reyes y Basoalto, Ricardo Eliecer Neftali
See Neruda, Pablo

Reymont, Wladyslaw (Stanislaw)
1868(?)-1925 .... **TCLC 5**
See also CA 104; DLB 332; EWL 3

Reynolds, John Hamilton 1794-1852 . **NCLC 146**
See also DLB 96

Reynolds, Jonathan 1942- .... **CLC 6, 38**
See also CA 65-68; CANR 28, 176

Reynolds, Joshua 1723-1792 .... **LC 15**
See also DLB 104

Reynolds, Michael S(hane) 1937-2000 . **CLC 44**
See also CA 65-68; 189; CANR 9, 89, 97

Reza, Yasmina 1959- .... **CLC 299; DC 34**
See also AAYA 69; CA 171; CANR 145; DFS 19; DLB 321

Reznikoff, Charles 1894-1976 .... **CLC 9; PC 124**
See also AMWS 14; CA 33-36; 61-64; CAP 2; CP 1, 2; DLB 28, 45; RGHL; WP

Rezzori, Gregor von
See Rezzori d'Arezzo, Gregor von

Rezzori d'Arezzo, Gregor von 1914-1998 ... **CLC 25**
See also CA 122; 136; 167

Rhine, Richard
See Silverstein, Alvin; Silverstein, Virginia B.

Rhodes, Eugene Manlove 1869-1934 . **TCLC 53**
See also CA 198; DLB 256; TCWW 1, 2

R'hoone, Lord
See Balzac, Honore de

Rhys, Jean 1890-1979 .. **CLC 2, 4, 6, 14, 19, 51, 124; SSC 21, 76**
See also BRWS 2; CA 25-28R; 85-88; CANR 35, 62; CDBLB 1945-1960; CD-WLB 3; CN 1, 2; DA3; DAM NOV; DLB 36, 117, 162; DNFS 2; EWL 3; LATS 1:1; MTCW 1, 2; MTFW 2005; NFS 19; RGEL 2; RGSF 2; RHW; TEA; WWE 1

Ribeiro, Darcy 1922-1997 .... **CLC 34**
See also CA 33-36R; 156; EWL 3

Ribeiro, Joao Ubaldo (Osorio Pimentel)
1941- .... **CLC 10, 67**
See also CA 81-84; CWW 2; EWL 3

Ribman, Ronald (Burt) 1932- .... **CLC 7**
See also CA 21-24R; CAD; CANR 46, 80; CD 5, 6

Ricci, Nino 1959- .... **CLC 70**
See also CA 137; CANR 130; CCA 1

Ricci, Nino Pio
See Ricci, Nino

Rice, Anne 1941- .... **CLC 41, 128**
See also AAYA 9, 53; AMWS 7; BEST 89:2; BPFB 3; CA 65-68; CANR 12, 36, 53, 74, 100, 133, 190; CN 6, 7; CPW; CSW; DA3; DAM POP; DLB 292; GL 3; GLL 2; HGG; MTCW 2; MTFW 2005; SUFW 2; YAW

Rice, Elmer (Leopold) 1892-1967 .... **CLC 7, 49; DC 44; TCLC 221**
See also CA 21-22; 25-28R; CAP 2; DAM DRAM; DFS 12; DLB 4, 7; EWL 3; IDTP; MAL 5; MTCW 1, 2; RGAL 4

Rice, Tim 1944- .... **CLC 21**
See also CA 103; CANR 46; DFS 7

Rice, Timothy Miles Bindon
See Rice, Tim

Rich, Adrienne 1929- .... **CLC 3, 6, 7, 11, 18, 36, 73, 76, 125; PC 5, 129**
See also AAYA 69; AMWR 2; AMWS 1; CA 9-12R; CANR 20, 53, 74, 128, 199; CDALBS; CP 1, 2, 3, 4, 5, 6, 7; CSW; CWP; DA3; DAM POET; DLB 5, 67; EWL 3; EXPP; FL 1:6; FW; MAL 5; MBL; MTCW 1, 2; MTFW 2005; PAB; PFS 15, 29, 39; RGAL 4; RGHL; WP

Rich, Adrienne Cecile
See Rich, Adrienne

Rich, Barbara
See Graves, Robert

Rich, Robert
See Trumbo, Dalton

Richard, Keith
See Richards, Keith

Richards, David Adams 1950- .... **CLC 59**
See also CA 93-96; CANR 60, 110, 156; CN 7; DAC; DLB 53; TCLE 1:2

Richards, I(vor) A(rmstrong) 1893-1979 ..... **CLC 14, 24**
See also BRWS 2; CA 41-44R; 89-92; CANR 34; CP 1, 2; DLB 27; EWL 3; MTCW 2; RGEL 2

Richards, Keith 1943- .... **CLC 17**
See also CA 107; CANR 77

Richardson, Anne
See Roiphe, Anne

Richardson, Dorothy Miller 1873-1957 .... **TCLC 3, 203**
See also BRWS 13; CA 104; 192; DLB 36; EWL 3; FW; RGEL 2

Richardson, Ethel Florence Lindesay
1870-1946 .... **TCLC 4**
See also CA 105; 190; DLB 197, 230; EWL 3; RGEL 2; RGSF 2; RHW

Richardson, Henrietta
See Richardson, Ethel Florence Lindesay

Richardson, Henry Handel
See Richardson, Ethel Florence Lindesay

Richardson, John 1796-1852 .... **NCLC 55**
See also CCA 1; DAC; DLB 99

Richardson, Samuel 1689-1761 ..... **LC 1, 44, 138, 204; WLC 5**
See also BRW 3; CDBLB 1660-1789; DA; DAB; DAC; DAM MST, NOV; DLB 154; RGEL 2; TEA; WLIT 3

Richardson, Willis 1889-1977 .... **HR 1:3**
See also BW 1; CA 124; DLB 51; SATA 60

Richardson Robertson, Ethel Florence Lindesay
See Richardson, Ethel Florence Lindesay

Richler, Mordecai 1931-2001 ... **CLC 3, 5, 9, 13, 18, 46, 70, 185, 271**
See also AITN 1; CA 65-68; 201; CANR 31, 62, 111; CCA 1; CLR 17; CN 1, 2, 3, 4, 5, 7; CWRI 5; DAC; DAM MST, NOV; DLB 53; EWL 3; MAICYA 1, 2; MTCW 1, 2; MTFW 2005; RGEL 2; RGHL; SATA 44, 98; SATA-Brief 27; TWA

Richter, Conrad (Michael) 1890-1968 . **CLC 30**
See also AAYA 21; AMWS 18; BYA 2; CA 5-8R; 25-28R; CANR 23; DLB 9, 212; LAIT 1; MAL 5; MTCW 1, 2; MTFW 2005; RGAL 4; SATA 3; TCWW 1, 2; TUS; YAW

Ricostranza, Tom
See Ellis, Trey

Riddell, Charlotte 1832-1906 .... **TCLC 40**
See also CA 165; DLB 156; HGG; SUFW

Riddell, Mrs. J. H.
See Riddell, Charlotte

Ridge, John Rollin 1827-1867 ..... **NCLC 82; NNAL**
See also CA 144; DAM MULT; DLB 175

Ridgeway, Jason
See Marlowe, Stephen

Ridgway, Keith 1965- .... **CLC 119**
See also CA 172; CANR 144

Riding, Laura
See Jackson, Laura

Riefenstahl, Berta Helene Amalia
1902-2003 .... **CLC 16, 190**
See also CA 108; 220

Riefenstahl, Leni
See Riefenstahl, Berta Helene Amalia

Riffe, Ernest
See Bergman, Ingmar

Riffe, Ernest Ingmar
See Bergman, Ingmar

Riggs, (Rolla) Lynn 1899-1954 .... **NNAL; TCLC 56**
See also CA 144; DAM MULT; DLB 175

Riis, Jacob A(ugust) 1849-1914 .... **TCLC 80**
See also CA 113; 168; DLB 23

Rikki
See Ducornet, Erica

Riley, James Whitcomb 1849-1916 ... **PC 48; TCLC 51**
See also CA 118; 137; DAM POET; MAI-CYA 1, 2; RGAL 4; SATA 17

Riley, Tex
See Creasey, John

Rilke, Rainer Maria 1875-1926 .... **PC 2; TCLC 1, 6, 19, 195**
See also CA 104; 132; CANR 62, 99; CD-WLB 2; DA3; DAM POET; DLB 81; EW 9; EWL 3; MTCW 1, 2; MTFW 2005; PFS 19, 27; RGWL 2, 3; TWA; WP

Rimbaud, Arthur 1854-1891 ... **NCLC 4, 35, 82, 227; PC 3, 57; WLC 5**
See also DA; DA3; DAB; DAC; DAM MST, POET; DLB 217; EW 7; GFL 1789 to the Present; LMFS 2; PFS 28; RGWL 2, 3; TWA; WP

Rukeyser, Muriel 1913-1980 . **CLC 6, 10, 15, 27; PC 12**
See also AMWS 6; CA 5-8R; 93-96; CANR 26, 60; CP 1, 2, 3; DA3; DAM POET; DLB 48; EWL 3; FW; GLL 2; MAL 5; MTCW 1, 2; PFS 10, 29; RGAL 4; SATA-Obit 22

Rule, Jane 1931-2007 .... **CLC 27, 265**
See also CA 25-28R; 266; CAAS 18; CANR 12, 87; CN 4, 5, 6, 7; DLB 60; FW

Rule, Jane Vance
See Rule, Jane

Rulfo, Juan 1918-1986 . **CLC 8, 80; HLC 2; SSC 25**
See also CA 85-88; 118; CANR 26; CD-WLB 3; DAM MULT; DLB 113; EWL 3; HW 1, 2; LAW; MTCW 1, 2; RGSF 2; RGWL 2, 3; WLIT 1

Rumi
See Rumi, Jalal al-Din

Rumi, Jalal al-Din 1207-1273 ..... **CMLC 20; PC 45, 123**
See also AAYA 64; RGWL 2, 3; WLIT 6; WP

Runeberg, Johan 1804-1877 .... **NCLC 41**

Runyon, (Alfred) Damon 1884(?)-1946 .... **TCLC 10**
See also CA 107; 165; DLB 11, 86, 171; MAL 5; MTCW 2; RGAL 4

Rush, Benjamin 1746-1813 .... **NCLC 251**
See also DLB 37

Rush, Norman 1933- .... **CLC 44, 306**
See also CA 121; 126; CANR 130; INT CA-126

Rushdie, Ahmed Salman
See Rushdie, Salman

Rushdie, Salman 1947- .... **CLC 23, 31, 55, 100, 191, 272; SSC 83; WLCS**
See also AAYA 65; BEST 89:3; BPFB 3; BRWS 4; CA 108; 111; CANR 33, 56, 108, 133, 192; CLR 125; CN 4, 5, 6, 7; CPW 1; DA3; DAB; DAC; DAM MST, NOV, POP; DLB 194, 323, 326; EWL 3; FANT; INT CA-111; LATS 1:2; LMFS 2; MTCW 1, 2; MTFW 2005; NFS 22, 23; RGEL 2; RGSF 2; TEA; WLIT 4

Rushforth, Peter 1945-2005 .... **CLC 19**
See also CA 101; 243

Rushforth, Peter Scott
See Rushforth, Peter

Ruskin, John 1819-1900 .... **TCLC 63**
See also BRW 5; BYA 5; CA 114; 129; CD-BLB 1832-1890; DLB 55, 163, 190; RGEL 2; SATA 24; TEA; WCH

Russ, Joanna 1937-2011 .... **CLC 15**
See also BPFB 3; CA 25-28R; CANR 11, 31, 65; CN 4, 5, 6, 7; DLB 8; FW; GLL 1; MTCW 1; SCFW 1, 2; SFW 4

Russ, Richard Patrick
See O'Brian, Patrick

Russell, George William 1867-1935 .. **TCLC 3, 10**
See also BRWS 8; CA 104; 153; CDBLB 1890-1914; DAM POET; DLB 19; EWL 3; RGEL 2

Russell, Jeffrey Burton 1934- .... **CLC 70**
See also CA 25-28R; CANR 11, 28, 52, 179

Russell, (Henry) Ken(neth Alfred) 1927- ..... **CLC 16**
See also CA 105

Russell, William Martin 1947- .... **CLC 60**
See also CA 164; CANR 107; CBD; CD 5, 6; DLB 233

Russell, Willy
See Russell, William Martin

Russo, Richard 1949- .... **CLC 181**
See also AMWS 12; CA 127; 133; CANR 87, 114, 194; NFS 25

Rutebeuf fl. c. 1249-1277 .... **CMLC 104**
See also DLB 208

Rutherford, Mark
See White, William Hale

Ruysbroeck, Jan van 1293-1381 . **CMLC 85**

Ruyslinck, Ward
See Belser, Reimond Karel Maria de

Ryan, Cornelius (John) 1920-1974 ... **CLC 7**
See also CA 69-72; 53-56; CANR 38

Ryan, Michael 1946- .... **CLC 65**
See also CA 49-52; CANR 109, 203; DLBY 1982

Ryan, Tim
See Dent, Lester

Rybakov, Anatoli (Naumovich) 1911-1998 .. **CLC 23, 53**
See also CA 126; 135; 172; DLB 302; RGHL; SATA 79; SATA-Obit 108

Rybakov, Anatolii (Naumovich)
See Rybakov, Anatoli (Naumovich)

Ryder, Jonathan
See Ludlum, Robert

Ryga, George 1932-1987 .... **CLC 14**
See also CA 101; 124; CANR 43, 90; CCA 1; DAC; DAM MST; DLB 60

Rymer, Thomas 1643(?)-1713 .... **LC 132**
See also DLB 101, 336

S. H.
See Hartmann, Sadakichi

S. L. C.
See Twain, Mark

S. S.
See Sassoon, Siegfried

Sa'adawi, al- Nawal
See El Saadawi, Nawal

Saadawi, Nawal El
See El Saadawi, Nawal

Saadiah Gaon 882-942 .... **CMLC 97**

Saba, Umberto 1883-1957 .... **TCLC 33**
See also CA 144; CANR 79; DLB 114; EWL 3; RGWL 2, 3

Sabatini, Rafael 1875-1950 .... **TCLC 47**
See also BPFB 3; CA 162; RHW

Sabato, Ernesto 1911-2011 .... **CLC 10, 23; HLC 2**
See also CA 97-100; CANR 32, 65; CD-WLB 3; CWW 2; DAM MULT; DLB 145; EWL 3; HW 1, 2; LAW; MTCW 1, 2; MTFW 2005

Sa-Carneiro, Mario de 1890-1916 ..... **TCLC 83**
See also DLB 287; EWL 3

Sacastru, Martin
See Bioy Casares, Adolfo

Sacher-Masoch, Leopold von 1836(?)-1895 . **NCLC 31**

Sachs, Hans 1494-1576 .... **LC 95**
See also CDWLB 2; DLB 179; RGWL 2, 3

Sachs, Marilyn 1927- .... **CLC 35**
See also AAYA 2; BYA 6; CA 17-20R; CANR 13, 47, 150; CLR 2; JRDA; MAI-CYA 1, 2; SAAS 2; SATA 3, 68, 164; SATA-Essay 110; WYA; YAW

Sachs, Marilyn Stickle
See Sachs, Marilyn

Sachs, Nelly 1891-1970 . **CLC 14, 98; PC 78**
See also CA 17-18; 25-28R; CANR 87; CAP 2; DLB 332; EWL 3; MTCW 2; MTFW 2005; PFS 20; RGHL; RGWL 2, 3

Sackler, Howard (Oliver) 1929-1982 ... **CLC 14**
See also CA 61-64; 108; CAD; CANR 30; DFS 15; DLB 7

Sacks, Oliver 1933- .... **CLC 67, 202**
See also CA 53-56; CANR 28, 50, 76, 146, 187, 230; CPW; DA3; INT CANR-28; MTCW 1, 2; MTFW 2005

Sacks, Oliver Wolf
See Sacks, Oliver

Sackville, Thomas 1536-1608 .... **LC 98**
See also DAM DRAM; DLB 62, 132; RGEL 2

Sadakichi
See Hartmann, Sadakichi

Sa'dawi, Nawal al-
See El Saadawi, Nawal

Sade, Donatien Alphonse Francois 1740-1814 .... **NCLC 3, 47**
See also DLB 314; EW 4; GFL Beginnings to 1789; RGWL 2, 3

Sade, Marquis de
See Sade, Donatien Alphonse Francois

Sadoff, Ira 1945- .... **CLC 9**
See also CA 53-56; CANR 5, 21, 109; DLB 120

Saetone
See Camus, Albert

Safire, William 1929-2009 .... **CLC 10**
See also CA 17-20R; 290; CANR 31, 54, 91, 148

Safire, William L.
See Safire, William

Safire, William Lewis
See Safire, William

Sagan, Carl 1934-1996 .... **CLC 30, 112**
See also AAYA 2, 62; CA 25-28R; 155; CANR 11, 36, 74; CPW; DA3; MTCW 1, 2; MTFW 2005; SATA 58; SATA-Obit 94

Sagan, Francoise 1935-2004 ..... **CLC 3, 6, 9, 17, 36**
See also CA 49-52; 231; CANR 6, 39, 73, 216; CWW 2; DLB 83; EWL 3; GFL 1789 to the Present; MTCW 1, 2; MTFW 2005; TWA

Sahgal, Nayantara (Pandit) 1927- .. **CLC 41**
See also CA 9-12R; CANR 11, 88; CN 1, 2, 3, 4, 5, 6, 7; DLB 323

Said, Edward W. 1935-2003 .... **CLC 123**
See also CA 21-24R; 220; CANR 45, 74, 107, 131; DLB 67, 346; MTCW 2; MTFW 2005

Saikaku, Ihara 1642-1693 .... **LC 141**
See also RGWL 3

Saikaku Ihara
See Saikaku, Ihara

Saint, H(arry) F. 1941- .... **CLC 50**
See also CA 127

St. Aubin de Teran, Lisa 1953- .... **CLC 36**
See also CA 118; 126; CANR 215; CN 6, 7; INT CA-126

Saint Birgitta of Sweden c. 1303-1373 .... **CMLC 24**

St. E. A. of M. and S
See Crowley, Edward Alexander

Sainte-Beuve, Charles Augustin 1804-1869 . **NCLC 5; PC 110**
See also DLB 217; EW 6; GFL 1789 to the Present

Saint-Exupery, Antoine de 1900-1944 .... **TCLC 2, 56, 169; WLC**
See also AAYA 63; BPFB 3; BYA 3; CA 108; 132; CLR 10, 142; DA3; DAM NOV; DLB 72; EW 12; EWL 3; GFL 1789 to the Present; LAIT 3; MAICYA 1, 2; MTCW 1, 2; MTFW 2005; NFS 30; RGWL 2, 3; SATA 20; TWA

Saint-Exupery, Antoine Jean Baptiste Marie Roger de
See Saint-Exupery, Antoine de

St. John, David
See Hunt, E. Howard

St. John, Henry 1678-1751 .... **LC 178**
See also DLB 101, 336

St. John, J. Hector
See Crevecoeur, J. Hector St. John de

Saint-John Perse
See Leger, Alexis Saint-Leger
Saintsbury, George (Edward Bateman)
1845-1933 .... **TCLC 31**
See also CA 160; DLB 57, 149
Sait Faik
See Abasiyanik, Sait Faik
Saki 1870-1916 .... **SSC 12, 115; TCLC 3;**
WLC 5
See also AAYA 56; BRWS 6; BYA 11; CA
104; 130; CANR 104; CDBLB 1890-
1914; DA; DA3; DAB; DAC; DAM MST,
NOV; DLB 34, 162; EXPS; LAIT 2;
MTCW 1; MTFW 2005; RGEL 2;
SSFS 1, 15; SUFW
Sala, George Augustus 1828-1895 ..... **NCLC**
46
Saladin 1138-1193 .... **CMLC 38**
Salama, Hannu 1936- .... **CLC 18**
See also CA 244; EWL 3
Salamanca, J(ack) R(ichard) 1922- . **CLC 4,**
15
See also CA 25-28R, 193; CAAE 193
Salas, Floyd Francis 1931- .... **HLC 2**
See also CA 119; CAAS 27; CANR 44, 75,
93; DAM MULT; DLB 82; HW 1, 2;
MTFW 2005
Sale, J. Kirkpatrick
See Sale, Kirkpatrick
Sale, John Kirkpatrick
See Sale, Kirkpatrick
Sale, Kirkpatrick 1937- .... **CLC 68**
See also CA 13-16R; CANR 10, 147
Salernitano, Masuccio c. 1420-c. 1475 .. **SSC**
152
Salinas, Luis Omar 1937- . **CLC 90; HLC 2**
See also AMWS 13; CA 131; CANR 81,
153; DAM MULT; DLB 82; HW 1, 2
Salinas (y Serrano), Pedro 1891(?)-1951 .....
TCLC 17, 212
See also CA 117; DLB 134; EWL 3
Salinger, J.D. 1919-2010 ..... **CLC 1, 3, 8, 12,**
55, 56, 138, 243, 318; SSC 2, 28, 65, 146;
WLC 5
See also AAYA 2, 36; AMW; AMWC 1;
BPFB 3; CA 5-8R; CANR 39, 129;
CDALB 1941-1968; CLR 18; CN 1, 2, 3,
4, 5, 6, 7; CPW 1; DA; DA3; DAB; DAC;
DAM MST, NOV, POP; DLB 2, 102, 173;
EWL 3; EXPN; LAIT 4; MAICYA 1, 2;
MAL 5; MTCW 1, 2; MTFW 2005; NFS
1, 30; RGAL 4; RGSF 2; SATA 67; SSFS
17; TUS; WYA; YAW
Salinger, Jerome David
See Salinger, J.D.
Salisbury, John
See Caute, (John) David
Sallust c. 86B.C.-35B.C. .... **CMLC 68**
See also AW 2; CDWLB 1; DLB 211;
RGWL 2, 3
Salter, James 1925- .... **CLC 7, 52, 59, 275;**
SSC 58
See also AMWS 9; CA 73-76; CANR 107,
160; DLB 130; SSFS 25
Saltus, Edgar (Everton) 1855-1921 . **TCLC 8**
See also CA 105; DLB 202; RGAL 4
Saltykov, Mikhail Evgrafovich 1826-1889 ...
NCLC 16
See also DLB 238:
Saltykov-Shchedrin, N.
See Saltykov, Mikhail Evgrafovich
Samarakis, Andonis
See Samarakis, Antonis
Samarakis, Antonis 1919-2003 .... **CLC 5**
See also CA 25-28R; 224; CAAS 16; CANR
36; EWL 3

Samigli, E.
See Schmitz, Aron Hector
Sanchez, Florencio 1875-1910 .... **TCLC 37**
See also CA 153; DLB 305; EWL 3; HW 1;
LAW
Sanchez, Luis Rafael 1936- .... **CLC 23**
See also CA 128; DLB 305; EWL 3; HW 1;
WLIT 1
Sanchez, Sonia 1934- . **BLC 1:3, 2:3; CLC 5,**
116, 215; PC 9
See also BW 2, 3; CA 33-36R; CANR 24,
49, 74, 115; CLR 18; CP 2, 3, 4, 5, 6, 7;
CSW; CWP; DA3; DAM MULT; DLB 41;
DLBD 8; EWL 3; MAICYA 1, 2; MAL 5;
MTCW 1, 2; MTFW 2005; PFS 26; SATA
22, 136; WP
Sancho, Ignatius 1729-1780 .... **LC 84**
Sand, George 1804-1876 ... **DC 29; NCLC 2,**
42, 57, 174, 234; WLC 5
See also DA; DA3; DAB; DAC; DAM
MST, NOV; DLB 119, 192; EW 6; FL 1:3;
FW; GFL 1789 to the Present; RGWL 2,
3; TWA
Sandburg, Carl 1878-1967 ..... **CLC 1, 4, 10,**
15, 35; PC 2, 41; WLC 5
See also AAYA 24; AMW; BYA 1, 3; CA
5-8R; 25-28R; CANR 35; CDALB 1865-
1917; CLR 67; DA; DA3; DAB; DAC;
DAM MST, POET; DLB 17, 54, 284;
EWL 3; EXPP; LAIT 2; MAICYA 1, 2;
MAL 5; MTCW 1, 2; MTFW 2005; PAB;
PFS 3, 6, 12, 33, 36; RGAL 4; SATA 8;
TUS; WCH; WP; WYA
Sandburg, Carl August
See Sandburg, Carl
Sandburg, Charles
See Sandburg, Carl
Sandburg, Charles A.
See Sandburg, Carl
Sanders, Ed 1939- .... **CLC 53**
See also BG 1:3; CA 13-16R; CAAS 21;
CANR 13, 44, 78; CP 1, 2, 3, 4, 5, 6, 7;
DAM POET; DLB 16, 244
Sanders, Edward
See Sanders, Ed
Sanders, James Edward
See Sanders, Ed
Sanders, Lawrence 1920-1998 .... **CLC 41**
See also BEST 89:4; BPFB 3; CA 81-84;
165; CANR 33, 62; CMW 4; CPW; DA3;
DAM POP; MTCW 1
Sanders, Noah
See Blount, Roy, Jr.
Sanders, Winston P.
See Anderson, Poul
Sandoz, Mari(e Susette) 1900-1966 . **CLC 28**
See also CA 1-4R; 25-28R; CANR 17, 64;
DLB 9, 212; LAIT 2; MTCW 1, 2; SATA
5; TCWW 1, 2
Sandys, George 1578-1644 .... **LC 80**
See also DLB 24, 121
Saner, Reg(inald Anthony) 1931- ...... **CLC 9**
See also CA 65-68; CP 3, 4, 5, 6, 7
Sankara 788-820 .... **CMLC 32**
Sannazaro, Jacopo 1456(?)-1530 .... **LC 8**
See also RGWL 2, 3; WLIT 7
Sansom, William 1912-1976 . **CLC 2, 6; SSC**
21
See also CA 5-8R; 65-68; CANR 42; CN 1,
2; DAM NOV; DLB 139; EWL 3; MTCW
1; RGEL 2; RGSF 2
Santayana, George 1863-1952 ...... **TCLC 40**
See also AMW; CA 115; 194; DLB 54, 71,
246, 270; DLBD 13; EWL 3; MAL 5;
RGAL 4; TUS
Santiago, Danny
See James, Daniel (Lewis)

Santillana, Inigo Lopez de Mendoza,
Marques de 1398-1458 .... **LC 111**
See also DLB 286
Santmyer, Helen Hooven 1895-1986 .... **CLC**
33; TCLC 133
See also CA 1-4R; 118; CANR 15, 33;
DLBY 1984; MTCW 1; RHW
Santoka, Taneda 1882-1940 .... **TCLC 72**
Santos, Bienvenido N(uqui) 1911-1996 ....
AAL; CLC 22; TCLC 156
See also CA 101; 151; CANR 19, 46; CP 1;
DAM MULT; DLB 312, 348; EWL;
RGAL 4; SSFS 19
Santos, Miguel
See Mihura, Miguel
Sapir, Edward 1884-1939 .... **TCLC 108**
See also CA 211; DLB 92
Sapper
See McNeile, Herman Cyril
Sapphire 1950- .... **CLC 99**
See also CA 262
Sapphire, Brenda
See Sapphire
Sappho fl. 6th cent. B.C.- . **CMLC 3, 67; PC**
5, 117
See also CDWLB 1; DA3; DAM POET;
DLB 176; FL 1:1; PFS 20, 31, 38; RGWL
2, 3; WLIT 8; WP
Saramago, Jose 1922-2010 ... **CLC 119, 275;**
HLCS 1
See also CA 153; CANR 96, 164, 210;
CWW 2; DLB 287, 332; EWL 3; LATS
1:2; NFS 27; SSFS 23
Sarduy, Severo 1937-1993 .... **CLC 6, 97;**
HLCS 2; TCLC 167
See also CA 89-92; 142; CANR 58, 81;
CWW 2; DLB 113; EWL 3; HW 1, 2;
LAW
Sargeson, Frank 1903-1982 ... **CLC 31; SSC**
99
See also CA 25-28R; 106; CANR 38, 79;
CN 1, 2, 3; EWL 3; GLL 2; RGEL 2;
RGSF 2; SSFS 20
Sarmiento, Domingo Faustino 1811-1888 ....
HLCS 2; NCLC 123
See also LAW; WLIT 1
Sarmiento, Felix Ruben Garcia
See Dario, Ruben
Saro-Wiwa, Ken(ule Beeson) 1941-1995 ......
CLC 114; TCLC 200
See also BW 2; CA 142; 150; CANR 60;
DLB 157, 360
Saroyan, William 1908-1981 .. **CLC 1, 8, 10,**
29, 34, 56; DC 28; SSC 21; TCLC 137;
WLC 5
See also AAYA 66; CA 5-8R; 103; CAD;
CANR 30; CDALBS; CN 1, 2; DA; DA3;
DAB; DAC; DAM DRAM, MST, NOV;
DFS 17; DLB 7, 9, 86; DLBY 1981; EWL
3; LAIT 4; MAL 5; MTCW 1, 2; MTFW
2005; NFS 39; RGAL 4; RGSF 2; SATA
23; SATA-Obit 24; SSFS 14; TUS
Sarraute, Nathalie 1900-1999 .. **CLC 1, 2, 4,**
8, 10, 31, 80; TCLC 145
See also BPFB 3; CA 9-12R; 187; CANR
23, 66, 134; CWW 2; DLB 83, 321; EW
12; EWL 3; GFL 1789 to the Present;
MTCW 1, 2; MTFW 2005; RGWL 2, 3
Sarton, May 1912-1995 .. **CLC 4, 14, 49, 91;**
PC 39; TCLC 120
See also AMWS 8; CA 1-4R; 149; CANR
1, 34, 55, 116; CN 1, 2, 3, 4, 5, 6; CP 1,
2, 3, 4, 5, 6; DAM POET; DLB 48; DLBY
1981; EWL 3; FW; INT CANR-34; MAL
5; MTCW 1, 2; MTFW 2005; RGAL 4;
SATA 36; SATA-Obit 86; TUS

Schwartz, Delmore (David) 1913-1966 . **CLC 2, 4, 10, 45, 87; PC 8; SSC 105**
See also AMWS 2; CA 17-18; 25-28R; CANR 35; CAP 2; DLB 28, 48; EWL 3; MAL 5; MTCW 1, 2; MTFW 2005; PAB; RGAL 4; TUS

Schwartz, Ernst
See Ozu, Yasujiro

Schwartz, John Burnham 1965- ..... **CLC 59**
See also CA 132; CANR 116, 188

Schwartz, Lynne Sharon 1939- .... **CLC 31**
See also CA 103; CANR 44, 89, 160, 214; DLB 218; MTCW 2; MTFW 2005

Schwartz, Muriel A.
See Eliot, T. S.

Schwartzman, Adam 1973- .... **CLC 318**
See also CA 307

Schwarz-Bart, Andre 1928-2006 ... **CLC 2, 4**
See also CA 89-92; 253; CANR 109; DLB 299; RGHL

Schwarz-Bart, Simone 1938- . **BLCS; CLC 7**
See also BW 2; CA 97-100; CANR 117; EWL 3

Schwerner, Armand 1927-1999 .... **PC 42**
See also CA 9-12R; 179; CANR 50, 85; CP 2, 3, 4, 5, 6; DLB 165

Schwitters, Kurt (Hermann Edward Karl Julius) 1887-1948 .... **TCLC 95**
See also CA 158

Schwob, Marcel (Mayer Andre) 1867-1905 . **TCLC 20**
See also CA 117; 168; DLB 123; GFL 1789 to the Present

Sciascia, Leonardo 1921-1989 . **CLC 8, 9, 41**
See also CA 85-88; 130; CANR 35; DLB 177; EWL 3; MTCW 1; RGWL 2, 3

Scoppettone, Sandra 1936- .... **CLC 26**
See also AAYA 11, 65; BYA 8; CA 5-8R; CANR 41, 73, 157; GLL 1; MAICYA 2; MAICYAS 1; SATA 9, 92; WYA; YAW

Scorsese, Martin 1942- ...... **CLC 20, 89, 207**
See also AAYA 38; CA 110; 114; CANR 46, 85

Scotland, Jay
See Jakes, John

Scott, Duncan Campbell 1862-1947 .. **TCLC 6**
See also CA 104; 153; DAC; DLB 92; RGEL 2

Scott, Evelyn 1893-1963 .... **CLC 43**
See also CA 104; 112; CANR 64; DLB 9, 48; RHW

Scott, F(rancis) R(eginald) 1899-1985 . **CLC 22**
See also CA 101; 114; CANR 87; CP 1, 2, 3, 4; DLB 88; INT CA-101; RGEL 2

Scott, Frank
See Scott, F(rancis) R(eginald)

Scott, Joan
See Scott, Joan Wallach

Scott, Joan W.
See Scott, Joan Wallach

Scott, Joan Wallach 1941- .... **CLC 65**
See also CA 293

Scott, Joanna 1960- .... **CLC 50**
See also AMWS 17; CA 126; CANR 53, 92, 168, 219

Scott, Joanna Jeanne
See Scott, Joanna

Scott, Paul (Mark) 1920-1978 ..... **CLC 9, 60**
See also BRWS 1; CA 81-84; 77-80; CANR 33; CN 1, 2; DLB 14, 207, 326; EWL 3; MTCW 1; RGEL 2; RHW; WWE 1

Scott, Ridley 1937- .... **CLC 183**
See also AAYA 13, 43

Scott, Sarah 1723-1795 .... **LC 44**
See also DLB 39

Scott, Sir Walter 1771-1832 ... **NCLC 15, 69, 110, 209, 241; PC 13; SSC 32; WLC 5**
See also AAYA 22; BRW 4; BYA 2; CD-BLB 1789-1832; CLR 154; DA; DAB; DAC; DAM MST, NOV, POET; DLB 93, 107, 116, 144, 159, 366; GL 3; HGG; LAIT 1; NFS 31; RGEL 2; RGSF 2; SSFS 10; SUFW 1; TEA; WLIT 3; YABC 2

Scotus, John Duns 1266(?)-1308 . **CMLC 59, 138**
See also DLB 115

Scribe, Augustin Eugene
See Scribe, (Augustin) Eugene

Scribe, (Augustin) Eugene 1791-1861 .... **DC 5; NCLC 16**
See also DAM DRAM; DLB 192; GFL 1789 to the Present; RGWL 2, 3

Scrum, R.
See Crumb, R.

Scudery, Georges de 1601-1667 .... **LC 75**
See also GFL Beginnings to 1789

Scudery, Madeleine de 1607-1701 . **LC 2, 58**
See also DLB 268; GFL Beginnings to 1789

Scum
See Crumb, R.

Scumbag, Little Bobby
See Crumb, R.

Seabrook, John
See Hubbard, L. Ron

Seacole, Mary Jane Grant 1805-1881 .... **NCLC 147**
See also DLB 166

Sealsfield, Charles 1793-1864 ..... **NCLC 233**
See also DLB 133, 186

Sealy, I(rwin) Allan 1951- .... **CLC 55**
See also CA 136; CN 6, 7

Search, Alexander
See Pessoa, Fernando

Seare, Nicholas
See Whitaker, Rod

Sebastian, Lee
See Silverberg, Robert

Sebastian Owl
See Thompson, Hunter S.

Sebestyen, Igen
See Sebestyen, Ouida

Sebestyen, Ouida 1924- .... **CLC 30**
See also AAYA 8; BYA 7; CA 107; CANR 40, 114; CLR 17; JRDA; MAICYA 1, 2; SAAS 10; SATA 39, 140; WYA; YAW

Sebold, Alice 1963- .... **CLC 193**
See also AAYA 56; CA 203; CANR 181; LNFS 1; MTFW 2005

Second Duke of Buckingham
See Villiers, George

Secundus, H. Scriblerus
See Fielding, Henry

Sedges, John
See Buck, Pearl S.

Sedgwick, Catharine Maria 1789-1867 .... **NCLC 19, 98, 238**
See also DLB 1, 74, 183, 239, 243, 254; FL 1:3; RGAL 4

Sedley, Sir Charles 1639-1701 .... **LC 168**
See also BRW 2; DLB 131; RGEL 2

Sedulius Scottus 9th cent. -c. 874 . **CMLC 86**

Seebohm, Victoria
See Glendinning, Victoria

Seelye, John (Douglas) 1931- .... **CLC 7**
See also CA 97-100; CANR 70; INT CA-97-100; TCWW 1, 2

Seferiades, Giorgos Stylianou
See Seferis, George

Seferis, George 1900-1971 .... **CLC 5, 11; TCLC 213**
See also CA 5-8R; 33-36R; CANR 5, 36; DLB 332; EW 12; EWL 3; MTCW 1; RGWL 2, 3

Segal, Erich 1937-2010 .... **CLC 3, 10**
See also BEST 89:1; BPFB 3; CA 25-28R; CANR 20, 36, 65, 113; CPW; DAM POP; DLBY 1986; INT CANR-20; MTCW 1

Segal, Erich Wolf
See Segal, Erich

Seger, Bob 1945- .... **CLC 35**

Seghers
See Radvanyi, Netty

Seghers, Anna
See Radvanyi, Netty

Seidel, Frederick 1936- .... **CLC 18**
See also CA 13-16R; CANR 8, 99, 180; CP 1, 2, 3, 4, 5, 6, 7; DLBY 1984

Seidel, Frederick Lewis
See Seidel, Frederick

Seifert, Jaroslav 1901-1986 . **CLC 34, 44, 93; PC 47**
See also CA 127; CDWLB 4; DLB 215, 332; EWL 3; MTCW 1, 2

Sei Shonagon c. 966-1017(?) .... **CMLC 6, 89**

Sejour, Victor 1817-1874 .... **DC 10**
See also DLB 50

Sejour Marcou et Ferrand, Juan Victor
See Sejour, Victor

Selby, Hubert, Jr. 1928-2004 ... **CLC 1, 2, 4, 8; SSC 20**
See also CA 13-16R; 226; CANR 33, 85; CN 1, 2, 3, 4, 5, 6, 7; DLB 2, 227; MAL 5

Self, Will 1961- .... **CLC 282**
See also BRWS 5; CA 143; CANR 83, 126, 171, 201; CN 6, 7; DLB 207

Self, William
See Self, Will

Self, William Woodward
See Self, Will

Selzer, Richard 1928- .... **CLC 74**
See also CA 65-68; CANR 14, 106, 204

Sembene, Ousmane
See Ousmane, Sembene

Senancour, Etienne Pivert de 1770-1846 ..... **NCLC 16**
See also DLB 119; GFL 1789 to the Present

Sender, Ramon (Jose) 1902-1982 ..... **CLC 8; HLC 2; TCLC 136**
See also CA 5-8R; 105; CANR 8; DAM MULT; DLB 322; EWL 3; HW 1; MTCW 1; RGWL 2, 3

Seneca, Lucius Annaeus c. 4B.C.-c. 65 .... **CMLC 6, 107; DC 5**
See also AW 2; CDWLB 1; DAM DRAM; DLB 211; RGWL 2, 3; TWA; WLIT 8

Seneca the Younger
See Seneca, Lucius Annaeus

Senghor, Leopold Sedar 1906-2001 ...... **BLC 1:3; CLC 54, 130; PC 25**
See also AFW; BW 2; CA 116; 125; 203; CANR 47, 74, 134; CWW 2; DAM MULT, POET; DNFS 2; EWL 3; GFL 1789 to the Present; MTCW 1, 2; MTFW 2005; PFS 36; TWA

Senior, Olive (Marjorie) 1941- .... **SSC 78**
See also BW 3; CA 154; CANR 86, 126; CN 6; CP 6, 7; CWP; DLB 157; EWL 3; RGSF 2

Senna, Danzy 1970- .... **CLC 119**
See also CA 169; CANR 130, 184

Sepheriades, Georgios
See Seferis, George

Serling, (Edward) Rod(man) 1924-1975 ...... **CLC 30**
See also AAYA 14; AITN 1; CA 162; 57-60; DLB 26; SFW 4

Serna, Ramon Gomez de la
See Gomez de la Serna, Ramon
Serote, Mongane Wally 1944- .... **PC 113**
See also BW 2, 3; CA 142; CANR 81; CP
5, 6, 7; DLB 125, 225
Serpieres
See Guillevic, (Eugene)
Service, Robert
See Service, Robert W.
Service, Robert W. 1874(?)-1958 ...... **PC 70;**
TCLC 15; WLC 5
See also BYA 4; CA 115; 140; CANR 84;
DA; DAB; DAC; DAM MST, POET;
DLB 92; PFS 10; RGEL 2; SATA 20
Service, Robert William
See Service, Robert W.
Servius c. 370-c. 431 .... **CMLC 120**
Seth, Vikram 1952- .... **CLC 43, 90, 277; PC**
118
See also BRWS 10; CA 121; 127; CANR
50, 74, 131; CN 6, 7; CP 5, 6, 7; DA3;
DAM MULT; DLB 120, 271, 282, 323;
EWL 3; INT CA-127; MTCW 2; MTFW
2005; WWE 1
Setien, Miguel Delibes
See Delibes Setien, Miguel
Seton, Cynthia Propper 1926-1982 . **CLC 27**
See also CA 5-8R; 108; CANR 7
Seton, Ernest (Evan) Thompson
1860-1946 .... **TCLC 31**
See also ANW; BYA 3; CA 109; 204; CLR
59; DLB 92; DLBD 13; JRDA; SATA 18
Seton-Thompson, Ernest
See Seton, Ernest (Evan) Thompson
Settle, Mary Lee 1918-2005 ..... **CLC 19, 61,**
273
See also BPFB 3; CA 89-92; 243; CAAS 1;
CANR 44, 87, 126, 182; CN 6, 7; CSW;
DLB 6; INT CA-89-92
Seuphor, Michel
See Arp, Jean
Seventeenth Earl of Oxford
See de Vere, Edward
Sevigne, Marie (de Rabutin-Chantal)
1626-1696 .... **LC 11, 144**
See also DLB 268; GFL Beginnings to
1789; TWA
Sevigne, Marie de Rabutin Chantal
See Sevigne, Marie (de Rabutin-Chantal)
Sewall, Samuel 1652-1730 .... **LC 38**
See also DLB 24; RGAL 4
Sexton, Anne 1928-1974 . **CLC 2, 4, 6, 8, 10,**
15, 53, 123; PC 2, 79; TCLC 252; WLC
5
See also AMWS 2; CA 1-4R; 53-56; CABS
2; CANR 3, 36; CDALB 1941-1968; CP
1, 2; DA; DA3; DAB; DAC; DAM MST,
POET; DLB 5, 169; EWL 3; EXPP; FL
1:6; FW; MAL 5; MBL; MTCW 1, 2;
MTFW 2005; PAB; PFS 4, 14, 30, 36, 40;
RGAL 4; RGHL; SATA 10; TUS
Sexton, Anne Harvey
See Sexton, Anne
Shaara, Jeff 1952- .... **CLC 119**
See also AAYA 70; CA 163; CANR 109,
172; CN 7; MTFW 2005
Shaara, Michael 1929-1988 .... **CLC 15**
See also AAYA 71; AITN 1; BPFB 3; CA
102; 125; CANR 52, 85; DAM POP;
DLBY 1983; MTFW 2005; NFS 26
Shackleton, C.C.
See Aldiss, Brian W.
Shacochis, Bob
See Shacochis, Robert G.
Shacochis, Robert G. 1951- .... **CLC 39**
See also CA 119; 124; CANR 100; INT CA-
124
Shadwell, Thomas 1641(?)-1692 .... **LC 114**
See also DLB 80; IDTP; RGEL 2

Shaffer, Anthony 1926-2001 .... **CLC 19**
See also CA 110; 116; 200; CBD; CD 5, 6;
DAM DRAM; DFS 13; DLB 13
Shaffer, Anthony Joshua
See Shaffer, Anthony
Shaffer, Peter 1926- .. **CLC 5, 14, 18, 37, 60,**
291; DC 7
See also BRWS 1; CA 25-28R; CANR 25,
47, 74, 118; CBD; CD 5, 6; CDBLB 1960
to Present; DA3; DAB; DAM DRAM,
MST; DFS 5, 13; DLB 13, 233; EWL 3;
MTCW 1, 2; MTFW 2005; RGEL 2; TEA
Shakespeare, William 1564-1616 . **PC 84, 89,**
98, 101, 128; WLC 5
See also AAYA 35; BRW 1; BRWR 3; CD-
BLB Before 1660; DA; DA3; DAB;
DAC; DAM DRAM, MST, POET; DFS
20, 21; DLB 62, 172, 263; EXPP; LAIT
1; LATS 1:1; LMFS 1; PAB; PFS 1, 2, 3,
4, 5, 8, 9, 35; RGEL 2; TEA; WLIT 3;
WP; WS; WYA
Shakey, Bernard
See Young, Neil
Shalamov, Varlam (Tikhonovich)
1907-1982 .... **CLC 18**
See also CA 129; 105; DLB 302; RGSF 2
Shamloo, Ahmad
See Shamlu, Ahmad
Shamlou, Ahmad
See Shamlu, Ahmad
Shamlu, Ahmad 1925-2000 .... **CLC 10**
See also CA 216; CWW 2
Shammas, Anton 1951- .... **CLC 55**
See also CA 199; DLB 346
Shandling, Arline
See Berriault, Gina
Shange, Ntozake 1948- . **BLC 1:3, 2:3; CLC**
8, 25, 38, 74, 126; DC 3
See also AAYA 9, 66; AFAW 1, 2; BW 2;
CA 85-88; CABS 3; CAD; CANR 27, 48,
74, 131, 208; CD 5, 6; CP 5, 6, 7; CWD;
CWP; DA3; DAM DRAM, MULT; DFS
2, 11; DLB 38, 249; FW; LAIT 4, 5; MAL
5; MTCW 1, 2; MTFW 2005; NFS 11;
RGAL 4; SATA 157; YAW
Shanley, John Patrick 1950- .... **CLC 75**
See also AAYA 74; AMWS 14; CA 128;
133; CAD; CANR 83, 154; CD 5, 6; DFS
23, 28
Shapcott, Thomas W(illiam) 1935- . **CLC 38**
See also CA 69-72; CANR 49, 83, 103; CP
1, 2, 3, 4, 5, 6, 7; DLB 289
Shapiro, Jane 1942- .... **CLC 76**
See also CA 196
Shapiro, Karl 1913-2000 .. **CLC 4, 8, 15, 53;**
PC 25
See also AMWS 2; CA 1-4R; 188; CAAS
6; CANR 1, 36, 66; CP 1, 2, 3, 4, 5, 6;
DLB 48; EWL 3; EXPP; MAL 5; MTCW
1, 2; MTFW 2005; PFS 3; RGAL 4
Sharp, William 1855-1905 .... **TCLC 39**
See also CA 160; DLB 156; RGEL 2;
SUFW
Sharpe, Thomas Ridley 1928- .... **CLC 36**
See also CA 114; 122; CANR 85; CN 4, 5,
6, 7; DLB 14, 231; INT CA-122
Sharpe, Tom
See Sharpe, Thomas Ridley
Shatrov, Mikhail .... **CLC 59**
Shaw, Bernard
See Shaw, George Bernard
Shaw, G. Bernard
See Shaw, George Bernard
Shaw, George Bernard 1856-1950 ... **DC 23;**
TCLC 3, 9, 21, 45, 205; WLC 5
See also AAYA 61; BRW 6; BRWC 1;
BRWR 2; CA 104; 128; CDBLB 1914-
1945; DA; DA3; DAB; DAC; DAM
DRAM, MST; DFS 1, 3, 6, 11, 19, 22;

DLB 10, 57, 190, 332; EWL 3; LAIT 3;
LATS 1:1; MTCW 1, 2; MTFW 2005;
RGEL 2; TEA; WLIT 4
Shaw, Henry Wheeler 1818-1885 . **NCLC 15**
See also DLB 11; RGAL 4
Shaw, Irwin 1913-1984 .... **CLC 7, 23, 34**
See also AITN 1; BPFB 3; CA 13-16R; 112;
CANR 21; CDALB 1941-1968; CN 1, 2,
3; CPW; DAM DRAM, POP; DLB 6,
102; DLBY 1984; MAL 5; MTCW 1, 21;
MTFW 2005
Shaw, Robert (Archibald) 1927-1978 .. **CLC**
5
See also AITN 1; CA 1-4R; 81-84; CANR
4; CN 1, 2; DLB 13, 14
Shaw, T. E.
See Lawrence, T. E.
Shawn, Wallace 1943- .... **CLC 41**
See also CA 112; CAD; CANR 215; CD 5,
6; DLB 266
Shaykh, Hanan al- 1945- .... **CLC 218**
See also CA 135; CANR 111, 220; CWW
2; DLB 346; EWL 3; WLIT 6
Shchedrin, N.
See Saltykov, Mikhail Evgrafovich
Shea, Lisa 1953- .... **CLC 86**
See also CA 147
Sheed, Wilfrid 1930-2011 .. **CLC 2, 4, 10, 53**
See also CA 65-68; CANR 30, 66, 181; CN
1, 2, 3, 4, 5, 6, 7; DLB 6; MAL 5; MTCW
1, 2; MTFW 2005
Sheed, Wilfrid John Joseph
See Sheed, Wilfrid
Sheehy, Gail 1937- .... **CLC 171**
See also CA 49-52; CANR 1, 33, 55, 92;
CPW; MTCW 1
Sheldon, Alice Hastings Bradley
1915(?)-1987 .... **CLC 48, 50**
See also CA 108; 122; CANR 34; DLB 8;
INT CA-108; MTCW 1; SCFW 1, 2; SFW
4
Sheldon, John
See Bloch, Robert (Albert)
Sheldon, Raccoona
See Sheldon, Alice Hastings Bradley
Shelley, Mary
See Shelley, Mary Wollstonecraft
Shelley, Mary Wollstonecraft 1797-1851 .....
NCLC 14, 59, 103, 170; SSC 92; WLC
5
See also AAYA 20; BPFB 3; BRW 3;
BRWC 2; BRWR 3; BRWS 3; BYA 5;
CDBLB 1789-1832; CLR 133; DA; DA3;
DAB; DAC; DAM MST, NOV; DLB 110,
116, 159, 178; EXPN; FL 1:3; GL 3;
HGG; LAIT 1; LMFS 1, 2; NFS 1, 37;
RGEL 2; SATA 29; SCFW 1, 2; SFW 4;
TEA; WLIT 3
Shelley, Percy Bysshe 1792-1822 . **NCLC 18,**
93, 143, 175; PC 14, 67; WLC 5
See also AAYA 61; BRW 4; BRWR 1; CD-
BLB 1789-1832; DA; DA3; DAB; DAC;
DAM MST, POET; DLB 96, 110, 158;
EXPP; LMFS 1; PAB; PFS 2, 27, 32, 36;
RGEL 2; TEA; WLIT 3; WP
Shepard, James R.
See Shepard, Jim
Shepard, Jim 1956- .... **CLC 36**
See also AAYA 73; CA 137; CANR 59, 104,
160, 199, 231; SATA 90, 164
Shepard, Lucius 1947- .... **CLC 34**
See also CA 128; 141; CANR 81, 124, 178;
HGG; SCFW 2; SFW 4; SUFW 2
Shepard, Sam 1943- ... **CLC 4, 6, 17, 34, 41,**
44, 169; DC 5
See also AAYA 1, 58; AMWS 3; CA 69-72;
CABS 3; CAD; CANR 22, 120, 140, 223;
CD 5, 6; DA3; DAM DRAM; DFS 3, 6,

7, 14; DLB 7, 212, 341; EWL 3; IDFW 3, 4; MAL 5; MTCW 1, 2; MTFW 2005; RGAL 4

Shepherd, Jean (Parker) 1921-1999 .. **TCLC 177**
See also AAYA 69; AITN 2; CA 77-80; 187

Shepherd, Michael
See Ludlum, Robert

Sherburne, Zoa (Lillian Morin) 1912-1995 . **CLC 30**
See also AAYA 13; CA 1-4R; 176; CANR 3, 37; MAICYA 1, 2; SAAS 18; SATA 3; YAW

Sheridan, Frances 1724-1766 .... **LC 7**
See also DLB 39, 84

Sheridan, Richard Brinsley 1751-1816 .. **DC 1; NCLC 5, 91; WLC 5**
See also BRW 3; CDBLB 1660-1789; DA; DAB; DAC; DAM DRAM, MST; DFS 15; DLB 89; WLIT 3

Sherman, Jonathan Marc 1968- ..... **CLC 55**
See also CA 230

Sherman, Martin 1941(?)- .... **CLC 19**
See also CA 116; 123; CAD; CANR 86; CD 5, 6; DFS 20; DLB 228; GLL 1; IDTP; RGHL

Sherwin, Judith Johnson
See Johnson, Judith

Sherwood, Frances 1940- .... **CLC 81**
See also CA 146, 220; CAAE 220; CANR 158

Sherwood, Robert E(mmet) 1896-1955 .. **DC 36; TCLC 3**
See also CA 104; 153; CANR 86; DAM DRAM; DFS 11, 15, 17; DLB 7, 26, 249; IDFW 3, 4; MAL 5; RGAL 4

Shestov, Lev 1866-1938 .... **TCLC 56**

Shevchenko, Taras 1814-1861 .... **NCLC 54**

Shiel, M. P. 1865-1947 .... **TCLC 8**
See also CA 106; 160; DLB 153; HGG; MTCW 2; MTFW 2005; SCFW 1, 2; SFW 4; SUFW

Shiel, Matthew Phipps
See Shiel, M. P.

Shields, Carol 1935-2003 . **CLC 91, 113, 193, 298; SSC 126**
See also AMWS 7; CA 81-84; 218; CANR 51, 74, 98, 133; CCA 1; CN 6, 7; CPW; DA3; DAC; DLB 334, 350; MTCW 2; MTFW 2005; NFS 23

Shields, David 1956- .... **CLC 97**
See also CA 124; CANR 48, 99, 112, 157

Shields, David Jonathan
See Shields, David

Shiga, Naoya 1883-1971 .. **CLC 33; SSC 23; TCLC 172**
See also CA 101; 33-36R; DLB 180; EWL 3; MJW; RGWL 3

Shiga Naoya
See Shiga, Naoya

Shilts, Randy 1951-1994 .... **CLC 85**
See also AAYA 19; CA 115; 127; 144; CANR 45; DA3; GLL 1; INT CA-127; MTCW 2; MTFW 2005

Shimazaki, Haruki 1872-1943 .... **TCLC 5**
See also CA 105; 134; CANR 84; DLB 180; EWL 3; MJW; RGWL 3

Shimazaki Toson
See Shimazaki, Haruki

Shirley, James 1596-1666 ...... **DC 25; LC 96**
See also DLB 58; RGEL 2

Sholem Aleykhem
See Rabinovitch, Sholem

Sholokhov, Mikhail 1905-1984 .... **CLC 7, 15**
See also CA 101; 112; DLB 272, 332; EWL 3; MTCW 1, 2; MTFW 2005; RGWL 2, 3; SATA-Obit 36

Sholokhov, Mikhail Aleksandrovich
See Sholokhov, Mikhail

Sholom Aleichem 1859-1916 ....
See Rabinovitch, Sholem

Shone, Patric
See Hanley, James

Showalter, Elaine 1941- .... **CLC 169**
See also CA 57-60; CANR 58, 106, 208; DLB 67; FW; GLL 2

Shreve, Susan
See Shreve, Susan Richards

Shreve, Susan Richards 1939- .... **CLC 23**
See also CA 49-52; CAAS 5; CANR 5, 38, 69, 100, 159, 199; MAICYA 1, 2; SATA 46, 95, 152; SATA-Brief 41

Shteyngart, Gary 1972- .... **CLC 319**
See also AAYA 68; CA 217; CANR 175

Shteyngart, Igor
See Shteyngart, Gary

Shue, Larry 1946-1985 .... **CLC 52**
See also CA 145; 117; DAM DRAM; DFS 7

Shu-Jen, Chou 1881-1936 . **SSC 20; TCLC 3**
See also CA 104; EWL 3

Shulman, Alix Kates 1932- .... **CLC 2, 10**
See also CA 29-32R; CANR 43, 199; FW; SATA 7

Shuster, Joe 1914-1992 .... **CLC 21**
See also AAYA 50

Shute, Nevil 1899-1960 .... **CLC 30**
See also BPFB 3; CA 102; 93-96; CANR 85; DLB 255; MTCW 2; NFS 9, 38; RHW 4; SFW 4

Shuttle, Penelope (Diane) 1947- .... **CLC 7**
See also CA 93-96; CANR 39, 84, 92, 108; CP 3, 4, 5, 6, 7; CWP; DLB 14, 40

Shvarts, Elena 1948-2010 .... **PC 50**
See also CA 147

Sidhwa, Bapsi 1939- ....
See Sidhwa, Bapsy (N.)

Sidhwa, Bapsy (N.) 1938- .... **CLC 168**
See also CA 108; CANR 25, 57; CN 6, 7; DLB 323; FW

Sidney, Mary 1561-1621 .... **LC 19, 39, 182**
See also DLB 167

Sidney, Sir Philip 1554-1586 . **LC 19, 39, 131, 197; PC 32**
See also BRW 1; BRWR 2; CDBLB Before 1660; DA; DA3; DAB; DAC; DAM MST, POET; DLB 167; EXPP; PAB; PFS 30; RGEL 2; TEA; WP

Sidney Herbert, Mary
See Sidney, Mary

Siegel, Jerome 1914-1996 .... **CLC 21**
See also AAYA 50; CA 116; 169; 151

Siegel, Jerry
See Siegel, Jerome

Sienkiewicz, Henryk (Adam Alexander Pius) 1846-1916 .... **TCLC 3**
See also CA 104; 134; CANR 84; DLB 332; EWL 3; RGSF 2; RGWL 2, 3

Sierra, Gregorio Martinez
See Martinez Sierra, Gregorio

Sierra, Maria de la O'LeJarraga Martinez
See Martinez Sierra, Maria

Sigal, Clancy 1926- .... **CLC 7**
See also CA 1-4R; CANR 85, 184; CN 1, 2, 3, 4, 5, 6, 7

Siger of Brabant 1240(?)-1284(?) . **CMLC 69**
See also DLB 115

Sigourney, Lydia H.
See Sigourney, Lydia Howard

Sigourney, Lydia Howard 1791-1865 . **NCLC 21, 87**
See also DLB 1, 42, 73, 183, 239, 243

Sigourney, Lydia Howard Huntley
See Sigourney, Lydia Howard

Sigourney, Lydia Huntley
See Sigourney, Lydia Howard

Siguenza y Gongora, Carlos de 1645-1700 . **HLCS 2; LC 8**
See also LAW

Sigurjonsson, Johann
See Sigurjonsson, Johann

Sigurjonsson, Johann 1880-1919 .. **TCLC 27**
See also CA 170; DLB 293; EWL 3

Sikelianos, Angelos 1884-1951 .... **PC 29; TCLC 39**
See also EWL 3; RGWL 2, 3

Silkin, Jon 1930-1997 .... **CLC 2, 6, 43**
See also CA 5-8R; CAAS 5; CANR 89; CP 1, 2, 3, 4, 5, 6; DLB 27

Silko, Leslie 1948- ..... **CLC 23, 74, 114, 211, 302; NNAL; SSC 37, 66, 151; WLCS**
See also AAYA 14; AMWS 4; ANW; BYA 12; CA 115; 122; CANR 45, 65, 118, 226; CN 4, 5, 6, 7; CP 4, 5, 6, 7; CPW 1; CWP; DA; DA3; DAC; DAM MST, MULT, POP; DLB 143, 175, 256, 275; EWL 3; EXPP; EXPS; LAIT 4; MAL 5; MTCW 2; MTFW 2005; NFS 4; PFS 9, 16; RGAL 4; RGSF 2; SSFS 4, 8, 10, 11; TCWW 1, 2

Silko, Leslie Marmon
See Silko, Leslie

Sillanpaa, Frans Eemil 1888-1964 .. **CLC 19**
See also CA 129; 93-96; DLB 332; EWL 3; MTCW 1

Sillitoe, Alan 1928-2010 ...... **CLC 1, 3, 6, 10, 19, 57, 148, 318**
See also AITN 1; BRWS 5; CA 9-12R, 191; CAAE 191; CAAS 2; CANR 8, 26, 55, 139, 213; CDBLB 1960 to Present; CN 1, 2, 3, 4, 5, 6; CP 1, 2, 3, 4, 5; DLB 14, 139; EWL 3; MTCW 1, 2; MTFW 2005; RGEL 2; RGSF 2; SATA 61

Silone, Ignazio 1900-1978 .... **CLC 4**
See also CA 25-28; 81-84; CANR 34; CAP 2; DLB 264; EW 12; EWL 3; MTCW 1; RGSF 2; RGWL 2, 3

Silone, Ignazione
See Silone, Ignazio

Siluriensis, Leolinus
See Jones, Arthur Llewellyn

Silver, Joan Micklin 1935- .... **CLC 20**
See also CA 114; 121; INT CA-121

Silver, Nicholas
See Faust, Frederick

Silverberg, Robert 1935- .... **CLC 7, 140**
See also AAYA 24; BPFB 3; BYA 7, 9; CA 1-4R; 186; CAAE 186; CAAS 3; CANR 1, 20, 36, 85, 140, 175; CLR 59; CN 6, 7; CPW; DAM POP; DLB 8; INT CANR-20; MAICYA 1, 2; MTCW 1, 2; MTFW 2005; SATA 13, 91; SATA-Essay 104; SCFW 1, 2; SFW 4; SUFW 2

Silverstein, Alvin 1933- .... **CLC 17**
See also CA 49-52; CANR 2; CLR 25; JRDA; MAICYA 1, 2; SATA 8, 69, 124

Silverstein, Shel 1932-1999 .... **PC 49**
See also AAYA 40; BW 3; CA 107; 179; CANR 47, 74, 81; CLR 5, 96; CWRI 5; JRDA; MAICYA 1, 2; MTCW 2; MTFW 2005; SATA 33, 92; SATA-Brief 27; SATA-Obit 116

Silverstein, Sheldon Allan
See Silverstein, Shel

Silverstein, Virginia B. 1937- .... **CLC 17**
See also CA 49-52; CANR 2; CLR 25; JRDA; MAICYA 1, 2; SATA 8, 69, 124

Silverstein, Virginia Barbara Opshelor
See Silverstein, Virginia B.

Sim, Georges
See Simenon, Georges

Simak, Clifford D(onald) 1904-1988 .... **CLC 1, 55**
See also CA 1-4R; 125; CANR 1, 35; DLB 8; MTCW 1; SATA-Obit 56; SCFW 1, 2; SFW 4

Simenon, Georges 1903-1989 ... **CLC 1, 2, 3, 8, 18, 47**
See also BPFB 3; CA 85-88; 129; CANR 35; CMW 4; DA3; DAM POP; DLB 72; DLBY 1989; EW 12; EWL 3; GFL 1789 to the Present; MSW; MTCW 1, 2; MTFW 2005; RGWL 2, 3

Simenon, Georges Jacques Christian
See Simenon, Georges

Simic, Charles 1938- .. **CLC 6, 9, 22, 49, 68, 130, 256; PC 69**
See also AAYA 78; AMWS 8; CA 29-32R; CAAS 4; CANR 12, 33, 52, 61, 96, 140, 210; CP 2, 3, 4, 5, 6, 7; DA3; DAM POET; DLB 105; MAL 5; MTCW 2; MTFW 2005; PFS 7, 33, 36; RGAL 4; WP

Simmel, Georg 1858-1918 .... **TCLC 64**
See also CA 157; DLB 296

Simmons, Charles (Paul) 1924- .... **CLC 57**
See also CA 89-92; INT CA-89-92

Simmons, Dan 1948- .... **CLC 44**
See also AAYA 16, 54; CA 138; CANR 53, 81, 126, 174, 204; CPW; DAM POP; HGG; SUFW 2

Simmons, James (Stewart Alexander) 1933- .... **CLC 43**
See also CA 105; CAAS 21; CP 1, 2, 3, 4, 5, 6, 7; DLB 40

Simmons, Richard
See Simmons, Dan

Simms, William Gilmore 1806-1870 . **NCLC 3, 241**
See also DLB 3, 30, 59, 73, 248, 254; RGAL 4

Simon, Carly 1945- .... **CLC 26**
See also CA 105

Simon, Claude 1913-2005 . **CLC 4, 9, 15, 39**
See also CA 89-92; 241; CANR 33, 117; CWW 2; DAM NOV; DLB 83, 332; EW 13; EWL 3; GFL 1789 to the Present; MTCW 1

Simon, Claude Eugene Henri
See Simon, Claude

Simon, Claude Henri Eugene
See Simon, Claude

Simon, Marvin Neil
See Simon, Neil

Simon, Myles
See Follett, Ken

Simon, Neil 1927- ...... **CLC 6, 11, 31, 39, 70, 233; DC 14**
See also AAYA 32; AITN 1; AMWS 4; CA 21-24R; CAD; CANR 26, 54, 87, 126; CD 5, 6; DA3; DAM DRAM; DFS 2, 6, 12, 18, 24, 27; DLB 7, 266; LAIT 4; MAL 5; MTCW 1, 2; MTFW 2005; RGAL 4; TUS

Simon, Paul 1941(?)- .... **CLC 17**
See also CA 116; 153; CANR 152

Simon, Paul Frederick
See Simon, Paul

Simonon, Paul 1956(?)- .... **CLC 30**

Simonson, Helen 1963- .... **CLC 318**
See also CA 307

Simonson, Rick CLC 70

Simpson, Harriette
See Arnow, Harriette (Louisa) Simpson

Simpson, Louis 1923- .. **CLC 4, 7, 9, 32, 149**
See also AMWS 9; CA 1-4R; CAAS 4; CANR 1, 61, 140; CP 1, 2, 3, 4, 5, 6, 7; DAM POET; DLB 5; MAL 5; MTCW 1, 2; MTFW 2005; PFS 7, 11, 14; RGAL 4

Simpson, Mona 1957- .... **CLC 44, 146**
See also CA 122; 135; CANR 68, 103, 227; CN 6, 7; EWL 3

Simpson, Mona Elizabeth
See Simpson, Mona

Simpson, N.F. 1919-2011 .... **CLC 29**
See also CA 13-16R; CBD; DLB 13; RGEL 2

Simpson, Norman Frederick
See Simpson, N.F.

Sinclair, Andrew (Annandale) 1935- .... **CLC 2, 14**
See also CA 9-12R; CAAS 5; CANR 14, 38, 91; CN 1, 2, 3, 4, 5, 6, 7; DLB 14; FANT; MTCW 1

Sinclair, Emil
See Hesse, Hermann

Sinclair, Iain 1943- .... **CLC 76**
See also BRWS 14; CA 132; CANR 81, 157; CP 5, 6, 7; HGG

Sinclair, Iain MacGregor
See Sinclair, Iain

Sinclair, Irene
See Griffith, D.W.

Sinclair, Julian
See Sinclair, May

Sinclair, Mary Amelia St. Clair (?)- ....
See Sinclair, May

Sinclair, May 1865-1946 .... **TCLC 3, 11**
See also CA 104; 166; DLB 36, 135; EWL 3; HGG; RGEL 2; RHW; SUFW

Sinclair, Roy
See Griffith, D.W.

Sinclair, Upton 1878-1968 .... **CLC 1, 11, 15, 63; TCLC 160; WLC 5**
See also AAYA 63; AMWS 5; BPFB 3; BYA 2; CA 5-8R; 25-28R; CANR 7; CDALB 1929-1941; DA; DA3; DAB; DAC; DAM MST, NOV; DLB 9; EWL 3; INT CANR-7; LAIT 3; MAL 5; MTCW 1, 2; MTFW 2005; NFS 6; RGAL 4; SATA 9; TUS; YAW

Sinclair, Upton Beall
See Sinclair, Upton

Singe, (Edmund) J(ohn) M(illington) 1871-1909 .... **WLC**

Singer, Isaac
See Singer, Isaac Bashevis

Singer, Isaac Bashevis 1904-1991 . **CLC 1, 3, 6, 9, 11, 15, 23, 38, 69, 111; SSC 3, 53, 80, 154; WLC 5**
See also AAYA 32; AITN 1, 2; AMW; AMWR 2; BPFB 3; BYA 1, 4; CA 1-4R; 134; CANR 1, 39, 106; CDALB 1941-1968; CLR 1; CN 1, 2, 3, 4; CWRI 5; DA; DA3; DAB; DAC; DAM MST, NOV; DLB 6, 28, 52, 278, 332, 333; DLBY 1991; EWL 3; EXPS; HGG; JRDA; LAIT 3; MAICYA 1, 2; MAL 5; MTCW 1, 2; MTFW 2005; RGAL 4; RGHL; RGSF 2; SATA 3, 27; SATA-Obit 68; SSFS 2, 12, 16, 27, 30; TUS; TWA

Singer, Israel Joshua 1893-1944 ... **TCLC 33**
See also CA 169; DLB 333; EWL 3

Singh, Khushwant 1915- .... **CLC 11**
See also CA 9-12R; CAAS 9; CANR 6, 84; CN 1, 2, 3, 4, 5, 6, 7; DLB 323; EWL 3; RGEL 2

Singleton, Ann
See Benedict, Ruth

Singleton, John 1968(?)- .... **CLC 156**
See also AAYA 50; BW 2, 3; CA 138; CANR 67, 82; DAM MULT

Siniavskii, Andrei
See Sinyavsky, Andrei (Donatevich)

Sinibaldi, Fosco
See Kacew, Romain

Sinjohn, John
See Galsworthy, John

Sinyavsky, Andrei (Donatevich) 1925-1997 . **CLC 8**
See also CA 85-88; 159; CWW 2; EWL 3; RGSF 2

Sinyavsky, Andrey Donatovich
See Sinyavsky, Andrei (Donatevich)

Sirin, V.
See Nabokov, Vladimir

Sissman, L(ouis) E(dward) 1928-1976 . **CLC 9, 18**
See also CA 21-24R; 65-68; CANR 13; CP 2; DLB 5

Sisson, C(harles) H(ubert) 1914-2003 .. **CLC 8**
See also BRWS 11; CA 1-4R; 220; CAAS 3; CANR 3, 48, 84; CP 1, 2, 3, 4, 5, 6, 7; DLB 27

Sitting Bull 1831(?)-1890 .... **NNAL**
See also DA3; DAM MULT

Sitwell, Dame Edith 1887-1964 .... **CLC 2, 9, 67; PC 3**
See also BRW 7; CA 9-12R; CANR 35; CDBLB 1945-1960; DAM POET; DLB 20; EWL 3; MTCW 1, 2; MTFW 2005; RGEL 2; TEA

Siwaarmill, H. P.
See Sharp, William

Sjoewall, Maj 1935- .... **CLC 7**
See also BPFB 3; CA 65-68; CANR 73; CMW 4; MSW

Sjowall, Maj
See Sjoewall, Maj

Skelton, John 1460(?)-1529 ... **LC 71; PC 25**
See also BRW 1; DLB 136; RGEL 2

Skelton, Robin 1925-1997 .... **CLC 13**
See also AITN 2; CA 5-8R; 160; CAAS 5; CANR 28, 89; CCA 1; CP 1, 2, 3, 4, 5, 6; DLB 27, 53

Skolimowski, Jerzy 1938- .... **CLC 20**
See also CA 128

Skram, Amalie (Bertha) 1846-1905 ... **TCLC 25**
See also CA 165; DLB 354

Skvorecky, Josef 1924- . **CLC 15, 39, 69, 152**
See also CA 61-64; CAAS 1; CANR 10, 34, 63, 108; CDWLB 4; CWW 2; DA3; DAC; DAM NOV; DLB 232; EWL 3; MTCW 1, 2; MTFW 2005

Skvorecky, Josef Vaclav
See Skvorecky, Josef

Slade, Bernard 1930- ....
See Newbound, Bernard Slade

Slaughter, Carolyn 1946- .... **CLC 56**
See also CA 85-88; CANR 85, 169; CN 5, 6, 7

Slaughter, Frank G(ill) 1908-2001 .. **CLC 29**
See also AITN 2; CA 5-8R; 197; CANR 5, 85; INT CANR-5; RHW

Slavitt, David R. 1935- .... **CLC 5, 14**
See also CA 21-24R; CAAS 3; CANR 41, 83, 166, 219; CN 1, 2; CP 1, 2, 3, 4, 5, 6, 7; DLB 5, 6

Slavitt, David Rytman
See Slavitt, David R.

Slesinger, Tess 1905-1945 .... **TCLC 10**
See also CA 107; 199; DLB 102

Slessor, Kenneth 1901-1971 .... **CLC 14**
See also CA 102; 89-92; DLB 260; RGEL 2

Slowacki, Juliusz 1809-1849 .... **NCLC 15**
See also RGWL 3

Small, David 1945- .... **CLC 299**
See also CLR 53; MAICYA 2; SATA 50, 95, 126, 183, 216; SATA-Brief 46

Smart, Christopher 1722-1771 ... **LC 3, 134; PC 13**
See also DAM POET; DLB 109; RGEL 2

Stafford, William 1914-1993 .. **CLC 4, 7, 29; PC 71**
See also AMWS 11; CA 5-8R; 142; CAAS 3; CANR 5, 22; CP 1, 2, 3, 4, 5; DAM POET; DLB 5, 206; EXPP; INT CANR-22; MAL 5; PFS 2, 8, 16; RGAL 4; WP

Stafford, William Edgar
See Stafford, William

Stagnelius, Eric Johan 1793-1823 . **NCLC 61**

Staines, Trevor
See Brunner, John (Kilian Houston)

Stairs, Gordon
See Austin, Mary Hunter

Stalin, Joseph 1879-1953 .... **TCLC 92**

Stampa, Gaspara c. 1524-1554 . **LC 114; PC 43**
See also RGWL 2, 3; WLIT 7

Stampflinger, K.A.
See Benjamin, Walter

Stancykowna
See Szymborska, Wislawa

Standing Bear, Luther 1868(?)-1939(?) .... **NNAL**
See also CA 113; 144; DAM MULT

Stanislavsky, Constantin 1863(?)-1938 .... **TCLC 167**
See also CA 118

Stanislavsky, Konstantin
See Stanislavsky, Constantin

Stanislavsky, Konstantin Sergeievich
See Stanislavsky, Constantin

Stanislavsky, Konstantin Sergeivich
See Stanislavsky, Constantin

Stanislavsky, Konstantin Sergeyevich
See Stanislavsky, Constantin

Stannard, Martin 1947- .... **CLC 44**
See also CA 142; CANR 229; DLB 155

Stanton, Elizabeth Cady 1815-1902 .. **TCLC 73**
See also CA 171; DLB 79; FL 1:3; FW

Stanton, Maura 1946- .... **CLC 9**
See also CA 89-92; CANR 15, 123; DLB 120

Stanton, Schuyler
See Baum, L. Frank

Stapledon, (William) Olaf 1886-1950 . **TCLC 22**
See also CA 111; 162; DLB 15, 255; SCFW 1, 2; SFW 4

Starbuck, George (Edwin) 1931-1996 . **CLC 53**
See also CA 21-24R; 153; CANR 23; CP 1, 2, 3, 4, 5, 6; DAM POET

Stark, Richard
See Westlake, Donald E.

Statius c. 45-c. 96 .... **CMLC 91**
See also AW 2; DLB 211

Staunton, Schuyler
See Baum, L. Frank

Stead, Christina (Ellen) 1902-1983 .. **CLC 2, 5, 8, 32, 80; TCLC 244**
See also BRWS 4; CA 13-16R; 109; CANR 33, 40; CN 1, 2, 3; DLB 260; EWL 3; FW; MTCW 1, 2; MTFW 2005; NFS 27; RGEL 2; RGSF 2; WWE 1

Stead, Robert J(ames) C(ampbell) 1880-1959 .... **TCLC 225**
See also CA 186; DLB 92; TCWW 1, 2

Stead, William Thomas 1849-1912 .... **TCLC 48**
See also BRWS 13; CA 167

Stebnitsky, M.
See Leskov, Nikolai (Semyonovich)

Steele, Richard 1672-1729 .. **LC 18, 156, 159**
See also BRW 3; CDBLB 1660-1789; DLB 84, 101; RGEL 2; WLIT 3

Steele, Timothy (Reid) 1948- .... **CLC 45**
See also CA 93-96; CANR 16, 50, 92; CP 5, 6, 7; DLB 120, 282

Steffens, (Joseph) Lincoln 1866-1936 . **TCLC 20**
See also CA 117; 198; DLB 303; MAL 5

Stegner, Wallace 1909-1993 . **CLC 9, 49, 81; SSC 27**
See also AITN 1; AMWS 4; ANW; BEST 90:3; BPFB 3; CA 1-4R; 141; CAAS 9; CANR 1, 21, 46; CN 1, 2, 3, 4, 5; DAM NOV; DLB 9, 206, 275; DLBY 1993; EWL 3; MAL 5; MTCW 1, 2; MTFW 2005; RGAL 4; TCWW 1, 2; TUS

Stegner, Wallace Earle
See Stegner, Wallace

Stein, Gertrude 1874-1946 ... **DC 19; PC 18; SSC 42, 105; TCLC 1, 6, 28, 48; WLC 5**
See also AAYA 64; AMW; AMWC 2; CA 104; 132; CANR 108; CDALB 1917-1929; DA; DA3; DAB; DAC; DAM MST, NOV, POET; DLB 4, 54, 86, 228; DLBD 15; EWL 3; EXPS; FL 1:6; GLL 1; MAL 5; MBL; MTCW 1, 2; MTFW 2005; NCFS 4; NFS 27; PFS 38; RGAL 4; RGSF 2; SSFS 5; TUS; WP

Steinbeck, John 1902-1968 . **CLC 1, 5, 9, 13, 21, 34, 45, 75, 124; SSC 11, 37, 77, 135; TCLC 135; WLC 5**
See also AAYA 12; AMW; BPFB 3; BYA 2, 3, 13; CA 1-4R; 25-28R; CANR 1, 35; CDALB 1929-1941; CLR 172; DA; DA3; DAB; DAC; DAM DRAM, MST, NOV; DLB 7, 9, 212, 275, 309, 332, 364; DLBD 2; EWL 3; EXPS; LAIT 3; MAL 5; MTCW 1, 2; MTFW 2005; NFS 1, 5, 7, 17, 19, 28, 34, 37, 39; RGAL 4; RGSF 2; RHW; SATA 9; SSFS 3, 6, 22; TCWW 1, 2; TUS; WYA; YAW

Steinbeck, John Ernst
See Steinbeck, John

Steinem, Gloria 1934- .... **CLC 63**
See also CA 53-56; CANR 28, 51, 139; DLB 246; FL 1:1; FW; MTCW 1, 2; MTFW 2005

Steiner, George 1929- .... **CLC 24, 221**
See also CA 73-76; CANR 31, 67, 108, 212; DAM NOV; DLB 67, 299; EWL 3; MTCW 1, 2; MTFW 2005; RGHL; SATA 62

Steiner, K. Leslie
See Delany, Samuel R., Jr.

Steiner, Rudolf 1861-1925 .... **TCLC 13**
See also CA 107

Stendhal 1783-1842 . **NCLC 23, 46, 178; SSC 27; WLC 5**
See also DA; DA3; DAB; DAC; DAM MST, NOV; DLB 119; EW 5; GFL 1789 to the Present; RGWL 2, 3; TWA

Stephen, Adeline Virginia
See Woolf, Virginia

Stephen, Sir Leslie 1832-1904 .... **TCLC 23**
See also BRW 5; CA 123; DLB 57, 144, 190

Stephen, Sir Leslie
See Stephen, Sir Leslie

Stephen, Virginia
See Woolf, Virginia

Stephens, James 1882(?)-1950 .... **SSC 50; TCLC 4**
See also CA 104; 192; DLB 19, 153, 162; EWL 3; FANT; RGEL 2; SUFW

Stephens, Reed
See Donaldson, Stephen R.

Stephenson, Neal 1959- .... **CLC 220**
See also AAYA 38; CA 122; CANR 88, 138, 195; CN 7; MTFW 2005; SFW 4

Steptoe, Lydia
See Barnes, Djuna

Sterchi, Beat 1949- .... **CLC 65**
See also CA 203

Sterling, Brett
See Bradbury, Ray; Hamilton, Edmond

Sterling, Bruce 1954- .... **CLC 72**
See also AAYA 78; CA 119; CANR 44, 135, 184; CN 7; MTFW 2005; SCFW 2; SFW 4

Sterling, George 1869-1926 .... **TCLC 20**
See also CA 117; 165; DLB 54

Stern, Gerald 1925- ... **CLC 40, 100; PC 115**
See also AMWS 9; CA 81-84; CANR 28, 94, 206; CP 3, 4, 5, 6, 7; DLB 105; PFS 26; RGAL 4

Stern, Richard (Gustave) 1928- .. **CLC 4, 39**
See also CA 1-4R; CANR 1, 25, 52, 120; CN 1, 2, 3, 4, 5, 6, 7; DLB 218; DLBY 1987; INT CANR-25

Sternberg, Josef von 1894-1969 ...... **CLC 20**
See also CA 81-84

Sterne, Laurence 1713-1768 . **LC 2, 48, 156; WLC 5**
See also BRW 3; BRWC 1; CDBLB 1660-1789; DA; DAB; DAC; DAM MST, NOV; DLB 39; RGEL 2; TEA

Sternheim, (William Adolf) Carl 1878-1942 .... **TCLC 8, 223**
See also CA 105; 193; DLB 56, 118; EWL 3; IDTP; RGWL 2, 3

Stetson, Charlotte Perkins
See Gilman, Charlotte Perkins

Stevens, Margaret Dean
See Aldrich, Bess Streeter

Stevens, Mark 1951- .... **CLC 34**
See also CA 122

Stevens, R. L.
See Hoch, Edward D.

Stevens, Wallace 1879-1955 .... **PC 6, 110; TCLC 3, 12, 45; WLC 5**
See also AMW; AMWR 1; CA 104; 124; CANR 181; CDALB 1929-1941; DA; DA3; DAB; DAC; DAM MST, POET; DLB 54, 342; EWL 3; EXPP; MAL 5; MTCW 1, 2; PAB; PFS 13, 16, 35, 41; RGAL 4; TUS; WP

Stevenson, Anne (Katharine) 1933- . **CLC 7, 33**
See also BRWS 6; CA 17-20R; CAAS 9; CANR 9, 33, 123; CP 3, 4, 5, 6, 7; CWP; DLB 40; MTCW 1; RHW

Stevenson, Robert Louis 1850-1894 .. **NCLC 5, 14, 63, 193; PC 84; SSC 11, 51, 126; WLC 5**
See also AAYA 24; BPFB 3; BRW 5; BRWC 1; BRWR 1; BYA 1, 2, 4, 13; CD-BLB 1890-1914; CLR 10, 11, 107; DA; DA3; DAB; DAC; DAM MST, NOV; DLB 18, 57, 141, 156, 174; DLBD 13; GL 3; HGG; JRDA; LAIT 1, 3; MAICYA 1, 2; NFS 11, 20, 33; RGEL 2; RGSF 2; SATA 100; SUFW; TEA; WCH; WLIT 4; WYA; YABC 2; YAW

Stevenson, Robert Louis Balfour
See Stevenson, Robert Louis

Stewart, J(ohn) I(nnes) M(ackintosh) 1906-1994 .... **CLC 7, 14, 32**
See also CA 85-88; 147; CAAS 3; CANR 47; CMW 4; CN 1, 2, 3, 4, 5; DLB 276; MSW; MTCW 1, 2

Stewart, Mary (Florence Elinor) 1916- . **CLC 7, 35, 117**
See also AAYA 29, 73; BPFB 3; CA 1-4R; CANR 1, 59, 130; CMW 4; CPW; DAB; FANT; RHW; SATA 12; YAW

Stewart, Mary Rainbow
See Stewart, Mary (Florence Elinor)

Stewart, Will
See Williamson, John Stewart

Stifle, June
See Campbell, Maria

Stifter, Adalbert 1805-1868 . NCLC 41, 198;
SSC 28
See also CDWLB 2; DLB 133; RGSF 2;
RGWL 2, 3

Still, James 1906-2001 .... CLC 49
See also CA 65-68; 195; CAAS 17; CANR
10, 26; CSW; DLB 9; DLBY 01; SATA
29; SATA-Obit 127

Sting 1951- .... CLC 26
See also CA 167

Stirling, Arthur
See Sinclair, Upton

Stitt, Milan 1941-2009 .... CLC 29
See also CA 69-72; 284

Stitt, Milan William
See Stitt, Milan

Stockton, Francis Richard 1834-1902 ....
TCLC 47
See also AAYA 68; BYA 4, 13; CA 108;
137; DLB 42, 74; DLBD 13; EXPS; MAI-
CYA 1, 2; SATA 44; SATA-Brief 32; SFW
4; SSFS 3; SUFW; WCH

Stockton, Frank R.
See Stockton, Francis Richard

Stoddard, Charles
See Kuttner, Henry

Stoker, Abraham
See Stoker, Bram

Stoker, Bram 1847-1912 .. SSC 62; TCLC 8,
144; WLC 6
See also AAYA 23; BPFB 3; BRWS 3; BYA
5; CA 105; 150; CDBLB 1890-1914; DA;
DA3; DAB; DAC; DAM MST; NOV;
DLB 304; GL 3; HGG; LATS 1:1; MTFW
2005; NFS 18; RGEL 2; SATA 29; SUFW;
TEA; WLIT 4

Stolz, Mary 1920-2006 .... CLC 12
See also AAYA 8, 73; AITN 1; CA 5-8R;
255; CANR 13, 41, 112; JRDA; MAICYA
1, 2; SAAS 3; SATA 10, 71, 133; SATA-
Obit 180; YAW

Stolz, Mary Slattery
See Stolz, Mary

Stone, Irving 1903-1989 .... CLC 7
See also AITN 1; BPFB 3; CA 1-4R; 129;
CAAS 3; CANR 1, 23; CN 1, 2, 3, 4;
CPW; DA3; DAM POP; INT CANR-23;
MTCW 1, 2; MTFW 2005; RHW; SATA
3; SATA-Obit 64

Stone, Lucy 1818-1893 .... NCLC 250
See also DLB 79, 239

Stone, Oliver 1946- .... CLC 73
See also AAYA 15, 64; CA 110; CANR 55,
125

Stone, Oliver William
See Stone, Oliver

Stone, Robert 1937- .... CLC 5, 23, 42, 175
See also AMWS 5; BPFB 3; CA 85-88;
CANR 23, 66, 95, 173; CN 4, 5, 6, 7;
DLB 152; EWL 3; INT CANR-23; MAL
5; MTCW 1; MTFW 2005

Stone, Robert Anthony
See Stone, Robert

Stone, Ruth 1915- .... PC 53
See also CA 45-48; CANR 2, 91, 209; CP
5, 6, 7; CSW; DLB 105; PFS 19, 40

Stone, Zachary
See Follett, Ken

Stoppard, Tom 1937- . CLC 1, 3, 4, 5, 8, 15,
29, 34, 63, 91; DC 6, 30; WLC 6
See also AAYA 63; BRWC 1; BRWR 2;
BRWS 1; CA 81-84; CANR 39, 67, 125;
CBD; CD 5, 6; CDBLB 1960 to Present;
DA; DA3; DAB; DAC; DAM DRAM,
MST; DFS 2, 5, 8, 11, 13, 16; DLB 13,

233; DLBY 1985; EWL 3; LATS 1:2;
LNFS 3; MTCW 1, 2; MTFW 2005;
RGEL 2; TEA; WLIT 4

Storey, David (Malcolm) 1933- . CLC 2, 4, 5,
8; DC 40
See also BRWS 1; CA 81-84; CANR 36;
CBD; CD 5, 6; CN 1, 2, 3, 4, 5, 6; DAM
DRAM; DLB 13, 14, 207, 245, 326; EWL
3; MTCW 1; RGEL 2

Storm, Hyemeyohsts 1935- .. CLC 3; NNAL
See also CA 81-84; CANR 45; DAM MULT

Storm, (Hans) Theodor (Woldsen)
1817-1888 . NCLC 1, 195; SSC 27, 106
See also CDWLB 2; DLB 129; EW; RGSF
2; RGWL 2, 3

Storni, Alfonsina 1892-1938 ...... HLC 2; PC
33; TCLC 5
See also CA 104; 131; DAM MULT; DLB
283; HW 1; LAW

Stoughton, William 1631-1701 .... LC 38
See also DLB 24

Stout, Rex (Todhunter) 1886-1975 .... CLC 3
See also AAYA 79; AITN 2; BPFB 3; CA
61-64; CANR 71; CMW 4; CN 2; DLB
306; MSW; RGAL 4

Stow, John 1525-1605 .... LC 186
See also DLB 132; RGEL 2

Stow, (Julian) Randolph 1935- . CLC 23, 48
See also CA 13-16R; CANR 33; CN 1, 2,
3, 4, 5, 6, 7; CP 1, 2, 3, 4; DLB 260;
MTCW 1; RGEL 2

Stowe, Harriet Beecher 1811-1896 .... NCLC
3, 50, 133, 195; SSC 159; WLC 6
See also AAYA 53; AMWS 1; CDALB
1865-1917; CLR 131; DA; DA3; DAB;
DAC; DAM MST; NOV; DLB 1, 12, 42,
74, 189, 239, 243; EXPN; FL 1:3; JRDA;
LAIT 2; MAICYA 1, 2; NFS 6; RGAL 4;
TUS; YABC 1

Stowe, Harriet Elizabeth Beecher
See Stowe, Harriet Beecher

Strabo c. 63B.C.-c. 21 .... CMLC 37, 121
See also DLB 176

Strachey, (Giles) Lytton 1880-1932 ... TCLC
12
See also BRWS 2; CA 110; 178; DLB 149;
DLBD 10; EWL 3; MTCW 2; NCFS 4

Stramm, August 1874-1915 .... PC 50
See also CA 195; EWL 3

Strand, Mark 1934- . CLC 6, 18, 41, 71; PC
63
See also AMWS 4; CA 21-24R; CANR 40,
65, 100; CP 1, 2, 3, 4, 5, 6, 7; DAM
POET; DLB 5; EWL 3; MAL 5; PAB;
PFS 9, 18; RGAL 4; SATA 41; TCLE 1:2

Stratton-Porter, Gene 1863-1924 .. TCLC 21
See also AMWS 20; ANW; BPFB 3; CA
112; 137; CLR 87; CWRI 5; DLB 221;
DLBD 14; MAICYA 1, 2; RHW; SATA
15

Stratton-Porter, Geneva Grace
See Stratton-Porter, Gene

Straub, Peter 1943- .... CLC 28, 107
See also AAYA 82; BEST 89:1; BPFB 3;
CA 85-88; CANR 28, 65, 109; CPW;
DAM POP; DLBY 1984; HGG; MTCW
1, 2; MTFW 2005; SUFW 2

Straub, Peter Francis
See Straub, Peter

Strauss, Botho 1944- .... CLC 22
See also CA 157; CWW 2; DLB 124

Strauss, Leo 1899-1973 .... TCLC 141
See also CA 101; 45-48; CANR 122

Streatfeild, Mary Noel
See Streatfeild, Noel

Streatfeild, Noel 1897(?)-1986 .... CLC 21
See also CA 81-84; 120; CANR 31; CLR
17, 83; CWRI 5; DLB 160; MAICYA 1,
2; SATA 20; SATA-Obit 48

Stribling, T(homas) S(igismund)
1881-1965 .... CLC 23
See also CA 189; 107; CMW 4; DLB 9;
RGAL 4

Strindberg, August 1849-1912 .... DC 18;
TCLC 1, 8, 21, 47, 231; WLC 6
See also CA 104; 135; DA; DA3; DAB;
DAC; DAM DRAM, MST; DFS 4, 9, 29;
DLB 259; EW 7; EWL 3; IDTP; LMFS
2; MTCW 2; MTFW 2005; RGWL 2, 3;
TWA

Strindberg, Johan August
See Strindberg, August

Stringer, Arthur 1874-1950 .... TCLC 37
See also CA 161; DLB 92

Stringer, David
See Roberts, Keith (John Kingston)

Stroheim, Erich von 1885-1957 .... TCLC 71

Strout, Elizabeth 1956- .... CLC 299
See also CA 178; CANR 154, 190; NFS 39

Strugatskii, Arkadii 1925-1991 .... CLC 27
See also CA 106; 135; DLB 302; SFW 4

Strugatskii, Arkadii Natanovich
See Strugatskii, Arkadii

Strugatskii, Boris 1933- .... CLC 27
See also CA 106; DLB 302; SFW 4

Strugatskii, Boris Natanovich
See Strugatskii, Boris

Strugatsky, Arkadii Natanovich
See Strugatskii, Arkadii

Strugatsky, Boris
See Strugatskii, Boris

Strugatsky, Boris Natanovich
See Strugatskii, Boris

Strummer, Joe 1952-2002 .... CLC 30

Strunk, William, Jr. 1869-1946 .... TCLC 92
See also CA 118; 164; NCFS 5

Stryk, Lucien 1924- .... PC 27
See also CA 13-16R; CANR 10, 28, 55,
110; CP 1, 2, 3, 4, 5, 6, 7

Stuart, Don A.
See Campbell, John W.

Stuart, Ian
See MacLean, Alistair

Stuart, Jesse (Hilton) 1906-1984 .. CLC 1, 8,
11, 14, 34; SSC 31
See also CA 5-8R; 112; CANR 31; CN 1,
2, 3; DLB 9, 48, 102; DLBY 1984; SATA
2; SATA-Obit 36

Stubblefield, Sally
See Trumbo, Dalton

Sturgeon, Theodore (Hamilton) 1918-1985 .
CLC 22, 39
See also AAYA 51; BPFB 3; BYA 9, 10;
CA 81-84; 116; CANR 32, 103; DLB 8;
DLBY 1985; HGG; MTCW 1, 2; MTFW
2005; SCFW; SFW 4; SUFW

Sturges, Preston 1898-1959 .... TCLC 48
See also CA 114; 149; DLB 26

Styron, William 1925-2006 . CLC 1, 3, 5, 11,
15, 60, 232, 244; SSC 25
See also AMW; AMWC 2; BEST 90:4;
BPFB 3; CA 5-8R; 255; CANR 6, 33, 74,
126, 191; CDALB 1968-1988; CN 1, 2,
3, 4, 5, 6, 7; CPW; CSW; DA3; DAM
NOV, POP; DLB 2, 143, 299; DLBY
1980; EWL 3; INT CANR-6; LAIT 2;
MAL 5; MTCW 1, 2; MTFW 2005; NCFS
1; NFS 22; RGAL 4; RGHL; RHW; TUS

Styron, William C.
See Styron, William

Styron, William Clark
See Styron, William

Su, Chien 1884-1918 .... TCLC 24
See also CA 123; EWL 3

Suarez Lynch, B.
See Bioy Casares, Adolfo; Borges, Jorge Luis

Suassuna, Ariano Vilar 1927- .... **HLCS 1**
See also CA 178; DLB 307; HW 2; LAW

Suckert, Kurt Erich
See Malaparte, Curzio

Suckling, Sir John 1609-1642 ..... **LC 75; PC 30**
See also BRW 2; DAM POET; DLB 58, 126; EXPP; PAB; RGEL 2

Suckow, Ruth 1892-1960 ..... **SSC 18; TCLC 257**
See also CA 193; 113; DLB 9, 102; RGAL 4; TCWW 2

Sudermann, Hermann 1857-1928 . **TCLC 15**
See also CA 107; 201; DLB 118

Sue, Eugene 1804-1857 .... **NCLC 1**
See also DLB 119

Sueskind, Patrick
See Suskind, Patrick

Suetonius c. 70-c. 130 .... **CMLC 60**
See also AW 2; DLB 211; RGWL 2, 3; WLIT 8

Su Hsuan-ying
See Su, Chien

Su Hsuean-ying
See Su, Chien

Sui Sin Far
See Eaton, Edith Maude

Sukenick, Ronald 1932-2004 .... **CLC 3, 4, 6, 48**
See also CA 25-28R; 209; 229; CAAE 209; CAAS 8; CANR 32, 89; CN 3, 4, 5, 6, 7; DLB 173; DLBY 1981

Suknaski, Andrew 1942- .... **CLC 19**
See also CA 101; CP 3, 4, 5, 6, 7; DLB 53

Sullivan, Vernon
See Vian, Boris

Sully Prudhomme, Rene-Francois-Armand 1839-1907 .... **TCLC 31**
See also CA 170; DLB 332; GFL 1789 to the Present

Sulpicius Severus c. 363-c. 425 .. **CMLC 120**

Su Man-shu
See Su, Chien

Sumarokov, Aleksandr Petrovich 1717-1777 .... **LC 104**
See also DLB 150

Summerforest, Ivy B.
See Kirkup, James

Summers, Andrew James
See Summers, Andy

Summers, Andy 1942- .... **CLC 26**
See also CA 255

Summers, Hollis (Spurgeon, Jr.) 1916- . **CLC 10**
See also CA 5-8R; CANR 3; CN 1, 2, 3; CP 1, 2, 3, 4; DLB 6; TCLE 1:2

Summers, (Alphonsus Joseph-Mary Augustus) Montague 1880-1948 .... **TCLC 16**
See also CA 118; 163

Sumner, Gordon Matthew
See Sting

Sun Tzu c. 400B.C.-c. 320B.C. .... **CMLC 56**

Surayya, Kamala
See Das, Kamala

Surayya Kamala
See Das, Kamala

Surdas c. 1478-c. 1583 .... **LC 163**
See also RGWL 2, 3

Surrey, Henry Howard 1517-1574 . **LC 121; PC 59**
See also BRW 1; RGEL 2

Surtees, Robert Smith 1805-1864 . **NCLC 14**
See also DLB 21; RGEL 2

Susann, Jacqueline 1921-1974 .... **CLC 3**
See also AITN 1; BPFB 3; CA 65-68; 53-56; MTCW 1, 2

Su Shi
See Su Shih

Su Shih 1037-1101 .... **CMLC 15, 139**
See also RGWL 2, 3

Suskind, Patrick 1949- .... **CLC 44, 182**
See also BPFB 3; CA 145; CWW 2

Suso, Heinrich c. 1295-1366 .... **CMLC 87**

Sutcliff, Rosemary 1920-1992 .... **CLC 26**
See also AAYA 10; BRWS 16; BYA 1, 4; CA 5-8R; 139; CANR 37; CLR 1, 37, 138; CPW; DAB; DAC; DAM MST, POP; JRDA; LATS 1:1; MAICYA 1, 2; MAIC-YAS 1; RHW; SATA 6, 44, 78; SATA-Obit 73; WYA; YAW

Sutherland, Efua (Theodora Morgue) 1924-1996 .... **BLC 2:3**
See also AFW; BW 1; CA 105; CWD; DLB 117; EWL 3; IDTP; SATA 25

Sutro, Alfred 1863-1933 .... **TCLC 6**
See also CA 105; 185; DLB 10; RGEL 2

Sutton, Henry
See Slavitt, David R.

Su Yuan-ying
See Su, Chien

Su Yuean-ying
See Su, Chien

Suzuki, D. T.
See Suzuki, Daisetz Teitaro

Suzuki, Daisetz T.
See Suzuki, Daisetz Teitaro

Suzuki, Daisetz Teitaro 1870-1966 .... **TCLC 109**
See also CA 121; 111; MTCW 1, 2; MTFW 2005

Suzuki, Teitaro
See Suzuki, Daisetz Teitaro

Svareff, Count Vladimir
See Crowley, Edward Alexander

Svevo, Italo
See Schmitz, Aron Hector

Swados, Elizabeth 1951- .... **CLC 12**
See also CA 97-100; CANR 49, 163; INT CA-97-100

Swados, Elizabeth A.
See Swados, Elizabeth

Swados, Harvey 1920-1972 .... **CLC 5**
See also CA 5-8R; 37-40R; CANR 6; CN 1; DLB 2, 335; MAL 5

Swados, Liz
See Swados, Elizabeth

Swan, Gladys 1934- .... **CLC 69**
See also CA 101; CANR 17, 39; TCLE 1:2

Swanson, Logan
See Matheson, Richard

Swarthout, Glendon (Fred) 1918-1992 . **CLC 35**
See also AAYA 55; CA 1-4R; 139; CANR 1, 47; CN 1, 2, 3, 4, 5; LAIT 5; NFS 29; SATA 26; TCWW 1, 2; YAW

Swedenborg, Emanuel 1688-1772 .... **LC 105**

Sweet, Sarah C.
See Jewett, Sarah Orne

Swenson, May 1919-1989 ..... **CLC 4, 14, 61, 106; PC 14**
See also AMWS 4; CA 5-8R; 130; CANR 36, 61, 131; CP 1, 2, 3, 4; DA; DAB; DAC; DAM MST, POET; DLB 5; EXPP; GLL 2; MAL 5; MTCW 1, 2; MTFW 2005; PFS 16, 30, 38; SATA 15; WP

Swift, Augustus
See Lovecraft, H. P.

Swift, Graham 1949- .... **CLC 41, 88, 233**
See also BRWC 2; BRWS 5; CA 117; 122; CANR 46, 71, 128, 181, 218; CN 4, 5, 6, 7; DLB 194, 326; MTCW 2; MTFW 2005; NFS 18; RGSF 2

Swift, Jonathan 1667-1745 .... **LC 1, 42, 101, 201; PC 9; WLC 6**
See also AAYA 41; BRW 3; BRWC 1; BRWR 1; BYA 5, 14; CDBLB 1660-1789; CLR 53, 161; DA; DA3; DAB; DAC; DAM MST, NOV, POET; DLB 39, 95, 101; EXPN; LAIT 1; NFS 6; PFS 27, 37; RGEL 2; SATA 19; TEA; WCH; WLIT 3

Swinburne, Algernon Charles 1837-1909 .... **PC 24; TCLC 8, 36; WLC 6**
See also BRW 5; CA 105; 140; CDBLB 1832-1890; DA; DA3; DAB; DAC; DAM MST, POET; DLB 35, 57; PAB; RGEL 2; TEA

Swinfen, Ann **CLC 34**
See also CA 202

Swinnerton, Frank (Arthur) 1884-1982 .... **CLC 31**
See also CA 202; 108; CN 1, 2, 3; DLB 34

Swinnerton, Frank Arthur 1884-1982 . **CLC 31**
See also CA 108; DLB 34

Swithen, John
See King, Stephen

Syjuco, Miguel 1976- .... **CLC 318**
See also CA 305

Sylvia
See Ashton-Warner, Sylvia (Constance)

Symmes, Robert Edward
See Duncan, Robert

Symonds, John Addington 1840-1893 .... **NCLC 34**
See also BRWS 14; DLB 57, 144

Symons, Arthur 1865-1945 .. **PC 119; TCLC 11, 243**
See also BRWS 14; CA 107; 189; DLB 19, 57, 149; RGEL 2

Symons, Julian (Gustave) 1912-1994 ... **CLC 2, 14, 32**
See also CA 49-52; 147; CAAS 3; CANR 3, 33, 59; CMW 4; CN 1, 2, 3, 4, 5; CP 1, 3, 4; DLB 87, 155; DLBY 1992; MSW; MTCW 1

Synge, Edmund John Millington
See Synge, John Millington

Synge, J. M.
See Synge, John Millington

Synge, John Millington 1871-1909 ..... **DC 2; TCLC 6, 37, 257**
See also BRW 6; BRWR 1; CA 104; 141; CDBLB 1890-1914; DAM DRAM; DFS 18; DLB 10, 19; EWL 3; RGEL 2; TEA; WLIT 4

Syruc, J.
See Milosz, Czeslaw

Szirtes, George 1948- .... **CLC 46; PC 51**
See also CA 109; CANR 27, 61, 117; CP 4, 5, 6, 7

Szymborska, Wislawa 1923- .. **CLC 99, 190; PC 44**
See also AAYA 76; CA 154; CANR 91, 133, 181; CDWLB 4; CWP; CWW 2; DA3; DLB 232, 332; DLBY 1996; EWL 3; MTCW 2; MTFW 2005; PFS 15, 27, 31, 34, 41; RGHL; RGWL 3

T. O., Nik
See Annensky, Innokenty (Fyodorovich)

Tabori, George 1914-2007 .... **CLC 19**
See also CA 49-52; 262; CANR 4, 69; CBD; CD 5, 6; DLB 245; RGHL

Tacitus c. 55-c. 117 .... **CMLC 56, 131**
See also AW 2; CDWLB 1; DLB 211; RGWL 2, 3; WLIT 8

Tadjo, Veronique 1955- .... **BLC 2:3**
See also DLB 360; EWL 3

Tagore, Rabindranath 1861-1941 .... **PC 8; SSC 48; TCLC 3, 53**
See also CA 104; 120; DA3; DAM DRAM, POET; DFS 26; DLB 323, 332; EWL 3;

MTCW 1, 2; MTFW 2005; PFS 18; RGEL 2; RGSF 2; RGWL 2, 3; TWA

Taine, Hippolyte Adolphe 1828-1893 . **NCLC 15**
See also EW 7; GFL 1789 to the Present

Talayesva, Don C. 1890-(?) .... **NNAL**

Talese, Gay 1932- .... **CLC 37, 232**
See also AITN 1; AMWS 17; CA 1-4R; CANR 9, 58, 137, 177; DLB 185; INT CANR-9; MTCW 1, 2; MTFW 2005

Tallent, Elizabeth 1954- .... **CLC 45**
See also CA 117; CANR 72; DLB 130

Tallmountain, Mary 1918-1997 .... **NNAL**
See also CA 146; 161; DLB 193

Tally, Ted 1952- .... **CLC 42**
See also CA 120; 124; CAD; CANR 125; CD 5, 6; INT CA-124

Talvik, Heiti 1904-1947 .... **TCLC 87**
See also EWL 3

Tamayo y Baus, Manuel 1829-1898 .. **NCLC 1**

Tammsaare, A(nton) H(ansen) 1878-1940 ... **TCLC 27**
See also CA 164; CDWLB 4; DLB 220; EWL 3

Tam'si, Tchicaya U
See Tchicaya, Gerald Felix

Tan, Amy 1952- .... **AAL; CLC 59, 120, 151, 257**
See also AAYA 9, 48; AMWS 10; BEST 89:3; BPFB 3; CA 136; CANR 54, 105, 132; CDALBS; CN 6, 7; CPW 1; DA3; DAM MULT, NOV, POP; DLB 173, 312; EXPN; FL 1:6; FW; LAIT 3, 5; MAL 5; MTCW 2; MTFW 2005; NFS 1, 13, 16, 31, 35; RGAL 4; SATA 75; SSFS 9; YAW

Tan, Amy Ruth
See Tan, Amy

Tandem, Carl Felix
See Spitteler, Carl

Tandem, Felix
See Spitteler, Carl

Tania B.
See Blixen, Karen

Tanizaki, Jun'ichiro 1886-1965 .. **CLC 8, 14, 28; SSC 21**
See also CA 93-96; 25-28R; DLB 180; EWL 3; MJW; MTCW 2; MTFW 2005; RGSF 2; RGWL 2

Tanizaki Jun'ichiro
See Tanizaki, Jun'ichiro

Tannen, Deborah 1945- .... **CLC 206**
See also CA 118; CANR 95

Tannen, Deborah Frances
See Tannen, Deborah

Tanner, William
See Amis, Kingsley

Tante, Dilly
See Kunitz, Stanley

Tao Lao
See Storni, Alfonsina

Tapahonso, Luci 1953- .... **NNAL; PC 65**
See also CA 145; CANR 72, 127, 214; DLB 175

Tarantino, Quentin 1963- ...... **CLC 125, 230**
See also AAYA 58; CA 171; CANR 125

Tarantino, Quentin Jerome
See Tarantino, Quentin

Tarassoff, Lev
See Troyat, Henri

Tarbell, Ida 1857-1944 .... **TCLC 40**
See also CA 122; 181; DLB 47

Tarbell, Ida Minerva
See Tarbell, Ida

Tarchetti, Ugo 1839(?)-1869 .... **SSC 119**

Tardieu d'Esclavelles,
   Louise-Florence-Petronille
See Epinay, Louise d'

Tarkington, (Newton) Booth 1869-1946 ....
TCLC 9
See also BPFB 3; BYA 3; CA 110; 143; CWRI 5; DLB 9, 102; MAL 5; MTCW 2; NFS 34; RGAL 4; SATA 17

Tarkovskii, Andrei Arsen'evich
See Tarkovsky, Andrei (Arsenyevich)

Tarkovsky, Andrei (Arsenyevich)
   1932-1986 .... **CLC 75**
See also CA 127

Tartt, Donna 1964(?)- .... **CLC 76**
See also AAYA 56; CA 142; CANR 135; LNFS 2; MTFW 2005

Tasso, Torquato 1544-1595 .... **LC 5, 94**
See also EFS 1:2, 2:1; EW 2; RGWL 2, 3; WLIT 7

Tate, (John Orley) Allen 1899-1979 . **CLC 2, 4, 6, 9, 11, 14, 24; PC 50**
See also AMW; CA 5-8R; 85-88; CANR 32, 108; CN 1; CP 1; DLB 4, 45, 63; DLBD 17; EWL 3; MAL 5; MTCW 1, 2; MTFW 2005; RGAL 4; RHW

Tate, Ellalice
See Hibbert, Eleanor Alice Burford

Tate, James 1943- .... **CLC 2, 6, 25**
See also CA 21-24R; CANR 29, 57, 114, 224; CP 1, 2, 3, 4, 5, 6, 7; DLB 5, 169; EWL 3; PFS 10, 15; RGAL 4; WP

Tate, James Vincent
See Tate, James

Tate, Nahum 1652(?)-1715 .... **LC 109**
See also DLB 80; RGEL 2

Tauler, Johannes c. 1300-1361 ..... **CMLC 37**
See also DLB 179; LMFS 1

Tavel, Ronald 1936-2009 .... **CLC 6**
See also CA 21-24R; 284; CAD; CANR 33; CD 5, 6

Taviani, Paolo 1931- .... **CLC 70**
See also CA 153

Tawada, Yoko 1960- .... **CLC 310**
See also CA 296

Taylor, Bayard 1825-1878 .... **NCLC 89**
See also DLB 3, 189, 250, 254, 366; RGAL 4

Taylor, C(ecil) P(hilip) 1929-1981 ... **CLC 27**
See also CA 25-28R; 105; CANR 47; CBD

Taylor, Charles 1931- .... **CLC 317**
See also CA 13-16R; CANR 11, 27, 164, 200

Taylor, Charles Margrave
See Taylor, Charles

Taylor, Edward 1642(?)-1729 .... **LC 11, 163; PC 63**
See also AMW; DA; DAB; DAC; DAM MST, POET; DLB 24; EXPP; PFS 31; RGAL 4; TUS

Taylor, Eleanor Ross 1920- .... **CLC 5**
See also CA 81-84; CANR 70

Taylor, Elizabeth 1912-1975 .. **CLC 2, 4, 29; SSC 100**
See also CA 13-16R; CANR 9, 70; CN 1, 2; DLB 139; MTCW 1; RGEL 2; SATA 13

Taylor, Frederick Winslow 1856-1915 ....
TCLC 76
See also CA 188

Taylor, Henry 1942- .... **CLC 44**
See also CA 33-36R; CAAS 7; CANR 31, 178; CP 6, 7; DLB 5; PFS 10

Taylor, Henry Splawn
See Taylor, Henry

Taylor, Kamala
See Markandaya, Kamala

Taylor, Mildred D. 1943- .... **CLC 21**
See also AAYA 10, 47; BW 1; BYA 3, 8; CA 85-88; CANR 25, 115, 136; CLR 9, 59, 90, 144; CSW; DLB 52; JRDA; LAIT 3; MAICYA 1, 2; MTFW 2005; SAAS 5; SATA 135; WYA; YAW

Taylor, Peter (Hillsman) 1917-1994 . **CLC 1, 4, 18, 37, 44, 50, 71; SSC 10, 84**
See also AMWS 5; BPFB 3; CA 13-16R; 147; CANR 9, 50; CN 1, 2, 3, 4, 5; CSW; DLB 218, 278; DLBY 1981, 1994; EWL 3; EXPS; INT CANR-9; MAL 5; MTCW 1, 2; MTFW 2005; RGSF 2; SSFS 9; TUS

Taylor, Robert Lewis 1912-1998 ..... **CLC 14**
See also CA 1-4R; 170; CANR 3, 64; CN 1, 2; SATA 10; TCWW 1, 2

Tchekhov, Anton
See Chekhov, Anton

Tchicaya, Gerald Felix 1931-1988 . **CLC 101**
See also CA 129; 125; CANR 81; EWL 3

Tchicaya U Tam'si
See Tchicaya, Gerald Felix

Teasdale, Sara 1884-1933 ... **PC 31; TCLC 4**
See also CA 104; 163; DLB 45; GLL 1; PFS 14; RGAL 4; SATA 32; TUS

Tecumseh 1768-1813 .... **NNAL**
See also DAM MULT

Tegner, Esaias 1782-1846 .... **NCLC 2**

Teilhard de Chardin, (Marie Joseph) Pierre
   1881-1955 .... **TCLC 9**
See also CA 105; 210; GFL 1789 to the Present

Temple, Ann
See Mortimer, Penelope (Ruth)

Tennant, Emma 1937- .... **CLC 13, 52**
See also BRWS 9; CA 65-68; CAAS 9; CANR 10, 38, 59, 88, 177; CN 3, 4, 5, 6, 7; DLB 14; EWL 3; SFW 4

Tenneshaw, S.M.
See Silverberg, Robert

Tenney, Tabitha Gilman 1762-1837 .. **NCLC 122, 248**
See also DLB 37, 200

Tennyson, Alfred 1809-1892 .. **NCLC 30, 65, 115, 202; PC 6, 101; WLC 6**
See also AAYA 50; BRW 4; BRWR 3; CD-BLB 1832-1890; DA; DA3; DAB; DAC; DAM MST, POET; DLB 32; EXPP; PAB; PFS 1, 2, 4, 11, 15, 19; RGEL 2; TEA; WLIT 4; WP

Teran, Lisa St. Aubin de
See St. Aubin de Teran, Lisa

Terence c. 184B.C.-c. 159B.C. ..... **CMLC 14, 132; DC 7**
See also AW 1; CDWLB 1; DLB 211; RGWL 2, 3; TWA; WLIT 8

Teresa de Jesus, St. 1515-1582 ... **LC 18, 149**

Teresa of Avila, St.
See Teresa de Jesus, St.

Terkel, Louis
See Terkel, Studs

Terkel, Studs 1912-2008 .... **CLC 38**
See also AAYA 32; AITN 1; CA 57-60; 278; CANR 18, 45, 67, 132, 195; DA3; MTCW 1, 2; MTFW 2005; TUS

Terkel, Studs Louis
See Terkel, Studs

Terry, C. V.
See Slaughter, Frank G(ill)

Terry, Megan 1932- .... **CLC 19; DC 13**
See also CA 77-80; CABS 3; CAD; CANR 43; CD 5, 6; CWD; DFS 18; DLB 7, 249; GLL 2

Tertullian c. 155-c. 245 .... **CMLC 29**

Tertz, Abram
See Sinyavsky, Andrei (Donatevich)

Tesich, Steve 1943(?)-1996 .... **CLC 40, 69**
See also CA 105; 152; CAD; DLBY 1983

Tesla, Nikola 1856-1943 .... **TCLC 88**
See also CA 157

Teternikov, Fyodor Kuzmich 1863-1927 ......
TCLC 9, 259
See also CA 104; DLB 295; EWL 3

Tevis, Walter 1928-1984 .... **CLC 42**
See also CA 113; SFW 4

Tey, Josephine
See Mackintosh, Elizabeth
Thackeray, William Makepeace 1811-1863 .
NCLC 5, 14, 22, 43, 169, 213; WLC 6
See also BRW 5; BRWC 2; CDBLB 1832-
1890; DA; DA3; DAB; DAC; DAM MST,
NOV; DLB 21, 55, 159, 163; NFS 13;
RGEL 2; SATA 23; TEA; WLIT 3
Thakura, Ravindranatha
See Tagore, Rabindranath
Thames, C. H.
See Marlowe, Stephen
Tharoor, Shashi 1956- .... **CLC 70**
See also CA 141; CANR 91, 201; CN 6, 7
Thelwall, John 1764-1834 .... **NCLC 162**
See also DLB 93, 158
Thelwell, Michael Miles 1939- .... **CLC 22**
See also BW 2; CA 101
Theo, Ion
See Theodorescu, Ion N.
Theobald, Lewis, Jr.
See Lovecraft, H. P.
Theocritus c. 310B.C.- .... **CMLC 45**
See also AW 1; DLB 176; RGWL 2, 3
Theodorescu, Ion N. 1880-1967 ...... **CLC 80**
See also CA 167; 116; CDWLB 4; DLB
220; EWL 3
Theriault, Yves 1915-1983 .... **CLC 79**
See also CA 102; CANR 150; CCA 1;
DAC; DAM MST; DLB 88; EWL 3
Therion, Master
See Crowley, Edward Alexander
Theroux, Alexander 1939- .... **CLC 2, 25**
See also CA 85-88; CANR 20, 63, 190; CN
4, 5, 6, 7
Theroux, Alexander Louis
See Theroux, Alexander
Theroux, Paul 1941- ... **CLC 5, 8, 11, 15, 28,
46, 159, 303**
See also AAYA 28; AMWS 8; BEST 89:4;
BPFB 3; CA 33-36R; CANR 20, 45, 74,
133, 179; CDALBS; CN 1, 2, 3, 4, 5, 6,
7; CP 1; CPW 1; DA3; DAM POP; DLB
2, 218; EWL 3; HGG; MAL 5; MTCW 1,
2; MTFW 2005; RGAL 4; SATA 44, 109;
TUS
Theroux, Paul Edward
See Theroux, Paul
Thesen, Sharon 1946- .... **CLC 56**
See also CA 163; CANR 125; CP 5, 6, 7;
CWP
Thespis fl. 6th cent. B.C.- .... **CMLC 51**
See also LMFS 1
Thevenin, Denis
See Duhamel, Georges
Thibault, Jacques Anatole Francois
See France, Anatole
Thiele, Colin 1920-2006 .... **CLC 17**
See also CA 29-32R; CANR 12, 28, 53,
105; CLR 27; CP 1, 2; DLB 289; MAI-
CYA 1, 2; SAAS 2; SATA 14, 72, 125;
YAW
Thiong'o, Ngugi Wa
See Ngugi wa Thiong'o
Thistlethwaite, Bel
See Wetherald, Agnes Ethelwyn
Thomas, Audrey (Callahan) 1935- .. **CLC 7,
13, 37, 107, 289; SSC 20**
See also AITN 2; CA 21-24R, 237; CAAE
237; CAAS 19; CANR 36, 58; CN 2, 3,
4, 5, 6, 7; DLB 60; MTCW 1; RGSF 2
Thomas, Augustus 1857-1934 .... **TCLC 97**
See also MAL 5
Thomas, D.M. 1935- .... **CLC 13, 22, 31, 132**
See also BPFB 3; BRWS 4; CA 61-64, 303;
CAAE 303; CAAS 11; CANR 17, 45, 75;
CDBLB 1960 to Present; CN 4, 5, 6, 7;

CP 1, 2, 3, 4, 5, 6, 7; DA3; DLB 40, 207,
299; HGG; INT CANR-17; MTCW 1, 2;
MTFW 2005; RGHL; SFW 4
Thomas, Donald Michael
See Thomas, D.M.
Thomas, Dylan 1914-1953 . **PC 2, 52; SSC 3,
44; TCLC 1, 8, 45, 105; WLC 6**
See also AAYA 45; BRWR 3; BRWS 1; CA
104; 120; CANR 65; CDBLB 1945-1960;
DA; DA3; DAB; DAC; DAM DRAM,
MST, POET; DLB 13, 20, 139; EWL 3;
EXPP; LAIT 3; MTCW 1, 2; MTFW
2005; PAB; PFS 1, 3, 8; RGEL 2; RGSF
2; SATA 60; TEA; WLIT 4; WP
Thomas, Dylan Marlais
See Thomas, Dylan
Thomas, (Philip) Edward 1878-1917 ...... **PC
53; TCLC 10**
See also BRW 6; BRWS 3; CA 106; 153;
DAM POET; DLB 19, 98, 156, 216; EWL
3; PAB; RGEL 2
Thomas, J. F.
See Fleming, Thomas
Thomas, Joyce Carol 1938- .... **CLC 35**
See also AAYA 12, 54; BW 2, 3; CA 113;
116; CANR 48, 114, 135, 206; CLR 19;
DLB 33; INT CA-116; JRDA; MAICYA
1, 2; MTCW 1, 2; MTFW 2005; SAAS 7;
SATA 40, 78, 123, 137, 210; SATA-Essay
137; WYA; YAW
Thomas, Lewis 1913-1993 .... **CLC 35**
See also ANW; CA 85-88; 143; CANR 38,
60; DLB 275; MTCW 1, 2
Thomas, M. Carey 1857-1935 ...... **TCLC 89**
See also FW
Thomas, Paul
See Mann, Thomas
Thomas, Piri 1928-2011 .. **CLC 17; HLCS 2**
See also CA 73-76; HW 1; LLW; SSFS 28
Thomas, R(onald) S(tuart) 1913-2000 . **CLC
6, 13, 48; PC 99**
See also BRWS 12; CA 89-92; 189; CAAS
4; CANR 30; CDBLB 1960 to Present;
CP 1, 2, 3, 4, 5, 6, 7; DAB; DAM POET;
DLB 27; EWL 3; MTCW 1; RGEL 2
Thomas, Ross (Elmore) 1926-1995 . **CLC 39**
See also CA 33-36R; 150; CANR 22, 63;
CMW 4
Thompson, Francis (Joseph) 1859-1907 ......
TCLC 4
See also BRW 5; CA 104; 189; CDBLB
1890-1914; DLB 19; RGEL 2; TEA
Thompson, Francis Clegg
See Mencken, H. L.
Thompson, Hunter S. 1937(?)-2005 . **CLC 9,
17, 40, 104, 229**
See also AAYA 45; BEST 89:1; BPFB 3;
CA 17-20R; 236; CANR 23, 46, 74, 77,
111, 133; CPW; CSW; DA3; DAM POP;
DLB 185; MTCW 1, 2; MTFW 2005;
TUS
Thompson, Hunter Stockton
See Thompson, Hunter S.
Thompson, James Myers
See Thompson, Jim
Thompson, Jim 1906-1977 .... **CLC 69**
See also BPFB 3; CA 140; CMW 4; CPW;
DLB 226; MSW
Thompson, Judith (Clare Francesca)
1954- .... **CLC 39**
See also CA 143; CD 5, 6; CWD; DFS 22;
DLB 334
Thomson, James 1700-1748 ... **LC 16, 29, 40**
See also BRWS 3; DAM POET; DLB 95;
RGEL 2
Thomson, James 1834-1882 .... **NCLC 18**
See also DAM POET; DLB 35; RGEL 2

Thoreau, Henry David 1817-1862 . **NCLC 7,
21, 61, 138, 207; PC 30; WLC 6**
See also AAYA 42; AMW; ANW; BYA 3;
CDALB 1640-1865; DA; DA3; DAB;
DAC; DAM MST; DLB 1, 183, 223, 270,
298, 366; LAIT 2; LMFS 1; NCFS 3;
RGAL 4; TUS
Thorndike, E. L.
See Thorndike, Edward L(ee)
Thorndike, Edward L(ee) 1874-1949 . **TCLC
107**
See also CA 121
Thornton, Hall
See Silverberg, Robert
Thorpe, Adam 1956- .... **CLC 176**
See also CA 129; CANR 92, 160; DLB 231
Thorpe, Thomas Bangs 1815-1878 .... **NCLC
183**
See also DLB 3, 11, 248; RGAL 4
Thubron, Colin 1939- .... **CLC 163**
See also CA 25-28R; CANR 12, 29, 59, 95,
171, 232; CN 5, 6, 7; DLB 204, 231
Thubron, Colin Gerald Dryden
See Thubron, Colin
Thucydides c. 455B.C.-c. 399B.C. ..... **CMLC
17, 117**
See also AW 1; DLB 176; RGWL 2, 3;
WLIT 8
Thumboo, Edwin Nadason 1933- .... **PC 30**
See also CA 194; CP 1
Thurber, James 1894-1961 ... **CLC 5, 11, 25,
125; SSC 1, 47, 137**
See also AAYA 56; AMWS 1; BPFB 3;
BYA 5; CA 73-76; CANR 17, 39; CDALB
1929-1941; CWRI 5; DA; DA3; DAB;
DAC; DAM DRAM, MST, NOV; DLB 4,
11, 22, 102; EWL 3; EXPS; FANT; LAIT
3; MAICYA 1, 2; MAL 5; MTCW 1, 2;
MTFW 2005; RGAL 4; RGSF 2; SATA
13; SSFS 1, 10, 19; SUFW; TUS
Thurber, James Grover
See Thurber, James
Thurman, Wallace (Henry) 1902-1934 . **BLC
1:3; HR 1:3; TCLC 6**
See also BW 1, 3; CA 104; 124; CANR 81;
DAM MULT; DLB 51
Tibullus c. 54B.C.-c. 18B.C. .... **CMLC 36**
See also AW 2; DLB 211; RGWL 2, 3;
WLIT 8
Ticheburn, Cheviot
See Ainsworth, William Harrison
Ticknor, George 1791-1871 .... **NCLC 255**
See also DLB 1, 59, 140, 235
Tieck, (Johann) Ludwig 1773-1853 ... **NCLC
5, 46; SSC 31, 100**
See also CDWLB 2; DLB 90; EW 5; IDTP;
RGSF 2; RGWL 2, 3; SUFW
Tiger, Derry
See Ellison, Harlan
Tilghman, Christopher 1946- .... **CLC 65**
See also CA 159; CANR 135, 151; CSW;
DLB 244
Tillich, Paul (Johannes) 1886-1965 ...... **CLC
131**
See also CA 5-8R; 25-28R; CANR 33;
MTCW 1, 2
Tillinghast, Richard (Williford) 1940- . **CLC
29**
See also CA 29-32R; CAAS 23; CANR 26,
51, 96; CP 2, 3, 4, 5, 6, 7; CSW
Tillman, Lynne (?)- .... **CLC 231, 312**
See also CA 173; CANR 144, 172
Timrod, Henry 1828-1867 .... **NCLC 25**
See also DLB 3, 248; RGAL 4
Tindall, Gillian (Elizabeth) 1938- ..... **CLC 7**
See also CA 21-24R; CANR 11, 65, 107;
CN 1, 2, 3, 4, 5, 6, 7
Ting Ling
See Chiang, Pin-chin

Vogel, Paula Anne
See Vogel, Paula A.

Voigt, Cynthia 1942- .... **CLC 30**
See also AAYA 3, 30; BYA 1, 3, 6, 7, 8;
CA 106; CANR 18, 37, 40, 94, 145; CLR
13, 48, 141; INT CANR-18; JRDA; LAIT
5; MAICYA 1, 2; MAICYAS 1; MTFW
2005; SATA 48, 79, 116, 160; SATA-Brief
33; WYA; YAW

Voigt, Ellen Bryant 1943- .... **CLC 54**
See also CA 69-72; CANR 11, 29, 55, 115,
171; CP 5, 6, 7; CSW; CWP; DLB 120;
PFS 23, 33

Voinovich, Vladimir 1932- . **CLC 10, 49, 147**
See also CA 81-84; CAAS 12; CANR 33,
67, 150; CWW 2; DLB 302; MTCW 1

Voinovich, Vladimir Nikolaevich
See Voinovich, Vladimir

Vollmann, William T. 1959- .... **CLC 89, 227**
See also AMWS 17; CA 134; CANR 67,
116, 185; CN 7; CPW; DA3; DAM NOV,
POP; DLB 350; MTCW 2; MTFW 2005

Voloshinov, V. N.
See Bakhtin, Mikhail Mikhailovich

Voltaire 1694-1778 . **LC 14, 79, 110; SSC 12,
112, 167; WLC 6**
See also BYA 13; DA; DA3; DAB; DAC;
DAM DRAM, MST; DLB 314; EW 4;
GFL Beginnings to 1789; LATS 1:1;
LMFS 1; NFS 7; RGWL 2, 3; TWA

von Aschendrof, Baron Ignatz
See Ford, Ford Madox

von Chamisso, Adelbert
See Chamisso, Adelbert von

von Daeniken, Erich 1935- .... **CLC 30**
See also AITN 1; CA 37-40R; CANR 17,
44

von Daniken, Erich
See von Daeniken, Erich

von dem Turlin, Heinrich
See Heinrich von dem Tuerlin

von Eschenbach, Wolfram c. 1170-c. 1220 ..
CMLC 5
See also CDWLB 2; DLB 138; EW 1;
RGWL 2, 3

von Hartmann, Eduard 1842-1906 ... **TCLC
96**

von Hayek, Friedrich August
See Hayek, F(riedrich) A(ugust von)

von Heidenstam, (Carl Gustaf) Verner
See Heidenstam, (Carl Gustaf) Verner von

von Heyse, Paul (Johann Ludwig)
See Heyse, Paul (Johann Ludwig von)

von Hofmannsthal, Hugo
See Hofmannsthal, Hugo von

von Horvath, Odon
See von Horvath, Odon

von Horvath, Odon
See von Horvath, Odon

von Horvath, Odon 1901-1938 ..... **TCLC 45**
See also CA 118; 184, 194; DLB 85, 124;
RGWL 2, 3

von Horvath, Oedoen
See von Horvath, Odon

von Kleist, Heinrich
See Kleist, Heinrich von

Vonnegut, Kurt, Jr.
See Vonnegut, Kurt

Vonnegut, Kurt 1922-2007 ... **CLC 1, 2, 3, 4,
5, 8, 12, 22, 40, 60, 111, 212, 254; SSC
8, 155; WLC 6**
See also AAYA 6, 44; AITN 1; AMWS 2;
BEST 90:4; BPFB 3; BYA 3, 14; CA
1-4R; 259; CANR 1, 25, 49, 75, 92, 207;
CDALB 1968-1988; CN 1, 2, 3, 4, 5, 6,
7; CPW 1; DA; DA3; DAB; DAC; DAM
MST, NOV, POP; DLB 2, 8, 152; DLBD
3; DLBY 1980; EWL 3; EXPN; EXPS;

LAIT 4; LMFS 2; MAL 5; MTCW 1, 2;
MTFW 2005; NFS 3, 28; RGAL 4;
SCFW 4; SFW 4; SSFS 5; TUS; YAW

Von Rachen, Kurt
See Hubbard, L. Ron

von Sternberg, Josef
See Sternberg, Josef von

Vorster, Gordon 1924- .... **CLC 34**
See also CA 133

Vosce, Trudie
See Ozick, Cynthia

Voznesensky, Andrei 1933-2010 . **CLC 1, 15,
57**
See also CA 89-92; CANR 37; CWW 2;
DAM POET; DLB 359; EWL 3; MTCW
1

Voznesensky, Andrei Andreievich
See Voznesensky, Andrei

Voznesensky, Andrey
See Voznesensky, Andrei

Wace, Robert c. 1100-c. 1175 ...... **CMLC 55**
See also DLB 146

Waddington, Miriam 1917-2004 ..... **CLC 28**
See also CA 21-24R; 225; CANR 12, 30;
CCA 1; CP 1, 2, 3, 4, 5, 6, 7; DLB 68

Wade, Alan
See Vance, Jack

Wagman, Fredrica 1937- .... **CLC 7**
See also CA 97-100; CANR 166; INT CA-
97-100

Wagner, Linda W.
See Wagner-Martin, Linda (C.)

Wagner, Linda Welshimer
See Wagner-Martin, Linda (C.)

Wagner, Richard 1813-1883 .. **NCLC 9, 119,
258**
See also DLB 129; EW 6

Wagner-Martin, Linda (C.) 1936- .. **CLC 50**
See also CA 159; CANR 135

Wagoner, David (Russell) 1926- .. **CLC 3, 5,
15; PC 33**
See also AMWS 9; CA 1-4R; CAAS 3;
CANR 2, 71; CN 1, 2, 3, 4, 5, 6, 7; CP 1,
2, 3, 4, 5, 6, 7; DLB 5, 256; SATA 14;
TCWW 1, 2

Wah, Fred(erick James) 1939- .... **CLC 44**
See also CA 107; 141; CP 1, 6, 7; DLB 60

Wahloo, Per 1926-1975 .... **CLC 7**
See also BPFB 3; CA 61-64; CANR 73;
CMW 4; MSW

Wahloo, Peter
See Wahloo, Per

Wain, John 1925-1994 ..... **CLC 2, 11, 15, 46**
See also BRWS 16; CA 5-8R; 145; CAAS
4; CANR 23, 54; CDBLB 1960 to Present;
CN 1, 2, 3, 4, 5; CP 1, 2, 3, 4, 5; DLB
15, 27, 139, 155; EWL 3; MTCW 1, 2;
MTFW 2005

Wajda, Andrzej 1926- .... **CLC 16, 219**
See also CA 102

Wakefield, Dan 1932- .... **CLC 7**
See also CA 21-24R; 211; CAAE 211;
CAAS 7; CN 4, 5, 6, 7

Wakefield, Herbert Russell 1888-1965 ....
TCLC 120
See also CA 5-8R; CANR 77; HGG; SUFW

Wakoski, Diane 1937- .... **CLC 2, 4, 7, 9, 11,
40; PC 15**
See also CA 13-16R; 216; CAAE 216;
CAAS 1; CANR 9, 60, 106; CP 1, 2, 3, 4,
5, 6, 7; CWP; DAM POET; DLB 5; INT
CANR-9; MAL 5; MTCW 2; MTFW
2005

Wakoski-Sherbell, Diane
See Wakoski, Diane

Walcott, Derek 1930- .... **BLC 1:3, 2:3; CLC
2, 4, 9, 14, 25, 42, 67, 76, 160, 282; DC
7; PC 46**
See also BW 2; CA 89-92; CANR 26, 47,
75, 80, 130, 230; CBD; CD 5, 6; CDWLB
3; CP 1, 2, 3, 4, 5, 6, 7; DA3; DAB; DAC;
DAM MST, MULT, POET; DLB 117,
332; DLBY 1981; DNFS 1; EFS 1:1, 2:2;
EWL 3; LMFS 2; MTCW 1, 2; MTFW
2005; PFS 6, 34, 39; RGEL 2; TWA;
WWE 1

Walcott, Derek Alton
See Walcott, Derek

Waldman, Anne 1945- .... **CLC 7**
See also BG 1:3; CA 37-40R; CAAS 17;
CANR 34, 69, 116, 219; CP 1, 2, 3, 4, 5,
6, 7; CWP; DLB 16

Waldman, Anne Lesley
See Waldman, Anne

Waldo, E. Hunter
See Sturgeon, Theodore (Hamilton)

Waldo, Edward Hamilton
See Sturgeon, Theodore (Hamilton)

Waldrop, Rosmarie 1935- .... **PC 109**
See also CA 101; CAAS 30; CANR 18, 39,
67; CP 6, 7; CWP; DLB 169

Walker, Alice 1944- .. **BLC 1:3, 2:3; CLC 5,
6, 9, 19, 27, 46, 58, 103, 167, 319; PC
30; SSC 5; WLCS**
See also AAYA 3, 33; AFAW 1, 2; AMWS
3; BEST 89:4; BPFB 3; BW 2, 3; CA 37-
40R; CANR 9, 27, 49, 66, 82, 131, 191;
CDALB 1968-1988; CN 4, 5, 6, 7; CPW;
CSW; DA; DA3; DAB; DAC; DAM MST,
MULT, NOV, POET, POP; DLB 6, 33,
143; EWL 3; EXPN; EXPS; FL 1:6; FW;
INT CANR-27; LAIT 3; MAL 5; MBL;
MTCW 1, 2; MTFW 2005; NFS 5; PFS
30, 34; RGAL 4; RGSF 2; SATA 31;
SSFS 2, 11; TUS; YAW

Walker, Alice Malsenior
See Walker, Alice

Walker, David Harry 1911-1992 ..... **CLC 14**
See also CA 1-4R; 137; CANR 1; CN 1, 2;
CWRI 5; SATA 8; SATA-Obit 71

Walker, Edward Joseph 1934-2004 . **CLC 13**
See also CA 21-24R; 226; CANR 12, 28,
53; CP 1, 2, 3, 4, 5, 6, 7; DLB 40

Walker, George F(rederick) 1947- . **CLC 44,
61**
See also CA 103; CANR 21, 43, 59; CD 5,
6; DAB; DAC; DAM MST; DLB 60

Walker, Joseph A. 1935-2003 .... **CLC 19**
See also BW 1, 3; CA 89-92; CAD; CANR
26, 143; CD 5, 6; DAM DRAM, MST;
DFS 12; DLB 38

Walker, Margaret 1915-1998 .... **BLC 1:3;
CLC 1, 6; PC 20; TCLC 129**
See also AFAW 1, 2; BW 2, 3; CA 73-76;
172; CANR 26, 54, 76, 136; CN 1, 2, 3,
4, 5, 6; CP 1, 2, 3, 4, 5, 6; CSW; DAM
MULT; DLB 76, 152; EXPP; FW; MAL
5; MTCW 1, 2; MTFW 2005; PFS 31;
RGAL 4; RHW

Walker, Ted
See Walker, Edward Joseph

Wallace, David Foster 1962-2008 .. **CLC 50,
114, 271, 281; SSC 68**
See also AAYA 50; AMWS 10; CA 132;
277; CANR 59, 133, 190; CN 7; DA3;
DLB 350; MTCW 2; MTFW 2005

Wallace, Dexter
See Masters, Edgar Lee

Wallace, (Richard Horatio) Edgar
1875-1932 .... **TCLC 57**
See also CA 115; 218; CMW 4; DLB 70;
MSW; RGEL 2

Wallace, Irving 1916-1990 .... **CLC 7, 13**
See also AITN 1; BPFB 3; CA 1-4R; 132;
CAAS 1; CANR 1, 27; CPW; DAM NOV,
POP; INT CANR-27; MTCW 1, 2

Wallant, Edward Lewis 1926-1962 .. **CLC 5, 10**
See also CA 1-4R; CANR 22; DLB 2, 28,
143, 299; EWL 3; MAL 5; MTCW 1, 2;
RGAL 4; RGHL

Wallas, Graham 1858-1932 .... **TCLC 91**

Waller, Edmund 1606-1687 ... **LC 86; PC 72**
See also BRW 2; DAM POET; DLB 126;
PAB; RGEL 2

Walley, Byron
See Card, Orson Scott

Walls, Jeannette 1960(?)- .... **CLC 299**
See also CA 242; CANR 220

Walpole, Horace 1717-1797 ... **LC 2, 49, 152**
See also BRW 3; DLB 39, 104, 213; GL 3;
HGG; LMFS 1; RGEL 2; SUFW 1; TEA

Walpole, Hugh 1884-1941 .... **TCLC 5**
See also CA 104; 165; DLB 34; HGG;
MTCW 2; RGEL 2; RHW

Walpole, Hugh Seymour
See Walpole, Hugh

Walrond, Eric (Derwent) 1898-1966 ...... **HR 1:3**
See also BW 1; CA 125; DLB 51

Walser, Martin 1927- .... **CLC 27, 183**
See also CA 57-60; CANR 8, 46, 145;
CWW 2; DLB 75, 124; EWL 3

Walser, Robert 1878-1956 ... **SSC 20; TCLC 18, 267**
See also CA 118; 165; CANR 100, 194;
DLB 66; EWL 3

Walsh, Gillian Paton
See Paton Walsh, Jill

Walsh, Jill Paton
See Paton Walsh, Jill

Walter, Villiam Christian
See Andersen, Hans Christian

Walter of Chatillon c. 1135-c. 1202 .. **CMLC 111**

Walters, Anna L(ee) 1946- .... **NNAL**
See also CA 73-76

Walther von der Vogelweide c. 1170-1228 ...
CMLC 56

Walton, Izaak 1593-1683 .... **LC 72**
See also BRW 2; CDBLB Before 1660;
DLB 151, 213; RGEL 2

Walzer, Michael 1935- .... **CLC 238**
See also CA 37-40R; CANR 15, 48, 127,
190

Walzer, Michael Laban
See Walzer, Michael

Wambaugh, Joseph, Jr. 1937- ..... **CLC 3, 18**
See also AITN 1; BEST 89:3; BPFB 3; CA
33-36R; CANR 42, 65, 115, 167, 217;
CMW 4; CPW 1; DA3; DAM NOV, POP;
DLB 6; DLBY 1983; MSW; MTCW 1, 2

Wambaugh, Joseph Aloysius
See Wambaugh, Joseph, Jr.

Wang Wei 699(?)-761(?) . **CMLC 100; PC 18**
See also TWA

Warburton, William 1698-1779 .... **LC 97**
See also DLB 104

Ward, Arthur Henry Sarsfield 1883-1959 ...
TCLC 28
See also AAYA 80; CA 108; 173; CMW 4;
DLB 70; HGG; MSW; SUFW

Ward, Douglas Turner 1930- .... **CLC 19**
See also BW 1; CA 81-84; CAD; CANR
27; CD 5, 6; DLB 7, 38

Ward, E. D.
See Lucas, E(dward) V(errall)

Ward, Mrs. Humphry 1851-1920 ....
See Ward, Mary Augusta
See also RGEL 2

Ward, Mary Augusta 1851-1920 .. **TCLC 55**
See Ward, Mrs. Humphry
See also DLB 18

Ward, Nathaniel 1578(?)-1652 .... **LC 114**
See also DLB 24

Ward, Peter
See Faust, Frederick

Warhol, Andy 1928(?)-1987 .... **CLC 20**
See also AAYA 12; BEST 89:4; CA 89-92;
121; CANR 34

Warner, Francis (Robert Le Plastrier)
1937- .... **CLC 14**
See also CA 53-56; CANR 11; CP 1, 2, 3, 4

Warner, Marina 1946- .... **CLC 59, 231**
See also CA 65-68; CANR 21, 55, 118; CN
5, 6, 7; DLB 194; MTFW 2005

Warner, Rex (Ernest) 1905-1986 .... **CLC 45**
See also CA 89-92; 119; CN 1, 2, 3, 4; CP
1, 2, 3, 4; DLB 15; RGEL 2; RHW

Warner, Susan (Bogert) 1819-1885 ... **NCLC 31, 146**
See also AMWS 18; DLB 3, 42, 239, 250,
254

Warner, Sylvia (Constance) Ashton
See Ashton-Warner, Sylvia (Constance)

Warner, Sylvia Townsend 1893-1978 ... **CLC 7, 19; SSC 23; TCLC 131**
See also BRWS 7; CA 61-64; 77-80; CANR
16, 60, 104; CN 1, 2; DLB 34, 139; EWL
3; FANT; FW; MTCW 1, 2; RGEL 2;
RGSF 2; RHW

Warren, Mercy Otis 1728-1814 ... **NCLC 13, 226**
See also DLB 31, 200; RGAL 4; TUS

Warren, Robert Penn 1905-1989 . **CLC 1, 4, 6, 8, 10, 13, 18, 39, 53, 59; PC 37; SSC 4, 58, 126; WLC 6**
See also AITN 1; AMW; AMWC 2; BPFB
3; BYA 1; CA 13-16R; 129; CANR 10,
47; CDALB 1968-1988; CN 1, 2, 3, 4;
CP 1, 2, 3, 4; DA; DA3; DAB; DAC;
DAM MST, NOV, POET; DLB 2, 48, 152,
320; DLBY 1980, 1989; EWL 3; INT
CANR-10; MAL 5; MTCW 1, 2; MTFW
2005; NFS 13; RGAL 4; RGSF 2; RHW;
SATA 46; SATA-Obit 63; SSFS 8; TUS

Warrigal, Jack
See Furphy, Joseph

Warshofsky, Isaac
See Singer, Isaac Bashevis

Warton, Joseph 1722-1800 . **LC 128; NCLC 118**
See also DLB 104, 109; RGEL 2

Warton, Thomas 1728-1790 .... **LC 15, 82**
See also DAM POET; DLB 104, 109, 336;
RGEL 2

Waruk, Kona
See Harris, (Theodore) Wilson

Warung, Price
See Astley, William

Warwick, Jarvis
See Garner, Hugh

Washington, Alex
See Harris, Mark

Washington, Booker T. 1856-1915 . **BLC 1:3; TCLC 10**
See also BW 1; CA 114; 125; DA3; DAM
MULT; DLB 345; LAIT 2; RGAL 4;
SATA 28

Washington, Booker Taliaferro
See Washington, Booker T.

Washington, George 1732-1799 .... **LC 25**
See also DLB 31

Wassermann, (Karl) Jakob 1873-1934 ....
TCLC 6
See also CA 104; 163; DLB 66; EWL 3

Wasserstein, Wendy 1950-2006 ...... **CLC 32, 59, 90, 183; DC 4**
See also AAYA 73; AMWS 15; CA 121;
129; 247; CABS 3; CAD; CANR 53, 75,
128; CD 5, 6; CWD; DA3; DAM DRAM;
DFS 5, 17, 29; DLB 228; EWL 3; FW;
INT CA-129; MAL 5; MTCW 2; MTFW
2005; SATA 94; SATA-Obit 174

Waterhouse, Keith 1929-2009 .... **CLC 47**
See also BRWS 13; CA 5-8R; 290; CANR
38, 67, 109; CBD; CD 6; CN 1, 2, 3, 4, 5,
6, 7; DLB 13, 15; MTCW 1, 2; MTFW
2005

Waterhouse, Keith Spencer
See Waterhouse, Keith

Waters, Frank (Joseph) 1902-1995 . **CLC 88**
See also CA 5-8R; 149; CAAS 13; CANR
3, 18, 63, 121; DLB 212; DLBY 1986;
RGAL 4; TCWW 1, 2

Waters, Mary C. CLC 70

Waters, Roger 1944- .... **CLC 35**

Watkins, Frances Ellen
See Harper, Frances Ellen Watkins

Watkins, Gerrold
See Malzberg, Barry N(athaniel)

Watkins, Gloria Jean
See hooks, bell

Watkins, Paul 1964- .... **CLC 55**
See also CA 132; CANR 62, 98, 231

Watkins, Vernon Phillips 1906-1967 .... **CLC 43**
See also CA 9-10; 25-28R; CAP 1; DLB
20; EWL 3; RGEL 2

Watson, Irving S.
See Mencken, H. L.

Watson, John H.
See Farmer, Philip Jose

Watson, Richard F.
See Silverberg, Robert

Watson, Rosamund Marriott 1860-1911 . **PC 117**
See also CA 207; DLB 240

Watson, Sheila 1909-1998 .... **SSC 128**
See also AITN 2; CA 155; CCA 1; DAC;
DLB 60

Watts, Ephraim
See Horne, Richard Henry Hengist

Watts, Isaac 1674-1748 .... **LC 98**
See also DLB 95; RGEL 2; SATA 52

Waugh, Auberon (Alexander) 1939-2001 ....
CLC 7
See also CA 45-48; 192; CANR 6, 22, 92;
CN 1, 2, 3; DLB 14, 194

Waugh, Evelyn 1903-1966 . **CLC 1, 3, 8, 13, 19, 27, 44, 107; SSC 41; TCLC 229; WLC 6**
See also AAYA 78; BPFB 3; BRW 7; CA
85-88; 25-28R; CANR 22; CDBLB 1914-
1945; DA; DA3; DAB; DAC; DAM MST,
NOV, POP; DLB 15, 162, 195, 352; EWL
3; MTCW 1, 2; MTFW 2005; NFS 13,
17, 34; RGEL 2; RGSF 2; TEA; WLIT 4

Waugh, Evelyn Arthur St. John
See Waugh, Evelyn

Waugh, Harriet 1944- .... **CLC 6**
See also CA 85-88; CANR 22

Ways, C.R.
See Blount, Roy, Jr.

Waystaff, Simon
See Swift, Jonathan

Webb, Beatrice 1858-1943 .... **TCLC 22**
See also CA 117; 162; DLB 190; FW

Webb, Beatrice Martha Potter
See Webb, Beatrice

Webb, Charles 1939- .... **CLC 7**
See also CA 25-28R; CANR 114, 188

Webb, Charles Richard
See Webb, Charles

Webb, Frank J. NCLC 143
See also DLB 50

Webb, James, Jr.
See Webb, James

Webb, James 1946- .... **CLC 22**
See also CA 81-84; CANR 156

Webb, James H.
See Webb, James

Webb, James Henry
See Webb, James

Webb, Mary Gladys (Meredith)
1881-1927 .... **TCLC 24**
See also CA 182; 123; DLB 34; FW; RGEL
2

Webb, Mrs. Sidney
See Webb, Beatrice

Webb, Phyllis 1927- .... **CLC 18; PC 124**
See also CA 104; CANR 23; CCA 1; CP 1,
2, 3, 4, 5, 6, 7; CWP; DLB 53

Webb, Sidney 1859-1947 .... **TCLC 22**
See also CA 117; 163; DLB 190

Webb, Sidney James
See Webb, Sidney

Webber, Andrew Lloyd
See Lloyd Webber, Andrew

Weber, Lenora Mattingly 1895-1971 ... **CLC
12**
See also CA 19-20; 29-32R; CAP 1; SATA
2; SATA-Obit 26

Weber, Max 1864-1920 .... **TCLC 69**
See also CA 109; 189; DLB 296

Webster, Augusta 1837-1894 .... **NCLC 230**
See also DLB 35, 240

Webster, John 1580(?)-1634(?) ..... **DC 2; LC
33, 84, 124; WLC 6**
See also BRW 2; CDBLB Before 1660; DA;
DAB; DAC; DAM DRAM, MST; DFS
17, 19; DLB 58; IDTP; RGEL 2; WLIT 3

Webster, Noah 1758-1843 ..... **NCLC 30, 253**
See also DLB 1, 37, 42, 43, 73, 243

Wedekind, Benjamin Franklin
See Wedekind, Frank

Wedekind, Frank 1864-1918 .. **TCLC 7, 241**
See also CA 104; 153; CANR 121, 122;
CDWLB 2; DAM DRAM; DLB 118; EW
8; EWL 3; LMFS 2; RGWL 2, 3

Weems, Mason Locke 1759-1825 ...... **NCLC
245**
See also DLB 30, 37, 42

Wehr, Demaris CLC 65

Weidman, Jerome 1913-1998 .... **CLC 7**
See also AITN 2; CA 1-4R; 171; CAD;
CANR 1; CD 1, 2, 3, 4, 5; DLB 28

Weil, Simone 1909-1943 .... **TCLC 23**
See also CA 117; 159; EW 12; EWL 3; FW;
GFL 1789 to the Present; MTCW 2

Weil, Simone Adolphine
See Weil, Simone

Weininger, Otto 1880-1903 .... **TCLC 84**

Weinstein, Nathan
See West, Nathanael

Weinstein, Nathan von Wallenstein
See West, Nathanael

Weir, Peter 1944- .... **CLC 20**
See also CA 113; 123

Weir, Peter Lindsay
See Weir, Peter

Weiss, Peter (Ulrich) 1916-1982 . **CLC 3, 15,
51; DC 36; TCLC 152**
See also CA 45-48; 106; CANR 3; DAM
DRAM; DFS 3; DLB 69, 124; EWL 3;
RGHL; RGWL 2, 3

Weiss, Theodore (Russell) 1916-2003 .. **CLC
3, 8, 14**
See also CA 9-12R, 189; 216; CAAE 189;
CAAS 2; CANR 46, 94; CP 1, 2, 3, 4, 5,
6, 7; DLB 5; TCLE 1:2

Welch, (Maurice) Denton 1915-1948 . **TCLC
22**
See also BRWS 8; CA 121; 148; RGEL 2

Welch, James 1940-2003 ...... **CLC 6, 14, 52,
249; NNAL; PC 62**
See also CA 85-88; 219; CANR 42, 66, 107;
CN 5, 6, 7; CP 2, 3, 4, 5, 6, 7; CPW;
DAM MULT, POP; DLB 175, 256; LATS
1:1; NFS 23; RGAL 4; TCWW 1, 2

Welch, James Phillip
See Welch, James

Weld, Angelina Grimke
See Grimke, Angelina Weld

Weldon, Fay 1931- . **CLC 6, 9, 11, 19, 36, 59,
122**
See also BRWS 4; CA 21-24R; CANR 16,
46, 63, 97, 137, 227; CDBLB 1960 to
Present; CN 3, 4, 5, 6, 7; CPW; DAM
POP; DLB 14, 194, 319; EWL 3; FW;
HGG; INT CANR-16; MTCW 1, 2;
MTFW 2005; RGEL 2; RGSF 2

Wellek, Rene 1903-1995 .... **CLC 28**
See also CA 5-8R; 150; CAAS 7; CANR 8;
DLB 63; EWL 3; INT CANR-8

Weller, Michael 1942- .... **CLC 10, 53**
See also CA 85-88; CAD; CD 5, 6

Weller, Paul 1958- .... **CLC 26**

Wellershoff, Dieter 1925- .... **CLC 46**
See also CA 89-92; CANR 16, 37

Welles, (George) Orson 1915-1985 . **CLC 20,
80**
See also AAYA 40; CA 93-96; 117

Wellman, John McDowell 1945- ..... **CLC 65**
See also CA 166; CAD; CD 5, 6; RGAL 4

Wellman, Mac
See Wellman, John McDowell; Wellman,
John McDowell

Wellman, Manly Wade 1903-1986 .. **CLC 49**
See also CA 1-4R; 118; CANR 6, 16, 44;
FANT; SATA 6; SATA-Obit 47; SFW 4;
SUFW

Wells, Carolyn 1869(?)-1942 .... **TCLC 35**
See also CA 113; 185; CMW 4; DLB 11

Wells, H. G. 1866-1946 ...... **SSC 6, 70, 151;
TCLC 6, 12, 19, 133; WLC 6**
See also AAYA 18; BPFB 3; BRW 6; CA
110; 121; CDBLB 1914-1945; CLR 64,
133; DA; DA3; DAB; DAC; DAM MST,
NOV; DLB 34, 70, 156, 178; EWL 3;
EXPS; HGG; LAIT 3; LMFS 2; MTCW
1, 2; MTFW 2005; NFS 17, 20, 36; RGEL
2; RGSF 2; SATA 20; SCFW 1, 2; SFW
4; SSFS 3, 34; SUFW; TEA; WCH; WLIT
4; YAW

Wells, Herbert George
See Wells, H. G.

Wells, Rosemary 1943- .... **CLC 12**
See also AAYA 13; BYA 7, 8; CA 85-88;
CANR 48, 120, 179; CLR 16, 69; CWRI
5; MAICYA 1, 2; SAAS 1; SATA 18, 69,
114, 156, 207, 237; YAW

Wells-Barnett, Ida B(ell) 1862-1931 .. **TCLC
125**
See also CA 182; DLB 23, 221

Welsh, Irvine 1958- .... **CLC 144, 276**
See also BRWS 17; CA 173; CANR 146,
196; CN 7; DLB 271

Welty, Eudora 1909-2001 . **CLC 319; SSC 1,
27, 51, 111; WLC 6**
See also AAYA 48; AMW; AMWR 1; BPFB
3; CA 9-12R; 199; CABS 1; CANR 32,
65, 128; CDALB 1941-1968; CN 1, 2, 3,
4, 5, 6, 7; CSW; DA; DA3; DAB; DAC;
DAM MST, NOV; DFS 26; DLB 2, 102,
143; DLBD 12; DLBY 1987, 2001; EWL

3; EXPS; HGG; LAIT 3; MAL 5; MBL;
MTCW 1, 2; MTFW 2005; NFS 13, 15;
RGAL 4; RGSF 2; RHW; SSFS 2, 10, 26;
TUS

Welty, Eudora Alice
See Welty, Eudora

Wendt, Albert 1939- .... **CLC 317**
See also CA 57-60; CN 3, 4, 5, 6, 7; CP 5,
6, 7; EWL 3; RGSF 2

Wen I-to 1899-1946 .... **TCLC 28**
See also EWL 3

Wentworth, Robert
See Hamilton, Edmond

Werfel, Franz (Viktor) 1890-1945 .. **PC 101;
TCLC 8, 248**
See also CA 104; 161; DLB 81, 124; EWL
3; RGWL 2, 3

Wergeland, Henrik Arnold 1808-1845 ....
NCLC 5
See also DLB 354

Werner, Friedrich Ludwig Zacharias
1768-1823 .... **NCLC 189**
See also DLB 94

Werner, Zacharias
See Werner, Friedrich Ludwig Zacharias

Wersba, Barbara 1932- .... **CLC 30**
See also AAYA 2, 30; BYA 6, 12, 13; CA
29-32R, 182; CAAE 182; CANR 16, 38;
CLR 3, 78; DLB 52; JRDA; MAICYA 1,
2; SAAS 2; SATA 1, 58; SATA-Essay 103;
WYA; YAW

Wertmueller, Lina 1928- .... **CLC 16**
See also CA 97-100; CANR 39, 78

Wescott, Glenway 1901-1987 . **CLC 13; SSC
35; TCLC 265**
See also CA 13-16R; 121; CANR 23, 70;
CN 1, 2, 3, 4; DLB 4, 9, 102; MAL 5;
RGAL 4

Wesker, Arnold 1932- .... **CLC 3, 5, 42**
See also CA 1-4R; CAAS 7; CANR 1, 33;
CBD; CD 5, 6; CDBLB 1960 to Present;
DAB; DAM DRAM; DLB 13, 310, 319;
EWL 3; MTCW 1; RGEL 2; TEA

Wesley, Charles 1707-1788 .... **LC 128**
See also DLB 95; RGEL 2

Wesley, John 1703-1791 .... **LC 88**
See also DLB 104

Wesley, Richard (Errol) 1945- .... **CLC 7**
See also BW 1; CA 57-60; CAD; CANR
27; CD 5, 6; DLB 38

Wessel, Johan Herman 1742-1785 .... **LC 7**
See also DLB 300

West, Anthony (Panther) 1914-1987 .... **CLC
50**
See also CA 45-48; 124; CANR 3, 19; CN
1, 2, 3, 4; DLB 15

West, C. P.
See Wodehouse, P. G.

West, Cornel 1953- .... **BLCS; CLC 134**
See also CA 144; CANR 91, 159; DLB 246

West, Cornel Ronald
See West, Cornel

West, Delno C(loyde), Jr. 1936- ...... **CLC 70**
See also CA 57-60

West, Dorothy 1907-1998 .... **HR 1:3; TCLC
108**
See also AMWS 18; BW 2; CA 143; 169;
DLB 76

West, Edwin
See Westlake, Donald E.

West, (Mary) Jessamyn 1902-1984 .. **CLC 7,
17**
See also CA 9-12R; 112; CANR 27; CN 1,
2, 3; DLB 6; DLBY 1984; MTCW 1, 2;
RGAL 4; RHW; SATA-Obit 37; TCWW
2; TUS; YAW

West, Morris L(anglo) 1916-1999 .... **CLC 6, 33**
See also BPFB 3; CA 5-8R; 187; CANR 24, 49, 64; CN 1, 2, 3, 4, 5, 6; CPW; DLB 289; MTCW 1, 2; MTFW 2005

West, Nathanael 1903-1940 ..... **SSC 16, 116; TCLC 1, 14, 44, 235**
See also AAYA 77; AMW; AMWR 2; BPFB 3; CA 104; 125; CDALB 1929-1941; DA3; DLB 4, 9, 28; EWL 3; MAL 5; MTCW 1, 2; MTFW 2005; NFS 16; RGAL 4; TUS

West, Owen
See Koontz, Dean

West, Paul 1930- .... **CLC 7, 14, 96, 226**
See also CA 13-16R; CAAS 7; CANR 22, 53, 76, 89, 136, 205; CN 1, 2, 3, 4, 5, 6, 7; DLB 14; INT CANR-22; MTCW 2; MTFW 2005

West, Rebecca 1892-1983 .. **CLC 7, 9, 31, 50**
See also BPFB 3; BRWS 3; CA 5-8R; 109; CANR 19; CN 1, 2, 3; DLB 36; DLBY 1983; EWL 3; FW; MTCW 1, 2; MTFW 2005; NCFS 4; RGEL 2; TEA

Westall, Robert (Atkinson) 1929-1993 . **CLC 17**
See also AAYA 12; BYA 2, 6, 7, 8, 9, 15; CA 69-72; 141; CANR 18, 68; CLR 13; FANT; JRDA; MAICYA 1, 2; MAICYAS 1; SAAS 2; SATA 23, 69; SATA-Obit 75; WYA; YAW

Westermarck, Edward 1862-1939 ..... **TCLC 87**

Westlake, Donald E. 1933-2008 .. **CLC 7, 33**
See also BPFB 3; CA 17-20R; 280; CAAS 13; CANR 16, 44, 65, 94, 137, 192; CMW 4; CPW; DAM POP; INT CANR-16; MSW; MTCW 2; MTFW 2005

Westlake, Donald E. Edmund
See Westlake, Donald E.

Westlake, Donald Edwin
See Westlake, Donald E.

Westlake, Donald Edwin Edmund
See Westlake, Donald E.

Westmacott, Mary
See Christie, Agatha

Weston, Allen
See Norton, Andre

Wetcheek, J. L.
See Feuchtwanger, Lion

Wetering, Janwillem van de
See van de Wetering, Janwillem

Wetherald, Agnes Ethelwyn 1857-1940 .... **TCLC 81**
See also CA 202; DLB 99

Wetherell, Elizabeth
See Warner, Susan (Bogert)

Whale, James 1889-1957 .... **TCLC 63**
See also AAYA 75

Whalen, Philip (Glenn) 1923-2002 .. **CLC 6, 29**
See also BG 1:3; CA 9-12R; 209; CANR 5, 39; CP 1, 2, 3, 4, 5, 6, 7; DLB 16; WP

Wharton, Edith 1862-1937 . **SSC 6, 84, 120; TCLC 3, 9, 27, 53, 129, 149; WLC 6**
See also AAYA 25; AMW; AMWC 2; AMWR 1; BPFB 3; CA 104; 132; CDALB 1865-1917; CLR 136; DA; DA3; DAB; DAC; DAM MST, NOV; DLB 4, 9, 12, 78, 189; DLBD 13; EWL 3; EXPS; FL 1:6; GL 3; HGG; LAIT 2, 3; LATS 1:1; MAL 5; MBL; MTCW 1, 2; MTFW 2005; NFS 5, 11, 15, 20, 37; RGAL 4; RGSF 2; RHW; SSFS 6, 7; SUFW; TUS

Wharton, Edith Newbold Jones
See Wharton, Edith

Wharton, James
See Mencken, H. L.

Wharton, William 1925-2008 .... **CLC 18, 37**
See also CA 93-96; 278; CN 4, 5, 6, 7; DLBY 1980; INT CA-93-96

Wheatley, Phillis 1753(?)-1784 ...... **BLC 1:3; LC 3, 50, 183; PC 3; WLC 6**
See also AFAW 1, 2; AMWS 20; CDALB 1640-1865; DA; DA3; DAC; DAM MST, MULT, POET; DLB 31, 50; EXPP; FL 1:1; PFS 13, 29, 36; RGAL 4

Wheatley Peters, Phillis
See Wheatley, Phillis

Wheelock, John Hall 1886-1978 ..... **CLC 14**
See also CA 13-16R; 77-80; CANR 14; CP 1, 2; DLB 45; MAL 5

Whim-Wham
See Curnow, (Thomas) Allen (Monro)

Whisp, Kennilworthy
See Rowling, J.K.

Whitaker, Rod 1931-2005 .... **CLC 29**
See also CA 29-32R; 246; CANR 45, 153; CMW 4

Whitaker, Rodney
See Whitaker, Rod

Whitaker, Rodney William
See Whitaker, Rod

White, Babington
See Braddon, Mary Elizabeth

White, E. B. 1899-1985 .... **CLC 10, 34, 39**
See also AAYA 62; AITN 2; AMWS 1; CA 13-16R; 116; CANR 16, 37; CDALBS; CLR 1, 21, 107; CPW; DA3; DAM POP; DLB 11, 22; EWL 3; FANT; MAICYA 1, 2; MAL 5; MTCW 1, 2; MTFW 2005; NCFS 5; RGAL 4; SATA 2, 29, 100; SATA-Obit 44; TUS

White, Edmund 1940- .... **CLC 27, 110**
See also AAYA 7; CA 45-48; CANR 3, 19, 36, 62, 107, 133, 172, 212; CN 5, 6, 7; DA3; DAM POP; DLB 227; MTCW 1, 2; MTFW 2005

White, Edmund Valentine III
See White, Edmund

White, Elwyn Brooks
See White, E. B.

White, Hayden V. 1928- .... **CLC 148**
See also CA 128; CANR 135; DLB 246

White, Patrick 1912-1990 . **CLC 3, 4, 5, 7, 9, 18, 65, 69; SSC 39; TCLC 176**
See also BRWS 1; CA 81-84; 132; CANR 43; CN 1, 2, 3, 4; DLB 260, 332; EWL 3; MTCW 1; RGEL 2; RGSF 2; RHW; TWA; WWE 1

White, Patrick Victor Martindale
See White, Patrick

White, Phyllis Dorothy James
See James, P.D.

White, T(erence) H(anbury) 1906-1964 .... **CLC 30**
See also AAYA 22; BPFB 3; BYA 4, 5; CA 73-76; CANR 37; CLR 139; DLB 160; FANT; JRDA; LAIT 1; MAICYA 1, 2; NFS 30; RGEL 2; SATA 12; SUFW 1; YAW

White, Terence de Vere 1912-1994 . **CLC 49**
See also CA 49-52; 145; CANR 3

White, Walter
See White, Walter F(rancis)

White, Walter F(rancis) 1893-1955 ...... **BLC 1:3; HR 1:3; TCLC 15**
See also BW 1; CA 115; 124; DAM MULT; DLB 51

White, William Hale 1831-1913 ... **TCLC 25**
See also CA 121; 189; DLB 18; RGEL 2

Whitehead, Alfred North 1861-1947 . **TCLC 97**
See also CA 117; 165; DLB 100, 262

Whitehead, Colson 1969- ..... **BLC 2:3; CLC 232**
See also CA 202; CANR 162, 211

Whitehead, E(dward) A(nthony) 1933- .... **CLC 5**
See also CA 65-68; CANR 58, 118; CBD; CD 5, 6; DLB 310

Whitehead, Ted
See Whitehead, E(dward) A(nthony)

Whiteman, Roberta J. Hill 1947- ...... **NNAL**
See also CA 146

Whitemore, Hugh (John) 1936- ...... **CLC 37**
See also CA 132; CANR 77; CBD; CD 5, 6; INT CA-132

Whitman, Sarah Helen (Power) 1803-1878 . **NCLC 19**
See also DLB 1, 243

Whitman, Walt 1819-1892 . **NCLC 4, 31, 81, 205; PC 3, 91; WLC 6**
See also AAYA 42; AMW; AMWR 1; CDALB 1640-1865; DA; DA3; DAB; DAC; DAM MST, POET; DLB 3, 64, 224, 250; EXPP; LAIT 2; LMFS 1; PAB; PFS 2, 3, 13, 22, 31, 39; RGAL 4; SATA 20; TUS; WP; WYAS 1

Whitman, Walter
See Whitman, Walt

Whitney, Isabella fl. 1565-fl. 1575 .. **LC 130; PC 116**
See also DLB 136

Whitney, Phyllis A. 1903-2008 .... **CLC 42**
See also AAYA 36; AITN 2; BEST 90:3; CA 1-4R; 269; CANR 3, 25, 38, 60; CLR 59; CMW 4; CPW; DA3; DAM POP; JRDA; MAICYA 1, 2; MTCW 2; RHW; SATA 1, 30; SATA-Obit 189; YAW

Whitney, Phyllis Ayame
See Whitney, Phyllis A.

Whittemore, (Edward) Reed, Jr. 1919- . **CLC 4**
See also CA 9-12R; 219; CAAE 219; CAAS 8; CANR 4, 119; CP 1, 2, 3, 4, 5, 6, 7; DLB 5; MAL 5

Whittier, John Greenleaf 1807-1892 . **NCLC 8, 59; PC 93**
See also AMWS 1; DLB 1, 243; PFS 36; RGAL 4

Whittlebot, Hernia
See Coward, Noel

Wicker, Thomas Grey
See Wicker, Tom

Wicker, Tom 1926- .... **CLC 7**
See also CA 65-68; CANR 21, 46, 141, 179

Wickham, Anna 1883-1947 .... **PC 110**
See also DLB 240

Wicomb, Zoë 1948- .... **BLC 2:3**
See also CA 127; CANR 106, 167; DLB 225

Wideman, John Edgar 1941- . **BLC 1:3, 2:3; CLC 5, 34, 36, 67, 122, 316; SSC 62**
See also AFAW 1, 2; AMWS 10; BPFB 4; BW 2, 3; CA 85-88; CANR 14, 42, 67, 109, 140, 187; CN 4, 5, 6, 7; DAM MULT; DLB 33, 143; MAL 5; MTCW 2; MTFW 2005; RGAL 4; RGSF 2; SSFS 6, 12, 24; TCLE 1:2

Wiebe, Rudy 1934- . **CLC 6, 11, 14, 138, 263**
See also CA 37-40R; CANR 42, 67, 123, 202; CN 1, 2, 3, 4, 5, 6, 7; DAC; DAM MST; DLB 60; RHW; SATA 156

Wiebe, Rudy Henry
See Wiebe, Rudy

Wieland, Christoph Martin 1733-1813 .... **NCLC 17, 177**
See also DLB 97; EW 4; LMFS 1; RGWL 2, 3

Wiene, Robert 1881-1938 .... **TCLC 56**

Wilson, August 1945-2005 ..... **BLC 1:3, 2:3; CLC 39, 50, 63, 118, 222; DC 2, 31; WLCS**
See also AAYA 16; AFAW 2; AMWS 8; BW 2, 3; CA 115; 122; 244; CAD; CANR 42, 54, 76, 128; CD 5, 6; DA; DA3; DAB; DAC; DAM DRAM, MST, MULT; DFS 3, 7, 15, 17, 24; DLB 228; EWL 3; LAIT 4; LATS 1:2; MAL 5; MTCW 1, 2; MTFW 2005; RGAL 4

Wilson, Brian 1942- .... **CLC 12**

Wilson, Colin 1931- .... **CLC 3, 14**
See also CA 1-4R, 315; CAAE 315; CAAS 5; CANR 1, 22, 33, 77; CMW 4; CN 1, 2, 3, 4, 5, 6; DLB 14, 194; HGG; MTCW 1; SFW 4

Wilson, Colin Henry
See Wilson, Colin

Wilson, Dirk
See Pohl, Frederik

Wilson, Edmund 1895-1972 . **CLC 1, 2, 3, 8, 24**
See also AMW; CA 1-4R; 37-40R; CANR 1, 46, 110; CN 1; DLB 63; EWL 3; MAL 5; MTCW 1, 2; MTFW 2005; RGAL 4; TUS

Wilson, Ethel Davis (Bryant) 1888(?)-1980 . **CLC 13**
See also CA 102; CN 1, 2; DAC; DAM POET; DLB 68; MTCW 1; RGEL 2

Wilson, Harriet
See Wilson, Harriet E. Adams

Wilson, Harriet E.
See Wilson, Harriet E. Adams

Wilson, Harriet E. Adams 1827(?)-1863(?) . **BLC 1:3; NCLC 78, 219**
See also DAM MULT; DLB 50, 239, 243

Wilson, John 1785-1854 .... **NCLC 5**
See also DLB 110

Wilson, John Anthony Burgess
See Burgess, Anthony

Wilson, John Burgess
See Burgess, Anthony

Wilson, Katharina CLC 65

Wilson, Lanford 1937-2011 .. **CLC 7, 14, 36, 197; DC 19**
See also CA 17-20R; CABS 3; CAD; CANR 45, 96; CD 5, 6; DAM DRAM; DFS 4, 9, 12, 16, 20; DLB 7, 341; EWL 3; MAL 5; TUS

Wilson, Robert M. 1941- .... **CLC 7, 9**
See also CA 49-52; CAD; CANR 2, 41; CD 5, 6; MTCW 1

Wilson, Robert McLiam 1964- .... **CLC 59**
See also CA 132; DLB 267

Wilson, Sloan 1920-2003 .... **CLC 32**
See also CA 1-4R; 216; CANR 1, 44; CN 1, 2, 3, 4, 5, 6

Wilson, Snoo 1948- .... **CLC 33**
See also CA 69-72; CBD; CD 5, 6

Wilson, Thomas 1523(?)-1581 .... **LC 184**
See also DLB 132, 236

Wilson, William S(mith) 1932- .... **CLC 49**
See also CA 81-84

Wilson, (Thomas) Woodrow 1856-1924 .... **TCLC 79**
See also CA 166; DLB 47

Winchelsea
See Finch, Anne

Winchester, Simon 1944- .... **CLC 257**
See also AAYA 66; CA 107; CANR 90, 130, 194, 228

Winchilsea, Anne (Kingsmill) Finch 1661-1720 ....
See Finch, Anne
See also RGEL 2

Winckelmann, Johann Joachim 1717-1768 . **LC 129**
See also DLB 97

Windham, Basil
See Wodehouse, P. G.

Wingrove, David 1954- .... **CLC 68**
See also CA 133; SFW 4

Winnemucca, Sarah 1844-1891 ... **NCLC 79; NNAL**
See also DAM MULT; DLB 175; RGAL 4

Winstanley, Gerrard 1609-1676 .... **LC 52**

Wintergreen, Jane
See Duncan, Sara Jeannette

Winters, Arthur Yvor
See Winters, Yvor

Winters, Janet Lewis
See Lewis, Janet

Winters, Yvor 1900-1968 . **CLC 4, 8, 32; PC 82**
See also AMWS 2; CA 11-12; 25-28R; CAP 1; DLB 48; EWL 3; MAL 5; MTCW 1; RGAL 4

Winterson, Jeanette 1959- ...... **CLC 64, 158, 307; SSC 144**
See also BRWS 4; CA 136; CANR 58, 116, 181; CN 5, 6, 7; CPW; DA3; DAM POP; DLB 207, 261; FANT; FW; GLL 1; MTCW 2; MTFW 2005; RHW; SATA 190

Winthrop, John 1588-1649 .... **LC 31, 107**
See also DLB 24, 30

Winthrop, Theodore 1828-1861 . **NCLC 210**
See also DLB 202

Winton, Tim 1960- .... **CLC 251; SSC 119**
See also AAYA 34; CA 152; CANR 118, 194; CN 6, 7; DLB 325; SATA 98

Wirth, Louis 1897-1952 .... **TCLC 92**
See also CA 210

Wiseman, Frederick 1930- .... **CLC 20**
See also CA 159

Wister, Owen 1860-1938 .... **SSC 100; TCLC 21**
See also BPFB 3; CA 108; 162; DLB 9, 78, 186; RGAL 4; SATA 62; TCWW 1, 2

Wither, George 1588-1667 .... **LC 96**
See also DLB 121; RGEL 2

Witkacy
See Witkiewicz, Stanislaw Ignacy

Witkiewicz, Stanislaw Ignacy 1885-1939 ..... **TCLC 8, 237**
See also CA 105; 162; CDWLB 4; DLB 215; EW 10; EWL 3; RGWL 2, 3; SFW 4

Wittgenstein, Ludwig (Josef Johann) 1889-1951 .... **TCLC 59**
See also CA 113; 164; DLB 262; MTCW 2

Wittig, Monique 1935-2003 .... **CLC 22**
See also CA 116; 135; 212; CANR 143; CWW 2; DLB 83; EWL 3; FW; GLL 1

Wittlin, Jozef 1896-1976 .... **CLC 25**
See also CA 49-52; 65-68; CANR 3; EWL 3

Wodehouse, P. G. 1881-1975 .... **CLC 1, 2, 5, 10, 22; SSC 2, 115; TCLC 108**
See also AAYA 65; AITN 2; BRWS 3; CA 45-48; 57-60; CANR 3, 33; CDBLB 1914-1945; CN 1, 2; CPW 1; DA3; DAB; DAC; DAM NOV; DLB 34, 162, 352; EWL 3; MTCW 1, 2; MTFW 2005; RGEL 2; RGSF 2; SATA 22; SSFS 10

Wodehouse, Pelham Grenville
See Wodehouse, P. G.

Woiwode, L.
See Woiwode, Larry

Woiwode, Larry 1941- .... **CLC 6, 10**
See also CA 73-76; CANR 16, 94, 192; CN 3, 4, 5, 6, 7; DLB 6; INT CANR-16

Woiwode, Larry Alfred
See Woiwode, Larry

Wojciechowska, Maia (Teresa) 1927-2002 ... **CLC 26**
See also AAYA 8, 46; BYA 3; CA 9-12R; 183; 209; CAAE 183; CANR 4, 41; CLR 1; JRDA; MAICYA 1, 2; SAAS 1; SATA 1, 28, 83; SATA-Essay 104; SATA-Obit 134; YAW

Wojtyla, Karol (Jozef)
See John Paul II, Pope

Wojtyla, Karol (Josef)
See John Paul II, Pope

Wolf, Christa 1929- .... **CLC 14, 29, 58, 150, 261**
See also CA 85-88; CANR 45, 123; CD-WLB 2; CWW 2; DLB 75; EWL 3; FW; MTCW 1; RGWL 2, 3; SSFS 14

Wolf, Naomi 1962- .... **CLC 157**
See also CA 141; CANR 110; FW; MTFW 2005

Wolfe, Gene 1931- .... **CLC 25**
See also AAYA 35; CA 57-60; CAAS 9; CANR 6, 32, 60, 152, 197; CPW; DAM POP; DLB 8; FANT; MTCW 2; MTFW 2005; SATA 118, 165; SCFW 2; SFW 4; SUFW 2

Wolfe, Gene Rodman
See Wolfe, Gene

Wolfe, George C. 1954- .... **BLCS; CLC 49**
See also CA 149; CAD; CD 5, 6

Wolfe, Thomas 1900-1938 .... **SSC 33, 113; TCLC 4, 13, 29, 61; WLC 6**
See also AMW; BPFB 3; CA 104; 132; CANR 102; CDALB 1929-1941; DA; DA3; DAB; DAC; DAM MST, NOV; DLB 9, 102, 229; DLBD 2, 16; DLBY 1985, 1997; EWL 3; MAL 5; MTCW 1, 2; NFS 18; RGAL 4; SSFS 18; TUS

Wolfe, Thomas Clayton
See Wolfe, Thomas

Wolfe, Thomas Kennerly
See Wolfe, Tom, Jr.

Wolfe, Tom, Jr. 1931- ... **CLC 1, 2, 9, 15, 35, 51, 147**
See also AAYA 8, 67; AITN 2; AMWS 3; BEST 89:1; BPFB 3; CA 13-16R; CANR 9, 33, 70, 104; CN 5, 6, 7; CPW; CSW; DA3; DAM POP; DLB 152, 185 185; EWL 3; INT CANR-9; LAIT 5; MTCW 1, 2; MTFW 2005; RGAL 4; TUS

Wolff, Geoffrey 1937- .... **CLC 41**
See also CA 29-32R; CANR 29, 43, 78, 154

Wolff, Geoffrey Ansell
See Wolff, Geoffrey

Wolff, Sonia
See Levitin, Sonia

Wolff, Tobias 1945- .. **CLC 39, 64, 172; SSC 63, 136**
See also AAYA 16; AMWS 7; BEST 90:2; BYA 12; CA 114; 117; CAAS 22; CANR 54, 76, 96, 192; CN 5, 6, 7; CSW; DA3; DLB 130; EWL 3; INT CA-117; MTCW 2; MTFW 2005; RGAL 4; RGSF 2; SSFS 4, 11, 35

Wolff, Tobias Jonathan Ansell
See Wolff, Tobias

Wolitzer, Hilma 1930- .... **CLC 17**
See also CA 65-68; CANR 18, 40, 172; INT CANR-18; SATA 31; YAW

Wollstonecraft, Mary 1759-1797 .. **LC 5, 50, 90, 147**
See also BRWS 3; CDBLB 1789-1832; DLB 39, 104, 158, 252; FL 1:1; FW; LAIT 1; RGEL 2; TEA; WLIT 3

Wonder, Stevie 1950- .... **CLC 12**
See also CA 111

Wong, Jade Snow 1922-2006 .... **CLC 17**
See also CA 109; 249; CANR 91; SATA 112; SATA-Obit 175

Wood, Ellen Price
See Wood, Mrs. Henry

Wood, Mrs. Henry 1814-1887 .... **NCLC 178**
See also CMW 4; DLB 18; SUFW

Wood, James 1965- .... **CLC 238**
See also CA 235; CANR 214
Woodberry, George Edward 1855-1930 ......
TCLC 73
See also CA 165; DLB 71, 103
Woodcott, Keith
See Brunner, John (Kilian Houston)
Woodruff, Robert W.
See Mencken, H. L.
Woodward, Bob 1943- .... **CLC 240**
See also CA 69-72; CANR 31, 67, 107, 176;
MTCW 1
Woodward, Robert Upshur
See Woodward, Bob
Woolf, Adeline Virginia
See Woolf, Virginia
Woolf, Virginia 1882-1941 .. **SSC 7, 79, 161;**
TCLC 1, 5, 20, 43, 56, 101, 123, 128,
268; WLC 6
See also AAYA 44; BPFB 3; BRW 7;
BRWC 2; BRWR 1; CA 104; 130; CANR
64, 132; CDBLB 1914-1945; DA; DA3;
DAB; DAC; DAM MST, NOV; DLB 36,
100, 162; DLBD 10; EWL 3; EXPS; FL
1:6; FW; LAIT 3; LATS 1:1; LMFS 2;
MTCW 1, 2; MTFW 2005; NCFS 2; NFS
8, 12, 28; RGEL 2; RGSF 2; SSFS 4, 12,
34; TEA; WLIT 4
Woollcott, Alexander (Humphreys)
1887-1943 .... **TCLC 5**
See also CA 105; 161; DLB 29
Woolman, John 1720-1772 .... **LC 155**
See also DLB 31
Woolrich, Cornell
See Hopley-Woolrich, Cornell George
Woolson, Constance Fenimore 1840-1894 ...
NCLC 82; SSC 90
See also DLB 12, 74, 189, 221; RGAL 4
Wordsworth, Dorothy 1771-1855 . **NCLC 25,**
138
See also DLB 107
Wordsworth, William 1770-1850 . **NCLC 12,**
38, 111, 166, 206; PC 4, 67; WLC 6
See also AAYA 70; BRW 4; BRWC 1; CD-
BLB 1789-1832; DA; DA3; DAB; DAC;
DAM MST, POET; DLB 93, 107; EXPP;
LATS 1:1; LMFS 1; PAB; PFS 2, 33, 38;
RGEL 2; TEA; WLIT 3; WP
Wotton, Sir Henry 1568-1639 .... **LC 68**
See also DLB 121; RGEL 2
Wouk, Herman 1915- .... **CLC 1, 9, 38**
See also BPFB 2, 3; CA 5-8R; CANR 6,
33, 67, 146, 225; CDALBS; CN 1, 2, 3,
4, 5, 6; CPW; DA3; DAM NOV, POP;
DLBY 1982; INT CANR-6; LAIT 4;
MAL 5; MTCW 1, 2; MTFW 2005; NFS
7; TUS
Wright, Charles 1932-2008 . **BLC 1:3; CLC**
49
See also BW 1; CA 9-12R; 278; CANR 26;
CN 1, 2, 3, 4, 5, 6, 7; DAM MULT,
POET; DLB 33
Wright, Charles 1935- .. **CLC 6, 13, 28, 119,**
146
See also AMWS 5; CA 29-32R; CAAS 7;
CANR 23, 36, 62, 88, 135, 180; CP 3, 4,
5, 6, 7; DLB 165; DLBY 1982; EWL 3;
MTCW 1, 2; MTFW 2005; PFS 10, 35
Wright, Charles Penzel, Jr.
See Wright, Charles
Wright, Charles Stevenson
See Wright, Charles
Wright, Frances 1795-1852 .... **NCLC 74**
See also DLB 73
Wright, Frank Lloyd 1867-1959 .. **TCLC 95**
See also AAYA 33; CA 174
Wright, Harold Bell 1872-1944 .. **TCLC 183**
See also BPFB 3; CA 110; DLB 9; TCWW
2

Wright, Jack R.
See Harris, Mark
Wright, James (Arlington) 1927-1980 . **CLC**
3, 5, 10, 28; PC 36
See also AITN 2; AMWS 3; CA 49-52; 97-
100; CANR 4, 34, 64; CDALBS; CP 1, 2;
DAM POET; DLB 5, 169, 342; EWL 3;
EXPP; MAL 5; MTCW 1, 2; MTFW
2005; PFS 7, 8; RGAL 4; TUS; WP
Wright, Judith 1915-2000 .. **CLC 11, 53; PC**
14
See also CA 13-16R; 188; CANR 31, 76,
93; CP 1, 2, 3, 4, 5, 6, 7; CWP; DLB 260;
EWL 3; MTCW 1, 2; MTFW 2005; PFS
8; RGEL 2; SATA 14; SATA-Obit 121
Wright, Judith Arundell
See Wright, Judith
Wright, L(aurali) R. 1939- .... **CLC 44**
See also CA 138; CMW 4
Wright, Richard 1908-1960 . **BLC 1:3; CLC**
1, 3, 4, 9, 14, 21, 48, 74; SSC 2, 109;
TCLC 136, 180; WLC 6
See also AAYA 5, 42; AFAW 1, 2; AMW;
BPFB 3; BW 1; BYA 2; CA 108; CANR
64; CDALB 1929-1941; DA; DA3; DAB;
DAC; DAM MST, MULT, NOV; DLB 76,
102; DLBD 2; EWL 3; EXPN; LAIT 3,
4; MAL 5; MTCW 1, 2; MTFW 2005;
NCFS 1; NFS 1, 7; RGAL 4; RGSF 2;
SSFS 3, 9, 15, 20; TUS; YAW
Wright, Richard B. 1937- .... **CLC 6**
See also CA 85-88; CANR 120; DLB 53
Wright, Richard Bruce
See Wright, Richard B.
Wright, Richard Nathaniel
See Wright, Richard
Wright, Rick 1945- .... **CLC 35**
Wright, Rowland
See Wells, Carolyn
Wright, Stephen 1946- .... **CLC 33**
See also CA 237; DLB 350
Wright, Willard Huntington 1888-1939 ....
TCLC 23
See also CA 115; 189; CMW 4; DLB 306;
DLBD 16; MSW
Wright, William 1930- .... **CLC 44**
See also CA 53-56; CANR 7, 23, 154
Wroblewski, David 1959- .... **CLC 280**
See also CA 283
Wroth, Lady Mary 1587-1653(?) ...... **LC 30,**
139; PC 38
See also DLB 121
Wu Ch'eng-en 1500(?)-1582(?) .... **LC 7**
Wu Ching-tzu 1701-1754 .... **LC 2**
Wulfstan c. 10th cent. -1023 . **CMLC 59, 135**
Wurlitzer, Rudolph 1938(?)- ... **CLC 2, 4, 15**
See also CA 85-88; CN 4, 5, 6, 7; DLB 173
Wyatt, Sir Thomas c. 1503-1542 . **LC 70; PC**
27
See also BRW 1; DLB 132; EXPP; PFS 25;
RGEL 2; TEA
Wycherley, William 1640-1716 .. **DC 41; LC**
8, 21, 102, 136
See also BRW 2; CDBLB 1660-1789; DAM
DRAM; DLB 80; RGEL 2
Wyclif, John c. 1330-1384 .... **CMLC 70**
See also DLB 146
Wylie, Elinor (Morton Hoyt) 1885-1928 . **PC**
23; TCLC 8
See also AMWS 1; CA 105; 162; DLB 9,
45; EXPP; MAL 5; RGAL 4
Wylie, Philip (Gordon) 1902-1971 .. **CLC 43**
See also CA 21-22; 33-36R; CAP 2; CN 1;
DLB 9; SFW 4
Wyndham, John
See Harris, John (Wyndham Parkes Lucas)
Beynon

Wyss, Johann David Von 1743-1818 . **NCLC**
10
See also CLR 92; JRDA; MAICYA 1, 2;
SATA 29; SATA-Brief 27
X, Malcolm
See Malcolm X
Xenophon c. 430B.C.-c. 354B.C. . **CMLC 17,**
137
See also AW 1; DLB 176; RGWL 2, 3;
WLIT 8
Xingjian, Gao 1940- .... **CLC 167, 315**
See also CA 193; DFS 21; DLB 330;
MTFW 2005; RGWL 3
Yakamochi 718-785 .... **CMLC 45; PC 48**
Yakumo Koizumi
See Hearn, Lafcadio
Yamada, Mitsuye (May) 1923- .... **PC 44**
See also CA 77-80
Yamamoto, Hisaye 1921-2011 ..... **AAL; SSC**
34
See also CA 214; DAM MULT; DLB 312;
LAIT 4; SSFS 14
Yamauchi, Wakako 1924- .... **AAL**
See also CA 214; DLB 312
Yan, Mo 1956(?)- .... **CLC 257**
See also CA 201; CANR 192; EWL 3;
RGWL 3
Yanez, Jose Donoso
See Donoso, Jose
Yanovsky, Basile S.
See Yanovsky, V(assily) S(emenovich)
Yanovsky, V(assily) S(emenovich)
1906-1989 .... **CLC 2, 18**
See also CA 97-100; 129
Yates, Richard 1926-1992 .... **CLC 7, 8, 23**
See also AMWS 11; CA 5-8R; 139; CANR
10, 43; CN 1, 2, 3, 4, 5; DLB 2, 234;
DLBY 1981, 1992; INT CANR-10; SSFS
24
Yau, John 1950- .... **PC 61**
See also CA 154; CANR 89; CP 4, 5, 6, 7;
DLB 234, 312; PFS 26
Yearsley, Ann 1753-1806 .... **NCLC 174**
See also DLB 109
Yeats, W. B.
See Yeats, William Butler
Yeats, William Butler 1865-1939 ...... **DC 33;**
PC 20, 51, 129; TCLC 1, 11, 18, 31, 93,
116; WLC 6
See also AAYA 48; BRW 6; BRWR 1; CA
104; 127; CANR 45; CDBLB 1890-1914;
DA; DA3; DAB; DAC; DAM DRAM,
MST, POET; DLB 10, 19, 98, 156, 332;
EWL 3; EXPP; MTCW 1, 2; MTFW
2005; NCFS 3; PAB; PFS 1, 2, 5, 7, 13,
15, 34; RGEL 2; TEA; WLIT 4; WP
Yehoshua, A. B. 1936- ...... **CLC 13, 31, 243**
See also CA 33-36R; CANR 43, 90, 145,
202; CWW 2; EWL 3; RGHL; RGSF 2;
RGWL 3; WLIT 6
Yehoshua, Abraham B.
See Yehoshua, A. B.
Yellow Bird
See Ridge, John Rollin
Yep, Laurence 1948- .... **CLC 35**
See also AAYA 5, 31; BYA 7; CA 49-52;
CANR 1, 46, 92, 161; CLR 3, 17, 54, 132;
DLB 52, 312; FANT; JRDA; MAICYA 1,
2; MAICYAS 1; SATA 7, 69, 123, 176,
213; WYA; YAW
Yep, Laurence Michael
See Yep, Laurence
Yerby, Frank G(arvin) 1916-1991 . **BLC 1:3;**
CLC 1, 7, 22
See also BPFB 3; BW 1, 3; CA 9-12R; 136;
CANR 16, 52; CN 1, 2, 3, 4, 5; DAM
MULT; DLB 76; INT CANR-16; MTCW
1; RGAL 4; RHW

Yesenin, Sergei Aleksandrovich
See Esenin, Sergei
Yevtushenko, Yevgeny Alexandrovich
See Yevtushenko, Yevgenyn
Yevtushenko, Yevgenyn 1933- ...... **CLC 1, 3, 13, 26, 51, 126; PC 40**
See also CA 81-84; CANR 33, 54; CWW 2; DAM POET; DLB 359; EWL 3; MTCW 1; PFS 29; RGHL; RGWL 2, 3
Yezierska, Anzia 1885(?)-1970 .... **CLC 46; SSC 144; TCLC 205**
See also CA 126; 89-92; DLB 28, 221; FW; MTCW 1; NFS 29; RGAL 4; SSFS 15
Yglesias, Helen 1915-2008 .... **CLC 7, 22**
See also CA 37-40R; 272; CAAS 20; CANR 15, 65, 95; CN 4, 5, 6, 7; INT CANR-15; MTCW 1
Y.O.
See Russell, George William
Yokomitsu, Riichi 1898-1947 .... **TCLC 47**
See also CA 170; EWL 3
Yolen, Jane 1939- .... **CLC 256**
See also AAYA 4, 22, 85; BPFB 3; BYA 9, 10, 11, 14, 16; CA 13-16R; CANR 11, 29, 56, 91, 126, 185; CLR 4, 44, 149; CWRI 5; DLB 52; FANT; INT CANR-29; JRDA; MAICYA 1, 2; MTFW 2005; NFS 30; SAAS 1; SATA 4, 40, 75, 112, 158, 194, 230; SATA-Essay 111; SFW 4; SSFS 29; SUFW 2; WYA; YAW
Yolen, Jane Hyatt
See Yolen, Jane
Yonge, Charlotte 1823-1901 .. **TCLC 48, 245**
See also BRWS 17; CA 109; 163; DLB 18, 163; RGEL 2; SATA 17; WCH
Yonge, Charlotte Mary
See Yonge, Charlotte
York, Jeremy
See Creasey, John
York, Simon
See Heinlein, Robert A.
Yorke, Henry Vincent 1905-1974 ..... **CLC 2, 13, 97**
See also BRWS 2; CA 85-88, 175; 49-52; DLB 15; EWL 3; RGEL 2
Yosano, Akiko 1878-1942 . **PC 11; TCLC 59**
See also CA 161; EWL 3; RGWL 3
Yoshimoto, Banana
See Yoshimoto, Mahoko
Yoshimoto, Mahoko 1964- .... **CLC 84**
See also AAYA 50; CA 144; CANR 98, 160; NFS 7; SSFS 15
Young, Al(bert James) 1939- .... **BLC 1:3; CLC 19**
See also BW 2, 3; CA 29-32R; CANR 26, 65, 109; CN 2, 3, 4, 5, 6, 7; CP 1, 2, 3, 4, 5, 6, 7; DAM MULT; DLB 33
Young, Andrew (John) 1885-1971 ..... **CLC 5**
See also CA 5-8R; CANR 7, 29; CP 1; RGEL 2
Young, Collier
See Bloch, Robert (Albert)
Young, Edward 1683-1765 .... **LC 3, 40**
See also DLB 95; RGEL 2
Young, Marguerite (Vivian) 1909-1995 .... **CLC 82**
See also CA 13-16; 150; CAP 1; CN 1, 2, 3, 4, 5, 6
Young, Neil 1945- .... **CLC 17**
See also CA 110; CCA 1
Young Bear, Ray A. 1950- . **CLC 94; NNAL**
See also CA 146; DAM MULT; DLB 175; MAL 5
Yourcenar, Marguerite 1903-1987 . **CLC 19, 38, 50, 87; TCLC 193**
See also BPFB 3; CA 69-72; CANR 23, 60, 93; DAM NOV; DLB 72; DLBY 1988; EW 12; EWL 3; GFL 1789 to the Present; GLL 1; MTCW 1, 2; MTFW 2005; RGWL 2, 3

Yuan, Chu 340(?)B.C.-278(?)B.C. ..... **CMLC 36**
Yu Dafu 1896-1945 .... **SSC 122**
See also DLB 328; RGSF 2
Yurick, Sol 1925- .... **CLC 6**
See also CA 13-16R; CANR 25; CN 1, 2, 3, 4, 5, 6, 7; MAL 5
Zabolotsky, Nikolai
See Zabolotsky, Nikolai Alekseevich
Zabolotsky, Nikolai Alekseevich 1903-1958 . **TCLC 52**
See also CA 116; 164; DLB 359; EWL 3
Zabolotsky, Nikolay Alekseevich
See Zabolotsky, Nikolai Alekseevich
Zagajewski, Adam 1945- .... **PC 27**
See also CA 186; DLB 232; EWL 3; PFS 25
Zakaria, Fareed 1964- .... **CLC 269**
See also CA 171; CANR 151, 189
Zalygin, Sergei -2000 .... **CLC 59**
Zalygin, Sergei (Pavlovich) 1913-2000 . **CLC 59**
See also DLB 302
Zamiatin, Evgenii
See Zamyatin, Evgeny Ivanovich
Zamiatin, Evgenii Ivanovich
See Zamyatin, Evgeny Ivanovich
Zamiatin, Yevgenii
See Zamyatin, Evgeny Ivanovich
Zamora, Bernice (B. Ortiz) 1938- . **CLC 89; HLC 2**
See also CA 151; CANR 80; DAM MULT; DLB 82; HW 1, 2
Zamyatin, Evgeny Ivanovich 1884-1937 ...... **SSC 89; TCLC 8, 37**
See also CA 105; 166; DLB 272; EW 10; EWL 3; RGSF 2; RGWL 2, 3; SFW 4
Zamyatin, Yevgeny Ivanovich
See Zamyatin, Evgeny Ivanovich
Zangwill, Israel 1864-1926 .. **SSC 44; TCLC 16**
See also CA 109; 167; CMW 4; DLB 10, 135, 197; RGEL 2
Zanzotto, Andrea 1921- .... **PC 65**
See also CA 208; CWW 2; DLB 128; EWL 3
Zappa, Francis Vincent, Jr. 1940-1993 . **CLC 17**
See also CA 108; 143; CANR 57
Zappa, Frank
See Zappa, Francis Vincent, Jr.
Zaturenska, Marya 1902-1982 .... **CLC 6, 11**
See also CA 13-16R; 105; CANR 22; CP 1, 2, 3
Zayas y Sotomayor, Maria de 1590-c. 1661 .... **LC 102; SSC 94**
See also RGSF 2
Zeami 1363-1443 .... **DC 7; LC 86**
See also DLB 203; RGWL 2, 3
Zelazny, Roger 1937-1995 .... **CLC 21**
See also AAYA 7, 68; BPFB 3; CA 21-24R; 148; CANR 26, 60, 219; CN 6; DLB 8; FANT; MTCW 1, 2; MTFW 2005; SATA 57; SATA-Brief 39; SCFW 1, 2; SFW 4; SUFW 1, 2
Zelazny, Roger Joseph
See Zelazny, Roger
Zephaniah, Benjamin 1958- .... **BLC 2:3**
See also CA 147; CANR 103, 156, 177; CP 5, 6, 7; DLB 347; SATA 86, 140, 189
Zhang Ailing
See Chang, Eileen
Zhdanov, Andrei Alexandrovich 1896-1948 .... **TCLC 18**
See also CA 117; 167
Zhou Shuren
See Lu Xun

Zhukovsky, Vasilii Andreevich
See Zhukovsky, Vasily (Andreevich)
Zhukovsky, Vasily (Andreevich) 1783-1852 .... **NCLC 35**
See also DLB 205
Ziegenhagen, Eric CLC 55
Zimmer, Jill Schary
See Robinson, Jill
Zimmerman, Robert
See Dylan, Bob
Zindel, Paul 1936-2003 .... **CLC 6, 26; DC 5**
See also AAYA 2, 37; BYA 2, 3, 8, 11, 14; CA 73-76; 213; CAD; CANR 31, 65, 108; CD 5, 6; CDALBS; CLR 3, 45, 85; DA; DA3; DAB; DAC; DAM DRAM, MST, NOV; DFS 12; DLB 7, 52; JRDA; LAIT 5; MAICYA 1, 2; MTCW 1, 2; MTFW 2005; NFS 14; SATA 16, 58, 102; SATA-Obit 142; WYA; YAW
Zinger, Yisroel-Yehoyshue
See Singer, Israel Joshua
Zinger, Yitskhok
See Singer, Isaac Bashevis
Zinn, Howard 1922-2010 .... **CLC 199**
See also CA 1-4R; CANR 2, 33, 90, 159
Zinov'Ev, A.A.
See Zinoviev, Alexander
Zinov'ev, Aleksandr
See Zinoviev, Alexander
Zinoviev, Alexander 1922-2006 .... **CLC 19**
See also CA 116; 133; 250; CAAS 10; DLB 302
Zinoviev, Alexander Aleksandrovich
See Zinoviev, Alexander
Zizek, Slavoj 1949- .... **CLC 188**
See also CA 201; CANR 171; MTFW 2005
Zobel, Joseph 1915-2006 .... **BLC 2:3**
Zoilus
See Lovecraft, H. P.
Zola, Emile 1840-1902 .... **SSC 109; TCLC 1, 6, 21, 41, 219; WLC 6**
See also CA 104; 138; DA; DA3; DAB; DAC; DAM MST, NOV; DLB 123; EW 7; GFL 1789 to the Present; IDTP; LMFS 1, 2; RGWL 2; TWA
Zola, Emile Edouard Charles Antione
See Zola, Emile
Zoline, Pamela 1941- .... **CLC 62**
See also CA 161; SFW 4
Zoroaster 628(?)B.C.-551(?)B.C. .. **CMLC 40**
Zorrilla y Moral, Jose 1817-1893 .. **NCLC 6**
Zoshchenko, Mikhail 1895-1958 ..... **SSC 15; TCLC 15**
See also CA 115; 160; EWL 3; RGSF 2; RGWL 3
Zoshchenko, Mikhail Mikhailovich
See Zoshchenko, Mikhail
Zuckmayer, Carl 1896-1977 .... **CLC 18; TCLC 191**
See also CA 69-72; DLB 56, 124; EWL 3; RGWL 2, 3
Zuk, Georges
See Skelton, Robin
Zukofsky, Louis 1904-1978 .. **CLC 1, 2, 4, 7, 11, 18; PC 11, 121**
See also AMWS 3; CA 9-12R; 77-80; CANR 39; CP 1, 2; DAM POET; DLB 5, 165; EWL 3; MAL 5; MTCW 1; RGAL 4
Zweig, Arnold 1887-1968 .... **TCLC 199**
See also CA 189; 115; DLB 66; EWL 3
Zweig, Paul 1935-1984 .... **CLC 34, 42**
See also CA 85-88; 113
Zweig, Stefan 1881-1942 .... **TCLC 17**
See also CA 112; 170; DLB 81, 118; EWL 3; RGHL
Zwingli, Huldreich 1484-1531 .... **LC 37**
See also DLB 179

Literary Criticism Series
Cumulative Topic Index

This index lists all topic entries in Gale's *Children's Literature Review* (CLR), *Classical and Medieval Literature Criticism* (CMLC), *Contemporary Literary Criticism* (CLC), *Drama Criticism* (DC), *Literature Criticism from 1400 to 1800* (LC), *Nineteenth-Century Literature Criticism* (NCLC), *Short Story Criticism* (SSC), and *Twentieth-Century Literary Criticism* (TCLC). The index also lists topic entries in the Gale Critical Companion Collection, which includes the following publications: *The Beat Generation* (BG), *Feminism in Literature* (FL), *Gothic Literature* (GL), and *Harlem Renaissance* (HR).

Topic Index

TCLC Cumulative Nationality Index

AMERICAN

Abbey, Edward **160**
Acker, Kathy **191**
Adams, Andy **56**
Adams, Brooks **80**
Adams, Henry (Brooks) **4, 52**
Addams, Jane **76**
Agee, James (Rufus) **1, 19, 180**
Aldrich, Bess (Genevra) Streeter **125**
Allen, Fred **87**
Anderson, Maxwell **2, 144**
Anderson, Sherwood **1, 10, 24, 123**
Anthony, Susan B(rownell) **84**
Antin, Mary **247**
Arendt, Hannah **193**
Arnow, Harriette **196**
Asch, Sholem **3, 251**
Atherton, Gertrude (Franklin Horn) **2**
Auden, W(ystan) H(ugh) **223**
Austin, Mary (Hunter) **25, 249**
Baker, Ray Stannard **47**
Baker, Carlos (Heard) **119**
Baldwin, James **229**
Bambara, Toni Cade **116**
Barnes, Djuna **212**
Barry, Philip **11**
Baum, L(yman) Frank **7, 132**
Beard, Charles A(ustin) **15**
Becker, Carl (Lotus) **63**
Belasco, David **3**
Bell, James Madison **43**
Benchley, Robert (Charles) **1, 55**
Benedict, Ruth (Fulton) **60**
Benét, Stephen Vincent **7**
Benét, William Rose **28**
Bettelheim, Bruno **143**
Bierce, Ambrose (Gwinett) **1, 7, 44**
Biggers, Earl Derr **65**
Bishop, Elizabeth **121**
Bishop, John Peale **103**
Black Elk **33**
Boas, Franz **56**
Bodenheim, Maxwell **44**
Bok, Edward W. **101**
Bonner, Marita **179**
Bourne, Randolph S(illiman) **16**
Bowles, Paul **209**
Boyd, James **115**
Boyd, Thomas (Alexander) **111**
Bradford, Gamaliel **36**
Brautigan, Richard **133**
Brennan, Christopher John **17**
Brennan, Maeve **124**
Brodkey, Harold (Roy) **123**
Brodsky, Joseph **219**
Bromfield, Louis (Brucker) **11**
Broun, Heywood **104**
Bryan, William Jennings **99**
Burroughs, Edgar Rice **2, 32**
Burroughs, William S(eward) **121**
Cabell, James Branch **6**
Cable, George Washington **4**

Cahan, Abraham **71**
Caldwell, Erskine (Preston) **117**
Campbell, Joseph **140**
Capote, Truman **164**
Cardozo, Benjamin N(athan) **65**
Carnegie, Dale **53**
Cather, Willa (Sibert) **1, 11, 31, 99, 132, 152, 264**
Chambers, Robert W(illiam) **41**
Chambers, (David) Whittaker **129**
Chandler, Raymond (Thornton) **1, 7, 179**
Chapman, John Jay **7**
Chase, Mary Ellen **124**
Chesnutt, Charles W(addell) **5, 39**
Childress, Alice **116**
Chopin, Katherine **5, 14, 127, 199**
Cobb, Irvin S(hrewsbury) **77**
Coffin, Robert P(eter) Tristram **95**
Cohan, George M(ichael) **60**
Comstock, Anthony **13**
Cotter, Joseph Seamon Sr. **28**
Cram, Ralph Adams **45**
Crane, (Harold) Hart **2, 5, 80**
Crane, Stephen (Townley) **11, 17, 32, 216**
Crawford, F(rancis) Marion **10**
Crothers, Rachel **19**
Cullen, Countée **4, 37, 220**
Cummings, E. E. **137**
Dahlberg, Edward **208**
Darrow, Clarence (Seward) **81**
Davis, Rebecca (Blaine) Harding **6, 267**
Davis, Richard Harding **24**
Day, Clarence (Shepard Jr.) **25**
Dent, Lester **72**
De Voto, Bernard (Augustine) **29**
Dewey, John **95**
Dickey, James **151**
Dixon, Thomas, Jr. **163**
di Donato, Pietro **159**
Dreiser, Theodore (Herman Albert) **10, 18, 35, 83**
Du Bois, W. E. B. **169**
Dulles, John Foster **72**
Dunbar, Paul Laurence **2, 12**
Duncan, Isadora **68**
Dunne, Finley Peter **28**
Eastman, Charles A(lexander) **55**
Eddy, Mary (Ann Morse) Baker **71**
Einstein, Albert **65**
Eliot, T.S. **236**
Erskine, John **84**
Farrell, James T. **228**
Faulkner, William **141**
Faust, Frederick (Schiller) **49**
Fenollosa, Ernest (Francisco) **91**
Fields, W. C. **80**
Fisher, Dorothy (Frances) Canfield **87**
Fisher, Rudolph **11, 255**
Fisher, Vardis **140**
Fitzgerald, F(rancis) Scott (Key) **1, 6, 14, 28, 55, 157**
Fitzgerald, Zelda (Sayre) **52**
Fletcher, John Gould **35**

Foote, Mary Hallock **108**
Ford, Henry **73**
Forten, Charlotte L. **16**
Freeman, Douglas Southall **11**
Freeman, Mary E(leanor) Wilkins **9**
Frost, Robert **236**
Fuller, Henry Blake **103**
Futrelle, Jacques **19**
Gale, Zona **7**
Gardner, John **195**
Garland, (Hannibal) Hamlin **3, 256**
Gibran, Kahlil **1, 9, 205**
Gilman, Charlotte (Anna) Perkins (Stetson) **9, 37, 117, 201**
Ginsberg, Allen **120**
Glasgow, Ellen (Anderson Gholson) **2, 7, 239**
Glaspell, Susan **55, 175**
Goldman, Emma **13**
Gordon, Caroline **241**
Green, Anna Katharine **63**
Grey, Zane **6**
Griffith, D(avid Lewelyn) W(ark) **68**
Griggs, Sutton (Elbert) **77**
Guest, Edgar A(lbert) **95**
Guiney, Louise Imogen **41**
Haley, Alex **147**
Hall, James Norman **23**
Hammett, Dashiell **187**
Handy, W(illiam) C(hristopher) **97**
Hansberry, Lorraine **192**
Harper, Frances Ellen Watkins **14, 217**
Harris, Joel Chandler **2**
Hartmann, Sadakichi **73**
Harte, (Francis) Bret(t) **1, 25**
Hawthorne, Julian **25**
Hearn, (Patricio) Lafcadio (Tessima Carlos) **9, 263**
Hecht, Ben **101**
Heller, Joseph **131, 151**
Hellman, Lillian (Florence) **119**
Hemingway, Ernest (Miller) **115, 203**
Henry, O. **1, 19**
Herbst, Josephine **243**
Hergesheimer, Joseph **11**
Heyward, (Edwin) DuBose **59**
Higginson, Thomas Wentworth **36**
Himes, Chester **139**
Holley, Marietta **99**
Holly, Buddy **65**
Holmes, Oliver Wendell Jr. **77**
Hopkins, Pauline Elizabeth **28, 251**
Horney, Karen (Clementine Theodore Danielsen) **71**
Howard, Robert E(rvin) **8**
Howe, Julia Ward **21**
Howells, William Dean **7, 17, 41**
Huneker, James Gibbons **65**
Hurston, Zora Neale **121, 131**
Ince, Thomas H. **89**
Isherwood, Christopher **227**
Jackson, Shirley **187**

451

TCLC-267 Title Index

ISBN-13: 978-1-4144-7047-4
ISBN-10: 1-4144-7047-9

90000

9 781414 470474